ROGET'S II
The New Thesaurus

BERKLEY BOOKS, NEW YORK

Preface

This book is a condensed version of *Roget's II: The New Thesaurus*, which is published by Houghton Mifflin Company. All the essential information contained in that work appears here in a new format. This book has been edited and designed to be as clear, accurate, and easy to use as the original hardcover book.

Introduction

Roget's II: The New Thesaurus represents a significant change from a traditional thesaurus, which groups words by association rather than by meaning. *Roget's II* is a thesaurus—a "treasury"—of synonyms.

The concept of synonymy is a difficult and complex one. In *Roget's II* words are listed as synonyms if they are closely equivalent in meaning even if they are not fully interchangeable in all contexts. Every entry is given a definition that is accurate for each word listed as a synonym for that entry. Many words have more than one definition, and separate lists of synonyms are given for each sense.

The simple and clear organization of *Roget's II* will help the user quickly and easily find a word expressing a particular meaning that is appropriate for the context. *Roget's II: The New Thesaurus* will serve its users well in selecting the right words to express thoughts precisely and to add color and variety to expression.

How to Use This Book

Types of Entry

Roget's II consists essentially of an alphabetical list of words that are identified by part of speech, defined, illustrated by an example phrase or sentence, and provided with a list of synonyms. These words are called *primary entries*. The word **gossip** is an example of such an entry with two distinct meanings:

> **gossip** *noun*
> 1. Idle, often sensational and groundless talk about others: *a tabloid full of gossip. According to gossip, they eloped.*
>   **Syns:** buzz, cry, hearsay, murmur, report, rumor, scuttlebutt (*Slang*), tattle, tittle-tattle, whispering, word.
> 2. A person habitually engaged in idle talk about others: *Our local gossip claimed we were getting a divorce.*
>   **Syns:** gossiper, gossipmonger, mumblenews, newsmonger, quidnunc, rumorer, rumormonger, scandalmonger, tabby, talebearer, tattle, tattler, tattletale, telltale, yenta (*Slang*).

Gossip in the sense "idle talk" (definition **1**) has 11 synonyms. Each of these words is also entered alphabetically in *Roget's II*, but identified only by a part of speech and a cross-reference (in SMALL CAPITAL LETTERS) to the primary entry **gossip.** No definition is given because each synonym has the same meaning as the primary entry. Such abbreviated entries are called *secondary entries*; the word **rumor,** a synonym of **gossip,** is an example:

> **rumor** *noun* GOSSIP.

Secondary entries are no less important than primary entries. A user who needs a word meaning "idle talk" and begins the search with one of the synonyms of **gossip** can, by looking up that synonym, find the primary entry and the other ten synonyms. One of these may be more appropriate than the word first considered.

It often happens that a word appears in synonym lists at several different primary entries. Cross-references to these entries are listed alphabetically under the secondary entry:

> **aspect** *noun*
> 1. APPEARANCE.
> 2. EXPRESSION.
> 3. FACE.
> 4. LIGHT[1].
> 5. PHASE.

This example shows that the word **aspect** can be found as a synonym at **appearance, expression, face, light[1],** and **phase,** reflecting the different shades of meaning that **aspect** can express.

Sometimes a secondary entry lists the same primary entry as a cross-reference more than once:

> **allow** *verb*
> 1. ACKNOWLEDGE.
> 2. ALLOT.
> 3, 4, 5. PERMIT.

Thus, at the primary entry **permit,** the word **allow** occurs in the synonym lists for three different senses:

> **permit** *verb*
> 1. To neither forbid nor prevent: *just permits the children to run wild.*
>   **Syns:** allow, have, leave[2], let, suffer, tolerate.
> 2. To give one's consent to: *permitted me to leave the office early.*
>   **Syns:** allow, authorize, consent, let, sanction.
> 3. To afford an opportunity for: *a job that permits me to advance.*
>   **Syns:** admit, allow, let.
> 4. ENABLE.

Because the cross-references at each secondary entry are listed in alphabetical order, the numbers assigned to them at the secondary entry (e.g., **allow**) do not necessarily match the numbers of the definitions under which they appear at the primary entry (e.g., **permit**). This arrangement should be kept in mind when using *Roget's II.*

A third kind of entry is called a *directional cross-reference.* It directs the user to the entry where more complete information is given:

> **amok** *adjective* SEE **amuck.**

ambush *verb*
1. To attack suddenly and without warning: *highwaymen who hid in thickets and ambushed passing travelers.*
   Syns: ambuscade, bushwhack, surprise, waylay.
2. LAY FOR at **lay**[1].

The second example shows that the synonyms of **lay for** can be found at the main entry **lay**[1].

In addition to the several kinds of main entries there are also *subentries*. The entry **lay for**, which appears at **lay**[1], is an example of a subentry. A subentry is listed under a main entry and not at its own alphabetical place. Most subentries are either verb phrases such as **lay for** that are listed under the simple verb or main entry words used as other parts of speech. **Lay**[1] contains several examples of the first kind:

lay[1] *verb*
1. To place in a designated setting: *The novel is laid in Italy.*
   Syn: set[1].
2. AIM.
3. ATTRIBUTE.
4. BET.
5. DRAFT.
6. GAMBLE.
7. PRESENT[2].
8, 9. SET[1].
lay aside *verb* SAVE.
lay away *verb*
1. BANK[1].
2. BURY.
3. SAVE.
lay by *verb* SAVE.
lay down *verb*
1. BET.
2. DEPOSIT.
3. DICTATE.
4. RELINQUISH.

lay for *verb*
Informal. To wait concealed in order to attack (someone): *The thieves threatened to lay for their accomplice if he double-crossed them.*
   Syns: ambuscade, ambush. —*Idioms* lay wait for, lie in wait for.
lay in *verb* SAVE.
lay into *verb* BEAT.
lay low *verb* HOLE UP at **hole.**
lay off *verb*
1. ABANDON.
2. STOP.
lay open *verb* REVEAL.
lay out *verb*
1. ARRANGE.
2. DESIGN.
3. PLOT.
4. SPEND.
lay over *verb* DEFER[1].
lay up *verb*
1. HOARD.
2. STOCKPILE.

The verb **import** is an example of the second kind:

import *noun*
1. The general sense or significance, as of an action, statement, etc.: *The import of his words did not register until much later.*
   Syns: amount, burden, drift, purport, substance. —*Idioms* sum and substance, sum total.
2. IMPORTANCE.
3. MEANING.
import *verb*
1. COUNT.
2. MEAN[1].

The two kinds of subentry can be combined. In such cases verb phrases immediately follow the simple verb and precede subentries that are not verbs; strict alphabetical order is therefore not observed for the entry as a whole. The verb phrases themselves, however, are in alphabetical order:

hold *verb*
1. To have and maintain in one's possession: *holds a controlling interest in the company.*
   Syns: hold back, keep, keep back, reserve, retain, withhold.
2. To maintain restraining control and possession of: *holding a material witness in protective custody.*
   Syns: detain, hold up.
3. ACCOMMODATE.
4. ASSERT.
5. BELIEVE.
6. COMMAND.
7. CONTAIN.
8. EMBRACE.
9. ENJOY.
10. FEEL.
11. GRIP.
12, 13. HAVE.
14. SUPPORT.

hold back *verb*
1. HINDER.
2. HOLD.
3. REPRESS.
4. RESTRAIN.

hold down *verb*
1. REPRESS.
2. RESTRAIN.

hold in *verb* RESTRAIN.

hold off *verb*
1. DEFER¹.
2. REFRAIN.

hold out *verb* ENDURE.

hold up *verb*
1. BEAR UP at **bear.**
2. DEFER¹.
3. DELAY.
4. HOLD.
5. ROB.
6. SKIN.
7. WASH.

hold *noun*
1. An act or means of holding something: *Keep a firm hold on your purse.*
   Syns: clasp, clench, clutch, grapple, grasp, grip.
2. A strong or powerful influence: *had a real hold on my emotions.*
   Syn: grip.

Many verb phrases have derived nouns, adjectives, or adverbs that are spelled as one word or hyphenated: **giveaway** from **give away**; **holdup** from **hold up**; **layout** from **lay out**; and **make-up** from **make up.** Unlike verb phrases, the derived words are found at their correct alphabetical places as main entries. **Holdup,** for example, comes between **holding(s)** and **hole,** and not as a subentry at **hold.**

Idioms

At many primary entries a list of idioms appears after the synonym list. An *idiom* is a phrase, often metaphorical in nature, that has a meaning equivalent to that of the main entry word. For example, *break bread* is an idiom meaning "eat," and it occurs after the list of synonyms at **eat.** Idioms are only included at the primary entries and do not appear as secondary entries at their own alphabetical places.

Variants

Some words have two or more spellings, which are called *variants.* All variant spellings of a word are given at the main entry and in the synonym lists. Some variants occur with equal frequency, and in *Roget's II* they are joined by *or*:

down-at-heel or **down-at-the-heel**

Some variants occur less frequently than the principal spelling, and these are introduced by *also*:

abeyance also **abeyancy** *noun*

Some words have more than one variant:

naive also **naïve, naif, naïf** *adjective*

Each variant spelling is entered at its own alphabetical place with a directional cross-reference to the principal spelling, unless the variant would be immediately adjacent to the main entry. Thus **abeyancy** is not a main entry because it would immediately follow **abeyance. Amok,** however, is separately entered, since it occurs several entries away from **amuck,** which is the principal spelling of the word.

Variant wordings for idioms appear in parentheses:

2. To come to the ground suddenly
and involuntarily: *I stumbled and
fell.*
Syns: drop, go down, pitch, plunge,
spill, sprawl, topple, tumble.
—*Idiom* take a fall (*or* header *or*
plunge *or* spill *or* tumble).

Homographs

A *homograph* is a word that is spelled the same as another word but differs in origin, meaning, and sometimes pronunciation. In *Roget's II* homographs are treated as distinct words, entered separately, and distinguished by superscript numerals:

bound[1] *verb* BOUNCE.
bound *noun*
1, 2. BOUNCE.
bound[2] *verb*
1. ADJOIN.
2. BORDER.
3. DETERMINE.
bound[3] *adjective* OBLIGED.

Cross-references to primary entries are identified by superscript numerals where necessary:

crumple *verb*
1. BEND.
2. WRINKLE[1].

Labels

Even though two words may be synonymous, they may not be equally appropriate in all contexts. *Roget's II* identifies words of restricted application with labels of various kinds. Words may be limited to a particular field (*Law*, *Chem.*), to a dialect (*Regional, Brit.*), or to a level of style or usage (*Informal, Poetic, Slang*); they may have limited occurrence (*Rare*) or not be a living part of Modern English (*Archaic*). Expressions from languages besides English are labeled with the appropriate language name (*French, Latin*).

In addition to the special labels mentioned above, every main entry is identified by its part of speech: *noun, verb, adjective, adverb, pronoun, interjection, preposition,* and *conjunction.* A list of all abbreviations used in *Roget's II* is given on the following page.

Abbreviations

Anat.	Anatomy
Archit.	Architecture
Austral.	Australian
Biol.	Biology
Bot.	Botany
Brit.	British
Can.	Canadian
Chem.	Chemistry
Eccles.	Ecclesiastical
Econ.	Economics
Ed.	Education
Eng.	English
esp.	especially
Geol.	Geology
Geom.	Geometry
Gk.	Greek
Hist.	History
Ir.	Irish
Jour.	Journalism
Ling.	Linguistics
Med.	Medicine
Mil.	Military
Motion Pic. & T.V.	Motion Pictures & Television
Mus.	Music
Myth.	Mythology
Naut.	Nautical
New Zeal.	New Zealand
Obs.	Obsolete
Path.	Pathology
Phon.	Phonetics
Physiol.	Physiology
Print.	Printing
Psychoanal.	Psychoanalysis
Psychol.	Psychology
Rhet.	Rhetoric
Rom.	Roman
Scot.	Scottish
usu.	usually
Vet. Med.	Veterinary Medicine
Zool.	Zoology

A

aback *adverb* UNAWARES.

abandon *verb*

1. To give up without intending to return or claim again: *abandoned his wife and children.*
   Syns: desert³, forsake, leave¹, quit, throw over, walk out on.

2. To cease trying to accomplish or continue: *abandoned her studies for lack of funds.*
   Syns: desist, discontinue, forswear (*also* foreswear), give up, lay off (*Slang*), quit, renounce, stop, swear off (*Informal*). —*Idioms* call it a day, call it quits, hang up the fiddle, have done with, throw in the towel.

3. ABDICATE.

4. GIVE OVER at **give**.

5. RELINQUISH.

abandon *noun*

1. A complete surrender of inhibitions: *playing the flute with abandon.*
   Syns: abandonment, incontinence, unrestraint, wantonness, wildness.

2. A careless, often reckless disregard for consequences: *rides his motorcycle with abandon.*
   Syns: heedlessness, thoughtlessness.

abandoned *adjective*

1. Having been given up and left alone: *an abandoned house.*
   Syns: derelict, deserted, destitute (*Obs.*), forlorn, forsaken, lorn (*Poetic*).

2. Lacking in moral restraint: *an abandoned brute.*
   Syns: dissolute, incontinent, licentious, profligate, unbridled, unconstrained, uncontrolled, ungoverned, uninhibited, unrestrained, wanton, wild.

abandonment *noun*

1. The act of forsaking: *his abandonment of his family.*
   Syn: desertion.

2. ABANDON.

3. ABDICATION.

abase *verb* HUMBLE.

abash *verb* EMBARRASS.

abashed *adjective* EMBARRASSED.

abashment *noun* EMBARRASSMENT.

abate *verb*

1. DECREASE.

2. SUBSIDE.

abatement *noun*

1. DECREASE.

2. DEDUCTION.

3. WANE.

abbreviate *verb*

1. SHORTEN.

2. TRUNCATE.

abdicate *verb*
To give up a possession, claim, or right: *The queen abdicated the throne in 1948.*
   Syns: abandon, cede, demit, hand over, quitclaim, relinquish, render (up), renounce, resign, surrender, waive, yield.

abdication *noun*
A giving up of a possession, claim, or right: *her abdication of her responsibilities.*
   Syns: abandonment, demission, quitclaim, renunciation, resignation, surrender, waiver.

abduct *verb* KIDNAP.

abecedarian *also* **abecedary** *noun* AMATEUR.

aberrance *or* **aberrancy** *noun* ABNORMALITY.

aberrant *adjective*

1. ABNORMAL.

2. ERRANT.

aberration *noun*
1. ABNORMALITY.
2. INSANITY.

abet *verb* HELP.

abeyance also **abeyancy** *noun*
The condition of being temporarily inactive: *hold a decision in abeyance; cancer kept in abeyance with chemotherapy.*
   Syns: dormancy, intermission, latency, quiescence (*also* quiescency), remission, suspension.

abeyant *adjective* LATENT.

abhor *verb* DESPISE.

abhorrence *noun*
1. HATE.
2. HORROR.

abhorrent *adjective* FILTHY.

abide *verb*
1, 2. ENDURE.
3. LIVE¹.
4. PAUSE.
5. REMAIN.

abide by *verb* FOLLOW.

abiding *adjective* CONTINUING.

ability *noun*
1. Physical, mental, financial, or legal power to perform: *had the ability to learn physics.*
   Syns: ableness, capability, capacity, competence (*also* competency), faculty, might.
2. Natural or acquired facility in a specific activity: *has fine technical ability.*
   Syns: adeptness, command, craft, expertise, expertism, expertness, knack, know-how (*Informal*), mastery, proficiency, skill.

abjuration *noun* RETRACTION.

abjure *verb* RETRACT.

ablaze *adjective* BLAZING.

able *adjective*
Having the ability to perform well: *an able attorney.*
   Syns: adept, au fait (*French*), capable, competent, good, proficient, qualified, skilled, skillful.

able-bodied *adjective*
Physically strong and healthy: *able-bodied young men helping to move the furniture.*
   Syns: strapping, sturdy.

ableness *noun* ABILITY.

abnormal *adjective*
Departing from the normal: *an abnormal fear of bats.*
   Syns: aberrant, anomalistic, anomalous, atypical (*also* atypic),

deviant, deviate, deviating, deviative, divergent, preternatural, unnatural.

abnormality *noun*
The condition of being abnormal: *an abnormality in his vision.*
   Syns: aberrance *or* aberrancy, aberration, anomalism, anomaly, deviance, deviancy, deviation, preternaturalness.

abode *noun* HOME.

abolish *verb*
1. To put an end to formally and with authority: *The Thirteenth Amendment abolished slavery.*
   Syns: abrogate, annihilate, annul, cancel, invalidate, negate, nullify, repeal, rescind, set aside, vitiate, void.
2. ANNIHILATE.

abolishment *noun* ABOLITION.

abolition *noun*
An often formal act of putting an end to: *the abolition of slavery.*
   Syns: abolishment, abrogation, annihilation, annulment, defeasance, extinguishment, invalidation, negation, nullification, repeal, rescindment, rescission.

abominable *adjective*
1. HATEFUL.
2. UNSPEAKABLE.

abominate *verb* HATE.

abomination *noun*
1, 2. HATE.

aboriginal *adjective* NATIVE.

abort *verb* MISCARRY.

abound *verb* TEEM¹.

abounding *adjective* ALIVE.

about *adverb*
1. APPROXIMATELY.
2. BACK.
3. BACKWARD.

about-face *verb* DOUBLE.

abracadabra *noun*
1, 2. GIBBERISH.

abrade *verb* CHAFE.

abridge *verb* TRUNCATE.

abridgment *noun* SYNOPSIS.

abrogate *verb* ABOLISH.

abrogation *noun* ABOLITION.

abrupt *adjective*
1. Happening quickly and without warning: *his abrupt departure for New York.*
   Syns: hasty, hurried, precipitant, precipitate, sudden.
2. Rudely unceremonious: *gave an abrupt, barely civil answer.*
   Syns: blunt, brief, brusque, crusty,

curt, gruff, short, short-spoken,
snippety, snippy.

3. STEEP[1].

abscond *verb* ESCAPE.

absence *noun*

1. Failure to be present: *his constant absence from meetings.*
   Syns: absentation, nonappearance, nonattendance.
2. The condition of lacking a usual or needed amount: *an absence of reliable information.*
   Syns: dearth, default (*Obs.*), defect, deficiency, lack, miss (*Regional*), want.

absent *adjective*

1. Not present: *absent from her office.*
   Syns: away, gone, missing, wanting.
2. Deficient in a usual or needed amount: *junk foods in which nutrition is absent.*
   Syns: lacking, wanting.

3. ABSENT-MINDED.

absentation *noun* ABSENCE.

absent-minded *adjective*

So lost in thought as to be unaware of one's surroundings: *an absent-minded professor.*
Syns: absent, abstracted, bemused, distrait, faraway, inattentive, inconscient, preoccupied. —*Idioms* a million miles away, off in the clouds.

absolute *adjective*

1. Having and exercising complete political power and control: *an absolute ruler.*
   Syns: absolutist (*also* absolutistic), arbitrary, autarchic (*also* autarchical), autocratic, despotic, dictatorial, monocratic, totalitarian, tyrannical (*also* tyrannic), tyrannous.

2. PERFECT.

3. PURE.

4. UNCONDITIONAL.

5. UTTER[2].

absolutely *adverb*

1. Without question: *absolutely the finest painting in the gallery.*
   Syns: certainly, doubtless, positively.

2. REALLY.

3. YES.

absolution *noun* FORGIVENESS.

absolutism *noun*

1. A government in which a single leader or party exercises absolute control over all citizens and every aspect of their lives: *Absolutism prevailed before the coup d'état.*
   Syns: autarchy, autocracy, dictatorship, monocracy.
2. A political doctrine advocating the principle of absolute rule: *a strong belief in absolutism held by reactionaries.*
   Syns: authoritarianism, autocracy, despotism, dictatorship, totalitarianism.

absolutist *also* **absolutistic** *adjective* ABSOLUTE.

absolve *verb*

1. CLEAR.
2. EXCUSE.

absorb *verb*

1. To take in and incorporate, esp. mentally: *quickly absorbed new ideas.*
   Syns: assimilate, digest, imbibe, insorb, soak up.
2. To occupy the full attention of: *His medical practice absorbed him.*
   Syns: consume, engross, immerse, monopolize, preoccupy.

absorbed *adjective*

Having one's thoughts fully occupied: *absorbed in painting.*
Syns: consumed, deep, engrossed, immersed, intent, preoccupied, rapt, wrapped up.

absorbent *adjective*

Having a capacity or tendency to absorb or soak up: *an absorbent fabric.*
Syns: absorptive, assimilating, assimilative, bibulous.

absorbing *adjective*

Catching and holding the full attention: *an absorbing book.*
Syns: consuming, engrossing, enthralling, gripping.

absorption *noun*

1. The process of absorbing and incorporating, esp. mentally: *her absorption of her mentor's opinions.*
   Syns: assimilation, digestion.
2. Total occupation of the attention or of the mind: *complete absorption in the work at hand.*
   Syns: engrossment, enthrallment, preoccupation.

absorptive *adjective* ABSORBENT.

abstain *verb* REFRAIN.

abstemious *adjective* TEMPERATE.

abstentious *adjective* TEMPERATE.

abstinence *noun* TEMPERANCE.

abstinent *adjective* TEMPERATE.

abstract *adjective*

1, 2. THEORETICAL.

abstract *noun* SYNOPSIS.

abstract *verb*
1. DETACH.
2. REVIEW.

abstracted *adjective* ABSENT-MINDED.

abstraction *noun* TRANCE.

abstruse *adjective* DEEP.

absurd *adjective* FOOLISH.

absurdity *noun* FOOLISHNESS.

abundance *noun* PLENTY.

abundant *adjective*
1. GENEROUS.
2. HEAVY.

abuse *verb*
1. To hurt or injure by maltreatment: *abused their lungs by smoking heavily.*
   Syns: ill-use, maltreat, mishandle, mistreat, misuse.
2. To use wrongly and improperly: *Some employees abused their privileges and arrived at noon.*
   Syns: misapply, misappropriate, misemploy, mishandle, misuse, pervert.
3. To take advantage of unfairly: *abused her hospitality by staying too long.*
   Syns: exploit, impose (on *or* upon), presume (on *or* upon), use (*Informal*).
4. REVILE.

abuse *noun*
1. Wrong, often corrupt use: *the abuse of power.*
   Syns: abusion (*Obs.*), misapplication, misappropriation, misemployment, mishandling, misuse, perversion.
2. Physically harmful treatment: *Child abuse is a crime.*
   Syns: maltreatment, mistreatment, misusage.
3. VITUPERATION.

abusion *noun* ABUSE.

abusive *adjective*
Of, relating to, or characterized by verbal abuse: *abusive remarks.*
   Syns: contumelious, invective, obloquious, opprobrious, reviling, scurrilous, vituperative.

abut *verb* ADJOIN.

abutting *adjective* ADJOINING.

abysmal *adjective*
1. DEEP.
2. YAWNING.

abyssal *adjective* YAWNING.

academic *adjective*
1. PEDANTIC.
2. THEORETICAL.

accede *verb* ASSENT.

accelerate *verb* SPEED UP at **speed.**

accent *noun*
1. EMPHASIS.
2. TONE.

accent *verb* EMPHASIZE.

accented *adjective* EMPHATIC.

accentuate *verb* EMPHASIZE.

accentuated *adjective* EMPHATIC.

accentuation *noun* EMPHASIS.

accept *verb*
1. To receive (something given or offered) willingly and gladly: *going to Sweden to accept the award.*
   Syns: embrace, take up, welcome.
2. To allow admittance, as to a group: *was accepted for membership in the country club.*
   Syns: admit, receive, take in.
3. APPROVE.
4. ASSENT.
5. BELIEVE.
6. ENDURE.
7. RECEIVE.
8. UNDERSTAND.

acceptable *adjective*
1. Capable of being accepted: *an acceptable applicant; an acceptable gift.*
   Syns: admissible, unobjectionable.
2. Of moderately good quality but less than excellent: *an acceptable dissertation by a capable student.*
   Syns: adequate, average, common, decent, fair, fairish, goodish, indifferent, O.K. (*Informal*), passable, respectable, satisfactory, sufficient, tidy (*Informal*), tolerable.

acceptance *noun*
1. The act or process of accepting: *his acceptance of the suggestion.*
   Syns: acquiescence, agreement, assent, consent, nod, yes.
2. Favorable regard: *The theory slowly gained acceptance.*
   Syns: approbation, approval, favor.

acceptant *adjective* RECEPTIVE.

acceptation *noun* MEANING.

accepted *adjective*
Generally approved or agreed upon: *accepted behavior.*
   Syns: conventional, orthodox, received, sanctioned.

acception *noun* MEANING.

acceptive *adjective* RECEPTIVE.

access *noun*
1. ADMISSION.
2. OUTBURST.
3. SEIZURE.

accessible *adjective*
1. APPROACHABLE.
2. OPEN.

accession *noun* ADDITION.

accessory *noun* ATTACHMENT.

accessory *adjective* AUXILIARY.

accident *noun*
1. An unexpected and usu. undesirable event: *a traffic accident.*
   Syns: casualty, contretemps, misadventure, mischance, misfortune, mishap.
2. CHANCE.

accidental *adjective*
1. Occurring unexpectedly: *an accidental meeting.*
   Syns: casual, chance, contingent, fluky, fortuitous, inadvertent, odd.
2. Not part of the real or essential nature of a thing: *The secondary plot was accidental to the novel.*
   Syns: adscititious (*also* acititious), adventitious, incident (*Archaic*), incidental, supervenient.

acclaim *verb* PRAISE.

acclaim *noun* PRAISE.

acclimate *verb*
1. ADAPT.
2. HARDEN.

acclimation *noun* ADAPTATION.

acclimatization *noun* ADAPTATION.

acclimatize *verb*
1. ADAPT.
2. HARDEN.

acclivity *noun* ASCENT.

accolade *noun* DISTINCTION.

accommodate *verb*
1. To have the room or capacity for: *a room that can accommodate a large crowd.*
   Syns: contain, hold.
2. ADAPT.
3. HARBOR.
4. HARMONIZE.
5. OBLIGE.

accommodating *adjective* OBLIGING.

accommodation *noun* ADAPTATION.

accompaniment *noun*
1. One that accompanies another: *Unemployment is an accompaniment of recessions.*
   Syns: associate, attendant, companion, concomitant.
2. Something added to another for embellishment or completion: *Croutons are a good accompaniment to soup.*
   Syns: augmentation, complement, enhancement, enrichment.

accompany *verb*
To be with or go with (another): *Thunder accompanies lightning. Jack accompanied his niece to the première.*
   Syns: attend, companion, company (*Rare*), consort (*Obs.*), escort.
   —*Idiom* go hand in hand with.

accompanying *adjective*
Occurring in company with: *war and its accompanying horrors.*
   Syns: attendant, attending, coincident, concomitant, concurrent.

accomplish *verb*
To succeed in doing: *accomplished her objective and won the race.*
   Syns: achieve, attain, gain, reach, realize, score.

accomplished *adjective*
Very proficient as a result of practice and study: *an accomplished musician.*
   Syns: finished, practiced, skilled.

accomplishment *noun*
1. Something completed successfully: *Winning the race was a real accomplishment.*
   Syns: achievement, acquirement, acquisition, attainment, effort, feat.
2. ACT.

accord *verb*
1, 2. AGREE.
3. CONFER.
4. GRANT.

accord *noun*
1, 2. AGREEMENT.
3. HARMONY.
4. TREATY.
5. UNANIMITY.

accordance *noun*
1. AGREEMENT.
2. CONFERMENT.

accordant *adjective*
1. AGREEABLE.
2. SYMMETRICAL.

accost *verb*
To approach for the purpose of speech: *was accosted by petitioners outside the door of the chamber.*
   Syns: greet, hail, salute.

accouchement *noun* BIRTH.

account *noun*
1. A statement of causes or motives: *She was asked to give an account for her tardiness.*
   Syns: explanation, justification, rationale, rationalization, reason.
   —*Idiom* why and wherefore.
2. A precise list of fees or charges: *My account has been paid in full.*

Syns: bill¹, invoice, reckoning, statement, tab.

3. ESTEEM.

4. SCORE.

5. STORY.

6. USE.

7. WORTH.

account *verb* REGARD.

account for *verb*

To offer reasons for or a cause of: *He had grown up in several different countries, which accounted for his unplaceable foreign accent.*

Syns: explain, justify, rationalize.

accountable *adjective*

1. EXPLAINABLE.

2. LIABLE.

accouter *verb* FURNISH.

accouterments *noun* OUTFIT.

accredit *verb*

1. ATTRIBUTE.

2. AUTHORIZE.

accretion *noun* BUILD-UP.

accrue *verb* ACCUMULATE.

acculturate *verb* SOCIALIZE.

accumulate *verb*

To bring together so as to increase in mass or number: *accumulated a great deal of money in a short time. Snow began to accumulate on the pavement.*

Syns: accrue, agglomerate, aggregate, amass, collect¹, cumulate, garner, gather, hive, pile up, roll up.

accumulation *noun*

1. A quantity accumulated: *an accumulation of junk in the attic.*

Syns: acervation, agglomeration, aggregation, amassment, assemblage, collection, congeries, cumulation, cumulus, garner, mass.

2. BUILD-UP.

accumulative *adjective*

Increasing, as in force, by successive additions: *the accumulative unhealthy effect of smoking.*

Syns: additive, additory, cumulative.

accuracy *noun*

1. Freedom from error: *checked the results for accuracy.*

Syns: accurateness, correctness, exactitude, exactness, preciseness, precision, rightness.

2. VERACITY.

accurate *adjective*

1. Having no errors: *an accurate calculation of expenses.*

Syns: correct, errorless.

2. Conforming to fact: *an accurate description of the house.*

Syns: correct, exact, faithful, precise, proper, right, rigorous, true, veracious, veridical.

accurateness *noun* ACCURACY.

accurse *verb* CURSE.

accursed *adjective* DAMNED.

accusal *noun* ACCUSATION.

accusant *noun*

1. ACCUSER.

2. COMPLAINANT.

accusation *noun*

A charging of someone with a misdeed: *an accusation that she had committed murder.*

Syns: accusal, accuse (*Obs.*), charge, denouncement, denunciation, imputation, incrimination, indictment (*Law*).

accusative *adjective* ACCUSATORIAL.

accusatorial *also* **accusatory** *adjective*

Containing, relating to, or involving an accusation: *pointing an accusatorial finger at the defendant.*

Syns: accusative, accusive, denunciative, denunciatory, incriminating, incriminative.

accuse *verb*

To make an accusation against: *accused the senator of accepting a bribe.*

Syns: arraign, charge (with), denounce, denunciate, incriminate, inculpate, indict, tax.

accuse *noun* ACCUSATION.

accused *noun*

Law. A person against whom an action is brought: *The accused pleaded innocent.*

Syns: defendant (*Law*), respondent (*Law*).

accuser *noun*

One that accuses: *confronted his accuser in open court.*

Syns: accusant, denouncer, denunciator, incriminator, indictor (*also* indicter).

accusive *adjective* ACCUSATORIAL.

accustom *verb*

To make familiar through constant practice or use: *She accustomed her eyes to the bright sunlight.*

Syns: acquaint (*Obs.*), condition, familiarize (*Archaic*), habituate, inure, wont.

accustomable *adjective* CUSTOMARY.

accustomary *adjective* CUSTOMARY.

accustomed *adjective*

1. Familiar through repetition: *crickets making their accustomed noises.*

Syns: chronic, habitual, routine.
2. CUSTOMARY.
accustomed to *adjective*
In the habit of: *He was a bachelor and accustomed to doing things his own way.*
Syns: used to, wont to.
ace¹ *noun* DAMN.
ace² *noun*
1. EXPERT.
2. TRUMP.
acerb *adjective*
1. BITING.
2. BITTER.
3. SARCASTIC.
4. SOUR.
acerbic *adjective*
1. BITING.
2. BITTER.
3. SARCASTIC.
4. SOUR.
acerbity *noun* SARCASM.
acervation *noun* ACCUMULATION.
acetous also **acetose** *adjective* SOUR.
ache *verb*
1. DESIRE.
2. FEEL.
3. HURT.
ache *noun* PAIN.
Acheronian *adjective* GLOOMY.
Acherontic *adjective* GLOOMY.
achieve *verb* ACCOMPLISH.
achievement *noun*
1. ACCOMPLISHMENT.
2. FEAT.
aching *adjective* PAINFUL.
acicular *adjective* POINTED.
aciculate *adjective* POINTED.
acid *adjective*
1. BITING.
2. SOUR.
acidic *adjective* BITING.
acidulous *adjective* SOUR.
acknowledge *verb*
1. To recognize, often reluctantly, the reality or truth of: *He acknowledged his mistake.*
Syns: admit, allow, avow, concede, confess, fess up (*Slang*), grant, own (up).
2. To express recognition of: *acknowledged his duty toward his family.*
Syns: admit, recognize.
acknowledgment also
acknowledgement *noun*
1. The act of admitting to something: *her acknowledgment of her error.*
Syns: admission, avowal, confession.
2. RECOGNITION.

acme *noun* CLIMAX.
acquaint *verb*
1. To make known socially: *The couple got acquainted at a party.*
Syns: introduce, present², quaint² (*Archaic*).
2. ACCUSTOM.
3. INFORM.
acquaintance *noun*
1. Personal knowledge derived from participation or observation: *has a more than passing acquaintance with baroque music.*
Syns: experience, familiarity.
2. A person whom one knows casually: *met several acquaintances on the street.*
Syns: acquaintant (*Obs.*), friend.
acquaintant *noun* ACQUAINTANCE.
acquainted *adjective* FAMILIAR.
acquiesce *verb* ASSENT.
acquiescence *noun*
1. ACCEPTANCE.
2. OBEDIENCE.
acquiescent *adjective*
1. PASSIVE.
2. WILLING.
acquire *verb* GET.
acquirement *noun* ACCOMPLISHMENT.
acquisition *noun* ACCOMPLISHMENT.
acquisitive *adjective* GREEDY.
acquisitiveness *noun* GREED.
acquit *verb*
1. ACT.
2. CLEAR.
acres *noun* LAND.
acrid *adjective*
1. BITING.
2. BITTER.
acridity *noun* RESENTMENT.
acrimonious *adjective* RESENTFUL.
acrimony *noun* RESENTMENT.
act *noun*
1. The process of doing: *the act of thinking.*
Syn: action.
2. Something done: *an act of bravery.*
Syns: accomplishment, action, actus, deed, doing, thing.
3. *Informal.* A display of insincere behavior: *Her concern is just an act.*
Syns: acting, dissemblance, masquerade, play-acting, pose, pretense, sham, show, simulation.
4. LAW.
5. SKETCH.
act *verb*
1. To play the part of: *acted Juliet in summer stock.*

Syns: do, enact, impersonate, perform, play-act, portray, represent.
2. To conduct oneself in a specified way: *always acts like a lady.*
Syns: acquit, bear, behave, carry, comport, demean[1], deport, disport, do, quit.
3. To behave affectedly or insincerely: *is usually just acting when he shows interest.*
Syns: affect, assume, counterfeit, dissemble, fake, feign, play-act, pose, pretend, put on, sham, simulate.
4. FUNCTION.
5. STAGE.

act for *verb*
To perform the duties of another: *In his brother's absence he acted for him.*
Syns: function, officiate, serve.

act up *verb*
1. MALFUNCTION.
2. MISBEHAVE.

actify *verb* ACTIVATE.

acting *adjective* TEMPORARY.

acting *noun*
1. The art and occupation of an actor: *went into acting as a profession.*
Syns: dramatics, play-acting, playing, stage.
2. ACT.

action *noun*
1, 2. ACT.
3. COMBAT.
4. LAWSUIT.

action *verb* SUE.

actions *noun* BEHAVIOR.

activate *verb*
To arouse to action: *trying to activate his wish to learn.*
Syns: actify, activize, actuate, dynamize, energize, galvanize, stimulate.

active *adjective*
1. In action or full operation: *an active volcano; an active imagination; an active savings account.*
Syns: alive, functioning, going, live[2], operative, running, working.
2. NIMBLE.
3. VIGOROUS.

activity *noun*
Energetic physical action: *growing fat from too much food and too little activity.*
Syns: exercise, exercising, exertion.

activize *verb* ACTIVATE.

actor *noun*
1. A theatrical performer: *an actor on Broadway.*
Syns: player, thespian.
2. PARTICIPANT.

actual *adjective*
1. Occurring or existing in act or fact: *The actual world as opposed to the ideal.*
Syns: existent, existing, extant.
2. In agreement or correspondence with fact: *made an actual contribution to the investigation.*
Syns: indisputable, real, true, undeniable.
3. Based on fact: *an actual account of what happened.*
Syns: factual, hard, sure-enough.

actuality *noun*
1. The state or fact of having reality: *ideas true in possibility but not in actuality.*
Syns: being, existence.
2. Something that exists: *turned my dream into an actuality.*
Syns: materiality, reality.
3. The quality of being factual: *The story was in actuality not true.*
Syns: fact, factuality, factualness, reality.

actualization *noun* EFFECT.

actualize *verb* REALIZE.

actually *adverb*
1. In point of fact: *She said she was working when actually she was reading a novel.*
Syns: genuinely, indeed, really.
2. NOW.
3. REALLY.

actuate *verb*
1. ACTIVATE.
2. DRIVE.
3. USE.

actus *noun* ACT.

acumen *noun* DISCERNMENT.

acuminate *verb* SHARPEN.

acuminate *adjective* POINTED.

acumination *noun* POINT.

acuminous *adjective* POINTED.

acute *adjective*
1. Possessing or displaying perceptions of great accuracy and sensitivity: *an acute observer of the passing scene.*
Syns: keen[1], perceptive, sensitive, sharp.
2. CRITICAL.
3. HIGH.
4. INCISIVE.
5. POINTED.
6. SHARP.

adage *noun* PROVERB.

adamant *adjective* STUBBORN.

adamantine *adjective* STUBBORN.

adapt *verb*
To make or become suitable to a particular situation or use: *The family quickly adapted to country life.*
Syns: acclimate, acclimatize, accommodate, adjust, conform, fashion, fit, reconcile (to *or* with), square, suit, tailor, tailor-make.

adaptable *adjective*
Capable of adapting or being adapted: *An adaptable person can live happily almost anywhere.*
Syns: adaptative, adaptive, adjustable, elastic, flexible, plastic, pliable, pliant, supple.

adaptation also **adaption** *noun*
1. The condition of being made suitable to an end: *the adaptation of the novel as a film.*
Syns: accommodation, adjustment, conformation.
2. Adjustment to a changing environment: *made a quick adaptation to the new job.*
Syns: acclimation, acclimatization.

adaptative *adjective* ADAPTABLE.
adaption *noun* SEE **adaptation**.
adaptive *adjective* ADAPTABLE.
adcititious *adjective* SEE **adscititious**.

add *verb*
1. To join so as to form a larger or more comprehensive entity: *added a new wing to the library.*
Syns: annex, append, plus.
2. To combine (figures) to form a sum: *adding the debit column in the ledger.*
Syns: cast, figure, foot (up), sum (up), summate, tally, tot² (up), total, totalize, tote² (up).

add up to *verb*
1. AMOUNT.
2. MEAN¹.

added *adjective* ADDITIONAL.

addition *noun*
1. The act or process of adding: *the waiter's addition of the price of the dinner and the tax.*
Syns: summation, totalization.
2. Something tending to augment something else: *The young lawyer proved a real addition to the staff.*
Syns: accession, augmentation.

additional *adjective*
1. Being an addition: *What additional information do you need?*
Syns: added, extra, fresh, further, more, new, other.
2. FURTHER.

additionally *adverb*
In addition: *Additionally he pleased us by the excellence of his work.*
Syns: also, besides, further, furthermore, item, more, still.
—*Idioms* as well, to boot.

additive *adjective*
1. Involving addition: *additive, not subtractive.*
Syns: additory, plus.
2. ACCUMULATIVE.

additory *adjective*
1. ACCUMULATIVE.
2. ADDITIVE.

addle *verb* CONFUSE.
addled *adjective* CONFUSED.

address *verb*
1. To direct speech to: *addressed her softly.*
Syns: speak (to), talk (to).
2. To talk to (an audience) formally: *addressed the meeting.*
Syns: bespeak (*Archaic*), lecture, prelect (*also* praelect), speak (to).
3. To bring an appeal or request to the attention of: *addressed the mayor for a solution to the problem.*
Syns: appeal (to), apply (to), approach, petition, sue.
4. To mark (a written communication) with its destination: *addressed the envelope.*
Syns: direct, superscribe.
5. APPLY.
6. COURT.
7. SEND.

address *noun*
1. A written inscription on a deliverable item giving its destination: *put the wrong address on the package.*
Syns: direction (*Archaic*), superscription.
2. BEARING.
3. DEXTERITY.
4. SPEECH.
5. TACT.

addresses *noun* COURTSHIP.
adduce *verb* PRESENT².
adept *adjective* EXPERT.
adept *noun* EXPERT.
adeptness *noun* ABILITY.
adequacy *noun* ENOUGH.
adequate *adjective*
1. ACCEPTABLE.
2. SUFFICIENT.
adhere *verb* BOND.
adherence *noun* BOND.
adherent *noun* FOLLOWER.

adhesion *noun* BOND.
adhesive *adjective* STICKY.
adieu *noun* PARTING.
ad interim *adjective* TEMPORARY.
adjacent *adjective* ADJOINING.
adjoin *verb*
To be contiguous or next to: *a lot that adjoins ours.*
   Syns: abut (on, upon, *or* against), border (on *or* upon), bound[2], butt[2] (on), join (*Informal*), juxtapose, meet[1], neighbor, touch, verge (on *or* upon).
adjoining *adjective*
Sharing a common boundary: *took adjoining rooms in the hotel.*
   Syns: abutting, adjacent, approximal, bordering, conterminous, contiguous, joined (*Informal*), juxtaposed, meeting, neighboring, next, touching.
adjourn *verb* DEFER[1].
adjournment *noun* DELAY.
adjudge *verb* JUDGE.
adjudicate *verb* JUDGE.
adjunct *noun* ATTACHMENT.
adjust *verb*
1. To alter (parts of a device) for proper functioning: *adjust the valves.*
   Syns: attune, fix, regulate, set[1], tune (up).
2. ADAPT.
adjustable *adjective* ADAPTABLE.
adjustment *noun* ADAPTATION.
adjutant *noun* ASSISTANT.
adjuvant *adjective* AUXILIARY.
ad-lib *adjective* EXTEMPORANEOUS.
  ad-lib *verb* IMPROVISE.
  ad-lib *noun* IMPROVISATION.
admeasure *verb* ALLOT.
administer *verb*
1. To have charge of (the affairs of others): *administer a colony.*
   Syns: administrate, direct, govern, head, manage, run, superintend.
2. To oversee the provision or execution of: *administer justice.*
   Syns: administrate, carry out, execute.
3. To provide as a remedy: *administer a sedative.*
   Syns: dispense, give (out).
4. GIVE.
administerial *adjective* ADMINISTRATIVE.
administrable *adjective* GOVERNABLE.
administrant *noun* EXECUTIVE.
administrate *verb*
1, 2. ADMINISTER.

administration *noun*
1. Authoritative control over the affairs of others: *was responsible for the administration of the province.*
   Syns: direction, government, management, superintendence.
2. The giving of a medication, esp. by prescribed dosage: *insisted on the administration of an antibiotic.*
   Syns: application, dispensation, dispensing.
administrational *adjective* ADMINISTRATIVE.
administrative *adjective*
Of, for, or relating to administration or administrators: *an administrative secretary.*
   Syns: administerial, administrational, executive, managerial, ministerial.
administrator *noun* EXECUTIVE.
admirable *adjective*
Deserving admiration: *She has some really admirable qualities.*
   Syns: commendable, estimable, laudable, meritable, meritorious, praiseworthy, worthy.
admiration *noun*
1. ESTEEM.
2. WONDER.
admire *verb*
1. To regard with great pleasure or approval: *admired the view.*
   Syns: appreciate, enjoy, relish.
2. To have a high opinion of: *admired him for his honesty.*
   Syns: consider, esteem, honor, regard, respect, value. —*Idiom* look up to.
admirer *noun*
1. One who ardently admires: *an admirer of Shakespeare's plays.*
   Syns: devotee, fan[2] (*Informal*), fancier, lover.
2. BEAU.
admissible *adjective*
1. ACCEPTABLE.
2. PERMISSIBLE.
admission *noun*
1. The state of being allowed entry: *her admission to college.*
   Syns: admittance, entrance[1], immission (*Archaic*), ingress (*also* ingression), introduction, intromission.
2. The right to enter or make use of: *It was months before he was allowed admission into the club's inner circle.*
   Syns: access, admittance, entrance[1],

entrée, entry, ingress (*also*
ingression).
3. ACKNOWLEDGMENT.

admit *verb*
1. To serve as a means of entrance for:
This ticket admits one adult.
Syns: immit (*Archaic*), intromit, let
in.
2. ACCEPT.
3, 4. ACKNOWLEDGE.
5. PERMIT.

admittance *noun*
1, 2. ADMISSION.

admix *verb* MIX.

admixture *noun* MIXTURE.

admonish *verb* CALL DOWN at **call**.

admonishing *adjective* CAUTIONARY.

admonishment *noun*
1. REBUKE.
2. WARNING.

admonition *noun*
1. REBUKE.
2. WARNING.

admonitory *adjective* CAUTIONARY.

ado *noun* FUSS.

adopt *verb*
1. To take, as another's idea, and make
one's own: *adopted a competitor's
sales techniques.*
Syns: embrace, espouse, take on (*or
up*).
2. PASS.

adopted *adjective* ASSUMED.

adoption *noun*
A ready taking up of something: *their
adoption of the latest fashions.*
Syns: embracement, embracing,
espousal.

adorable *adjective*
Easy to love: *an adorable baby.*
Syns: lovable, sweet.

adorant *adjective* REVERENT.

adoration *noun*
1. The act of adoring, esp. reverently:
prayed with solemn adoration.
Syns: idolization, reverence,
veneration, worship.
2. Deep and ardent affection: *his
adoration of his young wife.*
Syns: devotion, fancy (*Obs.*), love.

adore *verb*
1. To regard with great awe and
devotion: *a saint adored for his
kindness.*
Syns: idolize, revere, reverence,
venerate, worship.
2. To feel deep, devoted love for: *adored
her husband.*

Syns: affect[2] (*Archaic*), affection[1],
love, worship.
3. *Informal.* To like or enjoy
enthusiastically, often excessively:
She adores skiing.
Syns: delight in, dote on (*or upon*),
eat up (*Slang*), groove on (*Slang*),
love.

adoring *adjective* REVERENT.

adorn *verb*
1. To furnish with decorations: *a gown
adorned with lace.*
Syns: bedeck, deck (out), decorate,
dress (up), embellish, garnish,
ornament, trim.
2. GRACE.

adornment *noun*
Something that adorns: *jewels and other
adornments.*
Syns: decoration, embellishment,
garnishment, garniture, ornament,
ornamentation, trim, trimming.

adroit *adjective*
1. ARTFUL.
2. DEXTEROUS.
3. NEAT.

adroitness *noun* DEXTERITY.

adscititious *also* **adcititious** *adjective*
ACCIDENTAL.

adulate *verb* FLATTER.

adulation *noun* FLATTERY.

adulator *noun* SYCOPHANT.

adult *adjective* MATURE.

adulterant *noun* CONTAMINANT.

adulterate *verb*
To make impure or inferior by
deceptively adding foreign substances:
adulterated coffee.
Syns: debase, doctor (up), dope, load,
sophisticate.

adulterated *adjective* IMPURE.

adulteration *noun* CONTAMINATION.

adulterator *noun* CONTAMINANT.

adumbrate *verb*
1. To give an indication of something in
advance: *events that adumbrated later
developments.*
Syns: foreshadow, prefigure, presage.
2. DRAFT.
3. OBSCURE.
4. PREDICT.
5. SHADE.

adumbration *noun* SHADE.

advance *verb*
1. To cause to move forward or upward,
as toward a goal: *advance a worthy
cause.*

Syns: forward, foster, further, promote.
2. COME.
3. LEND.
4. PRESENT².
5. PROMOTE.
6. RISE.

advance *noun*
1. Forward movement: *recent advances in science; the advance of technology.*
  Syns: advancement, furtherance, headway, march¹, ongoing, progress, progression.
2. INCREASE.

advance *adjective*
Going before: *got advance warning of the storm's approach.*
  Syns: antecedent, anterior, precedent, preceding, prior.

advanced *adjective*
1. Ahead of current trends or customs: *had advanced ideas.*
  Syns: forward, precocious, progressive.
2. OLD.

advancement *noun*
1. A progression upward in rank: *a quick advancement in her career.*
  Syns: elevation, jump, promotion, upgrading.
2. ADVANCE.

advances *noun*
Preliminary actions intended to elicit a favorable response: *rejected her advances out of hand.*
  Syns: approach(es), overture(s).

advantage *noun*
1. A factor conducive to superiority and success: *Give the slow starters a 30-second advantage.*
  Syns: allowance, handicap, head start, odds, start, vantage.
2. A dominating position, as in a conflict: *had the advantage in the argument.*
  Syns: better¹, bulge (*Slang*), draw, drop, edge, forehand, jump, superiority, vantage. —*Idioms* inside track, upper hand.
3. Something beneficial: *gave the children many advantages.*
  Syns: benefit, blessing, boon¹, favor, gain, profit.
4. INTEREST.
5. USE.
6. WELFARE.

advantage *verb* BENEFIT.

advantageous *adjective*
1. BENEFICIAL.
2. PROFITABLE.

advent *noun*
1. APPROACH.
2. ARRIVAL.

adventitious *adjective* ACCIDENTAL.

adventure *noun*
An exciting, often hazardous undertaking: *a mountain-climbing adventure.*
  Syns: emprise (*also* emprize), enterprise, venture.

adventure *verb*
1. HAZARD.
2. RISK.

adventurer *noun*
1. One who engages in exciting, risky pursuits: *explorers and other adventurers.*
  Syns: daredevil, venturer.
2. MERCENARY.
3. SPECULATOR.

adventuresome *adjective*
ADVENTUROUS.

adventurous *adjective*
1. Taking or willing to take risks: *Adventurous pioneers settled the American West.*
  Syns: adventuresome, audacious, enterprising, venturesome, venturous.
2. DANGEROUS.

adventurousness *noun* DARING.

adversary *noun* OPPONENT.

adverse *adjective*
1. OPPOSING.
2. UNFAVORABLE.

adversity *noun* MISFORTUNE.

advert *verb* REFER.

advertent *adjective* ATTENTIVE.

advertise *also* **advertize** *verb*
1. To make known vigorously the positive features of (a product): *advertise a new camera.*
  Syns: ballyhoo (*Informal*), build up, cry (up), plug (*Informal*), promote, publicize, push (*Slang*), talk up.
2. To make (information) generally known: *The girl advertised her engagement by wearing a diamond ring.*
  Syns: blaze² (around), blazon, broadcast, bruit (about), disseminate, noise (about *or* abroad), promulgate. —*Idioms* spread far and wide, spread the word.
3. ANNOUNCE.

advertising *noun*
The act or profession of promoting something, as a product: *Advertising can be a lucrative occupation.*
  Syns: promotion, publicity.

advertize *verb* SEE **advertise**.
advice *noun*
An opinion as to a decision or course of action: *hopes to get sound advice before purchasing the house.*
    Syns: advisement, counsel, recommendation.
advice(s) *noun* NEWS.
advisable *adjective*
Worth doing, esp. for practical reasons: *Checking the data is advisable.*
    Syns: counselable (*also* counsellable), expedient, recommendable, well².
advise *verb*
1. To give recommendations to (someone) about a decision or course of action: *My attorney advised me to sue.*
    Syns: counsel, recommend.
2. CONFER.
3. INFORM.
advised *adjective*
1. Resulting from deliberation and careful thought: *a badly advised decision.*
    Syns: calculated, considered, deliberated, studied, studious (*Rare*), thought-out, weighed.
2. INFORMED.
advisement *noun*
1. A careful considering of a matter: *The judge took the case under advisement.*
    Syns: calculation, consideration, deliberation, lucubration (*Archaic*), study.
2. ADVICE.
adviser *also* **advisor** *noun*
One who advises another, esp. officially or professionally: *a financial adviser.*
    Syns: consultant, counsel, counselor (*also* counsellor), mentor.
advisory *adjective*
Giving advice: *the college advisory board.*
    Syns: consultative, consultatory, consulting.
advocate *verb* SUPPORT.
aegis *noun* PATRONAGE.
aeon *noun* SEE **eon**.
aerate *verb* AIR.
aerial *adjective*
1. AIRY.
2. FILMY.
3. LOFTY.
aerosphere *noun* AIR.
aery *adjective* FILMY.
aesthetic *or* **esthetic** *adjective*
TASTEFUL.

afeard *also* **afeared** *adjective*
AFRAID.
affability *noun* AMIABILITY.
affable *adjective*
1. AMIABLE.
2. GRACIOUS.
affair *noun*
1. BUSINESS.
2. LOVE.
3. MATTER.
4. PARTY.
affect¹ *verb*
To evoke a usu. strong mental or emotional response from: *a play that deeply affects its audience.*
    Syns: get (to) (*Informal*), impact, impress, influence, move, strike, sway, touch.
affect² *verb*
1. ADORE.
2. ASSUME.
affectation *noun*
Artificial behavior adopted to impress others: *That accent is mere affectation.*
    Syns: affectedness, airs, lug(s), mannerism, pretense.
affected¹ *adjective*
Emotionally aroused: *affected by a powerful novel.*
    Syns: impressed, inspired, moved, stirred, struck, swayed, touched.
affected² *adjective*
1. Artificially genteel: *put on an affected British accent.*
    Syns: artificial, la-di-da (*also* la-de-da) (*Informal*), lardy-dardy (*Slang*), mannered, precious, pretentious.
2. ARTIFICIAL.
3. CONCERNED.
affectedness *noun* AFFECTATION.
affecting *adjective*
Exciting a deep, usu. somber response: *an affecting climax to the story.*
    Syns: impressive, moving, poignant, stirring, touching.
affection¹ *noun*
1. ATTACHMENT.
2. EMOTION.
affection *verb* ADORE.
affection² *noun*
1. DISEASE.
2. QUALITY.
affectionate *adjective*
Feeling and expressing affection: *an affectionate parent.*
    Syns: affectionated (*Obs.*), affectuous (*Obs.*), doting, fond, loving.

affectionated *adjective*
AFFECTIONATE.

affective *adjective* EMOTIONAL.

affectivity *noun* EMOTION.

affectuous *adjective* AFFECTIONATE.

afferent *adjective* SENSORY.

affianced *adjective* ENGAGED.

affianced *noun* INTENDED.

affiliate *verb* ASSOCIATE.

affiliate *noun*
1. ASSOCIATE.
2. SUBSIDIARY.

affiliation *noun* ASSOCIATION.

affinity *noun* LIKENESS.

affirm *verb*
1. ASSERT.
2. CONFIRM.

affirmation *noun*
1. ASSERTION.
2. CONFIRMATION.

affirmative *adjective*
1. FAVORABLE.
2. POSITIVE.

affirmatory *adjective* FAVORABLE.

affix *verb*
1. ATTACH.
2. FIX.

afflation *noun*
1, 2. INSPIRATION.

afflatus *noun* INSPIRATION.

afflict *verb*
To bring great harm or suffering to:
afflicted with painful chronic ailments.
   Syns: agonize, curse, excruciate,
   plague, rack, scourge, smite, strike,
   torment, torture.

afflicted *adjective* MISERABLE.

affliction *noun*
1. BURDEN.
2. CURSE.
3. DISTRESS.

afflictive *adjective*
1. BITTER.
2. PAINFUL.

affluent *adjective* RICH.

afford *verb* OFFER.

affray *noun* BRAWL.

affright *verb* FRIGHTEN.

affright *noun* FEAR.

affront *verb* INSULT.

affront *noun* INDIGNITY.

afield *adverb* WRONG.

afire *adjective* BLAZING.

aflame *adjective* BLAZING.

à fond *adverb*
1, 2. COMPLETELY.

aforehand *adverb* EARLY.

aforetime *adverb* EARLIER.

afraid *adjective*
Filled with fear or terror: *was afraid of snakes.*
   Syns: afeard (*also* afeared)
   (*Regional*), aghast, apprehensive,
   ascared (*Chiefly Regional*), fearful,
   fearsome, frightened, petrified, scared.

afresh *adverb* NEW.

after *adjective*
1. BACK.
2. LATER.

after *adverb* LATER.

afterlife *noun* IMMORTALITY.

aftermath *noun* EFFECT.

afterward *also* **afterwards** *adverb*
LATER.

afterwhile *adverb* LATER.

again *adverb* NEW.

age *noun*
1. A particular time notable for its
   distinctive characteristics: *the
   Edwardian Age.*
   Syns: day(s), epoch, era, period,
   time(s).
2. *Informal.* A long time: *haven't seen
   you for ages.*
   Syns: eon (*also* aeon), eternity, long¹.
   —Idioms blue moon, dog's age,
   donkey's years, forever and a day,
   forever and ever, month of Sundays.
3. Old age: *the weakness and frailty of
   age.*
   Syns: agedness, caducity, elderliness,
   senectitude, senescence, years.

age *verb*
1. To grow old: *He is aging fast.*
   Syns: get along (*or* on), olden,
   senesce.
2. MATURE.

aged *adjective*
1. Brought to full flavor and richness by
   aging: *aged cheese.*
   Syns: matured, mellow, ripe, ripened.
2, 3. OLD.

agedness *noun* AGE.

ageless *adjective*
Existing unchanged forever: *the ageless
themes of love and hate.*
   Syns: dateless, eternal, eterne
   (*Archaic*), timeless.

agency *noun* MEANS.

agenda *noun* PROGRAM.

agent *noun* MEANS.

age-old *adjective* OLD.

agglomerate *verb* ACCUMULATE.

agglomeration *noun* ACCUMULATION.

aggrandize *verb*
1. EXALT.
2. INCREASE.

aggrandizement *noun* EXALTATION.

aggravate *verb*
1. ANNOY.
2. INTENSIFY.

aggravating *adjective* VEXATIOUS.

aggravation *noun*
1, 2. ANNOYANCE.
3. BOTHER.

aggregate *verb*
1. ACCUMULATE.
2. AMOUNT.

aggregate *noun*
1. TOTAL.
2. WHOLE.

aggregation *noun* ACCUMULATION.

aggress *verb* ATTACK.

aggression *noun*
1. *Psychoanal.* Hostile behavior: *could not control his aggression.*
   Syns: aggressiveness (*also* aggressivity), belligerence, belligerency, combativeness, contentiousness, hostility.
2. ATTACK.

aggressive *adjective*
1. Inclined to act in a hostile way: *an aggressive person, always ready to argue.*
   Syns: belligerent, combative, contentious, militant, offensive, pushy (*Informal*).
2. Marked by boldness and assertiveness: *an aggressive executive.*
   Syns: assertive, assertory, go-getting, hard-hitting.

aggressiveness *also* **aggressivity** *noun* AGGRESSION.

aggressor *noun*
One who starts a hostile action: *fought the foreign aggressors.*
   Syns: assailant, assailer, attacker.

aggrieve *verb*
1. DISTRESS.
2. WRONG.

aggroup *verb* GROUP.

aghast *adjective*
1. AFRAID.
2. SHOCKED.

agile *adjective* NIMBLE.

agility *also* **agileness** *noun*
The quality or state of being agile: *fielded all questions with agility.*
   Syns: dexterity, dexterousness, nimbleness, quickness.

agitate *verb*
1. To cause to move to and fro violently: *land and sea agitated by tremors.*
   Syns: churn, convulse, rock², shake.
2. To impair or destroy the composure of: *a mind agitated by grief.*
   Syns: bother, discombobulate (*Slang*), discompose, disquiet, disturb, flurry, fluster, perturb, rock², ruffle, shake (up), toss, unsettle, upset.
3. DISTURB.

agitation *noun*
1. The condition of being physically agitated: *a ship tossed by the agitation of the sea.*
   Syns: commotion, convulsion, turbulence, upset.
2. A state of discomposure: *almost incoherent from his agitation.*
   Syns: disquiet, dither, flap (*Slang*), flurry, fluster, flutter, lather (*Slang*), perturbation, stew (*Informal*), tumult, turmoil, upset.

agitator *noun*
One who agitates, esp. politically: *The British considered Samuel Adams an agitator.*
   Syns: fomenter, instigator.

agnate *adjective* RELATED.

agog *adjective* EAGER.

agonize *verb*
1. AFFLICT.
2. WRITHE.

agonizing *adjective* TORMENTING.

agony *noun* DISTRESS.

agree *verb*
1. To come to an understanding or to terms: *agreed on all major points.*
   Syns: accord, coincide, concord, concur, get together, harmonize.
2. To be compatible or in correspondence: *The copy agrees with the original.*
   Syns: accord, check out, comport, conform (to), consist, correspond, fit, gee (*Informal*), harmonize, jibe (*Informal*), match, quadrate, rhyme (*also* rime), square, tally.
3. ASSENT.

agreeability *noun* AMIABILITY.

agreeable *adjective*
1. To one's liking: *an agreeable change in your attitude.*
   Syns: favorable, good, gratifying, nice, pleasant, pleasing, pleasurable, welcome.

2. In keeping with one's needs or expectations: *a theory that was agreeable to current ideas.*
Syns: accordant (with), compatible, conformable (to), congenial, congruous, consistent, consonant (with *or* to), correspondent, corresponding.
3. AMIABLE.
4. WILLING.

agreeableness *noun* AMIABILITY.

agreed *adverb* YES.

agreement *noun*
1. The act or state of agreeing or conforming: *agreement between forecasts and sales.*
Syns: accordance, conformance, conformation, conformity, correspondence, tallying.
2. Harmonious mutual understanding: *We are in agreement on the issue.*
Syns: accord, chime, concord, concordance, concurrence, consonance, harmony, rapport, tune.
3. An act or state of agreeing between parties regarding a course of action: *an agreement with the union on overtime.*
Syns: accord, arrangement, bargain, deal (*Informal*), pact, understanding.
4. A legally binding arrangement between parties: *an author-publisher agreement.*
Syns: bond, compact[2], contract, convention, covenant, pact.
5. ACCEPTANCE.
6. TREATY.

agrestal *also* **agrestial** *adjective*
WILD.

agrestic *also* **agrestical** *adjective*
COUNTRY.

ahead *adverb* EARLY.

aid *verb* HELP.

aid *noun*
1. HELP.
2. HELPER.

aidant *adjective* HELPFUL.

aide *noun* ASSISTANT.

aidful *adjective* BENEFICIAL.

aiding *adjective*
1. AUXILIARY.
2. HELPFUL.

aidless *adjective* HELPLESS.

ail *verb* WORRY.

ailing *adjective* SICKLY.

ailment *noun*
1. DISEASE.
2. INDISPOSITION.

aim *verb*
1. To move (a weapon, blow, etc.) in the direction of someone or something: *aimed the gun at the bird.*
Syns: cast, direct, head, lay[1] (*Mil.*), level, point, present[2], set[1], train, turn, zero in.
2. To strive toward a goal: *aimed at a better education.*
Syns: aspire, seek. —*Idiom* set one's sights on.
3. INTEND.

aim *noun*
1. AMBITION.
2. INTENTION.
3. THRUST.

aimless *adjective*
Without aim, purpose, or intent: *an aimless conversation.*
Syns: desultory, objectless, purposeless.

air *noun*
1. The gaseous mixture enveloping the earth: *air polluted with smoke.*
Syns: aerosphere, atmosphere.
2. The celestial regions as seen from the earth: *Clouds filled the air.*
Syns: firmament, heaven(s), sky, welkin (*Archaic*).
3. A general impression produced by a predominant quality or characteristic: *exhibited an air of unease.*
Syns: ambiance (*also* ambience), atmosphere, aura, feel, feeling, mood, smell, tone.
4. BEARING.
5. MELODY.
6. WIND[1].

air *verb*
1. To expose to circulating air: *air a room.*
Syns: aerate, ventilate, wind[1].
2. To utter publicly: *air my opinions.*
Syns: blow off (*Slang*), come out with, express, put, state, vent, ventilate.

airless *adjective*
1. Oppressive due to a lack of fresh air: *a hot, airless room.*
Syns: breathless, close[1], stifling, stuffy.
2. Marked by an absence of circulating air: *couldn't run on airless days.*
Syns: breathless, breezeless, still, windless.

airs *noun* AFFECTATION.

airy *adjective*
1. Of or relating to air: *airy white clouds.*

Syns: aerial, atmospheric, pneumatic.
2. Exposed to or characterized by the presence of freely circulating air or wind: *an airy hillside.*
Syns: blowy, breezy, gusty, windy.
3. Displaying light-hearted nonchalance: *had an airy disregard for all rules.*
Syns: breezy, buoyant, corky (*Informal*), debonair (*also* debonaire), jaunty. —*Idiom* free and easy.
4. FILMY.
5. LOFTY.
akin *adjective* RELATED.
alabaster *also* **alabastrine** *adjective* FAIR.
à la mode *adjective* FASHIONABLE.
alarm *noun*
1. A signal that warns of imminent danger: *The troops responded to the alarm.*
Syns: alarum (*Archaic*), alert, tocsin, warning.
2. FEAR.
alarm *verb*
1. FRIGHTEN.
2. WARN.
alarming *adjective* FEARFUL.
alarmist *noun*
One who needlessly alarms others: *alarmists predicting global war.*
Syns: scaremonger, terrorist.
alarum *noun* ALARM.
albescent *adjective* FAIR.
alcoholic *adjective* HARD.
alert *adjective*
1. Vigilantly attentive: *alert to danger.*
Syns: observant, open-eyed, vigilant, wakeful, wary, watchful, wide-awake.
2. CLEVER.
alert *noun* ALARM.
alert *verb* WARN.
alertness *noun* AWARENESS.
alibi *noun* EXCUSE.
alien *adjective*
1, 2. FOREIGN.
alien *noun* FOREIGNER.
alien *verb* TRANSFER.
alienate *verb*
1. ESTRANGE.
2. TRANSFER.
alienation *noun*
1. ESTRANGEMENT.
2. INSANITY.
alight[1] *verb* LAND
alight on (or **upon**) *verb* COME ACROSS at **come**.
alight[2] *adjective* BLAZING.
alight on (or **upon**) *verb* SEE **alight**[1].

align *verb*
1. ALLY.
2. LINE.
aligned *adjective* ALLIED.
alike *adjective* LIKE[2].
alikeness *noun* LIKENESS.
aliment *noun* FOOD.
alimentary *adjective* NUTRITIVE.
alimentation *noun* LIVING.
alimony *noun* LIVING.
alive *adjective*
1. Marked by or exhibiting life: *The patient is still alive.*
Syns: animate, animated, live[2], living, vital.
2. Having existence or life: *the best chess player alive.*
Syns: around (*Informal*), existent, existing, extant, living.
3. Full of animation and activity: *a street alive with pedestrians.*
Syns: abounding, overflowing, replete, rife, teeming.
4. ACTIVE.
5. AWARE.
all *adjective* WHOLE.
all *noun* WHOLE.
all *adverb* PURELY.
all-around *adjective* SEE **all-round.**
allay *verb*
1. CALM.
2. RELIEVE.
allayment *noun* RELIEF.
allegation *noun* CLAIM.
allege *verb*
1. CLAIM.
2. PRESENT[2].
allegiance *noun* FIDELITY.
allegiant *adjective* FAITHFUL.
alleviate *verb* RELIEVE.
alleviation *noun* RELIEF.
alliance *noun*
1. An association, esp. of nations for a common cause: *a Western alliance against the Warsaw Pact countries.*
Syns: Anschluss (*German*), coalition, confederacy, confederation, federation, league, union.
2. ASSOCIATION.
allied *adjective*
1. Closely connected by or as if by a treaty: *Libya and its allied countries.*
Syns: aligned, confederated, federated, unified.
2. RELATED.
all in *adjective* EXHAUSTED.
all-inclusive *adjective* GENERAL.
allness *noun* COMPLETENESS.

allocate *verb*
1. ALLOT.
2. APPROPRIATE.
allocation *noun* ALLOTMENT.
allocution *noun* SPEECH.
allot *verb*
To set aside or distribute as a share: *Each sailor was allotted four ounces of grog.*
    Syns: admeasure, allocate, allow, apportion, assign, give, lot, mete (out), portion.
allotment *noun*
That which is allotted: *a gas allotment of 50 gallons a month.*
    Syns: allocation, allowance, cut (*Informal*), divvy (*Slang*), lot, measure, part, portion, quantum, quota, ration, share.
all-out *adjective*
1. THOROUGH.
2. UTTER².
all-overs *noun* JITTERS.
allow *verb*
1. ACKNOWLEDGE.
2. ALLOT.
3, 4, 5. PERMIT.
allowable *adjective* PERMISSIBLE.
allowance *noun*
1. ADVANTAGE.
2. ALLOTMENT.
3. CONCESSION.
4. PERMISSION.
alloyed *adjective* IMPURE.
all right *adverb* YES.
all-round also **all-around** *adjective*
1. GENERAL.
2. VERSATILE.
allude *verb* REFER.
allure *verb*
1. ATTRACT.
2. TEMPT.
    allure *noun* ATTRACTION.
allurement *noun*
1. ATTRACTION.
2. LURE.
alluring *adjective*
1. ATTRACTIVE.
2. SEDUCTIVE.
allusive *adjective* SUGGESTIVE.
alluvion *noun* FLOOD.
ally *verb*
1. To be formally associated, as by treaty: *That nation has allied itself with the Arabs.*
    Syns: align, confederate, federate, league.
2. ASSOCIATE.
    ally *noun*

1. One nation associated with another in a common cause: *England and America were allies against the Nazis.*
    Syns: coalitionist, confederate, leaguer.
2. ASSOCIATE.
almost *adverb* APPROXIMATELY.
alms *noun* DONATION.
almsman *noun* BEGGAR.
almswoman *noun* BEGGAR.
alone *adjective*
1. Lacking the company of others: *was alone after her husband's death.*
    Syns: companionless, lonely, lonesome, solitary, unaccompanied.
2. SOLITARY.
3. UNIQUE.
alone *adverb*
1. Without the presence or aid of another: *I'll finish the job alone.*
    Syns: single-handedly, solely, solo.
    —*Idioms* all by oneself, all by one's lonesome.
2. SOLELY.
aloneness *noun*
The quality or state of being alone: *Aloneness often engenders depression.*
    Syns: isolation, lonelihood, loneliness, loneness, solitude.
aloof *adjective*
1. COOL.
2. DETACHED.
aloofness *noun* DETACHMENT.
already *adverb*
1. EARLIER.
2. EVEN¹.
also *adverb* ADDITIONALLY.
alter *verb* CHANGE.
alterable *adjective* CHANGEABLE.
alterant *noun* CATALYST.
alteration *noun*
1. CHANGE.
2. CONVERSION.
altercation *noun* ARGUMENT.
alterity *noun* DIFFERENCE.
alternate *verb* ROTATE.
    alternate *noun* SUBSTITUTE.
alternation *noun* ROTATION.
alternative *noun* CHOICE.
altitude *noun* ELEVATION.
altitudinous *adjective* HIGH.
alto *adjective* LOW.
altogether *adverb*
1. COMPLETELY.
2. PURELY.
altruism *noun* BENEVOLENCE.
altruistic *adjective* BENEVOLENT.

amalgam *noun* MIXTURE.

amalgamate *verb* MIX.

amalgamation *noun* MIXTURE.

amaranthine *adjective* ENDLESS.

amaroidal *adjective* BITTER.

amass *verb* ACCUMULATE.

amassment *noun*
1. ACCUMULATION.
2. BUILD-UP.

amateur *noun*
One lacking professional skill and ease in a particular pursuit: *a foreign policy jeopardized by the mistakes of amateurs.*
   Syns: abecedarian (*also* abecedary), dabbler, dilettante, nonprofessional, smatterer, tyro, uninitiate.

amateurish *adjective*
Lacking the required professional skill: *an amateurish painting.*
   Syns: dilettante, dilettantish, dilettantist, jackleg (*Informal*), unskilled, unskillful.

amative *adjective* EROTIC.

amatory *adjective* EROTIC.

amaze *verb* SURPRISE.

  amaze *noun* WONDER.

amazement *noun* WONDER.

amazing *adjective* FABULOUS.

ambiance *also* **ambience** *noun*
1. AIR.
2. ENVIRONMENT.

ambidextrous *adjective*
1. INSINCERE.
2. VERSATILE.

ambience *noun* SEE **ambiance**.

ambiguity *noun*
1. An expression or term liable to more than one interpretation: *a political speech filled with ambiguities.*
   Syns: amphibology, double entendre, equivocality, equivocation, equivoque (*also* equivoke), tergiversation.
2. EQUIVOCATION.
3. VAGUENESS.

ambiguous *adjective*
1. Liable to more than one interpretation: *an ambiguous remark by the governor.*
   Syns: amphibological, cloudy, equivocal, nebulous, obscure, sibylline, uncertain, unclear, unexplicit, unintelligible, vague.
2. Not affording certainty: *an ambiguous position.*
   Syns: borderline, chancy, clouded, doubtable, doubtful, dubious, dubitable, equivocal, iffy (*Informal*), indecisive, indeterminate, open,

problematical (*also* problematic), questionable, uncertain, unclear, undecided, unsettled, unsure.
   —*Idioms* at issue, in doubt, in question, up in the air.

ambiguousness *noun* VAGUENESS.

ambit *noun*
1. CIRCUMFERENCE.
2. RANGE.

ambition *noun*
1. A strong desire to achieve something: *had an ambition to be a lawyer.*
   Syns: ambitiousness, aspiration.
2. Something strongly desired: *achieved his one ambition.*
   Syns: aim, goal, mark, object[1], objective.
3. The wish, power, and ability to begin and follow through with a plan or task: *a woman of great energy and ambition.*
   Syns: drive, enterprise, gumption (*Informal*), initiative, push (*Informal*).

ambitious *adjective*
Full of ambition: *an ambitious young artist.*
   Syns: aspiring, emulous.

ambitiousness *noun* AMBITION.

amble *verb* STROLL.

  amble *noun* WALK.

ambrosial *adjective* DELICIOUS.

ambulate *verb* WALK.

ambuscade *verb*
1. AMBUSH.
2. LAY FOR at **lay**[1].

ambush *verb*
1. To attack suddenly and without warning: *highwaymen who hid in thickets and ambushed passing travelers.*
   Syns: ambuscade, bushwhack, surprise, waylay.
2. LAY FOR at **lay**[1].

ameliorate *verb* IMPROVE.

amelioration *noun*
1. IMPROVEMENT.
2. PROGRESS.

amenable *adjective*
1. OBEDIENT.
2. RECEPTIVE.

amend *verb*
1. CORRECT.
2. IMPROVE.
3. REVISE.

amendment *noun*
1. IMPROVEMENT.
2. REVISION.

amends *noun* COMPENSATION.

amenities *noun*
Courteous acts that contribute to smoothness and ease in dealings and social relationships: *Even when he was angry, he observed the amenities.*
Syns: civilities, courtesies, pleasantries, proprieties.

amenity *noun*
1. Anything that increases physical comfort: *a sunny apartment with all the amenities.*
Syns: comfort, convenience, facility.
2. AMIABILITY.

ament *noun* FOOL.

amerce *verb* FINE².

amercement *noun* FINE².

amiability *noun*
The quality of being pleasant and friendly: *negotiations carried on in amiability; a woman of surprising amiability.*
Syns: affability, agreeability, agreeableness, amenity, amiableness, cordiality, friendliness, geniality, pleasantness.

amiable *adjective*
1. Pleasant and friendly: *met on the street and had an amiable conversation; found her to be an amiable companion.*
Syns: affable, agreeable, complaisant, cordial, easy, easygoing, genial, good-natured, good-tempered.
2. FRIENDLY.

amiableness *noun* AMIABILITY.

amicable *adjective*
1. FRIENDLY.
2. HARMONIOUS.

amical *adjective* HARMONIOUS.

amigo *noun* FRIEND.

amiss *adjective*
Not in accordance with what is usual or expected: *We knew something was amiss when he failed to keep the appointment.*
Syns: awry, wrong.

amiss *adverb* WRONG.

amnesiac *adjective* FORGETFUL.

amnesty *noun* FORGIVENESS.

amok *adjective* SEE **amuck.**

amorist *noun* GALLANT.

amorous *adjective*
1, 2. EROTIC.

amorousness *noun* LOVE.

amorphous *adjective* SHAPELESS.

amount *noun*
1. IMPORT.
2. QUANTITY.
3. TOTAL.

amount *verb*
1. To come to in number or quantity: *The total purchase amounts to ten dollars.*
Syns: add up to, aggregate, number, reach, run, total.
2. To be equivalent or tantamount: *criticism that amounted to rejection.*
Syns: constitute, correspond, equal.
—*Idiom* have all the earmarks.

amour *noun*
1, 2. LOVE.

amour-propre *noun*
1. EGOTISM.
2. PRIDE.

amphibological *adjective* AMBIGUOUS.

amphibology *noun* AMBIGUITY.

ample *adjective*
1. BROAD.
2. FULL.
3. GENEROUS.
4. ROOMY.

amplification *noun* EXPANSION.

amplify *verb*
1. ELABORATE.
2. ELEVATE.
3. INCREASE.

amplitude *noun*
1. BULK.
2, 3. SIZE.

amuck also **amok** *adjective* RUNAWAY.

amulet *noun* CHARM.

amuse *verb*
To occupy in an agreeable or pleasing way: *I amused myself with a game of solitaire.*
Syns: distract, divert, entertain, recreate.

amusement *noun*
1. The condition of being amused: *They perform music for their own amusement.*
Syns: distraction, diversion, entertainment, recreation.
2. Something, esp. a performance or show, designed to entertain: *A puppeteer provided amusement for the party.*
Syns: distraction, diversion, entertainment, recreation.

amusing *adjective*
1. Entertaining or pleasing: *an amusing game of bridge.*
Syns: distracting, diverting.
2. Arousing laughter: *a very amusing joke.*

Syns: comic, comical, droll, funny, humorous, killing (*Slang*), laughable, risible, zany.

analogize *verb* LIKEN.

analogon *noun* PARALLEL.

analogous *adjective* LIKE².

analogue *noun* PARALLEL.

analogy *noun* LIKENESS.

analysis *noun*

1. The separation of a whole into its parts for study: *a harmonic analysis of a Bach fugue.*
    Syns: breakdown, dissection, resolution.
2. A close or systematic study: *made an analysis of the election to determine why the victor had won.*
    Syns: examination, inspection, investigation, review, survey.

analytic also **analytical** *adjective* LOGICAL.

analyze *verb*

1. To separate into parts for study: *analyzed the ore and found it contained iron.*
    Syns: anatomize, break down, dissect, resolve.
2. To study closely or systematically: *analyzing Shakespeare's plays to find recurring motifs.*
    Syns: examine, inspect, investigate.

Ananias *noun* LIAR.

anarchy *noun* DISORDER.

anathema *noun*

1. CURSE.
2. HATE.

anathematize *verb* CURSE.

anatomize *verb* ANALYZE.

ancestor *noun*

1. A person from whom one is descended: *My ancestors were farmers.*
    Syns: antecedent, ascendant, father, forebear, forefather, progenitor.
2. A forerunner: *The harpsichord is the ancestor of the modern piano.*
    Syns: antecedent, precursor, predecessor, prototype.

ancestral *adjective*
Of or from one's ancestors: *lived in the ancestral home.*
    Syns: hereditary, inherited, patrimonial.

ancestry *noun*
One's ancestors or their character: *a young man of Italian-German ancestry.*
    Syns: birth, blood, bloodline, descent, extraction, family, genealogy, line,

lineage, origin, parentage, pedigree, seed.

anchor *verb* FASTEN.

ancient *adjective*

1. EARLY.
2. HIGH.
3. OLD.

ancient *noun* SENIOR.

ancillary *adjective* AUXILIARY.

anecdote *noun* YARN.

anemic *adjective*

1. PALE.
2. SICKLY.

anesthetic *adjective* INSENSITIVE.

anew *adverb* NEW.

anfractuous *adjective*

1. INDIRECT.
2. WINDING.

angel *noun*

1. INNOCENT.
2. PATRON.
3. SPONSOR.

angelic also **angelical** *adjective* INNOCENT.

anger *noun*
A strong feeling of displeasure or hostility: *Strong criticism often evokes anger.*
    Syns: indignation, irateness, ire.

anger *verb*

1. To cause to feel or show anger: *His condescending attitude angered her.*
    Syns: burn up (*Informal*), enrage, incense¹, infuriate, ire, madden, provoke, steam up (*Informal*).
    —*Idioms* make one hot under the collar, make one's blood boil, put one's back up, put one's dander up.
2. To be or become angry: *She angered at the slightest hint of criticism.*
    Syns: blow up (*Informal*), boil (over) (*Slang*), bristle, burn (up), explode, flare up, fume, rage, seethe. —*Idioms* blow a fuse, blow one's stack (*or* top), breathe fire, fly off the handle, get hot under the collar, get one's dander up, hit the ceiling, lose one's temper, see red.

angle *verb*

1. BEND.
2. BIAS.
3. HINT.

angle *noun*

1. LIGHT¹.
2. POINT OF VIEW.
3. WRINKLE².

angry *adjective*
Feeling or showing anger: *an angry*

*customer; an angry expression on his
face.*
    Syns: choleric, enraged, furious,
incensed, indignant, irate, ireful, mad,
maddened, seething, sore (*Informal*),
wrathful. —*Idioms* fit to be tied,
foaming at the mouth, hot under the
collar, in a rage (*or* temper).

angst *noun* ANXIETY.
anguish *noun* DISTRESS.
anguish *verb* DISTRESS.
angular *adjective* THIN.
anhydrous *adjective* DRY.
anima *noun* SPIRIT.
animal *adjective* PHYSICAL.
animalism *noun* PHYSICALITY.
animality *noun* PHYSICALITY.
animalize *verb* CORRUPT.
animate *verb*
1. ELATE.
2. ENCOURAGE.
3. FIRE.
4. LIGHT¹.
5. QUICKEN.
  animate *adjective*
1. ALIVE.
2. LIVELY.
animated *adjective*
1. ALIVE.
2. LIVELY.
animating *adjective* STIMULATING.
animation *noun*
1. ELATION.
2. ENERGY.
3. SPIRIT.
animosity *noun* ENMITY.
animus *noun*
1. ENMITY.
2. SPIRIT.
annals *noun* HISTORY.
annex *verb* ADD.
annihilate *verb*
1. To destroy all traces of: *A cholera
epidemic annihilated most of the
population.*
    Syns: abolish, blot out, clear,
eradicate, erase, exterminate,
extinguish, extirpate, liquidate,
obliterate, remove, root out, rub out,
snuff out, stamp out, uproot, wipe
out. —*Idioms* do away with, put an
end to.
2. To kill savagely and indiscriminately:
*The night raiders annihilated the
settlers.*
    Syns: butcher, decimate, massacre,
slaughter.
3, 4. ABOLISH.
5. OVERWHELM.

annihilation *noun*
1. Utter destruction: *the Nazis'
attempted annihilation of the Jewish
people.*
    Syns: eradication, extermination,
extinction, extinguishment,
extirpation, liquidation, obliteration.
2. ABOLITION.
annotation *noun* COMMENTARY.
announce *verb*
1. To bring to public notice: *The
management announced that Horowitz
would play a concert.*
    Syns: advertise (*also* advertize),
annunciate, broadcast, declare,
proclaim, promulgate, publish.
2. USHER IN at usher.
announcement *noun*
1. The act of announcing: *The press
listened attentively during the
President's announcement.*
    Syns: annunciation, broadcast,
declaration, proclamation,
promulgation, pronouncement,
publication.
2. A public statement: *an announcement
of a cease-fire.*
    Syns: declaration, edict, manifesto,
notice, proclamation, pronouncement.
annoy *verb*
1. To trouble the nerves or peace of
mind of, esp. by repeated vexations:
*The constant requests for a donation
finally began to annoy her.*
    Syns: aggravate (*Informal*), bother,
bug (*Slang*), chafe, disturb,
exasperate, fret, gall², get, irk, irritate,
nettle, peeve, provoke, ruffle, thorn,
vex. —*Idioms* get in one's hair, get on
one's nerves, get under one's skin.
2. To disturb by repeated attacks: *small
children annoying the cat by pulling its
tail.*
    Syns: bedevil, beleaguer, beset,
harass, harry, pester, plague, tease,
worry.
annoyance *noun*
1. Something that annoys: *Headaches
are a relatively minor annoyance.*
    Syns: aggravation (*Informal*),
besetment, bother, botheration,
botherment, irritant, irritation,
nuisance, peeve, plague.
2. The act of annoying: *used tactics of
annoyance to force the tenants to move.*
    Syns: bothering, harassment,
pestering, provocation, vexation.
3. The feeling of being annoyed: *He
won, much to his rival's annoyance.*

Syns: aggravation (*Informal*), bother, botheration, exasperation, irritation, vexation.

annoying *adjective* VEXATIOUS.

annul *verb*
1. ABOLISH.
2. CANCEL.

annular *adjective* ROUND.

annulment *noun* ABOLITION.

annunciate *verb* ANNOUNCE.

annunciation *noun* ANNOUNCEMENT.

anomalism *noun* ABNORMALITY.

anomalous *adjective* ABNORMAL.

anomaly *noun* ABNORMALITY.

anonymity *noun* OBSCURITY.

anonymous *adjective*
Having an unknown name or author: *anonymous authors; an anonymous letter.*
Syns: nameless, unnamed, unsigned.

anschauung *noun* INSTINCT.

Anschluss *noun* ALLIANCE.

answer *noun*
1. Something spoken or written as a return to a question, demand, etc.: *gave him a nasty answer.*
Syns: comeback (*Slang*), rejoinder, reply, response, retort.
2. Something worked out to explain, resolve, or provide a method for dealing with and settling a problem: *found the answer to the crossword puzzle.*
Syns: result, solution.

answer *verb*
1. To speak or act in response to: *answering a question; answered his letter. Answer when you're spoken to!*
Syns: rejoin, reply, respond, retort, return.
2. SATISFY.
3. SERVE.

answerable *adjective* LIABLE.

Antaean *adjective* GIANT.

antagonism *noun*
1. ANTIPATHY.
2. ENMITY.
3. OPPOSITION.

antagonist *noun* OPPONENT.

antagonistic *adjective* OPPOSING.

ante *noun* BET.

antecede *verb* PRECEDE.

antecedence *noun* PRECEDENCE.

antecedent *noun*
1, 2. ANCESTOR.
3. CAUSE.
4. PRECEDENT.

antecedent *adjective*
1. ADVANCE.
2. PAST.

antedate *verb* PRECEDE.

antediluvian *also* **antediluvial** *adjective*
1. EARLY.
2. OLD.

antediluvian *noun* SQUARE.

anterior *adjective*
1. ADVANCE.
2. PAST.

anthropoid *adjective* MANLIKE.

anthropomorphic *adjective* MANLIKE.

anthropomorphous *adjective* MANLIKE.

antic *noun* PRANK.

antic *adjective* FANTASTIC.

anticipant *adjective* EXPECTANT.

anticipate *verb*
1. EXPECT.
2. FORESEE.

anticipated *adjective* DUE.

anticipation *noun*
1. The condition of looking forward to something, esp. with eagerness: *a look of happy anticipation on the children's faces.*
Syns: expectancy (*also* expectance), expectation.
2. EXPECTATION.

anticipative *adjective* EXPECTANT.

anticipatory *adjective* EXPECTANT.

antidote *noun* REMEDY.

antipathetic *adjective*
1. Arousing deep-seated dislike: *an authoritarian person, in every way antipathetic.*
Syns: aversive, hateful, repellent, uncongenial, unsympathetic.
2. CONTRARY.
3. OPPOSING.

antipathy *noun*
1. A state of mind brought on by something that is antipathetic: *felt a real antipathy toward violent behavior.*
Syns: antagonism, aversion, hostility, repellence (*also* repellency).
2. ENMITY.

antipodal *adjective* OPPOSITE.

antipode *noun* OPPOSITE.

antipodean *adjective* OPPOSITE.

antipole *noun* OPPOSITE.

antiquated *adjective* OLD-FASHIONED.

antique *adjective*
1. OLD.
2. OLD-FASHIONED.

antiseptic *adjective* CLEAN.

antithesis *noun*
1. OPPOSITE.
2. OPPOSITION.

antithetical also **antithetic** *adjective*
1. CONTRARY.
2. OPPOSITE.
antonymous *adjective* CONTRARY.
anxiety *noun*
Anxious concern: *feeling anxiety about the outcome of the trial.*
   Syns: angst, anxiousness, care, disquiet, disquietude, distress, perturbation, unease, uneasiness, worry.
anxious *adjective*
1. In a state of uneasiness: *anxious about her high fever and pain.*
   Syns: concerned, disquieted, distressed, disturbed, nervous, troubled, uneasy, unsettled, worried.
2. EAGER.
anxiousness *noun* ANXIETY.
A-one *adjective* EXCELLENT.
apace *adverb* FAST.
apanage *noun* SEE **appanage**.
apart *adjective*
1. SOLITARY.
2. UNIQUE.
apart *adverb* SEPARATELY.
apartheid *noun* SEGREGATION.
apathetic *adjective*
Without emotion or interest: *renters apathetic about rising property taxes.*
   Syns: disinterested, impassive, indifferent, insensible, lethargic, listless, phlegmatic, stolid, unconcerned, uninterested, unresponsive.
apathy *noun*
Lack of emotion or interest: *looked at the excitement around him with complete apathy.*
   Syns: disinterest, disregard, impassivity, indifference, insensibility, lassitude, lethargy, listlessness, phlegm, stolidity, unconcern, unresponsiveness.
ape *verb* IMITATE.
ape *noun* THUG.
aperture *noun* HOLE.
apery *noun* MIMICRY.
apex *noun*
1. CLIMAX.
2. HEIGHT.
3. POINT.
aphonic *adjective* DUMB.
aphorism *noun* PROVERB.
aphoristic *adjective* PITHY.
aphrodisia *noun* DESIRE.
aphrodisiac *adjective* EROTIC.
aping *noun* MIMICRY.

apish *adjective* IMITATIVE.
aplomb *noun*
1. BALANCE.
2. CONFIDENCE.
apocalypse *noun* REVELATION.
apocalyptic also **apocalyptical** *adjective* FATEFUL.
apogee *noun* CLIMAX.
apologetic *adjective*
Expressing or inclined to express an apology: *an apologetic smile; an apologetic letter.*
   Syns: contrite, penitent, regretful, repentant, sorry.
apologetic *noun* APOLOGY.
apologia *noun* APOLOGY.
apology *noun*
1. A statement of acknowledgment expressing regret or asking pardon: *made an apology for being late.*
   Syns: excuse, regrets. —*Idiom* mea culpa.
2. A statement that justifies or defends past actions, policies, etc.: *The report was nothing more than an apology for capital punishment.*
   Syns: apologetic, apologia, defense, justification.
apostasy *noun* DEFECTION.
apostate *noun* DEFECTOR.
apostatize *verb* DEFECT.
apostle *noun* MISSIONARY.
apostolic *adjective* MISSIONARY.
apotheosis *noun* EXALTATION.
apotheosize *verb* EXALT.
appall *verb* DISMAY.
appalled *adjective* SHOCKED.
appalling *adjective*
1. FEARFUL.
2. TERRIBLE.
appanage also **apanage** *noun* BIRTHRIGHT.
apparatus *noun*
1. DEVICE.
2. OUTFIT.
apparel *noun* DRESS.
apparel *verb* DRESS.
apparent *adjective*
1. Readily seen, perceived, or understood: *exploded in anger for no apparent reason; a danger that was apparent at once; antagonism that was apparent to everyone.*
   Syns: clear, clear-cut, crystal-clear, distinct, evident, manifest, noticeable, obvious, patent, plain, visible. —*Idioms* in plain sight, in view.

2. Appearing as such but not necessarily so: *His apparent gruffness hid a deep kindness.*
   Syns: ostensible, outward, seeming, semblant, superficial.

apparently *adverb*
On the surface: *apparently calm but inwardly seething with rage.*
   Syns: evidently, seemingly. —*Idioms* on the face of it, to all outward appearances.

apparition *noun* GHOST.

appeal *noun*
   1. An earnest or urgent request: *made a frantic appeal for help.*
   Syns: beseechment, entreaty, imploration, plea, prayer, suit, supplication.
   2. An application to a higher authority, as for sanction or a decision: *about to make an appeal to the supreme court to review the case.*
   Syns: petition, suit.
   3. ATTRACTION.

appeal *verb*
   1. To make an earnest or urgent request: *appealed to passers-by to chase the mugger; appealed for help.*
   Syns: beg, beseech, conjure, entreat, implore, plead with, pray, supplicate.
   2. To make application to a higher authority: *appealing to the grievance committee to settle the problem.*
   Syns: apply, petition, sue.
   3. ADDRESS.
   4. ATTRACT.

appealer *noun*
One that asks a higher authority for something, as a favor or redress: *the latest appealer of the court's decision.*
   Syns: appellant, petitioner, suitor.

appealing *adjective* ATTRACTIVE.

appear *verb*
   1. To come into view: *A ship appeared on the horizon.*
   Syns: emerge, issue, loom, materialize, show, show up (*Informal*). —*Idioms* make (*or* put in) an appearance, meet (*or* strike) the eye.
   2. To have the appearance of: *He appeared to be sleeping, but he was wide awake.*
   Syns: look, seem, sound¹. —*Idiom* strike one as (being).
   3. DAWN.

appearance *noun*
   1. The act of coming into view: *the*

surprise appearance of an unexpected witness.
   Syns: emergence, materialization.
   2. The way something or someone looks: *Her elegant appearance showed good taste.*
   Syns: aspect, look(s), mien.
   3. ARRIVAL.
   4. IMAGE.

appease *verb*
   1. PACIFY.
   2. SATISFY.

appellant *noun* APPEALER.

appellation *noun* NAME.

appellative *noun* NAME.

append *verb* ADD.

appendage *noun* BRANCH.

appertain *verb*
   1. APPLY.
   2. BELONG.

appetence also **appetency** *noun*
   1. APPETITE.
   2. DESIRE.

appetent *adjective* EAGER.

appetite *noun*
   1. A desire for food or drink: *Though he has a healthy appetite, he is no glutton.*
   Syns: appetence (*also* appetency), hunger, stomach, taste, thirst.
   2. DESIRE.
   3. TASTE.

appetition *noun* DESIRE.

applaud *verb*
   1. To express approval, esp. by clapping: *The audience applauded the cast.*
   Syns: cheer, clap (for), root². —*Idiom* give someone a hand.
   2. PRAISE.

applause *noun*
   1. Approval expressed by clapping: *a round of applause at the end of the concert.*
   Syns: hand (*Informal*), ovation, plaudit.
   2. PRAISE.

apple-polish *verb* FAWN.

apple-polisher *noun* SYCOPHANT.

applesauce *noun* NONSENSE.

appliance *noun* DEVICE.

applicable *adjective* RELEVANT.

applicant *noun*
A person who applies for or seeks a job or position: *a job applicant; an applicant for admission to college.*
   Syns: aspirant, candidate, hopeful, petitioner, seeker.

application *noun*
1. A specific use: *Geometry has many practical applications.*
Syns: employment, implementation, operation, utilization.
2. A document used in applying, as for a job: *You'll have to fill out an application.*
Syn: form.
3. ADMINISTRATION.
4. DILIGENCE.
5. DUTY.
6. EXERCISE.
7. RELEVANCE.

apply *verb*
1. To devote (oneself or one's efforts): *Fred applied himself to his studies.*
Syns: address, bend, buckle, concentrate, dedicate, devote, direct, focus (on), give, turn.
2. To be pertinent: *This rule does not apply to you.*
Syns: appertain, bear on (*or upon*), concern, involve, pertain, refer, relate.
—*Idioms* have a bearing on, have to do with.
3. To ask for employment, acceptance, or admission: *applying for a job; applied to college.*
Syns: petition, put in (*Informal*), sign up.
4. ADDRESS.
5. APPEAL.
6. RESORT TO at **resort**.
7. USE.

appoint *verb*
1. To select for an office or position: *The board of directors appointed Martin president. Jane appointed herself my conscience.*
Syns: designate, make, name, nominate, tap¹ (*Slang*).
2. FURNISH.

appointee *noun*
A person who is appointed to an office or position: *a new consular appointee.*
Syns: designee, nominee.

appointment *noun*
1. The act of appointing to an office or position: *The appointment of a Chief Justice is an important decision.*
Syns: designation, naming, nomination.
2. ENGAGEMENT.
3. FURNISHING.
4. POSITION.

apportion *verb* ALLOT.

apportionment *noun* DISTRIBUTION.

apposite *adjective* RELEVANT.

appraisal *noun* ESTIMATE.

appraise *verb* ESTIMATE.

appraisement *noun* ESTIMATE.

appreciable *adjective* PERCEPTIBLE.

appreciate *verb*
1. To recognize the worth, quality, importance, etc., of: *Many art lovers appreciate Renoir.*
Syns: cherish, enjoy, esteem, go for (*Informal*), prize, relish, respect, savor, treasure, value.
2. ADMIRE.

appreciation *noun*
1. Recognition of worth, quality, importance, etc.: *a great appreciation of music and sculpture.*
Syns: admiration, awareness, comprehension, enjoyment, liking, receptivity, responsiveness, taste.
2. A being grateful: *expressed their appreciation with a small present.*
Syns: gratefulness, gratitude, thankfulness, thanks.
3. ESTEEM.

appreciative *adjective* GRATEFUL.

apprehend *verb*
1. ARREST.
2. FEAR.
3. KNOW.
4. PERCEIVE.
5. UNDERSTAND.

apprehension *noun*
1. ARREST.
2. GRASP.

apprehensive *adjective* AFRAID.

apprise also **apprize** *verb* INFORM.

approach *verb*
1. To come near in space or time: *approached the house; approaching three o'clock.*
Syn: near. —*Idioms* come close to, draw near to.
2. To make overtures to, esp. for the purpose of achieving a desired result: *approached the boss about a raise.*
Syns: address, sound¹.
3. ADDRESS.
4. RIVAL.
5. START.

approach *noun*
1. The act or fact of coming near: *The dog's barking announced the approach of the guests. Cold winds mark the approach of winter.*
Syns: advent, coming, convergence, imminence, nearness.
2. A method used in dealing with

something: *a new approach to solving the fuel shortage.*
Syns: attack, course, line, modus operandi (*Latin*), plan, procedure, tack, technique.

approachable *adjective*
Easily approached: *Despite his fame, he remained approachable and sympathetic.*
Syns: accessible, friendly, responsive, warm, welcoming.

approach(es) *noun* ADVANCES.

approaching *adjective* COMING.

approbate *verb* APPROVE.

approbation *noun* ACCEPTANCE.

approbatory *adjective*
COMPLIMENTARY.

appropriate *adjective*
1. Suitable for a particular person, condition, occasion, or place: *wore appropriate clothes to the wedding; music appropriate for that drama; an appropriate choice of words.*
Syns: apt, befitting, correct, felicitous, fit, fitting, happy, meet², proper, right, suited.
2. CONVENIENT.
3. JUST.

appropriate *verb*
1. To set aside for a specified purpose: *Congress appropriated money for public education.*
Syns: allocate, designate, earmark.
2. ASSUME.

appropriation *noun*
1. GRANT.
2. USURPATION.

approval *noun*
1. Official acceptance or permission: *receiving approval for the formation of a fact-finding committee.*
Syns: authorization, concurrence, consent, endorsement, O.K. (*Informal*), sanction.
2. ACCEPTANCE.
3. CONFIRMATION.

approve *verb*
1. To be favorably disposed toward: *They do not approve of gambling.*
Syns: accept, approbate, countenance, favor, go for, hold with, subscribe to. —*Idioms* take kindly to, think well (*or* highly) of.
2. CONFIRM.
3. PASS.

approximal *adjective* ADJOINING.

approximate *verb*
1. ESTIMATE.
2. RIVAL.

approximately *adverb*
Near to in quantity or amount: *Approximately 40 people came to the meeting.*
Syns: about, almost, nearly, roughly.

approximation *noun* ESTIMATE.

appulse *noun* COLLISION.

apropos *adjective* RELEVANT.

apt *adjective*
1. APPROPRIATE.
2. INCLINED.

aptitude *noun* TALENT.

aptness *noun* TALENT.

aquake *adjective* TREMULOUS.

aquiver *adjective* TREMULOUS.

arbiter *noun* JUDGE.

arbitrary *adjective*
1. Determined or marked by whim or caprice rather than reason: *The use of the color red to mean "stop" is arbitrary.*
Syns: capricious, chance, random, whimsical, willful.
2. Based on individual judgment or discretion: *made an arbitrary choice between two equally good alternatives.*
Syns: discretionary, judgmental, personal, subjective.
3. ABSOLUTE.

arbitrate *verb* JUDGE.

arbitrator *noun* JUDGE.

Arcadian *adjective* COUNTRY.

arcane *adjective* MYSTERIOUS.

arced *adjective* BENT.

archaic *adjective* OLD-FASHIONED.

arched *adjective* BENT.

archetypal *adjective* TYPICAL.

archetype *noun* ORIGINAL.

archetypic also **archetypical** *adjective*
TYPICAL.

archfiend *noun* FIEND.

architect *noun* ORIGINATOR.

arciform *adjective* BENT.

arctic *adjective* FRIGID.

ardent *adjective*
1. EAGER.
2. ENTHUSIASTIC.
3. HOT.
4. PASSIONATE.

ardor *noun*
1. ENTHUSIASM.
2. PASSION.

ardorless *adjective* FRIGID.

arduous *adjective*
1. BURDENSOME.
2. STEEP¹.

arduously *adverb* HARD.

area *noun*
1. A part of the earth's surface: *an agricultural area; an urban area.*
   Syns: belt, locality, neighborhood, quarter, region, tract. —*Idiom* neck of the woods.
2. A sphere of activity, study, or interest: *Comparative literature is his area.*
   Syns: arena, bag (*Slang*), department, domain, field, orbit, province, realm, scene (*Slang*), subject, terrain, territory, world.
3. LOCALITY.
4. NEIGHBORHOOD.

arena *noun* AREA.

argot *noun* DIALECT.

arguable *adjective* DEBATABLE.

argue *verb*
1. To put forth reasons for or against, often excitedly: *The senator argued in favor of the amendment. We argued the pros and cons of gas rationing.*
   Syns: contend, debate, dispute, moot.
2. To engage in a quarrel: *constantly argues with his wife.*
   Syns: bicker, contend, dispute, fight, hassle, quarrel, quibble, squabble, tiff, wrangle. —*Idioms* bandy (*or* have) words, cross swords, have it out, join (*or* take) issue, lock horns.
3. INDICATE.

argue into *verb* PERSUADE.

argument *noun*
1. A discussion, often heated, in which a difference of opinion is expressed: *regularly had arguments about money.*
   Syns: altercation, clash, contention, controversy, debate, disagreement, dispute, fight, hassle, polemic, quarrel, rhubarb (*Slang*), row², run-in, spat, squabble, tangle (*Informal*), tiff, unpleasantness, words, wrangle.
2. A course of reasoning: *The argument is that conservation will prevent shortages.*
   Syns: case, point, reason.
3. REASON.
4. SUBJECT.

argumentation *noun*
The presentation of an argument: *an attorney skilled in argumentation.*
   Syns: debate, disputation, forensics.

argumentative *adjective*
Given to arguing: *an argumentative old curmudgeon.*
   Syns: combative, contentious, disputatious, eristic, litigious, polemical, quarrelsome, scrappy.

argute *adjective* HIGH.

aria *noun* MELODY.

arid *adjective*
1. BORING.
2, 3. DRY.

ariose *adjective* MELODIOUS.

arise *verb*
1. BEGIN.
2. DAWN.
3. GET UP at get.
4. RISE.
5. STEM.

aristarch *noun* CRITIC.

aristocracy *noun* SOCIETY.

aristocratic *adjective* NOBLE.

aristoi *noun* SOCIETY.

arithmetic *noun* FIGURES.

arm *noun*
1, 2. BRANCH.

arm *verb* LOAD.

armistice *noun* TRUCE.

army *noun* CROWD.

aroma *noun*
1. FLAVOR.
2. FRAGRANCE.
3. SMELL.

aromatic *adjective* FRAGRANT.

aromatize *verb* SCENT.

around *adverb*
1. BACK.
2. BACKWARD.
3. THROUGH.

around *adjective* ALIVE.

around-the-clock *adjective* SEE round-the-clock.

arouse *verb*
1. To induce or elicit (a reaction or emotion): *Her magic tricks aroused wonder in the children.*
   Syns: awaken, foment, kindle, raise, rouse, stir¹ (up), waken.
2. INSPIRE.
3. PROVOKE.
4. WAKE.

arraign *verb* ACCUSE.

arrange *verb*
1. To put into a deliberate order: *arranging figures in sequential order.*
   Syns: array, assort, classify, dispose, distribute, group, marshal, order, organize, range, rank¹, sort, systematize.
2. To plan the details or arrangements of: *arranging a formal dinner for 12.*
   Syns: lay out, prepare, schedule, work out.
3. To come to an agreement about: *eventually arranged the terms of the cease-fire.*

Syns: conclude, fix, negotiate, set[1], settle.
4. HARMONIZE.
5. SETTLE.

arrangement *noun*
1. A way or condition of being arranged: *Every year we change the arrangement of the furniture.*
   Syns: disposal, disposition, distribution, formation, grouping, layout, line-up (*also* lineup), order, ordering, sequence.
2. AGREEMENT.

arrangements *noun*
Plans made in preparation for some undertaking: *We're making arrangements for our trip to Nassau.*
Syns: preparations, provisions.

arrant *adjective*
1. FLAGRANT.
2. SHAMELESS.
3. UTTER[2].

array *verb*
1. ARRANGE.
2. DRESS.

array *noun*
1. DISPLAY.
2. GROUP.

arrear or **arrears** *noun* DEBT.

arrearage *noun*
1, 2. DEBT.

arrears *noun* SEE **arrear.**

arrest *verb*
1. To take into custody as a prisoner: *got arrested for automobile theft.*
   Syns: apprehend, bag (*Slang*), bust (*Slang*), collar (*Slang*), detain, nab (*Slang*), pick up, pinch (*Slang*), run in, seize.
2. GRIP.
3. STOP.

arrest *noun*
1. A seizing and holding by law: *made five arrests yesterday; resisted arrest violently.*
   Syns: apprehension, bust (*Slang*), detention, nab (*Slang*), pickup, pinch, seizure.
2. STOP.

arresting *adjective* NOTICEABLE.
arrestive *adjective* NOTICEABLE.
arrival *noun*
1. The act of arriving: *the mayor's arrival at city hall.*
   Syns: advent, appearance, coming.
2. One that arrives: *a late arrival at the party.*

Syns: comer, incomer, visitor.
3. SUCCESS.

arrive *verb*
1. To come to a particular place: *arrived at the office at nine sharp.*
   Syns: blow in (*Slang*), check in (*Informal*), get in, pull in, reach, show up, turn up.
2. SUCCEED.

arrive at *verb*
To reach a goal or objective: *Management and the union arrived at an understanding.*
Syns: attain, gain, get to, hit on (*or* upon).

arrogance *noun*
The quality of being arrogant: *Even his walk showed his arrogance.*
Syns: disdain, haughtiness, hauteur, insolence (*also* insolency), loftiness, lordliness, overbearingness, presumption, pride, superciliousness, superiority.

arrogant *adjective*
Overly convinced of one's own superiority and importance: *An arrogant man treats others with condescension.*
Syns: disdainful, haughty, high-and-mighty, hoity-toity (*also* highty-tighty), insolent, lofty, lordly, overbearing, overweening, presumptuous, proud, supercilious, superior. —*Idiom* on one's high horse.

arrogate *verb* ASSUME.
arrogation *noun* USURPATION.
arrondi *adjective* BENT.
art *noun*
1. A skill in doing or performing that is attained by study, practice, or observation: *"The art of saying things well is useless to a man who has nothing to say."*—Macaulay.
   Syns: craft, expertise, knack, know-how (*Informal*), technique.
2. Deceitful cleverness: *used all the art at his disposal to manipulate his colleagues.*
   Syns: artfulness, artifice, craft, craftiness, cunning, foxiness, guile, wiliness.

artful *adjective*
1. Showing art or skill in performing or doing: *an artful rendition of a Chopin mazurka.*
   Syns: adroit, deft, dexterous, masterful, masterly, skillful.
2. Deceitfully clever: *used artful means to get exactly what she wanted.*

Syns: crafty, cunning, foxy, guileful, scheming, sly, tricky, wily.
artfulness *noun* ART.
article *noun*
1. ELEMENT.
2. OBJECT[1].
articulate *adjective*
1. ELOQUENT.
2. VOCAL.
  articulate *verb*
1. INTEGRATE.
2. PRONOUNCE.
3. SAY.
articulation *noun*
1. EXPRESSION.
2. VOICING.
artifice *noun*
1. ART.
2. TRICK.
artificial *adjective*
1. Made by human beings, not nature: *an artificial lake.*
  Syns: manmade, manufactured, synthetic.
2. Made to imitate something else: *artificial pearls; artificial flowers.*
  Syns: imitation, manmade, mock, pretend (*Informal*), sham, synthetic.
3. Not genuine or sincere: *an artificial display of affection.*
  Syns: affected, feigned, insincere, phony (*also* phoney) (*Informal*), pretended, spurious.
4. AFFECTED[2].
5. PLASTIC.
artistic *adjective* TASTEFUL.
artless *adjective*
1. Free from guile, cunning, or deceit: *the artless grace of a child.*
  Syns: guileless, ingenuous, innocent, naive (*also* naïve, naif, naïf), natural, simple, unaffected, unsophisticated, unstudied.
2. RUSTIC.
artsy *adjective* ARTY.
artsy-craftsy or **arty-crafty** *adjective* ARTY.
arty *adjective*
Pretentiously artistic: *arty movies.*
  Syns: artsy, artsy-craftsy (*or* arty-crafty), contrived, precious, pretentious.
arty-crafty *adjective* SEE **artsy-craftsy.**
aruspex *noun* SEE **haruspex.**
ascared *adjective* AFRAID.
ascend *verb*
1. To move upward on or along: *ascending a mountain.*

Syns: climb, go up, mount, scale[2].
2, 3. RISE.
ascendancy *noun* DOMINANCE.
ascendant *adjective* RULING.
ascendant *noun* ANCESTOR.
ascension *noun*
1. ASCENT.
2. RISE.
ascent *noun*
1. The act of moving upward on or along: *the mountaineer's ascent of the Matterhorn.*
  Syns: ascension, climb, climbing, mounting, scaling.
2. An upward slope: *climbed the steep ascent to the top of the hill.*
  Syns: acclivity, grade, gradient, rise, slope.
3. RISE.
ascertain *verb* DISCOVER.
ascribe *verb* ATTRIBUTE.
ascription *noun* ATTRIBUTION.
aseptic *adjective* BORING.
ashake *adjective* TREMULOUS.
ashen *adjective* PALE.
ashiver *adjective* TREMULOUS.
ashy *adjective* PALE.
aside *noun*
1, 2. DIGRESSION.
ask *verb*
1. To put a question to (someone): *He asked her what was wrong.*
  Syns: examine, inquire (*also* enquire) (of), interrogate, query, question, quiz.
2. To seek an answer to (a question): *You have to ask the right questions if you're going to learn.*
  Syns: pose, put, raise.
3. DEMAND.
4. INVITE.
5. REQUEST.
askance *adverb* SKEPTICALLY.
asleep *adjective*
1, 2. DEAD.
3. SLEEPING.
asomatous *adjective* IMMATERIAL.
aspect *noun*
1. APPEARANCE.
2. EXPRESSION.
3. FACE.
4. LIGHT[1].
5. PHASE.
asperity *noun* DIFFICULTY.
asperous *adjective* ROUGH.
asperse *verb* LIBEL.
aspersion *noun* LIBEL.
asphyxiate *verb* CHOKE.

aspirant *noun*
1. One who aspires: *All the aspirants for the presidency participated in the debate.*
   Syns: aspirer, hopeful, yearner.
2. APPLICANT.

aspiration *noun*
1. AMBITION.
2. DREAM.

aspire *verb*
1. To have a fervent hope or aspiration: *aspiring to great knowledge; aspires to become an actress.*
   Syns: dream, hope. —*Idioms* reach for the stars, set one's heart (*or* sights) on.
2. AIM.

aspirer *noun* ASPIRANT.

aspiring *adjective* AMBITIOUS.

ass *noun* FOOL.

assail *verb*
1. ATTACK.
2. REVILE.

assailable *adjective* VULNERABLE.

assailant *noun* AGGRESSOR.

assailer *noun* AGGRESSOR.

assailment *noun* ATTACK.

assault *verb*
1. ATTACK.
2. RAPE.
   assault *noun* ATTACK.

assay *verb*
1. ATTEMPT.
2. ESTIMATE.
3. TEST.
   assay *noun*
1. ATTEMPT.
2. TEST.

assemblage *noun*
1. ACCUMULATION.
2. ASSEMBLY.

assemble *verb*
1. To bring together: *assembling the staff for the meeting.*
   Syns: call, collect¹, convene, convoke, gather, get together, marshal, muster, round up, summon.
2. To come together: *A crowd quickly assembled to watch the motorcade.*
   Syns: aggroup, cluster, collect¹, congregate, convene, forgather (*also* foregather), gather, get together, muster.
3. MAKE.

assembly *noun*
1. A number of persons who have come or been gathered together: *an assembly of jurors waiting to be called.*

Syns: assemblage, body, company, conclave, congregation, congress, convocation, crowd, gathering, group, meeting, muster, troop.
2. CONVENTION.

assent *verb*
To respond affirmatively; receive with agreement or compliance: *The chairman immediately assented to the board's decision.*
Syns: accede (to), accept, acquiesce (in), agree, consent.
assent *noun* ACCEPTANCE.

assenting *adjective* FAVORABLE.

assert *verb*
1. To put into words positively and with conviction: *Some critics assert that he is the world's greatest pianist.*
   Syns: affirm, asseverate, aver, avouch, avow, declare, hold, maintain, state. —*Idiom* have it.
2. To defend, maintain, or insist on the recognition of (one's rights, for example): *She asserted her independence from the group.*
   Syns: claim, vindicate.
3. CLAIM.

assertion *noun*
1. The act of asserting positively: *bold assertions of cultural superiority.*
   Syns: affirmation, averment, avowal, declaration, statement.
2. CLAIM.

assertive *adjective*
1. AGGRESSIVE.
2. EMPHATIC.

assertory *adjective* AGGRESSIVE.

assess *verb*
1. ESTIMATE.
2. IMPOSE.

assessment *noun*
1. ESTIMATE.
2. TAX.

assets *noun* RESOURCES.

asseverate *verb* ASSERT.

assiduity *noun* DILIGENCE.

assiduous *adjective* DILIGENT.

assiduousness *noun* DILIGENCE.

assign *verb*
1. ALLOT.
2. ATTRIBUTE.
3. FIX.
4. STATION.
5. TRANSFER.

assignation *noun* ENGAGEMENT.

assignment *noun* ATTRIBUTION.

assimilate *verb*
1. ABSORB.
2. LIKEN.

assimilating *adjective* ABSORBENT.
assimilation *noun* ABSORPTION.
assimilative *adjective* ABSORBENT.
assist *verb* HELP.
assist *noun* HELP.
assistance *noun* HELP.
assistant *noun*
1. A person who holds a position auxiliary to another and assumes some of his responsibilities: *an editorial assistant; the colonel's office assistant.*
   Syns: adjutant, aide, auxiliary, coadjutant, coadjutor, lieutenant, second².
2. HELPER.

assisting *adjective* AUXILIARY.
assistive *adjective* HELPFUL.
assize *noun* LAW.
associate *verb*
1. To unite or be united in a relationship: *Mr. Elkins was associated with the firm of Harper and Brothers.*
   Syns: affiliate, ally, bind, combine, conjoin, connect, join, link, relate.
2. To come or bring together in one's mind or imagination: *I always associate lilacs with spring.*
   Syns: bracket, connect, correlate, couple, identify, link.
3. To keep company: *I told you not to associate with him; he's bad news.*
   Syns: consort, fraternize, hang out *(Slang)*, hobnob, run around *(Informal)*, troop (with). —*Idiom* rub elbows.

associate *noun*
1. One who is united in a relationship with another: *The politician's associates suffered the consequences when the scandal was exposed.*
   Syns: affiliate, ally, cohort *(Informal)*, colleague, confederate, copartner, fellow, partner.
2. One who keeps company with another: *One of his closest associates is a member of Congress.*
   Syns: buddy *(Informal)*, chum, companion, comrade, crony, mate, pal *(Informal)*.
3. ACCOMPANIMENT.

association *noun*
1. The state of being associated: *The architect and the builder work in close association.*
   Syns: affiliation, alliance, combination, conjunction, connection, cooperation, partnership.

2. CONFERENCE.
3. SUGGESTION.
4. UNION.

assort *verb*
1. To distribute into groups according to kinds: *assorted plates by size.*
   Syns: categorize, class, classify, group, pigeonhole, separate, sort, sort out.
2. ARRANGE.

assorted *adjective* VARIOUS.
assortment *noun*
A collection of various things: *Under the Christmas tree was piled a large assortment of packages.*
   Syns: conglomeration, diversity, gallimaufry, hodgepodge, jumble, medley, mélange *(also* melange*)*, miscellany, mishmash, olio, patchwork, salmagundi, variety. —*Idioms* grab bag, mixed bag.

assuage *verb*
1. PACIFY.
2. RELIEVE.

assuagement *noun* RELIEF.
assume *verb*
1. To take upon oneself: *He assumed responsibility for his widowed aunt.*
   Syns: incur, shoulder, tackle, take on, take over, take up, undertake.
2. To lay claim to for oneself or as one's right: *assumed the authority to close the office early.*
   Syns: appropriate, arrogate, commandeer, pre-empt *(also* preempt, preëmpt*)*, seize, take, usurp.
3. To take on or give a false appearance of: *assuming a sober, dignified expression.*
   Syns: affect², counterfeit, fake, feign, pretend, put on, simulate. —*Idiom* make believe.
4. ACT.
5. DON.
6. SUPPOSE.

assumed *adjective*
1. Being fictitious and not real: *an assumed name.*
   Syns: adopted, made-up, pseudonymic, pseudonymous.
2. PRESUMPTIVE.

assuming *adjective* PRESUMPTUOUS.
assumption *noun*
1. Something taken to be true without proof: *acted on the assumption that both countries were interested in world peace.*
   Syns: postulate, postulation, premise,

presumption, presupposition,
supposition, surmise, theory, thesis.
2. PRESUMPTION.
3. USURPATION.

assumptive *adjective*
1. PRESUMPTIVE.
2. PRESUMPTUOUS.

assurance *noun*
1. CONFIDENCE.
2. SAFETY.
3. WORD.

assure *verb*
1. CONVINCE.
2. GUARANTEE.

assured *adjective*
1. CONFIDENT.
2. SURE.

astonish *verb* SURPRISE.

astonishing *adjective*
1. FABULOUS.
2. STARTLING.

astound *verb* SURPRISE.

astounding *adjective*
1. FABULOUS.
2. STARTLING.

astral *adjective*
1. GRAND.
2. HIGHEST.

astrict *verb* CONSTRAIN.

astringent *adjective* BITTER.

astute *adjective* SHREWD.

astuteness *noun* DISCERNMENT.

asylum *noun*
1. COVER.
2. HOME.
3. REFUGE.

asymmetric also **asymmetrical**
adjective IRREGULAR.

asymmetry *noun* IRREGULARITY.

athirst *adjective*
1. EAGER.
2. THIRSTY.

atingle *adjective* THRILLED.

atman *noun* SPIRIT.

atmosphere *noun*
1, 2. AIR.
3. ENVIRONMENT.
4. FLAVOR.

atmospheric *adjective* AIRY.

atramentous *adjective* BLACK.

atrium *noun* COURT.

atrocious *adjective*
1. OFFENSIVE.
2. OUTRAGEOUS.

atrociousness *noun*
1. ENORMITY.
2. FLAGRANCY.

atrocity *noun*
1. ENORMITY.
2. FLAGRANCY.
3. OUTRAGE.

atrophy *noun* DETERIORATION.

attach *verb*
To join one thing to another: *the hinges
to which the door is attached.*
    Syns: affix, clip², connect, couple,
    fasten, fix, moor, secure.

attachment *noun*
1. Something that attaches as a
    supplementary part: *bought an
    attachment for the vacuum cleaner.*
    Syns: accessory, adjunct, supplement.
2. The condition of being closely tied to
    another by affection or faith: *felt a
    strong attachment for her friend.*
    Syns: affection¹, bond, devotion,
    fondness, love, loyalty, tie.

attack *verb*
1. To set upon with violent force:
    *Germany attacked the Soviet Union in
    1941.*
    Syns: aggress, assail, assault, beset,
    fall on (*or* upon), go at, have at, hit,
    pitch into (*Informal*), sail in (*or* into),
    storm, strike.
2. To start work on vigorously: *City
    Hall is attacking the problem of
    substandard housing.*
    Syns: go at, sail in (*or* into), tackle,
    wade in (*or* into).

attack *noun*
1. The act of attacking: *a sneak attack
    that left the city in ruins.*
    Syns: aggression, assailment, assault,
    offense, offensive, onrush, onset,
    onslaught, strike.
2. APPROACH.
3. SEIZURE.

attackable *adjective* VULNERABLE.

attacker *noun* AGGRESSOR.

attain *verb*
1. ACCOMPLISH.
2. ARRIVE AT at **arrive.**

attainable *adjective* AVAILABLE.

attainment *noun* ACCOMPLISHMENT.

attaint *noun* STAIN.

attempt *verb*
To make an attempt to do or make: *Let
me attempt to explain. She left without
attempting a retort.*
    Syns: assay, endeavor, essay, offer,
    seek, strive, try, undertake. —*Idioms*
    have a go at, have (*or make or take*) a
    shot at, make a stab at, take a crack
    (*or whack*) at.

attempt *noun*
1. An effort to do or make something: *the child's first awkward attempt to walk.*
   Syns: assay, endeavor, essay, offer, take (*Slang*), trial, try, undertaking.
2. EFFORT.

attend *verb*
1. ACCOMPANY.
2. FOLLOW.
3. HEAR.
4. SERVE.
5. TEND².

attend to *verb* SETTLE.

attendant *noun*
1. ACCOMPANIMENT.
2. HELPER.

attendant *adjective* ACCOMPANYING.

attending *adjective* ACCOMPANYING.

attention *noun*
1. Concentration of the mental powers on something: *The speaker held my full attention.*
   Syns: attentiveness, concentration, consideration, heedfulness.
2. NOTICE.

attentive *adjective*
1. Concentrating the mental powers on something: *an attentive audience.*
   Syns: advertent, heedful, intent, observant. —*Idioms* all ears (*or* eyes), on the ball.
2. Full of polite concern for the well-being of others: *very attentive to her guests.*
   Syns: considerate, courteous, gallant, polite, solicitous, thoughtful.

attentiveness *noun* ATTENTION.

attenuate *verb*
1. DILUTE.
2. ENERVATE.
3. THIN.

attenuate *adjective* THIN.

attest *verb*
1. CERTIFY.
2. CONFIRM.
3. INDICATE.
4. TESTIFY.

attestant *noun* WITNESS.

attestation *noun* CONFIRMATION.

attire *noun* DRESS.

attire *verb* DRESS.

attitude *noun*
1, 2. POSITION.
3. POSTURE.
4. SENTIMENT.

attitudinize *verb*
1. POSE.
2. POSTURE.

attract *verb*
1. To direct or impel to oneself by some quality or action: *A new celebrity attracted the crowd's attention. A handsome man attracts all eyes.*
   Syns: allure, appeal, draw, lure, magnetize, pull, take.
2. INTEREST.

attracting *adjective* ATTRACTIVE.

attraction *noun*
The power or quality of attracting: *the attraction of living in a big city. City life holds no attraction for the farm family. She is a woman of great attraction to men.*
   Syns: allure, allurement, appeal, attractiveness, call, charisma, charm, draw, enchantment, fascination, glamour (*also* glamor), lure, magnetism, pull, witchery.

attractive *adjective*
1. Pleasing to the eye or mind: *an attractive woman; an attractive offer.*
   Syns: alluring, appealing, attracting, bewitching, captivating, charming, come-hither, enchanting, engaging, enticing, entrancing, fascinating, fetching, glamorous (*also* glamourous), lovely, magnetic, prepossessing, pretty, sweet, taking, tempting, winning, winsome.
2. BEAUTIFUL.
3. BECOMING.

attractiveness *noun* ATTRACTION.

attribute *verb*
To regard as belonging to or resulting from another: *a painting attributed to da Vinci.*
   Syns: accredit, ascribe, assign, charge, credit, impute, lay¹, refer.

attribute *noun*
1. QUALITY.
2. SYMBOL.

attribution *noun*
The act of attributing: *the attribution of a previously unknown symphony to Mozart.*
   Syns: ascription, assignment, credit, imputation.

attrition *noun* PENITENCE.

attune *verb*
1, 2. ADJUST.
3. HARMONIZE.

atypical *also* **atypic** *adjective*
1. ABNORMAL.
2. UNUSUAL.

au courant *adjective* CONTEMPORARY.

audacious *adjective*
1. BRAVE.

2. DARING.
3. IMPUDENT.

audacity *noun*
1. DARING.
2. IMPUDENCE.

audience *noun*
1. HEARING.
2. PUBLIC.

audition *noun*
1, 2. HEARING.

au fait *adjective*
1. ABLE.
2. CORRECT.

aught *noun* NOTHING.

augment *verb* INCREASE.

augmentation *noun*
1. ACCOMPANIMENT.
2. ADDITION.
3. INCREASE.

augur *verb* PROPHESY.

augur *noun* PROPHET.

augury *noun* OMEN.

august *adjective*
1. EXALTED.
2. GRAND.

au naturel *adjective* NUDE.

aura *noun* AIR.

aureate *adjective* SONOROUS.

auricular *adjective* CONFIDENTIAL.

auriflamme *noun* SEE **oriflamme**.

aurora *noun* DAWN.

auspex *noun* PROPHET.

auspices *noun* PATRONAGE.

auspicious *adjective*
1. FAVORABLE.
2. OPPORTUNE.

austere *adjective*
1. BITTER.
2. BLEAK.

austerity *noun* SEVERITY.

autarchic also **autarchical** *adjective*
ABSOLUTE.

autarchy *noun* ABSOLUTISM.

authentic *adjective*
1. Not counterfeit or copied: *an authentic painting by Rembrandt.*
 Syns: bona fide, genuine, good, indubitable, original, real, true, undoubted, unquestionable.
2. Worthy of belief because of precision, faithfulness to an original, etc.: *an authentic re-creation of a Revolutionary War battle.*
 Syns: authoritative, convincing, credible, faithful, true, trustworthy, valid.

authenticate *verb*
1. CONFIRM.
2. PROVE.

authentication *noun* CONFIRMATION.

authenticity *noun*
The quality of being authentic: *recognized the authenticity of the painting.*
 Syns: genuineness, legitimacy, realness, truthfulness, validity.

author *noun* ORIGINATOR.

author *verb* PUBLISH.

authoritarian *adjective*
1. Characterized by or favoring absolute obedience to authority: *Nazi Germany was an authoritarian society.*
 Syns: autocratic, despotic, dictatorial, doctrinaire, totalitarian, tyrannical (*also* tyrannic).
2. DICTATORIAL.

authoritarian *noun*
One who imposes or favors absolute obedience to authority: *always felt his parents were authoritarians.*
 Syns: autocrat, despot, dictator, martinet, tyrant.

authoritarianism *noun* ABSOLUTISM.

authoritative *adjective*
1. Exercising authority: *an authoritative young executive.*
 Syns: commanding, dominant, lordly, masterful, mighty, powerful, weighty.
2. Having or arising from authority: *an authoritative interpretation of Mozart; an authoritative order.*
 Syns: conclusive, official, sanctioned, standard.
3. AUTHENTIC.

authority *noun*
1. The right and power to command, decide, rule, or judge: *The mayor has the authority to convene the school committee.*
 Syns: clout (*Informal*), command, control, domination, dominion, jurisdiction, mastery, might, power, prerogative, say-so (*Informal*), sway.
2. A person or group having the right and power to command, decide, rule, or judge: *governmental authorities; school authorities.*
 Syns: higher-up (*Informal*), official.
 —*Idiom* the powers that be.
3. EXPERT.
4. FACULTY.

authorization *noun* PERMISSION.

authorize *verb*
1. To give authority to: *I authorized my partner to negotiate in my behalf.*
 Syns: accredit, commission, empower, enable, entitle, license, qualify.
2. PERMIT.

autochthonous also **autochthonal,**
autochthonic *adjective* NATIVE.

autocracy *noun*
1, 2. ABSOLUTISM.

autocrat *noun* AUTHORITARIAN.

autocratic *adjective*
1. ABSOLUTE.
2. AUTHORITARIAN.

autograph *verb* SIGN.

automatic *adjective*
1. PERFUNCTORY.
2. SPONTANEOUS.

autonomous *adjective* FREE.

autonomy *noun* FREEDOM.

auxiliary *adjective*
1. Giving or able to give help or
support: *an auxiliary division of the
fire department.*
Syns: accessory, adjuvant, aiding,
ancillary, assisting, collateral,
contributory, helping, subsidiary.
2. Used or held in reserve: *an auxiliary
supply of oil; an auxiliary engine.*
Syns: back-up, emergency, reserve,
secondary, standby, supplemental,
supplementary.

auxiliary *noun* ASSISTANT.

avail *verb* PROFIT.

avail *noun* USE.

available *adjective*
Capable of being obtained or used: *All
the available information indicated that
war was imminent.*
Syns: attainable, disponible, gettable,
obtainable, procurable. —*Idiom* to be
had.

avarice *noun* GREED.

avaricious *adjective* GREEDY.

avenge *verb*
To exact revenge for: *avenged his sister's
death by killing her murderer.*
Syns: fix (*Informal*), pay back, pay
off, redress, repay, requite, vindicate.
—*Idioms* even the score, get even
with, pay back in full measure (*or* in
kind *or* in one's own coin), settle (*or*
square) accounts, take an eye for an
eye, wreak vengeance on.

avengement *noun* RETALIATION.

avenging *noun* RETALIATION.

avenue *noun* WAY.

aver *verb* ASSERT.

average *noun*
Something, as a type, number, quantity,
or degree, that represents a midpoint
between extremes on a scale of
valuation: *much more intelligent than the
average.*

Syns: mean[3], median, medium, norm,
par.

average *adjective*
1. ACCEPTABLE.
2. COMMON.
3. ORDINARY.

averment *noun* ASSERTION.

averse *adjective* INDISPOSED.

averseness *noun* INDISPOSITION.

aversion *noun*
1. ANTIPATHY.
2. DISGUST.
3. HORROR.

aversive *adjective* ANTIPATHETIC.

avert *verb*
1. PREVENT.
2. TURN.

avid *adjective*
1. EAGER.
2. GREEDY.
3. VORACIOUS.

avidity *noun* GREED.

avidness *noun* VORACITY.

avoid *verb*
To keep away from: *They drove through
the countryside, avoiding cities. Referees
must avoid taking sides.*
Syns: bypass, dodge, duck, elude,
escape, eschew, evade, get around,
shun. —*Idioms* fight shy of, give a
wide berth to, have no truck with,
keep (*or* stay *or* steer) clear of.

avoidance *noun* ESCAPE.

avoirdupois *noun* HEAVINESS.

avouch *verb* ASSERT.

avow *verb*
1. ACKNOWLEDGE.
2. ASSERT.

avowal *noun*
1. ACKNOWLEDGMENT.
2. ASSERTION.

await *verb* EXPECT.

awake *adjective*
1. AWARE.
2. WAKEFUL.

awake *verb* WAKE.

awaken *verb*
1. AROUSE.
2. WAKE.

award *noun*
1. REWARD.
2. TROPHY.

award *verb*
1. CONFER.
2. GRANT.

aware *adjective*
Marked by comprehension, cognizance,
and perception: *I am aware of my own
shortcomings.*

Syns: alive (to), awake (to), cognizant, conversant (with), hip (to) (*Slang*), knowing, mindful, sensible, sentient, wise[1] (to). —*Idiom* on to.

awareness *noun*
1. The condition of being aware: *His awareness of danger made him cautious.*
   Syns: alertness, cognizance, consciousness, perception, sense.
2. APPRECIATION.

awash *adjective* BIG.

away *adjective* ABSENT.

awe *noun* WONDER.

awful *adjective*
1. FEARFUL.
2. TERRIBLE.

awfully *adverb* VERY.

awkward *adjective*
1. Lacking dexterity and grace in physical movement: *an awkward girl with large hands and feet; an awkward dancer.*
   Syns: clumsy, gawky, graceless, inept, klutzy (*Slang*), lumbering, lumpish, ungainly, ungraceful. —*Idiom* all thumbs.
2. Difficult to handle or manage: *an awkward bundle to carry.*
   Syns: bulky, clumsy, cumbersome, cumbrous, inconvenient, unhandy, unmanageable, unwieldy.
3. Characterized by embarrassment and discomfort: *an awkward silence.*
   Syns: constrained, uncomfortable, uneasy.
4. EMBARRASSING.
5. UNFORTUNATE.
6. UNSKILLFUL.

awry *adjective* AMISS.

axiom *noun* LAW.

aye also **ay** *noun* YES.

aye also **ay** *adverb* YES.

B

babble *verb*
1. To talk rapidly, incoherently, or indistinctly: *babies babbling in their cribs.*
   Syns: blather, chatter, gabble, gibber, jabber, prate, prattle.
2. CHATTER.

babble *noun*
1. Unintelligible or foolish talk: *a babble of voices in the airport; a speech that was just so much babble.*
   Syns: blather, blatherskite, double-talk, gabble, gibberish, jabber, jabberwocky (*also* jabberwock), nonsense, prate, prattle, twaddle.
2. CHATTER.

babbling *adjective* LAUGHING.

babe *noun*
1. BABY.
2. INNOCENT.

babel *noun* NOISE.

baby *noun*
1. A very young child: *a tiny baby in its mother's arms.*
   Syns: babe, bambino, infant, neonate, newborn, nursling. —*Idiom* bundle of joy.
2. A person who behaves in a childish, weak, or spoiled way: *a real baby who is afraid to assert herself.*
   Syns: milksop, milquetoast, mollycoddle, weakling. —*Idiom* mama's boy (*or* girl).

baby *verb*
To treat with indulgence and often overtender care: *annoys her son by hovering over him and babying him.*
   Syns: cater to, coddle, cosset, indulge, mollycoddle, overindulge, pamper, spoil.

babyish *adjective*
1. Of or like a baby: *a lovely babyish face.*
   Syns: cherubic, childlike, infantile.
2. CHILDISH.

back *noun*
The part or area farthest from the front: *the back of the house.*
   Syns: posterior, rear[1], rearward.

back *verb*
1. To move in a reverse direction: *As she talked she kept backing slowly toward the door.*
   Syns: backtrack, fall back, retreat, retrocede, retrograde, retrogress. —*Idiom* retrace one's steps.
2. To present evidence in support of: *backed his claim by showing the receipts.*
   Syns: buttress, corroborate, justify, substantiate.
3. CONFIRM.
4. FINANCE.
5. SUPPORT.

back down (or **out**) *verb*
To abandon a former position or

commitment: *She accepted the invitation but backed down at the last minute.*
Syns: fink out (*Slang*), retreat.

back *adjective*
1. Located in the rear: *the back porch.*
Syns: after, hind, hindmost (*also* hindermost), posterior, postern, rear[1].
2. Distant from a center of activity: *back roads.*
Syn: outlying.

back *adverb*
1. In or toward a former location or condition: *going back to their hometown.*
Syns: about, around, backward (*also* backwards), rearward, round.
2. BACKWARD.

backbiting *adjective* LIBELOUS.
backbreaking *adjective* BURDENSOME.
backer *noun* PATRON.
backfire *verb*
To produce an unexpected and undesired result: *His elaborate plan to bypass his boss backfired.*
Syns: boomerang, bounce back, rebound.

background *noun* HISTORY.
backing *noun* PATRONAGE.
backland *noun* WILD.
backlog *noun* HOARD.
backside *noun* BOTTOM.
backslide *verb* RELAPSE.
backslide *noun* LAPSE.
backsliding *noun* LAPSE.
backtrack *verb* BACK.
back-up *adjective* AUXILIARY.
backward *adjective*
1. Directed or facing toward the back or rear: *a backward glance.*
Syns: retrograde, retrogressive.
2. Not progressing and developing as fast as others, as in economic and social aspects: *backward peoples; backward countries.*
Syns: behindhand, lagging, underdeveloped, undeveloped.
3. Having only a limited ability to learn and understand: *a backward child.*
Syns: dull, retarded, simple, simpleminded, slow, slow-witted, weakminded.
4. DEPRESSED.
5. IGNORANT.
6. MODEST.
7. UNPROGRESSIVE.

backward *also* **backwards** *adverb*
1. Toward the back: *jumped backward to avoid the oncoming taxi.*
Syns: about, around, back, rearward, round.
2. BACK.

bad *adjective*
1. Below a standard of quality: *a really bad book.*
Syns: bum (*Informal*), deficient, unsatisfactory. —*Idioms* below par, not up to scratch (*or* snuff).
2. Bringing, predicting, or characterized by misfortune: *a run of bad luck; bad times.*
Syns: evil, ill, inauspicious, unfavorable.
3. Impaired because of decay: *a bad apple.*
Syns: decayed, decomposed, putrid, rotten, spoiled.
4. EVIL.
5. HARMFUL.
6. NAUGHTY.
7. UNPLEASANT.
bad *noun* EVIL.
bad *adverb* HARD.
badge *noun* DECORATION.
badger *verb*
1. BAIT.
2. BESIEGE.
badland *noun* BARREN.
badly *adverb*
1. HARD.
2. WRONG.
bad-mannered *adjective* RUDE.
badness *noun* EVIL.
bad-tempered *adjective* ILL-TEMPERED.
baffle *verb* FRUSTRATE.
bag *verb*
1. ARREST.
2. BULGE.
3. TAKE.
bag *noun*
1. AREA.
2. FORTE.
3. WITCH.
baggage *noun* SLUT.
bail[1] *noun*
1. BOND.
2. BONDSMAN.
bail[2] *verb* DIP.
bail out *verb* EJECT.
bail[3] *verb* ROB.
bailsman *noun* BONDSMAN.
bairn *noun* CHILD.
bait *verb*
1. To torment with persistent insult or ridicule: *Neighborhood toughs baited minority groups with racist remarks.*
Syns: badger, bullyrag, heckle, hector, hound, needle (*Informal*), ride (*Informal*), taunt. —*Idiom* wave the red flag in front of the bull.

2. TANTALIZE.
 bait *noun* LURE.
bake *verb* BURN.
baking *adjective* HOT.
balance *noun*
 1. A stable state characterized by the cancellation of all forces by equal opposing forces: *Man has upset the balance of nature by destroying certain species.*
  Syns: counterpoise, equilibrium, equipoise, stasis.
 2. A stable, calm state of the emotions: *regained his balance slowly after the divorce.*
  Syns: aplomb, composure, cool (*Slang*), coolness, equanimity, poise, self-possession.
 3. What remains after a part has been used or subtracted: *a balance due of $50.*
  Syns: leavings, remainder, remains, remnant, residue, rest².
 4. PROPORTION.
balance *verb*
 1. To put in balance: *balancing the weights on both sides of the scale.*
  Syns: counterbalance, equalize, stabilize, steady.
 2. To act as an equalizing weight or force to: *Her basic kindness balances her quick temper.*
  Syns: compensate (for), counteract, counterbalance, counterpoise, countervail, make up (for), offset, set off.
 3. To place or be placed on a narrow or insecure surface: *balancing a glass on the edge of the table.*
  Syns: perch, poise.
 4. COMPARE.
 5. COMPENSATE.
balanced *adjective*
 1. FAIR.
 3. SANE.
 3, 4. SYMMETRICAL.
bald *adjective*
 1, 2. BARE.
balderdash *noun* NONSENSE.
bald-faced *adjective* SHAMELESS.
baleful *adjective*
 1. FATEFUL.
 2. MALIGN.
balk *verb* FRUSTRATE.
 balk *noun* BEAM.
balky *adjective* CONTRARY.
ball *noun* DANCE.
balloon *verb* BULGE.
ballot *verb* ELECT.
balloter *noun* ELECTOR.

ball up *verb*
 1. BOTCH.
 2. CONFUSE.
ballup *noun* DISORDER.
ballyhoo *verb*
 1. ADVERTISE.
 2. PROMOTE.
ballyhoo *noun* PROMOTION.
balm *verb* CALM.
balmy *adjective*
 1. FOOLISH.
 2. GENTLE.
baloney *also* **boloney** *noun*
NONSENSE.
bambino *noun* BABY.
bamboozle *verb* DECEIVE.
ban *verb*
 1. CENSOR.
 2. FORBID.
 ban *noun* FORBIDDANCE.
banal *adjective*
 1. INSIPID.
 2. TRITE.
banality *noun*
 1. CLICHÉ.
 2. INSIPIDITY.
band¹ *noun*
A thin strip of material or color: *wore a red band on her head.*
  Syns: bandeau, fillet, strip², stripe.
band *verb*
To encircle with or as if with a band: *The equator bands the earth. The waist on this dress is banded in velvet.*
  Syns: begird, belt, cincture, compass, encompass, engird, engirdle, gird, girdle, girt, ring.
band² *noun*
 1. A group of performers: *a band of actors touring the country.*
  Syns: company, corps, party, troop, troupe.
 2. GANG.
 3. GROUP.
 band *verb*
To assemble or join in a group: *The parents of the handicapped banded together to pressure the legislature.*
  Syns: combine, gang up (*Informal*), league, unite.
bandage *verb* DRESS.
bandeau *noun* BAND.¹
banderole *also* **banderol, bannerol** *noun* FLAG¹
bandy *verb* EXCHANGE.
bane *noun*
 1. CURSE.
 2. POISON.
 3. RUIN.

baneful *adjective*
1. FATEFUL.
2. VIRULENT.

bang *noun*
1. BLAST.
2. BLOW².
3. HIT.
4. REPORT.
5. SLAM.
6. THRILL.

bang *verb*
1. To strike, set down, or close in such a way as to make a loud noise: *banged the door behind him.*
    Syns: clap, crash, slam, whack.
2. BLAST.

bang *adverb* PRECISELY.

banish *verb*
1. To force to leave a country or place by official decree: *was banished for fomenting a rebellion.*
    Syns: deport, exile, expatriate, expel, ostracize, transport.
2. DISMISS.

banishment *noun* EXILE.

bank¹ *verb*
To place (money) in a bank: *banks her savings rather than keeping the money at home.*
    Syns: deposit, lay away, salt away (*Informal*), sock away (*Informal*).

bank on (or **upon**) *verb* DEPEND ON at **depend**.

bank² *noun* HEAP.

bank *verb* HEAP.

bankroll *verb* FINANCE.

bankrupt *verb* RUIN.

bankruptcy *noun* FAILURE.

banned *adjective* FORBIDDEN.

banner *noun* FLAG¹.

banner *adjective* EXCELLENT.

bannerol *noun* SEE **banderole**.

banquet *noun* FEAST.

bantam *adjective* LITTLE.

banter *verb* JOKE.

baptize *verb* NAME.

bar *noun*
1. Anything that impedes or prevents entry or passage: *His extreme conservatism is a bar to his acceptance by the workers.*
    Syns: barricade, barrier, block, hamper, hindrance, hurdle, impediment, obstacle, obstruction, snag, stop, traverse, wall.
2. COURT.
3. STICK.

bar *verb*
1. To shut in with or as if with bars: *In a rage, she barred herself in her room.*
    Syns: confine, lock, wall.

2. EXCLUDE.
3. OBSTRUCT.

barbarian *noun* BOOR.

barbarian *adjective*
1. COARSE.
2. UNCIVILIZED.

barbaric *adjective*
1. COARSE.
2. UNCIVILIZED.

barbarism *noun* CORRUPTION.

barbarity *noun* CRUELTY.

barbarous *adjective*
1. FIERCE.
2. UNCIVILIZED.

bard *noun* POET.

bare *adjective*
1. Without the usual covering: *a bare hillside.*
    Syns: bald, denuded, exposed, naked, nude.
2. Without addition, decoration, or qualification: *just the bare facts, please.*
    Syns: bald, dry, plain, simple, unadorned, unvarnished.
3. Just sufficient: *won the election by a bare majority.*
    Syns: mere, scant.
4. EMPTY.
5. MERE.
6. NUDE.

bare *verb*
1. To make bare: *bared his head to the sun.*
    Syns: denude, disrobe, divest, expose, strip¹, uncover.
2. REVEAL.

barefaced *adjective* SHAMELESS.

barely *adverb*
By a very little; almost not: *could barely hear the music through the static.*
    Syns: just, hardly, scarce.

bareness *noun* NUDITY.

bargain *noun*
1. An agreement, esp. one involving a sale or exchange: *kept his part of the bargain and mowed the lawn.*
    Syns: compact², contract, covenant, deal (*Informal*), transaction.
2. Something offered or bought at a low price: *a book that is a real bargain.*
    Syns: buy, giveaway (*Informal*), steal (*Slang*).
3. AGREEMENT.

bargain *verb*
1. HAGGLE.
2. CONTRACT.

bargain on (or **for**) *verb* EXPECT.

bark *verb*
1. CRACK.

2. SNAP.

bark *noun* REPORT.

barnacle *noun* PARASITE.

barnyard *adjective* OBSCENE.

baronial *adjective* GRAND.

baroque *adjective* ORNATE.

barrage *noun*
A concentrated outpouring, as of missiles, words, or blows: *was hit with a barrage of insults.*
    Syns: bombardment, burst, cannonade, fusillade, hail[1], salvo, shower, storm, volley.

barrage *verb*
To direct a barrage at: *barraging the speaker with questions.*
    Syns: bombard, cannonade, pepper, shower.

barrel *noun* HEAP.

barrel *verb* RUSH.

barren *adjective*
1. Unable to produce offspring: *a barren couple who plan to adopt.*
    Syns: childless, infecund, infertile, sterile.
2. Lacking or unable to produce growing plants or crops: *a barren desert; barren soil.*
    Syns: infertile, unproductive.
3. EMPTY.
4. FUTILE.

barren *noun*
A tract of unproductive land: *the pine barrens of New Jersey.*
    Syns: badland, desert[1], waste, wasteland, wilderness.

barrenness *noun*
1. EMPTINESS.
2. NOTHINGNESS.
3. STERILITY.

barricade *noun* BAR.

barrier *noun*
1. BAR.
2. WALL.

bar sinister *noun* STAIN.

basal *adjective*
1. ELEMENTARY.
2. RADICAL.

base¹ *noun*
1. The lowest or supporting part of structure: *built on a base of solid rock.*
    Syns: basis, bed, bottom, foot, footing, foundation, fundament, ground, groundwork, seat, substratum, underpinning.
2. A center of organization, supply, or activity: *the biggest army base in the East.*
    Syns: complex, headquarters, installation, station.

3, 4. BASIS.
5. THEME.

base *verb*
To take or serve as the basis for: *bases her opinions on facts; opinions based on facts.*
    Syns: build, establish, found, ground, predicate, rest[1], root in, seat.

base² *adjective*
1. LOWLY.
2. SHODDY.
3. SORDID.

baseborn *adjective*
1. ILLEGITIMATE.
2. LOWLY.

baseless *adjective*
Having no basis or foundation in fact: *a baseless accusation.*
    Syns: bottomless, groundless, idle, unfounded, unwarranted.

bash *noun*
1. BLAST.
2. BLOW².
3. PARTY.

bash *verb* HIT.

bashful *adjective* MODEST.

basic *adjective*
1. ELEMENTAL.
2. ELEMENTARY.
3. ESSENTIAL.
4. RADICAL.

basic *noun* ELEMENT.

basically *adverb* ESSENTIALLY.

basin *noun*
1. The region drained by a river system: *Much of the country lies within the Mississippi-Missouri basin.*
    Syn: watershed.
2. DEPRESSION.

basis *noun*
1. Anything on which something immaterial, such as an argument or charge, rests: *making decisions on the basis of expediency.*
    Syns: base[1], footing, foundation, ground, groundwork.
2. A fundamental principle or underlying concept: *Freedom of speech is a basis of democracy.*
    Syns: base[1], cornerstone, foundation, fundamental, root[1], rudiment.
3. A justifying fact or consideration: *made an accusation totally without basis.*
    Syns: foundation, justification, reason, warrant.
4. An established position from which to operate or deal with others: *We're on a friendly enough basis.*
    Syns: footing, status, terms.
5. BASE.

bask *verb* LUXURIATE.
bass *adjective* LOW.
bastard *adjective* ILLEGITIMATE.
bastardize *verb* CORRUPT.
bastardy *noun* ILLEGITIMACY.
baste *verb* BEAT.
bat[1] *noun* BENDER.
bat[2] *noun* WITCH.
bat[3] *verb* BLINK.
batch *noun* GROUP.
bate *verb* SUBSIDE.
bathe *verb*
1, 2. WASH.
bathetic *adjective*
1. SENTIMENTAL.
2. TRITE.
bathos *noun* SENTIMENTALITY.
batten *verb* CLEAN UP at **clean.**
batter *verb*
1. To injure or damage, as by abuse or heavy wear: *a house that was battered by the hurricane.*
   Syns: knock about, knock around, mangle, maul, rough up.
2. BEAT.
battle *noun*
1. An intense competition: *a political battle; a battle of wits.*
   Syns: struggle, vying.
2. COMBAT.
battle *verb* CONTEND.
battle-ax or **battle-axe** *noun* SCOLD.
batty *adjective* INSANE.
bauble *noun* NOVELTY.
bawd *noun* PROSTITUTE.
bawl *verb*
1. To cry loudly, as a healthy child does from pain or distress: *The unhappy infant kicked and bawled.*
   Syns: howl, wail, yowl.
2. CRY.
3. ROAR.
4. SHOUT.
bawl out *verb*
1. *Informal.* To reprimand loudly or harshly: *got bawled out for insubordination.*
   Syns: berate, rate[2], tell off (*Informal*), tongue-lash, wig (*Brit.*). —*Idioms* call on the carpet, give hell to.
2. CALL DOWN at **call.**
bawl *noun* ROAR.
bawling *noun* CRY.
bay[1] *noun*
A body of water partly enclosed by land but having a wide outlet to the sea: *sailboats bobbing in the blue water of the bay.*
   Syns: bight, cove.
bay[2] *verb* HOWL.

bazoo *noun* HISS.
be *verb*
1. To have reality or life: *I think, therefore I am.*
   Syns: breathe, exist, live[1], subsist.
2. EXIST.
beak *noun*
1. BILL[2].
2. NOSE.
beam *noun*
1. A large, oblong piece of wood or other material, used esp. for construction: *a dining-room ceiling featuring exposed beams.*
   Syns: balk, timber.
2. A series of particles or waves traveling close together in parallel paths: *A beam of light peeped through the curtains.*
   Syns: ray, shaft.
beam *verb*
1. To emit a bright light: *A hot sun beamed in the sky.*
   Syns: blaze[1], burn, gleam, glow, incandesce, radiate, shine.
2. SMILE.
beaming *adjective* BRIGHT.
bean *noun* HEAD.
bear *verb*
1. To hold up: *men bearing the burden of leadership in wartime.*
   Syns: carry, support, sustain.
2. To hold and turn over in the mind: *often bore grudges.*
   Syns: harbor, nurse.
3. To be endowed with as a visible characteristic or form: *sisters bearing a strong resemblance to their mother.*
   Syns: carry, display, exhibit, have, possess.
4. To give birth to: *a woman who has borne three children.*
   Syns: birth (*Chiefly Regional*), bring forth, deliver, have. —*Idiom* be brought abed (*or* to bed) of.
5. To bring forth (a product): *fruit trees that bear well.*
   Syns: produce, yield.
6. To exert pressure: *an old man bearing heavily on his cane.*
   Syns: press, push.
7. To proceed in a specified direction: *Bear right at the next intersection.*
   Syns: go, head, make, set out, strike out.
8. ACT.
9. BRING.
10, 11. CARRY.
12. ENDURE.
bear on (or **upon**) *verb* APPLY.

bear out *verb*
1. CONFIRM.
2. PROVE.

bear up *verb*
To withstand stress or difficulty: *bore up well during his mother's long illness.*
Syns: endure, hold up, stand up.

bearable *adjective*
Capable of being tolerated: *It's more discomfort than pain—quite bearable.*
Syns: endurable, sufferable, tolerable.

beard *verb* DEFY.

bearer *noun*
A person who carries messages or is sent on errands: *gave the bearer a receipt for the package.*
Syns: carrier, courier, messenger, runner.

bearing *noun*
1. Behavior through which one reveals one's personality: *a person of dignified bearing.*
Syns: address, air, demeanor, gest (*also* geste) (*Archaic*), manner, mien, port (*Archaic*), presence, style.
2. One's place and direction relative to one's surroundings: *can't find my bearing in this strange city.*
Syns: bearings, location, orientation, position, situation.
3. CONCERN.
4. HEADING.
5. RELEVANCE.

bearings *noun* BEARING.

beast *noun* FIEND.

beat *verb*
1. To hit heavily and repeatedly with violent blows: *mugged and beaten black and blue.*
Syns: baste, batter, belabor, buffet, drub, hammer, lambaste (*Slang*), pound, pummel, thrash, thresh (*Rare*). —*Idiom* rain blows on.
2. To punish with blows or lashes: *beat the boy for smoking.*
Syns: flog, hide², lay into, lick (*Slang*), thrash, trim (*Informal*), whip.
3. To shape, break, or flatten with repeated blows: *beat copper into bowls.*
Syns: forge¹, hammer, pound.
4. To mix rapidly to a frothy consistency: *beat egg whites for a meringue.*
Syns: whip, whisk.
5. To indicate (time or rhythm), as with repeated gestures or sounds: *a conductor beating the meter with his baton.*
Syns: count, mark.
6. To make rhythmic contractions, sounds, or movements: *His heart beat with excitement.*
Syns: palpitate, pulsate, pulse, throb.
7. DEFEAT.
8. FLAP.
9. GLARE.
10. NONPLUS.
11. SURPASS.

beat off *verb* PARRY.

beat *noun*
1. A repeated stroke or blow, esp. one that produces a sound: *the beat of galloping hoofs.*
Syns: clunk, pounding, thump.
2. A periodic contraction or sound of something coursing: *the beat of a heart.*
Syns: palpitation, pulsation, pulse, throb.
3. An area regularly covered, as by a policeman or reporter: *The Upper West Side is my beat.*
Syns: circuit, province, round, route.
4. RHYTHM.

beat *adjective* EXHAUSTED.

beating *noun*
1. A punishment dealt with blows or lashes: *gave him a beating for lying.*
Syns: flogging, hiding, licking (*Slang*), thrashing, whipping.
2. DEFEAT.

beatitude *noun* HAPPINESS.

beau *noun*
A man who courts a woman: *a flirt surrounded by beaus.*
Syns: admirer, courter, suitor, swain.

beau geste *noun* COURTESY.

beau ideal *noun* MODEL.

beauteous *adjective* BEAUTIFUL.

beautiful *adjective*
Having qualities that delight the eye: *the most beautiful face I ever saw.*
Syns: attractive, beauteous, bonny (*Scot.*), comely, fair, good-looking, gorgeous, handsome, lovely, pretty, pulchritudinous, ravishing, sightly. —*Idiom* easy on the eyes.

beautify *verb* GRACE.

beauty *noun*
1. A woman regarded as beautiful: *was a real beauty in her day.*
Syns: belle, doll (*Slang*), knockout (*Slang*), looker (*Slang*), lovely, stunner. —*Idiom* sight for sore eyes.
2. VIRTUE.

becalm *verb* CALM.

beckon *verb* COURT.

becloud *verb* OBSCURE.

beclouded *adjective* FILMY.

become *verb*
1. To come to be: *As time went on she became more and more like her mother. New York became my home.*
   Syns: come, get, grow, turn (out), wax.
2. FIT.
3. FLATTER.
4. SUIT.

becoming *adjective*
1. Pleasingly suited to the wearer: *wore a becoming hat.*
   Syns: attractive, flattering.
2. CORRECT.

becrush *verb* CRUSH.
bed *noun* BASE¹.
bed *verb*
1. HARBOR.
2. RETIRE.
3. TAKE.

bedamn *verb* SWEAR.
bedaub *verb* SMEAR.
bedaze *verb* DAZE.
bedazzle *verb* DAZE.
bedeck *verb* ADORN.
bedevil *verb*
1. ANNOY.
2. BESIEGE.

bedim *verb* OBSCURE.
bedlamite *adjective* INSANE.
bedog *verb* FOLLOW.
bedraggled *adjective* SHABBY.
bee *noun* FANCY.
beef *noun*
1. COMPLAINT.
2. GRIEVANCE.

beef *verb* COMPLAIN.
beef up *verb* INCREASE.
beetle *verb* HANG.
befall *verb*
1. CHANCE.
2, 3. COME.

befit *verb*
1. FIT.
2. SUIT.

befitting *adjective*
1. APPROPRIATE.
2. CONVENIENT.
3. CORRECT.

befog *verb* OBSCURE.
before *adverb*
1, 2. EARLIER.

beforehand *adverb*
1. EARLIER.
2. EARLY.

beforetime *adverb* EARLIER.
befoul *verb*
1. BLACKEN.
2. CONTAMINATE.
3. DIRTY.

befuddle *verb* CONFUSE.
befuddled *adjective* CONFUSED.
befuddlement *noun* DAZE.
beg *verb*
1. To ask or ask for as charity: *begging for quarters on street corners.*
   Syns: bum (*Slang*), cadge (*Informal*), mooch (*Slang*), panhandle (*Slang*).
2. APPEAL.

begats *noun*
1. GENEALOGY.
2. PROGENY.

beget *verb* FATHER.
beggar *noun*
1. One who begs habitually or for a living: *beggars and derelicts annoying passers-by.*
   Syns: almsman, almswoman, bummer¹ (*Slang*), cadger (*Informal*), mendicant, moocher (*Slang*), panhandler (*Slang*).
2. PAUPER.
3. SUPPLICANT.

beggary *noun*
1. The condition of being a beggar: *forced into beggary after years of unemployment.*
   Syns: mendicancy, mendicity.
2. POVERTY.

begin *verb*
1. To come into being: *Charity begins at home.*
   Syns: arise, commence, originate, start.
2. START.

beginner *noun*
One who is just starting to learn or do something: *As a beginner I played scales.*
   Syns: fledgling, freshman, initiate, innocent, neophyte, novice, novitiate (*also* noviciate), rookie (*Slang*), tenderfoot, tyro.

beginning *noun*
1. The act or process of bringing or being brought into existence: *assumed responsibility for the beginning of the strike.*
   Syns: commencement, genesis, inauguration, inception, initiation, kickoff (*Informal*), launching, leadoff, opening, start.
2. BIRTH.

beginning *adjective*
1. Indicating the start of something: *the beginning stages of the negotiations.*
   Syns: inceptive, initial, introductory.
2. EARLY.
3. ELEMENTARY.

begird *verb*
1. BAND¹.
2. SURROUND.

begrime *verb* DIRTY.
begrudge *verb* ENVY.
beguile *verb* DECEIVE.
beguiled *adjective* INFATUATED.
béguin *noun* INFATUATION.
behave *verb*
1, 2. ACT.
behavior *noun*
1. The manner in which one behaves:
*always on his best behavior when his
in-laws are there.*
Syns: actions, comportment, conduct,
demeanor, deportment, havings
(*Scot.*), havior (*Regional*), way.
2. The way in which a machine or other
thing performs or functions: *studying
the behavior of matter at extremely low
temperatures.*
Syns: functioning, operation,
performance, reaction, working.
behemoth *noun* GIANT.
behemothic *adjective* GIANT.
behest *noun* COMMAND.
behind *noun* BOTTOM.
  behind *adverb*
1. LATE.
2. SLOW.
behindhand *adjective*
1. BACKWARD.
2. LATE.
  behindhand *adverb*
1. LATE.
2. SLOW.
behold *verb* SEE.
beholden *adjective* OBLIGED.
beholder *noun* WATCHER.
behoove *verb* SUIT.
being *noun*
1. ACTUALITY.
2. EFFECT.
3. ESSENCE.
4. EXISTENCE.
5. HUMAN BEING.
6. THING.
belabor *verb* BEAT.
belated *adjective* LATE.
belatedness *noun* LATENESS.
belay *verb*
1, 2. STOP.
belch *verb* ERUPT.
beldam also **beldame** *noun* WITCH.
beleaguer *verb*
1. ANNOY.
2, 3. BESIEGE.
belie *verb*
1. DISTORT.
2. REFUTE.
belief *noun*
1. Mental acceptance of the truth or
actuality of something: *What she tells
you is not worthy of belief.*

Syns: credence, credit, faith.
2. Something believed or accepted as
true by a person: *It is her belief that
the end justifies the means.*
Syns: conviction, feeling, idea, mind,
notion, opinion, persuasion, position,
sentiment, view.
3. CONFIDENCE.
believable *adjective*
Worthy of being believed: *a completely
believable account of the biggest hurricane
in years.*
Syns: colorable, credible, creditable,
plausible.
believe *verb*
1. To regard (something) as true or real:
I don't believe a word he says.
Syns: accept, buy (*Slang*), go for
(*Slang*), swallow (*Slang*).
2. To have confidence in the
truthfulness of: *Do you believe her?*
Syns: credit, trust. —*Idiom* take at
one's word.
3. To have an opinion: *He believes that
jogging is good for his health.*
Syns: consider, deem, figure
(*Informal*), hold, opine, think.
—*Idiom* be of the opinion.
4. FEEL.
belittle *verb*
To think, represent, or speak of as small
or unimportant: *belittled the
accomplishments of his major political
opponent.*
Syns: decry, depreciate, derogate,
detract (from), discount, disparage,
downgrade, knock (*Slang*), minimize,
run down (*Informal*), talk down.
—*Idiom* make light (*or* little) of.
belittlement *noun*
The act or an instance of belittling: *a
belittlement of his sister's
accomplishments.*
Syns: depreciation, derogation,
detraction, disparagement.
belittling *adjective* DISPARAGING.
belle *noun* BEAUTY.
bellicose *adjective*
1. BELLIGERENT.
2. MILITARY.
bellicosity *noun*
1. BELLIGERENCE.
2. FIGHT.
belligerence *noun*
1. Warlike or hostile attitude or nature:
*greeted my suggestion with real
belligerence.*
Syns: bellicosity, belligerency,
combativeness, contentiousness,
hostility, pugnacity, truculence (*also*
truculency).

2. AGGRESSION.
3. FIGHT.

belligerency *noun*
1. AGGRESSION.
2. BELLIGERENCE.
3. CONFLICT.
4. FIGHT.

belligerent *adjective*
1. Having or showing an eagerness to fight: *a belligerent, loose-tongued drunkard.*
   Syns: bellicose, combative, contentious, hostile, pugnacious, quarrelsome, scrappy (*Informal*), truculent, warlike.
2. Of or engaged in warfare: *a belligerent nation.*
   Syns: combatant, fighting, warring. —*Idiom* at war.
3. AGGRESSIVE.

bellow *verb*
1. ROAR.
2. SHOUT.

bellow *noun* ROAR.

belly *verb* BULGE.

bellyache *verb* COMPLAIN.

bellyacher *noun* GROUCH.

belong *verb*
1. To be the property of a person or thing: *The necklace once belonged to her grandmother.*
   Syns: appertain, pertain.
2. To have a proper or suitable place: *The clean shirts belong in the bureau.*
   Syns: fit, go.

belongings *noun*
1. Those articles that belong to someone: *lost all her personal belongings in the fire.*
   Syns: effects, goods, possessions, stuff (*Informal*), things.
2. EFFECTS.

beloved *noun* DARLING.

beloved *adjective*
1. DARLING.
2. FAVORITE.

belt *noun*
1. AREA.
2. BLOW².
3. DRINK.

belt *verb*
1. BAND¹.
2. HIT.

bemask *verb* DISGUISE.

bemean *verb* HUMBLE.

bemire *verb* MUDDY.

bemired *adjective* MUDDY.

bemud *verb* MUDDY.

bemuse *verb* DAZE.

bemused *adjective* ABSENT-MINDED.

benchmark *noun* STANDARD.

bend *verb*
1. To swerve from a straight line: *a highway that bends to the left.*
   Syns: bow, crook, curve, round.
2. To cause to move, esp. at an angle: *The prism bent the emerging light rays.*
   Syns: angle, deflect, refract, turn.
3. To be unable to hold up: *a bridge that bent under the weight of the train.*
   Syns: break, cave in (*Informal*), collapse, crumple, fold (*Informal*), give, go. —*Idiom* give way.
4. APPLY.
5, 6. DISPOSE.
7. STOOP.

bend *noun*
Something bent: *the car rounding the bend.*
   Syns: bow, crook, curvation, curvature, curve, round, turn.

bender *noun*
Slang. A drinking bout: *went on a week's bender.*
   Syns: bat¹ (*Slang*), binge (*Slang*), booze, brannigan (*Slang*), carousal, carouse, compotation, drunk, tear¹ (*Slang*).

bending *adjective* CROOKED.

benediction *noun* GRACE.

benefact *verb* HELP.

benefaction *noun*
1. BENEVOLENCE.
2. DONATION.

benefactor *noun*
1. DONOR.
2. PATRON.

benefic *adjective* BENEFICIAL.

beneficence *noun*
1, 2. BENEVOLENCE.
3. DONATION.

beneficent *adjective* BENEFICIAL.

beneficial *adjective*
Affording benefit: *a beneficial climate.*
   Syns: advantageous, aidful (*Archaic*), benefic, beneficent, benignant, favorable, good, helpful, propitious, salutary, toward (*Rare*), useful.

benefit *verb*
1. To derive advantage: *benefited from the stock split.*
   Syns: advantage, capitalize (on), profit.
2. PROFIT.

benefit *noun*
1. ADVANTAGE.
2. FAVOR.
3. INTEREST.
4. USE.
5. WELFARE.

benevolence *noun*
1. Kindly, charitable interest in others: *ruled his subjects with benevolence.*
   Syns: altruism, beneficence, benevolentness, benignancy, charitableness, charity, good will, grace, kindliness, kindness.
2. A charitable deed: *was grateful for their financial benevolence.*
   Syns: benefaction, beneficence, benignity (*Archaic*), favor, kindness, oblation, office(s), philanthropy.

benevolent *adjective*
1. Characterized by kindness and concern for others: *a benevolent ruler.*
   Syns: benign, benignant, big, chivalrous, good, humane, humanitarian, kind, kindhearted, kindly.
2. Of or concerned with charity: *a benevolent fund.*
   Syns: altruistic, charitable, eleemosynary, philanthropic (*also* philanthropical).

benevolentness *noun* BENEVOLENCE.

benighted *adjective*
1. IGNORANT.
2. UNPROGRESSIVE.

benightedness *noun* IGNORANCE.

benign *adjective*
1. BENEVOLENT.
2. FAVORABLE.
3. KIND[1].

benignancy *noun* BENEVOLENCE.

benignant *adjective*
1. BENEFICIAL.
2. BENEVOLENT.
3. KIND[1].

benignity *noun* BENEVOLENCE.

bent *adjective*
1. Deviating from a straight line: *a bent tree limb.*
   Syns: arced, arched, arciform, arrondi (*French*), bowed, curved, curvilinear, rounded.
2. SET[1].

bent *noun*
1. An inclination to something: *a strong bent toward conservatism.*
   Syns: bias, disposition, leaning, partiality, penchant, predilection, predisposition, proclivity, proneness, propensity, squint, tendency, turn.
2. TALENT.

benumb *verb*
1. DAZE.
2. DEADEN.
3. PARALYZE.

benumbed *adjective*
1. DEAD.
2. DULL.

bequeath *verb*
1. HAND DOWN at **hand**.
2. LEAVE[1].

berate *verb* BAWL OUT at **bawl**.

bereave *verb* DEPRIVE.

berth *noun*
1. JOB.
2. PLACE.
3. POSITION.

berth *verb* HARBOR.

beseech *verb* APPEAL.

beseechment *noun* APPEAL.

beseem *verb* SUIT.

beset *verb*
1. ANNOY.
2. ATTACK.
3, 4. BESIEGE.
5. SURROUND.

besetment *noun* ANNOYANCE.

besides *adverb* ADDITIONALLY.

besiege *verb*
1. To surround with hostile troops: *besiege a fortress.*
   Syns: beleaguer, beset, blockade, invest (*Mil.*), siege.
2. To trouble persistently from or as if from all sides: *was besieged with complaints.*
   Syns: badger, bedevil, beleaguer, beset, harass, harry, hound, importune, pester, plague.
3. SURROUND.

besiegement *noun* SIEGE.

besmear *verb*
1. BLACKEN.
2. SMEAR.

besmirch *verb* BLACKEN.

besoil *verb* DIRTY.

besotted *adjective* DRUNK.

bespatter *verb*
1. BLACKEN.
2. SPLASH.
3. SPOT.

bespeak *verb*
1. ADDRESS.
2. BOOK.
3. INDICATE.

bespeckle *verb* SPECKLE.

besprinkle *verb* SPRINKLE.

best *adjective*
1. Surpassing all others in quality: *the best diamonds available.*
   Syns: bettermost (*Chiefly Regional*), optimal, optimum, superb, superlative, unsurpassed.
2. Much more than half: *The best part of the week is gone.*
   Syns: better[1], bettermost (*Chiefly Regional*), greater, larger, largest.

best *noun*
That which is superlative: *chose only the best among many paintings.*
 Syns: choice, cream, crème de la crème (*French*), elite (*also* élite), flower, pick, prize, top. —*Idioms* cream of the crop, flower of the flock, pick of the bunch, top cream.

best *verb*
1. DEFEAT.
2. SURPASS.
3. TRIUMPH.

bestain *verb* STAIN.

bestial *adjective* FIERCE.

bestialize *verb* CORRUPT.

bestow *verb*
1. CONFER.
2. DONATE.
3. GIVE.
4. HARBOR.

bestowal *noun* CONFERMENT.

bestride *verb* STRIDE.

bet *verb*
1. To make a bet on: *We bet on the winner.*
 Syns: gamble, game, lay¹, lay down, play, post, put, stake, wager. —*Idiom* take a flyer.
2. GAMBLE.

bet *noun*
1. Something valuable risked on an uncertain outcome: *My bet on the race is $50.*
 Syns: ante (*Slang*), pot (*Card Games*), stake, wager.
2. GAMBLE.

bête noire *noun* HATE.

bethink *verb* REMEMBER.

betide *verb*
1, 2. COME.

betimes *adverb*
1. EARLY.
2. NOW.

betoken *verb*
1. INDICATE.
2. PROMISE.

betray *verb*
1. To be treacherous to: *betrayed his comrades.*
 Syns: cross (up), double-cross (*Slang*), rat (on) (*Slang*), sell out (*Slang*).
2. To disclose in a breach of confidence: *betrayed my secret.*
 Syns: blab, discover (*Archaic*), divulge, expose, give away, let out, reveal, spill (*Informal*), tell, uncover, unveil. —*Idioms* let slip, let the cat out of the bag, spill the beans, tell all.
3, 4. DECEIVE.

betrayal *noun*
An act of betraying: *suffered betrayal to the Gestapo.*
 Syns: betrayment, double-cross (*Slang*), sellout (*Slang*), treachery. —*Idiom* Judas kiss.

betrayer *noun*
One who betrays: *a treacherous betrayer hanged by his comrades.*
 Syns: double-crosser (*Slang*), Judas, rat (*Slang*), traitor.

betrayment *noun* BETRAYAL.

betrothal *noun* ENGAGEMENT.

betrothed *adjective* ENGAGED.
 betrothed *noun* INTENDED.

betrothment *noun* ENGAGEMENT.

better¹ *adjective*
1. Of greater excellence than another: *This book is better than that one.*
 Syns: preferable, superior.
2. BEST.

better *verb*
1. IMPROVE.
2. SURPASS.

better *noun*
1. ADVANTAGE.
2. SUPERIOR.

better *adverb*
To a greater extent: *were better suited for the job than the others.*
 Syn: more.

better² *noun* SEE **bettor**.

betterment *noun*
1. IMPROVEMENT.
2. PROGRESS.

bettermost *adjective*
1, 2. BEST.

bettor *also* **better** *noun*
One who bets: *throngs of bettors at the race.*
 Syns: gambler, gamester, player, speculator.

bevel *adjective* BIAS.

beveled *adjective* BIAS.

bever *noun* BITE.

beverage *noun* DRINK.

bevy *noun* GROUP.

beware *verb* LOOK OUT at **look**.

bewilder *verb* CONFUSE.

bewildered *adjective* CONFUSED.

bewitch *verb*
1, 2. CHARM.

bewitched *adjective* INFATUATED.

bewitching *adjective*
1. ATTRACTIVE.
2. SEDUCTIVE.
3. WITCHING.

bias *noun*
1. An inclination for or against that

inhibits impartial judgment: *a decision influenced by personal bias.*
Syns: one-sidedness, partiality, prejudice, prepossession, tendentiousness.
2. BENT.

bias *verb*
1. To cause to have a prejudiced view: *His past experiences have biased his outlook.*
Syns: color, jaundice, prejudice, prepossess, warp.
2. To direct (material) to the interests of a particular group: *a magazine biased toward conservatives.*
Syns: angle, skew, slant.
3. DISPOSE.
4. INFLUENCE.

bias *adjective*
Angled at a slant: *a bias fold.*
Syns: bevel, beveled, biased (*also* biassed), diagonal, oblique, slanted, slanting.

biased *also* **biassed** *adjective*
1. Exhibiting bias: *a biased remark in favor of the tax.*
Syns: colored, one-sided, partial, partisan, prejudiced, prejudicial, prepossessed, tendentious.
2. BIAS.

bibelot *noun* NOVELTY.
bibulous *adjective* ABSORBENT.
bicker *verb* ARGUE.
bid *verb*
1. COMMAND.
2. GO.
3. INVITE.

bid *noun*
1. INVITATION.
2. OFFER.

biddable *adjective* OBEDIENT.
biddie *noun* SEE **biddy.**
bidding *noun* COMMAND.
biddy *also* **biddie** *noun* WITCH.
bide *verb*
1. LIVE¹.
2. PAUSE.
3. REMAIN.

biff *noun* BLOW².
biff *verb* HIT.
biform *adjective* DOUBLE.
bifurcate *verb* BRANCH.
big *adjective*
1. Notably above average in amount, size, or scope: *a big inheritance.*
Syns: considerable, extensive, good, great, healthy, large, large-scale, sizable (*also* sizeable), tidy (*Informal*).
2. Full to the point of flowing over: *eyes big with tears.*

Syns: awash, brimful, brimming, overflowing.
3. BENEVOLENT.
4. GENEROUS.
5. IMPORTANT.
6. MATURE.

big *noun* DIGNITARY.
Big Brother *noun* DICTATOR.
biggish *adjective* SIZABLE.
bighead *noun* EGOTISM.
bigheadedness *noun* EGOTISM.
big-hearted *adjective* GENEROUS.
big-heartedness *noun* GENEROSITY.
bight *noun* BAY¹.
big-league *adjective*
Being among the leaders of a particular class: *a big-league publisher.*
Syns: big-time (*Slang*), blue-chip, heavyweight (*Informal*), major, major-league.

bigness *noun* SIZE.
bigoted *adjective* INTOLERANT.
bigotry *noun* PREJUDICE.
big shot *noun* DIGNITARY.
big-time *adjective* BIG-LEAGUE.
big-timer *noun* DIGNITARY.
big wheel *noun* DIGNITARY.
bigwig *noun* DIGNITARY.
bilge *noun* NONSENSE.
bilk *verb* CHEAT.
bill¹ *verb*
To present a statement of fees or charges to: *Bill me next month.*
Syn: invoice.

bill *noun*
1. ACCOUNT.
2. PROGRAM.

bill² *noun*
1. The horny projection forming a bird's jaws: *The pelican has a large bill.*
Syn: beak.
2. The projecting rim on the front of a cap: *The bill shades my eyes.*
Syns: brim, peak, visor.

billet *verb* HARBOR.
billet *noun*
1. PLACE.
2. POSITION.

billingsgate *noun* VITUPERATION.
binary *adjective* DOUBLE.
bind *verb*
1. ASSOCIATE.
2. COMMIT.
3. DRESS.
4. TIE.

bind *noun* PREDICAMENT.
bine *noun* SHOOT.
binge *noun*
1. A period of uncontrolled self-indulgence: *a shopping binge.*

Syns: blowoff (*Informal*), fling, jag (*Slang*), orgy, rampage, spree.
2. BENDER.
bird *noun* HISS.
birdbrained *adjective* GIDDY.
bird-dog *verb* FOLLOW.
birth *noun*
1. The act or process of bringing forth young: *witnessed the birth of my son.*
Syns: accouchement (*French*), birthing (*Chiefly Regional*), childbearing, childbirth, delivery, labor, lying-in, parturition, travail.
2. The initial stage of a developmental process: *the birth of Christianity.*
Syns: beginning, commencement, dawn, dawning, genesis, inception, nascence (*also* nascency), onset, opening, origin, outset, spring, start.
3. ANCESTRY.
birth *verb* BEAR.
birthing *noun* BIRTH.
birthright *noun*
1. A privilege granted a person by virtue of birth: *Free speech is the birthright of Americans.*
Syns: appanage (*also* apanage), droit, perquisite, prerogative, right.
2. Any special privilege accorded a firstborn: *The estate was the eldest son's birthright.*
Syns: heritage, inheritance, legacy, patrimony.
bistered *adjective* DARK.
bit¹ *noun*
1. A tiny amount: *doesn't make a bit of difference.*
Syns: crumb, dab, dash, doit, dram, drop, fragment, grain, hoot, iota, jot, minim, mite, modicum, molecule, ounce, particle, scrap¹, scruple, shred, smidgen (*Informal*), smitch (*Informal*), snap, speck, spot (*Chiefly Brit. Informal*), tittle, whit.
2. A small portion of food: *a bit of cheese.*
Syns: bite, crumb, morsel, mouthful, piece.
3. A rather short period: *waited for a bit.*
Syns: space, spell³, stretch, time, while.
4. *Informal.* A particular kind of activity: *did the intellectual bit.*
Syn: routine. —*Idiom* song and dance.
bit² *verb* RESTRAIN.
bitch *verb* COMPLAIN.
bitchy *adjective* MALEVOLENT.

bite *verb*
1. To seize, as food, with the teeth: *The dog bit into the meat.*
Syns: champ (*also* chomp), gnash, gnaw.
2. To consume gradually, as by chemical reaction, friction, etc.: *acid biting into the silver.*
Syns: corrode, eat, erode, gnaw, wear, wear away.
3. STING.
bite *noun*
1. *Informal.* A light meal: *has a bite before bed every night.*
Syns: bever (*Chiefly Regional*), morsel, snack, snap (*Chiefly Brit. Regional*)
2. BIT¹.
3. EDGE.
biting *adjective*
1. So sharp as to cause mental pain: *biting criticism.*
Syns: acerb, acerbic, acid, acidic, acrid, caustic, cutting, incisive, mordacious, mordant, penetrating, pungent, scathing, slashing, stinging, truculent, vitriolic, vituperative.
2. INCISIVE.
bitter *adjective*
1. Having a noticeably sharp, pungent taste or smell: *a bitter wine.*
Syns: acerb, acerbic, acrid, amaroidal, astringent, austere (*Archaic*), harsh, sour.
2. Causing sharp, often prolonged discomfort: *the bitter climate of the Sahara.*
Syns: brutal, hard, harsh, rough, rugged, severe.
3. Difficult to accept: *the bitter truth.*
Syns: afflictive, distasteful, grievous, indigestible, painful, unpalatable.
4. FRIGID.
5. RESENTFUL.
bitter *verb* EMBITTER.
bitterness *noun* RESENTMENT.
bizarre *adjective*
1. ECCENTRIC.
2. FANTASTIC.
3. FREAKISH.
blab *verb*
1. BETRAY.
2. GOSSIP.
blab *noun* CHATTER.
blabber *verb* CHATTER.
blabber *noun* CHATTER.
blabby *adjective* GOSSIPY.
black *adjective*
1. Of the darkest achromatic visual value: *a black hat.*
Syns: atramentous, ebon (*Poetic*),

ebony, inky, jet[1], jet-black, jetty,
onyx, pitch-black, pitchy, sable,
sooty.
2. Having no light: *a black cave.*
Syns: caliginous (*Rare*), dark, inky,
pitch-dark.
3. DIRTY.
4. EVIL.
5. GLOOMY.
6. MALEVOLENT.

black *verb*
1. BRUISE.
2. DIRTY.

black out *verb*
1. To suffer temporary loss of
consciousness: *blacked out from lack
of oxygen.*
Syns: faint, keel over, pass out
(*Informal*), swoon.
2. CENSOR.

black-a-vised *adjective* DARK.

blackball *verb*
1. To exclude from normal social or
professional activities: *suspected
troublemakers blackballed from jobs.*
Syns: blacklist, boycott, ostracize,
shut out.
2. VETO.

blacken *verb*
1. To cast aspersions on: *blackened the
good name of a great statesman.*
Syns: befoul, besmear, besmirch,
bespatter, denigrate, dirty, smear,
smudge, smut, soil, stain, sully, taint,
tarnish. —*Idioms* give a black eye to,
throw mud on.
2. DIRTY.

black eye *noun*
1. A bruise surrounding the eye: *got a
black eye in the fight.*
Syns: mouse (*Slang*), shiner (*Slang*).
—*Idiom* eye in mourning.
2. STAIN.

black-hearted *adjective* MALEVOLENT.

blackish *adjective*
Somewhat black: *blackish clouds.*
Syns: dark, dusky.

blackjack *verb* COERCE.

blacklist *verb* BLACKBALL.

blackout *noun*
A temporary loss of consciousness:
suffered blackouts at high altitudes.
Syns: faint, swoon, syncope (*Path.*).
—*Idiom* dead faint.

blade *noun* EDGE.

blamable *also* **blameable** *adjective*
BLAMEWORTHY.

blame *verb*
1. To find fault with: *no one to blame
but myself.*
Syns: censure, condemn, criticize, cut

up (*Informal*), denounce, denunciate,
fault, pan (*Informal*), rap[1] (*Slang*),
reprehend, reprobate.
2. FIX.

blame *noun*
1. Responsibility for an error or crime:
The blame for the cover-up is mine.
Syns: culpability, fault, guilt, onus.
2. A finding fault: *said nothing to them
in the way of blame.*
Syns: censure, condemnation,
criticism, denunciation, reprehension,
reprobation.

blameable *adjective* SEE **blamable.**

blamed *adjective* DAMNED.

blameful *adjective* BLAMEWORTHY.

blameless *adjective*
1. EXEMPLARY.
2. INNOCENT.

blameworthy *adjective*
Deserving blame: *behavior that was
blameworthy if not criminal.*
Syns: blamable (*also* blameable),
blameful, censurable, culpable, guilty,
reprehensible. —*Idiom* at fault.

blanch *also* **blench** *verb* PALE.

blanched *adjective* PALE.

bland *adjective*
1. GENTLE.
2. INSIPID.
3. NEUTRAL.
4. SUAVE.

blandish *verb*
1. COAX.
2. FLATTER.

blandishment *noun* FLATTERY.

blandness *noun* INSIPIDITY.

blank *adjective* EXPRESSIONLESS.

blanket *verb* COVER

blankety-blank *adjective* DAMNED.

blankness *noun*
1, 2. EMPTINESS.

blare *verb*
1. GLARE.
2. SCREAM.

blare *noun* GLARE.

blaring *adjective* LOUD.

blarney *noun* FLATTERY.

blaspheme *verb* SWEAR.

blasphemous *adjective*
SACRILEGIOUS.

blasphemy *noun*
1. SACRILEGE.
2. SWEAR.

blast *noun*
1. A violent release of confined energy,
usu. accompanied by a loud sound
and shock waves: *a bomb blast.*
Syns: blowout, blowup, burst,
detonation, explosion, fulmination.

2. An earsplitting, explosive noise: *the blast of jet afterburners.*
Syns: bang, boom, burst, roar, thunder.

3. *Informal.* A big, exuberant party: *a pregraduation blast.*
Syns: bash (*Slang*), blowout (*Slang*), celebration, shindig (*Slang*).

blast *verb*
1. To make an earsplitting, explosive noise: *Jet fighters blasted off the runway.*
Syns: bang, boom, roar, thunder.

2. To spoil or destroy: *Our hopes have been blasted.*
Syns: blight, dash, nip, wreck.

3. EXPLODE.

4. OVERWHELM.

blasted *adjective* DAMNED.

blatant *adjective*
1. SHAMELESS.
2. VOCIFEROUS.

blather *verb* BABBLE.

blather *noun*
1. BABBLE.
2. NONSENSE.

blatherskite *noun* BABBLE.

blaze[1] *verb*
1. BEAM.
2. BURN.
3. GLARE.
4. SCREAM.

blaze *noun*
1. FIRE.
2. GLARE.

blaze[2] *verb* ADVERTISE.

blazing *adjective*
1. On fire: *The forest is blazing.*
Syns: ablaze, afire, aflame, alight[2], burning, comburent, conflagrant, fiery, flaming, flaring, ignited.
—*Idioms* in a blaze, in flames.

2. Extremely bright: *blazing sunlight.*
Syns: brilliant, dazzling, glaring, glary.

3. PASSIONATE.

blazon *verb* ADVERTISE.

bleach *verb* PALE.

bleak *adjective*
1. Cold and forbidding: *a bleak, silent man.*
Syns: austere, dour, grim, hard, harsh, severe.

2. GLOOMY.

blear *verb* OBSCURE.

blear *adjective* UNCLEAR.

bleary *adjective*
1. EXHAUSTED.
2. UNCLEAR.

bleed *verb* OOZE.

blemish *noun*
1. DEFECT.
2. STAIN.

blemish *verb* INJURE.

blench[1] *verb* FLINCH.

blench[2] *verb* SEE **blanch**.

blend *verb*
1. HARMONIZE.
2. MIX.

blend *noun* MIXTURE.

bless *verb*
1. SANCTIFY.
2. THANK.

blessed *adjective*
1. DAMNED.
2. HOLY.

blessedness *noun*
1. HAPPINESS.
2. HOLINESS.

blessing *noun*
1. ADVANTAGE.
2. GRACE.

blight *verb* BLAST.

blind *adjective*
1. Without the sense of sight: *was blind from birth.*
Syns: dark (*Regional*), eyeless, sightless, unseeing.

2. Unwilling or unable to perceive: *was blind to the danger.*
Syns: dull, purblind, uncomprehending, unperceptive.

3. Screened from the view of oncoming drivers: *a blind intersection.*
Syns: concealed, hidden.

4. DRUNK.

blind *verb* DAZE.

blind *noun*
A shelter for concealing hunters: *a duck blind.*
Syns: hide[1] (*Brit.*), stand.

blind alley *noun*
Informal. A course leading nowhere: *reached a blind alley in the negotiations.*
Syn: cul-de-sac. —*Idiom* dead-end street.

blindness *noun*
The condition of not being able to see: *suffered blindness after the accident.*
Syn: sightlessness.

blink *verb*
1. To open and close the eyes rapidly: *blinked in the glare.*
Syns: bat[3], nictitate (*also* nictate), twinkle (*Archaic*), wink.

2. To shine with intermittent gleams: *The ship's signal blinked in the night.*
Syns: coruscate, flash, flicker, glimmer, twinkle, wink.

blink at *verb*
To pretend not to see: *The senator merely blinked at the corruption.*
Syns: connive at, dissemble (*Obs.*), ignore, pass over, wink at. —*Idioms* be blind to, close (*or* shut) one's eyes to, look the other way, turn a blind eye to.

blink *noun*
1. A brief closing of the eyes: *One blink and the bird was gone.*
Syns: nictitation (*also* nictation), wink.
2. A sudden quick light: *saw a blink from the signal in the dark.*
Syns: coruscation, flash, flicker, glance¹, gleam, glimmer, glint, spark, twinkle, wink.
3. GLANCE¹.

blinker *noun* EYE.
blip *verb* SLAP.
blister *verb* SLAM.
blistering *adjective* HOT.
blithe *adjective*
1. GAY.
2. LIGHT².
blithesome *adjective* GAY.
bloated *adjective* POMPOUS.
bloc *noun* COMBINE.
block *verb*
1. FILL.
2. OBSTRUCT.
block out *verb*
1. To cut off from sight: *The trees block out the view.*
Syns: close¹, hide¹, obscure, obstruct, screen, shroud, shut out.
2. DRAFT.
block *noun*
1. BAR.
2. HEAD.
blockade *verb* BESIEGE.
blockhead *noun* DULLARD.
blockheaded *adjective* STUPID.
blocky *adjective* STOCKY.
blond also **blonde** *adjective* FAIR.
blood *noun*
1. The fluid circulated by the heart through the vascular system: *lost a lot of blood during the operation.*
Syns: claret (*Slang*), gore.
2. ANCESTRY.
3. MURDER.
blood bath *noun* MASSACRE.
bloodcurdling *adjective* HORRIBLE.
bloodhound *verb* DOG.
bloodless *adjective*
1. INSENSITIVE.
2, 3. PALE.
bloodletting *noun* MASSACRE.

bloodline *noun* ANCESTRY.
bloodshed *noun* MASSACRE.
bloodstained *adjective* BLOODY.
bloodsucker *noun* PARASITE.
bloodsucking *adjective* PARASITIC.
bloodthirsty *adjective* MURDEROUS.
bloody *adjective*
1. Of or covered with blood: *a bloody knife.*
Syns: bloodstained, ensanguined, gory, imbrued (*also* embrued).
2. Attended by or causing bloodshed: *a bloody battle.*
Syns: sanguinary, sanguineous.
3. MURDEROUS.
bloody *verb*
To cover with blood: *bloodied my hands while cleaning the fish.*
Syns: ensanguine, imbrue (*also* embrue).
bloom *noun*
1. The showy reproductive structure of a plant: *rose blooms.*
Syns: blossom, floret, flower.
2. A condition or time of vigor and freshness: *the bloom of Greek civilization.*
Syns: blossom, efflorescence, florescence, flower, flush, prime.
3. A fresh, rosy complexion: *was pale and had lost her bloom.*
Syns: blossom, blush, flush, glow.
bloom *verb*
1. To bear flowers: *roses blooming on the fence.*
Syns: blossom, blow³, burgeon, effloresce, flower.
2. FLOURISH.
bloomer *noun* BLUNDER.
blooming *adjective*
1. DAMNED.
2. FRESH.
3. RUDDY.
4. UTTER².
blooper *noun* BLUNDER.
blossom *noun*
1, 2, 3. BLOOM.
blossom *verb*
1. BLOOM.
2. FLOURISH.
blot *noun* STAIN.
blot out *verb*
1. ANNIHILATE.
2. CANCEL.
bloviate *verb* RANT.
blow¹ *verb*
1. To be in a state of motion, as air: *The wind is blowing.*
Syns: puff, winnow.
2. BOAST.

3. BOTCH.
4. EXPLODE.
5. GO.
6. PANT.
7. TREAT.
8. WASTE.
blow in *verb* ARRIVE.
blow off *verb* AIR.
blow out *verb* BURST.
blow up *verb*
1. ANGER.
2. BURST.
3. EXPLODE.
blow *noun*
1. BOAST.
2. WIND¹.
blow² *noun*
1. A sudden sharp, powerful stroke: *a blow on the head.*
  Syns: bang, bash (*Informal*), belt (*Slang*), biff (*Slang*), bop (*Informal*), clout, conk, crack, hit, lick, paste (*Slang*), pound, smack¹, smacker, sock (*Slang*), swat, thwack, wallop (*Informal*), welt (*Informal*), whack, whop.
2. SHOCK.
blow³ *verb* BLOOM.
blow-by-blow *adjective* DETAILED.
blower *noun* BRAGGART.
blowhard *noun* BRAGGART.
blowoff *noun* BINGE.
blowout *noun*
1, 2. BLAST.
blowup *noun*
1. BLAST.
2. OUTBURST.
blowy *adjective* AIRY.
blub *verb* CRY.
blubber *verb* CRY.
blubbering *noun* CRY.
bludgeon *verb* INTIMIDATE.
blue *adjective*
1. DEPRESSED.
2. RACY.
blue *verb* WASTE.
blue blood *noun* SOCIETY.
blue-blooded *adjective* NOBLE.
bluebottle *noun* POLICEMAN.
blue-chip *adjective* BIG-LEAGUE.
bluecoat *noun* POLICEMAN.
blue-eyed *adjective* FAVORITE.
bluenose *noun* PRUDE.
bluenosed *adjective* GENTEEL.
blueprint *noun* DESIGN.
blueprint *verb*
1, 2. DESIGN.
blue-ribbon *adjective* EXCELLENT.
blues *noun* GLOOM.
bluff *verb* DECEIVE.

blunder *noun*
A stupid, clumsy mistake: *a million-dollar manufacturing blunder.*
  Syns: bloomer (*Slang*), blooper (*Informal*), boner (*Slang*), bull, bungle, foozle, fumble, goof (*Slang*), miscue, rock¹, screw-up (*Slang*), stumble, trip.
blunder *verb*
1. To move awkwardly or clumsily: *blundered around in the dark and fell.*
  Syns: bumble¹, lurch, stumble, wallow.
2. BOTCH.
blunderer *noun*
A stupid, clumsy person: *a store mismanaged by blunderers.*
  Syns: blunderhead, botcher, bungler, foozler, fumbler. —*Idiom* bull in a china shop.
blunderhead *noun* BLUNDERER.
blunt *verb*
1. DEADEN.
2. DULL.
blunt *adjective*
1. ABRUPT.
2. DULL.
blur *verb* OBSCURE.
blurred *adjective* FILMY.
blurt *verb* EXCLAIM.
blurt *noun* EXCLAMATION.
blush *verb*
To become red in the face: *blushed with embarrassment.*
  Syns: color, crimson, flush, glow, mantle, redden.
blush *noun* BLOOM.
bluster *verb* ROAR.
board *verb*
1. HARBOR.
2. TAKE.
boards *noun* STAGE.
boast *verb*
1. To talk with excessive pride: *boasted about their wealth.*
  Syns: blow¹ (*Slang*), brag, crow, gasconade, rodomontade (*also* rhodomontade), vaunt.
2. COMMAND.
boast *noun*
An act of boasting: *big boasts about his strength.*
  Syns: blow¹ (*Slang*), brag, braggadocio, fanfaronade, gasconade, rodomontade (*also* rhodomontade).
boaster *noun* BRAGGART.
boastful *adjective*
Characterized by or given to boasting: *boastful remarks about his ability.*
  Syns: braggadocian, braggart, braggy, rodomontade (*also* rhodomontade).

bob *verb* TAP[1].
  bob *noun* TAP[1].
bobby *noun* POLICEMAN.
bodement *noun* OMEN.
bodiless *adjective* IMMATERIAL.
bodily *adjective*
Of or pertaining to the human body:
bodily organs; bodily cleanliness.
  Syns: corporal, corporeal, fleshly,
  personal, physical, somatic.
body *noun*
1. The physical frame of a dead person
   or animal: *lowered the body into the
   coffin.*
   Syns: cadaver, carcass, corpse,
   corpus, mort (*Rare*), remains, stiff
   (*Slang*).
2. The main part: *The body of the paper
   discusses nuclear energy.*
   Syns: bulk, corpus, substance.
3. A separate and distinct portion of
   matter: *celestial bodies.*
   Syns: mass, object[1].
4. ASSEMBLY.
5. FORCE.
6. GROUP.
7. HUMAN BEING.
8. QUANTITY.
  body *verb* REPRESENT.
boff *noun* HIT.
bog *verb* HINDER.
bogey *noun*
  SEE **bogy**.
boggle *verb*
1. BOTCH.
2. STAGGER.
bogie *noun* SEE **bogy**.
bogle *noun* GHOST.
bogus *adjective* COUNTERFEIT.
bogy also **bogey, bogie** *noun*
GHOST.
bohunk *noun* LUMP[1].
boil *verb*
1. To cook (food) in liquid heated to
   the point of steaming: *boiled the
   potatoes.*
   Syns: parboil, seethe (*Archaic*),
   simmer, stew.
2. To be in a state of emotional or
   mental turmoil: *was silently boiling
   over the delay.*
   Syns: bubble, burn, churn, ferment,
   moil, seethe, simmer, smolder.
3. ANGER.
4. RUSH.
boil away *verb* EVAPORATE.
boil down *verb*
To reduce in complexity or scope: *My
complaints can be boiled down to this.*
  Syn: simplify.

boiling *adjective* HOT.
boisterous *adjective* VOCIFEROUS.
bold *adjective*
1. Standing out prominently: *a bold
   handwriting.*
   Syns: conspicuous, prominent,
   pronounced.
2. BRAVE.
3. DARING.
4. IMPUDENT.
5. STEEP[1].
boldacious *adjective* IMPUDENT.
boldfaced *adjective* IMPUDENT.
boldness *noun*
1. DARING.
2. IMPUDENCE.
bollix up *verb* BOTCH.
boloney *noun* SEE **baloney**.
bolster *verb* SUSTAIN.
bolt *noun* JUMP.
  bolt *verb*
1. JUMP.
2. GULP.
3. RUN.
4. RUSH.
bomb *noun* FAILURE.
bombard *verb* BARRAGE.
bombardment *noun* BARRAGE.
bombastic *adjective* SONOROUS.
bombed *adjective* DRUNK.
bombinate *verb* HUM.
bombination *noun* HUM.
bona fide *adjective* AUTHENTIC.
bond *noun*
1. That which unites or binds: *the bond
   of matrimony.*
   Syns: knot, ligament, ligature, link,
   linkage, nexus, tie, vinculum, yoke.
2. The close physical union of two
   objects: *a tight bond between wall and
   wallpaper.*
   Syns: adherence, adhesion, cohesion.
3. *Law.* Money supplied for the
   temporary release of an arrested
   person that guarantees his
   appearance for trial: *Bond was set at
   $100,000.*
   Syn: bail[1].
4. AGREEMENT.
5. ATTACHMENT.
  bond *verb*
To hold fast to: *plastics bonded with
cement.*
  Syns: adhere (to), clag (*Brit.
  Regional*), cleave, cling, cohere, stick.
bonds *noun*
Something that physically confines the
legs or arms: *prisoners in bonds.*
  Syns: chains, fetters, gyves (*Archaic*),
  irons, manacles, restraints, shackles.

bondsman *noun*
One who posts bond: *The bondsman and the attorney conferred.*
    Syns: bail¹, bailsman.

bone-dry *adjective* DRY.

boner *noun* BLUNDER.

bone up *verb*
To study hard, esp. when pressed for time: *had to bone up for the examination.*
    Syns: cram (*Informal*), grind, mug up.
    —*Idiom* burn the midnight oil.

bong *verb* RING².

bonkers *adjective* INSANE.

bonny *adjective*
1. BEAUTIFUL.
2. GOOD.

bonus *noun* REWARD.

bony *adjective* THIN.

boo *noun* HISS.

booby trap *noun* PITFALL.

boodle *noun*
1. BRIBE.
2. FORTUNE.
3. PLUNDER.

boohoo *verb* CRY.

boohoos *noun* CRY.

book *noun*
A printed and bound work: *a book on birds.*
    Syns: tome, volume.

book *verb*
1. To claim in advance: *booked a room.*
    Syns: bespeak, engage, reserve.
2. LIST.

bookish *adjective*
1. PEDANTIC.
2. STUDIOUS.

booky *adjective* PEDANTIC.

boom *verb*
1. BLAST.
2. PROSPER.
3. RUMBLE.

boom *noun* BLAST.

boomerang *verb* BACKFIRE.

booming *adjective* FLOURISHING.

boon¹ *noun* ADVANTAGE.

boon² *adjective* GAY.

boor *noun*
An unrefined, rude person: *a boor who interrupted constantly.*
    Syns: barbarian, bosthoon (*Ir.*), bounder (*Chiefly Brit.*), chuff, churl, grobian, mucker, Philistine (*also* philistine), vulgarian, yahoo.

boorish *adjective* COARSE.

boost *verb*
1. ELEVATE.
2. PROMOTE.
3. RAISE.

boost *noun*
1. LIFT.
2, 3. INCREASE.

boot¹ *verb*
1. DISMISS.
2. EJECT.

boot *noun* THRILL.

boot² *noun* PROFIT.

bootleg *verb* SMUGGLE.

bootlegger *noun* SMUGGLER.

bootless *adjective* FUTILE.

bootlick *verb* FAWN.

booty *noun* PLUNDER.

booze *noun* BENDER.

booze *verb* DRINK.

boozed *adjective* DRUNK.

boozehound *noun* DRUNKARD.

boozer *noun* DRUNKARD.

boozy *adjective* DRUNK.

bop *verb* HIT.

bop *noun* BLOW².

border *noun*
1. A fairly narrow line or space forming a boundary: *a flower border around the sundial; the border of the property.*
    Syns: borderline (*also* border line), brim, brink, edge, edging, fringe, margin, perimeter (*Mil.*), periphery, rim, terminus (*Rare*), verge.
2. The line or area separating geopolitical units: *crossed the Canadian border.*
    Syns: borderland, boundary, march², marchland.

border *verb*
1. To put or form a border on: *Pansies border the flower beds.*
    Syns: bound², edge, fringe, margin, rim, skirt, verge.
2. ADJOIN.
3. RIVAL.

bordering *adjective* ADJOINING.

borderland *noun* BORDER.

borderline *also* **border line** *noun*
1. BORDER.
2. VERGE.

borderline *adjective* AMBIGUOUS.

bore *verb*
To fatigue with dullness or tedium: *Your stories bore me.*
    Syns: ennui, pall, tire, weary.

bore *noun* DRIP.

boreal *adjective* FRIGID.

boredom *noun*
The condition of being bored: *nearly died of boredom at the party.*
    Syns: ennui, tedium, yawn (*Informal*).

boresome *adjective* BORING.

boring *adjective*
Arousing no interest or curiosity: *a boring play.*

Syns: arid, aseptic, boresome, dreary (*also* drear), dry, dull, humdrum, irksome, monotonous, sterile, stuffy, tedious, tiresome, tiring, uninteresting, weariful, wearisome, weary.

bosky *adjective* SHADY.

bosom *noun* HEART.

bosom *verb* EMBRACE.

boss *noun*
1. Someone who directs and supervises workers: *The construction boss told the carpenters to build shelves in each office.*
   Syns: director, foreman, head, manager, overseer, superintendent, supervisor, taskmaster. —*Idiom* straw boss.
2. A professional politician who controls a party or political machine: *the boss of Tammany Hall.*
   Syns: chief, chieftain (*Slang*), leader, ringleader.
3. CHIEF.

boss *verb*
1. To command in an arrogant manner: *wouldn't let him boss her children.*
   Syns: dictate to, dominate, domineer, order (around), rule, tyrannize.
2. SUPERVISE.

boss *adjective*
1. EXCELLENT.
2. PRINCIPAL.

bossy *adjective* DICTATORIAL.

bosthoon *noun* BOOR.

botch *verb*
To harm irreparably through inept handling; make a mess of: *The mechanic botched the repair, and the car wouldn't run.*
Syns: ball up (*Slang*), blow¹ (*Slang*), blunder, boggle, bollix up (*Slang*), bungle, foul up (*Slang*), fumble, goof up (*Slang*), gum up (*Slang*), louse up (*Slang*), mess up, mishandle, mismanage, muck up, muddle, muff, screw up (*Slang*), snafu (*Slang*), spoil. —*Idiom* make a muck of.

botch *noun*
A ruinous state of disorder: *He really made a botch of his marriage.*
Syns: botchery, hash, mess, mess-up, muddle, mull¹, muss, shambles, snafu (*Slang*).

botcher *noun* BLUNDERER.

botchery *noun* BOTCH.

bother *verb*
1. AGITATE.
2. ANNOY.

bother *noun*
1. Needless trouble: *went through a lot of bother for nothing.*
   Syns: aggravation (*Informal*), botheration, bustle, fuss, pother, vexation.
2, 3. ANNOYANCE.

botheration *noun*
1, 2. ANNOYANCE.
3. BOTHER.

bothering *noun* ANNOYANCE.

botherment *noun* ANNOYANCE.

bothersome *adjective* VEXATIOUS.

bottom *noun*
1. A side or surface that is below or under: *put a sticker on the bottom of the drawer.*
   Syns: underneath, underside.
2. *Informal.* The part of one's back on which one rests in sitting: *gave him a playful swat on the bottom.*
   Syns: backside, behind, buttocks, derrière, fanny (*Slang*), posterior, rear¹ (*Informal*), rump, seat.
3. BASE¹.
4. CENTER.
5. LOW.

bottom *adjective*
1. Opposite to or farthest from the top: *the bottom drawer of the bureau.*
   Syns: lowermost, lowest, nethermost, undermost.
2. RADICAL.

bottomless *adjective* BASELESS.

boulevard *noun* WAY.

bounce *verb*
1. To spring back after colliding with something: *The ball bounced up and down.*
   Syn: rebound.
2. To move in a lively way: *bounced out of bed bright and early.*
   Syns: bound¹, jump, leap, spring.
3. DISMISS.
4. EJECT.

bounce back *verb* BACKFIRE.

bounce *noun*
1. An act of bouncing or a bouncing movement: *a bounce of the ball.*
   Syns: bound¹, rebound.
2. A sudden lively movement: *a quick bounce of her head.*
   Syns: bound¹, jump, leap, spring.
3. Capacity to bounce: *a ball with plenty of bounce.*
   Syns: resilience (*also* resiliency), spring, springiness.
4. RESILIENCE.
5. SPIRIT.

bouncy *adjective* LIVELY.

bound¹ *verb* BOUNCE.
 bound *noun*
  1, 2. BOUNCE.
bound² *verb*
  1. ADJOIN.
  2. BORDER.
  3. DETERMINE.
bound³ *adjective* OBLIGED.
boundary *noun* BORDER.
bounded *adjective* DEFINITE.
bounden *adjective* OBLIGED.
bounder *noun* BOOR.
boundless *adjective* ENDLESSNESS.
boundlessness *noun* INFINITY.
bound(s) *noun*
  1. END.
  2. LIMIT.
bounteous *adjective* GENEROUS.
bountiful *adjective* GENEROUS.
bountifulness *noun* PLENTY.
bounty *noun* REWARD.
bouquet *noun*
  1. Cut flowers that have been arranged
     in a usu. small bunch: *a bouquet of
     roses on the table.*
     Syns: nosegay, posy.
  2. COMPLIMENT.
  3. FRAGRANCE.
bout *noun*
  1. SIEGE.
  2. TURN.
boutade *noun* FANCY.
bow *verb*
  1. BEND.
  2. COME OUT at **come.**
  3. DEFER².
  4. STOOP.
  5. SUCCUMB.
 bow *noun*
  1. An inclination of the head or body,
     as in greeting, consent, courtesy,
     submission, or worship: *gave a bow of
     acknowledgment.*
     Syns: curtsy, genuflection, kowtow,
     nod, obeisance.
  2. BEND.
bowdlerize *verb* CENSOR.
bowed *adjective* BENT.
bowl over *verb* STAGGER.
box¹ *noun* PREDICAMENT.
box² *noun* SLAP.
 box *verb* SLAP.
boy *noun*
  Informal. A grown man, referred to
  familiarly, jokingly, or as a member of
  one's set or group: *had a night on the
  town with the boys.*
  Syns: chap, fellow.
boycott *verb* BLACKBALL.

boyfriend also **boy friend** *noun*
  Informal. A man who is the favored
  companion of a woman: *went to dinner
  with her boyfriend.*
  Syns: beau, fellow (*Informal*).
brace¹ *noun* COUPLE.
brace² *verb* GIRD.
 brace *noun* SUPPORT.
bracer *noun* TONIC.
bracing *adjective* TONIC.
bracket *noun* CLASS.
 bracket *verb* ASSOCIATE.
brag *verb* BOAST.
 brag *noun*
  1. BOAST.
  2. BRAGGART.
  brag *adjective* EXCELLENT.
braggadocian *adjective* BOASTFUL.
braggadocio *noun*
  1. BOAST.
  2. BRAGGART.
braggart *noun*
  One given to boasting: *just another self-
  important braggart.*
  Syns: blower (*Slang*), blowhard
  (*Slang*), boaster, brag, braggadocio,
  bragger, fanfaron (*Obs.*). —*Idiom* hot-
  air artist.
 braggart *adjective* BOASTFUL.
bragger *noun* BRAGGART.
braggy *adjective* BOASTFUL.
brain *noun*
  1. HEAD.
  2, 3. MIND.
brain child *noun* INVENTION.
brainless *adjective* MINDLESS.
brain(s) *noun* INTELLIGENCE.
brainsick *adjective* INSANE.
brainsickness *noun* INSANITY.
brainstorm *noun* INSPIRATION.
brainwash *verb* INDOCTRINATE.
brain wave *noun* INSPIRATION.
brainwork *noun* THOUGHT.
brainy *adjective* INTELLIGENT.
brake *verb* RESTRAIN.
branch *noun*
  1. Something resembling or structurally
     analogous to a tree branch: *The
     eastern branch of the road led to the
     city.*
     Syns: appendage, arm, fork, offshoot.
  2. An area of academic study that is
     part of a larger body of learning:
     Biology is a branch of science.
     Syns: discipline, specialty.
  3. A part of a family, tribe, or other
     group, or of such a group's language,
     that is believed to stem from a
     common ancestor: *Germanic is a
     branch of Indo-European.*

Syns: division, offshoot, subdivision.
4. A component of government that performs a given function: *the executive branch.*
　Syns: arm, division, organ, wing.
5. A small stream.
　Syns: brook[1], creek, run.
6. SUBSIDIARY.
branch *verb*
To separate into branches or branchlike parts: *The highway branches here.*
　Syns: bifurcate, diverge, divide, fork, ramify, subdivide.
brand *noun* MARK.
brand *verb*
1. MARK.
2. STIGMATIZE.
brandish *verb*
1. DISPLAY.
2. FLOURISH.
brand-new *adjective* FRESH.
brannigan *noun* BENDER.
brash *adjective*
1. PRESUMPTUOUS.
2. RASH[1].
3. TACTLESS.
brashness *noun*
1. PRESUMPTION.
2. TEMERITY.
brass *noun*
1. MONEY.
2. PRESUMPTION.
brassbound *adjective* STUBBORN.
brass-tacks *adjective* PITHY.
brassy *adjective*
1. PRESUMPTUOUS.
2. SHAMELESS.
brattle *verb* RATTLE.
brave *adjective*
Having or showing courage: *a brave effort to rescue the drowning child.*
　Syns: audacious, bold, courageous, dauntless, doughty, fearless, fortitudinous, gallant, game, gutsy (*Informal*), gutty, heroic, intrepid, mettlesome, plucky, stout, stouthearted, unafraid, undaunted, valiant, valorous.
　brave *verb* DEFY.
　brave *noun* BULLY.
braveness *noun* COURAGE.
bravery *noun* COURAGE.
braw *adjective* GOOD.
brawl *noun*
A quarrel or fight marked by very noisy, disorderly, and often violent behavior: *The party ended in a shameful brawl.*
　Syns: affray, broil, donnybrook, fracas, fray, free-for-all, melee (*also* mêlée), riot, row[2], ruckus (*Informal*), ruction, tumult, uproar.

brawl *verb*
To quarrel noisily: *The neighbors were constantly brawling.*
　Syns: broil, caterwaul, riot, squabble, wrangle.
brawn *noun* STRENGTH.
brawny *adjective*
1. MUSCULAR.
2. STRONG.
bray *verb* CRUSH.
brazen *adjective*
1. IMPUDENT.
2. PRESUMPTUOUS.
3. SHAMELESS.
brazenfaced *adjective* SHAMELESS.
brazenness *noun*
1. IMPUDENCE.
2. PRESUMPTION.
breach *noun*
1. An act or instance of breaking a law or regulation or of nonfulfillment of an obligation, promise, etc.: *was reproached for breach of good faith.*
　Syns: contravention, infraction, infringement, transgression, trespass, violation.
2. An opening, esp. in a solid structure: *Water poured through the breach in the dike.*
　Syns: break, cleft, gap, hole, perforation, rent[2], rupture.
3. An interruption in friendly relations: *a policy dispute that could create a breach between our two countries.*
　Syns: break, disaffection, estrangement, fissure, rent[2], rift, rupture, schism.
4. GAP.
breach *verb*
1. To make a hole or other opening in: *breached the walls during the attack.*
　Syns: break through, hole, perforate, pierce, puncture, rupture.
2. VIOLATE.
bread *noun*
1. FOOD.
2. LIVING.
3. MONEY.
breadth *noun* EXPANSE.
breadthen *verb* BROADEN.
break *verb*
1. To crack or split into two or more fragments by means of or as a result of force, a blow, or strain: *He's afraid he'll break his glasses. The mirror broke into hundreds of pieces.*
　Syns: cleave, disjoin, disjoint, fracture, rive, shatter, shiver, smash, splinter, sunder.
2. To become separated from: *At a*

certain speed space vehicles break free of the earth's gravity.
Syns: disengage, dissociate.
3. To make or become unusable or inoperative: *broke my watch; a typewriter that broke.*
Syns: bust (*Slang*), fail, ruin.
4. To impair severely the spirit, health, effectiveness, etc., of: *broke the enemy's resistance.*
Syns: crush, destroy, overwhelm, ruin, subdue.
5. To cut short; discontinue: *determined to break her smoking habit.*
Syns: cut out (*Slang*), give up, kick (*Slang*), leave off, stop.
6. To find the key to: *broke the Japanese military code and hastened the war's end.*
Syns: crack, decipher, puzzle out.
7. To interrupt regular activity for a short period: *We'll break for lunch at one.*
Syn: recess. —*Idioms* take a break, take a breather, take five.
8. BEND.
9. BREAKDOWN.
10. COME OUT at **come.**
11. COMMUNICATE.
12. DEMOTE.
13. DISOBEY.
14. DIVIDE.
15. GENTLE.
16. PENETRATE.
17. RUIN.
18. TURN.
19. VIOLATE.
break down *verb*
1. To collapse or shatter by or as if by breaking: *The firemen broke down the door.*
Syns: destroy, smash, tear down.
2. To give way mentally and emotionally: *She broke down from the pressure.*
Syns: break, cave in, collapse, crack (up), fold (*Informal*), snap.
3. ANALYZE.
4. CAVE IN at **cave.**
5. COLLAPSE.
6. DECAY.
7. FAIL.
break in *verb*
1. To enter forcibly and illegally: *Thieves broke in and stole the stereo.*
Syns: burglarize, housebreak, trespass.
2. INTERRUPT.
break off *verb*
1. SEPARATE.

2. SUSPEND.
break out *verb*
1. To become manifest suddenly and in full force: *In 1967 a war broke out in the Middle East.*
Syns: burst forth, erupt, explode, flare (up).
2. ESCAPE.
break through *verb* BREACH.
break up *verb*
1. To bring or come to a forced end: *The police may have to break up this fight. Their marriage broke up.*
Syns: halt[1], stop.
2. To reduce or become reduced to pieces or components: *Over the centuries rock breaks up into particles from erosion.*
Syns: crumble, decompose, disintegrate, dissolve, fragment, fragmentize.
3. *Slang.* To express great amusement or mirth: *The audience broke up at the comedienne's act.*
Syns: guffaw, howl (*Slang*), roar.
4. DIVIDE.
5. SEPARATE.
break *noun*
1. A cessation of continuity or regularity: *a break in the conversation.*
Syns: discontinuity, disruption, interruption, pause, suspension.
2. A pause or interval, as from work or duty: *going to take a coffee break.*
Syns: breather (*Informal*), intermission, recess, respite, rest[1], time-out.
3, 4. BREACH.
5. CRACK.
6. ESCAPE.
7. GAP.
8. OPPORTUNITY.
breakable *adjective* FRAGILE.
breakage *noun*
An act, instance, or consequence of breaking: *wholesale breakage of china during the move.*
Syns: damage, destruction, impairment, wreckage.
breakdown *noun*
1. A sudden sharp decline in mental, emotional, or physical health: *Stress caused a complete breakdown.*
Syns: collapse, crackup (*Informal*).
2. ANALYSIS.
3. COLLAPSE.
4. DECAY.
5. FAILURE.
breakneck *adjective* FAST.
breakout *noun* ESCAPE.
breast *noun* HEART.

breath *noun*
1. The act or process of breathing: *the runner's labored breath.*
   Syn: respiration.
2. Air breathed out, evidenced by vapor, odor, or heat: *could see my breath in the frosty air.*
   Syn: exhalation.
3. Air breathed in: *took an audible breath.*
   Syn: inhalation.
4. TRACE.

breathe *verb*
1. To draw air into the lungs in the process of respiration: *breathing rapidly from exertion.*
   Syns: inhale, inspire.
2. To expel air in the process of respiration: *breathed out loudly.*
   Syns: exhale, expire.
3. To breathe in and out: *breathing deeply.*
   Syn: respire.
4. BE.
5. CONFIDE.

breather *noun* BREAK.

breathless *adjective*
1, 2. AIRLESS.

breed *verb*
1. FATHER.
2. GENERATE.
3. GROW.
4. REPRODUCE.

breed *noun* KIND².

breeding *noun* REPRODUCTION.

breeze *noun*
1. A gentle wind: *We went sailing, but there was no breeze.*
   Syn: zephyr.
2. *Informal.* An easily accomplished task: *Chopping onions is a breeze with a food processor.*
   Syns: cinch (*Informal*), pushover (*Informal*), snap (*Informal*), walkaway (*Informal*), walkover (*Informal*). —*Idioms* child's play, duck soup.
3. WIND¹.

breeze *verb*
Informal. To move swiftly and effortlessly: *two young girls breezing down the street.*
   Syns: waltz, zip.

breezeless *adjective* AIRLESS.

breezy *adjective*
1, 2. AIRY.

briary *adjective* SEE **briery.**

bribe *noun*
Money, property, or a favor given, offered, or promised to a person in a position of trust as an inducement to dishonest behavior: *offered the judge a bribe to find in his favor.*
   Syns: boodle (*Slang*), fix, graft, payoff (*Informal*), payola (*Slang*).

bribe *verb*
To give, offer, or promise a bribe to: *tried to bribe the senator to vote in favor of the tax law.*
   Syns: buy, buy off, fix, pay off (*Informal*). —*Idioms* grease someone's palm (*or* hand), tickle someone's palm (*or* hand).

bridal *noun* WEDDING.

bridle *verb* RESTRAIN.

brief *adjective*
1. Not long in time or duration: *Spring is all too brief.*
   Syn: short.
2. Marked by or consisting of few words: *a brief explanation.*
   Syns: compendious, concise, condensed, laconic, lean², short, succinct, summary, terse. —*Idiom* to the point.
3. ABRUPT.
4. QUICK.

brief *noun* SYNOPSIS.

brief *verb* TRUNCATE.

briery also **briary** *adjective* THORNY.

brig *noun* JAIL.

bright *adjective*
1. Giving off or reflecting light readily or in large amounts: *a bright brass doorknob; bright, sparkling diamonds.*
   Syns: beaming, brilliant, effulgent, incandescent, irradiant, lambent, lucent, luminous, lustrous, radiant, refulgent, shining.
2. CHEERFUL.
3. CLEVER.
4. COLORFUL.
5. FAVORABLE.

brighten *verb*
1. CLEAR.
2. LIGHT¹.

brilliance also **brilliancy** *noun*
1. FIRE.
2. GLITTER.

brilliant *adjective*
1. BRIGHT.
2. FAVORABLE.
3. INTELLIGENT.

brim *noun* BORDER.

brimful *adjective*
1. BIG.
2. FULL.

brimming *adjective*
1. BIG.
2. FULL.

bring *verb*
1. To cause to come along with oneself: *Soldiers brought the prisoner back for questioning.*
   Syns: bear, carry, convey, fetch, take.
2. To achieve a certain price: *His stamp collection should bring $1,000.*
   Syns: bring in, fetch (*Informal*), realize, sell for.
3. CAUSE.
4. PERSUADE.

bring about *verb* CAUSE.

bring around *verb*
1. PERSUADE.
2. REVIVE.

bring down *verb*
1. DROP.
2. OVERTHROW.

bring forth *verb* BEAR.

bring in *verb*
1. BRING.
2. RETURN.

bring off *verb* EFFECT.

bring on *verb* PRECIPITATE.

bring out *verb* PUBLISH.

bring up *verb*
1. To take care of and educate (a child): *was brought up by conservative parents.*
   Syns: raise, rear².
2. BROACH.
3. REFER.

brink *noun*
1. BORDER.
2. VERGE.

brio *noun* SPIRIT.

brisk *adjective*
1. NIMBLE.
2. VIGOROUS.

brisky *adjective* VIGOROUS.

bristle *verb*
1. ANGER.
2. TEEM¹.

brittle *adjective* FRAGILE.

broach *verb*
To put forward a topic for discussion: *did not know how to broach the subject tactfully.*
   Syns: bring up, introduce, moot, put forth, raise.

broad *adjective*
1. Extending over a large area from side to side: *broad shoulders; a broad smile.*
   Syn: wide.
2. Large in expanse: *a broad, velvety lawn.*
   Syns: ample, expansive, extended, extensive, spacious.
3. Not narrow or conservative in thought, expression, or conduct: *a woman of broad views on social reform.*
   Syns: broad-minded, liberal, open-minded, progressive, tolerant.
4. GENERAL.
5. RACY.
6. UNSUBTLE.

broadcast *verb*
1. ADVERTISE.
2. ANNOUNCE.

broadcast *noun* ANNOUNCEMENT.

broaden *verb*
1. To make or become broad or broader: *The turnpike broadens at the tollgate.*
   Syns: breadthen, widen.
2. EXTEND.

broad-minded *adjective* BROAD.

broadness *noun* WIDTH.

broad-spectrum *adjective* GENERAL.

Brobdingnagian *adjective* GIANT.

broil *noun* BRAWL.

broil *verb*
1. BRAWL.
2. BURN.

broiling *adjective* HOT.

broke *adjective* POOR.

broken-down *adjective* SHABBY.

broker *noun* GO-BETWEEN.

bromide *noun* CLICHÉ.

bromidic *adjective* TRITE.

Bronx cheer *noun* HISS.

brood *noun*
1. PROGENY.
2. YOUNG.

brood *verb*
To turn over in the mind, moodily and at length: *He's brooding about his decline in popularity and worrying about the upcoming election.*
   Syns: despond, dwell on (*or* upon), fret, mope, stew (over *or* about) (*Informal*), worry. —*Idiom* be in a brown study.

brook¹ *noun* BRANCH.

brook² *verb* ENDURE.

brotherhood *noun* FRIENDSHIP.

brouhaha *noun* SENSATION.

browbeat *verb* INTIMIDATE.

browbeater *noun* BULLY.

brown-nose *verb* FAWN.

browse *verb*
1. To look through reading matter casually: *browsed through the magazine looking at advertisements.*
   Syns: dip into, flip (through), glance at (*or* over *or* through), leaf through,

riffle through, run through, scan, skim, thumb through.

2. To go through a place, viewing or inspecting in a leisurely way: *browsing around in the department store.*
   Syns: roam, stroll, wander.

bruise *verb*
To make or receive a bruise or bruises on: *bruised his shoulder when he fell off the horse; skin that bruises easily.*
   Syns: black, contuse.

bruit *verb*
1. ADVERTISE.
2. NOISE.

brume *noun* HAZE.

brummagem *noun* COPY.

brunet also **brunette** *adjective* DARK.

brush *noun*
1. Light and momentary contact with another person or thing: *a brush of her fingers on the piano keys.*
   Syns: flick, glance[1], graze, skim.
2. A brief, hostile exposure to or contact with something, as danger, opposition, etc.: *has frequent brushes with the law.*
   Syns: clash, encounter, run-in, skirmish.

brush *verb*
To make light and momentary contact with, as in passing: *His arm brushed mine in the elevator.*
   Syns: flick, glance[1], graze, kiss, shave, skim.

brusque *adjective* ABRUPT.

brutal *adjective* BITTER.

brutality *noun* CRUELTY.

brutalize *verb* CORRUPT.

bubble *noun* ILLUSION.

bubble *verb*
1. BOIL.
2. FOAM.

buck[1] *verb* CONTEST.

buck up *verb* ENCOURAGE.

buck[3] *verb* CRUSH.

bucket *verb* RUSH.

buckle *verb*
1. APPLY.
2. CAVE IN at **cave**.

buckram *adjective* STIFF.

bucks *noun* MONEY.

bucolic *adjective* COUNTRY.

bud *noun*
1. CHILD.
2. GERM.

buddy *noun* ASSOCIATE.

budge *verb* STIR[1].

budget *noun* QUANTITY.

buff *verb* GLOSS.

buffet *noun* SLAP

buffet *verb*
1. BEAT.
2. SLAP.

bug *noun*
1. DEFECT.
2. ENTHUSIAST.
3. GERM.

bug *verb*
1. ANNOY.
2. TAP[2].

bugbear *noun*
1. GHOST.
2. HATE.

buggy *adjective* INSANE.

bughouse *adjective* INSANE.

bugs *adjective* INSANE.

build *verb*
1. To make or form (a structure): *built a skyscraper; built a sand castle for the children.*
   Syns: construct, erect, put up, raise, rear[2].
2. BASE[1].
3. MAKE.
4. RISE.

build in *verb*
To construct or include as an integral or permanent part: *Be sure to build in the sum allowed for cost overruns.*
   Syns: incorporate, integrate.

build up *verb*
1. ADVERTISE.
2. GAIN.
3. INCREASE.
4. PROMOTE.

build *noun* CONSTITUTION.

builder *noun*
1. A person or business that makes or builds something: *the builder of a house; an automobile builder.*
   Syns: constructor, erector, maker, manufacturer.
2. A person instrumental in the growth of something, esp. in its early stages: *one of the builders of the space age.*
   Syns: contributor, creator, developer, pioneer.

building *noun*
A usu. permanent construction, as a house, store, etc.: *put up a 25-story building on the site.*
   Syns: edifice, pile, structure.

build-up also **buildup** *noun*
1. The result or product of building up: *the build-up of ashes in the fireplace; the build-up of tensions during the strike.*

Syns: accretion, accumulation, amassment, development, enlargement, increase, increment, multiplication, proliferation.

2. PROMOTION.

built *adjective* SHAPELY.

built-in *adjective*

1. Constructed as a nondetachable part of a larger unit: *a built-in bookcase.*
   Syns: component, constituent, incorporated.

2. Forming an essential element: *a built-in sense of danger.*
   Syns: congenital, constitutional, inborn, inbred, inherent, innate, intrinsic, natural.

bulge *noun*

1. A part that protrudes or extends outward: *a bulge under his jacket indicating a pistol.*
   Syns: jut, knob, knot, projection, protrusion, protuberance.

2. ADVANTAGE.

bulge *verb*

To curve outward past the normal or usual limit: *Money and cosmetics are making her purse bulge.*
   Syns: bag, balloon, belly, jut, overhang, pouch, project, protrude, protuberate, stand out, stick out.

bulk *noun*

1. Great extent, amount, or dimension: *Whales have monstrous bulk.*
   Syns: amplitude, magnitude, mass, size, volume.

2. BODY.

3. QUANTITY.

4. WEIGHT.

bulky *adjective*

1. Extremely large; having great mass: *a bulky volume of poetry.*
   Syns: massive, oversize (*also* oversized).

2. Having a large body, esp. in girth: *a bulky man having trouble climbing the stairs.*
   Syns: hulking, hulky, stout.

3. AWKWARD.

bull *noun*

1. BLUNDER.

2. NONSENSE.

3. POLICEMAN.

bulldogged *adjective* OBSTINATE.
bulldoggish *adjective* OBSTINATE.
bulldoggy *adjective* OBSTINATE.
bulldoze *verb*

1. INTIMIDATE.

2. PUSH.

bulldozer *noun* BULLY.
bullet *verb* RUSH.

bullheaded *adjective* OBSTINATE.
bullheadedness *noun* OBSTINACY.
bullwork *noun* LABOR.
bully *noun*

One who is habitually cruel to smaller or weaker people: *A swaggering bully is often a real coward.*
   Syns: brave (*Obs.*), browbeater, bulldozer, hector, intimidator.

bully *verb* INTIMIDATE.
bully *adjective* EXCELLENT.

bullyrag *verb*

1. BAIT.

2. INTIMIDATE.

bum *verb*

1. BEG.

2. IDLE.

bum *noun* WASTREL.
bum *adjective* BAD.

bumble¹ *verb* BLUNDER.
bumble² *verb* HUM.
bumble *noun* HUM.
bumbling *adjective* UNSKILLFUL.
bummer¹ *noun* BEGGAR.
bummer² *noun* SHAME.

bump *verb*

1. To proceed with sudden, abrupt movements: *an old car bumping down the road.*
   Syns: jerk, jolt.

2. COLLIDE.

3. DEMOTE.

4. EJECT.

bump into *verb* COME ACROSS at come.

bump off *verb* MURDER.

bump *noun*

1. A small raised area of skin resulting from a light blow, an insect sting, etc.: *Wasp bites cause bumps.*
   Syns: bunch, knob, knot, lump¹, swelling.

2. An unevenness or elevation on a surface: *a bump in the road.*
   Syns: hump, knob, lump¹, nub, protuberance.

3. COLLISION.

bump-off *noun* MURDER.

bunch *noun*

1. BUMP.

2. CROWD.

3, 4. GROUP.

buncombe *noun* SEE bunkum¹.

bundle *noun*

1. FORTUNE.

2. GROUP.

bungle *verb* BOTCH.
bungle *noun* BLUNDER.
bungler *noun* BLUNDERER.
bunk¹ *verb* HARBOR.

bunk² *noun* NONSENSE.

bunk³ *verb* ESCAPE.

bunkum¹ also **buncombe** *noun* NONSENSE.

bunkum² *adjective* HEALTHY.

Bunyanesque *adjective* GIANT.

buoy *verb* ELATE.

 buoy up *verb* SUSTAIN.

buoyancy *noun* RESILIENCE.

buoyant *adjective* AIRY.

bur *verb & noun* SEE **burr**.

burble *verb* WASH.

burbling *adjective* LAUGHING.

burden *noun*
  1. Something carried physically: *the camel's burden of spices.*
     Syns: cargo, freight, haul, impost, load.
  2. Something hard to bear physically or emotionally: *the burden of a guilty conscience.*
     Syns: affliction, cross, trial.
  3. A duty or responsibility that is a source of anxiety, worry, or hardship: *the burden of supporting dependent relatives.*
     Syns: millstone, onus, tax, weight.
  4. IMPORT.

burden *verb* CHARGE.

burdensome *adjective*
  Imposing a severe test of bodily or spiritual strength: *burdensome farm chores.*
     Syns: arduous, backbreaking, demanding, difficult, effortful, exacting, exigent, formidable, hard, heavy, laborious, onerous, oppressive, rigorous, rough, severe, taxing, tough, trying, weighty.

burg *noun* CITY.

burgeon *verb*
  1. BLOOM.
  2. RISE.

burglarize *verb* BREAK IN at **break**.

burial *noun*
  An act of placing a body in a grave or tomb: *Burial immediately followed the funeral.*
     Syns: entombment, inhumation, interment.

buried *adjective* ULTERIOR.

burke *verb* SKIRT.

burlesque *noun* MOCKERY.

 burlesque *verb* IMITATE.

burly *adjective* MUSCULAR.

burn *verb*
  1. To undergo combustion: *Wood shavings burn readily.*
     Syns: blaze¹, combust, conflagrate, flame (up), flare.

  2. To undergo or cause to undergo damage by or as if by fire: *burned the rug with a cigarette.*
     Syns: char, scorch, sear, singe.
  3. To feel or look hot: *He's burning with fever.*
     Syns: bake, broil, roast, scorch, swelter.
  4. ANGER.
  5. BEAM.
  6. BOIL.
  7. IRRITATE.
  8. STING.

burn out *verb* RUN DOWN at **run**.

burn up *verb* ANGER.

burn *noun*
  Damage that results from burning: *a burn in the tablecloth.*
     Syns: char, scorch, sear, singe.

burning *adjective*
  1. Of immediate import: *a burning issue; burning needs.*
     Syns: crying, exigent, imperative, importunate, instant, pressing, urgent.
  2. BLAZING.
  3. HOT.
  4. PASSIONATE.

burnish *verb* GLOSS.

burr also **bur** *verb* HUM.

 burr also **bur** *noun* HUM.

burrow *noun* HOLE.

burst *verb*
  1. To come open or fly apart suddenly and violently, as from internal pressure: *The balloon burst.*
     Syns: blow out, blow up, bust (*Informal*), explode, pop.
  2. EXPLODE.

burst forth *verb* BREAK OUT at **break**.

burst *noun*
  1. BARRAGE.
  2, 3. BLAST.
  4. OUTBURST.

bursting *adjective*
  1. EAGER.
  2. FULL.

bury *verb*
  1. To place (a corpse) in or as if in a grave: *bury the dead.*
     Syns: entomb, inhume, inter, lay away (*Informal*). —*Idiom* lay to rest.
  2. DEFEAT.
  3. HIDE¹.

bush *noun* WILD.

 bush *verb* EXHAUST.

 bush up *verb* HIDE¹.

bushed *adjective* EXHAUSTED.

bushel *noun* HEAP.

bushwhack *verb* AMBUSH.

business *noun*
1. Activity pursued as a livelihood: *Her business is advertising.*
   Syns: calling, employ (*Archaic*), employment, job, line, occupation, pursuit, racket (*Slang*), trade, vocation, work.
2. Commercial, industrial, or professional activity in general: *laws regulating business; when business is slow.*
   Syns: commerce, industry, trade, trading, traffic.
3. Something that concerns or involves one personally: *Do you think that's any of your business?*
   Syns: affair, concern, lookout.
4. COMPANY.
5. PATRONAGE.

businesslike *adjective*
1. Showing characteristics advantageous to or of use in business: *businesslike procedures.*
   Syns: efficient, methodical, systematic (*also* systematical).
2. SERIOUS.

businessperson *noun* DEALER.

buss *noun* KISS.
   buss *verb* KISS.

bust *verb*
1. ARREST.
2. BREAK.
3. BURST.
4. DEMOTE.
5. GENTLE.
6. RUIN.
7. SLAP.
   bust *noun*
1. ARREST.
2, 3. FAILURE.
4. SLAP.

busted *adjective* POOR.

bustle *noun*
1. BOTHER.
2. STIR¹.
   bustle *verb*
1. FUSS.
2. RUSH.

busy *adjective*
1. Involved in activity or work: *Call when you're not so busy.*
   Syns: employed, engaged, occupied.
2. Excessively filled with detail: *a busy advertising layout.*
   Syns: cluttered, crowded, fussy.
   busy *verb*
To make busy: *busying myself with legal matters.*
   Syns: engage, engross, occupy.

busybody *noun*
1. MEDDLER.
2. SNOOP.

but *adverb* SOLELY.

butcher *verb* ANNIHILATE.
   butcher *noun* MURDERER.

butchery *noun* MASSACRE.

butt¹ *noun* PUSH.
   butt in *verb*
1. INTRUDE.
2. MEDDLE.

butt² *verb* ADJOIN.

butt³ *noun*
1. DUPE.
2. JOKE.

butt⁴ *noun* END.

butter *verb* SMEAR.
   butter up *verb* FLATTER.

buttinsky *noun* MEDDLER.

buttocks *noun* BOTTOM.

button-down *adjective* CONVENTIONAL.

buttress *noun* SUPPORT.
   buttress *verb* BACK.

buy *verb*
1. To acquire in exchange for money or something of equal value: *bought a house.*
   Syn: purchase.
2. BELIEVE.
3. BRIBE.
   buy off *verb* BRIBE.
   buy *noun*
1. Something bought or capable of being bought: *a major buy in cotton futures.*
   Syn: purchase.
2. BARGAIN.

buyable *adjective* CORRUPTIBLE.

buyer *noun* PATRON.

buzz *verb*
1. GOSSIP.
2. HUM.
3. TELEPHONE.
   buzz *noun*
1. CALL.
2. GOSSIP.
3. HUM.

by-and-by *noun* FUTURE.

bygone *adjective* OLD-FASHIONED.

bypass *verb*
1. AVOID.
2, 3. SKIRT.

by-product *noun* DERIVATIVE.

by-sitter *noun* WATCHER.

bystander *noun* WATCHER.

byword *noun* PROVERB.

Byzantine *adjective* COMPLEX.

C

cabal *noun* PLOT.
cabalistic *adjective* MYSTERIOUS.
cabbage *noun* MONEY.
cache *verb* HIDE[1]
cachinnate *verb* LAUGH.
cachinnation *noun* LAUGH.
cackle *verb* LAUGH.
 cackle *noun* LAUGH.
cacophonous also **cacophonic,
 cacophonical** *adjective*
 INHARMONIOUS.
cadaver *noun* BODY.
cadaverous *adjective*
 1. GHASTLY.
 2. PALE.
 3. WASTED.
cadence also **cadency** *noun*
 RHYTHM.
cadenced *adjective* RHYTHMICAL.
cadency *noun* SEE **cadence.**
cadge *verb* BEG.
cadger *noun* BEGGAR.
caducity *noun* AGE.
cage *verb* ENCLOSE.
cagey also **cagy** *adjective* SHREWD.
Cain *noun* MURDERER.
cajole *verb* COAX.
cake *verb* HARDEN.
calaboose *noun* JAIL.
calamitous *adjective* FATAL.
calamity *noun* DISASTER.
calculate *verb*
 1. To ascertain by mathematics:
 *astronomers calculating the positions of
 the planets.*
 Syns: cast, cipher, compute, figure
 (out), reckon.
 2. COUNT.
 3. ESTIMATE.
calculated *adjective*
 1. Planned, weighed, or estimated in
 advance: *took a calculated risk.*
 Syns: considered, deliberate,
 intentional, premeditated.
 2. ADVISED.
calculating *adjective*
 Coldly planning to achieve selfish aims:
 a calculating and shrewd businessman.
 Syns: designing, scheming.
calculation *noun*
 1. The act, process, or result of
 calculating: *made a quick calculation
 of the cost.*

 Syns: computation, figuring,
 reckoning.
 2. ADVISEMENT.
 3. CAUTION.
calendar *noun* PROGRAM.
caliber *noun*
 1. CLASS.
 2. MERIT.
 3. QUALITY.
caliginous *adjective* BLACK.
call *verb*
 1. To demand to appear, come, or
 assemble: *calling the doctor; called a
 meeting.*
 Syns: convene, convoke, muster, send
 for, summon.
 2. To describe with a word or term:
 called me a liar.
 Syns: characterize, designate, label,
 style, tag, term.
 3. ASSEMBLE.
 4. ESTIMATE.
 5. NAME.
 6. PREDICT.
 7. ROAR.
 8. TELEPHONE.
 9. VISIT.
call down *verb*
Informal. To criticize for a fault or
offense: *got called down for failing to
meet the deadline.*
 Syns: admonish, bawl out (*Informal*),
 castigate, chastise, chew out (*Slang*),
 chide, dress down, lambaste (*Slang*),
 rap[1] (*Informal*), rebuke, reprimand,
 reproach, reprove, scold, tax, upbraid.
 —*Idioms* bring (*or* call *or* take) to
 task, haul (*or* rake) over the coals, let
 someone have it, rap on (*or* over) the
 knuckles.
call for *verb*
 1. To be a proper or sufficient occasion
 for: *This calls for champagne.*
 Syns: justify, occasion, warrant.
 2, 3. DEMAND.
call off *verb* CANCEL.
call *noun*
 1. A telephone communication: *Give
 him a call when you arrive.*
 Syns: buzz (*Informal*), ring[1]
 (*Informal*).
 2. ATTRACTION.
 3. CAUSE.
 4. DEMAND.
 5. SHOUT.
 6. VISIT.
called-for *adjective* REQUIRED.
call girl *noun* PROSTITUTE.

calligraphic *adjective* GRAPHIC.
calling *noun*
1. BUSINESS.
2. VOCATION.
callous *adjective* COLD-BLOODED.
calm *adjective*
1. Not excited or emotionally agitated: *spoke in a calm voice.*
 Syns: composed, placid, serene, tranquil, unruffled.
2. COOL.
3. STILL.
calm *noun*
1. Lack of emotional agitation: *kept his calm during the emergency.*
 Syns: calmness, composure, cool (*Slang*), equanimity, head, sang-froid, serenity, tranquillity *or* tranquility.
2. STILLNESS.
calm *verb*
1. To make or become calm: *calmed her fears.*
 Syns: allay, balm, becalm, compose, lull, quiet, settle, soothe, still, tranquilize (*also* tranquillize).
2. PACIFY.
calm down *verb* PACIFY.
calmness *noun* CALM.
calumniate *verb* LIBEL.
calumnious *adjective* LIBELOUS.
calumny *noun* LIBEL.
camouflage *verb* DISGUISE.
campaign *noun* DRIVE.
campestral *adjective* COUNTRY.
camp follower *noun* PROSTITUTE.
can *verb*
1. CONSERVE.
2. DISMISS.
can *noun* JAIL.
canard *noun* LIE².
cancel *verb*
1. To remove or invalidate by or as if by running a line through or wiping clean: *canceled checks; going to cancel his magazine subscription; an order canceled by the President.*
 Syns: annul, blot out, cross out, erase, expunge, rub out, scratch out, strike out, undo, vacate (*Law*), wipe out, x out.
2. To decide not to go ahead with (something previously arranged): *canceled the concert because of illness.*
 Syns: call off, drop, kill (*Slang*), scratch (*Informal*), scrub (*Informal*).
3. To make ineffective by applying an opposite force or amount: *Two opposing votes cancel each other.*
 Syns: counteract, neutralize.
4. ABOLISH
cancellation *noun* ERASURE.

candid *adjective* FRANK.
candidate *noun* APPLICANT.
candy *verb* SWEETEN.
candyman *noun* PUSHER.
cane *noun* STICK.
canker *verb*
1. CORRUPT.
2. POISON.
cannonade *noun* BARRAGE.
cannonade *verb* BARRAGE.
canny *adjective*
1. ECONOMICAL.
2. SHARP.
canon *noun* LAW.
canonical *adjective* ORTHODOX.
cant¹ *verb*
1. INCLINE.
2. LURCH.
cant *noun* INCLINATION.
cant² *noun*
1. DIALECT.
2. LANGUAGE.
cantankerous *adjective* ILL-TEMPERED.
canted *adjective* INCLINED.
cap *verb*
1. CLIMAX.
2. COVER.
3. TOP.
capability *noun* ABILITY.
capable *adjective* ABLE.
capacious *adjective*
1. FULL.
2. ROOMY.
capacity *noun*
1. ABILITY.
2. GRASP.
caper *verb* GAMBOL.
caper *noun* PRANK.
capital *adjective*
1. EXCELLENT.
2. FLAGRANT.
3. PRIMARY.
capital *noun*
1. FUNDS.
2. RESOURCES.
capitalist *noun* FINANCIER.
capitalize *verb*
1. BENEFIT.
2. FINANCE.
capitulate *verb* SUCCUMB.
capitulation *noun* SURRENDER.
caprice *noun* FANCY.
capricious *adjective*
1. Following no predictable pattern: *a capricious flirt; a capricious storm; capricious stock-market fluctuations.*
 Syns: changeable, erratic, fantastic (*also* fantastical), fickle, freakish, inconsistent, inconstant, lubricious,

mercurial, temperamental, ticklish,
uncertain, unpredictable, unstable,
unsteady, variable, volatile,
whimsical.
2. ARBITRARY.
captain *verb* LEAD.
captious *adjective* CRITICAL.
captivate *verb* CHARM.
captivated *adjective* INFATUATED.
captivating *adjective* ATTRACTIVE.
capture *verb*
1. To obtain possession or control of:
   The Dodgers captured the pennant.
   Syns: cop (*Slang*), gain, get, take,
   win.
2. TAKE.
carcass *noun* BODY.
card *noun* JOKER.
cardboard *adjective* STIFF.
cardinal *adjective*
1. PIVOTAL.
2. PRIMARY.
care *noun*
1. A cause of worry: *Her main care is
   how to support the family.*
   Syns: concern, trouble. —*Idiom* thorn
   in one's side.
2. Cautious attentiveness: *handled the
   glass with care.*
   Syns: carefulness, caution,
   gingerliness, heed, heedfulness,
   regard.
3. The function of watching, guarding,
   or overseeing: *left the keys to the
   house in his care.*
   Syns: charge, custody, guardianship,
   keeping, superintendence,
   supervision, trust.
4. ANXIETY.
5. THOROUGHNESS.
6. TREATMENT.
care *verb*
To have an objection: *I don't care if you
go.*
   Syns: mind, object2.
care for *verb* TEND2.
carefree *adjective* LIGHT2.
careful *adjective*
1. Cautiously attentive: *gave the will a
   careful reading.*
   Syns: heedful, mindful, observant,
   watchful.
2. Showing or marked by attentiveness
   to all aspects or details: *a careful
   worker; fine, careful work.*
   Syns: meticulous, painstaking,
   scrupulous.
3. WARY.
carefulness *noun*
1. CARE.
2. CAUTION.

careless *adjective*
1. Lacking or marked by a lack of care:
   hurt her by a careless remark.
   Syns: feckless, heedless, inattentive,
   thoughtless, unconcerned, unmindful.
2. Indifferent to correctness, accuracy,
   or neatness: *a careless writer.*
   Syns: messy, slapdash, slipshod,
   sloppy, slovenly, untidy.
caress *verb*
To touch or stroke affectionately: *patted
and caressed the little boy.*
   Syns: cuddle, fondle, pet1.
careworn *adjective* HAGGARD.
cargo *noun* BURDEN.
caricature *noun* MOCKERY.
caritas *noun* GRACE.
cark *verb*
1, 2. WORRY.
carnage *noun* MASSACRE.
carnal *adjective* PHYSICAL.
carnality *noun* PHYSICALITY.
carol *verb* SING.
carom *also* **carrom** *verb* GLANCE1.
carousal *noun* BENDER.
carouse *verb* REVEL.
carouse *noun* BENDER.
carp *verb* QUIBBLE.
carp at *verb* NAG.
carper *noun* CRITIC.
carping *adjective* CRITICAL.
carriage *noun*
1. POSTURE.
2. TRANSPORTATION.
carrier *noun* BEARER.
carrom *verb* SEE **carom.**
carry *verb*
1. To move while supporting: *carried
   the groceries into the house.*
   Syns: bear, convey, lug, schlep
   (*Slang*), tote1 (*Informal*), transport.
2. To hold on one's person: *I never
   carry much money.*
   Syns: bear, have, pack (*Informal*),
   possess.
3. To have as an accompaniment,
   condition, or consequence: *a crime
   that carries a heavy penalty.*
   Syns: entail, involve.
4. To have for sale: *All drugstores carry
   aspirin.*
   Syns: keep, stock.
5. ACT.
6, 7. BEAR.
8. BRING.
9, 10. COMMUNICATE.
11. CONDUCT.
12. EXTEND.
13. PASS.
14. SUPPORT.

carry away *verb*
To move or excite greatly: *completely carried away by the music.*
  Syns: enrapture, send (*Slang*), thrill, transport.

carry off *verb*
1. KIDNAP.
2. KILL.

carry on *verb*
1. To continue without halting despite difficulties or setbacks: *carried on with her work as if he hadn't said a word.*
  Syns: go on, hang on, keep going, keep on, persevere, persist.
2. CONDUCT.
3. ENTHUSE.
4. MISBEHAVE.
5. PARTICIPATE.
6. WAGE.

carry out *verb*
1. ADMINISTER.
2. EFFECT.
3. ENFORCE.
4. WAGE.

carry through *verb* EFFECT.

cartel *noun*
1, 2. COMBINE.

carve *verb* CUT.

Casanova *noun*
1. GALLANT.
2. PHILANDERER.

case *noun*
1. ARGUMENT.
2. EXAMPLE.
3. LAWSUIT.

case *verb* EXAMINE.

caseharden *verb* HARDEN.

casehardened *adjective* HARD.

cash *noun* MONEY.

cashier *verb* DISMISS.

Cassandra *noun* PESSIMIST.

cast *verb*
1. ADD.
2. AIM.
3. CALCULATE.
4. DESIGN.
5. MISCARRY.
6. SHED.
7. THROW.

cast about *verb* SEEK.

cast away *verb* WRECK.

cast down *verb*
1. DEPRESS.
2. DISAPPOINT.

cast out *verb* DISMISS.

cast *noun*
1. EXPRESSION.
2, 3. FORM.
4. KIND².
5. PROPHECY.

6. THROW.
7. TINT.

castigate *verb* CALL DOWN at **call**.

castrate *verb* STERILIZE.

castration *noun* STERILIZATION.

casual *adjective*
1. ACCIDENTAL.
2. EASYGOING.

casualness *noun* INFORMALITY.

casualty *noun*
1. ACCIDENT.
2. FATALITY.
3. VICTIM.

casuistry *noun* FALLACY.

cataclysm *noun*
1. DISASTER.
2. FLOOD.
3. REVOLUTION.

cataclysmic also **cataclysmal** *adjective* FATAL.

catacomb *noun* GRAVE¹.

catalogue also **catalog** *verb* LIST¹.

catalogue also **catalog** *noun* LIST¹.

catalyst *noun*
An agent that stimulates or precipitates a reaction, development, or change: *a biochemical catalyst used in testing; was a catalyst for good.*
  Syns: alterant, ferment, leaven, leavening, yeast.

cataract *noun* FLOOD.

catastrophe *noun* DISASTER.

catastrophic *adjective* FATAL.

catcall *noun* HISS.

catch *verb*
1. To get hold of (something moving): *The outfielder caught the fly ball.*
  Syns: clutch, grab, nab, seize, snatch. —*Idiom* lay hands on.
2. To gain control of or an advantage over by or as if by trapping: *hoping to catch her in her own lies.*
  Syns: enmesh, ensnare, entangle, entrap, snare, tangle, trammel, trap, web.
3. To become or cause to become stuck or lodged: *The bone caught in his throat.*
  Syns: fix, lodge, stick.
4. To perceive, esp. barely or fleetingly: *caught a glimpse of the President's motorcade.*
  Syns: descry, detect, discern, espy, get (*Informal*), spot, spy.
5. CONTRACT.
6. FASTEN.
7. HIT.
8. SEIZE.
9. SNAP.
10, 11, 12. TAKE.

13. UNDERSTAND.

catch on verb UNDERSTAND.

catch up verb

1. To come up even with (another): *running hard to catch up with the other joggers.*
   Syn: overtake.
2. GRIP.
3. INVOLVE.

catch noun

1. The act of catching, esp. a sudden taking and holding: *retrieved the flyaway hat with a leaping catch.*
   Syns: clutch, grab, seizure, snatch.
2. A device for fastening or for checking motion: *The catch of my necklace broke.*
   Syns: clasp, fastener, hook.
3. *Informal.* A tricky or unsuspected condition: *an offer so generous that I'm sure there's a catch to it.*
   Syns: rub, snag.
4. *Informal.* A person or thing worth catching: *was considered quite a catch in his day.*
   Syns: plum, prize.

catching adjective COMMUNICABLE.

catechism noun TEST.

catechization noun TEST.

categorical adjective DEFINITE.

categorize verb

1. ASSORT.
2. CLASS.

category noun CLASS.

cater to verb

1. BABY.
2. HUMOR.

caterwaul verb BRAWL.

catharsis noun PURIFICATION.

cathartic adjective ELIMINATIVE.

catholic adjective UNIVERSAL.

catholicon noun PANACEA.

catlike adjective STEALTHY.

catnap noun NAP.

 catnap verb NAP.

cat's-paw also **cats-paw** noun PAWN².

cause noun

1. That which produces an effect: *Scientists are seeking the cause of cancer.*
   Syns: antecedent, reason.
2. A basis for an action or decision: *gave his wife cause to be angry.*
   Syns: ground, motivation, motive, reason, spring.
3. That which provides a reason or justification: *no cause for alarm.*
   Syns: call, justification, necessity, occasion.

4. A goal or set of interests served with dedication: *working in the cause of peace.*
   Syn: crusade.
5. LAWSUIT.

cause verb
To be the cause of: *a loss that caused pain. Drunken drivers often cause accidents.*
   Syns: bring about, effect, effectuate, engender, generate, induce, ingenerate, lead to, make, occasion, produce, result in, secure. —*Idioms* bring to pass (*or* effect), give rise to.

caustic adjective

1. BITING.
2. SARCASTIC.

causticity noun SARCASM.

caution noun

1. Careful forethought to avoid harm or risk: *climbed the icy steps with caution.*
   Syns: calculation, carefulness, circumspection, gingerliness, precaution, wariness.
2. CARE.
3. EXAMPLE.
4. PRUDENCE.
5. WARNING.

caution verb WARN.

cautionary adjective
Giving warning: *sent him a cautionary letter before he filed suit.*
   Syns: admonishing, admonitory, monitory, warning.

cautious adjective WARY.

cave noun
A hollow beneath the earth's surface: *Water trickled out of the cave.*
   Syns: cavern, grotto.

cave in verb

1. To fall in: *The roof caved in from the heavy snow.*
   Syns: break down, buckle, collapse, give, go.
2. BEND.
3. BREAK DOWN at break.
4. COLLAPSE.

caveat noun WARNING.

cavern noun CAVE.

cavernous adjective

1. HOLLOW.
2. YAWNING.

cavil verb QUIBBLE.

caviler noun CRITIC.

caviling adjective CRITICAL.

cavity noun HOLE.

cavort verb GAMBOL.

cease verb

1. CLOSE¹.
2. SUSPEND.

3, 4. STOP.
cease *noun* END.
cease-fire *noun* TRUCE.
ceaseless *adjective* CONTINUAL.
cede *verb*
1. ABDICATE.
2. TRANSFER.
ceiling *noun*
1. LIMIT.
2. MAXIMUM.
celebrate *verb*
1. To mark (a day or event) with
   ceremonies of respect, festivity, or
   rejoicing: *We always celebrate
   Christmas with prayers and carols.*
   Syns: commemorate, keep, observe,
   solemnize.
2. To show happy satisfaction in an
   event, esp. by merrymaking:
   celebrated by giving a party.
   Syns: rejoice, revel. —*Idioms* kill the
   fatted calf, make merry.
3. HONOR.
celebrated *adjective* EMINENT.
celebration *noun*
1. The act of observing a day or event
   with ceremonies: *the celebration of
   Passover.*
   Syns: commemoration, observance.
2. The act of showing happy satisfaction
   in an event: *During the graduation
   celebration speeches were made.*
   Syns: festivity, merrymaking,
   rejoicing, revelry, revels.
3. BLAST.
celebrity *noun*
1. A famous person: *All the celebrities
   arrived for the première of the play.*
   Syns: hero, luminary, name, notable,
   personage. —*Idioms* big name, person
   of note.
2. FAME.
celeritous *adjective* FAST.
celerity *noun*
1. HASTE.
2. SPEED.
celestial *adjective*
1, 2. HEAVENLY.
censor *verb*
1. To examine (material) and remove
   parts considered harmful or improper
   for publication or transmission:
   censoring the prisoner's mail.
   Syns: bowdlerize, expurgate, screen.
2. To keep from being published or
   transmitted: *censored the news story.*
   Syns: ban, black out, hush up, stifle,
   suppress. —*Idiom* put the lid on.
censorious *adjective* CRITICAL.
censurable *adjective* BLAMEWORTHY.

censure *verb*
1. BLAME.
2. DEPLORE.
censure *noun* BLAME.
center *noun*
1. A point or area equidistant from all
   sides of something: *put the flowers in
   the center of the table.*
   Syns: middle, midpoint, midst.
2. A point of origin from which ideas,
   influences, etc., emanate: *tried to get
   to the center of the problem.*
   Syns: bottom, core, focus, heart, hub,
   quick, root[1].
3. A place of concentrated activity,
   influence, or importance: *New York is
   a great urban center.*
   Syns: focus, headquarters, heart, hub,
   seat.
center *verb* CONCENTRATE.
center *adjective* CENTRAL.
central *adjective*
1. At, in, near, or being the center: *the
   central part of the state.*
   Syns: center, medial, median, mid,
   middle.
2. MIDDLE.
3. PIVOTAL.
cerebral *adjective*
1. INTELLECTUAL.
2. MENTAL.
cerebrate *verb*
1. PONDER.
2. THINK.
cerebration *noun* THOUGHT.
ceremonial *adjective* RITUAL.
ceremonial *noun* CEREMONY.
ceremonious *adjective*
Fond of or given to ceremony: *The
Japanese are a ceremonious people.*
   Syns: conventional, courtly, formal,
   polite, punctilious.
ceremoniousness *noun* CEREMONY.
ceremony *noun*
1. A formal act or set of acts prescribed
   by ritual: *performed the wedding
   ceremony.*
   Syns: ceremonial, liturgy, observance,
   office (*Eccles.*), rite, ritual, service.
2. Strict observance of social
   conventions: *welcomed the pope with
   great ceremony.*
   Syns: ceremoniousness, formality,
   protocol.
3. RITUAL.
certain *adjective*
1. Sure to happen: *certain death.*
   Syns: inescapable, inevitable,
   unavoidable.
2. Established beyond a doubt: *It is
   absolutely certain that chaos will result.*

Syns: inarguable, incontestable, incontrovertible, indisputable, indubitable, irrefutable, positive, sure, undeniable, undisputable, unquestionable.

3. DEFINITE.

4. FIRM[1].

5, 6. SURE.

certainly *adverb*
1. ABSOLUTELY.
2. YES.

certainty *noun*
1. A clearly established fact: *It is by no means a certainty that a virus causes cancer.*
Syn: cinch (*Slang*). —*Idiom* sure thing.
2. SURENESS.

certify *verb*
1. To confirm formally as true, accurate, or genuine: *This letter certifies that the bearer was employed by us.*
Syns: attest, testify, vouch for, witness. —*Idiom* bear witness to.
2. GUARANTEE.

certitude *noun* SURENESS.

cessation *noun*
1. END.
2, 3. STOP.

cesspit *noun* PIT.

cesspool *noun* PIT.

chafe *verb*
1. To make (the skin) raw by or as if by friction: *chafed her knee when she fell on the concrete.*
Syns: abrade, excoriate, fret, gall[1].
2. ANNOY.
3. FUSS.

chaff *verb* JOKE.

chafing *adjective* IMPATIENT.

chagrin *noun* EMBARRASSMENT.
chagrin *verb* EMBARRASS.

chagrined *adjective* EMBARRASSED.

chain *noun*
1. RUN.
2. SERIES.

chains *noun* BONDS.

challenge *verb*
1. CONTEST.
2. DARE.
3. DEFY.
4. RIVAL.

challenge *noun*
1. DARE.
2. DEFIANCE.
3. OBJECTION.

champ *also* **chomp** *verb*
1. BITE.
2. CHEW.

champion *adjective* EXCELLENT.
champion *verb* SUPPORT.

chance *noun*
1. The quality shared by random, unintended, or unpredictable events or this quality regarded as the cause of such events: *left the result up to chance.*
Syns: fortuitousness, fortuity, fortune, hap[1] (*Archaic*), hazard, luck.
2. The likelihood of a given event occurring: *There's very little chance that he'll win the election.*
Syns: likeliness, odds, outlook, probability, prospect.
3. An unexpected random event: *We met quite by chance.*
Syns: accident, fluke, fortuity, hap[1] (*Archaic*), happenstance (*also* happenchance).
4. OPPORTUNITY.
5. RISK.

chance *verb*
1. To take place by chance: *It chanced that she was there too.*
Syns: befall, hap[1] (*Archaic*), happen.
2. HAZARD.

chance on (or **upon**) *verb* COME ACROSS at **come**.

chance *adjective*
1. ACCIDENTAL.
2. ARBITRARY.

chancy *adjective*
1. AMBIGUOUS.
2. DANGEROUS.

change *verb*
1. To make or become different: *a series of events that will change the world.*
Syns: alter, modify, mutate, turn, vary.
2. To give up in return for something else: *"Would you change places with me?" I asked.*
Syns: commute, exchange, interchange, substitute, swap (*also* swop) (*Informal*), switch, trade.
3. To leave or discard for another: *changed planes in Chicago; changed the subject.*
Syns: shift, switch.
4. STERILIZE.

change *noun*
1. The process or result of making or becoming different: *The change in her personality was amazing.*
Syns: alteration, modification, mutation, permutation, variation.
2. The process or result of giving a different form or appearance: *cultural changes resulting from occupation by foreign troops.*
Syns: conversion, metamorphosis,

transfiguration, transformation,
translation, transmutation.
3. The act of exchanging or
substituting: *a change of clothes.*
Syns: commutation, exchange,
interchange, shift, substitution, swap
(*also* swop) (*Informal*), switch, trade,
transposition (*also* transposal).

changeable *adjective*
1. Capable of or liable to change:
changeable fall weather.
Syns: alterable, fluid, mutable,
uncertain, unsettled, unstable,
unsteady, variable, variant, various
(*Archaic*).
2. CAPRICIOUS.
3. MOBILE.

changeover *noun*
1. CONVERSION.
2. TRANSITION.

channel *verb* CONDUCT.

chant *verb* SING.

chaos *noun* DISORDER.

chaotic *adjective* CONFUSED.

char *verb* BURN.
char *noun* BURN.

character *noun*
1. The combination of emotional,
intellectual, and moral qualities that
distinguishes an individual: *Goodness
is the foundation of the great man's
character.*
Syns: complexion, disposition, make-
up (*also* makeup), nature.
2. Moral or ethical strength: *a person of
real character.*
Syns: fiber, honesty, integrity,
principles, probity, rectitude.
3. A person portrayed in fiction or
drama: *the cast of characters.*
Syns: persona, personage.
4. *Informal.* A person who is
appealingly odd or curious: *an old
character talking to the pigeons.*
Syns: card (*Slang*), oddball (*Slang*),
oddity, original, quiz.
5. A conventional mark used in a
writing system: *Chinese characters are
used in Japanese texts.*
Syns: sign, symbol.
6. DIGNITARY.
7. QUALITY.
8. REFERENCE.
9. REPUTATION.

characteristic *adjective* DISTINCTIVE.
characteristic *noun*
1. HABIT.
2. QUALITY.

characterize *verb*
1. CALL.
2. DISTINGUISH.

charade *noun* PRETENSE.

charge *verb*
1. To place a burden or heavy load on:
The ship's hold was charged with coal.
Syns: burden, cumber, encumber,
freight, lade, load, saddle, tax, weigh,
weight.
2. To cause to be filled with a particular
mood or tone: *an atmosphere charged
with excitement.*
Syns: freight, impregnate, permeate,
pervade, saturate, suffuse, transfuse.
3. ACCUSE.
4. ATTRIBUTE.
5. COMMAND.
6. COMMIT.
7. ENTRUST.
8. FILL.
9. LOAD.

charge *noun*
1. A swift advance or attack: *a cavalry
charge.*
Syns: race, rush.
2. ACCUSATION.
3. CARE.
4. COMMAND.
5. COST.
6. DEPENDENT.
7. DUTY.
8. LOAD.
9. TOLL[1].

charisma *noun* ATTRACTION.

charitable *adjective*
1. HUMANITARIAN.
2. TOLERANT.

charitableness *noun*
1. BENEVOLENCE.
2. TOLERANCE.

charity *noun*
1. BENEVOLENCE.
2. DONATION.
3. GRACE.
4. TOLERANCE.

charlatan *noun* FAKE.

charm *verb*
1. To act upon with or as if with magic:
*charms the authorities into waiving the
regulations.*
Syns: bewitch, enchant, ensorcel,
enthrall, entrance[2], spell[2], spellbind,
witch.
2. To please greatly or irresistibly:
*charmed the audience with the pas de
deux.*
Syns: beguile, bewitch, captivate,
enchant, entrance[2], fascinate.

charm *noun*
1. A small object worn or kept for its
supposed magical power: *wore a
good-luck charm.*

Syns: amulet, fetish, juju, periapt, phylactery (*Archaic*), talisman.
2. ATTRACTION.

charmer *noun* SEDUCER.

charming *adjective*
1. ATTRACTIVE.
2. DELIGHTFUL.

chart *noun* TABLE.

chart *verb*
1. DESIGN.
2. PLOT.

charter *verb* HIRE.

chary *adjective*
1. ECONOMICAL.
2. WARY.

chase *verb* PURSUE.

chase *noun* PURSUIT.

chaste *adjective*
Morally beyond reproach, esp. in sexual conduct: *a chaste nun.*
Syns: decent, modest, nice, pure, virtuous.

chasten *verb* CORRECT.

chastise *verb* CALL DOWN at **call.**

chastity *noun*
The condition of being chaste: *Victorian ideas of chastity.*
Syns: decency, modesty, purity, virtue, virtuousness.

chat *noun*
1. CHATTER.
2. CONVERSATION.

chat *verb* CONVERSE¹.

chattel *noun* FURNISHING.

chattels *noun* EFFECTS.

chatter *verb*
1. To talk volubly, persistently, and usu. inconsequentially: *chattered for hours about his operation.*
Syns: babble, blabber, clack, gab (*Informal*), gas (*Slang*), go on (*Informal*), jabber, jaw (*Slang*), palaver, prate, prattle, rattle on, run on, spiel (*Slang*), yak (*Slang*).
—*Idioms* run off at the mouth, shoot the breeze (*or* the bull).
2. BABBLE.
3. RATTLE.

chatter *noun*
Incessant and usu. inconsequential talk: *I don't have time for chatter, so I'll get right to the point.*
Syns: babble, blab, blabber, chat, chitchat, gab (*Informal*), jabber, palaver, prate, prattle, yak (*Slang*).
—*Idiom* small talk.

chatty *adjective*
1. CONVERSATIONAL.
2. TALKATIVE.

chaw *verb* CHEW.

cheap *adjective*
1. Low in price: *Tomatoes are cheap in August.*
Syns: inexpensive, low, low-cost, low-priced.
2. SHODDY.
3. STINGY.

cheapen *verb*
1. DEBASE.
2. DEPRECIATE.

cheapskate *also* **cheap skate** *noun*
MISER.

cheat *verb*
1. To get money or something else from by deceitful trickery: *cheated the American Indians out of their land.*
Syns: bilk (*Slang*), chisel (*Slang*), cozen, defraud, diddle (*Slang*), do (*Slang*), flimflam (*Slang*), gull, gyp (*also* gip) (*Informal*), mulct, rook (*Slang*), stick (*Slang*), sting (*Slang*), swindle, take, trim (*Informal*), victimize.
2. PHILANDER.

cheat *noun*
1. An act of cheating: *He pulled off a big cheat when he sold us that car.*
Syns: flimflam (*Slang*), fraud, gyp (*Informal*), swindle.
2. A person who cheats: *is a sneak and a cheat.*
Syns: cheater, chiseler (*Slang*), crook (*Informal*), diddler (*Slang*), flimflammer (*Slang*), gyp (*Informal*), gypper (*Informal*), sharper, swindler, trickster.

cheater *noun* CHEAT.

check *noun*
1. EXAMINATION.
2. STOP.

check *verb*
1. EXAMINE.
2. FRUSTRATE.
3. RESTRAIN.
4. STOP.
5, 6. TEST.

check in *verb* ARRIVE.

check out *verb*
1. AGREE.
2. DIE.

checkmate *verb* FRUSTRATE.

checkup *noun*
1, 2. EXAMINATION.

cheek *noun*
1. IMPUDENCE.
2. PRESUMPTION.

cheekiness *noun* PRESUMPTION.

cheeky *adjective*
1. IMPUDENT.
2. PRESUMPTUOUS.

cheer *noun* HAPPINESS.
  cheer *verb*
  1. APPLAUD.
  2. DELIGHT.
cheer (on) *verb* ENCOURAGE.
cheer (up) *verb* ENCOURAGE.
cheerful *adjective*
  1. Being in or showing good spirits:
    gave a cheerful wave of the hand to the
    onlookers.
    Syns: bright, cheery, chipper
    (*Informal*), happy, lighthearted,
    sunny.
  2. GLAD.
cheerfulness *noun* HAPPINESS.
cheering *adjective* ENCOURAGING.
cheerless *adjective* GLOOMY.
cheery *adjective*
  1. CHEERFUL.
  2. GLAD.
cheesy *adjective* SHODDY.
chef *noun* COOK.
chef d'oeuvre *noun* MASTERPIECE.
cherish *verb*
  1. To have the highest regard for:
    cherished their friendship.
    Syns: prize, treasure. —*Idiom* hold
    dear.
  2. APPRECIATE.
cherubic *adjective* BABYISH.
chew *verb*
  To bite and grind with the teeth: *Many*
  athletes chew tobacco.
    Syns: champ (*also* chomp), chaw
    (*Regional*), chump[2], crump, crunch,
    masticate, munch.
chew out *verb* CALL DOWN at **call.**
chew over *verb* PONDER.
chic *adjective* FASHIONABLE.
chicanery *noun* INDIRECTION.
chicken *noun* COWARD.
  chicken *adjective* COWARDLY.
chicken feed *noun* PEANUTS.
chickenhearted *adjective* COWARDLY.
chide *verb* CALL DOWN at **call.**
chiding *noun* REBUKE.
chief *adjective*
  1. PRIMARY.
  2. PRINCIPAL.
  chief *noun*
  1. One who is highest in rank or
    authority: *makes out a weekly report*
    for his chief.
    Syns: boss, chieftain, director, head,
    headman, hierarch, honcho
    (*Informal*), leader, master. —*Idioms*
    cock of the walk, first fiddle.
  2. BOSS.
chieftain *noun*
  1. BOSS.
  2. CHIEF.

child *noun*
  1. A young person between birth and
    puberty: *a group of children with their*
    teacher.
    Syns: bairn (*Scot.*), bud, innocent,
    juvenile, kid (*Informal*), moppet, tot[1],
    youngster.
  2. DESCENDANT.
  3. INNOCENT.
  4. MINOR.
childbearing *noun* BIRTH.
childbirth *noun* BIRTH.
childish *adjective*
  Of or characteristic of a child, esp. in
  immaturity: *childish, sulking behavior.*
    Syns: babyish, immature, infantile,
    juvenile, puerile.
childless *adjective* BARREN.
childlike *adjective* BABYISH.
children *noun* DESCENDANTS.
chill *adjective*
  1, 2. COLD.
  chill *noun* COLD.
chilliness *noun* COLD.
chilly *adjective*
  1. COLD.
  2. COOL.
chime *noun* AGREEMENT.
  chime *verb* RING[2].
chime in *verb* INTERRUPT.
chimera *noun* ILLUSION.
chimerical *also* **chimeric** *adjective*
  1. ILLUSIVE.
  2. IMAGINARY.
chink *noun* CRACK.
chintzy *adjective* GAUDY.
chip in *verb*
  1. CONTRIBUTE.
  2. INTERRUPT.
chipper *adjective*
  1. CHEERFUL.
  2. LIVELY.
chisel *verb* CHEAT.
chiseler *noun* CHEAT.
chitchat *noun* CHATTER.
chivalric *adjective* GALLANT.
chivalrous *adjective*
  1. BENEVOLENT.
  2. GALLANT.
  3. GRACIOUS.
chivalrousness *noun* GALLANTRY.
chivalry *noun* GALLANTRY.
choate *adjective* COMPLETE.
chockablock FULL.
chock-full *also* **chuck-full**, **choke-full**
  adjective FULL.
choice *noun*
  1. The act of choosing: *Did price*
    influence your choice?

Syns: election, option, preference, selection.

2. The power or right of choosing: *I had no choice but to accept his decision.*
   Syns: alternative, option.
3. BEST.
4. ELECT.
5. WILL[1].

choice *adjective*
1. Of fine quality: *had a choice glass of wine.*
   Syns: fine, first-class, prime, select, superior, top-quality.
2. DELICATE.
3. SELECT.

choke *verb*
1. To interfere with or stop the normal breathing of, esp. by constricting the windpipe: *choked the victim to death.*
   Syns: strangle, throttle.
2. To stop the breathing of: *a tight collar that almost chokes him.*
   Syns: asphyxiate, smother, stifle, suffocate.
3. FILL.
4. REPRESS.

choke-full *adjective*
   SEE **chock-full.**

choking *noun* REPRESSION.

choler *noun*
1. FURY.
2. TEMPER.

choleric *adjective*
1. ANGRY.
2. TESTY.

chomp *verb* SEE **champ.**

choose *verb*
1. To make a choice from a number of alternatives: *You'll have to choose which cities you most want to visit.*
   Syns: cull, elect, opt for, pick (out), select, single out.
2. To have the desire or inclination to: *I can do exactly as I choose.*
   Syns: desire, like[1], please, want, will[1], wish. —*Idioms* have a mind, see fit.

choosy *adjective* NICE.

chop[1] *verb*
1. CUT.
2. CUT BACK at **cut.**
   chop *noun* SLAP.

chop[2] *verb* SWERVE.

chore *noun*
1, 2. TASK.

chortle *verb* CHUCKLE.

chosen *adjective* SELECT.

chow *noun* FOOD.

   chow *verb* EAT.

christen *verb* NAME.

chronic *adjective*
1. Of long duration: *suffering from chronic feelings of doubt.*
   Syns: continuing, lingering, persistent, prolonged, protracted.
2. Subject to a disease or habit for a long time: *a chronic alcoholic; a chronic liar.*
   Syns: confirmed, habitual, habituated, inveterate.
3. ACCUSTOMED.

chronicle *noun*
1. HISTORY.
2. STORY.

chubby *adjective* PLUMP[1].

chuck[1] *verb*
1. DISCARD.
2. EJECT.

chuck[2] *noun* FOOD.

chuck[3] *verb* CHUCKLE.

chuck-full *adjective*
   SEE **chock-full.**

chuckle *verb*
   To laugh quietly: *The baby chuckled while playing with his toys.*
   Syns: chortle, chuck[3] (*Obs.*).

chuff *noun*
1. BOOR.
2. MISER.
   chuff *adjective* GLUM.

chuffy *adjective* GLUM.

chum *noun* ASSOCIATE.

chummy *adjective*
1. FAMILIAR.
2. FRIENDLY.

chump[1] *noun* DUPE.

chump[2] *verb* CHEW.

chunk *noun* LUMP[1].

chunky *adjective* STOCKY.

church *noun* FAITH.

   church *adjective* SPIRITUAL.

churchly *adjective* SPIRITUAL.

churchman *noun* PREACHER.

churl *noun* BOOR.

churlish *adjective* COARSE.

churn *verb*
1. AGITATE.
2. BOIL.

chutzpah *noun* TEMERITY.

cinch *noun*
1. BREEZE.
2. CERTAINTY.
   cinch *verb* GUARANTEE.

cincture *verb* BAND[1].

cinerarium *noun* GRAVE[1].

cipher *verb* CALCULATE.

   cipher *noun* NONENTITY.

circle *noun*
1. A closed plane curve everywhere equidistant from a fixed point or

something shaped like this: *a bracelet that looks like a circle of diamonds.*
Syns: circuit, gyre, orb (*Archaic*), ring¹, wheel.

2. A course, process, or journey that ends where it began or repeats itself: *drove full circle—Boston to New York and back.*
Syns: circuit, cycle, orbit, round, tour, turn.

3. A group of people sharing an interest, activity, or achievement: *popular in musical circles.*
Syns: crowd, group, set².

4. CROWD.

circle *verb*
1. SURROUND.
2. TURN.

circuit *noun*
1. BEAT.
2, 3. CIRCLE.
4. CIRCUMFERENCE.
5. CONFERENCE.
6. REVOLUTION.

circuitous *adjective* INDIRECT.

circular *adjective*
1. INDIRECT.
2. ROUND.

circulate *verb*
1. DISTRIBUTE.
2. FLOW.
3. GET ABOUT at **get.**

circulation *noun* REVOLUTION.

circumference *noun*
A line around a closed figure or area: *walked around the circumference of the property.*
Syns: ambit, circuit, compass, perimeter, periphery.

circumlocutional *adjective* TAUTOLOGICAL.

circumlocutionary *adjective* TAUTOLOGICAL.

circumlocutious *adjective* TAUTOLOGICAL.

circumlocutory *adjective* TAUTOLOGICAL.

circumnavigate *verb* SKIRT.

circumscribe *verb* LIMIT.

circumscribed *adjective* RESTRICTED.

circumscription *noun*
1, 2. RESTRICTION.

circumspect *adjective* WARY.

circumspection *noun*
1. CAUTION.
2. PRUDENCE.

circumstance *noun*
1. One of the conditions or facts attending an event and having some bearing on it: *Tell me the circumstances under which you left.*

Syns: detail, fact, factor, particular.

2. Something that happens: *a victim of circumstance.*
Syns: event, happening, incident, occurrence.

3. EVENT.

circumstances *noun* CONDITIONS.

circumstantial *adjective* DETAILED.

circumvent *verb*
1, 2. SKIRT.

circumvolution *noun* REVOLUTION.

cite *verb*
1. NAME.
2. PRESENT².

citify *verb*
To imbue with city ways, manners, and customs: *After living in New York for six months she became thoroughly citified.*
Syns: metropolitanize, urbanize.

citizen *noun*
A person owing loyalty to and entitled to the protection of a given state: *an American citizen arrested on suspicion of spying.*
Syns: national, subject.

city *noun*
A large and important town: *The city of Budapest straddles the Danube.*
Syns: burg (*Informal*), metropolis, municipality.

city *adjective*
Of, in, or belonging to a city: *city government; city life.*
Syns: metropolitan, municipal, urban.

civic *adjective* PUBLIC.

civil *adjective*
1. COURTEOUS.
2. PUBLIC.

civilities *noun* AMENITIES.

civility *noun*
1, 2. COURTESY.

civilization *noun* CULTURE.

civilize *verb* SOCIALIZE.

civilized *adjective* CULTURED.

civilizing *adjective* CULTURAL.

clack *noun* SNAP.

clack *verb*
1. CHATTER.
2. RATTLE.
3. SNAP.

clacket *verb* SNAP.

clad *verb*
1. DRESS.
2. FACE.

clag *verb* BOND.

claggy *adjective* STICKY.

claim *verb*
1. To assert one's right to: *claimed his share of the profits.*
Syn: demand. —*Idiom* lay claim to.

2. To state to be true: *claims she can write poetry and novels with equal ease.*
Syns: allege, assert, contend, declare, maintain, say.
3. ASSERT.

claim *noun*
1. A legitimate or supposed right to demand something as one's rightful due: *the Arabs' claim to lands conquered by Israel; keyboard virtuosity as her claim to fame.*
Syns: dibs (*Slang*), pretense, pretension, title.
2. A statement of something as fact: *an advertisement that makes false claims.*
Syns: allegation, assertion, contention, declaration.
3. INTEREST.

claimant *noun*
1. One who sets forth a claim to a royal title: *The Comte de Paris is the claimant to the throne of France.*
Syns: claimer, pretender.
2. COMPLAINANT.

claimer *noun* CLAIMANT.
clamber *verb* SCRAMBLE.
clamor *verb* ROAR.
clamor *noun*
1. NOISE.
2. ROAR.
3. VOCIFERATION.
clamorous *adjective* VOCIFEROUS.
clampdown *noun* SUPPRESSION.
clan *noun* FAMILY.
clandestine *adjective* SECRET.
clandestinely *adverb* SECRETLY.
clap *verb*
1. APPLAUD.
2. BANG.
3. CRACK.
claptrap *noun* NONSENSE.
claret *noun* BLOOD.
clarification *noun*
1. EXPLANATION.
2. PURIFICATION.
clarified *adjective* REFINED.
clarify *verb*
1. To make clear or clearer: *tried to clarify the point of law for his client.*
Syns: clear, clear up, elucidate, illuminate. —*Idiom* shed (*or* throw) light on (*or* upon).
2. REFINE.
clarity *noun*
1. The quality of being clear and easy to perceive or understand: *a photograph remarkable for its clarity; an actor renowned for the clarity of his speech.*
Syns: clearness, distinctness,

limpidity, lucidity, perspicuity, plainness.
2. PURITY.

clash *verb*
1. To strike together with a loud, harsh noise: *cymbals clashing.*
Syns: crash, smash.
2. CONFLICT.

clash *noun*
1. A loud striking together: *a clash of cymbals.*
Syns: crash, smash.
2. ARGUMENT.
3. BRUSH.
4. CONFLICT.

clashing *adjective* CONFLICTING.
clasp *noun*
1. CATCH.
2. EMBRACE.
3. HOLD.
clasp *verb*
1. EMBRACE.
2. GRASP.
class *noun*
1. A subdivision of a larger group: *the class of concertgoers who enjoy chamber music.*
Syns: category, classification, order, set².
2. A division of persons or things by quality, rank, or grade: *a painter of the highest class.*
Syns: bracket, caliber, grade, league (*Informal*), order, rank¹, tier.
3. *Slang.* High style in quality, manner, or dress: *a new restaurant with real class.*
Syns: quality, refinement.
4. QUALITY.

class *verb*
1. To assign to a class or classes: *classed farmers separately from those whose work entails only service.*
Syns: categorize, classify, grade, group, pigeonhole, place, rank¹, rate¹.
2. ASSORT.

classic *adjective*
1. TYPICAL.
2. VINTAGE.
classical *adjective*
1. TYPICAL.
2. VINTAGE.
classification *noun* CLASS.
classified *adjective* CONFIDENTIAL.
classify *verb*
1. ARRANGE.
2. ASSORT.
3. CLASS.
classy *adjective* FASHIONABLE.
clatter *verb* RATTLE.

clean *adjective*
1. Free from dirt, stain, or impurities: *clean clothing; clean water.*
   Syns: antiseptic, cleanly, immaculate, spotless, stainless, unsoiled, unsullied.
2. Without imperfections or blemishes: *the clean lines of a fine antique.*
   Syns: perfect, regular.
3. Not lewd or obscene: *a clean joke.*
   Syns: decent, modest, wholesome.
4, 5. INNOCENT.
6. SPORTSMANLIKE.

clean *verb*
1. REFINE.
2. TIDY.

clean out *verb*
1. EMPTY.
2. RUIN.

clean up *verb*
Informal. To make a large profit: *cleaned up on the stock market.*
   Syns: batten, profit. —*Idiom* make a killing.

clean *adverb* COMPLETELY.
cleaner *noun* PURIFIER.
cleaning *noun* PURIFICATION.
cleanliness *noun* PURITY.
cleanly *adjective* CLEAN.
   cleanly *adverb* FAIR.
cleanness *noun* PURITY.
cleanse *verb*
1. PURIFY.
2. REFINE.
cleanser *noun* PURIFIER.
cleansing *noun* PURIFICATION.
clear *adjective*
1. Free from what obscures or dims: *a glass of clear, sediment-free claret.*
   Syns: limpid, lucid, pellucid, transparent.
2. Free from clouds, mist, etc.: *a clear day.*
   Syns: cloudless, fair, fine[1], sunny, unclouded.
3. Free from flaws or blemishes: *a clear, radiant complexion.*
   Syns: flawless, unblemished, unbroken, unmarked.
4. Free from obstructions: *The road ahead is clear.*
   Syns: open, unimpeded, unobstructed.
5. Freed from contact or connection: *The rope is clear of the scaffolding.*
   Syns: disengaged, free, unfastened.
6. APPARENT.
7. DECIDED.
8. EMPTY.
9. SHARP.
10. TRANSPARENT.
11. UNSUBTLE.

clear *verb*
1. To become brighter or fairer: *If the weather clears, we can enjoy the picnic.*
   Syns: brighten, clear up.
2. To free from an entanglement: *cleared himself from the unsatisfactory relationship.*
   Syns: disengage, disentangle, extricate, untangle.
3. To rid of obstructions: *cleared the streets for the motorcade.*
   Syn: open.
4. To free from a charge or imputation of guilt: *The jury cleared the defendant of the murder charge.*
   Syns: absolve, acquit, disculpate, exculpate, exonerate, purge (*Law*), vindicate.
5. To pass by or over safely or successfully: *Our car barely cleared the snowdrift.*
   Syns: hurdle, negotiate.
6. ANNIHILATE.
7. CLARIFY.
8. EMPTY.
9. PASS.
10. RETURN.
11. RID.
12. SETTLE.
13. TIDY.

clear out *verb* RUN.
clear up *verb*
1. CLARIFY.
2. CLEAR.
3. RESOLVE.

clear *adverb*
Informal. All the way: *From here you can see clear to the park.*
   Syns: completely, entirely, fully.
clearance *noun* ELIMINATION.
clear-cut *adjective*
1. APPARENT.
2. DECIDED.
3. DEFINITE.
4. INCISIVE.
clearness *noun* CLARITY.
clear-sightedness *noun* DISCERNMENT.
cleave *verb*
1. BREAK.
2. CUT.
3. TEAR[1].
cleft *noun*
1. BREACH.
2. CRACK.
clemency *noun* GRACE.
clement *adjective* TOLERANT.
clench *verb* GRASP.
   clench *noun* HOLD.
clergyman *noun* PREACHER.

cleric *noun* PREACHER.

clerical *noun* PREACHER.

clerk *noun* PREACHER.

clever *adjective*
1. Mentally quick and original: *The child is clever but not brilliant.*
   Syns: alert, bright, intelligent, keen¹, quick-witted, sharp, sharp-witted, smart. —*Idiom* smart as a tack (*or* whip).
2. Amusing or pleasing because of wit or originality: *made the audience laugh with a few clever, offbeat comparisons.*
   Syns: scintillating, smart, sparkling, sprightly, witty.
3. DEXTEROUS.
4. SHARP.

clew *noun* SEE clue.

cliché *noun*
A trite expression or idea: *a short story marred by clichés.*
   Syns: banality, bromide, commonplace, platitude, stereotype, truism.

cliché *adjective* TRITE.

click *noun* SNAP.

click *verb*
1. RELATE.
2. SNAP.
3. SUCCEED.

client *noun* PATRON.

clientele *noun* PATRONAGE.

climacteric *adjective* CRITICAL.

climactic *adjective*
Of or constituting a climax: *The climactic moment of the event was the presentation of the award.*
   Syns: crowning, culminating, peak.

climate *noun*
1. ENVIRONMENT.
2. TEMPER.

climatize *verb* HARDEN.

climax *noun*
1. The highest point or state: *a public figure at the climax of his popularity.*
   Syns: acme, apex, apogee, crest, crown, culmination, height, meridian, payoff (*Informal*), peak, pinnacle, summit, zenith.
2. MAXIMUM.

climax *verb*
To reach or bring to a climax: *The movie climaxes with realistic scenes of an invasion.*
   Syns: cap, crown, culminate, peak, top off.

climb *verb*
1. ASCEND.
2. RISE.

climb *noun* ASCENT.

climbing *noun* ASCENT.

clinch *verb*
1. EMBRACE.
2. GRASP.

clinch *noun* EMBRACE.

clincher *noun* TRUMP.

cling *verb* BOND.

clink *noun* JAIL.

clip¹ *verb*
1. CUT BACK at cut.
2. HIT.
3. SKIN.

clip *noun*
1. SLAP.
2. SPEED.

clip² *verb*
1. ATTACH.
2. EMBRACE.

clitter *verb* RATTLE.

cloak *verb*
1. CLOTHE.
2. COVER.
3. DISGUISE.
4. WRAP.

cloak *noun*
1. FAÇADE.
2. WRAP.

cloak-and-dagger *adjective* SECRET.

clobber *verb*
1. DEFEAT.
2. HIT.
3. OVERWHELM.

clobbering *noun* DEFEAT.

clock *verb* TIME.

clod *noun*
1. DRIP.
2, 3. LUMP¹.

clog *verb* FILL.

cloggy *adjective* STICKY.

cloister *verb* SECLUDE.

cloistered *adjective* SECLUDED.

clomp *verb* THUD.

close¹ *adjective*
1. Not far from another in space, time, or relation: *an airport that is close to town; a birthday close to my own.*
   Syns: immediate, near, near-at-hand, nearby, nigh, proximate. —*Idioms* at hand, under one's nose, within a stone's throw, within hailing distance.
2. Nearly equivalent or even: *a close race; a close election.*
   Syns: neck-and-neck (*Informal*), tight.
3. Not deviating from correctness, accuracy, or completeness: *keeping a close watch on the prisoner.*
   Syns: exact, faithful, full, rigorous, strict.

4. AIRLESS.
5. FAMILIAR.
6. STINGY.
7. TACITURN.
8. TAUT.
9. THICK.
10. TIGHT.

close *verb*
1. To move an appropriate barrier into (an opening): *Close the door behind you.*
   Syns: put to, shut.
2. To bring or come to a natural or proper end: *She closes letters with greetings. The play closed after ten performances.*
   Syns: cease, complete, conclude, consummate, end, finish, terminate, ultimate, wind up (*Informal*), wrap up. —*Idiom* put (*or* set) a period to.
3. To come together: *His arms closed around her in a tight embrace.*
   Syns: converge, meet¹.
4. BLOCK OUT at **block.**
5. FILL.

close in *verb*
To surround and advance upon: *The skyscrapers seemed to close in on us.*
   Syns: enclose, envelop, fence, hedge, hem.

close off *verb* ISOLATE.
close out *verb* SELL OFF at **sell.**
close *noun*
1, 2. END.

close *adverb*
To a point near in time, space, or relation: *stuck close together; standing close by.*
   Syns: hard, near, nearby, nigh.
close² *noun* COURT.
close-at-hand *adjective* CONVENIENT.
close-by *adjective* CONVENIENT.
close-fisted *adjective* STINGY.
close-minded *adjective*
1. INTOLERANT.
2. OBSTINATE.
close-mouthed *adjective* TACITURN.
closet *verb* IMPRISON.
closing *adjective* LAST¹.
closing *noun* END.
closure *noun* END.
clot *verb* COAGULATE.
clothe *verb*
1. To cover as if with clothes: *trees clothed in leafy splendor.*
   Syns: cloak, drape, mantle, robe.
2. DRESS.
3. WRAP.
clothes *noun* DRESS.
clothing *noun* DRESS.

cloud *verb* OBSCURE.
cloud *noun* CROWD.
clouded *adjective* AMBIGUOUS.
cloudiness *noun* VAGUENESS.
cloudless *adjective* CLEAR.
cloudy *adjective*
1. AMBIGUOUS.
2. CLEAR.
clout *noun*
1. AUTHORITY.
2. BLOW².
3. INFLUENCE.
4. MUSCLE.
clout *verb* HIT.
clown *noun* JOKER.
clown *verb* JOKE.
cloy *verb* SATIATE.
club *noun* UNION.
clue also **clew** *noun*
1. HINT.
2. LEAD.
clump *noun*
1. GROUP.
2. LUMP¹.
clump *verb*
1. LUMP¹.
2. THUD.
clumsy *adjective*
1, 2. AWKWARD.
3. TACTLESS.
4. UNSKILLFUL.
clunk *noun* BEAT.
clunk *verb* THUD.
cluster *noun* GROUP.
cluster *verb* ASSEMBLE.
clutch *noun*
1. CATCH.
2. GROUP.
3. HOLD.
clutch *verb*
1. CATCH.
2. GRASP.
clutching *adjective* JEALOUS.
clutter *noun* DISORDER.
cluttered *adjective* BUSY.
coadjutant *noun* ASSISTANT.
coadjute *verb* COOPERATE.
coadjutor *noun* ASSISTANT.
coadjuvancy *noun* COOPERATION.
coagency *noun* COOPERATION.
coagulate *verb*
To change or be changed from a liquid into a soft, semisolid, or solid mass: *Egg white coagulates when heated.*
   Syns: clot, congeal, gelatinize, jell, set¹.
coalesce *verb* COMBINE.
coalition *noun*
1. ALLIANCE.

2. COMBINE.
3. UNIFICATION.
coalitionist *noun* ALLY.
coarse *adjective*
1. Lacking in delicacy or refinement: *coarse language; coarse manners; a coarse person who offended others.*
   Syns: barbarian, barbaric, boorish, churlish, crass, crude, earthy, gross, ill-bred, Philistine (*also* philistine), raw, rough, rude, tasteless, uncivilized, uncouth, uncultivated, unpolished, unrefined, vulgar.
2. Consisting of or covered with large particles: *coarse sand.*
   Syns: grainy, granular, gritty, rough.
3. CRUDE.
4. OBSCENE.
5. ROUGH.
coast *verb* SLIDE.
coax *verb*
To persuade or try to persuade by gentle, persistent urging or flattery: *She succeeded in coaxing her parents to buy her a car.*
   Syns: blandish, cajole, soft-soap (*Informal*), sweet-talk (*Informal*), wheedle.
cockcrow *noun* DAWN.
cock-eyed *adjective*
1. DRUNK.
2. FOOLISH.
coddle *verb* BABY.
coefficient *adjective* COOPERATIVE.
coequal *noun* PEER².
coerce *verb*
1. To compel by pressure or threats: *coerced them into the car at gunpoint.*
   Syns: blackjack, dragoon, force, hijack (*also* highjack) (*Informal*), shotgun (*Informal*), strong-arm (*Informal*).
2. FORCE.
coerced *adjective* FORCED.
coercion *noun* FORCE.
coercive *adjective* FORCIBLE.
coetaneous *adjective* CONTEMPORARY.
coeval *adjective* CONTEMPORARY.
coeval *noun* CONTEMPORARY.
coexistent *adjective* CONTEMPORARY.
coextensive *adjective* PARALLEL.
cogent *adjective*
1. CONVINCING.
2. SOUND².
cogitate *verb*
1. CONSIDER.
2. PONDER.
3. REASON.
4. THINK.

cogitation *noun* THOUGHT.
cogitative *adjective* THOUGHTFUL.
cognate *adjective* RELATED.
cognizance *noun*
1. AWARENESS.
2. NOTICE.
cognizant *adjective* AWARE.
cognomen *noun* NAME.
cohere *verb* BOND.
coherence *noun* CONSISTENCY.
cohesion *noun* BOND.
cohort *noun*
1. ASSOCIATE.
2. FOLLOWER.
coil *verb* WIND².
coincide *verb*
1. To occur at the same time: *The two events coincided.*
   Syn: concur.
2. AGREE.
coincident *adjective*
1. ACCOMPANYING.
2. SIMULTANEOUS.
cold *adjective*
1. Marked by a low temperature: *a cold night.*
   Syns: chill, chilly, cool, nippy, shivery.
2. Not affected by or showing emotion: *a cold person unable to respond.*
   Syns: cold-blooded, emotionless, unaffected, unemotional.
3. Lacking all friendliness and warmth: *a cold farewell.*
   Syns: chill, emotionless, frigid, glacial, icy.
4. FRIGID.
5. GLOOMY.
6. UNCONSCIOUS.
cold *noun*
Relative lack of warmth: *the winter cold.*
   Syns: chill, chilliness, coldness, coolness, coolth.
cold-blooded *adjective*
1. Totally lacking in compassion: *a cold-blooded killer.*
   Syns: callous, cold-hearted, compassionless, hard-boiled (*Informal*), hardened, hardhearted, heartless, obdurate, stonyhearted, unfeeling. —*Idiom* cold of heart.
2. COLD.
cold-hearted *adjective* COLD-BLOODED.
coldness *noun* COLD.
cold shoulder *noun* SNUB.
cold-shoulder *verb* SNUB.
collaborate *verb* COOPERATE.
collaboration *noun* COOPERATION.
collaborative *adjective* COOPERATIVE.

collapse *verb*
1. To suddenly lose all health or strength: *collapsed from exhaustion.*
   Syns: break down, cave in, conk out (*Slang*), crack, crack up (*Informal*), drop, give out, give way, succumb.
2. To undergo sudden financial failure: *The stock market collapsed.*
   Syns: break, bust, crash, fail, fold (*Informal*), go under. —*Idioms* go bust, go on the rocks, go to the wall.
3. BEND.
4, 5. BREAK DOWN at **break**.
6. CAVE IN at **cave**.
7. SURRENDER.
collapse *noun*
1. An abrupt, disastrous failure: *the 1929 stock-market collapse.*
   Syns: breakdown, crash, debacle, smash, smashup, wreck.
2. BREAKDOWN.
3. FALL.
collar *verb* ARREST.
collate *verb* COMPARE.
collateral *adjective*
1. AUXILIARY.
2. PARALLEL.
3. SUBORDINATE.
colleague *noun*
1. ASSOCIATE.
2. PEER².
collect¹ *verb*
1. ACCUMULATE.
2, 3. ASSEMBLE.
4. COMPOSE.
collect² *noun* PRAYER.
collected *adjective* COOL.
collection *noun*
1. ACCUMULATION.
2. GROUP.
collide *verb*
To come together or come up against with force: *The two cars collided.*
   Syns: bump, crash.
collision *noun*
Violent, forcible contact between two or more things: *the collision of the two spacecraft.*
   Syns: appulse, bump, concussion, crash, impact, jar, jolt, percussion, shock, smash, wallop.
colloquial *adjective* CONVERSATIONAL.
colloquialist *noun* CONVERSATIONALIST.
colloquist *noun* CONVERSATIONALIST.
colloquium *noun* CONFERENCE.
colloquy *noun* CONVERSATION.
collude *verb* PLOT.
collusion *noun* PLOT.
colony *noun* POSSESSION.

colophon *noun* MARK.
color *noun*
1. The property by which the sense of vision can distinguish between objects, as a red apple and a green apple, that are very similar or identical in form and size: *Red, yellow, and blue are primary colors.*
   Syns: hue, shade, tone.
2. Something that imparts color: *painted the room using a new washable color.*
   Syns: colorant, coloring, dye, dyestuff, pigment, stain, tincture.
3. COMPLEXION.
4. FAÇADE.
5. VERISIMILITUDE.
color *verb*
1. To impart color to: *colored the shingles brown.*
   Syns: dye, stain, tint.
2. To give a deceptively attractive appearance to: *color a lie.*
   Syns: gild, gloss, gloze (over), palliate, sugarcoat, varnish, veneer, whitewash. —*Idioms* lend a good color to, paper over the cracks, put a gloss on, put a good face on.
3. BIAS.
4. BLUSH.
5. DIP.
6. DISTORT.
colorable *adjective* BELIEVABLE.
colorant *noun* COLOR.
coloration *noun* COMPLEXION.
colored *adjective* BIASED.
colorful *adjective*
1. Full of color: *a colorful bed of pansies.*
   Syns: bright, gay, showy, vivid.
2. Evoking strong mental images through distinctiveness: *colorful writing; a colorful character.*
   Syns: picturesque, vivid.
coloring *noun*
1. COLOR.
2. COMPLEXION.
3. FAÇADE.
colorless *adjective*
1. DULL.
2. NEUTRAL.
3. PALE.
colorlessness *noun* INSIPIDITY.
colors *noun* FLAG¹.
colossal *adjective* GIANT.
column *noun* LINE.
comb *verb* SCOUR.
combat *noun*
A hostile encounter between opposing military forces: *sent the infantry into combat.*
   Syns: action, battle, engagement.

combat *verb*
1. CONTEND.
2. CONTEST.
3. RESIST.

combatant *noun* FIGHTER.

combatant *adjective* BELLIGERENT.

combative *adjective*
1. AGGRESSIVE.
2. ARGUMENTATIVE.
3. BELLIGERENT.

combativeness *noun*
1. AGGRESSION.
2. BELLIGERENCE.
3. FIGHT.

combinate *verb* COMBINE.

combination *noun*
1. The result of combining: *Water is a combination of hydrogen and oxygen.*
   Syns: conjugation, melding, unification, union.
2. ASSOCIATION.
3. COMBINE.

combinational *adjective*
Of, relating to, or tending to produce combination: *the combinational tendencies of these substances.*
   Syns: combinative, combinatorial, combinatory, conjugational, conjugative.

combinative *adjective*
COMBINATIONAL.

combinatorial *adjective*
COMBINATIONAL.

combinatory *adjective*
COMBINATIONAL.

combine *verb*
1. To bring or come together into a united whole: *combine oxygen with hydrogen; artistic expression combined with technique.*
   Syns: coalesce, combinate, compound, concrete, conjoin, conjugate, connect, couple, join, link, marry, meld, unite, wed, yoke.
2. ASSOCIATE.
3. BAND².
4. EMBODY.
5. MIX.

combine *noun*
1. A group of individuals united in a common cause: *a combine of citizens demanding tax relief.*
   Syns: bloc, cartel, coalition, combination, faction, party, ring¹.
2. A combination of businesses closely interconnected for common profit: *a large oil combine.*
   Syns: cartel, pool, syndicate, trust.

combined *adjective*
Joined together into a whole: *the combined influences of poverty and inflation.*
   Syns: conjoint, fused, melded.

comburent *adjective* BLAZING.

combust *verb* BURN.

come *verb*
1. To take place: *Will war come?*
   Syns: befall, betide, come about, come off, develop, hap¹ (*Archaic*), happen, occur, pass, transpire.
2. To take place at a set time: *Christmas comes on December 25.*
   Syns: fall, occur.
3. To happen to one: *Depression came to her quickly.*
   Syns: befall, betide.
4. To go forward, esp. toward a conclusion: *This project is coming just fine.*
   Syns: advance, come along, get along, march¹, move (along), proceed, progress.
5. To have as one's home or place of origin: *I come from Virginia.*
   Syns: hail², originate.
6. BECOME.
7. STEM.

come about *verb* COME.

come across *verb*
1. To find or meet by chance: *come across the lost sock; come across an old friend.*
   Syns: alight on (*or* upon) (*Archaic*), bump into (*Informal*), chance on (*or* upon), come on (*or* upon), find, happen on (*or* upon), light on (*or* upon), run across, run into, stumble on (*or* upon), tumble (on). —*Idiom* meet up with.
2. CONTRIBUTE.

come along *verb* COME.

come around (*or* **round**) *verb*
RECOVER.

come back *verb* RETURN.

come by *verb*
1. GET.
2. VISIT.

come in *verb*
1. ENTER.
2. RUN.

come into *verb* INHERIT.

come off *verb*
1. COME.
2. SUCCEED.

come on (*or* **upon**) *verb* COME ACROSS at **come**.

come out *verb*
1. To be made public: *didn't want the whole story to come out.*
   Syns: break, get out, leak (out), out, transpire. —*Idiom* come to light.

2. To make one's formal entry, as into society: *came out at the debutante ball.*
Syns: bow, debut (*also* début).

come out with *verb* AIR.
come over *verb* VISIT.
come through *verb*
1. CONTRIBUTE.
2. SUCCEED.
3. SURVIVE.
comeback *noun*
1. A return to former prosperity or status: *made a political comeback.*
Syn: recovery.
2. ANSWER.
3. RETORT.
comedian *noun* JOKER.
comedown *noun* DESCENT.
comedy *noun* HUMOR.
come-hither *adjective* ATTRACTIVE.
comely *adjective*
1. BEAUTIFUL.
2. CORRECT.
come-on *noun* LURE.
comer *noun*
1. *Informal.* One showing much promise: *The young executive is a real comer.*
Syn: up-and-comer. —*Idioms* man (*or* woman) on the way up, rising star.
2. ARRIVAL.
comestible *adjective* EDIBLE.
comestible *noun* FOOD.
comeuppance *also* **comeupance** *noun* DUE.
comfort *verb*
1. To give hope to in time of grief or pain: *comforted the widow.*
Syns: consolate (*Obs.*), console, solace, soothe.
2. RELIEVE.
comfort *noun*
1. A consoling in time of grief or pain: *gave comfort to the bereaved.*
Syns: consolation, solace.
2. AMENITY.
3. PROSPERITY.
comfortable *adjective*
1. Affording pleasurable ease: *a comfortable new house.*
Syns: comfy (*Informal*), cozy (*also* cosy), easeful, easy, snug, soft (*Informal*).
2. PROSPEROUS.
3. SUFFICIENT.
comfortless *adjective* UNCOMFORTABLE.
comfy *adjective* COMFORTABLE.
comic *noun* JOKER.
comic *adjective*
1. AMUSING.

2. LAUGHABLE.
comical *adjective*
1. AMUSING.
2. LAUGHABLE.
comicality *also* **comicalness** *noun* HUMOR.
coming *adjective*
1. In the relatively near future: *the coming years.*
Syns: approaching, forthcoming, upcoming.
2. *Informal.* Showing great promise: *Roller discos are the coming thing.*
Syns: promising, up-and-coming.
3. FLOURISHING.
4. FOLLOWING.
5. FUTURE.
coming *noun*
1. APPROACH.
2. ARRIVAL.
coming-out *noun* PRESENTATION.
command *verb*
1. To give orders to: *commanded the brigade to attack.*
Syns: bid, charge, direct, enjoin, instruct, order, require, tell.
2. To be possessed of: *commands great prestige; commands five languages.*
Syns: boast, enjoy, have, hold, possess.
3. DOMINATE.
4. LEAD.
command *noun*
1. An authoritative indication to be obeyed: *gave the command to fire.*
Syns: behest, bidding, charge, commandment, dictate, direction, directive, injunction, instruction, mandate, order, word.
2. ABILITY.
3. AUTHORITY.
4. DOMINATION.
5. LEAD.
6. TECHNIQUE.
commandeer *verb*
1. ASSUME.
2. SEIZE.
commandeering *noun* SEIZURE.
commanding *adjective*
1. AUTHORITATIVE.
2. DOMINANT.
commandment *noun* COMMAND.
comme il faut *adjective* CORRECT.
commemorate *verb*
1. CELEBRATE.
2. MEMORIALIZE.
commemoration *noun*
1. CELEBRATION.
2. MEMORIAL.
commemorative *adjective* MEMORIAL.

commence *verb*
1. BEGIN.
2. DAWN.
3. START.

commencement *noun*
1. BEGINNING.
2. BIRTH.

commend *verb*
1. COMPLIMENT.
2. ENTRUST.
3. PRAISE.

commendable *adjective* ADMIRABLE.

commendation *noun*
1. COMPLIMENT.
2. PRAISE.

commendatory *adjective*
COMPLIMENTARY.

commensurable *adjective*
1. PROPORTIONAL.
2. SYMMETRICAL.

commensurate *adjective*
1. PROPORTIONAL.
2. SYMMETRICAL.

comment *noun*
1. An expression of fact or opinion: *made a positive comment about the party.*
   Syns: note, obiter dictum, observation, remark.
2. COMMENTARY.
3. REVIEW.
4. WORD.

comment *verb*
To make observations: *commented on the artist's technique.*
Syns: note, observe, remark.

commentary *noun*
1. Critical explanation or analysis: *commentaries on the Old Testament.*
   Syns: annotation, comment, exegesis, interpretation, note.
2. A narrative of experiences undergone by the writer: *Caesar's Commentaries on the Gallic War.*
   Syns: memoir, reminiscence.
3. REVIEW.

commentator *noun* CRITIC.
commerce *noun* BUSINESS.
commingle *verb* MIX.
commiserable *adjective* PITIFUL.
commiserate *verb* FEEL.
commiseration *noun* PITY.
commiserative *adjective*
SYMPATHETIC.

commission *verb* AUTHORIZE.
commission *noun* MISSION.

commit *verb*
1. To be responsible for or guilty of (an error or crime): *committed murder.*
   Syns: perpetrate, pull off (*Informal*).
2. To place officially in confinement: *commit a criminal to prison.*
   Syns: consign, institutionalize, send up (*Informal*).
3. To be morally bound to do: *was committed to defend his country.*
   Syns: bind, charge, obligate, pledge.
4. ENTRUST.

commitment *noun* DUTY.
committal *noun* DUTY.
commix *verb* MIX.
commodious *adjective* ROOMY.
commodities *noun* GOODS.

common *adjective*
1. Belonging to, shared by, or applicable to all alike: *National security is a common concern for Americans.*
   Syns: communal, conjoint, general, intermutual, joint, mutual, public.
2. Occurring quite often: *Traffic accidents are common phenomena.*
   Syns: everyday, familiar, frequent, ordinary, regular, routine, widespread.
3. To be expected: *the common problems of city life.*
   Syns: average, commonplace, general, matter-of-course, normal, ordinary, typical (*also* typic), usual.
4. ACCEPTABLE.
5. EASYGOING.
6. GENERAL.
7. INFERIOR.
8. LOWLY.
9. NOTORIOUS.
10. ORDINARY.
11. SHODDY.

common *noun*
A tract of cultivated land belonging to and used by a community: *picnics on the town common.*
Syn: green.

commonage *noun* COMMONALTY.

commonalty *also* **commonality** *noun*
The common people: *laws protecting both the nobility and the commonalty.*
Syns: commonage, commoners, commons, crowd, masses, mob, plebeians, plebs, populace, public, ruck¹. —*Idiom* third estate.

commoners *noun* COMMONALTY.
commonly *adverb* USUALLY.

commonplace *adjective*
1. COMMON.
2. EVERYDAY.
3. ORDINARY.
4. TRITE.

commonplace *noun*
1. CLICHÉ.
2. USUAL.

commons *noun* COMMONALTY.

common sense *noun*
The ability to make sensible decisions: *had enough common sense to study hard.*
Syns: gumption, judgment, sense, wisdom. —*Idiom* horse sense.

commonsensible *adjective* SANE.

commonsensical *adjective* SANE.

commotion *noun*
1. AGITATION.
2. DISTURBANCE.

communal *adjective* COMMON.

communalize *verb* SOCIALIZE.

communicable *adjective*
1. Capable of transmission by infection: *measles and other communicable diseases.*
Syns: catching, contagious, infectious, taking.
2. OUTGOING.

communicate *verb*
1. To make known: *communicate information.*
Syns: break, carry, convey, disclose, get across, impart, pass, report, tell, transmit.
2. To cause (a disease) to pass to another or others: *typhus communicated from one to another.*
Syns: carry, convey, give, pass, spread, transmit.
3. EXPRESS.
4. RELATE.
5. SAY.

communication *noun*
1. The exchange of ideas by writing, speech, or signals: *Good communication is essential to a successful business.*
Syns: communion, converse[1] (*Rare*), intercommunication, intercourse.
2. Something communicated, as information: *I have read your latest communication.*
Syns: message, word.
3. TOUCH.

communicative *adjective* OUTGOING.

communion *noun*
1. COMMUNICATION.
2. FAITH.

community *noun* PUBLIC.

commutation *noun* CHANGE.

commute *verb*
1. CHANGE.
2. CONVERT.

comp *noun* PASS.

compact[1] *adjective*
1. PITHY.
2. THICK.
3. TIGHT.

compact[2] *noun*
1. AGREEMENT.
2. BARGAIN.

compactness *noun* THICKNESS.

companion *noun*
1. ACCOMPANIMENT.
2. ASSOCIATE.
3. MATE.

companion *verb* ACCOMPANY.

companionable *adjective*
Liking company: *a companionable person.*
Syns: convivial, sociable, social.

companionless *adjective* ALONE.

companionship *noun* COMPANY.

company *noun*
1. A commercial organization: *a new computer company.*
Syns: business, concern, corporation, enterprise, establishment, firm[2], house, outfit.
2. A person or persons visiting one: *had company for dinner.*
Syns: guest, visitant, visitor.
3. A pleasant association among people: *enjoyed their company.*
Syns: companionship, fellowship, society.
4. ASSEMBLY.
5. BAND[2].

company *verb* ACCOMPANY.

comparable *adjective* LIKE[2].

comparative *adjective*
Being such by comparison with some standard: *comparative affluence.*
Syn: relative.

compare *verb*
1. To examine so as to note the similarities and differences of: *compare prices; compare one poet's verse with another's.*
Syns: balance, collate.
2. To be equal or alike: *These concerts compare well with last season's.*
Syns: correspond (to), equal, match, measure up (to), parallel, stack up (*Informal*), touch.
3. LIKEN.

comparison *noun* LIKENESS.

compass *noun*
1. CIRCUMFERENCE.
2. GRASP.
3. RANGE.

compass *verb*
1. SURROUND.
2. UNDERSTAND.

compassion *noun* PITY.

compassionate *adjective*
1. HUMANITARIAN.
2. PITYING.

3. SYMPATHETIC.
compassionate verb FEEL.
compassionless adjective COLD-BLOODED.
compatible adjective AGREEABLE.
compatriot noun COUNTRYMAN.
compeer noun PEER².
compel verb FORCE.
compendious adjective BRIEF.
compensate verb
1. To make up for the defects of: *His lack of height was compensated by agility.*
   Syns: balance, counterbalance, counterpoise, countervail, neutralize, offset, outweigh, redeem, set off.
2. To give compensation to: *They were compensated for their travel expenses.*
   Syns: indemnify, pay, recompense, redress, reimburse, remunerate, repay, requite.
3. BALANCE.
4. PAY.
compensation noun
1. Something to make up for loss or damage: *compensation for work-related injuries.*
   Syns: amends, indemnification, indemnity, offset, quittance, recompense, redress, remuneration, reparation, requital, restitution, satisfaction, setoff.
2. PAYMENT.
compensative adjective COMPENSATORY.
compensatory adjective
Affording compensation: *was awarded compensatory damages.*
   Syns: compensative, indemnificatory, remunerative.
compete verb
To strive against (others) for victory: *competed against the best athletes in the Olympics.*
   Syns: contend, contest, rival, vie.
competence also **competency** noun
1. ABILITY.
2. FACULTY.
competent adjective
1. ABLE.
2. EQUAL.
3. SUFFICIENT.
competition noun
1. A struggle with others for victory or supremacy: *competition between political parties; cutthroat competition between auto dealers.*
   Syns: contest, corrivalry, race, rivality, rivalry, strife, striving, war, warfare. —*Idiom* tug of war.

2. A trial of skill or ability: *an archery competition.*
   Syns: contest, meet¹.
3. COMPETITOR.
competitive adjective
Given to competition: *a competitive business.*
   Syns: competitory, emulous, vying.
competitor noun
One that competes: *competitors for that market.*
   Syns: competition, contender, contestant, corrival, opponent, rival.
competitory adjective COMPETITIVE.
complain verb
To express negative feelings, esp. of dissatisfaction or resentment: *complained about the inadequate service.*
   Syns: beef (*Slang*), bellyache (*Slang*), bitch (*Slang*), gripe (*Informal*), grouch, grouse (*Informal*), grumble, kick (*Informal*), murmur, whine, yawp (*also* yaup).
complainant noun
One that makes a formal complaint, esp. in court: *The complainant has filed suit.*
   Syns: accusant, claimant, plaintiff (*Law*).
complainer noun GROUCH.
complaint noun
1. An expression of dissatisfaction: *received many complaints about the car.*
   Syns: beef (*Slang*), grievance, gripe (*Informal*), grumble.
2. DISEASE.
3. INDISPOSITION.
complaisant adjective
1. AMIABLE.
2. OBLIGING.
complement noun
1. Something that completes another: *An attractively set table is a complement to fine food.*
   Syns: completion, expletive (*Rare*), supplement.
2. ACCOMPANIMENT.
complement verb
To fill in what is lacking and make perfect: *A good wine complements any meal.*
   Syns: complete, fill out, round off, round out, supplement.
complemental adjective COMPLEMENTARY.
complementary adjective
Forming or serving as a complement: *wall colors complementary to the decor.*
   Syns: complemental, completing, supplemental.

complete *adjective*
1. Lacking nothing essential or normal: *developed a complete strategy.*
   Syns: choate, entire, full, intact, integral, perfect, whole.
2. Not shortened by omissions: *a complete anthology.*
   Syns: unabridged, uncut, unexpurgated.
3. Having reached completion: *The novel is at last complete.*
   Syns: completed, concluded, done, ended, finished, terminated, through.
   —*Idiom* all wrapped up.
4. ROUND.
5. THOROUGH.
6. UTTER².
7. WHOLE.

complete *verb*
1. CLOSE¹.
2. COMPLEMENT.

completed *adjective* COMPLETE.

completely *adverb*
1. To the fullest extent: *completely wrong.*
   Syns: à fond (*French*), altogether, clean (*Informal*), dead, entirely, flat, fully, quite, thoroughly, well², wholly.
   —*Idiom* through and through.
2. In a complete manner: *completely investigated the crash.*
   Syns: à fond (*French*), exhaustively, intensively, thoroughly. —*Idioms* in and out, inside out, up and down.
3. CLEAR.

completeness *noun*
The state of being entirely whole: *maintained the completeness of his empire.*
Syns: allness, entireness, entirety, integrity, oneness, totality, wholeness.

completing *adjective*
COMPLEMENTARY.

completion *noun*
1. COMPLEMENT.
2. END.

complex *adjective*
1. Consisting of two or more interconnected parts: *complex flower structures.*
   Syns: composite, compound.
2. Difficult to understand due to intricacy: *Inflation is a complex problem.*
   Syns: Byzantine, complicated, convòluted, daedal, daedalian, elaborate, gordian, intricate, involute, involved, knotty, labyrinthine, perplexing, tangled.

complex *verb* COMPLICATE.

complex *noun*
1. A usu. large entity composed of interconnected parts: *the military-industrial complex.*
   Syns: complexus, system.
2. *Informal.* An exaggerated concern: *had a complex about flying.*
   Syns: hangup (*Informal*), preoccupation, prepossession.
3. BASE¹.

complexion *noun*
1. Skin tone, esp. of the face: *a dark complexion.*
   Syns: color, coloration, coloring.
2. CHARACTER.
3. DISPOSITION.

complexity *noun*
Something complex: *the complexities of nuclear physics.*
Syns: complication, intricacy.

complexus *noun* COMPLEX.

compliance also **compliancy** *noun* OBEDIENCE.

compliant *adjective* OBEDIENT.

complicate *verb*
To make complex, intricate, or perplexing: *a crisis complicated by a lack of communication.*
Syns: complex, embarrass, entangle, mix up, perplex, ravel, snarl¹, tangle.

complicated *adjective*
1. COMPLEX.
2. ELABORATE.

complication *noun* COMPLEXITY.

compliment *verb*
1. To pay a compliment to: *complimented the pianist on his performance.*
   Syns: commend, praise, recommend.
   —*Idiom* take off one's hat to.
2. FLATTER.
3. PRAISE.

compliment *noun*
An expression of admiration or congratulation: *deserved compliments on her scholarly work.*
Syns: bouquet, commendation, orchid(s), praise, tribute.

complimentary *adjective*
1. Serving to compliment: *complimentary remarks.*
   Syns: approbatory, commendatory.
2. FREE.

compliment(s) *noun*
1. COURTESY.
2. PRAISE.

comply *verb* FOLLOW.

complying *adjective* OBEDIENT.

component *noun* ELEMENT.

component *adjective* BUILT-IN.

comport *verb*
1. ACT.
2. AGREE.

comportment *noun* BEHAVIOR.

compose *verb*
1. To form by artistic effort: *composed a piano sonata.*
   Syns: create, indite, produce, write.
2. To bring one's emotions under control: *composed herself in spite of the danger.*
   Syns: collect[1], contain, control, cool (down), restrain, simmer down.
3. CALM.
4. CONSTITUTE.

composed *adjective*
1. CALM.
2. COOL.

composite *adjective* COMPLEX.

composition *noun*
1. Something that is the result of creative effort: *a composition for flute and oboe; a composition in black and red.*
   Syns: opus, piece, production, work.
2. A relatively brief discourse written esp. as an exercise: *a composition for English class.*
   Syns: essay, paper, theme.
3. COMPROMISE.

compos mentis *adjective* SANE.

composure *noun*
1. BALANCE.
2. CALM.

compotation *noun* BENDER.

compound *adjective* COMPLEX.
compound *verb*
1. COMBINE.
2. MIX.
compound *noun* MIXTURE.

comprehend *verb*
1. CONTAIN.
2. KNOW.
3. UNDERSTAND.

comprehensible *adjective*
UNDERSTANDABLE.

comprehension *noun*
1. APPRECIATION.
2. GRASP.

comprehensive *adjective* GENERAL.

compress *verb*
1. CONTRACT.
2. CROWD.
3. SQUEEZE.

compression *noun* CONSTRICTION.

comprise *verb*
1. CONSTITUTE.
2. CONTAIN.

compromise *noun*
A settlement of differences through mutual concession: *a union-management compromise.*
   Syns: composition, give-and-take, medium, mid-course.

compromise *verb*
1. To make a concession: *were unable to compromise on the wording of the treaty.*
   Syn: concede. —*Idioms* give and take, go fifty-fifty, meet halfway.
2. RISK.

compulsory *adjective*
1. FORCED.
2. REQUIRED.

compunction *noun*
1. PENITENCE.
2. QUALM.

compunctious *adjective* REMORSEFUL.

computation *noun*
1. CALCULATION.
2. FIGURES.

compute *verb*
1. CALCULATE.
2. COUNT.

comrade *noun* ASSOCIATE.

comradeship *noun* FRIENDSHIP.

con *verb*
1. EXAMINE.
2. MEMORIZE.
3. STUDY.

concatenate *verb* INTEGRATE.

concave *adjective* HOLLOW.

concavity *noun* DEPRESSION.

conceal *verb*
1. COVER.
2. HIDE[1].

concealed *adjective*
1. BLIND.
2. ULTERIOR.

concealment *noun* SECRECY.

concede *verb*
1. ACKNOWLEDGE.
2. COMPROMISE.
3. GIVE IN at give.
4. GRANT.

conceit *noun*
1. EGOTISM.
2. FANCY.
conceit *verb* LIKE[1].

conceited *adjective*
1. EGOTISTICAL.
2. VAIN.

conceivable *adjective*
1. EARTHLY.
2. PROBABLE.

conceive *verb*
1. IMAGINE.
2. UNDERSTAND.

concentrate *verb*
1. To direct toward a common center:

The enemy concentrated its firepower on the inner city.
Syns: center, converge, focalize, focus.
2. APPLY.

concentrated *adjective*
1. Not diffused or dispersed: *Concentrated effort is required.*
Syns: exclusive, fixed, intensive, undivided, unswerving, whole.
2. HEAVY.
3. STRONG.

concentration *noun*
1. A converging at a common center: *heavy troop concentrations on the border.*
Syns: confluence, conflux, convergence.
2. ATTENTION.

concept *noun* IDEA.
conception *noun* IDEA.
conceptual *adjective* IMAGINARY.
concern *noun*
1. A feeling of being personally interested in: *You are the object of our concern.*
Syns: concernment, interest, interestedness, regard.
2. A connecting relation: *a matter of no concern to our plans.*
Syns: bearing, concernment, pertinence (*also* pertinency), relevance (*also* relevancy).
3. BUSINESS.
4. CONSIDERATION.
5. CARE.
6. COMPANY.
7. GADGET.
8. IMPORTANCE.

concern *verb*
1. APPLY.
2. WORRY.

concerned *adjective*
1. Having concern: *All those concerned attended the meeting.*
Syns: affected[2], interested, involved.
2. ANXIOUS.

concernment *noun*
1, 2. CONCERN.
3. IMPORTANCE.

concert *noun* HARMONY.
concession *noun*
An accommodation made in the light of special or extenuating circumstances: *made a concession due to her inexperience.*
Syn: allowance.

conciliate *verb*
1. PACIFY.
2. RECONCILE.

conciliation *noun* RECONCILIATION.

concise *adjective* BRIEF.
conclave *noun* ASSEMBLY.
conclude *verb*
1. ARRANGE.
2. CLOSE[1].
3. DECIDE.
4. INFER.
5. SETTLE.

concluded *adjective* COMPLETE.
concluding *adjective* LAST[1].
conclusion *noun*
1. DECISION.
2. DEDUCTION.
3, 4. END.

conclusive *adjective*
1. AUTHORITATIVE.
2. DECISIVE.
3. DEFINITIVE.

conclusively *adverb* LAST[1].
concoct *verb* INVENT.
concomitant *adjective* ACCOMPANYING.
concomitant *noun* ACCOMPANIMENT.
concord *verb* AGREE.
concord *noun*
1. AGREEMENT.
2, 3. HARMONY.
4. TREATY.

concordance *noun* AGREEMENT.
concordant *adjective* SYMMETRICAL.
concourse *noun* JUNCTION.
concrete *adjective*
1. PHYSICAL.
2. REAL.

concrete *verb*
1. COMBINE.
2. HARDEN.

concupiscence *noun* DESIRE.
concupiscent *adjective* EROTIC.
concupiscible *adjective* DESIRABLE.
concur *verb*
1. AGREE.
2. COINCIDE.

concurrence *noun* AGREEMENT.
concurrent *adjective*
1. ACCOMPANYING.
2. CONTEMPORARY.
3. PARALLEL.
4. UNANIMOUS.

concursion *noun* JUNCTION.
concussion *noun* COLLISION.
condemn *verb*
1. To pronounce judgment against: *condemned the dissidents to hard labor.*
Syns: damn, doom, sentence.
2. BLAME.
3. DEPLORE.

condemnation *noun* BLAME.

condemnatory *adjective*
Containing or imposing a
condemnation: *a condemnatory decree.*
Syn: condemning.

condemned *adjective*
Sentenced to terrible, irrevocable
punishment: *a condemned man on death
row.*
Syns: doomed, fated, foredoomed,
lost.

condemning *adjective*
CONDEMNATORY.

condensation *noun* SYNOPSIS.

condense *verb* THICKEN.

condensed *adjective* BRIEF.

condescend *verb*
1. To descend to a level considered
inappropriate to one's dignity:
condescended to empty the garbage.
Syns: deign, stoop, vouchsafe.
2. To treat in a superciliously indulgent
manner: *a snob who condescended to
all the neighbors.*
Syns: patronize, talk down (to).

condescendence *noun*
CONDESCENSION.

condescending *adjective*
Exhibiting condescension: *a
condescending snob.*
Syn: patronizing.

condescension *noun*
Superciliously indulgent treatment, esp.
of those considered inferior: *His overt
condescension toward us is repellent.*
Syns: condescendence, patronization,
patronizing.

condiment *noun* FLAVORING.

condition *noun*
1. Manner of being or form of
existence: *a patient in a weakened
condition; a house restored to its
former condition.*
Syns: mode, posture, situation, state,
status.
2. Something indispensable: *Eating is a
condition to survival.*
Syns: essential, must, necessity,
precondition, prerequisite,
requirement, requisite, sine qua non.
3. PROVISION.
4. TRIM.

condition *verb* ACCUSTOM.

conditional *adjective*
1. Depending on or containing a
condition or conditions: *a conditional
surrender.*
Syns: provisional, provisionary,
provisory, qualified, tentative.
2. DEPENDENT.

conditioned *adjective* DEPENDENT.

conditions *noun*
Existing surroundings that affect an
activity: *poor working conditions.*
Syns: circumstances, environment.

condonable *adjective* PARDONABLE.

condonation *noun* FORGIVENESS.

condone *verb* FORGIVE.

conduce *verb* CONTRIBUTE.

conducive *adjective* CONTRIBUTIVE.

conduct *verb*
1. To control the course of (an activity):
*conduct the affairs of state; conduct an
experiment.*
Syns: carry on, direct, manage,
operate, steer, supervise.
2. To serve as a conduit: *Most metals
conduct electricity.*
Syns: carry, channel, convey,
transmit.
3. GUIDE.
4. WAGE.

conduct *noun* BEHAVIOR.

conductor *noun* GUIDE.

confab *noun* CONFERENCE.

confab *verb* CONFER.

confabulate *verb*
1. CONFER[1].
2. CONVERSE[1].

confabulation *noun*
1. CONFERENCE.
2. CONVERSATION.
3. DELIBERATION.

confabulator *noun*
CONVERSATIONALIST.

confabulatory *adjective*
CONVERSATIONAL.

confederacy *noun* ALLIANCE.

confederate *verb* ALLY.

confederate *noun*
1. ALLY.
2. ASSOCIATE.

confederated *adjective* ALLIED.

confederation *noun*
1. ALLIANCE.
2. UNION.

confer *verb*
1. To meet and exchange views to reach
a decision: *confer with one's
associates.*
Syns: advise (with), confab
(*Informal*), confabulate, consult,
parley, powwow, talk.
2. To give formally or officially:
conferred honors on them.
Syns: accord, award, bestow, grant,
present[2].

conferee also **conferree** *noun*
One who participates in a conference:
nine conferees on the panel.
Syns: deliberant, discussant,
discussor.

conference *noun*
1. A meeting for the exchange of views: *a teachers' conference.*
   Syns: colloquium, discussion, powwow, seminar. —*Idiom* rap session.
2. An exchanging of views: *needed several hours of conference with each student.*
   Syns: confab (*Informal*), confabulation, discussion, rap[1] (*Slang*), ventilation.
3. A group of athletic teams that play each other: *Southern Conference football clubs.*
   Syns: association, circuit, league.
4. CONFERMENT.
5. CONVENTION.
6. DELIBERATION.

conferment *noun*
The act of conferring, as of an honor: *conferment of an honorary doctorate.*
   Syns: accordance, bestowal, conference, conferral, presentation.

conferral *noun* CONFERMENT.

conferree *noun* SEE **conferee.**

confess *verb* ACKNOWLEDGE.

confession *noun* ACKNOWLEDGMENT.

confessor *noun* CONFIDANT.

confidant *also* **confidante** *noun*
One in whom secrets are confided: *her closest friend and confidant.*
   Syns: confessor, repository.

confide *verb*
1. To tell in confidence: *confided my secret to her.*
   Syns: breathe, whisper.
2. ENTRUST.

confidence *noun*
1. Absolute certainty in the trustworthiness of another: *had confidence in the President.*
   Syns: belief, faith, reliance, trust.
2. A firm belief in one's own powers: *had a lot of confidence.*
   Syns: aplomb, assurance, self-assurance, self-confidence, self-possession.
3. SURENESS.

confident *adjective*
1. Having a firm belief in one's own powers: *a confident man.*
   Syns: assured, secure, self-assured, self-confident, self-possessed.
2. SURE.

confidential *adjective*
1. Known about by very few: *a confidential executive decision.*
   Syns: auricular, hush-hush (*Informal*), inside (*Slang*), private, privy (*Archaic*).

2. Indicating intimacy and mutual trust: *drew me aside in a confidential way.*
   Syns: familiar, intimate[1], privy (*Obs.*).
3. Of or being information available only to authorized persons: *confidential government documents.*
   Syns: classified, privileged (*Law*), restricted.

configuration *noun* FORM.

confine *verb*
1. BAR.
2. IMPRISON.
3. JAIL.
4. LIMIT.

confinement *noun* RESTRICTION.

confine(s) *adjective*
1. END.
2. LIMIT.

confining *adjective* TIGHT.

confirm *verb*
1. To assure the certainty or validity of: *a suspicion confirmed by evidence.*
   Syns: attest, authenticate, back (up), bear out, corroborate, justify, substantiate, testify (to), validate, verify, warrant.
2. To make valid and binding by a formal legal act: *Congress must confirm the treaty.*
   Syns: affirm, approve, ratify.
3. To make firmer in a particular conviction or habit: *scandals that confirmed their distrust of politicians.*
   Syns: fortify, harden, strengthen.
4. PROVE.

confirmation *noun*
1. An act of confirming officially: *Senate confirmation of the treaty.*
   Syns: affirmation, approval, ratification.
2. That which confirms: *found in the ledger confirmation of fraud.*
   Syns: attestation, authentication, corroboration, evidence, proof, substantiation, testament, testimonial, testimony, validation, verification.

confirmed *adjective*
1. Firmly established by long standing: *confirmed habits difficult to break.*
   Syns: entrenched, hard-shell (*also* hard-shelled), ingrained, inveterate, irradicable, set[1], settled.
2. CHRONIC.

confiscate *verb* SEIZE.

confiscation *noun* SEIZURE.

conflagrant *adjective* BLAZING.

conflagrate *verb* BURN.

conflagration *noun* FIRE.

conflict *noun*
1. A state of open, prolonged fighting: *the conflict in Vietnam.*

Syns: belligerency, hostilities, strife, war, warfare.
2. A state of disagreement and disharmony: *family conflicts.*
Syns: clash, contention, difficulty, disaccord, discord, dissension, dissent, dissentience, dissidence, dissonance, friction, inharmony, strife, variance.

conflict *verb*
To fail to be in accord: *Your story conflicts with hers.*
Syns: clash, contradict, disaccord, discord, jar (with). —*Idiom* go (or run) counter to.

conflicting *adjective*
In sharp opposition: *conflicting statements.*
Syns: clashing, disconsonant, discrepant, incongruent, incongruous, inconsistent.

confluence *noun*
1. CONCENTRATION.
2. JUNCTION.

conflux *noun* CONCENTRATION.

conform *verb*
1. ADAPT.
2. AGREE.
3. CONVENTIONALIZE.
4. FOLLOW.
5. HARMONIZE.

conform to *verb* FIT.

conformable *adjective*
1. AGREEABLE.
2. OBEDIENT.

conformance *noun*
1. AGREEMENT.
2. OBEDIENCE.

conformation *noun*
1. ADAPTATION.
2. AGREEMENT.

conformist *adjective* CONVENTIONAL.

conformity *noun*
1. AGREEMENT.
2. CONSISTENCY.
3. OBEDIENCE.

confound *verb*
1, 2. CONFUSE.
3. EMBARRASS.
4. NONPLUS.

confounded *adjective*
1. DAMNED.
2. EMBARRASSED.
3. SHOCKED.

confront *verb*
1. To meet face-to-face, esp. defiantly: *enemy troops confronting each other.*
Syns: accost, encounter, face, front.
2. ENCOUNTER.

confrontation *noun*
A face-to-face, usu. hostile meeting: *a*

confrontation between union and management.
Syns: encounter, face-off.

confuse *verb*
1. To cause to be unclear in mind or intent: *The purpose of camouflage is to confuse the enemy. I was totally confused by the complex memorandum. The heavy traffic confused the novice driver.*
Syns: addle, befuddle, bewilder, confound, discombobulate (*Slang*), dizzy, fuddle, mix up, perplex, throw. —*Idiom* make one's head reel (or swim or whirl).
2. To put into total disorder: *had hopelessly confused his finances.*
Syns: ball up (*Slang*), disorder, jumble, mess up, muddle, scramble, snafu (*Slang*), snarl[1].
3. To take (one thing) mistakenly for another: *confused aggressiveness with ruthlessness.*
Syns: confound, misdeem, mistake, mix up.
4. EMBARRASS.

confused *adjective*
1. Characterized by physical confusion: *a confused sea of faces; a confused pile of clothes.*
Syns: chaotic, confusional, disordered, helter-skelter, higgledy-piggledy, jumbled, mixed-up, muddled, topsy-turvy, upside-down.
2. Mentally uncertain: *I am totally confused by this problem.*
Syns: addled, befuddled, bewildered, discombobulated (*Slang*). —*Idiom* turned around.

confusedness *noun* DISORDER.

confusion *noun*
1. DISORDER.
2. EMBARRASSMENT.

confusional *adjective* CONFUSED.

confute *verb* REFUTE.

congeal *verb*
1. COAGULATE.
2. HARDEN.

congener *noun* PARALLEL.

congenial *adjective*
1. AGREEABLE.
2. FRIENDLY.
3. GRACIOUS.
4. GRATEFUL.
5. HARMONIOUS.

congenital *adjective*
1. BUILT-IN.
2. CONSTITUTIONAL.
3. INNATE.

congeries *noun* ACCUMULATION.

congest *verb* FILL.

conglomeration *noun* ASSORTMENT.
congratulate *verb* PRIDE.
congregate *verb* ASSEMBLE.
congregation *noun* ASSEMBLY.
congress *noun*
1. ASSEMBLY.
2. CONVENTION.
3. UNION.
congruity *noun* CONSISTENCY.
congruous *adjective*
1. AGREEABLE.
2. SYMMETRICAL.
conjectural *adjective* SUPPOSED.
conjecture *verb* GUESS.
conjecture *noun*
1. GUESS.
2. THEORY.
conjectured *adjective* PRESUMPTIVE.
conjoin *verb*
1. ASSOCIATE.
2. COMBINE.
conjoint *adjective*
1. COMBINED.
2. COMMON.
conjugal *adjective* MARITAL.
conjugality *noun* MARRIAGE.
conjugate *verb* COMBINE.
conjugation *noun* COMBINATION.
conjugational *adjective*
COMBINATIONAL.
conjugative *adjective*
COMBINATIONAL.
conjunction *noun* ASSOCIATION.
conjuration *noun*
1, 2. MAGIC.
conjure *verb* APPEAL.
conjury *noun*
1, 2. MAGIC.
conk *noun*
1. BLOW².
2. HEAD.
conk out *verb*
1. COLLAPSE.
2. FAIL.
connate *adjective* RELATED.
connatural *adjective*
1. CONSTITUTIONAL.
2. RELATED.
connect *verb*
1, 2. ASSOCIATE.
3. ATTACH.
4. COMBINE.
5. RELATE.
connection *noun*
1. ASSOCIATION.
2. CONTACT.
3. JOINT.
4. RELATION.
5. SUGGESTION.
conniption *noun* TEMPER.

connivance also **connivence** *noun*
PLOT.
connive *verb* PLOT.
connive at *verb* BLINK AT at **blink**.
connivence *noun* SEE **connivance**.
connotation *noun* SUGGESTION.
connote *verb* MEAN¹.
connubial *adjective* MARITAL.
connubiality *noun* MARRIAGE.
conquer *verb*
1. DEFEAT.
2. TRIUMPH.
conquering *adjective* VICTORIOUS.
conqueror *noun*
One that conquers: *the conqueror of
Wales.*
   Syns: conquistador, master, victor,
   winner.
conquest *noun*
The act of conquering: *the Norman
Conquest.*
   Syns: triumph, victory, win.
conquistador *noun* CONQUEROR.
consanguineous also **consanguine**
adjective RELATED.
conscienceless *adjective*
UNSCRUPULOUS.
conscious *adjective* MINDFUL.
consciousness *noun* AWARENESS.
conscript *verb* DRAFT.
conscription *noun* DRAFT.
consecrate *verb*
1. DEVOTE.
2. SANCTIFY.
consecrated *adjective* SACRED.
consecution *noun*
1. ORDER.
2. SERIES.
consecutive *adjective*
Following one after another in an
orderly pattern: *It was cloudy for six
consecutive days.*
   Syns: sequent, sequential, serial,
   subsequent, subsequential, succedent,
   succeeding, successional, successive.
consensus *noun* UNANIMITY.
consent *noun*
1. ACCEPTANCE.
2. PERMISSION.
consent *verb*
1. ASSENT.
2. PERMIT.
consequence *noun*
1. EFFECT.
2. IMPORTANCE.
consequent *adjective* LOGICAL.
consequential *adjective*
1. IMPORTANT.
2. INFLUENTIAL.
conservancy *noun* CONSERVATION.

conservation *noun*
The careful guarding of an asset: *wildlife conservation.*
   Syns: conservancy, husbandry, management, preserval, preservation.

conservative *adjective*
1. Strongly favoring retention of the existing order: *a conservative politician.*
   Syns: orthodox, right, rightist, right-wing, Tory, traditionalist (*also* traditionalistic).
2. Kept within sensible limits: *a conservative estimate; conservative attire.*
   Syns: discreet, moderate, reasonable, restrained, temperate.
3. PRESERVATIVE.

conservative *noun*
One who strongly favors retention of the existing order: *a political conservative.*
   Syns: fundamentalist, praetorian, rightist, right-winger, Tory.

conservator *noun* GUARDIAN.

conservatory *adjective*
PRESERVATIVE.

conserve *verb*
1. To protect (an asset) from loss or destruction: *conserve energy.*
   Syns: husband, preserve, save.
2. To prepare (food) for storage and future use: *conserve strawberries.*
   Syns: can, preserve, put up.

consider *verb*
1. To think about seriously: *considered all the options first.*
   Syns: cogitate, entertain, excogitate, study, think over.
2. ADMIRE.
3. BELIEVE.
4. DEAL.
5. LOOK.
6. REGARD.

considerable *adjective*
1. BIG.
2. IMPORTANT.

considerably *adverb*
To a considerable extent: *sales considerably higher than forecast.*
   Syns: far, quite, well². —*Idioms* by a long shot (*or* way), by a wide margin, by far.

considerate *adjective* ATTENTIVE.

considerately *adverb*
In a considerate manner: *Treat your parents considerately.*
   Syns: solicitously, well².

consideration *noun*
1. Thoughtful attention: *consideration for the feelings of others.*

   Syns: concern, regard, solicitude, thoughtfulness.
2. ADVISEMENT.
3. ATTENTION.
4. ESTEEM.
5. PAYMENT.

considered *adjective*
1. ADVISED.
2. CALCULATED.

consign *verb*
1. COMMIT.
2. ENTRUST.
3. SEND.

consist *verb*
1. To have as an inherent basis: *The beauty of the style consists in its simplicity.*
   Syns: dwell, exist, inhere, lie¹, repose, reside, rest¹.
2. AGREE.

consist of *verb* CONSTITUTE.

consistency *also* **consistence** *noun*
Logical agreement among things or parts: *The statements lack consistency.*
   Syns: coherence, conformity, congruity, correspondence.

consistent *adjective*
1. Remaining continually unchanged: *a consistent advocate of reform.*
   Syns: constant, invariable, same, unchanging, unfailing.
2. AGREEABLE.

consistently *adverb* USUALLY.

consolate *verb* COMFORT.

consolation *noun* COMFORT.

console *verb* COMFORT.

consolidation *noun* UNIFICATION.

consonance *noun*
1. AGREEMENT.
2. HARMONY.

consonant *adjective*
1. AGREEABLE.
2. HARMONIOUS.

consort *verb*
1. ACCOMPANY.
2. ASSOCIATE.

consort *noun* SPOUSE.

conspicuous *adjective*
1. BOLD.
2. NOTICEABLE.

conspiracy *noun* PLOT.

conspire *verb* PLOT.

constable *noun* POLICEMAN.

constancy *noun* FIDELITY.

constant *adjective*
1. CONSISTENT.
2. CONTINUAL.
3. EVEN¹.
4. FAITHFUL.

consternate *verb* DISMAY.

consternation *noun*
1. DISMAY.
2. FEAR.
constituent *adjective* BUILT-IN.
constituent *noun* ELEMENT.
constitute *verb*
1. To be the constituent parts of: *Ten members constitute a quorum.*
   Syns: compose, comprise, consist of, form, make, make up.
2. AMOUNT.
3. ENACT.
4. ESTABLISH.
5. FOUND.
constitution *noun*
Bodily type: *a strong constitution.*
   Syns: build, habit (*Rare*), habitus, physique.
constitutional *adjective*
1. Of or arising from the most basic structure of an individual: *constitutional weaknesses.*
   Syns: congenital, connatural, elemental, inborn, inbred, indigenous, indwelling, ingenerate, ingrained, inherent, innate, intrinsic.
2. ESSENTIAL.
constitutional *noun*
A usu. brief and regular journey on foot, esp. for exercise: *a morning constitutional through the park.*
   Syns: hike, turn, walk.
constitutive *adjective* ESSENTIAL.
constrain *verb*
1. To check the freedom and spontaneity of: *a friendship now constrained by tension.*
   Syns: astrict, constrict, cramp, inhibit.
2. CROWD.
3. FORCE.
4. RESTRAIN.
5. SQUEEZE.
constrained *adjective*
1. AWKWARD.
2. FORCED.
3. RESERVED.
constrainment *noun* RESTRICTION.
constraint *noun*
1. FORCE.
2, 3. RESTRICTION.
constrict *verb*
1. To render narrow or narrower: *constricted blood vessels.*
   Syns: constringe, narrow.
2. CONSTRAIN.
3. CONTRACT.
4. SQUEEZE.

constriction *noun*
1. A becoming narrow or narrower: *a constriction of the small bowel.*
   Syn: stricture (*Path.*).
2. A compressing of something: *The tight collar produced a painful constriction of my neck.*
   Syns: compression, squeeze, squeezing.
constringe *verb*
1. CONSTRICT.
2. SQUEEZE.
construct *verb*
1. BUILD.
2. MAKE.
construction *noun* EXPLANATION.
constructor *noun* BUILDER.
construe *verb*
1. EXPLAIN.
2. INTERPRET.
3. TRANSLATE.
consuetude *noun* CONVENTION.
consult *verb* CONFER.
consultant *noun* ADVISER.
consultation *noun* DELIBERATION.
consultative *adjective* ADVISORY.
consultatory *adjective* ADVISORY.
consulting *adjective* ADVISORY.
consume *verb*
1. To eat completely or entirely: *consumed eight pancakes in a flash.*
   Syns: devour, dispatch, eat up, polish off (*Informal*), punish (*Informal*), put away, shift.
2. To do away with completely and destructively: *a body consumed with cancer; a building consumed by flames.*
   Syns: devour, eat, eat up, swallow (up), waste.
3. ABSORB.
4. EAT.
5. EXHAUST.
6. GO.
7, 8. WASTE.
consumed *adjective* ABSORBED.
consumer *noun*
One who consumes goods and services: *gas consumers.*
   Syns: customer, user.
consuming *adjective* ABSORBING.
consummate *verb* CLOSE[1].
consummate *adjective*
1. PERFECT.
2. UTTER[2].
consummation *noun*
1. END.
2. FULFILLMENT.
consumption *noun*
1. A quantity consumed: *Gas consumption has markedly increased.*

Syns: usage, use.
2. TUBERCULOSIS.

consumptive *adjective*
1. Tending to consume and destroy: *tasks consumptive of my time; a consumptive fire.*
   Syns: desolating, ravaging, wasting.
2. TUBERCULAR.

contact *noun*
1. A coming together so as to be touching: *body contact.*
   Syns: contingence, touch.
2. An acquaintance who is in a position to help: *received the information from a government contact.*
   Syns: connection (*Slang*), source.
3. TOUCH.

contact *verb*
1. To bring into or make contact with: *a burn where the acid contacted his body.*
   Syn: touch.
2. REACH.

contagion *noun* POISON.

contagious *adjective* COMMUNICABLE.

contain *verb*
1. To have within: *Orange juice contains vitamin C.*
   Syns: have, hold.
2. To have as an integral part: *The estate contains a manor house and grounds.*
   Syns: comprehend, comprise, embody, embrace, encompass, have, include, involve, subsume, take in.
3. ACCOMMODATE.
4. COMPOSE.

contaminant *noun*
One that contaminates: *sewage and other contaminants.*
   Syns: adulterant, adulterator, contamination, contaminator, impurity, poison, pollutant.

contaminate *verb*
1. To make physically impure: *water contaminated with radioactive wastes.*
   Syns: befoul, foul, poison, pollute.
2. TAINT.

contaminated *adjective* IMPURE.

contaminating *adjective* UNWHOLESOME.

contamination *noun*
1. The state of being contaminated: *radioactive contamination.*
   Syns: adulteration, pollution.
2. CONTAMINANT.

contaminative *adjective* UNWHOLESOME.

contaminator *noun* CONTAMINANT.

contemn *verb* DESPISE.

contemplate *verb*
1. INTEND.
2. LOOK.
3. PONDER.

contemplative *adjective* THOUGHTFUL.

contemporanean *noun*
1, 2. CONTEMPORARY.

contemporanean *adjective* CONTEMPORARY.

contemporaneous *adjective* CONTEMPORARY.

contemporary *adjective*
1. Belonging to the same period of time as another: *a fact documented by two contemporary sources.*
   Syns: coetaneous, coeval, coexistent, concurrent, contemporanean, contemporaneous, synchronic (*also* synchronical), synchronous.
2. Modern: *was very contemporary in his thinking.*
   Syns: au courant (*French*), mod (*Informal*), up-to-date, up-to-the-minute.
3. PRESENT[1].
4. SIMULTANEOUS.

contemporary *noun*
1. One of the same time or age as another: *a contemporary of Tolstoy.*
   Syns: coeval, contemporanean.
2. A person of the present age: *Shostakovich and other contemporaries.*
   Syns: contemporanean, modern.

contemporize *verb* MODERNIZE.

contempt *noun*
1. DEFIANCE.
2. DESPISAL.

contempt *verb* DESPISE.

contemptible *adjective*
1. FILTHY.
2. SORDID.

contemptuous *adjective* DEFIANT.

contend *verb*
1. To strive in opposition to: *contended with heavy traffic; two nations contending for nuclear superiority.*
   Syns: battle, combat, fight, oppugn, struggle, tilt, vie, war, wrestle.
2, 3. ARGUE.
4. CLAIM.
5. COMPETE.

contender *noun* COMPETITOR.

content *adjective* FULFILLED.

contention *noun*
1. ARGUMENT.
2. CLAIM.
3. CONFLICT.
4. THESIS.

contentious *adjective*
1. AGGRESSIVE.
2. ARGUMENTATIVE.
3. BELLIGERENT.

contentiousness *noun*
1. AGGRESSION.
2. BELLIGERENCE.
3. FIGHT.

conterminous *adjective* ADJOINING.

contest *verb*
1. To take a stand against: *contested the court ruling.*
   Syns: buck[1], challenge, combat, dispute, fight, oppose, recalcitrate, resist, traverse.
2. COMPETE.

contest *noun*
1, 2. COMPETITION.

contestant *noun* COMPETITOR.

contestation *noun* THESIS.

contested *adjective* DEBATABLE.

contexture *noun* TEXTURE.

contiguous *adjective* ADJOINING.

continent *adjective* TEMPERATE.

contingence *noun* CONTACT.

contingency *noun* POSSIBILITY.

contingent *adjective*
1. ACCIDENTAL.
2. DEPENDENT.

continual *adjective*
Existing or occurring without interruption or end: *were irritated by their continual complaints.*
   Syns: ceaseless, constant, continuous, endless, eternal, everlasting, incessant, interminable, nonstop, perpetual, relentless, round-the-clock (*also* around-the-clock), timeless, unceasing, unending, uninterrupted, unremitting.

continuance *noun*
An uninterrupted course: *were concerned about the continuance of the symptoms.*
   Syns: continuation, persistence (*also* persistency), run.

continuation *noun*
1. Uninterrupted existence or succession: *a continuation of the hostilities.*
   Syns: continuity, continuum, duration, endurance, persistence (*also* persistency).
2. CONTINUANCE.

continue *verb*
1. To go on after an interruption: *I continued working after lunch.*
   Syns: pick up, recommence, renew, reopen, restart, resume, take up.
2. ENDURE.

continuing *adjective*
1. Existing or remaining in the same state for an indefinitely long time: *enjoyed a continuing friendship with them.*
   Syns: abiding, enduring, inveterate, lasting, long-lasting, long-lived, long-standing, old, perdurable, perennial.
2. CHRONIC.

continuity *noun* CONTINUATION.

continuous *adjective* CONTINUAL.

continuum *noun* CONTINUATION.

contort *verb* DEFORM.

contour *noun* OUTLINE.

contra *noun* OPPOSITE.

contraband *verb* SMUGGLE.

contrabandist *noun* SMUGGLER.

contract *verb*
1. To enter into a formal agreement: *contracted with local workers to harvest the cucumbers.*
   Syns: bargain, covenant.
2. To become affected with a disease: *contracted diphtheria.*
   Syns: catch, develop, get, sicken, take. —*Idiom* come down with.
3. To reduce in size by or as if by drawing together: *contract an arm muscle.*
   Syns: compress, constrict, shrink.
4. PLEDGE.

contract *noun*
1. AGREEMENT.
2. BARGAIN.

contradict *verb*
1. CONFLICT.
2. DENY.

contradiction *noun* DENIAL.

contradictory *adjective* OPPOSITE.

contradictory *noun* OPPOSITE.

contradistinction *noun*
1. CONTRAST.
2. OPPOSITION.

contradistinguish *verb* CONTRAST.

contraposition *noun*
1. OPPOSITE.
2. OPPOSITION.

contraption *noun*
1. DEVICE.
2. GADGET.

contrariety *noun* OPPOSITION.

contrarious *adjective* CONTRARY

contrary *adjective*
1. Characterized by a natural or innate opposition: *a policy contrary to ethical principles.*
   Syns: antipathetic, antithetical (*also* antithetic), antonymous, opposite, repugnant (*Logic*).
2. Given to acting in opposition to

others: *a contrary person who refused
to conform.*
Syns: balky, contrarious (*Rare*),
difficult, froward, impossible, ornery,
perverse, wayward.
3. OPPOSITE.
contrary *noun*
1. OPPOSITE.
2. OPPOSITION.
contrast *verb*
To compare so as to reveal differences:
a poem contrasting good and evil.
Syns: contradistinguish, set off
(against).
contrast *noun*
Striking difference between compared
individuals: *the contrast between father
and son.*
Syns: contradistinction, counterpoint.
contravene *verb*
1. DENY.
2. VIOLATE.
contravention *noun* BREACH.
contretemps *noun* ACCIDENT.
contribute *verb*
1. To give in common with others: *All
employees contributed to the retirement
fund.*
Syns: chip in (*Informal*), come across
(*Slang*), come through (*Informal*),
donate, kick in (*Slang*), subscribe.
2. To have a share in (an act, result,
etc.); have a hand in: *All of us
contributed to the cost overrun.*
Syns: conduce (to *or* toward), partake
(in), share (in).
3. DONATE.
contribution *noun* DONATION.
contributive *adjective*
Tending to contribute to a result:
*factors contributive to international
tension.*
Syn: conducive.
contributor *noun*
1. BUILDER.
2. DONOR.
3. PATRON.
contributory *adjective* AUXILIARY.
contrite *adjective*
1. APOLOGETIC.
2. REMORSEFUL.
contriteness *noun* PENITENCE.
contrition *noun* PENITENCE.
contrivance *noun*
1. DEVICE.
2. GADGET.
3. INVENTION.
contrive *verb*
1. DESIGN.
2. INVENT.

contrived *adjective* ARTY.
control *verb*
1. To exercise authority or influence
over: *The Romans controlled a huge
empire.*
Syns: direct, dominate, govern, rule.
—*Idioms* be at the helm, be in the
driver's seat, hold sway over, hold the
reins.
2. COMPOSE.
3. GOVERN.
control *noun*
1. AUTHORITY.
2. DOMINATION.
3. GOVERNMENT.
4. RESERVE.
controllable *adjective* GOVERNABLE.
controlled *adjective* RESERVED.
controlling *adjective* DOMINANT.
controversy *noun* ARGUMENT.
controvert *verb* DENY.
contumacious *adjective* DEFIANT.
contumacy *noun* DEFIANCE.
contumelious *adjective*
1. ABUSIVE.
2. IMPUDENT.
contumely *noun*
1. INDIGNITY.
2. VITUPERATION.
contuse *verb* BRUISE.
conundrum *noun* MYSTERY.
convalesce *verb* RECOVER.
convene *verb*
1, 2. ASSEMBLE.
3. CALL.
convenience *noun* AMENITY.
convenience *noun* OBLIGE.
convenient *adjective*
1. Suited to one's end or purpose: *found
a convenient excuse not to go.*
Syns: appropriate, befitting,
expedient, fit, good, meet² (*Archaic*),
proper, suitable, tailor-made, useful.
2. Being within easy reach: *found a
convenient location for the shelves.*
Syns: close-at-hand, close-by, handy,
near-at-hand, nearby.
convention *noun*
1. A formal assemblage of the members
of a group: *a medical convention.*
Syns: assembly, conference, congress,
convocation, meeting.
2. An accepted way of doing something:
social conventions.
Syns: consuetude, form, usage.
3. AGREEMENT.
4. TREATY.
conventional *adjective*
1. Conforming to established practice or
standards: *conventional attire; a
conventional view of society.*

Syns: button-down (*Informal*), conformist, establishmentarian, orthodox, square (*Slang*), straight (*Slang*), traditional.

2. ACCEPTED.
3. CEREMONIOUS.

conventionalize *verb*
To make conventional: *conventionalized decorating schemes.*
Syns: conform, stylize.

converge *verb*
1. CLOSE¹.
2. CONCENTRATE.

convergence *noun*
1. APPROACH.
2. CONCENTRATION.
3. JUNCTION.

conversant *adjective*
1. AWARE.
2. FAMILIAR.

conversation *noun*
Spoken exchange: *a telephone conversation with a friend.*
Syns: chat, colloquy, confabulation, converse¹, coze, dialogue (*also* dialog), parley, talk.

conversational *adjective*
1. In the style of conversation: *a conversational narrative.*
Syns: chatty, colloquial, confabulatory, informal.
2. TALKATIVE.

conversationalist also **conversationist** *noun*
One given to conversation: *an excellent conversationalist at parties.*
Syns: colloquialist, colloquist, confabulator, discourser, talker.

converse¹ *verb*
To engage in spoken exchange: *conversed softly in the corner.*
Syns: chat, confabulate, coze, discourse, speak, talk, visit (*Informal*).

converse *noun*
1. COMMUNICATION.
2. CONVERSATION.

converse² *adjective* OPPOSITE.
converse *noun* OPPOSITE.

conversion *noun*
1. A usu. physical change of one thing into another: *the company's conversion from domestic to military production.*
Syns: alteration, changeover, shift, transformation.
2. A fundamental change in one's beliefs: *conversion from the Methodist to the Catholic faith.*
Syns: metanoia, rebirth, regeneration.
3. CHANGE.

convert *verb*
1. To change into a different form, substance, or state: *convert water into ice; convert a country from democracy to police state.*
Syns: commute, metamorphize, metamorphose, mutate, transfer, transfigure, transform, translate, transmogrify, transmute, transpose, transubstantiate.
2. To convince (another) to adopt a particular faith or belief: *Missionaries converted the islanders to Christianity.*
Syns: lead, persuade.

convey *verb*
1. BRING.
2. CARRY.
3, 4. COMMUNICATE.
5. CONDUCT.
6. EXPRESS.
7. PASS.
8. SAY.
9. TRANSFER.

conveyance *noun*
1. GRANT.
2. LARCENY.
3. TRANSPORTATION.

conviction *noun*
1. BELIEF.
2. SURENESS.

convince *verb*
1. To cause (another) to believe something: *Convince me that I'm wrong!*
Syns: assure, persuade, satisfy, win over.
2. PERSUADE.

convincing *adjective*
1. Serving to convince: *a convincing argument.*
Syns: cogent, persuasive, satisfactory, satisfying, solid, sound², telling.
2. AUTHENTIC.

convivial *adjective*
1. COMPANIONABLE.
2. FRIENDLY.
3. SOCIAL.

convocation *noun*
1. ASSEMBLY.
2. CONVENTION.

convoke *verb*
1. ASSEMBLE.
2. CALL.

convoluted *adjective* COMPLEX.
convulse *verb* AGITATE.

convulsion *noun*
1. AGITATION.
2. REVOLUTION.
3. THROE.

cook *verb*
To prepare (food) for eating by the use of heat: *cooked his steak rare.*
Syn: do.

cook up *verb* INVENT.
cook *noun*
A person who prepares food for eating: *an excellent cook.*
 Syns: chef, cuisinier.
cool *adjective*
1. Not easily excited, even under pressure: *a cool and controlled person.*
 Syns: calm, collected, composed, cool-headed, detached, dispassionate, even[1], even-tempered, imperturbable, nonchalant, unflappable (*Slang*), unruffled.
2. Not friendly, sociable, or warm in manner: *a shy, cool person.*
 Syns: aloof, chilly, distant, frosty, offish, remote, reserved, reticent, solitary, standoffish, unapproachable, uncommunicative, undemonstrative, withdrawn.
3. COLD.
4. MARVELOUS.
cool *verb* COMPOSE.
cool *noun*
1. BALANCE.
2. CALM.
3. NONCHALANCE.
cooler *noun* JAIL.
cool-headed *adjective* COOL.
coolie also **cooly** *noun* LABORER.
coolness *noun*
1. BALANCE.
2. COLD.
coolth *noun* COLD.
cooly *noun* SEE **coolie.**
coop *verb* ENCLOSE.
coop *noun* JAIL.
cooperant *adjective* COOPERATIVE.
cooperate *verb*
To work together toward a common end: *The two agencies cooperated on the energy policy.*
 Syns: coadjute, collaborate.
cooperation *noun*
1. Joint work toward a common end: *mutual cooperation among the allies to achieve peace.*
 Syns: coadjuvancy, coagency, collaboration, synergy, teamwork.
2. ASSOCIATION.
cooperative *adjective*
Working together toward a common end: *a cooperative effort.*
 Syns: coefficient, collaborative, cooperant, synergetic.
coordinate also **co-ordinate** *verb*
1, 2. HARMONIZE.
cop *noun* POLICEMAN.
cop *verb*
1. CAPTURE.
2. STEAL.

copartner *noun* ASSOCIATE.
copious *adjective*
1. GENEROUS.
2. HEAVY.
copper *noun* POLICEMAN.
copulate *verb* TAKE.
copy *noun*
1. An inferior substitute imitating an original: *an inexpensive copy of the tiara.*
 Syns: brummagem, ersatz, imitation, pinchbeck, simulacrum (*also* simulacre), simulation.
2. Something closely resembling another: *copies of Louis XV furniture.*
 Syns: duplicate, facsimile, reduplication, replica, replication, reproduction. —*Idiom* carbon copy.
3. LIKENESS.
copy *verb*
1. To make a copy of: *copied an original design.*
 Syns: duplicate, image, imitate, reduplicate, replicate, reproduce.
2. FOLLOW.
coquet *verb* FLIRT.
coquetry *noun* FLIRTATION.
coquette *noun* FLIRT.
coquettish *adjective* FLIRTATIOUS.
cordial *adjective*
1. AMIABLE.
2. GRACIOUS.
cordiality *noun* AMIABILITY.
core *noun*
1. CENTER.
2. HEART.
corkscrew *verb* WIND[2].
corky *adjective* AIRY.
corner *noun*
1. MONOPOLY.
2. PREDICAMENT.
cornerstone *noun* BASIS.
corny *adjective* TRITE.
corollary *noun* EFFECT.
corporal *adjective* BODILY.
corporation *noun* COMPANY.
corporeal *adjective*
1. BODILY.
2. PHYSICAL.
corps *noun*
1. BAND[2].
2. FORCE.
corpse *noun* BODY.
corpselike *adjective* GHASTLY.
corpulent *adjective* FAT.
corpus *noun*
1, 2. BODY.
3. QUANTITY.

correct *verb*
1. To make right what is wrong: *correct an error.*
   Syns: amend, emend, mend, rectify, remedy, right.
2. To castigate for the purpose of improving: *correct a child for being rude.*
   Syns: chasten, chastise, rebuke, reprove.
3. PUNISH.

correct *adjective*
1. Conforming to accepted standards: *correct social behavior.*
   Syns: au fait (*French*), becoming, befitting, comely, comme il faut (*French*), decent, decorous, de rigueur (*French*), nice, proper, respectable, right, seemly.
2, 3. ACCURATE.
4. APPROPRIATE.

correction *noun* PUNISHMENT.

corrective *adjective*
Tending to correct: *took corrective measures to ease the tension.*
Syns: emendatory, reformatory, remedial.

corrective *noun* REMEDY.

correctly *adverb* FAIR.

correctness *noun*
1. ACCURACY.
2. DECENCY.
3. VERACITY.

correlate *verb* ASSOCIATE.

correlate *noun* PARALLEL.

correlation *noun* RELATION.

correspond *verb*
1. AGREE.
2. AMOUNT.
3. COMPARE.

correspond to *verb* FIT.

correspondence *noun*
1. AGREEMENT.
2. CONSISTENCY.

correspondent *noun* PARALLEL.

correspondent *adjective* AGREEABLE.

corresponding *adjective*
1. AGREEABLE.
2. LIKE².

corrival *noun* COMPETITOR.

corrivalry *noun* COMPETITION.

corroborate *verb*
1. BACK.
2. CONFIRM.
3. PROVE.

corroboration *noun* CONFIRMATION.

corrode *verb* BITE.

corrosive *adjective*
1. CORRUPTIVE.
2. SARCASTIC.

corrosiveness *noun* SARCASM.

corrupt *adjective*
1. Utterly reprehensible in nature or behavior: *a corrupt parent who debased the child.*
   Syns: degenerate, depraved, flagitious, miscreant, nefarious, perverse, rotten, unhealthy, villainous.
2. Marked by dishonesty, esp. in matters of public trust: *corrupt police officers who accepted bribes.*
   Syns: crooked, dishonest, venal.
3. Ruthlessly seeking personal advantage: *corrupt politicians who line their pockets at taxpayers' expense.*
   Syns: mercenary, praetorian, unethical, unprincipled, unscrupulous, venal.

corrupt *verb*
1. To ruin utterly in character or quality: *public taste corrupted by pornography.*
   Syns: animalize, bastardize, bestialize, brutalize, canker, debase, debauch, demoralize, deprave, pervert, stain, vitiate, warp.
2. To subject (someone having the public's trust) to improper influence: *The mob corrupted the city council.*
   Syns: buy, purchase.
3. TAINT.

corrupted *adjective*
Lowered in character or quality: *a man corrupted by his lust for power.*
Syns: debased, debauched, depraved, perverted, vitiated. —*Idiom* gone to the dogs.

corruptible *adjective*
Capable of being bribed: *a corruptible congressman—easy pickings for the mob.*
Syns: buyable, purchasable, venal.

corrupting *adjective* UNWHOLESOME.

corruption *noun*
1. Immoral, degrading acts or habits: *condemned the luxury and corruption of the ruling classes.*
   Syns: depravity, immorality, turpitude, vice, wickedness.
2. Departure from what is legally, ethically, and morally correct: *impeached for corruption in high office.*
   Syns: corruptness, crookedness, dishonesty, improbity.
3. A term whose form offends against established usage standards: *Many writers consider "finalize" a corruption of good English.*
   Syns: barbarism, solecism, vulgarism.

corruptive *adjective*
Serving to corrupt: *The presence of drugs was a corruptive factor.*
　Syns: corrosive, injurious.
corruptness *noun* CORRUPTION.
coruscate *verb*
1. BLINK.
2. FLASH.
coruscation *noun* BLINK.
cosmic *adjective* UNIVERSAL.
cosmopolitan *adjective*
1. SOPHISTICATED.
2. UNIVERSAL.
cosmos *noun* UNIVERSE.
cosset *verb* BABY.
cost *noun*
1. An amount paid or to be paid for a purchase: *The cost of the dress is $60.*
　Syns: charge, price, tab.
2. Something expended to obtain a benefit or desired result: *Production costs offset sales.*
　Syns: disbursement, expense, expenditure, outlay.
3. A loss sustained in the accomplishment of or as the result of something: *a revolution brought about at the cost of many lives.*
　Syns: expense, price, sacrifice, toll[1].
cost *verb*
To require a specified price: *The painting costs $10,000.*
　Syns: go for, sell for.
cost-free *adjective* FREE.
costive *adjective* STINGY.
costly *adjective*
1. Bringing a high price: *costly paintings.*
　Syns: dear, expensive, high, high-priced. —*Idiom* high as smoke.
2. VALUABLE.
costume *noun* DISGUISE.
cosy *adjective* SEE **cozy.**
cotton *verb*
1. FAWN.
2. GET ALONG at **get.**
couch *verb* PHRASE.
counsel *verb* ADVISE.
counsel *noun*
1. ADVICE.
2. ADVISER.
3. DELIBERATION.
counselable also **counsellable** *adjective* ADVISABLE.
counselor or **counsellor** *noun* ADVISER.
count *verb*
1. To note (items) one by one so as to get a total: *Count your change.*
　Syns: calculate, compute, enumerate,

number, numerate, reckon, tale, tally, tell off.
2. To be of significance or importance: *an opinion that counts for naught; felt that honesty counted too.*
　Syns: import, matter, signify, weigh.
3. BEAT.
count on *verb*
1. DEPEND ON at **depend.**
2. EXPECT.
count out *verb* EXCLUDE.
count *noun*
A noting of items one by one: *kept an accurate count of the words.*
　Syns: numeration, reckoning, tab, tally.
countenance *noun*
1. EXPRESSION.
2, 3. FACE.
countenance *verb*
1. APPROVE.
2. ENCOURAGE.
counter *noun*
1. OPPOSITE.
2. RETORT.
counter *verb*
1. OPPOSE.
2. RETALIATE.
counter *adjective* OPPOSITE.
counteract *verb*
1. BALANCE.
2. CANCEL.
counteraction *noun* RETALIATION.
counteragent *noun* REMEDY.
counterattack *noun* RETALIATION.
counterbalance *verb*
1, 2. BALANCE.
3. COMPENSATE.
counterblow *noun* RETALIATION.
counterfactual *adjective* FALSE.
counterfeit *adjective*
Fraudulently or deceptively imitative: *counterfeit bills; counterfeit love.*
　Syns: bogus, ersatz, fake, false, fraudulent, phony (also phoney) (*Informal*), pseudo, sham, spurious, supposititious, suppositious.
counterfeit *verb*
1. To make a fraudulent copy of: *counterfeited the signature on the check.*
　Syns: fake, falsify, forge[1].
2. ACT.
3. ASSUME.
counterfeit *noun*
A fraudulent imitation: *The painting is a clever counterfeit of an old master.*
　Syns: fake, forgery, phony (also phoney) (*Informal*), sham.
countermeasure *noun* REMEDY.

counterpart *noun*
1. One holding a position corresponding to that of one in another organization or hierarchy: *Each foreign diplomat was seated next to his American counterpart at the banquet.*
   Syn: vis-à-vis. —*Idiom* opposite number.
2. PARALLEL.

counterpoint *noun* CONTRAST.

counterpoise *noun* BALANCE.

counterpoise *verb*
1. BALANCE.
2. COMPENSATE.

counterstroke *noun* RETALIATION.

countertype *noun* PARALLEL.

countervail *verb*
1. BALANCE.
2. COMPENSATE.

countless *adjective* INCALCULABLE.

country *noun*
1. A rural area: *a farm in the country.*
   Syn: countryside. —*Idiom* God's country.
2. STATE.
3. TERRITORY.

country *adjective*
Of or pertaining to the countryside: *a quiet country scene.*
   Syns: agrestic (*also* agrestical), Arcadian, bucolic, campestral, hick (*Informal*), pastoral, provincial, rural, rustic.

countryman *noun*
A person who is from one's own country: *The President addressed his countrymen.*
   Syn: compatriot. —*Idiom* fellow citizen.

countryside *noun* COUNTRY.

couple *noun*
1. Two items of the same kind together: *a couple of pistols; sang a couple of songs.*
   Syns: brace¹, doublet, pair.
2. PAIR.

couple *verb*
1. ASSOCIATE.
2. ATTACH.
3. COMBINE.

couple with *verb* TAKE.

coupling *noun* JOINT.

courage *noun*
The quality of mind enabling one to face danger or hardship resolutely: *a soldier decorated for courage in battle.*
   Syns: braveness, bravery, courageousness, dauntlessness, fearlessness, fortitude, gallantry, guts (*Slang*), heart, intrepidity, mettle, moxie (*Slang*), nerve, pluck,

resolution, spirit, spunk (*Informal*), valiancy (*also* valiance), valor.

courageous *adjective* BRAVE.

courageousness *noun* COURAGE.

courier *noun* BEARER.

course *verb*
1, 2. FLOW.

course *noun*
1. APPROACH.
2. HEADING.
3. SERIES.

court *verb*
1. To attempt to gain the affection of: *court a girl.*
   Syns: address, pursue, romance (*Informal*), rush, spark, sue (*Archaic*), woo.
2. To solicit (danger) playfully and provocatively, often unwittingly: *courted economic disaster; a stunt pilot who courted death.*
   Syns: beckon, invite, provoke, tempt, toy (with).

court *noun*
1. An area partially or entirely enclosed by walls or buildings: *My window opens onto a court.*
   Syns: atrium, close², courtyard, curtilage, enclosure, quad, quadrangle, yard.
2. A judicial assembly: *called the court to order.*
   Syns: bar, lawcourt, tribunal.

courteous *adjective*
1. Characterized by good manners: *a courteous person who took my coat.*
   Syns: civil, genteel, mannerly, polite, well-bred, well-mannered.
2. ATTENTIVE.

courteousness *noun* COURTESY.

courter *noun* BEAU.

courtesan *noun* PROSTITUTE.

courtesies *noun* AMENITIES.

courtesy *noun*
1. Well-mannered behavior toward others: *common courtesy.*
   Syns: civility, courteousness, politeness.
2. A courteous act: *Little courtesies like thank-you notes are important.*
   Syn: civility.
3. An act requiring special generosity: *received free drinks by courtesy of the airline.*
   Syns: beau geste, compliment(s), favor, indulgence.

courtier *noun* SYCOPHANT.

courting *noun* COURTSHIP.

courtliness *noun* GALLANTRY.

courtly *adjective*
1. CEREMONIOUS.

2. GALLANT.
3. GRACIOUS.

courtship *noun*
Romantic attentions: *a long courtship before marriage.*
    Syns: addresses, courting, suit.

courtyard *noun* COURT.

cove *noun* BAY¹.

covenant *noun*
1. AGREEMENT.
2. PROMISE.

covenant *verb*
1. CONTRACT.
2. PLEDGE.

cover *verb*
1. To extend over the surface of: *Snow covered the ground.*
    Syns: blanket, cap, overcast, overlay, spread over.
2. *Jour.* To observe, analyze, and relate the details of (an event): *covered the elections.*
    Syn: report.
3. To prevent (something) from being known: *tried to cover up the scandal.*
    Syns: cloak, conceal, enshroud, hide¹, hush (up), mask, shroud, veil.
    —*Idioms* keep under cover, keep under wraps, veil in secrecy.
4. TRAVERSE.

cover up *verb* DISGUISE.

cover *noun*
1. Something that physically protects, esp. from danger: *sought cover in the house from the attackers.*
    Syns: asylum, covert, harbor, harborage, haven, protection, refuge, retreat, sanctuary, shelter.
2. FAÇADE.
3. PRETENSE.

coverage *noun*
Jour. The extent to which an event is reported: *election coverage.*
    Syn: reportage.

covert *adjective*
1. SECRET.
2. ULTERIOR.

covert *noun*
1. COVER.
2. HIDE-OUT.

covet *verb*
1. DESIRE.
2. ENVY.

covetous *adjective*
1. ENVIOUS.
2. GREEDY.

covetousness *noun*
1. ENVY.
2. GREED.

cow *verb* INTIMIDATE.

coward *noun*
An ignoble, uncourageous person: *a coward who deserted his comrades under fire.*
    Syns: chicken (*Slang*), craven, dastard, funk² (*Chiefly Brit.*), poltroon (*Archaic*), yellow-belly (*Slang*). —*Idiom* gutless wonder.

cowardice *noun*
Ignoble lack of courage: *desertion and other acts of cowardice.*
    Syns: cowardliness, cravenness, dastardliness, faint-heartedness, funk² (*Chiefly Brit.*), gutlessness, poltroonery, pusillanimity, unmanliness, yellowness (*Slang*).
    —*Idioms* white feather, yellow streak.

cowardliness *noun* COWARDICE.

cowardly *adjective*
Ignobly lacking in courage: *cowardly turncoats.*
    Syns: chicken (*Slang*), chickenhearted, craven, dastardly, faint-hearted, gutless, lily-livered, pusillanimous, unmanly, yellow (*Slang*), yellow-bellied (*Slang*).

coy *adjective*
1. FLIRTATIOUS.
2. MODEST.

coze *verb* CONVERSE¹.

coze *noun* CONVERSATION.

cozen *verb*
1. CHEAT.
2. DECEIVE.

cozy *also* **cosy** *adjective*
COMFORTABLE.

crab *noun* GROUCH.

crabbed *adjective* ILL-TEMPERED.

crabby *adjective* ILL-TEMPERED.

crack *noun*
1. A usu. narrow partial opening caused by splitting and rupture: *a crack in the ice.*
    Syns: break, chink, cleft, fissure, rift, split.
2. *Informal.* A flippant or sarcastic remark: *made a crack about women drivers.*
    Syns: cut (*Informal*), dig, jab, quip, wisecrack.
3. BLOW².
4. FLASH.
5. REPORT.
6. TRY.

crack *verb*
1. To make a sudden sharp, explosive noise: *The rifle cracked in the silent woods.*
    Syns: bark, clap, pop, snap.

2. To undergo partial breaking: *The ice cracked under my weight.*
   Syns: fissure, rupture, snap, split.
3. BREAK.
4. BREAK DOWN at **break**.
5. COLLAPSE.
crack *adjective* EXPERT.
crack up *verb*
1. COLLAPSE.
2. CRASH.
crackajack *adjective & noun* SEE **crackerjack**.
crackdown *noun* SUPPRESSION.
cracked *adjective* INSANE.
crackerjack *also* **crackajack** *adjective* EXPERT.
crackerjack *also* **crackajack** *noun* EXPERT.
crackers *adjective* INSANE.
crackle *verb*
To make a series of short, sharp noises: *The fire crackled as it consumed the dry branches.*
   Syns: crepitate, splutter, sputter.
crackpot *noun*
An insanely foolish or strange person: *a crackpot who wrote incoherent letters to the President.*
   Syns: crank, cuckoo, ding-a-ling (*Informal*), dingbat (*Informal*), eccentric, harebrain, kook (*Slang*), loon, loony (*also* luny), lunatic, nut (*Slang*), screwball, weirdie (*also* weirdy, weirdo) (*Slang*).
crackup *noun*
1. BREAKDOWN.
2. CRASH.
cracky *adjective* INSANE.
craft *noun*
1. ABILITY.
2, 3. ART.
4. INDIRECTION.
craftiness *noun*
1. ART.
2. INDIRECTION.
craftsmanship *noun* WORK.
crafty *adjective* ARTFUL.
cragged *adjective* ROUGH.
craggy *adjective* ROUGH.
cram *verb*
1. BONE UP.
2, 3. CROWD.
crammed *adjective* FULL.
cramp *verb* CONSTRAIN.
cramp *noun* RESTRICTION.
cramped *adjective* TIGHT.
crank *noun*
1. CRACKPOT.
2. GROUCH.
cranky *adjective* ILL-TEMPERED.

crap *noun* NONSENSE.
crappy *adjective* SHODDY.
crapulence *noun* DRUNKENNESS.
crapulent *adjective* DRUNK.
crapulous *adjective* DRUNK.
crash *noun*
1. A wrecking of a vehicle: *a plane crash.*
   Syns: crackup, pileup, smash, smashup, wreck.
2. CLASH.
3. COLLAPSE.
4. COLLISION.
5. SLAM.
crash *verb*
1. To undergo wrecking: *The plane crashed.*
   Syns: crack up (*Informal*), pile up, smash, smash up.
2. BANG.
3. CLASH.
4. COLLAPSE.
5. COLLIDE.
6. RETIRE.
crash *adjective*
Informal. Designed to meet emergency needs as quickly as possible: *a crash program to save energy; a hospital crash tray.*
   Syns: hurry-up, rush.
crashing *adjective* UTTER².
crass *adjective* COARSE.
crave *verb*
1. DESIRE.
2. LUST.
craven *adjective* COWARDLY.
craven *noun* COWARD.
cravenness *noun* COWARDICE.
craving *noun* DESIRE.
crawl *verb*
1. To move along in a crouching or prone position: *soldiers crawling through barbed-wire obstacles.*
   Syns: creep, slide, snake, worm.
2. To advance slowly: *Time crawls.*
   Syns: creep, drag, inch.
3. To experience a repugnant tingling sensation: *a person who made my skin crawl.*
   Syns: creep, formicate. —*Idiom* have the creeps.
4. TEEM¹.
crawl *noun*
A very slow rate of speed: *Time passed at a crawl.*
   Syn: creep. —*Idiom* snail's pace.
crawly *adjective*
Experiencing a repugnant tingling sensation: *My skin felt crawly after the horror movie.*

Syns: creepy (*Informal*), goose-
pimply.
craze *verb* DERANGE.
craze *noun*
1. ENTHUSIASM.
2. FASHION.
crazed *adjective* INSANE.
craziness *noun*
1. FOOLISHNESS.
2. INSANITY.
crazy *adjective*
1. ENTHUSIASTIC.
2. FOOLISH.
3. INSANE.
cream *noun* BEST.
cream *verb*
1. FOAM.
2. OVERWHELM.
creamy *adjective* FRESH.
crease *noun*
1. FOLD.
2. LINE.
create *verb*
1. COMPOSE.
2. FOUND.
3. PRODUCE.
creation *noun*
1. FOUNDATION.
2. MYTH.
3. UNIVERSE.
creative *adjective* INVENTIVE.
creativity *noun* INVENTION.
creator *noun*
1. BUILDER.
2. ORIGINATOR.
creature *noun* HUMAN BEING.
credence *noun* BELIEF.
credible *adjective*
1. AUTHENTIC.
2. BELIEVABLE.
credit *verb*
1. ATTRIBUTE.
2. BELIEVE.
credit *noun*
1. ATTRIBUTION.
2. BELIEF.
3. RECOGNITION.
creditable *adjective*
1. BELIEVABLE.
2. HONORABLE.
creed *noun*
1. FAITH.
2. RELIGION.
creek *noun* BRANCH.
creep *verb*
1, 2, 3. CRAWL.
4. SNEAK.
creep *noun* CRAWL.
creepy *adjective* CRAWLY.

crème de la crème *noun*
1. BEST.
2. SOCIETY.
crepehanger *noun* PESSIMIST.
crepitate *verb* CRACKLE.
crest *noun*
1. CLIMAX.
2. HEIGHT.
3. MAXIMUM.
cretin *noun* FOOL.
crew *noun* FORCE.
crib *verb* PIRATE.
cribber *noun* PIRATE.
crime *noun*
1. A serious breaking of the public law:
*Car theft and armed robbery are
crimes.*
Syns: felony (*Law*), illegality,
misdeed, offense, trespass, violation.
2. A wicked act: *white-collar crimes such
as stealing supplies.*
Syns: diablerie (*also* diablery), evil,
evildoing, iniquity, misdeed, offense,
sin, tort, transgression, wrong,
wrongdoing.
3. Something that offends one's sense of
propriety, fairness, or justice: *It is a
crime to waste food.*
Syns: outrage, sin.
4. SHAME.
criminal *adjective*
Of, involving, or being a crime: *criminal
activities such as extortion and blackmail.*
Syns: illegal, illegitimate, illicit,
lawless, unlawful, wrongful.
criminal *noun*
One who commits a crime: *killers and
other criminals.*
Syns: felon (*Law*), lawbreaker,
malefactor, offender.
crimp *verb* WRINKLE[1].
crimple *verb* WRINKLE[1].
crimson *verb* BLUSH.
crinkle *noun*
1. FOLD.
2. LINE.
crinkle *verb* WRINKLE[1].
cripple *verb*
1. To deprive of, or of the use of, a limb
or bodily member: *was badly crippled
in the crash.*
Syns: dismember, maim, mutilate.
2. DISABLE.
crisis *noun*
1. A highly volatile, dangerous situation
requiring immediate remedial action:
*The Middle East situation has reached
the point of crisis.*
Syns: emergency, extremity. —*Idiom*
flash point.

2. A decisive point: *decided to adopt a new lifestyle as the result of a midlife crisis.*
   Syns: crossroad(s), exigency (*also* exigence), head, juncture, pass.
   —*Idioms* turning point, zero hour.
crisscross *verb* CROSS.
criterion *noun* - STANDARD.
critic *noun*
   1. A person who evaluates and reports on the worth of something: *an art critic.*
      Syns: commentator, judge, reviewer.
   2. A person who finds fault, often severely and willfully: *a chronic critic of everyone.*
      Syns: aristarch, carper, caviler, criticizer, faultfinder, hypercritic, knocker (*Slang*), momus.
critical *adjective*
   1. Inclined to judge too severely: *an unnecessarily critical attitude.*
      Syns: captious, carping, caviling, censorious, faultfinding, hypercritical, overcritical.
   2. Characterized by careful and exact evaluation: *a critical appraisal of the athlete's abilities.*
      Syns: discerning, discriminating, penetrating.
   3. So serious as to be at the point of crisis: *a critical shortage of fuel.*
      Syns: acute, climacteric, crucial, desperate, dire, exigent.
criticism *noun*
   1. BLAME.
   2. REVIEW.
criticize *verb*
   1. BLAME.
   2. REVIEW.
criticizer *noun* CRITIC.
critique *noun* REVIEW.
critique *verb* REVIEW.
croak *verb* DIE.
crocked *adjective* DRUNK.
crone *noun* WITCH.
crony *noun* ASSOCIATE.
crook *verb* BEND.
crook *noun*
   1. BEND.
   2. CHEAT.
crooked *adjective*
   1. Having bends, curves, or angles: *a crooked tree limb; a crooked country lane.*
      Syns: bending, curved, curving, devious, twisting.
   2. CORRUPT.
   3. IRREGULAR.

crookedness *noun*
   1. CORRUPTION.
   2. IRREGULARITY.
crop *verb*
   1. CUT BACK at **cut**.
   2. GLEAN.
   3. TRUNCATE.
crop *noun* HARVEST.
cropping *noun* HARVEST.
cross *verb*
   1. To go across: *crossed the ocean.*
      Syns: transit, transverse, traverse.
   2. To pass through or over: *at the corner where Elm crosses Main Street.*
      Syns: crisscross, crosscut, cut across, decussate, intercross, intersect.
   3. BETRAY.
cross out *verb* CANCEL.
cross *noun* BURDEN.
cross *adjective* ILL-TEMPERED.
crosscut *verb* CROSS.
cross-examine *verb* INTERROGATE.
cross-eye *noun* SQUINT.
cross-eyed *adjective* SQUINTY.
crossing *adjective* TRANSVERSE.
cross-interrogate *verb* INTERROGATE.
cross-question *verb* INTERROGATE.
crossroad(s) *noun* CRISIS.
crosswise *adjective* TRANSVERSE.
crouch *verb*
   To stoop low with the limbs pulled in close to the body: *crouched behind the tree and listened.*
      Syns: huddle, hunch, hunker, squab (*Brit. Regional*), squat.
crow *verb*
   1. BOAST.
   2. EXULT.
crowd *noun*
   1. An enormous number of persons gathered together: *An enthusiastic crowd surrounded the President.*
      Syns: crush, drove, flock, horde, mass, mob, multitude, swarm, throng.
   2. A very large number of things grouped together: *a crowd of insects.*
      Syns: army, cloud, drove, flock, host, legion, multitude, rout[1] (*Archaic*), scores.
   3. A particular social group: *invited only our crowd.*
      Syns: bunch (*Informal*), circle, gang, set[2].
   4. ASSEMBLY.
   5. CIRCLE.
   6. COMMONALTY.
crowd *verb*
   1. To congregate closely around or

against: *The fans crowded around the singer.*
Syns: cram, crush, flock, jam, mob, press, squash, squeeze.
2. To fill to excess by compressing or squeezing tightly: *Commuters crowded the bus.*
Syns: cram, jam, jam-pack (*Informal*), load, mob, pack, stuff.
3. To act on with a steady pushing force: *The passengers crowded each other in the subway.*
Syns: compress, constrain, crush, mash, press, push, squash, squeeze.

crowded *adjective*
1. BUSY.
2. FULL.
3. THICK.
4. TIGHT.

crown *verb*
1. CLIMAX.
2. TOP.

crown *noun*
1. CLIMAX.
2. HEIGHT.

crowning *adjective* CLIMACTIC.

crucial *adjective*
1. CRITICAL.
2. DECISIVE.

crucible *noun* TRIAL.

crucify *verb* TORTURE.

crude *adjective*
1. In a natural state and still not prepared for use: *crude oil; crude ore.*
Syns: impure, native, raw, unprocessed, unrefined.
2. Displaying a lack of knowledge or skill: *crude attempts to negotiate.*
Syns: coarse, inexpert.
3. COARSE.
4. OBSCENE.
5. RUDE.

cruel *adjective*
1. So intense as to cause extreme suffering: *cruel hurricane winds.*
Syns: ferocious, fierce, savage, vicious.
2. FIERCE.

cruelty *noun*
A cruel act or an instance of cruel behavior: *the cruelty of an Eastern potentate.*
Syns: barbarity, brutality, ferocity, inhumanity, truculence (*also* truculency), viciousness.

crumb *noun*
1, 2. BIT[1].

crumble *verb* BREAK UP at **break.**

crummy *also* **crumby** *adjective*
SHODDY.

crump *verb* CHEW.

crumple *verb*
1. BEND.
2. WRINKLE[1].

crunch *verb*
1. CHEW.
2. GRIND.

crusade *noun*
1. CAUSE.
2. DRIVE.

crush *verb*
1. To press forcefully so as to break up into a pulpy mass: *crushed mint leaves.*
Syns: becrush, mash, mush (up), pulp, squash.
2. To break up into tiny particles: *crushed the iron ore.*
Syns: bray, buck[2], granulate, granulize, grind, mill, powder, pulverize, triturate.
3. BREAK.
4, 5. CROWD.
6. OVERWHELM.
7. SQUEEZE.
8. SUPPRESS.

crush *noun*
1. CROWD.
2. INFATUATION.

crust *noun* PRESUMPTION.

crusty *adjective*
1. ABRUPT.
2. OBSCENE.

crutch *noun* SUPPORT.

cry *verb*
1. To make inarticulate sounds of grief or pain, usu. accompanied by tears: *The child cried after falling down.*
Syns: bawl, blub, blubber, boohoo, howl, keen[2], sob, wail, weep, yowl.
2. ADVERTISE.
3. EXCLAIM.
4. ROAR.
5. SHOUT.

cry *noun*
1. A fit of crying: *had a good cry after the funeral.*
Syns: bawling, blubbering, boohoos, tears, wailing, weeping. —*Idiom* flood of tears.
2. A rallying term used by proponents of a cause: *"Freedom!" was the cry of the revolutionaries.*
Syn: motto. —*Idioms* battle cry, call to arms (*or* battle), rallying cry, war cry.
3. DEMAND.
4. FASHION.
5. GOSSIP.

crying *adjective*
1. BURNING.
2. OUTRAGEOUS.
crypt *noun* GRAVE[1].
crystal-clear *adjective*
1. APPARENT.
2. TRANSPARENT.
crystalline *adjective* TRANSPARENT.
cuckoo *noun* CRACKPOT.
 cuckoo *adjective* INSANE.
cuddle *verb*
1. CARESS.
2. SNUGGLE.
cue *noun* HINT.
cuff *noun* SLAP.
 cuff *verb* SLAP.
cuisinier *noun* COOK.
cul-de-sac *noun* BLIND ALLEY.
cull *verb*
1. CHOOSE.
2. GLEAN.
culminate *verb* CLIMAX.
culminating *adjective* CLIMACTIC.
culmination *noun*
1. CLIMAX.
2. FULFILLMENT.
culpability *noun* BLAME.
culpable *adjective* BLAMEWORTHY.
cultivate *verb*
1. GROW.
2. NURSE.
3. PROMOTE.
4. TILL.
cultivated *adjective* CULTURED.
cultivation *noun* CULTURE.
cultural *adjective*
Promoting culture: *cultural pursuits such
as supporting the local orchestra.*
 Syns: civilizing, edifying, enlightening,
 humanizing, refining.
culture *noun*
1. Enlightenment and excellent taste
resulting from intellectual
development: *a person of great charm
and culture.*
 Syns: cultivation, polish, refinement.
2. The total product of human creativity
and intellect at a particular time: *the
culture of ancient Greece.*
 Syns: civilization, Kultur (*German*).
 culture *verb* TILL.
cultured *adjective*
Characterized by discriminating taste
and broad knowledge as a result of
development or education: *a cultured
man.*
 Syns: civilized, cultivated,
 enlightened, polished, refined,
 urbane, well-bred.
cumber *verb* CHARGE.

cumbersome *adjective*
1. AWKWARD.
2. HEAVY.
cumbrous *adjective* AWKWARD.
cumshaw *noun* GRATUITY.
cumulate *verb* ACCUMULATE.
cumulation *noun* ACCUMULATION.
cumulative *adjective* ACCUMULATIVE.
cumulus *noun* ACCUMULATION.
cunning *adjective* ARTFUL.
 cunning *noun*
1. ART.
2. DECEIT.
cupidity *noun* GREED.
curative *adjective*
Serving to cure: *curative drugs.*
 Syns: curing, healing, polychrestic,
 remedial, restorative, therapeutic.
 curative *noun* REMEDY.
curb *verb* RESTRAIN.
cure *noun*
1. An agent used to restore health: *had
found no cure for cancer.*
 Syns: elixir, medicament, medicant,
 medication, medicine, nostrum,
 pharmacon, physic, polychrest,
 remedy.
2. REMEDY.
 cure *verb*
To rectify an undesirable or unhealthy
condition: *cure a cold; cure a sick
economy.*
 Syns: heal, remedy.
cure-all *noun* PANACEA.
cureless *adjective* HOPELESS.
curing *adjective* CURATIVE.
curiosity *noun*
1. Mental acquisitiveness: *intellectual
curiosity.*
 Syns: inquisitiveness, interest.
 —*Idioms* inquiring mind, thirst for
 knowledge.
2. Undue interest in the affairs of
others: *The neighbors' curiosity is
irritating.*
 Syns: nosiness (*Informal*), prying,
 snoopiness (*Informal*).
curious *adjective*
1. Eager to acquire knowledge: *was
curious about the origins of man.*
 Syns: disquisitive, inquiring (*also
 enquiring*), inquisitive, investigative,
 questioning.
2. Unduly interested in the affairs of
others: *a curious neighbor.*
 Syns: inquisitive, inquisitorial,
 inquisitory, nosy (*also nosey*)
 (*Informal*), prying, snoopy (*Informal*).
3. ECCENTRIC.
4. FUNNY.

curl *verb*
1. WAVE.
2. WIND[2].
currency *noun* MONEY.
current *adjective*
1. MODERN.
2. PRESENT[1].
3. PREVAILING.
current *noun* FLOW.
currently *adverb* NOW.
curse *noun*
1. A denunciation invoking a wish or threat of evil or injury: *the dying prisoner's curse against his captors.*
   Syns: anathema, damnation, execration, imprecation, malediction, malison (*Archaic*).
2. A cause of suffering or harm: *Mankind's greatest curse is poverty.*
   Syns: affliction, bane, evil, ill, plague, scourge, woe.
3. JINX.
4. SWEAR.
curse *verb*
1. To invoke evil or injury upon: *cursed my bad luck.*
   Syns: accurse (*Rare*), anathematize, damn, execrate (*Archaic*), imprecate, maledict (*Rare*). —*Idiom* call down evil on.
2. AFFLICT.
3. SWEAR.
cursed also **curst** *adjective* DAMNED.
cursive *adjective* SMOOTH.
cursiveness *noun* FLUENCY.
cursory *adjective* SUPERFICIAL.
curst *adjective* SEE **cursed**.
curt *adjective* ABRUPT.
curtail *verb* CUT BACK at **cut**.
curtailment *noun* CUTBACK.
curtains *noun* DEATH.
curtilage *noun* COURT.
curtsy *noun* BOW.
curvaceous *adjective* SHAPELY.
curvation *noun* BEND.
curvature *noun* BEND.
curve *verb*
1. BEND.
2. WAVE.
curve *noun* BEND.
curved *adjective*
1. BENT.
2. CROOKED.
curvesome *adjective* SHAPELY.
curvilinear *adjective* BENT.
curving *adjective* CROOKED.
curvy *adjective* SHAPELY.
cusp *noun* POINT.
cuspate also **cuspated, cusped** *adjective* POINTED.

cuspidate also **cuspidated** *adjective* POINTED.
cuss *verb* SWEAR.
cuss *noun* SWEAR.
cussword *noun* SWEAR.
custodian *noun* GUARDIAN.
custody *noun* CARE.
custom *noun*
1. A habitual way of behaving: *Social custom varies from country to country.*
   Syns: habit, habitude, manner, practice, praxis, usage, use, way, wont.
2. PATRONAGE.
custom *adjective*
Made according to the specifications of the buyer: *a custom sports car.*
   Syns: custom-built, customized, custom-made, custom-tailored, made-to-order, tailor-made.
customarily *adverb* USUALLY.
customary *adjective*
Commonly practiced or used: *took his customary route to work.*
   Syns: accustomable (*Obs.*), accustomary (*Archaic*), accustomed, habitual, regular, usual.
custom-built *adjective* CUSTOM.
customer *noun*
1. CONSUMER.
2. PATRON.
customized *adjective* CUSTOM.
custom-made *adjective* CUSTOM.
custom-tailored *adjective* CUSTOM.
cut *verb*
1. To penetrate with a sharp edge: *cut my finger with a razor blade.*
   Syns: gash, incise, pierce, slash, slit.
2. To separate into parts with or as if with a sharp-edged instrument: *cut a cake into twelve slices.*
   Syns: carve, cleave, dissever, sever, slice, split.
3. To bring down, as with a saw or ax: *cut timber.*
   Syns: chop[1], fell[1], hew.
4. *Informal.* To fail to attend on purpose: *cut classes.*
   Syns: mooch (*Chiefly Brit. Regional*), skip. —*Idioms* go A.W.O.L., play hooky (*or* truant), skip out on, take French leave.
5. CUT BACK at **cut**.
6. DILUTE.
7. SNUB.
8. SWERVE.
cut across *verb* CROSS.
cut back *verb*
To decrease, as in length or amount, by or as if by severing or excising: *cut back expenses ruthlessly.*

Syns: chop¹, clip¹, crop, curtail, cut, cut down, lop¹, lower², pare, reduce, shear, slash, trim.

cut down *verb*
1. CUT BACK at **cut**.
2. DROP.

cut in *verb*
1. INTERRUPT.
2. INTRUDE.

cut off *verb*
1. HEAD OFF at **head**.
2. ISOLATE.
3. KILL.

cut out *verb*
1. BREAK.
2. GO.
3. SUPPLANT.

cut up *verb*
1. BLAME.
2. MISBEHAVE.

cut *noun*
1. The result of cutting: *a long cut on his cheek from a duel.*
   Syns: gash, incision, slash, slice, slit, split.
2. A part severed from a whole: *a good cut of beef.*
   Syns: piece, portion, section, segment, slice.
3. *Informal.* An unexcused absence: *No cuts are allowed in his class.*
   Syns: hooky (*Informal*), skip, truancy. —*Idiom* French leave.
4. ALLOTMENT.
5. CRACK.
6. KIND².
7. SNUB.

cut *adjective* DILUTE.

cut-and-dried *adjective* ROUTINE.

cutback *noun*
The act or process of decreasing in length, amount, duration, etc.: *a cutback in production.*
   Syns: curtailment, decrease, reduction, slash.

cut-off *noun* STOP.

cutthroat *noun* MURDERER.

cutthroat *adjective* MURDEROUS.

cutting *adjective* BITING.

cutup *noun* JOKER.

cycle *noun* CIRCLE.

cyclic *also* **cyclical** *adjective* RECURRENT.

cyclopean *adjective* GIANT.

cynic *noun*
A person who expects only the worst from people: *Life's experiences had rendered him a cynic.*
   Syns: man-hater, misanthrope, misanthropist.

cynical *adjective*
Marked by or displaying contemptuous mockery of the motives or virtues of others: *a cynical attitude toward society.*
   Syns: ironic (*also* ironical), sardonic, wry.

D

dab¹ *verb* SMEAR.

dab *noun*
1. BIT¹.
2. SMEAR.

dab² *noun* EXPERT.

dabbler *noun* AMATEUR.

dad *noun* FATHER.

daddy *noun* FATHER.

daedal *adjective* COMPLEX.

daedalian *adjective* COMPLEX.

daffy *adjective* INSANE.

daft *adjective* INSANE.

dainty *adjective*
1. DELICATE.
2. NICE.

dainty *noun* DELICACY.

dalliance *noun*
1, 2. FLIRTATION.

dally *verb*
1. DELAY.
2, 3. FLIRT.

damage *noun*
1. BREAKAGE.
2. HARM.

damage *verb* INJURE.

damaging *adjective* HARMFUL.

damn *verb*
1. CONDEMN.
2. CURSE.
3. SWEAR.

damn *noun*
Informal. The least bit: *His opinion isn't worth a damn.*
   Syns: ace¹, hoot, iota, jot, ounce, rap², shred, straw, whit.

damn *adjective* DAMNED.

damnation *noun* CURSE.

damned *adjective*
1. Condemned, esp. to hell: *damned souls.*
   Syns: doomed, lost. —*Idiom* gone to blazes.
2. So annoying or detestable as to

deserve condemnation: *The damned car won't start.*
Syns: accursed, blamed, blankety-blank (*Informal*), blasted (*Slang*), blessed, blooming (*Slang*), confounded, cursed (*also* curst), damn, darn, execrable, infernal, ruddy (*Slang*).
3. UTTER².

damp *adjective*
Slightly wet: *damp ground; a damp sponge.*
Syns: dank, moist.

dampen *verb*
1. MUFFLE.
2. WASH.

dance *verb*
1. To move rhythmically to music, using patterns of steps or gestures: *often dances alone to the radio.*
Syns: foot (it), hoof (*Slang*), step. —*Idioms* cut a rug, trip the light fantastic.
2. GAMBOL.

dance *noun*
A party or gathering for dancing: *went to a dance at the country club.*
Syns: ball, hop (*Slang*).

dancer *noun*
A person who dances, esp. professionally: *ballet dancer.*
Syns: hoofer (*Slang*), terpsichorean.

dandy *adjective*
1. EXCELLENT.
2. MARVELOUS.

danger *noun*
Exposure to possible harm, loss, or injury: *High flood waters put the town in danger.*
Syns: endangerment, hazard, imperilment, jeopardy, peril, risk. —*Idiom* thin ice.

danger *verb* ENDANGER.

dangerous *adjective*
1. Involving possible risk, loss, or injury: *a dangerous climb.*
Syns: adventurous, chancy, hairy (*Slang*), hazardous, jeopardous, parlous (*Archaic*), perilous, risky, treacherous, unsafe, venturous.
2. GRIEVOUS.

dangle *verb* HANG.

dank *adjective* DAMP.

dap *verb* GLANCE¹.

dapple *verb* SPECKLE.

dare *verb*
1. To call on another to do something requiring boldness: *He dared her to say he was a liar.*
Syns: challenge, defy. —*Idiom* throw down the gauntlet.

2. DEFY.

dare *noun*
An act of taunting another to do something bold or rash: *I did it on a dare.*
Syns: challenge, stump (*Informal*).

daredevil *noun* ADVENTURER.

daredevil *adjective* DARING.

daring *adjective*
Taking or willing to take risks: *a daring test pilot.*
Syns: adventurous, audacious, bold, daredevil, venturesome, venturous.

daring *noun*
Willingness to take risks: *an officer with nerve and daring.*
Syns: adventurousness, audacity, boldness.

dark *adjective*
1. Deficient in brightness: *kept the sickroom dark and quiet.*
Syns: dim, dusky, murky (*also* mirky), obscure, tenebrous.
2. Of a complexion tending toward brown or black: *a tall, dark man.*
Syns: bistered, black-a-vised, brunet (*also* brunette), dusky, swarthy.
3. Characterized by or expressive of a foreboding somberness: *gave me a dark scowl and left the room; dark, angry clouds in the distance.*
Syns: lowering (*also* louring), lowery (*also* loury), overhanging, sullen.
4. BLACK.
5. BLACKISH.
6. BLIND.
7. GLOOMY.

dark *noun*
Absence or deficiency of light: *groping around in the dark for his glasses.*
Syns: darkness, dimness, duskiness, obscurity, tenebrosity.

darken *verb* SHADE.

darkness *noun* DARK.

darling *noun*
1. A person who is much loved: *Hello, my darling.*
Syns: beloved, dear, honey, love, sweet, sweetheart, truelove. —*Idiom* light of one's life.
2. FAVORITE.

darling *adjective*
1. Regarded with much love and tenderness: *a darling child.*
Syns: beloved, dear, loved, precious.
2. DELIGHTFUL.
3. FAVORITE.

darn *adjective* DAMNED.

dart *verb*
1. FLY.
2. RUSH.

dash *verb*
1. BLAST.
2. RUN.
3. RUSH.
4. SPLASH.
dash *noun*
1. SPIRIT.
2. TRACE.
3. VIGOR.
dashing *adjective*
1. FASHIONABLE.
2. LIVELY.
dastard *noun* COWARD.
dastardliness *noun* COWARDICE.
dastardly *adjective* COWARDLY.
data *noun* INFORMATION.
date *noun* ENGAGEMENT.
date *verb* SEE.
dated *adjective* OLD-FASHIONED.
dateless *adjective* AGELESS.
daub *verb* SMEAR.
daub *noun* SMEAR.
daunt *verb* DISMAY.
dauntless *adjective* BRAVE.
dauntlessness *noun* COURAGE.
dawdle *verb* DELAY.
dawn *noun*
1. The first appearance of daylight in the morning: *Farmers often get up before dawn.*
   Syns: aurora (*Poetic*), cockcrow, dawning, daybreak, dayspring (*Poetic*), morn (*Poetic*), morning, sunrise, sunup. —*Idioms* break of day, crack of dawn, first light.
2. BIRTH.
dawn *verb*
To begin to appear or develop: *A new era in science dawned with the theory of relativity.*
   Syns: appear, arise, commence, emerge, originate.
dawn on (or **upon**) *verb* REGISTER.
dawning *noun*
1. BIRTH.
2. DAWN.
daybreak *noun* DAWN.
day(s) *noun* AGE.
dayspring *noun* DAWN.
daze *verb*
1. To confuse with bright light: *The spotlight dazed her, and she shielded her eyes.*
   Syns: bedazzle, blind, dazzle.
2. To stun the senses, as with a heavy blow, a shock, or fatigue: *bewildered and dazed after the bombing.*
   Syns: bedaze, bemuse, benumb, maze (*Archaic*), stupefy.

daze *noun*
A stunned or bewildered condition: *fell flat and lay on the ground in a daze.*
   Syns: befuddlement, fog, maze (*Archaic*), muddle, stupor, trance.
dazzle *verb* DAZE.
dazzle *noun* GLARE.
dazzling *adjective* BLAZING.
dead *adjective*
1. No longer alive: *Dead men tell no tales.*
   Syns: asleep, deceased, defunct, demised, departed, extinct, gone, late, lifeless, perished. —*Idioms* at rest, pushing up daisies, with one's fathers.
2. Lacking physical feeling or sensitivity: *Her frostbitten toes felt dead.*
   Syns: asleep, benumbed, insensible, insensitive, numb, numbed, unfeeling.
3. EXHAUSTED.
4. UTTER².
5. VANISHED.
dead *adverb*
1. COMPLETELY.
2. DIRECTLY.
3. PRECISELY.
deaden *verb*
1. To render less sensitive: *a topical anesthetic to deaden the pain.*
   Syns: benumb, blunt, desensitize, dull, numb. —*Idiom* take the edge off.
2. MUFFLE.
deadliness *noun* FATALITY.
deadlock *noun* TIE.
deadly *adjective*
1. Causing or tending to cause death: *Cyanide is a deadly poison.*
   Syns: deathly, fatal, lethal, mortal, vital (*Archaic*).
2. GHASTLY.
3. VIRULENT.
deadpan *adjective* EXPRESSIONLESS.
deafening *adjective* LOUD.
deal *verb*
1. To be occupied or concerned: *Astronomy deals with heavenly bodies.*
   Syns: consider, take up, treat. —*Idiom* have to do with.
2. DISTRIBUTE.
3. GIVE.
4. PUSH.
deal in *verb* SELL.
deal with *verb*
To behave in a specified way toward: *dealt with his assistants as equals.*
   Syns: handle, treat.
deal *noun*
1. An indefinite amount or extent: *has a*

good deal of money; is a great deal thinner.
Syns: lot, quantity.
2. AGREEMENT.

dealer *noun*
1. A person engaged in buying and selling: *a diamond dealer.*
Syns: businessperson, merchandiser, merchant, trader, tradesman, trafficker.
2. PUSHER.

dear *noun* DARLING.
dear *adjective*
1. COSTLY.
2. DARLING.
3. FAVORITE.

dearth *noun* ABSENCE.

death *noun*
1. The act or fact of dying: *the hour of her death; the death of a dream.*
Syns: curtains (*Slang*), decease, demise, dissolution, extinction, passing, quietus. —*Idioms* eternal rest, Grim Reaper, Pale Horse.
2. FATALITY.

deathless *adjective* IMMORTAL.
deathlessness *noun* IMMORTALITY.
deathlike *adjective* GHASTLY.
deathly *adjective*
1, 2. DEADLY.

debacle *noun* COLLAPSE.
debar *verb* EXCLUDE.
debark *verb* LAND.
debase *verb*
1. To lower in character or quality: *debasing language by misusing it.*
Syns: cheapen, degrade, demean², downgrade.
2. ADULTERATE.
3. CORRUPT.

debased *adjective* CORRUPTED.
debatable *adjective*
In doubt or dispute: *a debatable theory.*
Syns: arguable, contested, disputable, disputed, doubtful, moot, mootable, problematical (*also* problematic), questionable, uncertain.

debate *verb* ARGUE.
debate *noun*
1. ARGUMENT.
2. ARGUMENTATION.

debauch *verb*
1. CORRUPT.
2. SEDUCE.

debauched *adjective* CORRUPTED.
debaucher *noun* SEDUCER.
debauching *noun* SEDUCTION.
debauchment *noun* SEDUCTION.
debilitate *verb* ENERVATE.
debilitated *adjective* RUN-DOWN.

debilitation *noun* INFIRMITY.
debility *noun* INFIRMITY.
debonair *also* **debonaire** *adjective*
AIRY.

debt *noun*
1. Something, such as money, owed by one person to another: *a debt of $500; a debt of gratitude.*
Syns: arrear *or* arrears, arrearage, due, indebtedness, liability.
2. A condition of owing something to another: *can't seem to get out of debt.*
Syns: arrearage, indebtedness, liability, obligation, obligement.

debunk *verb* DISCREDIT.
debut *also* **début** *verb* COME OUT at come.

decadence *noun* DETERIORATION.
decamp *verb* ESCAPE.
decampment *noun* ESCAPE.
decant *verb* POUR.

decay *verb*
To become or cause to become rotten or unsound: *a tooth decaying from neglect.*
Syns: break down, decompose, deteriorate, molder, putrefy, putresce, rot, spoil, turn. —*Idioms* go bad, go to pot, go to seed.

decay *noun*
The condition of being decayed: *the complete decay of civilization.*
Syns: breakdown, decomposition, deterioration, putrefaction, putrescence, putridness, rot, spoilage.

decayed *adjective* BAD.
decaying *adjective* SHABBY.
decease *noun* DEATH.
decease *verb* DIE.
deceased *adjective* DEAD.

deceit *noun*
The act or practice of deceiving: *a pious man on the Sabbath who is full of deceit during the week.*
Syns: cunning, deceitfulness, deception, double-dealing, duplicity, guile.

deceitful *adjective* DISHONEST.
deceitfulness *noun* DECEIT.

deceive *verb*
To cause to accept what is false, esp. by trickery or misrepresentation: *An inexperienced person is easily deceived.*
Syns: bamboozle (*Informal*), beguile, betray, bluff, cozen, delude, double-cross (*Slang*), dupe, fool, four-flush (*Slang*), have, hoodwink, humbug, mislead, take in, trick. —*Idioms* lead astray, play false, pull the wool over someone's eyes, put something over on, take for a ride.

decency *noun*
1. Conformity to recognized standards, as of conduct or appearance: *behaved with decency.*
   Syns: correctness, decorum, propriety, seemliness.
2. A sense of propriety or rightness: *had the decency to resign.*
   Syns: conscience, grace.
3. CHASTITY.

decent *adjective*
1. *Informal.* Proper in appearance: *bought a decent suit of clothes.*
   Syns: presentable, respectable.
2. ACCEPTABLE.
3. CHASTE.
4. CLEAN.
5. CORRECT.

deception *noun*
1. An action meant to deceive: *guilty of lies and deception.*
   Syns: dodge, imposture, ruse, sell (*Slang*), sleight, stratagem, subterfuge, take-in, trick.
2. DECEIT.

deceptive *adjective* FALLACIOUS.

decide *verb*
1. To make up or cause to make up one's mind: *Have you decided to buy the house?*
   Syns: conclude, determine, resolve, settle.
2. JUDGE.

decided *adjective*
1. Without any doubt: *The dinner was a decided success.*
   Syns: clear, clear-cut, definite, distinct, pronounced, unquestionable.
2. DECISIVE.
3. DEFINITE.
4. SET[1].

decidedness *noun* DECISION[1].

deciding *adjective* DECISIVE.

decimate *verb* ANNIHILATE.

decimation *noun* RUIN.

decipher *verb*
1. BREAK.
2. EXPLAIN.
3. RESOLVE.

decision *noun*
1. A position reached after consideration: *When you've made a decision, please let me know.*
   Syns: conclusion, determination, resolution.
2. Unwavering firmness of character or action: *a woman of extraordinary decision.*
   Syns: decidedness, decisiveness, determination, firmness, resoluteness, resolution, resolve.

decisive *adjective*
1. Determining or having the power to determine an outcome: *The decisive vote was cast.*
   Syns: conclusive, crucial, deciding, determinative.
2. Not hesitating or wavering: *took decisive action to end the strike.*
   Syns: decided, determined, firm[1], resolute.

decisiveness *noun* DECISION.

deck *verb*
1. ADORN.
2. DROP.

deck out *verb* DRESS UP at **dress.**

declamation *noun*
1. ORATORY.
2. SPEECH.

declamatory *adjective*
1. ORATORICAL.
2. SONOROUS.

declaration *noun*
1, 2. ANNOUNCEMENT.
3. ASSERTION.

declare *verb*
1. ANNOUNCE.
2. ASSERT.
3. CLAIM.
4. SAY.

déclassé also **declassed** *adjective* LOWLY.

declension *noun* DETERIORATION.

declination *noun*
1. DETERIORATION.
2. FAILURE.

decline *verb*
1. To be unwilling to accept, consider, or receive: *always declines offers of help.*
   Syns: dismiss, nix (*Slang*), refuse, reject, spurn, turn down. —*Idiom* turn thumbs down on.
2. DETERIORATE.
3. DROP.
4. FADE.

decline *noun*
1. DETERIORATION.
2. DROP.
3. FAILURE.
4. FALL.

declivity *noun* DROP.

decompose *verb*
1. BREAK UP at **break.**
2. DECAY.

decomposed *adjective* BAD.

decomposition *noun* DECAY.

decontaminate *verb* STERILIZE.

decorate *verb* ADORN.

decoration *noun*
1. An emblem of honor worn on one's

clothing: *wore all his decorations when he put on his full-dress suit.*
Syns: badge, medal.
2. ADORNMENT.

decorous *adjective* CORRECT.

decorticate *verb* SKIN.

decorum *noun*
1. DECENCY.
2. MANNERS.

decrease *verb*
To grow or cause to grow gradually less: *The amount of grain harvested this year has decreased because of bad weather.*
Syns: abate, diminish, drain, dwindle, ebb, lessen, let up, peter out, rebate (*Rare*), reduce, tail off, taper off.

decrease *noun*
1. The act or process of decreasing: *a steady decrease in the number of students in the department.*
Syns: abatement, decrement, diminishment, diminution, letup, reduction.
2. CUTBACK.

decree *noun*
1. LAW.
2. RULING.
decree *verb* DICTATE.

decrement *noun* DECREASE.

decrepit *adjective*
1. INFIRM.
2. SHABBY.

decrepitude *noun* INFIRMITY.

decretum *noun* LAW.

decry *verb* BELITTLE.

decrying *adjective* DISPARAGING.

decumbent *adjective* FLAT.

decussate *verb* CROSS.

dedicate *verb*
1. APPLY.
2. DEVOTE.

dedicated *adjective* SACRED.

deduce *verb* INFER.

deduct *verb*
1. To take away (a quantity) from another quantity: *will deduct the medical costs from her taxable income.*
Syns: discount, knock off (*Informal*), subtract, take, take off.
2. INFER.

deduction *noun*
1. An amount deducted: *a legitimate tax deduction.*
Syns: abatement, discount, rebate, reduction.
2. A position arrived at by reasoning from premises or general principles: *The result bore out the deduction he had made.*

Syns: conclusion, illation, inference, judgment.

deed *noun* ACT.
deed *verb* TRANSFER.

deem *verb* BELIEVE.

de-emphasize *verb* SOFT-PEDAL.

deep *adjective*
1. Extending far downward or inward from a surface: *a deep hole; a deep drawer.*
Syns: abysmal, profound.
2. Beyond the understanding of an average mind: *a deep mystery.*
Syns: abstruse, esoteric, heavy (*Slang*), profound, recondite.
3. Resulting from or affecting one's innermost feelings: *a deep love; deep sorrow.*
Syns: deep-felt, intense, profound, strong.
4. ABSORBED.
5. LOW.

deepen *verb* INTENSIFY.

deep-felt *adjective* DEEP.

deepness *noun*
1, 2. DEPTH.

defamation *noun* LIBEL.

defamatory *adjective* LIBELOUS.

defame *verb* LIBEL.

default *noun*
1. ABSENCE.
2. FAILURE.
default *verb* FAIL.

defeasance *noun* ABOLITION.

defeat *verb*
1. To win a victory over, as in battle or a competition: *The Allies defeated the Axis powers in World War II.*
Syns: beat, best, bury (*Slang*), clobber (*Slang*), conquer, down (*Informal*), drub (*Slang*), lick (*Slang*), overcome, rout², shellac (*Slang*), smear (*Slang*), subdue, thrash, trim (*Informal*), triumph (over), trounce, vanquish, whip (*Informal*), worst.
—*Idioms* carry (*or* win) the day, get the better (*or* best) of, go someone one better.
2. FRUSTRATE.

defeat *noun*
The act of defeating or the condition of being defeated: *suffered total defeat by the enemy.*
Syns: beating, clobbering (*Slang*), drubbing (*Slang*), licking (*Informal*), overthrow, rout², shellacking (*Slang*), thrashing, trimming (*Informal*), whipping (*Informal*).

defect *noun*
1. Something that mars the appearance

or causes inadequacy or failure: *a speech defect.*
   Syns: blemish, bug (*Slang*), fault, flaw, imperfection, shortcoming.
2. ABSENCE.
3. SHORTAGE.

defect *verb*
To abandon one's cause or party usu. to join another: *defected from the Soviet Union and sought asylum in Switzerland.*
   Syns: apostatize, desert[3], rat (*Slang*), run out (*Slang*), tergiversate, turn. —*Idioms* change sides, turn one's coat.

defection *noun*
An instance of defecting from or abandoning a cause: *expected his defection.*
   Syns: apostasy, recreancy, tergiversation.

defective *adjective*
1. Having a defect or defects: *bought a book that turned out to be defective.*
   Syns: faulty, flawed, imperfect.
2. DEFICIENT.

defector *noun*
A person who has defected: *a defector from the Soviet Union.*
   Syns: apostate, rat (*Slang*), recreant, renegade, runagate (*Archaic*), tergiversator, turncoat.

defend *verb*
1. To keep safe from danger, attack, or harm: *used an alarm system to defend his home against burglars.*
   Syns: fend (*Archaic*), guard, protect, safeguard, secure, shield.
2. To support against arguments, attack, or criticism: *constantly has to defend his opinions and actions.*
   Syns: justify, maintain, vindicate. —*Idioms* speak up for, stand up for, stick up for.

defendable *adjective* TENABLE.
defendant *noun* ACCUSED.
defense *noun*
1. The act or a means of defending: *taking measures for the defense of the country.*
   Syns: guard, protection, safeguard, security, shield, ward.
2. APOLOGY.

defenseless *adjective* HELPLESS.
defensible *adjective*
1. JUSTIFIABLE.
2. TENABLE.

defer[1] *verb*
To put off until a later time: *deferred writing the letter until she knew when she would leave.*
   Syns: adjourn, delay, hold off, hold

up, lay over, postpone, remit, shelve, stay[1], suspend, table, wait (*Informal*), waive. —*Idioms* put on ice, set aside.

defer[2] *verb*
To conform to the will or judgment of another, esp. out of respect or courtesy: *deferred to his better judgment.*
   Syns: bow, submit, yield. —*Idioms* give ground, give place, give way.

deference *noun* HONOR.

deferential *adjective*
Marked by courteous submission or respect: *deferential behavior.*
   Syns: dutiful, obeisant, respectful.

deferment *noun* DELAY.
deferral *noun* DELAY.
defiance *noun*
1. The disposition boldly to defy or resist authority or an opposing force: *often exhibited defiance toward his parents.*
   Syns: contempt, contumacy, despite, recalcitrance (*also* recalcitrancy), unruliness.
2. Behavior or an act that is intentionally provocative: *failure to comply that can only be called defiance.*
   Syns: challenge, provocation.

defiant *adjective*
Marked by defiance: *a defiant attitude; defiant words.*
   Syns: contemptuous, contumacious, recalcitrant, unruly.

deficiency also **deficience** *noun*
SHORTAGE.

deficient *adjective*
1. Lacking an essential element: *deficient in awareness of the world around her.*
   Syns: defective, incomplete, lacking, wanting.
2. INSUFFICIENT.

deficit *noun* SHORTAGE.
defile *verb*
1. TAINT.
2, 3. VIOLATE.

defiled *adjective* IMPURE.
definite *adjective*
1. Clearly, fully, and sometimes emphatically expressed: *a definite statement that he would not run for re-election.*
   Syns: categorical, clear-cut, decided, explicit, express, positive, precise, specific, unambiguous, unequivocal.
2. Known positively: *The time of his departure is not definite.*
   Syns: certain, positive, sure. —*Idiom* for certain.

3. Having distinct limits: *will stay for a short but definite period.*
Syns: bounded, determinate, fixed, limited.
4. DECIDED.

definitive *adjective*
Serving the function of deciding or settling with finality: *a definitive biography that answers all the questions.*
Syns: conclusive, determinative, final.

deflect *verb*
1. BEND.
2. TURN.

deflorate *verb* VIOLATE.

deflower *verb* VIOLATE.

deform *verb*
To alter and spoil the natural form or appearance of: *Rage deformed his face.*
Syns: contort, disfigure, distort, misshape, twist.

deformity *noun*
A disfiguring abnormality of shape or form: *scoliosis and other deformities.*
Syns: disfigurement, malformation.

defraud *verb* CHEAT.

deft *adjective*
1. ARTFUL.
2. DEXTEROUS.
3. NEAT.

deftness *noun* DEXTERITY.

defunct *adjective*
1. DEAD.
2. VANISHED.

defy *verb*
1. To confront boldly and courageously: *an innovator who defies tradition at every turn.*
Syns: beard, brave, challenge, dare, face, front, outdare. —*Idioms* fly in the face of, hurl defiance at, shake one's fist at, snap one's fingers at, stand up to, thumb one's nose at.
2. DARE.
3. DISOBEY.

degeneracy *noun* DETERIORATION.

degenerate *adjective* CORRUPT.

degenerate *verb* DETERIORATE.

degeneration *noun*
1. DETERIORATION.
2. RUIN.

degradation *noun* DEMOTION.

degrade *verb*
1. DEBASE.
2. DEMOTE.
3. HUMBLE.

degraded *adjective* IMPURE.

degree *noun*
1. One of the units in a course, as on an ascending or descending scale: *moved up slowly and by degrees.*

Syns: grade, level, notch, peg, rung, stage, step.
2. Relative intensity or amount, as of a quality or attribute: *a high degree of accuracy; various degrees of ability.*
Syns: extent, magnitude, measure, portion, proportion.

dehydrate *verb* DRY.

dehydrated *adjective* DRY.

deific *adjective* DIVINE¹.

deign *verb* CONDESCEND.

deject *verb* DEPRESS.

dejected *adjective* DEPRESSED.

dejection *noun* GLOOM.

delay *verb*
1. To cause to be later or slower than expected or desired: *delayed by urgent business.*
Syns: detain, hang up, hold up, retard, set back, slow (down *or* up).
2. To go or move slowly so that progress is hindered: *didn't hurry but didn't delay either.*
Syns: dally, dawdle, dilly-dally, drag, lag, linger, loiter, poke, procrastinate, tarry, trail. —*Idioms* drag one's feet, mark time, take one's time.
3. DEFER¹.

delay *noun*
1. The condition or fact of being made late or slow: *a delay caused by rush-hour traffic.*
Syns: detainment, holdup, lag, retardation.
2. The act of putting off or the condition of being put off: *a delay of 15 minutes.*
Syns: adjournment, deferment, deferral, postponement, stay¹, suspension.

delectable *adjective*
1. DELICIOUS.
2. DELIGHTFUL.

delectate *verb* DELIGHT.

delectation *noun*
1. DELIGHT.
2. ENJOYMENT.

delegate *noun* REPRESENTATIVE.

delegation *noun* MISSION.

delete *verb* DROP.

deleterious *adjective* HARMFUL.

deletion *noun* ERASURE.

deliberate *verb*
1. PONDER.
2. REASON.

deliberate *adjective*
1. Done or said on purpose: *a deliberate lie.*
Syns: intended, intentional, voluntary, willful, willing, witting.

2. Careful and slow in acting, moving, or deciding: *walked with a deliberate step.*
   Syns: leisurely, measured, unhurried.
3. CALCULATED.

deliberated *adjective* ADVISED.

deliberation *noun*
1. An exchange of views in an attempt to reach a decision: *the deliberations of the steering committee.*
   Syns: confabulation, conference, consultation, counsel, parley.
2. THOUGHT.

deliberative *adjective* THOUGHTFUL.

delicacy *noun*
Something fine and delicious, esp. a food: *Caviar is a real delicacy.*
   Syns: dainty, goody (*Informal*), morsel, tidbit, treat.

delicate *adjective*
1. Appealing to refined taste: *prepared a delicate meal.*
   Syns: choice, dainty, elegant, exquisite, fine¹.
2. So slight as to be difficult to notice or appreciate: *a delicate difference.*
   Syns: fine¹, finespun, nice, refined, subtle.
3. Showing sensitivity and skill in dealing with others: *too delicate to tell him the gossip we had heard about him.*
   Syns: diplomatic, discreet, politic, sensitive, tactful.
4. Requiring great tact or skill: *a delicate subject.*
   Syns: sensitive, ticklish, touch-and-go, touchy, tricky.
5. FINE.
6. FRAGILE.
7. INFIRM.

delicious *adjective*
1. Highly pleasing, esp. to the sense of taste: *a perfectly delicious pâté.*
   Syns: ambrosial, delectable, heavenly, luscious, savory, scrumptious (*Slang*), tasteful (*Rare*), tasty, toothsome, yummy (*Slang*).
2. DELIGHTFUL.

delight *noun*
A feeling of extreme gratification aroused by something good or desired: *listened to the concert with delight.*
   Syns: delectation, enjoyment, joy, pleasure, relish.

delight *verb*
1. To give great or keen pleasure to: *a view that delights the eye.*
   Syns: cheer, delectate, enchant, gladden, gratify, joy (*Archaic*), please, pleasure, tickle.

2. REJOICE.

delight in *verb* ADORE.

delighted *adjective* GLAD.

delightful *adjective*
Giving great pleasure or delight: *a Renoir that is the most delightful painting in the collection.*
   Syns: charming, darling (*Informal*), delectable, delicious, enchanting, heavenly, luscious.

delimit *verb*
1. DETERMINE.
2. LIMIT.

delimitate *verb*
1. DETERMINE.
2. LIMIT.

delineate *verb* REPRESENT.

delineation *noun*
1. OUTLINE.
2. REPRESENTATION.

delineative *adjective* DESCRIPTIVE.

delinquency *noun* FAILURE.

deliquesce *verb* MELT.

delirious *adjective* FRANTIC.

deliver *verb*
1. BEAR.
2, 3. GIVE.
4. RESCUE.

deliverance *noun* RESCUE.

delivery *noun*
1. The act of delivering or the condition of being delivered: *only one mail delivery a day.*
   Syns: surrender, transfer.
2. BIRTH.
3. RESCUE.

delude *verb* DECEIVE.

deluge *verb*
1, 2. FLOOD.

deluge *noun* FLOOD.

delusion *noun* ILLUSION.

delusive *adjective*
1. FALLACIOUS.
2. ILLUSORY.

delusory *adjective*
1. FALLACIOUS.
2. ILLUSORY.

delve *verb*
1. DIG.
2. EXPLORE.

delving *noun* INQUIRY.

demand *verb*
1. To ask for urgently or insistently: *demanding better working conditions.*
   Syns: call for, exact, insist on (or upon), require, requisition. —*Idiom* cry out for.
2. To have as a need or prerequisite: *The work of a lawyer demands an analytical mind and patience.*

Syns: ask, call for, entail, involve, necessitate, require, take.

demand *noun*
1. The act of demanding: *wouldn't pay up on demand.*
   Syns: call, claim, cry, exaction, requisition.
2. Something asked for or needed: *Submit your demands in writing.*
   Syns: exigency (*also* exigence), need, requirement, want.

demanding *adjective*
1. Requiring great effort: *a demanding job.*
   Syns: exacting, exigent, taxing, tough.
2. BURDENSOME.
3. SEVERE.

demarcate *verb* DETERMINE.
demean[1] *verb* ACT.
demean[2] *verb*
1. DEBASE.
2. HUMBLE.

demeanor *noun*
1. BEARING.
2. BEHAVIOR.

demented *adjective* INSANE.
dementia *noun* INSANITY.
demise *noun* DEATH.
demise *verb* DIE.
demised *adjective* DEAD.
demission *noun* ABDICATION.
demit *verb*
1. ABDICATE.
2. RETIRE.

demobilize *verb* DISCHARGE.
democratic *adjective* POPULAR.
demolish *verb*
1, 2. DESTROY.

demonstrate *verb*
1. PROVE.
2. SHOW.

demonstration *noun* DISPLAY.
demoralize *verb* CORRUPT.
demoralizing *adjective*
UNWHOLESOME.

demote *verb*
To lower in rank or grade: *was demoted from captain to lieutenant.*
Syns: break, bump (*Informal*), bust (*Slang*), degrade, downgrade, reduce.

demotion *noun*
The act or an instance of demoting: *received a demotion for insubordination.*
Syns: degradation, downgrading, reduction.

demure *adjective* MODEST.
demureness *noun* MODESTY.
den *noun*
1. HIDE-OUT.
2. HOLE.

denial *noun*
1. A refusal to grant the truth of a statement or charge: *The article drew an immediate denial from the mayor.*
   Syns: contradiction, disaffirmation, disclaimer, gainsaying, negation, rejection, traversal (*Law*).
2. REFUSAL.

denigrate *verb* BLACKEN.
denominate *verb* NAME.
denomination *noun*
1. FAITH.
2. NAME.
3. RELIGION.

denotative *adjective* DESIGNATIVE.
denote *verb*
1. DESIGNATE.
2. MEAN[1].

denotive *adjective* DESIGNATIVE.
denounce *verb*
1. ACCUSE.
2. BLAME.

denouncement *noun* ACCUSATION.
denouncer *noun* ACCUSER.
dense *adjective*
1. STUPID.
2. THICK.

density *noun* THICKNESS.
denude *verb*
1. BARE.
2. STRIP[1].

denuded *adjective* BARE.
denunciate *verb*
1. ACCUSE.
2. BLAME.

denunciation *noun*
1. ACCUSATION.
2. BLAME.

denunciative *adjective*
ACCUSATORIAL.
denunciator *noun* ACCUSER.
denunciatory *adjective*
ACCUSATORIAL.
deny *verb*
1. To refuse to admit the truth, reality, value, or worth of: *You can't deny that he's an arrogant man.*
   Syns: contradict, contravene, controvert, disaffirm, gainsay, negate, negative, traverse (*Law*).
2. REFUSE.
3. REPUDIATE.

depart *verb*
1. DEVIATE.
2. DIE.
3. GO.

departed *adjective* DEAD.
departing *adjective* PARTING.
department *noun* AREA.

departure *noun*
1. The act of leaving: *The hour of departure is here.*
   Syns: egress, exit, exodus, going, leaving, withdrawal (*also* withdrawment).
2. DEVIATION.

depend *verb* HANG.

depend on (or **upon**) *verb*
1. To place trust or confidence in: *You can depend on me.*
   Syns: bank on (or upon) (*Informal*), count on, reckon on (or upon), rely on (or upon), trust (in).
2. To be determined by or contingent on something unknown, uncertain, or changeable: *Whether he goes back to jail depends on whether he violates parole.*
   Syns: hang on (or upon), hinge on (or upon), rest on (or upon), turn on (or upon).
3. EXPECT.

dependable *adjective*
Capable of being depended upon: *a dependable worker who is always punctual.*
   Syns: reliable, responsible, solid, trustworthy, trusty.

dependant *adjective* SEE **dependent**.

dependency *noun* POSSESSION.

dependent also **dependant** *adjective*
1. Determined or to be determined by someone or something else: *The result is dependent on many circumstances.*
   Syns: conditional, conditioned, contingent, relative (to), reliant, subject (to).
2. SUBORDINATE.

dependent *noun*
A person who relies on another for support: *will receive a tax deduction for each dependent.*
   Syns: charge, ward.

depict *verb* REPRESENT.

depiction *noun* REPRESENTATION.

depictive *adjective* DESCRIPTIVE.

deplete *verb*
1. To lessen or weaken severely, as by removing something essential: *Our supplies are depleted.*
   Syns: drain, exhaust, impoverish, sap, use up.
2. DRY UP at **dry**.

depleted *adjective* POOR.

deplorable *adjective*
Worthy of severe disapproval: *a deplorable lack of manners.*
   Syns: disgraceful, opprobrious, shameful, unfortunate.

deplore *verb*
1. To feel or express strong disapproval of: *deplores all forms of violence.*
   Syns: censure, condemn, reprehend, reprobate.
2. REGRET.

depone *verb* TESTIFY.

deponent *noun* WITNESS.

deport *verb*
1. ACT.
2. BANISH.

deportation *noun* EXILE.

deportment *noun* BEHAVIOR.

depose *verb* TESTIFY.

deposit *verb*
1. To put down, esp. in layers, by a natural process: *The river deposits silt that forms sandbars.*
   Syns: lay down, precipitate.
2. BANK[1].

deposit *noun*
1. Matter that settles on a bottom or collects on a surface by a natural process: *a muddy deposit in the riverbed.*
   Syns: dregs, lees, precipitate, precipitation, sediment.
2. A partial or initial payment: *put down a deposit on a mink coat.*
   Syn: down payment.

deposition *noun* TESTIMONY.

depository *noun*
A place where something is deposited for safekeeping: *found a secure depository for the silver.*
   Syns: magazine, repository, store, storehouse.

deprave *verb* CORRUPT.

depraved *adjective*
1. CORRUPT.
2. CORRUPTED.

depravity *noun* CORRUPTION.

deprecate *verb* DISAPPROVE.

deprecatory also **deprecative** *adjective* DISPARAGING.

depreciate *verb*
1. To become or make less in price or value: *used cars that steadily depreciate; depreciating the U.S. dollar.*
   Syns: cheapen, devaluate, devalue, downgrade, lower[2], mark down, reduce, write down.
2. BELITTLE.

depreciating *adjective* DISPARAGING.

depreciation *noun*
1. A lowering in price or value: *a depreciation in the value of real estate.*
   Syns: devaluation, markdown, reduction.
2. BELITTLEMENT.

depreciative *adjective* DISPARAGING.
deprecatory *adjective* DISPARAGING.
depredate *verb*
1. DEVASTATE.
2. SACK².
depress *verb*
1. To make sad or gloomy: *Returning from the funeral to an empty house depressed her deeply.*
    Syns: cast down, deject, dispirit, oppress, sadden, weigh down.
2. LOWER².
depressed *adjective*
1. In low spirits: *The news left me depressed for several days.*
    Syns: blue (*Informal*), dejected, dispirited, down, downcast, downhearted, dull, gloomy, heavy-hearted, low, melancholic, melancholy, sad, saddened, spiritless, tristful (*Archaic*), unhappy. —*Idioms* down in (*or* at) the mouth, in the depths.
2. Economically and socially below standard: *a program of aid to depressed areas.*
    Syns: backward, deprived, disadvantaged, impoverished, underprivileged.
depressing *adjective* SAD.
depression *noun*
1. An area sunk below its surroundings: *a depression in the road.*
    Syns: basin, concavity, dip, hollow, sag, sink.
2. A period of decreased business activity and high unemployment: *All signs pointed to a depression.*
    Syns: recession, slump.
3. GLOOM.
deprival *noun* DEPRIVATION.
deprivation *noun*
The condition of being deprived of what one once had or ought to have: *living in poverty and deprivation.*
    Syns: deprival, dispossession, divestiture, loss, privation.
deprive *verb*
To take or keep something away from: *The poll tax deprived many of their right to vote.*
    Syns: bereave, dispossess, divest, rob, strip¹.
deprived *adjective* DEPRESSED.
depth *noun*
1. The extent or measurement downward from a surface: *dove to a depth of 100 feet.*
    Syns: deepness, drop.
2. Intellectual penetration or range:

showed an amazing depth of knowledge.
    Syns: deepness, profoundness, profundity.
deputy *noun* REPRESENTATIVE.
derange *verb*
1. To make insane: *One survivor of the ordeal was permanently deranged by prolonged confinement in the collapsed mine.*
    Syns: craze, distract, madden, unbalance, unhinge.
2. DISORDER.
3. UPSET.
deranged *adjective* INSANE.
derangement *noun* INSANITY.
derelict *adjective*
1. ABANDONED.
2. NEGLIGENT.
dereliction *noun* FAILURE.
deride *verb* RIDICULE.
de rigueur *adjective* CORRECT.
derision *noun* RIDICULE.
derivate *adjective* SEE **derivative.**
derivation *noun*
1. DERIVATIVE.
2. ORIGIN.
derivational *adjective* DERIVATIVE.
derivative also **derivate** *adjective*
Stemming from an original source: *Derivative problems of economic instability include unemployment and devaluation of the dollar.*
    Syns: derivational, derived, secondary.
derivative *noun*
Something derived from another: *a televison series that is a derivative of a novel; an anesthesia that is a curare derivative.*
    Syns: by-product, derivation, descendant, offshoot, outgrowth, spin-off.
derive *verb*
1. To arrive at through reasoning: *derived the formula through a set of equations.*
    Syns: educe, evolve, excogitate.
2. To obtain from another source: *We derive our surname from Gaelic.*
    Syns: draw, get, take.
3. DESCEND.
4. STEM.
derived *adjective*
1. DERIVATIVE.
2. DESCENDING.
derogate *verb* BELITTLE.
derogation *noun* BELITTLEMENT.
derogatory *adjective* DISPARAGING.
derrière *noun* BOTTOM.

descend *verb*
1. To bring oneself down to a lower level of behavior: *Don't descend to his level and be underhanded.*
    Syns: sink, stoop.
2. To have hereditary derivation: *a family that descends from George III.*
    Syns: derive, issue, spring. —*Idiom* trace one's descent.
3. DETERIORATE.
4. DROP.
5. FALL.

descendant *noun*
1. One descended directly from the same parents or ancestors: *Elizabeth II is a descendant of George III.*
    Syns: child, offspring, scion.
2. DERIVATIVE.

descendant *adjective* SEE **descendent**.

descendants *noun*
Those descended from another: *Many cultivated plants are the descendents of unremarkable wildflowers.*
    Syns: begats (*Slang*), brood, children, get, issue, offspring, posterity, progeny, scions, seed.

descendent also **descendant** *adjective*
1, 2, 3. DESCENDING.

descending *adjective*
1. Moving down: *read the names in descending order; the descending escalator.*
    Syns: descendent (*also* descendant), downward.
2. Having a down slope: *a descending mountain stream.*
    Syns: descendent (*also* descendant).
3. Proceeding by descent from an ancestor: *a line descending from kings.*
    Syns: derived, descendent (*also* descendant).

descent *noun*
1. A sudden drop to a lower condition or status: *a marked descent in presidential prestige.*
    Syns: comedown, down, downfall, downgrade.
2. ANCESTRY.
3, 4. FALL.

describe *verb*
1. To give a verbal account of: *described the accident for the police officer.*
    Syns: narrate, recite, recount, rehearse, relate, report.
2. REPRESENT.

description *noun*
1. KIND[2].
2. REPRESENTATION.
3. STORY.

descriptive *adjective*
Serving to describe: *descriptive narrative augmenting the photographs.*
    Syns: delineative, depictive, graphic, representative.

descry *verb*
1. CATCH.
2. DISCERN.
3. NOTICE.

desecrate *verb* VIOLATE.

desecrated *adjective* IMPURE.

desecration *noun* SACRILEGE.

desegregate *verb* INTEGRATE.

desegregation *noun* INTEGRATION.

desensitize *verb* DEADEN.

desert[1] *noun* BARREN.

desert[2] *noun* DUE.

desert[3] *verb*
1. ABANDON.
2. DEFECT.

deserted *adjective*
1. ABANDONED.
2. LONELY.

desertion *noun* ABANDONMENT.

deserve *verb* EARN.

deserved *adjective* JUST.

desiccate *verb*
1. DRY.
2. DRY UP at **dry**.

desiccated *adjective* DRY.

design *verb*
1. To form a strategy for: *designed an elaborate propaganda campaign.*
    Syns: blueprint, cast, chart, contrive, devise, dope out (*Informal*), draw up, frame, plan, project. —*Idiom* lay plans.
2. To work out and arrange the parts or details of: *design a new town.*
    Syns: blueprint, lay out, map (out), plan, set out.
3. INTEND.

design *noun*
1. A method for making, doing, or accomplishing something: *a design for a civic center; a grand design for energy conservation.*
    Syns: blueprint, idea, layout, plan, project, schema, scheme, strategy. —*Idiom* game plan.
2. FIGURE.
3. INTENTION.

designate *verb*
1. To make known or identify, as by signs: *Barriers designated the border crossing.*
    Syns: denote, indicate, point out, show, specify.
2. APPOINT.
3. APPROPRIATE.

4. CALL.
5. NAME.

designation *noun*
1. APPOINTMENT.
2. NAME.

designative *adjective*
Serving to designate or indicate:
applause designative of approval.
   Syns: denotative, denotive,
   designatory, exhibitive, indicative,
   indicatory.

designatory *adjective* DESIGNATIVE.

designee *noun* APPOINTEE.

designing *adjective* CALCULATING.

desirable *adjective*
Arousing erotic desire: *a desirable girl.*
   Syns: concupiscible (*Archaic*),
   desireful (*Archaic*), sexy (*Slang*).

desire *verb*
1. To have a strong longing for: *He
   gave her everything her heart desired.
   We only desire peace.*
   Syns: ache, covet, crave, hanker,
   hone² (for *or* after) (*Regional*), long²,
   pant, yearn for (*or* after), wish.
2. CHOOSE.

desire *noun*
1. A strong wish for what promises
   enjoyment or pleasure: *his desire for
   power; a desire for affection.*
   Syns: appetence (*also* appetency),
   appetite, appetition, craving, hunger,
   itch, longing, lust, yearning, yen
   (*Informal*).
2. Sexual hunger: *mistook physical desire
   for love.*
   Syns: aphrodisia, concupiscence,
   eroticism, itch, lust, lustfulness,
   passion, prurience (*also* pruriency).

desireful *adjective* DESIRABLE.

desirous *adjective* GREEDY.

desist *verb*
1. ABANDON.
2. STOP.

desolate *verb* DEVASTATE.

desolate *adjective* LONELY.

desolating *adjective* CONSUMPTIVE.

desolation *noun* EMPTINESS.

despair *verb*
To lose all hope: *despaired of ever
escaping the prison.*
   Syns: despond, give up.

despair *noun*
Utter lack of hope: *was in a state of
despair just before committing suicide.*
   Syns: desperateness, desperation,
   despond, despondency (*also*
   despondence), hopelessness. —*Idioms*
   cave of despair, slough of despond.

despairful *adjective* DESPONDENT.

despairing *adjective* DESPONDENT.

desperate *adjective*
1. CRITICAL.
2. DESPONDENT.
3. INTENSE.

desperateness *noun* DESPAIR.

desperation *noun* DESPAIR.

despicable *adjective*
1. FILTHY.
2. INFAMOUS.
3. SORDID.

despisable *adjective* FILTHY.

despisal *noun*
The feeling of despising: *his despisal of
the idle rich.*
   Syns: contempt, despisement, despite,
   disdain, scorn.

despise *verb*
1. To regard with utter contempt and
   disdain: *despised his opponents.*
   Syns: abhor, contemn, contempt
   (*Archaic*), disdain, scorn, scout²,
   sneer (at). —*Idioms* have no use for,
   look down on (*or* upon), view with a
   scornful eye, want no part of.
2. HATE.

despisement *noun* DESPISAL.

despite *noun*
1. DEFIANCE.
2. DESPISAL.
3. INDIGNITY.

despiteful *adjective* MALEVOLENT.

despitefulness *noun* MALEVOLENCE.

despoil *verb* SACK².

despond *verb*
1. BROOD.
2. DESPAIR.

despond *noun* DESPAIR.

despondency *also* **despondence** *noun*
1. DESPAIR.
2. GLOOM.

despondent *adjective*
Having lost all hope: *was despondent
after the divorce.*
   Syns: despairful, despairing,
   desperate, forlorn, hopeless.

despot *noun*
1. AUTHORITARIAN.
2. DICTATOR.

despotic *adjective*
1. ABSOLUTE.
2. AUTHORITARIAN.

despotism *noun*
1. ABSOLUTISM.
2. TYRANNY.

destine *verb* FATE.

destined *adjective* FATED.

destiny *noun* FATE.

destitute *adjective*
1. ABANDONED.

2. EMPTY.

3. POOR.

destitution *noun* POVERTY.

destroy *verb*

1. To cause the complete ruin or wreckage of: *paintings destroyed by fire; drugs that destroyed her health; news that destroyed his hopes.*
   Syns: demolish, dynamite, finish, ruin, ruinate (*Regional*), shatter, sink, smash, total, torpedo, undo, wrack, wreck. —*Idiom* put the kibosh on.

2. To break up so that reconstruction is impossible: *destroy a condemned building.*
   Syns: demolish, dismantle, knock down, level, pull down, pulverize, raze, rubble, tear down.

3. BREAK.

4. BREAK DOWN at **break.**

5. KILL.

6. MURDER.

destroyer *noun* RUIN.

destruction *noun*

1. The state of being destroyed: *a tornado that left destruction in its path.*
   Syns: devastation, havoc, ruin, ruination, wrack, wreck, wreckage. —*Idiom* wrack and ruin.

2. BREAKAGE.

3, 4. RUIN.

destructive *adjective*

1. Having the capability or effect of damaging irreparably: *a destructive ice storm; drugs that are destructive influences on youth.*
   Syns: pernicious, ruinous, shattering.

2. FATAL.

desuetude *noun* OBSOLETENESS.

desultory *adjective*

1. AIMLESS.

2. RANDOM.

detach *verb*

1. To separate one thing from another thing: *detached the side panels from the truck.*
   Syns: disconnect, disengage, uncouple.

2. To remove from association with: *could not detach himself from his past.*
   Syns: abstract, disassociate, dissociate, withdraw.

detached *adjective*

1. Lacking interest in one's surroundings or worldly affairs: *took a detached view of the conflict.*
   Syns: aloof, disinterested, incurious, indifferent, unconcerned, uninterested.

2. COOL.

3. NEUTRAL.

4. SOLITARY.

detachment *noun*

1. The act or process of detaching: *detachment of a freight car from a train.*
   Syns: disconnection, disengagement, separation, uncoupling.

2. Dissociation from one's surroundings or worldly affairs: *viewed the crisis with cold detachment.*
   Syns: aloofness, distance, remoteness.

3. *Mil.* A unit of troops on special assignment: *an honor-guard detachment.*
   Syn: detail (*Mil.*).

4. DIVISION.

5. FAIRNESS.

6. FORCE.

detail *noun*

1. A small, often specialized element of a whole: *asked to see the details of the contract.*
   Syns: item, particular, punctilio, technicality. —*Idiom* fine print.

2. CIRCUMSTANCE.

3. DETACHMENT.

4. ELEMENT.

   detail *verb* STIPULATE.

detailed *adjective*

Characterized by attention to detail: *a detailed account of the trip.*
   Syns: blow-by-blow, circumstantial, full, itemized, minute[1], particular, particularized, thorough.

detain *verb*

1. ARREST.

2. DELAY.

3. HOLD.

detainment *noun* DELAY.

detect *verb* CATCH.

detectable *adjective* PERCEPTIBLE.

detective *noun*

A person whose work is investigating crimes or obtaining hidden evidence or information: *hired a detective to get the needed facts.*
   Syns: dick (*Slang*), eye (*Informal*), gumshoe (*Slang*), investigator, Javert, sleuth (*Informal*).

detention *noun* ARREST.

deter *verb*

1. DISSUADE.

2. PREVENT.

deteriorate *verb*

1. To become lower in quality, character, or condition: *a school system rapidly deteriorating; mental health that had deteriorated.*
   Syns: decline, degenerate, descend, disimprove, disintegrate, retrograde,

sink, worsen. —*Idioms* get no better
fast, go to the bad.
2. DECAY.
3. FADE.
deterioration *noun*
1. Descent to a lower level or condition:
*concerned about widespread moral
deterioration.*
Syns: atrophy, decadence, declension,
declination, decline, degeneracy,
degeneration, disintegration,
worsening.
2. DECAY.
3. FAILURE.
4. RUIN.
determent *noun* PREVENTION.
determinate *adjective*
1. DEFINITE.
2. RESTRICTED.
determination *noun*
1, 2. DECISION.
3. RULING.
determinative *adjective*
1. DECISIVE.
2. DEFINITIVE.
3. FATEFUL.
determine *verb*
1. To fix the limits of: *Surveyors
determined the property boundaries.*
Syns: bound^2, delimit, delimitate,
demarcate, limit, mark out (*or* off),
measure.
2. DECIDE.
3. DISCOVER.
4. JUDGE.
determined *adjective*
1. DECISIVE.
2. FIRM^1.
3. SET^1.
deterrence *noun* PREVENTION.
deterrent *adjective* PREVENTIVE.
deterring *adjective* PREVENTIVE.
detest *verb* HATE.
detestable *adjective*
1. FILTHY.
2. INFAMOUS.
detestation *noun*
1, 2. HATE.
detonate *verb* EXPLODE.
detonation *noun* BLAST.
detour *verb* SKIRT.
detract *verb* BELITTLE.
detracting *adjective*
1. DISPARAGING.
2. LIBELOUS.
detraction *noun*
1. BELITTLEMENT.
2. LIBEL.
detractive *adjective* LIBELOUS.
detractory *adjective* LIBELOUS.

detriment *noun*
1. DISADVANTAGE.
2. HARM.
detrimental *adjective* HARMFUL.
de trop *adjective* SUPERFLUOUS.
devaluate *verb* DEPRECIATE.
devaluation *noun* DEPRECIATION.
devalue *verb* DEPRECIATE.
devastate *verb*
To destroy completely while conquering
or occupying: *The invaders devastated
the villages in their path.*
Syns: depredate, desolate, ravage,
spoil (*Obs.*), spoliate, strip^1, waste.
—*Idiom* lay waste.
devastation *noun*
1. DESTRUCTION.
2. RUIN.
develop *verb*
1. To bring (a product, idea, etc.) into
being: *developed gasoline from coal.*
Syns: generate, produce.
2. To be disclosed gradually: *As the plot
developed, the story got better.*
Syns: evolve, unfold.
3. To come gradually to have: *develop a
taste for caviar.*
Syn: form.
4. COME.
5. CONTRACT.
6, 7. ELABORATE.
8. GAIN.
9. MATURE.
developed *adjective* MATURE.
developer *noun* BUILDER.
development *noun*
1. A progression from a simple form to
a more complex one: *the development
of man.*
Syns: evolution, evolvement, growth,
progress, unfolding.
2. BUILD-UP.
3. EVENT.
4. PROGRESS.
deviance *noun* ABNORMALITY.
deviancy *noun* ABNORMALITY.
deviant *noun*
One whose sexual behavior differs from
the accepted norm: *an aggressive deviant
who had to be institutionalized.*
Syns: deviate, pervert.
deviant *adjective* ABNORMAL.
deviate *verb*
1. To turn away from a prescribed
course of action or conduct: *never
deviated from the truth.*
Syns: depart, digress, diverge, err,
stray, swerve.
2. DIGRESS.
deviate *noun* DEVIANT.
deviate *adjective* ABNORMAL.

deviating *adjective*
1. ABNORMAL.
2. ERRANT.

deviation *noun*
1. A departing from what is prescribed: *tolerated no deviation from preflight procedures.*
    Syns: aberration, departure, divergence (*also* divergency), diversion.
2. ABNORMALITY.
3. DIGRESSION.

deviative *adjective* ABNORMAL.

device *noun*
1. Something, as a machine, devised for a particular function: *a new food-processing device.*
    Syns: apparatus, appliance, contraption, contrivance.
2. FIGURE.
3. INVENTION.
4. TRICK.

devilish *adjective* FIENDISH.

devious *adjective*
1. CROOKED.
2. ERRATIC.
3. UNDERHAND.

deviousness *noun* INDIRECTION.

devise *verb*
1. DESIGN.
2. INVENT.
3. LEAVE¹.

devitalize *verb* ENERVATE.

devoid *adjective*
1, 2. EMPTY.

devolve *verb* FALL.

devote *verb*
1. To give over by or as if by vow to a higher purpose: *a nun who devoted her life to Christ.*
    Syns: consecrate, dedicate, hallow.
2. APPLY.

devoted *adjective* SACRED.

devotee *noun*
1. One zealously devoted to a religion: *a devotee of Zen.*
    Syns: fanatic, sectary, votary.
2. ADMIRER.
3. ENTHUSIAST.

devotion *noun*
1. ADORATION.
2. ATTACHMENT.

devour *verb*
1, 2. CONSUME.
3. EAT.
4. EAT UP at **eat**.
5. WASTE.

devout *adjective* HOLY.

dexterity *noun*
1. Skillfulness in the use of the hands or body: *performed with dexterity on the parallel bars.*
    Syns: address, adroitness, deftness, dexterousness, prowess, readiness, skill, sleight.
2. AGILITY.

dexterous *adjective*
1. Exhibiting or possessing skill and ease in performance: *dexterous handling of the sports car.*
    Syns: adroit, clever, deft, facile, handy, nimble, slick.
2. ARTFUL.

dexterousness *noun*
1. AGILITY.
2. DEXTERITY.

diablerie *also* **diablery** *noun*
1. CRIME.
2. MISCHIEF.

diabolic *also* **diabolical** *adjective* FIENDISH.

diagonal *adjective* BIAS.

dial *verb* TELEPHONE.

dial *noun* FACE.

dialect *noun*
1. An often regional form of a language not considered standard: *Cockney is a dialect of English.*
    Syns: argot, cant², jargon, lingo, patois, vernacular.
2, 3. LANGUAGE.

dialogue *also* **dialog** *noun* CONVERSATION.

diametric *adjective* OPPOSITE.

diamond *noun* TREASURE.

diaphanous *adjective* FILMY.

diatribe *noun* TIRADE.

dibs *noun* CLAIM.

dick *noun* DETECTIVE.

dicker *verb* HAGGLE.

dictate *verb*
To set forth expressly and authoritatively: *The victors dictated the surrender terms.*
    Syns: decree, fix, impose, lay down, ordain, prescribe. —*Idioms* call the tune (*or* signals *or* shots), lay it on the line.

dictate to *verb* BOSS.

dictate *noun*
1. COMMAND.
2. RULE.

dictative *adjective* DICTATORIAL.

dictator *noun*
1. An absolute ruler, esp. one who is harsh and oppressive: *Stalin was a bloody dictator.*
    Syns: Big Brother, despot, führer (*also* fuehrer) (*German*), oppressor, totalitarian, tyrant. —*Idioms* man on

dictatorial | dig

horseback, strong man, tinhorn
dictator.
2. AUTHORITARIAN.

dictatorial *adjective*
1. Tending to dictate: *a dictatorial
executive who imposed his will on
everyone.*
Syns: authoritarian, bossy, dictative,
doctrinaire, dogmatic, domineering,
imperious, magisterial, masterful,
overbearing, peremptory.
2. ABSOLUTE.
3. AUTHORITARIAN.

dictatorship *noun*
1, 2. ABSOLUTISM.
3. TYRANNY.

diction *noun* WORDING.

dictionary *noun* VOCABULARY.

didactic also **didactical** *adjective*
MORAL.

diddle *verb*
1. CHEAT.
2. IDLE.
3. MESS AROUND at **mess.**

diddler *noun* CHEAT.

die *verb*
1. To cease living: *She died at an early
age.*
Syns: check out (*Slang*), croak
(*Slang*), decease, demise, depart,
drop, expire, go, kick in (*Slang*), kick
off (*Slang*), pass away, pass (on),
perish, pop off (*Informal*), succumb.
—*Idioms* bite the dust, breathe one's
last, cash in one's chips, depart this
life, give up the ghost, go to one's
grave, kick the bucket, meet one's
end (*or* Maker), pass on to the Great
Beyond, take a cab, turn up one's
toes.
2. *Theol.* To experience spiritual death:
*Those who believe in God shall never
die.*
Syn: perish.
3. FADE.
4. SUBSIDE.

die out (or **away**) *verb* DISAPPEAR.

die-hard also **diehard** *noun*
REACTIONARY.

die-hard also **diehard** *adjective*
1. REACTIONARY.
2. STUBBORN.

differ *verb*
1. To be unlike or dissimilar: *The two
prime ministers differed in every
aspect.*
Syns: disagree, vary. —*Idiom* be at
variance.
2. To be of different opinion: *politicians
differing on national health insurance.*

Syns: disaccord, disagree, discord,
dissent, vary.

difference *noun*
1. The condition of being unlike or
dissimilar: *noted the vast difference
between liberals and conservatives.*
Syns: alterity, discrepancy (*also*
discrepance), disparity, dissimilarity,
dissimilitude, distinction,
divarication, divergence (*also*
divergency), unlikeness.
2. GAP.
3. VARIATION.

different *adjective*
1. Not like another in nature, quality,
amount, or form: *two different ways
of working; two brothers who could not
have been more different.*
Syns: disparate, dissimilar, divergent,
diverse, unlike, variant, various.
2. FRESH.

differentiate *verb*
1, 2. DISTINGUISH.

differentiation *noun* DISTINCTION.

difficile *adjective* DIFFICULT.

difficult *adjective*
1. Not easy to do, achieve, or master: *a
difficult problem; a difficult climb.*
Syns: difficile, hard, knotty,
laborious, serious, slavish, sticky
(*Informal*), tall, tough, uphill.
2. BURDENSOME.
3. CONTRARY.
4. INCONVENIENT.

difficultly *adverb* HARD.

difficulty *noun*
1. Something that obstructs progress
and requires great effort to overcome:
*His chief difficulty was a physical
weakness. The negotiators ran into
difficulty.*
Syns: asperity, hardship, rigor,
vicissitude. —*Idioms* a hard nut to
crack, a hard row to hoe, heavy
sledding.
2. TROUBLE.

diffidence *noun* MODESTY.

diffident *adjective* MODEST.

diffuse *verb* SPREAD.

diffuse *adjective* WORDY.

dig *verb*
1. To break, turn over, or remove
(earth, sand, etc.) with or as if with a
tool: *dig for carrots; dig through a
trunk for winter clothes.*
Syns: delve (*Archaic*), excavate, grub,
shovel, spade.
2. To make by digging: *dig a well.*
Syns: excavate, scoop, shovel, spade.
3. To thrust against or into: *dug me in
the ribs.*

Syns: jab, jog, nudge, poke, prod.
4. ENJOY.
5. EXPLORE.
6. LIVE¹.
7. RAM.
8. UNDERSTAND.
dig up (or **out**) verb UNCOVER.
dig noun
1. An act of thrusting into or against, as to attract attention: *gave me a sharp dig in the ribs and pointed to the crowd.*
   Syns: jab, nudge, poke, stab.
2. CRACK.
digest verb ABSORB.
digestion noun ABSORPTION.
dignification noun EXALTATION.
dignify verb
1. EXALT.
2. GRACE.
dignitary noun
An important, influential person: *State Department dignitaries.*
   Syns: big, big shot (*Slang*), big-timer (*Slang*), big wheel (*Slang*), bigwig (*Informal*), character, eminence, heavyweight (*Informal*), leader, lion, luminary, muckamuck (*also* mucketymuck) (*Slang*), nabob, notability, notable, personage, personality, somebody (*Informal*), someone (*Informal*), VIP (*Informal*).
dignity noun HONOR.
digress verb
1. To turn aside from the main subject in writing or speaking: *The senator had the annoying habit of digressing from the main theme of his speeches.*
   Syns: deviate, divagate, diverge, excurse, stray, wander. —*Idiom* go off at (*or* on) a tangent.
2. DEVIATE.
digression noun
1. The act of digressing: *His statements on monetary policy, by way of digression, are very misleading.*
   Syns: aside, divagation, parenthesis.
2. An instance of digressing: *His aunt used to break off now and then into a brief digression about the old days.*
   Syns: aside, deviation, discursion, divagation, divergence (*also* divergency), ecbole (*Rhet.*), episode, excursion, excursus, irrelevancy, parenthesis, tangent.
digressive adjective
Marked by or given to digression: *a digressive remark; an author who is habitually digressive.*
   Syns: discursive, episodic, excursive,

parenthetic (*also* parenthetical), tangential.
digs noun HOME.
dilapidated adjective
1. SHABBY.
2. RUINOUS.
dilate verb ELABORATE.
dilatory adjective SLOW.
dilemma noun PREDICAMENT.
dilettante noun AMATEUR.
dilettante adjective AMATEURISH.
dilettantish adjective AMATEURISH.
dilettantist adjective AMATEURISH.
diligence noun
Steady attention and effort, as to one's occupation: *worked with real diligence to finish the project.*
   Syns: application, assiduity, assiduousness, industriousness, industry, sedulousness.
diligent adjective
Characterized by steady attention and effort: *made a diligent search for the missing book.*
   Syns: assiduous, industrious, sedulous, studious.
dilly-dally verb DELAY.
dilute adjective
Lower than normal in strength or concentration due to admixture: *dilute wine.*
   Syns: cut, diluted, thin, washy, watered, watered-down, waterish, watery, weak.
dilute verb
To lessen the strength of by or as if by admixture: *The impact of his thesis was diluted by poor organization and bad writing. He always dilutes his drink with a splash of soda.*
   Syns: attenuate, cut, thin, water (down), weaken.
diluted adjective DILUTE.
dim verb
1. DULL.
2. OBSCURE.
dim adjective
1. DARK.
2. DULL.
3. FILMY.
4. UNCLEAR.
dimensions noun SIZE.
diminish verb DECREASE.
diminishment noun DECREASE.
diminution noun DECREASE.
diminutive adjective TINY.
dimness noun DARK.
dimwit noun DULLARD.
dimwitted adjective
1. MINDLESS.
2. STUPID.

din *noun* NOISE.
ding-a-ling *noun* CRACKPOT.
dingbat *noun* CRACKPOT.
dinge *noun* GLOOM.
dingy *adjective* SHABBY.
dip *verb*
1. To plunge briefly in or into a liquid:
   She dipped a piece of bread into her soup.
   Syns: douse, duck, dunk, immerge,
   immerse, souse, submerge, submerse.
2. To immerse in a coloring solution:
   dip Easter eggs.
   Syns: color, dye.
3. To take a substance, as liquid, from a
   container by plunging the hand or a
   utensil into it: *dipped water from the
   leaky boat; dipped punch from the
   bowl.*
   Syns: bail², lade, ladle, scoop up.
4. DROP.
5. FALL.
6. PAWN¹.
dip into *verb* BROWSE.
dip *noun*
1. DEPRESSION.
2. FALL.
3. PLUNGE.
diplomacy *noun* TACT.
diplomatic *adjective* DELICATE.
dippy *adjective* FOOLISH.
dire *adjective*
1. CRITICAL.
2. FATEFUL.
3. FEARFUL.
direct *adjective*
1. Proceeding or lying in an
   uninterrupted line or course: *a direct
   path across the fields.*
   Syns: straight, straightforward,
   through.
2. Of unbroken descent or lineage: *a
   direct descendant of King David.*
   Syn: lineal.
3. FRANK.
4. IMMEDIATE.
5. INTIMATE¹.
direct *verb*
1. ADDRESS.
2. ADMINISTER.
3. AIM.
4. APPLY.
5. COMMAND.
6. CONDUCT.
7. CONTROL.
8. GUIDE.
direct *adverb*
1, 2. DIRECTLY.
3. PRECISELY.
direction *noun*
1. ADDRESS.

2. ADMINISTRATION.
3. COMMAND.
4. GOVERNMENT.
5. GUIDANCE.
directive *noun* COMMAND.
directly *adverb*
1. In a direct line: *went directly to
   Atlanta; flew directly north.*
   Syns: dead, direct, due, right,
   straight.
2. With precision or absolute
   conformity: *hit him directly on the
   kneecap.*
   Syns: dead, direct, exactly, fair, flush,
   just, precisely, right, smack-dab
   (*Slang*), square, straight.
3. Without delay: *I'll see you at the
   restaurant directly.*
   Syns: forthwith, immediately, instant
   (*Poetic*), now. —*Idioms* at once, first
   off, right away (*or* off), straight away
   (*or* off).
4. IMMEDIATELY.
director *noun*
1. BOSS.
2. CHIEF.
3. EXECUTIVE.
4. GUIDE.
direful *adjective*
1. FATEFUL.
2. FEARFUL.
dirt *noun*
1. FILTH.
2. OBSCENITY.
dirtiness *noun*
1. The condition or state of being dirty:
   the dirtiness of the slum apartment.
   Syns: filth, filthiness, foulness,
   griminess, uncleanliness, uncleanness.
2. IMPURITY.
3. OBSCENITY.
dirty *adjective*
1. Covered or stained with or as if with
   dirt or other impurities: *sending the
   dirty clothes to the laundry.*
   Syns: black, filthy, grimy, grubby,
   smutty, soiled, soily, unclean,
   uncleanly.
2. OBSCENE.
3. ROUGH.
dirty *verb*
1. To make dirty: *dirtied the cuffs of his
   shirt when he changed his typewriter
   ribbon.*
   Syns: befoul, begrime, besoil, black,
   blacken, smudge, smutch, soil.
2. BLACKEN.
disable *verb*
1. To render powerless or motionless by
   inflicting severe injury: *veterans*

*disabled in the war; disabled the tank
with a carefully placed grenade.*
Syns: cripple, immobilize,
incapacitate, knock out (*Informal*),
paralyze, prostrate. —*Idioms* lay low,
put out of action (*or* commission).
2. UNFIT.

disaccord *noun* CONFLICT.
  disaccord *verb*
  1. CONFLICT.
  2. DIFFER.

disacknowledge *verb* REPUDIATE.

disadvantage *noun*
An unfavorable condition, circumstance,
or characteristic: *One of the
disadvantages of the car is its enormous
gas consumption.*
  Syns: detriment, drawback, handicap,
minus, shortcoming.

disadvantaged *adjective* DEPRESSED.

disadvantageous *adjective*
  1. INCONVENIENT.
  2. UNFAVORABLE.

disaffect *verb*
  1. DISLIKE.
  2. ESTRANGE.

disaffection *noun*
  1. BREACH.
  2. DISLIKE.
  3. ESTRANGEMENT.

disaffirm *verb* DENY.

disaffirmation *noun* DENIAL.

disagree *verb*
  1, 2. DIFFER.

disagreeable *adjective*
  1. ILL-TEMPERED.
  2. UNPLEASANT.

disagreement *noun*
  1. ARGUMENT.
  2. GAP.

disallow *verb*
  1. FORBID.
  2. REFUSE.

disallowance *noun*
  1. FORBIDDANCE.
  2. REFUSAL.

disappear *verb*
  1. To pass out of sight either gradually
or suddenly: *The top of the skyscraper
disappeared in the fog.*
  Syns: evanesce, evanish, evaporate,
fade, vanish.
  2. To cease to exist: *The ancient
Egyptian people disappeared long ago.*
  Syns: die out (*or* away), expire.

disappearance *noun*
The act or an example of passing out of
sight: *The sudden disappearance of the
financier is causing speculation about his
honesty.*

Syns: evanescence, evanishment,
evanition, evaporation, fade-out.

disappoint *verb*
To cause unhappiness by failing to
satisfy the hopes, desires, or
expectations of: *The candidate's speech
disappointed his supporters.*
  Syns: cast down, discontent,
disgruntle, dishearten, dissatisfy, let
down.

disappointing *adjective*
Disturbing because of failure to
measure up to a standard or produce
the desired results: *disappointing test
scores; a disappointing state of affairs.*
  Syns: disheartening, dissatisfying,
sorry, unlucky.

disappointment *noun*
Unhappiness caused by the failure of
one's hopes, desires, or expectations:
*will feel keen disappointment when his
application is rejected.*
  Syns: discontent, discontentment,
disgruntlement, disheartenment,
dissatisfaction, letdown, regret.

disapprobation *noun* DISAPPROVAL.

disapproval *noun*
Unfavorable opinion or judgment:
*couldn't keep the tone of disapproval out
of her voice.*
  Syns: disapprobation, displeasure.

disapprove *verb*
  1. To have or express an unfavorable
opinion: *Why do you disapprove of the
new fashions?*
  Syns: deprecate, discountenance,
disesteem, disfavor, frown on (*or*
upon), object² (to). —*Idioms* hold no
brief for, not go for, take a dim view
of, take exception to.
  2. REFUSE.

disarrange *verb*
  1. DISORDER.
  2. TOUSLE.

disarranged *adjective* DISORDERED.

disarrangement *noun* DISORDER.

disarray *noun* DISORDER.
  disarray *verb* DISORDER.

disassemble *verb* TAKE DOWN at
take.

disassociate *verb* DETACH.

disaster *noun*
An occurrence inflicting widespread
destruction and distress: *It took a long
time to recover from the disaster caused
by the flood.*
  Syns: calamity, cataclysm,
catastrophe, tragedy.

disastrous *adjective* FATAL.

disavow *verb* REPUDIATE.

disbelief *noun*
The refusal or reluctance to believe:
looked at me in pure disbelief.
   Syns: discredit, incredulity, unbelief.
disbelieve *verb*
To give no credence to: *We disbelieve
their story as mere rumor.*
   Syns: discredit, misbelieve, unbelieve.
   —*Idioms* set no store by, take no
stock in.
disbelieving *adjective* INCREDULOUS.
disburden *verb*
1. RID.
2. UNLOAD.
disbursal *noun* DISTRIBUTION.
disburse *verb*
1. DISTRIBUTE.
2. SPEND.
disbursement *noun* COST.
discard *verb*
To let go or get rid of as being no
longer of use, value, etc.: *plans to
discard all the linens in the old trunk.*
   Syns: chuck[1] (*Informal*), dispose of,
ditch, dump, jettison, junk, scrap[1],
shuck (off), throw away, throw out.
discard *noun* DISPOSAL.
discarnate *adjective* IMMATERIAL.
discern *verb*
1. To perceive and fix the identity of:
*We could barely discern a sail on the
horizon.*
   Syns: descry, distinguish, make out,
pick out, spot.
2. CATCH.
3. DISTINGUISH.
discernible *adjective* PERCEPTIBLE.
discerning *adjective*
1. CRITICAL.
2. WISE[1].
discernment *noun*
Skill in perceiving, discriminating, or
judging: *She hires her assistants with
such discernment that none ever
disappoints her.*
   Syns: acumen, astuteness, clear-
sightedness, discrimination, eye,
keenness, nose, penetration,
perceptiveness, percipience,
perspicacity, sagacity, sageness,
shrewdness, wit.
discharge *verb*
1. To release from military duty: *will be
discharged from the army next week.*
   Syns: demobilize, muster out,
separate.
2. To pass or pour out into: *The Illinois
River discharges into the Mississippi.*
   Syns: emit, empty, flow, issue, vent,
void.

3. DISMISS.
4. EXCUSE.
5. FREE.
6. FULFILL.
7. SETTLE.
8. SHOOT.
9. UNLOAD.
discharge *noun* DISMISSAL.
disciple *noun* FOLLOWER.
disciplinary *adjective* PUNISHING.
discipline *noun*
1. BRANCH.
2. PUNISHMENT.
discipline *verb*
1. EDUCATE.
2. PUNISH.
disclaim *verb* REPUDIATE.
disclaimer *noun* DENIAL.
disclose *verb*
1. COMMUNICATE.
2. REVEAL.
disclosure *noun* REVELATION.
discolor *verb* STAIN.
discombobulate *verb*
1. AGITATE.
2. CONFUSE.
discombobulated *adjective*
CONFUSED.
discomfiture *noun* EMBARRASSMENT.
discomfort *noun*
1, 2. INCONVENIENCE.
discomfort *verb*
1. EMBARRASS.
2. INCONVENIENCE.
discompose *verb* AGITATE.
discomposure *noun* EMBARRASSMENT.
disconcert *verb* EMBARRASS.
disconcerted *adjective* EMBARRASSED.
disconcertion *noun* EMBARRASSMENT.
disconcertment *noun*
EMBARRASSMENT.
disconnect *verb* DETACH.
disconnection *noun* DETACHMENT.
disconsonant *adjective*
1. CONFLICTING.
2. INCONGRUOUS.
discontent *verb* DISAPPOINT.
discontent *noun* DISAPPOINTMENT.
discontentment *noun*
DISAPPOINTMENT.
discontinue *verb*
1. ABANDON.
2. STOP.
3. SUSPEND.
discontinuity *noun* BREAK.
discord *noun* CONFLICT.
discord *verb*
1. CONFLICT.
2. DIFFER.

discordant *adjective*
1. HARSH.
2. INCONGRUOUS.
3, 4. INHARMONIOUS.

discount *verb*
1. BELITTLE.
2. DEDUCT.
3. WRITE OFF at write.

discount *noun* DEDUCTION.

discountenance *verb*
1. DISAPPROVE.
2. EMBARRASS.

discourage *verb*
1. To make less hopeful or enthusiastic: *The magnitude of the problem discouraged me.*
   Syns: dishearten, dispirit.
2. DISSUADE.

discouraging *adjective*
Tending to make less hopeful or enthusiastic: *read a discouraging analysis of the current economic situation.*
   Syns: disheartening, dispiriting.

discourse *noun*
1. A formal, lengthy exposition of a topic: *wrote a discourse on trade deficits.*
   Syns: disquisition, dissertation, treatise.
2. SPEECH.

discourse *verb* CONVERSE¹.

discourser *noun* CONVERSATIONALIST.

discourteous *adjective* RUDE.

discover *verb*
1. To obtain knowledge or awareness of something not known before, as through observation, study, etc.: *discovered that the world is round.*
   Syns: ascertain, determine, find out, hear, learn.
2. BETRAY.
3. REVEAL.

discovery *noun*
Something that has been discovered: *Radium is one of the great discoveries of science.*
   Syns: find, finding, strike.

discredit *verb*
1. To cause to be no longer believed or valued: *new evidence that discredits previous research.*
   Syns: debunk, explode, puncture, shoot down. —*Idioms* knock the bottom out of, shoot full of holes.
2. DISBELIEVE.
3. DISGRACE.
4. REFUTE.

discredit *noun*
1. DISBELIEF.
2. DISGRACE.

discreditable *adjective* DISGRACEFUL.

discreet *adjective*
1. CONSERVATIVE.
2. DELICATE.

discrepancy also **discrepance** *noun*
1. DIFFERENCE.
2. GAP.

discrepant *adjective*
1. CONFLICTING.
2. INCONGRUOUS.

discrete *adjective*
1. DISTINCT.
2. INDIVIDUAL.

discretely *adverb* SEPARATELY.

discreteness *noun* INDIVIDUALITY.

discretion *noun* WILL¹.

discretionary *adjective*
1. ARBITRARY.
2. OPTIONAL.

discriminate *verb*
1. To act on the basis of prejudice: *Some employers used to discriminate against workers for union activity.*
   Syn: prejudice (against).
2, 3. DISTINGUISH.

discriminate *adjective* DISCRIMINATING.

discriminating *adjective*
1. Able to recognize small differences or draw fine distinctions: *discriminating in his choice of food and wine.*
   Syns: discriminate, discriminative, discriminatory, select, selective.
2. CRITICAL.

discrimination *noun*
1. The ability to distinguish, esp. to recognize small differences or draw fine distinctions: *choice of furniture that shows little artistic discrimination.*
   Syns: refinement, selectiveness, selectivity.
2. DISTINCTION.

discriminative *adjective* DISCRIMINATING.

discriminatory *adjective* DISCRIMINATING.

disculpate *verb* CLEAR.

discursion *noun* DIGRESSION.

discursive *adjective* DIGRESSIVE.

discuss *verb*
1. To speak together and exchange ideas and opinions about: *discussing the pros and cons of nuclear power.*
   Syns: hash over (*Informal*), kick around (*Informal*), knock about (*Informal*), knock around (*Informal*), moot, talk over, thrash out, thresh out, toss about (*Informal*), toss around (*Informal*). —*Idiom* go into a huddle.
2. EAT.

discussant *noun* CONFEREE.

discussion *noun*
1, 2. CONFERENCE.

discussor *noun* CONFEREE.

disdain *noun*
1. ARROGANCE.
2. DESPISAL.
disdain *verb* DESPISE.

disdainful *adjective* ARROGANT.

disease *noun*
A pathological condition of mind or body: *a disease of the eyes.*
Syns: affection², ailment, complaint, disorder, ill, illness, infirmity, malady, sickness.

disembark *verb* LAND.

disembarrass *verb* RID.

disembodied *adjective* IMMATERIAL.

disencumber *verb* RID.

disengage *verb*
1. BREAK.
2. CLEAR.
3. DETACH.
4. UNDO.

disengaged *adjective* CLEAR.

disengagement *noun* DETACHMENT.

disentangle *verb* CLEAR.

disesteem *noun* DISGRACE.
disesteem *verb* DISAPPROVE.

disfavor *noun* DISLIKE.
disfavor *verb* DISAPPROVE.

disfigure *verb* DEFORM.

disfigurement *noun* DEFORMITY.

disgorge *verb* ERUPT.

disgrace *noun*
Loss of or damage to one's reputation: *a public official who had to resign in disgrace.*
Syns: discredit, disesteem, dishonor, disrepute, ignominy, obloquy, opprobrium, shame. —*Idioms* bad name (*or* odor), ill repute.
disgrace *verb*
To damage in reputation: *disgraced his family with his arrest for drug dealing.*
Syns: discredit, dishonor, shame. —*Idioms* be a reproach to, put to the blush.

disgraceful *adjective*
1. Meriting or causing shame or dishonor: *a disgraceful secret that is being withheld from the public; disgraceful behavior.*
Syns: discreditable, dishonorable, disreputable, ignominious, obloquious, opprobrious, shabby, shameful.
2. DEPLORABLE.

disgracefulness *noun* INFAMY.

disgruntle *verb* DISAPPOINT.

disgruntlement *noun* DISAPPOINTMENT.

disguise *verb*
To change or modify so as to prevent recognition of the true identity or character of: *disguised her interest with a blasé attitude.*
Syns: bemask, camouflage, cloak, cover up, dissemble, dissimulate, mask, masquerade, sleek.
disguise *noun*
1. Clothes or other personal effects, such as make-up, used to conceal one's identity: *will wear the disguise of a witch to the fancy-dress ball.*
Syn: costume.
2. FAÇADE.

disguisement *noun* FAÇADE.

disgust *verb*
To offend the senses or feelings of: *The sight of the cockroach scurrying around disgusted her.*
Syns: nauseate, repel, repulse, revolt, sicken. —*Idiom* turn one's stomach.
disgust *noun*
Extreme repugnance excited by something offensive: *behavior that arouses disgust.*
Syns: aversion, loathing, repulsion.

disgusted *adjective* SICK.

disgusting *adjective*
1. FILTHY.
2. OFFENSIVE.

disharmonic *adjective* INHARMONIOUS.

disharmonious *adjective* INHARMONIOUS.

dishearten *verb*
1. DISAPPOINT.
2. DISCOURAGE.

disheartening *adjective*
1. DISAPPOINTING.
2. DISCOURAGING.

disheartenment *noun* DISAPPOINTMENT.

dishevel *verb* TOUSLE.

disheveled *adjective* MESSY.

dishonest *adjective*
1. Given to or marked by deliberate concealment or misrepresentation of the truth: *a sneaky, dishonest manipulator of people; a dishonest answer to the question.*
Syns: deceitful, lying, mendacious, shifty, untruthful, unveridical.
2. CORRUPT.

dishonesty *noun*
1. Lack of integrity: *mistrust him because of his fundamental dishonesty.*
Syn: improbity.

2. CORRUPTION.
3. INDIRECTION.
dishonor *noun* DISGRACE.
dishonor *verb* DISGRACE.
dishonorable *adjective* DISGRACEFUL.
dishonorableness *noun* INFAMY.
disimpassioned *adjective* COOL.
disimprove *verb* DETERIORATE.
disinclination *noun*
1. DISLIKE.
2. INDISPOSITION.
disinclined *adjective* INDISPOSED.
disinfect *verb* STERILIZE.
disingenuity *noun* INSINCERITY.
disingenuous *adjective*
1. INSINCERE.
2. UNDERHAND.
disingenuousness *noun*
INSINCERITY.
disintegrate *verb*
1. BREAK UP at **break.**
2. DETERIORATE.
disintegration *noun*
1. DETERIORATION.
2. RUIN.
disinterest *noun*
1. APATHY.
2. FAIRNESS.
disinterested *adjective*
1. APATHETIC.
2. DETACHED.
3. NEUTRAL.
disinterestedness *noun* FAIRNESS.
disjoin *verb*
1. BREAK.
2. DIVIDE.
disjoint *verb*
1. BREAK.
2. DIVIDE.
dislike *verb*
To have a feeling of aversion for: *The two men heartily dislike each other.*
Syns: disaffect (*Archaic*), disrelish, mislike. —*Idiom* have no use for.
dislike *noun*
An attitude or feeling of aversion: *had a real dislike for folk music.*
Syns: disaffection, disfavor, disinclination, disrelish, distaste.
dislocate *verb*
1. DISTURB.
2. SLIP.
disloyal *adjective* FAITHLESS.
disloyalty *noun* FAITHLESSNESS.
dismal *adjective*
1, 2. GLOOMY.
3. SAD.
dismantle *verb*
1. DESTROY.
2. TAKE DOWN at **take.**

dismay *verb*
To deprive of courage or the power to act as a result of fear, anxiety, or disgust: *The news of plummeting stock prices dismayed speculators.*
Syns: appall, consternate, daunt, horrify, shake, shock.
dismay *noun*
A sudden or complete loss of courage in the face of trouble or danger: *looked at me in dismay when she learned she needed surgery.*
Syn: consternation.
dismayed *adjective* SHOCKED.
dismember *verb*
1. CRIPPLE.
2. TAKE DOWN at **take.**
dismiss *verb*
1. To end the employment of: *Workers who habitually arrive late are first warned, then dismissed.*
Syns: boot[1] (*Slang*), bounce (*Slang*), can (*Slang*), cashier, discharge, drop, fire (*Informal*), sack[1] (*Slang*), terminate. —*Idioms* give someone his walking papers, give someone the ax, give someone the gate, give someone the pink slip, let go.
2. To direct or allow to leave: *When the bell rang, the teacher dismissed the class.*
Syn: send away. —*Idioms* send about one's business, send packing, show the door to.
3. To rid one's mind of: *She thought of chasing the bus but dismissed the idea when another bus came into view.*
Syns: banish, cast out, dispel, kiss off (*Slang*), shut out.
4. DECLINE.
5. DROP.
6. EJECT.
dismissal *noun*
1. The act of dismissing or the condition of being dismissed from employment: *deeply resented his dismissal.*
Syns: discharge, firing (*Informal*), sack[1] (*Slang*), termination. —*Idioms* the boot, the bounce.
2. EJECTION.
dismount *verb* TAKE DOWN at **take.**
disobedience *noun*
The condition or practice of not obeying: *Disobedience was quickly punished in that household.*
Syns: insubordination, noncompliance, unruliness.
disobedient *adjective*
Refusing or failing to obey: *a disobedient child.*

Syns: insubordinate, lawless,
uncompliant, unruly.

disobey *verb*
To refuse or fail to obey: *disobeying
instructions.*
　Syns: break, defy, disregard, flout,
transgress, violate. —*Idiom* pay no
attention (*or* mind) to.

disorder *noun*
1. A lack of order or regular
arrangement: *We found the
burglarized apartment in disorder.*
　Syns: ballup (*Slang*), chaos, clutter,
confusedness, confusion,
disarrangement, disarray,
disorderliness, disorganization,
huddle, jumble, mess, mix-up,
muddle, scramble, snafu (*Slang*),
snarl[1], topsy-turviness, tumble,
turmoil.
2. A lack of civil order or peace:
*Looting and disorder prevailed during
the blackout.*
　Syns: anarchy, lawlessness, misrule.
3. DISEASE.
4. SICKNESS.

disorder *verb*
1. To put out of proper order: *Father
warned us not to disorder the books
and papers on his desk.*
　Syns: derange, disarrange, disarray,
disorganize, disrupt, disturb, jumble,
mess up, mix up, muddle, tumble,
unsettle, upset.
2. CONFUSE.
3. DISRUPT.
4. TOUSLE.
5. UPSET.

disordered *adjective*
1. In a condition of disorder: *disordered
schedules; disordered finances.*
　Syns: disarranged, disorganized,
disrupted.
2. CONFUSED.
3. INSANE.

disordering *noun* UPSET.
disorderliness *noun* DISORDER.
disorderly *adjective*
1. Lacking regular or logical order: *the
disorderly closet of a teen-ager.*
　Syns: messy, unsystematic.
2. Upsetting civil order or peace: *The
police moved to disperse the disorderly
crowd.*
　Syns: riotous, rowdy, unruly.

disorganization *noun*
1. DISORDER.
2. UPSET.

disorganize *verb* DISORDER.
disorganized *adjective* DISORDERED.
disown *verb* REPUDIATE.

disparage *verb* BELITTLE.
disparagement *noun* BELITTLEMENT.
disparaging *adjective*
Tending or intending to belittle: *made
disparaging comments about the other
editors.*
　Syns: belittling, decrying, deprecatory
(*also* deprecative), depreciating,
depreciative, depreciatory, derogatory,
detracting, pejorative, slighting,
uncomplimentary.

disparate *adjective* DIFFERENT.
disparity *noun*
1. DIFFERENCE.
2. GAP.
3. INEQUALITY.

dispassion *noun* FAIRNESS.
dispassionate *adjective*
1. FAIR.
2. NEUTRAL.

dispassionately *adverb* FAIRLY.
dispassionateness *noun* FAIRNESS.
dispatch *verb*
1. CONSUME.
2. KILL.
3. SEND.

dispatch *noun* HASTE.
dispel *verb*
1. DISMISS.
2. LIFT.
3. SCATTER.

dispensation *noun*
1. ADMINISTRATION.
2. DISTRIBUTION.

dispense *verb*
1. ADMINISTER.
2. DISTRIBUTE.
3. EXCUSE.

dispensing *noun* ADMINISTRATION.
disperse *verb*
1. DISTRIBUTE.
2. LIFT.
3. SCATTER.
4. SPREAD.

dispirit *verb*
1. DEPRESS.
2. DISCOURAGE.

dispirited *adjective* DEPRESSED.
dispiriting *adjective*
1. DISCOURAGING.
2. GLOOMY.

displace *verb*
1. DISTURB.
2. SUPPLANT.

display *verb*
1. To make a public and usu.
ostentatious show of: *displayed her
trophies on a pedestal; displaying his
trim figure to best advantage.*
　Syns: brandish, disport, exhibit,

expose, flash, flaunt, parade, show,
show off, sport.
2. BEAR.
3. EXPRESS.
4. REVEAL.
5. SHOW.

display noun
1. An act of showing or displaying: *a display of articles for sale; a display of force.*
   Syns: demonstration, exhibit, exhibition, manifestation, show.
2. An impressive or ostentatious exhibition: *The lottery winner made a display of his new wealth.*
   Syns: array, panoply, parade, pomp, spectacle.

displease verb OFFEND.
displeasing adjective UNPLEASANT.
displeasure noun DISAPPROVAL.
displeasure verb OFFEND.
disponible adjective AVAILABLE.
disport verb
1. ACT.
2. DISPLAY.
3. PLAY.
disport noun PLAY.
disposal noun
1. The act of getting rid of something useless or used up: *Garbage disposal is a municipal function.*
   Syns: discard, dumping, elimination, jettison, riddance.
2. ARRANGEMENT.
dispose verb
1. To influence or be influenced in a certain direction: *His friendliness disposed me to like him.*
   Syns: bend, bias, incline, predispose, sway.
2. ARRANGE.
dispose of verb
1. DISCARD.
2. SETTLE.
disposed adjective INCLINED.
disposition noun
1. A person's customary manner of emotional response: *an affectionate disposition.*
   Syns: complexion, humor, kidney, nature, temper, temperament.
   —*Idiom* frame of mind.
2. ARRANGEMENT.
3. BENT.
4. CHARACTER.
5. SENTIMENT.
dispossess verb DEPRIVE.
dispossession noun DEPRIVATION.
disproportion noun INEQUALITY.
disprove verb REFUTE.
disputable adjective DEBATABLE.

disputation noun ARGUMENTATION.
disputatious adjective ARGUMENTATIVE.
dispute verb
1. ARGUE.
2. CONTEST.
dispute noun ARGUMENT.
disputed adjective DEBATABLE.
disqualify verb UNFIT.
disquiet verb AGITATE.
disquiet noun
1. AGITATION.
2. ANXIETY.
3. RESTLESSNESS.
disquieted adjective ANXIOUS.
disquietude noun
1. ANXIETY.
2. RESTLESSNESS.
disquisition noun DISCOURSE.
disquisitive adjective CURIOUS.
disregard verb
1. IGNORE.
2, 3. NEGLECT.
disregard noun
1. APATHY.
2. NEGLECT.
3. THOUGHTLESSNESS.
disrelish verb DISLIKE.
disrelish noun DISLIKE.
disremember verb FORGET.
disreputable adjective DISGRACEFUL.
disrepute noun DISGRACE.
disrespect noun
1. Lack of proper respect: *accused of disrespect for failing to salute the flag.*
   Syns: incivility, irreverence, lese majesty (*also* lèse majesté).
2. IMPUDENCE.
disrespectful adjective
Having or showing a lack of respect: *It is disrespectful to talk loudly in church.*
   Syns: irreverent, uncivil.
disrobe verb
1. BARE.
2. STRIP[1].
disrobed adjective NUDE.
disrupt verb
1. To break up the order or progress of: *Hecklers disrupted the council meeting.*
   Syns: disturb, upset. —*Idiom* play havoc with.
2. DISORDER.
disrupted adjective DISORDERED.
disruption noun
1. BREAK.
2. UPSET.
disruptive adjective DISTURBING.
dissatisfaction noun DISAPPOINTMENT.
dissatisfy verb DISAPPOINT.

dissatisfying *adjective*
DISAPPOINTING.
dissect *verb* ANALYZE.
dissection *noun* ANALYSIS.
dissemblance *noun* ACT.
dissemble *verb*
1. ACT.
2. BLINK AT at **blink**.
3. DISGUISE.
disseminate *verb*
1. ADVERTISE.
2. DISTRIBUTE.
dissension *noun* CONFLICT.
dissent *verb* DIFFER.
 dissent *noun* CONFLICT.
dissenter *noun* SEPARATIST.
dissentience *noun* CONFLICT.
dissertation *noun*
1. DISCOURSE.
2. THESIS.
disserve *verb* INJURE.
disservice *noun* INJUSTICE.
dissever *verb* CUT.
dissidence *noun* CONFLICT.
dissident *noun* SEPARATIST.
dissimilar *adjective* DIFFERENT.
dissimilarity *noun* DIFFERENCE.
dissimilitude *noun* DIFFERENCE.
dissimulate *verb* DISGUISE.
dissipate *verb*
1. LIFT.
2. SCATTER.
3. WASTE.
dissociate *verb*
1. BREAK.
2. DETACH.
dissolute *adjective*
1. ABANDONED.
2. FAST.
dissoluteness *noun* LICENSE.
dissolution *noun*
1. DEATH.
2. LICENSE.
dissolve *verb*
1. BREAK UP at **break**.
2. FADE.
3. FADE OUT at **fade**.
4. MELT.
 dissolve *noun* FADE-OUT.
dissonance *noun* CONFLICT.
dissonant *adjective*
1. INCONGRUOUS.
2. INHARMONIOUS.
dissuade *verb*
To persuade (a person) not to do
something: *tried to dissuade the
President from taking military action.*
 Syns: deter, discourage, divert.
 —*Idiom* talk out of.

distaff *noun* FEMININITY.
distaff *adjective* FEMININE.
distance *noun*
1. The fact or condition of being far
removed or apart: *Because of its
distance Helena was an appropriate
island of exile.*
 Syns: farness, remoteness.
2. An extent, measured or unmeasured,
of linear space: *Favorable winds
propelled the ship a great distance
before sunset.*
 Syns: length, piece (*Regional*), space,
stretch, way.
3. DETACHMENT.
4. EXPANSE.
5. REMOVE.
distant *adjective*
1. Far from others in space, time, or
relationship: *faint light from distant
parts of the universe; crumbled remains
of the distant past.*
 Syns: far, faraway, far-flung, far-off,
remote, removed. —*Idiom* at a
distance.
2. COOL.
distaste *noun* DISLIKE.
distasteful *adjective*
1. BITTER.
2. UNPALATABLE.
distill *verb* DRIP.
distinct *adjective*
1. Distinguished from others by nature
or qualities: *The design used two
compatible but distinct colors.*
 Syns: discrete, diverse, separate,
several, various.
2. APPARENT.
3. DECIDED.
4. SHARP.
distinction *noun*
1. The act or an instance of
distinguishing: *The statistics make no
distinction between part-time and full-
time employees.*
 Syns: differentiation, discrimination,
separation.
2. Recognition of achievement or
superiority or a sign of this:
graduated with distinction.
 Syns: accolade, honor, kudos, laurels.
3. DIFFERENCE.
4. EMINENCE.
5. VIRTUE.
distinctive *adjective*
Serving to identify or set apart an
individual or group: *a bird's distinctive
markings; a distinctive behavior pattern.*
 Syns: characteristic, distinguishing,
individual, peculiar, typical (*also
typic*), vintage.

distinctiveness *noun* INDIVIDUALITY.
distinctness *noun* CLARITY.
distinguish *verb*
1. To recognize as being different: *could not distinguish fear from cowardice.*
    Syns: differentiate, discern, discriminate, know, separate, tell.
2. To make noticeable or different: *Simple, clean-cut forms distinguish the work of this architect.*
    Syns: characterize, differentiate, discriminate, individualize, mark, qualify, set apart, signalize, singularize.
3. To cause to be eminent or recognized: *He distinguished himself as a statesman.*
    Syns: elevate, ennoble, exalt, honor, signalize.
4. DISCERN.
5. NOTICE.

distinguished *adjective* EMINENT.
distinguishing *adjective* DISTINCTIVE.
distort *verb*
1. To give an inaccurate view of by representing falsely or misleadingly: *propagandists who distort facts.*
    Syns: belie, color, falsify, load, misrepresent, misstate, pervert, twist, warp, wrench. —*Idiom* give a false coloring to.
2. DEFORM.

distract *verb*
1. AMUSE.
2. DERANGE.

distracting *adjective* AMUSING.
distraction *noun*
1, 2. AMUSEMENT.
distrait *adjective* ABSENT-MINDED.
distraught *adjective* INSANE.
distress *verb*
1. To cause suffering or painful sorrow to: *The news of the child's death distressed her deeply.*
    Syns: afflict, aggrieve, anguish, grieve, pain.
2. WORRY.

distress *noun*
1. A state of physical or mental suffering: *respiratory distress; felt great distress over the death of her father.*
    Syns: affliction, agony, anguish, hurt, misery, pain, woe.
2. The condition of being in need of immediate assistance: *a swimmer in distress.*
    Syns: exigency (*also* exigence), trouble. —*Idiom* hot water.
3. ANXIETY.

distressed *adjective* ANXIOUS.

distressful *adjective* DISTURBING.
distressing *adjective* DISTURBING.
distribute *verb*
1. To give out in portions or shares: *The government distributed land to settlers willing to plant it.*
    Syns: deal, disburse, dispense, divide, divvy (*Slang*), dole out, measure out, parcel, portion, share.
2. To pass (something) out: *distributing handbills on the street.*
    Syns: circulate, disperse, disseminate, hand out.
3. ARRANGE.
4. SPREAD.

distribution *noun*
1. The act of distributing or the condition of being distributed: *Attorneys supervised the distribution of the property among the heirs.*
    Syns: apportionment, disbursal, dispensation, division.
2. ARRANGEMENT.

distrust *noun*
Lack of trust: *looked at the new device with distrust.*
    Syns: doubt, doubtfulness, mistrust, suspicion.
distrust *verb*
To lack trust or confidence in: *Distrusting banks, he kept his cash in a shoebox.*
    Syns: doubt, misdoubt, mistrust, suspect.

distrustful *adjective*
Lacking trust or confidence: *distrustful of strangers.*
    Syns: doubtful, doubting, dubious, mistrustful, suspicious, untrusting.

disturb *verb*
1. To alter the settled state or position of: *The earthquake disturbed the rocks and started a landslide.*
    Syns: agitate, dislocate, displace, move, shake, shift.
2. AGITATE.
3. ANNOY.
4. DISORDER.
5. DISRUPT.

disturbance *noun*
An interruption of regular procedure or of public peace: *A disturbance at the back of the hall made the speaker pause.*
    Syns: agitation, commotion, fuss, rumpus, stir[1], to-do (*Informal*), tumult, turbulence, uproar.

disturbed *adjective* ANXIOUS.
disturbing *adjective*
Troubling to the mind or emotions: *a disturbing turn of events in Southwest Asia.*

Syns: disruptive, distressing, distressful, intrusive, troublesome, unsettling, upsetting.

disunion *noun*
1, 2. DIVISION.

disunite *verb*
1. DIVIDE.
2. ESTRANGE.

disuse *noun* OBSOLETENESS.

ditch *verb* DISCARD.

dither *noun* AGITATION.

dither *verb* HESITATE.

dithyrambic *adjective* PASSIONATE.

divagate *verb* DIGRESS.

divagation *noun*
1, 2. DIGRESSION.

divarication *noun* DIFFERENCE.

dive *verb*
1. FALL.
2. PLUNGE.

dive *noun*
1, 2. FALL.
3. JOINT.
4. PLUNGE.

diverge *verb*
1. BRANCH.
2. DEVIATE.
3. DIGRESS.

divergence *also* **divergency** *noun*
1. DEVIATION.
2. DIFFERENCE.
3. DIGRESSION.
4. DIVISION.

divergent *adjective*
1. ABNORMAL.
2. DIFFERENT.

divers *adjective*
1. GENERAL.
2. SEVERAL.
3. VARIOUS.

diverse *adjective*
1. DIFFERENT.
2. DISTINCT.
3. GENERAL.
4. VARIOUS.

diverseness *noun* VARIETY.

diversified *adjective*
1. GENERAL.
2. VARIOUS.

diversion *noun*
1, 2. AMUSEMENT.
3. DEVIATION.
4. PLAY.

diversity *noun*
1. ASSORTMENT.
2. VARIETY.

divert *verb*
1. AMUSE.
2. DISSUADE.
3. TURN.

diverting *adjective* AMUSING.

divest *verb*
1. BARE.
2. DEPRIVE.

divestiture *noun* DEPRIVATION.

divide *verb*
1. To make a division into parts, sections, or branches: *Berlin is divided into four sectors.*
   Syns: break up, part, partition, section, segment, separate.
2. To become or cause to become apart one from another: *Many families in Border States were divided over the issue of slavery. A great schism divided the Christian church.*
   Syns: break, detach, disjoin, disjoint, disunite, divorce, separate, split.
   —*Idioms* part company, set at odds.
3. DISTRIBUTE.

dividend *noun* REWARD.

divine[1] *adjective*
1. Of, from, like, or being a god or God: *the divine will; divine inspiration.*
   Syns: deific, godlike, godly, heavenly.
2. In the service or worship of God or a god: *divine rites.*
   Syns: holy, religious, sacred.
3. MARVELOUS.

divine *noun* PREACHER.

divine[2] *verb*
1. FORESEE.
2. PROPHESY.

diviner *noun* PROPHET.

divinitory *adjective* PROPHETICAL.

division *noun*
1. The act or an instance of separating one thing from another: *a division of Church and State.*
   Syns: detachment, disunion, divorce, divorcement, partition, separation, split-up.
2. One of the parts into which something is divided: *a company with European and U.S. divisions.*
   Syns: member, parcel, part, piece, portion, section, segment, subdivision.
3. The condition of being divided, as in opinion: *a nation rent by wide division over the Vietnam conflict.*
   Syns: divergence (*also* divergency), disunion, split.
4, 5. BRANCH.
6. DISTRIBUTION.
7. SUBSIDIARY.

divorce *verb*
1. To terminate a marriage through legal action: *He divorced his wife.*
   Syn: unmarry.

2. DIVIDE.
divorce *noun* DIVISION.
divorcement *noun* DIVISION.
divulge *verb* BETRAY.
divvy *verb* DISTRIBUTE.
divvy *noun* ALLOTMENT.
dizziness *noun*
A sensation of whirling or falling:
suffers dizziness when climbing on ladders.
   Syns: giddiness, lightheadedness, vertigo, wooziness.
dizzy *adjective*
1. Having a sensation of whirling or falling: *too dizzy to get on the merry-go-round again.*
   Syns: giddy, lightheaded, reeling, vertiginous, woozy. —*Idioms* going around in circles, seeing double.
2, 3. GIDDY.
4. STEEP¹.
dizzy *verb* CONFUSE.
dizzying *adjective*
1. GIDDY.
2. STEEP¹.
do *verb*
1, 2. ACT.
3. CHEAT.
4. COOK.
5. MANAGE.
6. PERFORM.
7, 8. SERVE.
9. STAGE.
10. TRAVERSE.
do for *verb* SERVE.
do in *verb*
1. EXHAUST.
2. KILL.
3. MURDER.
do up *verb* WRAP.
do *noun* PARTY.
docile *adjective* GENTLE.
docket *noun* PROGRAM.
doctor *verb*
1. ADULTERATE.
2. FIX.
3. TREAT.
doctrinaire *adjective*
1. Devoted to certain doctrines without regard to practicability: *persisted in a doctrinaire faith in the free market even when it wasn't working.*
   Syns: dogmatic, theoretical (*also* theoretic).
2. AUTHORITARIAN.
3. DICTATORIAL.
doctrine *noun*
A principle taught or advanced for belief, as by a religious or philosophical group: *the doctrines of the church.*
   Syns: dogma, teaching, tenet.

doddering *adjective* SENILE.
doddery *adjective* SENILE.
dodge *noun*
   DECEPTION.
dodge *verb*
1. AVOID.
2. EVADE.
doff *verb* REMOVE.
dog *verb*
1. To follow closely or persistently: *The toddler dogged my footsteps all day.*
   Syns: bloodhound, heel¹, tag, trail.
2. FOLLOW.
dogged *adjective* OBSTINATE.
doggedness *noun* OBSTINACY.
dogma *noun* DOCTRINE.
dogmatic *adjective*
1. DICTATORIAL.
2. DOCTRINAIRE.
dog-tired *adjective* EXHAUSTED.
doing *noun* ACT.
doit *noun* BIT¹.
doldrums *noun* GLOOM.
dole *noun* RELIEF.
dole out *verb* DISTRIBUTE.
doleful *adjective*
1, 2. SORROWFUL.
dolefulness *noun* GLOOM.
dolittle *noun* WASTREL.
doll *noun* BEAUTY.
doll up *verb* DRESS UP at **dress.**
dolorous *adjective*
1, 2. SORROWFUL.
dolt *noun* DULLARD.
doltish *adjective* STUPID.
domain *noun* AREA.
dome *noun* HEAD.
domestic *adjective*
1. Of or pertaining to the family or household: *cooking, cleaning, and other domestic chores.*
   Syns: familial, family, home, homely, household.
2. Trained or bred to live with and be of use to human beings: *a domestic cat that reverted to the wild.*
   Syns: domesticated, domesticized, tame.
3. Of, from, or within a country's own territory: *domestic political issues; domestic wines.*
   Syns: home, internal, national, native.
domesticate *verb*
To train to live with and be of use to human beings: *tried to domesticate a jaguar.*
   Syns: domesticize, gentle, master, tame.
domesticated *adjective* DOMESTIC.
domesticize *verb* DOMESTICATE.

domesticized *adjective* DOMESTIC.
domicile *noun* HOME.
domicile also **domiciliate** *verb*
1. HARBOR.
2. LIVE!.
dominance *noun*
1. The condition or fact of being dominant: *a currency of unquestionable dominance in the international money markets.*
   Syns: ascendancy, domination, predominance, pre-eminence (*also* preeminence, preëminence), preponderance (*also* preponderancy), prepotency, supremacy.
2. DOMINATION.
dominant *adjective*
1. Exercising controlling power or influence: *a dominant new dynasty.*
   Syns: commanding, controlling, dominating, dominative, governing, regnant, ruling.
2. PRIMARY.
3. RULING.
dominate *verb*
1. To occupy the pre-eminent position in: *The Yankees dominated the American League for years.*
   Syns: predominate, preponderate, prevail, reign, rule. —*Idioms* have the ascendancy, reign supreme.
2. To rise above, esp. so as to afford a view of: *A high water tower dominates the town.*
   Syns: command, overlook, tower above.
3. BOSS.
4. CONTROL.
domination *noun*
1. The act of exercising controlling power or the condition of being so controlled: *the former domination of Africa by colonial powers.*
   Syns: command, control, dominance, dominion, mastery, rule, sway.
2. AUTHORITY.
3. DOMINANCE.
domineer *verb* BOSS.
domineering *adjective* DICTATORIAL.
dominion *noun*
1. AUTHORITY.
2. DOMINATION.
3. OWNERSHIP.
don *verb*
To put (an article of clothing) on one's person: *donned overalls for the dirty work ahead.*
   Syns: assume, get on, pull on, put on, slip into, slip on.

donate *verb*
1. To present as a gift to a charity or cause: *donated a painting to the church bazaar.*
   Syns: bestow, contribute, give, hand out.
2. CONTRIBUTE.
donation *noun*
Something given to a charity or cause: *a donation of $2,000 to the Red Cross.*
   Syns: alms, benefaction, beneficence, charity, contribution, gift, handout, offering.
donator *noun* DONOR.
done *adjective*
1. COMPLETE.
2, 3. THROUGH.
done for *adjective* THROUGH.
done in *adjective* EXHAUSTED.
Don Juan *noun*
1. GALLANT.
2. PHILANDERER.
3. SEDUCER.
donnish *adjective* PEDANTIC.
donnybrook *noun* BRAWL.
donor *noun*
A person who gives to a charity or cause: *a generous donor to the Red Cross.*
   Syns: benefactor, contributor, donator, giver, grantor, subscriber.
do-nothing *adjective* LAZY.
do-nothing *noun* WASTREL.
doodad *noun* GADGET.
doodle *verb* MESS AROUND at **mess.**
doohickey *noun* GADGET.
doom *noun* FATE.
doom *verb*
1. CONDEMN.
2. FATE.
doomed *adjective* CONDEMNED.
doomful *adjective* FATEFUL.
doomsayer *noun* PESSIMIST.
dope *noun*
1. DRUG.
2. FOOL.
dope *verb*
1. ADULTERATE.
2. DRUG.
dope out *verb*
1. DESIGN.
2. RESOLVE.
doped *adjective* DRUGGED.
dopey also **dopy** *adjective*
LETHARGIC.
dopeyness also **dopiness** *noun*
LETHARGY.
dopy *adjective* SEE **dopey.**
dormancy *noun* ABEYANCE.

dormant *adjective*
1. LATENT.
2. SLEEPING.
dose *verb* DRUG.
dot *noun* POINT.
dot *verb* SPECKLE.
dotage *noun* SENILITY.
dote on *verb* ADORE.
doting *adjective*
1. AFFECTIONATE.
2. SENILE.
double *adjective*
1. Composed of two parts or things: *a double window; a double pleat.*
   Syns: biform, binary, dual, duple, duplex, duplicate, geminate, twofold.
2. Twice as much or as large: *took a double dose of the painkiller.*
   Syns: doubled, twofold.
3. Characterized by duplicity: *a scoundrel's double tongue.*
   Syns: double-dealing, double-faced, Iscariotic *or* Iscariotical, treacherous, two-faced.
4. TWIN.
double *noun*
1. One exactly resembling another: *ordinary people who happen to be the doubles of celebrities.*
   Syns: duplicate, image, picture, portrait, ringer (*Slang*). —*Idiom* spitting image.
2. MATE.
double *verb*
1. To make or become twice as great: *She got a big raise that doubled her salary. The price of gold more than doubled in the 1970's.*
   Syns: duplicate, redouble.
2. To turn sharply around: *The runner had to double back to pick up the dropped baton.*
   Syns: about-face, reverse.
3. FOLD.
double-cross *verb*
1. BETRAY.
2. DECEIVE.
double-cross *noun* BETRAYAL.
doubled *adjective* DOUBLE.
double-dealing *adjective* DOUBLE.
double-dealing *noun* DECEIT.
double entendre *noun* AMBIGUITY.
double-faced *adjective* DOUBLE.
doublet *noun* COUPLE.
double-talk *noun*
1. BABBLE.
2. GIBBERISH.
doubt *verb*
1. To be uncertain, disbelieving, or skeptical about: *The new data made*

the scientists doubt their original assumptions.
   Syns: mistrust, question. —*Idiom* have one's doubts.
2. DISTRUST.
doubt *noun*
1. A lack of conviction or certainty: *A prior record of perjury cast doubt on his truthfulness. The commander regarded the battle plan with growing doubt.*
   Syns: doubtfulness, dubiety, dubiousness, incertitude, mistrust, question, skepticism, suspicion, uncertainty, wonder.
2. DISTRUST.
doubtable *adjective* AMBIGUOUS.
doubter *noun* SKEPTIC.
doubtful *adjective*
1. Experiencing doubt: *I am doubtful about your plans.*
   Syns: dubious, skeptical, uncertain, undecided, unsure. —*Idiom* in doubt.
2. Not likely: *It is doubtful that our team will win.*
   Syns: improbable, questionable, unlikely.
3. AMBIGUOUS.
4. DEBATABLE.
5. DISTRUSTFUL.
6. SHADY.
doubtfulness *noun*
1. DISTRUST.
2. DOUBT.
doubting *adjective* DISTRUSTFUL.
doubting Thomas *noun* SKEPTIC.
doubtless *adverb* ABSOLUTELY.
dough *noun* MONEY.
doughty *adjective* BRAVE.
dour *adjective*
1. BLEAK.
2. GLUM.
douse *verb*
1. DIP.
2. EXTINGUISH.
3. REMOVE.
4. WET.
dovetail *verb* FIT.
dowdy *adjective*
1. OLD-FASHIONED.
2. TACKY².
dower *verb* GIFT.
down *adjective*
1. DEPRESSED.
2. SICK.
3. SLOW.
down *verb*
1. DEFEAT.
2. DROP.
3. SWALLOW.
down *noun* DESCENT.

down-and-out *noun* PAUPER.
down-at-heel or **down-at-the-heel**
adjective SHABBY.
downcast *adjective* DEPRESSED.
downfall *noun*
1. DESCENT.
2. FALL.
3. RUIN.
downgrade *verb*
1. BELITTLE.
2. DEBASE.
3. DEMOTE.
4. DEPRECIATE.
downgrade *noun* DESCENT.
downgrading *noun* DEMOTION.
downhearted *adjective* DEPRESSED.
down payment *noun* DEPOSIT.
downright *adjective*
1. FRANK.
2. UTTER².
downslide *noun* FALL.
downswing *noun* FALL.
down-to-earth *adjective* REALISTIC.
downturn *noun* FALL.
downward *adjective* DESCENDING.
doze *verb* NAP.
doze *noun* NAP.
dozy *adjective* SLEEPY.
drab¹ *adjective*
1, 2. DULL.
drab² *noun* WITCH.
draft *noun*
1. Compulsory enrollment in military
service: *rioting students opposed to the
draft.*
Syns: conscription, induction, levy.
2. A preliminary plan or version, as of a
written work: *finished a first draft of
her novel.*
Syns: outline, rough, skeleton, sketch.
3. DRINK.
4. PULL.
draft *verb*
1. To enroll compulsorily in military
service: *was drafted into the army for
four years.*
Syns: conscript, induct, levy. —*Idiom*
call to the colors.
2. To devise and set down: *The
committee drafted a national health-
insurance program.*
Syns: draw up, formulate, frame, lay¹.
3. To draw up a preliminary plan or
version of: *He drafted his speech
quickly, then began to revise.*
Syns: adumbrate, block out, outline,
rough in, rough out, sketch.
drag *noun*
1. DRINK.

2. INFLUENCE.
3. PULL.
drag *verb*
1. CRAWL.
2. DELAY.
3. PULL.
4. TRAIL.
drag down *verb* EARN.
dragging *adjective*
1. LONG¹.
2. SLOW.
draggle *verb* TRAIL.
dragoon *verb* COERCE.
drain *verb*
1. To remove (a liquid) by a steady,
gradual process: *We drained the water
from the cistern with a siphon.*
Syns: draw off, let out, pump, tap².
2. DECREASE.
3. DEPLETE.
4. DRY UP at **dry.**
5. EXHAUST.
6. FATIGUE.
drained *adjective*
1. EXHAUSTED.
2. RUN-DOWN.
dram *noun*
1. BIT¹.
2. DROP.
dramatic *adjective*
1. Of or pertaining to drama or the
theater: *a dramatic performance.*
Syns: dramaturgic, histrionic,
theatrical (*also* theatric), thespian.
2. Suggesting drama or a stage
performance, as in emotionality or
suspense: *made a dramatic entrance in
a swirling cape.*
Syns: histrionic, melodramatic,
sensational, spectacular, theatrical
(*also* theatric).
dramaticism *noun* THEATRICALISM.
dramatics *noun*
1. ACTING.
2. THEATRICS.
dramatize *verb* STAGE.
dramaturgic *adjective* DRAMATIC.
drape *verb*
1. CLOTHE.
2. SPRAWL.
draw *verb*
1. ATTRACT.
2. DERIVE.
3. EVOKE.
4. INFER.
5. POUR.
6. PULL.
7. RETURN.
draw back *verb* RETREAT.
draw down *verb* EARN.

draw in *verb* WITHDRAW.
draw in (or **into**) *verb* ENGAGE.
draw off *verb* DRAIN.
draw out *verb* LENGTHEN.
draw up *verb*
1. DESIGN.
2. DRAFT.
draw *noun*
1. ADVANTAGE.
2. ATTRACTION.
3, 4. PULL.
5. TIE.
drawback *noun* DISADVANTAGE.
drawn-out *adjective* LONG¹.
dread *noun*
1. FEAR.
2. WONDER.
dread *verb* FEAR.
dreadful *adjective*
1. FEARFUL.
2. TERRIBLE.
dreadfully *adverb* VERY.
dream *noun*
1. An illusory mental image: *bad
dreams; can't distinguish dreams from
reality.*
   Syns: fancy, fantasy (*also* phantasy),
   fiction, figment, illusion, phantasm
   (*also* phantasma), reverie, vision.
   —*Idiom* figment (*or* creature) of the
   imagination.
2. A fervent hope, wish, or goal: *the
dream of a national homeland.*
   Syns: aspiration, ideal.
3. ILLUSION.
dream *verb*
1. To experience dreams or daydreams:
*spent her time dreaming instead of
working.*
   Syns: fantasize, moon, muse¹.
   —*Idiom* go woolgathering.
2. ASPIRE.
dream up *verb* INVENT.
dreamer *noun*
A person inclined to be imaginative or
idealistic but impractical: *Ashley Wilkes
was a true dreamer.*
   Syns: idealist, utopian, visionary.
dreamy *adjective*
1. Given to daydreams or reverie: *a
dreamy, quiet child in a world of his
own.*
   Syns: moony, otherworldly, visionary,
   woolgathering. —*Idiom* in the clouds.
2. MARVELOUS.
dreary *also* **drear** *adjective*
1. BORING.
2. GLOOMY.
dregs *noun*
1. DEPOSIT.
2. TRASH¹.

drench *verb*
1. POUR.
2. WET.
drenched *adjective* WET.
dress *verb*
1. To put clothes on: *She dressed her
children warmly.*
   Syns: apparel, array, attire, clad,
   clothe, garb, garment, invest (*Rare*),
   tog (*Informal*).
2. To apply therapeutic materials to (a
wound): *used a handkerchief to dress
his cut.*
   Syns: bandage, bind.
3. ADORN.
4. TILL.
dress down *verb* CALL DOWN at **call**.
dress up *verb*
To dress in formal or special clothing:
all dressed up in a new suit.
   Syns: deck out, doll up (*Slang*), slick
   (up) (*Informal*), tog out (*Informal*),
   tog up (*Informal*), trick out, trick up.
dress *noun*
1. Articles worn to cover the body:
expensive dress.
   Syns: apparel, attire, clothes,
   clothing, duds (*Informal*), garb,
   garments, habiliments, raiment,
   threads (*Slang*), togs (*Informal*).
2. A set or style of clothing: *Edwardian
dress.*
   Syns: getup, guise, outfit, rig, turnout.
3. A one-piece, skirted outer garment
for women and children: *long and
short dresses.*
   Syns: frock, gown.
dressy *adjective* FORMAL.
dribble *verb*
1. DRIP.
2. DROOL.
dribble *noun* DRIP.
driblet *noun* DROP.
drift *verb*
1. HEAP.
2. ROVE.
3. SLIDE.
4. WASH.
drift *noun*
1. FLOW.
2. HEAP.
3. THRUST.
drill *noun* PRACTICE.
drill *verb*
1. EXERCISE.
2. INDOCTRINATE.
drink *verb*
1. To take into the mouth and swallow
(a liquid): *We drank tea and ate
biscuits.*

Syns: imbibe, quaff, sip, sup, swig
(*Informal*), toss down, toss off.
—*Idiom* wet one's whistle.
2. To take alcoholic liquor, esp.
excessively or habitually: *Strict
Hindus do not drink.*
Syns: booze (*Slang*), guzzle, imbibe,
liquor up (*Slang*), lush (*Slang*), nip[2],
soak (*Slang*), tank up (*Slang*), tipple.
—*Idioms* bend the elbow, hit the
bottle, take a drop.
3. To salute by raising and drinking
from a glass: *We drank to the memory
of old friends.*
Syns: pledge, toast. —*Idiom* raise a
glass to.
4. To take in (moisture or liquid): *The
parched earth drank in the rain.*
Syns: absorb, imbibe, soak up, sop
(up).
drink *noun*
1. Any liquid that is fit for drinking:
supplied us with food and drink.
Syns: beverage, drinkable, liquor,
potable.
2. An act of drinking or the amount
swallowed: *She paused to take a drink
from her wine glass.*
Syns: belt (*Slang*), draft, drag,
potation, pull, quaff, sip, sup, swig
(*Informal*), swill.
drinkable *noun* DRINK.
drip *verb*
To fall or let fall in drops of liquid:
Water dripped from the leaky faucet.
Syns: distill, dribble, drop, trickle,
weep.
drip *noun*
1. The process or sound of dripping:
heard the slow drip of a leaky faucet.
Syns: dribble, drop, trickle.
2. *Slang.* An unpleasant, tiresome
person: *an old drip who spoiled all our
fun.*
Syns: bore, clod, jerk (*Slang*), pill
(*Slang*), poop (*Slang*).
drippy *adjective* SENTIMENTAL.
drive *verb*
1. To force to move or advance with
or as if with blows or pressure: *The
fire drove residents from their homes.*
Syns: propel, push, ram, shove,
thrust.
2. To urge to move along: *driving the
cattle to slaughter.*
Syns: herd, run.
3. To set or keep going: *a mill driven
by wind power.*
Syns: actuate, impel, mobilize,
move, propel, run.

4. To run and control (a motor
vehicle): *drove the car to work.*
Syns: motor, pilot, tool (*Informal*),
wheel.
5. HUNT.
6. IMPRESS.
7. LABOR.
8. PLUNGE.
9. RAM.
10. WORK.
drive *noun*
1. A trip in a motor vehicle: *a Sunday
drive.*
Syns: ride, spin (*Informal*), whirl
(*Informal*).
2. An organized effort to accomplish a
purpose: *a fund-raising drive.*
Syns: campaign, crusade, push.
3. An aggressive readiness to undertake
taxing efforts: *a young executive with
a lot of drive.*
Syns: enterprise, getup, get-up-and-go
(*Informal*), hustle, punch, push
(*Informal*), snap (*Informal*), steam,
vigor.
4. AMBITION.
5. WAY.
drivel *noun*
1. DROOL.
2. NONSENSE.
drivel *verb* DROOL.
driveling *adjective* INSIPID.
driver *noun*
A person who operates a motor vehicle:
a reckless driver.
Syns: motorist, operator.
driving *adjective* VIGOROUS.
droit *noun* BIRTHRIGHT.
droll *adjective* AMUSING.
drollery *noun* HUMOR.
drollness *noun* HUMOR.
drone[1] *noun* WASTREL.
drone[2] *verb* HUM.
drone *noun* HUM.
drool *verb*
To let saliva run from the mouth:
Basset hounds drool.
Syns: dribble, drivel, salivate, slaver,
slobber.
drool *noun*
Saliva running from the mouth: *The
nurse wiped the drool from the patient's
face.*
Syns: drivel, salivation, slaver,
slobber.
droop *verb*
1. SLOUCH.
2. WILT.
drop *noun*
1. A quantity of liquid falling or resting

in a spherical mass: *Drops of perspiration stood out on her forehead.*
Syns: driblet, droplet, globule.
2. A small amount of liquor: *had only a drop of brandy left.*
Syns: dram, nip², sip, shot, slug¹ (*Informal*), snort (*Slang*), tot¹.
3. BIT¹.
4. DRIP.
5, 6. FALL.
7. A downward slope or distance: *a sheer drop to the canyon floor.*
Syns: decline, declivity, descent, fall.
8. ADVANTAGE.
9. DEPTH.
drop *verb*
1. To go from a more erect posture to a less erect posture: *dropped to his knees before the king.*
Syns: fall, sink, slump.
2. To slope downward: *The ocean floor drops sharply at the continental shelf.*
Syns: decline, descend, dip, fall, fall off, sink.
3. To cause to fall, as from a shot or blow: *The hunter dropped his prey with a single shot. The boxer dropped his opponent with a right hook.*
Syns: bring down, cut down, deck, down, fell¹, flatten, floor, ground, knock down, level, prostrate, throw. —*Idiom* lay low.
4. To cease consideration or treatment of: *Let's drop the matter.*
Syns: dismiss, give over, give up, skip. —*Idioms* have done with, wash one's hands of.
5. To take or leave out: *We have to drop two illustrations from the book for lack of space.*
Syns: delete, eliminate, omit, remove.
6. To suffer the loss of: *dropped a lot of money at the race track.*
Syns: forfeit, lose. —*Idiom* kiss good-by to.
7. CANCEL.
8. COLLAPSE.
9. DIE.
10. DISMISS.
11. DRIP.
12, 13, 14. FALL.
15. LOWER².
drop by *verb* VISIT.
drop in *verb* VISIT.
droplet *noun* DROP.
drop-off *noun* FALL.
drop off *verb* SLIP.
drossy *adjective* WORTHLESS.
droughty *adjective* DRY.

drove *noun*
1, 2. CROWD.
drown *verb* FLOOD.
drowsy *adjective* SLEEPY.
drub *verb*
1. BEAT.
2. DEFEAT.
3. OVERWHELM.
4. SLAM.
drubbing *noun*
1. DEFEAT.
2. TROUNCING.
drudge *verb* GRIND.
drudgery *noun* LABOR.
drug *noun*
1. A substance used in the treatment of disease: *Aspirin is a common drug for headaches.*
Syns: medicament, medication, medicine.
2. A narcotic substance, esp. one that is addictive: *arrested for dealing illictly in drugs.*
Syns: dope (*Informal*), narcotic, opiate.
drug *verb*
To administer or add a drug to: *drugged the patient to induce sleep.*
Syns: dope (*Informal*), dose, medicate, narcotize, physic (*Archaic*).
drugged *adjective*
Stupefied, intoxicated, or otherwise influenced by the taking of drugs: *The drugged bum lay in a heap in the filthy doorway.*
Syns: doped (*Informal*), high (*Slang*), hopped-up (*Slang*), spaced-out (*Slang*), stoned (*Slang*), turned-on (*Slang*), wiped-out (*Slang*), zonked (*Slang*).
drunk *adjective*
Intoxicated with alcoholic liquor: *too drunk to walk a straight line.*
Syns: besotted, blind (*Slang*), bombed (*Slang*), boozed (*Slang*), boozy (*Slang*), cock-eyed (*Slang*), crapulent, crapulous, crocked (*Slang*), drunken, high (*Slang*), inebriate, inebriated, lit up (*Slang*), loaded (*Slang*), looped (*Slang*), pickled (*Slang*), pixilated (*Slang*), plastered (*Slang*), potted (*Slang*), sloshed (*Slang*), smashed (*Slang*), sodden (*Slang*), soused (*Slang*), stewed (*Slang*), stinking (*Slang*), tight (*Slang*), tipsy (*Slang*), zonked (*Slang*). —*Idioms* drunk as a skunk, half-seas over, high as a kite, in one's cups, three sheets to the wind.

drunk noun
1. BENDER.
2. DRUNKARD.

drunkard noun
A person who is habitually drunk: a self-admitted drunkard who refused treatment.
Syns: boozehound (Slang), boozer (Slang), drunk, inebriate, lush (Slang), rummy¹ (Slang), soak (Slang), sot, souse (Slang), sponge (Slang), stiff (Slang), tippler.

drunken adjective DRUNK.

drunkenness noun
The condition of being intoxicated with alcoholic liquor: the drunkenness of an old wino.
Syns: crapulence, inebriation, inebriety, insobriety, intoxication.

dry adjective
1. Having little or no liquid or moisture: The laundry was dry by morning.
Syns: anhydrous, arid, bone-dry, dehydrated, desiccated, moistureless, parched, waterless.
2. Having little or no precipitation: a dry climate.
Syns: arid, droughty, rainless, thirsty.
3. With little or no emotion or expression: dealing out facts in a dry, mechanical way.
Syns: impassive, matter-of-fact, unemotional.
4. BARE.
5. BORING.
6. DULL.
7. HARSH.
8. SOUR.
9. THIRSTY.

dry verb
1. To make or become free of moisture: drying dishes; a soap that dries out the skin.
Syns: dehydrate, desiccate, exsiccate, parch.
2. HARDEN.

dry up verb
1. To make or become no longer fresh or shapely because of loss of moisture: The cut flowers wilted and dried up in the hot sun.
Syns: mummify, mummy, sear, shrivel, wither, wizen.
2. To make or become no longer active or productive: When he went into exile, his imagination simply dried up.
Syns: deplete, desiccate, drain, give out, play out, run dry, run out.

dryness noun
1. INSIPIDITY.
2. TEMPERANCE.

dual adjective
1. DOUBLE.
2. TWIN.

dub¹ verb NAME.

dub² noun LUMP¹.

dubiety noun DOUBT.

dubious adjective
1. AMBIGUOUS.
2. DISTRUSTFUL.
3. DOUBTFUL.
4. RACY.

dubiously adverb SKEPTICALLY.

dubiousness noun DOUBT.

dubitable adjective AMBIGUOUS.

duck verb
1. AVOID.
2. DIP.
3. EVADE.

ductile adjective MALLEABLE.

ductility noun FLEXIBILITY.

dud noun FAILURE.

dudgeon noun OFFENSE.

duds noun DRESS.

due adjective
1. Owed as a debt: The rent is due on the first of each month. The bookkeeper tallied the accounts due.
Syns: outstanding, owed, owing, payable, receivable, unpaid, unsettled.
2. Known to be about to arrive: not home, but due shortly.
Syns: anticipated, expected, scheduled.
3. JUST.

due noun
1. Something justly deserved: Give the devil his due.
Syns: comeuppance (also comeupance) (Informal), desert², lumps, recompense, reward, wage(s). —Idioms just deserts, what is coming to one, what one has coming.
2. DEBT.

due adverb DIRECTLY.

duel verb RESIST.

dulcet adjective MELODIOUS.

dulcify verb PACIFY.

dull adjective
1. Lacking responsiveness or alertness: senses grown dull with fatigue; a dull stupor.
Syns: benumbed, insensible, insensitive, numb, unresponsive, wooden.
2. Not physically sharp or keen: a dull blade.
Syn: blunt.

3. Lacking liveliness, charm, or surprise: *a competent but dull performance by a veteran actor.*
Syns: colorless, drab¹, dry, earthbound (*also* earth-bound), flat, lackluster, lifeless, lusterless, matter-of-fact, spiritless, pedestrian, prosaic, unimaginative, uninspired.
4. Lacking vividness in color: *a dull brown.*
Syns: dim, drab¹, flat, muddy, murky (*also* mirky).
5. Lacking gloss and luster: *a dull finish on the cabinet.*
Syns: flat, lackluster, lusterless, mat (*also* matte).
6. BACKWARD.
7. BLIND.
8. BORING.
9. DEPRESSED.
10. INSENSITIVE.
11. SLOW.
dull *verb*
1. To make or become less sharp-edged: *Misuse will dull the scissors.*
Syns: blunt, turn. —*Idiom* take the edge off.
2. To make or become less keen or responsive: *afraid that television might dull the minds of viewers.*
Syns: dim, hebetate, stupefy.
3. DEADEN.
4. OBSCURE.
dullard *noun*
A mentally dull person: *had to tell the dullard four times to close the door.*
Syns: blockhead (*Slang*), dimwit (*Slang*), dolt, dumbbell (*Slang*), dunce, numskull (*also* numbskull), thickhead.
dullness *noun*
1. INSIPIDITY.
2. LETHARGY.
dumb *adjective*
1. Lacking the power or faculty of speech: *A disease in childhood left her deaf and dumb.*
Syns: aphonic, inarticulate, mute, speechless, voiceless.
2. SPEECHLESS.
3. STUPID.
dumbbell *noun* DULLARD.
dumbfound *verb* SEE **dumfound.**
dumbfounded *adjective* SEE **dumfounded.**
dumbness *noun* SILENCE.
dumfound *also* **dumbfound** *verb* STAGGER.
dumfounded *also* **dumbfounded** *adjective* SHOCKED.

dump *verb*
1. DISCARD.
2. SELL OFF at **sell.**
3. UNLOAD.
dumping *noun* DISPOSAL.
dumps *noun* GLOOM.
dumpy *adjective* STOCKY.
dunce *noun* DULLARD.
dunk *verb* DIP.
duo *noun* PAIR.
dupable *adjective* EASY.
dupe *noun*
A person who is easily deceived or victimized: *became the dupe of a clever swindler.*
Syns: butt³, chump¹ (*Slang*), fool, gudgeon (*Slang*), gull, mark, monkey (*Slang*), mug (*Brit.*), patsy (*Slang*), pigeon (*Slang*), pushover (*Informal*), sap¹ (*Slang*), sucker (*Slang*), tool, victim. —*Idioms* easy mark, fall guy.
dupe *verb* DECEIVE.
duple *adjective* DOUBLE.
duplex *adjective* DOUBLE.
duplicate *noun* DOUBLE.
duplicate *verb*
1. COPY.
2. DOUBLE.
duplicate *adjective* DOUBLE.
duplicitous *adjective* UNDERHAND.
duplicity *noun* DECEIT.
duration *noun*
1. CONTINUATION.
2. LIFE.
3. TERM.
duress *noun* FORCE.
dusk *noun* EVENING.
duskiness *noun* DARK.
dusky *adjective*
1. BLACKISH.
2, 3. DARK.
dust *verb*
1. RUSH.
2. SPRINKLE.
dust off *verb* MURDER.
dusting *noun* TROUNCING.
dusty *adjective* FINE¹.
Dutch *noun* TROUBLE.
dutiful *adjective* DEFERENTIAL.
duty *noun*
1. An act or course of action that is demanded of one, as by position, custom, law, or religion: *It is the duty of the physician to heal the sick.*
Syns: charge, commitment, committal, imperative, must, need, obligation, responsibility.
2. The condition of being put to use: *a cleanser for heavy kitchen duty.*

Syns: application, employment,
service, use, utilization.
3. TASK.
4. TAX.
dwarf *adjective* TINY.
dwell *verb*
1. CONSIST.
2. LIVE[1].
  dwell on (or **upon**) *verb* BROOD.
dwelling *noun* HOME.
dwindle *verb* DECREASE.
dye *noun* COLOR.
  dye *verb*
1. COLOR.
2. DIP.
dyestuff *noun* COLOR.
dynamic also **dynamical** *adjective*
1. ENERGETIC.
2. FORCEFUL.
3. VIGOROUS.
dynamite *verb* DESTROY.
dynamize *verb* ACTIVATE.
dynamo *noun* EAGER BEAVER.
dysphoria *noun* GLOOM.

E

eager *adjective*
Intensely desirous or interested:
*executives eager for profits; eager football
fans.*
  Syns: agog, anxious, appetent, ardent,
athirst, avid, bursting, impatient,
keen[1], raring (*Informal*), solicitous,
thirsting, thirsty. —*Idioms* champing
at the bit, ready and willing.
eager beaver *noun*
Informal. An intensely energetic,
enthusiastic person: *eager beavers who
couldn't wait to get started.*
  Syns: dynamo (*Informal*), energumen,
go-getter (*Informal*), hustler, live wire
(*Slang*).
ear *noun* HEARING.
earlier *adverb*
1. At a time in the past: *had heard that
rumor earlier.*
  Syns: aforetime (*Archaic*), already,
before, beforetime (*Rare*), erstwhile
(*Archaic*), formerly, heretofore, once.
2. Up to this time: *straightened out what
had earlier been a mess.*
  Syns: heretofore, yet.

3. Until then: *You'll hear from me on
Monday and not earlier.*
  Syns: before, beforehand.
earliest *adjective* FIRST.
early *adjective*
1. At or near the start of a period,
development, or series: *early stages of
cancer.*
  Syns: beginning, first, initial.
2. Of, existing, or occurring in a distant
period: *Early man discovered fire.*
  Syns: ancient, antediluvian (*also
antediluvial*), primitive, primordial.
3. Developing, occurring, or appearing
before the expected time: *an early
death; an early robin.*
  Syns: precocious, premature,
untimely.
  early *adverb*
Before the expected time: *She arrived
early.*
  Syns: aforehand (*Chiefly Regional*),
ahead, beforehand, betimes. —*Idioms*
ahead of time, in advance, with time
to spare.
earmark *verb* APPROPRIATE.
earn *verb*
1. To receive, as wages, for one's labor:
earned $20,000 a year.
  Syns: drag down (*Slang*), draw down,
gain, get, make, pull down, win.
—*Idioms* earn (*or* make) a living,
earn one's keep, make one's way.
2. To acquire as a result of one's
behavior or effort: *He has earned our
respect through his bravery.*
  Syns: deserve, gain, get, merit, rate[1]
(*Informal*), win.
3. RETURN.
earnest *adjective*
1. GRAVE[2].
2. SERIOUS.
  earnest *noun.*
1. PAWN[1].
2. SERIOUSNESS.
earnestness *noun* SERIOUSNESS.
earnings *noun* WAGE(S).
earshot *noun* HEARING.
earth *noun*
The celestial body where humans live:
The spacecraft orbited the earth.
  Syn: world.
earthbound also **earth-bound**
adjective
1. DULL.
2. EARTHLY.
earthen *adjective*
1. EARTHLY.
2. EARTHY.
earthiness *noun* PHYSICALITY.
earthlike *adjective* EARTHY.

earthly *adjective*
1. Pertaining to or characteristic of the earth or of human life on earth: *totally occupied with earthly pursuits.*
   Syns: earthbound (*also* earth-bound), earthen, earthy, mundane, secular, tellurian, telluric, temporal, terrene, terrestrial, worldly.
2. Capable of being anticipated, considered, or imagined: *There is no earthly reason for us to go.*
   Syns: conceivable, imaginable, likely, mortal, possible, thinkable. —*Idioms* humanly possible, within the bounds (*or* realm *or* range) of possibility.

earthquake *noun* TREMOR.

earthy *adjective*
1. Consisting of or resembling soil: *the earthy smell of the woods after a rain.*
   Syns: earthen, earthlike, terrene, terrestrial.
2. COARSE.
3. EARTHLY.

ease *noun*
1. Freedom from constraint, embarrassment, or awkwardness: *the ease of her approach to a stranger.*
   Syns: easiness, informality, naturalness, poise, spontaneity, unrestraint.
2. The ability to perform without apparent effort: *translated the document with ease.*
   Syns: easiness, effortlessness, facileness, facility, readiness.
3. PROSPERITY.
4. RELIEF.
5. REST¹.

ease *verb*
1. To reduce in tension, pressure, or rigidity: *The pull of the current eased as the tide turned. I eased off on the anchor line.*
   Syns: lax, let up, loose, loosen, relax, slack, slacken, untighten.
2. To make less difficult: *Use short cuts to ease and speed your work.*
   Syns: expedite, facilitate. —*Idioms* clear (*or* prepare) the way for, grease the wheels, open the door for (*or* to).
3. To maneuver gently and slowly into place: *ease a pie into the oven.*
   Syns: glide, slide, slip.
4. EDGE.
5. RELIEVE.

ease off *verb*
1. SUBSIDE.
2. WEAKEN.

easeful *adjective* COMFORTABLE.

easiness *noun*
1, 2. EASE.

easy *adjective*
1. Posing no difficulty: *an easy solution to the problem.*
   Syns: effortless, facile, ready, simple, smooth, snap (*Informal*). —*Idioms* easy as ABC, easy as falling off a log, easy as one-two-three, easy as pie, like taking candy from a baby, nothing to it.
2. Easily imposed on or tricked: *an easy target for swindlers.*
   Syns: dupable, exploitable, gullible, naive (*also* naïve, naif, naïf), susceptible.
3. AMIABLE.
4. COMFORTABLE.
5. EASYGOING.
6. GRADUAL.
7. LIGHT².
8. PROSPEROUS.
9. SMOOTH.
10. TOLERANT.
11. WANTON.

easygoing *adjective*
1. Unconstrained by rigid standards: *an easygoing person who never worried.*
   Syns: casual, common (*Chiefly Regional*), easy, easy-osey (*also* easy-osie) (*Scot.*), informal, laid-back (*Slang*), relaxed.
2. AMIABLE.

easy-osey *also* **easy-osie** *adjective* EASYGOING.

easy street *also* **Easy Street** *noun* PROSPERITY.

eat *verb*
1. To take (food) into the body as nourishment: *ate a hearty dinner.*
   Syns: chow (*Slang*), consume, devour, discuss (*Rare*), fare (*Rare*), grub (*Slang*), ingest, meal, partake (of). —*Idioms* break bread, have (*or* take) a bite, take nourishment.
2. BITE.
3. CONSUME.

eat up *verb*
1. To be avidly interested in: *She just eats up gossip.*
   Syns: devour, feast (on), relish. —*Idiom* eat up with a greasy spoon.
2. ADORE.
3, 4. CONSUME.
5. EXHAUST.

eatable *adjective* EDIBLE.

eats *noun* FOOD.

eavesdrop *verb* SPY.

ebb *verb*
1. DECREASE.
2. RECEDE.

3. SUBSIDE.

ebb *noun* WANE.

ebb *adjective* SHALLOW.

ebbing *noun* FAILURE.

ebon *adjective* BLACK.

ebony *adjective* BLACK.

ebullient *adjective* EXUBERANT.

ecbole *noun* DIGRESSION.

eccentric *adjective*
Deviating from the customary: *an eccentric person; eccentric habits.*
    Syns: bizarre, curious, erratic, freakish, idiosyncratic, odd, oddball (*Informal*), peculiar, quaint[1], queer, quirky, rum (*also* rummy) (*Brit. Slang*), singular, strange, unusual, weird.

eccentric *noun* CRACKPOT.

eccentricity *noun*
Peculiar behavior: *Living as a recluse is just one of his eccentricities.*
    Syns: idiosyncrasy, peculiarity, quirk, singularity.

ecclesiastic *noun* PREACHER.

ecclesiastical *adjective* SPIRITUAL.

echinate *adjective* THORNY.

echo *noun*
1. Repetition of sound via reflection from a surface: *heard an echo of the cry across the canyon.*
    Syns: rebound, repercussion, resounding, reverberation.
2. Imitative reproduction, as of the style of another: *paintings that were echoes of the Impressionists.*
    Syns: reflection, repetition, reflex.
3. One who mindlessly imitates another: *He is but an echo of the king's wishes.*
    Syns: imitator, mimic, parrot.

echo *verb*
1. To send back the sound of: *The canyon echoed her cry.*
    Syns: rebound, re-echo, reflect, repeat, resound, reverberate.
2. To copy (another) slavishly: *corporate minions who merely echoed the style of the president; a composition that echoes Brahms.*
    Syns: image, imitate, mimic, mirror, parrot, reflect, repeat.

echoic *adjective*
Imitating sounds: *The word "cuckoo" is echoic of the bird's call.*
    Syns: imitative, onomatopoeic (*also* onomatopoetic).

echoism *noun*
The formation of words in imitation of sounds: *The word "buzz" is an example of echoism.*
    Syns: onomatopoeia (*also* onomatopoësis).

eclipse *verb* OBSCURE.

economical *adjective*
Careful in the use of material resources: *an economical shopper.*
    Syns: canny, chary, forehanded, frugal, provident, prudent, saving, Scotch, sparing, stewardly, thrifty, wary.

economize *verb*
To use without wasting: *economize on gas by making fewer trips.*
    Syns: save, spare. —*Idiom* keep within compass.

economy *noun*
Careful use of material resources: *One must practice economy when buying food.*
    Syns: forehandedness, frugality, providence, prudence, thrift, thriftiness.

ecstasy *noun* HEAVEN.

ecumenical *adjective* UNIVERSAL.

edacious *adjective*
1. GREEDY.
2. VORACIOUS.

edacity *noun* VORACITY.

eddy *verb* SWIRL.

edge *noun*
1. The cutting part of a sharp instrument: *the edge of a sword.*
    Syn: blade. —*Idiom* cutting edge.
2. A cutting quality: *His voice had an edge to it.*
    Syns: bite, incisiveness, keenness, sharpness, sting. —*Idiom* cutting edge.
3. ADVANTAGE.
4. BORDER.
5. VERGE.

edge *verb*
1. To advance carefully and gradually: *edged my way across the crowded room.*
    Syns: ease, sidle.
2. BORDER.
3. SHARPEN.

edge in *verb* INSINUATE.

edging *noun* BORDER.

edgy *adjective*
Feeling or exhibiting nervous tension: *The pilots were edgy before the mission.*
    Syns: fidgety, jittery (*Informal*), jumpy, goosey (*also* goosy) (*Informal*), nervous, nervy (*Chiefly Brit.*), restive, restless, skittish, tense, twitchy, uneasy, up tight (*also* uptight) (*Slang*). —*Idioms* a bundle of nerves, all wound up, on edge, on the ragged edge.

edible *adjective*
Fit to be eaten: *edible fare.*
    Syns: comestible, eatable, esculent.

edible(s) *noun* FOOD.
edict *noun*
1. ANNOUNCEMENT.
2. LAW.
3. RULING.
edification *noun* ILLUMINATION.
edifice *noun* BUILDING.
edify *verb* ILLUMINATE.
edifying *adjective*
1. CULTURAL.
2. EDUCATIONAL.
educable *adjective*
Capable of being educated: *retarded yet educable children.*
Syns: instructible, teachable.
educand *noun* STUDENT.
educate *verb*
1. To impart knowledge and skill to: *educate our children.*
Syns: discipline, instruct, teach, train, tutor.
2. INFORM.
educated *adjective*
1. Having an education: *an educated person.*
Syns: enlightened, informed, instructed, lettered, literate.
2. INFORMED.
education *noun*
1. The act, process, or art of imparting knowledge and skill: *great advances in public education.*
Syns: instruction, pedagogics, pedagogy, schooling, teaching, training, tuition, tutelage, tutoring.
2. Known facts, ideas, and skills that have been imparted: *received a good education; a man of education.*
Syns: erudition, instruction, knowledge, learning, scholarship, science.
educational *adjective*
Serving to educate or inform: *educational TV programs.*
Syns: edifying, educative, enlightening, informative, instructional, instructive.
educationist *noun* EDUCATOR.
educative *adjective* EDUCATIONAL.
educator *noun*
One who educates: *high-school and college educators.*
Syns: educationist (*Chiefly Brit.*), instructor, pedagogist, pedagogue, teacher.
educe *verb*
1. DERIVE.
2. EVOKE.
eerie *also* **eery** *adjective* WEIRD.
effacement *noun* ERASURE.

effect *noun*
1. Something brought about by a cause: *The effect of good advertising was increased sales.*
Syns: aftermath, consequence, corollary, event, fruit, harvest, issue, outcome, precipitate, result, resultant, sequel, sequence, sequent, upshot.
—*Idiom* end product.
2. The power or capacity to produce a desired result: *Our advice had no effect on them.*
Syns: effectiveness, efficacy, efficiency, influence, potency.
3. The condition of being in full force or operation: *The law goes into effect tomorrow.*
Syns: actualization, being, realization.
effect *verb*
1. To carry to a successful conclusion: *effected reunification of the country.*
Syns: bring off, carry out, carry through, effectuate, execute, put through, swing (*Slang*). —*Idiom* bring to a happy issue.
2. CAUSE.
3. ENFORCE.
effective *adjective*
1. Producing or able to produce a desired effect: *an effective reprimand; an antitoxin effective against snakebite.*
Syns: effectual, efficacious, efficient, productive, virtuous (*Rare*).
2. EFFICIENT.
3. FORCEFUL.
4. In effect: *The law is effective immediately.*
Syn: operative.
effectiveness *noun*
1. EFFECT.
2. EFFICIENCY.
effects *noun*
1. One's portable property: *The deceased's effects are here.*
Syns: belongings, chattels, goods, lares and penates, movables (*also* moveables) (*Law*), possessions, things.
2. BELONGINGS.
effectual *adjective* EFFECTIVE.
effectuate *verb*
1. CAUSE.
2. EFFECT.
effectuation *noun* PERFORMANCE.
effeminacy *noun*
The quality of being effeminate: *a man who projected an air of effeminacy.*
Syns: effeminateness, femininity, womanishness.

effeminate *adjective*
Having qualities more appropriate to
women than to men: *He had a high,
effeminate voice.*
   Syns: epicene, feminine, sissified,
swish (*Slang*), unmanly, womanish.
effeminate *verb*
To make effeminate: *Luxurious living
effeminated their manners.*
   Syns: effeminize, feminize.
effeminateness *noun* EFFEMINACY.
effeminize *verb* EFFEMINATE.
effervesce *verb* FOAM.
effervescent *adjective* EXUBERANT.
efficacious *adjective* EFFECTIVE.
efficacy *noun*
  1. EFFECT.
  2. EFFICIENCY.
efficiency *noun*
  1. The quality of being efficient: *tested
the fuel efficiency of the engine.*
   Syns: effectiveness, efficacy,
performance, productivity.
  2. EFFECT.
efficient *adjective*
  1. Acting effectively with minimal
waste: *an efficient motor; an efficient
secretary.*
   Syns: effective, high-performance,
productive, proficient.
  2. BUSINESSLIKE.
  3. EFFECTIVE.
effloresce *verb* BLOOM.
efflorescence *noun* BLOOM.
effort *noun*
  1. The use of energy to do something:
This job isn't worth the effort.
   Syns: endeavor, exertion, pains,
strain[1], striving, struggle, trouble,
while. —*Idiom* elbow grease.
  2. An earnest try: *Please make an effort
to be prompt.*
   Syns: attempt, endeavor, essay, trial.
  3. ACCOMPLISHMENT.
  4. TASK.
effortful *adjective*
  1. BURDENSOME.
  2. FORCED.
effortless *adjective*
  1. EASY.
  2. SMOOTH.
effortlessness *noun* EASE.
effrontery *noun*
  1. IMPUDENCE.
  2. PRESUMPTION.
effulgent *adjective* BRIGHT.
effuse *verb* POUR.
egg on *verb* PROVOKE.
ego *noun*
  1. EGOTISM.

  2. PRIDE.
  3. SELF.
egocentric *adjective*
  1. Concerned with the person rather
than with society: *an egocentric
philosophy advocating the virtue of
selfishness.*
   Syns: egoistic (*also* egoistical),
individualist, individualistic.
  2. EGOTISTICAL.
egocentric *noun* EGOTIST.
egocentricity *noun* EGOISM.
egocentrism *noun* EGOISM.
egoism *noun*
  1. Concern only for oneself: *His egoism
precluded any thought for the feelings
of others.*
   Syns: egocentricity, egocentrism, self-
absorption, self-centeredness,
selfishness.
  2, 3. EGOTISM.
egoist *noun* EGOTIST.
egoistic *also* **egoistical** *adjective*
  1. EGOCENTRIC.
  2. EGOTISTICAL.
egomaniac *noun* EGOTIST.
egomaniacal *adjective* EGOTISTICAL.
egotism *noun*
  1. An exaggerated belief in one's own
importance: *a person consumed by
egotism.*
   Syns: bighead (*Informal*),
bigheadedness (*Informal*), egoism,
self-importance, swelled head
(*Informal*).
  2. A regarding of oneself with undue
favor: *His incessant boasting is
evidence of egotism.*
   Syns: amour-propre, conceit, ego,
egoism, ego trip (*Slang*), narcissism
(*also* narcism), pride, vainglory,
vainness, vanity.
egotist *noun*
A conceited, self-centered person: *an
egotist who constantly aggrandized his
abilities.*
   Syns: egocentric, egoist, egomaniac,
narcissist. —*Idioms* no modest violet,
the big It, the only pebble on the
beach.
egotistical *or* **egotistic** *adjective*
  1. Thinking too highly of oneself: *an
egotistical person who thought he was
never wrong.*
   Syns: conceited, narcissistic, stuck-up
(*Informal*), swellheaded (*Informal*),
vainglorious.
  2. Concerned only with oneself: *an
egotistical executive absorbed with his
own advancement.*

Syns: egocentric, egoistic (*also* egoistical), egomaniacal, self-absorbed, self-centered, selfish, self-seeking, self-serving. —*Idiom* all wrapped up in oneself.

ego trip *noun* EGOTISM.

egregious *adjective* FLAGRANT.

egress *noun* DEPARTURE.

eidolon *noun* GHOST.

ejaculate *verb* EXCLAIM.

ejaculation *noun* EXCLAMATION.

eject *verb*
1. To put out by force: *eject a heckler from the meeting.*
Syns: boot[1] (out) (*Slang*), bounce (*Slang*), bump, chuck[1] (*Informal*), dismiss, evict, expel, kick out (*Slang*), oust, throw out. —*Idioms* give someone his walking papers, give the old heave-ho, send packing, show someone the door, throw out on one's ear.
2. To catapult oneself from a disabled aircraft: *The pilot ejected at 20,000 feet.*
Syns: bail out, jump.
3. ERUPT.

ejection *noun*
The act of ejecting or the state of being ejected: *ejection from the apartment.*
Syns: dismissal, ejectment, eviction, expulsion, ouster. —*Idioms* the boot, the bounce, the chuck.

ejectment *noun* EJECTION.

elaborate *adjective*
1. Complexly detailed: *an elaborate carving.*
Syns: complicated, fancy, intricate.
2. COMPLEX.

elaborate *verb*
1. To express at greater length or in greater detail: *said he was leaving and refused to elaborate. Will you elaborate your point?*
Syns: amplify, develop, dilate (on), enlarge (on), expand (on), expatiate (on), labor.
2. To disclose bit by bit: *gradually elaborated the true nature of the plan.*
Syns: develop, evolve. —*Idioms* fill in the details, go into detail.

élan *noun* SPIRIT.

elapse *verb* GO.

elastic *adjective*
1, 2. FLEXIBLE.

elasticity *noun*
1. FLEXIBILITY.
2. RESILIENCE.

elate *verb*
To raise the spirits of: *Winning the gold medal elated the team.*

Syns: animate, buoy (up), elevate, exalt, exhilarate, flush, inspire, inspirit, lift, uplift.

elate *adjective* ELATED.

elated *adjective*
Feeling great delight and joy: *The commanders were elated by the victory.*
Syns: elate, elevated, exalted, exhilarated, flushed, inspired, overjoyed, turned-on (*Slang*), uplifted.

elatedness *noun* ELATION.

elation *noun*
1. High spirits: *felt great elation at winning the regatta.*
Syns: animation, elatedness, euphoria, exaltation, exhilaration, inspiration, lift, uplift.
2. *Psychiatry.* An exaggerated feeling of well-being and pleasure: *mood swings ranging from elation to depression.*
Syns: euphoria (*Psychiatry*), exaltation, intoxication.

elbowroom *noun* FREEDOM.

elder *noun*
1, 2. SENIOR.
3. SUPERIOR.

elder *adjective* SENIOR.

elderliness *noun* AGE.

elderly *adjective* OLD.

elect *verb*
1. To select by vote for an office: *elect a new president.*
Syns: ballot, vote (in).
2. CHOOSE.

elect *noun*
One that is selected: *Only the elect can belong to that club.*
Syns: choice, pick, select.

elect *adjective* SELECT.

election *noun* CHOICE.

elective *adjective* OPTIONAL.

elector *noun*
One who votes: *The electors have cast their ballots.*
Syns: balloter, voter.

electrifying *adjective* STARTLING.

eleemosynary *adjective* BENEVOLENT.

elegance *noun*
Refined, effortless beauty of manner, form, and style: *He noticed her unaffected elegance.*
Syns: grace, polish, urbanity.

elegant *adjective*
1. Of such tasteful beauty as to elicit admiration: *an elegant gown; an elegant woman.*
Syns: exquisite, graceful.
2. DELICATE.

element *noun*
1. A fundamental, irreducible

constituent of a whole: *studied the
elements of music.*
Syns: basic, essential, fundamental,
rudiment. —*Idiom* part and parcel.
2. One of the individual entities
contributing to a whole: *the
grammatical elements of a sentence;
ambition as a key element to success.*
Syns: component, constituent, factor,
ingredient, integrant, part. —*Idiom*
building block.
3. An individually considered portion of
a whole: *dissected the argument
element by element.*
Syns: article, detail, item, particular,
point.

elemental *adjective*
1. Of or being an irreducible element:
*elemental aspects of existence such as
birth and death.*
Syns: basic, elementary, essential,
fundamental, primitive, ultimate,
underlying.
2. CONSTITUTIONAL.

elementary *adjective*
1. Of or treating the simplest aspects:
an elementary math text.
Syns: basal, basic, beginning,
rudimental, rudimentary.
2. ELEMENTAL.

elephantine *adjective*
1. GIANT.
2. HEAVY.
3. PONDEROUS.

elevate *verb*
1. To move (something) to a higher
position: *The nurse elevated the
patient's bed. Cranes elevated the
crates onto the ship.*
Syns: boost, hoist, lift, pick up, raise,
take up, uphold, uplift, upraise.
2. To increase markedly in level or
intensity, esp. of sound: *The musician
elevated the instrument's volume.*
Syns: amplify, heighten, raise.
3. DISTINGUISH.
4. ELATE.
5. EXALT.
6. PROMOTE.

elevated *adjective*
1. Being positioned above a given level:
an elevated train.
Syns: lifted, raised, uplifted, upraised,
uprisen.
2. Being on a high intellectual or moral
level: *elevated opinions on human
rights.*
Syns: high-minded, moral, noble.
3. Abnormally increased, esp. in
intensity: *an elevated fever.*
Syns: heightened, high, raised.

4. Exceedingly dignified in form, tone,
or style: *elevated prose.*
Syns: eloquent, exalted, grand, high,
high-flown, lofty.
5. ELATED.
6. EXALTED.
7. GRAND.
8. TALL.

elevation *noun*
1. The distance of something from a
given level: *the elevation of the land
above sea level.*
Syns: altitude, height.
2. ADVANCEMENT.
3. EXALTATION.

elicit *verb* EVOKE.

eligibility *noun* QUALIFICATION.

eligible *adjective*
1. Satisfying the requirements, as for
selection: *eligible varsity players;
eligible voters.*
Syns: fit, fitted, qualified, suitable,
worthy.
2. Deemed suitable for marriage: *an
eligible bachelor.*
Syns: marriable (*Archaic*),
marriageable.

eligibleness *noun* QUALIFICATION.

eliminant *adjective* ELIMINATIVE.

eliminate *verb*
1. To get rid of, esp. by banishment or
execution: *The dictator has eliminated
all opposition.*
Syns: eradicate, liquidate, remove,
purge, wipe out. —*Idioms* do away
with, put an end to.
2. *Physiol.* To discharge (wastes or
foreign substances) from the body:
*The kidneys function to eliminate
bodily wastes.*
Syns: evacuate, excrete, purge (*Med.*).
3. DROP.
4. EXCLUDE.

elimination *noun*
1. The act or process of eliminating:
elimination of all opposing voices.
Syns: clearance, eradication,
liquidation, purge, removal, riddance.
2. *Physiol.* The act or process of
discharging bodily wastes or foreign
substances: *The liver aids in the
elimination of alcohol from the system.*
Syns: evacuation, excretion,
purgation.
3. DISPOSAL.

eliminative *adjective*
Of, relating to, or tending to eliminate:
*the eliminative organs of the body; drugs
serving eliminative functions.*
Syns: cathartic, eliminant,

eliminatory, evacuant, evacuative, excretory, purgative.

eliminatory *adjective* ELIMINATIVE.

elite also **élite** *noun*
1. BEST.
2. SOCIETY.

elitist also **élitist** *adjective* SNOBBISH.

elitist also **élitist** *noun* SNOB.

elixir *noun* CURE.

elocution *noun* ORATORY.

elocutionary *adjective* ORATORICAL.

elongate *verb* LENGTHEN.

elongate *adjective* LONG¹.

elongated *adjective* LONG¹.

elongation *noun* EXTENSION.

eloquence *noun*
Vivid, effective, or persuasive communication in speech or artistic performance: *gave the oration with eloquence.*
Syns: eloquentness, expression, expressiveness, expressivity, facundity.

eloquent *adjective*
1. Fluently persuasive and forceful: *an eloquent rebuttal.*
Syns: articulate, facund, fluent, silver-tongued, smooth-spoken.
2. ELEVATED.
3. EXPRESSIVE.

eloquentness *noun* ELOQUENCE.

elucidate *verb* CLARIFY.

elucidation *noun* EXPLANATION.

elucidative *adjective* EXPLANATORY.

elude *verb*
1. AVOID.
2. ESCAPE.
3. LOSE.

elusion *noun* ESCAPE.

elusive *adjective* EVASIVE.

emaciated *adjective* WASTED.

emanate *verb* STEM.

emancipate *verb* FREE.

emancipated *adjective* FREE.

emancipation *noun* LIBERTY.

embark *verb* START.

embarrass *verb*
1. To cause (a person) to be self-consciously distressed: *Personal questions embarrass me.*
Syns: abash, chagrin, confound, confuse, discomfort, disconcert, discountenance, faze, mortify, put out, rattle (*Informal*). —Idioms put on the spot, put to the blush.
2. COMPLICATE.

embarrassed *adjective*
Distressed and ill at ease: *I am embarrassed by my child's misbehavior.*
Syns: abashed, chagrined,
confounded, disconcerted, mortified, put-out, rattled (*Informal*).

embarrassing *adjective*
Causing self-conscious distress: *asked embarrassing questions about the divorce.*
Syns: awkward, incommodious, mortifying.

embarrassment *noun*
1. Self-conscious distress: *a face red with embarrassment; financial embarrassment.*
Syns: abashment, chagrin, confusion, discomfiture, discomposure, disconcertion, disconcertment.
2. EXCESS.

embed also **imbed** *verb* FIX.

embellish *verb*
1. ADORN.
2. GRACE.

embellishment *noun* ADORNMENT.

embitter *verb*
To make or become bitter: *Their hard life has embittered them.*
Syns: bitter, sour.

embittered *adjective* RESENTFUL.

emblem *noun* SYMBOL.

emblematic also **emblematical** *adjective* SYMBOLIC.

embodiment *noun*
A physical entity typifying an abstraction: *a soldier who was the very embodiment of courage.*
Syns: incarnation, personification, prosopopeia (*also* prosopopoeia) (*Rhet.*), substantiation.

embody *verb*
1. To represent (an abstraction) in or as if in bodily form: *The general embodies the spirit of revolution and freedom.*
Syns: exteriorize, externalize, incarnate, manifest, materialize, objectify, personalize, personify, substantiate.
2. To make a part of a united whole: *a judicial system embodying much of Roman law.*
Syns: combine, incorporate, integrate.
3. CONTAIN.
4. REPRESENT.

embolden *verb* ENCOURAGE.

embrace *verb*
1. To put one's arms around affectionately: *She embraced her husband.*
Syns: bosom (*Archaic*), clasp, clinch (*Slang*), clip² (*Brit. Regional*), enfold (*also* infold), hold, hug, press, squeeze.
2. ACCEPT.

3. ADOPT.
4. CONTAIN.

embrace noun
The act of embracing: *held his wife in a warm embrace.*
Syns: clasp, clinch (*Slang*), hug, squeeze.

embracement noun ADOPTION.

embracing noun ADOPTION.

embrangle verb INVOLVE.

embroil verb INVOLVE.

embroilment noun ENTANGLEMENT.

embrue verb SEE **imbrue.**

embrued adjective SEE **imbrued.**

embryo noun GERM.

emend verb
1. CORRECT.
2. REVISE.

emendate verb REVISE.

emendation noun REVISION.

emendatory adjective CORRECTIVE.

emerge verb
1. APPEAR.
2. DAWN.

emergency noun CRISIS.

emergency adjective AUXILIARY.

emigrant noun
One who emigrates: *an island full of Southeast Asian emigrants.*
Syns: immigrant, migrant, transmigrant.

emigrate verb
To leave one's native land and to settle in another: *In 1908 he emigrated to America from Italy.*
Syns: immigrate, migrate, transmigrate.

emigration noun
Departure from one's native land to settle in another: *the emigration of Soviet Jews to Israel.*
Syns: exodus, immigration, migration, transmigration.

émigré noun
1. One forced to emigrate, usu. for political reasons: *Paris was the new home for many White Russian émigrés.*
Syns: exile, expatriate, expellee.
2. FOREIGNER.

eminence noun
1. A position of exalted, widely recognized importance: *a man of eminence in medicine.*
Syns: distinction, eminency (*Obs.*), glory, illustriousness, luster, mark, notability, note, pre-eminence (*also* preeminence, preëminence), prestige, prominence (*also* prominency), renown.

2. DIGNITARY.
3. HILL.

eminency noun
1. EMINENCE.
2. FORTE.

eminent adjective
Widely known and esteemed: *an eminent statesman and scholar.*
Syns: celebrated, distinguished, famed, famous, great, illustrious, lustrous, notable, noted, pre-eminent (*also* preeminent, preëminent), prestigious, prominent, redoubtable, renowned.

eminently adverb VERY.

emit verb
1. To discharge material, as vapor or fumes, usu. suddenly and violently: *a geyser emitting steam.*
Syns: give, give forth, give off, give out, issue, let off, let out, release, send forth, throw off, vent.
2. DISCHARGE.
3. SHED.

emolument noun WAGE(S).

emote verb EMOTIONALIZE.

emotion noun
A complex and usu. strong subjective response, as love, hate, etc.: *a person of emotion, not reason.*
Syns: affection[1], affectivity, feeling, sentiment.

emotionable adjective EMOTIONAL.

emotional adjective
1. Readily stirred by emotion: *an emotional person who cried a lot.*
Syns: emotionable, feeling, sensitive, sentient.
2. Relating to, arising from, or appealing to the emotions: *an emotional appeal for help.*
Syns: affective, emotive, moving.

emotionalize verb
To make an emotional display: *a mother emotionalizing over her sick child.*
Syns: emote, gush.

emotionless adjective
1, 2. COLD.

emotive adjective EMOTIONAL.

empathetic adjective
UNDERSTANDING.

empathize verb
1. IDENTIFY.
2. SYMPATHIZE.

empathy noun SYMPATHY.

emphasis noun
Special weight placed upon something considered important: *a strong emphasis on foreign languages.*
Syns: accent, accentuation, stress.

emphasize *verb*
To accord emphasis to: *a school emphasizing academic discipline.*
   Syns: accent, accentuate, feature, italicize, play up (*Informal*), point up, stress, underline, underscore.
   —*Idioms* bear down hard on (*or* upon), lay stress on (*or* upon).

emphatic *adjective*
1. Expressed or performed with emphasis: *My answer is an emphatic "No"!*
   Syns: accented, accentuated, forceful, resounding, underlined, underscored.
2. Bold and definite in character: *an emphatic gesture of disapproval.*
   Syns: assertive, forceful, insistent.

emphatically *adverb* FLATLY.

emplacement *noun* POSITION.

employ *verb*
1. To obtain the use or services of: *employed a new secretary.*
   Syns: engage, hire, retain, take on.
   —*Idiom* put on the payroll.
2. USE.

employ *noun*
1. BUSINESS.
2. EMPLOYMENT.

employable *adjective*
1. OPEN.
2. USABLE.

employe also **employé** *noun* SEE **employee**.

employed *adjective*
1. Having a job: *statistics on employed women.*
   Syns: hired, jobholding, working.
2. BUSY.

employee also **employe, employé** *noun*
One who is employed by another: *a company of 100 employees.*
   Syns: hireling, jobholder, worker.

employer *noun*
One that employs persons for wages: *The employer must withhold Social Security taxes.*
   Syn: hirer.

employment *noun*
1. The act of employing for wages: *investigated the company's methods of employment.*
   Syns: engagement, engaging, hire, hiring.
2. The state of being employed: *No person in our employment will betray trade secrets.*
   Syns: employ, hire.
3. APPLICATION.
4. BUSINESS.

5. DUTY.
6. EXERCISE.

empoison *verb* POISON.

emporium *noun* STORE.

empower *verb*
1. AUTHORIZE.
2. ENABLE.

emprise also **emprize** *noun*
ADVENTURE.

emptiness *noun*
1. Total absence of matter: *The emptiness of the city in early morning is depressing.*
   Syns: vacancy, vacuity, vacuum.
2. Total lack of ideas, meaning, or substance: *the emptiness of political rhetoric.*
   Syns: barrenness, blankness, hollowness, vacancy, vacuity.
3. A desolate sense of loss: *He felt only emptiness after she left him.*
   Syns: blankness, desolation, hollowness, vacuum, void.
4. NOTHINGNESS.

empty *adjective*
1. Containing nothing: *an empty cupboard; an empty apartment.*
   Syns: bare, clear, devoid (of), stark, vacant, vacuous, void.
2. Lacking value, use, or substance: *an empty life.*
   Syns: hollow, idle, nugatory, otiose, vacant, vain.
3. Lacking a desirable element: *writing empty of insight; a person empty of feeling.*
   Syns: barren (of), destitute (of), devoid (of), innocent (of), void (of), wanting. —*Idiom* in want of.
4. VACANT.

empty *verb*
1. To remove the contents of: *emptied the cellar of combustible materials.*
   Syns: clean out, clear, evacuate, vacate, void.
2. DISCHARGE.

empty-headed *adjective*
1. GIDDY.
2. VACANT.

emulate *verb* FOLLOW.

emulative *adjective* IMITATIVE.

emulous *adjective*
1. AMBITIOUS.
2. COMPETITIVE.

enable *verb*
1. To give the means, ability, or opportunity to do: *Modern medicine has enabled us to prolong life.*
   Syns: empower, permit.
2. AUTHORIZE.

enact *verb*
1. To cause to be by official action: *laws enacted by Congress.*
   Syns: constitute, establish, legislate, make.
2. ACT.
3. ESTABLISH.
4. STAGE.

enactment *noun* LAW.

enamored *adjective* INFATUATED.

enceinte *adjective* PREGNANT.

enchant *verb*
1, 2. CHARM.
3. DELIGHT.

enchanting *adjective*
1. ATTRACTIVE.
2. DELIGHTFUL.

enchantment *noun* ATTRACTION.

enchantress *noun*
1. SEDUCTRESS.
2. WITCH.

encircle *verb* SURROUND.

enclose *verb*
1. To confine within a limited area: *convicts enclosed within prison walls; cattle enclosed in feedlots.*
   Syns: cage, coop (in *or* up), fence (in), hem (in *or* about *or* around), immure, mew (up), mure (*Rare*), pen², shut in, wall (in *or* up).
2. CLOSE IN at close¹.
3. SURROUND.

enclosure *noun* COURT.

encompass *verb*
1. CONTAIN.
2. SURROUND.

encounter *verb*
1. To come up against: *They encountered enormous obstacles in the peace talks.*
   Syns: confront, face, meet¹, run into.
2. CONFRONT.
3. ENGAGE.
4. MEET¹.

encounter *noun*
1. BRUSH.
2. CONFRONTATION.

encourage *verb*
1. To impart strength and confidence to: *The doctor's report has encouraged me.*
   Syns: buck up (*Informal*), cheer (up), enhearten, hearten, nerve, perk².
2. To impart courage, inspiration, and resolution to: *encouraged the students to try harder.*
   Syns: animate, cheer (on), embolden, inspirit, inspire, motivate, stimulate.
3. To lend supportive approval to: *The government encouraged the peace initiative.*
   Syns: countenance, favor, smile on (*or* upon).
4. PROMOTE.

encouragement *noun*
1. Something that encourages: *The prospect of a bonus is encouragement to produce a good product.*
   Syns: inspiration, motivation, stimulation.
2. INVITATION.

encouraging *adjective*
Inspiring confidence or hope: *Increased trade with China is an encouraging sign.*
   Syns: cheering, heartening, hopeful, likely, promising, roseate, rose-colored, rosy.

encumber *verb*
1. CHARGE.
2. HINDER.

end *noun*
1. A demarcation point or boundary beyond which something does not extend or occur: *Buffalo lies at the eastern end of Lake Erie. I am at the end of my patience.*
   Syns: bound(s), confine(s), limit, limitation.
2. A concluding or terminating: *the end of the fighting.*
   Syns: cease, cessation, close¹, closing, closure, completion, conclusion, consummation, ending, finish, period, stop, termination, terminus, wind-up (*Informal*), wrap-up. —*Idioms* end of the line, stopping point.
3. The last part: *the end of the performance.*
   Syns: close¹, conclusion, ending, finale, finish, last¹, termination, wind-up (*Informal*), wrap-up.
4. Residual matter: *broken candle ends.*
   Syns: butt⁴, fragment, scrap¹, shard, remnant.
5. INTENTION.
6. TAIL.

end *verb* CLOSE¹.

endanger *verb*
To subject to danger or destruction: *Drunken driving endangers lives.*
   Syns: danger (*Archaic*), imperil, jeopard, jeopardize, jeopardy, menace, peril, risk.

endangerment *noun* DANGER.

endeavor *verb* ATTEMPT.

endeavor *noun*
1. ATTEMPT.
2, 3. EFFORT.

ended *adjective* COMPLETE.

endemic *adjective*
1. INDIGENOUS.
2. NATIVE.

ending *noun*
1., 2. END.

endless *adjective*
1. Having no ends or limits: *an endless stretch of sandy beach; endless patience.*
   Syns: boundless, immeasurable, infinite, limitless, measureless, unbounded, unlimited.
2. Enduring for all time: *endless truths.*
   Syns: amaranthine, ceaseless, eternal, eterne (*Archaic*), everlasting, immortal, never-ending, perpetual, unending, world-without-end.
3. CONTINUAL.

endlessness *noun*
The quality or state of having no end: *the endlessness of human suffering.*
   Syns: eternality, eternalness, eternity, everlastingness, foreverness, perpetuity, world-without-end.

endmost *adjective* LAST[1].

endorse *verb*
1. PROVE.
2. SIGN.

endow *verb* GIFT.

endowed *adjective* GIFTED.

endue *verb* GIFT.

endurable *adjective* BEARABLE.

endurance *noun*
1. The quality or power of withstanding hardship or stress: *lacked the endurance needed for long-distance running.*
   Syn: stamina. —*Idiom* staying power.
2. CONTINUATION.

endure *verb*
1. To carry on through despite hardships: *enduring an Arctic winter.*
   Syns: sweat out, tough out.
2. To put up with: *couldn't endure such insolence.*
   Syns: abide, accept, bear, brook[2], go, lump[2] (*Informal*), stand (for), stomach, suffer, support, sustain, swallow, take, tolerate. —*Idioms* take it, take it lying down.
3. To remain in existence or in a certain state for an indefinitely long time: *stone buildings that endure for centuries.*
   Syns: abide, continue, go on, hold out, last[2], persist.
4. BEAR UP at bear.

enduring *adjective* CONTINUING.

enemy *noun*
One who is hostile to or opposes the purposes or interests of another: *lost his job because he made enemies of his colleagues.*
   Syns: foe, opponent.

energetic *adjective*
1. Possessing, exerting, or displaying energy: *an energetic worker; an energetic attempt to win the race.*
   Syns: active, dynamic (*also* dynamical), forceful, kinetic, lively, peppy (*Informal*), sprightly, strenuous, vigorous.
2. VIGOROUS.

energize *verb* ACTIVATE.

energizing *adjective* TONIC.

energumen *noun* EAGER BEAVER.

energy *noun*
Capacity or power for work or vigorous activity: *We all lacked the energy to do the dishes. He ran about with furious energy.*
   Syns: animation, force, get-up-and-go (*Informal*), go (*Informal*), might, pep (*Informal*), potency, puissance, sprightliness, steam, strength, vigor, vim, zip (*Informal*).

enervate *verb*
To lessen or deplete the nerve, energy, or strength of: *enervated by the humidity; enervated by the crisis.*
   Syns: attenuate, debilitate, devitalize, enfeeble, sap[2], undo, undermine, unnerve, weaken.

enervated *adjective* RUN-DOWN.

enfeeble *verb* ENERVATE.

enfeebled *adjective* RUN-DOWN.

enfold *also* **infold** *verb*
1. EMBRACE.
2. WRAP.
3. WRAP UP at wrap.

enforce *verb*
To compel observance of: *Policemen enforce the law.*
   Syns: carry out, effect, execute, implement, invoke. —*Idioms* put into action, put in force, put (*or* set) in motion.

engage *verb*
1. To get and hold the attention of: *The striking billboard engaged many passers-by.*
   Syns: involve, occupy.
2. To come or bring together and interlock: *The teeth of the two gear wheels engaged smoothly.*
   Syns: intermesh, mesh.
3. To involve (someone) in an activity: *engaged him in conversation.*
   Syns: draw in (*or* into), entangle.
4. To enter into conflict with: *Armored units advanced and engaged the enemy.*
   Syns: encounter, meet[1], take on (*Informal*). —*Idiom* do (*or* join) battle with.

5. BOOK.
6. BUSY.
7. EMPLOY.
8. PARTICIPATE.
9. PLEDGE.
10. TIE UP at tie.

engaged *adjective*
1. Pledged to marry: *gave a party for the engaged couple.*
   Syns: affianced, betrothed, intended, plighted.
2. BUSY.

engagement *noun*
1. The act or condition of being pledged to marry: *announced their engagement at a party.*
   Syns: betrothal, betrothment, espousal, troth.
2. A commitment to appear at a certain time and place: *had several engagements for the weekend.*
   Syns: appointment, assignation, date (*Informal*), rendezvous, tryst.
3. COMBAT.
4. EMPLOYMENT.

engaging *adjective* ATTRACTIVE.
engaging *noun* EMPLOYMENT.

engender *verb*
1. CAUSE.
2. GENERATE.
3. PRODUCE.

engineer *verb* WANGLE.
engird *verb* BAND[1].
engirdle *verb* BAND[1].
englut *verb* GULP.
engorge *verb* GULP.
engorgement *noun* SATIATION.

engrave *verb*
1. To cut (a design or inscription) into a hard surface, esp. for printing: *engraved a copper plate for making calling cards.*
   Syns: etch, grave[3], incise.
2. To produce a deep impression on: *The scene of the accident was engraved in his memory ever after.*
   Syns: etch, fix, grave[3], impress, imprint, inscribe, stamp.

engross *verb*
1. ABSORB.
2. BUSY.
3. WRITE.

engrossed *adjective* ABSORBED.
engrossing *adjective* ABSORBING.
engrossment *noun* ABSORPTION.

engulf *verb*
1. FLOOD.
2. OVERWHELM.

enhance *verb*
1. FLATTER.
2. GRACE.
3. INTENSIFY.
4. PROMOTE.

enhancement *noun*
ACCOMPANIMENT.

enhearten *verb* ENCOURAGE.
enigma *noun* MYSTERY.

enjoin *verb*
1. COMMAND.
2. FORBID.

enjoy *verb*
1. To receive pleasure from: *enjoy good food.*
   Syns: dig (*Slang*), like[1], relish, savor.
2. To have the use or benefit of: *Women did not enjoy the right to vote until early in the 20th century.*
   Syns: have, hold, possess.
3. ADMIRE.
4. APPRECIATE.
5. COMMAND.

enjoyable *adjective*
Affording enjoyment: *The movie proved so enjoyable that we saw it twice.*
   Syns: gratifying, pleasant, pleasing, pleasurable.

enjoyment *noun*
1. The condition of responding pleasurably to something: *A sudden headache put an end to her enjoyment of the party.*
   Syns: delectation, pleasure.
2. APPRECIATION.
3. DELIGHT.

enkindle *verb*
1. FIRE.
2. LIGHT[1].

enlarge *verb*
1. ELABORATE.
2. INCREASE.

enlargement *noun*
1. BUILD-UP.
2. EXPANSION.
3, 4. INCREASE.

enlighten *verb*
1. ILLUMINATE.
2. INFORM.

enlightened *adjective*
1. CULTURED.
2. EDUCATED.
3. INFORMED.

enlightening *adjective*
1. CULTURAL.
2. EDUCATIONAL.

enlightenment *noun* ILLUMINATION.
enlist *verb* JOIN.

enliven *verb*
1. LIGHT[1].
2. QUICKEN.

enlivening *adjective* STIMULATING.

enmesh *verb*
1. CATCH.
2. INVOLVE.

enmeshment *noun* ENTANGLEMENT.

enmity *noun*
Deep-seated hatred, as between longtime opponents or rivals: *felt bitter enmity toward the oppressor.*
 Syns: animosity, animus, antagonism, antipathy, hostility.

ennoble *verb*
1. DISTINGUISH.
2. EXALT.

ennui *verb* BORE.

ennui *noun* BOREDOM.

enormity *noun*
1. The quality of passing all moral bounds: *the enormity of the crime of matricide.*
 Syns: atrociousness, atrocity, heinousness, monstrousness.
2. FLAGRANCY.
3. OUTRAGE.

enormous *adjective*
1. GIANT.
2. OUTRAGEOUS.

enormousness *noun*
The quality of being enormous: *the enormousness of the blue whale.*
 Syns: hugeness, immensity, magnitude, tremendousness, vastness.

enough *adjective* SUFFICIENT.

enough *noun*
An adequate quantity: *Give me enough to eat.*
 Syns: adequacy, sufficiency, sufficient.

enounce *verb* STATE.

enquire *verb* SEE **inquire.**

enquirer *noun* SEE **inquirer.**

enquiring *adjective* SEE **inquiring.**

enquiry *noun* SEE **inquiry.**

enrage *verb* ANGER.

enraged *adjective*
1. ANGRY.
2. FURIOUS.

enrapture *verb* CARRY AWAY at carry.

enrich *verb* FERTILIZE.

enrichment *noun* ACCOMPANIMENT.

enroll *verb*
1. JOIN.
2. LIST[1].

ensanguine *verb* BLOODY.

ensanguined *adjective* BLOODY.

ensconce *verb*
1. ESTABLISH.
2. HIDE[1].

ensemble *adverb* TOGETHER.

enshroud *verb*
1. COVER.
2. WRAP.

ensign *noun* FLAG[1].

enslave *verb*
To make a slave of: *The Romans often enslaved their conquered enemies.*
 Syns: enthrall, subject, subjugate.

enslavement *noun* SLAVERY.

ensnare *verb*
1. CATCH.
2. INVOLVE.

ensnarement *noun* ENTANGLEMENT.

ensnarl *verb*
1. ENTANGLE.
2. INVOLVE.

ensorcel *verb* CHARM.

ensue *verb* FOLLOW.

ensuing *adjective* FOLLOWING.

ensure also **insure** *verb* GUARANTEE.

enswathe *verb* WRAP UP at **wrap.**

entail *verb*
1. CARRY.
2. DEMAND.

entangle *verb*
1. To twist together so that separation is difficult: *The cat batted and entangled the spool of thread.*
 Syns: ensnarl, foul, intertangle, snarl[1], tangle.
2. CATCH.
3. COMPLICATE.
4. ENGAGE.
5. INVOLVE.

entanglement *noun*
1. The condition of being entangled or implicated: *romantic entanglements.*
 Syns: embroilment, enmeshment, ensnarement, involvement.
2. TANGLE.

enter *verb*
1. To come or go into (a place): *He opened the door and entered. The ship entered the harbor.*
 Syns: come in, go in, ingress, penetrate, put in (*Naut.*). —*Idioms* gain entrance (*or* entry), set foot in.
2. JOIN.
3. POST.
4. START.

enterprise *noun*
1. ADVENTURE.
2. AMBITION.
3. COMPANY.
4. DRIVE.
5. PROJECT.

enterprising *adjective* VIGOROUS.

entertain *verb*
1. AMUSE.

2. CONSIDER.
3. HEAR OF at **hear**.

entertainment *noun* AMUSEMENT.

enthrall *verb*
1. CHARM.
2. ENSLAVE.
3. GRIP.

enthralling *adjective* ABSORBING.

enthrallment *noun* ABSORPTION.

enthuse *verb*
Informal. To show enthusiasm: *He enthused over my new stereo.*
Syns: carry on, rave, rhapsodize.

enthusiasm *noun*
1. Passionate devotion to or interest in a cause, subject, etc.: *His enthusiasm for butterfly collecting persisted throughout life.*
Syns: ardor, fervor, fire, passion, zeal, zealousness.
2. A subject or activity that inspires lively interest: *The game of mahjong was one of the many enthusiasms of the 1920's.*
Syns: craze, mania, passion, rage.

enthusiast *noun*
A person who is ardently devoted to a particular subject or activity: *roller-skating enthusiasts.*
Syns: bug (*Slang*), devotee, fan² (*Informal*), fanatic, fiend (*Slang*), freak (*Slang*), maniac, nut (*Slang*), zealot.

enthusiastic *adjective*
Showing or having enthusiasm: *enthusiastic applause; enthusiastic about the new movie.*
Syns: ardent, crazy (*Informal*), fervent, glowing, gung ho (*Slang*), keen¹, mad (*Informal*), nutty (*Informal*), warm, zealous.

entice *verb* TEMPT.

enticement *noun* LURE.

enticer *noun* SEDUCER.

enticing *adjective*
1. ATTRACTIVE.
2. SEDUCTIVE.

entire *adjective*
1. COMPLETE.
2. GOOD.
3. ROUND.
4. WHOLE.

entirely *adverb*
1. CLEAR.
2. COMPLETELY.
3. SOLELY.

entireness *noun* COMPLETENESS.

entirety *noun*
1. COMPLETENESS.
2. WHOLE.

entitle *verb*
1. AUTHORIZE.
2. NAME.

entity *noun*
1. EXISTENCE.
2. SYSTEM.
3. THING.

entomb *verb* BURY.

entombment *noun* BURIAL.

entourage *noun* RETINUE.

entrance¹ *noun*
1. The act of entering: *Courtiers stood awaiting the entrance of the king.*
Syns: entry, ingress (*also* ingression).
2, 3. ADMISSION.

entrance² *verb*
1, 2. CHARM.

entrancing *adjective* ATTRACTIVE.

entrap *verb* CATCH.

entreat *verb* APPEAL.

entreaty *noun* APPEAL.

entrée *noun* ADMISSION.

entrench *verb* FIX.

entrenched *adjective* CONFIRMED.

entrust *also* **intrust** *verb*
1. To give over to another for care, use, or performance: *entrusted the task to his aides; entrust one's soul to God.*
Syns: commend, commit, confide, consign, hand over, relegate, turn over. —*Idiom* give in trust (*or* charge).
2. To place a trust upon: *entrusted his aides with the task.*
Syns: charge, trust.

entry *noun*
1. An item inserted, as in a diary, register, or reference book: *There were no entries in her journal for the next week.*
Syns: insertion, posting.
2. ADMISSION.
3. ENTRANCE¹.

entwine *verb* WIND².

enucleate *verb* EXPLAIN.

enumerate *verb*
1. To name or specify one by one: *Town meetings give ordinary citizens a chance to enumerate their complaints.*
Syns: itemize, list¹, numerate, tick off.
2. COUNT.

enunciate *verb*
1. PRONOUNCE.
2. STATE.

envelop *verb*
1. CLOSE IN at close¹.
2. SURROUND.
3. WRAP.
4. WRAP UP at **wrap**.

envenom *verb* POISON.

envious *adjective*
Resentfully or painfully desirous of
another's advantages: *envious of his
brother's success with women.*
   Syns: covetous, green-eyed, invidious
(*Obs.*), jealous.

enviousness *noun* ENVY.

environ *verb* SURROUND.

environment *noun*
1. A surrounding area: *visited the new
national capital and its backwoods
environment.*
   Syns: environs, locale, locality,
surroundings, vicinity.
2. The totality of surrounding
conditions and circumstances
affecting growth or development:
*plants able to survive in the desert
environment; a social environment that
encouraged racial prejudice.*
   Syns: ambiance (*also* ambience),
atmosphere, climate, medium, milieu,
mise en scène (*French*), surroundings,
world.
3. CONDITIONS.

environs *noun*
1. ENVIRONMENT.
2. LIMIT.
3. SKIRTS.

envisage *verb* IMAGINE.

envision *verb*
1. FORESEE.
2. IMAGINE.

envy *noun*
Resentful or painful desire for another's
advantages: *The rich boy's fine clothing
and toys provoked envy among his poorer
classmates.*
   Syns: covetousness, enviousness,
invidiousness (*Obs.*), jealousy.

envy *verb*
To feel envy for: *She envied her friend's
good fortune.*
   Syns: begrudge, covet, grudge.

enwrap *verb*
1. WRAP.
2. WRAP UP at **wrap.**

eon *also* **aeon** *noun* AGE.

ephemeral *adjective* TRANSITORY.

epicene *adjective* EFFEMINATE.

epicure *noun* SYBARITE.

epicurean *adjective*
1. SENSUOUS.
2. SYBARITIC.

epidemic *noun* OUTBREAK.

epidermis *noun* SKIN.

epigrammic *also* **epigrammical**
adjective PITHY.

episode *noun*
1. DIGRESSION.
2. EVENT.

episodic *adjective* DIGRESSIVE.

epistle *noun* LETTER.

epithet *noun* SWEAR.

epitome *noun* SYNOPSIS.

epitomize *verb*
1. REPRESENT.
2. REVIEW.

epoch *noun* AGE.

equable *adjective* EVEN[1].

equal *adjective*
1. Agreeing exactly in value, quantity,
or effect: *The meter is equal to 39.37
inches.*
   Syns: equivalent, even[1], identical,
same, tantamount. —*Idioms* on a par,
one and the same.
2. Having the necessary strength or
ability: *not equal to the task.*
   Syns: competent, qualified, up
(*Informal*).
3. Just to all parties: *All citizens are
entitled to equal treatment in courts of
law.*
   Syns: equitable, even[1], evenhanded,
fair.

equal *noun* PEER[2].

equal *verb*
1. To do or make something equal to:
*He equaled the world's record in the
mile run.*
   Syns: match, meet[1], tie.
2. AMOUNT.
3. COMPARE.
4. EQUALIZE.

equality *noun* EQUIVALENCE.

equalize *verb*
1. To make equal: *The goal of the
program was to equalize economic
opportunities for the poor.*
   Syns: equal, equate, even[1], level,
square.
2. BALANCE.

equanimity *noun*
1. BALANCE.
2. CALM.

equate *verb*
1. EQUALIZE.
2. LIKEN.

equilibrium *noun* BALANCE.

equip *verb* FURNISH.

equipment *noun* OUTFIT.

equipoise *noun* BALANCE.

equitable *adjective*
1. EQUAL.
2. FAIR.

equitableness *noun*
1. FAIRNESS.
2. JUSTICE.

equitably *adverb* FAIRLY.

equity *noun* JUSTICE.

equivalence *also* **equivalency** *noun*
The state of being equivalent: *Einstein asserted the equivalence of mass and energy.*
> **Syns:** equality, par, parity, sameness.

equivalent *adjective*
1. EQUAL.
2. LIKE².

equivalent *noun* PEER².

equivocal *adjective*
1, 2. AMBIGUOUS.
3. EVASIVE.
4. SHADY.

equivocality *noun* AMBIGUITY.

equivocalness *noun* VAGUENESS.

equivocate *verb*
1. To use evasive or deliberately vague language: *The candidate had to equivocate on several issues he knew little about.*
> **Syns:** hedge, pussyfoot (*Slang*), shuffle, tergiversate, waffle (*Informal*), weasel. —*Idioms* beat about (*or* around) the bush, mince words.
2. To stray from truthfulness or sincerity: *By concealing the facts he was equivocating, if not actually lying.*
> **Syns:** palter, prevaricate.

equivocating *adjective* EVASIVE.

equivocation *noun*
1. The use or an instance of equivocal language: *a speech full of equivocation.*
> **Syns:** ambiguity, equivoque (*also* equivoke), tergiversation.
2. AMBIGUITY.
3. FALLACY.

equivoque *also* **equivoke** *noun*
1. AMBIGUITY.
2. EQUIVOCATION.

era *noun* AGE.

eradicate *verb*
1. ANNIHILATE.
2. ELIMINATE.

eradication *noun*
1. ANNIHILATION.
2. ELIMINATION.

erase *verb*
1. ANNIHILATE.
2. CANCEL.
3. MURDER.

erasure *noun*
The act of erasing or the condition of being erased: *the erasure of his name from the roster.*
> **Syns:** cancellation, deletion, effacement, expunction, obliteration.

erect *adjective*
Directed or pointed upward: *erect posture; a frightened cat's erect hair.*
> **Syns:** raised, upraised, upright, upstanding.

erect *verb*
1. To raise upright: *We erected the Christmas tree and decorated it.*
> **Syns:** pitch, put up, raise, rear², set up, upraise, uprear.
2. BUILD.

erector *noun* BUILDER.

eristic *adjective* ARGUMENTATIVE.

erode *verb* BITE.

erotic *adjective*
1. Of, concerning, or promoting sexual love or desire: *erotic art.*
> **Syns:** amative, amatory, amorous, aphrodisiac, sexual, sexy (*Slang*).
2. Feeling or devoted to sexual love or desire: *a highly erotic nature.*
> **Syns:** amorous, concupiscent, horny (*Slang*), libidinous, lustful, passionate, prurient, sexy (*Slang*).

eroticism *noun* DESIRE.

err *verb*
1. To make an error or mistake: *must have erred while adding up the bill.*
> **Syns:** miscue, mistake, slip, slip up (*Informal*), stumble, trip. —*Idiom* pull a boner.
2. DEVIATE.

errable *adjective* FALLIBLE.

errand *noun* MISSION.

errant *adjective*
1. Traveling about, esp. in search of adventure: *a knight errant.*
> **Syns:** itinerant, roaming, roving, wandering.
2. Straying from a proper course or standard: *Errant pupils are kept after school.*
> **Syns:** aberrant, deviating, erring.
3. FALLIBLE.

erratic *adjective*
1. Without a fixed or regular course: *erratic movements.*
> **Syns:** devious, stray, wandering.
2. CAPRICIOUS.
3. ECCENTRIC.

erratum *noun* ERROR.

erring *adjective* ERRANT.

erroneous *adjective*
1. Containing an error or errors: *erroneous information.*
> **Syns:** fallacious, false, inaccurate, incorrect, mistaken, off, unsound, untrue, wrong. —*Idioms* all wet, in

error, off base, off (*or* wide of) the
mark, off the track.
2. FALSE.

erroneousness *noun* FALLACY.

error *noun*
1. An act or thought that
unintentionally deviates from what is
correct, right, or true: *an error in
logic; a printer's error.*
Syns: erratum, lapse, miscue, misstep,
mistake, slip, slip-up (*Informal*), trip.
2. FALLACY.
3. MISCALCULATION.

errorless *adjective* ACCURATE.

ersatz *adjective* COUNTERFEIT.
ersatz *noun* COPY.

erstwhile *adjective* LATE.
erstwhile *adverb* EARLIER.

eruct *verb* ERUPT.

erudite *adjective* LEARNED.

erudition *noun* EDUCATION.

erupt *verb*
1. To send forth (confined matter)
violently: *The geyser erupts steam
periodically.*
Syns: belch, disgorge, eject, eruct,
expel, extravasate (*Geol.*), spew.
2. BREAK OUT at **break**.

eruption *noun*
1. The act of emerging violently from
limits or restraints: *the eruption of
lava and ash from a volcano.*
Syns: explosion, outbreak, outburst.
2. OUTBURST.

escalate *verb* RISE.

escape *verb*
1. To break loose and leave suddenly, as
from confinement or from a difficult
or threatening situation: *escaped from
a prison cell.*
Syns: abscond, break out, bunk³
(*Brit.*), decamp, flee, fly, get away,
run away, skip. —*Idioms* cut and run,
do a bunk (*Brit.*), fly the coop, give
the slip, slip the cable, take flight,
take it on the lam.
2. To fail to be fixed by the mind,
memory, or senses: *His name escapes
me at the moment.*
Syns: elude, slip away (from).
3. AVOID.

escape *noun*
1. The act or an instance of escaping, as
from confinement or difficulty: *The
thief made his escape by crawling
through an air-conditioning duct.*
Syns: break, breakout, decampment,
escapement, flight, getaway, slip
(*Slang*).
2. The act, an instance, or a means of

avoiding: *Bankruptcy seemed the only
escape from his creditors.*
Syns: avoidance, elusion (*Rare*),
evasion.
3. Freedom from worry, care, or
unpleasantness: *The movie is suitable
for those seeking lighthearted escape.*
Syns: forgetfulness, oblivion.

escaped *adjective* FUGITIVE.

escapee *noun* FUGITIVE.

escapement *noun* ESCAPE.

eschew *verb* AVOID.

escort *verb*
1. ACCOMPANY.
2. GUIDE.

esculent *adjective* EDIBLE.
esculent *noun* FOOD.

esoteric *adjective* DEEP.

especial *adjective* SPECIAL.

espousal *noun*
1. ADOPTION.
2. ENGAGEMENT.
3. WEDDING.

espouse *verb*
1. ADOPT.
2. MARRY.

esprit *noun*
1. MORALE.
2. SPIRIT.

esprit de corps *noun* MORALE.

espy *verb*
1. CATCH.
2. NOTICE.

essay *noun*
1. ATTEMPT.
2. COMPOSITION.
3. EFFORT.
4. TEST.

essay *verb*
1. ATTEMPT.
2. TEST.

essence *noun*
1. A basic trait or set of traits that
define and establish the character of
something: *Free enterprise is the
essence of capitalism.*
Syns: being, essentia, essentiality,
nature, pith, quintessence,
quintessential, texture.
2. HEART.

essentia *noun* ESSENCE.

essential *adjective*
1. Constituting or forming part of the
essence of something: *We have meat
and the other essential ingredients for
beef stew.*
Syns: basic, constitutional,
constitutive, fundamental, integral,
vital.
2. Incapable of being dispensed with:

Fresh vegetables are essential to good nutrition.
Syns: imperative, indispensable, necessary, necessitous, required, requisite.
3. ELEMENTAL.
essential *noun*
1. CONDITION.
2. ELEMENT.
essentiality *noun* ESSENCE.
essentially *adverb*
In regard to the essence of a matter: *Essentially what the bargain hunter wants is something for nothing.*
Syns: basically, fundamentally.
—*Idioms* at bottom, at heart, au fond (French), in essence.
establish *verb*
1. To place securely in a position or condition: *It took time to establish himself socially in the community.*
Syns: ensconce, fix, install, seat, settle.
2. To put in force by legal authority: *a bill establishing import quotas on certain classes of goods.*
Syns: constitute, enact, promulgate.
3. BASE[1].
4. ENACT.
5. FOUND.
6. PROVE.
establishment *noun*
1. COMPANY.
2. FOUNDATION.
establishmentarian *adjective*
CONVENTIONAL.
estate *noun*
1. HOLDING(S).
2. LAND.
esteem *noun*
A feeling of deference, approval, and liking: *a professor held in great esteem.*
Syns: account, admiration, appreciation, consideration, estimation, favor, honor, regard, respect.
esteem *verb*
1. ADMIRE.
2. APPRECIATE.
3. REGARD.
esthetic *adjective* SEE **aesthetic.**
estimable *adjective*
1. ADMIRABLE.
2. HONORABLE.
estimate *verb*
1. To make a judgment as to the worth or value of: *How do you estimate that man's abilities?*
Syns: appraise, assay, assess, calculate, evaluate, gauge (*also* gage),

judge, rate[1], size up (*Informal*), valuate, value. —*Idiom* take the measure of.
2. To calculate approximately: *Police estimated the crowd at six thousand.*
Syns: approximate, call, place, put, reckon, set[1].
estimate *noun*
1. The act or result of judging the worth or value of something or someone: *a correct estimate of the enemy's resources.*
Syns: appraisal, appraisement, assessment, estimation, evaluation, judgment, valuation.
2. A rough or tentative calculation: *The contractor gave us an estimate of the cost of the work.*
Syns: approximation, estimation.
estimation *noun*
1. ESTEEM.
2, 3. ESTIMATE.
estrange *verb*
To make distant, hostile, or unsympathetic: *They were once friends, but political differences estranged them.*
Syns: alienate, disaffect, disunite.
—*Idiom* set at odds.
estrangement *noun*
1. The act of estranging or the condition of being estranged: *a critical attitude that caused their permanent estrangement.*
Syns: alienation, disaffection.
2. BREACH.
estrus *also* **oestrus** *noun* HEAT.
etceteras *noun* ODDS AND ENDS.
etch *verb*
1, 2. ENGRAVE.
eternal *adjective*
1. Without beginning or end: *God is conceived as an eternal, changeless being.*
Syns: illimitable, infinite, sempiternal.
2. AGELESS.
3. CONTINUAL.
4. ENDLESS.
eternality *noun* ENDLESSNESS.
eternalize *verb* IMMORTALIZE.
eternalness *noun* ENDLESSNESS.
eterne *adjective*
1. AGELESS.
2. ENDLESS.
eternity *noun*
1. The totality of time without beginning or end: *At death we are launched back into eternity.*
Syns: forever, foreverness, infinity, sempiternity.
2. AGE.

3. ENDLESSNESS.
4. IMMORTALITY.
eternize *verb* IMMORTALIZE.
ethereal *adjective* FILMY.
ethic *noun*
A principle of right or good conduct or a body of such principles: *the Protestant ethic.*
Syns: morality, morals, mores.
ethical *adjective*
In accordance with principles of right or good conduct: *Taking credit for someone else's work is not ethical.*
Syns: moral, principled, proper, right, righteous, right-minded.
ethicalness *noun* ETHICS.
ethics *noun*
The moral quality of a course of action: *I question the ethics of reviewing a performance without attending it.*
Syns: ethicalness, propriety, righteousness, rightness.
ethos *noun* PSYCHOLOGY.
etiolate *verb* PALE.
etiquette *noun* MANNERS.
eulogize *verb* PRAISE.
euphonic *adjective* MELODIOUS.
euphonious *adjective* MELODIOUS.
euphoria *noun*
1, 2. ELATION.
evacuant *adjective* ELIMINATIVE.
evacuate *verb*
1. ELIMINATE.
2. EMPTY.
evacuation *noun* ELIMINATION.
evacuative *adjective* ELIMINATIVE.
evade *verb*
1. To avoid fulfilling or answering completely: *The mayor neatly evaded questions about the scandal.*
Syns: dodge, duck, sidestep.
2. AVOID.
3. LOSE.
evaluate *verb* ESTIMATE.
evaluation *noun* ESTIMATE.
evanesce *verb* DISAPPEAR.
evanescence *noun* DISAPPEARANCE.
evanescent *adjective* TRANSITORY.
evangelical *adjective* MISSIONARY.
evangelist *noun* MISSIONARY.
evangelize *verb* PREACH.
evanish *verb* DISAPPEAR.
evanishment *noun* DISAPPEARANCE.
evanition *noun* DISAPPEARANCE.
evaporate *verb*
1. To pass off as vapor, esp. due to being heated: *Alcohol evaporates quickly.*
Syns: boil away, vaporize, volatilize.
2. DISAPPEAR.

evaporation *noun* DISAPPEARANCE.
evasion *noun* ESCAPE.
evasive *adjective*
1. Characterized by or exhibiting evasion: *timid, evasive animals.*
Syns: elusive, slippery.
2. Deliberately ambiguous or vague: *His evasive answer to the question led us to believe he had something to hide.*
Syns: equivocal, equivocating, hedging, pussyfooting (*Slang*), shifty.
eve *noun* EVENING.
even¹ *adjective*
1. Having no irregularities, roughness, or indentations: *even boards. Ivory has a hard, even surface.*
Syns: flat, flush, level, planate, plane, smooth, straight.
2. On the same plane or line: *The top of the boy's head was even with his father's chin.*
Syns: flush, level.
3. Having no variations: *an even rate of speed.*
Syns: constant, equable, regular, steady, unchanging, uniform, unvarying.
4. Owing or being owed nothing: *Pay me back and we'll be even.*
Syns: quit, square.
5. Being an exact amount or number: *an even dollar.*
Syns: exact, square. —*Idiom* on the nose.
6. COOL.
7, 8. EQUAL.
9. FAIR.
even *verb*
1. To make even, smooth, or level: *evened the ground with a bulldozer.*
Syns: flatten, flush, level, plane, smooth.
2. EQUALIZE.
even *adverb*
1. To a more extreme degree: *an even worse condition.*
Syns: still, yet.
2. At the very time: *Even now he persists in a suicidal course.*
Syn: already.
3. Not just this but also: *unhappy, even weeping; a horrible, even unspeakable act.*
Syns: indeed, truly, verily. —*Idiom* not to mention.
4. In the same manner: *He can study hard even as his classmates do.*
Syns: exactly, just, precisely. —*Idiom* as well.
even² *noun* EVENING.

evenhanded *adjective* EQUAL.

evening *noun*
The period between afternoon and nighttime: *usually eat dinner at seven in the evening.*
   Syns: dusk, eve (*Poetic*), even² (*Archaic*), eventide (*Poetic*), gloaming (*Poetic*), nightfall, twilight, vesper (*Archaic*).

event *noun*
1. Something significant that happens: *The chief event of the year for Edna was a trip to China and Japan.*
   Syns: circumstance, development, episode, happening, incident, news, occasion, occurrence, thing.
2. CIRCUMSTANCE.
3. EFFECT.
4. FACT.

even-tempered *adjective* COOL.

eventide *noun* EVENING.

eventual *adjective* POTENTIAL.

eventuality *noun* POSSIBILITY.

everlasting *adjective*
1. CONTINUAL.
2. ENDLESS.

everlastingness *noun*
1. ENDLESSNESS.
2. IMMORTALITY.

everyday *adjective*
1. Of or suitable for ordinary days or routine occasions: *an everyday suit; everyday chores.*
   Syns: commonplace, mundane, prosaic, quotidian, workaday, workday.
2. COMMON.

evict *verb* EJECT.

eviction *noun* EJECTION.

evidence *noun*
1. CONFIRMATION.
2. SIGN.

evidence *verb* SHOW.

evident *adjective* APPARENT.

evidently *adverb* APPARENTLY.

evil *adjective*
1. Morally objectionable: *repented of his evil deeds.*
   Syns: bad, black, immoral, iniquitous, nefarious, peccant, reprobate, sinful, vicious, wicked, wrong.
2. BAD.
3. HARMFUL.
4. MALEVOLENT.
5. OFFENSIVE.

evil *noun*
1. That which is morally bad or objectionable: *a villain whose heart is blackened with evil.*
   Syns: sin, wickedness, wrong.

2. Whatever is destructive or harmful: *The reconstruction of the burned city showed that good can come out of evil.*
   Syns: bad, badness, ill.
3. CRIME.
4. CURSE.

evildoing *noun* CRIME.

evince *verb* SHOW.

evocative *adjective* SUGGESTIVE.

evoke *verb*
To call forth or bring out (something latent, hidden, or unexpressed): *a clown whose wry face always evokes laughter and applause.*
   Syns: draw, educe, elicit.

evolution *noun*
1. DEVELOPMENT.
2. MOVEMENT.

evolve *verb*
1. DERIVE.
2. DEVELOP.
3. ELABORATE.

evolvement *noun* DEVELOPMENT.

evulse *verb* PULL.

exact *adjective*
1. ACCURATE.
2. CLOSE¹.
3. EVEN¹.
4. PRECISE.
5. STRICT.

exact *verb*
1. DEMAND.
2. EXTORT.
3. IMPOSE.

exacting *adjective*
1. BURDENSOME.
2. DEMANDING.
3. NICE.
4. SEVERE.

exaction *noun*
1. DEMAND.
2. TOLL¹.

exactitude *noun*
1. ACCURACY.
2. VERACITY.

exactly *adverb*
1. EVEN¹.
2. PRECISELY.

exactness *noun*
1. ACCURACY.
2. VERACITY.

exaggerate *verb*
To make (something) seem greater than is actually the case: *Some anglers tend to exaggerate the size of the fish they catch.*
   Syns: hyperbolize, inflate, magnify, overcharge, overstate, stretch.
   —*Idioms* blow up out of proportion, lay it on thick, stretch the truth.

exaggeration *noun*
The act or an instance of exaggerating:

*The headline "World War Imminent"
turned out to be a gross exaggeration.*
Syns: hyperbole, hyperbolism,
magnification, overstatement. —*Idiom*
tall talk.

exalt *verb*
1. To raise to a high position or status:
*best sellers that exalt physical fitness
as a cure-all for modern ills.*
Syns: aggrandize, apotheosize,
dignify, elevate, ennoble, glorify,
magnify, uplift. —*Idiom* put on a
pedestal.
2. DISTINGUISH.
3. ELATE.
4. HONOR.
5. PRAISE.

exaltation *noun*
1. The act of raising to a high position
or status or the condition of being so
raised: *the exaltation of materialism.*
Syns: aggrandizement, apotheosis,
dignification, elevation, glorification,
sublimation.
2, 3. ELATION.
4. PRAISE.

exalted *adjective*
1. Raised to or occupying a high
position or rank: *dared not hope to
see such an exalted personage as the
queen herself.*
Syns: august, elevated, grand, high-
ranking, lofty, sublime.
2. ELATED.
3. ELEVATED.
4. GRAND.

exam *noun*
1. EXAMINATION.
2. TEST.

examination *noun*
1. The act of examining carefully: *A
close examination of the knife revealed
traces of human blood.*
Syns: check, checkup, inspection,
perusal, scrutiny, study.
2. A medical inquiry into a patient's
state of health: *went for an eye
examination.*
Syns: checkup, exam (*Informal*).
3. ANALYSIS.
4. TEST.

examine *verb*
1. To look at carefully or critically: *An
expert examined the handwriting and
declared it a forgery.*
Syns: case (*Slang*), check, con, go
over, inspect, peruse, scrutinize,
study, survey, traverse, view. —*Idiom*
give a going over.
2. ANALYZE.

3. ASK.
4, 5. TEST.

example *noun*
1. One that is representative of a group
or class: *Hungary is an example of a
landlocked nation.*
Syns: case, illustration, instance,
representative, sample, specimen.
2. An instance that warns or
discourages prospective imitators: *Let
this punishment be an example to all
shoplifters.*
Syns: caution, lesson, warning.
3. MODEL.
4. PRECEDENT.
example *verb* INSTANCE.

exasperate *verb* ANNOY.
exasperation *noun* ANNOYANCE.
excavate *verb*
1, 2. DIG.
exceed *verb*
1. To go beyond the limits of: *In
sending the pupil home the teacher
exceeded his authority.*
Syns: overreach, overrun, overstep,
surpass.
2. SURPASS.

excel *verb* SURPASS.
excellence *noun*
1. The quality of being exceptionally
good of its kind: *her excellence at
both the violin and the keyboard.*
Syns: fineness, superbness,
superiority.
2. VIRTUE.

excellent *adjective*
Exceptionally good of its kind: *an
excellent portrait, showing her just as she
is; excellent wines.*
Syns: A-one (*Informal*), banner, blue-
ribbon, boss (*Slang*), brag, bully
(*Informal*), capital, champion, dandy
(*Informal*), fine¹, first-class, first-rate,
great, prime, quality, sovereign,
splendid, super (*Slang*), superb,
superior, swell (*Informal*), terrific
(*Informal*), tiptop, top, topflight,
topnotch (*Informal*).

except *verb*
1. EXCLUDE.
2. OBJECT².

exceptionable *adjective*
OBJECTIONABLE.
exceptional *adjective*
1. OUTSTANDING.
2. RARE.

exceptionally *adverb*
1. UNUSUALLY.
2. VERY.

excess *noun*
1. A condition of going or being beyond what is needed, desired, or appropriate: *baggage in excess of the weight limit; an excess of qualified job applicants.*
   Syns: embarrassment, excessiveness, overabundance, plethora, superabundance, superfluity, surfeit, surplus.
2. Immoderate indulgence, as in food or drink: *warned by his doctor to avoid excess.*
   Syns: intemperance, overindulgence.
3. SURPLUS.

excess *adjective* SUPERFLUOUS.

excessive *adjective*
Exceeding a normal or reasonable limit: *excessive taxes; an excessive amount of salt.*
   Syns: exorbitant, extravagant, extreme, immoderate, inordinate, overmuch, undue. —*Idioms* out of all bounds, out of sight.

excessiveness *noun* EXCESS.

exchange *verb*
1. To give and receive: *The delegates exchanged ideas at an informal dinner.*
   Syns: bandy, interchange.
2. CHANGE.

exchange *noun* CHANGE.

excite *verb*
1. INSPIRE.
2. PROVOKE.

excited *adjective* THRILLED.

excitement *noun* HEAT.

exclaim *verb*
To speak suddenly or sharply, as from surprise or emotion: *"Watch out!" she exclaimed.*
   Syns: blurt (out), cry, ejaculate, rap out.

exclamation *noun*
A sudden, sharp utterance: *an exclamation of astonishment.*
   Syns: blurt, ejaculation, outcry.

exclude *verb*
To keep from being admitted, included, or considered: *a club that excluded certain people from membership.*
   Syns: bar, count out, debar, eliminate, except, keep out, rule out.

exclusive *adjective*
1. Not divided among or shared with others: *exclusive publishing rights; your exclusive function.*
   Syns: single, sole.
2. Catering to, used by, or admitting only the wealthy or socially superior: *an exclusive hotel; an exclusive neighborhood.*
   Syns: fancy, posh (*Informal*), ritzy (*Slang*), swank (*also* swanky).
3. CONCENTRATED.
4. SELECT.

excogitate *verb*
1. CONSIDER.
2. DERIVE.

excoriate *verb*
1. CHAFE.
2. SLAM.

excorticate *verb* SKIN.

excrete *verb* ELIMINATE.

excretion *noun* ELIMINATION.

excretory *adjective* ELIMINATIVE.

excruciate *verb* AFFLICT.

excruciating *adjective* TORMENTING.

exculpate *verb*
1. CLEAR.
2. FORGIVE.

exculpation *noun* FORGIVENESS.

excurse *verb* DIGRESS.

excursion *noun*
1. DIGRESSION.
2. TRIP.

excursionist *noun* TOURIST.

excursive *adjective* DIGRESSIVE.

excursus *noun* DIGRESSION.

excusable *adjective*
1. JUSTIFIABLE.
2. PARDONABLE.

excuse *verb*
1. To free from an obligation or duty: *The teacher excused the sick boy from class.*
   Syns: absolve, discharge, dispense, exempt, let off, relieve, spare.
2. FORGIVE.
3. JUSTIFY.

excuse *noun*
1. An explanation offered to justify an action or make it better understood: *used a prior engagement as an excuse to leave early.*
   Syns: alibi (*Informal*), plea, pretext.
2. APOLOGY.

exec *noun* EXECUTIVE.

execrable *adjective* DAMNED.

execrate *verb*
1. CURSE.
2. HATE.
3. SWEAR.

execration *noun* CURSE.

execute *verb*
1. ADMINISTER.
2. EFFECT.
3. ENFORCE.
4. FULFILL.
5. INTERPRET.
6. PERFORM.

execution *noun*
1. INTERPRETATION.
2. PERFORMANCE.

executive *noun*
A person having administrative or managerial authority in an organization: *a brash young executive in the advertising business.*
Syns: administrant, administrator, director, exec (*Informal*), manager, officer, official.

executive *adjective* ADMINISTRATIVE.

exegesis *noun*
1. COMMENTARY.
2. EXPLANATION.

exegetic *adjective* EXPLANATORY.

exemplar *noun* MODEL.

exemplary *adjective*
1. Beyond reproach: *has lived an exemplary life.*
Syns: blameless, good, lily-white, irreprehensible, irreproachable, unblamable.
2. IDEAL.

exemplify *verb*
1. INSTANCE.
2. REPRESENT.

exempt *verb* EXCUSE.

exercise *noun*
1. The act of putting into play: *Conformity is stifling to any free exercise of intellect.*
Syns: application, employment, exertion, operation, play, usage, use.
2. ACTIVITY.
3. PRACTICE.

exercise *verb*
1. To bring to bear steadily or forcefully: *exercised a strong influence on his generation.*
Syns: exert, ply, put out, throw, wield.
2. To subject to forms of exertion in order to train, strengthen, or condition: *He exercised every morning at a local gym. The teacher exercised the child by assigning extra problems.*
Syns: drill, practice, work out.
3. FULFILL.
4. USE.

exercising *noun* ACTIVITY.

exert *verb* EXERCISE.

exertion *noun*
1. ACTIVITY.
2. EFFORT.
3. EXERCISE.

exhalation *noun* BREATH.

exhale *verb* BREATHE.

exhaust *verb*
1. To use all of: *Faced with the heavy*

expenses of city life, he soon had exhausted his money.
Syns: consume, drain, eat up, finish, play out, polish off (*Informal*), run through, spend, use up.
2. To make extremely tired: *The long day of work in the fields exhausted us.*
Syns: bush (*Slang*), do in (*Slang*), fag (out) (*Slang*), gruel, knock out (*Informal*), poop (out) (*Slang*), tire out, tucker (*Informal*), wear out.
—*Idioms* run ragged, take it out of.
3. DEPLETE.
4. GO.

exhausted *adjective*
Extremely tired: *exhausted after a long day at the office.*
Syns: all in (*Informal*), beat (*Informal*), bleary, bushed (*Slang*), dead (*Informal*), dog-tired, done in (*Slang*), drained, fagged (out) (*Slang*), fatigued, pooped (out) (*Slang*), tired out, tuckered (out) (*Informal*), wearied, weariful, weary, worn, worn-down, worn-out. —*Idioms* all in, ready to drop.

exhausting *adjective* TIRING.

exhaustion *noun*
The condition of being extremely tired: *labored to exhaustion.*
Syns: fatigue, lassitude, tire, tiredness, weariness.

exhaustive *adjective* THOROUGH.

exhaustively *adverb* COMPLETELY.

exhibit *verb*
1. BEAR.
2. DISPLAY.
3. SHOW.

exhibit *noun*
1. DISPLAY.
2. EXHIBITION.

exhibition *noun*
1. A large public display, as of goods, works of art, etc.: *went to an exhibition of old prints at the museum.*
Syns: exhibit, exposition, show.
2. DISPLAY.

exhibitive *adjective* DESIGNATIVE.

exhilarant *adjective* INSPIRING.

exhilarate *verb* ELATE.

exhilarated *adjective* ELATED.

exhilarating *adjective* INSPIRING.

exhilaration *noun* ELATION.

exhort *verb* URGE.

exigency *also* **exigence** *noun*
1. CRISIS.
2. DEMAND.
3. DISTRESS.
4. NEED.

exigent *adjective*
1. BURDENSOME.
2. BURNING.
3. CRITICAL.
4. DEMANDING.

exiguous *adjective* MEAGER.

exile *noun*
1. Enforced removal from one's native country by official decree: *Convicted revolutionaries were given the choice of imprisonment or exile.*
   Syns: banishment, deportation, expatriation, ostracism.
2. ÉMIGRÉ.

exile *verb* BANISH.

exist *verb*
1. To have being or actuality: *a town that has existed since the Middle Ages.*
   Syns: be, subsist.
2. BE.
3. CONSIST.

existence *noun*
1. The fact or state of existing: *questioning the existence of God; laws in existence for centuries.*
   Syns: actuality, being, entity.
2. ACTUALITY.
3. LIFE.
4. THING.

existent *adjective*
1. ACTUAL.
2. ALIVE.
3. PRESENT[1].

existent *noun* THING.

existing *adjective*
1. ACTUAL.
2. ALIVE.
3. PRESENT[1].

exit *noun* DEPARTURE.

exit *verb* GO.

exodus *noun*
1. DEPARTURE.
2. EMIGRATION.

exonerate *verb* CLEAR.

exorbitant *adjective* EXCESSIVE.

exotic *adjective* FOREIGN.

expand *verb*
1. ELABORATE.
2. EXTEND.
3. INCREASE.
4. SPREAD.

expanse *noun*
A wide and open area, as of land, sky, or water: *crossed the vast expanse of the prairie.*
   Syns: breadth, distance, expansion, reach, space, spread, stretch, sweep.

expansible *adjective* EXTENSIBLE.

expansile *adjective* EXTENSIBLE.

expansion *noun*
1. The act of increasing in dimensions, scope, or inclusiveness: *the gradual westward expansion of the empire.*
   Syns: amplification, enlargement, extension, spread.
2. EXPANSE.

expansive *adjective*
1. BROAD.
2. GENERAL.
3. OUTGOING.

expatiate *verb* ELABORATE.

expatriate *verb* BANISH.

expatriate *noun* ÉMIGRÉ.

expatriation *noun* EXILE.

expect *verb*
1. To anticipate confidently: *The weatherman expects rain for the weekend.*
   Syns: anticipate, await, bargain on (*or* for), count on (*Informal*), depend on (*or* upon), figure on, look for.
2. REQUIRE.

expectancy *also* **expectance** *noun*
1. ANTICIPATION.
2. EXPECTATION.

expectant *adjective*
1. Having or marked by expectation: *An expectant pause followed her question.*
   Syns: anticipant, anticipative, anticipatory.
2. PREGNANT.

expectation *noun*
1. Something expected: *That he would succeed was his confident expectation.*
   Syns: anticipation, expectancy (*also* expectance), prospect.
2. ANTICIPATION.

expected *adjective* DUE.

expecting *adjective* PREGNANT.

expediency *also* **expedience** *noun*
1. MAKESHIFT.
2. RESORT.

expedient *noun*
1. MAKESHIFT.
2. RESORT.

expedient *adjective*
1. ADVISABLE.
2. CONVENIENT.

expedite *verb*
1. EASE.
2. SPEED UP at **speed**.

expedition *noun* HASTE.

expeditiousness *noun* HASTE.

expel *verb*
1. BANISH.
2. EJECT.
3. ERUPT.

expellee *noun* ÉMIGRÉ.

expend *verb*
1. GO.
2. SPEND.

expenditure *noun* COST.

expense *noun*
1, 2. COST.

expensive *adjective* COSTLY.

experience *verb*
1. To participate in or partake of personally: *experience a change of heart; must experience a toboggan ride to know what it is like.*
   Syns: go through, have, know, meet with, prove (*Archaic*), see, suffer, taste, undergo. —*Idiom* run up against.
2, 3. FEEL.

experience *noun* ACQUAINTANCE.

experienced *adjective*
Skilled or knowledgeable through long practice: *An experienced carpenter never splinters wood.*
   Syns: old, practiced, seasoned, versed, veteran. —*Idiom* knowing the ropes.

experiment *noun* TEST.
experiment *verb* TEST.

experimental *adjective* PILOT.

experimentation *noun* TEST.

expert *noun*
A person with a high degree of knowledge or skill in a particular field: *Only an expert can detect certain art forgeries.*
   Syns: ace² (*Informal*), adept, authority, crackerjack (*also* crackajack) (*Slang*), dab² (*Brit. Informal*), master, proficient, whiz (*also* whizz) (*Slang*), wizard. —*Idiom* past master.

expert *adjective*
Having or demonstrating a high degree of knowledge or skill: *an expert marksman.*
   Syns: adept, crack, crackerjack (*also* crackajack) (*Slang*), master, masterful, masterly, proficient.

expertise *noun* ABILITY.
expertism *noun* ABILITY.
expertness *noun* ABILITY.

expiative *adjective* PURGATIVE.

expire *verb*
1. BREATHE.
2. DIE.
3. DISAPPEAR.
4. GO.
5. LAPSE.

explain *verb*
1. To make understandable: *The poet read, pausing occasionally to explain a rare word or obscure symbol.*
   Syns: construe, decipher, enucleate (*Archaic*), explicate, expound, illustrate, interpret, spell out. —*Idiom* put into plain English.
2. ACCOUNT FOR at **account**.
3. RESOLVE.

explain away *verb* JUSTIFY.

explainable *adjective*
Capable of being accounted for: *Her mistakes are explainable in terms of inexperience.*
   Syns: accountable, explicable.

explanation *noun*
1. Something that serves to explain or clarify: *wrote for an explanation of a complicated tax law.*
   Syns: clarification, construction, elucidation, exegesis, explication, exposition, illumination, interpretation.
2. ACCOUNT.

explanative *adjective* EXPLANATORY.

explanatory *adjective*
Serving to explain: *issued the declaration with some explanatory remarks.*
   Syns: elucidative, exegetic, explanative, explicative, explicatory, expositive, expository, hermeneutic, interpretive.

expletive *noun*
1. COMPLEMENT.
2. SWEAR.

explicable *adjective* EXPLAINABLE.
explicate *verb* EXPLAIN.
explication *noun* EXPLANATION.
explicative *adjective* EXPLANATORY.
explicatory *adjective* EXPLANATORY.
explicit *adjective* DEFINITE.

explode *verb*
1. To release or cause to release energy suddenly and violently, esp. with a loud noise: *The bomb exploded in midair. The dynamite was exploded with an electric fuse.*
   Syns: blast, blow¹, blow up, burst, detonate, fire, fulminate, go off, touch off.
2. To increase or expand suddenly, rapidly, or without control: *feared that without natural checks on growth the population would explode.*
   Syns: mushroom, snowball.
3. ANGER.
4. BREAK OUT at **break**.
5. BURST.
6. DISCREDIT.

exploit *verb*
1. ABUSE.
2. MANIPULATE.
3. USE.

exploit *noun* FEAT.

exploitable *adjective* EASY.
exploration *noun*
The act or an instance of exploring or investigating: *the exploration of the Arctic; an exploration of the mentality of a criminal.*
   Syns: investigation, probe, reconnaissance.
explore *verb*
To go into or through for the purpose of making discoveries or acquiring information: *explored the upper Amazon; exploring the chances for a compromise.*
   Syns: delve (into), dig (into), inquire (*also* enquire) (into), investigate, look into, probe, reconnoiter, scout[1].
explosion *noun*
1. BLAST.
2. ERUPTION.
3. OUTBURST.
4. REPORT.
expose *verb*
1. To lay open, as to something undesirable or injurious: *Cracks around the windows exposed us to a frigid draft.*
   Syns: subject, uncover. —*Idiom* open the door to.
2. BARE.
3. BETRAY.
4. DISPLAY.
5. REVEAL.
exposé *noun* REVELATION.
exposed *adjective*
1. BARE.
2. OPEN.
exposition *noun*
1. EXHIBITION.
2. EXPLANATION.
expositive *adjective* EXPLANATORY.
expository *adjective* EXPLANATORY.
expostulate *verb* OBJECT[2].
expostulation *noun* OBJECTION.
exposure *noun*
The condition of being laid open to something undesirable or injurious: *exposure to ridicule.*
   Syns: liability, openness, susceptibility, vulnerability, vulnerableness.
expound *verb* EXPLAIN.
express *verb*
1. To give expression to, as by gestures, facial aspects, or bodily posture: *a smirk that expressed smug self-satisfaction; expressing indifference with a shrug.*
   Syns: communicate, convey, display, manifest.
2. AIR.
3. PHRASE.

4. SAY.
5. SQUEEZE.
express *adjective*
1. DEFINITE.
2. SPECIFIC.
expression *noun*
1. The act or an instance of expressing in words: *His views found expression in a series of essays.*
   Syns: articulation, statement, utterance, vent, voice.
2. Something that takes the place of words in communicating a thought or feeling: *squeezed her hand as an expression of affection.*
   Syns: gesture, indication, sign, token.
3. A word or group of words forming a unit and conveying meaning: *used an idiomatic expression.*
   Syns: locution, phrase.
4. A disposition of the facial features that conveys meaning, feeling, or mood: *Her kindly expression showed that we were not to take her harsh words too seriously.*
   Syns: aspect, cast, countenance, face, look, visage.
5. ELOQUENCE.
expressionless *adjective*
Lacking expression: *the expressionless face of the weary cashier.*
   Syns: blank, deadpan (*Slang*), inexpressive, pokerfaced.
expressive *adjective*
Effectively conveying meaning, feeling, or mood: *expressive hands; an expressive gesture.*
   Syns: eloquent, meaning, meaningful, significant.
expressiveness *noun* ELOQUENCE.
expressivity *noun* ELOQUENCE.
expropriate *verb* SEIZE.
expropriation *noun* SEIZURE.
expunction *noun* ERASURE.
expunge *verb* CANCEL.
expurgate *verb*
1. CENSOR.
2. PURIFY.
expurgation *noun* PURIFICATION.
expurgatory *also* **expurgatorial** *adjective* PURGATIVE.
exquisite *adjective*
1. DELICATE.
2. ELEGANT.
exsiccate *verb* DRY.
extant *adjective*
1. ACTUAL.
2. ALIVE.
extemporaneous *adjective*
Spoken, performed, or composed with

little or no preparation or forethought: *added a few extemporaneous remarks to his prepared speech; extemporaneous decisions.*

Syns: ad-lib (*Informal*), extemporary, extempore, impromptu, improvised, offhand, off-the-cuff (*Informal*), snap, spur-of-the-moment, unrehearsed.

extemporary *adjective*
EXTEMPORANEOUS.

extempore *adjective*
EXTEMPORANEOUS.

extemporization *noun*
IMPROVISATION.

extemporize *verb* IMPROVISE.

extend *verb*
1. To make or become more comprehensive or inclusive: *extended the nation's boundaries; extended the right to vote to include all adult citizens.*
Syns: broaden, expand, widen.
2. To proceed on a certain course or for a certain distance: *The coast extends northward from here. God's love extends to the smallest creatures.*
Syns: carry, go, lead, reach, run, stretch.
3. GO.
4. INCREASE.
5. LENGTHEN.
6. OFFER.
7. SPREAD.

extended *adjective*
1. BROAD.
2. GENERAL.
3. LONG[1].

extendible *adjective* EXTENSIBLE.
extensible *adjective*
Capable of being extended or expanded: *an extensible ladder; a frog's extensible tongue.*
Syns: expansible, expansile, extendible, extensile, stretch, stretchable.

extensile *adjective* EXTENSIBLE.
extension *noun*
1. The act of making something longer or the condition of being made longer: *the extension of the ladder.*
Syns: elongation, production (*Geom.*), prolongation, protraction.
2. A part added to a main structure: *building an extension to the library.*
Syns: annex, arm, wing.
3. EXPANSION.
4. RANGE.

extensive *adjective*
1. BIG.
2. BROAD.
3. GENERAL.

extent *noun*
1. The measure of how far or long something goes in space, time, or degree: *the indefinite extent of outer space; was at fault to a considerable extent.*
Syns: length, reach, span, stretch.
2. DEGREE.
3. RANGE.
4, 5. SIZE.

extenuate *verb*
1. To conceal or make light of a fault or offense: *a breach of trust that could be neither forgiven nor extenuated.*
Syns: gloss over, gloze over, palliate, whitewash.
2. THIN.

exteriorize *verb* EMBODY.
exterminate *verb* ANNIHILATE.
extermination *noun* ANNIHILATION.
externalize *verb* EMBODY.
extinct *adjective*
1. DEAD.
2. VANISHED.

extinction *noun*
1. ANNIHILATION.
2. DEATH.

extinguish *verb*
1. To cause to stop burning or giving light: *extinguished the fire with water; extinguished all lamps.*
Syns: douse, put out, quench, snuff² (out).
2. ANNIHILATE.
3. SUPPRESS.

extinguishment *noun*
1. ABOLITION.
2. ANNIHILATION.

extirpate *verb* ANNIHILATE.
extirpation *noun* ANNIHILATION.
extol *verb*
1. HONOR.
2. PRAISE.

extort *verb*
To obtain by coercion or intimidation: *bullies who extort money and favors from smaller children.*
Syns: exact, gouge, shake down (*Informal*), squeeze, wrench, wrest, wring.

extra *adjective*
1. ADDITIONAL.
2. SUPERFLUOUS.

extra *adverb* VERY.
extract *verb*
1. GLEAN.
2. PULL.

extraction *noun* ANCESTRY.
extramundane *adjective*
SUPERNATURAL.

extraneous *adjective*
1. FOREIGN.
2. IRRELEVANT.

extraordinarily *adverb* UNUSUALLY.

extraordinary *adjective* RARE.

extrasensory *adjective*
SUPERNATURAL.

extravagance also **extravagancy**
noun
1. Excessive or imprudent expenditure: *a small income that made comfort difficult and extravagance impossible.*
   Syns: lavishness, prodigality, profligacy, squander, waste, wastefulness.
2. LUXURY.

extravagant *adjective*
1. Characterized by excessive or imprudent spending: *an extravagant fellow who soon squandered his fortune.*
   Syns: lavish, prodigal, profligate, spendthrift, wasteful.
2. EXCESSIVE.
3. PROFUSE.

extravasate *verb* ERUPT.

extreme *adjective*
1. Most distant or remote from a center: *comets whose orbits reach the extreme limits of the solar system.*
   Syns: farthermost, farthest, furthermost, furthest, outermost, outmost, ultimate, utmost, uttermost.
2. Of the greatest or highest degree: *taking extreme care; extreme heat.*
   Syns: utmost, uttermost.
3. Holding esp. political views that deviate drastically and fundamentally from conventional or traditional beliefs: *the party of the extreme right.*
   Syns: extremist, fanatical (*also* fanatic), far-out (*Slang*), rabid, radical, revolutionary, ultra.
4. EXCESSIVE.

extreme *noun*
1. Either of the two points at the ends of a spectrum or range: *experienced the extremes of joy and despair.*
   Syns: extremity, limit.
2. LENGTH.

extremist *noun*
One who holds extreme views or advocates extreme measures: *Extremists of both the left and right opposed a moderate solution.*
   Syns: fanatic, radical, revolutionary (*also* revolutionist), ultra.

extremist *adjective* EXTREME.

extremity *noun*
1. CRISIS.
2. EXTREME.

extricate *verb* CLEAR.

extrinsic *adjective* FOREIGN.

extroverted *adjective* OUTGOING.

exuberant *adjective*
1. Full of joyful, unrestrained high spirits: *bright and varied colors that expressed her exuberant personality.*
   Syns: ebullient, effervescent, high-spirited, sparkling, vivacious.
2. PROFUSE.

exude *verb* OOZE.

exult *verb*
1. To feel or express an uplifting joy over a success or victory: *The victorious army exulted in its capture of the town.*
   Syns: crow, glory, jubilate, triumph.
2. REJOICE.

exultance also **exultancy** *noun*
EXULTATION.

exultant *adjective*
Feeling or expressing an uplifting joy over a success or victory: *The goal posts were torn down by exultant spectators after the game.*
   Syns: jubilant, triumphant.

exultation *noun*
The act or condition of feeling an uplifting joy over a success or victory: *The winning candidate's headquarters was full of the exultation of victory.*
   Syns: exultance (*also* exultancy), jubilance, jubilation, triumph.

exuviate *verb* SHED.

eye *noun*
1. An organ of vision: *She has blue eyes.*
   Syns: blinker (*Slang*), orb (*Poetic*).
2. DETECTIVE.
3. DISCERNMENT.
4. LOOK.
5. LOOP.
6. THICK.
7. WATCH.

eye *verb*
1. GAZE.
2. LOOK.
3. WATCH.

eye-catching *adjective* NOTICEABLE.

eyeless *adjective* BLIND.

eye opener *noun* REVELATION.

eyes *noun*
1. POINT OF VIEW.
2. VISION.

eyesight *noun* VISION.

eyewash *noun* NONSENSE.

eyewitness *noun* WITNESS.

F

fable *noun*
1. FICTION.
2. MYTH.
3. YARN.

fabric *noun* TEXTURE.

fabricate *verb*
1. FAKE.
2. INVENT.
3. MAKE.

fabricator *noun* LIAR.

fabulous *adjective*
1. So remarkable as to elicit disbelief: *the fabulous endurance of a marathon runner.*
   Syns: amazing, astonishing, astounding, fantastic (*also* fantastical), incredible, marvelous (*also* marvellous), miraculous, phenomenal, prodigious, stupendous, unbelievable, wonderful, wondrous.
2. MARVELOUS.
3. MYTHICAL.

façade *also* **facade** *noun*
1. *Archit.* The forward outer surface of a building: *the famous façade of the Supreme Court building.*
   Syns: face, front, frontage, frontal, frontispiece (*Archit.*).
2. A deceptive outward appearance: *put on a façade of respectability.*
   Syns: cloak, color, coloring, cover, disguise, disguisement, face, front, gloss, guise, mask, masquerade, pretense, pretext, put-on (*Slang*), semblance, show, veil, veneer, window-dressing (*also* window dressing). —*Idiom* false colors.

face *noun*
1. The front surface of the head: *turned her face toward the camera; cattle with white faces.*
   Syns: countenance, features, kisser (*Slang*), map (*Slang*), mug (*Slang*), muzzle, pan (*Slang*), puss (*Slang*), visage.
2. A facial contortion indicating displeasure, disgust, pain, etc.: *made a face at the teacher.*
   Syns: grimace, mop (*Archaic*), moue, mouth, mow (*also* mowe), mug (*Slang*). —*Idiom* wry face (*or* mouth).
3. An outward appearance: *The face of the city has changed.*

Syns: aspect, countenance, look, physiognomy, surface, view, visage.
4. The outer layer covering something: *the face of the earth.*
   Syns: surface, top.
5. The marked outer surface of an instrument: *the face of a clock.*
   Syn: dial.
6. The level of credit or respect at which one is regarded by others: *They hushed up the scandal to save face.*
   Syns: prestige, standing, status.
7. EXPRESSION.
8, 9. FAÇADE.
10. PRESUMPTION.

face *verb*
1. To have the face or front turned in a specific direction: *Face the class. The house faces the ocean.*
   Syns: front, look on (*or* upon).
2. To furnish with a covering of a different material: *a house faced with rock veneer.*
   Syns: clad, sheathe, side, skin.
3. CONFRONT.
4. DEFY.
5. ENCOUNTER.

face lifting *also* **facelift** *noun* RENEWAL.

face-off *noun* CONFRONTATION.

facet *noun* PHASE.

facetious *adjective* HUMOROUS.

facile *adjective*
1. DEXTEROUS.
2. EASY.
3. GLIB.
4. NIMBLE.

facileness *noun* EASE.

facilitate *verb* EASE.

facility *noun*
1. AMENITY.
2. EASE.
3. FLUENCY.

facsimile *noun*
1. COPY.
2. LIKENESS.

fact *noun*
1. Something having real, demonstrable existence: *distinguish between fact and fiction.*
   Syns: event, phenomenon.
2. ACTUALITY.
3. CIRCUMSTANCE.

faction *noun* COMBINE.

factitious *adjective* PLASTIC.

factor *noun*
1. CIRCUMSTANCE.
2. ELEMENT.

facts *noun* INFORMATION.

factual *adjective* ACTUAL.
factuality *noun* ACTUALITY.
factualness *noun* ACTUALITY.
facultative *adjective* OPTIONAL.
faculty *noun*
1. Conferred power: *The states now have the faculty to redefine their penal codes.*
   Syns: authority, competence (*also* competency) (*Law*), right.
2. ABILITY.
3. TALENT.
facund *adjective* ELOQUENT.
facundity *noun* ELOQUENCE.
facy *adjective* IMPUDENT.
fad *noun* FASHION.
fade *verb*
1. To lose strength or power: *His health and vitality faded after fifty.*
   Syns: decline, deteriorate, fail, fizzle (out) (*Informal*), flag², languish, wane, waste (*away*), weaken. —*Idioms* go downhill, hit the skids, sink into a decline.
2. To become inaudible: *The sound of his footsteps gradually faded.*
   Syns: die (*away, out, or down*), fade out.
3. To disappear gradually by or as if by dispersal of particles: *The rainbow faded. The riders faded into the distance. Our hopes for peace are fading.*
   Syns: dissolve, melt (*away*). —*Idiom* do a fade-out.
4. DISAPPEAR.
fade out *verb*
1. *Motion Pic. & T.V.* To make (a film image) disappear gradually: *The camera faded out the last shot of the beach.*
   Syn: dissolve (*Motion Pic. & T.V.*).
2. FADE.
fade *noun* FADE-OUT.
fadeaway *noun* FADE-OUT.
faded *adjective* SHABBY.
fade-out *noun*
1. *MotionPic.&T.V.* The gradual disappearance, esp. of a film image: *ended the love scene with a classic fade-out.*
   Syns: dissolve (*MotionPic.&T.V.*), fade (*MotionPic.&T.V.*), fadeaway (*MotionPic.&T.V.*).
2. DISAPPEARANCE.
fag *noun* LABOR.
fag *verb*
1. EXHAUST.
2. LABOR.
fagged *adjective* EXHAUSTED.

fail *verb*
1. To prove deficient or insufficient: *The heating-oil supply failed in mid-winter.*
   Syns: give out, run out. —*Idioms* fall (*or* run) short, run dry.
2. To be unsuccessful: *The attack failed.*
   Syns: fall down (*Informal*), fall through, flop (*Informal*), flummox (*Slang*). —*Idioms* fail of success, fall short of success.
3. To cease functioning properly: *The brakes failed.*
   Syns: break down, conk out, give out.
4. To receive less than a passing grade: *failed the course.*
   Syns: flunk (*Informal*), wash out (*of*).
5. To not do (something necessary): *The defendant failed to appear in court. You have failed to meet your payments.*
   Syns: default, neglect, omit.
6. BREAK.
7. COLLAPSE.
8. FADE.
failing *noun* WEAKNESS.
fail-safe *adjective* FOOLPROOF.
failure *noun*
1. The condition of not achieving the desired end: *the candidate's failure to win the election.*
   Syns: unsuccess, unsuccessfulness.
2. One that fails completely: *The play was a failure. I am a failure as a writer.*
   Syns: bomb (*Slang*), bust (*Slang*), dud (*Informal*), fiasco, flop (*Informal*), lemon (*Informal*), loser, washout.
3. A cessation of proper mechanical functions: *a power failure.*
   Syns: breakdown, outage.
4. Nonperformance of what ought to be done: *Failure to pay taxes can result in a stiff fine.*
   Syns: default, delinquency, dereliction, neglect, nonfeasance (*Law*), omission.
5. A marked loss of strength or effectiveness: *experienced failure of physical stamina in his later years.*
   Syns: declination, decline, deterioration, ebbing, weakening.
6. The condition of being financially insolvent: *bank failures in 1929.*
   Syns: bankruptcy, bust (*Slang*), insolvency.
7. SHORTAGE.
fain *adjective* WILLING.
fainéancy *also* **fainéance** *noun* LAZINESS.
fainéant *adjective* LAZY.
fainéant *noun* WASTREL.

faint *adjective*
1. So lacking in strength as to be barely audible: *faint cries for help.*
   Syns: feeble, muted, weak.
2. GENTLE.
3. UNCLEAR.
faint *verb* BLACK OUT at **black.**
faint *noun* BLACKOUT.
faint-hearted *adjective* COWARDLY.
faint-heartedness *noun* COWARDICE.
faintly *adverb*
In a barely audible way: *whispered faintly from her sickbed.*
   Syns: feebly, weakly.
fair *adjective*
1. Having light hair: *Mother and daughter are very fair.*
   Syns: blond (*also* blonde), fair-haired, towheaded.
2. Of a moderately white color: *fair skin.*
   Syns: alabaster (*also* alabastrine), albescent, ivory, light[1], pale.
3. Neither favorable nor unfavorable: *had a fair chance to survive.*
   Syns: balanced, even[1], fifty-fifty (*Informal*), sporting (*Informal*).
4. Free from bias in judgment: *a fair judge.*
   Syns: dispassionate, equitable, fair-minded, impartial, indifferent, just, liberal, nonpartisan, objective, square, unbiased, unprejudiced.
   —*Idiom* fair and square.
5. ACCEPTABLE.
6. BEAUTIFUL.
7. CLEAR.
8. EQUAL.
9. FAVORABLE.
10. SPORTSMANLIKE.
fair *adverb*
In a fair, sporting manner: *play fair.*
   Syns: cleanly, correctly, fairly, properly.
fair-haired *adjective*
1. FAIR.
2. FAVORITE.
fairish *adjective* ACCEPTABLE.
fairly *adverb*
1. In a just way: *settled the dispute fairly.*
   Syns: dispassionately, equitably, justly.
2. To some extent: *felt fairly well but not terrific.*
   Syns: pretty, rather. —*Idiom* more or less.
3. FAIR.
4. REALLY.
fair-minded *adjective* FAIR.

fair-mindedness *noun* FAIRNESS.
fairness *noun*
The quality or state of being just and unbiased: *a judge noted for her scrupulous fairness.*
   Syns: detachment, disinterest, disinterestedness, dispassion, dispassionateness, equitableness, fair-mindedness, impartiality, justice, justness, nonpartisanship, objectiveness, objectivity.
faith *noun*
1. Those who accept and practice a particular religious belief: *All faiths participated in the ecumenical service.*
   Syns: church, communion, creed, denomination, persuasion, sect.
2. BELIEF.
3. CONFIDENCE.
4. RELIGION.
faithful *adjective*
1. Adhering firmly and devotedly, as to a person, a cause, or a duty: *a faithful party member; a faithful spouse.*
   Syns: allegiant, constant, fast, firm[1], loyal, liege, resolute, staunch, steadfast, steady, true.
2. ACCURATE.
3. AUTHENTIC.
4. CLOSE[1].
faithless *adjective*
Not true to duty or obligation: *a faithless lover; a faithless quisling.*
   Syns: disloyal, false, false-hearted, perfidious, recreant, traitorous, treacherous, unfaithful, untrue.
faithlessness *noun*
Betrayal, esp. of a moral obligation: *the faithlessness of a cheating spouse.*
   Syns: disloyalty, falseness, falsity, infidelity, perfidiousness, perfidy, unfaithfulness.
fake *verb*
1. To impart a false character to (something) by alteration: *fake the results of an experiment.*
   Syns: fabricate, falsify, fictionalize.
2. To contrive and present as genuine: *You're not really hurt; you're faking.*
   Syns: feign, pretend, simulate.
   —*Idioms* make believe, make out like, put on an act.
3. ACT.
4. ASSUME.
5. COUNTERFEIT.
6. IMPROVISE.
fake *noun*
1. One who is not what he claims to be: *He's not a doctor; he's a fake.*
   Syns: charlatan, faker, fraud, humbug, impostor, mountebank,

phony (*also* phoney) (*Informal*), pretender, quack.
2. COUNTERFEIT.
fake *adjective* COUNTERFEIT.
faker *noun* FAKE.
fall *verb*
1. To move downward in response to gravity: *Apples fell from the tree.*
   Syns: descend, drop.
2. To come to the ground suddenly and involuntarily: *I stumbled and fell.*
   Syns: drop, go down, pitch, plunge, spill, sprawl, topple, tumble.
   —*Idiom* take a fall (*or* header *or* plunge *or* spill *or* tumble).
3. To undergo a sharp, rapid descent in value or price: *That stock fell 40 points in one day of trading.*
   Syns: dip, dive, drop, nose-dive, plummet, plunge, sink, skid, slump, tumble. —*Idiom* take a sudden downturn (*or* downtrend).
4. To undergo moral deterioration: *Society has fallen into decay.*
   Syns: sink, slip, vitiate. —*Idiom* go bad (*or* wrong).
5. To come as by lot or inheritance: *Child support often falls to the father. The estate fell to the eldest son.*
   Syns: devolve, pass.
6. COME.
7, 8. DROP.
9. SUBSIDE.
10. SURRENDER.
fall back *verb*
1. BACK.
2. RETREAT.
fall down *verb* FAIL.
fall off *verb*
1. DROP.
2. SLIP.
3. SUBSIDE.
fall on (*or* **upon**) *verb* ATTACK.
fall through *verb* FAIL.
fall *noun*
1. The act of dropping from a height: *the fall of the satellite to the earth.*
   Syns: descent, drop.
2. A sudden involuntary drop to the ground: *had a bad fall on the ice.*
   Syns: dive, header (*Slang*), nose-dive, pitch, plunge, spill, sprawl, tumble.
3. A disastrous, overwhelming defeat or ruin: *the fall of the dynasty.*
   Syns: collapse, downfall, toppling, Waterloo.
4. A usu. swift downward trend, as in prices: *a fall in stock prices.*
   Syns: decline, descent, dip, dive, downslide, downswing, downturn,

drop, drop-off, plunge, skid, slide, slump, tumble.
5. DROP.
fallacious *adjective*
1. Containing fundamental errors in reasoning: *a fallacious syllogism; fallacious logic.*
   Syns: false, illogical, invalid, sophistic, specious, spurious.
2. Tending to lead one into error: *a fallacious argument.*
   Syns: deceptive, delusive, delusory, misleading.
3. ERRONEOUS.
fallaciousness *noun* FALLACY.
fallacy *noun*
1. An erroneous or false idea: *an educational philosophy grounded on fallacy.*
   Syns: erroneousness, error, fallaciousness, falsehood, falseness, falsity, untruth.
2. Plausible but invalid reasoning: *The fallacy of the hypothesis negates the conclusions.*
   Syns: casuistry, equivocation, sophism, sophistry, speciousness, spuriousness.
fallback *noun* RETREAT.
fall guy *noun* SCAPEGOAT.
fallible *adjective*
Liable to err: *The President is fallible too.*
   Syns: errable, errant.
false *adjective*
1. Devoid of truth: *The rumor is false.*
   Syns: counterfactual, erroneous, inaccurate, incorrect, specious, truthless, unsound, untruthful, wrong.
   —*Idiom* way off the mark.
2. COUNTERFEIT.
3. ERRONEOUS.
4. FAITHLESS.
5. FALLACIOUS.
false-hearted *adjective* FAITHLESS.
falsehood *noun*
1. FALLACY.
2. LIE².
3. MENDACITY.
falseness *noun*
1. FAITHLESSNESS.
2. FALLACY.
falsifier *noun* LIAR.
falsify *verb*
1. COUNTERFEIT.
2. DISTORT.
3. FAKE.
4. LIE².
falsity *noun*
1. FAITHLESSNESS.

2. FALLACY.
3. LIE[2].
falter *verb*
1. HESITATE.
2. LURCH.
faltering *adjective* HESITANT.
fame *noun*
1. Wide recognition for one's deeds: *a star whose fame was worldwide.*
   Syns: celebrity, famousness, notoriety, renown, reputation, repute.
2. NOTORIETY.
famed *adjective*
1. EMINENT.
2. FAMOUS.
familial *adjective* DOMESTIC.
familiar *adjective*
1. Having good knowledge of: *familiar with the roads here; familiar with that case.*
   Syns: acquainted, conversant, up on (*Informal*), versant, versed.
2. Very closely associated: *familiar companions.*
   Syns: chummy (*Informal*), close[1], friendly, intimate[1], thick (*Informal*), tight (*Slang*). —*Idiom* hand and glove.
3. COMMON.
4. CONFIDENTIAL.
5. PRESUMPTUOUS.
familiar *noun* FRIEND.
familiarity *noun*
1. ACQUAINTANCE.
2. PRESUMPTION.
familiarize *verb* ACCUSTOM.
family *noun*
1. A group of people sharing common ancestry: *The British royal family includes descendants of Queen Victoria.*
   Syns: clan, house, kindred, lineage, stock, tribe. —*Idioms* kith and kin, one's own flesh and blood.
2. A group of usu. related people living together as a unit: *a family of three.*
   Syns: house, household, ménage.
3. ANCESTRY.
family *adjective* DOMESTIC.
famished *adjective* RAVENOUS.
famous *adjective*
1. Widely known and discussed: *a famous newscaster.*
   Syns: famed, leading, notorious, popular, well-known.
2. EMINENT.
3. NOTORIOUS.
famousness *noun* FAME.
fan[1] *verb* SEARCH.
fan out *verb* SPREAD.

fan[2] *noun*
1. ADMIRER.
2. ENTHUSIAST.
fanatic *noun*
1. DEVOTEE.
2. ENTHUSIAST.
3. EXTREMIST.
fanatical *also* **fanatic** *adjective* EXTREME.
fancied *adjective* IMAGINARY.
fancier *noun* ADMIRER.
fanciful *adjective*
1. Appealing to fancy: *fanciful Baroque fountains in the park.*
   Syns: fancy, fantastic (*also* fantastical), imaginative, whimsical.
2. FICTITIOUS.
3. IMAGINARY.
fancy *noun*
1. An impulsive, often illogical turn of mind: *had a sudden fancy to take up hang gliding.*
   Syns: bee, boutade, caprice, conceit, freak, humor, impulse, megrim, notion, vagary, whim, whimsy (*also* whimsey). —*Idiom* bee in one's bonnet.
2. ADORATION.
3. DREAM.
4. IMAGINATION.
5. LIKING.
fancy *verb*
1. IMAGINE.
2. LIKE[1].
fancy *adjective*
1. ELABORATE.
2. EXCLUSIVE.
3. FANCIFUL.
fancy-dress *adjective* FORMAL.
fanfaron *noun* BRAGGART.
fanfaronade *noun* BOAST.
fanny *noun* BOTTOM.
fans *noun* PUBLIC.
fantasize *verb*
1. DREAM.
2. IMAGINE.
fantastic *also* **fantastical** *adjective*
1. Conceived or done with no reference to reality or common sense: *a fantastic alibi.*
   Syns: antic, bizarre, far-fetched, grotesque.
2. CAPRICIOUS.
3. FABULOUS.
4. FANCIFUL.
5. FICTITIOUS.
6. FOOLISH.
7. IMAGINARY.
fantasy *also* **phantasy** *noun*
1. DREAM.

2. ILLUSION.

3. IMAGINATION.

4. MYTH.

far *adjective* DISTANT.

far *adverb* CONSIDERABLY.

faraway *adjective*

1. ABSENT-MINDED.

2. DISTANT.

farce *noun* MOCKERY.

farceur also **farcer** *noun* JOKER.

farcical *adjective* LAUGHABLE.

fare *verb*

1. EAT.

2. GO.

3. MANAGE.

fare *noun* FOOD.

farewell *adjective* PARTING.

farewell *noun* PARTING.

far-fetched *adjective* FANTASTIC.

far-flung *adjective* DISTANT.

farness *noun* DISTANCE.

far-off *adjective* DISTANT.

far-out *adjective* EXTREME.

far-reaching *adjective* GENERAL.

far-sighted *adjective* VISIONARY.

far-sightedness *noun* VISION.

farthermost *adjective* EXTREME.

farthest *adjective* EXTREME.

fascinate *verb*

1. CHARM.

2. GRIP.

fascinating *adjective* ATTRACTIVE.

fascination *noun* ATTRACTION.

fashion *noun*

1. The current custom: *Shorter dresses
   are now the fashion.*
   Syns: craze, cry, fad, furor, mode,
   rage, style, thing, trend, vogue.
   —*Idioms* the in thing, the last word,
   the latest thing.

2. STYLE.

3. WAY.

fashion *verb*

1. ADAPT.

2. MAKE.

fashionable *adjective*
Being or in accordance with the current
fashion: *a fashionable fur; a fashionable
little restaurant.*
   Syns: à la mode, chic, classy (*Slang*),
   dashing, in (*Slang*), modish, posh
   (*Informal*), sharp (*Slang*), smart,
   snappy (*Informal*), stylish, swank
   (*also* swanky), swish (*Chiefly Brit.*),
   tonish, tony (*also* toney), trendy
   (*Informal*), trig, with-it (*Slang*).
   —*Idioms* all the rage, right up to the
   minute.

fast *adjective*

1. Characterized by great celerity: *a fast
   freight train; a fast pace.*
   Syns: breakneck, celeritous, fleet[1],
   hell-for-leather (*Informal*), quick,
   rapid, speedy, swift. —*Idioms* fleet as
   the wind, quick as lightning (*or
   thought*), swift as an arrow.

2. Given to heedless, unrestrained
   pursuit of pleasure: *led a fast but
   short life devoted to booze, girls, and
   gambling.*
   Syns: dissolute, gay, rakehell, rakish,
   wild. —*Idiom* fast and loose.

3. Permanently resistive to fading: *a fast
   dye.*
   Syn: indelible.

4. FAITHFUL.

5. QUICK.

6. SURE.

7. TIGHT.

8. WANTON.

fast *adverb*

1. In a rapid way: *Run—fast! I need the
   statistics fast. The fire is spreading
   fast.*
   Syns: apace, flat-out (*Informal*), hell-
   for-leather (*Informal*), lickety-split,
   posthaste, pronto (*Informal*), quick.
   —*Idioms* full tilt, in a flash, in
   nothing flat, lightning fast, like a bat
   out of hell, like a blue streak, like a
   flash, like a house on fire, like a shot,
   like a streak, like greased lightning,
   like wildfire.

2. TIGHT.

fasten *verb*

1. To make secure: *fasten your seat belts.*
   Syns: anchor, catch, fix, moor, secure.
   —*Idiom* make fast.

2. ATTACH.

3, 4. FIX.

5. TIE.

fastener *noun* CATCH.

fastidious *adjective* NICE.

fastigium *noun* HEIGHT.

fat *adjective*

1. Having too much flesh: *a fat person.*
   Syns: corpulent, fatty, fleshy, gross,
   obese, overblown, overweight,
   porcine, portly, stout, weighty.

2. FATTY.

3. PROFITABLE.

4. REMOTE.

5. THICK.

fat *noun*

1. Adipose tissue: *soap made of animal
   fat.*
   Syn: suet.

2. SURPLUS.

fatal *adjective*
1. Causing ruin or destruction: *Trusting the enemy was a fatal error.*
   Syns: calamitous, cataclysmic (*also* cataclysmal), catastrophic, destructive, disastrous, fateful, ruinous.
2. DEADLY.
3. FATEFUL.

fatality *noun*
1. The quality or condition of causing death: *The fatality of cancer is on the upswing.*
   Syns: deadliness, lethality, lethalness, mortality.
2. A termination of life, usu. as the result of an accident or a disaster: *ten fatalities in the crash.*
   Syns: casualty, death.

fate *noun*
1. That which is inevitably destined: *His fate was to become a king.*
   Syns: destiny, kismet, lot, portion, predestination.
2. A predestined tragic end: *Execution is often the fate of dissidents.*
   Syns: doom, foredoom (*Rare*).

fate *verb*
1. To determine the future of in advance: *The gods fated the ascendancy of Athens.*
   Syns: destine, foredestine, foreordain, predestinate, predestine, predetermine, preordain.
2. To predestine to a tragic end: *This escape plan is fated to fail.*
   Syns: doom, foredoom.

fated *adjective*
1. Governed and decided by or as if by fate: *his fated lot.*
   Syns: destined, fateful, foreordained, predestined, predetermined.
2. CONDEMNED.

fateful *adjective*
1. So critically decisive as to affect the future: *the fateful Yalta Conference.*
   Syns: fatal, determinative, momentous.
2. Portending future disaster: *fateful warnings of a nuclear holocaust.*
   Syns: apocalyptic (*also* apocalyptical), baleful, baneful, dire, direful, doomful, fire-and-brimstone, grave², hellfire, ominous, unlucky.
3. FATAL.
4. FATED.

father *noun*
1. A male parent: *He was the father of nine children. I have to ask Father.*
   Syns: dad (*Informal*), daddy, sire.
2. ANCESTOR.
3. ORIGINATOR.

father *verb*
1. To be the biological father of: *a man who fathered nine children.*
   Syns: beget, breed, get, procreate, sire.
2. PRODUCE.

fatherless *adjective* ILLEGITIMATE.
fatherlike *adjective* FATHERLY.
fatherly *adjective*
Like a father: *He took a fatherly interest in his late brother's children.*
   Syns: fatherlike, paternal.

fathom *verb*
1. KNOW.
2. UNDERSTAND.

fathomable *adjective* UNDERSTANDABLE.
fatidic *also* **fatidical** *adjective* PROPHETIC.
fatigue *noun* EXHAUSTION.
fatigue *verb*
To diminish the strength and energy of: *The long flight fatigued me.*
   Syns: drain, tire, wear, wear down, wear out, weary.

fatigued *adjective* EXHAUSTED.
fatiguing *adjective* TIRING.
fatty *adjective*
1. Having the qualities of fat: *a fatty residue in the saucepan.*
   Syns: fat, greasy, oily, oleaginous, unctuous.
2. FAT.

fatuous *adjective* MINDLESS.
fault *noun*
1. BLAME.
2. DEFECT.
3. WEAKNESS.
fault *verb* BLAME.
faultfinder *noun*
1. CRITIC.
2. GROUCH.
faultfinding *adjective* CRITICAL.
faultless *adjective*
1. INNOCENT.
2. PERFECT.
faulty *adjective* DEFECTIVE.
favor *noun*
1. A kindly act: *do a favor for a friend.*
   Syns: benefit (*Archaic*), grace, indulgence, kindness, service. —*Idiom* good turn.
2. Favorable, preferential bias: *curried favor with the congressman.*
   Syns: favoritism, partiality, partialness, preference.
3. ACCEPTANCE.
4. ADVANTAGE.
5. BENEVOLENCE.

6. COURTESY.

7. ESTEEM.

favor *verb*

1. To be similar to, as in appearance: *John favors his father.*
  Syns: feature (*Informal*), liken (to), resemble, take after.

2. To treat with inordinate gentleness and care: *The wounded soldier favored his right leg.*
  Syn: spare. —*Idiom* handle (*or* treat) with kid gloves.

3. To show partiality toward (someone): *The jurors seemed to favor the defendant. Some parents favor sons over daughters.*
  Syn: prefer. —*Idiom* play favorites.

4. APPROVE.

5. ENCOURAGE.

6. GRACE.

7. OBLIGE.

favorable *adjective*

1. Indicative of future success: *a favorable economic climate for investment; favorable omens.*
  Syns: auspicious, benign, bright, brilliant, fair, fortunate, good, propitious.

2. Disposed to favor one over another: *We received favorable treatment after the payoff.*
  Syns: partial, preferential.

3. Giving assent: *received a favorable reply to the request.*
  Syns: affirmative, affirmatory, assenting, positive.

4. AGREEABLE.

5. BENEFICIAL.

6. OPPORTUNE.

favored *adjective*

1, 2. FAVORITE.

favorite *adjective*

1. Given special, usu. doting treatment: *His favorite daughter could do no wrong.*
  Syns: beloved, blue-eyed, darling, dear, fair-haired, favored, loved, pet¹, precious.

2. Being a favorite: *her favorite song.*
  Syns: favored, popular, preferred, well-liked.

favorite *noun*

1. One liked or preferred above all others: *He is the current matinee favorite.*
  Syns: darling, pet¹. —*Idiom* apple of one's eye.

2. A competitor regarded as the most likely winner: *the favorite in the Kentucky Derby.*

  Syns: pot (*Brit. Slang*), shoo-in (*Informal*).

favoritism *noun* FAVOR.

fawn *verb*

To support slavishly every opinion or suggestion of a superior: *an assistant who fawned on the president and fulfilled his every desire.*
  Syns: apple-polish (*Informal*), bootlick, brown-nose (*Slang*), cotton, grovel, honey (up), kowtow, slaver, truckle. —*Idioms* curry favor, dance attendance, kiss someone's feet, lick someone's boots, slobber all over, suck up to.

faze *verb* EMBARRASS.

fealty *noun* FIDELITY.

fear *noun*

Great agitation and anxiety caused by the expectation or the realization of danger: *a fear of heights; felt great fear during the hijacking.*
  Syns: affright (*Archaic*), alarm, consternation, dread, fearfulness, fright, funk² , horror, panic, terror, trepidation. —*Idioms* cold feet (*or* sweat), fear and trembling.

fear *verb*

To be afraid of: *feared the steep climb; feared her attacker.*
  Syns: apprehend, dread. —*Idioms* be in fear and trembling, have one's heart in one's mouth.

fearful *adjective*

1. Causing or able to cause fear: *spent a fearful night as a hostage; fearful stillness before the tornado.*
  Syns: alarming, appalling, awful, dire, direful, dreadful, fearsome, formidable, frightening, frightful, ghastly, redoubtable, scary (*Informal*), terrible, tremendous.

2. AFRAID.

3. TERRIBLE.

fearfulness *noun* FEAR.

fearless *adjective* BRAVE.

fearlessness *noun* COURAGE.

fearsome *adjective*

1. AFRAID.

2. FEARFUL.

feasible *adjective* POSSIBLE.

feast *noun*

A large meal elaborately prepared or served: *staged a traditional Hawaiian feast for the mainland visitors.*
  Syns: banquet, feed (*Informal*), junket, spread.

feast *verb* EAT UP at **eat**.

feat *noun*

1. A great or heroic deed: *acrobatic feats.*

Syns: achievement, exploit, gest *or* geste (*Archaic*), masterstroke, stunt, tour de force (*French*).

2. ACCOMPLISHMENT.
3. TRICK.

feather *noun* KIND².
featherbrained *adjective* GIDDY.
featly *adjective* NIMBLE.
feature *noun*
  1. A prominent article in a periodical: *a front-page feature on the assassination.*
    Syns: lead (*Jour.*), leader (*Chiefly Brit.*). —*Idiom* feature story.
  2. QUALITY.
feature *verb*
  1. EMPHASIZE.
  2. FAVOR.
  3. IMAGINE.
features *noun* FACE.
febrile *adjective* HOT.
feckless *adjective*
  1. CARELESS.
  2. IRRESPONSIBLE.
fecund *adjective*
  1, 2. FERTILE.
fecundate *verb* FERTILIZE.
fecundity *noun* FERTILITY.
federate *verb* ALLY.
federated *adjective* ALLIED.
federation *noun*
  1. ALLIANCE.
  2. UNION.
fed up *adjective* SICK.
fee *noun*
  1. TOLL¹.
  2. WAGE(S).
feeble *adjective*
  1. FAINT.
  2. INFIRM.
  3. TENUOUS.
feeble-minded *adjective*
  1. FOOLISH.
  2. STUPID.
feebleness *noun* INFIRMITY.
feebly *adverb* FAINTLY.
feed *verb*
  1. LIVE¹.
  2. NOURISH.
  3. PROMOTE.
feed *noun* FEAST.
feel *verb*
  1. To be physically aware of through the senses: *felt a sharp pain.*
    Syns: experience, have.
  2. To undergo an emotional reaction: *The team felt the first flush of victory.*
    Syns: experience, have, know, savor, taste.
  3. To view in a certain way: *I feel that this is the wrong approach. We feel it*

advisable to wait. She felt he was entirely mistaken.
    Syns: believe, hold, sense, think.
  4. To experience or express compassion: *I feel for the families of the crash victims.*
    Syns: ache (for), commiserate (with), compassionate, pity, sympathize (with), yearn. —*Idiom* be sorry for.
  5. GROPE.
  6. PERCEIVE.
  7. TOUCH.
feel out *verb*
To test the attitude of: *Let's feel out his opinion on that issue first.*
    Syns: probe, sound¹. —*Idioms* put out feelers, send up a trial balloon.
feel *noun*
  1. AIR.
  2, 3. TOUCH.
feeler *noun*
Something, as a remark, used to determine the attitude of another: *put out peace feelers.*
    Syn: probe. —*Idiom* trial balloon.
feeling *noun*
  1. Intuitive cognition: *I have a feeling that she's going to leave him.*
    Syns: hunch, idea, impression, intuition, suspicion. —*Idioms* funny (*or* intuitive) feeling, sneaking suspicion.
  2. AIR.
  3. BELIEF.
  4. EMOTION.
  5. SENSATION.
  6. SENSITIVENESS.
  7. SENTIMENT.
  8, 9, 10. TOUCH.
feeling *adjective* EMOTIONAL.
feign *verb*
  1. ACT.
  2. ASSUME.
  3. FAKE.
feigned *adjective* ARTIFICIAL.
feint *noun* TRICK.
felicitous *adjective* APPROPRIATE.
feline *adjective* STEALTHY.
fell¹ *verb*
  1. CUT.
  2. DROP.
fell² *adjective* FIERCE.
fell³ *noun* HIDE².
fellow *noun*
  1. ASSOCIATE.
  2. HUMAN BEING.
  3. MATE.
  4. PEER².

fellowship *noun*
1. COMPANY.
2. UNION.
felon *noun* CRIMINAL.
felony *noun* CRIME.
female *adjective* FEMININE.
femaleness *noun* FEMININITY.
feminality *noun* FEMININITY.
feminine *adjective*
1. Of, relating to, or characteristic of women: *a musical, feminine laugh; feminine fashions.*
   Syns: distaff, female, muliebral, womanly.
2. EFFEMINATE.
feminineness *noun* FEMININITY.
femininity *noun*
1. The quality or condition of being feminine: *a woman whose attitude and appearance projected true femininity.*
   Syns: femaleness, feminality, feminineness, womanity, womanliness, womanness.
2. Women in general: *laws disadvantageous to femininity.*
   Syns: distaff, womankind, womenfolk. —*Idiom* the fair (*or* weaker*) sex.
3. EFFEMINACY.
feminize *verb* EFFEMINATE.
femme fatale *noun* SEDUCTRESS.
fen *noun* SWAMP.
fenagle *verb* SEE **finagle**.
fence *verb*
1. CLOSE IN at close[1].
2. ENCLOSE.
3. WALL.
fend *verb*
1. DEFEND.
2. MANAGE.
fend off *verb* PARRY.
feral *adjective*
1. FIERCE.
2. SAVAGE.
ferment *verb* BOIL.
ferment *noun*
1. CATALYST.
2. UNREST.
ferocious *adjective*
1. CRUEL.
2. FIERCE.
3. MURDEROUS.
ferocity *noun*
1. CRUELTY.
2. INTENSITY.
fertile *adjective*
1. Capable of reproducing: *a woman still fertile after 50.*
   Syns: fecund, productive, proliferous (*Biol.*), prolific, spawning.

2. Characterized by great productivity: *fertile farm land; a brain fertile with unique ideas.*
   Syns: fecund, fruitful, productive, prolific, rich.
3. RESOURCEFUL.
fertility *noun*
The quality or state of being fertile: *increased the fertility of the soil with chemical nutrients.*
   Syns: fecundity, fruitfulness, productivity, richness.
fertilize *verb*
To make fertile: *fertilized the fields.*
   Syns: enrich, fecundate.
fervency *noun* PASSION.
fervent *adjective*
1. ENTHUSIASTIC.
2. PASSIONATE.
fervid *adjective*
1. Characterized by intense emotion and activity: *a man of fervid artistic imagination.*
   Syns: burning, fevered, feverish, heated, hectic.
2. PASSIONATE.
fervidity *noun* PASSION.
fervidness *noun* PASSION.
fervor *noun*
1. ENTHUSIASM.
2, 3. HEAT.
4. PASSION.
Fescennine *adjective* OBSCENE.
fess up *verb* ACKNOWLEDGE.
festinate *verb* RUSH.
festive *adjective*
1. GAY.
2. GLAD.
3. MERRY.
festivity *noun*
1. CELEBRATION.
2. GAIETY.
3. PARTY.
fetch *verb*
1, 2. BRING.
fetching *adjective* ATTRACTIVE.
fete also **fête** *noun* PARTY.
fetid *adjective* SMELLY.
fetish *noun*
1. CHARM.
2. THING.
fetter *verb* HAMPER.
fetters *noun* BONDS.
fettle *noun* TRIM.
fevered *adjective*
1. FERVID.
2. HOT.
feverish *adjective*
1. FERVID.
2. HOT.

feverous *adjective* HOT.
fiasco *noun* FAILURE.
fib *verb* LIE².
fib *noun* LIE².
fibber *noun* LIAR.
fibbery *noun* MENDACITY.
fiber *noun*
1. CHARACTER.
2. TEXTURE.
3. THREAD.
fibril also **fibrilla** *noun* THREAD.
fibster *noun* LIAR.
fickle *adjective* CAPRICIOUS.
fiction *noun*
1. A narrative not based on fact: *short stories and other fiction.*
   Syns: fable, story.
2. DREAM.
3. LIE².
4. MYTH.
fictional *adjective* FICTITIOUS.
fictionalize *verb* FAKE.
fictitious *adjective*
Consisting or suggestive of fiction: *fictional characters in a novel.*
   Syns: fanciful, fantastic (*also* fantastical), fictional, fictive, invented, made-up.
fictive *adjective* FICTITIOUS.
fiddle *verb*
1. To move one's fingers or hands in a nervous or aimless fashion: *fiddled with her papers; fiddling around with the dials of the television set.*
   Syns: fidget, fool, monkey, play, putter (around), tinker, toy, trifle, twiddle.
2. TAMPER.
fiddle away *verb* IDLE.
fiddle-faddle *noun* FROTH.
fidelity *noun*
1. Faithfulness or devotion to a person, a cause, obligations, or duties: *The captain expected the full fidelity of his crew.*
   Syns: allegiance, constancy, fealty, loyalty, steadfastness.
2. VERACITY.
fidget *verb* FIDDLE.
fidgets *noun* JITTERS.
fidgety *adjective* EDGY.
field *noun* AREA.
fiend *noun*
1. A perversely bad, cruel, or wicked person: *a fiend who tormented and killed his prisoners.*
   Syns: archfiend, beast, ghoul, monster, ogre, tiger, vampire.
   —*Idiom* devil incarnate.
2. ENTHUSIAST.

fiendish *adjective*
Perversely bad, cruel, or wicked: *took fiendish pleasure in torturing his victims.*
   Syns: devilish, diabolic (*also* diabolical), ghoulish, hellish (*Informal*), infernal, ogreish, satanic (*also* satanical).
fierce *adjective*
1. Showing or suggesting a disposition to be violently destructive without scruple or restraint: *a fierce interrogator; fierce cannibals.*
   Syns: barbarous, bestial, cruel, fell², feral, ferocious, inhuman, savage, truculent, vicious, wolfish.
2. CRUEL.
3. HEAVY.
4. HIGH.
5. INTENSE.
6. MURDEROUS.
fiercely *adverb* HARD.
fierceness *noun* INTENSITY.
fiery *adjective*
1. BLAZING.
2. HOT.
3. PASSIONATE.
4. SPIRITED.
fifty-fifty *adjective* FAIR.
fight *verb*
1. ARGUE.
2. CONTEND.
3. CONTEST.
4. RESIST.
fight *noun*
1. A physical conflict involving two or more: *a disagreement that is bound to lead to a fight; saw a dreadful fight with knives and fists.*
   Syns: fisticuffs, fray, run-in, scrap², scuffle, tussle.
2. The power or will to fight: *There's a lot of fight left in her.*
   Syns: bellicosity, belligerence, belligerency, combativeness, contentiousness, pugnacity, pugnaciousness, scrap².
3. ARGUMENT.
fighter *noun*
One who engages in a combat or struggle: *a fighter for freedom.*
   Syns: combatant, soldier, warrior.
fighting *adjective* BELLIGERENT.
figment *noun*
1. DREAM.
2. MYTH.
figure *noun*
1. An element or component in a decorative composition: *a tapestry with a floral figure.*

Syns: design, device, motif, motive, pattern.
2. FORM.
figure *verb*
1. ADD.
2. BELIEVE.
3. CALCULATE.
figure on *verb* EXPECT.
figure out *verb*
1. RESOLVE.
2. WORK.
figures *noun*
Arithmetic calculations: *a good head for figures.*
Syns: arithmetic, computation, numbers.
figuring *noun* CALCULATION.
filament *noun* THREAD.
filch *verb* STEAL.
file *noun* LINE.
fill *verb*
1. To make or become full; put into as much as can be held: *fill a theater; filled a sack with grain.*
Syns: charge, freight, heap, load, pack, pile.
2. To plug up something, as a hole, space, or container: *fill a tooth; filled the cracks with cement.*
Syns: block, choke, clog, close¹, congest, plug, stop (up).
3. To occupy the whole of; be found throughout: *The smell of flowers filled the room.*
Syns: imbue, permeate, pervade, suffuse.
4. SATISFY.
fill in *verb* SUBSTITUTE.
fill out *verb* COMPLEMENT.
fille de joie *noun* PROSTITUTE.
fillet *noun* BAND¹.
fill-in *noun* SUBSTITUTE.
fillip *noun* STIMULUS.
film *noun* HAZE.
filmy *adjective*
1. So light and insubstantial as to resemble air or a thin film: *a filmy chiffon dress.*
Syns: aerial, aery, airy, diaphanous, ethereal, gauzy, gossamer (*also* gossamery), sheer², transparent, vaporous (*also* vapory).
2. Covered by or as if by a thin coating or film: *filmy lights in the distance.*
Syns: beclouded, blurred, dim, hazy, misty.
filth *noun*
1. Foul or dirty matter: *Flies carry filth.*
Syns: dirt, grime, muck.
2. DIRTINESS.
3. OBSCENITY.

filthiness *noun*
1. DIRTINESS.
2. OBSCENITY.
filthy *adjective*
1. Heavily soiled; very dirty or unclean: *a filthy pair of shoes.*
Syns: foul, nasty, squalid, vile.
2. So objectionable as to elicit despisal: *a filthy trick.*
Syns: abhorrent, contemptible, despicable, despisable, detestable, disgusting, foul, loathsome, low, lousy (*Slang*), mean², nasty, obnoxious, odious, reprehensible, repugnant, rotten, shabby, sorry, vile, wretched
3. DIRTY.
4. OBSCENE.
finagle *also* **fenagle** *verb*
1. MANEUVER.
2. WANGLE.
final *adjective*
1. DEFINITIVE.
2, 3. LAST¹.
finale *noun* END.
finally *adverb*
1. AT LAST at last¹.
2. LAST¹.
finance *verb*
To supply capital to or for: *finance the renovation of an old house.*
Syns: back, bankroll (*Slang*), capitalize, fund, grubstake, stake (*Informal*), subsidize. —*Idiom* put up money for.
finances *noun* FUNDS.
financial *adjective*
Of or relating to finances or those who deal in finances: *a financial adviser.*
Syns: fiscal, monetary, pecuniary.
financier *noun*
One who is occupied with or expert in large-scale financial affairs: *an internationally famous financier.*
Syns: capitalist, moneyman (*Informal*).
find *verb*
1. To look for and discover: *Help me find my glasses.*
Syns: locate, pinpoint, spot.
2. COME ACROSS at come.
find out *verb* DISCOVER.
find *noun* DISCOVERY.
finding *noun* DISCOVERY.
fine¹ *adjective*
1. Able to make or detect effects of great subtlety or precision: *a fine eye for color.*
Syns: delicate, nice, subtle.
2. Consisting of small particles: *fine buckwheat flour.*

Syns: dusty, powdery, pulverous, pulverulent, small (*Brit. Regional*).
3. CLEAR.
4, 5. DELICATE.
6. EXCELLENT.
fine² *noun*
A sum of money levied as punishment for an offense: *a fine for overtime parking. Failure to file an income-tax return results in a fine set by law.*
Syns: amercement, mulct, penalty.
fine *verb*
To impose a fine on: *fined them a large sum for failing to comply with the law.*
Syns: amerce, mulct, penalize.
fineness *noun* EXCELLENCE.
finespun *adjective* DELICATE.
finesse *verb*
1. TRUMP.
2. WANGLE.
finest *noun* POLICEMAN.
finger *verb*
1. PLACE.
2. TOUCH.
finical *adjective* NICE.
finicky *adjective* NICE.
finish *verb*
1. CLOSE¹.
2. DESTROY.
3. EXHAUST.
4. GO.
5. KILL.
6. MURDER.
7. RUN.
finish off *verb* KILL.
finish *noun*
1, 2. END.
finished *adjective*
1. ACCOMPLISHED.
2. COMPLETE.
3, 4. THROUGH.
fink *noun* INFORMER.
fink *verb* INFORM.
fink out *verb* BACK DOWN at **back**.
fire *noun*
1. The visible signs of combustion: *a huge fire at the refinery.*
Syns: blaze¹, conflagration, flame(s), flare-up.
2. Liveliness and vivacity of imagination: *poetry of divine fire.*
Syns: genius, inspiration.
3. Exceptional brightness and clarity, as of a cut and polished stone: *a diamond with extraordinary fire.*
Syns: brilliance (*also* brilliancy), luminosity, radiance.
4. ENTHUSIASM.
5. PASSION.

fire *verb*
1. To arouse the emotions of; make ardent: *fired by righteous indignation.*
Syns: animate, enkindle, impassion, inspire, kindle, stir¹ (up).
2. DISMISS.
3. EXPLODE.
4. LIGHT¹.
5, 6. SHOOT.
7. THROW.
fire-and-brimstone *adjective*
1. FATEFUL.
2. PASSIONATE.
fired up *adjective* THRILLED.
firing *noun* DISMISSAL.
firm¹ *adjective*
1. Unyielding to pressure or force: *firm muscles.*
Syns: hard, incompressible, solid.
2. Indicating or possessing determination, resolution, or persistence: *a firm intention to do the right thing.*
Syns: determined, resolute, tough, unbending, uncompromising, unyielding.
3. In a definite and final form; not likely to change: *a firm price.*
Syns: certain, fixed, flat, set¹, settled, straight.
4. DECISIVE.
5. FAITHFUL.
6. SOUND.
7. SURE.
8. TIGHT.
firm² *noun* COMPANY.
firmament *noun* AIR.
firmness *noun*
1. DECISION.
2. SOUNDNESS.
3. STABILITY.
first *adjective*
1. Preceding all others in time: *America's first space flight.*
Syns: earliest, initial, maiden, original, pioneer, primary, prime.
2. EARLY.
3. PRIMARY.
first-class *adjective*
1. CHOICE.
2. EXCELLENT.
firsthand *adjective*
1. IMMEDIATE.
2. INTIMATE¹.
first-rate *adjective* EXCELLENT.
fiscal *adjective* FINANCIAL.
fish *verb* HINT.
fishwife *noun* SCOLD.
fishy *adjective* SHADY.

fissure *noun*
1. BREACH.
2. CRACK.
fissure *verb* CRACK.
fisticuffs *noun* FIGHT.
fit *verb*
1. To conform to another, esp. in size and shape: *two boards that fit together; a shoe that fits.*
Syn: dovetail.
2. To be in keeping with: *a dress that fits the occasion.*
Syns: become, befit, conform to, correspond to, go with, match, suit. —*Idiom* hit the spot.
3. ADAPT.
4. AGREE.
5. BELONG.
6. PREPARE.
fit up (or **out**) *verb*
1, 2. FURNISH.
fit *noun*
1. ERUPTION.
2. TEMPER.
fit *adjective*
1. APPROPRIATE.
2. CONVENIENT.
3. ELIGIBLE.
4. HEALTHY.
fitful *adjective* INTERMITTENT.
fitness *noun*
1. QUALIFICATION.
2. TRIM.
fitted *adjective* ELIGIBLE.
fitting *adjective*
1. APPROPRIATE.
2. JUST.
fitting *noun* FURNISHING.
fix *verb*
1. To ascribe (a misdeed, error, etc.) to: *fixed the blame on me.*
Syns: affix, assign, blame, fasten, impute, pin on, place, saddle (on).
2. To implant so deeply as to make change nearly impossible: *Racial prejudice was fixed in their minds.*
Syns: embed (*also* imbed), entrench, fasten, infix, ingrain, lodge, root¹.
3. To restore to proper condition or functioning: *fix some torn clothes.*
Syns: doctor, fix up (*Informal*), mend, overhaul, patch, repair, revamp, right. —*Idiom* set right.
4. To prearrange the outcome of (a contest) unlawfully: *fix a football game; fix an election.*
Syn: tamper (with). —*Idiom* pack the deck.
5. ADJUST.
6. ARRANGE.
7. ATTACH.
8. AVENGE.
9. BRIBE.
10. CATCH.
11. DICTATE.
12. ENGRAVE.
13. ESTABLISH.
14. FASTEN.
15. PREPARE.
16. SETTLE.
17. STERILIZE.
fix up *verb*
1. *Informal.* To improve in appearance, esp. by refurbishing: *fix up old toys by repainting them; decorators fixing up an old house.*
Syns: smarten (up), spruce (up).
2. FIX.
fix *noun*
1. BRIBE.
2. PREDICAMENT.
fixation *noun* THING.
fixed *adjective*
1. Firmly in position: *There are no fixed objects in space.*
Syns: immobile, immovable, stationary, steadfast, unmovable, unmoving.
2. CONCENTRATED.
3. DEFINITE.
4. FIRM.
5. RESTRICTED.
6. SET¹.
fizz *noun* FOAM.
fizz *verb*
1. FOAM.
2. HISS.
fizzle *verb*
1. FADE.
2. HISS.
flabbergast *verb* STAGGER.
flabby *adjective* LIMP.
flaccid *adjective* LIMP.
flag¹ *noun*
Fabric used esp. as a symbol: *salute our country's flag.*
Syns: banderole (*also* banderol, bannerol), banner, colors, ensign, jack, oriflamme (*also* auriflamme), pennant, pennon, standard, streamer.
flag *verb* SIGNAL.
flag² *verb*
1. FADE.
2. WILT.
flagging *adjective* SLOW.
flagitious *adjective* CORRUPT.
flagrancy or **flagrance** *noun*
The quality or state of being flagrant: *the flagrancy of his crimes.*

flagrant *adjective*

1. Conspicuously bad or offensive: *a flagrant attempt at price fixing; flagrant debauchery.*
   Syns: arrant, capital, egregious, glaring, gross, rank2.
2. OUTRAGEOUS.

flagrantness *noun* FLAGRANCY.

flail *verb* THRASH.

flair *noun* TALENT.

flamboyant *adjective*
1. ORNATE.
2. SHOWY.

flame *verb* BURN.

flame(s) *noun* FIRE.

flaming *adjective*
1. BLAZING.
2. PASSIONATE.

flank *noun* SIDE.

flap *verb*
1. To move (wings, arms, etc.) up and down: *The gull flapped its heavy wings.*
   Syns: beat, flitter, flop, flutter, waggle, wave.
2. To move or cause to move about while being fixed at one edge: *a naval ensign flapping in the breeze; flapped the signal flags.*
   Syns: flitter, flutter, fly, wave.
3. FLY.

flap *noun* AGITATION.

flare *verb*
1. BREAK OUT at **break**.
2. BURN.
3. FLY.

flare up *verb* ANGER.

flare-up *noun*
1. FIRE.
2. OUTBURST.

flaring *adjective* BLAZING.

flash *verb*
1. To emit light suddenly in rays or sparks: *Jagged streaks of lightning flashed. Diamond tiaras were flashing in the candlelight.*
   Syns: coruscate, glance1, gleam, glimmer, glint, glisten, glister (*Poetic*), glitter, scintillate, shimmer, spangle, sparkle, twinkle.
2. BLINK.
3. DISPLAY.
4. RUSH.

flash *noun*
1. A very brief time: *was gone in a flash.*
   Syns: crack, instant, jiffy (*also* jiff) (*Informal*), minute2, moment, second1, tick (*Brit. Informal*), trice,

twinkle, twinkling, wink. —*Idioms* split second, the twinkling of an eye.
2. BLINK.
3. GLITTER.

flashy *adjective* GAUDY.

flat *adjective*
1. Lying down: *I am flat on my back in bed.*
   Syns: decumbent, horizontal, procumbent, prone, prostrate, recumbent.
2. Having lost tang or effervescence: *a flat champagne.*
   Syn: stale.
3. Lacking an appetizing flavor: *a flat, starchy meal.*
   Syns: flavorless, insipid, tasteless.
4, 5, 6. DULL.
7. EVEN.
8. FIRM.
9. UTTER2.

flat *adverb*
1. COMPLETELY.
2. FLATLY.

flatfoot *noun* POLICEMAN.

flatly *adverb*
In a direct, positive manner: *denied it flatly.*
   Syns: emphatically, flat, flat-out (*Regional*), positively.

flatness *noun* INSIPIDITY.

flat-out *adjective* UTTER2.

flat-out *adverb*
1. FAST.
2. FLATLY.

flatten *verb*
1. DROP.
2. EVEN1.

flatter *verb*
1. To compliment excessively and ingratiatingly: *sycophants who flattered the king's mistress.*
   Syns: adulate, blandish, butter up (*Informal*), glaver (*Obs.*), honey, oil (*Informal*), slaver, soft-soap (*Informal*), sweet-talk (*Informal*).
2. To look good on or with: *a gown that flatters the figure.*
   Syns: become, compliment, enhance, suit. —*Idiom* put in the best light.

flatterer *noun* SYCOPHANT.

flattering *adjective* BECOMING.

flattery *noun*
Excessive, ingratiating praise: *a person blinded by flattery.*
   Syns: adulation, blandishment, blarney, incense2, oil (*Informal*), slaver (*Archaic*). —*Idioms* honeyed words, soft soap.

flatulent *adjective* INFLATED.

flaunt *verb* DISPLAY.

flavor *noun*
1. A distinctive property of a substance affecting the gustatory sense: *meat permeated with the flavor of garlic.*
   Syns: relish, sapor, savor, smack², taste, twang.
2. A distinctive yet intangible quality deemed typical of a given thing: *a city imbued with the flavor of the Orient.*
   Syns: aroma, atmosphere, savor, smack².
3. FLAVORING.

flavor *verb*
1. To impart flavor to: *flavored the sauce with herbs and wine.*
   Syn: season.
2. SMACK².

flavoring *noun*
A substance that imparts taste: *lemon flavoring.*
   Syns: condiment, flavor, seasoning.

flavorless *adjective* FLAT.
flavorlessness *noun* INSIPIDITY.
flaw *noun* DEFECT.
flawed *adjective* DEFECTIVE.
flawless *adjective*
1. CLEAR.
2. GOOD.
3. PERFECT.

flay *verb* SLAM.
fleck *verb* SPECKLE.
fledgling *noun* BEGINNER.
flee *verb* ESCAPE.
fleecy *adjective* HAIRY.
fleeing *adjective* TRANSITORY.
fleer *verb* SNEER.
  fleer at *verb* RIDICULE.
  fleer *noun* SNEER.
fleet¹ *verb* RUSH.
  fleet *adjective* FAST.
fleet² *adjective* SHALLOW.
fleeting *adjective* TRANSITORY.
fleetness *noun* HASTE.
Fleet Street *noun* PRESS.
flesh *noun* MANKIND.
fleshless *adjective* THIN.
fleshliness *noun* PHYSICALITY.
fleshly *adjective*
1. BODILY.
2. PHYSICAL.

fleshy *adjective* FAT.
flexibility *noun*
The quality or state of being flexible: *measured the flexibility of the aluminum.*
   Syns: ductility, elasticity, flexibleness, flexure (*Obs.*), give (*Informal*), malleability, plasticity, pliability, pliableness, pliancy, resilience (*also* resiliency), springiness, suppleness.

flexible *also* **flexile** *adjective*
1. Easily altered or influenced: *the flexible mind of the diplomat.*
   Syns: elastic, malleable, plastic, pliable, pliant.
2. Capable of withstanding stress without injury: *a flexible girder.*
   Syns: elastic, plastic, resilient, springy, supple.
3. MALLEABLE.

flexibleness *noun* FLEXIBILITY.
flexile *adjective* SEE **flexible**.
flexuous *also* **flexuose** *adjective*
1. MALLEABLE.
2. WINDING.

flexure *noun* FLEXIBILITY.
flick *noun* BRUSH.
  flick *verb* BRUSH.
flicker *verb*
1. BLINK.
2. FLUTTER.
  flicker *noun* BLINK.
flight *noun* ESCAPE.
flighty *adjective* GIDDY.
flimflam *verb* CHEAT.
  flimflam *noun* CHEAT.
flimflammer *noun* CHEAT.
flimsy *adjective*
1. IMPLAUSIBLE.
2. TENUOUS.

flinch *verb*
To draw away involuntarily, usu. due to fear or disgust: *flinched at the sight of the carnage.*
   Syns: blench¹, quail, recoil, shrink, shy¹, squinch, start, wince.

fling *noun*
1. BINGE.
2. THROW.
3. TRY.
  fling *verb* THROW.

flip *verb*
1. BROWSE.
2. TOSS.

flip *adjective*
1. GLIB.
2. IMPUDENT.

flirt *verb*
1. To make amorous advances without serious intentions: *a girl who flirted with all the boys.*
   Syns: coquet, dally, toy, trifle.
2. To treat lightly or flippantly: *a stunt pilot who flirted with death.*
   Syns: dally (with), play (with), toy (with), trifle (with).

flirt *noun*
A woman who leads men on: *Scarlett O'Hara—the epitome of a flirt.*
   Syns: coquette, vamp.

flirtation *noun*
1. The practice of flirting: *Dancing and flirtation were their chief amusements.*
Syns: coquetry, dalliance.
2. A usu. brief romance entered into lightly or frivolously: *It's not love; it's just another flirtation.*
Syn: dalliance.

flirtatious *adjective*
Given to flirting: *a flirtatious belle.*
Syns: coquettish, coy, flirty.

flirty *adjective* FLIRTATIOUS.

flit *verb*
1. FLUTTER.
2. FLY.
3. RUSH.

flitter *verb*
1, 2. FLAP.
3. FLUTTER.

float *verb*
1. FLY.
2. WASH.

flock *noun*
1, 2. CROWD.

flock *verb* CROWD.

flog *verb* BEAT.

flogging *noun* BEATING.

flood *noun*
1. An abundant, usu. overwhelming flow: *a flood following the storm; a flood of tears.*
Syns: alluvion, cataclysm, cataract, deluge, freshet, inundation, Niagara, overflow, spate, torrent.
2. FLOW.

flood *verb*
1. To flow over completely: *The storm flooded our basement. Tears flooded my face.*
Syns: deluge, drown, engulf, flush, inundate, overflow, submerge, whelm.
2. To affect as if by an outpouring of water: *The White House was flooded with angry telegrams.*
Syns: deluge, overwhelm, whelm.
3. POUR.

floor *verb*
1. DROP.
2. STAGGER.

floozy also **floozey** *noun* SLUT.

flop *verb*
1. To drop or sink heavily and noisily: *He flopped into the chair.*
Syns: flump, plop, plump[2], plunk.
2. FAIL.
3. FLAP.
4. RETIRE.
5. SLOUCH.

flop *noun* FAILURE.

floppy *adjective* LIMP.

florescence *noun* BLOOM.

floret *noun* BLOOM.

florid *adjective*
1. ORNATE.
2. RUDDY.

flounce *verb* STRUT.

flounder *verb* WALLOW.

flourish *verb*
1. To grow rapidly and luxuriantly: *Most flowers flourish in full sunlight.*
Syns: bloom, blossom, thrive.
2. To be in one's prime: *an artist who flourished in the late 14th century.*
Syns: flower, shine. —*Idioms* cut a figure, make a splash.
3. To wield boldly and dramatically: *a drum major flourishing his baton.*
Syns: brandish, sweep, wave.
4. PROSPER.

flourishing *adjective*
Improving, growing, or succeeding steadily: *a flourishing business.*
Syns: booming, coming (*Informal*), healthy, prospering, prosperous, roaring, robust, thrifty, thriving. —*Idiom* going strong.

flout *verb* DISOBEY.

flow *verb*
1. To move freely as a liquid: *blood flowing through the veins.*
Syns: circulate, course, run, stream.
2. To come forth or emit in abundance: *Food parcels for the tornado victims flowed in. Tears flowed.*
Syns: course, gush, pour, rush, stream, surge, well[1].
3. To proceed with ease, esp. of expression: *Churchill's resplendent prose flowed on and on.*
Syns: glide, roll, sail.
4. DISCHARGE.
5. STEM.
6. TEEM.

flow *noun*
Something suggestive of running water: *a flow of sympathy; a steady flow of complaints.*
Syns: current, drift, flood, flux, rush, spate, stream, tide.

flower *noun*
1. BEST.
2, 3. BLOOM.
4. SOCIETY.

flower *verb*
1. BLOOM.
2. FLOURISH.

flowing *adjective* SMOOTH.

fluency *noun*
Ready skill in expression: *achieved fluency in Russian.*
Syns: cursiveness, facility, fluidity.

fluent *adjective*
1. ELOQUENT.
2. SMOOTH.

fluff *noun* LAPSE.

fluid *adjective*
1. CHANGEABLE.
2. MOBILE.
3. SMOOTH.

fluidity *noun* FLUENCY.

fluke *noun* CHANCE.

fluky *adjective* ACCIDENTAL.

flummox *verb*
1. FAIL.
2. NONPLUS.

flump *verb* FLOP.

flunk *verb* FAIL.

flurry *verb* AGITATE.

flurry *noun*
1. AGITATION.
2. STIR¹.

flush *verb*
1. BLUSH.
2. ELATE.
3. EVEN¹.
4. FLOOD.

flush *noun*
1, 2. BLOOM.
3. GLOW.

flush *adjective*
1, 2. EVEN¹.
3. RICH.
4. RUDDY.

flushed *adjective*
1. ELATED.
2. RUDDY.

fluster *verb* AGITATE.

fluster *noun* AGITATION.

flutter *verb*
1. To move quickly and intermittently in a nervous, excited way: *The children fluttered around the birthday cake.*
   Syns: flicker, flit, flitter, hover.
2, 3. FLAP.
4. FLY.

flutter *noun* AGITATION.

flux *noun* FLOW.

flux *verb* MELT.

fly *verb*
1. To move through the air with or as if with wings: *Gulls flew over the beach.*
   Syns: flap, flit, flutter, sail, wing.
2. To pass quickly and lightly through the air: *Storm clouds flew past us.*
   Syns: dart, float, sail, shoot, skim.
3. To react explosively or suddenly: *flew into a towering rage.*
   Syn: flare (up).
4. ESCAPE.
5. FLAP.

6, 7. RUN.
8. RUSH.

flying *adjective* QUICK.

foam *noun*
A mass of bubbles in or on the surface of a liquid: *Foam rose on the beer.*
   Syns: fizz, froth, head, lather, spume, suds, yeast.

foam *verb*
To form or cause to form foam: *The beer foamed in the glass.*
   Syns: bubble, cream, effervesce, fizz, froth, lather, spume.

foamy *adjective*
Consisting of or resembling foam: *Winds churned the sea into a foamy spray.*
   Syns: frothy, lathery, spumy, sudsy.

fob *verb* FOIST.

focalize *verb* CONCENTRATE.

focus *noun* CENTER.

focus *verb*
1. APPLY.
2. CONCENTRATE.

foe *noun* ENEMY.

fog *noun*
1. DAZE.
2. HAZE.

fog *verb* OBSCURE.

foggy *adjective* UNCLEAR.

fogy *noun* SQUARE.

foible *noun* WEAKNESS.

foil *verb* FRUSTRATE.

foist *verb*
1. To offer or put into circulation (an inferior or spurious item): *tried to foist damaged merchandise on his customers.*
   Syns: fob (off), palm off, pass off.
2. IMPOSE.
3. INSINUATE.

fold *noun*
A line made by the doubling of one part over another: *the folds of a curtain.*
   Syns: crease, crinkle, pleat, plica, plication, ply, rimple, ruck², wrinkle¹.

fold *verb*
1. To bend together or crease so that one part lies over another: *folded the paper in thirds.*
   Syns: double, pleat, plicate, ruck².
2. BEND.
3. BREAK DOWN at **break**.
4. COLLAPSE.
5. SUCCUMB.

folklore *noun* LORE.

follow *verb*
1. To move behind (another) in the same direction: *She followed me into the room.*

Syns: heel[1], pursue, trail. —*Idioms* camp on the heel of, follow in the trail of, follow on the heel of.

2. To keep (another) under surveillance by moving along behind: *The police followed the suspect home.*
Syns: bedog, bird-dog, dog, shadow, tail (*Informal*), trail, track.

3. To take as a model: *He tried to follow his father's high standards.*
Syns: copy, emulate, model, pattern (on, upon, *or* after). —*Idioms* follow in the footsteps of, follow suit, follow the example of.

4. To act in conformity with: *follow the rules; was just following orders.*
Syns: abide by, adhere (to), comply (with), conform (to), keep, mind, obey, observe.

5. To occur after (another) in time: *The reign of Elizabeth II followed the reign of George VI.*
Syns: follow on, succeed, supervene. —*Idiom* follow on the heels of.

6. To occur as a consequence: *If you do that, it follows that you will be caught.*
Syns: attend, ensue, result.

7. UNDERSTAND.

follow on *verb* FOLLOW.

follow through *verb* FOLLOW UP at **follow.**

follow up *verb*
To strengthen the effect of (an action) by further action: *followed up the barrage with an assault.*
Syns: follow through (on), pursue.

follower *noun*
One who supports and adheres to another: *Lenin's followers.*
Syns: adherent, cohort, disciple, henchman, partisan, satellite, supporter.

following *adjective*
Occurring right after another: *On the following day he quit.*
Syns: coming, ensuing, next.

following *noun*
1. PUBLIC.
2. RETINUE.

folly *noun* FOOLISHNESS.

foment *verb* AROUSE.

fomenter *noun* AGITATOR.

fond *adjective* AFFECTIONATE.

fondle *verb* CARESS.

fondness *noun*
1. ATTACHMENT.
2. TASTE.

food *noun*
1. Something fit to be eaten: *delicious food.*

Syns: bread, chow (*Slang*), chuck[2] (*Regional*), comestible, eats (*Slang*), edible(s), esculent, fare, foodstuff, grub (*Slang*), meat, nurture, peck[2], provisions, sustenance. —*Idioms* daily bread, meat and drink.

2. That which sustains the mind or spirit: *a passion that found its food in music.*
Syns: aliment, nourishment, nutriment, pabulum, pap, sustenance.

foodstuff *noun* FOOD.

fool *noun*
1. One deficient in judgment and good sense: *acted like a fool over her.*
Syns: ass, dope (*Informal*), goose (*Informal*), idiot, imbecile, jackass, jerk (*Slang*), mooncalf, nincompoop, ninny, nitwit (*Informal*), numskull (*also* numbskull), schmo (*also* schmoe) (*Slang*), schmuck (*Slang*), simple, simpleton, tomfool, turkey (*Slang*).

2. A mentally deficient person: *had the mentality of a fool.*
Syns: ament, cretin, gander[1] (*Informal*), half-wit, idiot, imbecile, moron, natural, simpleton.

3. DUPE.

fool *verb*
1. DECEIVE.
2. FIDDLE.
3. JOKE.
4. TAMPER.

fool around *verb*
1. MESS AROUND at **mess.**
2. PHILANDER.

fool away *verb* WASTE.

foolery *noun* FOOLISHNESS.

foolhardy *adjective* RASH[1].

foolish *adjective*
1. So senseless as to be laughable: *a foolish land-speculation scheme.*
Syns: absurd, balmy (*Slang*), cock-eyed (*Slang*), crazy, dippy (*Slang*), fantastic (*also* fantastical), feeble-minded, harebrained, idiotic, insane, jerky (*Slang*), loony (*also* luny) (*Informal*), loopy (*Informal*), lunatic, mad, nonsensical, preposterous, sappy (*Slang*), silly, softheaded, tomfool, unearthly, wacky (*also* whacky) (*Slang*), zany.

2. MINDLESS.

foolishness *noun*
The condition of being foolish: *The utter foolishness of that marketing plan is embarrassing.*
Syns: absurdity, craziness, folly, foolery, idiocy, insanity, lunacy,

preposterousness, senselessness,
silliness, tomfoolery.

foolproof *adjective*
Designed so as to be impervious to
human error or misuse: *a foolproof
detonator.*
Syn: fail-safe.

foot *verb*
1. ADD.
2. DANCE.
3. WALK.
foot *noun* BASE¹.

footfall *noun* TREAD.

footing *noun*
1. BASE¹.
2, 3. BASIS.
4. PLACE.

footstep *noun* TREAD.

foozle *noun* BLUNDER.

foozler *noun* BLUNDERER.

forage *verb* SCOUR.

foray *noun* INVASION.

foray *verb* INVADE.

forbear *verb* REFRAIN.

forbearance *noun*
1. PATIENCE.
2. TOLERANCE.

forbearant *adjective* TOLERANT.

forbearing *adjective*
1. PATIENT.
2. TOLERANT.

forbid *verb*
To refuse to allow: *The law forbids tax
evasion. The guard forbade them entry.*
Syns: ban, disallow, enjoin, inhibit,
interdict, outlaw, prohibit, proscribe.

forbiddance *noun*
A refusal to allow: *protested that
nation's forbiddance of racial mingling.*
Syns: ban, disallowance, interdiction,
prohibition, proscription, taboo (*also*
tabu).

forbidden *adjective*
Not allowed: *Smoking is forbidden.*
Syns: banned, impermissible,
prohibited, taboo (*also* tabu),
verboten.

forbidding *adjective*
So disagreeably austere as to discourage
approach: *a forbidding look; forbidding
castle walls.*
Syns: inhospitable, unhospitable,
uninviting.

force *noun*
1. Power used to overcome resistance:
used force to obtain a confession.
Syns: coercion, constraint, duress,
pressure, strength, violence.
2. The capacity to exert an influence:

*The force of the speaker's personality
moved the crowd to an ovation.*
Syns: forcefulness, magnetism, power,
vigor, vitality.
3. A group of people organized for a
particular purpose: *a work force; a
police force.*
Syns: body, corps, crew, detachment,
team, unit.
4. ENERGY.
5. IMPACT.
6. MUSCLE.

force *verb*
1. To cause (a person or thing) to act or
move in spite of resistance: *Tear gas
forced the fugitives out of their hiding
place.*
Syns: coerce, compel, constrain,
make, oblige, pressure.
2. COERCE.
3. RAPE.

forced *adjective*
1. Done under force: *roads built with
forced labor.*
Syns: coerced, compulsory,
constrained.
2. Not natural or spontaneous: *She
greeted us with a forced smile.*
Syns: effortful, labored, strained.

forceful *adjective*
1. Full of or displaying force: *a forceful
speaker.*
Syns: dynamic (*also* dynamical),
effective, powerful, strong, vigorous.
2, 3. EMPHATIC.
4. ENERGETIC.

forcefully *adverb* HARD.

forcefulness *noun* FORCE.

forcible *adjective*
Accomplished by force: *forcible seizure
of American sailors.*
Syns: coercive, strong-arm (*Informal*),
violent.

forcibly *adverb* HARD.

fore *noun* FRONT.

forearm *verb* GIRD.

forebear *noun* ANCESTOR.

forebode *verb* THREATEN.

forecast *verb* PREDICT.

forecast *noun* PREDICTION.

foredestine *verb* FATE.

foredoom *verb* FATE.

foredoom *noun* FATE.

foredoomed *adjective* CONDEMNED.

forefather *noun* ANCESTOR.

forefend *verb* SEE forfend.

foregather *verb* SEE forgather.

forego *verb* SEE forgo.

foregoing *adjective*
1. LAST[1].
2. PAST.

forehand *noun* ADVANTAGE.

forehanded *adjective* ECONOMICAL.

forehandedness *noun* ECONOMY.

foreign *adjective*
1. Of, from, or characteristic of another place or part of the world: *foreign species of plants; a foreign accent.*
   Syns: alien, exotic, outlandish (*Archaic*), strange.
2. Not part of the essential nature of a thing: *Jealousy is foreign to his nature.*
   Syns: alien, extraneous, extrinsic.

foreigner *noun*
A person coming from another country: *a foreigner who came to the U.S. in 1910.*
   Syns: alien, émigré, newcomer, outlander, outsider, stranger.

foreknow *verb* FORESEE.

foreman *noun* BOSS.

foremost *adjective*
1. PRIMARY.
2. PRINCIPAL.

forenoon *noun* MORNING.

forensics *noun* ARGUMENTATION.

foreordain *verb* FATE.

foreordained *adjective* FATED.

forepart *noun* FRONT.

forerun *verb* PRECEDE.

foresee *verb*
To know in advance: *difficulties that no one could foresee.*
   Syns: anticipate, divine[2], envision, foreknow, see.

foreshadow *verb*
1. ADUMBRATE.
2. PROMISE.

foresight *noun*
1. PRUDENCE.
2. VISION.

forestall *verb* PREVENT.

forestalling *noun* PREVENTION.

forestalling *adjective* PREVENTIVE.

forestallment *noun* PREVENTION.

foreswear *verb* SEE **forswear**.

foresworn *adjective* SEE **forsworn**.

foretaste *noun* TASTE.

foretell *verb*
1. PREDICT.
2. PROPHESY.

foreteller *noun* PROPHET.

foretelling *noun*
1. PREDICTION.
2. PROPHECY.

forethink *verb* PREMEDITATE.

forethought *noun* PRUDENCE.

foretoken *noun* OMEN.

foretoken *verb* PROMISE.

forever *noun* ETERNITY.

foreverness *noun*
1. ENDLESSNESS.
2. ETERNITY.

forewarn *verb*
1. THREATEN.
2. WARN.

forewarning *noun*
1. THREAT.
2. WARNING.

foreword *noun* INTRODUCTION.

forfeit *verb* DROP.

forfend also **forefend** *verb* PREVENT.

forgather also **foregather** *verb* ASSEMBLE.

forge[1] *verb*
1. BEAT.
2. COUNTERFEIT.
3. MAKE.

forge[2] *verb* PLUNGE.

forgery *noun* COUNTERFEIT.

forget *verb*
To fail to remember: *I always forget his name.*
   Syn: disremember. —*Idiom* draw a blank.

forgetful *adjective*
Unable to remember: *Anyone who's that forgetful should write things down.*
   Syn: amnesiac.

forgetfulness *noun* ESCAPE.

forgivable *adjective* PARDONABLE.

forgive *verb*
To grant forgiveness for a fault, offense, or injury: *It was an insulting remark, but I forgave him.*
   Syns: condone, excuse, exculpate, pardon, remit. —*Idiom* forgive and forget.

forgiveness *noun*
The act or an instance of forgiving: *forgiveness for all our sins.*
   Syns: absolution, amnesty, condonation, exculpation, pardon, remission.

forgo also **forego** *verb* RELINQUISH.

fork *noun* BRANCH.

fork *verb* BRANCH.

fork out *verb* SPEND.

forlorn *adjective*
1. ABANDONED.
2. DESPONDENT.
3. LONELY.

form *noun*
1. The external outline of a thing: *a cake in the form of a guitar.*
   Syns: cast, configuration, figure, format, pattern, shape.

2. A model for making a mold:
Concrete is poured into forms.
Syns: cast, matrix.
3. APPLICATION.
4. CONVENTION.
5. RITUAL.
6. TRIM.

form *verb*
1. To give form to by or as if by
pressing and kneading: *used his hands
to form the clay into a statue.*
Syns: model, mold, shape.
2. CONSTITUTE.
3. DEVELOP.

formal *adjective*
1. Requiring elegant clothes and fine
manners: *a formal dance.*
Syns: dressy, fancy-dress, full-dress.
2. CEREMONIOUS.
3. RITUAL.

formalistic *adjective* PEDANTIC.

formality *noun*
1. CEREMONY.
2. RITUAL.

format *noun* FORM.

formation *noun* ARRANGEMENT.

former *adjective*
1. LATE.
2. PAST.

formerly *adverb* EARLIER.

formicate *verb*
1. CRAWL.
2. TEEM[1].

formidable *adjective*
1. BURDENSOME.
2. FEARFUL.

formless *adjective* SHAPELESS.

formulaic *adjective* ROUTINE.

formulate *verb*
1. DRAFT.
2. INVENT.
3. PHRASE.

forsake *verb* ABANDON.

forsaken *adjective* ABANDONED.

forswear also **foreswear** *verb*
1. ABANDON.
2. LIE[2].

forsworn or **foresworn** *adjective*
PERJURIOUS.

forte *noun*
Something at which a person excels:
*She's all right as a cook, but writing is
her forte.*
Syns: bag (*Slang*), eminency,
medium, métier, specialty, thing
(*Slang*). —*Idioms* long suit, strong
point (*or* suit).

forthcoming *adjective* COMING.

forthright *adjective*
1. FRANK.
2. PLAIN.

forthwith *adverb* DIRECTLY.

fortify *verb*
1. CONFIRM.
2. GIRD.

fortitude *noun* COURAGE.

fortitudinous *adjective* BRAVE.

fortuitous *adjective* ACCIDENTAL.

fortuitousness *noun* CHANCE.

fortuity *noun*
1, 2. CHANCE.

fortunate *adjective*
1. FAVORABLE.
2. HAPPY.

fortunateness *noun* LUCK.

fortune *noun*
1. A large sum of money: *made a
fortune in gold mining.*
Syns: boodle (*Slang*), bundle (*Slang*),
mint, pile (*Slang*), wad (*Informal*).
—*Idioms* pretty penny, tidy sum.
2. CHANCE.
3. LUCK.
4. RESOURCES.
5. RICHES.

forward *verb*
1. ADVANCE.
2. SEND.

forward *adjective*
1. ADVANCED.
2. IMPUDENT.

forwardness *noun* IMPUDENCE.

fossil *noun* SQUARE.

foster *verb*
1. ADVANCE.
2. NURSE.
3. PROMOTE.

foul *adjective*
1, 2. FILTHY.
3. INFAMOUS.
4. OBSCENE.
5. OFFENSIVE.
6. SMELLY.

foul *verb*
1. CONTAMINATE.
2. ENTANGLE.

foul up *verb* BOTCH.

foulness *noun*
1. DIRTINESS.
2. IMPURITY.

foul-smelling *adjective* SMELLY.

found *verb*
1. To bring into existence formally: *My
grandfather founded the university.*
Syns: constitute, create, establish,
institute, organize, originate, set up,
start.
2. BASE[1].

foundation *noun*
1. The act of founding or establishing: *the foundation of a scholarship fund.*
   Syns: creation, establishment, institution.
2. BASE¹.
3, 4, 5. BASIS.

foundational *adjective* RADICAL.
founder¹ *noun* ORIGINATOR.
founder² *verb* SINK.
fount *noun* ORIGIN.
fountain *noun* ORIGIN.
fountainhead *noun* ORIGIN.
four-flush *verb* DECEIVE.
fourth estate *noun* PRESS.
foxiness *noun* ART.
foxy *adjective* ARTFUL.
fracas *noun* BRAWL.
fractional *adjective* PARTIAL.
fractious *adjective* UNRULY.
fractiousness *noun* UNRULINESS.
fracturable *adjective* FRAGILE.
fracture *verb* BREAK.
fragile *adjective*
1. Easily broken or damaged: *a fragile piece of glassware.*
   Syns: breakable, brittle, delicate, fracturable, frangible.
2. INFIRM.

fragility *noun* INFIRMITY.
fragment *noun*
1. BIT¹.
2. END.

fragment *verb* BREAK UP at **break**.
fragmentary *adjective* PARTIAL.
fragmentize *verb* BREAK UP at **break**.
fragrance *noun*
A sweet or pleasant odor: *the fragrance of a fresh rose.*
   Syns: aroma, bouquet, perfume, redolence, scent.

fragrant *adjective*
Having a pleasant odor: *a fragrant bouquet.*
   Syns: aromatic, perfumed, redolent, scented.

frail *adjective* INFIRM.
frailty *noun*
1. INFIRMITY.
2. WEAKNESS.

frame *verb*
1. DESIGN.
2. DRAFT.
3. MAKE.

frangible *adjective* FRAGILE.
frank *adjective*
Speaking or spoken freely and sincerely: *a frank statement of his objections.*
   Syns: candid, direct, downright, forthright, honest, open, plainspoken, straight, straightforward, straight-from-the-shoulder (*Informal*), undisguised.

frantic *adjective*
Marked by extreme excitement, confusion, or agitation: *frantic with worry; a frantic scramble for seats.*
   Syns: delirious, frenetic, frenzied, mad, madding (*Obs.*), rabid, wild.

frantically *adverb* HARD.
fraternity *noun* UNION.
fraternize *verb* ASSOCIATE.
fraud *noun*
1. CHEAT.
2. FAKE.

fraudulent *adjective* COUNTERFEIT.
fray *noun*
1. BRAWL.
2. FIGHT.

freak *noun*
1. A person or animal that is abnormally formed: *freaks exhibited in the circus sideshow.*
   Syns: monster, monstrosity, oddity.
2. ENTHUSIAST.
3. FANCY.

freakish *adjective*
1. Resembling a freak: *a person of freakish appearance.*
   Syns: bizarre, freaky, grotesque, monstrous.
2. CAPRICIOUS.
3. ECCENTRIC.

freaky *adjective* FREAKISH.
freckle *verb* SPECKLE.
free *adjective*
1. Costing nothing: *a free ticket to the ball game.*
   Syns: complimentary, cost-free, gratis, gratuitous, on-the-house (*Slang*).
2. At liberty; not imprisoned or enslaved: *Slaves became free with Lincoln's Emancipation Proclamation.*
   Syns: emancipated, liberated, manumitted, released.
3. Having political independence: *Jamaica is now a free country.*
   Syns: autonomous, independent, sovereign.
4. CLEAR.
5. GENEROUS.
6, 7. LOOSE.
8. OUTSPOKEN.
9. UNRESERVED.
10. VOLUNTARY.

free *verb*
To set at liberty: *freeing a man from prison.*

Syns: discharge, emancipate, liberate, loose, manumit, release, spring (*Slang*). —*Idiom* let loose.

freebie also **freebee** *noun* PASS.

freedom *noun*
1. The condition of being politically free: *granted the colony its freedom.*
  Syns: autonomy, independence, liberty, sovereignty.
2. Ease of movement: *a coat that gives the wearer plenty of freedom.*
  Syns: elbowroom, latitude, play, swing.
3, 4. LIBERTY.

free-for-all *noun* BRAWL.
freehanded *adjective* GENEROUS.
freehandedness *noun* GENEROSITY.
freeloader *noun* PARASITE.
freeloading *adjective* PARASITIC.
free-speaking *adjective* OUTSPOKEN.
free-spoken *adjective*
1. OUTSPOKEN.
2. TALKATIVE.

freeway *noun* WAY.
freezing *adjective* FRIGID.
freight *noun* BURDEN.
freight *verb*
1, 2. CHARGE.
3. FILL.

frenetic *adjective* FRANTIC.
frenzied *adjective* FRANTIC.
frenziedly *adverb* HARD.
frequent *verb*
To visit regularly: *We frequented the park on Saturday mornings.*
  Syns: hang around (*Informal*), hang out (*Slang*), haunt, resort to.

frequent *adjective* COMMON.
frequently *adverb* USUALLY.
fresh *adjective*
1. Not previously known or used: *fresh evidence; a fresh coat of paint.*
  Syns: brand-new, different, new.
2. Bright and clear; not dull or faded: *the fresh complexion of a young girl.*
  Syns: blooming, creamy, glowing, peaches-and-cream.
3. ADDITIONAL.
4. IMPUDENT.
5. NEW.

freshen *verb*
1. REFRESH.
2. TIDY.

freshet *noun* FLOOD.
freshman *noun* BEGINNER.
freshness *noun* NOVELTY.
fret *verb*.
1. ANNOY.
2. BROOD.
3. CHAFE.
4. FUSS.

fretful *adjective*
1. IMPATIENT.
2. IRRITABLE.

fribbling *adjective* GIDDY.
friction *noun* CONFLICT.
friend *noun*
1. A person whom one knows well, likes, and trusts: *He's been my friend since high school.*
  Syns: amigo (*Spanish*), confidant, familiar, intimate[1], mate, sidekick (*Slang*).
2. ACQUAINTANCE.
3. PATRON.

friendliness *noun* AMIABILITY.
friendly *adjective*
1. Of or befitting a friend or friends: *a friendly letter; friendly cooperation.*
  Syns: amiable, amicable, chummy (*Informal*), congenial, convivial, neighborly, sympathetic, warmhearted.
2. APPROACHABLE.
3. FAMILIAR.
4. HARMONIOUS.

friendship *noun*
The condition of being friends: *Our friendship has survived many arguments.*
  Syns: brotherhood, comradeship, intimacy.

fright *noun*
1. FEAR.
2. MESS.

fright *verb* FRIGHTEN.
frighten *verb*
To fill with fear: *The explosion frightened me. A small child frightens easily.*
  Syns: affright (*Archaic*), alarm, fright (*Archaic*), panic, scare, scarify (*Regional*), shake up (*Informal*), startle, terrify, terrorize. —*Idioms* make one's blood run cold, make one's hair stand on end, scare silly (*or* spitless *or* stiff), scare the daylights out of.

frightened *adjective* AFRAID.
frightening *adjective* FEARFUL.
frightful *adjective*
1. FEARFUL.
2. TERRIBLE.
3. UNSPEAKABLE.

frightfulness *noun* UGLINESS.
frigid *adjective*
1. Very cold: *a frigid January day.*
  Syns: arctic, bitter, boreal, freezing, frore (*Archaic*), frory (*Archaic*),

frosty, gelid, glacial, icy, polar,
wintry.

2. Deficient in or lacking sexual desire:
*a frigid person unable to respond to
love.*
Syns: ardorless, cold, inhibited,
passionless, unresponsive.

3. COLD.

frill *noun* LUXURY.

fringe *noun*
1. BORDER.
2. SKIRTS.
fringe *verb* BORDER.

frippery *noun* FROTH.

frisk *verb*
1. GAMBOL.
2. SEARCH.
frisk *noun* SHAKEDOWN.

fritter away *verb* WASTE.

frivolity *noun* FROTH.

frivolous *adjective* GIDDY.

frock *noun* DRESS.

frolic *verb*
1. GAMBOL.
2. REVEL.
frolic *noun* PRANK.

front *noun*
1. The part of an object, person, etc.,
facing the viewer: *a blouse with tucks
down the front; spilled gravy down his
front.*
Syns: fore, forepart.
2, 3. FAÇADE.
front *verb*
1. CONFRONT.
2. DEFY.
3. FACE.

frontage *noun* FAÇADE.

frontal *adjective* FAÇADE.

frontispiece *noun* FAÇADE.

front-runner *noun* LEADER.

frore *adjective* FRIGID.

frory *adjective* FRIGID.

frosty *adjective*
1. COOL.
2. FRIGID.

froth *noun*
1. Something lacking substance or
depth: *The play was nothing but froth.*
Syns: fiddle-faddle (*Slang*), frippery,
frivolity, trivia, triviality.
2. FOAM.
froth *verb* FOAM.

frothy *adjective*
1. Amusing but essentially empty and
frivolous: *a frothy new comedy.*
Syn: light².
2. FOAMY.
3. GIDDY.

froward *adjective* CONTRARY.

frown *verb*
To wrinkle one's brow, as in thought,
puzzlement, or displeasure: *frowns when
he's angry.*
Syns: glare, glower, lower¹ (*also* lour),
scowl. —*Idiom* look black.

frown on (or **upon**) *verb* DISAPPROVE.

frown *noun*
The act of wrinkling the brow, as in
thought, puzzlement, or displeasure:
With a frown, she refused to shake hands.
Syns: glare, glower, lower¹ (*also* lour),
scowl. —*Idiom* black look.

frowsy *adjective* MOLDY.

frugal *adjective* ECONOMICAL.

frugality *noun* ECONOMY.

fruit *noun*
1. EFFECT.
2. HARVEST.

fruitage *noun* HARVEST.

fruitfulness *noun* FERTILITY.

fruition *noun* FULFILLMENT.

fruitless *adjective* FUTILE.

fruitlessness *noun* FUTILITY.

fruity *adjective* INSANE.

frumpish *adjective* TACKY².

frustrate *verb*
To prevent from accomplishing a
purpose: *A poor memory frustrated his
efforts to become an actor.*
Syns: baffle, balk, check, checkmate,
defeat, foil, stymie, thwart. —*Idiom*
cut the ground from under.

fuddle *verb* CONFUSE.

fuddy-duddy *noun* SQUARE.

fudge *verb* MUDDLE.

fuehrer *noun* SEE **führer**.

fugacious *adjective* TRANSITORY.

fugitive *noun*
One who flees, as from home,
confinement, captivity, justice, etc.: *a
fugitive from jail.*
Syns: escapee, refugee, runaway.
fugitive *adjective*
1. Fleeing or having fled, as from home,
confinement, captivity, justice, etc.: *a
manhunt for fugitive convicts.*
Syns: escaped, runaway.
2. TRANSITORY.

führer *also* **fuehrer** *noun* DICTATOR.

fulfill *verb*
1. To carry out the functions,
requirements, or terms of: *fulfilling
her official duties; fulfilled my side of
the bargain.*
Syns: discharge, execute, exercise,
implement, perform. —*Idiom* live up
to.
2. SATISFY.

fulfilled *adjective*
Having achieved satisfaction, as of one's goal: *She felt fulfilled when she reached the top of her profession.*
  Syns: content, gratified, happy, satisfied.

fulfillment *noun*
The condition of being fulfilled: *dreams that could never reach fulfillment.*
  Syns: consummation, culmination, fruition, realization.

full *adjective*
1. Completely filled: *a full pail; a room full of people.*
  Syns: brimful, brimming, bursting, chockablock, chock-full (*also* chuck-full, choke-full), crammed, crowded, jam-full, jammed, jam-packed (*Informal*), loaded, packed, replete, stuffed, trig (*Brit. Regional*).
2. Of full measure; not narrow or restricted: *a full skirt.*
  Syns: ample, capacious, voluminous, wide.
3. CLOSE¹.
4. COMPLETE.
5. DETAILED.
6. ROUND.

full-blooded *adjective*
1. RUDDY.
2. THOROUGHBRED.

full-blown *adjective* MATURE.

full-dress *adjective*
1. FORMAL.
2. THOROUGH.

full-fledged *adjective* MATURE.

full-grown *adjective* MATURE.

full-strength *adjective* STRAIGHT.

fully *adverb.*
1. CLEAR.
2. COMPLETELY.

fulminate *verb* EXPLODE.

fulmination *noun*
1. BLAST.
2. TIRADE.

fulsome *adjective* UNCTUOUS.

fumble *verb*
1. BOTCH.
2. GROPE.
3. MUDDLE.

fumble *noun* BLUNDER.

fumbler *noun* BLUNDERER.

fume *verb* ANGER.

fume *noun* STATE.

fun *noun*
1. GAIETY.
2, 3. PLAY.

fun *verb*
1, 2. JOKE.

function *noun*
1. The proper activity of a person or thing: *the function of a teacher; the function of a carburetor.*
  Syns: job, purpose, role (*also* rôle).
2. PARTY.

function *verb*
1. To react in a specified way: *He functioned well in the crisis.*
  Syns: act, behave, operate, take, work.
2. ACT FOR at act.
3. WORK.

functional *adjective* PRACTICAL.

functioning *noun* BEHAVIOR.

functioning *adjective* ACTIVE.

fund *verb* FINANCE.

fundament *noun* BASE¹.

fundamental *adjective*
1. ELEMENTAL.
2. ESSENTIAL.
3. RADICAL.

fundamental *noun*
1. BASIS.
2. ELEMENT.
3. LAW.

fundamentalist *noun* CONSERVATIVE.

fundamentally *adverb* ESSENTIALLY.

funds *noun*
The monetary resources of a government, organization, or individual: *state government funds; had insufficient funds to pay for the elaborate banquet.*
  Syns: capital, finances, moneys.

funk¹ *verb* SMELL.

funk² *noun*
1. COWARD.
2. COWARDICE.
3. FEAR.
4. GLOOM.

funniness *noun* HUMOR.

funny *adjective*
1. Causing puzzlement; perplexing: *That's a funny way to behave when you're paid a compliment.*
  Syns: curious, kooky (*Slang*), odd, peculiar, queer, strange, weird.
2. AMUSING.
3. HUMOROUS.
4. LAUGHABLE.
5. QUAINT¹.

funny *noun* JOKE.

fur *noun* HIDE².

furbish *verb*
1. GLOSS.
2. RENEW.

furious *adjective*
1. Full of or marked by extreme anger: *He was furious when I criticized him.*
  Syns: enraged, inflamed, infuriated, rabid, raging, ranting, raving.

—*Idioms* foaming at the mouth, in a
towering rage.
2. ANGRY.
3. HEAVY.
4. HIGH.
furiously *adverb* HARD.
furlough *noun* VACATION.
furnish *verb*
1. To supply what is needed for some
activity or purpose: *furnished their
new house.*
Syns: accouter, appoint, equip, fit up
(*or* out), gear, outfit, rig (out *or* up),
turn out.
2. GIVE.
furnishing *noun*
A piece of equipment for comfort or
convenience: *a chair or other furnishing.*
Syns: appointment, chattel, fitting,
movable (*also* moveable).
furor *noun.*
1. FASHION.
2. FURY.
furrow *noun* LINE.
furry *adjective* HAIRY.
further *adjective*
1. Going beyond what currently exists:
without further ado.
Syns: additional, subsequent, ulterior.
2. ADDITIONAL.
further *verb* ADVANCE.
further *adverb* ADDITIONALLY.
furtherance *noun* ADVANCE.
furthermore *adverb* ADDITIONALLY.
furthermost *adjective* EXTREME.
furthest *adjective* EXTREME.
furtive *adjective*
1. SLY.
2. STEALTHY.
furtiveness *noun* STEALTH.
fury *noun*
1. Violent or unrestrained anger: *He
smashed the glass in his fury.*
Syns: choler, furor, ire, rage, wrath,
wrathfulness.
2. INTENSITY.
3. SCOLD.
fuse *verb*
1. MELT.
2. MIX.
fused *adjective* COMBINED.
fusillade *noun* BARRAGE.
fusion *noun* MIXTURE.
fuss *noun*
1. Busy and useless activity: *Can't we
give a party without a lot of fuss?*
Syns: ado, to-do (*Informal*).
2. BOTHER.
3. DISTURBANCE.

fuss *verb*
1. To be nervously or uselessly active:
She fussed in the kitchen all afternoon.
Syns: bustle, mess around (*Slang*),
pother, putter (around).
2. To worry over trifles: *no need to fuss
about a bad dream.*
Syns: chafe, fret, stew, take on.
3. NAG.
fussy *adjective*
1. BUSY.
2. NICE.
fustian *adjective* SONOROUS.
fusty *adjective*
1. MOLDY.
2. OLD-FASHIONED.
futile *adjective*
Having no useful result: *a futile effort to
engage him in conversation.*
Syns: barren, bootless, fruitless,
ineffective, ineffectual, unavailing,
unsuccessful, useless, vain. —*Idiom* in
vain.
futility *noun*
The condition or quality of being
useless or ineffective: *a war that was an
exercise in futility.*
Syns: fruitlessness, ineffectiveness,
ineffectuality, ineffectualness,
inefficacy, uselessness.
future *noun*
1. Time that is yet to be: *We'll face that
problem some time in the future.*
Syns: by-and-by, hereafter. —*Idiom*
time to come.
2. Chance of success or advancement: *a
job with no future.*
Syns: outlook, prospect.
future *adjective*
Being or occurring in the time ahead:
postponed the meeting to a future date.
Syns: coming, later, subsequent.
fuzz *noun* POLICEMAN.
fuzzy *adjective* UNCLEAR.

G

gab *verb* CHATTER.
gab *noun* CHATTER.
gabble *verb* BABBLE.
gabble *noun* BABBLE.
gabby *adjective* TALKATIVE.
gad about (*or* **around**) *verb* ROVE.

gadget *noun*
Informal. A small, specialized mechanical device: *a gadget for peeling potatoes.*
  Syns: concern (*Informal*), contraption, contrivance, doodad (*Informal*), doohickey (*Informal*), gimmick (*Informal*), gismo (*also* gizmo) (*Slang*), jigger, thing, thingamabob (*also* thingumabob) (*Informal*), thingamajig (*also* thingumajig) (*Informal*), widget (*Informal*).

gag *noun* JOKE.
gag *verb* REPRESS.
gaga *adjective*
1. GIDDY.
2. INSANE.
gage *noun & verb* SEE **gauge**.
gaiety *noun*
1. A state of joyful exuberance: *the gaiety of the holidays; a house that rang with the gaiety of children.*
  Syns: glee, gleefulness, hilarity, jocularity, jocundity, jollity, joviality, jovialness, merriment, mirth.
2. Joyful, exuberant activity: *a weekend of unrestrained gaiety.*
  Syns: festivity, fun, jollity, merriment, merrymaking, revel, reveling, revelry, whoopee (*Slang*).
gain *verb*
1. To achieve an increment of gradually: *gain weight; gain speed.*
  Syns: build up, develop, increase.
2. ARRIVE AT at **arrive.**
3. CAPTURE.
4, 5. EARN.
6. GET.
7. RECOVER.
8. RETURN.
gain *noun*
1. Something earned, won, or otherwise acquired: *a net gain of $5 per share.*
  Syns: profit, return.
2. ADVANTAGE.
gainsay *verb* DENY.
gainsaying *noun* DENIAL.
gala *noun* PARTY.
gala *adjective* MERRY.
gale *noun* WIND[1].
gall[1] *noun* RESENTMENT.
gall *verb*
1. ANNOY.
2. CHAFE.
gall[2] *noun*
1. IMPUDENCE.
2. PRESUMPTION.
gallant *adjective*
1. Respectfully attentive, esp. to women: *gallant conduct.*

  Syns: chivalric, chivalrous, courtly.
2. BRAVE.
3. GRACIOUS.
gallant *noun*
A man amorously attentive to women: *a flirtatious gallant keeping an eye out for pretty young things.*
  Syns: amorist, Casanova, Don Juan, Lothario, Romeo. —*Idioms* gay blade, lady's man (*also* ladies' man).
gallantry *noun*
1. Respectful attention, esp. toward women: *true gentlemen, noted for gallantry.*
  Syns: chivalrousness, chivalry, courtliness.
2. COURAGE.
3. HEROISM.
gallimaufry *noun* ASSORTMENT.
galling *adjective* VEXATIOUS.
gallivant *verb* ROVE.
galumph or **gallumph** *verb* LUMP[1].
galvanize *verb*
1. ACTIVATE.
2. PROVOKE.
gamble *verb*
1. To take a risk in the hope of gaining advantage: *gambled in cotton futures.*
  Syns: speculate, venture.
2. To put up as a stake in a game or speculation: *gambled her half of the estate against his.*
  Syns: bet, go, lay[1], risk, set[1], stake, venture, wager. —*Idiom* put one's money on.
3. BET.
gamble *noun*
1. A venture depending on chance: *His gamble was that the market would rise.*
  Syns: bet, speculation, wager.
2. RISK.
gambler *noun* BETTOR.
gambol *verb*
To leap and skip about playfully: *children gamboling on the lawn.*
  Syns: caper, cavort, dance, frisk, frolic, prance, rollick, romp.
game *verb* BET.
game *noun* PLAY.
game *adjective*
1. BRAVE.
2. WILLING.
gamester *noun* BETTOR.
gander[1] *noun* FOOL.
gander[2] *noun* GLANCE[1].
gang *noun*
1. An organized group of criminals, hoodlums, or wrongdoers: *the City Hall gang; a gang of car thieves.*
  Syns: band[2], mob (*Informal*), pack, ring[1].

2. CROWD.

gang up *verb* BAND[2].

gangling *adjective*
Tall, thin, and awkwardly built: *danced reluctantly with a gangling youth.*
   Syns: gangly, lanky, loose-jointed, rangy, spindling, spindly.

gangly *adjective* GANGLING.

gaol *noun* JAIL.

gaoler *noun* JAILER.

gap *noun*
1. An interval during which continuity is suspended: *a gap in the manuscript.*
   Syns: breach, break, hiatus, interim, lacuna, void.
2. A marked lack of correspondence or agreement: *a gap between revenue and spending; the generation gap.*
   Syns: difference, disagreement, discrepancy (*also* discrepance), disparity, incongruity, inconsistency.
3. BREACH.

gap *verb* YAWN.

gape *verb*
1. GAZE.
2, 3. YAWN.

gape *noun* GAZE.

gaping *adjective* YAWNING.

garb *noun* DRESS.

garb *verb* DRESS.

garden *adjective* ORDINARY.

garden-variety *adjective* ORDINARY.

gargantuan *adjective* GIANT.

garish *adjective* GAUDY.

garment *verb* DRESS.

garments *noun* DRESS.

garner *verb*
1. ACCUMULATE.
2. GATHER.
3. GLEAN.

garner *noun* ACCUMULATION.

garnish *verb* ADORN.

garnishment *noun* ADORNMENT.

garniture *noun* ADORNMENT.

garrulous *adjective* TALKATIVE.

gas *noun* SCREAM.

gas *verb* CHATTER.

gasconade *verb* BOAST.

gasconade *noun* BOAST.

gash *verb* CUT.

gash *noun* CUT.

gasp *verb*
1. To utter in a breathless manner: *gasped a warning and fainted.*
   Syns: heave, pant.
2. PANT.

gate *noun* TAKE.

gate money *noun* TAKE.

gather *verb*
1. To collect ripe crops: *gather peaches.*

   Syns: garner, harvest, reap.
2. ACCUMULATE.
3, 4. ASSEMBLE.
5. GLEAN.
6. GROUP.
7. INFER.

gathering *noun*
1. ASSEMBLY.
2. HARVEST.
3. JUNCTION.

gauche *adjective* UNSKILLFUL.

gaudy *adjective*
Tastelessly showy: *a gaudy disco; gaudy clothes.*
   Syns: chintzy, flashy, garish, glaring, loud, meretricious, tacky[2], tawdry, tinsel.

gauge *also* **gage** *noun* STANDARD.

gauge *also* **gage** *verb*
1. ESTIMATE.
2. MEASURE.

gaum *noun* LUMP[1].

gaunt *adjective*
1. THIN.
2. WASTED.

gaunt *verb* THIN.

gauzy *adjective* FILMY.

gawk *noun* LUMP[1].

gawk *verb* GAZE.

gawky *adjective* AWKWARD.

gay *adjective*
1. Characterized by joyful exuberance: *a gay companion; a gay Christmas party.*
   Syns: blithe, blithesome, boon[2], festive, gleeful, jocund, jolly, jovial, lighthearted, merry, mirthful.
2. Pertaining to, characteristic of, or exhibiting sexual desire for others of one's own sex: *the Gay Rights Movement.*
   Syns: homophile, homosexual.
3. COLORFUL.
4. FAST.
5. GLAD.

gaze *verb*
1. To look intently and fixedly: *gazed in awe at the Alps.*
   Syns: eye, gape, gawk (*Informal*), glare, goggle, ogle, peer[1], stare, yawp (*also* yaup) (*Regional*). —*Idioms* gaze open-mouthed, rivet the eyes on.
2. LOOK.

gaze *noun*
1. An intent, fixed look: *was disconcerted by his penetrating gaze.*
   Syns: gape, peer[1], stare.
2. LOOK.

gear *noun* OUTFIT.

gear *verb* FURNISH.

gee *verb* AGREE.

gelastic *adjective* LAUGHABLE.
gelatinize *verb* COAGULATE.
gelatinous *adjective* THICK.
geld *verb* STERILIZE.
gelding *noun* STERILIZATION.
gelid *adjective* FRIGID.
gelt *noun* MONEY.
gem *noun* TREASURE.
geminate *adjective* DOUBLE.
gendarme *noun* POLICEMAN.
genealogy *noun*
1. A written record of ancestry: *studied her family's genealogy.*
   Syns: begats (*Slang*), pedigree.
   —*Idiom* family tree.
2. ANCESTRY.
general *adjective*
1. Belonging or pertaining to the whole: *a general change in society.*
   Syns: common, generic, universal.
2. Covering a wide scope: *general discontent.*
   Syns: all-inclusive, all-round (*also* all-around), broad, broad-spectrum, comprehensive, expansive, extended, extensive, far-ranging, far-reaching, global, inclusive, large, overall, sweeping, wide-ranging, wide-reaching, widespread.
3. Not limited to a single class: *general merchandise.*
   Syns: divers, diverse, diversified, sundry.
4, 5. COMMON.
6. POPULAR.
generalize *verb* UNIVERSALIZE.
generate *verb*
1. To give rise to a particular development: *strict policies generating employee discontent.*
   Syns: breed, cause, engender, hatch, induce, provoke, spawn, stir[1] (up), touch off.
2. DEVELOP.
3. PRODUCE.
generic *adjective* GENERAL.
generosity *noun*
The quality or state of being generous: *a philanthropist whose generosity was famed.*
   Syns: big-heartedness, freehandedness, generousness, great-heartedness, liberality, magnanimity, magnanimousness, munificence, openhandedness.
generous *adjective*
1. Willing to give of oneself and one's possessions: *He is a generous contributor. That's generous of you.*
   Syns: big, big-hearted, great-hearted,

large-hearted, magnanimous, unselfish.
2. Characterized by bounteous giving: *a generous divorce settlement; was generous with her money.*
   Syns: free, freehanded, handsome, liberal, munificent, openhanded, unsparing, unstinting.
3. Characterized by abundance: *a generous serving of potatoes.*
   Syns: abundant, ample, bounteous, bountiful, copious, liberal, plenteous, plentiful.
generousness *noun* GENEROSITY.
genesis *noun*
1. BEGINNING.
2. BIRTH.
genial *adjective*
1. AMIABLE.
2. GRACIOUS.
geniality *noun* AMIABILITY.
genius *noun*
1. FIRE.
2. TALENT.
genteel *adjective*
1. Marked by excessive concern for propriety and good form: *a genteel abhorrence of plain speaking.*
   Syns: bluenosed, missish, old-maidish, precise, prim, prissy, proper, prudish, puritanical, strait-laced, stuffy (*Informal*), tight-laced, Victorian. —*Idiom* prim and proper.
2. COURTEOUS.
gentility *noun* SOCIETY.
gentle *adjective*
1. Of a kindly, considerate character: *a gentle mother.*
   Syns: mild, soft, softhearted, tender[1], tenderhearted.
2. Free from severity or violence, as in movement: *a gentle summer breeze.*
   Syns: balmy, bland, delicate, faint, mild, smooth, soft.
3. Easily managed or handled: *a gentle horse.*
   Syns: docile, meek, mild, tame.
4. GRADUAL.
5. LIGHT[2].
gentle *verb*
1. To make (an animal) docile: *gentled a wild horse.*
   Syns: break, bust (*Slang*), tame.
2. DOMESTICATE.
3. PACIFY.
gentry *noun* SOCIETY.
genuflection *noun* BOW.
genuine *adjective*
1. Devoid of any hypocrisy or pretense: *genuine grief.*
   Syns: heartfelt, heart-whole, hearty,

honest, real, sincere, true, unaffected, unfeigned.
2. AUTHENTIC.

genuinely *adverb* ACTUALLY.

genuineness *noun* AUTHENTICITY.

germ *noun*
1. *Med.* A minute organism usu. producing disease: *influenza germs.*
   Syns: bug (*Informal*), microbe, microorganism (*also* micro-organism).
2. A source of further growth and development: *germs of doubt; the germ of a new idea.*
   Syns: bud, embryo, kernel, nucleus, seed, spark.

germane *adjective* RELEVANT.

germaneness *noun* RELEVANCE.

gest or **geste** *noun*
1. BEARING.
2. FEAT.

gestation *noun* PREGNANCY.

geste *noun* SEE **gest**.

gesticulate *verb* GESTURE.

gesticulation *noun* GESTURE.

gesture *noun*
1. An expressive, meaningful bodily movement: *made an emphatic gesture of disapproval.*
   Syns: gesticulation, indication, motion, sign, signal.
2. EXPRESSION.

gesture *verb*
To make bodily motions so as to convey an idea or complement speech: *gestured to me to be quiet; gestured as she described the accident.*
   Syns: gesticulate, motion, sign, signal, signalize. —*Idiom* give the high sign.

get *verb*
1. To come into possession of: *Where did you get that expensive car?*
   Syns: acquire, come by, gain, land, obtain, pick up, procure, secure, win.
2. To cause to be in a certain state or to undergo a particular experience or action: *got ready; get the car washed; got her angry.*
   Syns: have, make.
3. AFFECT.
4. ANNOY.
5. BECOME.
6. CAPTURE.
7. CATCH.
8. CONTRACT.
9. DERIVE.
10, 11. EARN.
12. FATHER.
13. LEARN.
14. REACH.
15. RUN.
16. TAKE.
17. UNDERSTAND.

get about *verb*
To become known far and wide: *The news got about very quickly.*
   Syns: circulate, get around, go around, spread, travel. —*Idiom* make the rounds.

get across *verb* COMMUNICATE.

get ahead *verb* SUCCEED.

get along *verb*
1. To live or act together in harmony: *a family that got along well.*
   Syns: cotton (*Informal*), get on, harmonize. —*Idiom* hit it off.
2. AGE.
3. COME.
4. MANAGE.

get around *verb*
1. AVOID.
2. GET ABOUT at **get**.
3. SKIRT.

get away *verb*
1. ESCAPE.
2. GO.

get behind *verb* SUPPORT.

get by *verb* MANAGE.

get in *verb* ARRIVE.

get off *verb* START.

get on *verb.*
1. AGE.
2. DON.
3. GET ALONG at **get**.
4. SUCCEED.

get out *verb*
1. COME OUT at **come**.
2. RUN.

get to *verb* ARRIVE AT at **arrive**.

get together *verb*
1. AGREE.
2, 3. ASSEMBLE.

get up *verb*
1. To leave one's bed: *got up at seven.*
   Syns: arise, pile out, rise, roll out, turn out, uprise. —*Idiom* rise and shine.
2. To adopt a standing posture: *The football player got up after being tackled.*
   Syns: rise, stand up, uprise, upspring. —*Idiom* get to one's feet.

get *noun* PROGENY.

getaway *noun* ESCAPE.

gettable *adjective* AVAILABLE.

getup *noun* DRESS.

get-up-and-go *noun*
1. DRIVE.
2. ENERGY.

gewgaw *noun* NOVELTY.

ghastly *adjective*
1. Shockingly repellent: *the ghastly sight of starving refugee children.*
   Syns: grim, grisly, gruesome, hideous, horrible, horrid, lurid, macabre.
2. Gruesomely suggestive of ghosts or death: *A ghastly figure loomed up. The dying man had a ghastly pallor.*
   Syns: cadaverous, corpselike, deadly, deathlike, deathly, ghostlike, ghostly, mortuary, spectral.
3. FEARFUL.
4. TERRIBLE.

ghost *noun*
1. A supernatural being: *thought she saw the ghost of her great-grandmother.*
   Syns: apparition, bogle, bogy (*also* bogey, bogie), bugbear (*Archaic*), eidolon, haunt (*Regional*), phantasm (*also* phantasma), phantom, revenant, shade, shadow, specter, spectrum, spirit, spook, umbra, visitant, wraith.
2. SHADE.

ghost *verb*
To write for and credit authorship to another: *She ghosted the queen's autobiography.*
   Syns: ghostwrite, spook (*Slang*).

ghostlike *adjective* GHASTLY.
ghostly *adjective* GHASTLY.
ghostwrite *verb* GHOST.
ghoul *noun* FIEND.
ghoulish *adjective* FIENDISH.

giant *noun*
One that is extraordinarily large and powerful: *a giant of a linebacker; a literary giant; a giant among corporations.*
   Syns: behemoth, Goliath, jumbo, leviathan, mammoth, monster, titan, whopper.

giant *adjective*
Of extraordinary size and power: *a giant football player; a giant interlocking conglomerate.*
   Syns: Antaean, behemothic, Brobdingnagian, Bunyanesque, colossal, cyclopean, elephantine, enormous, gargantuan, gigantean, gigantesque, gigantic, herculean, heroic, huge, immense, jumbo, leviathan, mammoth, massive, massy (*Archaic*), mastodonic, mighty, monster, monstrous, monumental, mountainous, planetary, prodigious, pythonic, stupendous, titan, titanic, tremendous, vast, walloping (*Informal*), whopping.

gibber *verb* BABBLE.

gibberish *noun*
1. Wordy, unclear jargon: *couldn't understand government gibberish.*
   Syns: abracadabra, double talk, gobbledygook (*also* gobbledegook), jabberwocky (*also* jabberwock), mumbo jumbo.
2. Esoteric, formulaic, and often incomprehensible speech relating to the occult: *the gibberish of witches.*
   Syns: abracadabra, hocus-pocus, mumbo jumbo.
3. BABBLE.

gibbet *verb* HANG.
gibe at *verb* RIDICULE.
giddiness *noun* DIZZINESS.

giddy *adjective*
1. Given to lighthearted silliness: *giddy youngsters.*
   Syns: birdbrained (*Slang*), dizzy (*Informal*), empty-headed, featherbrained, flighty, fribbling, frivolous, frothy, gaga (*Slang*), harebrained, lightheaded, scatterbrained, silly, skittish. —*Idiom* giddy as a goose.
2. Producing dizziness or vertigo: *a giddy height.*
   Syns: dizzy, dizzying, vertiginous.
3. DIZZY.

gift *noun*
1. Something bestowed freely: *The platter was a wedding gift.*
   Syns: handsel (*also* hansel) (*Chiefly Brit.*), present², presentation.
2. DONATION.
3. TALENT.

gift *verb*
1. To present with a quality, trait, or power: *The Lord has gifted us with good health.*
   Syns: dower, endow, endue, gird, invest.
2. GIVE.

gifted *adjective*
Having talent: *a gifted pianist.*
   Syns: endowed, talented.

gig *noun* POSITION.
gigantean *adjective* GIANT.
gigantesque *adjective* GIANT.
gigantic *adjective* GIANT.

giggle *verb*
To laugh in a stifled way: *children giggling in class.*
   Syns: snicker (*also* snigger), tehee *or* tee-hee, titter.

giggle *noun*
A stifled laugh: *had a fit of giggles.*
   Syns: snicker (*also* snigger), tehee *or* tee-hee, titter.

gild *verb*
1. COLOR.
2. SWEETEN.

gimcrack *noun* NOVELTY.

gimmick *noun*
1. GADGET.
2. TRICK.
3. WRINKLE².

ginger *noun* SPIRIT.

gingerliness *noun* CAUTION.

gingerly *adjective* WARY.

gip *verb* SEE **gyp.**

gird *verb*
1. To prepare (oneself) for action: *soldiers girding themselves for the forthcoming battle.*
   Syns: brace², forearm, fortify, ready, steel, strengthen. —*Idiom* gird one's loins.
2. BAND¹.
3. GIFT.
4. SURROUND.

girdle *verb*
1. BAND¹.
2. SURROUND.

gismo also **gizmo** *noun* GADGET.

gist *noun* HEART.

give *verb*
1. To make a gift of: *gave the children candy; was given an expensive watch.*
   Syns: bestow, gift (*Chiefly Brit.*), give away, hand out, present².
2. To relinquish to the possession or control of another: *gave them the cottage for a week; give me the scissors.*
   Syns: deliver, furnish, hand, hand over, provide, supply, transfer, turn over.
3. To mete out by means of some action: *give a spanking.*
   Syns: administer, deal (out), deliver.
4. ALLOT.
5. APPLY.
6. BEND.
7. CAVE IN at **cave.**
8. COMMUNICATE.
9. DONATE.
10. EMIT.
11. GRANT.
12. HAVE.
13. SPEND.
14. STAGE.

give away *verb*
1. BETRAY.
2. GIVE.

give back *verb*
1. RESTORE.
2. RETURN.

give forth *verb* EMIT.

give in *verb*
To cease opposition: *finally saw that he had lost the election and gave in.*
   Syns: concede, yield.

give off *verb* EMIT.

give out *verb*
1. COLLAPSE.
2. DRY UP at **dry.**
3. EMIT.
4, 5. FAIL.
6. RUN DOWN at **run.**

give over *verb*
1. To yield (oneself) unrestrainedly, as to a particular impulse: *gave herself over to uncontrolled sobbing.*
   Syns: abandon, give up, surrender.
2. DROP.

give up *verb*
1. ABANDON.
2. BREAK.
3. DESPAIR.
4. DROP.
5. GIVE OVER at **give.**

give *noun* FLEXIBILITY.

give-and-take *noun* COMPROMISE.

giveaway *noun* BARGAIN.

given *adjective* INCLINED.

giver *noun* DONOR.

gizmo *noun* SEE **gismo.**

glacial *adjective*
1. COLD.
2. FRIGID.

glad *adjective*
1. Providing joy and pleasure: *a glad occasion; glad tidings.*
   Syns: cheerful, cheery, festive, gay, joyful, joyous, pleasing.
2. Eagerly compliant: *I am glad to help.*
   Syns: delighted, happy, pleased, proud (*Chiefly Regional*), ready, tickled.
3. MERRY.

gladden *verb* DELIGHT.

gladness *noun* HAPPINESS.

gladsome *adjective* MERRY.

glamorous also **glamourous** *adjective* ATTRACTIVE.

glamour also **glamor** *noun* ATTRACTION.

glance¹ *verb*
1. To strike a surface at such an angle as to be deflected: *bullets glancing off the armor plating.*
   Syns: carom (*also* carrom) (off), dap, glint (*Archaic*), graze, ricochet, skim, skip.
2. BROWSE.
3. BRUSH.
4. FLASH.
5. GLIMPSE.

glance at (or **over** or **through**) *verb*
BROWSE.

glance *noun*
1. A quick look: *took a glance at the book.*
   Syns: blink, gander² (*Slang*), glimpse, peek, peep, squiz (*Austral. & New Zeal.*).
2. BLINK.
3. BRUSH.

glance² *verb* GLOSS.

glare *verb*
1. To stare fixedly and angrily: *glared at me with obvious resentment.*
   Syns: glower, lower¹ (*also* lour), scowl. —*Idiom* look daggers.
2. To be projected with blinding intensity: *a desert sun that glared mercilessly.*
   Syns: beat (down), blare, blaze¹.
3. To be obtrusively conspicuous: *errors glaring from the page.*
   Syns: stand out, stick out. —*Idioms* hit someone in the eye, hit (*or* stare) someone in the face, stick out like a sore thumb.
4. FROWN.
5. GAZE.

glare *noun*
1. A fixed, angry stare: *looked at me with a ferocious glare.*
   Syns: glower, scowl.
2. An intense, blinding light: *Sunglasses will decrease the glare.*
   Syns: blare, blaze¹, dazzle.
3. FROWN.

glaring *adjective*
1. BLAZING.
2. FLAGRANT.
3. GAUDY.

glassy *adjective* GLOSSY.

glaver *verb* FLATTER.

glaze *noun* GLOSS.

glaze *verb* GLOSS.

gleam *noun* BLINK.

gleam *verb*
1. BEAM.
2. FLASH.
3. GLOW.

gleaming *adjective* GLOSSY.

glean *verb*
1. To gather (grain) left by reapers: *gleaned a huge wheat crop.*
   Syns: crop (*Brit. Regional*), harvest, reap.
2. To collect (something) bit by bit: *gleaned the true facts through long investigation.*
   Syns: cull, extract, garner, gather, pick up.

glee *noun* GAIETY.

gleeful *adjective* GAY.

gleefulness *noun* GAIETY.

glib *adjective*
Characterized by ready but often insincere or superficial discourse: *glib commercials; a glib denial.*
   Syns: facile, flip (*Informal*), glossy, silver-tongued, slick, vocative, voluble.

glide *verb*
1. To move smoothly, continuously, and effortlessly: *sharks gliding about in search of prey.*
   Syns: glissade, lapse (*Poetic*), slick, slide, slip, slither.
2. EASE.
3. FLOW.
4. SNEAK.

glimmer *noun* BLINK.

glimmer *verb*
1. BLINK.
2. FLASH.

glimpse *verb*
To look briefly and quickly: *glimpsed at the photos but quickly pushed them away.*
   Syns: glance¹, glint, peek, peep.

glimpse *noun* GLANCE¹.

glint *noun*
1. BLINK.
2. GLITTER.
3. GLOSS.

glint *verb*
1. FLASH.
2. GLANCE¹.
3. GLIMPSE.

glissade *verb* GLIDE.

glisten *verb* FLASH.

glisten *noun* GLITTER.

glistening *adjective* GLOSSY.

glister *verb* FLASH.

glister *noun* GLITTER.

glitter *noun*
1. Sparkling, brilliant light: *the glitter of diamonds.*
   Syns: flash, glint, glisten, glister (*Poetic*), scintillation, shimmer, sparkle.
2. Brilliant, showy splendor: *the opulence and glitter of the Romanov court.*
   Syns: brilliance (*also* brilliancy), glory, magnificence, resplendence *or* resplendency, sparkle, sumptuousness.
3. A small, sparkling decoration: *Christmas costumes decorated with glitter.*
   Syns: sequin, spangle.

glitter *verb* FLASH.

gloaming *noun* EVENING.

global *adjective.*
1. GENERAL.
2. UNIVERSAL.
globoid *adjective* ROUND.
globular *adjective* ROUND.
globule *noun* DROP.
gloom *noun*
A feeling or spell of dismally low spirits: *could not dispel his gloom after the funeral.*
   Syns: blues (*Informal*), dejection, depression, despondency (*also* despondence), dinge, doldrums, dolefulness, dumps (*Informal*), dysphoria, funk² (*Chiefly Brit.*), glumness, heavy-heartedness, melancholy, mopes, mournfulness, sadness, suds (*Informal*), unhappiness.
gloom *verb* OBSCURE.
glooming *adjective* GLOOMY.
gloomy *adjective*
1. Dark and depressing: *a gloomy, rainy day.*
   Syns: Acheronian, Acherontic, black, bleak, blue, cheerless, cold, dismal, dispiriting, dreary (*also* drear), glooming, glum (*Brit. Regional*), joyless, somber (*also* sombre), tenebrific.
2. Marked by little hopefulness: *gloomy predictions of a recession.*
   Syns: dark, dismal, pessimistic.
3. DEPRESSED.
4. GLUM.
5. SAD.
glorification *noun*
1. EXALTATION.
2. PRAISE.
glorify *verb*
1. EXALT.
2. HONOR.
3. PRAISE.
glorious *adjective*
1. Marked by extraordinary elegance, beauty, and splendor: *the glorious palace of Versailles.*
   Syns: gorgeous, magnificent, proud, resplendent, splendorous *or* splendrous, sublime, superb.
2. MARVELOUS.
glory *noun*
1. Something meriting the highest praise or regard: *the glory that was Rome; the glory of the Presidency.*
   Syns: grandeur, grandiosity, grandness, greatness, majesty, splendor.
2. EMINENCE.

3. GLITTER.
glory *verb* EXULT.
gloss *noun*
1. A radiant brightness or glow, usu. due to light reflected from a smooth surface: *the gloss of satin and pearls by candlelight.*
   Syns: glaze, glint, luster, polish, sheen, shine.
2. FAÇADE.
gloss *verb*
1. To give a gleaming luster to, usu. through friction: *gloss furniture with wax.*
   Syns: buff, burnish, furbish, glance², glaze, polish, shine, sleek.
2. COLOR.
gloss over *verb* EXTENUATE.
glossy *adjective*
1. Having a high, radiant sheen: *glossy beads.*
   Syns: glassy, gleaming, glistening, lustrous, polished, shining, shiny.
2. GLIB.
glow *verb*
1. To shine brightly and steadily but without a flame: *red-hot coals glowing in the grate; lights glowing from windows.*
   Syns: gleam, incandesce.
2. BEAM.
glow *noun*
1. A feeling of pervasive emotional warmth: *saw the glow of first love in her eyes; felt the glow of victory.*
   Syns: blush, flush, radiance.
2. BLOOM.
glower *verb*
1. FROWN.
2. GLARE.
glower *noun*
1. FROWN.
2. GLARE.
glowing *adjective*
1. ENTHUSIASTIC.
2. FRESH.
3. RUDDY.
gloze *verb* COLOR.
gloze over *verb* EXTENUATE.
gluey *adjective* STICKY.
glum *adjective*
1. Broodingly and sullenly unhappy: *a glum, petulant loser.*
   Syns: chuff (*Regional*), chuffy (*Brit. Regional*), dour, gloomy, morose, mumpish, saturnine, sour, sulky, sullen, surly.
2. GLOOMY.
glumness *noun* GLOOM.

glut *verb* SATIATE.
glut *noun* SURPLUS.
glutinous *adjective* VISCOUS.
glutted *adjective* SATIATED.
gluttonous *adjective* GREEDY.
gnash *verb*
1. BITE.
2. GRIND.
gnaw *verb*
1, 2. BITE.
gnawing *adjective* SHARP.
go *verb*
1. To move along a particular course:
We were going along a narrow road.
Syns: fare (*Archaic*), journey, pass,
proceed, push on, repair, travel,
wend (*Archaic*).
2. To move or proceed away from a
place: *We must go now.*
Syns: blow¹ (*Slang*), cut out
(*Slang*), depart, exit, get away, get
off, go away, leave¹, pull out, push
off (*Informal*), quit, remove (*Poetic*),
retire, run, run along, shove off
(*Slang*), split (*Slang*), take off
(*Slang*), withdraw. —*Idioms* beat it,
hit the road, take one's leave.
3. To be depleted: *All my money is
gone.*
Syns: consume, exhaust, expend,
finish, run through, spend, use (up),
wash up. —*Idiom* go down the
drain.
4. To move toward a termination: *The
pain is going now.*
Syns: elapse, go away, go by, expire,
pass, pass away.
5. To change or fluctuate within limits:
The prices go from $20 to $50.
Syns: extend, range, run, vary.
6. To make an offer of: *was willing to
go $50 for the antique teapot.*
Syns: bid, offer.
7. BEAR.
8. BELONG.
9. BEND.
10. CAVE IN at **cave**.
11. DIE.
12. EXTEND.
13. FIT.
14. GAMBLE.
15. PROSPER.
16. RESORT TO at **resort**.
17. SUCCEED.
18. WORK.
go along *verb* PLAY ALONG at **play**.
go around *verb*
1. GET ABOUT at **get**.
2. SKIRT.

go at *verb*
1, 2. ATTACK.
go away *verb*
1, 2. GO.
go by *verb* GO.
go down *verb*
1. FALL.
2. SURRENDER.
go for *verb*
1. APPRECIATE.
2. APPROVE.
3. BELIEVE.
4. COST.
go in *verb* ENTER.
go off *verb* EXPLODE.
go on *verb*
1. CARRY ON at **carry**.
2. CHATTER.
3. ENDURE.
go over *verb*
1. EXAMINE.
2. REVIEW.
3. SUCCEED.
go through *verb* EXPERIENCE.
go under *verb*
1. COLLAPSE.
2. SURRENDER.
go up *verb* ASCEND.
go with *verb* FIT.
go *noun*
1. ENERGY.
2. SIEGE.
3. TRY.
4. TURN.
go *adjective* READY.
goad *verb* PROVOKE.
goal *noun*
1. AMBITION.
2. INTENTION.
goat *noun* SCAPEGOAT.
gob¹ *noun*
1. HEAP.
2. LUMP¹.
gob² *noun* MOUTH.
gob³ *noun* SAILOR.
gobble *verb* GULP.
gobble *noun* SWALLOW.
gobbledygook also **gobbledegook**
noun GIBBERISH.
go-between *noun*
Someone who acts as an intermediate
agent in a transaction: *He was the go-
between in negotiations with the
kidnappers.*
Syns: broker, interagent, interceder,
intercessor, intermediary,
intermediate, intermediator, mediator,
middleman.
godforsaken also **Godforsaken**
adjective LONELY.

godlike *adjective* DIVINE[1].
godly *adjective*
1. DIVINE[1].
2. HOLY.
go-getter *noun* EAGER BEAVER.
go-getting *adjective* AGGRESSIVE.
goggle *verb* GAZE.
going *noun* DEPARTURE.
 going *adjective* ACTIVE.
goldbrick *verb* IDLE.
golden ager *noun* SENIOR.
Goliath *noun* GIANT.
gone *adjective*
1. ABSENT.
2. DEAD.
3. INFATUATED.
4. LOST.
5. PREGNANT.
good *adjective*
1. Well above average: *a good student;
 good workmanship.*
 Syns: high-grade, nice.
2. Having pleasant, desirable qualities:
 a good chap.
 Syns: bonny (*Scot.*), braw (*Scot.*),
 goodly, nice. —*Idiom* good as gold.
3. In excellent condition: *a good tooth.*
 Syns: entire, flawless, intact, perfect,
 sound[2], unblemished, unbroken,
 undamaged, unhurt, unimpaired,
 uninjured, unmarred, whole.
4. ABLE.
5. AGREEABLE.
6. AUTHENTIC.
7. BENEFICIAL.
8. BENEVOLENT.
9. BIG.
10. CONVENIENT.
11. EXEMPLARY.
12. FAVORABLE.
13. ROUND.
good *noun*
1. The quality or state of being morally
 sound: *Good triumphed over evil.*
 Syns: goodness, morality, probity,
 rectitude, righteousness, rightness,
 uprightness, virtue, virtuousness.
2. INTEREST.
3. WELFARE.
good-by or **good-bye** *noun* PARTING.
 good-by or **good-bye** *adjective*
 PARTING.
good-for-nothing *noun* WASTREL.
 good-for-nothing *adjective*
 WORTHLESS.
good-hearted *adjective* KIND[1].
goodish *adjective* ACCEPTABLE.
good-looking *adjective* BEAUTIFUL.
goodly *adjective*
1. GOOD.
2. SIZABLE.

good-natured *adjective* AMIABLE.
goodness *noun* GOOD.
goods *noun*
1. Products bought and sold in
 commerce: *inventoried all the goods in
 the store.*
 Syns: commodities, line, merchandise,
 wares.
2. BELONGINGS.
3. EFFECTS.
good-tempered *adjective* AMIABLE.
good will *noun* BENEVOLENCE.
goody *noun* DELICACY.
gooey *adjective*
1. SENTIMENTAL.
2. STICKY.
goof *noun* BLUNDER.
 goof off *verb* IDLE.
 goof up *verb* BOTCH.
goon *noun* THUG.
goose *noun* FOOL.
goose-pimply *adjective* CRAWLY.
goosey also **goosy** *adjective* EDGY.
gordian *adjective* COMPLEX.
gore *noun* BLOOD.
gorge *verb* SATIATE.
gorged *adjective* SATIATED.
gorgeous *adjective*
1. BEAUTIFUL.
2. GLORIOUS.
gorilla *noun* THUG.
gory *adjective* BLOODY.
gossamer also **gossamery** *adjective*
 FILMY.
gossip *noun*
1. Idle, often sensational and groundless
 talk about others: *a tabloid full of
 gossip. According to gossip, they
 eloped.*
 Syns: buzz, cry, hearsay, murmur,
 report, rumor, scuttlebutt (*Slang*),
 tattle, tittle-tattle, whispering, word.
2. A person habitually engaged in idle
 talk about others: *Our local gossip
 claimed we were getting a divorce.*
 Syns: gossiper, gossipmonger,
 mumblenews, newsmonger, quidnunc,
 rumorer, rumormonger,
 scandalmonger, tabby, talebearer,
 tattle, tattler, tattletale, telltale, yenta
 (*Slang*).
gossip *verb*
To engage in or spread gossip: *gossiped
about the President's private life.*
 Syns: buzz, blab, noise (about or
 abroad), rumor, talk, tattle, tittle-
 tattle. —*Idiom* tell tales out of school.
gossiper *noun* GOSSIP.
gossipmonger *noun* GOSSIP.

gossipy *adjective*
Inclined to gossip: *a gossipy old crone.*
  Syns: blabby, talebearing, taletelling.

gouge *verb*
1. EXTORT.
2. SKIN.

govern *verb*
1. To exercise the authority of a sovereign: *Catherine the Great thought she governed in an enlightened manner.*
  Syns: overrule, reign, rule, sway.
  —*Idioms* wear the crown, wield the scepter.
2. To keep the mechanical operation of (a device) within proper parameters: *a valve governing fuel intake.*
  Syns: control, regulate.
3. ADMINISTER.
4. CONTROL.

governable *adjective*
Capable of being governed: *a docile, governable people; a financial situation that while bad was still governable.*
  Syns: administrable, controllable, handleable, manageable.

governance *noun*
1, 2. GOVERNMENT.

governing *adjective* DOMINANT.

government *noun*
1. A system by which a political unit is controlled: *The United States has a democratic form of government.*
  Syns: governance, regìme, rule.
2. The continuous exercise of authority over a political unit: *was active in the government of the province.*
  Syns: administration, control, direction, governance, rule.
3. ADMINISTRATION.

governmental *adjective*
Of or relating to government: *governmental agencies.*
  Syns: gubernatorial, regulatory.

gown *noun* DRESS.

grab *verb*
1. CATCH.
2. GRASP.
3. GRIP.
4. SEIZE.

grab *noun* CATCH.

grabble *verb* GROPE.

grabby *adjective* GREEDY.

grace *noun*
1. Kind, forgiving, or compassionate treatment of or disposition toward others: *forgiven by the grace of the king.*
  Syns: caritas, charity, clemency, leniency (*also* lenience), lenity, mercifulness, mercy.

2. Temporary immunity from penalties: *a day of grace before enforcing the new law.*
  Syns: respite, reprieve.
3. A short prayer said at meals: *said grace before dinner.*
  Syns: benediction, blessing, thanks, thanksgiving.
4. BENEVOLENCE.
5. DECENCY.
6. ELEGANCE.
7. FAVOR.

grace *verb*
1. To lend dignity or honor to by an act or favor: *The prime minister graced our gathering with his august presence.*
  Syns: dignify, favor, honor.
2. To endow with beauty and elegance by way of a notable addition: *Magnificent gold candlesticks graced an already opulent table.*
  Syns: adorn, beautify, embellish, enhance, ornament, set off.

graceful *adjective*
1. ELEGANT.
2. SMOOTH.

graceless *adjective* AWKWARD.

gracious *adjective*
1. Characterized by kindness and warm, unaffected courtesy: *a gracious attitude toward everyone.*
  Syns: affable, congenial, cordial, genial, sociable.
2. Characterized by elaborate but usu. formal courtesy: *gracious old-world manners.*
  Syns: chivalrous, courtly, gallant, knightly, stately.

gradation *noun*
1, 2. SHADE.

gradational *adjective* GRADUAL.

grade *noun*
1. ASCENT.
2. CLASS.
3. GRADE.
4. QUALITY.

grade *verb* CLASS.

gradient *noun*
1. ASCENT.
2. INCLINATION.

gradual *adjective*
1. Proceeding very slowly by degrees: *a gradual shift in Sino-Soviet policy.*
  Syns: gradational, piecemeal, step-by-step.
2. Not steep or abrupt: *a gradual slope.*
  Syns: easy, gentle, moderate.

graft *noun* BRIBE.

grain *noun* BIT[1].

grainy *adjective* COARSE.

grand *adjective*
1. Large and impressive in size, scope, or extent: *The view of the Winter Palace is indeed grand.*
   Syns: august, baronial, grandiose, imposing, lordly, magnific (*Obs.*), magnificent, majestic, noble, princely, regal, royal, stately, sublime, superb.
2. Marked by magnificently lavish ceremony and display: *The inaugural ball is a truly grand occasion.*
   Syns: impressive, regal, splendid, stately.
3. Very broad and noble in character, scope, or grasp: *the Secretary of State's grand design for peace.*
   Syns: astral, elevated, exalted, lofty.
4. ELEVATED.
5. EXALTED.

grandeur *noun* GLORY.
grandiloquent *adjective* SONOROUS.
grandiose *adjective*
1. GRAND.
2. POMPOUS.

grandiosity *noun* GLORY.
grandness *noun* GLORY.
grant *verb*
1. To let have as a favor or privilege: *granted them a hearing.*
   Syns: accord, award, concede, give, vouchsafe.
2. ACKNOWLEDGE.
3. CONFER.
4. TRANSFER.

grant *noun*
1. Something, as a gift, granted for a definite purpose: *the foundation's grant for medical research.*
   Syns: appropriation, subsidy, subvention.
2. A making over of legal ownership or title: *the court's grant of the property to her.*
   Syns: conveyance (*Law*), transfer.

grantor *noun* DONOR.
granular *adjective* COARSE.
granulate *verb* CRUSH.
granulize *verb* CRUSH.
graphic *adjective*
1. Of or pertaining to representation by means of writing: *graphic communication.*
   Syns: calligraphic, scriptural, written.
2. Of or pertaining to representation by drawings or pictures: *a textbook's graphic aids.*
   Syns: illustrative, photographic, pictographic, pictorial.
3. Described verbally in sharp and accurate detail: *a graphic account of the battle.*
   Syns: lifelike, photographic, pictorial, picturesque, realistic, vivid.
4. DESCRIPTIVE.

grapple *noun* HOLD.
grapple *verb* WRESTLE.
grasp *verb*
1. To take firmly with the hand and maintain a hold on: *grasped the handrail of the moving escalator.*
   Syns: clasp, clench, clinch, clutch, grab, grip, hang on, seize.
2. UNDERSTAND.

grasp *noun*
1. The ability or power to seize or attain: *a goal within their grasp.*
   Syns: capacity, compass, range, reach, scope.
2. Intellectual hold: *a grasp of practical politics.*
   Syns: apprehension, comprehension, grip, mastery, savvy (*Slang*), understanding.
3. GRIP.
4. HOLD.

grasping *adjective* GREEDY.
grate *verb* SCRAPE.
grateful *adjective*
1. Showing or feeling gratitude: *a grateful glance; grateful for your understanding.*
   Syns: appreciative, obliged, thankful.
2. Affording pleasure or comfort: *the grateful quiet of evening.*
   Syns: congenial, gratifying, satisfying, welcome.

gratefulness *noun* APPRECIATION.
gratified *adjective* FULFILLED.
gratify *verb*
1. DELIGHT.
2. HUMOR.

gratifying *adjective*
1. AGREEABLE.
2. ENJOYABLE.
3. GRATEFUL.

grating *adjective* HARSH.
gratis *adjective* FREE.
gratitude *noun* APPRECIATION.
gratuitous *adjective*
1. FREE.
2. WANTON.

gratuity *noun*
A material favor or gift, usu. money, given in return for service: *Gratuities must be reported with taxable income.*
   Syns: cumshaw, lagniappe (*Informal*), largess (*also* largesse), perk[1] (*Slang*), perquisite, tip[3].

gravamen *noun* HEART.

grave¹ *noun*
A burial place or receptacle for human remains: *graves decorated with floral pieces.*
  Syns: catacomb, cinerarium, crypt, mausoleum, ossuary, sepulcher, sepulture (*Archaic*), tomb, vault¹.

grave² *adjective*
1. Having great consequence or weight: *a grave problem.*
  Syns: heavy, momentous, serious, severe, weighty.
2. Full of or marked by dignity and seriousness: *had a grave expression when he told me I needed surgery.*
  Syns: earnest, sedate, serious, sober, solemn, somber (*also* sombre), staid.
3. FATEFUL.
4. GRIEVOUS.

grave³ *verb*
1, 2. ENGRAVE.

gravid *adjective* PREGNANT.
gravidation *noun* PREGNANCY.
gravidity *noun* PREGNANCY.
gravitate *verb* SETTLE.
gravity *noun*
1. The condition of being grave and of involving serious consequences: *the gravity of her accusation.*
  Syns: momentousness, seriousness, severity, weightiness.
2. High seriousness of manner or bearing: *the gravity of courtroom procedure.*
  Syns: sobriety, solemnness, solemnity, somberness.
3. HEAVINESS.

gray matter *noun* HEAD.
graze *verb*
1. BRUSH.
2. GLANCE¹.

graze *noun* BRUSH.
greasy *adjective* FATTY.
great *adjective*
1. BIG.
2. EMINENT.
3. EXCELLENT.

greater *adjective*
1. BEST.
2. HIGHER.

great-hearted *adjective* GENEROUS.
great-heartedness *noun*
GENEROSITY.
greatness *noun*
1. GLORY.
2. PREGNANCY.
3. SIZE.

greed *noun*
Excessive desire for more than one needs or deserves: *the greed of speculators that feeds on small investors.*
  Syns: acquisitiveness, avarice, avariciousness, avidity, covetousness, cupidity, rapacity.

greedy *adjective*
1. Having a strong urge to obtain or possess something, esp. material wealth, in quantity: *foreclosures that enriched greedy landowners.*
  Syns: acquisitive, avaricious, avid, covetous, desirous, grabby (*Informal*), grasping, hungry, rapacious.
2. Wanting to eat or drink more than one can reasonably consume: *a greedy boy hunched over an overfilled plate.*
  Syns: edacious, gluttonous, hoggish, piggish, ravenous, voracious.

green *adjective*
1. INEXPERIENCED.
2. YOUNG.

green *noun* COMMON.
greenbacks *noun* MONEY.
green-eyed *adjective* ENVIOUS.
greenness *noun*
1. INEXPERIENCED.
2. YOUTH.

greet *verb*
1. To address in a friendly and respectful way: *greeted each guest individually.*
  Syns: hail², salute, welcome.
2. To present with a specified reaction: *greeted our proposal with scorn.*
  Syns: meet¹, react to, respond to.

greeting *noun*
An expression, in words or gestures, marking a meeting of persons: *had a friendly greeting for all.*
  Syns: salutation, salute, welcome.

gregarious *adjective*
1. OUTGOING.
2. SOCIAL.

grief *noun*
Mental anguish or pain caused by loss or despair: *showing grief openly at the funeral.*
  Syns: heartache, heartbreak, sorrow, woe.

grievance *noun*
1. A circumstance regarded as a cause for protest or complaint: *legislation aimed at the remedy of basic grievances.*
  Syns: beef (*Informal*), gripe (*Informal*), kick (*Informal*). —*Idiom* bone to pick.
2. COMPLAINT.

grieve *verb*
1. To feel, show, or express grief: *grieved deeply over the death of her husband.*
   Syns: lament, mourn, sorrow, suffer.
2. DISTRESS.

grievous *adjective*
1. Causing or marked by danger, pain, etc.: *sustained a grievous wound.*
   Syns: dangerous, grave², serious, severe.
2. BITTER.
3. SORROWFUL.

grill *verb* INTERROGATE.

grim *adjective*
1. Having or showing uncompromising determination or resolution in purpose or action: *a grim will to succeed.*
   Syns: implacable, hard-shell (*also* hard-shelled), inexorable, intransigent, merciless, remorseless, unbending, unrelenting, unyielding.
2. BLEAK.
3. GHASTLY.

grimace *noun* FACE.

grimace *verb*
To contort one's face to indicate displeasure, disgust, pain, etc.: *grimaced like a monkey when he saw the bills.*
   Syns: mop (*Archaic*), mouth, mow, mug (*Slang*). —*Idioms* make (*or* pull) a face, make faces.

grime *noun* FILTH.

griminess *noun* DIRTINESS.

grimy *adjective* DIRTY.

grin *verb* SMILE.

grin *noun* SMILE.

grind *verb*
1. To rub together noisily: *ground his teeth in rage.*
   Syns: crunch, gnash.
2. To do tedious, laborious, and sometimes menial work: *grinding away to support his family.*
   Syns: drudge, grub, plod, slave, slog, toil.
3. BONE UP.
4. CRUSH.

grind *noun*
Informal. A habitual, laborious, often tiresome course of action: *tired of the daily grind—to work and straight home again.*
   Syns: groove, routine, rut, treadmill. —*Idiom* the beaten path.

grip *noun*
1. Firm control: *has a good grip on her emotions; seems to have lost his grip on reality.*

Syns: grasp, handle, hold.
2. GRASP.
3, 4. HOLD.
5. THROE.

grip *verb*
1. To compel the attention, interest, imagination, etc., of: *a scene that gripped the entire audience.*
   Syns: arrest, catch up, enthrall, fascinate, grab (*Informal*), hold, mesmerize, rivet, spellbind, transfix.
2. GRASP.

gripe *verb* COMPLAIN.

gripe *noun*
1. COMPLAINT.
2. GRIEVANCE.

griper *noun* GROUCH.

gripping *adjective* ABSORBING.

grisly *adjective* GHASTLY.

gritty *adjective* COARSE.

grobian *noun* BOOR.

groom *verb* TIDY.

groove *noun* GRIND.

groove on *verb* ADORE.

groovy *adjective* MARVELOUS.

grope *verb*
To reach about or search blindly or uncertainly: *groping for the light switch; groped for the answer to the question.*
   Syns: feel (around), fumble, grabble, poke around.

gross *adjective*
1. COARSE.
2. FAT.
3. FLAGRANT.
4. OBSCENE.
5. WHOLE.

gross *noun* WHOLE.

gross *verb* RETURN.

grossness *noun* FLAGRANCY.

grotesque *adjective*
1. FANTASTIC.
2. FREAKISH.

grouch *verb* COMPLAIN.

grouch *noun*
A person who habitually complains or grumbles: *Her upstairs neighbor is an old grouch who bangs on the floor at the smallest noise.*
   Syns: bellyacher (*Slang*), complainer, crab (*Informal*), crank (*Informal*), faultfinder, griper (*Informal*), grouser (*Informal*), growler, grumbler, grump, kicker (*Informal*), sorehead (*Slang*), sourpuss (*Slang*).

grouchy *adjective* ILL-TEMPERED.

ground *noun*
1. BASE¹.

2. BASIS.
3. CAUSE.
4. REASON.

ground *verb*
1. BASE¹.
2. DROP.

groundless *adjective* BASELESS.

groundlessly *adverb* UNFOUNDEDLY.

groundwork *noun*
1. BASE¹.
2. BASIS.

group *noun*
1. A number of individuals making up or considered a unit: *a group of men standing on the corner; a group of islands off the coast of Alaska.*
   Syns: array, batch, body, bunch (*Informal*), bundle, clump, cluster, clutch, collection, knot, lot, set².
2. A usu. small number of individuals: *The waiter asked how many were in the group.*
   Syns: band², bevy, bunch (*Informal*), party.
3. ASSEMBLY.

group *verb*
1. To come or bring into a group or groups: *travelers grouping with their tour guide in the hotel lobby.*
   Syns: aggroup, assemble, cluster, collect, gather.
2. ARRANGE.
3. ASSORT.
4. CLASS.

grouping *noun* ARRANGEMENT.

grouse *verb* COMPLAIN.

grouser *noun* GROUCH.

grow *verb*
1. To bring into existence and foster the development of: *grows orchids as a hobby; a farm where corn and apples are grown.*
   Syns: breed, cultivate, produce, propagate, raise.
2. BECOME.
3. INCREASE.
4. MATURE.

growl *verb* RUMBLE.

growler *noun* GROUCH.

grown *adjective* MATURE.

grown-up *adjective* MATURE.

growth *noun*
1. DEVELOPMENT.
2. INCREASE.

grub *verb*
1. DIG.
2. EAT.
3. GRIND.

grub *noun* FOOD.

grubby *adjective* DIRTY.

grubstake *verb* FINANCE.

grudge *verb* ENVY.

gruel *verb* EXHAUST.

gruesome *adjective* GHASTLY.

gruff *adjective*
1. ABRUPT.
2. HOARSE.

grumble *verb*
1. COMPLAIN.
2. MUTTER.
3. RUMBLE.

grumble *noun*
1. COMPLAINT.
2. MUTTER.

grumbler *noun* GROUCH.

grump *noun* GROUCH.

grumpy *adjective* ILL-TEMPERED.

grunt *verb* MUTTER.

grunt *noun* MUTTER.

guarantee *noun*
1. An assumption of responsibility, as one given by a manufacturer, for the quality, worth, or durability of a product: *a stereo with a one-year guarantee.*
   Syns: surety, warrant, warranty.
2. PROMISE.
3. WORD.

guarantee *verb*
1. To render certain: *His family connections guarantee his success in business.*
   Syns: assure, cinch (*Slang*), ensure (*also* insure), secure, warrant.
2. To assume responsibility for the quality, worth, or durability of: *The factory guaranteed the dishwasher for three years.*
   Syns: certify, guaranty, warrant.
3. SECURE.

guarantor *noun* SPONSOR.

guaranty *noun*
1. PAWN¹.
2. SPONSOR.

guaranty *verb* GUARANTEE.

guard *verb* DEFEND.

guard *noun*
1. A person or special body of persons assigned to provide protection, keep watch over, etc.: *a bank guard; the palace guard.*
   Syns: lookout, picket, sentry, ward, watch.
2. DEFENSE.

guardian *noun*
A person who is legally responsible for

the person or property of another considered by law to be incompetent to manage his affairs: *was appointed as the child's guardian under the parents' will.*
   Syns: conservator (*Law*), custodian, keeper, warden.
guardianship *noun* CARE.
gubernatorial *adjective* GOVERNMENTAL.
gudgeon *noun* DUPE.
guerdon *noun* REWARD.
guerdon *verb* REWARD.
guess *verb*
To draw an inference on the basis of inconclusive evidence or insufficient information: *We can only guess that he had a motive for the crime.*
   Syns: conjecture, infer, presume, suppose, surmise.
guess *noun*
A judgment, estimate, or opinion arrived at by guessing: *All this is merely a guess on my part.*
   Syns: conjecture, presumption, supposition, surmise.
guest *noun* COMPANY.
guffaw *verb* BREAK UP at **break**.
guidance *noun*
An act or instance of guiding: *a tax program administered under the guidance of the Secretary of the Treasury.*
   Syns: direction, lead, leadership, management.
guide *noun*
Something or someone that shows the way: *Let your conscience be your guide. Her designer friend is her guide in choosing clothes.*
   Syns: conductor, director, lead, leader, mentor, pilot.
guide *verb*
To show the way to: *Sailors once used the stars to guide them. He guided me to my seat.*
   Syns: conduct, direct, escort, lead, pilot, route, shepherd, show, steer, usher.
guild *noun* UNION.
guile *noun*
1. ART.
2. DECEIT.
guileful *adjective*
1. ARTFUL.
2. UNDERHAND.
guileless *adjective* ARTLESS.
guilt *noun* BLAME.
guiltless *adjective* INNOCENT.

guilty *adjective* BLAMEWORTHY.
guise *noun*
1. DRESS.
2. FAÇADE.
gull *noun* DUPE.
gull *verb* CHEAT.
gullible *adjective* EASY.
gulosity *noun* VORACITY.
gulp *verb*
To swallow (food or drink) greedily or rapidly in large amounts: *Too busy to take a full hour, she had to gulp down her lunch.*
   Syns: bolt, englut, engorge, gobble, guttle, guzzle, ingurgitate, swill, wolf.
gulp *noun* SWALLOW.
gummy *adjective* STICKY.
gumption *noun*
1. AMBITION.
2. COMMON SENSE.
gumshoe *noun* DETECTIVE.
gumshoe *verb* SNEAK.
gum up *verb* BOTCH.
gun *verb* SHOOT.
gung ho *adjective* ENTHUSIASTIC.
gurge *verb* SWIRL.
gurgle *verb* WASH.
gurgling *adjective* LAUGHING.
gush *verb*
1. EMOTIONALIZE.
2. FLOW.
gushy *adjective* SENTIMENTAL.
gust *noun*
1. OUTBURST.
2. WIND[1].
gusto *noun* ZEST.
gusty *adjective* AIRY.
gut *adjective* INNER.
gutless *adjective* COWARDLY.
gutlessness *noun* COWARDICE.
guts *noun* COURAGE.
gutsy *adjective* BRAVE.
guttle *verb* GULP.
gutty *adjective* BRAVE.
guzzle *verb*
1. DRINK.
2. GULP.
gyp also **gip** *verb* CHEAT.
gyp *noun*
1, 2. CHEAT.
gypper *noun* CHEAT.
gyrate *verb*
1. SPIN.
2. TURN.
gyration *noun* REVOLUTION.
gyre *noun* CIRCLE.
gyves *noun* BONDS.

H

habiliments *noun* DRESS.
habit *noun*
1. An activity done without thinking:
has a habit of pulling his ear.
Syns: characteristic, pattern, trait.
2. Clothing worn by members of a
religious order: *a nun dressed in her
habit.*
Syns: robes, vestments.
3. CONSTITUTION.
4. CUSTOM.
habit *verb* INHABIT.
habitable *adjective* LIVABLE.
habitat *noun* HOME.
habitation *noun* HOME.
habitual *adjective*
1. ACCUSTOMED.
2. CHRONIC.
habituate *verb* ACCUSTOM.
habituated *adjective* CHRONIC.
habitude *noun* CUSTOM.
habitus *noun* CONSTITUTION.
hackneyed *adjective* TRITE.
hag *noun*
1, 2. WITCH.
haggard *adjective*
Pale and exhausted because of worry,
sleeplessness, etc.: *always looks haggard
in the morning.*
Syns: careworn, gaunt, hollow-eyed,
toilworn, wan, worn.
haggle *verb*
To argue about the terms, as of a sale:
preferred being overcharged to haggling.
Syns: bargain, dicker, higgle,
huckster, palter.
ha-ha *noun* JOKE.
hail¹ *noun* BARRAGE.
hail² *verb*
1. COME.
2. GREET.
3. HONOR.
hair *noun* SHADE.
hair-raising *adjective* HORRIBLE.
hairy *adjective*
1. Covered with hair: *a hairy animal; a
hairy chest.*
Syns: fleecy, furry, hirsute, pilose,
woolly.
2. DANGEROUS.
halcyon *adjective* STILL.
hale *adjective* HEALTHY.
haleness *noun* HEALTH.
halfhearted *adjective* TEPID.
half-wit *noun* FOOL.

half-witted *adjective* STUPID.
halloa also **halloa** *verb* ROAR.
halloo also **halloa** *noun* SHOUT.
hallow *verb*
1. DEVOTE.
2. SANCTIFY.
hallowed *adjective*
1. HOLY.
2. SACRED.
hallowedness *noun* HOLINESS.
hallucination *noun*
1. An illusion of perceiving something
that does not really exist: *LSD-
induced hallucinations.*
Syns: phantasmagoria (*also*
phantasmagory), trip (*Slang*).
2. ILLUSION.
hallucinatory *adjective* ILLUSIVE.
halt¹ *verb*
1. BREAK UP at **break**.
2, 3. STOP.
halt *noun*
1, 2. STOP.
halt² *verb*
1. HESITATE.
2. LIMP.
halting *adjective* HESITANT.
hammer *verb*
1, 2. BEAT.
3. STAMMER.
hamper *verb*
1. To restrict the activity or free
movement of: *Hampered by leg irons,
the escaped convicts were soon
overtaken.*
Syns: fetter, hamstring, handcuff,
hobble, hog-tie (*also* hogtie), leash,
manacle, shackle, tie down, trammel.
2. HINDER.
hamper *noun* BAR.
hamstring *verb* HAMPER.
hand *verb*
1. GIVE.
2. PASS.
hand down *verb*
1. To convey (something) from one
generation to the next: *The farm was
handed down from father to son.*
Syns: bequeath, hand on, pass (along
or on), transmit.
2. RETURN.
hand on *verb* HAND DOWN at **hand**.
hand out *verb*
1. DISTRIBUTE.
2. DONATE.
3. GIVE.
hand over *verb*
1. ABDICATE.
2. ENTRUST.
3. GIVE.

hand *noun*
1. APPLAUSE.
2. HELP.
3. LABORER.
4. PHASE.
5. SIDE.

handcuff *verb* HAMPER.

handicap *noun*
1. ADVANTAGE.
2. DISADVANTAGE.

handle *verb*
1. To use with or as if with the hands: *He handles an ax like a born woodsman.*
   Syns: manipulate, ply, wield.
2. DEAL WITH at **deal**.
3. OPERATE.
4. SELL.
5. TOUCH.

handle *noun*
1. GRIP.
2. NAME.

handleable *adjective* GOVERNABLE.

handout *noun*
1. DONATION.
2. RELIEF.

handsel also **hansel** *noun* GIFT.

handsome *adjective*
1. BEAUTIFUL.
2. GENEROUS.

handy *adjective*
1. CONVENIENT.
2. DEXTEROUS.
3. PRACTICAL.

hang *verb*
1. To fasten or be fastened at one point with no support from below: *hang decorations on a Christmas tree; clothes hanging in a closet.*
   Syns: dangle, depend (from), sling, suspend.
2. To execute by suspending by the neck: *a murderer sentenced to be hanged.*
   Syns: gibbet, noose, stretch (*Archaic*), string up (*Informal*), swing (*Informal*), turn off (*Rare*).
3. To incline downward or over: *hung his head in shame; children hanging from bus windows.*
   Syns: beetle, bend (over), jut, lean¹ (over), overhang.
4. To remain stationary over a place or object: *black clouds hanging in the sky.*
   Syns: hover, poise.
5. THREATEN.

hang around *verb* FREQUENT.

hang on *verb*
1. CARRY ON at **carry**.
2. GRASP.

hang on (or **upon**) *verb* DEPEND ON at **depend**.

hang out *verb*
1. ASSOCIATE.
2. FREQUENT.

hang up *verb* DELAY.

hang *noun*
Informal. The proper method for doing, using, or handling something: *get the hang of using a food processor.*
   Syns: knack, swing (*Informal*), trick.

hanger-on *noun* PARASITE.

hanging *adjective*
Hung or appearing to be hung from a support: *a hanging plant.*
   Syns: pendulous, pensile, suspended.

hangout *noun* HAUNT.

hangup *noun* COMPLEX.

hanker *verb* DESIRE.

hansel *noun* SEE **handsel**.

hap¹ *verb*
1. CHANCE.
2. COME.

hap *noun*
1, 2. CHANCE.

hap² *noun* WRAP.

hap *verb* WRAP UP at **wrap**.

haphazard *adjective* RANDOM.

hapless *adjective* UNFORTUNATE.

happen *verb*
1. CHANCE.
2. COME.

happen on (or **upon**) *verb* COME ACROSS at **come**.

happenchance *noun* SEE **happenstance**.

happening *noun*
1. CIRCUMSTANCE.
2. EVENT.

happenstance also **happenchance** *noun* CHANCE.

happiness *noun*
A condition of supreme well-being and good spirits: *felt great happiness on her wedding day.*
   Syns: beatitude, blessedness, cheer, cheerfulness, gladness, joy.

happy *adjective*
1. Characterized by luck or good fortune: *a happy outcome to a tense situation.*
   Syns: fortunate, lucky, providential.
2. CHEERFUL.
3. FULFILLED.
4. GLAD.
5. MERRY.

harangue *verb* RANT.

harangue *noun* TIRADE.

harass *verb*
1. ANNOY.

2. BESIEGE.

3. RAID.

harassment *noun* ANNOYANCE.

harbor *noun* COVER.

harbor *verb*

1. To give refuge to: *harbored escaped convicts.*
   Syns: haven (*Rare*), house, shelter.

2. To provide with often temporary lodging: *harbored the migrant workers in barracks.*
   Syns: accommodate, bed, berth, bestow (*Archaic*), billet, board, bunk¹, domicile (*also* domiciliate), house, put up, quarter, room.

3. BEAR.

harborage *noun* COVER.

hard *adjective*

1. Physically toughened so as to have great endurance: *a lean, hard farmer who was used to 14-hour days.*
   Syns: casehardened, hard-bitten, hardened, hardfisted, hardhanded, hardy, rugged, tough. —*Idiom* hard (*or* tough) as nails.

2. Containing alcohol: *hard liquor.*
   Syns: alcoholic, spirituous, strong.

3. ACTUAL.

4. BITTER.

5. BLEAK.

6. BURDENSOME.

7. DIFFICULT.

8. FIRM.

9. HEAVY.

10. INSENSITIVE.

11. REALISTIC.

12. RESENTFUL.

13. SEVERE.

hard *adverb*

1. With intense energy and force: *hit the baseball hard.*
   Syns: forcefully, forcibly, vigorously. —*Idioms* hammer and tongs, tooth and nail, with might and main.

2. In such a way as to inflict hardship or difficulty: *Things went hard for her after the divorce.*
   Syns: bad (*Informal*), badly, sour (*Informal*).

3. In a violent, strenuous way: *fought hard; storm winds blowing hard.*
   Syns: fiercely, frantically, frenziedly, furiously.

4. With effort: *breathing hard after running.*
   Syns: arduously, difficultly, heavily.

5. CLOSE¹.

hard-bitten *adjective* HARD.

hard-boiled *adjective*

1. COLD-BLOODED.

2. REALISTIC.

harden *verb*

1. To make or become physically hard: *a cement that hardens quickly.*
   Syns: cake, concrete, congeal, dry, indurate, petrify, set¹, solidify.

2. To make resistant to hardship, esp. through continued exposure: *Life in the outback hardened the settlers.*
   Syns: acclimate, acclimatize, caseharden, climatize, indurate, season, stiffen, toughen.

3. CONFIRM.

hardened *adjective*

1. COLD-BLOODED.

2. HARD.

hard-eyed *adjective* REALISTIC.

hardfisted *adjective*

1. HARD.

2. STINGY.

hardhanded *adjective* HARD.

hardheaded *adjective*

1. OBSTINATE.

2. REALISTIC.

hardheadedness *noun* OBSTINACY.

hardhearted *adjective*
COLD-BLOODED.

hard-hitting *adjective* AGGRESSIVE.

hardly *adverb* BARELY.

hard-shell *also* **hard-shelled** *adjective*

1. CONFIRMED.

2. GRIM.

hardship *noun* DIFFICULTY.

hardy *adjective*

1. HARD.

2. STRONG.

harebrain *noun* CRACKPOT.

harebrained *adjective*

1. FOOLISH.

2. GIDDY.

hark *verb*

1. HEAR.

2. LISTEN.

harken *verb* SEE **hearken**.

harlot *noun* PROSTITUTE.

harm *noun*
The action or result of inflicting loss or pain: *did harm to the hostages.*
   Syns: damage, detriment, hurt, injury, mischief, outrage.

harm *verb* INJURE.

harmful *adjective*
Causing harm or injury: *The sun's rays can be harmful when exposure is excessive.*
   Syns: bad, damaging, deleterious, detrimental, evil, hurtful, injurious.

harmless *adjective*

1. Devoid of hurtful qualities: *asked a few harmless questions.*
   Syns: innocent, innocuous, inoffensive, unoffensive.

2. Incapable of inflicting injury: *a harmless garter snake*.
   Syns: hurtless, innocuous.
3. INNOCENT.

harmonic *adjective* HARMONIOUS.

harmonious *adjective*
1. Exhibiting accord in feeling or action: *a harmonious relationship between father and son*.
   Syns: amicable, amical, congenial, friendly.
2. Characterized by harmony of sound: *a harmonious piano-violin duet*.
   Syns: consonant, harmonic, musical, symphonic.
3. SYMMETRICAL.

harmonize *verb*
1. To bring into accord: *a leader who harmonized numerous factions into a solid front*.
   Syns: accommodate, attune, conform, coordinate (*also* co-ordinate), integrate, proportion, reconcile, tune.
2. To combine and adapt in order to attain a particular effect: *harmonized the wall hangings with the room decor*.
   Syns: arrange, blend, coordinate (*also* co-ordinate), integrate, orchestrate, synthesize, unify.
3, 4. AGREE.
5. GET ALONG at get.

harmony *noun*
1. Pleasing agreement, as of musical sounds: *three-part harmony*.
   Syns: accord, concert, concord, consonance (*Mus.*), tune.
2. The state of individuals who are in utter agreement: *family harmony*.
   Syns: concord, rapport, unity.
   —*Idiom* meeting of minds.
3. AGREEMENT.
4. PROPORTION.

harpy *noun* SCOLD.

harrow *verb* SACK².

harrowing *adjective* TORMENTING.

harry *verb*
1. ANNOY.
2. BESIEGE.
3. RAID.

harsh *adjective*
1. Disagreeable to the sense of hearing: *He had a harsh, parade-ground voice*.
   Syns: discordant, dry, grating, hoarse, jarring, rasping, raspy, raucous, rough, rugged, squawky, strident.
2, 3. BITTER.
4. BLEAK.
5. ROUGH.

harshness *noun* SEVERITY.

harum-scarum *adjective* RASH¹.

haruspex *also* **aruspex** *noun*
PROPHET.

harvest *noun*
1. The act or process of bringing in a crop: *Thanksgiving culminates the harvest*.
   Syns: cropping, gathering, harvesting, reaping.
2. The produce gathered from the land: *a huge cucumber harvest*.
   Syns: crop, fruit, fruitage, yield.
3. EFFECT.

harvest *verb*
1. GATHER.
2. GLEAN.

harvesting *noun* HARVEST.

hash *noun* BOTCH.

hash over *verb* DISCUSS.

hassle *noun* ARGUMENT.

hassle *verb* ARGUE.

haste *noun*
1. Rapidness of movement or activity: *left the room in great haste*.
   Syns: celerity, dispatch, expedition, expeditiousness, fleetness, hurry, hustle (*Informal*), rapidity, speed, speediness, swiftness.
2. Careless, headlong action: *Haste makes waste*.
   Syns: hastiness, hurriedness, precipitance (*also* precipitancy), precipitation, rashness, rush.

haste *verb* RUSH.

hasten *verb*
1. RUSH.
2. SPEED UP at speed.

hastiness *noun* HASTE.

hasty *adjective*
1. ABRUPT.
2. PRECIPITATE.
3. QUICK.
4. RASH¹.

hatch *verb*
1. GENERATE.
2. INVENT.
3. PRODUCE.

hate *verb*
To regard with extreme dislike and hostility: *hated the enemy*.
   Syns: abominate, despise, detest, execrate, loathe.

hate *noun*
1. Extreme hostility and dislike: *looked at me with undisguised hate*.
   Syns: abhorrence, abomination, detestation, hatred, loathing, repugnance (*also* repugnancy), repulsion, revulsion.
2. An object of extreme dislike: *A pet hate of mine is laziness*.

Syns: abomination, anathema, bête noire (*French*), bugbear, detestation.
—*Idiom* black beast.

hateable *adjective* HATEFUL.

hateful *adjective*
1. Eliciting or deserving hate: *a hateful child who tortures animals.*
   Syns: abominable, hateable, horrid, odious.
2. ANTIPATHETIC.
3. MALEVOLENT.

hatred *noun* HATE.

haughtiness *noun* ARROGANCE.

haughty *adjective* ARROGANT.

haul *noun*
1. BURDEN.
2. PULL.

haul *verb* PULL.

haunt *verb*
1. To recur to continually: *The fear of failure haunted him.*
   Syns: obsess, torment, trouble, weigh on (*or* upon).
2. FREQUENT.

haunt *noun*
1. A frequently visited place: *His favorite haunt is the clubhouse.*
   Syns: hangout (*Informal*), rendezvous, resort. —*Idiom* stamping ground.
2. GHOST.
3. HOME.

hauteur *noun* ARROGANCE.

haut monde *noun* SOCIETY.

have *verb*
1. To keep at one's disposal: *I have a savings account. We have property on the shore.*
   Syns: hold, own, possess, retain.
2. To organize and carry out (an activity): *have a dinner party; have a parade.*
   Syns: give, hold, stage.
3, 4. BEAR.
5. CARRY.
6. COMMAND.
7, 8. CONTAIN.
9. DECEIVE.
10. ENJOY.
11. EXPERIENCE.
12, 13. FEEL.
14. GET.
15. PARTICIPATE.
16. PERMIT.
17. TAKE.

have at *verb* ATTACK.

haven *noun*
1. COVER.
2. HOME.

haven *verb* HARBOR.

have-not *noun* PAUPER.

havings *noun* BEHAVIOR.

havior *noun* BEHAVIOR.

havoc *noun* DESTRUCTION.

havoc *verb* SACK².

hawk *verb* PEDDLE.

hazard *verb*
1. To run the risk of: *hazard frostbite in the cold.*
   Syns: adventure, chance, risk, venture.
2. PRESUME.
3. RISK.

hazard *noun*
1. CHANCE.
2. DANGER.
3. RISK.

hazardous *adjective* DANGEROUS.

haze *noun*
A thick, heavy atmospheric condition offering reduced visibility due to the presence of suspended particles: *a haze of cigar smoke.*
   Syns: brume, film, fog, mist, murk (*also* mirk), smaze.

haze *verb* OBSCURE.

hazy *adjective*
1. FILMY.
2. TURBID.
3. UNCLEAR.

head *noun*
1. The uppermost part of the body: *He had a handsome oval head.*
   Syns: bean (*Slang*), block (*Slang*), conk (*Slang*), dome (*Slang*), noddle, noggin (*Slang*), noodle (*Slang*), nut (*Slang*), pate, poll.
2. The seat of the faculty of intelligence and reason: *used her head and found the solution.*
   Syns: brain, gray matter (*Informal*), mind, upper story (*Informal*), upperworks (*Informal*).
3. *Informal.* A term or terms in large type introducing a text: *The head was set in 24-point type.*
   Syns: heading, headline.
4. BOSS.
5. CALM.
6. CHIEF.
7. CRISIS.
8. FOAM.
9. MIND.
10. TALENT.

head *verb*
1. ADMINISTER.
2. AIM.
3. BEAR.

head off *verb*
1. To block the progress of and force to

change direction: *A posse headed off the robbers at the pass.*
Syns: cut off, intercept.
2. PREVENT.

head *adjective* PRINCIPAL.

header *noun*
1. FALL.
2. PLUNGE.

heading *noun*
1. The compass direction in which a ship or aircraft moves: *checked the heading of the enemy destroyer.*
Syns: bearing, course, vector.
2. HEAD.

headline *noun* HEAD.

headlong *adjective* RASH[1].

headman *noun* CHIEF.

headquarters *noun*
1. BASE[1].
2. CENTER.

headshaker *noun* SKEPTIC.

head start *noun* ADVANTAGE.

headstrong *adjective* OBSTINATE.

headway *noun* ADVANCE.

heal *verb* CURE.

heal-all *noun* PANACEA.

healing *adjective* CURATIVE.

health *noun*
The condition of being physically and mentally sound: *A proper diet is essential to good health.*
Syns: haleness, healthiness, heartiness, soundness, wholeness.

healthful *adjective*
1. Promoting good health: *Jogging is a healthful exercise.*
Syns: healthy, hygienic, salubrious, salutary, wholesome.
2. HEALTHY.

healthiness *noun* HEALTH.

healthy *adjective*
1. Having good health: *a healthy child.*
Syns: bunkum[2] (*Regional*), fit, hale, healthful (*Rare*), hearty, right, sound[2], well[2], whole, wholesome.
—*Idioms* fit as a fiddle, hale and hearty, in fine fettle, sound as a dollar.
2. BIG.
3. FLOURISHING.
4. HEALTHFUL.

heap *noun*
1. A group of things gathered haphazardly: *a heap of ironing on the table; a heap of beer cans.*
Syns: agglomeration, bank[2], drift, hill, mass, mess, mound, mountain, pile, pyramid, ruck[1], shock, stack, tumble.
2. *Informal.* A great deal: *learned a heap from him; a heap of troubles.*

Syns: barrel (*Informal*), lot, mass, mountain, much, pack, peck[1] (*Informal*), pile (*Informal*), plenty, power (*Regional*), sight (*Chiefly Regional*), wealth, world.
3. *Informal.* An indeterminately great amount or number: *has a heap of money; had heaps of good ideas.*
Syns: bushel (*Informal*), gob[1] (*Informal*), jillion (*Informal*), load (*Informal*), lot, million, multiplicity, oodle (*Informal*), passel (*Regional*), peck[1] (*Informal*), ream, scad (*Informal*), slew (*also* slue) (*Informal*), trillion, wad (*Informal*), zillion (*Informal*).

heap *verb*
1. To put into a disordered pile: *heaped the rags on the garage floor.*
Syns: bank[2], drift, hill, lump[1], mound, pile (up), stack.
2. To fill to overflowing: *heaped his plate with food.*
Syns: lade, load, pile.
3. SHOWER.

hear *verb*
1. To perceive by ear, usu. attentively: *Hear my advice before you act.*
Syns: attend, hark, hearken (*also* harken) (*Poetic & Archaic*), heed, listen. —*Idioms* bend an ear, give a hear to, give an ear to, lend one's ear.
2. DISCOVER.

hear of *verb*
To receive (an idea) and take it into consideration: *I won't even hear of apologizing!*
Syns: entertain, think of. —*Idiom* turn a willing ear.

hearing *noun*
1. The sense by which sound is perceived: *keen hearing.*
Syns: audition, ear.
2. Range of audibility: *Don't say that within their hearing!*
Syns: earshot, sound[1].
3. A chance to be heard: *At least give me a hearing.*
Syns: audience, audition.
4. TRIAL.

hearken *also* **harken** *verb*
1. HEAR.
2. LISTEN.

hearsay *noun* GOSSIP.

heart *noun*
1. *Anat.* The circulatory organ of the body: *The patient's heart stopped.*
Syn: ticker (*Slang*).
2. The seat of a person's innermost emotions and feelings: *knew in my heart that I had failed.*

Syns: bosom, breast, soul. —*Idioms* bottom of one's heart, cockles of one's heart, one's heart of hearts.

3. The most central and material part: *the heart of the matter.*
Syns: core, essence, gist, gravamen, kernel, marrow, meat, nub, pith, quintessence, root[1], soul, spirit, stuff, substance.

4, 5. CENTER.

6. COURAGE.

heartache *noun* GRIEF.

heartbreak *noun* GRIEF.

hearten *verb* ENCOURAGE.

heartening *adjective* ENCOURAGING.

heartfelt *adjective* GENUINE.

heartiness *noun* HEALTH.

heartless *adjective* COLD-BLOODED.

heart-whole *adjective* GENUINE.

hearty *adjective*
1. GENUINE.
2. HEALTHY.

heat *noun*
1. Intense warmth: *the summer's heat.*
Syns: fervor (*Poetic*), hot (*Regional*), hotness, torridness.
2. Intensity of feeling or reaction: *retorted with some heat when cross-examined.*
Syns: excitement, fervor, warmth.
3. A regular period of sexual excitement in female mammals: *a cat in heat.*
Syns: estrus (*also* oestrus), rut, season.
4. POLICEMAN.

heat *verb*
To make hot: *The broiling sun heated the sand.*
Syns: heat up, hot (up) (*Chiefly Brit.*).

heat up *verb* HEAT.

heated *adjective*
1. FERVID.
2. HOT.

heave *verb*
1. GASP.
2. PANT.
3. THROW.
4. TOSS.

heave *noun*
1. LIFT.
2. THROW.

heaven *noun*
A state of elated bliss: *I was in heaven when living in Hawaii.*
Syns: ecstasy, paradise, rapture, transport. —*Idioms* cloud nine, seventh heaven.

heavenly *adjective*
1. Of or relating to heaven: *heavenly angels.*

Syns: celestial, paradisaical *or* paradisiacal.
2. Of or relating to the heavens: *The moon and the stars are heavenly bodies.*
Syns: celestial, empyrean.
3. DELICIOUS.
4. DELIGHTFUL.
5. DIVINE[1].
6. MARVELOUS.

heaven(s) *noun* AIR.

heavily *adverb*
1. HARD.
2. WEARILY.

heaviness *noun*
1. The state or quality of being physically heavy: *dieted to lose excess heaviness.*
Syns: avoirdupois (*Informal*), gravity (*Rare*), heftiness, massiveness, ponderosity, ponderousness, weight, weightiness.
2. PREGNANCY.

heavy *adjective*
1. Having a relatively great weight: *a heavy piano.*
Syns: burdensome, heavyweight, hefty, massive, ponderous, weighty.
2. Large in number or yield: *heavy amounts of paperwork; a heavy crop of asparagus.*
Syns: abundant, copious, substantial, voluminous.
3. Intensely sustained, esp. in activity: *heavy artillery fire.*
Syns: concentrated, fierce, furious, heightened, intense, intensive.
4. Indulging in drink to an excessive degree: *a heavy drinker.*
Syns: hard, two-fisted (*Informal*).
5. Not readily digested because of richness: *a heavy meal; heavy dough.*
Syn: rich.
6. Having a solid, compact build: *a heavy wrestler.*
Syns: heavyset, hefty, thick, thickbodied, thickset.
7. Unwieldy, esp. due to excess weight: *heavy Victorian furniture.*
Syns: cumbersome, elephantine, lumpish, ponderous.
8. Burdened by a weighty load: *trees heavy with peaches.*
Syns: heavy-laden, loaded (down).
9. BURDENSOME.
10. DEEP.
11. GRAVE.
12. HIGH.
13. PREGNANT.
14. ROUGH.
15. SEVERE.

16, 17. THICK.

heavy *noun*
A mean, worthless character in a story or play: *played the heavy in a western.*
 Syns: scoundrel, villain.

heavy-handed *adjective*
1. PONDEROUS.
2. UNSKILLFUL.

heavy-hearted *adjective* DEPRESSED.

heavy-heartedness *noun* GLOOM.

heavy-laden *adjective* HEAVY.

heavyset *adjective* HEAVY.

heavyweight *adjective*
1. BIG-LEAGUE.
2. HEAVY.
 heavyweight *noun* DIGNITARY.

hebetate *verb* DULL.

hebetude *noun* LETHARGY.

hebetudinous *adjective*
1. LETHARGIC.
2. STUPID.

hecatomb *noun* SACRIFICE.

heckle *verb* BAIT.

hectic *adjective*
1. FERVID.
2. HOT.

hector *verb*
1. BAIT.
2. INTIMIDATE.
 hector *noun* BULLY.

hedge *verb*
1. CLOSE IN at **close**¹.
2. EQUIVOCATE.
3. SKIRT.
4. SURROUND.

hedging *adjective* EVASIVE.

hedonic *adjective* SYBARITIC.

hedonist *noun* SYBARITE.

hedonistic *adjective* SYBARITIC.

heebie-jeebies *noun* JITTERS.

heed *noun*
1. CARE.
2. NOTICE.
 heed *verb* HEAR.

heedful *adjective*
1. ATTENTIVE.
2. CAREFUL.
3. MINDFUL.

heedfulness *noun*
1. ATTENTION.
2. CARE.

heedless *adjective*
1. CARELESS.
2. MINDLESS.

heedlessness *noun* ABANDON.

heehaw *noun* LAUGH.
 heehaw *verb* LAUGH.

heel¹ *verb*
1. DOG.
2. FOLLOW.

heel² *verb* INCLINE.

heftiness *noun* HEAVINESS.

hefty *adjective*
1, 2. HEAVY.
3. SEVERE.

height *noun*
1. The highest point: *scaled the mountain to its very height.*
 Syns: apex, crest, crown, fastigium, peak, roof, summit, top, vertex.
2. CLIMAX.
3. ELEVATION.

heighten *verb*
1. ELEVATE.
2. INTENSIFY.
3. RISE.

heightened *adjective*
1. ELEVATED.
2. HEAVY.

heinous *adjective* OUTRAGEOUS.

heinousness *noun* ENORMITY.

heir *verb* INHERIT.

heist *verb* ROB.
 heist *noun* ROBBERY.

hell *noun*
Excruciating punishment: *subjected the concentration-camp inmates to pure hell.*
 Syns: persecution, torment, torture.
 —*Idioms* living hell, tortures of the damned.
 hell *verb*
1. REVEL.
2. RUSH.

hellfire *adjective* FATEFUL.

hell-for-leather *adjective* FAST.
 hell-for-leather *adverb* FAST.

hellish *adjective* FIENDISH.

helotry *noun* SLAVERY.

help *verb*
1. To give support or assistance: *The lifeguard helped the exhausted swimmer.*
 Syns: abet, aid, assist, benefact, help out, succor. —*Idioms* give (*or* lend) a hand, give a leg up.
2. IMPROVE.
 help out *verb* HELP.
 help *noun*
1. The act or an instance of helping: *Welfare provides help for the needy.*
 Syns: aid, assist, assistance, hand, relief, succor, support.
2. HELPER.

helper *noun*
A person who helps: *After a year as a helper he was made foreman.*
 Syns: aid, assistant, attendant, help.

helpful *adjective*
1. Affording support or assistance: *helpful advice.*

Syns: aidant, aiding, assistive, serviceable, supportive.
2. BENEFICIAL.

helping noun SERVING.
  helping adjective AUXILIARY.

helpless adjective
1. Unable to manage for oneself: *The dying patient was helpless in his attempt to speak.*
  Syns: impotent, incapable, paralyzed, powerless.
2. Devoid of help or protection: *helpless hostages.*
  Syns: aidless, defenseless, unprotected.

helplessly adverb
Without regard to desire or inclination: *a nation drifting helplessly toward anarchy.*
  Syns: inextricably, perforce, willy-nilly.

helter-skelter adjective CONFUSED.

hem verb
1. CLOSE IN at close¹.
2. ENCLOSE.
3. SURROUND.

henchman noun FOLLOWER.

henpeck verb NAG.

herald verb USHER IN at usher.

herculean adjective GIANT.

herd verb DRIVE.

hereafter noun FUTURE.

hereditary adjective
1. ANCESTRAL.
2. INNATE.

heretic noun SEPARATIST.

heretofore adverb
1, 2. EARLIER.

heritage noun
1. Something immaterial, as a style or philosophy, that is passed from one generation to another: *The heritage of ancient Greece is reflected in Western thought.*
  Syns: inheritance, legacy, tradition.
2. BIRTHRIGHT.

hermeneutic adjective EXPLANATORY.

hermetic adjective SECLUDED.

hero noun
1. A person revered esp. for noble courage: *Sergeant York was one of the heroes of World War I.*
  Syn: paladin. —*Idiom* man of the hour.
2. CELEBRITY.

heroic adjective
1. BRAVE.
2. GIANT.

heroism noun
The quality or state of being heroic: *a rescue that was an act of heroism.*
  Syns: gallantry, prowess, valiancy (*also* valiance), valor, valorousness.

hesitancy noun HESITATION.

hesitant adjective
Given to or exhibiting hesitation: *A hesitant leader is an ineffective one.*
  Syns: faltering, halting, hesitating, indecisive, irresolute, pendulous, tentative, timid, uncertain, undecisive, vacillant, vacillating (*also* vacillatory), wavering, wobbly.

hesitate verb
To be irresolute in acting or doing: *The witness hesitated before answering the question.*
  Syns: dither, falter, halt², pause, shilly-shally, stagger, vacillate, waver.

hesitating adjective HESITANT.

hesitation noun
The act or an instance of hesitating: *Hesitation in foreign-policy decision-making can be disastrous.*
  Syns: hesitancy, indecision, indecisiveness, irresolution, shilly-shally, to-and-fro, vacillation, wavering.

Hessian noun MERCENARY.

heterogeneity noun VARIETY.

heterogeneous adjective VARIOUS.

hew verb CUT.

hex noun
1. JINX.
2. WITCH.

hiatus noun GAP.

hick adjective COUNTRY.

hidden adjective
1. BLIND.
2. SECLUDED.
3. ULTERIOR.

hide¹ verb
1. To put or keep out of sight: *They hid the stolen jewels in an abandoned mine shaft.*
  Syns: bury, bush up (*Chiefly Regional*), cache, conceal, ensconce, occult, plant (*Informal*), secrete, stash.
2. BLOCK OUT at block.
3. COVER.
4. OBSCURE.

hide out verb HOLE UP at hole.
hide noun
1. BLIND.
2. HIDE-OUT.

hide² noun
The skin of an animal: *trappers selling hides.*

Syns: fell³, fur, jacket, pelt¹.
hide *verb* BEAT.
hideaway *noun* HIDE-OUT.
hidebound *adjective* INTOLERANT.
hideous *adjective*
1. GHASTLY.
2. UGLY.
hideousness *noun* UGLINESS.
hide-out *noun*
A hiding place: *The robbers' hide-out was deep in the desert.*
   Syns: covert, den, hide¹, hideaway, lair.
hiding *noun* BEATING.
hierarch *noun* CHIEF.
hifalutin *adjective* SEE **highfalutin.**
higgle *verb* HAGGLE.
higgledy-piggledy *adjective*
CONFUSED.
high *adjective*
1. Having a rather great upward projection: *a high building; high French windows.*
   Syns: altitudinous, long¹ (*Rare*), tall.
2. Elevated in pitch: *a high voice; high notes.*
   Syns: acute (*Mus.*), argute, high-pitched, piercing, piping, shrieky, shrill, shrilly, treble.
3. Long past: *high antiquity.*
   Syns: ancient, immemorial, remote, removed.
4. Intensely violent in sustained velocity: *high winds.*
   Syns: fierce, furious, heavy, strong.
5. COSTLY.
6. DRUGGED.
7. DRUNK.
8, 9. ELEVATED.
10. TALL.
high *noun* THRILL.
high-and-mighty *adjective*
ARROGANT.
highball *verb* RUSH.
highborn *adjective* NOBLE.
highbred *adjective*
1. NOBLE.
2. THOROUGHBRED.
highbrow *adjective* INTELLECTUAL.
higher *adjective*
1. Being at a rank above another: *The clerk had to consult with a higher official.*
   Syns: senior, superior.
2. Being at a height or level above another: *a higher rock stratum.*
   Syns: greater, over, superior.
higher-up *noun*
1. AUTHORITY.
2. SUPERIOR.

highest *adjective*
1. Pre-eminent in rank or position: *rumors that were denied at the highest levels.*
   Syns: astral, highest-ranking, stratospheric, top-drawer (*Informal*), top-ranking.
2. TOP.
highest-ranking *adjective* HIGHEST.
highfalutin or **hifalutin** also
 highfaluting *adjective*
1. POMPOUS.
2. SONOROUS.
high-flown *adjective*
1. ELEVATED.
2. SONOROUS.
high-grade *adjective* GOOD.
high-hat *noun* SNOB.
high-hat *adjective* SNOBBISH.
highjack *verb* SEE **hijack.**
high-minded *adjective* ELEVATED.
high-performance *adjective*
EFFICIENT.
high-pitched *adjective* HIGH.
high-priced *adjective* COSTLY.
high-ranking *adjective* EXALTED.
high-sounding *adjective* SONOROUS.
high-spirited *adjective*
1. EXUBERANT.
2. SPIRITED.
hightail *verb* RUN.
highty-tighty *adjective* SEE
hoity-toity.
highway *noun* WAY.
hijack also **highjack** *verb* COERCE.
hike *noun*
1. CONSTITUTIONAL.
2, 3. INCREASE.
hike *verb* RAISE.
hilarious *adjective* PRICELESS.
hilarity *noun* GAIETY.
hill *noun*
1. A natural land elevation: *The palace stood on a hill overlooking a lake.*
   Syns: eminence, projection, prominence (*also* prominency), rise.
2. HEAP.
hill *verb* HEAP.
hind *adjective* BACK.
hinder *verb*
To interfere with the progress of: *Demands on both sides hindered resolution of the conflict.*
   Syns: bog (down), encumber, hamper, hold back, impede, obstruct, overslaugh, retard. —*Idiom* get in the way of.
hindmost also **hindermost** *adjective*
1. BACK.
2. LAST¹.

hindrance *noun* BAR.
hinge on (or **upon**) *verb* DEPEND ON at **depend**.
hint *noun*
1. A subtle pointing out: *Give me a hint to the solution of this puzzle.*
   Syns: clue (*also* clew), cue, indication, intimation, suggestion.
2. A subtle quality underlying or felt to underlie a situation, action, or person: *wanted to avoid any hint of nepotism.*
   Syns: implication, inkling, innuendo, suspicion, undertone.
3. SHADE.
4. TRACE.
hint
1. To convey an idea by indirect, subtle means: *hinted at a breakthrough in negotiations.*
   Syns: imply, innuendo, insinuate, intimate[2], suggest. —*Idiom* drop a hint.
2. To try to obtain, usu. by subtleness and cunning: *kept hinting for an invitation to the party.*
   Syns: angle, fish.
hip *adjective* AWARE.
hire *verb*
1. To engage the temporary use of (something) for a fee: *hired a bus for the school trip.*
   Syns: charter, lease, let, rent[1].
2. EMPLOY.
hire *noun*
1, 2. EMPLOYMENT.
3. WAGE(S).
hired *adjective* EMPLOYED.
hireling *noun*
1. EMPLOYEE.
2. MERCENARY.
hirer *noun* EMPLOYER.
hiring *noun* EMPLOYMENT.
hirsute *adjective* HAIRY.
hiss *verb*
To make a sharp sibilant sound: *The coiled snake hissed and then struck. Air hissed from the tire.*
   Syns: fizz, fizzle, sibilate, sizzle, swish, whisk, whiz (*also* whizz), whoosh.
hiss *noun*
Any derisive sound of disapproval: *Hisses filled the auditorium.*
   Syns: bazoo, bird (*Slang*), boo, Bronx cheer (*Slang*), catcall, hoot, raspberry (*Slang*), razz (*Slang*).
historic *adjective* IMPORTANT.
history *noun*
1. A chronological record of past events: *the history of Western Europe.*
   Syns: annals, chronicle.
2. Past events surrounding a person or thing: *He has a history of heart disease.*
   Syns: background, past. —*Idiom* past history.
3. STORY.
histrionic *adjective* DRAMATIC.
histrionics *noun* THEATRICS.
hit *verb*
1. To deliver (a powerful blow) suddenly and sharply: *The boxer hit his opponent on the jaw.*
   Syns: bash (*Informal*), belt (*Slang*), biff (*Slang*), bop (*Informal*), catch, clip[1] (*Informal*), clobber (*Slang*), clout, knock, paste (*Slang*), pop, slam, slog, slug[2] (*Slang*), smack[1], smash, smite, sock (*Slang*), strike, swat, wallop (*Informal*), whack, wham. —*Idioms* let someone have it, sock it to someone.
2. ATTACK.
3. MURDER.
4. OCCUR.
5. ROB.
hit back *verb* RETALIATE.
hit on (or **upon**) *verb*
1. ARRIVE AT at **arrive**.
2. TAKE.
hit *noun*
1. A dazzling, often sudden instance of success: *a Broadway hit.*
   Syns: bang, boff, sleeper (*Informal*), smash (*Informal*), ten-strike (*Informal*), wow (*Informal*). —*Idioms* bell ringer, smash hit.
2. BLOW[2].
3. PULL.
hitch *verb*
1. LIMP.
2. MARRY.
hitch *noun*
1. TIME.
2. TURN.
hit-or-miss *adjective* RANDOM.
hive *verb* ACCUMULATE.
hoard *verb*
To store up (supplies or money), usu. well beyond one's needs: *was arrested for hoarding coffee and selling it on the black market.*
   Syns: lay up, squirrel, stash, stockpile, treasure.
hoard *noun*
A supply stored or hidden for future use: *kept a hoard of food in his bomb shelter.*
   Syns: backlog, hoarding, inventory, reserve, reservoir, stock, stockpile, store, treasure. —*Idiom* nest egg.

hoarding *noun* HOARD.

hoarse *adjective*
1. Low and grating in sound: *spoke in a hoarse whisper.*
  Syns: croaking, croaky, gruff, husky, roupy (*Chiefly Scot.*).
2. HARSH.

hoary *adjective* OLD.

hobble *verb*
1. HAMPER.
2. LIMP.

hobnob *verb* ASSOCIATE.

hock *verb* PAWN[1].

hocus-pocus *noun* GIBBERISH.

hodgepodge *noun* ASSORTMENT.

hoggish *adjective* GREEDY.

hog-tie also **hogtie** *verb* HAMPER.

hoi polloi *noun* TRASH[1].

hoist *verb* ELEVATE.
  hoist *noun* LIFT.

hoity-toity also **highty-tighty** *adjective* ARROGANT.

hold *verb*
1. To have and maintain in one's possession: *holds a controlling interest in the company.*
  Syns: hold back, keep, keep back, reserve, retain, withhold.
2. To maintain restraining control and possession of: *holding a material witness in protective custody.*
  Syns: detain, hold up.
3. ACCOMMODATE.
4. ASSERT.
5. BELIEVE.
6. COMMAND.
7. CONTAIN.
8. EMBRACE.
9. ENJOY.
10. FEEL.
11. GRIP.
12, 13. HAVE.
14. SUPPORT.

hold back *verb*
1. HINDER.
2. HOLD.
3. REPRESS.
4. RESTRAIN.

hold down *verb*
1. REPRESS.
2. RESTRAIN.

hold in *verb* RESTRAIN.

hold off *verb*
1. DEFER[1].
2. REFRAIN.

hold out *verb* ENDURE.

hold up *verb*
1. BEAR UP at **bear.**
2. DEFER[1].
3. DELAY.

4. HOLD.
5. ROB.
6. SKIN.
7. WASH.

hold *noun*
1. An act or means of holding something: *Keep a firm hold on your purse.*
  Syns: clasp, clench, clutch, grapple, grasp, grip.
2. A strong or powerful influence: *had a real hold on my emotions.*
  Syn: grip.

holder *noun* OWNER.

holding(s) *noun*
Something, as land and assets, legally possessed: *The company has vast holdings in South Africa.*
  Syns: estate, possessions, property.

holdup *noun*
1. DELAY.
2. ROBBERY.

hole *noun*
1. A space in an otherwise solid mass: *a hole in the ground.*
  Syns: cavity, hollow, vacuity, void.
2. An open space allowing passage: *rats running through a hole in the baseboard.*
  Syns: aperture, opening, orifice, outlet, vent.
3. A hollow place used as an animal's dwelling: *chipmunk holes.*
  Syns: burrow, den, lair.
4. An ugly, squalid dwelling: *refugees subsisting in filthy holes.*
  Syns: hovel, hut, shanty.
5. BREACH.
6. PREDICAMENT.

hole *verb* BREACH.

hole up *verb*
To shut oneself up in secrecy: *The bandits holed up in a sleazy motel.*
  Syns: hide out, lair, lay low. —*Idioms* go underground, lie low.

holiday *noun* VACATION.

holiness *noun*
The quality of being holy or sacred: *the holiness of a religious shrine.*
  Syns: blessedness, hallowedness, sacredness, sanctity.

holler *verb*
1. ROAR.
2. SHOUT.
  holler *noun* SHOUT.

hollow *adjective*
1. Curving inward: *a tired face with hollow cheeks.*
  Syns: cavernous, concave, indented.
2. EMPTY.

hollow *noun*
1. DEPRESSION.
2. HOLE.
hollow-eyed *adjective* HAGGARD.
hollowness *noun*
1, 2. EMPTINESS.
holy *adjective*
1. Deeply concerned with God and the beliefs and practice of religion: *saints and other holy men.*
    Syns: devout, godly, pietistic, pious, religious.
2. Regarded with particular reverence or respect: *the Holy Grail.*
    Syns: blessed, hallowed, sacred, sacrosanct, sanctified.
3. DIVINE[1].
homage *noun* HONOR.
home *noun*
1. A building or shelter where one lives: *a modest home on the edge of town.*
    Syns: abode, digs (*Informal*), domicile, dwelling, habitation, house, lodgings, place.
2. The natural environment of an animal or plant: *Florida is the home of the alligator.*
    Syns: habitat, haunt. —*Idiom* stamping ground.
3. An institution that provides care and shelter: *a home for wayward boys; a home for the aged.*
    Syns: asylum, haven, hospice, refuge, retreat.
home *adjective*
1, 2. DOMESTIC.
homely *adjective*
1. DOMESTIC.
2. PLAIN.
3. RUSTIC.
homespun *adjective* RUSTIC.
homicidal *adjective* MURDEROUS.
homicide *noun*
1. MURDER.
2. MURDERER.
homilize *verb* PREACH.
hominoid *adjective* MANLIKE.
homo *noun* HUMAN BEING.
homophile *adjective* GAY.
Homo sapiens *noun* MANKIND.
homosexual *adjective* GAY.
honcho *noun* CHIEF.
hone[1] *verb* SHARPEN.
hone[2] *verb* DESIRE.
honed *adjective* SHARP.
honest *adjective*
1. Having or marked by uprightness in principle and action: *an honest man; an honest business.*
    Syns: honorable, incorruptible,

righteous, straight-shooting (*Informal*), true, upright, upstanding. —*Idiom* on the up and up.
2. FRANK.
3. GENUINE.
honesty *noun*
1. The quality of being honest: *a man respected for his honesty.*
    Syns: honor, incorruptibility (*also* incorruptibleness), integrity, rectitude, uprightness.
2. CHARACTER.
honey *verb*
1. FAWN.
2. FLATTER.
3. SWEETEN.
honey *noun* DARLING.
honky-tonk *noun* JOINT.
honor *noun*
1. Great respect or high public esteem accorded as a right or as due: *Only a head of state receives the honor of a 21-gun salute.*
    Syns: deference, homage, obeisance.
2. A person's high standing among others: *had to fight to protect his honor.*
    Syns: dignity, prestige, reputation, repute, status. —*Idiom* good name (*or* report).
3. DISTINCTION.
4. ESTEEM.
5. HONESTY.
honor *verb*
1. To pay tribute or homage to: *a country honoring its heroes.*
    Syns: acclaim, celebrate, exalt, extol, glorify, hail[2], laud, magnify, panegyrize, praise, venerate. —*Idiom* sing someone's praises.
2. ADMIRE.
3. DISTINGUISH.
4. GRACE.
honorable *adjective*
1. Deserving honor or respect: *Teaching is an honorable occupation.*
    Syns: creditable, estimable, reputable, respectable, worthy.
2. HONEST.
honorarium *noun* REWARD.
hood *noun* THUG.
hoodlum *noun* THUG.
hoodoo *noun* JINX.
hoodwink *verb* DECEIVE.
hooey *noun* NONSENSE.
hoof *verb*
1. DANCE.
2. WALK.
hoofer *noun* DANCER.
hoo-hah *noun* SENSATION.

hook *verb* STEAL.
  hook *noun* CATCH.
hooker *noun* PROSTITUTE.
hookup *noun* RELATION.
hooky *noun* CUT.
hooligan *noun* THUG.
hoosegow *noun* JAIL.
hoot *noun*
  1. BIT[1].
  2. DAMN.
  3. HISS.
  4. SCREAM.
hop *noun*
  1. DANCE.
  2. SKIP.
  hop *verb* SKIP.
hope *verb* ASPIRE.
hopeful *adjective* ENCOURAGING.
  hopeful *noun*
  1. APPLICANT.
  2. ASPIRANT.
hopeless *adjective*
  1. Offering no hope or expectation of
     improvement: *an illness that seemed
     hopeless.*
     Syns: cureless, impossible, incurable,
     irremediable, irreparable.
  2. DESPONDENT.
hopelessness *noun* DESPAIR.
hopped-up *adjective* DRUGGED.
horde *noun* CROWD.
horizon *noun* KEN.
horizontal *adjective* FLAT.
horn in *verb*
  1. INTRUDE.
  2. MEDDLE.
horny *adjective* EROTIC.
horrendous *adjective* TERRIBLE.
horrible *adjective*
  1. Causing great horror: *a horrible
     scream.*
     Syns: bloodcurdling, hair-raising,
     horrid, horrific, horrifying, terrific,
     terrifying.
  2. GHASTLY.
  3. TERRIBLE.
horrid *adjective*
  1. GHASTLY.
  2. HATEFUL.
  3. HORRIBLE.
horrific *adjective* HORRIBLE.
horrified *adjective* SHOCKED.
horrify *verb* DISMAY.
horrifying *adjective* HORRIBLE.
horror *noun*
  1. A feeling of fear and repugnance:
     *experienced horror at the sight of
     blood.*

  Syns: abhorrence, aversion, repulsion,
  revulsion.
  2. FEAR.
horrorstruck *adjective* SHOCKED.
horse around *verb* MISBEHAVE.
horseplay *verb* MISBEHAVE.
hospice *noun* HOME.
host *noun* CROWD.
hostile *adjective*
  1. Feeling or showing unfriendliness:
     had a hostile attitude toward authority.
     Syns: inimicable, inimical, unfriendly.
  2. BELLIGERENT.
hostilities *noun* CONFLICT.
hostility *noun*
  1. AGGRESSION.
  2. ANTIPATHY.
  3. BELLIGERENCE.
  4. ENMITY.
hot *adjective*
  1. Marked by much heat: *a hot oven; a
     hot day.*
     Syns: ardent, baking, blistering,
     boiling, broiling, burning, fiery,
     heated, red-hot, scalding, scorching,
     sizzling, sultry, sweltering, torrid.
  2. Being at a higher temperature than is
     normal or desirable: *a hot forehead.*
     Syns: febrile, fevered, feverish,
     feverous, hectic, pyretic.
  3. *Informal.* Of great current interest: *a
     hot topic.*
     Syns: live[2], red-hot.
  4. MARVELOUS.
  hot *noun* HEAT.
  hot *verb* HEAT.
hot-blooded *adjective* PASSIONATE.
hotfoot *verb* RUN.
hotheaded *adjective* RASH[1].
hotness *noun* HEAT.
hot-tempered *adjective* TESTY.
hot water *noun* TROUBLE.
hound *verb*
  1. BAIT.
  2. BESIEGE.
house *noun*
  1. COMPANY.
  2, 3. FAMILY.
  4. HOME.
  house *verb*
  1, 2. HARBOR.
housebreak *verb* BREAK IN at **break.**
house-cleaning *noun* SHAKEUP.
household *noun* FAMILY.
  household *adjective* DOMESTIC.
housing *noun* SHELTER.
hovel *noun* HOLE.
hover *verb*
  1. FLUTTER.
  2. HANG.

howl *verb*
1. To utter or emit a long, mournful, plaintive sound: *a dog howling at the moon.*
   Syns: bay², ululate, wail, yowl.
2. CRY.
3. BAWL.
4. BREAK UP at **break**.

howl *noun*
1. A long, mournful cry: *heard the howl of a wolf.*
   Syns: moan, ululation, wail, yowl.
2. SCREAM.

hub *noun* CENTER.

hubbub *noun* NOISE.

huckster *verb*
1. HAGGLE.
2. PEDDLE.

huddle *verb* CROUCH.

huddle *noun* DISORDER.

hue *noun*
1. COLOR.
2. SHADE.
3. TINT.

huff *noun*
1. OFFENSE.
2. TEMPER.

huff *verb* PANT.

hug *verb* EMBRACE.

hug *noun* EMBRACE.

huge *adjective* GIANT.

hugeness *noun* ENORMOUSNESS.

huggermugger or **hugger-mugger** *adjective* SECRET.

huggermugger or **hugger-mugger** *noun* SECRECY.

huggermugger or **hugger-mugger** *adverb* SECRETLY.

hugger-muggery *noun* SECRECY.

hulk *noun* LUMP¹.

hulk *verb* LUMP¹.

hulking *adjective* BULKY.

hulky *adjective* BULKY.

hullabaloo also **hullaballoo** *noun*
1. NOISE.
2. VOCIFERATION.

hum *verb*
To make a continuous low-pitched droning sound: *The radio hummed briefly after being turned on.*
   Syns: bombinate, bumble², burr (*also* bur), buzz, drone², whir, whiz (*also* whizz).

hum *noun*
A continuous low-pitched droning sound: *the steady hum of a roomful of sewing machines.*
   Syns: bombination, bumble², burr (*also* bur), buzz, drone², whir, whiz (*also* whizz).

human *adjective*
1. Of or characteristic of human beings or mankind: *the caprices of human conduct.*
   Syn: mortal.
2. HUMANITARIAN.

human *noun* HUMAN BEING.

human being *noun*
A member of the human race: *freedom for all human beings.*
   Syns: being, body (*Informal*), creature, fellow, homo, human, individual, life, man, mortal, party (*Informal*), person, personage, soul.

humane *adjective*
1. BENEVOLENT.
2. HUMANITARIAN.

humanitarian *adjective*
1. Concerned with human welfare and the alleviation of suffering: *The governor spared the prisoner out of humanitarian considerations.*
   Syns: charitable, compassionate, human, humane, merciful.
2. BENEVOLENT.

humanity *noun* MANKIND.

humanizing *adjective* CULTURAL.

humankind *noun* MANKIND.

humanoid *adjective* MANLIKE.

humble *adjective*
1. Having or expressing feelings of humility: *had a humble opinion of his own aptitude.*
   Syns: lowly, meek, modest, unassuming, unpresuming.
2. Of little distinction: *my humble abode.*
   Syns: lowly, mean², modest, simple, undistinguished, unpretentious.
3. LOWLY.

humble *verb*
To deprive of esteem, self-worth, or effectiveness: *humbled his opponent in the debate.*
   Syns: abase, bemean, degrade, demean², humiliate. —*Idioms* bring low, take down a peg or two.

humbleness *noun* MODESTY.

humbug *verb* DECEIVE.

humbug *noun* FAKE.

humdrum *adjective* BORING.

humdrum *noun* MONOTONY.

humid *adjective* STICKY.

humiliate *verb* HUMBLE.

humility *noun* MODESTY.

Humist *noun* SKEPTIC.

humor *noun*
1. The quality of being laughable or comical: *finally saw the humor of the situation.*
   Syns: comedy, comicality (*also*

comicalness), drollery, drollness, funniness, humorousness, wit, wittiness.
2. DISPOSITION.
3. FANCY.
4. MOOD.

humor *verb*
To comply with the wishes or ideas of (another): *humored the cook and stayed out of the kitchen.*
Syns: cater to, gratify, indulge, oblige. —*Idioms* give in (*or* way) to, go along with.

humorist *noun* JOKER.

humorous *adjective*
1. Intended to excite laughter or amusement: *humorous comments.*
Syns: facetious, funny, jesting, jocose, jocular, witty.
2. AMUSING.

humorousness *noun* HUMOR.

humorsome *adjective* MOODY.

hump *noun* BUMP.
hump *verb* STOOP.

hunch *verb*
1. CROUCH.
2. STOOP.
hunch *noun*
1. FEELING.
2. LUMP[1].

hunger *noun*
1. APPETITE.
2. DESIRE.
hunger *verb* LUST.

hungry *adjective*
1. GREEDY.
2. RAVENOUS.

hunk *noun*
1, 2. LUMP[1].

hunker *verb*
1. CROUCH.
2. SQUAT.

hunks *noun* MISER.

hunky-dory *adjective* MARVELOUS.

hunt *verb*
To look for and pursue (game) in order to capture or kill it: *We hunt deer in November.*
Syns: drive, stalk, run.
hunt down *verb* RUN DOWN at **run**.
hunt up *verb* SEEK.

hurdle *noun*
1. BAR.
2. JUMP.
hurdle *verb*
1. CLEAR.
2. JUMP.

hurl *verb* THROW.
hurl *noun* THROW.

hurried *adjective*
1, 2. ABRUPT.
3. QUICK.

hurriedness *noun* HASTE.

hurry *verb*
1. RUSH.
2. SPEED UP at **speed**.
hurry *noun* HASTE.

hurry-up *adjective* CRASH.

hurt *verb*
1. To cause physical damage to: *hurt his eye when he broke his glasses.*
Syns: injure, wound.
2. To have or cause a feeling of physical pain or discomfort: *Does your back still hurt?*
Syns: ache, pain.
3. INJURE.
hurt *noun*
1. DISTRESS.
2. HARM.

hurtful *adjective*
1. HARMFUL.
2. PAINFUL.

hurtle *verb* SHOOT.

hurtless *adjective* HARMLESS.

husband *verb* CONSERVE.

husbandry *noun* CONSERVATION.

hush *verb*
1. COVER.
2. REPRESS.
3. SILENCE.
hush up *verb* CENSOR.
hush *noun*
1. SILENCE.
2. STILLNESS.
hush *adjective* SILENT.

hushed *adjective* SOFT.

hush-hush *adjective*
1. CONFIDENTIAL.
2. SECRET.

hussy *noun* SLUT.

hustle *noun*
1. DRIVE.
2. HASTE.
hustle *verb* RUSH.

hustler *noun* EAGER BEAVER.

hut *noun* HOLE.

hygienic *adjective* HEALTHFUL.

hymeneal *adjective* MARITAL.

hype *verb* PROMOTE.
hype *noun* PROMOTION.

hyperbole *noun* EXAGGERATION.

hyperbolism *noun* EXAGGERATION.

hyperbolize *verb* EXAGGERATE.

hypercritic *noun* CRITIC.

hypercritical *adjective* CRITICAL.

hypernormal *adjective*
PRETERNATURAL.

hypnotic *adjective* SLEEPY.
hypnotic *noun* SOPORIFIC.
hypocrisy *noun*
A show or expression of feelings or beliefs one does not actually hold or possess: *the hypocrisy of condemning graft when you're taking kickbacks.*
Syns: hypocriticalness, pecksniffery, pharisaism (*also* phariseeism), sanctimony (*also* sanctimoniousness), tartuffery, two-facedness.
hypocrite *noun*
A person who practices hypocrisy: *a hypocrite who prays on Sunday and cheats customers on Monday.*
Syns: pharisee, phony (*also* phoney) (*Informal*), tartuffe (*also* tartufe).
hypocritical *adjective*
Of or practicing hypocrisy: *hypocritical praise; a hypocritical rogue.*
Syns: pecksniffian, pharisaic (*also* pharisaical), sanctimonious, tartuffian, two-faced.
hypocriticalness *noun* HYPOCRISY.
hypogeal *also* **hypogean, hypogeous** *adjective* UNDERGROUND.
hypothecate *verb* PAWN[1].
hypothesis *noun* THEORY.
hypothetical *also* **hypothetic** *adjective*
1. SUPPOSED.
2. THEORETICAL.

I

icy *adjective*
1. COLD.
2. FRIGID.
idea *noun*
1. That which exists in the mind as the product of careful mental activity: *a novel idea about energy conservation.*
Syns: concept, conception, image, perception, thought.
2. The gist of a specific action or situation: *What's the idea of shouting?*
Syns: import, meaning, point, purport, significance (*also* significancy).
3. BELIEF.
4. DESIGN.
5. FEELING.
ideal *noun*
1. DREAM.

2. MODEL.
ideal *adjective*
1. Conforming to an ultimate form of perfection or excellence: *the ideal vacation.*
Syns: exemplary, model, perfect, supreme.
2. IDEALISTIC.
3. THEORETICAL.
idealist *noun* DREAMER.
idealistic *adjective*
1. Showing a tendency to envision things in perfect but unrealistic form: *an idealistic but disastrously naive approach to foreign policy.*
Syns: ideal, utopian, visionary.
2. Not compatible with reality: *an idealistic view of controlling inflation.*
Syns: quixotic, romantic, starry-eyed, unrealistic, utopian, visionary.
identic *adjective* SAME.
identical *adjective*
1. EQUAL.
2. PRECISE.
3. SAME.
identicalness *noun* SAMENESS.
identify *verb*
1. To associate or affiliate oneself closely with a person or group: *couldn't identify with the play's hero.*
Syns: empathize, relate (to), sympathize.
2. ASSOCIATE.
3. MARK.
4. PLACE.
identity *noun*
1. The set of behavioral or personal characteristics by which an individual is recognizable: *watching a child develop its own identity.*
Syns: individualism, individuality, personality, selfhood.
2. SAMENESS.
idiocy *noun*
1. FOOLISHNESS.
2. NONSENSE.
idiom *noun* LANGUAGE.
idiosyncrasy *noun* ECCENTRICITY.
idiosyncratic *adjective* ECCENTRIC.
idiot *noun*
1, 2. FOOL.
idiotic *adjective* FOOLISH.
idle *adjective*
1. Not occupied or put to use: *idle machines.*
Syns: inactive, unemployed, unused, vacant.
2. BASELESS.
3. EMPTY.
4. INACTIVE.

5. LAZY.

idle *verb*
1. To pass time without working or in avoiding work: *He idled while his parents slaved.*
   Syns: bum (around) (*Informal*), diddle, goldbrick (*Slang*), goof off (*Slang*), laze, lazy, loaf, loiter, lounge, shirk.
2. To pass (time) without working or in avoiding work: *idled the hours away.*
   Syns: fiddle away, trifle, waste, while (away), wile (away).
3. TIE UP at **tie.**

idleness *noun*
1. INACTION.
2. LAZINESS.

idler *noun* WASTREL.
idolization *noun* ADORATION.
idolize *verb* ADORE.
iffy *adjective* AMBIGUOUS.
ignis fatuus *noun* ILLUSION.
ignite *verb* LIGHT[1].
ignited *adjective* BLAZING.
ignoble *adjective*
1. LOWLY.
2. SORDID.

ignominious *adjective* DISGRACEFUL.
ignominy *noun* DISGRACE.
ignorance *noun*
1. The condition of being ignorant; lack of knowledge or learning: *Ignorance is unusual in modern Western society.*
   Syns: benightedness, illiteracy, nescience.
2. The condition of being uninformed: *her ignorance of the new tax structure.*
   Syns: innocence, nescience, unfamiliarity.

ignorant *adjective*
1. Without education or knowledge: *ignorant youths who dropped out of school.*
   Syns: illiterate, nescient, uneducated, unlearned, unschooled, untaught.
2. Exhibiting lack of education or knowledge: *ignorant nomads at odds with a machine-age culture.*
   Syns: backward, benighted, primitive, unenlightened.
3. Not aware or informed: *ignorant of the change in plans.*
   Syns: innocent, oblivious, unacquainted, unaware, unconscious, unenlightened, unfamiliar, uninformed, unknowing, unwitting.
   —*Idiom* in the dark.

ignore *verb*
1. To refuse to pay attention to (a person); treat with contempt: *greeted her but ignored me.*

Syns: disregard, neglect, slight, snub.
   —*Idiom* give someone the go-by.
2. BLINK AT at **blink.**

ilk *noun* KIND[2].
ill *adjective*
1. BAD.
2. SICK.

ill *noun*
1. CURSE.
2. DISEASE.
3. EVIL.

ill-advised *adjective* UNWISE.
illation *noun* DEDUCTION.
ill-behaved *adjective* NAUGHTY.
ill-bred *adjective*
1. COARSE.
2. RUDE.

ill-chosen *adjective* UNFORTUNATE.
ill-considered *adjective*
1. PRECIPITATE.
2. UNWISE.

illegal *adjective*
1. Prohibited by law: *an illegal tax deduction.*
   Syns: illegitimate, illicit, lawless, outlawed, unlawful, wrongful.
2. CRIMINAL.

illegality *noun*
1. The state or quality of being illegal: *the illegality of a labor contract.*
   Syns: illegitimacy, illicitness, unlawfulness.
2. CRIME.

illegitimacy *noun*
1. The condition of being of illegitimate birth: *His illegitimacy made him the target of cruel jokes.*
   Syn: bastardy.
2. ILLEGALITY.

illegitimate *adjective*
1. Born out of wedlock: *her illegitimate son.*
   Syns: baseborn, bastard, fatherless, misbegotten, natural, spurious, unlawful.
2. CRIMINAL.
3. ILLEGAL.

ill-fated *adjective* UNFORTUNATE.
ill-favored *adjective*
1. OBJECTIONABLE.
2. UGLY.

illiberal *adjective* INTOLERANT.
illicit *adjective*
1. CRIMINAL.
2. ILLEGAL.
3. UNLAWFUL.

illicitness *noun* ILLEGALITY.
illimitable *adjective* ETERNAL.
illiteracy *noun* IGNORANCE.
illiterate *adjective* IGNORANT.

ill-judged *adjective* UNWISE.
ill-kempt *adjective* MESSY.
ill-looking *adjective* UGLY.
ill-mannered *adjective* RUDE.
illness *noun*
1. DISEASE.
2. SICKNESS.
illogical *noun*
1. FALLACIOUS.
2. UNREASONABLE.
ill-starred *adjective* UNFORTUNATE.
ill-suited *adjective* UNFIT.
ill-tempered *adjective*
Having or showing a bad temper: *ill-tempered employees; an ill-tempered reply.*
   Syns: bad-tempered, cantankerous, crabbed, crabby, cranky, cross, disagreeable, grouchy, grumpy, irascible, irritable, mean[2] (*Informal*), nasty, peevish, petulant, querulous, ratty (*Chiefly Brit.*), runty (*Regional*), snappish, surly, testy, ugly (*Informal*), waspish.
ill-timed *adjective* INCONVENIENT.
illume *verb*
1, 2. ILLUMINATE.
illuminate *verb*
1. To provide, cover, or fill with light: *A bonfire illuminated the clearing.*
   Syns: illume (*Poetic*), illumine, light[1], lighten.
2. To enable (one) to understand, esp. in a spiritual sense: *a sermon that illumined me.*
   Syns: edify, enlighten, illume (*Poetic*), illumine, instruct.
3. CLARIFY.
illumination *noun*
1. The act of physically illuminating or the condition of being filled with light: *presided at the illumination of the nation's official Christmas tree.*
   Syns: light[1], lighting.
2. The condition of being informed spiritually: *illumination experienced through meditation.*
   Syns: edification, enlightenment, instruction.
3. EXPLANATION.
4. LIGHT[1].
illumine *verb*
1, 2. ILLUMINATE.
ill-use *verb* ABUSE.
illusion *noun*
1. An erroneous perception of reality: *optical illusions caused by trick mirrors.*
   Syns: delusion, hallucination, ignis

fatuus, mirage, phantasm (*also* phantasma), will-o'-the-wisp.
2. A fantastic, impracticable plan or desire: *had grand illusions of changing the world.*
   Syns: bubble, chimera, dream, fantasy (*also* phantasy), pipe dream, rainbow. —*Idiom* castle in the air.
3. DREAM.
illusive *adjective*
1. Of, pertaining to, or in the nature of an illusion; lacking reality: *the mental patient's illusive perceptions.*
   Syns: chimerical (*also* chimeric), hallucinatory, illusory.
2. ILLUSORY.
illusory *adjective*
1. Tending to deceive; of the nature of an illusion: *illusory wage gains.*
   Syns: delusive, delusory, illusive.
2. ILLUSIVE.
illustrate *verb*
1. EXPLAIN.
2. INSTANCE.
3. REPRESENT.
illustration *noun* EXAMPLE.
illustrative *adjective* GRAPHIC.
illustrious *adjective* EMINENT.
illustriousness *noun* EMINENCE.
ill will *noun* MALEVOLENCE.
image *noun*
1. The character projected by someone to the public: *a politician concerned about his image.*
   Syns: appearance, impression.
2. DOUBLE.
3. IDEA.
4. LIKENESS.
5. REFLECTION.
image *verb*
1. COPY.
2. ECHO.
3. IMAGINE.
4. REFLECT.
5. REPRESENT.
imaginable *adjective* EARTHLY.
imaginary *adjective.*
Existing only in the imagination: *an imaginary playmate.*
   Syns: chimerical (*also* chimeric), conceptual, fancied, fanciful, fantastic (*also* fantastical), imagined, notional, unreal.
imagination *noun*
The power of the mind to form images: *Children have great imagination in playing.*
   Syns: fancy, fantasy (*also* phantasy), imaginativeness. —*Idiom* flight of fancy.

imaginative *adjective* FANCIFUL.
imaginativeness *noun* IMAGINATION.
imagine *verb*
To form mental images of: *imagined that she had seen the murder; couldn't imagine what it was like.*
   Syns: conceive, envisage, envision, fancy, fantasize, feature (*Informal*), image, picture, see, think, vision, visualize.
imagined *adjective* IMAGINARY.
imbecile *noun*
  1, 2. FOOL.
imbed *verb* SEE embed.
imbibe *verb*
  1. ABSORB.
  2, 3, 4. DRINK.
imbrue *also* **embrue** *verb* BLOODY.
imbrued *also* **embrued** *adjective* BLOODY.
imbue *verb* FILL.
imitate *verb*
  1. To copy (the manner or expression of another), esp. in an exaggerated or mocking way: *He imitated the teacher behind her back.*
    Syns: ape, burlesque, mimic, mock, parody, take off (*Informal*), travesty.
    —*Idiom* do a takeoff on.
  2. COPY.
  3. ECHO.
imitation *noun*
  1. COPY.
  2. MIMICRY.
  3. TAKEOFF.
imitation *adjective* ARTIFICIAL.
imitative *adjective*
  1. Copying another in an inferior or obsequious way: *executives imitative of their president; a forgery imitative of a Rembrandt.*
    Syns: apish, emulative, slavish.
  2. ECHOIC.
imitator *noun* ECHO.
immaculate *adjective* CLEAN.
immaterial *adjective*
  1. Having no body, form, or substance: *immaterial apparitions.*
    Syns: asomatous, bodiless, discarnate, disembodied, incorporeal, insubstantial, metaphysical (*also* metaphysic), nonphysical, spiritual, unbodied, uncorporal, unsubstantial.
  2. IRRELEVANT.
immature *adjective*
  1. CHILDISH.
  2. YOUNG.
immeasurable *adjective*
  1. ENDLESS.
  2. INCALCULABLE.

immediate *adjective*
  1. Marked by the absence of any intervention: *The police had immediate evidence of a plot.*
    Syns: direct, firsthand, primary.
  2. CLOSE¹.
immediately *adverb*
  1. Without intermediary: *Their yard is immediately behind ours.*
    Syn: directly.
  2. DIRECTLY.
immemorial *adjective* HIGH.
immense *adjective* GIANT.
immensity *noun* ENORMOUSNESS.
immerge *verb* DIP.
immerse *verb*
  1. ABSORB.
  2. DIP.
immersed *adjective* ABSORBED.
immigrant *noun* EMIGRANT.
immigrate *verb* EMIGRATE.
immigration *noun* EMIGRATION.
imminence *noun* APPROACH.
imminent *adjective* MOMENTARY.
immission *noun* ADMISSION.
immit *verb* ADMIT.
immobile *adjective*
  1. FIXED.
  2. MOTIONLESS.
immobilize *verb*
  1. DISABLE.
  2. TIE UP at **tie.**
immoderate *adjective* EXCESSIVE.
immolate *verb* SACRIFICE.
immolation *noun* SACRIFICE.
immoral *adjective*
  1. EVIL.
  2. IMPURE.
immorality *noun* CORRUPTION.
immortal *adjective*
  1. Not being subject to death: *prayed for his immortal soul.*
    Syns: deathless, undying.
  2. ENDLESS.
immortality *noun*
Endless life after death: *believed in the immortality of the soul.*
    Syns: afterlife, deathlessness, eternity, everlastingness, world-without-end.
    —*Idiom* everlasting life.
immortalize *verb*
To cause to last endlessly: *a colossal statue that immortalizes the memory of our fallen heroes.*
    Syns: eternalize, eternize, perpetuate.
immovable *adjective* FIXED.
immune *adjective* RESISTANT.
immunity *noun* RESISTANCE.

immure *verb*
1. ENCLOSE.
2. JAIL.
immutable *adjective* INFLEXIBLE.
imp *noun* MISCHIEF.
impact *noun*
1. The strong effect exerted by one person or thing on another: *The impact of the oil embargo is still being felt by the consumer.*
   Syns: force, repercussion.
2. COLLISION.
3. WALLOP.
impact *verb* AFFECT[1].
impair *verb* INJURE.
impairment *noun* BREAKAGE.
impalpable *adjective* IMPERCEPTIBLE.
impart *verb* COMMUNICATE.
impartial *adjective*
1. FAIR.
2. NEUTRAL.
impartiality *noun* FAIRNESS.
impassable *adjective* INSUPERABLE.
impassible *adjective* INSENSITIVE.
impassion *verb* FIRE.
impassioned *adjective* PASSIONATE.
impassive *adjective*
1. APATHETIC.
2. DRY.
3. INSENSITIVE.
impassivity *noun* APATHY.
impatient *adjective*
1. Being unable to endure irritation or opposition: *an impatient person who could not abide incompetence.*
   Syns: chafing, fretful.
2. EAGER.
3. INTOLERANT.
impeccable *adjective* PERFECT.
impecunious *adjective* POOR.
impecuniousness *noun* POVERTY.
impede *verb*
1. HINDER.
2. OBSTRUCT.
impediment *noun* BAR.
impel *verb*
1. DRIVE.
2. PROVOKE.
impend *verb* THREATEN.
impending *adjective* MOMENTARY.
impenetrable *adjective* INCOMPREHENSIBLE.
impenitent *adjective* REMORSELESS.
imperative *adjective*
1. BURNING.
2. ESSENTIAL.
3. REQUIRED.
imperative *noun* DUTY.
imperceptible *adjective*
1. Incapable of being apprehended by the mind or the senses: *imperceptible variations in the patient's breathing. Color is imperceptible to the touch.*
   Syns: impalpable, imponderable, inappreciable, indiscernible, indistinguishable, insensible, intangible, invisible, unappreciable, undistinguishable, unnoticeable, unobservable.
2. So minute as to be undiscernible: *imperceptible particles in liquid suspension.*
   Syns: infinitesimal, microscopic.
imperfect *adjective* DEFECTIVE.
imperfection *noun* DEFECT.
imperil *verb* ENDANGER.
imperilment *noun* DANGER.
imperious *adjective* DICTATORIAL.
impermanent *adjective* TEMPORARY.
impermissible *adjective* FORBIDDEN.
impersonal *adjective* NEUTRAL.
impersonate *verb*
1. ACT.
2. POSE.
impersonator *noun* MIMIC.
impertinence *noun* IMPUDENCE.
impertinent *adjective*
1. IMPUDENT.
2. IRRELEVANT.
imperturbability *noun* NONCHALANCE.
imperturbable *adjective* COOL.
impervious *adjective* RESISTANT.
imperviousness *noun* RESISTANCE.
impetuous *adjective*
1. PRECIPITATE.
2. RASH[1].
impetus *noun* STIMULUS.
impignorate *verb* PAWN[1].
impishness *noun* MISCHIEF.
implacable *adjective* GRIM.
implausible *adjective*
Not plausible or believable: *an implausible alibi.*
   Syns: flimsy, improbable, inconceivable, incredible, shaky, thick, thin, unbelievable, unconceivable, unconvincing, unsubstantial, weak.
implement *verb*
1. ENFORCE.
2. FULFILL.
3. USE.
implement *noun* TOOL.
implementation *noun* APPLICATION.
implicate *verb* INVOLVE.
implication *noun* HINT.
implicit *adjective*
1. Conveyed indirectly without words or

speech: *Those companies reached an implicit agreement to fix prices.*
Syns: implied, inferred, tacit, undeclared, understood, unexpressed, unsaid, unspoken, unuttered, wordless. —*Idiom* taken for granted.
2. Involved in the essential nature of something but not shown or developed: *Suspicion is implicit in that tone of voice.*
Syns: practical, virtual.
3. Having no reservations: *I have implicit trust in you.*
Syns: unconditional, undoubting, unhesitating, unquestioning, unreserved, wholehearted.
implied *adjective* IMPLICIT.
imploration *noun* APPEAL.
implore *verb* APPEAL.
imply *verb*
1. To lead to by logical inference: *His aims imply a good deal of effort.*
Syns: indicate, point to, suggest.
2. HINT.
impolite *adjective* RUDE.
impolitic *adjective*
1. TACTLESS.
2. UNWISE.
imponderable *adjective* IMPERCEPTIBLE.
import *noun*
1. The general sense or significance, as of an action, statement, etc.: *The import of his words did not register until much later.*
Syns: amount, burden, drift, purport, substance. —*Idioms* sum and substance, sum total.
2. IMPORTANCE.
3. MEANING.
import *verb*
1. COUNT.
2. MEAN[1].
importance *noun*
The quality or state of being important: *Energy conservation is a matter of great importance.*
Syns: concern, concernment, consequence, import, moment, significance (*also* significancy), weight, weightiness.
important *adjective*
1. Having great significance: *an important news story.*
Syns: big, consequential, considerable, historic, large, material, meaningful, momentous, significant, substantial, weighty.
2. INFLUENTIAL.
importunate *adjective* BURNING.

importune *verb* BESIEGE.
impose *verb*
1. To establish and apply as compulsory: *imposed a tax on imported oil.*
Syns: assess, exact, levy, put.
2. To force (another) to accept a burden: *Don't try to impose that hard job on me!*
Syns: foist, inflict, saddle, stick (*Slang*).
3. ABUSE.
4. DICTATE.
5. INFLICT.
imposing *adjective* GRAND.
imposition *noun*
An excessive, unwelcome burden: *Unannounced house guests are an imposition on the hostess.*
Syns: infliction, intrusion.
impossible *adjective*
1. Not capable of happening or being done: *impossible dreams; an impossible plan.*
Syns: impracticable, impractical, irrealizable, unattainable, unfeasible, unrealizable, unthinkable, unworkable. —*Idioms* beyond the bounds of possibility (*or* reason), out of the question.
2. CONTRARY.
3. HOPELESS.
4. INCREDIBLE.
5. UNBEARABLE.
impost *noun*
1. BURDEN.
2. TAX.
impostor *noun* FAKE.
imposture *noun* DECEPTION.
impotence *noun* INEFFECTUALITY.
impotent *adjective*
1. HELPLESS.
2. INEFFECTUAL.
impoverish *verb*
1. DEPLETE.
2. RUIN.
impoverished *adjective*
1. DEPRESS.
2, 3. POOR.
impoverishment *noun* POVERTY.
impracticable *adjective*
1. Incapable of being used or availed of to advantage: *chose an impracticable route through the desert.*
Syns: impractical, unnegotiable, unserviceable, unusable, unworkable, useless.
2. IMPOSSIBLE.
impractical *adjective*
1. Incapable of dealing efficiently with

practical matters: *a complex,
impractical solution to the problem.*
Syns: ivory-tower, ivory-towered,
ivory-towerish.
IMPOSSIBLE.
IMPRACTICABLE.

precate *verb*
CURSE.
SWEAR.

precation *noun* CURSE.

pregnable *adjective* INVINCIBLE.

pregnate *verb* CHARGE.

press *verb*
To fix (an idea) in someone's mind
by re-emphasis and repetition:
*impressed the necessity of water safety
in the minds of the children.*
Syns: drive, inculcate, pound.
AFFECT[1].
ENGRAVE.

npress *noun* IMPRESSION.

pressed *adjective* AFFECTED[1].

pressible *adjective* SENSITIVE.

pression *noun*
The visible effect made on a surface
by pressure: *saw the impression of a
heavy boot in the sand.*
Syns: impress, imprint, indent,
indentation, print, stamp.
Print. The entire number of copies of
a publication printed from a single
typesetting: *the third impression of a
book.*
Syn: printing.
FEELING.
IMAGE.

pressionable *adjective* SENSITIVE.

pressionistic *adjective*
UGGESTIVE.

pressive *adjective*
AFFECTING.
GRAND.

print *verb* ENGRAVE.

nprint *noun* IMPRESSION.

prison *verb*
To enclose so as to hinder or prohibit
escape: *We were imprisoned in the
house during the blizzard.*
Syns: closet, confine, isolate, shut up.
JAIL.

probable *adjective*
DOUBTFUL.
IMPLAUSIBLE.

probity *noun*
CORRUPTION.
DISHONESTY.

promptu *adjective*
XTEMPORANEOUS.

mpromptu *noun* IMPROVISATION.

improper *adjective*
1. Not suited to circumstances: *wore
improper attire for church.*
Syns: inappropriate, inapt, inept,
incongruous, malapropos, unapt,
unbecoming, unbefitting, unfitting,
unseemly, unsuitable. —*Idiom* out of
place.
2. Not in keeping with conventional
mores: *nothing improper about going
alone; used improper language when
drunk.*
Syns: indecent, indecorous, indelicate,
unbecoming, unbefitting, unseemly,
untoward. —*Idiom* out of line.

impropriety *noun*
1. The condition of being improper: *the
impropriety of speaking one's mind at
the wrong time.*
Syns: inappropriateness, unfitness,
unseemliness, unsuitability,
unsuitableness.
2. An improper act or statement: *barred
from the club after his improprieties at
the dance.*
Syns: indecency, indecorum,
indelicacy.

improve *verb*
1. To advance to a more desirable state:
Practice will improve your golf game.
Syns: ameliorate, amend, better[1],
help, meliorate, upgrade.
2. RECOVER.

improvement *noun*
1. Something that improves: *made
improvements in the working
conditions.*
Syns: amelioration, amendment,
betterment, melioration, upgrading.
2. PROGRESS.

improvident *adjective*
1. Reckless esp. in the use of material
resources: *ended his life as a pauper
due to his improvident lifestyle.*
Syns: thriftless, unthrifty.
2. UNWISE.

improvisation *noun*
Something improvised: *The speech was a
skillful improvisation.*
Syns: ad-lib (*Informal*),
extemporization, impromptu.

improvise *verb*
To compose or recite without
preparation: *He had to improvise the
monologue on camera.*
Syns: ad-lib (*Informal*), extemporize,
fake (*Slang*), make up. —*Idiom* wing
it.

improvised *adjective*
EXTEMPORANEOUS.

imprudent *adjective* UNWISE.

impudence *also* **impudency** *noun*
The state or quality of being impudent: *made to apologize for his impudence.*
Syns: audacity, boldness, brazenness, cheek, disrespect, effrontery, forwardness, gall[2], impertinence, insolence (*also* insolency), nerve (*Informal*), rudeness, sauce (*Informal*), sauciness.

impudent *adjective*
Rude and disrespectful: *was reproved for being impudent; made an impudent remark; an impudent child who never obeyed.*
Syns: audacious, bold, boldacious (*Brit. Regional*), brazen, cheeky, contumelious, facy (*Brit. Regional*), flip (*Informal*), forward, fresh (*Informal*), impertinent, insolent, malapert, nervy (*Informal*), pert, presumptuous, sassy, saucy, smart, smart-alecky (*Informal*), wise[1].

impulse *noun*
1. FANCY.
2. STIMULUS.

impulsive *adjective*
1. PRECIPITATE.
2. RASH[1].
3. SPONTANEOUS.

impure *adjective*
1. Ceremonially or religiously unfit: *communion vessels made impure by vandalism.*
   Syns: contaminated, defiled, desecrated, polluted, unclean.
2. Not chaste or moral: *confessed to thinking impure thoughts.*
   Syns: immoral, unchaste, unclean, uncleanly.
3. Mixed with other substances: *impure gold.*
   Syns: adulterated, alloyed, degraded.
4. CRUDE.

impurity *noun*
1. Impure condition: *Smog increases the impurity of the air.*
   Syns: dirtiness, foulness, pollution, uncleanness, unwholesomeness.
2. CONTAMINANT.

imputation *noun*
1. ACCUSATION.
2. ATTRIBUTION.

impute *verb*
1. ATTRIBUTE.
2. FIX.

in *adjective* FASHIONABLE.

inability *noun*
Lack of ability or capacity: *has a real inability to follow a diet.*

Syns: incapability, incapacity, powerlessness.

inaccessible *adjective*
1. Unable to be reached: *His house is distant and inaccessible.*
   Syns: unapproachable, unattainable, unreachable. —*Idioms* beyond reach, out of the way.
2. INCONVENIENT.

inaccurate *adjective*
1. ERRONEOUS.
2. FALSE.

inaction *noun*
A lack of action or activity: *Danger forced him out of his inaction.*
Syns: idleness, inactivity, inertness, lethargy, stagnation, torpor.

inactive *adjective*
1. Marked by a lack of action or activity: *an inactive volcano; an invalid leading an inactive life.*
   Syns: idle, inert, inoperative.
2. IDLE.
3. SLEEPING.

inactivity *noun* INACTION.

inadequacy *noun* INEFFECTUALITY.

inadequate *adjective*
1. Lacking capability: *felt inadequate to the task.*
   Syns: incapable, incompetent, unequal, unfit, unqualified.
2. INEFFECTUAL.
3. INSUFFICIENT.

inadmissible *adjective* OBJECTIONABLE.

inadvertent *adjective*
1. ACCIDENTAL.
2. UNINTENTIONAL.

inalterable *adjective* INFLEXIBLE.

inane *adjective* INSIPID.

inaneness *noun* INSIPIDITY.

inanity *noun* INSIPIDITY.

inapplicable *adjective* IRRELEVANT.

inappreciable *adjective* IMPERCEPTIBLE.

inappropriate *adjective*
1. IMPROPER.
2. UNFIT.
3. UNFORTUNATE.

inappropriateness *noun* IMPROPRIETY.

inapt *adjective*
1. IMPROPER.
2. INEFFICIENT.
3. UNFIT.

inarguable *adjective* CERTAIN.

inarticulate *adjective* DUMB.

inattentive *adjective* ABSENT-MINDED.

inaugural *noun* INITIATION.

inaugurate *verb*
1. INITIATE.
2. INTRODUCE.
3. START.

inauguration *noun*
1. BEGINNING.
2. INITIATION.

inauspicious *adjective* BAD.

inborn *adjective*
1. BUILT-IN.
2. CONSTITUTIONAL.
3. INNATE.

inbred *adjective*
1. BUILT-IN.
2. CONSTITUTIONAL.

incalculable *adjective*
Too great to be calculated: *an incalculable number of mosquitoes.*
   Syns: countless, immeasurable, incomputable, inestimable, infinite, innumerable, measureless, uncountable.

incandesce *verb*
1. BEAM.
2. GLOW.

incandescent *adjective* BRIGHT.

incapability *noun*
1. INABILITY.
2. INEFFECTUALITY.

incapable *adjective*
1. HELPLESS.
2. INADEQUATE.
3. INEFFICIENT.

incapacitate *verb* DISABLE.

incapacity *noun* INABILITY.

incarcerate *verb* JAIL.

incarnate *verb* EMBODY.

incarnation *noun* EMBODIMENT.

incautious *adjective* IRRESPONSIBLE.

incense[1] *verb* ANGER.

incense[2] *noun* FLATTERY.

incensed *adjective* ANGRY.

incentive *noun* STIMULUS.

inception *noun*
1. BEGINNING.
2. BIRTH.

inceptive *adjective* BEGINNING.

incertitude *noun* DOUBT.

incessant *adjective* CONTINUAL.

inch *verb* CRAWL.

inchoate *adjective* SHAPELESS.

incident *noun*
1. CIRCUMSTANCE.
2. EVENT.

incident *adjective* ACCIDENTAL.

incidental *adjective* ACCIDENTAL.

incise *verb*
1. CUT.
2. ENGRAVE.

incision *noun* CUT.

incisive *adjective*
1. Having or suggesting keen, discerning intellect: *an incisive analysis of the problem.*
   Syns: acute, biting, clear-cut, penetrating, perceptive, probing, sharp, shrewd, trenchant.
2. BITING.

incisiveness *noun* EDGE.

incitation *noun* STIMULUS.

incite *verb* PROVOKE.

incitement *noun* STIMULUS.

incivility *noun* DISRESPECT.

inclination *noun*
1. Deviation from a particular direction: *an inclination of 45° from the horizontal.*
   Syns: cant[1], gradient, incline, slope, slant, tilt.
2. TALENT.
3. TASTE.

incline *verb*
1. To depart or cause to depart from true vertical or horizontal: *The flagpole inclines toward the roof.*
   Syns: cant[1], heel[2], lean[1], list[2], rake[2], slant, slope, tilt, tip[2].
2. DISPOSE.
3. TEND[1].

incline *noun* INCLINATION.

inclined *adjective*
1. Departing from true vertical or horizontal: *an inclined plane.*
   Syns: canted, pitched, sloped, sloping, tilted, tilting, tipped.
2. Having or showing a tendency or likelihood: *inclined to take offense easily.*
   Syns: apt, disposed, given, liable, likely, prone, susceptible.
3. WILLING.

include *verb* CONTAIN.

inclusive *adjective* GENERAL.

incomer *noun* ARRIVAL.

incommode *verb* INCONVENIENCE.

incommodious *adjective*
1. EMBARRASSING.
2. INCONVENIENT.

incommunicable *adjective*
1. RESERVED.
2. UNSPEAKABLE.

incomparable *adjective* UNIQUE.

incompatible *adjective*
INCONGRUOUS.

incompetent *adjective*
1. Totally incapable of doing a job: *weed out a few incompetent employees.*
   Syns: unfit, unqualified.
2. INADEQUATE.
3. INEFFICIENT.

incomplete *adjective* DEFICIENT.
incompliance or **incompliancy** *noun*
OBSTINACY.
incompliant *adjective* OBSTINATE.
incomprehensible *adjective*
Incapable of being grasped by the
intellect or understanding: *spoke an
incomprehensible dialect; a decision that
is incomprehensible to me.*
   Syns: impenetrable, unfathomable,
uncomprehensible, unintelligible.
incompressible *adjective* FIRM[1].
incomputable *adjective*
INCALCULABLE.
inconceivable *adjective*
1. IMPLAUSIBLE.
2. INCREDIBLE.
incongruent *adjective*
1. CONFLICTING.
2. INCONGRUOUS.
incongruity *noun* GAP.
incongruous *adjective*
1. Made up of parts or qualities that are
   disparate or otherwise markedly
   lacking in consistency: *a hodgepodge
   of incongruous literary styles.*
   Syns: disconsonant, discordant,
   discrepant, dissonant, incompatible,
   incongruent, inconsistent.
2. CONFLICTING.
3. IMPROPER.
inconquerable *adjective* INVINCIBLE.
inconscient *adjective*
ABSENT-MINDED.
inconscious *adjective* UNCONSCIOUS.
inconsequence *noun*
1. INDIFFERENCE.
2. PETTINESS.
inconsequent *adjective* PETTY.
inconsequential *adjective*
1. LITTLE.
2. PETTY.
inconsiderable *adjective* PETTY.
inconsiderate *adjective*
THOUGHTLESS.
inconsiderateness *noun*
THOUGHTLESSNESS.
inconsideration *noun*
THOUGHTLESSNESS.
inconsistency *noun* GAP.
inconsistent *adjective*
1. CAPRICIOUS.
2. CONFLICTING.
3. INCONGRUOUS.
inconsonant *adjective*
INHARMONIOUS.
inconspicuous *adjective*
Not readily noticed or seen: *an
inconspicuous flaw; a former public figure*

who now lived an inconspicuous life as a
private citizen.
   Syns: obscure, unconspicuous,
unnoticeable, unobtrusive. —*Idiom*
having (or keeping) a low profile.
inconstant *adjective* CAPRICIOUS.
incontestable *adjective* CERTAIN.
incontinence *noun* ABANDON.
incontinent *adjective* ABANDONED.
incontrovertible *adjective* CERTAIN.
inconvenience *noun*
1. The state or quality of being
   inconvenient: *the inconvenience caused
   by poor lighting.*
   Syns: discomfort, inconveniency,
   trouble.
2. Something that causes difficulty,
   trouble, or lack of ease: *Rising before
   dawn was an inconvenience.*
   Syn: discomfort.
inconvenience *verb*
To cause inconvenience for:
inconvenienced her by arriving late.
   Syns: discomfort, incommode, put
out, trouble.
inconveniency *noun* INCONVENIENCE.
inconvenient *adjective*
1. Not accessible or handy: *an
   inconvenient location for a shop.*
   Syns: inaccessible, unhandy.
2. Causing difficulty, trouble, or
   discomfort: *Being without modern
   plumbing was inconvenient.*
   Syns: difficult, disadvantageous,
   discomforting, incommodious,
   troublesome.
3. Not occurring at a favorable time: *an
   inconvenient appointment.*
   Syns: ill-timed, inopportune,
   untimely.
4. AWKWARD.
incorporate *verb*
1. BUILD IN at build.
2. EMBODY.
incorporated *adjective* BUILT-IN.
incorporeal *adjective* IMMATERIAL.
incorrect *adjective*
1. ERRONEOUS.
2. FALSE.
incorruptibility also **incorruptibleness**
noun HONESTY.
incorruptible *adjective* HONEST.
incorruptibleness *noun* SEE
incorruptibility.
increase *verb*
1. To make or become greater or larger:
   *increased her income; difficulties that
   seemed to increase daily.*
   Syns: aggrandize, amplify, augment,
   beef up (*Slang*), build up, enlarge,

expand, extend, grow, magnify,
mount, multiply, run up, snowball,
swell, upsurge, wax.
2, 3. GAIN.
4. RISE.
increase *noun*
1. The act of increasing or rising:
*seasonal increases in sales; property
values showing an increase; an increase
in enemy infiltration.*
Syns: augmentation, boost,
enlargement, growth, hike, jump,
multiplication, rise, upswing, upturn.
2. The amount by which something is
increased: *a wage increase of $50 per
month.*
Syns: advance, boost, enlargement,
hike, increment, jump, raise, rise.
3. BUILD-UP.
incredible *adjective*
1. Not to be believed: *an incredible
blunder; a weapon of incredible power.*
Syns: impossible, inconceivable,
preposterous, unbelievable,
unimaginable, unthinkable. —*Idioms*
beyond belief, contrary to all reason.
2. FABULOUS.
3. IMPLAUSIBLE.
incredulity *noun* DISBELIEF.
incredulous *adjective*
Refusing or reluctant to believe: *trying
to reassure incredulous customers.*
Syns: disbelieving, leery (*Informal*),
questioning, skeptical, unbelieving.
increment *noun*
1. BUILD-UP.
2. INCREASE.
incriminate *verb* ACCUSE.
incriminating *adjective*
ACCUSATORIAL.
incrimination *noun* ACCUSATION.
incriminative *adjective*
ACCUSATORIAL.
incriminator *noun* ACCUSER.
inculcate *verb*
1. IMPRESS.
2. INDOCTRINATE.
inculpate *verb* ACCUSE.
incumbency *noun* TENURE.
incur *verb* ASSUME.
incurable *adjective* HOPELESS.
incurious *adjective* DETACHED.
incursion *noun* INVASION.
indebted *adjective* OBLIGED.
indebtedness *noun* DEBT.
indecency *noun*
1. IMPROPRIETY.
2. OBSCENITY.

indecent *adjective*
1. IMPROPER.
2. OBSCENE.
indecision *noun* HESITATION.
indecisive *adjective*
1. AMBIGUOUS.
2. HESITANT.
indecisiveness *noun* HESITATION.
indecorous *adjective* IMPROPER.
indecorum *noun* IMPROPRIETY.
indeed *adverb*
1. ACTUALLY.
2. EVEN[1].
3. REALLY.
indefatigable *adjective* TIRELESS.
indefectible *adjective* PERFECT.
indefensible *adjective* INEXCUSABLE.
indefinable *adjective* UNSPEAKABLE.
indefinite *adjective*
1. Lacking precise limits: *plans to be
away for an indefinite period.*
Syns: indeterminate, inexact,
undetermined.
2. Marked by lack of firm decision or
commitment; of questionable
outcome: *vacation plans that are still
indefinite.*
Syns: open, uncertain, undecided,
undetermined, unresolved, unsettled,
unsure, vague. —*Idiom* up in the air.
3. UNCLEAR.
indefiniteness *noun* VAGUENESS.
indelible *adjective* FAST.
indelicacy *noun* IMPROPRIETY.
indelicate *adjective*
1. IMPROPER.
2. TACTLESS.
indemnification *noun*
COMPENSATION.
indemnificatory *adjective*
COMPENSATORY.
indemnify *verb* COMPENSATE.
indemnity *noun* COMPENSATION.
indent *noun* IMPRESSION.
indentation *noun* IMPRESSION.
indented *adjective* HOLLOW.
independence *noun*
1. The capacity to manage one's own
affairs, make one's own judgments,
and provide for oneself: *showed her
independence by getting a job and
moving out.*
Syns: self-determination, self-reliance,
self-sufficiency.
2. FREEDOM.
independent *adjective*
1. Free from the influence, guidance, or
control of others: *an independent
mind.*

Syns: self-contained, self-reliant, self-sufficient.

2. Able to support oneself financially: *a job that made her independent.*
Syns: self-sufficient, self-supporting.

3. FREE.

indescribable *adjective*
UNSPEAKABLE.

indeterminate *adjective*
1. AMBIGUOUS.
2. INDEFINITE.

index *noun* SIGN.

indicate *verb*
1. To give grounds for believing in the existence or presence of: *High unemployment usually indicates a sick economy.*
Syns: argue, attest, bespeak, betoken, mark, point to, testify, witness.

2. DESIGNATE.
3. IMPLY.
4. PROMISE.
5. SHOW.

indication *noun*
1. EXPRESSION.
2. GESTURE.
3. HINT.
4. SIGN.

indicative *adjective*
1. DESIGNATIVE.
2. SYMBOLIC.

indicator *noun* SIGN.

indicatory *adjective* DESIGNATIVE.

indict *verb* ACCUSE.

indicter *noun* SEE **indictor**.

indictment *noun* ACCUSATION.

indictor also **indicter** *noun* ACCUSER.

indifference *noun*
1. Lack of importance: *Their approval is a matter of complete indifference to me.*
Syns: inconsequence, insignificance (*also* insignificancy), unimportance.

2. APATHY.

indifferent *adjective*
1. ACCEPTABLE.
2. APATHETIC.
3. DETACHED.
4. FAIR.

indigence also **indigency** *noun*
POVERTY.

indigenous *adjective*
1. Existing, born, or produced naturally in a land or region: *plants indigenous to the New World; a disease indigenous to the Far East.*
Syns: endemic, native.

2. CONSTITUTIONAL.

indigent *adjective* POOR.

indigent *noun* PAUPER.

indigestible *adjective* BITTER.

indignant *adjective* ANGRY.

indignation *noun* ANGER.

indignity *noun*
An act that offends a person's sense of pride or dignity: *suffered the indignity of being ignored by his own children.*
Syns: affront, contumely, despite, insult, offense, outrage. —*Idiom* slap in the face.

indirect *adjective*
1. Not taking a direct or straight line or course: *made an indirect approach to the painful subject.*
Syns: anfractuous, circuitous, circular, oblique, roundabout, tortuous.

2. UNDERHAND.

indirection *noun*
Lack of straightforwardness and honesty in action: *achieve a goal by indirection.*
Syns: chicanery, craft, craftiness, deviousness, dishonesty, shadiness, slyness, sneakiness, trickery, trickiness, underhandedness.

indiscernible *adjective*
IMPERCEPTIBLE.

indiscriminate *adjective* RANDOM.

indispensable *adjective* ESSENTIAL.

indisposed *adjective*
1. Not inclined or willing to do or undertake: *indisposed to interfere in their quarrel.*
Syns: averse, disinclined, loath (*also* loth), reluctant, unwilling.

2. SICKLY.

indisposition *noun*
1. A minor illness, esp. one of a temporary nature: *lost a day's work because of an indisposition.*
Syns: ailment, complaint, rockiness.

2. The state of not being disposed or inclined: *The slowness of her response revealed an indisposition to help.*
Syns: averseness, disinclination, reluctance, unwillingness.

3. SICKNESS.

indisputable *adjective*
1. ACTUAL.
2. CERTAIN.

indistinct *adjective* UNCLEAR.

indistinctive *adjective* NEUTRAL.

indistinguishable *adjective*
IMPERCEPTIBLE.

indite *verb*
1. COMPOSE.
2. WRITE.

individual *adjective*
1. Being or related to a distinct entity: *the individual words that make up a sentence.*

Syns: discrete, separate, single, singular.
2. DISTINCTIVE.
3. PERSONAL.
4. SPECIAL.

individual *noun*
1. HUMAN BEING.
2. THING.

individualism *noun* IDENTITY.

individualist *adjective* EGOCENTRIC.

individualistic *adjective* EGOCENTRIC.

individuality *noun*
1. The quality of being individual: *a slowly emerging sense of individuality.*
Syns: discreteness, distinctiveness, particularity, separateness, singularity.
2. IDENTITY.

individualize *verb* DISTINGUISH.

indocile *adjective* UNRULY.

indoctrinate *verb*
1. To instruct in a body of doctrine or belief: *lectures intended to indoctrinate soldiers with patriotic ideas.*
Syns: drill, inculcate, instill.
2. To teach to accept a system of thought uncritically: *prisoners indoctrinated by a system of rewards and punishments.*
Syns: brainwash, propagandize.

indolence *noun* LAZINESS.

indolent *adjective* LAZY.

indomitable *adjective*
1. INSUPERABLE.
2. UNRULY.

indubitable *adjective*
1. AUTHENTIC.
2. CERTAIN.

induce *verb*
1. CAUSE.
2. GENERATE.
3. PERSUADE.

inducement *noun*
1. INVITATION.
2. LURE.

induct *verb*
1. DRAFT.
2. INITIATE.

induction *noun*
1. DRAFT.
2. INITIATION.

inductive *adjective* PRELIMINARY.

indulge *verb*
1. BABY.
2. HUMOR.
3. LUXURIATE.
4. PARTICIPATE.
5. SATISFY.

indulgence *noun*
1. COURTESY.
2. FAVOR.
3. TOLERANCE.

indulgent *adjective*
1. OBLIGING.
2. TOLERANT.

indurate *verb*
1, 2. HARDEN.

industrious *adjective* DILIGENT.

industriousness *noun* DILIGENCE.

industry *noun*
1. BUSINESS.
2. DILIGENCE.

indwelling *adjective* CONSTITUTIONAL.

inebriate *verb*
To make drunk: *a brandy that inebriates with one sip.*
Syn: intoxicate.

inebriate *adjective* DRUNK.

inebriate *noun* DRUNKARD.

inebriated *adjective* DRUNK.

inebriation *noun* DRUNKENNESS.

inebriety *noun* DRUNKENNESS.

ineffable *adjective* UNSPEAKABLE.

ineffective *adjective*
1. FUTILE.
2. INEFFECTUAL.

ineffectiveness *noun*
1. FUTILITY.
2. INEFFECTUALITY.

ineffectual *adjective*
1. Not having the desired effect: *an ineffectual remedy for inflation.*
Syns: ineffective, inefficacious, inefficient.
2. Not capable of accomplishing anything: *an ineffectual leader.*
Syns: impotent, inadequate, powerless, weak.
3. FUTILE.
4. USELESS.

ineffectuality *noun*
1. The condition or state of being incapable of accomplishing or effecting anything: *showed her ineffectuality in getting the cooperation of the community.*
Syns: impotence, inadequacy, incapability, ineffectiveness, ineffectualness, inefficacy, powerlessness.
2. FUTILITY.

ineffectualness *noun*
1. FUTILITY.
2. INEFFECTUALITY.

inefficacious *adjective* INEFFECTUAL.

inefficacy *noun*
1. FUTILITY.
2. INEFFECTUALITY.

inefficient *adjective*
1. Lacking the qualities, as efficiency or

skill, required to produce desired results: *inefficient workers.*
Syns: inapt, incapable, incompetent, inept, inexpert, unapt, unskilled, unskillful, unworkmanlike.
2. INEFFECTUAL.

inelastic *adjective* RIGID.
inelegant *adjective* TACKY².
inenarrable *adjective* UNSPEAKABLE.
inept *adjective*
1. AWKWARD.
2. IMPROPER.
3. INEFFICIENT.
4. UNFORTUNATE.
5. UNSKILLFUL.

inequality *noun*
1. The condition or fact of being unequal, as in age, rank, or degree: *the inequality between the rich and the poor.*
Syns: disparity, disproportion.
2. IRREGULARITY.

inequitable *adjective* UNFAIR.
inequitableness *noun* INJUSTICE.
inequity *noun* INJUSTICE.
inert *adjective* INACTIVE.
inertness *noun* INACTION.
inescapable *adjective* CERTAIN.
inessential *adjective* UNNECESSARY.
inestimable *adjective*
1. INCALCULABLE.
2. VALUABLE.

inevitable *adjective* CERTAIN.
inexact *adjective*
1. INDEFINITE.
2. LOOSE.

inexcusable *adjective*
Impossible to excuse, pardon, or justify: *an inexcusable insult.*
Syns: indefensible, unforgivable, unjustifiable, unpardonable.

inexhaustibility *noun* INFINITY.
inexhaustible *adjective* TIRELESS.
inexorable *adjective*
1. GRIM.
2. STUBBORN.

inexpensive *adjective* CHEAP.
inexperience *noun*
Lack of experience and the knowledge gained from it: *will make allowances for her inexperience.*
Syns: greenness, inexpertness.

inexperienced *adjective*
Lacking experience and the knowledge gained from it: *Inexperienced employees are seldom paid more than the minimum wage.*
Syns: green, inexpert, raw, unpracticed, unseasoned, untried, unversed.

inexpert *adjective*
1. CRUDE.
2. INEFFICIENT.
3. INEXPERIENCED.

inexpertness *noun* INEXPERIENCE.
inexplicable *adjective*
That cannot be explained: *an inexplicable burst of anger.*
Syns: unaccountable, unexplainable.

inexpressible *adjective* UNSPEAKABLE.
inexpressive *adjective*
EXPRESSIONLESS.
inextricably *adverb* HELPLESSLY.
infallible *adjective* SURE.
infamous *adjective*
1. Deserving strong condemnation: *guilty of an infamous crime.*
Syns: abhorrent, despicable, detestable, foul, perfidious, reprehensible, shocking, vile.
2. NOTORIOUS.

infamy *noun*
1. The condition of being infamous: *President Roosevelt said that December 7, 1941, was a day that would live in infamy.*
Syns: disgracefulness, dishonorableness, odiousness, perfidy, shamefulness, villainy, wickedness.
2. NOTORIETY.

infancy *noun* MINORITY.
infant *noun*
1. BABY.
2. MINOR.

infant *adjective* YOUNG.
infantile *adjective*
1. BABYISH.
2. CHILDISH.

infatuated *adjective*
Affected with intense romantic attraction: *a prince infatuated with a chorus girl.*
Syns: beguiled, bewitched, captivated, enamored, gone (*Slang*), mashed (*Slang*), smitten.

infatuation *noun*
An extravagant, short-lived romantic attachment: *an infatuation with her geography professor.*
Syns: béguin (*French*), crush (*Informal*), passion.

infect *verb*
1. POISON.
2. TAINT.

infectious *adjective* COMMUNICABLE.
infecund *adjective* BARREN.
infecundity *noun* STERILITY.
infelicitous *adjective* UNFORTUNATE.
infer *verb*
1. To draw a conclusion from evidence

or reasoning: *Am I to infer that you're not going?*
Syns: conclude, deduce, deduct, draw, gather, judge.
2. GUESS.

inference *noun* DEDUCTION.

inferior *adjective*
1. Of mediocre quality: *The inferior cloth quickly disintegrated.*
Syns: common, low-grade, low-quality, mean², miserable, second-class, second-rate, substandard.
2. MINOR.

inferior *noun* SUBORDINATE.

infernal *adjective*
1. DAMNED.
2. FIENDISH.

inferred *adjective*
1. IMPLICIT.
2. PRESUMPTIVE.

infertile *adjective*
1, 2. BARREN.

infertility *noun* STERILITY.

infidelity *noun* FAITHLESSNESS.

infiltrate *verb* INSINUATE.

infinite *adjective*
1. ENDLESS.
2. ETERNAL.
3. INCALCULABLE.

infiniteness *noun* INFINITY.

infinitesimal *adjective*
IMPERCEPTIBLE.

infinity *noun*
1. The state or quality of being infinite: *Nature's variety is close to infinity.*
Syns: boundlessness, inexhaustibility, infiniteness, limitlessness.
2. ETERNITY.

infirm *adjective*
1. Not physically strong: *too infirm to resume his daily walks.*
Syns: decrepit, delicate, feeble, fragile, frail, insubstantial, puny, unsound, unsubstantial, weak, weakly.
2. INSECURE.

infirmity *noun*
1. The condition of being infirm or physically weak: *Infirmity often comes with old age.*
Syns: debilitation, debility, decrepitude, feebleness, fragility, frailty, unsoundness, weakliness, weakness.
2. DISEASE.
3. SICKNESS.
4. WEAKNESS.

infix *verb* FIX.

inflame *verb*
1. IRRITATE.
2. PROVOKE.

inflamed *adjective* FURIOUS.

inflammation *noun* IRRITATION.

inflate *verb* EXAGGERATE.

inflated *adjective*
Filled up with or as if with something insubstantial: *has a highly inflated ego.*
Syns: flatulent, overblown, tumescent, tumid, turgid, windy (*Chiefly Scot.*).

inflatus *noun* INSPIRATION.

inflection *noun* TONE.

inflexible *adjective*
1. Incapable of changing or being modified: *inflexible standards of performance.*
Syns: immutable, inalterable, invariable, ironclad, rigid, stiff, unalterable, unchangeable, unpliant, unyielding.
2. RIGID.
3. STUBBORN.

inflict *verb*
1. To cause to undergo or bear, as something unwelcome or damaging: *inflicting punishment; a storm that inflicted widespread destruction.*
Syns: impose, play, visit, wreak.
2. IMPOSE.

infliction *noun* IMPOSITION.

influence *noun*
1. The power to produce an effect by indirect means: *a special-interest group with influence on Capitol Hill.*
Syns: clout (*Informal*), drag (*Slang*), leverage, pull (*Slang*), sway, weight.
2. EFFECT.

influence *verb*
1. To have an effect or impact upon: *Don't let him influence your decision.*
Syns: bias, prejudice, sway.
2. AFFECT¹.

influential *adjective*
Having or exercising influence: *one of our more influential citizens.*
Syns: consequential, important, powerful, weighty.

infold *verb* SEE **enfold.**

inform *verb*
1. To cause to know about or be aware of: *Inform everyone of the change in schedule. Was he informed of his rights?*
Syns: acquaint, advise, apprise (*also* apprize) (of), educate, enlighten, notify, tell.
2. To give incriminating information about others, esp. to the authorities: *The thief informed on his accomplice.*

Syns: fink (*Slang*), rat (*Slang*), sing (*Slang*), snitch (*Slang*), squeal (*Slang*), stool (*Slang*), talk, tattle. —*Idiom* blow the whistle.

informal *adjective*
1. Not formal or ceremonious: *an informal gathering of close friends; wore informal attire.*
   Syns: simple, unceremonious, unpretentious.
2. CONVERSATIONAL.
3. EASYGOING.

informality *noun*
1. Lack or avoidance of formality: *a candlelight supper served with charming informality.*
   Syns: casualness, naturalness, simplicity, unceremoniousness.
2. EASE.

informant *noun* INFORMER.

information *noun*
1. Knowledge about a specific subject or situation: *gathering information for a biography.*
   Syns: data, facts, intelligence.
2. KNOWLEDGE.

informative *adjective* EDUCATIONAL.

informed *adjective*
1. Provided with information; made aware: *able to give an informed opinion; one of our best-informed officials.*
   Syns: advised, educated, enlightened, instructed, knowledgeable.
2. EDUCATED.

informer *noun*
One who gives incriminating information about others: *He's a paid informer.*
   Syns: fink (*Slang*), informant, rat (*Slang*), snitch (*also* snitcher) (*Slang*), squealer (*Slang*), stoolie (*Slang*), stool pigeon (*Slang*), tattler, tattletale, tipster.

infra *adverb* LATER.

infraction *noun* BREACH.

infrequent *adjective*
Rarely occurring or appearing: *Our parties are infrequent these days. He is an infrequent visitor.*
   Syns: occasional, rare, scarce, sporadic, uncommon, unusual. —*Idiom* few and far between.

infrequently *adverb*
At rare intervals: *I now go to Europe infrequently if at all.*
   Syns: little, rarely, seldom. —*Idioms* hardly (*or* scarcely) ever, once in a blue moon.

infringement *noun* BREACH.

infuriate *verb* ANGER.

infuriated *adjective* FURIOUS.

ingenerate *adjective*
1. CONSTITUTIONAL.
2. INNATE.

ingenerate *verb* CAUSE.

ingenious *adjective*
1. INVENTIVE.
2. RESOURCEFUL.

ingénue *noun* INNOCENT.

ingenuity *noun* INVENTION.

ingenuous *adjective* ARTLESS.

ingest *verb*
1. EAT.
2. SWALLOW.

ingestion *noun* SWALLOW.

ingrain *verb* FIX.

ingrained *adjective*
1. CONFIRMED.
2. CONSTITUTIONAL.

ingratiating *adjective* INSINUATING.

ingratiative *adjective* INSINUATING.

ingredient *noun* ELEMENT.

ingress *verb* ENTER.

ingress *also* **ingression** *noun*
1, 2. ADMISSION.
3. ENTRANCE[1].

ingurgitate *verb* GULP.

inhabit *verb*
To live in (a place): *Nomads inhabited the steppes.*
   Syns: habit (*Archaic*), occupy, people, populate.

inhabitable *adjective* LIVABLE.

inhalation *noun*
1. BREATH.
2. INSPIRATION.

inhale *verb* BREATHE.

inharmonic *also* **inharmonical** *adjective* INHARMONIOUS.

inharmonious *adjective*
1. Characterized by unpleasant discordance of sound: *an inharmonious performance by the student band.*
   Syns: cacophonous (*also* cacophonic, cacophonical), discordant, disharmonic, disharmonious, dissonant, inharmonic (*also* inharmonical), rude, unharmonious, unmusical.
2. Devoid of harmony and accord: *He had an inharmonious relationship with his mother.*
   Syns: discordant, inconsonant, uncongenial, unharmonious.

inharmony *noun* CONFLICT.

inhere *verb* CONSIST.

inherent *adjective*
1. BUILT-IN.
2. CONSTITUTIONAL.

inherit *verb*
To receive (property) from one who has died: *inherited the farm from his late father.*
Syns: come into, heir (*Chiefly Regional*).

inheritance *noun*
1. BIRTHRIGHT.
2. HERITAGE.

inherited *adjective*
1. ANCESTRAL.
2. INNATE.

inhibit *verb*
1. CONSTRAIN.
2. FORBID.
3. RESTRAIN.

inhibited *adjective* FRIGID.
inhospitable *adjective* FORBIDDING.
inhospitableness *noun* UNWELCOME.
inhospitality *noun* UNWELCOME.
inhuman *adjective* FIERCE.
inhumanity *noun* CRUELTY.
inhumation *noun* BURIAL.
inhume *verb* BURY.
inimicable *adjective* HOSTILE.
inimical *adjective* HOSTILE.
iniquitous *adjective* EVIL.

iniquity *noun*
1. CRIME.
2. INJUSTICE.

initial *adjective*
1. BEGINNING.
2. EARLY.
3. FIRST.

initiate *verb*
1. To admit formally into membership or office, as with ritual: *initiated pledges into the fraternity.*
Syns: inaugurate, induct, install, instate, invest.
2. INTRODUCE.
3. START.

initiate *noun* BEGINNER.

initiation *noun*
1. The act or process of formally admitting a person to membership or office: *the initiation of new sorority pledges.*
Syns: inaugural, inauguration, induction, installation, instatement, investiture.
2. BEGINNING.

initiative *noun* AMBITION.
injudicious *adjective* UNWISE.
injunction *noun* COMMAND.

injure *verb*
1. To spoil the soundness or perfection

of: *an official who injured his credibility by lying.*
Syns: blemish, damage, disserve, harm, hurt, impair, mar, prejudice, tarnish, vitiate.
2. HURT.

injurious *adjective*
1. CORRUPTIVE.
2. HARMFUL.
3. LIBELOUS.

injury *noun*
1. HARM.
2. INJUSTICE.

injust *adjective* UNFAIR.

injustice *noun*
1. Lack of justice: *an attorney general who saw injustice and tried to remedy it.*
Syns: inequitableness, inequity, iniquity (*Scot. Law*), unfairness, unjustness, wrong.
2. An act that is not just: *By lying he did himself and others an injustice.*
Syns: disservice, injury, wrong.
—*Idiom* raw deal.

inkhorn *adjective* PEDANTIC.
inkling *noun* HINT.

inky *adjective*
1, 2. BLACK.

inlying *adjective* INNER.

innate *adjective*
1. Possessed at birth: *innate cardiovascular abnormalities; innate talent.*
Syns: congenital, hereditary, inborn, ingenerate, inherited, innative, native, natural.
2. BUILT-IN.
3. CONSTITUTIONAL.

innative *adjective* INNATE.

inner *adjective*
1. Located farther in: *an inner room.*
Syns: inlying, inside, interior, internal, intestine (*Obs.*).
2. Of, pertaining to, or arising from one's mental or spiritual being: *has inner conflicts.*
Syns: gut (*Slang*), interior, internal, intestine, intimate[1], inward, visceral, viscerous.
3. Being closer to a center of power and influence: *the inner circles of the organization.*
Syn: inside (*Slang*).

innerve *verb* PROVOKE.
innings *noun* TURN.
innocence *noun* IGNORANCE.

innocent *adjective*
1. Free from evil and corruption: *innocent little children.*

Syns: angelic (*also* angelical), clean, lily-white, pure, unblemished, undefiled, uncorrupted, unstained, unsullied, untainted, virginal. —*Idiom* pure as the driven snow.

2. Free from guilt or blame: *innocent of all charges; innocent victims.*
Syns: blameless, clean (*Slang*), faultless, guiltless, harmless. —*Idiom* in the clear.

3. ARTLESS.

4. EMPTY.

5. HARMLESS.

6. IGNORANT.

7. LAWFUL.

innocent *noun*

1. A pure, uncorrupted person: *a woman who had the beguiling look of a young innocent.*
Syns: angel, lamb, virgin.

2. A guileless, unsophisticated person: *a foreign-policy adviser who was a mere innocent in dealing with the Soviets.*
Syns: babe (*Slang*), child, ingénue, naive (*also* naïve, naif, naïf), unsophisticate. —*Idiom* babe in the woods.

3. BEGINNER.

4. CHILD.

innocuous *adjective*

1, 2. HARMLESS.

3. INSIPID.

innovation *noun* NOVELTY.

innovative *adjective*

1. INVENTIVE.

2. NEW.

innuendo *noun*

1. HINT.

2. INSINUATION.

innuendo *verb* HINT.

innumerable *adjective* INCALCULABLE.

inobtrusive *adjective* QUIET.

inoffensive *adjective* HARMLESS.

inoperative *adjective* INACTIVE.

inopportune *adjective* INCONVENIENT.

inordinate *adjective* EXCESSIVE.

inquest *noun* INQUIRY.

inquietude *noun* RESTLESSNESS.

inquire *also* **enquire** *verb*

1. ASK.

2. EXPLORE.

inquirer *also* **enquirer** *noun*
One who inquires: *avoided reporters and other inquirers.*
Syns: inquisitor, querier, questioner.

inquiring *also* **enquiring** *adjective* CURIOUS.

inquiry *also* **enquiry** *noun*

1. A seeking of knowledge, data, or the

truth about something: *an inquiry as to the cause of the patient's death.*
Syns: delving, inquest, inquisition, investigation, probe, quest.

2. A request for data: *The company receives many inquiries about the cost of books.*
Syns: interrogation, interrogatory (*Law*), query, question.

inquisition *noun* INQUIRY.

inquisitive *adjective*

1, 2. CURIOUS.

inquisitiveness *noun* CURIOSITY.

inquisitor *noun*

1. One who conducts an official inquiry, usu. with no regard for human rights: *The captured spy was tortured by his inquisitors.*
Syns: interrogator, questioner.

2. INQUIRER.

inquisitorial *adjective* CURIOUS.

inquisitory *adjective* CURIOUS.

inroad *noun* INVASION.

insalubrious *adjective* UNWHOLESOME.

insalutary *adjective* UNWHOLESOME.

insane *adjective*

1. Afflicted with or exhibiting irrationality and mental unsoundness: *The assassin was diagnosed insane by two psychiatrists.*
Syns: batty (*Slang*), bedlamite, bonkers (*Slang*), brainsick, buggy (*Slang*), bughouse (*Slang*), bugs (*Slang*), cracked, crackers (*Chiefly Brit. Slang*), cracky (*Chiefly Brit. Slang*), crazed, crazy, cuckoo, daffy (*Informal*), daft, demented, deranged, disordered, distraught, fruity (*Slang*), gaga (*Slang*), loco (*Slang*), loony (*also* luny) (*Informal*), lunatic, mad, maniac, maniacal, mental (*Chiefly Brit.*), mindless, moonstruck (*also* moonstricken), non compos mentis (*Law*), nuts (*Slang*), nutty (*Informal*), off, screwy (*Slang*), touched, unbalanced, unsound, wacky (*also* whacky) (*Slang*), witless, wrong. —*Idioms* around the bend, crazy as a loon, mad as a hatter, not all there, nutty as a fruitcake, off one's rocker, out of one's head (*or* mind), sick in the head, stark raving mad, unsound of mind.

2. FOOLISH.

insaneness *noun* INSANITY.

insanity *noun*

1. Serious mental illness or disorder impairing a person's capacity to function normally and safely: *Wild*

fears and suspicions were the first signs of his approaching insanity.
Syns: aberration, alienation, brainsickness, craziness, dementia, derangement, insaneness, lunacy, madness, mania, psychopathy, unbalance.
2. FOOLISHNESS.

inscribe *verb*
1. ENGRAVE.
2. LIST[1].
3. SIGN.
4. WRITE.

insecure *adjective*
1. Inadequately protected: *Without the military police the air base would be insecure.*
Syns: unguarded, unprotected, unsafe.
2. Lacking stability: *an insecure peace; an insecure ally.*
Syns: infirm (*Rare*), insubstantial, shaky, tottery, unstable, unsteady, unsure, weak, wobbly.

insecurity *noun* INSTABILITY.
insensate *adjective* INSENSITIVE.
insensibility *noun* APATHY.
insensible *adjective*
1. APATHETIC.
2. DEAD.
3. DULL.
4. IMPERCEPTIBLE.
5. INSENSITIVE.
6. UNCONSCIOUS.

insensitive *adjective*
1. Lacking passion and emotion: *turned an insensitive ear to our pleas.*
Syns: anesthetic, bloodless, dull, hard, insensate, insensible. —*Idiom* as hard as nails.
2. Not capable of being affected or impressed: *I am totally insensitive to flattery.*
Syns: impassible, impassive, insusceptible, unimpressionable, unsusceptible.
3. DEAD.
4. DULL.

insert *verb*
1. INTRODUCE.
2. POST.

insertion *noun* ENTRY.
inside *adjective*
1. CONFIDENTIAL.
2, 3. INNER.
4. INTIMATE[1].

insight *noun*
1. INSTINCT.
2. WISDOM.

insignificance also **insignificancy** *noun* INDIFFERENCE.

insignificant *adjective* LITTLE.
insincere *adjective*
1. Not being what one purports to be: *insincere flattery; an insincere person not to be trusted.*
Syns: ambidextrous, disingenuous, left-handed, mala fide (*Latin*).
2. ARTIFICIAL.

insincerity *noun*
Lack of sincerity: *was shocked by their insincerity.*
Syns: disingenuity, disingenuousness, uncandor.

insinuate *verb*
1. To introduce gradually and slyly: *A spy has insinuated himself into government circles. She insinuated her beliefs into every policy discussion.*
Syns: edge in, foist, infiltrate, wind[2] (into), work (into), worm.
2. HINT.

insinuating *adjective*
1. Provoking a change of outlook and esp. gradual doubt and suspicion: *made insinuating remarks about his competence.*
Syns: insinuative, suggestive.
2. Purposefully contrived to gain favor: *the insinuating smiles of courtiers.*
Syns: ingratiating, ingratiative, saccharine, sugary.

insinuation *noun*
An artful, indirect hint: *made insinuations that he had cheated on the exam.*
Syn: innuendo.

insinuative *adjective* INSINUATING.
insipid *adjective*
1. Lacking the qualities requisite for spiritedness and originality: *an insipid soap opera.*
Syns: banal, bland, driveling, inane, innocuous, jejune, namby-pamby, vapid, washy, waterish, watery, wishy-washy (*Informal*).
2. FLAT.

insipidity *noun*
The state or quality of being insipid: *the insipidity of the play; the insipidity of her cooking.*
Syns: banality, blandness, colorlessness, dullness, dryness, flatness, flavorlessness, inaneness, inanity, insipidness, jejunity, vapidity.

insipidness *noun* INSIPIDITY.
insist *verb*
1. To take and maintain a stand obstinately: *He still insisted on the truth of his story.*
Syns: persevere, persist.

2. To solicit insistently: *The prime minister insisted that the king abdicate. You insisted upon my going to the party.*
 Syns: press, pressure, prod, urge.
insist on (or **upon**) *verb* DEMAND.
insistence *also* **insistency** *noun*
 1. The state or quality of being insistent: *The attorney's insistence on learning the truth saved his client.*
 Syns: perseverance, persistence (*also* persistency).
 2. Urgent solicitation: *We signed this contract only at your insistence.*
 Syns: instance (*Archaic*), plying, pressing, prodding, urgence, urgency, urging.
insistent *adjective*
 1. Obstinately maintaining a stand: *insistent denials of all guilt.*
 Syns: perseverant, persevering, persistent, persisting, unremitting.
 2. EMPHATIC.
insobriety *noun* DRUNKENNESS.
insolence *also* **insolency** *noun*
 1. ARROGANCE.
 2. IMPUDENCE.
insolent *adjective*
 1. ARROGANT.
 2. IMPUDENT.
insolvency *noun* FAILURE.
insorb *verb* ABSORB.
inspect *verb*
 1. ANALYZE.
 2. EXAMINE.
 3. SEARCH.
inspection *noun*
 1. ANALYSIS.
 2. EXAMINATION.
inspiration *noun*
 1. *Theol.* Divine guidance and motivation imparted directly: *received inspiration through prayer and contemplation.*
 Syns: afflation, afflatus, inflatus.
 2. The act of breathing in: *counted the rate of the patient's inspirations.*
 Syns: afflation, inhalation.
 3. A sudden, exciting thought: *had an inspiration to change lifestyles.*
 Syns: brainstorm, brain wave.
 4. ELATION.
 5. ENCOURAGEMENT.
 6. FIRE.
inspirational *adjective* INSPIRING.
inspire *verb*
 1. To elicit a strong emotional response from: *a woman capable of inspiring a man's devotion; conduct inspiring only disgust.*

 Syns: arouse, excite, prompt, provoke, stimulate, stir[1]. —*Idiom* stir the blood of.
 2. BREATHE.
 3. ELATE.
 4. ENCOURAGE.
 5. FIRE.
inspired *adjective*
 1. AFFECTED[1].
 2. ELATED.
inspiring *adjective*
 Providing inspiration: *an inspiring sermon.*
 Syns: exhilarant, exhilarating, inspirational, intoxicating, rousing, stirring.
inspirit *verb*
 1. ELATE.
 2. ENCOURAGE.
inspissate *verb* THICKEN.
instability *noun*
 1. The quality or condition of being erratic and undependable: *the instability of the bond market; the instability of the new government.*
 Syns: insecurity, precariousness, shakiness, unstability, unstableness.
 2. UNSTABLENESS.
install *verb*
 1. ESTABLISH.
 2. INITIATE.
 3. POSITION.
installation *noun*
 1. BASE[1].
 2. INITIATION.
instance *verb*
 1. To demonstrate and clarify with examples: *The author's true intent is instanced in these quotations.*
 Syns: example, exemplify, illustrate.
 2. NAME.
instance *noun*
 1. EXAMPLE.
 2. INSISTENCE.
 3. LAWSUIT.
instant *noun*
 1. A particular interval of time that is limited and often crucial: *At the very instant the general fell ill, the enemy attacked.*
 Syns: juncture, moment, point.
 2. FLASH.
 instant *adjective* BURNING.
 instant *adverb* DIRECTLY.
instate *verb* INITIATE.
instatement *noun* INITIATION.
instigate *verb* PROVOKE.
instigation *noun* STIMULUS.
instigator *noun* AGITATOR.
instill *verb* INDOCTRINATE.

instinct *noun*
1. The power to discern the true nature of a person or situation: *Instinct warned me never to trust him.*
   Syns: anschauung (*German*), insight, intuitiveness, intuition. —*Idiom* sixth sense.
2. TALENT.

instinctive *adjective*
1. Derived from or prompted by a natural tendency or impulse: *The cornered animal drew back with instinctive fear. My instinctive feeling is that he's a crook.*
   Syns: instinctual, intuitive, visceral.
2. SPONTANEOUS.

instinctual *adjective* INSTINCTIVE.

institute *verb*
1. FOUND.
2. INTRODUCE.
institute *noun* LAW.

institution *noun* FOUNDATION.

institutionalize *verb* COMMIT.

instruct *verb*
1. COMMAND.
2. EDUCATE.
3. ILLUMINATE.

instructed *adjective*
1. EDUCATED.
2. INFORMED.

instructible *adjective* EDUCABLE.

instruction *noun*
1. COMMAND.
2, 3. EDUCATION.
4. ILLUMINATION.

instructional *adjective* EDUCATIONAL.
instructive *adjective* EDUCATIONAL.
instructor *noun* EDUCATOR.

instrument *noun*
1. MEANS.
2. PAWN².
3. TOOL.

instrumentality *noun* MEANS.
instrumentation *noun* MEANS.
insubordinate *adjective* DISOBEDIENT.
insubordination *noun* DISOBEDIENCE.

insubstantial *adjective*
1. IMMATERIAL.
2. INFIRM.
3. INSECURE.
4. TENUOUS.

insufferable *adjective* UNBEARABLE.

insufficiency also **insufficience** *noun* SHORTAGE.

insufficient *adjective*
Not enough to meet a demand or requirement: *Men cannot work on insufficient rations.*
   Syns: deficient, inadequate, scanty, scarce, short, shy¹, skimpy, wanting.

insular *adjective*
1. LOCAL.
2. REMOTE.

insulate *verb* ISOLATE.

insult *verb*
To cause resentment or hurt by callous, rude behavior: *The drunken guest insulted the hostess.*
   Syns: affront, offend, outrage. —*Idioms* add insult to injury, give offense to.
insult *noun* INDIGNITY.

insuperable *adjective*
1. Incapable of being negotiated or overcome: *were confronted with insuperable problems.*
   Syns: impassable, indomitable, insurmountable, unsurmountable.
2. INVINCIBLE.

insupportable *adjective* UNBEARABLE.
insure *verb* SEE **ensure.**
insurgence *noun* REBELLION.
insurgency *noun* REBELLION.
insurgent *adjective* REBELLIOUS.
insurgent *noun* REBEL.

insurmountable *adjective* INSUPERABLE.

insurrect *verb* REBEL.
insurrection *noun* REBELLION.
insurrectionist *noun* REBEL.
insusceptible *adjective* INSENSITIVE.

intact *adjective*
1. COMPLETE.
2. GOOD.

intangible *adjective* IMPERCEPTIBLE.

integral *adjective*
1. COMPLETE.
2. ESSENTIAL.
integral *noun* SYSTEM.

integrant *noun* ELEMENT.

integrate *verb*
1. To make into a whole by joining a system of parts: *a political party that had integrated both liberal and conservative elements.*
   Syns: articulate, concatenate, unify.
2. To open to all people regardless of race: *worked to integrate the schools.*
   Syn: desegregate.
3. BUILD IN at **build.**
4. EMBODY.
5, 6. HARMONIZE.
integrate *noun* SYSTEM.

integration *noun*
The act, process, or result of abolishing racial segregation: *school integration.*
   Syn: desegregation.

integrity *noun*
1. CHARACTER.
2. COMPLETENESS.

3. HONESTY.
4. SOUNDNESS.
integument *noun* SKIN.
intellect *noun*
1. INTELLIGENCE.
2. MIND.
intellective *adjective* MENTAL.
intellectual *adjective*
1. Appealing to or engaging the intellect: *an intellectual discussion.*
   Syns: cerebral, highbrow (*Informal*), sophisticated, thoughtful.
2. INTELLIGENT.
3. MENTAL.
intellectual *noun* MIND.
intelligence *noun*
1. The faculty of thinking, reasoning, and acquiring and applying knowledge: *A woman of her intelligence would make a good Supreme Court justice.*
   Syns: brain(s) (*Informal*), brainpower (*Informal*), intellect, mentality, mind, smarts (*Slang*), sense, understanding, wit.
2. INFORMATION.
3. NEWS.
intelligent *adjective*
1. Having or showing intelligence, often of a high order: *an intelligent child; a book for an intelligent readership.*
   Syns: brainy (*Informal*), brilliant, intellectual, knowing, knowledgeable.
2. CLEVER.
3. LOGICAL.
intelligible *adjective*
UNDERSTANDABLE.
intemperance *noun* EXCESS.
intend *verb*
1. To have in mind as a goal or purpose: *We intend to sell the house.*
   Syns: aim, contemplate, design, mean¹, mind (*Chiefly Regional*), plan, propose, project, purpose.
2. MEAN¹.
intended *noun*
A person to whom one is engaged to be married: *took his intended to meet his mother.*
   Syns: betrothed, affianced.
intended *adjective*
1. DELIBERATE.
2. ENGAGED.
intense *adjective*
1. Extreme in degree, strength, or effect: *an intense struggle of wills.*
   Syns: desperate, fierce, furious, terrible, vehement, violent.
2. DEEP.
3. HEAVY.

intensify *verb*
To increase in intensity or severity: *intensified their efforts; pain that intensified every minute.*
   Syns: aggravate, deepen, enhance, heighten, mount, redouble.
intensity *noun*
Exceptionally great concentration, power, or force, esp. in activity: *a hurricane of staggering intensity.*
   Syns: ferocity, fierceness, fury, pitch, severity, vehemence, violence.
intensive *adjective*
1. CONCENTRATED.
2. HEAVY.
3. THOROUGH.
intensively *adverb* COMPLETELY.
intent *noun*
1. INTENTION.
2, 3. MEANING.
4. THRUST.
intent *adjective*
1. ABSORBED.
2. ATTENTIVE.
3. SET¹.
intention *noun*
What one intends to do or achieve: *It was not my intention to offend you.*
   Syns: aim, design, end, goal, intent, mark, meaning, plan, point, purpose, target, view. —*Idiom* end in view.
intentional *adjective*
1. CALCULATED.
2. DELIBERATE.
inter *verb* BURY.
interagent *noun* GO-BETWEEN.
interceder *noun* GO-BETWEEN.
intercept *verb* HEAD OFF at **head.**
intercessor *noun* GO-BETWEEN.
interchange *verb*
1. CHANGE.
2. EXCHANGE.
interchange *noun* CHANGE.
intercommunication *noun*
1. COMMUNICATION.
2. TOUCH.
interconnection *noun* RELATION.
intercourse *noun* COMMUNICATION.
interdependence *noun* RELATION.
interdict *verb* FORBID.
interdict *noun* SANCTION.
interdiction *noun*
1. FORBIDDANCE.
2. SANCTION.
interest *noun*
1. Something that contributes to or increases one's well-being: *always considered the interest of his clients.*
   Syns: advantage, benefit, good, profit.
2. A right or legal share in something:

*own a half interest in a computer
company.*
   Syns: claim, portion, stake, title.
3. CONCERN.
4. CURIOSITY.
interest *verb*
To arouse the interest and attention of:
Archaeology has always interested me.
   Syns: attract, intrigue, turn on
   (*Slang*). —*Idiom* get one going.
interested *adjective* CONCERNED.
interestedness *noun* CONCERN.
interfere *verb* MEDDLE.
interference *noun* MEDDLING.
interfering *adjective* MEDDLING.
interim *adjective*
1, 2. TEMPORARY.
   interim *noun* GAP.
interior *adjective*
1, 2. INNER.
interject *verb* INTRODUCE.
interlard *adjective* INTRODUCE.
interlope *verb* INTRUDE.
intermediary *noun*
1. GO-BETWEEN.
2. MEANS.
intermediate *adjective* MIDDLE.
   intermediate *noun* GO-BETWEEN.
intermediator *noun* GO-BETWEEN.
interment *noun* BURIAL.
intermesh *verb* ENGAGE.
interminable *adjective* CONTINUAL.
intermingle *verb* MIX.
intermission *noun*
1. ABEYANCE.
2. BREAK.
intermittent *adjective*
Happening or appearing now and then:
*intermittent showers; intermittent
outbreaks of violence.*
   Syns: fitful, occasional, periodic (*also*
   periodical), sporadic.
intermix *verb* MIX.
intermutual *adjective* COMMON.
intern *verb* JAIL.
internal *adjective*
1. DOMESTIC.
2, 3. INNER.
interpolate *verb* INTRODUCE.
interpose *verb* INTRODUCE.
interpret *verb*
1. To perform according to one's artistic
   conception: *How did she interpret the
   role of Lady Macbeth?*
   Syns: execute, play, render.
2. To understand in a particular way:
   *We didn't know how to interpret her
   remark.*

   Syns: construe, read, take.
3. EXPLAIN.
interpretation *noun*
1. One's artistic conception as shown by
   the rendering of a dramatic role,
   musical composition, etc.: *an unusual
   interpretation of Beethoven's
   "Appassionata" Sonata.*
   Syns: execution, performance,
   reading, realization, rendition.
2. COMMENTARY.
3. EXPLANATION.
interpretive *adjective* EXPLANATORY.
interrelation *noun* RELATION.
interrelationship *noun* RELATION.
interrogate *verb*
1. To question thoroughly and
   relentlessly to verify facts:
   interrogated the captured soldier.
   Syns: cross-examine, cross-
   interrogate, cross-question, grill
   (*Informal*), third-degree. —*Idioms*
   give someone the third degree, put on
   the grill.
2. ASK.
interrogation *noun* INQUIRY.
interrogator *noun* INQUISITOR.
interrogatory *noun* INQUIRY.
interrupt *verb*
1. To interject remarks or questions into
   another's discourse: *Hecklers
   interrupted the speech.*
   Syns: break in, chime in, chip in, cut
   in.
2. SUSPEND.
interruption *noun* BREAK.
intersect *verb* CROSS.
intertangle *verb* ENTANGLE.
intervention *noun* MEDDLING.
intestine *adjective*
1, 2. INNER.
intimacy *noun* FRIENDSHIP.
intimate[1] *adjective*
1. Characterized by a close and
   thorough acquaintance: *has an
   intimate knowledge of drug dealing.*
   Syns: direct, firsthand, inside,
   personal.
2. CONFIDENTIAL.
3. FAMILIAR.
   intimate *noun* FRIEND.
   intimate *adjective* INNER.
intimate[2] *verb* HINT.
intimation *noun*
1. HINT.
2. SHADE.
intimidate *verb*
To domineer or drive into compliance

by the use of threats, force, etc.: *mob members intimidating local merchants.*
  Syns: bludgeon, browbeat, bulldoze, bully, bullyrag, cow, hector, strongarm (*Informal*), threaten.

intimidation *noun* THREAT.

intimidator *noun* BULLY.

intolerable *adjective* UNBEARABLE.

intolerance *noun* PREJUDICE.

intolerant *adjective*
1. Not tolerant of the beliefs, opinions, etc., of others: *an intolerant old-line conservative.*
  Syns: bigoted, close-minded, hidebound, illiberal, narrow, narrow-minded, small-minded.
2. Not able or willing to tolerate or endure with equanimity: *intolerant of everything unfamiliar.*
  Syns: impatient, unforbearing.

intonation *noun* TONE.

intoxicate *verb* INEBRIATE.

intoxicating *adjective* INSPIRING.

intoxication *noun*
1. DRUNKENNESS.
2. ELATION.

intractability *noun* OBSTINACY.

intractable *adjective* OBSTINATE.

intransigence or **intransigency** *noun* OBSTINACY.

intransigent *adjective*
1. GRIM.
2. OBSTINATE.

intrepid *adjective* BRAVE.

intrepidity *noun* COURAGE.

intricacy *noun* COMPLEXITY.

intricate *adjective*
1. COMPLEX.
2. ELABORATE.

intrigue *noun*
1, 2. PLOT.

intrigue *verb*
1. INTEREST.
2. PLOT.

intrinsic *adjective*
1. BUILT-IN.
2. CONSTITUTIONAL.

introduce *verb*
1. To bring into currency, use, fashion, or practice: *Automobiles were introduced for commercial use in the twentieth century.*
  Syns: inaugurate, initiate, institute, launch, originate, usher in.
2. To put or set into, between, or among another or other things: *introduced some suspense into the novel.*

  Syns: insert, interject, interlard, interpolate, interpose.
3. To begin (something) with preliminary or prefatory material: *introduced the poem with a dedication.*
  Syns: lead, precede, preface, usher in.
4. ACQUAINT.
5. BROACH.
6. USHER IN at **usher.**

introduction *noun*
1. A short section of preliminary remarks: *explains his work methods in the introduction.*
  Syns: foreword, overture, preamble, preface, prelude, prolegomenon, prologue.
2. ADMISSION.

introductory *adjective*
1. Serving to introduce a subject, person, etc.: *a few introductory remarks before the program.*
  Syns: prefatory (*also* prefatorial), preliminary, preparatory, prolegomenous.
2. BEGINNING.
3. PRELIMINARY.

intromission *noun* ADMISSION.

intromit *verb* ADMIT.

intrude *verb*
To force or come in as an improper or unwanted element : *won't make the mistake of intruding myself on your guests.*
  Syns: butt in, cut in, horn in, interlope, obtrude.

intrusion *noun* IMPOSITION.

intrusive *adjective*
1. DISTURBING.
2. MEDDLING.

intrust *verb* SEE **entrust.**

intuit *verb* PERCEIVE.

intuition *noun*
1. FEELING.
2. INSTINCT.

intuitive *adjective* INSTINCTIVE.

intuitiveness *noun* INSTINCT.

inumbrate *verb* SHADE.

inundate *verb* FLOOD.

inundation *noun* FLOOD.

inure *verb* ACCUSTOM.

inutile *adjective*
1. USELESS.
2. WORTHLESS.

invade *verb*
To enter in order to attack, plunder, destroy, or conquer: *The Nazis invaded Czechoslovakia.*

Syns: foray (into), overrun, raid, swarm over.

invalid *adjective* FALLACIOUS.

invalidate *verb* ABOLISH.

invalidation *noun* ABOLITION.

invaluable *adjective* VALUABLE.

invariable *adjective*
1. CONSISTENT.
2. INFLEXIBLE.

invasion *noun*
An act of invading, esp. by military forces: *the Roman invasion of Britain.*
  Syns: foray, incursion, inroad, raid.

invective *noun*
1. SWEAR.
2. VITUPERATION.

invective *adjective* ABUSIVE.

inveigh *verb* OBJECT².

inveigle *verb* TEMPT.

inveiglement *noun* LURE.

inveigler *noun* SEDUCER.

invent *verb*
To use ingenuity in making, developing, or achieving: *a gang that invented a remote-control bomb.*
  Syns: concoct, contrive, cook up (*Informal*), devise, dream up, fabricate, formulate, hatch, make up, think up. *—Idiom* come up with.

invented *adjective* FICTITIOUS.

invention *noun*
1. Something invented: *The cotton gin was a vitally important invention for the South's economy.*
  Syns: brain child (*Informal*), contrivance, device.
2. The power or ability to invent: *a dress designer of amazing invention.*
  Syns: creativity, ingenuity, inventiveness, originality.
3. MYTH.

inventive *adjective*
1. Characterized by or productive of new things or new ideas: *an inventive mind; inventive solutions to the energy problem.*
  Syns: creative, ingenious, innovative, original.
2. NEW.
3. RESOURCEFUL.

inventiveness *noun* INVENTION.

inventor *noun* ORIGINATOR.

inventory *noun* HOARD.

inveracity *noun* LIE².

inverse *verb* REVERSE.

inversion *noun* REVERSAL.

invert *verb* REVERSE.

inverted *adjective* UPSIDE-DOWN.

invest *verb*
1. BESIEGE.
2. DRESS.
3. GIFT.
4. INITIATE.
5. WRAP.
6. WRAP UP at wrap.

investigate *verb*
1. ANALYZE.
2. EXPLORE.

investigation *noun*
1. ANALYSIS.
2. EXPLORATION.
3. INQUIRY.

investigative *adjective* CURIOUS.

investigator *noun* DETECTIVE.

investiture *noun* INITIATION.

inveterate *adjective*
1. CHRONIC.
2. CONFIRMED.
3. CONTINUING.

invidious *adjective*
1. ENVIOUS.
2. LIBELOUS.

invidiousness *noun* ENVY.

invigorating *adjective* TONIC.

invincible *adjective*
Incapable of being conquered, overrun, or subjugated: *an invincible foe; an invincible fortress.*
  Syns: impregnable, inconquerable, insuperable, unconquerable.

inviolability *noun* SANCTITY.

inviolable *adjective* SACRED.

invisible *adjective* IMPERCEPTIBLE.

invitation *noun*
1. A spoken or written request for someone to take part or be present: *sent out the wedding invitations.*
  Syn: bid.
2. A tendency to cause or bring on: *Reckless driving is an invitation to disaster.*
  Syns: encouragement, inducement.

invite *verb*
1. To request that someone take part in or be present at a particular occasion: *Let's invite them to dinner.*
  Syns: ask, bid.
2. COURT.

inviting *adjective* SEDUCTIVE.

invocate *verb* PRAY.

invocation *noun* PRAYER.

invoice *noun* ACCOUNT.

invoice *verb* BILL¹.

invoke *verb* ENFORCE.

involute *adjective* COMPLEX.

involve *verb*
1. To draw in such a way that extrication is difficult: *a local skirmish that could involve the major powers.*
Syns: catch up, embrangle, embroil, enmesh, ensnare, ensnarl, entangle, implicate, suck in (*Informal*).
2. APPLY.
3. CARRY.
4. CONTAIN.
5. DEMAND.
6. ENGAGE.

involved *adjective*
1. COMPLEX.
2. CONCERNED.

involvement *noun*
1. ENTANGLEMENT.
2. PARTICIPATION.

inward *adjective* INNER.

iota *noun*
1. BIT¹.
2. DAMN.

irascibility *noun* TEMPER.

irascible *adjective*
1. ILL-TEMPERED.
2. TESTY.

irascibleness *noun* TEMPER.

irate *adjective* ANGRY.

irateness *noun* ANGER.

ire *noun*
1. ANGER.
2. FURY.

ire *verb* ANGER.

ireful *adjective* ANGRY.

irenic *adjective* PEACEABLE.

irk *verb* ANNOY.

irksome *adjective*
1. BORING.
2. VEXATIOUS.

iron *verb* PRESS.

iron *adjective* STUBBORN.

ironbound *adjective* ROUGH.

ironclad *adjective* INFLEXIBLE.

ironic also **ironical** *adjective* CYNICAL.

irons *noun* BONDS.

irradiant *adjective* BRIGHT.

irradiate *verb* SHED.

irradicable *adjective* CONFIRMED.

irrational *adjective*
1. MINDLESS.
2. UNREASONABLE.

irrationality *noun* UNREASON.

irrealizable *adjective* IMPOSSIBLE.

irrefutable *adjective* CERTAIN.

irregular *adjective*
Not straight, uniform, or symmetrical: *an irregular coastline; irregular teeth.*

Syns: asymmetric (*also* asymmetrical), crooked, jagged, uneven.

irregularity *noun*
Lack of smoothness or regularity: *the irregularity of the terrain.*
Syns: asymmetry, crookedness, inequality, jaggedness, roughness, unevenness.

irrelevancy *noun* DIGRESSION.

irrelevant *adjective*
Not relevant or pertinent to the subject; not applicable: *tells us about the weather, which is irrelevant to the question we asked.*
Syns: extraneous, immaterial, impertinent, inapplicable. —*Idioms* beside the point, neither here nor there, off target.

irremediable *adjective* HOPELESS.

irreparable *adjective* HOPELESS.

irreprehensible *adjective* EXEMPLARY.

irreproachable *adjective* EXEMPLARY.

irresolute *adjective* HESITANT.

irresolution *noun* HESITATION.

irresponsible *adjective*
Lacking or showing a lack of a sense of responsibility: *irresponsible actions.*
Syns: feckless, incautious, reckless.

irreverence *noun* DISRESPECT.

irreverent *adjective* DISRESPECTFUL.

irreversible *adjective* IRREVOCABLE.

irrevocable *adjective*
That cannot be revoked or undone: *My decision is irrevocable.*
Syns: irreversible, unalterable. —*Idiom* beyond recall.

irritable *adjective*
1. Easily annoyed: *Hot, sticky weather always makes me irritable.*
Syns: fretful, peevish, petulant, prickish, querulent, querulous, snappish, snappy, waspish. —*Idiom* out of sorts.
2. ILL-TEMPERED.

irritant *noun* ANNOYANCE.

irritate *verb*
1. To cause to become sore or inflamed: *Smoke irritates my eyes.*
Syns: burn, inflame, sting.
2. ANNOY.

irritating *adjective* VEXATIOUS.

irritation *noun*
1. An instance of irritating, as of a part of the body: *Aspirin sometimes causes stomach irritation.*
Syns: inflammation, soreness.
2, 3. ANNOYANCE.

Iscariotic or **Iscariotical** *adjective*
1. DOUBLE.
2. TREASONOUS.

J

isochronal also **isochronic,**
isochronous *adjective* RECURRENT.

isolate *verb*
1. To set apart from a group: *trying to isolate a suspected carcinogen.*
   Syns: close off, cut off, insulate, seclude, segregate, separate, sequester.
2. IMPRISON.

isolate *adjective* SOLITARY.

isolated *adjective*
1. LOCAL.
2. REMOTE.
3. SOLITARY.

isolation *noun*
1. The act or process of isolating: *the isolation of cancer patients.*
   Syns: segregation, separation, sequestration.
2. ALONENESS.

issue *verb*
1. APPEAR.
2. DESCEND.
3. DISCHARGE.
4. EMIT.
5. PUBLISH.
6. STEM.

issue *noun*
1. EFFECT.
2. PROBLEM.
3. PROGENY.
4. PUBLICATION.

italicize *verb* EMPHASIZE.

itch *noun*
1, 2. DESIRE.

itch for *verb* LUST.

item *noun*
1. A usu. brief detail of news or information: *The morning paper has an item about their divorce.*
   Syns: bit, paragraph, piece, squib, story.
2. DETAIL.
3. ELEMENT.
4. OBJECT¹.

item *adverb* ADDITIONALLY.

itemize *verb* ENUMERATE.

itemized *adjective* DETAILED.

iterate *verb* REPEAT.

iteration *noun* REPETITION.

iterative *adjective* REPETITIVE.

itinerant *adjective*
1. ERRANT.
2. MIGRANT.
3. NOMADIC.

ivory *adjective* FAIR.

ivory-tower *adjective* IMPRACTICAL.

ivory-towered *adjective*
IMPRACTICAL.

ivory-towerish *adjective*
IMPRACTICAL.

jab *verb* DIG.

jab *noun*
1. CRACK.
2. DIG.

jabber *verb*
1. BABBLE.
2. CHATTER.

jabber *noun*
1. BABBLE.
2. CHATTER.

jabberwocky also **jabberwock** *noun*
1. BABBLE.
2. GIBBERISH.

jack *noun*
1. FLAG¹.
2. MONEY.
3. SAILOR.

jack *verb* RAISE.

jackass *noun* FOOL.

jacket *noun* HIDE².

jackleg *adjective* AMATEURISH.

jacktar *noun* SAILOR.

jade *noun* SLUT.

jag *noun* BINGE.

jagged *adjective*
1. IRREGULAR.
2. ROUGH.

jaggedness *noun* IRREGULARITY.

jail *noun*
A place for the confinement of persons in lawful detention: *was sent to jail for murder.*
   Syns: brig, calaboose (*Slang*), can (*Slang*), clink (*Slang*), cooler (*Slang*), coop (*Slang*), gaol (*Chiefly Brit.*), hoosegow (*Slang*), joint (*Slang*), jug (*Slang*), keep, lockup (*Informal*), pen³ (*Slang*), penitentiary, pokey¹ (*Slang*), prison, slammer (*Slang*), stir² (*Slang*). —*Idioms* big house (*also* Big House), house of correction (*or* detention), rock pile.

jail *verb*
To put in jail: *will jail the suspect for attempted robbery.*
   Syns: confine, immure, imprison, incarcerate, intern, lock up.

jailer also **jailor** *noun*
A guard or keeper of a prison: *a jailer in the state penitentiary.*
   Syns: gaoler (*Chiefly Brit.*), turnkey, warden, warder (*Brit.*). —*Idiom* The Man.

jam *verb*
1, 2. CROWD.
jam *noun* PREDICAMENT.
jam-full *adjective* FULL.
jammed *adjective* FULL.
jam-pack *verb* CROWD.
jam-packed *adjective* FULL.
jape *noun* JOKE.
jar *verb* CONFLICT.
jar *noun* COLLISION.
jargon *noun*
1. DIALECT.
2. LANGUAGE.
jarring *adjective* HARSH.
jaundice *verb* BIAS.
jaunt *noun* TRIP.
jaunty *adjective* AIRY.
Javert *noun* DETECTIVE.
jaw *verb* CHATTER.
jealous *adjective*
1. Fearful of the loss of position or affection: *a jealous husband.*
   Syns: clutching, possessive.
2. ENVIOUS.
jealousy *noun* ENVY.
jeer at *verb* RIDICULE.
jejune *adjective* INSIPID.
jejunity *noun* INSIPIDITY.
jell *verb* COAGULATE.
jeopard *verb* ENDANGER.
jeopardize *verb* ENDANGER.
jeopardous *adjective* DANGEROUS.
jeopardy *noun* DANGER.
jeopardy *verb* ENDANGER.
jeremiad *noun* TIRADE.
jerk *verb*
1. To move or cause to move with a sudden, abrupt motion: *jerked the window open. His head jerked forward onto his chest.*
   Syns: lurch, snap, tug, twitch, wrench, yank (*Informal*).
2. BUMP.
jerk *noun*
1. A sudden pull: *opened the door with a jerk.*
   Syns: lurch, snap, tug, twitch, wrench, yank (*Informal*).
2. DRIP.
3. FOOL.
jerky *adjective* FOOLISH.
jest *verb*
1, 2. JOKE.
jest *noun*
1, 2. JOKE.
jester *noun* JOKER.
jesting *adjective* HUMOROUS.
jet¹ *adjective* BLACK.
jet² *noun* SPURT.
jet *verb* SPURT.

jet-black *adjective* BLACK.
jettison *noun* DISPOSAL.
jettison *verb* DISCARD.
jetty *adjective* BLACK.
jibe *verb* AGREE.
jiffy *also* **jiff** *noun* FLASH.
jig *noun* TRICK.
jigger *noun* GADGET.
jiggle *verb* SHAKE.
jillion *noun* HEAP.
jim-jams *noun* JITTERS.
jimmies *noun* JITTERS.
jinx *noun*
Informal. Something or someone believed to bring bad luck: *His teammates considered him a jinx.*
   Syns: curse, hex, hoodoo.
jitters *noun*
Informal. A state of nervous restlessness or agitation: *got the jitters at the thought of going to the dentist.*
   Syns: all-overs (*Chiefly Regional*), fidgets, heebie-jeebies (*Slang*), jim-jams (*Slang*), jimmies (*Slang*), jumps (*Informal*), shakes, shivers, tremble(s), whim-whams (*also* wim-wams), willies (*Slang*).
jittery *adjective* EDGY.
jive *verb* JOKE.
job *noun*
1. BUSINESS.
2. FUNCTION.
3. POSITION.
4, 5. TASK.
jobholder *noun* EMPLOYEE.
jobholding *adjective* EMPLOYED.
jobless *adjective* WORKLESS.
jockey *verb* MANEUVER.
jocular *adjective* HUMOROUS.
jocularity *noun* GAIETY.
jocund *adjective* GAY.
jocundity *noun* GAIETY.
jog *verb*
1. DIG.
2. TROT.
jog *noun* TROT.
joggle *verb* SHAKE.
join *verb*
1. To become a member of: *wants to join the tennis club.*
   Syns: enlist (in), enroll (in), enter, muster (in), sign up (*or* on).
2. ADJOIN.
3. ASSOCIATE.
4. COMBINE.
joined *adjective* ADJOINING.
joining *noun* JOINT.
joint *noun*
1. A point or position at which two or

more things are joined: *a gas leak at the joint in the pipe.*
Syns: connection, coupling, joining, junction, juncture, seam, union.
2. *Slang.* A disreputable or run-down bar or restaurant: *a cheap, sleazy joint.*
Syns: dive (*Slang*), honky-tonk (*Slang*).
3. JAIL.
joint *adjective* COMMON.
jointly *adverb* TOGETHER.
joke *noun*
1. Words or actions intended to excite laughter or amusement: *opened the speech with a joke.*
Syns: funny (*Informal*), gag (*Informal*), ha-ha (*Slang*), jape, jest, quip, witticism.
2. An object of amusement or laughter: *The employees consider their inept boss a joke.*
Syns: butt³, jest, laughingstock, mockery.
3. PRANK.
4. SCREAM.
joke *verb*
1. To make jokes; behave playfully: *joking with his friends.*
Syns: clown (around) (*Informal*), fool (around) (*Informal*), fun, jest.
2. To tease or mock good-humoredly: *joked him about his shyness with girls.*
Syns: banter, chaff, fun, jest, jive (*Slang*), josh, kid (*Informal*), rag (*Slang*), razz (*Slang*), rib (*Slang*), ride (*Informal*).
joker *noun*
A person whose words or actions provoke or are intended to provoke amusement or laughter: *His uncle is quite a joker.*
Syns: card (*Informal*), clown, comedian, comic, cutup (*Informal*), farceur (*also* farcer), humorist, jester, jokester, wag², wit, zany.
jokester *noun* JOKER.
jollity *noun*
1, 2. GAIETY.
jolly *adjective* GAY.
jolt *verb*
1. BUMP.
2. STARTLE.
jolt *noun*
1. COLLISION.
2. SHOCK.
jolting *adjective* STARTLING.
josh *verb* JOKE.
jot *noun*
1. BIT¹.
2. DAMN.

journey *verb*
1. To make or go on a journey: *journeying to Spain; journeyed through the mountains.*
Syns: pass, peregrinate, travel, trek, trip (*Rare*). —*Idiom* hit the road.
2. GO.
joust *noun* TILT.
jovial *adjective* GAY.
joviality *noun* GAIETY.
jovialness *noun* GAIETY.
joy *noun*
1. DELIGHT.
2. HAPPINESS.
joy *verb*
1. DELIGHT.
2. REJOICE.
joyful *adjective*
1. GLAD.
2. MERRY.
joyless *adjective* SAD.
joyous *adjective*
1. GLAD.
2. MERRY.
jubilance *noun* EXULTATION.
jubilant *adjective* EXULTANT.
jubilate *verb* EXULT.
jubilation *noun* EXULTATION.
Judas *noun* BETRAYER.
judge *verb*
1. To make a decision about (a controversy, dispute, etc.) after deliberation, as in a court of law: *The jury judged the merits of the case.*
Syns: adjudge, adjudicate, arbitrate, decide, decree, determine, referee, rule, umpire.
2. ESTIMATE.
3. INFER.
judge *noun*
1. A public official who decides cases brought before a court of law in order to administer justice: *a judge in the appellate court.*
Syns: justice, magistrate.
2. A person, usu. appointed, who decides the issues or results, or supervises the conduct, of a competition or conflict: *a judge in the skating championships.*
Syns: arbiter, arbitrator, ref (*Slang*), referee, ump (*Slang*), umpire.
3. CRITIC.
judgment *noun*
1. COMMON SENSE.
2. DEDUCTION.
3. ESTIMATE.
4. RULING.
5. SENTENCE.
judgmental *adjective* ARBITRARY.

judicious *adjective* SANE.
jug *noun* JAIL.
juju *noun* CHARM.
jumble *verb*
1. CONFUSE.
2. DISORDER.
3. SHUFFLE.
jumble *noun*
1. ASSORTMENT.
2. DISORDER.
jumbled *adjective* CONFUSED.
jumbo *noun* GIANT.
jumbo *adjective* GIANT.
jump *verb*
1. To move off the ground by a muscular effort of the legs and feet: *jumped three feet into the air.*
   Syns: hurdle, leap, spring, vault².
2. To move suddenly and involuntarily: *always jumps when the telephone rings.*
   Syns: bolt, start, startle.
3. EJECT.
4. PROMOTE.
5. RAISE.
jump *noun*
1. The act of jumping: *gave a jump for joy.*
   Syns: hurdle, leap, spring, vault².
2. A sudden and involuntary movement: *woke up with a jump.*
   Syns: bolt, start, startle.
3. ADVANCEMENT.
4. ADVANTAGE.
5. BOUNCE.
6, 7. INCREASE.
jumps *noun* JITTERS.
jumpy *adjective* EDGY.
junction *noun*
1. The act or fact of coming together: *St. Louis is near the junction of the Mississippi and Missouri rivers.*
   Syns: concourse, concursion, confluence, convergence, gathering, meeting.
2. JOINT.
juncture *noun*
1. CRISIS.
2. INSTANT.
3. JOINT.
jungle *noun* TANGLE.
junior *noun* SUBORDINATE.
junk *verb* DISCARD.
junket *noun*
1. FEAST.
2. TRIP.
jurisdiction *noun* AUTHORITY.
jus *noun* LAW.
just *adjective*
1. Consistent with prevailing or accepted standards or circumstances: *Many believe that execution is never a just punishment.*
   Syns: appropriate, deserved, due, fitting, merited, right, rightful, suitable.
2. FAIR.
3. SOUND.
just *adverb*
1. Only a moment ago: *just walked in.*
   Syns: newly, recently.
2. BARELY.
3. EVEN¹.
4. MERELY.
5. PURELY.
justice *noun*
1. The state, action, or principle of treating all persons equally in accordance with the law: *Justice prevailed at the trial.*
   Syns: equitableness, equity. —*Idiom* due process.
2. FAIRNESS.
3. JUDGE.
justifiable *adjective*
Capable of being justified: *a justifiable reaction.*
   Syns: defensible, excusable, tenable.
justification *noun*
1. ACCOUNT.
2. APOLOGY.
3. BASIS.
4. CAUSE.
justify *verb*
1. To show to be just, right, or valid: *He lamely tried to justify his mistaken conduct.*
   Syns: excuse, explain away, rationalize, vindicate. —*Idiom* make a case for.
2. ACCOUNT FOR at **account.**
3. BACK.
4. CALL FOR at **call.**
5. CONFIRM.
6. DEFEND.
justly *adverb* FAIRLY.
justness *noun* FAIRNESS.
jut *verb*
1. BULGE.
2. HANG.
jut *noun* BULGE.
juvenescence *noun* YOUTH.
juvenile *adjective*
1. CHILDISH.
2. YOUNG.
juvenile *noun* CHILD.
juvenility *noun*
1. YOUNG.
2. YOUTH.
juxtapose *verb* ADJOIN.
juxtaposed *adjective* ADJOINING.

K

kaput *adjective* THROUGH.
keel over *verb* BLACK OUT at **black**.
keen¹ *adjective*
1. ACUTE.
2. CLEVER.
3. EAGER.
4. ENTHUSIASTIC.
5. MARVELOUS.
6. SHARP.
keen² *verb* CRY.
keenness *noun*
1. DISCERNMENT.
2. EDGE.
keep *verb*
1. To persevere in some condition, action, or belief: *keep quiet; kept a busy schedule.*
   Syns: maintain, retain, stay with.
2. To have or put in a customary place: *keeps the pots in the kitchen.*
   Syns: stash, store.
3. To remain fresh and unspoiled: *The soufflé won't keep.*
   Syns: last², stay¹.
4. CARRY.
5. CELEBRATE.
6. FOLLOW.
7. HOLD.
8. REFRAIN.
9. RESTRAIN.
10. SAVE.
11. SUPPORT.
keep back *verb*
1. HOLD.
2. RESTRAIN.
keep off *verb* PARRY.
keep on *verb* CARRY ON at **carry**.
keep out *verb* EXCLUDE.
keep up *verb* MAINTAIN.
keep *noun*
1. JAIL.
2. LIVING.
keeper *noun* GUARDIAN.
keeping *noun* CARE.
keepsake *noun* REMEMBRANCE.
ken *noun*
The extent of one's perception, understanding, knowledge, or vision: *The speaker went into technical details beyond the ken of the audience.*
   Syns: horizon, purview, range, reach, scope.
ken *verb*
1. SEE.
2. UNDERSTAND.

kernel *noun*
1. GERM.
2. HEART.
3. SEED.
key *noun* TICKET.
key *adjective*
1. PIVOTAL.
2. PRIMARY.
kibitzer *noun* MEDDLER.
kick *verb*
1. BREAK.
2. COMPLAIN.
3. OBJECT².
kick around *verb* DISCUSS.
kick in *verb*
1. CONTRIBUTE.
2. DIE.
kick off *verb*
1. DIE.
2. START.
kick out *verb* EJECT.
kick *noun*
1. *Slang.* A temporary concentration of interest: *He's on a science-fiction kick.*
   Syns: binge (*Slang*), thing (*Slang*), trip (*Slang*).
2. *Slang.* A stimulating or intoxicating effect: *quite a kick in that martini.*
   Syns: punch (*Informal*), sting (*Informal*), wallop.
3. GRIEVANCE.
4. OBJECTION.
5. THRILL.
6. WRINKLE².
kicker *noun*
1. GROUCH.
2. WRINKLE².
kickoff *noun* BEGINNING.
kid *noun* CHILD.
kid *verb* JOKE.
kidnap *verb*
To seize and detain (a person) unlawfully: *Terrorists kidnapped the ambassador.*
   Syns: abduct, carry off, snatch (*Slang*), spirit away.
kidney *noun* DISPOSITION.
kill *verb*
1. To cause the death of: *Famine killed thousands.*
   Syns: carry off, cut off, destroy, dispatch, do in (*Informal*), finish, finish off (*Informal*), slay, zap (*Slang*). —*Idioms* lay low, put an end to, put to sleep.
2. CANCEL.
3. MURDER.
killer *noun* MURDERER.

killing *noun* MURDER.

killing *adjective*
1. AMUSING.
2. PRICELESS.

kilter *noun* TRIM.

kin *noun*
1. One's relatives collectively: *His kin thought he was dead.*
   Syns: kindred, kinsfolk (*also* kinfolk).
2. RELATIVE.

kind[1] *adjective*
Having or showing a tender, considerate, and helping nature: *a kind person; a kind gesture.*
   Syns: benign, benignant, good-hearted, kindhearted, kindly.

kind[2] *noun*
A class that is defined by the common attribute or attributes possessed by all its members: *the kind of people who dress for dinner; flowers of every kind.*
   Syns: breed, cast, cut, description, feather, ilk, lot, manner, mold, nature, order, persuasion, sort, species, stamp, stripe, type, variety.

kindhearted *adjective* KIND[1].

kindle *verb*
1. AROUSE.
2. FIRE.
3. LIGHT[1].
4. PROVOKE.

kindliness *noun* BENEVOLENCE.

kindly *adjective* KIND[1].

kindness *noun*
1. The quality or state of being kind: *impossible to repay their kindness.*
   Syn: benignity (*also* benignancy).
2. BENEVOLENCE.
3. FAVOR.

kindred *noun*
1. FAMILY.
2. KIN.

kindred *adjective* RELATED.

kinetic *adjective* ENERGETIC.

kinsfolk *also* **kinfolk** *noun* KIN.

kinsman *noun* RELATIVE.

kinswoman *noun* RELATIVE.

kismet *noun* FATE.

kiss *verb*
1. To touch or caress with the lips, esp. as a sign of passion or affection: *I kissed her good-bye.*
   Syns: buss, osculate, peck[2], smack[1], smooch.
2. BRUSH.

kiss off *verb* DISMISS.

kiss *noun*
The act or an instance of kissing: *gave me a kiss.*
   Syns: buss, peck[2], smack[1], smacker, smooch.

kisser *noun* FACE.

klutz *noun* LUMP[1].

klutzy *adjective* AWKWARD.

knack *noun*
1. ABILITY.
2. ART.
3. HANG.
4. TALENT.

knead *verb* WORK.

knell *verb* RING[2].

knickknack *noun* NOVELTY.

knifelike *adjective* SHARP.

knightly *adjective* GRACIOUS.

knob *noun*
1. BULGE.
2, 3. BUMP.

knock *verb*
1. BELITTLE.
2. HIT.
3. TAP[1].

knock about *verb*
1. BATTER.
2. DISCUSS.

knock around *verb*
1. BATTER.
2. DISCUSS.

knock down *verb*
1. DESTROY.
2. DROP.

knock off *verb*
1. DEDUCT.
2. MURDER.
3. ROB.

knock over *verb*
1. OVERTURN.
2. ROB.

knock out *verb*
1. DISABLE.
2. EXHAUST.

knock *noun* TAP[1].

knockabout *adjective* ROUGH.

knocker *noun* CRITIC.

knockout *noun* BEAUTY.

knot *noun*
1. BOND.
2. BULGE.
3. BUMP.
4. GROUP.
5. TANGLE.

knot *verb* TIE.

knotty *adjective*
1. COMPLEX.
2. DIFFICULT.

know *verb*
1. To perceive directly with the intellect: *He knows quantum mechanics.*

Syns: apprehend, comprehend,
fathom, grasp, understand.
2. DISTINGUISH.
3. EXPERIENCE.
4. FEEL.
5. RECOGNIZE.

knowable *adjective*
UNDERSTANDABLE.

know-how *noun*
1. ABILITY.
2. ART.

knowing *adjective*
1. AWARE.
2. INTELLIGENT.
3. SHREWD.
4. WISE¹.

know-it-all *noun* SMART ALECK.

knowledge *noun*
1. That which is known; the sum of
what has been perceived, discovered,
or inferred: *new additions to our
knowledge about the universe.*
Syns: information, lore, wisdom.
2. EDUCATION.

knowledgeable *adjective*
1. INFORMED.
2. INTELLIGENT.

kook *noun* CRACKPOT.

kooky *adjective* FUNNY.

kowtow *noun* BOW.
kowtow *verb* FAWN.

kudize *verb* PRAISE.

kudos *noun*
1. DISTINCTION.
2. PRAISE.

Kultur *noun* CULTURE.

L

label *noun* TICKET.
label *verb*
1. CALL.
2. MARK.
3. TICKET.

labor *noun*
1. Physical exertion that is usu. difficult
and exhausting: *a life full of labor and
little rest.*
Syns: bullwork, drudgery, fag, moil,
sweat, toil, travail, work. —*Idioms*
lick (*or* stroke) of work, sweat of
one's brow.
2. BIRTH.

labor *verb*
1. To exert one's mental or physical
powers, usu. under difficulty and to
the point of exhaustion: *The child
labored over his homework. My father
labored all his life to support us.*
Syns: drive, fag, moil, strain¹, strive,
sweat, toil, travail, tug, work. —*Idiom*
break one's back (*or* neck).
2. ELABORATE.
3. TILL.
4. WORK.

labored *adjective*
1. FORCED.
2. PONDEROUS.

laborer *noun*
One who labors: *migrant farm laborers.*
Syns: coolie (*also* cooly), hand,
operative, roustabout, worker,
workhand, workingman, workman.
—*Idiom* beast of burden.

laborious *adjective*
1. BURDENSOME.
2. DIFFICULT.

labyrinth *noun* TANGLE.

labyrinthine *adjective* COMPLEX.

lachrymose *adjective* TEARFUL.

lack *verb*
To be without what is needed, required,
or essential: *a house that lacks indoor
plumbing; a school that lacks discipline.*
Syns: need, require, want.

lack *noun*
1. ABSENCE.
2. SHORTAGE.

lackadaisical *adjective* LANGUID.

lacking *adjective*
1. ABSENT.
2. DEFICIENT.

lackluster *adjective*
1, 2. DULL.

laconic *adjective* BRIEF.

lacuna *noun* GAP.

lade *verb*
1. CHARGE.
2. DIP.
3. HEAP.

la-di-da *also* **la-de-da** *adjective*
AFFECTED².

ladies' man *noun* SEE lady's man.

ladle *verb* DIP.

ladykiller *noun* PHILANDERER.

lady's man *also* **ladies' man** *noun*
PHILANDERER.

lag *verb* DELAY.

lag *noun*
1. DELAY.
2. LAGGARD.

lag *adjective* LAST¹.

laggard *noun*
One that lags: *That child is a real laggard on field trips. The company was a laggard in the drive to conserve energy.*
   Syns: lag, lingerer, loiterer, poke, slowpoke (*Informal*), straggler.
   —*Idiom* slow coach.
laggard *adjective* SLOW.
lagging *adjective*
1. BACKWARD.
2. SLOW.
lagniappe *noun* GRATUITY.
laid-back *adjective* EASYGOING.
laid up *adjective* SICK.
lair *noun*
1. HIDE-OUT.
2. HOLE.
lair *verb* HOLE UP at **hole.**
lamb *noun* INNOCENT.
lambaste *verb*
1. BEAT.
2. CALL DOWN at **call.**
lambasting *noun* TROUNCING.
lambent *adjective* BRIGHT.
lament *verb* GRIEVE.
lamentable *adjective* SORROWFUL.
lamia *noun* WITCH.
lamina *noun* SKIN.
lampoon *noun* SATIRE.
lancinating *adjective* SHARP.
land *noun*
1. *Law.* Usu. extensive real estate: *an English noble who owned land in Scotland.*
   Syns: acres, estate, property.
2. STATE.
land *verb*
1. To come to rest on the ground: *The jet landed. When I fell, I landed on my back.*
   Syns: alight[1], light[2], set down, settle, touch down.
2. To come ashore from a seacraft: *The D-day invasion forces landed on the Normandy beaches.*
   Syns: debark, disembark.
3. GET.
language *noun*
1. A system of terms used by a people sharing a history and culture: *Polish, Russian, and Serbo-Croatian are Slavic languages.*
   Syns: dialect, speech, tongue, vernacular.
2. Specialized expressions indigenous to a particular field, subject, trade, or subculture: *Chemical engineers speak their own language. The language of the social sciences is often unintelligible to the uninitiated.*

   Syns: cant[2], dialect, idiom, jargon, lexicon, terminology, vernacular, vocabulary.
languid *adjective*
1. Lacking energy and vitality: *gave a languid wave of her hand.*
   Syns: lackadaisical, languishing, languorous, limp, lymphatic, spiritless.
2. Showing weariness: *was obviously languid after her long nap.*
   Syns: languorous, leaden, listless.
languidness *noun* LETHARGY.
languish *verb*
1. To waste away from longing or grief: *When her husband was killed, she languished and died.*
   Syns: pine (away), wither.
2. FADE.
languishing *adjective* LANGUID.
languor *noun* LETHARGY.
languorous *adjective*
1, 2. LANGUID.
lanky *adjective* GANGLING.
lap *verb*
1, 2. WASH.
lapse *noun*
1. A minor mistake: *a brief lapse of memory.*
   Syns: fluff (*Informal*), slip (*Informal*), slip-up (*Informal*).
2. A slipping from a higher or better condition to a lower or poorer one: *a lapse into senility; another lapse into vulgarity.*
   Syns: backslide, backsliding, recidivation, recidivism, relapse.
3. ERROR.
lapse *verb*
1. *Law.* To become void, esp. through passage of time or an omission: *The insurance policy lapsed because we failed to renew it.*
   Syns: expire, run out.
2. GLIDE.
3. RELAPSE.
4. SUBSIDE.
larcener *noun*
A person who steals: *a larcener who specializes in automobiles.*
   Syns: larcenist, purloiner, stealer, thief.
larcenist *noun* LARCENER.
larcenous *adjective*
Tending to larceny: *larcenous white-collar workers who stole supplies.*
   Syns: sticky-fingered, thieving, thievish.
larceny *noun*
The crime of taking someone else's

property without consent: *convicted of larceny.*
  Syns: conveyance (*Archaic*), lifting (*Informal*), pinching (*Slang*), purloining, steal, stealing, theft, thievery, thieving.
lardy-dardy *adjective* AFFECTED[2].
lares and penates *noun* EFFECTS.
large *adjective*
  1. BIG.
  2. GENERAL.
  3. IMPORTANT.
large-hearted *adjective* GENEROUS.
largeish *adjective* SEE **largish**.
largeness *noun* SIZE.
larger *adjective* BEST.
large-scale *adjective* BIG.
largess also **largesse** *noun* GRATUITY.
largest *adjective* BEST.
largish also **largeish** *adjective* SIZABLE.
lark *noun* PRANK.
lash *verb*
  1. SLAM.
  2. WAG[1].
lassitude *noun*
  1. APATHY.
  2. EXHAUSTION.
  3. LETHARGY.
last[1] *adjective*
  1. Coming after all others: *the last act.*
    Syns: closing, concluding, final, terminal.
  2. Of or relating to a terminative condition, stage, or point: *the last days of Pompeii; a last farewell; last rites.*
    Syns: final, lag (*Rare*), latter, terminal, ultimate.
  3. Bringing up the rear: *the last car in the line.*
    Syns: endmost, hindmost (*also* hindermost), lattermost, rearmost.
  4. Next before the present one: *last night.*
    Syns: foregoing, latter, preceding, previous.
last *noun* END.
at last *adverb*
After a considerable length of time, usu. after a delay: *We arrived at last.*
  Syns: finally, ultimately. —*Idiom* at long last.
last *adverb*
In conclusion: *Last, we ask you to find this defendant guilty.*
  Syns: conclusively, finally, lastly.
last[2] *verb*
  1. ENDURE.

  2. KEEP.
  3. SURVIVE.
lasting *adjective* CONTINUING.
lastly *adverb* LAST[1].
late *adjective*
  1. Not being on time: *was late for the appointment; sent late condolences.*
    Syns: behindhand, belated, overdue, tardy.
  2. Having been such previously: *the company's late president, now retired; the late capital of that nation.*
    Syns: erstwhile, former, old, once, one-time (*also* onetime), past, previous, quondam, sometime, whilom.
  3. DEAD.
late *adverb*
  1. Not on time: *arrived late.*
    Syns: behind, behindhand.
  2. Not long ago: *As late as last night the hostages had not been released.*
    Syns: lately, latterly, recently. —*Idiom* of late.
  3. SLOW.
lately *adverb* LATE.
latency *noun* ABEYANCE.
lateness *noun*
The quality or condition of not being on time: *Please forgive the lateness of my arrival.*
  Syns: belatedness, tardiness.
latent *adjective*
  1. Existing in a temporarily inactive and hidden form: *latent cancer.*
    Syns: abeyant, dormant, quiescent, remissive, remittent.
  2. POTENTIAL.
later *adjective*
  1. Following something else in time: *Later developments vindicated my predictions.*
    Syns: after, posterior, postliminary, subsequent, subsequential.
  2. FUTURE.
later *adverb*
At a subsequent time: *I'll finish later. Later we left the club and went home.*
  Syns: after, afterward (*also* afterwards), afterwhile, infra, latterly, next. —*Idioms* after a while, by and by, later on.
lather *noun*
  1. AGITATION.
  2. FOAM.
  3. SWEAT.
lather *verb*
  1. FOAM.
  2. SWEAT.
lathery *adjective* FOAMY.

latitude *noun*
1. FREEDOM.
2. LIBERTY.
3. ROOM.

latter *adjective*
1, 2. LAST¹.

latter-day *adjective* MODERN.

latterly *adverb*
1. LATE.
2. LATER.

lattermost *adjective* LAST¹.

laud *verb*
1. HONOR.
2, 3. PRAISE.

laudable *adjective* ADMIRABLE.

laudation *noun*
1, 2. PRAISE.

laugh *verb*
To express amusement, mirth, or scorn by smiling and emitting loud, inarticulate sounds: *laughed at the comedian.*
    Syns: cachinnate, cackle, heehaw.
    —*Idioms* die laughing, laugh one's head off, roll in the aisles, split one's sides.

laugh at *verb* RIDICULE.

laugh *noun*
1. An act of laughing: *gave a hearty laugh.*
    Syns: cachinnation, cackle, heehaw, laughter.
2. SCREAM.

laughable *adjective*
1. Deserving laughter: *a laughable matter.*
    Syns: comic, comical, farcical, funny, gelastic, laughing, ludicrous, risible.
2. AMUSING.

laughing *adjective*
1. Emitting a murmuring sound felt to resemble a laugh: *laughing brooks.*
    Syns: babbling, burbling, gurgling, rippling.
2. LAUGHABLE.

laughingstock *noun* JOKE.

laughter *noun* LAUGH.

launch *verb*
1. INTRODUCE.
2. START.

launching *noun* BEGINNING.

laurels *noun* DISTINCTION.

lave *verb* WASH.

lavish *adjective*
1. EXTRAVAGANT.
2. LUXURIOUS.
3. PROFUSE.

lavish *verb* SHOWER.

lavishness *noun* EXTRAVAGANCE.

law *noun*
1. The formal product of a legislative or judicial body: *federal and state laws.*
    Syns: act, assize (*Eng. Hist.*), enactment, jus (*Latin*), legislation, lex, measure, statute.
2. A principle governing the affairs of man within or among political units: *the law of nations; maritime law.*
    Syns: canon, decree, decretum, edict, institute, ordinance, precept, prescription, regulation, rule.
3. A broad and basic rule or truth: *the laws of decency; the laws of physics.*
    Syns: axiom, fundamental, principle, theorem, universal.
4. POLICEMAN.

law *verb* SUE.

lawbreaker *noun* CRIMINAL.

lawcourt *noun* COURT.

lawful *adjective*
Within, allowed by, or sanctioned by the law: *lawful entry; a lawful marriage.*
    Syns: innocent, legal, legit (*Slang*), legitimate, licit.

lawfulness *noun* LEGALITY.

lawless *adjective*
1. CRIMINAL.
2. DISOBEDIENT.
3. ILLEGAL.
4. UNLAWFUL.

lawlessness *noun* DISORDER.

lawsuit *noun*
A legal proceeding to demand justice or enforce a right: *The lawsuit was heard in the superior court.*
    Syns: action (*Law*), case (*Law*), cause (*Law*), instance, suit (*Law*).

lax *verb* EASE.

lax *adjective*
1. LOOSE.
2. NEGLIGENT.
3. TOLERANT.

laxity *noun* NEGLIGENCE.

laxness *noun* NEGLIGENCE.

lay¹ *verb*
1. To place in a designated setting: *The novel is laid in Italy.*
    Syn: set¹.
2. AIM.
3. ATTRIBUTE.
4. BET.
5. DRAFT.
6. GAMBLE.
7. PRESENT².
8, 9. SET¹.

lay aside *verb* SAVE.

lay away *verb*
1. BANK¹.
2. BURY.

3. SAVE.
lay by *verb* SAVE.
lay down *verb*
1. BET.
2. DEPOSIT.
3. DICTATE.
4. RELINQUISH.
lay for
Informal. To wait concealed in order to attack (someone): *The thieves threatened to lay for their accomplice if he double-crossed them.*
　　Syns: ambuscade, ambush. —*Idioms* lay wait for, lie in wait for.
lay in *verb* SAVE.
lay into *verb* BEAT.
lay low *verb* HOLE UP at **hole**.
lay off *verb*
1. ABANDON.
2. STOP.
lay open *verb* REVEAL.
lay out *verb*
1. ARRANGE.
2. DESIGN.
3. PLOT.
4. SPEND.
lay over *verb* DEFER¹.
lay up *verb*
1. HOARD.
2. STOCKPILE.
lay² *adjective* PROFANE.
layout *noun*
1. ARRANGEMENT.
2. DESIGN.
laze *verb* IDLE.
laze *noun* LAZINESS.
laziness *noun*
The quality or state of being lazy: *Laziness and carelessness have no place in editorial work.*
　　Syns: fainéancy (*also* fainéance), idleness, indolence, laze, loafing, shiftlessness, sloth, slothfulness, sluggishness.
lazy *adjective*
Resistant to exertion and activity: *a lazy procrastinator.*
　　Syns: do-nothing, fainéant, idle, indolent, shiftless, slothful, trifling (*Chiefly Regional*). —*Idioms* bone lazy, born tired, lazy as Ludlam's dog.
lazy *verb* IDLE.
lazybones *noun* WASTREL.
leach *verb* OOZE.
lead *verb*
1. To have authoritative charge of: *This man has led his troops well.*
　　Syns: captain, command, officer.
2. To go through (life) in a certain way: *She has led a full and varied life.*

Syns: live¹, pass, pursue.
3. CONVERT.
4. EXTEND.
5. GUIDE.
6. INTRODUCE.
lead off *verb* START.
lead to *verb* CAUSE.
lead *noun*
1. A piece of information useful in a search: *had picked up a strong lead in the hunt for the killer.*
　　Syns: clue (*also* clew), scent.
2. The capacity to lead others: *a young captain who took the lead in battle.*
　　Syns: command, leadership.
3. The main performer in a theatrical production: *was the lead in the play.*
　　Syns: principal, protagonist, star.
4. FEATURE.
5. GUIDANCE.
6. GUIDE.
leaden *adjective* LANGUID.
leader *noun*
1. A leading contestant: *the leader in the marathon.*
　　Syns: front-runner, number one (*Informal*).
2. BOSS.
3. CHIEF.
4. DIGNITARY.
5. FEATURE.
6. GUIDE.
leadership *noun*
1. GUIDANCE.
2. LEAD.
leading *adjective*
1. FAMOUS.
2. PRIMARY.
leadoff *noun* BEGINNING.
leaf *verb* BROWSE.
league *noun*
1. ALLIANCE.
2. CLASS.
3. CONFERENCE.
4. UNION.
league *verb*
1. ALLY.
2. BAND².
leaguer *noun* ALLY.
leak *verb* COME OUT at **come**.
lean¹ *verb*
1. HANG.
2. INCLINE.
3. TEND¹.
lean² *adjective*
1. BRIEF.
2. THIN.
3. TIGHT.
lean *verb* THIN.
leaning *noun* BENT.

leap *verb*
1. BOUNCE.
2. JUMP.
leap *noun*
1. BOUNCE.
2. JUMP.
learn *verb*
1. To gain knowledge or mastery of by study: *learn French.*
   Syns: get, master, pick up.
2. DISCOVER.
3. MEMORIZE.
learned *adjective*
Having or showing profound knowledge and scholarship: *a learned man.*
   Syns: erudite, scholarly, scholastic, wise[1].
learner *noun* STUDENT.
learning *noun* EDUCATION.
lease *verb* HIRE.
leash *verb* HAMPER.
leave[1] *verb*
1. To give (property) to another person after one's death: *My aunt left me a house and $100.*
   Syns: bequeath (*Law*), devise (*Law*), legate, will[2].
2. ABANDON.
3. GO.
4. QUIT.
leave off *verb*
1. BREAK.
2. STOP.
leave[2] *noun*
1. PERMISSION.
2. VACATION.
leave *verb* PERMIT.
leaven *noun* CATALYST.
leavening *noun* CATALYST.
leave-taking *noun* PARTING.
leaving *noun* DEPARTURE.
leavings *noun* BALANCE.
lecher *noun* WANTON.
lecture *verb* ADDRESS.
lecture *noun* SPEECH.
leech *noun* PARASITE.
leery *adjective* INCREDULOUS.
lees *noun* DEPOSIT.
leeway *noun*
1. LIBERTY.
2. ROOM.
left-handed *adjective* INSINCERE.
leftover *adjective* REMAINING.
legacy *noun*
1. BIRTHRIGHT.
2. HERITAGE.
legal *adjective* LAWFUL.
legality *noun*
The state or quality of being within the

law: *The legality of your actions is suspect.*
   Syns: lawfulness, legitimacy, legitimateness, licitness.
legalize *verb*
To make lawful: *tried to legalize marijuana.*
   Syns: legitimate, legitimatize, legitimize.
legate *verb* LEAVE[1].
legation *noun* MISSION.
legend *noun*
1. LORE.
2. MYTH.
legendary *adjective* MYTHICAL.
legerdemain *noun* MAGIC.
legion *noun* CROWD.
legion *adjective* MANY.
legislate *verb* ENACT.
legislation *noun* LAW.
legit *adjective* LAWFUL.
legitimacy *noun*
1. AUTHENTICITY.
2. LEGALITY.
legitimate *adjective*
1. LAWFUL.
2. TRUE.
legitimate *verb* LEGALIZE.
legitimateness *noun* LEGALITY.
legitimatize *verb* LEGALIZE.
legitimize *verb* LEGALIZE.
leisure *noun* REST[1].
leisurely *adjective* DELIBERATE.
lemon *noun* FAILURE.
lend *verb*
To supply (money), esp. on credit: *refused to lend her any cash.*
   Syns: advance, loan.
length *noun*
1. The ultimate point to which an action, thought, discussion, or policy is carried: *will go to any length to free the hostages.*
   Syns: extreme, limit.
2. DISTANCE.
3. EXTENT.
lengthen *verb*
To make or become longer: *lengthened the table by inserting a leaf; relapses that lengthened her convalescence.*
   Syns: draw out, elongate, extend, produce (*Geom.*), prolong, prolongate, protract, spin out, stretch (out).
lengthy *adjective*
1, 2. LONG[1].
leniency *also* **lenience** *noun*
1. GRACE.
2. TOLERANCE.
lenient *adjective* TOLERANT.
lenity *noun* GRACE.

lentitude *noun* LETHARGY.
lese majesty *also* **lèse majesté** *noun*
DISRESPECT.
lessen *verb*
1. DECREASE.
2. RELIEVE.
lesser *adjective* MINOR.
lesson *noun* EXAMPLE.
let *verb*
1. HIRE.
2, 3, 4. PERMIT.
let down *verb*
1. DISAPPOINT.
2. LOWER².
let in *verb* ADMIT.
let off *verb*
1. EMIT.
2. EXCUSE.
let out *verb*
1. BETRAY.
2. DRAIN.
3. EMIT.
let up *verb*
1. DECREASE.
2. EASE.
3. SUBSIDE.
letdown *noun* DISAPPOINTMENT.
lethal *adjective* DEADLY.
lethargic *adjective*
1. Lacking mental and physical
alertness and activity: *lethargic,
overtranquilized patients.*
Syns: dopey (*also* dopy) (*Slang*),
hebetudinous, sluggish, stupid, torpid.
2. APATHETIC.
lethargy *noun*
1. A deficiency in mental and physical
alertness and activity: *The
overmedicated patient sank into a state
of lethargy.*
Syns: dopeyness (*also* dopiness)
(*Slang*), dullness, hebetude,
languidness, languor, lassitude,
lentitude (*Archaic*), sluggishness,
stupor, torpidity, torpidness, torpor.
2. APATHY.
3. INACTION.
letter *noun*
1. A written communication directed to
another: *I wrote a letter to my son.*
Syns: epistle, missive, note.
2. The literal meaning of something: *the
letter of the law.*
Syns: literality, literalness.
lettered *adjective* EDUCATED.
lettuce *noun* MONEY.
letup *noun*
1. DECREASE.
2. WANE.

level *adjective*
1, 2. EVEN¹.
level *noun* DEGREE.
level *verb*
1. AIM.
2. DESTROY.
3. DROP.
4. EQUALIZE.
5. EVEN.
levelheaded *adjective* SANE.
leverage *noun* INFLUENCE.
leviathan *noun* GIANT.
leviathan *adjective* GIANT.
levy *noun*
1. DRAFT.
2. TAX.
levy *verb*
1. DRAFT.
2. IMPOSE.
lewd *adjective* OBSCENE.
lewdness *noun* OBSCENITY.
lex *noun* LAW.
lexicon *noun*
1. LANGUAGE.
2, 3. VOCABULARY.
liability *noun*
1, 2. DEBT.
3. EXPOSURE.
liable *adjective*
1. Legally obligated: *a bill to make
parents liable for a child's vandalism.*
Syns: accountable, answerable,
responsible.
2. Tending to incur: *liable to asthma
attacks.*
Syns: open, prone, subject,
susceptible, vulnerable.
3. INCLINED.
liar *noun*
One who tells lies: *a notorious liar whom
no one believed.*
Syns: Ananias, fabricator, falsifier,
fibber, fibster, perjurer, prevaricator,
storyteller. —*Idiom* false witness.
libel *noun*
The expression of injurious, malicious
statements about someone: *Those
remarks about the senator's taking
payoffs are libel.*
Syns: aspersion, calumny, defamation,
detraction, scandal, slander. —*Idioms*
character assassination, malicious
falsehood.
libel *verb*
To make defamatory statements about:
libeled his rival on the Senate floor.
Syns: asperse, calumniate, defame,
malign, scandal, scandalize, slander,
slur, spatter, tear down, vilify.
—*Idioms* cast aspersions on, sling
mud on.

libelous *adjective*
Damaging to the reputation: *libelous remarks for which we brought suit.*
Syns: backbiting, calumnious, defamatory, detracting, detractive, detractory, injurious, invidious, maligning, scandalous, slanderous, vilifying.

liberal *adjective*
1. Favoring civil liberties and social progress: *holds liberal political opinions.*
Syns: liberalistic, progressive.
2. BROAD.
3. FAIR.
4, 5. GENEROUS.

liberal *noun*
A person with liberal political opinions: *The liberals will debate the conservatives.*
Syns: liberalist, progressive.

liberalist *noun* LIBERAL.
liberalistic *adjective* LIBERAL.
liberality *noun* GENEROSITY.
liberate *verb* FREE.
liberated *adjective* FREE.
liberation *noun* LIBERTY.
libertine *adjective* WANTON.
libertine *noun* WANTON.
libertinism *noun* LICENSE.

liberty *noun*
1. The state of not being in confinement or servitude: *a prisoner given his liberty when he received his parole.*
Syns: emancipation, freedom, liberation, manumission.
2. Departure from normal rules or procedures: *too much liberty in her translation of Homer.*
Syns: freedom, latitude, leeway, license.
3. FREEDOM.

libidinous *adjective* EROTIC.

license *noun*
1. Legal permission to do something: *You need a license to operate a car.*
Syns: permit, warrant. —*Idiom* piece of paper.
2. Excessive freedom; lack of restraint: *Unrestricted behavior can turn to license.*
Syns: dissoluteness, dissolution, libertinism, licentiousness, profligacy.
3. LIBERTY.
4. PERMISSION.

license *verb* AUTHORIZE.
licentious *adjective* ABANDONED.
licentiousness *noun* LICENSE.
licit *adjective* LAWFUL.
licitness *noun* LEGALITY.

lick *verb*
1. BEAT.
2. DEFEAT.
lick *noun* BLOW[2].
lickety-split *adverb* FAST.
licking *noun*
1. BEATING.
2. DEFEAT.
3. TROUNCING.

lie[1] *verb*
1. To be or place oneself in a prostrate or recumbent position: *He lay under the oak tree and read.*
Syns: lie down, recline, repose, stretch out.
2. CONSIST.
3. REST[1].

lie down *verb*
1. LIE[1].
2. REST[1].

lie[2] *noun*
An untrue declaration: *spread lies about the star's personal life.*
Syns: canard, falsehood, falsity, fib, fiction, inveracity, misrepresentation, misstatement, prevarication, story, tale, untruth, whopper. —*Idioms* barefaced lie, cock-and-bull story, fish story, tall story (*or* tale).

lie *verb*
To make untrue declarations: *lied about his whereabouts on the night of the murder.*
Syns: falsify, fib, forswear (*also* foreswear), perjure, prevaricate.

liege *adjective* FAITHFUL.
lieu *noun* PLACE.
lieutenant *noun* ASSISTANT.

life *noun*
1. The period during which someone or something exists: *his brief, unhappy life; a warranty good for the life of the car.*
Syns: duration, existence, lifetime, term. —*Idiom* one's born days.
2. HUMAN BEING.
3. SPIRIT.

lifeless *adjective*
1. DEAD.
2. DULL.

lifelike *adjective*
1. GRAPHIC.
2. REALISTIC.

lifetime *noun* LIFE.

lift *verb*
1. To disappear by or as if by rising: *waiting for the fog to lift.*
Syns: dispel, disperse, dissipate, scatter.

2. To take back or remove: *lifted the ban on smoking.*
Syns: recall, repeal, rescind, reverse, revoke.
3. ELATE.
4. ELEVATE.
5. RISE.
6. STEAL.
7. TAKE OFF at **take.**

lift *noun*
1. An instance of lifting or being lifted: *Give me a lift onto the saddle.*
Syns: boost, heave, hoist.
2. ELATION.
3. THRILL.

lifted *adjective* ELEVATED.
lifting *noun* LARCENY.
liftoff *noun* TAKEOFF.
ligament *noun* BOND.
ligature *noun* BOND.

light¹ *noun*
1. Electromagnetic radiation that makes vision possible: *enough light so we could read.*
Syns: illumination, luminosity.
2. A way of considering a matter: *now sees the problem in a new light.*
Syns: angle, aspect, slant, standpoint, viewpoint. —*Idioms* frame of reference, vantage point.
3. ILLUMINATION.
4. VISION.

light *verb*
1. To cause to burn or undergo combustion: *Light the fire.*
Syns: enkindle, fire, ignite, kindle, torch (*Slang*). —*Idioms* set fire to, set on fire (*or* afire).
2. To make lively or animated: *smiles lighting their faces.*
Syns: animate, brighten, enliven.
3. ILLUMINATE.

light *adjective* FAIR.

light² *adjective*
1. Having little weight; not heavy: *a light suitcase; a light jacket.*
Syns: lightweight, weightless. —*Idiom* light as a feather.
2. Of small intensity: *a light breeze; a light tap at the door.*
Syns: gentle, moderate, slight, soft.
3. Free from care or worry: *a light heart; a light mood.*
Syns: blithe, carefree, debonair, lighthearted, sprightly.
4. Requiring little effort or exertion: *light chores; light exercise.*
Syns: easy, moderate.
5. FROTHY.
6. WANTON.

light *verb* LAND.
light on (*or* **upon**) *verb* COME ACROSS at **come.**

lighten *verb*
1. ILLUMINATE.
2. RELIEVE.

lightheaded *adjective*
1. DIZZY.
2. GIDDY.

lightheadedness *noun* DIZZINESS.

lighthearted *adjective*
1. CHEERFUL.
2. GAY.
3. LIGHT².

lighting *noun* ILLUMINATION.

lightweight *adjective* LIGHT².

like¹ *verb*
1. To find agreeable: *Do you like this kind of music?*
Syns: conceit (*Rare*), fancy, take to.
2. CHOOSE.
3. ENJOY.

like² *adjective*
Possessing the same or almost the same characteristics: *two sisters of like opinions.*
Syns: alike, analogous, comparable, corresponding, equivalent, parallel, similar, uniform.

likeliness *noun* CHANCE.

likely *adjective*
1. EARTHLY.
2. ENCOURAGING.
3. INCLINED.
4. PRESUMPTIVE.

liken *verb*
1. To represent as similar: *Some liken politics to a game of chess.*
Syns: analogize, assimilate, compare, equate, match, parallel.
2. FAVOR.

likeness *noun*
1. A representation of a person or thing: *The photo is a very good likeness of you.*
Syns: copy, facsimile, image, replica.
2. The quality or state of being alike: *the amazing likeness between Edward and his brother.*
Syns: affinity, alikeness, analogy, comparison, resemblance, similarity, similitude.

liking *noun*
1. A desire for a particular thing or activity: *Maybe this will be more to your liking.*
Syns: fancy, mind, pleasure, will¹.
2. APPRECIATION.

lilliputian *adjective* TINY.
lily-livered *adjective* COWARDLY.

lily-white *adjective*
1. EXEMPLARY.
2. INNOCENT.

limit *noun*
1. The boundary surrounding a certain area: *a house outside the city limits.*
   Syns: bound(s), confine(s), environs, precinct(s).
2. The greatest amount or number allowed: *a speed limit of 30 miles an hour.*
   Syns: ceiling, limitation, maximum.
3. END.
4. EXTREME.
5. LENGTH.

limit *verb*
1. To place a limit on: *limiting the number of free coupons; research limited to the laboratory.*
   Syns: circumscribe, confine, delimit, delimitate, restrict.
2. DETERMINE.

limitation *noun*
1. END.
2. LIMIT.
3, 4. RESTRICTION.

limited *adjective*
1. DEFINITE.
2, 3. LOCAL.
4. NARROW.
5. QUALIFIED.
6. RESTRICTED.

limitless *adjective* ENDLESS.
limitlessness *noun* INFINITY.
limn *verb* REPRESENT.
limp *verb*
1. To walk in a lame way: *The quarterback limped off the field.*
   Syns: halt², hitch, hobble.
2. MUDDLE.

limp *adjective*
1. Lacking in stiffness or firmness: *a limp shirt collar.*
   Syns: flabby, flaccid, floppy.
2. LANGUID.

limpid *adjective*
1. CLEAR.
2. TRANSPARENT.

limpidity *noun* CLARITY.
line *noun*
1. A group of people or things arranged in a row: *a long line at the bus stop.*
   Syns: column, file, queue, rank¹, row¹, string, tier.
2. An indentation or seam on the skin, esp. on the face: *needed more and more make-up to hide the lines.*
   Syns: crease, crinkle, furrow, wrinkle¹.
3. An official or prescribed plan or course of action: *adhering to the party line.*
   Syns: policy, procedure, program.
4. ANCESTRY.
5. APPROACH.
6. BUSINESS.
7. GOODS.

line *verb*
To place in or form a line or lines: *lines his pencils on the table.*
   Syns: align, line up, range.

line up *verb* LINE.
lineage *noun*
1. ANCESTRY.
2. FAMILY.

lineal *adjective* DIRECT.
line-up *also* **lineup** *noun*
1. ARRANGEMENT.
2. PROGRAM.
3. TICKET.

linger *verb*
1. DELAY.
2. PAUSE.
3. REMAIN.

lingerer *noun* LAGGARD.
lingering *adjective* CHRONIC.
lingo *noun* DIALECT.
link *verb*
1, 2. ASSOCIATE.
3. COMBINE.

link *noun*
1. BOND.
2. RELATION.

linkage *noun* BOND.
lion *noun* DIGNITARY.
lip *verb* WASH.
liquefy *verb* MELT.
liquidate *verb*
1. ANNIHILATE.
2. ELIMINATE.
3. MURDER.
4. SETTLE.

liquidation *noun*
1. ANNIHILATION.
2. ELIMINATION.

liquor *noun* DRINK.
liquor up *verb* DRINK.
list¹ *verb*
1. To register in or as if in a book: *list names on the honor roll.*
   Syns: book, catalogue (*also* catalog), enroll, inscribe. —*Idiom* set (*or* write) down.
2. ENUMERATE.

list *noun*
A series of names, words, etc., printed or written down: *keeps a list of her friends' birthdays.*
   Syns: catalogue (*also* catalog), register, roll, roster, schedule.

list² *verb* INCLINE.
list³ *verb* LISTEN.
listen *verb*
1. To make an effort to hear something: *He's such a fine violinist that everyone listens carefully.*
   Syns: hark, hearken (*also* harken) (*Poetic & Archaic*), list³ (*Poetic*).
   —*Idioms* bend (*or* lend) an ear, give ear to.
2. HEAR.
listless *adjective*
1. APATHETIC.
2. LANGUID.
listlessness *noun* APATHY.
literal *adjective*
Employing the very same words as another: *a literal transcription of the witnesses' reports.*
   Syns: verbatim, verbal, word-for-word. —*Idiom* true to the letter.
literality *noun* LETTER.
literalness *noun* LETTER.
literate *adjective* EDUCATED.
litigable *adjective*
Subject to a lawsuit: *not enough evidence to make the case litigable.*
   Syns: prosecutable, triable.
litigate *verb* SUE.
litigious *adjective* ARGUMENTATIVE.
litter *noun* YOUNG.
little *adjective*
1. Notably below average in amount, size, or scope: *bought a little sports car.*
   Syns: bantam, petite, small, smallish.
2. Not of great importance: *Every little thing upsets him.*
   Syns: inconsequential, insignificant, trivial, unimportant. —*Idiom* of no account.
3. NARROW.
4. SMALL.
little *adverb* INFREQUENTLY.
lit up *adjective* DRUNK.
liturgical *adjective* RITUAL.
liturgy *noun* CEREMONY.
livable *also* **liveable** *adjective*
Fit to live in: *a livable apartment house.*
   Syns: habitable, inhabitable, lodgeable.
live¹ *verb*
1. To have as one's domicile, usu. for an extended period: *had lived in Europe for ten years.*
   Syns: abide, bide, dig (*Slang*), domicile (*also* domiciliate), dwell, reside.
2. To maintain existence in a certain

way: *lived on fast foods and sodas; a propaganda machine that lived on lies.*
   Syns: feed, subsist.
3. BE.
4. LEAD.
live² *adjective*
1. ACTIVE.
2. ALIVE.
3. HOT.
liveable *adjective* SEE **livable.**
livelihood *noun* LIVING.
liveliness *noun* SPIRIT.
lively *adjective*
1. Very brisk, alert, and high-spirited: *a lively personality.*
   Syns: animate, animated, bouncy, chipper, dashing, peppy (*Informal*), pert, spirited, vivacious. —*Idioms* bright-eyed and bushy-tailed, full of life.
2. ENERGETIC.
3. VIGOROUS.
liven *verb* QUICKEN.
live wire *noun* EAGER BEAVER.
livid *adjective* PALE.
living *adjective*
1, 2. ALIVE.
living *noun*
The means needed to support life: *earned a comfortable living by selling real estate.*
   Syns: alimentation, alimony, bread, keep, livelihood, maintenance, salt, subsistence, support, sustenance, upkeep. —*Idiom* bread and butter.
load *noun*
1. A quantity of explosives put into a weapon: *a high-powered rifle capable of firing heavy loads; missiles armed with multiple nuclear loads.*
   Syn: charge.
2. BURDEN.
3. HEAP.
load *verb*
1. To put (explosive material) into a weapon: *load a rifle.*
   Syns: arm, charge.
2. ADULTERATE.
3. CHARGE.
4. CROWD.
5. DISTORT.
6. FILL.
7. HEAP.
loaded *adjective*
1. DRUNK.
2. FULL.
3. HEAVY.
4. RICH.
loaf *verb* IDLE.
loafer *noun* WASTREL.
loafing *noun* LAZINESS.

loan *verb* LEND.
loath also **loth** *adjective* INDISPOSED.
loathe *verb* HATE.
loathing *noun*
1. DISGUST.
2. HATE.
loathsome *adjective*
1. FILTHY.
2. OFFENSIVE.
local *adjective*
1. Confined to a particular location or
site: *local problems of no concern to
the federal government; a local
infection.*
Syns: isolated, limited, localized,
restricted.
2. Having the restricted outlook often
characteristic of geographic isolation:
*took a local, not a global, view of the
monetary crisis.*
Syns: insular, limited, narrow,
narrow-minded, parochial, provincial,
small-town.
locale *noun*
1. ENVIRONMENT.
2. LOCALITY.
3. SCENE.
locality *noun*
1. A particular geographic area: *wanted
to live in a locality near the city.*
Syns: locale, location, place.
2. A surrounding site: *searched for the
stolen car in the locality of the
waterfront.*
Syns: area, neighborhood, vicinity.
3. AREA.
4. ENVIRONMENT.
5. NEIGHBORHOOD.
localized *adjective* LOCAL.
locate *verb*
1. FIND.
2. POSITION.
location *noun*
1. BEARING.
2. LOCALITY.
3. POINT.
4. POSITION.
lock *verb* BARB.
lock up *verb* JAIL.
lockup *noun* JAIL.
loco *adjective* INSANE.
locus *noun*
1. POINT.
2. POSITION.
locution *noun* EXPRESSION.
lodge *verb*
1. CATCH.
2. FIX.
lodgeable *adjective* LIVABLE.
lodging *noun* SHELTER.

lodgings *noun* HOME.
loftiest *adjective* TOP.
loftiness *noun* ARROGANCE.
lofty *adjective*
1. Imposingly high: *The cathedral's
central feature is its magnificent lofty
spire.*
Syns: aerial, airy, sky-high,
skyscraping, towering.
2. ARROGANT.
3. ELEVATED.
4. EXALTED.
5. GRAND.
6. TALL.
logic *noun*
1. Exact, valid, and rational reasoning:
used logic to solve life's problems.
Syns: ratiocination, rationality,
reason.
2. SENSE.
logical *adjective*
1. Consistent with reason and intellect:
*gave the class a logical explanation for
the phenomena.*
Syns: consequent, intelligent,
rational, reasonable, sensible.
2. Able to reason validly: *a logical mind.*
Syns: analytic (*also* analytical),
ratiocinative, rational.
loiter *verb*
1. DELAY.
2. IDLE.
loiterer *noun* LAGGARD.
loll *verb*
1, 2. SLOUCH.
3. SPRAWL.
lone *adjective*
1. Alone in a given category: *This
dolmen is the lone example of
prehistoric monuments in our village.*
Syns: one, only, particular, separate,
single, sole, solitary, unique. —*Idioms*
first and last, one and only.
2. SINGLE.
3. SOLITARY.
lonelihood *noun* ALONENESS.
loneliness *noun* ALONENESS.
lonely *adjective*
1. Empty of people: *a dark, lonely road.*
Syns: deserted, desolate, forlorn,
godforsaken (*also* Godforsaken),
lonesome, unfrequented.
2. Dejected due to the awareness of
being alone: *a lonely, unwanted child
relegated to foster homes.*
Syns: forlorn, lonesome, lorn
(*Poetic*).
3. ALONE.
4. REMOTE.
loneness *noun* ALONENESS.

lonesome *adjective*
1. ALONE.
2, 3. LONELY.
4. REMOTE.

long¹ *adjective*
1. Having great physical length: *a long distance.*
   Syns: elongate, elongated, extended, lengthy.
2. Extending tediously beyond a standard duration: *a long, boring play.*
   Syns: dragging, drawn-out, lengthy, long-drawn (*also* long-drawn-out), overlong, prolonged, protracted.
3. Having many syllables: *long words.*
   Syns: multisyllabic, polysyllabic, sesquipedalian.
4. HIGH.

long *noun* AGE.

long² *verb* DESIRE.

long-drawn *also* **long-drawn-out** *adjective* LONG¹.

longing *noun*
1. DESIRE.
2. DREAM.

long-lasting *adjective* CONTINUING.
long-lived *adjective* CONTINUING.
long-standing *adjective* CONTINUING.
long-suffering *adjective* PATIENT.
long-suffering *noun* PATIENCE.
longwinded *adjective* WORDY.

look *verb*
1. To use the power of vision: *Look before you cross the street.*
   Syns: observe, perceive, watch.
2. To direct the eyes on an object: *She looked at the child with a smile.*
   Syns: consider, contemplate, eye, gaze (at, on, *or* upon), regard, view.
3. To be sure that: *Look that you don't arrive too late.*
   Syns: mind, see, watch.
4. APPEAR.

look after *verb* TEND².
look for *verb*
1. EXPECT.
2. SEEK.

look in *verb* VISIT.
look into *verb* EXPLORE.
look on (or **upon**) *verb* FACE.
look out *verb*
To be careful: *Look out for ice on the steps.*
   Syns: beware, mind, watch out.
   —*Idioms* be on guard, be on the lookout, keep an eye peeled, take care (*or* heed).

look over *verb* SURVEY.
look up *verb* VISIT.
look *noun*
1. An act of directing the eyes on an object: *took a close look at the merchandise.*
   Syns: eye, gaze, regard, sight, view.
2. EXPRESSION.
3. FACE.

looker *noun* BEAUTY.
looker-on *noun* WATCHER.
lookout *noun*
1. The act of carefully watching: *kept a constant lookout for enemy aircraft.*
   Syns: surveillance, vigil, vigilance, watch. —*Idiom* watch and ward.
2. A high structure commanding a wide view: *a concentration camp surrounded with high fences and lookouts.*
   Syns: observatory, outlook, overlook.
3. BUSINESS.
4. GUARD.
5. VIEW.

look(s) *noun* APPEARANCE.
loom *verb*
1. APPEAR.
2. THREATEN.

loon *noun* CRACKPOT.
loony *also* **luny** *adjective*
1. FOOLISH.
2. INSANE.

loony *also* **luny** *noun* CRACKPOT.
loop *noun*
A length of line folded over and joined at the ends so as to form a curve or circle: *a loop of ribbon.*
   Syns: eye, ring¹.

looped *adjective* DRUNK.
loopy *adjective* FOOLISH.
loose *adjective*
1. Able to move about at will without bounds or restraint: *The fence is down and the cattle are loose. Two escaped convicts are loose.*
   Syns: free, unconfined, unrestrained.
   —*Idioms* at liberty, free as a bird, on the loose.
2. Not tautly bound to something else: *a loose anchor line.*
   Syns: lax, relaxed, slack.
3. Lacking literal exactness: *a loose translation.*
   Syns: free, inexact.
4. WANTON.

loose *verb*
1. EASE.
2. FREE.
3. SHOOT.
4. UNDO.

loose-jointed *adjective* GANGLING.
loosen *verb*
1. EASE.
2. UNDO.

loot *verb*
1. To rob on a large scale: *The rioting mob looted many stores.*
   Syns: plunder, ransack.
2. SACK².
loot *noun* PLUNDER.
lop¹ *verb*
1. CUT BACK at **cut**.
2. TRUNCATE.
lop² *verb*
1, 2. SLOUCH.
lope *verb*
1. SKIP.
2. TROT.
lope *noun* TROT.
loquacious *adjective* TALKATIVE.
lordliness *noun* ARROGANCE.
lordly *adjective*
1. ARROGANT.
2. AUTHORITATIVE.
3. GRAND.
lore *noun*
1. A body of traditional beliefs and notions accumulated about a particular subject: *World War II lore; sea lore.*
   Syns: folklore, legend, myth, mythology, mythos, tradition.
2. KNOWLEDGE.
lorn *adjective*
1. ABANDONED.
2. LONELY.
lose *verb*
1. To be unable to find: *I've lost my wallet.*
   Syns: mislay, misplace.
2. To fail to take advantage of: *lost a good chance to explain.*
   Syns: miss, waste. —*Idioms* let slip by, let slip through one's fingers, lose out on.
3. To get away from (a pursuer): *The hunted criminal managed to lose the police in traffic.*
   Syns: elude, evade, shake (off), throw off. —*Idiom* give someone the slip.
4. DROP.
loser *noun*
1. FAILURE.
2. UNFORTUNATE.
loss *noun*
1. The act or an instance of losing something: *was troubled by the loss of her keys.*
   Syns: mislaying, misplacement, misplacing.
2. DEPRIVATION.
lost *adjective*
1. No longer in one's possession: *My keys are lost.*
   Syns: gone, missing.

2. CONDEMNED.
3. VANISHED.
lot *noun*
1. A piece of land: *bought a cemetery lot.*
   Syns: parcel, plot, tract.
2. ALLOTMENT.
3. DEAL.
4. FATE.
5. GROUP.
6, 7. HEAP.
8. KIND².
lot *verb* ALLOT.
loth *adjective* SEE **loath.**
Lothario *noun* GALLANT.
loud *adjective*
1. Marked by extremely high volume and intensity of sound: *loud yells; a loud rock band.*
   Syns: blaring, deafening, roaring, stentorian, stentorious.
2. GAUDY.
loudmouthed *adjective* VOCIFEROUS.
lounge *verb* IDLE.
lour *verb & noun* SEE **lower¹.**
louring *adjective* SEE **lowering.**
loury *adjective* SEE **lowery.**
louse up *verb* BOTCH.
lousy *adjective*
1. FILTHY.
2. SHODDY.
lout *noun* LUMP¹.
lovable *adjective* ADORABLE.
love *noun*
1. The passionate affection and desire felt by lovers for each other: *Their love knew no bounds.*
   Syns: amorousness, amour, passion.
2. An intimate sexual relationship between two people: *couldn't discuss this latest illicit love.*
   Syns: affair, amour, love affair, romance.
3. A strong, enthusiastic liking for something: *a love of the sea.*
   Syns: love affair, passion.
4. ADORATION.
5. ATTACHMENT.
6. DARLING.
love *verb*
1, 2. ADORE.
love affair *noun*
1, 2. LOVE.
loved *adjective*
1. DARLING.
2. FAVORITE.
lovely *adjective*
1. ATTRACTIVE.
2. BEAUTIFUL.
lovely *noun* BEAUTY.

lover *noun*
1. A person's regular sexual partner: *He has been her lover for years.*
   Syn: paramour.
2. ADMIRER.

loving *adjective* AFFECTIONATE.

low *adjective*
1. Cut to reveal the wearer's neck, chest, and back: *a revealingly low bodice.*
   Syns: low-cut, low-necked (*also* low-neck), plunging.
2. *Mus.* Being a sound produced by a relatively small frequency of vibrations: *The instrument was capable of very low pitches.*
   Syns: alto (*Mus.*), bass, deep, low-pitched.
3. CHEAP.
4. DEPRESSED.
5. FILTHY.
6. MINOR.
7. SICKLY.
8. SOFT.
9. SORDID.

low *noun*
A very low level, position, or degree: *The stock market reached an all-time low.*
   Syn: bottom. —*Idiom* rock bottom.

low-cost *adjective* CHEAP.
low-cut *adjective* LOW.
low-down *adjective* SORDID.
lower[1] *also* **lour** *verb*
1. FROWN.
2. GLARE.
3. THREATEN.

lower *also* **lour** *noun* FROWN.
lower[2] *verb*
1. To cause to descend: *The soldier lowered the flag.*
   Syns: depress, drop, let down, take down.
2. CUT BACK at cut.
3. DEPRECIATE.

lower *adjective* MINOR.
lowering *also* **louring** *adjective* DARK.
lowermost *adjective* BOTTOM.
lowery *also* **loury** *adjective* DARK.
lowest *adjective* BOTTOM.
low-grade *adjective* INFERIOR.
low-key *also* **low-keyed** *adjective* SOFT.
lowly *adjective*
1. Lacking high station or birth: *a lowly peasant; the lowly masses.*
   Syns: base[2], baseborn, common, déclassé (*also* declassed), humble, ignoble, mean[2], ordinary, plebeian, unwashed, vulgar.
2, 3. HUMBLE.

low-necked *also* **low-neck** *adjective* LOW.
low-pitched *adjective* LOW.
low-priced *adjective* CHEAP.
low-quality *adjective* INFERIOR.
loyal *adjective* FAITHFUL.
loyalty *noun*
1. ATTACHMENT.
2. FIDELITY.

lubricious *adjective*
1. CAPRICIOUS.
2. SLICK.

lucent *adjective* BRIGHT.
lucid *adjective*
1. CLEAR.
2. SANE.

lucidity *noun*
1. CLARITY.
2. SANITY.

lucidness *noun* SANITY.
luck *noun*
1. Success attained as a result of chance: *It was just my luck to find the money.*
   Syns: fortunateness, fortune, luckiness. —*Idiom* good luck (*or* fortune).
2. CHANCE.

luck *verb* RISK.
luckiness *noun* LUCK.
luckless *adjective* UNFORTUNATE.
lucky *adjective* HAPPY.
lucrative *adjective* PROFITABLE.
lucre *noun* MONEY.
lucubrate *verb* STUDY.
lucubration *noun* ADVISEMENT.
ludicrous *adjective* LAUGHABLE.
lug *verb* CARRY.
lug *noun* LUMP[1].
lug(s) *noun* AFFECTATION.
lugubrious *adjective* SORROWFUL.
lukewarm *adjective* TEPID.
lull *verb* CALM.
lull *noun* STILLNESS.
lumber *verb* LUMP[1].
lumbering *adjective* AWKWARD.
luminary *noun*
1. CELEBRITY.
2. DIGNITARY.

luminosity *noun*
1. FIRE.
2. LIGHT[1].

luminous *adjective* BRIGHT.
lummox *noun* LUMP[1].
lump[1] *noun*
1. An irregularly shaped mass of indefinite size: *a lump of sugar; lumps of dirt all over the floor.*
   Syns: chunk, clod, clump, gob[1], hunch, hunk, nugget, wad.

2. A large, ungainly, and dull-witted person: *a dumb lump of a man.*
   Syns: bohunk (*Slang*), clod, dub² (*Slang*), gaum (*Regional*), gawk, hulk, hunk, klutz (*Slang*), lout, lug (*Slang*), lummox, meatball (*Slang*), meathead (*Slang*), oaf, ox.

3, 4. BUMP.

lump *verb*
1. To move heavily: *linebackers lumping across the field.*
   Syns: clump, galumph *or* gallumph, hulk, lumber, stump.
2. HEAP.

lump² *verb* ENDURE.

lumpish *adjective*
1. AWKWARD.
2. HEAVY.

lumps *noun* DUE.

lunacy *noun*
1. FOOLISHNESS.
2. INSANITY.

lunatic *adjective*
1. FOOLISH.
2. INSANE.

lunatic *noun* CRACKPOT.

lunge *verb*
1, 2. PLUNGE.

luny *adjective & noun* SEE **loony.**

lurch *verb*
1. To lean suddenly, unsteadily, and erratically from the vertical axis: *The deck lurched back and forth in the heavy swells.*
   Syns: cant¹, pitch, roll, seesaw, tilt, yaw.
2. To walk unsteadily: *The drunk lurched out of the bar and into the alley.*
   Syns: falter, reel, stagger, stammer, stumble, teeter, totter, weave, wobble.
3. BLUNDER.
4. JERK.

lurch *noun* JERK.

lure *noun*
1. Something that attracts, esp. with the promise of pleasure or reward: *Her beauty was an irresistible lure to men.*
   Syns: allurement, come-on, enticement, inducement, inveiglement, seduction, temptation.
2. Something that leads one into a place or situation from which escape is difficult: *The lure of fast money drew him into gambling.*
   Syns: bait, snare, trap.
3. ATTRACTION.

lure *verb*
1. ATTRACT.
2. TEMPT.

lurid *adjective*
1. GHASTLY.
2. PALE.

lurk *verb* SNEAK.

luscious *adjective*
1. DELICIOUS.
2. DELIGHTFUL.

lush *noun* DRUNKARD.

lush *verb* DRINK.

lush *adjective*
1. LUXURIOUS.
2. PROFUSE.
3. THICK.

lust *verb*
To have a greedy, obsessive desire: *an executive who lusted only for power and money.*
   Syns: crave, hunger (*after or* for), itch for, thirst.

lust *noun*
1, 2. DESIRE.

luster *noun*
1. EMINENCE.
2. GLOSS.

lusterless *adjective*
1, 2. DULL.

lustful *adjective*
1. EROTIC.
2. LUSTY.

lustfulness *noun* DESIRE.

lustral *adjective* PURGATIVE.

lustrate *verb* PURIFY.

lustration *noun* PURIFICATION.

lustrative *adjective* PURGATIVE.

lustratory *adjective* PURGATIVE.

lustrous *adjective*
1. BRIGHT.
2. EMINENT.
3. GLOSSY.

lusty *adjective*
1. Full of vigor: *a healthy, lusty man who worked and played hard.*
   Syns: lustful (*Archaic*), red-blooded, robust, vigorous, vital.
2. STRONG.

luxuriant *adjective*
1. LUXURIOUS.
2. PROFUSE.
3. THICK.

luxuriate *verb*
To take extravagant pleasure: *Oh, to luxuriate in the warmth of a Pacific island!*
   Syns: bask, indulge, revel, roll, rollick, wallow.

luxurious *adjective*
Characterized by extravagant, ostentatious magnificence: *The luxurious yacht featured a lapis lazuli table.*
   Syns: lavish, lush, luxuriant, opulent,

palatial, plush, plushy (*Informal*), rich.

luxury *noun*
Something costly and unnecessary: *a fur coat that is a real luxury.*
   Syns: extravagance (*also* extravagancy), frill.

lying *adjective* DISHONEST.

lying-in *noun* BIRTH.

lymphatic *adjective* LANGUID.

lyric *adjective* POETIC.

lyricism *noun* POETRY.

M

macabre *adjective*
1. GHASTLY.
2. MORBID.

machinate *verb* PLOT.

machination *noun* PLOT.

macho *adjective* MANLY.

macrocosm *noun* UNIVERSE.

macrocosmos *noun* UNIVERSE.

mad *adjective*
1. ANGRY.
2. ENTHUSIASTIC.
3. FOOLISH.
4. FRANTIC.
5. INSANE.

mad-brained *adjective* RASH[1].

madcap *adjective* RASH[1].

madden *verb*
1. ANGER.
2. DERANGE.

maddened *adjective* ANGRY.

madding *adjective* FRANTIC.

made-to-order *adjective* CUSTOM.

made-up *adjective*
1. ASSUMED.
2. FICTITIOUS.

mad-headed *adjective* RASH[1].

madness *noun* INSANITY.

Maecenas *noun* PATRON.

magazine *noun* DEPOSITORY.

magic *noun*
1. The use of supernatural powers to influence or predict events: *By magic the door opened at the command of the long-bearded old man.*
   Syns: conjuration, conjury, sorcery, sortilege, thaumaturgy, theurgy,

witchcraft, witchery, witching, wizardry.
2. The use of skillful tricks and deceptions to produce entertainingly baffling effects: *a show of magic for children.*
   Syns: conjuration, conjury, legerdemain, prestidigitation. —*Idiom* sleight of hand.

magic also **magical** *adjective*
1. Having or brought about by supernatural powers: *a magic wand; a magic transformation.*
   Syns: thaumaturgic, wizardly.
2. WITCHING.

magisterial *adjective* DICTATORIAL.

magistrate *noun* JUDGE.

magnanimity *noun* GENEROSITY.

magnanimous *adjective* GENEROUS.

magnanimousness *noun* GENEROSITY.

magnetic *adjective* ATTRACTIVE.

magnetism *noun*
1. ATTRACTION.
2. FORCE.

magnetize *verb* ATTRACT.

magnific *adjective* GRAND.

magnification *noun*
1. EXAGGERATION.
2. PRAISE.

magnificence *noun* GLITTER.

magnificent *adjective*
1. GLORIOUS.
2. GRAND.
3. OUTSTANDING.

magnify *verb*
1. EXAGGERATE.
2. EXALT.
3. HONOR.
4. INCREASE.
5. PRAISE.
6. RISE.

magniloquent *adjective* SONOROUS.

magnitude *noun*
1. BULK.
2. DEGREE.
3. ENORMOUSNESS.
4, 5. SIZE.

magnum opus *noun* MASTERPIECE.

maiden *adjective* FIRST.

maim *verb* CRIPPLE.

main *adjective* PRIMARY.

maintain *verb*
1. To keep in a condition of good repair, efficiency, or use: *maintained fitness with daily exercise.*
   Syns: keep up, preserve, sustain.
2. ASSERT.
3. CLAIM.
4. DEFEND.

5. KEEP.

6, 7. SUPPORT.

maintenance *noun* LIVING.

majestic *adjective* GRAND.

majesty *noun* GLORY.

major *adjective*

1. BIG-LEAGUE.

2. PRIMARY.

major-league *adjective* BIG-LEAGUE.

make *verb*

1. To create by forming, combining, or altering materials: *made a house from logs; making a sandwich.*
   Syns: assemble, build, construct, fabricate, fashion, forge¹, frame, manufacture, mold, produce, put together, shape.

2. APPOINT.

3. BEAR.

4. CAUSE.

5. CONSTITUTE.

6. EARN.

7. ENACT.

8. FORCE.

9. GET.

10. PREPARE.

11. PRODUCE.

12. TRAVERSE.

make out *verb*

1. DISCERN.

2. MANAGE.

3. PROSPER.

4. UNDERSTAND.

make over *verb* TRANSFER.

make up *verb*

1. BALANCE.

2. CONSTITUTE.

3. IMPROVISE.

4. INVENT.

make-believe *noun* PRETENSE.

maker *noun*

1. BUILDER.

2. ORIGINATOR.

makeshift *noun*

Something used temporarily or reluctantly when other means are not available: *Lacking a bat, the boys used a broom handle as a makeshift.*
   Syns: expediency (*also* expedience), expedient, shift, stopgap.

make-up *also* **makeup** *noun*

CHARACTER.

maladroit *adjective*

1. TACTLESS.

2. UNSKILLFUL.

malady *noun* DISEASE.

mala fide *adjective* INSINCERE.

malapert *adjective* IMPUDENT.

malapert *noun* SMART ALECK.

malapropos *adjective* IMPROPER.

malarkey *also* **malarky** *noun*

NONSENSE.

male *adjective* MANLY.

maledict *verb* CURSE.

malediction *noun* CURSE.

malefactor *noun* CRIMINAL.

malevolence *noun*

A desire to harm others or to see others suffer: *Out of sheer malevolence he refused to help lost travelers who knocked on his door to ask directions.*
   Syns: despitefulness (*Archaic*), ill will, malice, maliciousness, malignancy (*also* malignance), malignity, spite, spitefulness.

malevolent *adjective*

Characterized by intense ill will or spite: *a malevolent hatred of anyone who dared to challenge him.*
   Syns: bitchy (*Slang*), black, black-hearted, despiteful (*Archaic*), evil, hateful (*Rare*), malicious, malign, malignant, mean², nasty, poisonous, spiteful, venomous, vicious, wicked.

malformation *noun* DEFORMITY.

malfunction *verb*

To work improperly due to mechanical difficulties: *The bank's accounting system came to a halt when the central computer malfunctioned.*
   Syns: act up (*Informal*), misbehave.

malice *noun* MALEVOLENCE.

malicious *adjective* MALEVOLENT.

maliciousness *noun* MALEVOLENCE.

malign *verb* LIBEL.

malign *adjective*

1. Strongly suggestive of great harm, menace, or evil: *the executioner's malign expression.*
   Syns: baleful, sinister.

2. MALEVOLENT.

malignancy *also* **malignance** *noun*

MALEVOLENCE.

malignant *adjective*

1. MALEVOLENT.

2. VIRULENT.

maligning *adjective* LIBELOUS.

malignity *noun* MALEVOLENCE.

malism *noun* PESSIMISM.

malison *noun* CURSE.

malleability *noun* FLEXIBILITY.

malleable *adjective*

1. Capable of being shaped, bent, or drawn out, as by hammering or pressure: *Gold and copper are malleable metals.*
   Syns: ductile, flexible (*also* flexile), flexuous (*also* flexuose), moldable,

plastic, pliable, pliant, supple,
workable.
2. FLEXIBLE.
malodorous *adjective* SMELLY.
maltreat *verb* ABUSE.
maltreatment *noun* ABUSE.
mammoth *noun* GIANT.
mammoth *adjective* GIANT.
man *noun*
1. HUMAN BEING.
2. MANKIND.
Man *noun* POLICEMAN.
manacle *verb* HAMPER.
manacles *noun* BONDS.
manage *verb*
1. To progress or perform adequately,
esp. in difficult circumstances: *The
trail looked steep, but the hiker assured
his friends that he could manage.*
Syns: do, fare, fend, get along, get
by, make out (*Informal*), muddle
through (*Chiefly Brit.*), shift, stagger
(on *or* along). —*Idioms* make do,
make shift.
2. ADMINISTER.
3. CONDUCT.
manageable *adjective* GOVERNABLE.
management *noun*
1. ADMINISTRATION.
2. CONSERVATION.
3. GUIDANCE.
manager *noun*
1. BOSS.
2. EXECUTIVE.
managerial *adjective*
ADMINISTRATIVE.
mandate *noun* COMMAND.
mandatory *adjective* REQUIRED.
maneuver *noun*
1. MOVEMENT.
2. TACTIC[1].
3. TRICK.
maneuver *verb*
1. To direct the course of carefully:
*maneuvered the great ship into the
dock.*
Syns: navigate, pilot, steer. —*Idiom*
back and fill.
2. To take clever or cunning steps to
achieve one's goals: *schemed and
maneuvered to get promoted.*
Syns: finagle (*also* fenagle)
(*Informal*), jockey. —*Idiom* pull
strings (*or* wires).
3. MANIPULATE.
4. MOVE.
manful *adjective* MANLY.
mangle *verb*
1. BATTER.
2. PRESS.

mangy *adjective* SHABBY.
manhandle *verb* SLAP AROUND at
slap.
man-hater *noun* CYNIC.
mania *noun*
1. ENTHUSIASM.
2. INSANITY.
3. THING.
maniac *noun* ENTHUSIAST.
maniac *adjective* INSANE.
maniacal *adjective* INSANE.
manifest *verb*
1. EMBODY.
2. EXPRESS.
3. SHOW.
manifest *adjective* APPARENT.
manifestation *noun*
1. DISPLAY.
2. SIGN.
manifesto *noun* ANNOUNCEMENT.
manipulate *verb*
1. To control to one's own advantage by
artful or indirect means: *She
manipulates people by helping her by
pretending to be overworked.*
Syns: exploit, maneuver, play.
2. HANDLE.
3. WORK.
mankind *noun*
The human race: *A nuclear war might
destroy all mankind.*
Syns: flesh, Homo sapiens, humanity,
humankind, man, universe, world.
manlike *adjective*
Resembling a man or human being:
*reports of a furry, manlike creature living
in the forest.*
Syns: anthropoid, anthropomorphic,
anthropomorphous, hominoid,
humanoid.
manly *adjective*
Of, characteristic of, or befitting the
male sex: *manly self-reliance; paying
manly attentions to the ladies.*
Syns: macho, male, manful,
masculine, virile.
manmade *adjective*
1, 2. ARTIFICIAL.
manner *noun*
1. BEARING.
2. CUSTOM.
3. KIND[2].
4. STYLE.
mannered *adjective* AFFECTED[2].
mannerism *noun* AFFECTATION.
mannerly *adjective* COURTEOUS.
manners *noun*
Socially correct behavior: *minding his
manners.*
Syns: decorum, etiquette, mores,

proprieties. —*Idioms* good form,
p's and q's.
manslaying *noun* MURDER.
mantic *adjective* PROPHETIC.
mantle *verb*
1. BLUSH.
2. CLOTHE.
man-to-man *adjective* PLAIN.
manufacture *verb* MAKE.
manufactured *adjective* ARTIFICIAL.
manufacturer *noun* BUILDER.
manumission *noun* LIBERTY.
manumit *verb* FREE.
manumitted *adjective* FREE.
many *adjective*
Amounting to or consisting of a large,
indefinite number: *Many sails dotted the
horizon.*
   Syns: legion, multitudinous, myriad,
numerous, voluminous. —*Idiom* quite
a few.
many-sided *adjective* VERSATILE.
map *noun* FACE.
map *verb*
1. DESIGN.
2. PLOT.
mar *verb* INJURE.
maraud *verb* RAID.
marbles *noun* SANITY.
march[1] *verb*
1. COME.
2. STRIDE.
march *noun* ADVANCE.
march[2] *noun* BORDER.
marchland *noun* BORDER.
margin *noun*
1. BORDER.
2. MINIMUM.
3. ROOM.
margin *verb* BORDER.
marine *adjective*
1. Of or relating to the seas or oceans:
marine life; marine exploration.
   Syns: maritime, oceanic, pelagic,
thalassic.
2. NAUTICAL.
mariner *noun* SAILOR.
marital *adjective*
Of, relating to, or typical of marriage:
the marital bond; marital difficulties.
   Syns: conjugal, connubial, hymeneal,
married, matrimonial, nuptial,
spousal, wedded.
maritime *adjective*
1. MARINE.
2. NAUTICAL.
mark *noun*
1. A name or other device placed on
merchandise to signify its ownership

or manufacture: *The maker's mark
was nearly invisible.*
   Syns: brand, colophon, trademark.
2. AMBITION.
3. DUPE.
4. EMINENCE.
5. INTENTION.
6. NOTICE.
7. QUALITY.
8. SIGN.
9. STANDARD.
10. TARGET.
mark *verb*
1. To set off by or as if by a mark
indicating ownership or manufacture:
*marked each product with the company
seal.*
   Syns: brand, identify, label, tag.
2. BEAT.
3. DISTINGUISH.
4. INDICATE.
5. NOTICE.
6, 7. SHOW.
8. TARGET.
  mark down *verb* DEPRECIATE.
  mark out (or off) *verb* DETERMINE.
markdown *noun* DEPRECIATION.
marked *adjective* NOTICEABLE.
marker *noun* TICKET.
market *verb* SELL.
marketability *noun* SELL.
marketableness *noun* SELL.
marriable *adjective* ELIGIBLE.
marriage *noun*
1. The state of being united as husband
and wife: *seldom quarreled during
their long marriage.*
   Syns: conjugality, connubiality,
matrimony, wedlock.
2. WEDDING.
marriageable *adjective* ELIGIBLE.
married *adjective* MARITAL.
marrow *noun* HEART.
marrowy *adjective* PITHY.
marry *verb*
1. To join or be joined in marriage: *He
married his high-school sweetheart.
They married after a brief courtship.*
   Syns: espouse, hitch (*Slang*), mate,
wed. —*Idiom* tie the knot.
2. COMBINE.
marsh *noun* SWAMP.
marshal *verb*
1. ARRANGE.
2. ASSEMBLE.
3. MOBILIZE.
marshland *noun* SWAMP.
martial *adjective*
1, 2. MILITARY.
martinet *noun* AUTHORITARIAN.

marvel *noun*
One that evokes great surprise and admiration: *such natural marvels as the Grand Canyon; a prose style that is a marvel of precision.*
   Syns: miracle, phenomenon, prodigy, sensation, stunner, wonder, wonderment. —*Idioms* one for the books, the eighth wonder of the world.
marvel *verb* WONDER.
marveling *noun* WONDER.
marvelous *also* **marvellous** *adjective*
1. Particularly excellent: *had a marvelous time in Europe.*
   Syns: cool (*Slang*), dandy (*Informal*), divine[1] (*Informal*), dreamy (*Informal*), fabulous (*Informal*), glorious, groovy (*Slang*), heavenly (*Informal*), hot (*Slang*), hunky-dory (*Slang*), keen[1] (*Slang*), neat (*Slang*), nifty (*Slang*), ripping, sensational, splendid, super (*Informal*), superb, swell (*Informal*), terrific, tremendous (*Informal*), wonderful. —*Idiom* out of this world.
2. FABULOUS.
masculine *adjective* MANLY.
mash *verb*
1. CROWD.
2. CRUSH.
mashed *adjective* INFATUATED.
mask *noun* FAÇADE.
  mask *verb*
1. COVER.
2. DISGUISE.
masquerade *noun*
1. ACT.
2. FAÇADE.
  masquerade *verb*
1. DISGUISE.
2. POSE.
mass *noun*
1. ACCUMULATION.
2. BODY.
3. BULK.
4. CROWD.
5, 6. HEAP.
7. WEIGHT.
massacre *noun*
The savage killing of many victims: *a massacre during the revolution.*
   Syns: blood bath, bloodletting, bloodshed, butchery, carnage, pogrom, slaughter.
  massacre *verb*
1. ANNIHILATE.
2. OVERWHELM.
massacrer *noun* MURDERER.
masses *noun* COMMONALTY.

massive *adjective*
1. BULKY.
2. GIANT.
3. HEAVY.
massiveness *noun* HEAVINESS.
massy *adjective* GIANT.
master *noun*
1. CHIEF.
2. CONQUEROR.
3. EXPERT.
4. ORIGINAL.
5. OWNER.
  master *verb*
1. DOMESTICATE.
2. LEARN.
3. TRIUMPH.
master *adjective* EXPERT.
masterful *adjective*
1. ARTFUL.
2. AUTHORITATIVE.
3. DICTATORIAL.
4. EXPERT.
masterly *adjective*
1. ARTFUL.
2. EXPERT.
masterpiece *noun*
An outstanding and ingenious work: *a novel that is a real masterpiece.*
   Syns: chef d'oeuvre (*French*), magnum opus, masterwork, tour de force (*French*).
masterstroke *noun* FEAT.
masterwork *noun* MASTERPIECE.
mastery *noun*
1. ABILITY.
2. AUTHORITY.
3. DOMINATION.
4. GRASP.
masticate *verb* CHEW.
mastodonic *adjective* GIANT.
mat *also* **matte** *adjective* DULL.
match *noun*
1. MATE.
2. PARALLEL.
  match *verb*
1. AGREE.
2. COMPARE.
3. EQUAL.
4. FIT.
5. LIKEN.
6. OPPOSE.
matchless *adjective* UNIQUE.
mate *noun*
1. One of a matched pair of things: *The mate of this glove is missing.*
   Syns: companion, double, fellow, match, twin.
2. ASSOCIATE.
3. FRIEND.
4. SPOUSE.

mate *verb*
1. MARRY.
2. TAKE.

material *noun*
1. That from which things are or can be made: *built a crude shelter out of materials at hand; a novelist in search of material.*
   Syns: matter, stuff, substance.
   —*Idiom* grist for one's mill.
2. MATTER.
3. TIMBER.

material *adjective*
1. IMPORTANT.
2. PHYSICAL.
3. RELEVANT.

materialistic *adjective*
Of or preoccupied with material rather than spiritual or intellectual things: *the materialistic goal of amassing property.*
   Syns: mundane, sensual, temporal, worldly.

materiality *noun*
1. ACTUALITY.
2. MATTER.

materialization *noun* APPEARANCE.

materialize *verb*
1. APPEAR.
2. EMBODY.
3. REALIZE.

materials *noun* OUTFIT.

materiel or **matériel** *noun* OUTFIT.

matrimonial *adjective* MARITAL.

matrimony *noun* MARRIAGE.

matrix *noun* FORM.

matte *adjective* SEE **mat.**

matter *noun*
1. That which occupies space and can be perceived by the senses: *a universe consisting of matter and energy.*
   Syns: material, materiality, substance.
2. Something to be done, considered, or dealt with: *There are several matters left before we can adjourn.*
   Syns: affair, thing.
3. MATERIAL.
4. SUBJECT.

matter *verb* COUNT.

matter-of-course *adjective* COMMON.

matter-of-fact *adjective*
1. DRY.
2. DULL.
3. REALISTIC.

maturate *verb* MATURE.

mature *adjective*
Having reached full growth and development: *mature fruit, ready for picking.*
   Syns: adult, big, developed, full-

blown, full-fledged, full-grown, grown, grown-up, ripe. —*Idiom* of age.

mature *verb*
To bring or come to full development: *He matured the wine in vats in his cellar. As a teen-ager she matured slowly.*
   Syns: age, develop, grow, maturate, mellow, ripe (*Chiefly Regional*), ripen.

matured *adjective* AGED.

maudlin *adjective* SENTIMENTAL.

maudlinism *noun* SENTIMENTALITY.

maul *verb* BATTER.

mausoleum *noun* GRAVE¹.

mawkish *adjective* SENTIMENTAL.

mawkishness *noun* SENTIMENTALITY.

maxim *noun* PROVERB.

maximal *adjective* MAXIMUM.

maximum *adjective*
Greatest in quantity or highest in degree that has been or can be attained: *An inflated balloon reaches its maximum size just before bursting.*
   Syns: maximal, top, topmost, upside (*Informal*), ultimate, utmost.

maximum *noun*
1. The greatest quantity or highest degree attainable: *Desert temperatures are at a maximum in late afternoon and then fall sharply.*
   Syns: ceiling, climax, crest, outside, peak, top, ultimate. —*Idiom* ne plus ultra.
2. LIMIT.

maybe *adverb*
Possibly but not certainly: *Maybe it will rain, and maybe not.*
   Syns: perchance, perhaps.

maze *verb* DAZE.

maze *noun*
1. DAZE.
2. TANGLE.

mazuma *noun* MONEY.

meager *adjective*
1. Conspicuously deficient in quantity, fullness, or extent: *a meager diet of rice and broth; a meager living.*
   Syns: exiguous, measly (*Slang*), poor, puny, scant, scanty, skimpy, spare, sparse, stingy.
2. THIN.

meal *verb* EAT.

mean¹ *verb*
1. To have or convey a particular idea: *We discussed what the poem meant. A red light means to stop.*
   Syns: add up to, connote, denote, import, intend, signify, spell¹.
2. INTEND.

mean² *adjective*
1. FILTHY.

2. HUMBLE.
3. ILL-TEMPERED.
4. INFERIOR.
5. LOWLY.
6. MALEVOLENT.
7. NARROW.
8. SICKLY.
9. SORDID.
10. STINGY.
11. TROUBLESOME.

mean³ *noun* AVERAGE.
mean *adjective* MIDDLE.

meander *verb*
1. ROVE.
2. STROLL.
3. WIND².

meandering *adjective* WINDING.
meandrous *adjective* WINDING.

meaning *noun*
1. That which is signified by a word or expression: *Synonyms are words having the same meaning.*
   Syns: acceptation, acception, import, intent, message, purport, sense, significance (*also* significancy), signification, value.
2. INTENTION.

meaning *adjective* EXPRESSIVE.

meaningful *adjective*
1. EXPRESSIVE.
2. IMPORTANT.
3. PREGNANT.

meaningless *adjective* MINDLESS.

means *noun*
1. That by which something is accomplished or some end achieved: *We built a rope bridge and by this means crossed the gorge.*
   Syns: agency, agent, instrument, instrumentality, instrumentation, intermediary, mechanism, medium, organ.
2. RESOURCES.

measliness *noun* PETTINESS.

measly *adjective*
1. MEAGER.
2. PETTY.

measure *noun*
1. ALLOTMENT.
2. DEGREE.
3. LAW.
4. MEASUREMENT.
5. MODERATION.
6. MOVE.
7. RHYTHM.
8. SIZE.
9. STANDARD.

measure *verb*
1. To ascertain the dimensions, quantity, or capacity of: *measured the room with a yardstick.*
   Syns: gauge (*also* gage), mete (*Archaic*). —*Idiom* take the measure of.
2. DETERMINE.

measure out *verb* DISTRIBUTE.
measure up *verb* COMPARE.

measured *adjective*
1. DELIBERATE.
2. RHYTHMICAL.

measureless *adjective*
1. ENDLESS.
2. INCALCULABLE.

measurement *noun*
The act or process of ascertaining dimensions, quantity, or capacity: *equipment used in the measurement of the speed of light.*
   Syns: measure, mensuration, metrology.

meat *noun*
1. FOOD.
2. HEART.

meatball *noun* LUMP¹.
meathead *noun* LUMP¹.
meaty *adjective* PITHY.
mechanical *adjective* PERFUNCTORY.
mechanism *noun* MEANS.
medal *noun* DECORATION.

meddle *verb*
1. To intervene officiously or indiscreetly in the affairs of others: *tried to keep her mother-in-law from meddling in her life.*
   Syns: butt in (*Slang*), horn in (*Slang*), interfere.
2. TAMPER.

meddler *noun*
1. A person given to intruding in other people's affairs: *A hopeless meddler, she took sides in every family quarrel on the block.*
   Syns: busybody, buttinsky (*Slang*), kibitzer (*Informal*), pragmatic, quidnunc.
2. SNOOP.

meddlesome *adjective* MEDDLING.

meddling *noun*
The act or an instance of interfering: *constant meddling in the colony's internal politics.*
   Syns: interference, intervention.

meddling *adjective*
Given to intruding in other people's affairs: *a meddling mother who can't let her daughter lead a life of her own.*
   Syns: interfering, intrusive, meddlesome, obtrusive, officious.

media *noun* PRESS.

medial *adjective*
1. CENTRAL.
2. MIDDLE.

median *noun* AVERAGE.
median *adjective*
1. CENTRAL.
2. MIDDLE.

mediator *noun* GO-BETWEEN.
medicament *noun*
1. CURE.
2. DRUG.

medicant *noun* CURE.
medicate *verb* DRUG.
medication *noun*
1. CURE.
2. DRUG.

medicine *noun*
1. CURE.
2. DRUG.

meditate *verb* PONDER.
meditation *noun* THOUGHT.
meditative *adjective*
1. PENSIVE.
2. THOUGHTFUL.

medium *noun*
1. AVERAGE.
2. COMPROMISE.
3. ENVIRONMENT.
4. FORTE.
5. MEANS.

medium-priced *adjective* POPULAR.
medley *noun* ASSORTMENT.
meek *adjective*
1. GENTLE.
2. HUMBLE.

meet¹ *verb*
1. To come together face-to-face by
   arrangement: *met with the child's
   teacher; met him for lunch.*
   Syns: encounter, rendezvous.
2. ADJOIN.
3. CLOSE¹.
4. ENCOUNTER.
5. ENGAGE.
6. EQUAL.
7. GREET.
8. SATISFY.

meet with *verb* EXPERIENCE.
meet *noun* COMPETITION.
meet² *adjective*
1. APPROPRIATE.
2. CONVENIENT.

meeting *noun*
1. ASSEMBLY.
2. CONVENTION.
3. JUNCTION.

meeting *adjective* ADJOINING.
megacosm *noun* UNIVERSE.
megrim *noun* FANCY.
melancholic *adjective* DEPRESSED.

melancholy *adjective*
1. DEPRESSED.
2. SAD.

melancholy *noun* GLOOM.
mélange also **melange** *noun*
ASSORTMENT.
meld *verb* COMBINE.
melded *adjective* COMBINED.
melding *noun* COMBINATION.
melee also **mêlée** *noun* BRAWL.
meliorate *verb* IMPROVE.
melioration *noun*
1. IMPROVEMENT.
2. PROGRESS.

mellow *adjective*
1. AGED.
2. RESONANT.

mellow *verb* MATURE.
melodia *noun* MELODY.
melodic *adjective* MELODIOUS.
melodious *adjective*
1. Having or producing a pleasing
   melody: *a melodious and lilting
   passage in the scherzo; the melodious
   flute.*
   Syns: ariose, melodic, musical,
   tuneful.
2. Resembling or having the effect of
   music, esp. pleasing music: *As she
   recited she varied the pitch in a richly
   melodious voice.*
   Syns: dulcet, euphonic, euphonious,
   melodic, musical, tuneful.

melodramatic *adjective* DRAMATIC.
melodramatics *noun* THEATRICS.
melody *noun*
A pleasing succession of musical tones
forming a usu. brief aesthetic unit:
picked out a simple melody on his guitar.
   Syns: air, aria, melodia, note (*Poetic*),
   strain², tune.

melt *verb*
1. To change from a solid to a liquid:
   *Plastic bowls will melt in the oven. We
   melted the butter in a saucepan.*
   Syns: deliquesce, dissolve, flux, fuse,
   liquefy, run, thaw.
2. FADE.

member *noun* DIVISION.
memento *noun* REMEMBRANCE.
memoir *noun* COMMENTARY.
memorial *noun*
Something, as a structure or custom,
serving to honor or keep alive a
memory: *The poet's house is preserved as
a memorial.*
   Syns: commemoration, monument,
   remembrance.

memorial *adjective*
Serving to honor or keep alive a

memory: *a memorial ceremony at the graves of the war dead.*
Syn: commemorative.

memorialize *verb*
To honor or keep alive the memory of: *A plaque at the base of the bridge memorialized the workmen killed in its construction.*
Syn: commemorate.

memorize *verb*
To commit to memory: *memorized her lines for the play.*
Syns: con, learn.

memory *noun*
1. The power of retaining and recalling past experience: *a poor memory for names.*
   Syns: recall, recollection, remembrance, reminiscence.
2. An act or instance of remembering: *The old friends traded memories of school days.*
   Syns: recollection, remembrance, reminiscence.

menace *verb*
1. ENDANGER.
2. THREATEN.
menace *noun*
1, 2. THREAT.

menacing *adjective* THREATENING.
ménage *noun* FAMILY.

mend *verb*
1. CORRECT.
2. FIX.
3. RECOVER.

mendacious *adjective* DISHONEST.
mendaciousness *noun* MENDACITY.

mendacity *noun*
The practice of lying: *The prosecutor exposed the witness' mendacity by making her contradict herself.*
Syns: falsehood, fibbery, mendaciousness, perjury, truthlessness, untruthfulness, unveracity.

mendicancy *noun* BEGGARY.
mendicant *noun* BEGGAR.
mendicity *noun* BEGGARY.
menial *adjective* SERVILE.
mensuration *noun* MEASUREMENT.

mental *adjective*
1. Relating to or performed by the mind: *mental arithmetic; such mental events as dreams.*
   Syns: cerebral, intellective, intellectual, psychic (*also* psychical), psychological.
2. INSANE.

mentality *noun*
1. INTELLIGENCE.
2. PSYCHOLOGY.

mention *verb*
1. NAME.
2. REFER.

mentor *noun*
1. ADVISER.
2. GUIDE.

mephitic or **mephitical** *adjective*
1. POISONOUS.
2. SMELLY.

mercenary *adjective* CORRUPT.
mercenary *noun*
A free-lance fighter: *mercenaries fighting in Africa.*
Syns: adventurer, Hessian, hireling. —*Idiom* soldier of fortune.

merchandise *noun* GOODS.
merchandise *verb* SELL.
merchandiser *noun* DEALER.
merchant *noun* DEALER.
merchant *verb* SELL.

merciful *adjective*
1. HUMANITARIAN.
2. TOLERANT.

mercifulness *noun* GRACE.

merciless *adjective*
1. Having or showing no mercy: *a merciless Gestapo interrogator.*
   Syns: pitiless, remorseless, unmerciful. —*Idiom* without an ounce of pity.
2. GRIM.

mercurial *adjective* CAPRICIOUS.
mercy *noun* GRACE.

mere *adjective*
1. Being what is specified and nothing more: *a mere mortal.*
   Syns: bare, very.
2. BARE.

merely *adverb*
Nothing more than: *Merely thinking of home makes me nostalgic.*
Syns: just, only.

meretricious *adjective* GAUDY.
merge *verb* MIX.
meridian *noun* CLIMAX.

merit *noun*
1. A level of superiority that is usu. high: *a book of merit.*
   Syns: caliber, quality, stature, value, virtue, worth.
2. VIRTUE.
merit *verb* EARN.

meritable *adjective* ADMIRABLE.
merited *adjective* JUST.
meritorious *adjective* ADMIRABLE.

merriment *noun*
1, 2. GAIETY.

merry *adjective*
1. Marked by festal celebration: *had a merry Christmas.*
Syns: festive, gala, glad, gladsome, happy, joyful, joyous.
2. GAY.
merrymaking *noun*
1. CELEBRATION.
2. GAIETY.
mesh *noun*
1. TANGLE.
2. WEB.
mesh *verb* ENGAGE.
mesmerize *verb* GRIP.
mess *noun*
1. An unsightly object: *That old abandoned house is a mess.*
Syns: fright, monstrosity, sight, ugliness, ugly.
2. BOTCH.
3. DISORDER.
4. HEAP.
5. SERVING.
mess *verb*
1. TAMPER.
2. TOUSLE.
mess around (or **about**) *verb*
1. *Informal.* To waste time by engaging in aimless activity: *While the diplomats were messing around, the world moved to the brink of war.*
Syns: diddle, doodle, fool around (*Informal*), puddle, putter.
2. FUSS.
3. PHILANDER.
mess up *verb*
1. BOTCH.
2. CONFUSE.
3. DISORDER.
message *noun*
1. COMMUNICATION.
2. MEANING.
messenger *noun* BEARER.
mess-up *noun* BOTCH.
messy *adjective*
1. Marked by an absence of cleanliness and order: *a messy house; messy attire.*
Syns: disheveled, ill-kempt, mussy, slipshod, slobbery, sloppy, slovenly, unkempt, untidy.
2. CARELESS.
3. DISORDERLY.
metamorphize *verb* CONVERT.
metamorphose *verb*
1. CONVERT.
2. REVOLUTIONIZE.
metamorphosis *noun* CHANGE.
metanoia *noun* CONVERSION.

metaphysical also **metaphysic** *adjective*
1. IMMATERIAL.
2. SUPERNATURAL.
mete *verb*
1. ALLOT.
2. MEASURE.
meter *noun* RHYTHM.
method *noun*
1. Systematic arrangement and design: *tried to find some sort of method in this madness.*
Syns: order, orderliness, pattern, plan, system.
2. A systematic body of procedures and techniques characteristic of a field or discipline: *the scientific method.*
Syn: methodology.
3. WAY.
methodical also **methodic** *adjective*
Arranged or proceeding in a set, systematized pattern: *methodical, cogently expressed arguments.*
Syns: orderly, regular, systematic (*also* systematical).
methodize *verb*
To arrange in an orderly manner: *developed a set of emergency procedures and methodized them.*
Syns: order, organize, systematize, systemize.
methodology *noun* METHOD.
meticulous *adjective*
1. CAREFUL.
2. NICE.
meticulousness *noun*
THOROUGHNESS.
métier *noun* FORTE.
metrical also **metric** *adjective*
RHYTHMICAL.
metrology *noun* MEASUREMENT.
metropolis *noun* CITY.
metropolitan *adjective* CITY.
metropolitanize *verb* CITIFY.
mettle *noun* COURAGE.
mettlesome *adjective*
1. BRAVE.
2. SPIRITED.
mew *verb* ENCLOSE.
microbe *noun* GERM.
microorganism also **micro-organism** *noun* GERM.
microscopic *adjective* IMPERCEPTIBLE.
mid *adjective*
1. CENTRAL.
2. MIDDLE.
mid-course *noun* COMPROMISE.
middle *adjective*
1. Not extreme: *took the middle course in the negotiations.*

Syns: central, intermediate, mean³, medial, median, mid, middle-of-the-road, middle-road, midway.
2. CENTRAL.
middle *noun* CENTER.
middleman *noun* GO-BETWEEN.
middle-of-the-road *adjective* MIDDLE.
middle-road *adjective* MIDDLE.
midget *adjective* TINY.
midpoint *noun* CENTER.
midst *noun*
1. CENTER.
2. THICK.
midway *adjective* MIDDLE.
mien *noun*
1. APPEARANCE.
2. BEARING.
miff *noun* OFFENSE.
might *noun*
1. ABILITY.
2. AUTHORITY.
3. STRENGTH.
mighty *adjective*
1. AUTHORITATIVE.
2. GIANT.
3. POWERFUL.
mighty *adverb* VERY.
migrant *noun* EMIGRANT.
migrant *adjective*
1. Moving from one area to another in search of work: *migrant farm workers.*
   Syns: itinerant, migratory.
2. MIGRATORY.
migrate *verb*
1. To change habitat seasonally: *geese migrating from Canada to Florida every fall.*
   Syn: transmigrate.
2. EMIGRATE.
migration *noun* EMIGRATION.
migrational *adjective* MIGRATORY.
migrative *adjective* MIGRATORY.
migratory *adjective*
1. Moving from one habitat to another on a seasonal basis: *Swallows are migratory birds.*
   Syns: migrant, migrational, migrative, mobile, transmigratory.
2. MIGRANT.
mild *adjective*
1. Free from extremes in temperature: *a mild climate.*
   Syns: moderate, temperate.
2, 3, 4. GENTLE.
milden *verb* PACIFY.
milieu *noun* ENVIRONMENT.
militant *adjective* AGGRESSIVE.
militaristic *adjective* MILITARY.
militarize *verb*
To assemble, equip, and train for war:

During the war the population was totally militarized.
Syn: mobilize.
military *adjective*
1. Pertaining to, characteristic of, or performed by troops: *saluted with military precision; military science and tactics.*
   Syns: martial, soldierly.
2. Of, pertaining to, or inclined toward war: *military actions on the border.*
   Syns: bellicose, martial, militaristic, warlike.
milksop *noun* BABY.
mill *noun* WORKS.
mill *verb* CRUSH.
million *noun* HEAP.
millstone *noun* BURDEN.
milquetoast *noun* BABY.
mime *noun* MIMIC.
mimetism *noun* MIMICRY.
mimic *noun*
1. A performer skilled at copying the manner or expression of another: *a renowned mimic whose take-offs were hilarious.*
   Syns: impersonator, mime.
2. ECHO.
mimic *verb*
1. ECHO.
2. IMITATE.
mimicry *noun*
The act, practice, or art of copying the manner or expression of another: *an actor who was an expert at mimicry.*
Syns: apery, aping, imitation, mimetism.
mind *noun*
1. A person of great mental ability: *He is one of the greatest minds of this century.*
   Syns: brain (*Slang*), head (*Slang*), intellect, intellectual, thinker.
2. BELIEF.
3. HEAD.
4. INTELLIGENCE.
5. LIKING.
6. PSYCHOLOGY.
7. SANITY.
mind *verb*
1. CARE.
2. FOLLOW.
3. INTEND.
4. LOOK.
5. LOOK OUT at **look.**
6. NOTICE.
7. REMEMBER.
8. TEND².
mind-blowing *adjective* STAGGERING.

mind-boggling *adjective*
STAGGERING.
minded *adjective* WILLING.
mindful *adjective*
1. Tending toward awareness and appreciation: *a person mindful of the feelings of others.*
   Syns: conscious, heedful, observant, observative, observing, thoughtful.
2. AWARE.
3. CAREFUL.
mindless *adjective*
1. Displaying a complete lack of forethought and good sense: *The wrecked car is the handiwork of my mindless teen-age son.*
   Syns: brainless, dimwitted (*Slang*), fatuous, foolish, senseless, silly, simple, unintelligent, weak-minded, witless.
2. Lacking rational direction or purpose: *Mindless violence is always shocking.*
   Syns: irrational, meaningless, pointless, purposeless, senseless.
   —*Idiom* without rhyme or reason.
3. Showing no concern, attention, or regard: *plunged on, mindless of the danger.*
   Syns: heedless, unheeding, unmindful.
4. INSANE.
mingle *verb*
1. MIX.
2. SOCIALIZE.
miniature *noun* MODEL.
miniature *adjective* TINY.
minim *noun* BIT[1].
minimal *adjective*
Comprising the least possible: *was exposed to minimal radiation; the minimal accepted dosage.*
   Syns: minimum, smallest.
minimize *verb* BELITTLE.
minimum *noun*
The least possible quantity or degree: *systems that reduced the probability of error to a minimum.*
   Syn: margin.
minimum *adjective* MINIMAL.
minister *noun* PREACHER.
minister *verb* SERVE.
minister *to verb* TEND[2].
ministerial *adjective* ADMINISTRATIVE.
ministry *noun* MISSION.
minor *adjective*
1. Of subordinate standing or importance: *minor government officials.*
   Syns: inferior, lesser, low, lower[2], minor-league, petty, secondary, small,

small-fry (*Informal*), small-time (*Informal*), under.
2. *Law.* Not yet a legal adult: *left his estate to one minor child.*
   Syn: underage[2].
minor *noun*
Law. One who is not yet legally of age: *was arrested for contributing to the delinquency of a minor.*
   Syns: child, infant (*Law*).
minority *noun*
The state or period of being under legal age: *an heir still in his minority.*
   Syns: infancy (*Law*), nonage.
minor-league *adjective* MINOR.
mint *noun* FORTUNE.
minus *noun* DISADVANTAGE.
minute[1] *adjective* DETAILED.
minute[2] *noun* FLASH.
minutiae *noun* TRIVIA.
miracle *noun*
1. An event inexplicable by the laws of nature: *Many miracles are attributed to Our Lady of Lourdes.*
   Syn: wonder.
2. MARVEL.
miraculous *adjective*
1. FABULOUS.
2. SUPERNATURAL.
mirage *noun* ILLUSION.
mire *noun* SWAMP.
mirk *noun & verb* SEE **murk.**
mirky *adjective* SEE **murky.**
mirror *noun* MODEL.
mirror *verb*
1. ECHO.
2. REFLECT.
mirth *noun* GAIETY.
mirthful *adjective* GAY.
miry *adjective* MUDDY.
misadventure *noun* ACCIDENT.
misanthrope *noun* CYNIC.
misanthropist *noun* CYNIC.
misapplication *noun* ABUSE.
misapply *verb* ABUSE.
misapprehend *verb* MISUNDERSTAND.
misapprehension *noun*
MISUNDERSTANDING.
misappropriate *verb* ABUSE.
misappropriation *noun* ABUSE.
misbegotten *adjective* ILLEGITIMATE.
misbehave *verb*
1. To behave in a rowdy or unruly fashion: *The children had to be disciplined because they misbehaved.*
   Syns: act up (*Informal*), carry on, cut up (*Informal*), horse around (*Informal*), horseplay.
2. MALFUNCTION.

misbehavior *noun*
Improper, often rude behavior: *was punished for his misbehavior in church.*
Syns: misconduct, misdoing, naughtiness, wrongdoing.

misbelieve *verb* DISBELIEVE.

miscalculate *verb*
To calculate wrongly: *The pilot miscalculated the air speed.*
Syns: misestimate, misjudge, misreckon.

miscalculation *noun*
A wrong calculation: *The cost overrun is due to a miscalculation of production time.*
Syns: error, misjudgment, misreckoning.

miscarry
1. To go wrong: *The marketing strategy miscarried and sales suffered.*
Syns: misfire, miss. —*Idioms* fall short, go amiss (*or* astray), miss the mark.
2. To bring forth a nonviable fetus prematurely: *The mother miscarried during the first trimester.*
Syns: abort, cast (*Brit.&Vet.Med.*), slip (*Vet.Med.*).

miscellaneous *adjective* VARIOUS.

miscellany *noun* ASSORTMENT.

mischance *noun* ACCIDENT.

mischief *noun*
1. Annoying yet harmless, usu. playful acts: *The mischief that toddlers can get into is endless.*
Syns: diablerie (*also* diablery), impishness, prankishness, roguery, roguishness, sportiveness.
2. One who causes minor trouble or damage: *The child was a real mischief in school.*
Syns: imp, prankster, rascal, rogue, scamp.
3. HARM.

misconceive *verb* MISUNDERSTAND.

misconception *noun*
MISUNDERSTANDING.

misconduct *noun* MISBEHAVIOR.

misconstrue *verb* MISUNDERSTAND.

miscreant *adjective* CORRUPT.

miscue *noun*
1. BLUNDER.
2. ERROR.

miscue *verb* ERR.

misdeed *noun*
1, 2. CRIME.

misdeem *verb*
1. CONFUSE.
2. MISJUDGE.

misdoing *noun* MISBEHAVIOR.

misdoubt *verb* DISTRUST.

mise en scène *noun*
1. ENVIRONMENT.
2. SCENE.

misemploy *verb* ABUSE.

misemployment *noun* ABUSE.

miser *noun*
A stingy person: *a miser who wouldn't spend a penny on his family.*
Syns: cheapskate (*also* cheap skate) (*Slang*), chuff, hunks, muckworm, niggard, Scrooge, skinflint (*Slang*), stiff (*Slang*), tightwad (*Slang*). —*Idiom* penny pincher.

miserable *adjective*
1. Suffering from usu. prolonged anguish: *miserable, half-starved prisoners.*
Syns: woebegone (*also* wobegone) (*Archaic*), woeful (*also* woful), wretched.
2. *Informal.* Having a painful ailment: *was just miserable with a bad cold.*
Syns: afflicted, suffering, wretched.
3. INFERIOR.

miserable *noun* UNFORTUNATE.

miserly *adjective* STINGY.

misery *noun*
1. A state of prolonged anguish and privation: *The misery of the refugees is heartbreaking.*
Syns: suffering, unhappiness, woe, wretchedness.
2. DISTRESS.
3. PAIN.

misestimate *verb*
1. MISCALCULATE.
2. MISJUDGE.

misfire *verb* MISCARRY.

misfortunate *adjective*
UNFORTUNATE.

misfortune *noun*
1. Bad fortune: *Be brave in times of misfortune. She had the misfortune to marry a faithless man.*
Syns: adversity, unluck (*Chiefly Regional*), unluckiness.
2. ACCIDENT.

misgiving *noun* QUALM.

mishandle *verb*
1, 2. ABUSE.
3. BOTCH.

mishandling *noun* ABUSE.

mishap *noun* ACCIDENT.

mishmash *noun* ASSORTMENT.

misinterpret *verb* MISUNDERSTAND.

misinterpretation *noun*
MISUNDERSTANDING.

misjudge
1. To make a mistake in judging: *I misjudged his true character.*

Syns: misdeem, misestimate, misread.
2. MISCALCULATE.

misjudgment *noun* MISCALCULATION.
mislay *verb* LOSE.
mislaying *noun* LOSS.
mislead *verb* DECEIVE.
mislike *verb* DISLIKE.
mismanage *verb* BOTCH.
misplace *verb* LOSE.
misplacement *noun* LOSS.
misplacing *noun* LOSS.
misread *verb* MISJUDGE.
misreckon *verb* MISCALCULATE.
misreckoning *noun*
MISCALCULATION.
misrepresent *verb* DISTORT.
misrepresentation *noun* LIE².
misrule *noun* DISORDER.
miss *verb*
1. LOSE.
2. MISCARRY.
miss *noun* ABSENCE.
misshape *verb* DEFORM.
missing *adjective*
1. ABSENT.
2. LOST.
mission *noun*
1. An assignment one is sent to carry
out: *on a mission of mercy.*
Syns: commission, errand, office,
task.
2. A diplomatic office or headquarters
in a foreign country: *the Soviet
mission to the U.N.*
Syns: delegation, legation, post,
ministry.
3. VOCATION.
missionary *noun*
A person doing religious or charitable
work in a foreign country: *missionaries
spreading the faith.*
Syns: apostle, evangelist, missioner.
—*Idioms* field preacher, propagator of
the faith.
missionary *adjective*
Of missionaries or their work: *off to
Africa on a missionary assignment.*
Syns: apostolic, evangelical.
missioner *noun* MISSIONARY.
missish *adjective* GENTEEL.
missive *noun* LETTER.
misstate *verb* DISTORT.
misstatement *noun* LIE².
misstep *noun* ERROR.
mist *noun* HAZE.
mist *verb* OBSCURE.
mistake *noun* ERROR.
mistake *verb*
1. CONFUSE.

2. ERR.
3. MISUNDERSTAND.
mistaken *adjective* ERRONEOUS.
mistreat *verb* ABUSE.
mistreatment *noun* ABUSE.
mistrust *noun*
1. DISTRUST.
2. DOUBT.
mistrust *verb*
1. DISTRUST.
2. DOUBT.
mistrustful *adjective* DISTRUSTFUL.
misty *adjective*
1. FILMY.
2. UNCLEAR.
misunderstand *verb*
To understand incorrectly: *completely
misunderstood the instructions.*
Syns: misapprehend, misconceive,
misconstrue, misinterpret, mistake.
misunderstanding *noun*
A failure to understand correctly: *a
misunderstanding about what he was to
do.*
Syns: misapprehension,
misconception, misinterpretation.
—*Idiom* false impression.
misusage *noun* ABUSE.
misuse *verb*
1, 2. ABUSE.
misuse *noun* ABUSE.
mite *noun* BIT¹.
mitigate *verb* RELIEVE.
mitigation *noun* RELIEF.
mix *verb*
To put together into one mass so that
the constituent parts are more or less
homogeneous: *mixing eggs, butter, and
sugar into a batter.*
Syns: admix, amalgamate, blend,
combine, commingle, commix,
compound, fuse, intermingle,
intermix, merge, mingle, stir¹.
mix up *verb*
1. COMPLICATE.
2, 3. CONFUSE.
4. DISORDER.
mix *noun* MIXTURE.
mixed *adjective* VARIOUS.
mixed-up *adjective* CONFUSED.
mixture *noun*
Something produced by mixing: *a
mixture of flour and milk; yarn that is a
mixture of wool and nylon.*
Syns: admixture, amalgam,
amalgamation, blend, compound,
fusion, mix.
mix-up *noun* DISORDER.
moan *noun* HOWL.

mob *noun*
1. COMMONALTY.
2. CROWD.
3. GANG.
mob *verb*
1, 2. CROWD.
mobile *adjective*
1. Capable of moving or being moved from place to place: *a mobile home; a mobile hospital.*
   Syns: movable (*also* moveable), moving, transportable, traveling.
2. Changing easily, as in expression: *a mobile face.*
   Syns: changeable, fluid, plastic.
3. MIGRATORY.
mobilize *verb*
1. To assemble, prepare, or put into operation, as for war or a similar emergency: *mobilized the troops; trying to mobilize public opinion.*
   Syns: marshal, muster, organize, rally.
2. DRIVE.
3. MILITARIZE.
mock *verb*
1. IMITATE.
2. RIDICULE.
mock *noun* MOCKERY.
mock *adjective* ARTIFICIAL.
mockery *noun*
1. A false, derisive, or impudent imitation of something: *The trial was a mockery of justice.*
   Syns: burlesque, caricature, farce, mock, parody, sham, travesty.
2. JOKE.
3. RIDICULE.
mod *adjective* CONTEMPORARY.
mode *noun*
1. CONDITION.
2. FASHION.
3. STYLE.
model *noun*
1. A small-scale representation of something: *a model of a proposed skyscraper; a model of an oldtime sailing vessel.*
   Syn: miniature. —*Idiom* pocket edition.
2. One that is worthy of imitation or duplication: *My aunt was a model of ladylike behavior.*
   Syns: beau ideal, example, exemplar, ideal, mirror, paradigm, pattern, phenomenon, standard.
model *verb*
1. FOLLOW.
2. FORM.

model *adjective*
1. IDEAL.
2. TYPICAL.
moderate *adjective*
1. Not excessive or extreme in amount, degree, or force: *drives at moderate speeds; antiques for sale at moderate prices.*
   Syns: modest, reasonable, temperate.
2. CONSERVATIVE.
3. GRADUAL.
4, 5. LIGHT².
6. MILD.
moderate *verb*
1. To make or become less severe or extreme: *In later years he moderated his views.*
   Syns: mute, soften, subdue, tame, temper, tone down.
2. SUBSIDE.
moderateness *noun* MODERATION.
moderation *noun*
Avoidance of extremes of opinion, feeling, or personal conduct: *was advised to eat and drink with moderation.*
   Syns: measure, moderateness, temperance.
modern *adjective*
Of or pertaining to recent times or the present: *a course in modern history; studies modern languages.*
   Syns: current, latter-day, modern-day.
modern *noun* CONTEMPORARY.
modern-day *adjective* MODERN.
modernize *verb*
To make modern in appearance or style: *modernized their colonial house.*
   Syns: refurbish, rejuvenate, renovate, restore, revamp, update.
modest *adjective*
1. Reticent or reserved in manner: *too modest to speak up for herself.*
   Syns: backward, bashful, coy, demure, diffident, retiring, self-effacing, shy¹, timid.
2. Not elaborate or showy, as in appearance or style: *a modest little house; a modest gift.*
   Syns: plain, simple, unostentatious, unpretentious.
3. CHASTE.
4. CLEAN.
5. HUMBLE.
6. MODERATE.
modesty *noun*
1. Reserve in speech, behavior, or dress: *a woman of unaffected modesty.*
   Syns: demureness, diffidence, reticence.
2. Lack of vanity or self-importance:

*The famous scientist never lost his
modesty.*
Syns: humbleness, humility.
3. Lack of ostentation or pretension:
*amazed at the modesty of their
lifestyle.*
Syns: plainness, simplicity,
unostentatiousness,
unpretentiousness.
4. CHASTITY.

modicum *noun* BIT[1].
modification *noun* CHANGE.
modified *adjective* QUALIFIED.
modify *verb* CHANGE.
modish *adjective* FASHIONABLE.
modus *noun* WAY.
modus operandi *noun*
1. APPROACH.
2. WAY.
moil *verb*
1. BOIL.
2. LABOR.
 moil *noun* LABOR.
moist *adjective* DAMP.
moisten *verb* WASH.
moistureless *adjective* DRY.
mold *noun* KIND[2].
 mold *verb*
1. FORM.
2. MAKE.
moldable *adjective* MALLEABLE.
molder *verb* DECAY.
moldy *adjective*
Smelling of mildew or decay: *We held
our noses against the moldy air in the
cluttered attic.*
Syns: frowsy, fusty, musty, putrid,
rank[2].
molecule *noun* BIT[1].
moll *noun* PROSTITUTE.
mollify *verb* PACIFY.
mollycoddle *noun* BABY.
 mollycoddle *verb* BABY.
molt *verb* SHED.
moment *noun*
1. FLASH.
2. IMPORTANCE.
3. INSTANT.
momentary *adjective*
1. About to occur at any moment: *We
awaited her momentary return.*
Syns: imminent, impending,
proximate.
2. TRANSITORY.
momentous *adjective*
1. FATEFUL.
2. GRAVE[2].
3. IMPORTANT.
momentousness *noun* GRAVITY.
momus *noun* CRITIC.

monetary *adjective* FINANCIAL.
money *noun*
Something, as coins, printed bills, etc.,
used as a medium of exchange: *counted
out the money and paid the waiter.*
Syns: brass (*Brit. Slang*), bread
(*Slang*), bucks (*Slang*), cabbage
(*Slang*), cash, currency, dough
(*Slang*), gelt (*Slang*), greenbacks, jack
(*Slang*), lettuce (*Slang*), lucre,
mazuma (*Slang*), moola *or* moolah
(*Slang*), pelf, scratch (*Slang*),
wampum. —*Idioms* green stuff, long
green.
moneyed *adjective* RICH.
moneymaking *adjective* PROFITABLE.
moneyman *noun* FINANCIER.
moneys *noun* FUNDS.
moniker *or* **monicker** *noun* NAME.
monition *noun* WARNING.
monitory *adjective* CAUTIONARY.
monkey *noun* DUPE.
 monkey *verb*
1. FIDDLE.
2. TAMPER.
monkeyshine *noun* PRANK.
monocracy *noun* ABSOLUTISM.
monocratic *adjective* ABSOLUTE.
monopolize *verb*
1. ABSORB.
2. TIE UP at **tie**.
monopoly *noun*
Exclusive control or possession: *efforts
to break the monopoly of the utility
companies.*
Syn: corner.
monotone *noun* MONOTONY.
monotonous *adjective* BORING.
monotony *noun*
A tiresome lack of variety: *the monotony
of his office routine.*
Syns: humdrum, monotone, sameness,
tediousness, tedium.
monster *noun*
1. FIEND.
2. FREAK.
3. GIANT.
 monster *adjective* GIANT.
monstrosity *noun*
1. FREAK.
2. MESS.
3. OUTRAGE.
monstrous *adjective*
1. FREAKISH.
2. GIANT.
3, 4. OUTRAGEOUS.
monstrousness *noun* ENORMITY.
monument *noun* MEMORIAL.
monumental *adjective* GIANT.

mooch *verb*
1. BEG.
2. CUT.

moocher *noun* BEGGAR.

mood *noun*
1. A temporary state of mind or feeling: *Bad weather puts her in a gloomy mood.*
   Syns: humor, spirits, temper, vein. —*Idiom* frame of mind.
2. AIR.
3. TEMPER.

moody *adjective*
Given to changeable emotional states, esp. of anger or gloom: *The pressures of work make her moody.*
   Syns: humorsome, notional, temperamental.

moola or **moolah** *noun* MONEY.

moon *verb* DREAM.

mooncalf *noun* FOOL.

moonstruck also **moonstricken**
adjective INSANE.

moony *adjective* DREAMY.

moor *verb*
1. ATTACH.
2. FASTEN.

moot *verb*
1. BROACH.
2. DISCUSS.

   moot *adjective* DEBATABLE.

mootable *adjective* DEBATABLE.

mop *noun* FACE.

   mop *verb* GRIMACE.

mope *verb*
1. BROOD.
2. SULK.

mopes *noun* GLOOM.

moppet *noun* CHILD.

moral *adjective*
1. Inclined to teach or moralize excessively: *a tiresomely moral lecture.*
   Syns: didactic (*also* didactical), moralizing, preachy.
2. ELEVATED.
3. ETHICAL.

   moral *noun*
   The principle taught by a fable, parable, etc.: *The moral is not to waste one's youth.*
   Syns: lesson, precept.

morale *noun*
A strong sense of enthusiasm and dedication to a common goal that unites a group: *The morale of the troops is superb.*
   Syns: esprit, esprit de corps.

morality *noun*
1. ETHIC.
2. GOOD.

moralize *verb*
To indulge in moral reflection, usu. pompously: *loves to moralize.*
   Syns: preach, sermonize.

morals *noun* ETHIC.

morass *noun*
1. SWAMP.
2. TANGLE.

morbid *adjective*
Susceptible to or marked by preoccupation with unwholesome matters: *a morbid fascination with death.*
   Syns: macabre, sick, sickly, unhealthy, unwholesome.

mordacious *adjective* BITING.

mordacity *noun* SARCASM.

mordancy *noun* SARCASM.

mordant *adjective*
1. BITING.
2. SARCASTIC.

more *adjective* ADDITIONAL.

   more *adverb*
   1. ADDITIONALLY.
   2. BETTER¹.

mores *noun*
1. ETHIC.
2. MANNERS.

morn *noun* DAWN.

morning *noun*
1. The time of day from sunrise to noon: *worked all morning, then ate lunch.*
   Syn: forenoon.
2. DAWN.

moron *noun* FOOL.

morose *adjective* GLUM.

morsel *noun*
1. BIT¹.
2. BITE.
3. DELICACY.

mort *noun* BODY.

mortal *adjective*
1. DEADLY.
2. EARTHLY.
3. HUMAN.

   mortal *noun* HUMAN BEING.

mortality *noun* FATALITY.

mortgage *verb* PAWN¹.

mortified *adjective* EMBARRASSED.

mortify *verb* EMBARRASS.

mortifying *adjective* EMBARRASSING.

mortuary *adjective* GHASTLY.

mosey *verb* STROLL.

mossback *noun*
1. REACTIONARY.
2. SQUARE.

most *adverb* VERY.

motif *noun* FIGURE.

motion *noun*
1. The act or process of moving: *made a sudden motion in his sleep.*
   Syns: move, movement, stir[1].
2. GESTURE.
motion *verb* GESTURE.
motionless *adjective*
Not moving: *sitting motionless at the desk.*
   Syns: immobile, stationary, still, stock-still.
motivate *verb*
1. ENCOURAGE.
2. PROVOKE.
motivation *noun*
1. CAUSE.
2. ENCOURAGEMENT.
motive *noun*
1. CAUSE.
2. FIGURE.
motley *adjective*
1. MULTICOLORED.
2. VARIOUS.
motor *verb* DRIVE.
motorist *noun* DRIVER.
mottle *verb* SPECKLE.
motto *noun* CRY.
moue *noun* FACE.
mound *noun* HEAP.
mound *verb* HEAP.
mount *verb*
1. ASCEND.
2. INCREASE.
3. INTENSIFY.
4, 5, 6. RISE.
mountain *noun*
1, 2. HEAP.
mountainous *adjective* GIANT.
mountebank *noun* FAKE.
mounting *noun*
1. ASCENT.
2. RISE.
mourn *verb* GRIEVE.
mournful *adjective*
1, 2. SORROWFUL.
mournfulness *noun* GLOOM.
mouse *noun* BLACK EYE.
mouse *verb* SNEAK.
mouth *noun*
1. The opening in the body through which food is ingested: *put a spoonful of ice cream in his mouth.*
   Syns: gob[2] (*Slang*), puss (*Slang*), trap (*Slang*).
2. FACE.
3. SPEAKER.
mouth *verb*
1. GRIMACE.
2. RANT.
mouthful *noun* BIT[1].

mouthpiece *noun* SPEAKER.
mouthwatering *adjective* TANTALIZING.
movable *also* **moveable** *adjective* MOBILE.
movable *also* **moveable** *noun* FURNISHING.
movables *also* **moveables** *noun* EFFECTS.
move *verb*
1. To go or cause to go from one place to another: *moved away from the railing; moved the lamp closer.*
   Syns: maneuver, remove, shift, transfer.
2. To change one's residence, place of business, etc.: *We moved here last October.*
   Syns: relocate, remove, transfer.
3. AFFECT[1].
4. COME.
5. DISTURB.
6. DRIVE.
7. PROVOKE.
8, 9. STIR[1].
move *noun*
1. An action calculated to achieve an end: *Changing jobs was a wise move.*
   Syns: maneuver, measure, procedure, step, tactic[1].
2. MOTION.
3. MOVEMENT.
4. REMOVAL.
moveable *adjective & noun* SEE **movable.**
moveables *noun* SEE **movables.**
moved *adjective* AFFECTED[1].
movement *noun*
1. A calculated change in position: *troop movements; the movements of a dance.*
   Syns: evolution, maneuver, move, turn.
2. MOTION.
moving *adjective*
1. AFFECTING.
2. EMOTIONAL.
3. MOBILE.
mow *verb* GRIMACE.
mow *also* **mowe** *noun* FACE.
moxie *noun* COURAGE.
Mrs. Grundy *noun* PRUDE.
much *noun* HEAP.
muchly *adverb* VERY.
mucilaginous *adjective* VISCOUS.
muck *noun*
1. FILTH.
2. SLIME.
muck *verb* MUDDY.
muck up *verb* BOTCH.

muckamuck also **mucketymuck** *noun*
DIGNITARY.

mucker *noun* BOOR.

mucketymuck *noun* SEE **muckamuck**.

muckworm *noun* MISER.

mucky *adjective*
1. SLIMY.
2. STICKY.

mucro *noun* POINT.

mucronate *adjective* POINTED.

mucronation *noun* POINT.

muddle *verb*
1. To proceed or perform in an unsteady, faltering manner: *He muddled on clearly unprepared to recite.*
   Syns: fudge, fumble, limp, shuffle, stagger, stumble.
2. BOTCH.
3. CONFUSE.
4. DISORDER.

muddle through *verb* MANAGE.

muddle *noun*
1. BOTCH.
2. DAZE.
3. DISORDER.

muddled *adjective* CONFUSED.

muddy *adjective*
1. Covered or soiled with mud: *a muddy road; muddy shoes.*
   Syns: bemired, miry.
2. DULL.
3. TURBID.

muddy *verb*
To soil with mud: *muddied the clean floor.*
   Syns: bemire, bemud (*Archaic*), muck (up).

mudslinging *noun* SMEAR.

muff *verb* BOTCH.

muffle *verb*
1. To decrease or dull the sound of: *The trumpeter muffled his horn to give a sad, blues quality to his playing.*
   Syns: dampen, deaden, mute, stifle.
2. REPRESS.

mug *noun*
1. DUPE.
2, 3. FACE.
4. TOUGH.

mug *verb* GRIMACE.

muggy *adjective* STICKY.

mulct *verb*
1. CHEAT.
2. FINE².

mulct *noun* FINE².

muleheaded *adjective* OBSTINATE.

muley *adjective* OBSTINATE.

muliebral *adjective* FEMININE.

mulish *adjective* OBSTINATE.

mulishness *noun* OBSTINACY.

mull¹ *noun* BOTCH.

mull² *verb* PONDER.

multicolored *adjective*
Having many different colors: *a cheerful multicolored bedspread.*
   Syns: motley, polychromatic (*also* polychromic, polychromous), polychrome, varicolored, variegated, versicolor (*also* versicolored).

multifaceted *adjective* VERSATILE.

multifarious *adjective* VARIOUS.

multifariousness *noun* VARIETY.

multiformity *noun* VARIETY.

multiloquent *adjective* TALKATIVE.

multiplication *noun*
1. BUILD-UP.
2. INCREASE.
3. REPRODUCTION.

multiplicity *noun*
1. HEAP.
2. VARIETY.

multiply *verb*
1. INCREASE.
2. REPRODUCE.
3. RISE.

multisyllabic *adjective* LONG¹.

multitude *noun*
1, 2. CROWD.

multitudinous *adjective* MANY.

multivocal *adjective* VOCIFEROUS.

mum *adjective* SPEECHLESS.

mumble *verb* MUTTER.

mumble *noun* MURMUR.

mumblenews *noun* GOSSIP.

mumbo jumbo *noun*
1, 2. GIBBERISH.

mummify *verb* DRY UP at **dry**.

mummy *verb* DRY UP at **dry**.

mumpish *adjective* GLUM.

mun *verb* MUST.

munch *verb* CHEW.

mundane *adjective*
1. EARTHLY.
2. EVERYDAY.
3. MATERIALISTIC.

municipal *adjective* CITY.

municipality *noun* CITY.

munificence *noun* GENEROSITY.

munificent *adjective* GENEROUS.

murder *verb*
To take the life of (a person or persons) unlawfully: *murdered his parents.*
   Syns: bump off (*Slang*), destroy, do in (*Slang*), dust off (*Slang*), erase (*Slang*), finish, hit (*Slang*), kill, knock off (*Slang*), liquidate, off (*Slang*), put away, rub out (*Slang*), slay, waste (*Slang*), wipe out (*Informal*), zap (*Slang*).

murder *noun*
The crime of murdering someone: *convicted of first-degree murder.*
　　Syns: blood, bump-off (*Slang*), homicide, killing, manslaying, slaying.
murderer *noun*
One who murders another: *arrested the murderer.*
　　Syns: butcher, Cain, cutthroat, homicide, killer, manslayer, massacrer, slaughterer, slayer, triggerman (*Slang*). —*Idiom* hit man.
murderous *adjective*
Eager for bloodshed: *a murderous pirate.*
　　Syns: bloodthirsty, bloody, cutthroat, ferocious, fierce, homicidal, sanguinary, sanguineous, slaughterous.
mure *verb* ENCLOSE.
murk *also* **mirk** *noun* HAZE.
murk *also* **mirk** *verb* OBSCURE.
murky *also* **mirky** *adjective*
1. DARK.
2. DULL.
3. TURBID.
murmur *noun*
1. A low, indistinct, and often continuous sound: *the murmur of the sea; the approving murmurs of the listeners.*
　　Syns: mumble, sigh, sough, susurration, whisper.
2. GOSSIP.
3. MUTTER.
murmur *verb*
1. To make a low, continuous, and indistinct sound: *The wind murmured through the trees.*
　　Syns: sigh, sough, whisper.
2. COMPLAIN.
3, 4. MUTTER.
muscle *noun*
1. Effective means of influencing, compelling, or punishing: *putting muscle in law enforcement.*
　　Syns: clout (*Informal*), force, power, weight.
2. STRENGTH.
muscle *verb*
To force one's way into a place or situation: *muscled his way through the crowd; muscled into our conversation.*
　　Syns: push, shove, strong-arm.
muscular *adjective*
Characterized by marked muscular development; powerfully built: *a muscular boxer; a strong, muscular physique.*
　　Syns: brawny, burly, robust, sinewy, sturdy.

muse[1] *verb*
1. DREAM.
2. PONDER.
muse *noun* TRANCE.
muse[2] *noun* POET.
museful *adjective* THOUGHTFUL.
mush *verb* CRUSH.
mush *noun* SENTIMENTALITY.
mushiness *noun* SENTIMENTALITY.
mushroom *verb* EXPLODE.
mushy *adjective*
1. SENTIMENTAL.
2. SOFT.
musical *adjective*
1. HARMONIOUS.
2. MELODIOUS.
musician *noun* PLAYER.
musicianer *noun* PLAYER.
musico *noun* PLAYER.
musing *adjective* PENSIVE.
muskeg *noun* SWAMP.
muss *verb* TOUSLE.
muss *noun* BOTCH.
mussy *adjective* MESSY.
must *verb*
To be required or compelled to do: *You simply must answer that letter.*
　　Syns: need, mun (*Brit. Regional*). —*Idioms* have got to, have to, must needs.
must *noun*
1. CONDITION.
2. DUTY.
muster *verb*
1, 2. ASSEMBLE.
3. CALL.
4. JOIN.
5. MOBILIZE.
muster out *verb* DISCHARGE.
muster *noun* ASSEMBLY.
musty *adjective*
1. MOLDY.
2. TRITE.
mutable *adjective* CHANGEABLE.
mutate *verb*
1. CHANGE.
2. CONVERT.
mutation *noun* CHANGE.
mute *adjective*
1. DUMB.
2. SPEECHLESS.
mute *verb*
1. MODERATE.
2. MUFFLE.
muted *adjective* FAINT.
muteness *noun* SILENCE.
mutilate *verb* CRIPPLE.
mutineer *noun* REBEL.
mutineer *verb* REBEL.
mutinize *verb* REBEL.

mutinous *adjective* REBELLIOUS.
mutiny *noun* REBELLION.
  mutiny *verb* REBEL.
mutter *verb*
1. To speak or utter indistinctly, as by lowering the voice or partially closing the mouth: *Don't mutter—speak up.*
  Syns: mumble, murmur, whisper.
  —*Idiom* swallow one's words.
2. To complain in low, indistinct tones: *The crowd muttered in disapproval.*
  Syns: grumble, grunt, murmur, rumble.
mutter *noun*
A low, indistinct utterance of complaint: *a mutter of angry voices.*
  Syns: grumble, grunt, murmur, rumble.
mutual *adjective*
1. Having the same relationship each to the other: *mutual affections.*
  Syns: reciprocal, reciprocative.
2. COMMON.
muzzle *noun* FACE.
myriad *adjective* MANY.
mysterious *adjective*
Difficult to explain or understand: *He has some mysterious power over women.*
  Syns: arcane, cabalistic, mystic, mystical, mystifying, unaccountable, unexplainable, unfathomable.
mystery *noun*
Anything that arouses curiosity or perplexes because it is unexplained, inexplicable, or secret: *Her whereabouts remains a mystery. The location of the lost continent of Atlantis is an unsolved mystery.*
  Syns: conundrum, enigma, puzzle, puzzlement, puzzler, riddle. —*Idiom* question mark.
mystic *adjective* MYSTERIOUS.
mystical *adjective* MYSTERIOUS.
mystifying *adjective* MYSTERIOUS.
myth *noun*
1. A traditional story or tale dealing with ancestors, heroes, supernatural events, etc., that has no proven factual basis but attempts to explain beliefs, practices, or natural phenomena: *The myth told how mankind was given the gift of fire by the gods.*
  Syns: fable, legend.
2. Any fictitious idea accepted as part of an ideology by an uncritical group; a received idea: *the myth of a pure race.*

  Syns: creation, fantasy (*also* phantasy), fiction, figment, invention.
3. LORE.
mythical *also* **mythic** *adjective*
Of or existing only in myths: *the mythical unicorn; the mythical golden cities of Cibola.*
  Syns: fabulous, legendary, mythological (*also* mythologic).
mythological *also* **mythologic** *adjective* MYTHICAL.
mythology *noun* LORE.
mythos *noun* LORE.

N

nab *verb*
1. ARREST.
2. CATCH.
  nab *noun*
1. ARREST.
2. POLICEMAN.
nabob *noun* DIGNITARY.
nag *verb*
To scold or find fault constantly: *always nagging me about something or other.*
  Syns: carp (at), fuss (at), henpeck, peck², pick (on).
naif *also* **naïf** *adjective & noun* SEE **naive.**
nail *verb* TAKE.
naive *also* **naïve, naif, naïf** *adjective*
1. ARTLESS.
2. EASY.
  naive *also* **naïve, naif, naïf** *noun*
INNOCENT.
naked *adjective*
1. BARE.
2. NUDE.
nakedness *noun* NUDITY.
namby-pamby *adjective* INSIPID.
name *noun*
1. The word or words by which one is called and identified: *gave his son two names; recalled the name of the book.*
  Syns: appellation, appellative, cognomen, denomination, designation, handle (*Slang*), moniker *or* monicker (*Slang*), nomen, style, tag (*Slang*).
2. CELEBRITY.
3. REPUTATION.

name *verb*
1. To give a name or title to: *named the baby after his father.*
   Syns: baptize, call, christen, denominate, designate, dub[1], entitle, style, term, title.
2. To refer to by name: *She spoke of her previous jobs, naming several.*
   Syns: cite, instance, mention, specify.
3. APPOINT.

nameless *adjective*
1. ANONYMOUS.
2. OBSCURE.

namelessness *noun* OBSCURITY.

namely *adverb*
That is to say: *You must improve your manners, namely, your eating habits.*
Syns: scilicet, videlicet. —*Idiom* to wit.

naming *noun* APPOINTMENT.

nap *noun*
A brief sleep: *takes a nap after lunch.*
Syns: catnap, doze, siesta.

nap *verb*
To sleep for a brief period: *napped for an hour before dinner.*
Syns: catnap, doze (off), nod (off), siesta. —*Idiom* catch (*or* grab) forty winks.

narcissism *also* **narcism** *noun*
EGOTISM.

narcissist *noun* EGOTIST.

narcissistic *adjective*
1. EGOTISTICAL.
2. VAIN.

narcotic *noun*
1. DRUG.
2. SOPORIFIC.

narcotic *adjective* SLEEPY.

narcotize *verb* DRUG.

narrate *verb* DESCRIBE.

narrative *noun* STORY.

narrow *adjective*
1. Not broad or elevated in scope or understanding: *unappreciated by the narrow provincials of her home town.*
   Syns: limited, little, mean[2], narrow-minded, paltry, petty, small, small-minded.
2. INTOLERANT.
3. LOCAL.
4. STINGY.
5. TIGHT.

narrow *verb* CONSTRICT.

narrow-minded *adjective*
1. INTOLERANT.
2. LOCAL.
3. NARROW.

nascence *also* **nascency** *noun*
BIRTH.

nasty *adjective*
1, 2. FILTHY.
3. ILL-TEMPERED.
4. MALEVOLENT.
5. OBSCENE.
6. OFFENSIVE.

nation *noun* STATE.

national *noun* CITIZEN.

national *adjective*
1. DOMESTIC.
2. PUBLIC.

nationalize *verb* SOCIALIZE.

native *adjective*
1. Belonging to one because of the place or circumstances of one's birth: *our native land; her native language.*
   Syns: aboriginal, autochthonous (*also* autochthonal, autochthonic), endemic, indigenous.
2. CRUDE.
3. DOMESTIC.
4. INDIGENOUS.
5. INNATE.
6. WILD.

natural *adjective*
1. Produced by nature; not artificial or manmade: *natural foods.*
   Syns: organic, unadulterated. —*Idiom* pure as the driven snow.
2. ARTLESS.
3. BUILT-IN.
4. ILLEGITIMATE.
5. INNATE.
6. REALISTIC.
7. RUSTIC.
8. WILD.

natural *noun* FOOL.

naturalistic *adjective* REALISTIC.

naturally *adverb* USUALLY.

naturalness *noun*
1. EASE.
2. INFORMALITY.

nature *noun*
1. CHARACTER.
2. DISPOSITION.
3. ESSENCE.
4. KIND[2].
5. UNIVERSE.

naughtiness *noun* MISBEHAVIOR.

naughty *adjective*
Misbehaving, often in a troublesome way: *a naughty child.*
Syns: bad, ill-behaved, out-of-line (*Informal*).

nauseate *verb* DISGUST.

nauseating *adjective*
1. OFFENSIVE.
2. UNSPEAKABLE.

nautical *adjective*
Of or relating to sea navigation: *nautical charts and instruments.*
  Syns: marine, maritime, navigational.
navigable *adjective* PASSABLE.
navigate *verb* MANEUVER.
navigational *adjective* NAUTICAL.
navigator *noun* SAILOR.
nay *noun*
1, 2. NO.
nay *adverb*
1. EVEN[1].
2. NO.
near *adjective* CLOSE[1].
near *verb* APPROACH.
near *adverb* CLOSE[1].
near-at-hand *adjective*
1. CLOSE[1].
2. CONVENIENT.
nearby *adjective*
1. CLOSE[1].
2. CONVENIENT.
nearby *adverb* CLOSE[1].
nearly *adverb* APPROXIMATELY.
nearness *noun* APPROACH.
neat *adjective*
1. In good order or clean condition: *a neat room; a neat appearance.*
  Syns: orderly, shipshape, snug, spic-and-span, spruce, taut, tidy, tight (*Regional*), trig, trim, well-groomed.
  —*Idiom* neat as a pin.
2. Well done or executed: *a neat turn of phrase.*
  Syns: adept, adroit, deft, skillful.
3. MARVELOUS.
4. STRAIGHT.
neaten *verb*
1, 2. TIDY.
nebbish *noun* NONENTITY.
nebulous *adjective* AMBIGUOUS.
necessary *adjective*
1. ESSENTIAL.
2. REQUIRED.
necessitate *verb* DEMAND.
necessitous *adjective*
1. ESSENTIAL.
2. POOR.
necessity *noun*
1. CAUSE.
2. CONDITION.
3. NEED.
neck-and-neck *adjective* CLOSE[1].
need *noun*
1. A condition in which something necessary or desirable is required or wanted: *patients in need of nursing.*
  Syns: exigency (*also* exigence), necessity.
2. DEMAND.

3. DUTY.
4. POVERTY.
need *verb*
1. LACK.
2. MUST.
neediness *noun* POVERTY.
needle *noun* PRICK.
needle *verb* BAIT.
needless *adjective* UNNECESSARY.
needy *adjective* POOR.
ne'er-do-well *noun* WASTREL.
nefarious *adjective*
1. CORRUPT.
2. EVIL.
negate *verb*
1. ABOLISH.
2. DENY.
negation *noun*
1. ABOLITION.
2. DENIAL.
negative *adjective* UNFAVORABLE.
negative *verb*
1. DENY.
2. VETO.
neglect *verb*
1. To fail to care for or give proper attention to: *neglected her children.*
  Syns: disregard, slight.
2. To avoid the fulfillment of: *neglected their duty.*
  Syns: disregard, shirk, slack. —*Idiom* let slide.
3. FAIL.
4. IGNORE.
neglect *noun*
1. An act or instance of neglecting: *parents' neglect of their responsibility; property ruined through neglect.*
  Syns: disregard, oversight, slight.
2. FAILURE.
neglectful *adjective* NEGLIGENT.
negligence *noun*
The state or quality of being negligent: *mine operators charged with negligence.*
  Syns: laxity, laxness, remissness, slackness.
negligent *adjective*
Guilty of neglect; lacking due care or concern: *negligent ship's officers who disregarded warnings about icebergs.*
  Syns: derelict, lax, neglectful, remiss, slack.
negligible *adjective*
1. PETTY.
2. REMOTE.
negotiable *adjective* PASSABLE.
negotiate *verb*
1. ARRANGE.
2. CLEAR.
negotiation *noun* TALK.

neighbor *verb* ADJOIN.
neighborhood *noun*
1. A rather small part of a geographic unit considered in regard to its inhabitants or distinctive characteristics: *a well-known Italian neighborhood.*
   Syns: area, locality, quarter.
2. *Informal.* Approximate size or amount: *priced in the neighborhood of fifty dollars.*
   Syns: order, range, vicinity.
3. AREA.
4. LOCALITY.

neighboring *adjective* ADJOINING.
neighborly *adjective* FRIENDLY.
neonate *noun* BABY.
neophyte *noun* BEGINNER.
nephalism *noun* TEMPERANCE.
nerve *noun*
1. COURAGE.
2. IMPUDENCE.
3. PRESUMPTION.
   nerve *verb* ENCOURAGE.
nervous *adjective*
1. ANXIOUS.
2. EDGY.
nervy *adjective*
1. EDGY.
2. IMPUDENT.
3. PRESUMPTUOUS.
nescience *noun*
1, 2. IGNORANCE.
nescient *adjective* IGNORANT.
nestle *verb* SNUGGLE.
Nestor *noun* SAGE.
net[1] *verb* TAKE.
   net *noun* WEB.
net[2] *verb* RETURN.
nethermost *adjective* BOTTOM.
netting *noun* WEB.
nettle *verb* ANNOY.
nettlesome *adjective*
1. THORNY.
2. VEXATIOUS.
network *noun*
1, 2. WEB.
neuter *verb* STERILIZE.
   neuter *adjective* NEUTRAL.
neutral *adjective*
1. Not inclining toward or actively taking either side in a matter under dispute: *strove to be neutral in the cold war.*
   Syns: impartial, neuter, nonaligned, nonpartisan, unbiased, uncommitted, uninvolved, unprejudiced. —*Idiom* on the fence.
2. Without definite or distinctive characteristics: *His neutral personality contrasted with her flamboyant one.*
   Syns: bland, colorless, indistinctive.
3. Feeling or showing no strong emotional involvement: *a neutral approach to a controversial issue.*
   Syns: detached, disinterested, dispassionate, impersonal.
neutralize *verb*
1. CANCEL.
2. COMPENSATE.
never-ending *adjective* ENDLESS.
new *adjective*
1. Showing marked departure from previous practice: *a new style of painting.*
   Syns: fresh, innovative, inventive, newfangled, novel, original, unfamiliar, unprecedented.
2. ADDITIONAL.
3. FRESH.
4. PRESENT[1].
new *adverb*
Once more: *new-remembered pleasures.*
   Syns: afresh, again, anew.
newborn *noun* BABY.
newcomer *noun* FOREIGNER.
newfangle *noun* NOVELTY.
newfangled *adjective* NEW.
newly *adverb* JUST.
newness *noun* NOVELTY.
news *noun*
1. New information, esp. about recent events and happenings: *just got the news of the hurricane.*
   Syns: advice(s), intelligence, tidings, word.
2. EVENT.
newsmonger *noun* GOSSIP.
next *adjective*
1. ADJOINING.
2. FOLLOWING.
   next *adverb* LATER.
nexus *noun* BOND.
Niagara *noun* FLOOD.
nice *adjective*
1. Very difficult to please: *was nice to a fault about his appearance.*
   Syns: choosy, dainty, exacting, fastidious, finical, finicky, fussy, meticulous, particular, persnickety, picky.
2. AGREEABLE.
3. CHASTE.
4. CORRECT.
5. DELICATE.
6. FINE[1].
7, 8. GOOD.
niche *noun* PLACE.
nictitate *verb* BLINK.

nictitation noun BLINK.

nifty adjective MARVELOUS.

niggard noun MISER.

niggard adjective STINGY.

niggardly adjective STINGY.

niggle verb QUIBBLE.

niggling adjective PETTY.

nigh adverb CLOSE¹.

nigh adjective CLOSE¹.

night noun
The period of time between sunset and
sunrise: *will return tomorrow night.*
   Syns: nighttide, nighttime.

night adjective NIGHTLY.

nightfall noun EVENING.

nightly adjective
Of or occurring during the night: *nightly
prowlings.*
   Syns: night, nocturnal.

nighttide noun NIGHT.

nighttime noun NIGHT.

nihility noun NOTHINGNESS.

nil noun NOTHING.

nimble adjective
1. Moving or performing quickly,
   lightly, and easily: *nimble feet.*
   Syns: active, agile, brisk, facile,
   featly, quick, spry.
2. AGILE.
3. DEXTEROUS.

nimbleness noun AGILITY.

nincompoop noun FOOL.

ninny noun FOOL.

nip¹ verb
1. RUSH.
2. SNAP.
3. STEAL.

nip² noun DROP.

nip verb DRINK.

nippy adjective COLD.

nit-pick verb QUIBBLE.

nitwit noun FOOL.

nix verb
1. DECLINE.
2. VETO.

nix noun NOTHING.

nix adverb NO.

no noun
1. A negative response: *The proposal
   produced only noes.*
   Syns: nay, refusal, rejection.
2. A negative vote or voter: *The noes
   carried the day.*
   Syn: nay.

no adverb
Not so: *No, I won't be there.*
   Syns: nay, nix (*Slang*), nope (*Slang*).
   —*Idioms* nothing doing, no way.

noble adjective
1. Of high birth or social position: *a
   noble family; noble ladies of the court.*
   Syns: aristocratic, blue-blooded,
   highborn, highbred, patrician,
   thoroughbred, well-born.
2. ELEVATED.
3. GRAND.

nobody pronoun
No person: *Nobody stayed after the
lecture.*
   Syn: no one.

nobody noun NONENTITY.

nocturnal adjective NIGHTLY.

nod noun
1. ACCEPTANCE.
2. BOW.

nod verb NAP.

nodding adjective SLEEPY.

noddle noun HEAD.

noggin noun HEAD.

no-good noun WASTREL.

no-good adjective WORTHLESS.

noise noun
1. Sounds or a sound, esp. when loud,
   confused, or disagreeable: *deafened by
   the noise in the subway.*
   Syns: babel, clamor, din, hubbub,
   hullabaloo (*also* hullaballoo),
   pandemonium, racket, rumpus,
   tumult, uproar.
2. SOUND¹.

noise verb
1. To spread as news: *It was noised
   about that he would be appointed to the
   post.*
   Syns: bruit (about), report.
2. ADVERTISE.
3. GOSSIP.

noiseless adjective SILENT.

noisome adjective SMELLY.

nomadic adjective
Leading the life of a person without a
fixed domicile; moving from place to
place: *a nomadic tribe.*
   Syns: itinerant, peripatetic, roaming,
   roving, vagabond, vagrant, wandering.

nomen noun NAME.

nominate verb APPOINT.

nomination noun APPOINTMENT.

nominee noun APPOINTEE.

nonage noun MINORITY.

nonaligned adjective NEUTRAL.

nonappearance noun ABSENCE.

nonattendance noun ABSENCE.

nonchalance noun
The state or quality of being
nonchalant: *An assumed nonchalance
concealed his agitation.*

Syns: cool (*Slang*), imperturbability, sang-froid.

nonchalant *adjective* COOL.

noncommittal *adjective* RESERVED.

noncompliance *noun* DISOBEDIENCE.

non compos mentis *adjective* INSANE.

nonconformist *noun* SEPARATIST.

nonentity *noun*
A totally insignificant person: *a colorless nonentity overlooked by everyone.*
Syns: cipher, nebbish (*Slang*), nobody, nothing, pip-squeak, shrimp (*Slang*), zero, zilch (*Slang*).

nonessential *adjective* UNNECESSARY.

nonesuch *noun* NONPAREIL.

nonexistence *noun* NOTHINGNESS.

nonfeasance *noun* FAILURE.

no-nonsense *adjective* SERIOUS.

nonpareil *noun*
A person or thing so excellent as to have no equal or match: *the nonpareil of singers.*
Syns: nonesuch, paragon, phoenix.

nonpareil *adjective* UNIQUE.

nonpartisan *adjective*
1. FAIR.
2. NEUTRAL.

nonpartisanship *noun* FAIRNESS.

nonphysical *adjective* IMMATERIAL.

nonplus *verb*
To make incapable of finding something to think, do, or say: *was nonplussed by their audacity.*
Syns: beat (*Slang*), confound, flummox (*Slang*), stick (*Informal*), stump (*Informal*). —*Idiom* put someone at a loss.

nonprofessional *noun* AMATEUR.

nonresistant *adjective* PASSIVE.

nonresisting *adjective* PASSIVE.

nonsense *noun*
1. Something that does not have or make sense: *was completely ignorant and held views that were utter nonsense.*
Syns: applesauce (*Slang*), balderdash, baloney (*also* boloney) (*Slang*), bilge, blather, bull (*Slang*), bunk² (*Slang*), bunkum¹ (*also* buncombe), claptrap, crap (*Slang*), drivel, eyewash, hooey (*Slang*), idiocy, malarkey (*also* malarky) (*Slang*), piffle, pishposh, poppycock, rigmarole (*also* rigamarole), stuff, tomfoolery, tommyrot (*Informal*), trash¹, twaddle.
2. BABBLE.

nonsensical *adjective* FOOLISH.

nonstop *adjective* CONTINUAL.

noodle *noun* HEAD.

no one *pronoun* NOBODY.

noose *verb* HANG.

nope *adverb* NO.

norm *noun* AVERAGE.

normal *adjective* COMMON.

normally *adverb* USUALLY.

nose *noun*
1. The structure on the human face that contains the nostrils and organs of smell and forms the beginning of the respiratory tract: *a snub nose.*
Syns: beak (*Informal*), nozzle (*Slang*), proboscis, schnozzle (*Slang*), smeller (*Informal*), snoot (*Slang*), snout (*Slang*).
2. DISCERNMENT.
3. SMELL.

nose *verb*
1. SMELL.
2. SNOOP.

nose out *verb* RUN DOWN at run.

nose-dive *noun*
1. FALL.
2. PLUNGE.

nose-dive *verb* FALL.

nosey *adjective* SEE **nosy**.

nosiness *noun* CURIOSITY.

nostrum *noun* CURE.

nosy *also* **nosey** *adjective* CURIOUS.

notability *noun*
1. DIGNITARY.
2. EMINENCE.

notable *adjective* EMINENT.

notable *noun*
1. CELEBRITY.
2. DIGNITARY.

notably *adverb* VERY.

notation *noun* NOTE.

notch *verb* SCORE.

notch *noun* DEGREE.

note *noun*
1. A brief record written as an aid to the memory: *made a note of what was said.*
Syns: memo, memorandum, notation.
2. COMMENT.
3. COMMENTARY.
4. EMINENCE.
5. LETTER.
6. MELODY.
7. NOTICE.

note *verb*
1. COMMENT.
2. NOTICE.

noted *adjective* EMINENT.

nothing *noun*
1. No thing; not anything: *I have nothing to say. The fire left us with nothing.*

Syns: aught (*Archaic*), nil, nix (*Slang*), zilch (*Slang*).
2. NONENTITY.
3. NOTHINGNESS.
4. OBSCURITY.
nothing *adjective* WORTHLESS.
nothingness *noun*
1. Absence of anything perceptible: *The building was reduced to nothingness by the atomic bomb.*
Syns: nihility, nonexistence, nothing, vacuity.
2. Empty, unfilled space: *looked out into the nothingness of the Arctic night.*
Syns: barrenness, emptiness, void.
notice *noun*
1. The act of noting, observing, or taking into account: *took notice of the youth's performance and promoted him.*
Syns: attention, cognizance, heed, mark, note, observance, observation, regard, remark.
2. ANNOUNCEMENT.
3. REVIEW.
notice *verb*
To perceive with a special effort of the senses or the mind: *noticed a change in the old man's expression.*
Syns: descry, distinguish, espy, mark, mind, note, observe, remark, see.
noticeable *adjective*
1. Readily attracting notice: *a noticeable swelling in her right leg; a noticeable increase in East-West tension.*
Syns: arresting, arrestive, conspicuous, eye-catching, marked, observable, outstanding, pointed, prominent, remarkable, salient, signal, striking. —*Idiom* sticking out like a sore thumb.
2. APPARENT.
3. PERCEPTIBLE.
notify *verb* INFORM.
notion *noun*
1. BELIEF.
2. FANCY.
notional *adjective*
1. IMAGINARY.
2. MOODY.
notoriety *noun*
1. Unfavorable, usu. unsavory renown: *a disbarred lawyer of great notoriety.*
Syns: fame, infamy, notoriousness.
2. FAME.
notorious *adjective*
1. Known widely and unfavorably: *a notorious crook.*
Syns: common, famous (*Archaic*), infamous.
2. FAMOUS.

notoriousness *noun* NOTORIETY.
nourish *verb*
1. To sustain (a living organism) with food: *Well-balanced meals nourished the growing children.*
Syn: feed.
2. NURSE.
nourishing *adjective* NUTRITIOUS.
nourishment *noun* FOOD.
novel *adjective*
1. NEW.
2. UNUSUAL.
novelty *noun*
1. The quality of being novel: *He tired of the game after the novelty wore off.*
Syns: freshness, newness, originality.
2. A new, unusual thing: *Edison's light bulb was at first merely an interesting novelty.*
Syns: innovation, newfangle (*Archaic*).
3. A small, showy article: *a store that sold rings, key chains, and other novelties.*
Syns: bauble, bibelot, gewgaw, gimcrack, knickknack, toy, trifle, trinket, whatnot.
novice *noun*
1. An entrant who has not yet taken the final vows of a religious order: *a novice in a convent.*
Syn: novitiate (*also* noviciate) (*Eccles.*).
2. BEGINNER.
novitiate *also* **noviciate** *noun*
1. BEGINNER.
2. NOVICE.
now *noun*
The current time: *Now is the time to begin.*
Syns: nowadays, present[1], today.
now *adjective* PRESENT[1].
now *adverb*
1. At the present; these days: *Air travel is much faster now with the supersonic transports.*
Syns: nowadays, today. —*Idiom* in this day and age.
2. At this moment: *I'm on the phone now.*
Syns: actually, currently. —*Idiom* just (or right) now.
3. At times: *a ballet that was now adagio, now allegro.*
Syns: betimes, periodically. —*Idioms* ever and again, ever and anon, now and again, now and then.
4. DIRECTLY.
nowadays *noun* NOW.
nowadays *adverb* NOW.

noxious *adjective* VIRULENT.
nozzle *noun* NOSE.
nuance *noun* SHADE.
nub *noun*
1. BUMP.
2. HEART.
nucleus *noun* GERM.
nude *adjective*
1. Not wearing any clothes: *nude models.*
   Syns: au naturel, bare, disrobed, naked, stripped, unclad, unclothed, undressed. —*Idioms* bare as a newborn babe, in one's birthday suit, in the altogether (*or* buff *or* raw), naked as a jaybird, stark naked, without a stitch.
2. BARE.
nudeness *noun* NUDITY.
nudge *verb* DIG.
nudge *noun* DIG.
nudity *noun*
   The state of being without clothes: *The artist found nudity an appealing subject.*
   Syns: bareness, nakedness, nudeness, undress.
nugatory *adjective* EMPTY.
nugget *noun* LUMP[1].
nuisance *noun* ANNOYANCE.
nullification *noun* ABOLITION.
nullify *verb* ABOLISH.
numb *verb*
1. DEADEN.
2. PARALYZE.
numb *adjective*
1. DEAD.
2. DULL.
numbed *adjective* DEAD.
number *verb*
1. AMOUNT.
2. COUNT.
number-one *adjective* PRIMARY.
number one *noun* LEADER.
numbers *noun* FIGURES.
numbskull *noun* SEE **numskull**.
numerate *verb*
1. COUNT.
2. ENUMERATE.
numeration *noun* COUNT.
numerous *adjective* MANY.
numinous *adjective* SPIRITUAL.
numskull also **numbskull** *noun*
1. DULLARD.
2. FOOL.
nuptial *noun* WEDDING.
nuptial *adjective* MARITAL.
nurse *verb*
1. To promote and sustain the development of: *agitators who nursed discontent into open revolution.*
   Syns: cultivate, foster, nourish, nurture.
2. BEAR.
nursling *noun* BABY.
nurture *verb* NURSE.
nurture *noun* FOOD.
nut *noun*
1. CRACKPOT.
2. ENTHUSIAST.
3. HEAD.
nutrient *adjective* NUTRITIOUS.
nutriment *noun* FOOD.
nutritional *adjective* NUTRITIVE.
nutritious *adjective*
   Providing nourishment: *served the children nutritious and satisfying meals.*
   Syns: nourishing, nutrient, nutritive.
nutritive *adjective*
1. Of or relating to food or nutrition: *the nutritive system of a plant.*
   Syns: alimentary, nutritional.
2. NUTRITIOUS.
nuts *adjective* INSANE.
nutty *adjective*
1. ENTHUSIASTIC.
2. INSANE.
nuzzle *verb* SNUGGLE.

O

oaf *noun* LUMP[1].
oath *noun* SWEAR.
obdurate *adjective*
1. COLD-BLOODED.
2. STUBBORN.
obedience *noun*
1. The quality or state of willingly carrying out the wishes of others: *The commander wanted absolute obedience from the troops.*
   Syns: acquiescence, compliance (*also* compliancy), submission.
2. The action of willingly carrying out the wishes of others: *obedience to the law.*
   Syns: conformance, conformity, obeyance, observance.
obedient *adjective*
   Willing to carry out the wishes of others: *an obedient child.*
   Syns: amenable, biddable, compliant, complying, conformable, submissive,

tractable. —*Idiom* toeing the mark (*or* line).

obeisance *noun*
1. BOW.
2. HONOR.

obeisant *adjective* DEFERENTIAL.

obese *adjective* FAT.

obey *verb* FOLLOW.

obeyance *noun* OBEDIENCE.

obfuscate *verb* OBSCURE.

obiter dictum *noun* COMMENT.

object¹ *noun*
1. Something having material existence: *Place the object directly beneath the lens.*
   Syns: article, item, thing.
2. AMBITION.
3. BODY.
4. THING.

object² *verb*
1. To express opposition by argument: *The defense attorney objected to that line of questioning.*
   Syns: except, expostulate, inveigh, kick (*Informal*), protest, remonstrate, squawk (*Informal*). —*Idiom* raise a squawk, take exception to.
2. CARE.
3. DISAPPROVE.

objectify *verb* EMBODY.

objection *noun*
The act of expressing strong or reasoned opposition: *The forest was cut down despite the objections of conservationists.*
   Syns: challenge, expostulation, kick (*Informal*), protest, protestation, remonstrance, remonstration, squawk (*Informal*).

objectionable *adjective*
Arousing disapproval: *objectionable behavior.*
   Syns: exceptionable, ill-favored, inadmissible, unacceptable, undesirable, unwanted, unwelcome.

objective *noun* AMBITION.

objective *adjective*
1. FAIR.
2. PHYSICAL.
3. REALISTIC.

objectiveness *noun* FAIRNESS.

objectivity *noun* FAIRNESS.

objectless *adjective*
1. AIMLESS.
2. RANDOM.

oblation *noun*
1. BENEVOLENCE.
2. OFFERING.

obligate *verb* COMMIT.

obligated *adjective* OBLIGED.

obligation *noun*
1. DEBT.
2. DUTY.

obligatory *adjective* REQUIRED.

oblige *verb*
1. To perform a service or a courteous act: *You will oblige me if you will keep this matter quiet.*
   Syns: accommodate, convenience, favor.
2. FORCE.
3. HUMOR.

obliged *adjective*
1. Owing something, as gratitude or appreciation, to another: *I felt obliged to help him after he had helped me.*
   Syns: beholden, bound², bounden, indebted, obligated. —*Idiom* under obligation.
2. GRATEFUL.

obligement *noun* DEBT.

obliging *adjective*
Ready to do favors for another: *an obliging person, always willing to help.*
   Syns: accommodating, agreeable, complaisant, indulgent.

oblique *adjective*
1. BIAS.
2. INDIRECT.

obliterate *verb* ANNIHILATE.

obliteration *noun*
1. ANNIHILATION.
2. ERASURE.

oblivion *noun* ESCAPE.

oblivious *adjective* IGNORANT.

obloquious *adjective*
1. ABUSIVE.
2. DISGRACEFUL.

obloquy *noun*
1. DISGRACE.
2. TIRADE.
3. VITUPERATION.

obnoxious *adjective* FILTHY.

obscene *adjective*
1. Offensive to accepted standards of decency: *obscene jokes.*
   Syns: barnyard, coarse, crude, crusty, dirty, Fescennine, filthy, foul, gross, indecent, lewd, nasty, profane, rank², raunchy (*Slang*), raw, rocky, scatological (*also* scatologic), scurrilous, smutty.
2. OUTRAGEOUS.

obsceneness *noun* OBSCENITY.

obscenity *noun*
1. The quality or state of being obscene: *a campaign to eradicate obscenity from films.*
   Syns: dirtiness, filthiness, indecency,

lewdness, obsceneness, raunchiness (*Slang*).
2. Something that is offensive to accepted standards of decency: *four-letter words and other obscenities.*
Syns: dirt, filth, profanity, smut.

obscure *verb*
1. To make dim or indistinct: *Swirling snow obscured the road. Smog had obscured the view.*
Syns: adumbrate, becloud, bedim, befog, blear, blur, cloud, dim, dull, eclipse, fog, gloom, haze, mist, murk (*also* mirk), obfuscate, overcast, overshadow, shadow.
2. To conceal in obscurity: *details obscured in a maze of legal jargon.*
Syns: hide¹, submerge.
3. BLOCK OUT at **block.**

obscure *adjective*
1. Unknown by name: *an obscure writer; an obscure disease.*
Syns: nameless, unheard-of.
2. AMBIGUOUS.
3. DARK.
4. INCONSPICUOUS.
5. REMOTE.
6. UNCLEAR.

obscured *adjective* ULTERIOR.
obscurity *noun*
1. The quality or state of being obscure: *a leader who rose from obscurity to notoriety.*
Syns: anonymity, namelessness, nothing.
2. DARK.
3. VAGUENESS.

obsequious *adjective* SERVILE.
observable *adjective*
1. NOTICEABLE.
2. PERCEPTIBLE.

observance *noun*
1. CELEBRATION.
2. CEREMONY.
3. NOTICE.
4. OBEDIENCE.
5. WATCH.

observant *adjective*
1. ALERT.
2. ATTENTIVE.
3. MINDFUL.

observation *noun*
1. COMMENT.
2. NOTICE.
3. WATCH.

observative *adjective* MINDFUL.
observatory *noun* LOOKOUT.
observe *verb*
1. CELEBRATE.
2. COMMENT.

3. FOLLOW.
4. LOOK.
5. NOTICE.
6. WATCH.

observer *noun* WATCHER.
observing *adjective* MINDFUL.
obsess *verb*
1. HAUNT.
2. POSSESS.

obsession *noun* THING.
obsolesce *verb*
To make or become obsolete: *As surgical procedures obsolesce they are no longer used.*
Syns: obsolete, outdate, superannuate.

obsolescence *noun*
The process of becoming obsolete: *Building new roads retards the obsolescence of our highway system.*
Syn: obsoletion.

obsolete *adjective*
No longer in use: *obsolete weaponry; obsolete Middle English words.*
Syn: superseded. —*Idioms* in mothballs, on the shelf.

obsolete *verb* OBSOLESCE.
obsolete *noun* OBSOLETISM.
obsoleteness *noun*
The quality or state of being obsolete: *words that had fallen into obsoleteness.*
Syns: desuetude, disuse, obsoletion, obsoletism.

obsoletion *noun*
1. OBSOLESCENCE.
2. OBSOLETENESS.

obsoletism *noun*
1. Something that is obsolete: *prose full of archaisms and obsoletisms.*
Syn: obsolete.
2. OBSOLETENESS.

obstacle *noun* BAR.
obstinacy *also* **obstinance** *noun*
The quality or state of being stubbornly unyielding: *The prime minister's obstinacy was a hindrance to the peace talks.*
Syns: bullheadedness, doggedness, hardheadedness, incompliance *or* incompliancy, intractability, intransigence *or* intransigency, mulishness, pertinacity, perverseness, perversity, pigheadedness, refractoriness, stubbornness, willfulness.

obstinate *adjective*
1. Tenaciously unwilling to yield: *an obstinate man who never apologized.*
Syns: bulldogged, bulldoggish, bulldoggy, bullheaded, close-minded, dogged, hardheaded, headstrong,

incompliant, intractable, intransigent,
muleheaded, muley, mulish,
pertinacious, perverse, pigheaded,
refractory, stiff-necked, stubborn,
tenacious, tough, willful.
2. STUBBORN.

obstreperous *adjective*
1. UNRULY.
2. VOCIFEROUS.

obstreperousness *noun* UNRULINESS.

obstruct *verb*
1. To stop or prevent passage of:
obstructed the vote by filibustering.
Syns: bar, block, impede, overslaugh.
—*Idiom* stand in the way of.
2. BLOCK OUT at **block.**
3. HINDER.

obstruction *noun* BAR.

obtain *verb* GET.

obtainable *adjective* AVAILABLE.

obtrude *verb* INTRUDE.

obtrusive *adjective* MEDDLING.

obtuse *adjective* STUPID.

obviate *verb* PREVENT.

obviation *noun* PREVENTION.

obvious *adjective*
1. APPARENT.
2. UNSUBTLE.

occasion *noun*
1. The general point at which an event
occurs: *We met on several occasions.*
Syn: time. —*Idiom* point in time.
2. CAUSE.
3. EVENT.
4. OPPORTUNITY.
5. PARTY.

occasion *verb*
1. CALL FOR at **call.**
2. CAUSE.

occasional *adjective*
1. INFREQUENT.
2. INTERMITTENT.

occult *verb* HIDE[1].

occupancy *noun* TENURE.

occupation *noun*
1. BUSINESS.
2. TENURE.

occupied *adjective* BUSY.

occupy *verb*
1. To seize and move into by force:
*Terrorists have attacked and occupied
the embassy.*
Syn: take over.
2. BUSY.
3. ENGAGE.
4. INHABIT.
5. TIE UP at **tie.**

occur *verb*
1. To enter a person's mind: *It occurred
to him that he was on the wrong street.*

Syns: hit, strike. —*Idiom* cross one's
mind.
2, 3. COME.

occurrence *noun*
1. CIRCUMSTANCE.
2. EVENT.
3. PRESENCE.

oceanic *adjective* MARINE.

odd *adjective*
1. ACCIDENTAL.
2. ECCENTRIC.
3. FUNNY.
4. QUAINT[1].

oddball *adjective*
1. ECCENTRIC.
2. QUAINT[1].

oddity *noun*
1. CHARACTER.
2. FREAK.

oddments *noun* ODDS AND ENDS.

odds *noun*
1. ADVANTAGE.
2. CHANCE.

odds and ends *noun*
Articles too small or numerous to be
specified: *a box in the closet in which she
kept odds and ends.*
Syns: etceteras, oddments, sundries.

odious *adjective*
1. FILTHY.
2. HATEFUL.

odiousness *noun* INFAMY.

odor *noun* SMELL.

oestrus *noun* SEE **estrus.**

off *adjective*
1. ERRONEOUS.
2. INSANE.
3. REMOTE.
4. SLOW.

off *verb* MURDER.

offbeat *adjective* UNUSUAL.

off-color *adjective*
1. RACY.
2. SICKLY.

offend *verb*
1. To be very disagreeable to: *Bad
manners offend me.*
Syns: displease, displeasure (*Archaic*),
turn off (*Slang*). —*Idioms* give
offense, not set right (*or* well) with.
2. To violate a moral or divine law:
offended against the word of the Lord.
Syns: sin, transgress, trespass.
3. INSULT.

offender *noun* CRIMINAL.

offense *noun*
1. Extreme displeasure caused by an
insult or slight: *took offense at the
least provocation.*
Syns: dudgeon, huff, miff, pique,

resentment, umbrage. —*Idiom* ruffled
feathers.
2. ATTACK
3, 4. CRIME.
5. INDIGNITY.
offensive *adjective*
1. Extremely unpleasant to the senses or
feelings: *offensive odors; offensive
language.*
Syns: atrocious, disgusting, evil, foul,
loathsome, nasty, nauseating,
repellent, repulsive, revolting,
sickening, ugly, unwholesome, vile.
2. AGGRESSIVE.
3. UNPLEASANT.
offensive *noun* ATTACK.
offer *verb*
1. To put before another for
acceptance: *offering us cookies;
offered his sympathy to the widow;
offered us his help.*
Syns: extend, present², proffer,
tender², volunteer. —*Idioms* come
forward with, lay at someone's feet.
2. To make (something) readily
available: *a college offering a broad
curriculum.*
Syns: afford, provide. —*Idiom* place
(or put) at one's disposal.
3. ATTEMPT.
4. GO.
5. PROPOSE.
offer *noun*
1. Something offered: *made him an offer
of $4,000 for the car; had numerous
job offers.*
Syns: bid, proffer, proposal, tender².
2. ATTEMPT.
offering *noun*
1. A presentation made to a deity as an
act of worship: *made sacrifices and
other offerings to the gods.*
Syn: oblation.
2. DONATION.
3. SACRIFICE.
offhand *adjective* EXTEMPORANEOUS.
office *noun*
1. CEREMONY.
2. MISSION.
3. POSITION.
officer *noun*
1. EXECUTIVE.
2. POLICEMAN.
officer *verb* LEAD.
office(s) *noun* BENEVOLENCE.
official *adjective* AUTHORITATIVE.
official *noun*
1. AUTHORITY.
2. EXECUTIVE.
officiate *verb* ACT FOR at **act.**

officious *adjective* MEDDLING.
offish *adjective*
1. COOL.
2. SICKLY.
offset *verb*
1. BALANCE.
2. COMPENSATE.
offset *noun* COMPENSATION.
offshoot *noun*
1, 2. BRANCH.
3. SHOOT.
offspring *noun*
1. DESCENDANT.
2. PROGENY.
off-the-cuff *adjective*
EXTEMPORANEOUS.
ogle *verb* GAZE.
ogre *noun* FIEND.
ogreish *adjective* FIENDISH.
oil *noun* FLATTERY.
oil *verb* FLATTER.
oily *adjective*
1. FATTY.
2. UNCTUOUS.
O.K. or OK *adjective* ACCEPTABLE.
O.K. or OK *adverb* YES.
okeydoke *also* **okeydokey** *adverb*
YES.
old *adjective*
1. Far along in life or time: *an old lady
in her nineties.*
Syns: advanced, aged, elderly, olden
(*Archaic & Poetic*), oldish, senior.
—*Idiom* getting on (or along) in
years.
2. Belonging to, existing, or occurring in
times long past: *an old castle; an old
tale.*
Syns: ancient, aged, age-old,
antediluvian (*also* antediluvial),
antique, hoary, olden (*Archaic &
Poetic*), timeworn, venerable.
—*Idioms* old as Methuselah, old as
time, old as the hills.
3. CONTINUING.
4. EXPERIENCED.
5. LATE.
6. OLD-FASHIONED.
olden *adjective*
1, 2. OLD.
olden *verb* AGE.
older *adjective* SENIOR.
oldfangled *adjective* OLD-FASHIONED.
old-fashioned *adjective*
Of a style or method formerly in vogue:
an old-fashioned refrigerator.
Syns: antiquated, antique, archaic,
bygone, dated, dowdy, fusty, old,
oldfangled, old-time, outdated,

outmoded, out-of-date, passé, stale, vintage.

oldish *adjective* OLD.

old maid *noun* PRUDE.

old-maidish *adjective* GENTEEL.

oldster *noun* SENIOR.

old-time *adjective* OLD-FASHIONED.

old-timer *noun*
1. SENIOR.
2. VETERAN.

oleaginous *adjective*
1. FATTY.
2. UNCTUOUS.

olfaction *noun* SMELL.

olio *noun* ASSORTMENT.

omen *noun*
A phenomenon that serves as a sign or warning of some future good or evil: *The crash seemed to be an omen of trouble to come.*
   Syns: augury, bodement, foretoken, portent, presage, prognostic, prognostication. —*Idiom* writing (*or* handwriting) on the wall.

ominous *adjective* FATEFUL.

omission *noun* FAILURE.

omit *verb*
1. DROP.
2. FAIL.

omnipresent *adjective* UNIVERSAL.

omnivorous *adjective* VORACIOUS.

on-again-off-again *adjective* UNEVEN.

once *adjective* LATE.
 once *adverb* EARLIER.

once-over *noun* SHAKEDOWN.

one *adjective* LONE.

one-dimensional *adjective* SUPERFICIAL.

oneness *noun*
1. COMPLETENESS.
2. SAMENESS.
3. UNIQUENESS.
4, 5. UNITY.

onerous *adjective* BURDENSOME.

one-sided *adjective* BIASED.

one-sidedness *noun* BIAS.

one-time *also* **onetime** *adjective* LATE.

one-up *verb* TRUMP.

ongoing *noun* ADVANCE.

only *adjective*
1. LONE.
2. UNIQUE.
 only *adverb*
1. MERELY.
2. SOLELY.

onomatopoeia *also* **onomatopoësis** *noun* ECHOISM.

onomatopoeic *also* **onomatopoetic** *adjective* ECHOIC.

onomatopoësis *noun* SEE onomatopoeia.

onomatopoetic *adjective* SEE onomatopoeic.

onrush *noun* ATTACK.

onset *noun*
1. ATTACK.
2. BIRTH.

onslaught *noun* ATTACK.

on-the-house *adjective* FREE.

onus *noun*
1. BLAME.
2. BURDEN.
3. STAIN.
4. TASK.

onyx *adjective* BLACK.

oodle *noun* HEAP.

oomph *noun* SPIRIT.

ooze *verb*
To flow or leak out slowly: *blood oozing from a cut.*
   Syns: bleed, exude, leach, percolate, seep, transude, transpire, weep.

ooze *noun* SLIME.

oozy *adjective* SLIMY.

ope *verb* OPEN.

open *adjective*
1. Having no protecting or concealing cover: *cooking over an open fire.*
   Syns: exposed, uncovered, unprotected.
2. Not restricted or confined to few: *open enrollment; open competition.*
   Syns: open-door, public, unrestricted.
3. Available for use: *Only two possibilities remain open.*
   Syns: accessible, employable, operative, practicable, usable.
4. AMBIGUOUS.
5. CLEAR.
6. FRANK.
7. INDEFINITE.
8. LIABLE.
9. RECEPTIVE.
10. UNRESERVED.

open *verb*
1. To become or cause to become open: *The door suddenly opened. Let's open the package.*
   Syns: ope, unclose, undo.
2. CLEAR.
3. SPREAD.
4. START.

open-door *adjective* OPEN.

open-eyed *adjective* ALERT.

openhanded *adjective* GENEROUS.

openhandedness *noun* GENEROSITY.

opening *noun*
1. BEGINNING.

2. BIRTH.
3. HOLE.
4. OPPORTUNITY.

open-minded *adjective*
1. BROAD.
2. RECEPTIVE.

openness *noun* EXPOSURE.

operate *verb*
1. To control or direct the functioning of: *operate the movie projector.*
   Syns: handle, run, use, work.
2. CONDUCT.
3. FUNCTION.
4. WORK.

operation *noun*
1. APPLICATION.
2. BEHAVIOR.
3. EXERCISE.

operative *noun*
1. LABORER.
2. SPY.

operative *adjective*
1. ACTIVE.
2. EFFECTIVE.
3. OPEN.

operator *noun*
1. DRIVER.
2. SPECULATOR.

opiate *noun*
1. DRUG.
2. SOPORIFIC.

opine *verb* BELIEVE.

opinion *noun* BELIEF.

opponent *noun*
1. One that opposes another in a battle, contest, controversy, or debate: *legislation that found rabid opponents in Congress.*
   Syns: adversary, antagonist, opposer, opposition.
2. COMPETITOR.
3. ENEMY.
4. RESISTER.

opportune *adjective*
Occurring at a fitting or advantageous time: *Wait for the opportune moment.*
   Syns: auspicious, favorable, propitious, prosperous, seasonable, timely, well-timed.

opportunity *noun*
A favorable or advantageous combination of circumstances: *a job with opportunities for advancement.*
   Syns: break (*Informal*), chance, occasion, opening, shot (*Informal*).

oppose *verb*
1. To place in opposition or be in opposition to: *oppose a liberal and a conservative in the debate; two armies opposing each other.*
   Syns: counter, match, pit, play off.
   —*Idioms* bump heads with, meet head-on, set (*or* be) at odds, set (*or* be) at someone's throat, trade blows (*or* punches).
2. CONTEST.

opposed *adjective* OPPOSING.

opposer *noun* OPPONENT.

opposing *adjective*
1. Acting against or in opposition: *opposing forces; opposing interests.*
   Syns: adverse, antagonistic, antipathetic, opposed.
2. OPPOSITE.

opposite *adjective*
1. Diametrically opposed: *The democrat and the autocrat hold opposite political views.*
   Syns: antipodal, antipodean, antithetical (*also* antithetic), contradictory, contrary, converse², counter, diametric, opposing, polar, reverse.
2. CONTRARY.

opposite *noun*
That which is diametrically opposed to another: *Love and hate are opposites.*
   Syns: antipode, antipole, antithesis, contra, contradictory, contraposition, contrary, converse², counter, polarity, reverse.

opposition *noun*
1. The condition of being in conflict: *the basic opposition of good and evil.*
   Syns: antithesis, antagonism, contradistinction, contraposition, contrariety, contrary, polarity.
2. OPPONENT.
3. RESISTANCE.

oppress *verb*
1. DEPRESS.
2. WRONG.

oppressive *adjective* BURDENSOME.

oppressor *noun* DICTATOR.

opprobrious *adjective*
1. ABUSIVE.
2. DEPLORABLE.
3. DISGRACEFUL.

opprobrium *noun* DISGRACE.

oppugn *verb* CONTEND.

opt for *verb* CHOOSE.

optic *adjective* VISUAL.

optical *adjective* VISUAL.

optimal *adjective* BEST.

optimism *noun*
A tendency to expect a favorable

outcome or to dwell on hopeful aspects: *didn't let the bad news shake his optimism.*
   Syns: Pollyannaism, sanguineness, sanguinity.

optimist *noun*
One who expects a favorable outcome or dwells on hopeful aspects: *was an optimist about his team's chances for the pennant.*
   Syns: Pangloss, Pollyanna.

optimistic *adjective*
Expecting a favorable outcome or dwelling on hopeful aspects: *an optimistic estimate of future oil discoveries.*
   Syns: Panglossian, Pollyannaish, roseate, rosy, sanguine, upbeat (*Informal*). —*Idioms* looking on the bright side, looking through rose-colored glasses.

optimum *adjective* BEST.

option *noun*
1, 2. CHOICE.

optional *adjective*
Not compulsory or automatic: *Radios and whitewall tires are optional features in new cars.*
   Syns: discretionary, elective, facultative.

opulent *adjective*
1. LUXURIOUS.
2. PROFUSE.

opus *noun*
1. COMPOSITION.
2. PUBLICATION.

oracle *noun* PROPHECY.

oracular *adjective* PROPHETIC.

oral *adjective*
1. Expressed or transmitted in speech: *an oral message; home remedies known by oral tradition.*
   Syns: spoken, unwritten, verbal, word-of-mouth.
2. VOCAL.

oration *noun* SPEECH.

orator *noun*
A public speaker: *known as a silver-tongued orator.*
   Syn: rhetorician.

oratorical *adjective*
Of or relating to the art of public speaking: *The candidate's oratorical gifts helped him win.*
   Syns: declamatory, elocutionary, rhetorical.

oratory *noun*
The art of public speaking: *Political leaders must be skilled at oratory.*
   Syns: declamation, elocution, rhetoric.

orb *noun*
1. CIRCLE.
2. EYE.

orbit *noun*
1. AREA.
2. CIRCLE.
3. RANGE.

orchestrate *verb* HARMONIZE.

orchid(s) *noun* COMPLIMENT.

ordain *verb* DICTATE.

ordeal *noun* TRIAL.

order *noun*
1. A way in which things follow each other in space or time: *The child could recite the months of the year in the proper order.*
   Syns: consecution, procession, sequence, succession.
2. ARRANGEMENT.
3, 4. CLASS.
5. COMMAND.
6. KIND².
7. METHOD.
8. NEIGHBORHOOD.
9. SERIES.
10. TRIM.
11. UNION.

order *verb*
1. ARRANGE.
2. BOSS.
3. COMMAND.
4. METHODIZE.

ordering *noun* ARRANGEMENT.

orderliness *noun* METHOD.

orderly *adjective*
1. METHODICAL.
2. NEAT.

ordinance *noun* LAW.

ordinariness *noun* USUALNESS.

ordinary *adjective*
1. Being of no special quality or type: *an ordinary response; an ordinary rodent.*
   Syns: average, common, commonplace, garden, garden-variety, plain, run-of-the-mill, stock, unexceptional.
2, 3. COMMON.
4. LOWLY.

ordinary *noun* USUAL.

organ *noun*
1. BRANCH.
2. MEANS.

organic *adjective* NATURAL.

organization *noun* UNION.

organize *verb*
1. ARRANGE.

2. FOUND.
3. METHODIZE.
4. MOBILIZE.
orgy *noun* BINGE.
orientation *noun* BEARING.
orifice *noun* HOLE.
oriflamme also **auriflamme** *noun*
FLAG[1].
origin *noun*
1. A point of origination: *words of
Russian origin. The origin of the
American Revolution lay in France.*
Syns: derivation, fount, fountain,
fountainhead, provenance,
provenience, root[1], rootstock, source,
spring, well[1].
2. ANCESTRY.
3. BIRTH.
original *adjective*
1. Not derived from something else: *an
original play, not an adaptation.*
Syns: primary, prime, primitive.
2. AUTHENTIC.
3. FIRST.
4. INVENTIVE.
5. NEW.
6. RADICAL.
original *noun*
1. A first form from which varieties
arise or imitations are made: *Copies
of the portrait lack the vivid colors of
the original.*
Syns: archetype, master, protoplast
(*Rare*), prototype.
2. CHARACTER.
originality *noun*
1. INVENTION.
2. NOVELTY.
originate *verb*
1. BEGIN.
2. COME.
3. DAWN.
4. FOUND.
5. INTRODUCE.
6. PRODUCE.
7. STEM.
originator *noun*
One that creates, founds, or originates:
*the originator of the slogan; the originator
of the new company.*
Syns: architect, author, creator,
father, founder[1], inventor, maker,
patriarch.
orison *noun* PRAYER.
ornament *verb*
1. ADORN.
2. GRACE.
ornament *noun* ADORNMENT.
ornamentation *noun* ADORNMENT.

ornate *adjective*
Elaborately and heavily ornamented: *an
ornate hall with a marble portal, arched
ceilings, wrought-iron balconies, and
statuary.*
Syns: baroque, flamboyant, florid,
rococo.
ornery *adjective* CONTRARY.
orotund *adjective*
1. RESONANT.
2. SONOROUS.
orthodox *adjective*
1. Adhering to beliefs or practices
approved by authority or tradition:
*held an orthodox view of papal
infallibility; an orthodox putting
stance.*
Syns: canonical, received, sanctioned,
time-honored.
2. ACCEPTED.
3. CONSERVATIVE.
4. CONVENTIONAL.
oscillate *verb* SWING.
osculate *verb* KISS.
ossuary *noun* GRAVE[1].
ostensible *adjective* APPARENT.
ostentation *noun* PRETENTIOUSNESS.
ostentatious *adjective* SHOWY.
ostracism *noun* EXILE.
ostracize *verb*
1. BANISH.
2. BLACKBALL.
other *adjective* ADDITIONAL.
otherworldly *adjective*
1. DREAMY.
2. SPIRITUAL.
otiose *adjective* EMPTY.
ounce *noun*
1. BIT[1].
2. DAMN.
oust *verb* EJECT.
ouster *noun* EJECTION.
out *adjective* SLEEPING.
out *verb* COME OUT at **come.**
outage *noun* FAILURE.
out-and-out *adjective* UTTER[2].
outbreak *noun*
1. A sudden increase in something, as
the occurrence of a disease: *an
outbreak of influenza.*
Syns: epidemic, plague, rash[2].
2. ERUPTION.
3. OUTBURST.
outburst *noun*
1. A sudden, violent expression, as of
emotion: *calmed down and apologized
for his intemperate outburst.*

Syns: access, blowup, burst, eruption, explosion, fit, flare-up, gust, outbreak.
2. ERUPTION.

outcome *noun* EFFECT.

outcry *noun*
1. EXCLAMATION.
2. VOCIFERATION.

outdate *verb* OBSOLESCE.

outdated *adjective* OLD-FASHIONED.

outdo *verb* SURPASS.

outermost *adjective* EXTREME.

outfit *noun*
1. Things needed for a task, journey, or other purpose: *Goggles are an essential part of a skier's outfit.*
   Syns: accouterments, apparatus, equipment, gear, materials, materiel *or* matériel, paraphernalia, rig, tackle, turnout.
2. COMPANY.
3. DRESS.

outfit *verb* FURNISH.

outgoing *adjective*
Disposed to be open, sociable, and talkative: *a friendly and outgoing young man.*
   Syns: communicable, communicative, expansive, extroverted, gregarious, unreserved.

outgrowth *noun* DERIVATIVE.

outlander *noun* FOREIGNER.

outlandish *adjective* FOREIGN.

outlast *verb*
To live, exist, or remain longer than: *A stone house will outlast any number of wooden ones.*
   Syns: outlive, outwear, survive.

outlaw *verb* FORBID.

outlawed *adjective* ILLEGAL.

outlay *noun* COST.

outlay *verb* SPEND.

outlet *noun*
1. HOLE.
2. STORE.

outline *noun*
1. A line marking and shaping the outer form of an object: *We saw the outline of a deer among the trees.*
   Syns: contour, delineation, profile, silhouette.
2. DRAFT.

outline *verb* DRAFT.

outlive *verb* OUTLAST.

outlook *noun*
1. CHANCE.
2. FUTURE.
3. LOOKOUT.
4. POINT OF VIEW.
5. POSTURE.

6. PREDICTION.
7. VIEW.

outlying *adjective* BACK.

outmaneuver *verb* OUTWIT.

outmatch *verb* SURPASS.

outmoded *adjective* OLD-FASHIONED.

outmost *adjective* EXTREME.

out-of-date *adjective*
1. OLD-FASHIONED.
2. TACKY².

out-of-line *adjective* NAUGHTY.

out-of-the-way *adjective* REMOTE.

output *noun* YIELD.

outrage *noun*
1. A monstrous offense or evil: *the outrages committed in the Nazi death camps.*
   Syns: atrocity, enormity, monstrosity.
2. CRIME.
3. HARM.
4. INDIGNITY.

outrage *verb*
1. INSULT.
2. RAPE.
3. WRONG.

outrageous *adjective*
1. Disgracefully and grossly offensive: *outrageous violations of the Geneva Convention.*
   Syns: atrocious, crying, enormous (*Archaic*), flagrant, heinous, monstrous, scandalous, shocking.
2. Beyond all reason: *charged an outrageous sum to repair the clock.*
   Syns: monstrous, obscene, preposterous, ridiculous, shocking, unconscionable, unreasonable.
   —*Idioms* out of bounds, out of sight.

outrageousness *noun* FLAGRANCY.

outright *adjective* UTTER².

outset *noun* BIRTH.

outshine *verb* SURPASS.

outside *adjective* REMOTE.

outside *noun* MAXIMUM.

outsider *noun* FOREIGNER.

outskirts *noun* SKIRTS.

outsmart *verb* OUTWIT.

outspoken *adjectiv*
Speaking or spoken without reserve: *She's outspoken but not rude.*
   Syns: free, free-speaking, free-spoken, vocal.

outstanding *adjective*
1. Far above others in quality or excellence: *outstanding athletes; outstanding accomplishments.*
   Syns: exceptional, magnificent, pre-eminent (*also* preeminent, preëminent), standout, surpassing, towering, transcendent.

2. DUE.
3. NOTICEABLE.
4. PRIMARY.

outstretch *verb*
1. REACH.
2. SPREAD.

outstrip *verb* SURPASS.
outthink *verb* OUTWIT.
outward *adjective* APPARENT.
outwear *verb* OUTLAST.
outweigh *verb* COMPENSATE.
outwit *verb*
To get the better of by cleverness or cunning: *The police outwitted the master criminal.*
   Syns: outmaneuver, outsmart, outthink, overreach.

oval *adjective*
Resembling an egg in shape: *an oval table; an oval face.*
   Syns: ovate, oviform, ovoid (*also* ovoidal).

ovate *adjective* OVAL.
ovation *noun* APPLAUSE.
over *adjective* HIGHER.
over *adverb*
1, 2. THROUGH.
3. UNDULY.

overabundance *noun* EXCESS.
overage *noun* SURPLUS.
overall *adjective* GENERAL.
overbearing *adjective*
1. ARROGANT.
2. DICTATORIAL.

overbearingness *noun* ARROGANCE.
overblown *adjective*
1. FAT.
2. INFLATED.

overcast *verb*
1. COVER.
2. OBSCURE.

overcharge *verb*
1. EXAGGERATE.
2. SKIN.

overcome *verb*
1. DEFEAT.
2. OVERWHELM.
3. TRIUMPH.

overconfidence *noun* PRESUMPTION.
overconfident *adjective*
PRESUMPTUOUS.
overcritical *adjective* CRITICAL.
overdue *adjective* LATE.
overflow *verb* FLOOD.
overflow *noun*
1. FLOOD.
2. SURPLUS.

overflowing *adjective*
1. ALIVE.
2. BIG.

overhang *verb*
1. BULGE.
2. HANG.
3. THREATEN.

overhanging *adjective*
1. DARK.
2. THREATENING.

overhaul *verb*
1. FIX.
2. PASS.

overhaul *noun* SHAKEUP.
overindulge *verb* BABY.
overindulgence *noun* EXCESS.
overjoyed *adjective* ELATED.
overlay *verb* COVER.
overlong *adjective* LONG¹.
overlook *verb*
1. DOMINATE.
2. SUPERVISE.
3. SURVEY.

overlook *noun* LOOKOUT.
overmuch *adjective* EXCESSIVE.
overmuch *noun* SURPLUS.
overmuch *adverb* UNDULY.
overpower *verb*
1, 2. OVERWHELM.

overpowering *adjective* TOWERING.
overreach *verb*
1. EXCEED.
2. OUTWIT.

overrule *verb* GOVERN.
overrun *verb*
1. EXCEED.
2. INVADE.

overrun *noun* SURPLUS.
oversee *verb*
1. SUPERVISE.
2. SURVEY.

overseer *noun* BOSS.
overshadow *verb* OBSCURE.
oversight *noun* NEGLECT.
oversize *also* **oversized** *adjective*
BULKY.
overslaugh *verb*
1. HINDER.
2. OBSTRUCT.

oversleep *verb* SLEEP IN at **sleep.**
overstate *verb* EXAGGERATE.
overstatement *noun* EXAGGERATION.
overstep *verb* EXCEED.
overstock *noun* SURPLUS.
oversupply *noun* SURPLUS.
overtake *verb*
1. CATCH UP at **catch.**
2. PASS.

overthrow *verb*
1. To bring about the downfall of:
Religious zealots succeeded in overthrowing the government.

Syns: bring down, overturn, subvert, topple, tumble, unhorse.
2. OVERTURN.

overthrow *noun* DEFEAT.
overture *noun* INTRODUCTION.
overture(s) *noun* ADVANCES.
overturn *verb*
1. To turn or cause to turn from a vertical or horizontal position: *Rough seas overturned several sailboats.*
Syns: knock over, overthrow, topple, turn over, upset.
2. OVERTHROW.

overview *noun* SURVEY.
overweening *adjective* ARROGANT.
overweight *adjective* FAT.
overwhelm *verb*
1. To render totally ineffective by decisive defeat: *All resistance was overwhelmed by the blitzkrieg attack. Our team overwhelmed the visitors 20 to 1.*
Syns: annihilate (*Informal*), blast (*Slang*), clobber (*Slang*), cream (*Slang*), drub, massacre (*Informal*), overpower, shellac (*Slang*), smear (*Slang*), smother, steamroller, thrash, trounce, wallop (*Informal*).
2. To affect deeply or completely, as with emotion: *Grief overwhelmed the bereaved parents.*
Syns: crush, engulf, overcome, overpower, prostrate.
3. FLOOD.

overwhelming *adjective*
1. STAGGERING.
2. TOWERING.

oviform *adjective* OVAL.
ovoid *also* **ovoidal** *adjective* OVAL.
owed *adjective* DUE.
owing *adjective* DUE.
own *verb*
1. ACKNOWLEDGE.
2. HAVE.

owner *noun*
A person who has legal title to property: *the owner of a large estate.*
Syns: holder, master, possessor, proprietor.

ownership *noun*
1. Legal right to the possession of a thing: *Ownership of the factory passed to the nephew.*
Syns: dominion, possession, proprietorship, title.
2. POSSESSION.

OX *noun* LUMP[1].

P

pabulum *noun* FOOD.
pace *noun* SPEED.
pace *verb* WALK.
pacific *also* **pacifical** *adjective* PEACEABLE.
pacifist *also* **pacifistic** *adjective* PEACEABLE.
pacify *verb*
To ease the anger or agitation of: *She managed to pacify the irate customer by offering a full refund.*
Syns: appease, assuage, calm, calm down, conciliate, dulcify, gentle, milden, mollify, placate, propitiate, soften, soothe, sweeten. —*Idiom* pour oil on troubled waters.

pack *verb*
1. CARRY.
2. CROWD.
3. FILL.
pack *noun*
1. GANG.
2. HEAP.
package *verb* WRAP.
packed *adjective*
1. FULL.
2. THICK.
pact *noun*
1. AGREEMENT.
2. TREATY.
paddy *noun* POLICEMAN.
pain *noun*
1. A sensation of physical discomfort occurring as the result of disease or injury: *a pain in my left ankle.*
Syns: ache, misery (*Informal*), pang, smart, soreness, stitch, throe, twinge.
2. DISTRESS.
3. THORN.
pain *verb*
1. DISTRESS.
2. HURT.
painful *adjective*
1. Marked by, causing, or experiencing physical pain: *a painful back injury.*
Syns: aching, afflictive, hurtful, smarting, sore.
2. BITTER.
pains *noun*
1. EFFORT.
2. THOROUGHNESS.
painstaking *adjective* CAREFUL.
painstaking *noun* THOROUGHNESS.

pair *noun*
1. Two persons united, as by marriage: *toasted the happy pair.*
   Syns: couple, duo, twosome.
2. COUPLE.

paired *adjective* TWIN.

pal *noun* ASSOCIATE.

paladin *noun* HERO.

palatial *adjective* LUXURIOUS.

palaver *noun* CHATTER.

palaver *verb* CHATTER.

pale *adjective*
1. Lacking color: *a pale face.*
   Syns: ashen, ashy, blanched, bloodless, cadaverous, colorless, livid, lurid, pallid, pasty, sallow, wan, waxen.
2. Being weak in quality or substance: *a pale, uninspiring campaign speech.*
   Syns: anemic, bloodless, pallid, waterish, watery.
3. FAIR.

pale *verb*
To lose normal coloration; turn pale: *He paled when he read the telegram.*
   Syns: blanch (*also* blench), bleach, etiolate, wan.

palinode *verb* RETRACT.

palinode *noun* RETRACTION.

pall *verb* BORE.

palliate *verb*
1. COLOR.
2. EXTENUATE.
3. RELIEVE.

pallid *adjective*
1, 2. PALE.

palm off *verb* FOIST.

palp *verb* TOUCH.

palpability *noun* TANGIBILITY.

palpable *adjective*
1. PERCEPTIBLE.
2. TANGIBLE.

palpate *verb* TOUCH.

palpation *noun* TOUCH.

palpitate *verb* BEAT.

palter *verb*
1. EQUIVOCATE.
2. HAGGLE.

paltriness *noun* PETTINESS.

paltry *adjective*
1. NARROW.
2. PETTY.
3. SHODDY.

pamper *verb* BABY.

pan *verb* BLAME.

pan out *verb* SUCCEED.

pan *noun* FACE.

panacea *noun*
Something believed to cure all human disorders: *Money is not the panacea for human suffering.*
   Syns: catholicon, cure-all, heal-all.

pandemic *adjective* UNIVERSAL.

pandemonium *noun* NOISE.

panegyrize *verb*
1. HONOR.
2. PRAISE.

pang *noun*
1. PAIN.
2. PRICK.

Pangloss *noun* OPTIMIST.

Panglossian *adjective* OPTIMISTIC.

panhandle *verb* BEG.

panhandler *noun* BEGGAR.

panic *noun*
1. FEAR.
2. SCREAM.

panic *verb* FRIGHTEN.

panoply *noun* DISPLAY.

pant *verb*
1. To breathe hard: *was panting after climbing six flights of stairs.*
   Syns: blow[1], gasp, heave, huff, puff.
2. DESIRE.
3. GASP.

pap *noun* FOOD.

paper *noun* COMPOSITION.

pappy *adjective* SOFT.

par *noun*
1. AVERAGE.
2. EQUIVALENCE.

parade *noun*
1. DISPLAY.
2. REVIEW.

parade *verb* DISPLAY.

paradigm *noun* MODEL.

paradigmatic *adjective* TYPICAL.

paradisaical *or* **paradisiacal** *adjective* HEAVENLY.

paradise *noun* HEAVEN.

paradisiacal *adjective* SEE paradisaical.

paragon *noun* NONPAREIL.

paragraph *noun* ITEM.

parallel *adjective*
1. Lying in the same plane and not intersecting: *Railroad tracks are parallel.*
   Syns: coextensive, collateral, concurrent. —*Idiom* side by side.
2. LIKE[2].

parallel *noun*
Something closely resembling or analogous to something else: *The rank of army captain is the parallel of the rank of navy lieutenant.*
   Syns: analogon, analogue, congener, correlate, correspondent, counterpart, countertype, match.

parallel *verb*
1. COMPARE.
2. LIKEN.

paralyze *verb*
1. To render helpless, as by emotion: *Sudden fear paralyzed him.*
   Syns: benumb, numb, stun, stupefy.
   —*Idioms* cut the ground from under, knock the props out from under.
2. DISABLE.

paralyzed *adjective* HELPLESS.
paramount *adjective* PRIMARY.
paramour *noun* LOVER.
paraphernalia *noun* OUTFIT.
paraphrase *noun*
   A restating of something in other, esp. simpler, words: *will write a paraphrase of the Latin text.*
   Syns: rendering, restatement, rewording, translation, version.

paraphrase *verb*
   To express the meaning of in other, esp. simpler, words: *paraphrased a passage from the Bible.*
   Syns: rephrase, restate, reword, translate.

parasite *noun*
   One who depends on another for support without reciprocating: *a king surrounded by parasites.*
   Syns: barnacle, bloodsucker, freeloader (*Slang*), hanger-on, leech, sponge.

parasitic also **parasitical** *adjective*
   Of or characteristic of a parasite: *leads a parasitic existence.*
   Syns: bloodsucking, freeloading (*Slang*).

parboil *verb* BOIL.
parcel *noun*
1. DIVISION.
2. LOT.

parcel *verb* DISTRIBUTE.
parch *verb* DRY.
parched *adjective*
1. DRY.
2. THIRSTY.

pardon *verb* FORGIVE.
pardon *noun* FORGIVENESS.
pardonable *adjective*
   Admitting of forgiveness or pardon: *a pardonable offense; spoke with pardonable pride.*
   Syns: condonable, excusable, forgivable, venial.

pare *verb* CUT BACK at cut.
parent *verb* PRODUCE.
parentage *noun* ANCESTRY.
parenthesis *noun*
1, 2. DIGRESSION.

parenthetic also **parenthetical** *adjective* DIGRESSIVE.
parity *noun* EQUIVALENCE.
parlance *noun* WORDING.
parley *noun*
1. CONVERSATION.
2. DELIBERATION.
3. TALK.

parley *verb* CONFER.
parlous *adjective* DANGEROUS.
parochial *adjective* LOCAL.
parody *noun*
1. MOCKERY.
2. TAKEOFF.

parody *verb* IMITATE.
paroxysm *noun*
1, 2. THROE.

parrot *noun* ECHO.
parrot *verb* ECHO.
parry *verb*
   To turn or drive away: *He stood, sword in hand, ready to parry his opponent's attack.*
   Syns: beat off, fend off, keep off, repel, repulse, ward off.

parsimonious *adjective* STINGY.
parson *noun* PREACHER.
part *noun*
1. One's proper or expected function in a common effort: *Everyone must do his part.*
   Syns: piece, role (*also* rôle), share.
2. ALLOTMENT.
3. DIVISION.
4. ELEMENT.
5. SECTION.
6. SIDE.

part *verb*
1. DIVIDE.
2. SEPARATE.

part *adjective* PARTIAL.
partake *verb*
1. CONTRIBUTE.
2. EAT.
3. PARTICIPATE.

partial *adjective*
1. Pertaining to or affecting only a part; not total: *a partial solution; partial success.*
   Syns: fractional, fragmentary, part.
2. BIASED.
3. FAVORABLE.

partiality *noun*
1. BENT.
2. BIAS.
3. FAVOR.
4. TASTE.

partialness *noun* FAVOR.

participant *noun*
One who participates: *prizes for all participants in the tournament.*
   Syns: actor, party.

participate *verb*
To involve oneself in (an activity): *participated in a lively conversation.*
   Syns: carry on, engage, have, indulge, partake. —*Idiom* take part.

participation *noun*
The act or fact of participating: *trying to increase participation in the political process.*
   Syns: involvement, sharing.

particle *noun* BIT[1].

particular *noun*
  1. CIRCUMSTANCE.
  2. DETAIL.
  3. ELEMENT.

particular *adjective*
  1. DETAILED.
  2. LONE.
  3. NICE.
  4. SPECIAL.

particularity *noun* INDIVIDUALITY.
particularize *verb* STIPULATE.
particularized *adjective* DETAILED.

parting *noun*
A separation of two or more people: *feeling sad at their parting.*
   Syns: adieu, farewell, good-by *or* good-bye, leave-taking.

parting *adjective*
Of, done, given, or said on departing: *parting words; a parting gift.*
   Syns: departing, farewell, good-by *or* good-bye, valedictory.

partisan *noun* FOLLOWER.
partisan *adjective* BIASED.

partition *noun*
  1. DIVISION.
  2. WALL.

partition *verb*
  1. DIVIDE.
  2. WALL.

partner *noun*
  1. ASSOCIATE.
  2. SPOUSE.

partnership *noun* ASSOCIATION.
parturiency *noun* PREGNANCY.
parturient *adjective* PREGNANT.
parturition *noun* BIRTH.

party *noun*
  1. A large or important social gathering: *a party at the White House.*
    Syns: affair, bash (*Slang*), do (*Slang*), festivity, fete (*also* fête), function, gala, occasion, soiree (*also* soirée).
  2. BAND[2].
  3. COMBINE.

  4. GROUP.
  5. HUMAN BEING.
  6. PARTICIPANT.

pass *verb*
  1. To catch up with and move past: *cars passing us on all sides.*
    Syns: overhaul, overtake.
  2. To cause to be transferred from one to another: *Pass your plate for seconds. Did you pass the word along?*
    Syns: convey, hand (over), transmit.
  3. To be accepted or approved: *The motion passed by a wide margin.*
    Syns: carry, clear.
  4. To accept officially: *The Senate voted to pass the resolution.*
    Syns: adopt, approve.
  5. COME.
  6, 7. COMMUNICATE.
  8. DIE.
  9. FALL.
  10, 11. GO.
  12. HAND DOWN at **hand.**
  13. LEAD.
  14. POSE.
  15. SPEND.
  16. SURPASS.
  17. TRAVERSE.

pass away *verb*
  1. DIE.
  2. GO.

pass off *verb* FOIST.
pass out *verb* BLACK OUT at **black.**
pass over *verb* BLINK AT at **blink.**

pass *noun*
  1. A free ticket entitling one to transportation or admission: *a movie pass for students.*
    Syns: comp (*Informal*), freebie (*also* freebee) (*Slang*).
  2. CRISIS.

passable *adjective*
  1. Capable of being passed, traversed, or crossed: *The highways are passable for the first time since the blizzard.*
    Syns: navigable, negotiable.
  2. ACCEPTABLE.

passage *noun*
  1. SECTION.
  2. TRANSITION.

passé *adjective* OLD-FASHIONED.
passel *noun* HEAP.
passing *adjective* TRANSITORY.
passing *noun* DEATH.

passion *noun*
  1. Powerful, intense emotion: *a sermon filled with passion; shows no passion in his acting.*

Syns: ardor, fervency, fervidity, fervidness, fervor, fire. —*Idiom* fire and brimstone.
2. DESIRE.
3, 4. ENTHUSIASM.
5. INFATUATION.
6, 7. LOVE.
8. TEMPER.

passionate *adjective*
1. Fired with intense feeling: *a passionate rebuttal.*
Syns: ardent, blazing, burning, dithyrambic, fervent, fervid, fiery, fire-and-brimstone, flaming, hot-blooded, impassioned, perfervid, red-hot, scorching, torrid.
2. EROTIC.

passionless *adjective* FRIGID.

passive *adjective*
Submitting without objection or resistance: *remained passive when sentence was passed.*
Syns: acquiescent, nonresistant, nonresisting, resigned, submissive, yielding.

past *adjective*
1. Just gone by or elapsed: *lunched together several times during the past year.*
Syns: antecedent, anterior, foregoing, former, precedent, preceding, previous, prior.
2. LATE.

past *noun*
1. A former period of time or of one's life: *You can't relive the past.*
Syns: yesterday, yesteryear, yore.
—*Idioms* bygone days, days gone by, the good old days, the old days.
2. HISTORY.

paste *verb* HIT.
paste *noun* BLOW[2].
pastoral *adjective* COUNTRY.
pasty *adjective* PALE.
patch *verb* FIX.
patchwork *noun* ASSORTMENT.
patchy *adjective* UNEVEN.
pate *noun* HEAD.
patent *adjective*
1. APPARENT.
2. UNSUBTLE.
paternal *adjective* FATHERLY.
path *noun* WAY.
pathetic *adjective* PITIFUL.
patience *noun*
The capacity of enduring hardship or inconvenience without complaint: *needed real patience not to respond to his insults.*

Syns: forbearance, long-suffering, resignation.

patient *adjective*
Enduring or capable of enduring hardship or inconvenience without complaint: *a quiet and patient mother of four.*
Syns: forbearing, long-suffering, resigned.

patois *noun* DIALECT.
patriarch *noun* ORIGINATOR.
patrician *adjective* NOBLE.
patriciate *noun* SOCIETY.
patrimonial *adjective* ANCESTRAL.
patrimony *noun* BIRTHRIGHT.
patrol *verb* POLICE.
patrolman *noun* POLICEMAN.
patron *noun*
1. A person who supports or champions an activity, institution, etc.: *a patron of the arts.*
Syns: angel (*Informal*), backer, benefactor, contributor, friend, Maecenas, sponsor, supporter.
2. One who buys goods or services: *a regular patron known to all the dealers.*
Syns: buyer, client, customer, purchaser.

patronage *noun*
1. Aid or support given by a patron: *hoped to gain the patronage of the rich and influential.*
Syns: aegis, auspices, backing, sponsorship, patronization.
2. The commercial transactions of customers with a supplier: *a shop with a large patronage.*
Syns: business, custom, trade, traffic.
3. Customers or patrons collectively: *sending announcements of the sale to the patronage.*
Syn: clientele.
4. The political appointments or jobs that are at the disposal of those in power: *dispensed patronage to the party regulars in her ward.*
Syns: pork (*Slang*), spoils.

patronization *noun*
1. CONDESCENSION.
2. PATRONAGE.

patronize *verb*
1. To act as a patron to: *patronized all the worthy causes in the community.*
Syns: sponsor, support.
2. CONDESCEND.

patronizing *noun* CONDESCENSION.
patronizing *adjective* CONDESCENDING.

patsy *noun*
1. DUPE.
2. SCAPEGOAT.
pattern *noun*
1. FIGURE.
2. FORM.
3. HABIT.
4. METHOD.
5. MODEL.
pattern *verb* FOLLOW.
paucity *noun* SHORTAGE.
pauper *noun*
An impoverished person: *paupers begging on street corners.*
    Syns: beggar, down-and-out, have-not, indigent.
pauper *verb* RUIN.
pause *verb*
1. To stop temporarily and remain, as if reluctant to leave: *paused for a while at a small café.*
    Syns: abide, bide, linger, tarry, wait.
2. HESITATE.
pause *noun* BREAK.
pawn¹ *noun*
Something given to guarantee the repayment of a loan or the fulfillment of an obligation: *left her jewels as pawns for her brother's debt.*
    Syns: earnest, guaranty, pledge, security, token, warrant.
pawn *verb*
To give or deposit as a pawn: *pawned his typewriter for the price of a meal.*
    Syns: dip (*Brit. Slang*), hock (*Informal*), hypothecate, impignorate, mortgage, pignorate, pledge, pop (*Brit. Slang*).
pawn² *noun*
A person used or controlled by others: *was a pawn in the struggle for political control.*
    Syns: cat's-paw (*also* cats-paw), instrument, puppet, stooge, tool.
pay *verb*
1. To give payment to in return for goods or services rendered: *was prepared to pay him $100 for the chair.*
    Syns: compensate, recompense, remunerate.
2. COMPENSATE.
3. RETURN.
4. SETTLE.
5. SPEND.
pay back *verb* AVENGE.
pay off *verb*
1. AVENGE.
2. BRIBE.
pay *noun* WAGE(S).
payable *adjective* DUE.

payment *noun*
Something given in exchange for goods or services rendered: *required immediate payment for the delivery.*
    Syns: compensation, consideration, recompense, remuneration.
payoff *noun*
1. BRIBE.
2. CLIMAX.
payola *noun* BRIBE.
peaceable *adjective*
Inclined or disposed to peace; not quarrelsome or unruly: *met in a peaceable spirit.*
    Syns: irenic, pacific (*also* pacifical), pacifist (*also* pacifistic), peaceful.
peaceful *adjective* PEACEABLE.
peaches-and-cream *adjective* FRESH.
peacock *verb* STRUT.
peak *noun*
1. CLIMAX.
2. HEIGHT.
3. MAXIMUM.
peak *adjective* CLIMACTIC.
peak *verb* CLIMAX.
peaked *adjective* SICKLY.
peaky *adjective* SICKLY.
peal *verb* RING².
peanuts *noun*
Slang. A small or trifling amount of money: *sold his car for peanuts.*
    Syns: chicken feed (*Slang*), two bits (*Informal*).
pearl *noun* TREASURE.
peccant *adjective* EVIL.
peck¹ *noun*
1, 2. HEAP.
peck² *noun*
1. FOOD.
2. KISS.
peck *verb*
1. KISS.
2. NAG.
pecksniffery *noun* HYPOCRISY.
pecksniffian *adjective* HYPOCRITICAL.
peculiar *adjective*
1. DISTINCTIVE.
2. ECCENTRIC.
3. FUNNY.
peculiarity *noun*
1. ECCENTRICITY.
2. QUALITY.
pecuniary *adjective* FINANCIAL.
pedagogics *noun* EDUCATION.
pedagogist *noun* EDUCATOR.
pedagogue *noun* EDUCATOR.
pedagogy *noun* EDUCATION.
pedantic *also* **pedantical** *adjective*
    Characterized by a narrow concern for

book learning and formal rules, without knowledge or experience of practical matters: *a pedantic attention to details.*
Syns: academic, bookish, booky, donnish, formalistic, inkhorn, quodlibetic, scholastic.

peddle *verb*
1. To travel about selling goods: *loaded the trunk with apples and went peddling.*
Syns: hawk, huckster, vend.
2. PUSH.
3. SELL.

pedestrian *adjective* DULL.

pedigree *noun*
1. ANCESTRY.
2. GENEALOGY.

peek *verb* GLIMPSE.
peek *noun* GLANCE[1].
peel *noun* SKIN.
peel *verb* SKIN.
peep *verb* GLIMPSE.
peep *noun* GLANCE[1].
peer[1] *verb* GAZE.
peer *noun* GAZE.
peer[2] *noun*
One that is very similar to another in rank or position: *doctors' competency reviewed by their peers. She is the peer of any tennis player on the professional circuit.*
Syns: coequal, colleague, compeer, equal, equivalent, fellow.

peerless *adjective* UNIQUE.
peeve *verb* ANNOY.
peeve *noun* ANNOYANCE.
peevish *adjective*
1. ILL-TEMPERED.
2. IRRITABLE.

peewee *adjective* TINY.
peg *noun* DEGREE.
pejorative *adjective* DISPARAGING.
pelagic *adjective* MARINE.
pelf *noun* MONEY.
pellucid *adjective* CLEAR.
pelt[1] *noun* HIDE[2].
pelt[2] *verb* RUSH.
pen[1] *verb* PUBLISH.
pen[2] *verb* ENCLOSE.
pen[3] *noun* JAIL.
penalize *verb* FINE[2].
penalty *noun*
1. FINE[2].
2. SANCTION.

penchant *noun* BENT.
pendulous *adjective*
1. HANGING.
2. HESITANT.

penetrate *verb*
1. To pass into or through by overcoming resistance: *Enemy sappers penetrated our defenses. The cold penetrated his bones.*
Syns: break (through), perforate, pierce, puncture.
2. ENTER.

penetrating *adjective*
1. BITING.
2. CRITICAL.
3. INCISIVE.

penetration *noun* DISCERNMENT.

penitence *also* **penitency** *noun*
A feeling of regret for one's sins or misdeeds: *didn't know how to express his penitence.*
Syns: attrition, compunction, contriteness, contrition, remorse, remorsefulness, repentance, rue.

penitent *adjective*
1. APOLOGETIC.
2. REMORSEFUL.

penitential *adjective* REMORSEFUL.
penitentiary *noun* JAIL.
pennant *noun* FLAG[1].
penniless *adjective* POOR.
pennon *noun* FLAG[1].
penny-pinching *adjective* STINGY.
pensile *adjective* HANGING.
pension *verb* RETIRE.
pensive *adjective*
1. Suggestive of or expressing deep, often melancholy thoughtfulness: *a pensive expression.*
Syns: meditative, musing, tristful (*Archaic*), wistful.
2. THOUGHTFUL.

penumbra *noun* SHADE.
penurious *adjective*
1. POOR.
2. STINGY.

penury *noun* POVERTY.
people *noun* PUBLIC.
people *verb* INHABIT.
pep *noun*
1. ENERGY.
2. SPIRIT.

pepper *verb*
1. BARRAGE.
2. SPECKLE.

peppery *adjective*
1. SPIRITED.
2. TESTY.

peppy *adjective*
1. ENERGETIC.
2. LIVELY.
3. VIGOROUS.

perambulate *verb* STROLL.

perambulation *noun* WALK.
perceivable *adjective*
1. PERCEPTIBLE.
2. VISIBLE.
perceive *verb*
1. To be intuitively aware of: *could easily perceive her unexpressed hostility.*
   Syns: apprehend (*Obs.*), feel, intuit, sense. —*Idioms* feel in one's bones, get vibrations.
2. LOOK.
3. SEE.
perceptible *adjective*
1. Capable of being noticed or apprehended mentally: *speaks with a perceptible edge in her voice when angry; underwent a perceptible change in outlook.*
   Syns: appreciable, detectable, discernible, noticeable, observable, palpable, perceivable.
2. VISIBLE.
perception *noun*
1. AWARENESS.
2. IDEA.
perceptive *adjective*
1. ACUTE.
2. INCISIVE.
perceptiveness *noun* DISCERNMENT.
perch *verb* BALANCE.
perchance *adverb* MAYBE.
percipience *noun* DISCERNMENT.
percolate *verb* OOZE.
percussion *noun* COLLISION.
perdurable *adjective* CONTINUING.
peregrinate *verb*
1. JOURNEY.
2. ROVE.
peremptory *adjective* DICTATORIAL.
perennial *adjective* CONTINUING.
perfect *adjective*
1. Supremely excellent in quality or nature: *a perfect diamond; a perfect performance.*
   Syns: absolute, consummate, faultless, flawless, impeccable, indefectible, unflawed.
2. CLEAN.
3. COMPLETE.
4. GOOD.
5. IDEAL.
6. PURE.
7. ROUND.
8. UTTER².
perfect *verb*
To bring to perfection or completion: *The architect worked to perfect his design.*

Syns: polish, refine, smooth. —*Idiom* smooth off the rough edges.
perfection *noun* VIRTUE.
perfervid *adjective* PASSIONATE.
perfidious *adjective*
1. FAITHLESS.
2. INFAMOUS.
perfidiousness *noun*
1. FAITHLESSNESS.
2. TREACHERY.
perfidy *noun*
1. FAITHLESSNESS.
2. INFAMY.
3. TREACHERY.
perforate *verb*
1. BREACH.
2. PENETRATE.
perforation *noun*
1. BREACH.
2. PRICK.
perforce *adverb* HELPLESSLY.
perform *verb*
1. To begin and carry through to completion: *perform an acrobatic feat.*
   Syns: do, execute, prosecute, pull off (*Informal*).
2. ACT.
3. FULFILL.
4. STAGE.
performance *noun*
1. The act of beginning and carrying through to completion: *in the performance of his duty.*
   Syns: effectuation, execution, prosecution.
2. BEHAVIOR.
3. EFFICIENCY.
4. INTERPRETATION.
performer *noun* PLAYER.
perfume *noun* FRAGRANCE.
perfume *verb* SCENT.
perfumed *adjective* FRAGRANT.
perfunctory *adjective*
Performed or performing automatically and impersonally: *gave me a perfunctory nod as he passed.*
   Syns: automatic, mechanical.
perhaps *adverb* MAYBE.
perhaps *noun* THEORY.
periapt *noun* CHARM.
peril *noun* DANGER.
peril *verb* ENDANGER.
perilous *adjective* DANGEROUS.
perimeter *noun*
1. BORDER.
2. CIRCUMFERENCE.
period *noun*
1. A specific length of time characterized by the occurrence of

certain conditions or events: *a period
of sunshine.*
   Syns: season, span, term.
2. An interval regarded as a distinct
evolutionary or developmental unit:
Picasso's blue period.
   Syns: phase, stage.
3. AGE.
4. END.
5. TIME.
periodic *also* **periodical** *adjective*
1. INTERMITTENT.
2. RECURRENT.
periodically *adverb* NOW.
peripatetic *adjective* NOMADIC.
periphery *noun*
1. BORDER.
2. CIRCUMFERENCE.
periphrastic *adjective* WORDY.
perish *verb*
1, 2. DIE.
perished *adjective* DEAD.
perjure *verb* LIE².
perjured *adjective* PERJURIOUS.
perjurer *noun* LIAR.
perjurious *adjective*
  Marked by lying under oath: *perjurious
witnesses; perjurious testimony.*
   Syns: forsworn (*also* foresworn),
perjured.
perjury *noun* MENDACITY.
perk¹ *noun* GRATUITY.
perk² *verb* ENCOURAGE.
perk up *verb* RECOVER.
permeate *verb*
1. CHARGE.
2. FILL.
permissible *adjective*
  Capable of being allowed: *It is
permissible to smoke here.*
   Syns: admissible, allowable.
permission *noun*
  Approval for an action, esp. as granted
by one in authority: *gave them
permission to smoke.*
   Syns: allowance, authorization,
consent, leave², license, permit,
sanction.
permit *verb*
1. To neither forbid nor prevent: *just
permits the children to run wild.*
   Syns: allow, have, leave², let, suffer,
tolerate.
2. To give one's consent to: *permitted
me to leave the office early.*
   Syns: allow, authorize, consent, let,
sanction.
3. To afford an opportunity for: *a job
that permits me to advance.*

   Syns: admit, allow, let.
4. ENABLE.
permit *noun*
1. LICENSE.
2. PERMISSION.
permutation *noun* CHANGE.
pernicious *adjective*
1. DESTRUCTIVE.
2. VIRULENT.
perorate *verb* RANT.
perpendicular *adjective* VERTICAL.
perpetrate *verb* COMMIT.
perpetual *adjective*
1. CONTINUAL.
2. ENDLESS.
perpetuate *verb* IMMORTALIZE.
perpetuity *noun* ENDLESSNESS.
perplex *verb*
1. COMPLICATE.
2. CONFUSE.
perplexing *adjective* COMPLEX.
perquisite *noun*
1. BIRTHRIGHT.
2. GRATUITY.
persecute *verb* WRONG.
persecution *noun* HELL.
perseverance *noun* INSISTENCE.
perseverant *adjective* INSISTENT.
persevere *verb*
1. CARRY ON at **carry.**
2. INSIST.
persevering *adjective* INSISTENT.
persist *verb*
1. CARRY ON at **carry.**
2. ENDURE.
3. INSIST.
4. SURVIVE.
persistence *also* **persistency** *noun*
1. CONTINUANCE.
2. CONTINUATION.
3. INSISTENCE.
persistent *adjective*
1. CHRONIC.
2. INSISTENT.
3. STUBBORN.
persisting *adjective* INSISTENT.
persnickety *adjective* NICE.
person *noun* HUMAN BEING.
persona *noun* CHARACTER.
personage *noun*
1. CELEBRITY.
2. CHARACTER.
3. DIGNITARY.
4. HUMAN BEING.
personal *adjective*
1. Belonging to, pertaining to, or
affecting a particular person: *personal
loyalties.*
   Syn: individual.

2. ARBITRARY.
3. BODILY.
4. INTIMATE[1].
5. PRIVATE.

personality noun
1. DIGNITARY.
2. IDENTITY.

personalize verb EMBODY.

personification noun EMBODIMENT.

personify verb
1. EMBODY.
2. REPRESENT.

perspective noun VIEW.

perspicacious adjective SHREWD.

perspicacity noun DISCERNMENT.

perspicuity noun CLARITY.

perspire verb SWEAT.

perspiring adjective SWEATY.

persuade verb
1. To succeed in causing (a person) to act in a certain way: *persuaded the President to veto the bill. Nothing could persuade her to forgive him.*
   Syns: argue into, bring, bring around, convince, get, induce, prevail on (*or* upon), sell (on), talk into.
2. CONVERT.
3. CONVINCE.

persuasion noun
1. BELIEF.
2. FAITH.
3. KIND[2].
4. RELIGION.

persuasive adjective CONVINCING.

pert adjective
1. IMPUDENT.
2. LIVELY.

pertain verb
1. APPLY.
2. BELONG.

pertinacious adjective
1. OBSTINATE.
2. STUBBORN.

pertinacity noun OBSTINACY.

pertinence also **pertinency** noun
1. CONCERN.
2. RELEVANCE.

pertinent adjective RELEVANT.

perturb verb AGITATE.

perturbation noun AGITATION.

perusal noun EXAMINATION.

peruse verb EXAMINE.

pervade verb
1. CHARGE.
2. FILL.

perverse adjective
1. CONTRARY.
2. CORRUPT.
3. OBSTINATE.

perverseness noun OBSTINACY.

perversion noun ABUSE.

perversity noun OBSTINACY.

pervert verb
1. ABUSE.
2. CORRUPT.
3. DISTORT.

pervert noun DEVIANT.

perverted adjective CORRUPTED.

pesky adjective TROUBLESOME.

pessimism noun
The doctrine that this world is evil: *a philosophy grounded on pessimism.*
   Syn: malism.

pessimist noun
A prophet of misfortune or disaster: *pessimists predicting a nuclear holocaust.*
   Syns: Cassandra, crepehanger, doomsayer, worrywart (*Informal*).
   —*Idioms* calamity howler, prophet of doom and gloom.

pessimistic adjective GLOOMY.

pester verb
1. ANNOY.
2. BESIEGE.

pestering noun ANNOYANCE.

pestilent adjective VIRULENT.

pestilential adjective VIRULENT.

pet[1] verb CARESS.
   pet noun FAVORITE.
   pet adjective FAVORITE.

pet[2] verb SULK.

petechia noun STIGMA.

peter out verb DECREASE.

petite adjective LITTLE.

petition noun APPEAL.
   petition verb
1. ADDRESS.
2. APPEAL.
3. APPLY.

petitioner noun
1. APPEALER.
2. APPLICANT.

petrified adjective AFRAID.

petrify verb
1. HARDEN.
2. WITHER.

pettifog verb QUIBBLE.

pettiness noun
Contemptible unimportance: *The pettiness of his criticism is incredible.*
   Syns: inconsequence, measliness (*Slang*), paltriness, smallness, triviality, trivialness.

petty adjective
1. Contemptibly unimportant: *the petty concerns of bored socialites.*
   Syns: inconsequent, inconsequential, inconsiderable, measly (*Slang*),

negligible, niggling, paltry, picayune, piddling, small, small-minded, trifling, trivial, unconsequential, unconsidered.
2. MINOR.
3. NARROW.

petulant *adjective*
1. ILL-TEMPERED.
2. IRRITABLE.

phantasm also **phantasma** *noun*
1. DREAM.
2. GHOST.
3. ILLUSION.

phantasmagoria also **phantasmagory** *noun* HALLUCINATION.

phantasy *noun* SEE **fantasy.**

phantom *noun* GHOST.

pharisaic also **pharisaical** *adjective* HYPOCRITICAL.

pharisaism also **phariseeism** *noun* HYPOCRISY.

pharisee *noun* HYPOCRITE.

phariseeism *noun* SEE **pharisaism.**

pharmacon *noun* CURE.

phase *noun*
1. The particular angle from which something is considered: *examined the problem from the practical phase.*
   Syns: aspect, facet, hand, respect, side.
2. PERIOD.

phenomenal *adjective*
1. FABULOUS.
2. PHYSICAL.

phenomenon *noun*
1. FACT.
2. MARVEL.
3. MODEL.

philander *verb*
To be sexually unfaithful to another: *a husband well known for philandering.*
   Syns: cheat, fool around (*Informal*), mess around (*Informal*), play around (*Informal*), womanize.

philander *noun* PHILANDERER.

philanderer *noun*
A man who philanders: *Edward VII was a notorious philanderer.*
   Syns: Casanova, Don Juan, ladykiller (*Slang*), lady's man (*also* ladies' man), philander, wolf (*Slang*), womanizer. —*Idioms* man on the make, skirt chaser.

philanthropic also **philanthropical** *adjective* BENEVOLENT.

philanthropy *noun* BENEVOLENCE.

philippic *noun* TIRADE.

Philistine also **philistine** *noun* BOOR.

Philistine also **philistine** *adjective* COARSE.

philosopher *noun* THINKER.

phlegm *noun* APATHY.

phlegmatic *adjective* APATHETIC.

phoenix *noun* NONPAREIL.

phone *verb* TELEPHONE.

phony also **phoney** *adjective*
1. ARTIFICIAL.
2. COUNTERFEIT.

phony also **phoney** *noun*
1. COUNTERFEIT.
2. FAKE.
3. HYPOCRITE.

photographic *adjective*
1, 2. GRAPHIC.

phrase *verb*
To convey in language or words of a particular form: *He phrased the promise so as to give himself an escape.*
   Syns: couch, express, formulate, put, word.

phrase *noun*
1. EXPRESSION.
2. WORDING.

phraseology *noun* WORDING.

phrasing *noun* WORDING.

phthisic also **phthisical** *adjective* TUBERCULAR.

phthisic *noun* TUBERCULOSIS.

phthisis also **phthisic** *noun* TUBERCULOSIS.

phylactery *noun* CHARM.

physic *noun* CURE.

physic *verb* DRUG.

physical *adjective*
1. Composed of or relating to things that occupy space and can be perceived by the senses: *a physical barrier; physical changes in the landscape.*
   Syns: concrete, corporeal, material, objective, phenomenal, sensible, substantial, tangible.
2. Relating to the desires and appetites of the body: *It was purely physical attraction.*
   Syns: animal, carnal, fleshly, sensual.
3. BODILY.

physicality *noun*
A preoccupation with the body and satisfaction of its desires: *was struck by his sheer physicality.*
   Syns: animalism, animality, carnality, earthiness, fleshliness, sensuality.

physiognomy *noun* FACE.

physique *noun* CONSTITUTION.

picayune *adjective* PETTY.

pick *noun*
1. BEST.
2. ELECT.

pick verb
1. CHOOSE.
2. NAG.
pick off verb SHOOT.
pick out verb DISCERN.
pick up verb
1. ARREST.
2. CONTINUE.
3. ELEVATE.
4. GET.
5. GLEAN.
6. LEARN.
picket noun GUARD.
pickle noun PREDICAMENT.
pickled adjective DRUNK.
pick-me-up noun TONIC.
pickup noun ARREST.
picky adjective NICE.
pictographic adjective GRAPHIC.
pictorial adjective
1, 2. GRAPHIC.
picture verb
1. IMAGINE.
2. REPRESENT.
picture noun
1. DOUBLE.
2. REPRESENTATION.
picturesque adjective
1. COLORFUL.
2. GRAPHIC.
piddling adjective PETTY.
piece noun
1. BIT[1].
2. COMPOSITION.
3. CUT.
4. DISTANCE.
5. DIVISION.
6. ITEM.
7. PART.
piecemeal adjective GRADUAL.
pierce verb
1. BREACH.
2. CUT.
3. PENETRATE.
piercing adjective
1. HIGH.
2. SHARP.
pietistic adjective HOLY.
piffle noun NONSENSE.
pig noun POLICEMAN.
pigeon noun DUPE.
pigeonhole verb
1. ASSORT.
2. CLASS.
piggish adjective GREEDY.
pigheaded adjective OBSTINATE.
pigheadedness noun OBSTINACY.
pigment noun COLOR.
pigmy adjective SEE **pygmy**.

pignorate verb PAWN[1].
pile noun
1. BUILDING.
2. FORTUNE.
3, 4. HEAP.
pile verb
1, 2. HEAP.
pile in verb RETIRE.
pile out verb GET UP at **get**.
pile up verb
1. ACCUMULATE.
2. CRASH.
3. WRECK.
pileup noun CRASH.
pilfer verb STEAL.
pill noun DRIP.
pillage verb SACK[2].
pillage noun PLUNDER.
pilose adjective HAIRY.
pilot noun GUIDE.
pilot verb
1. DRIVE.
2. GUIDE.
3. MANEUVER.
pilot adjective
Constituting a tentative model for
future experiment or development: *a
pilot project in urban renewal.*
 Syns: experimental, test, trial.
pinch verb
1. ARREST.
2. SCRIMP.
3. STEAL.
pinch noun ARREST.
pinchbeck noun COPY.
pinch-hit verb SUBSTITUTE.
pinch hitter noun SUBSTITUTE.
pinching adjective STINGY.
pinching noun LARCENY.
pine verb LANGUISH.
pinnacle noun CLIMAX.
pin on verb FIX.
pinpoint noun POINT.
pinpoint verb
1. FIND.
2. PLACE.
pint-size also **pint-sized** adjective
TINY.
pioneer noun BUILDER.
pioneer adjective FIRST.
pious adjective HOLY.
pip noun SEED.
pipe dream noun ILLUSION.
pip-squeak noun NONENTITY.
piquant adjective PUNGENT.
pique noun OFFENSE.
pique verb PROVOKE.
pirate noun
 One who illicitly reproduces the artistic

work of another: *a pirate who lifted a chapter from another writer's book.*
   Syns: cribber (*Informal*), plagiarist.
   —*Idiom* literary pirate.
pirate *verb*
To reproduce (the artistic work of another) illicitly: *She pirated another director's ideas and used them in the play.*
   Syns: crib (*Informal*), plagiarize.
pirouette *verb* SPIN.
pishposh *noun* NONSENSE.
pit *noun*
1. A place known for its great filth or corruption: *Upright citizens considered the red-light district to be a pit.*
   Syns: cesspit, cesspool, sink. —*Idiom* Augean stable.
2. SEED.
pit *verb* OPPOSE.
pitch *verb*
1. ERECT.
2. FALL.
3. LURCH.
4. PLUNGE.
5. SEED.
6. THROW.
7. TOSS.
pitch into *verb* ATTACK.
pitch *noun*
1. FALL.
2. INTENSITY.
3. PROMOTION.
4. THROW.
pitch-black *adjective* BLACK.
pitch-dark *adjective* BLACK.
pitched *adjective* INCLINED.
pitchy *adjective* BLACK.
piteous *adjective*
1. PITIFUL.
2. PITYING.
pitfall *noun*
A source of danger or difficulty not easily foreseen and avoided: *The possibility of being kidnapped is one of the pitfalls of being wealthy.*
   Syns: booby trap, trap.
pith *noun*
1. ESSENCE.
2. HEART.
pithy *adjective*
Precisely meaningful and tersely cogent: *gave a pithy summary of our foreign policy.*
   Syns: aphoristic, brass-tacks, compact¹, epigrammatic (*also* epigrammical), marrowy, meaty.
   —*Idiom* down to brass tacks.
pitiful *adjective*
1. Arousing or deserving pity: *a pitiful abandoned baby.*

   Syns: commiserable, pathetic, piteous, pitiable, poor, rueful, ruthful (*Archaic*).
2. PITYING.
pitiless *adjective* MERCILESS.
pity *noun*
1. Sympathetic, sad concern for someone in misfortune: *felt great pity for the poor.*
   Syns: commiseration, compassion, sympathy.
2. SHAME.
pity *verb* FEEL.
pitying *adjective*
Feeling or expressing pity: *didn't give a single pitying thought for the wounded.*
   Syns: compassionate, piteous (*Archaic*), pitiful (*Archaic*), ruthful (*Archaic*), sympathetic.
pivot *verb*
1. SWING.
2. TRAVERSE.
3. TURN.
pivotal *adjective*
Dominant in importance or influence: *the pivotal piece of evidence in the case; the pivotal character in the play.*
   Syns: cardinal, central, key.
pixilated *adjective* DRUNK.
placate *verb* PACIFY.
place *noun*
1. The function or position customarily occupied by another: *I was sent on the trip in her place.*
   Syns: lieu, room (*Archaic*), stead.
2. A particular position in a designated order of importance: *secured a top place in the executive echelon.*
   Syns: berth, billet, slot, spot.
3. Positioning of one individual vis-à-vis others: *A person in your place should know better.*
   Syns: footing, position, rank¹, situation, standing, station, status.
4. The proper or designated location: *everything in its place.*
   Syn: niche.
5. HOME.
6. LOCALITY.
7. POINT.
8. POSITION.
place *verb*
1. To establish the identification of: *He looks familiar, but I can't place him.*
   Syns: finger, identify, pinpoint, recognize. —*Idiom* put one's finger on.
2. CLASS.

3. ESTIMATE.
4. FIX.
5. RUN.
6. SET[1].

placement *noun* POSITION.

placid *adjective*
1. CALM.
2. STILL.

placidity *noun* STILLNESS.

plagiarist *noun* PIRATE.

plagiarize *verb* PIRATE.

plague *noun*
1. ANNOYANCE.
2. CURSE.
3. OUTBREAK.

plague *verb*
1. AFFLICT.
2. ANNOY.
3. BESIEGE.

plaguy also **plaguey** *adjective*
VEXATIOUS.

plain *adjective*
1. Executed without pretense or
   obfuscation: *plain dealings with our*
   allies.
   Syns: forthright, man-to-man,
   straightforward, straight-shooting,
   undissembling, unmannered,
   unreserved. —*Idioms* plain and open,
   shooting straight from the hip.
2. Not handsome or beautiful: *a plain*
   face.
   Syns: homely, unattractive, uncomely,
   unlovely. —*Idioms* not much for
   looks, not much to look at, plain as a
   mud fence, short on looks.
3. APPARENT.
4. BARE.
5. MODEST.
6. ORDINARY.
7. PURE.
8. STRAIGHT.
9. UNSUBTLE.

plainness *noun*
1. CLARITY.
2. MODESTY.

plainspoken *adjective* FRANK.

plaintiff *noun* COMPLAINANT.

plaintive *adjective* SORROWFUL.

plan *noun*
1. APPROACH.
2. DESIGN.
3. INTENTION.
4. METHOD.

plan *verb*
1, 2. DESIGN.
3. INTEND.

planate *adjective* EVEN[1].

plane *adjective* EVEN[1].

plane *verb* EVEN[1].

planetary *adjective*
1. GIANT.
2. UNIVERSAL.

plangent *adjective* RESONANT.

plant *verb*
1. HIDE[1].
2. SEED.

plant *noun* WORKS.

plaster *verb* SMEAR.

plastered *adjective* DRUNK.

plastic *adjective*
1. Marked by unnaturalness, pretension,
   and often a slavish love of fads: *the*
   plastic world of Madison Avenue hype;
   plastic, superficial socialites.
   Syns: artificial, factitious, synthetic.
2, 3. FLEXIBLE.
4. MALLEABLE.
5. MOBILE.

plasticity *noun* FLEXIBILITY.

platform *noun* STAGE.

platitude *noun* CLICHÉ.

platitudinous *adjective* TRITE.

plaudit *noun*
1. APPLAUSE.
2. PRAISE.

plausibility *noun* VERISIMILITUDE.

plausible *adjective* BELIEVABLE.

play *verb*
1. To occupy oneself with amusement
   or diversion: *children playing after*
   school.
   Syns: disport, recreate, sport.
2. To be performed: *The show is playing*
   in London.
   Syns: run, show.
3. To make music: *The pianist played in*
   Carnegie Hall.
   Syn: perform.
4. BET.
5. FIDDLE.
6. FLIRT.
7. INFLICT.
8. INTERPRET.
9. MANIPULATE.

play along *verb*
Informal. To agree to cooperate or
participate: *I played along and drove the*
getaway car.
Syn: go along (with).

play around *verb* PHILANDER.

play down *verb* SOFT-PEDAL.

play off *verb* OPPOSE.

play out *verb*
1. To cause (a line) to become longer
   and less taut: *played out the anchor*
   line.
   Syns: unroll, unwind.
2. DRY UP at **dry**.

3. EXHAUST.
4. RUN DOWN at run.

play up *verb* EMPHASIZE.

play *noun*
1. Activity engaged in for relaxation and amusement: *Children need time for play.*
   Syns: disport, diversion, fun, recreation, sport.
2. Actions taken as a joke: *It was done all in play.*
   Syns: fun, game, sport. —*Idiom* fun and games.
3. EXERCISE.
4. FREEDOM.
5. ROOM.
6. TRICK.

play-act *verb*
1, 2. ACT.

play-acting *noun*
1. ACT.
2. ACTING.

player *noun*
1. One who plays a musical instrument: *The players in the orchestra were tuning up.*
   Syns: musician, musicianer, musico, performer.
2. ACTOR.
3. BETTOR.

playing *noun* ACTING.

plaything *noun* TOY.

plea *noun*
1. APPEAL.
2. EXCUSE.

plead with *verb* APPEAL.

pleasant *adjective*
1. AGREEABLE.
2. ENJOYABLE.

pleasantness *noun* AMIABILITY.

pleasantries *noun* AMENITIES.

please *verb*
1. To be satisfactory to: *This job pleases me.*
   Syns: satisfy, suit.
2. CHOOSE.
3. DELIGHT.

pleased *adjective* GLAD.

pleasing *adjective*
1. AGREEABLE.
2. ENJOYABLE.
3. GLAD.

pleasurable *adjective*
1. AGREEABLE.
2. ENJOYABLE.

pleasure *noun*
1. DELIGHT.
2. ENJOYMENT.
3. LIKING.

4. WILL[1].

pleasure *verb* DELIGHT.

pleat *noun* FOLD.

pleat *verb* FOLD.

plebeian *adjective* LOWLY.

plebeians *noun* COMMONALTY.

plebs *noun* COMMONALTY.

pledge *verb*
1. To guarantee by a solemn promise: *The couple pledged their undying love.*
   Syns: covenant, plight[2], promise, swear, vow. —*Idioms* give one's word of honor, solemnly swear.
2. To assume an obligation: *The benefactor pledged to pay the girl's way through school.*
   Syns: contract, engage, promise, undertake.
3. COMMIT.
4. DRINK.
5. PAWN[1].
6. SECURE.

pledge *noun*
1. PAWN[1].
2. PROMISE.
3. TOAST.

plenitude *noun* PLENTY.

plenteous *adjective* GENEROUS.

plenteousness *noun* PLENTY.

plentiful *adjective* GENEROUS.

plenty *noun*
1. Prosperity and a sufficiency of life's necessities: *America is a land of plenty.*
   Syns: abundance, bounteousness, bountifulness, plenitude, plenteousness.
2. HEAP.

pleonastic *adjective*
1. TAUTOLOGICAL.
2. WORDY.

plethora *noun* EXCESS.

pliability *noun* FLEXIBILITY.

pliable *adjective*
1. FLEXIBLE.
2. MALLEABLE.

pliableness *noun* FLEXIBILITY.

pliancy *noun* FLEXIBILITY.

pliant *adjective*
1. FLEXIBLE.
2. MALLEABLE.

plica *noun* FOLD.

plicate *verb* FOLD.

plication *noun* FOLD.

plight[1] *noun* PREDICAMENT.

plight[2] *verb* PLEDGE.

plighted *adjective* ENGAGED.

plod *verb*
1. To walk heavily, slowly, and with

difficulty: *Troops loaded with heavy packs plodded through the mud.*
Syns: slog, slop, toil, trash² (*Brit. Regional*), trudge, wade.
2. GRIND.

plop *verb* FLOP.

plot *noun*
1. The series of events and relationships forming the basis of a composition: *a novel with a complex plot and subplot.*
Syns: intrigue, story. —*Idiom* story line.
2. A secret plan to achieve an evil or illegal end: *a plot to hijack an airliner.*
Syns: cabal, collusion, connivance (*also* connivence), conspiracy, intrigue, machination, scheme.
3. LOT.

plot *verb*
1. To show graphically the direction or location of, as by using coordinates: *The navigator plotted the bomber's course.*
Syns: chart, lay out, map (out).
2. To work out a secret plan to achieve an evil or illegal end: *Revolutionaries plotted the overthrow of the government.*
Syns: collude, connive, conspire, intrigue, machinate, practice (against *or* with) (*Obs.*), scheme.

plow *verb* TURN.

ploy *noun* TRICK.

pluck *noun* COURAGE.

pluck *verb* PULL.

plucky *adjective* BRAVE.

plug *verb*
1. ADVERTISE.
2. FILL.
3. PROMOTE.
4. SHOOT.

plum *noun*
1. CATCH.
2. REWARD.

plumb *adjective* VERTICAL.

plummet *verb* FALL.

plump¹ *adjective*
Well-rounded and usu. short in physique: *a plump lady.*
Syns: chubby, plumpish, plumpy, podgy, puddy, pudgy, roly-poly, rotund, round, tubby, zaftig *or* zoftig. —*Idiom* plump as a dumpling (*or* partridge).

plump² *verb* FLOP.

plump for *verb* SUPPORT.

plumpish *adjective* PLUMP¹.

plumpy *adjective* PLUMP¹.

plunder *noun*
Goods or property seized unlawfully,

esp. by a victor in wartime: *The marauders ransacked the castle and carried their plunder back to their tents.*
Syns: boodle (*Slang*), booty, loot, pillage, prize, spoils.

plunder *verb*
1. LOOT.
2. SACK².

plunge *verb*
1. To move or thrust at, under, or into the midst of with sudden force: *The duck plunged under water. The senator plunged into the crowd to shake hands.*
Syns: dive, lunge, wade in (*or* into).
2. To move or advance against strong resistance: *He bent his head and plunged into the wind.*
Syns: drive, forge², lunge, pitch.
3, 4. FALL.
5. RAM.

plunge *noun*
1. The act of plunging suddenly downward into or as if into water: *took a plunge off the high board into the lake.*
Syns: dive, header (*Informal*), nose-dive, swoop.
2. The act of swimming: *longed for a refreshing plunge in the pool after work.*
Syns: dip, swim.
3, 4. FALL.

plunging *adjective* LOW.

plunk *verb* FLOP.

plus *verb* ADD.

plus *adjective* ADDITIVE.

plush *adjective* LUXURIOUS.

plushy *adjective* LUXURIOUS.

ply *noun* FOLD.

ply *verb*
1. EXERCISE.
2. HANDLE.

plying *noun* INSISTENCE.

pneuma *noun* SPIRIT.

pneumatic *adjective* AIRY.

podgy *adjective* PLUMP¹.

poem *noun*
1. A metrical composition: *read Byron's poems.*
Syns: poesy (*Archaic*), poetry, rhyme (*also* rime), verse.
2. POETRY.

poesy *noun* POEM.

poet *noun*
Someone who writes verse: *Pushkin is Russia's greatest poet.*
Syns: bard, muse².

poetic *also* **poetical** *adjective*
Of, pertaining to, or having the

characteristics of poetry: *poetic works;
poetic diction.*
   Syn: lyric.

poetry *noun*
1. Something likened to verse, as in
form or style: *Her dance movements
were sheer poetry.*
   Syns: lyricism, poem.
2. POEM.

pogrom *noun* MASSACRE.

poignant *adjective*
1. AFFECTING.
2. PUNGENT.

point *noun*
1. A sharp or tapered end: *the point of
a stiletto; the point of a yucca leaf.*
   Syns: acumination (*Biol.*), apex,
cusp, mucro (*Biol.*), mucronation
(*Biol.*), tip[1].
2. A very small mark: *A point of light
fell on the screen.*
   Syns: dot, pinpoint, spot.
3. A particular portion of space chosen
for something: *The beginning is a
good point at which to start.*
   Syns: location, locus, place, spot.
4. ARGUMENT.
5. ELEMENT.
6. IDEA.
7. INSTANT.
8. INTENTION.
9. SUBJECT.
10. VERGE.

point *verb*
1. To mark with punctuation: *pointed
the text.*
   Syn: punctuate.
2. AIM.

point out *verb*
1. DESIGNATE.
2. REFER.

point to *verb*
1. IMPLY.
2. INDICATE.

point up *verb* EMPHASIZE.

pointed *adjective*
1. Having an end tapering to a point:
*pointed yucca leaves; a pointed quill;
pointed bamboo stakes.*
   Syns: acicular, aciculate, acuminate
(*Biol.*), acuminous (*Biol.*), acute,
cuspate (*also* cuspated, cusped),
cuspidate (*also* cuspidated) (*Biol.*),
mucronate (*Biol.*), pointy, sharp.
2. NOTICEABLE.

pointer *noun* TIP[3].

pointless *adjective* MINDLESS.

point of view *noun*
The position from which something is

observed or considered: *You must live in
China for some time to understand the
Chinese point of view on world affairs.*
   Syns: angle, eyes, outlook, slant,
standpoint, view, viewpoint.

pointy *adjective* POINTED.

poise *noun*
1. BALANCE.
2. EASE.

poise *verb*
1. BALANCE.
2. HANG.

poison *noun*
1. Anything that is injurious,
destructive, or fatal: *Rhubarb leaves
contain a deadly poison. Her life was
ruined by the poison of pernicious
gossip.*
   Syns: bane, contagion, toxin, venom,
virus.
2. CONTAMINANT.

poison *verb*
1. To have a destructive effect on:
Jealousy poisoned their love.
   Syns: canker, empoison (*Archaic*),
envenom, infect.
2. CONTAMINATE.

poison *adjective* POISONOUS.

poisonous *adjective*
1. Capable of injuring or killing by
poison: *a poisonous snake; poisonous
chemicals; a poisonous atmosphere in
the office.*
   Syns: mephitic *or* mephitical, poison,
toxic, toxicant, venomous, virulent.
2. MALEVOLENT.

poke *verb*
1. To cause to stick out: *A seal poked its
head out of the water.*
   Syns: push, shove, thrust.
2. DELAY.
3. DIG.
4. SNOOP.

poke around *verb* GROPE.

poke *noun*
1. DIG.
2. LAGGARD.

pokerfaced *adjective* EXPRESSIONLESS.

pokey[1] *noun* JAIL.

pokey[2] *adjective* SEE **poky.**

poky also **pokey** *adjective* SLOW.

polar *adjective*
1. FRIGID.
2. OPPOSITE.

polarity *noun*
1. OPPOSITE.
2. OPPOSITION.

polemic *noun* ARGUMENT.

polemical *adjective* ARGUMENTATIVE.

police *verb*
1. To maintain or keep in order with or as if with police: *plainclothesmen policing the campus.*
   Syn: patrol.
2. TIDY.

police *noun* POLICEMAN.

policeman *noun*
A member of a law-enforcement agency: *Policemen direct traffic.*
   Syns: bluebottle (*Brit.*), bluecoat, bobby (*Brit. Slang*), bull (*Slang*), constable (*Brit.*), cop (*Informal*), copper (*Slang*), finest, flatfoot (*Slang*), fuzz (*Slang*), gendarme (*Slang*), heat (*Slang*), law (*Informal*), Man (*Slang*), nab (*Slang*), officer, paddy (*Slang*), patrolman, peeler (*Obs. Brit. Slang*), pig (*Slang*), police, rozzer (*Brit. Slang*), trap (*Brit.*).
   —*Idioms* John Law, peace officer, police officer.

policy *noun* LINE.

polish *verb*
1. GLOSS.
2. PERFECT.
3. TOUCH UP at touch.

polish off *verb*
1. CONSUME.
2. EXHAUST.

polish *noun*
1. CULTURE.
2. ELEGANCE.
3. GLOSS.

polished *adjective*
1. CULTURED.
2. GLOSSY.

polite *adjective*
1. CEREMONIOUS.
2. COURTEOUS.

politeness *noun* COURTESY.
politic *adjective* DELICATE.
polity *noun* STATE.
poll *noun* HEAD.
pollutant *noun* CONTAMINANT.

pollute *verb*
1. CONTAMINATE.
2. TAINT.

polluted *adjective* IMPURE.

pollution *noun*
1. CONTAMINATION.
2. IMPURITY.

Pollyanna *noun* OPTIMIST.
Pollyannaish *adjective* OPTIMISTIC.
Pollyannaism *noun* OPTIMISM.
poltroon *noun* COWARD.
poltroonery *noun* COWARDICE.
polychrest *noun* CURE.
polychrestic *adjective* CURATIVE.

polychromatic also **polychromic, polychromous** *adjective*
MULTICOLORED.

polychrome *adjective*
MULTICOLORED.

polychromic *adjective* SEE **polychromatic.**

polychromous *adjective* SEE **polychromatic.**

polymorphism *noun* VARIETY.
polysyllabic *adjective* LONG¹.
pomp *noun* DISPLAY.
pomposity *noun* PRETENTIOUSNESS.

pompous *adjective*
Characterized by an exaggerated show of dignity or self-importance: *a pompous old fool.*
   Syns: bloated, grandiose, highfalutin or hifalutin (*also* highfaluting) (*Informal*), pretentious, puffed-up, puffy, self-important, stuffy.

ponder *verb*
To consider carefully and at length: *pondered the problem as he drove along. The jurors pondered the defendant's testimony.*
   Syns: cerebrate, chew over, cogitate, contemplate, deliberate, meditate, mull², muse¹, reflect (on), revolve, ruminate, think over, think through, turn over, weigh. —*Idioms* cudgel one's brains, put on one's thinking cap.

ponderosity *noun* HEAVINESS.

ponderous *adjective*
1. Lacking fluency or gracefulness: *a ponderous history of Bronze Age agriculture.*
   Syns: elephantine, heavy-handed, labored.
2, 3. HEAVY.

ponderousness *noun* HEAVINESS.
pool *noun* COMBINE.
poop *verb* EXHAUST.
poop out *verb* RUN DOWN at run.
poop *noun* DRIP.
pooped *adjective* EXHAUSTED.

poor *adjective*
1. Having little or no money or wealth: *too poor to eat regularly.*
   Syns: broke (*Informal*), busted (*Slang*), destitute, impecunious, impoverished, indigent, necessitous, needy, penniless, penurious, poverty-stricken, strapped (*Informal*).
   —*Idioms* down and out, hard up, on one's uppers.
2. Lacking desirable elements or constituents: *poor soil.*

Syns: depleted, impoverished.
3. MEAGER.
4. PITIFUL.
5. SHODDY.
poorly *adjective* SICKLY.
pop *verb*
1. BURST.
2. CRACK.
3. HIT.
4. PAWN[1].
pop in *verb* VISIT.
pop off *verb* DIE.
pop *noun* REPORT.
poppycock *noun* NONSENSE.
populace *noun* COMMONALTY.
popular *adjective*
1. Of, representing, or carried on by people at large: *held popular elections.*
Syns: democratic, general, public.
2. Suited to or within the means of ordinary people: *seats available at popular prices.*
Syns: medium-priced, modest, reasonable.
3. FAMOUS.
4. FAVORITE.
populate *verb* INHABIT.
porcine *adjective* FAT.
pork *noun* PATRONAGE.
port *noun* BEARING.
portent *noun* OMEN.
portion *verb*
1. ALLOT.
2. DISTRIBUTE.
portion *noun*
1. ALLOTMENT.
2. CUT.
3. DIVISION.
4. FATE.
5. INTEREST.
6. SERVING.
portly *adjective* FAT.
portrait *noun* DOUBLE.
portraiture *noun* REPRESENTATION.
portray *verb*
1. ACT.
2. REPRESENT.
portrayal *noun* REPRESENTATION.
pose *verb*
1. To assume a particular position, as for a portrait: *The family posed in front of the fireplace.*
Syns: posture, sit.
2. To represent oneself in a given character or as other than what one is: *The confidence man posed as a wealthy count.*
Syns: attitudinize, impersonate, masquerade, pass, posture. —*Idiom* pass oneself off as.

3. ACT.
4. ASK.
5. POSTURE.
6. PROPOSE.
pose *noun*
1. ACT.
2. POSITION.
3. POSTURE.
posh *adjective*
1. EXCLUSIVE.
2. FASHIONABLE.
posit *verb* SUPPOSE.
position *noun*
1. The place where a person or thing is located: *The positions of the guards are reassigned each day. The position of the boxwood is undesirable.*
Syns: emplacement, location, locus, placement, site, situation.
2. The way in which one is placed or arranged: *in a sitting position.*
Syns: attitude, pose, posture.
3. A post of employment: *a top position with a brokerage firm.*
Syns: appointment, berth, billet, gig (*Slang*), job, office, place, situation, slot, spot.
4. BEARING.
5. BELIEF.
6. PLACE.
7. POSTURE.
position *verb*
To place in proper position or location: *positioned the shrubs in a circle.*
Syns: install, locate, put, set[1], site, situate.
positive *adjective*
1. Of a constructive nature: *positive suggestions for improving our service.*
Syns: affirmative, upbeat (*Informal*).
2. CERTAIN.
3, 4. DEFINITE.
5. FAVORABLE.
6. SURE.
7. UTTER[2].
positively *adverb*
1. ABSOLUTELY.
2. FLATLY.
3. REALLY.
possess *verb*
1. To dominate the mind or thoughts of: *Delusions of omnipotence possessed him.*
Syn: obsess.
2. BEAR.
3. CARRY.
4. COMMAND.
5. ENJOY.
6. HAVE.

possession *noun*
1. The fact of possessing: *Possession of the property is being contested.*
Syns: ownership, proprietorship, title.
2. An area subject to rule by an outside power: *Cuba was once a possession of Spain.*
Syns: colony, dependency, province, territory.
3. OWNERSHIP.

possessions *noun*
1. BELONGINGS.
2. EFFECTS.
3. HOLDING(S).

possessive *adjective*
1. Having or showing a tendency to control or dominate: *a possessive mother.*
Syn: possessory.
2. JEALOUS.

possessor *noun* OWNER.

possessory *adjective* POSSESSIVE.

possibility *noun*
Something that may occur or be done: *Rain is a possibility for the weekend.*
Syns: contingency, eventuality.

possible *adjective*
1. Capable of occurring or being done: *There are four possible solutions to the problem.*
Syns: feasible, practicable, viable, workable. —*Idiom* within reach.
2. Capable of favorable development: *a possible source of cheap fuel.*
Syn: potential.
3. EARTHLY.
4. POTENTIAL.
5. PROBABLE.

post *verb*
1. To place on a list or in a record: *posted all payments in the ledger.*
Syns: enter, insert, record, register.
2. BET.
3. SCORE.
4. STATION.

post *noun*
1. MISSION.
2. STATION.

posterior *adjective*
1. BACK.
2. LATER.

posterior *noun*
1. BACK.
2. BOTTOM.

posterity *noun* PROGENY.

postern *adjective* BACK.

posthaste *adverb* FAST.

posthumous *adjective*
Occurring or done after death: *posthumous publication of his memoirs.*

Syns: post-mortem, post-obit (*also* post-obituary).

posting *noun*
1. ENTRY.
2. STATION.

postliminary *adjective* LATER.

post-mortem *adjective* POSTHUMOUS.

post-obit *also* **post-obituary** *adjective* POSTHUMOUS.

postpone *verb* DEFER[1].

postponement *noun* DELAY.

postulate *verb* SUPPOSE.

postulate *noun* ASSUMPTION.

postulation *noun* ASSUMPTION.

posture *noun*
1. The way in which a person holds or carries his body: *learning good posture.*
Syns: attitude, carriage, pose, stance.
2. A frame of mind affecting one's thoughts or behavior: *a posture of defenseless womanhood.*
Syns: attitude, outlook, position, stance.
3. CONDITION.
4. POSITION.

posture *verb*
1. To assume an exaggerated or unnatural attitude or pose: *postured whenever a photographer came near.*
Syns: attitudinize, pose. —*Idiom* strike an attitude.
2, 3. POSE.

pot *noun*
1. BET.
2. FAVORITE.

potable *noun* DRINK.

potation *noun* DRINK.

potency *noun*
1. EFFECT.
2. ENERGY.
3. STRENGTH.

potent *adjective*
1. POWERFUL.
2, 3. STRONG.

potential *adjective*
1. Capable of being but not yet in existence: *a potential buyer; a potential threat.*
Syns: eventual, latent, possible.
2. POSSIBLE.

potential *noun*
The inherent capacity for growth or development: *a potential for artistry that has never been realized.*
Syn: potentiality.

potentiality *noun* POTENTIAL.

pother *noun* BOTHER.
pother *verb*
1. FUSS.
2. WORRY.
potted *adjective* DRUNK.
pouch *verb* BULGE.
pound *verb*
1, 2. BEAT.
3. IMPRESS.
pound *noun* BLOW².
pounding *noun* BEAT.
pour *verb*
1. To cause (a liquid) to flow in a steady stream: *pouring milk from the carton.*
   Syns: decant, draw (off), effuse.
2. To rain heavily: *It started to pour just as I left for work.*
   Syns: drench, teem². —*Idioms* come down in buckets (*or* sheets *or* torrents), rain cats and dogs.
3. To come or go in large numbers: *The army poured into enemy territory.*
   Syns: flood, swarm, teem¹, throng, troop.
4. FLOW.
pout *verb*
1. BULGE.
2. SULK.
poverty *noun*
The condition of being extremely poor: *government aid to those living in poverty.*
   Syns: beggary, destitution, impecuniousness, impoverishment, indigence (*also* indigency), need, neediness, penury, privation, want.
   —*Idiom* distressed (*or* reduced *or* straitened) circumstances.
poverty-stricken *adjective* POOR.
powder *verb*
1. CRUSH.
2. SPRINKLE.
powdery *adjective* FINE¹.
power *noun*
1. AUTHORITY.
2. FORCE.
3. HEAP.
4. MUSCLE.
5. STRENGTH.
powerful *adjective*
1. Having or able to exert great power: *a powerful nation.*
   Syns: mighty, potent, puissant.
2. AUTHORITATIVE.
3. FORCEFUL.
4. INFLUENTIAL.
5. SEVERE.
6. STRONG.
powerfulness *noun* STRENGTH.

powerless *adjective*
1. HELPLESS.
2. INEFFECTUAL.
powerlessness *noun*
1. INABILITY.
2. INEFFECTUALITY.
powwow *noun* CONFERENCE.
powwow *verb* CONFER.
practic *adjective* REALISTIC.
practicable *adjective*
1. OPEN.
2. POSSIBLE.
3. PRACTICAL.
practical *adjective*
1. Serving or capable of serving a useful purpose: *A wrist watch is one piece of jewelry that is practical.*
   Syns: functional, handy, practicable, serviceable, useful, utilitarian.
2. Resulting from experience or practice: *has a practical knowledge of the shoe business.*
   Syns: practiced, veteran.
3. IMPLICIT.
4. REALISTIC.
practice *verb*
1. To do or perform repeatedly so as to master: *practice the shot-put; practice the violin.*
   Syn: rehearse.
2. To work at, esp. as a profession: *practices law.*
   Syn: pursue.
3. EXERCISE.
4. PLOT.
5. USE.
practice *noun*
1. Repetition of an action so as to develop or maintain one's skill: *It takes years of practice to play the cello.*
   Syns: drill, exercise, rehearsal, study, training.
2. A working at a profession or occupation: *began the practice of medicine.*
   Syn: pursuit.
3. CUSTOM.
practiced *adjective*
1. ACCOMPLISHED.
2. EXPERIENCED.
3. PRACTICAL.
praelect *verb* SEE **prelect**.
praetorian *adjective* CORRUPT.
praetorian *noun* CONSERVATIVE.
pragmatic *noun* MEDDLER.
pragmatic also **pragmatical** *adjective* REALISTIC.
praise *noun*
1. An expression of warm approval:

emphatic in their praise of his
performance.
Syns: acclaim, acclamation, applause,
commendation, compliment(s), kudos,
laudation, plaudit.
2. The honoring of God, as in worship:
a hymn of praise.
   Syns: exaltation, glorification,
laudation, magnification.
3. COMPLIMENT.

praise *verb*
1. To express warm approval of: *His
partner praises him to the skies.*
   Syns: acclaim, applaud, commend,
compliment, kudize (*Informal*), laud.
2. To honor (God) in religious worship:
*Praise God, from whom all blessings
flow.*
   Syns: eulogize, exalt, extol, glorify,
laud, magnify, panegyrize. —*Idiom*
pay homage to.
3. COMPLIMENT.
4. HONOR.

praiseworthy *adjective* ADMIRABLE.
prance *verb* GAMBOL.
prank *noun*
A mischievous act: *Halloween pranks.*
   Syns: antic, caper, frolic, joke, lark,
monkeyshine, shenanigan, tomfoolery,
trick. —*Idiom* high jinks.
prankishness *noun* MISCHIEF.
prankster *noun* MISCHIEF.
prate *verb*
1. BABBLE.
2. CHATTER.
prate *noun*
1. BABBLE.
2. CHATTER.
prattle *verb*
1. BABBLE.
2. CHATTER.
prattle *noun*
1. BABBLE.
2. CHATTER.
praxis *noun* CUSTOM. .
pray *verb*
1. To offer a reverent petition to God or
a god: *praying for a bountiful harvest.*
   Syns: invocate (*Archaic*), supplicate.
2. APPEAL.
prayer *noun*
1. The act of praying: *hands clasped in
prayer.*
   Syns: invocation, supplication.
2. A formula of words used in praying:
said many prayers for peace.
   Syns: collect2, orison, rogation.
3. APPEAL.
4. SUPPLICANT.

prayerful *adjective*
Deeply concerned with God and the
beliefs and practice of religion: *a
prayerful and exemplary life.*
   Syns: devotional, devout, godly,
pious.
preach *verb*
1. To deliver (a sermon or sermons),
esp. as a vocation: *preached the
gospel.*
   Syns: evangelize, homilize, sermonize.
2. MORALIZE.
preacher *noun*
A person ordained for service in a
Christian church: *a marriage performed
by a preacher.*
   Syns: churchman, clergyman, cleric,
clerical, clerk (*Archaic*), divine1,
ecclesiastic, minister, parson, reverend
(*Informal*).
preachy *adjective* MORAL.
preamble *noun* INTRODUCTION.
precariousness *noun*
1. INSTABILITY.
2. UNSTABLENESS.
precaution *noun*
1. CAUTION.
2. PRUDENCE.
precede *verb*
1. To come, exist, or occur prior to in
time: *Her birthday precedes mine.*
   Syns: antecede, antedate, forerun,
predate.
2. INTRODUCE.
precedence also **precedency** *noun*
The act, condition, or right of
preceding: *Her career takes precedence
over her family.*
   Syns: antecedence, priority. —*Idiom*
right of way.
precedent *noun*
A closely similar case in existence or in
the past: *a ruling without precedent in
legal history.*
   Syns: antecedent, example.
precedent *adjective*
1. ADVANCE.
2. PAST.
preceding *adjective*
1. ADVANCE.
2. LAST1.
3. PAST.
precept *noun*
1. LAW.
2. MORAL.
precinct(s) *noun* LIMIT.
precious *adjective*
1. AFFECTED2.
2. ARTY.

3. DARLING.
4. FAVORITE.
5. VALUABLE.

precipitance also **precipitancy** *noun*
HASTE.

precipitant *adjective*
1. ABRUPT.
2. RASH[1].

precipitate *verb*
1. To cause to happen suddenly or unexpectedly: *The heckling precipitated a riot.*
   Syns: bring on, prompt, spur.
2. DEPOSIT.

precipitate *adjective*
1. Lacking due thought or consideration: *forced to make a precipitate decision.*
   Syns: hasty, ill-considered, impetuous, impulsive, rash[1], reckless.
2. ABRUPT.
3. RASH[1].
4. STEEP[1].

precipitate *noun*
1. DEPOSIT.
2. EFFECT.

precipitation *noun*
1. DEPOSIT.
2. HASTE.

precipitous *adjective*
1. RASH[1].
2. STEEP[1].

precise *adjective*
1. Strictly distinguished from others: *at that precise moment.*
   Syns: exact, identical, very.
2. ACCURATE.
3. DEFINITE.
4. GENTEEL.

precisely *adverb*
1. Without the slightest deviation in any respect: *precisely at 3:00 A.M.*
   Syns: bang (*Informal*), dead, direct, directly, exactly, right, smack[1] (*Informal*), square, straight.
2. DIRECTLY.
3. EVEN[1].

preciseness *noun* ACCURACY.
precision *noun* ACCURACY.
preclude *verb* PREVENT.
preclusion *noun* PREVENTION.
precocious *adjective*
1. ADVANCED.
2. EARLY.

precondition *noun* CONDITION.
preconsider *verb* PREMEDITATE.
precursor *noun* ANCESTOR.
predate *verb* PRECEDE.
predecessor *noun* ANCESTOR.

predeliberate *verb* PREMEDITATE.
predestinate *verb* FATE.
predestination *noun* FATE.
predestine *verb* FATE.
predestined *adjective* FATED.
predetermine *verb*
1. FATE.
2. PREMEDITATE.

predetermined *adjective* FATED.
predicament *noun*
A difficult, embarrassing situation: *got into a real predicament when he wrecked his fiancée's car.*
   Syns: bind (*Informal*), box[1], corner, dilemma, fix, hole, jam (*Informal*), pickle (*Informal*), plight[1], quagmire, scrape (*Slang*), soup (*Slang*), spot (*Informal*). —**Idioms** deep water, hot spot, hot water, a spot of trouble, trouble in paradise.

predicate *verb* BASE[1].
predict *verb*
To tell about or make known (future events) in advance, esp. by means of special knowledge or inference: *predicting the collapse of the government.*
   Syns: adumbrate, call, forecast, foretell, prognosticate.

prediction *noun*
The act of predicting: *listened to the weather predictions.*
   Syns: forecast, foretelling, outlook, prognosis, prognostication, projection.

predictive *adjective*
Of or relating to prediction: *the weather forecaster's predictive methods.*
   Syns: prognostic, prognosticative.

predilection *noun* BENT.
predispose *verb* DISPOSE.
predisposition *noun*
1. BENT.
2. TASTE.

predominance *noun* DOMINANCE.
predominant *adjective* RULING.
predominate *verb* DOMINATE.
pre-eminence also **preeminence, preëminence** *noun*
1. DOMINANCE.
2. EMINENCE.

pre-eminent also **preeminent, preëminent** *adjective*
1. EMINENT.
2. OUTSTANDING.
3. PRIMARY.

pre-empt also **preempt, preëmpt** *verb* ASSUME.
pre-emption also **preemption, preëmption** *noun* USURPATION.
preen *verb* PRIDE.

preface noun INTRODUCTION.
preface verb INTRODUCE.
prefatory also **prefatorial** adjective
1. INTRODUCTORY.
2. PRELIMINARY.
prefer verb FAVOR.
preferable adjective BETTER[1].
preference noun
1. CHOICE.
2. FAVOR.
preferential adjective FAVORABLE.
preferred adjective FAVORITE.
prefigure verb
1. ADUMBRATE.
2. PROMISE.
pregnable adjective VULNERABLE.
pregnancy noun
The condition of carrying a developing fetus within the uterus: *a difficult pregnancy.*
   Syns: gestation, gravidation (*Obs.*), gravidity, greatness (*Archaic*), heaviness (*Archaic*), parturiency.
pregnant adjective
1. Carrying a developing fetus within the uterus: *She's three months pregnant.*
   Syns: enceinte, expectant, expecting, gone, gravid, heavy (*Archaic*), parturient. —*Idioms* big (*or* heavy) with child, in a family way, with child.
2. Conveying hidden or unexpressed meaning: *a pregnant silence.*
   Syns: meaningful, significant, suggestive.
prejudice noun
1. Irrational suspicion or hatred of a particular group, race, or religion: *prejudice against women.*
   Syns: bigotry, intolerance.
2. BIAS.
prejudice verb
1. BIAS.
2. DISCRIMINATE.
3. INFLUENCE.
4. INJURE.
prejudiced adjective BIASED.
prejudicial adjective BIASED.
prelect also **praelect** verb ADDRESS.
prelection noun SPEECH.
preliminary adjective
1. Prior to or preparing for the main matter, action, or business: *a preliminary statement.*
   Syns: inductive, introductory, prefatory (*also* prefatorial), preparatory, prolegomenous.
2. INTRODUCTORY.
3. ROUGH.

prelude noun INTRODUCTION.
premature adjective EARLY.
premeditate verb
To consider and plan in advance: *She premeditated her strategy.*
   Syns: forethink, preconsider, predeliberate, predetermine.
premeditated adjective CALCULATED.
premier adjective PRIMARY.
premise noun ASSUMPTION.
premise verb SUPPOSE.
preoccupation noun
1. ABSORPTION.
2. COMPLEX.
preoccupied adjective
1. ABSENT-MINDED.
2. ABSORBED.
preoccupy verb ABSORB.
preordain verb FATE.
preparation noun
The condition of being made ready beforehand: *adequate preparation in case of disaster or accident.*
   Syns: preparedness, readiness.
preparations noun ARRANGEMENTS.
preparatory adjective
1. INTRODUCTORY.
2. PRELIMINARY.
prepare verb
1. To cause to be ready, as for use, consumption, or a special purpose: *preparing dinner.*
   Syns: fit, fix, make, ready.
2. ARRANGE.
prepared adjective READY.
preparedness noun PREPARATION.
preponderance also **preponderancy** noun
1. DOMINANCE.
2. WEIGHT.
preponderate verb DOMINATE.
prepossess verb BIAS.
prepossessed adjective BIASED.
prepossessing adjective ATTRACTIVE.
prepossession noun
1. BIAS.
2. COMPLEX.
preposterous adjective
1. FOOLISH.
2. OUTRAGEOUS.
preposterousness noun FOOLISHNESS.
prepotency noun DOMINANCE.
prepotent adjective RULING.
prerequisite noun CONDITION.
prerogative noun
1. AUTHORITY.
2. BIRTHRIGHT.

presage *verb*
1. ADUMBRATE.
2. PROMISE.
3. USHER IN at **usher**.
presage *noun* OMEN.
prescience *noun* VISION.
prescient *adjective* VISIONARY.
prescribe *verb* DICTATE.
prescript *noun* RULE.
prescription *noun* LAW.
presence *noun*
1. The condition or fact of being present: *A reddish dust indicated the presence of termites.*
   Syn: occurrence.
2. BEARING.
present[1] *noun* NOW.
present *adjective*
In existence now: *present trends; the present generation.*
   Syns: contemporary, current, existent, existing, new, now, present-day.
present[2] *verb*
1. To bring forward and quote for formal consideration: *a brief that presented all the precedents to the court for review.*
   Syns: adduce, advance, allege (*Archaic*), cite, lay[1].
2. ACQUAINT.
3. AIM.
4. CONFER.
5. GIVE.
6. OFFER.
7. STAGE.
present *noun* GIFT.
presentable *adjective* DECENT.
presentation *noun*
1. The instance or occasion of being presented for the first time to society: *the presentation of this season's debutantes.*
   Syn: coming-out (*Informal*).
2. CONFERMENT.
3. GIFT.
present-day *adjective* PRESENT[1].
preserval *noun* CONSERVATION.
preservation *noun* CONSERVATION.
preservative *adjective*
Able to preserve: *Arizona has a dry, preservative climate.*
   Syns: conservative, conservatory, preservatory, protective.
preservatory *adjective* PRESERVATIVE.
preserve *verb*
1, 2. CONSERVE.
3. MAINTAIN.
preserve *noun* RESERVATION.

press *verb*
1. To smooth by applying heat and pressure: *press shirts.*
   Syns: iron, mangle.
2. BEAR.
3, 4. CROWD.
5. EMBRACE.
6. INSIST.
7. PUSH.
8. SQUEEZE.
9. URGE.
press *noun*
Journalists and journalism in general: *The press covered the President's speech. We advocate freedom of the press.*
   Syns: Fleet Street (*Brit.*), fourth estate, media.
pressing *adjective* BURNING.
pressing *noun* INSISTENCE.
pressure *noun*
1. The act, condition, or effect of exerting force on someone or something: *Excessive pressure on the job caused her breakdown. The engine pylon sheared off under pressure in the wind tunnel.*
   Syns: strain[1], stress, tension.
2. FORCE.
pressure *verb*
1. FORCE.
2. INSIST.
3. PRESSURIZE.
pressurize *verb*
To maintain normal air pressure in: *The cockpit is pressurized for high-altitude flying.*
   Syn: pressure.
prestidigitation *noun* MAGIC.
prestige *noun*
1. EMINENCE.
2. FACE.
3. HONOR.
prestigious *adjective* EMINENT.
presumable *adjective* PRESUMPTIVE.
presume *verb*
1. To have the courage to put forward, as an idea, esp. when rebuff or criticism is likely: *I wouldn't even presume to explain his motives.*
   Syns: hazard, pretend, venture.
2. ABUSE.
3. GUESS.
4. SUPPOSE.
presumed *adjective* PRESUMPTIVE.
presuming *adjective* PRESUMPTUOUS.
presumption *noun*
1. Excessive and arrogant self-confidence: *has the presumption to accept the invitation for me.*

Syns: assumption, brashness, brass (*Informal*), brazenness, cheek, cheekiness, crust (*Slang*), effrontery, face, familiarity, gall², nerve (*Informal*), overconfidence, presumptuousness, temerity, uppitiness (*Informal*).
2. ARROGANCE.
3. ASSUMPTION.
4. GUESS.

presumptive *adjective*
1. Based on probability or presumption: *the heiress presumptive to the throne.*
Syns: assumptive, likely, presumable, probable. —*Idiom* taken for granted.
2. Based on inference, not fact: *The enemy's presumptive intentions cannot yet be verified.*
Syns: assumed, conjectured, inferred, presumed, supposed.
3. PRESUMPTUOUS.

presumptuous *adjective*
1. Having or exhibiting excessive and arrogant self-confidence: *a disrespectful, presumptuous pip-squeak.*
Syns: assuming, assumptive, brash, brassy (*Informal*), brazen, cheeky, familiar, nervy (*Informal*), overconfident, presuming, presumptive (*Archaic*), pushy (*Informal*), uppity (*also* uppish) (*Informal*).
2. ARROGANT.
3. IMPUDENT.

presumptuousness *noun*
PRESUMPTION.

presuppose *verb* SUPPOSE.

presupposition *noun* ASSUMPTION.

pretend *verb*
1. ACT.
2. ASSUME.
3. FAKE.
4. PRESUME.

pretend *adjective* ARTIFICIAL.

pretended *adjective* ARTIFICIAL.

pretender *noun*
1. CLAIMANT.
2. FAKE.

pretense *noun*
1. The presentation of something false as true: *Their protestations of innocence were sheer pretense.*
Syns: charade, make-believe, pretension.
2. A professed rather than a real reason: *a secret agent who entered the country on the pretense of being a diplomat.*
Syns: cover, pretension, pretext.

3. ACT.
4. AFFECTATION.
5. CLAIM.
6. FAÇADE.

pretension *noun*
1. CLAIM.
2, 3. PRETENSE.
4. PRETENTIOUSNESS.

pretentious *adjective*
1. AFFECTED².
2. ARTY.
3. POMPOUS.
4. SHOWY.

pretentiousness *noun*
Boastful self-importance: *The rock star's press conference was the height of pretentiousness.*
Syns: ostentation, pomposity, pretension.

preternatural *adjective*
1. Greatly exceeding or departing from the normal course of nature: *a hurricane of preternatural force and violence.*
Syns: hypernormal, supernatural, unnatural.
2. ABNORMAL.
3. SUPERNATURAL.

preternaturalness *noun*
ABNORMALITY.

pretext *noun*
1. EXCUSE.
2. FAÇADE.
3. PRETENSE.

pretty *adjective*
1. ATTRACTIVE.
2. BEAUTIFUL.

pretty *adverb* FAIRLY.

prevail *verb*
1. DOMINATE.
2. TRIUMPH.

prevail on (or **upon**) *verb* PERSUADE.

prevailing *adjective*
1. Most generally existing or encountered at a given time: *The prevailing view is that war is imminent.*
Syns: current, prevalent, regnant, rife, widespread.
2. RULING.

prevalence *noun* USUALNESS.

prevalent *adjective* PREVAILING.

prevaricate *verb*
1. EQUIVOCATE.
2. LIE².

prevarication *noun* LIE².

prevaricator *noun* LIAR.

prevent *verb*
To prohibit from occurring by advance planning or action: *Crisis management*

is an unreliable way of preventing war.
Mass inoculations prevented an epidemic.
Syns: avert, deter, forestall, forfend
(*also* forefend), head off, obviate,
preclude, rule out, stave off, turn
aside, ward (off). —*Idiom* nip in the
bud.

preventative *adjective* SEE
preventive.

prevention *noun*
The act of preventing: *prevention of war*
through balance of power.
Syns: determent, deterrence,
forestalling, forestallment, obviation,
preclusion.

preventive *also* **preventative**
adjective
1. Intended to prevent: *took preventive*
measures to avoid a conflict.
Syns: deterrent, deterring,
forestalling.
2. *Med.* Defending against disease:
preventive dentistry.
Syns: prophylactic, protective.

previous *adjective*
1. LAST[1].
2. LATE.
3. PAST.

prey *noun* VICTIM.

price *noun*
1, 2. COST.

priceless *adjective*
1. Extremely funny: *That joke is just*
priceless!
Syns: hilarious, killing (*Informal*),
rich (*Informal*), screaming (*Slang*),
sidesplitting, slaying (*Slang*).
2. VALUABLE.

prick *noun*
1. A sudden, sharp, painful feeling: *felt*
a prick of remorse.
Syns: pang, prickle, stab, sting.
2. A small mark or hole made by a
sharp, pointed object: *looked for*
telltale needle pricks in the suspected
addict's arm.
Syns: perforation, puncture, stab.
3. A sharp, pointed object: *the pricks on*
a cactus.
Syns: needle, prickle, thorn.
prick *verb* URGE.

prickish *adjective* IRRITABLE.

prickle *noun*
1, 2. PRICK.

prickly *adjective*
1, 2. THORNY.

pride *noun*
1. A sense of one's own dignity or
worth: *had to respond to save his*
pride.

Syns: amour-propre, ego, self-esteem,
self-regard, self-respect.
2. ARROGANCE.
3. EGOTISM.

pride *verb*
To be proud of (oneself) because of
some accomplishment, achievement,
etc.: *prides herself on her organizational*
ability.
Syns: congratulate, preen.

prideful *adjective* PROUD.

prier *also* **pryer** *noun* SNOOP.

prim *adjective* GENTEEL.

primary *adjective*
1. Most important, influential, or
significant: *the primary duty of an*
employee; the primary leader of the
opposition.
Syns: capital, cardinal, chief,
dominant, first, foremost, key,
leading, main, major, number-one
(*Informal*), outstanding, paramount,
pre-eminent (*also* preeminent,
preëminent), premier, prime,
principal, top.
2. FIRST.
3. IMMEDIATE.
4. PRIMITIVE.
5. ORIGINAL.
6. RADICAL.

prime *noun*
1. BLOOM.
2. YOUTH.

prime *adjective*
1. CHOICE.
2. EXCELLENT.
3. FIRST.
4. ORIGINAL.
5. PRIMARY.

primed *adjective* READY.

primeval *adjective* PRIMITIVE.

primitive *adjective*
1. Of or pertaining to early stages in the
evolution of human culture: *a*
primitive society.
Syns: primary, primeval.
2. EARLY.
3. ELEMENTAL.
4. IGNORANT.
5. ORIGINAL.
6. RUDE.
7. UNCIVILIZED.

primordial *adjective* EARLY.

princely *adjective* GRAND.

principal *adjective*
1. Having or exercising authority: *the*
principal carpenter on that job.
Syns: boss, chief, foremost, head.
2. PRIMARY.

principal *noun* LEAD.

principle noun LAW.
principled adjective ETHICAL.
principles noun CHARACTER.
print noun
1. IMPRESSION.
2. TRACK.
printing noun
1. IMPRESSION.
2. PUBLICATION.
prior adjective
1. ADVANCE.
2. PAST.
priority noun PRECEDENCE.
prison noun JAIL.
prissy adjective GENTEEL.
private adjective
1. Belonging or confined to a particular person or group as opposed to the public or the government: *private property.*
   Syns: personal, privy.
2. CONFIDENTIAL.
privation noun
1. DEPRIVATION.
2. POVERTY.
privileged adjective CONFIDENTIAL.
privy adjective
1, 2. CONFIDENTIAL.
3. PRIVATE.
prize noun
1. BEST.
2. CATCH.
3. PLUNDER.
4. REWARD.
5. TREASURE.
6. TROPHY.
prize verb
1. APPRECIATE.
2. CHERISH.
probability noun CHANCE.
probable adjective
1. Likely to happen or to be true: *The probable consequences are frightening.*
   Syns: conceivable, possible.
2. PRESUMPTIVE.
probe noun
1. EXPLORATION.
2. FEELER.
3. INQUIRY.
probe verb
1. EXPLORE.
2. FEEL OUT at feel.
probing adjective INCISIVE.
probity noun
1. CHARACTER.
2. GOOD.
problem noun
A situation that presents difficulty, uncertainty, or perplexity: *dealing with the unemployment problem.*
   Syns: issue, question. —*Idioms* can of worms, hornet's nest.
problematical also **problematic** adjective
1. AMBIGUOUS.
2. DEBATABLE.
proboscis noun NOSE.
procedure noun
1. APPROACH.
2. LINE.
proceed verb
1. COME.
2. GO.
3. STEM.
procession noun ORDER.
proclaim verb
1. ANNOUNCE.
2. SHOW.
3. USHER IN at usher.
proclamation noun
1, 2. ANNOUNCEMENT.
proclivity noun BENT.
procrastinate verb DELAY.
procreant adjective REPRODUCTIVE.
procreate verb
1. FATHER.
2. PRODUCE.
3. REPRODUCE.
procreation noun REPRODUCTION.
procreative adjective REPRODUCTIVE.
procumbent adjective FLAT.
procurable adjective AVAILABLE.
procure verb GET.
prod verb
1. DIG.
2. INSIST.
3. URGE.
prod noun
1. PUSH.
2. STIMULUS.
prodding noun INSISTENCE.
prodigal adjective
1. EXTRAVAGANT.
2. PROFUSE.
prodigal noun WASTREL.
prodigality noun EXTRAVAGANCE.
prodigious adjective
1. FABULOUS.
2. GIANT.
prodigy noun MARVEL.
produce verb
1. To cause to come into existence: *produce an alternative energy plan.*
   Syns: create, engender, father, generate, hatch, make, originate, parent, procreate, sire, spawn.
   —*Idioms* bring to pass, give birth (or rise) to.

2. BEAR.
3. CAUSE.
4. COMPOSE.
5. DEVELOP.
6. GROW.
7. LENGTHEN.
8. MAKE.
9. RETURN.

product   *noun*
1. Something produced by human effort: *the product of an active imagination.*
   Syn: production.
2. YIELD.

production   *noun*
1. COMPOSITION.
2. EXTENSION.
3. PRODUCT.
4. YIELD.

productive   *adjective*
1. EFFECTIVE.
2. EFFICIENT.
3, 4. FERTILE.

productivity   *noun*
1. EFFICIENCY.
2. FERTILITY.

profanation   *noun*   SACRILEGE.
profane   *adjective*
1. Not religious in subject matter, form, or use: *sacred and profane music.*
   Syns: lay², secular, temporal, worldly.
2. OBSCENE.
3. SACRILEGIOUS.

profane   *verb*   VIOLATE.
profanity   *noun*   OBSCENITY.
proffer   *verb*   OFFER.
proffer   *noun*   OFFER.
proficiency   *noun*   ABILITY.
proficient   *adjective*
1. ABLE.
2. EFFICIENT.
3. EXPERT.

proficient   *noun*   EXPERT.
profile   *noun*   OUTLINE.
profit   *verb*
1. To be an advantage to: *It would profit you to learn to drive.*
   Syns: avail, benefit, boot² (*Archaic*), serve. —*Idiom* stand someone in good stead.
2. BENEFIT.
3. CLEAN UP at **clean.**

profit   *noun*
1. ADVANTAGE.
2. GAIN.
3. INTEREST.
4. USE.

profitable   *adjective*
Affording profit: *a profitable business.*

Syns: advantageous, fat, lucrative, moneymaking, remunerative.
profligacy   *noun*
1. EXTRAVAGANCE.
2. LICENSE.

profligate   *adjective*
1. ABANDONED.
2. EXTRAVAGANT.

profligate   *noun*
1. WANTON.
2. WASTREL.

profound   *adjective*
1, 2, 3. DEEP.

profoundness   *noun*   DEPTH.
profundity   *noun*
1. DEPTH.
2. WISDOM.

profuse   *adjective*
1. Given to or marked by unrestrained abundance: *profuse apologies.*
   Syns: extravagant, exuberant, lavish, lush, luxuriant, opulent, prodigal, profusive, riotous, superabundant.
2. THICK.

profusive   *adjective*   PROFUSE.
progenitive   *adjective*   REPRODUCTIVE.
progenitor   *noun*   ANCESTOR.
progeny   *noun*
A group consisting of those descended directly from the same parents or ancestors: *Queen Victoria's progeny sat on many European thrones.*
   Syns: begats (*Slang*), brood, get, issue, offspring, posterity, seed.

prognosis   *noun*   PREDICTION.
prognostic   *adjective*   PREDICTIVE.
prognostic   *noun*   OMEN.
prognosticate   *verb*   PREDICT.
prognostication   *noun*
1. OMEN.
2. PREDICTION.

prognosticative   *adjective*
PREDICTIVE.

program   *noun*
1. An organized list of procedures, activities, events, etc.: *On our program is a visit to Chinatown.*
   Syns: agenda, calendar, docket, line-up (*also* lineup), schedule, timetable. —*Idiom* order of the day.
2. A printed list of the order of events and other pertinent information for a public performance: *Why isn't her name on the program?*
   Syns: bill¹, prospectus, syllabus.
3. LINE.

program   *verb*   SCHEDULE.
progress   *noun*
1. Steady improvement, as of an

individual or a society: *progress in the economy of developing countries.*
Syns: amelioration, betterment, development, improvement, melioration.
2. ADVANCE.
3. DEVELOPMENT.
progress *verb* COME.
progression *noun* ADVANCE.
progressive *adjective*
1. ADVANCED.
2. BROAD.
3. LIBERAL.
progressive *noun* LIBERAL.
prohibit *verb* FORBID.
prohibited *adjective* FORBIDDEN.
prohibition *noun* FORBIDDANCE.
project *noun*
1. Something undertaken, esp. something requiring extensive planning and work: *a five-year research project.*
Syns: enterprise, undertaking, venture.
2. DESIGN.
project *verb*
1. BULGE.
2. DESIGN.
3. INTEND.
4. SHED.
5. SHOOT.
projection *noun*
1. BULGE.
2. HILL.
3. PREDICTION.
prolegomenon *noun* INTRODUCTION.
prolegomenous *adjective*
1. INTRODUCTORY.
2. PRELIMINARY.
proliferate *verb* REPRODUCE.
proliferation *noun*
1. BUILD-UP.
2. REPRODUCTION.
proliferous *adjective* FERTILE.
prolific *adjective*
1, 2. FERTILE.
prolix *adjective* WORDY.
prolixity *noun* WORDINESS.
prolixness *noun* WORDINESS.
prologue *noun* INTRODUCTION.
prolong *verb* LENGTHEN.
prolongate *verb* LENGTHEN.
prolongation *noun* EXTENSION.
prolonged *adjective*
1. CHRONIC.
2. LONG¹.
promenade *verb* STROLL.
promenade *noun* WALK.

prominence also **prominency** *noun*
1. EMINENCE.
2. HILL.
prominent *adjective*
1. BOLD.
2. EMINENT.
3. NOTICEABLE.
promise *noun*
A declaration that one will or will not do a certain thing: *made a promise to repay the debt but defaulted; gave her his promise that he would return.*
Syns: covenant, guarantee, pledge, vow.
promise *verb*
1. To give reason for expecting: *dark clouds that promised rain.*
Syns: betoken, foreshadow, foretoken, indicate, prefigure, presage.
2, 3. PLEDGE.
promising *adjective*
1. COMING.
2. ENCOURAGING.
promote *verb*
1. To raise in rank: *promoted him from corporal to sergeant.*
Syns: advance, elevate, jump, raise, upgrade.
2. To help bring about: *believed that TV violence promotes real violence.*
Syns: cultivate, encourage, feed, foster.
3. To increase or seek to increase the importance or reputation of by favorable publicity: *His press agent promoted the movie in feature stories.*
Syns: ballyhoo (*Informal*), boost, build up, enhance, hype (*Slang*), plug (*Informal*), publicize, puff, tout.
4. ADVANCE.
5. ADVERTISE.
promotion *noun*
1. A systematic effort to increase the importance or reputation of by favorable publicity: *spent $100,000 in promotion of the new product.*
Syns: ballyhoo (*Informal*), build-up (*also* buildup) (*Informal*), hype (*Slang*), pitch (*Slang*), publicity, puffery.
2. ADVANCEMENT.
3. ADVERTISING.
prompt *adjective* PUNCTUAL.
prompt *verb*
1. INSPIRE.
2. PRECIPITATE.
3. URGE.
promulgate *verb*
1. ADVERTISE.

2. ANNOUNCE.
3. ESTABLISH.

promulgation *noun* ANNOUNCEMENT.

prone *adjective*
1. FLAT.
2. INCLINED.
3. LIABLE.

proneness *noun* BENT.

pronounce *verb*
To produce or make (speech sounds): *She pronounced her vowels with a southern drawl.*
  Syns: articulate, enunciate, say, utter¹, vocalize.

pronounced *adjective*
1. BOLD.
2. DECIDED.

pronouncement *noun*
1, 2. ANNOUNCEMENT.
3. RULING.

pronto *adverb* FAST.

proof *noun*
1. CONFIRMATION.
2. REASON.
3. TEST.

proof *adjective* RESISTANT.

prop *noun* SUPPORT.

prop *verb* SUSTAIN.

propagandize *verb* INDOCTRINATE.

propagate *verb*
1. GROW.
2. REPRODUCE.

propagation *noun* REPRODUCTION.

propel *verb*
1, 2. DRIVE.
3. SHOOT.
4. URGE.

propensity *noun* BENT.

proper *adjective*
1. ACCURATE.
2. APPROPRIATE.
3. CONVENIENT.
4. CORRECT.
5. ETHICAL.
6. GENTEEL.

properly *adverb* FAIR.

property *noun*
1. HOLDING(S).
2. LAND.
3. QUALITY.

prophecy *noun*
Something that is foretold by or as if by supernatural means: *The priest's prophecy was that the deposed king would regain his throne.*
  Syns: cast, foretelling, oracle, vaticination, vision.

prophesier *noun* PROPHET.

prophesy *verb*
To tell about or make known (future events) by or as if by supernatural means: *prophesied the end of civilization.*
  Syns: augur, divine², foretell, soothsay, vaticinate.

prophet *noun*
A person who foretells future events by or as if by supernatural means: *When the flood came just as he predicted, the old man was revered as a prophet.*
  Syns: augur, auspex, diviner, foreteller, haruspex (*also* aruspex), prophesier, seer¹, soothsayer, sibyl.

prophetic *also* **prophetical** *adjective*
Of or relating to the foretelling of events by or as if by supernatural means: *an old fortune teller believed to have prophetic powers.*
  Syns: divinitory, fatidic (*also* fatidical), mantic, oracular, sibylline, vatic (*also* vatical), vaticinal.

prophylactic *adjective* PREVENTIVE.

propitiate *verb* PACIFY.

propitious *adjective*
1. BENEFICIAL.
2. FAVORABLE.
3. OPPORTUNE.

proportion *noun*
1. Satisfying arrangement marked by even distribution of elements, as in a design: *sculpture of excellent proportion.*
  Syns: balance, harmony, symmetry.
2. DEGREE.

proportion *verb* HARMONIZE.

proportional *adjective*
1. Properly or correspondingly related in size, amount, or scale: *Happiness is not always proportional to virtue.*
  Syns: commensurable, commensurate, proportionate. —*Idiom* in proportion.
2. SYMMETRICAL.

proportionate *adjective*
1. PROPORTIONAL.
2. SYMMETRICAL.

proportions *noun* SIZE.

proposal *noun*
1. Something that is put forward for consideration: *a daring proposal to abolish the income tax.*
  Syns: proposition, submission, suggestion.
2. OFFER.

propose *verb*
1. To advance, as an idea, for consideration: *He proposed a trip to New York.*

Syns: offer, pose, propound, put forth, submit, suggest.
2. INTEND.
proposition *noun* PROPOSAL.
propound *verb* PROPOSE.
proprieties *noun*
1. AMENITIES.
2. MANNERS.
proprietor *noun* OWNER.
proprietorship *noun*
1. OWNERSHIP.
2. POSSESSION.
propriety *noun*
1. DECENCY.
2. ETHICS.
prosaic *adjective*
1. DULL.
2. EVERYDAY.
proscenium *noun* STAGE.
proscribe *verb* FORBID.
proscription *noun* FORBIDDANCE.
prosecutable *adjective* LITIGABLE.
prosecute *verb*
1. PERFORM.
2. SUE.
3. WAGE.
prosecution *noun* PERFORMANCE.
prosopopeia also **prosopopoeia** *noun* EMBODIMENT.
prospect *noun*
1. CHANCE.
2. EXPECTATION.
3. FUTURE.
4. VIEW.
prospectus *noun* PROGRAM.
prosper *verb*
To fare well: *The aerospace industry prospered during the 1960's.*
Syns: boom, flourish, go, make out (*Slang*), score (*Informal*), thrive. —*Idioms* do (*or* fare) well, get (*or* go) somewhere, go great guns, go strong.
prospering *adjective* FLOURISHING.
prosperity *noun*
1. Steady good fortune or financial security: *a struggling small businessman's dream of prosperity.*
Syns: comfort, ease, easy street (*also* Easy Street) (*Slang*), prosperousness. —*Idioms* comfortable (*or* easy) circumstances, the good life.
2. WELFARE.
prosperous *adjective*
1. Enjoying steady good fortune or financial security: *fashionable new clothes that befit a prosperous young man.*
Syns: comfortable, easy, well-fixed

(*Informal*), well-heeled (*Slang*), well-off, well-to-do. —*Idioms* comfortably off, in clover, on easy street.
2. FLOURISHING.
3. OPPORTUNE.
prosperousness *noun* PROSPERITY.
prostitute *noun*
A woman who engages in sexual intercourse for payment: *studied the psychological profiles of prostitutes.*
Syns: bawd, call girl, camp follower, courtesan, fille de joie (*French*), harlot, hooker (*Slang*), moll (*Slang*), streetwalker, whore. —*Idioms* lady of the night, lady of pleasure, scarlet woman, soiled dove.
prostrate *verb*
1. DISABLE.
2. DROP.
3. OVERWHELM.
prostrate *adjective* FLAT.
protagonist *noun* LEAD.
protean *adjective* VERSATILE.
protect *verb* DEFEND.
protection *noun*
1. COVER.
2. DEFENSE.
protective *adjective*
1. PRESERVATIVE.
2. PREVENTIVE.
pro tem *adjective* TEMPORARY.
pro tempore *adjective* TEMPORARY.
protest *verb* OBJECT².
protest *noun* OBJECTION.
protestation *noun* OBJECTION.
protocol *noun* CEREMONY.
protoplast *noun* ORIGINAL.
prototypal *adjective* TYPICAL.
prototype *noun*
1. ANCESTOR.
2. ORIGINAL.
prototypic or **prototypical** *adjective* TYPICAL.
protract *verb* LENGTHEN.
protracted *adjective*
1. CHRONIC.
2. LONG¹.
protraction *noun* EXTENSION.
protrude *verb* BULGE.
protrusion *noun* BULGE.
protuberance *noun*
1. BULGE.
2. BUMP.
protuberate *verb* BULGE.
proud *adjective*
1. Properly valuing oneself, one's honor, or one's dignity: *Poor but proud, he would not accept charity.*

Syns: prideful, self-esteeming, self-respecting.
2. ARROGANT.
3. GLORIOUS.
4. GLAD.

prove *verb*
1. To establish as true or genuine: *He proved his identity with a birth certificate.*
   Syns: authenticate, bear out, confirm, corroborate, demonstrate, endorse, establish, show, substantiate, validate, verify.
2. EXPERIENCE.
3. TEST.
prove out *verb* WASH.
provenance *noun* ORIGIN.
provenience *noun* ORIGIN.
proverb *noun*
A usu. pithy and familiar statement expressing an observation or principle generally accepted as wise or true: *"A cat in gloves catches no mice"* is a well-known proverb.
   Syns: adage, aphorism, byword, maxim, saw, saying.
provide *verb*
1. GIVE.
2. OFFER.
provide for *verb* SUPPORT.
providence *noun* ECONOMY.
provident *adjective* ECONOMICAL.
providential *adjective* HAPPY.
province *noun*
1. AREA.
2. BEAT.
3. POSSESSION.
provincial *adjective*
1. COUNTRY.
2. LOCAL.
provision *noun*
A restricting or modifying element: *a treaty with many provisions.*
   Syns: condition, proviso, qualification, reservation, specification, stipulation, string (*Informal*), term(s).
provisional *adjective*
1. CONDITIONAL.
2. TEMPORARY.
provisionary *adjective* CONDITIONAL.
provisions *noun*
1. ARRANGEMENTS.
2. FOOD.
proviso *noun* PROVISION.
provisory *adjective* CONDITIONAL.
provocation *noun*
1. ANNOYANCE.

2. DEFIANCE.
3. STIMULUS.
provoke *verb*
1. To stir to action or feeling: *The insult provoked her to leave abruptly. His carelessness often provoked her to anger.*
   Syns: arouse, egg on, excite, galvanize, goad, impel, incite, inflame, innerve, inspire, instigate, kindle, motivate, move, pique, rouse, spur, stimulate, work up.
2. ANGER.
3. ANNOY.
4. COURT.
5. GENERATE.
provoking *adjective* VEXATIOUS.
prowess *noun*
1. DEXTERITY.
2. HEROISM.
prowl *verb* SNEAK.
proximate *adjective*
1. CLOSE¹.
2. MOMENTARY.
prude *noun*
A person who is too much concerned with being proper, modest, or righteous: *prudes who read the most improper ideas into the most innocent words.*
   Syns: bluenose, Mrs. Grundy, old maid, puritan, Victorian.
prudence *noun*
1. The exercise of good judgment or common sense in practical matters: *showed a good deal of prudence when she chose the shop.*
   Syns: caution, circumspection, foresight, forethought, precaution.
2. ECONOMY.
prudent *adjective*
1. ECONOMICAL.
2. SANE.
3. WARY.
prudish *adjective* GENTEEL.
prurience also **pruriency** *noun* DESIRE.
prurient *adjective* EROTIC.
pry *verb* SNOOP.
pryer *noun* SEE **prier**.
prying *adjective* CURIOUS.
  prying *noun* CURIOSITY.
pseudo *adjective* COUNTERFEIT.
pseudonymic *adjective* ASSUMED.
pseudonymous *adjective* ASSUMED.
psyche *noun*
1. PSYCHOLOGY.
2. SPIRIT.
psychic also **psychical** *adjective* MENTAL.

psychological *adjective* MENTAL.
psychology *noun*
The thought processes characteristic of an individual or group: *A good detective tries to understand the psychology of the criminal.*
  Syns: ethos, mentality, mind, psyche.
  —*Idioms* mind set, what makes someone tick.
psychopathy *noun* INSANITY.
public *adjective*
1. Of, concerning, or affecting the community or the people: *the public good.*
  Syns: civic, civil, national.
2. COMMON.
3. OPEN.
4. POPULAR.
public *noun*
1. Persons as an organized body: *rights and freedoms guaranteed to the public.*
  Syns: community, people, society.
2. The body of persons who admire a public personality, esp. an entertainer: *His public demanded an encore from the singer.*
  Syns: audience, fans (*Informal*), following.
3. COMMONALTY.
publication *noun*
1. The act or process of publishing printed matter: *The publication of a newly discovered piece by Mozart is a major event.*
  Syns: issue, printing, publishing.
2. An issue of printed material offered for sale or distribution: *a new publication on the breeding habits of wild deer.*
  Syns: opus, title, volume, work.
3. ANNOUNCEMENT.
publicity *noun*
1. ADVERTISING.
2. PROMOTION.
publicize *verb*
1. ADVERTISE.
2. PROMOTE.
publish *verb*
1. To present for circulation, exhibit, or sale: *published a new one-volume edition.*
  Syns: bring out, issue, put out.
2. To be the author of (a published work or works): *She published a biography of Marx.*
  Syns: author, pen[1], write.
3. ANNOUNCE.
publishing *noun* PUBLICATION.
puddle *verb* MESS AROUND at **mess**.
puddy *adjective* PLUMP[1].

pudgy *adjective* PLUMP[1].
puerile *adjective* CHILDISH.
puff *verb*
1. BLOW[1].
2. PANT.
3. PROMOTE.
puff *noun* PULL.
puffed-up *adjective* POMPOUS.
puffery *noun* PROMOTION.
puffy *adjective* POMPOUS.
pugnacious *adjective* BELLIGERENT.
pugnaciousness *noun* FIGHT.
pugnacity *noun*
1. BELLIGERENCE.
2. FIGHT.
puissance *noun* ENERGY.
puissant *adjective*
1. POWERFUL.
2. STRONG.
pulchritudinous *adjective* BEAUTIFUL.
pule *verb* WHINE.
pull *verb*
1. To exert force so as to move something toward the source of the force: *The boy pulled her hair. Everyone pulled on the rope.*
  Syns: drag, draw, haul, tow, tug.
2. To remove from a fixed position: *pull a tooth.*
  Syns: evulse, extract, pluck, tear[1].
3. ATTRACT.
pull down *verb*
1. DESTROY.
2. EARN.
pull in *verb*
1. ARRIVE.
2. RESTRAIN.
pull off *verb*
1. COMMIT.
2. PERFORM.
pull on *verb* DON.
pull out *verb* GO.
pull through *verb* SURVIVE.
pull *noun*
1. The action or process of pulling: *gave the cord a pull.*
  Syns: jerk, tug.
2. The act of drawing or pulling a load: *increased the pull of the tractor by shifting gears.*
  Syns: draft, draw, haul, traction.
3. An inhalation, as of a cigar, pipe, or cigarette: *took a pull on his meerschaum.*
  Syns: drag (*Informal*), draw, hit (*Slang*), puff.
4. ATTRACTION.
5. DRINK.
6. INFLUENCE.

pullback *noun* RETREAT.
pullout *noun* RETREAT.
pullulate *verb* TEEM[1].
pulp *verb* CRUSH.
pulpous *adjective* SOFT.
pulpy *adjective* SOFT.
pulsate *verb* BEAT.
pulsating *adjective* RHYTHMICAL.
pulsation *noun* BEAT.
pulse *noun* BEAT.
 pulse *verb* BEAT.
pulverize *verb*
 1. CRUSH.
 2. DESTROY.
pulverous *adjective* FINE[1].
pulverulent *adjective* FINE[1].
pummel *verb* BEAT.
pump *verb* DRAIN.
punch *noun*
 1. DRIVE.
 2. KICK.
 3. WALLOP.
punctilio *noun* DETAIL.
punctilious *adjective* CEREMONIOUS.
punctual *adjective*
 Occurring, acting, or performed exactly
 at the time appointed: *a punctual
 arrival.*
 Syns: prompt, timely. —*Idioms* on
  the dot, on time.
punctuate *verb* POINT.
puncture *verb*
 1. BREACH.
 2. DISCREDIT.
 3. PENETRATE.
 puncture *noun* PRICK.
pundit *noun* SAGE.
pungent *adjective*
 1. Affecting the organs of taste or smell
  with a strong and often harsh
  sensation: *a pungent smell; a pungent
  flavor.*
  Syns: piquant, poignant (*Archaic*),
  sharp.
 2. BITING.
punish *verb*
 1. To subject (one) to a penalty for a
  wrong: *punished them for playing
  hooky.*
  Syns: correct, discipline.
 2. CONSUME.
punishing *adjective*
 Inflicting or aiming to inflict
 punishment: *took punishing action
 against the rebels.*
 Syns: disciplinary, punitive, punitory.
punishment *noun*
 A penalty imposed for wrongdoing: *The

punishment for armed robbery is a prison
term.*
 Syns: correction, discipline, punition.
punition *noun* PUNISHMENT.
punitive *adjective* PUNISHING.
punitory *adjective* PUNISHING.
punk *noun* TOUGH.
puny *adjective*
 1. INFIRM.
 2. MEAGER.
pup *noun* SQUIRT.
pupil *noun* STUDENT.
puppet *noun* PAWN[2].
puppy *noun* SQUIRT.
purblind *adjective* BLIND.
purchasable *adjective* CORRUPTIBLE.
purchase *verb*
 1. BUY.
 2. CORRUPT.
 purchase *noun* BUY.
purchaser *noun* PATRON.
pure *adjective*
 1. Free from extraneous elements: *pure
  brilliance; pure necessity; pure gold.*
  Syns: absolute, perfect, plain, sheer[2],
  unadulterated, undiluted, unmixed.
 2. CHASTE.
 3. INNOCENT.
 4. STRAIGHT.
 5. UTTER[2].
 pure *verb* PURIFY.
 pure *adverb* VERY.
pureblooded *adjective*
 THOROUGHBRED.
purebred *adjective* THOROUGHBRED.
purely *adverb*
 Without exception; in its entirety: *Any
 such resemblance is purely coincidental.*
 Syns: all, altogether, just, quite,
 utterly, wholly. —*Idioms* in all, in
 toto.
pureness *noun* PURITY.
purgation *noun*
 1. ELIMINATION.
 2. PURIFICATION.
purgative *adjective*
 1. Serving to purify of sin: *Confession is
  a purgative rite in the Russian Church.*
  Syns: expiative, expiatory,
  expurgatory (*also* expurgatorial),
  lustral, lustrative, lustratory,
  purgatorial, purifying.
 2. ELIMINATIVE.
purgatorial *adjective* PURGATIVE.
purge *verb*
 1. CLEAR.
 2, 3. ELIMINATE.
 4. PURIFY.
 purge *noun* ELIMINATION.

purificant *noun* PURIFIER.
purification *noun*
1. The act or process of removing physical impurities: *water purification.*
   Syns: clarification, cleaning, cleansing.
2. A freeing from sin, guilt, or defilement: *purification of mind and soul through confession.*
   Syns: catharsis, cleansing, expurgation, lustration, purgation.
purificator *noun* PURIFIER.
purified *adjective* REFINED.
purifier *noun*
Something that purifies: *Water purifiers are needed in some places.*
   Syns: cleaner, cleanser, purificant, purificator.
purify *verb*
1. To free from sin, guilt, or defilement: *prayed that her soul would be purified.*
   Syns: cleanse, expurgate, lustrate, pure (*Obs.*), purge.
2. REFINE.
purifying *adjective* PURGATIVE.
puritan *noun* PRUDE.
puritanical *adjective* GENTEEL.
purity *noun*
1. The condition of being clean and free of contaminants: *tested the purity of the town's water supply.*
   Syns: clarity, cleanliness, cleanness, pureness, taintlessness.
2. CHASTITY.
purloin *verb* STEAL.
purloiner *noun* LARCENER.
purloining *noun* LARCENY.
purport *noun*
1. IDEA.
2. IMPORT.
3. MEANING.
4. THRUST.
purpose *noun*
1. FUNCTION.
2. INTENTION.
purpose *verb* INTEND.
purposeless *adjective*
1. AIMLESS.
2. MINDLESS.
3. RANDOM.
pursual *noun* PURSUIT.
pursuance *noun* PURSUIT.
pursue *verb*
1. To follow (another) with the intent of overtaking and capturing: *The police pursued the armed robbers across town.*
   Syns: chase, run after. —*Idioms* be (*or* go) in hot pursuit, give chase.
2. COURT.

3. FOLLOW.
4. FOLLOW UP at **follow.**
5. LEAD.
6. PRACTICE.
pursuing *noun* PURSUIT.
pursuit *noun*
1. The following of another in an attempt to overtake and capture: *in pursuit of the hijackers.*
   Syn: chase. —*Idiom* hot pursuit.
2. An attempting to accomplish or attain: *life, liberty, and the pursuit of happiness.*
   Syns: pursual, pursuance, pursuing, quest, search.
3. BUSINESS.
4. PRACTICE.
purview *noun*
1. KEN.
2. RANGE.
push *verb*
1. To do or achieve by forcing obstacles out of one's way: *pushed his way through the crowd; pushed energy legislation through Congress.*
   Syns: bulldoze (*Slang*), press, ram, shoulder, shove.
2. *Slang.* To engage in the illicit sale of (narcotics): *pushing heroin on the street.*
   Syns: deal, peddle, shove.
3. ADVERTISE.
4. BEAR.
5. CROWD.
6. DRIVE.
7. MUSCLE.
8. POKE.
push off *verb* GO.
push on *verb* GO.
push *noun*
1. An act or instance of using force so as to propel ahead: *gave him a quick push off the diving board.*
   Syns: butt¹, prod, shove, thrust.
2. AMBITION.
3, 4. DRIVE.
5. STIMULUS.
pusher *noun*
Slang. A person who sells narcotics illegally: *heroin and cocaine pushers.*
   Syns: candyman (*Slang*), dealer.
pushover *noun*
1. BREEZE.
2. DUPE.
3. RUNAWAY.
pushy *adjective*
1. AGGRESSIVE.
2. PRESUMPTUOUS.
pusillanimity *noun* COWARDICE.
pusillanimous *adjective* COWARDLY.

puss *noun*
1. FACE.
2. MOUTH.
pussyfoot *verb*
1. EQUIVOCATE.
2. SNEAK.
pussyfooting *adjective* EVASIVE.
put *verb*
1. AIR.
2. ASK.
3. BET.
4. ESTIMATE.
5. IMPOSE.
6. PHRASE.
7. POSITION.
8. SET¹.
9. TRANSLATE.
put away *verb*
1. CONSUME.
2. MURDER.
put by *verb* SAVE.
put down *verb* SUPPRESS.
put forth *verb*
1. BROACH.
2. PROPOSE.
put in *verb*
1. APPLY.
2. ENTER.
3. SERVE.
4. SPEND.
put on *verb*
1. ACT.
2. ASSUME.
3. DON.
4. STAGE.
put out *verb*
1. EMBARRASS.
2. EXERCISE.
3. EXTINGUISH.
4. INCONVENIENCE.
5. PUBLISH.
put through *verb* EFFECT.
put to *verb* CLOSE¹.
put together *verb* MAKE.
put up *verb*
1. BUILD.
2. CONSERVE.
3. ERECT.
4. HARBOR.
putative *adjective* REPUTED.
put-on *noun* FAÇADE.
put-out *adjective* EMBARRASSED.
putrefaction *noun* DECAY.
putrefy *verb* DECAY.
putresce *verb* DECAY.
putrescence *noun* DECAY.
putrid *adjective*
1. BAD.
2. MOLDY.

putridness *noun* DECAY.
putter *verb*
1. FIDDLE.
2. FUSS.
3. MESS AROUND at **mess.**
puzzle *noun* MYSTERY.
 puzzle out *verb* BREAK.
puzzlement *noun* MYSTERY.
puzzler *noun* MYSTERY.
pygmy also **pigmy** *adjective* TINY.
pyramid *noun* HEAP.
pyretic *adjective* HOT.
pythonic *adjective* GIANT.

Q

quack *noun* FAKE.
quad *noun* COURT.
quadrangle *noun* COURT.
quadrate *adjective* SQUARE.
 quadrate *verb* AGREE.
quaff *verb* DRINK.
 quaff *noun* DRINK.
quag *noun* SWAMP.
quaggy *adjective* SOFT.
quagmire *noun*
1. PREDICAMENT.
2. SWAMP.
quail *verb* FLINCH.
quaint¹ *adjective*
1. Agreeably curious, esp. in an old-
fashioned or unusual way: *an old
house with quaint, meandering
stairways.*
 Syns: funny, odd, oddball (*Informal*).
2. ECCENTRIC.
quaint² *verb* ACQUAINT.
quake *verb*
1, 2. SHAKE.
 quake *noun* TREMOR.
quaking *adjective* TREMULOUS.
quaky *adjective* TREMULOUS.
qualification *noun*
1. The quality or state of being eligible:
*His qualification for the senate is
unquestioned.*
 Syns: eligibility, eligibleness, fitness,
suitableness.
2. PROVISION.
qualified *adjective*
1. Not total, unlimited, or

wholehearted: *a qualified plan for expansion.*
   Syns: limited, modified, reserved, restricted.
2. ABLE.
3. CONDITIONAL.
4. ELIGIBLE.
5. EQUAL.
qualify *verb*
1. AUTHORIZE.
2. DISTINGUISH.
quality *noun*
1. A distinctive element: *Honesty is her finest quality.*
   Syns: affection², attribute, character, characteristic, feature, mark, peculiarity, property, savor, trait.
2. Degree of excellence: *yard goods of low quality.*
   Syns: caliber, class, grade.
3. CLASS.
4. MERIT.
5. SOCIETY.
   quality *adjective* EXCELLENT.
qualm *noun*
A feeling of uncertainty about the fitness or correctness of an action: *I had qualms about passing on the story.*
   Syns: compunction, misgiving, reservation, scruple.
quantity *noun*
1. A measurable whole: *a large quantity of coal; a small quantity of evidence.*
   Syns: amount, body, budget, bulk, corpus, quantum.
2. DEAL.
quantum *noun*
1. ALLOTMENT.
2. QUANTITY.
quarrel *noun* ARGUMENT.
   quarrel *verb* ARGUE.
quarrelsome *adjective*
1. ARGUMENTATIVE.
2. BELLIGERENT.
quarter *noun*
1. One of four equal parts of something: *Each took a quarter of the profit.*
   Syn: quartern.
2. AREA.
3. NEIGHBORHOOD.
   quarter *verb* HARBOR.
quarterage *noun* SHELTER.
quartern *noun* QUARTER.
quash *verb* SUPPRESS.
quashing *noun* REPRESSION.
quaver *verb* SHAKE.
   quaver *noun* TREMOR.
queer *adjective*
1. ECCENTRIC.
2. FUNNY.

quell *verb* SUPPRESS.
quench *verb*
1. EXTINGUISH.
2. REPRESS.
3. SUPPRESS.
quenching *noun* REPRESSION.
querier *noun* INQUIRER.
querulent *adjective* IRRITABLE.
querulous *adjective*
1. ILL-TEMPERED.
2. IRRITABLE.
query *noun* INQUIRY.
   query *verb* ASK.
quest *noun*
1. INQUIRY.
2. PURSUIT.
   quest *verb* SEEK.
question *noun*
1. DOUBT.
2. INQUIRY.
3. PROBLEM.
   question *verb*
1. ASK.
2. DOUBT.
questionable *adjective*
1. AMBIGUOUS.
2. DEBATABLE.
3. DOUBTFUL.
4. SHADY.
questioner *noun*
1. INQUIRER.
2. INQUISITOR.
questioning *adjective*
1. CURIOUS.
2. INCREDULOUS.
questioningly *adverb* SKEPTICALLY.
queue *noun* LINE.
quibble *verb*
1. To raise unnecessary or trivial objections: *always quibbling about the silliest things.*
   Syns: carp, cavil, niggle, nit-pick (*Informal*), pettifog. —*Idiom* pick to pieces.
2. ARGUE.
quick *adjective*
1. Accomplished in very little time: *a quick visit.*
   Syns: brief, fast, flying, hasty, hurried, speedy.
2. FAST.
3. NIMBLE.
   quick *noun* CENTER.
   quick *adverb* FAST.
quicken *verb*
1. To make alive: *Sun and showers quicken plants.*
   Syns: animate, enliven, liven, vivify.
2. SPEED UP at **speed**.

quickening *adjective* STIMULATING.
quickness *noun*
1. AGILITY.
2. SPEED.
quick-tempered *adjective* TESTY.
quick-witted *adjective* CLEVER.
quidnunc *noun*
1. GOSSIP.
2. MEDDLER.
quiescence also **quiescency** *noun*
ABEYANCE.
quiescent *adjective* LATENT.
quiet *adjective*
1. Not showy or obtrusive: *a room
   decorated in a quiet, pleasing style.*
   Syns: inobtrusive, restrained,
   subdued, tasteful, unobtrusive.
2. SILENT.
3. SOFT.
4. STILL.
quiet *noun*
1. SILENCE.
2. STILLNESS.
quiet *verb*
1. CALM.
2. SILENCE.
quiet *adverb* STILL.
quieten *verb* SILENCE.
quietness *noun* SILENCE.
quietude *noun* SILENCE.
quietus *noun* DEATH.
quintessence *noun*
1. ESSENCE.
2. HEART.
quintessential *adjective* TYPICAL.
quintessential *noun* ESSENCE.
quip *noun*
1. CRACK.
2. JOKE.
quirk *noun* ECCENTRICITY.
quirky *adjective* ECCENTRIC.
quit *verb*
1. To relinquish one's engagement in or
   occupation with: *quit his job; quit
   drinking.*
   Syns: leave[1], resign, terminate.
2, 3. ABANDON.
4. ACT.
5. GO.
6. STOP.
quit *adjective* EVEN[1].
quitclaim *noun* ABDICATION.
quitclaim *verb* ABDICATE.
quite *adverb*
1. COMPLETELY.
2. CONSIDERABLY.
3. PURELY.
quittance *noun* COMPENSATION.
quiver *verb* SHAKE.
quiver *noun* TREMOR.

quivering *adjective* TREMULOUS.
quivery *adjective* TREMULOUS.
quixotic *adjective* IDEALISTIC.
quiz *verb*
1. ASK.
2. RIDICULE.
quiz *noun*
1. CHARACTER.
2. TEST.
quodlibetic *adjective* PEDANTIC.
quondam *adjective* LATE.
quota *noun* ALLOTMENT.
quotidian *adjective* EVERYDAY.

R

rabble *noun* TRASH[1].
rabid *adjective*
1. EXTREME.
2. FRANTIC.
3. FURIOUS.
race *noun*
1. CHARGE.
2. COMPETITION.
race *verb* RUSH.
rack *verb*
1. AFFLICT.
2. TORTURE.
racket *noun*
1. BUSINESS.
2. NOISE.
racy *adjective*
Bordering on indelicacy or impropriety:
shocked the ladies by telling a racy story.
   Syns: blue, broad, dubious, off-color,
   risqué, salty, scabrous, spicy,
   suggestive.
radiance *noun*
1. FIRE.
2. GLOW.
radiant *adjective* BRIGHT.
radiate *verb*
1. BEAM.
2. SHED.
3. SPREAD.
radical *adjective*
1. Arising from or going to the root or
   source: *radical differences that can
   make activism and reason
   incompatible.*
   Syns: basal, basic, bottom,

foundational, fundamental, original, primary, underlying.
2. EXTREME.
radical *noun* EXTREMIST.
rag *verb* JOKE.
ragamuffin *noun* TATTERDEMALION.
rage *noun*
1. ENTHUSIASM.
2. FASHION.
3. FURY.
rage *verb* ANGER.
ragged *adjective*
1. ROUGH.
2. TATTERED.
raggedy *adjective* TATTERED.
raging *adjective*
1. FURIOUS.
2. ROUGH.
rags *noun* TATTERS.
ragtag also **ragtag and bobtail** *noun* TRASH[1].
raid *noun* INVASION.
raid *verb*
1. To make a surprise attack on: *Apaches raided the outpost to discourage further expansion.*
   Syns: harass, harry, maraud.
2. INVADE.
rail at (or **against**) *verb* REVILE.
railing *noun* VITUPERATION.
raiment *noun* DRESS.
rain *verb* SHOWER.
rainbow *noun* ILLUSION.
rainless *adjective* DRY.
raise *verb*
1. To increase in amount: *raised prices; raised my rent.*
   Syns: boost, hike, increase, jack (up), jump, up.
2. AROUSE.
3. ASK.
4. BRING UP at **bring**.
5. BROACH.
6. BUILD.
7, 8. ELEVATE.
9. ERECT.
10. GROW.
11. PROMOTE.
raise *noun* INCREASE.
raised *adjective*
1, 2. ELEVATED.
3. ERECT.
rake[1] *noun* WANTON.
rake[2] *verb* INCLINE.
rakehell *adjective* FAST.
rakish *adjective* FAST.
rally *verb*
1. MOBILIZE.
2. RECOVER.
rally *noun* RECOVERY.

ram *verb*
1. To cause to penetrate with force: *rammed the bayonet into the target.*
   Syns: dig, drive, plunge, run, sink, stab, stick, thrust.
2. DRIVE.
3. PUSH.
ramble *verb*
1. ROVE.
2. STROLL.
ramble *noun* WALK.
ramify *verb* BRANCH.
rampage *noun* BINGE.
ramshackle *adjective* RUINOUS.
rancor *noun* RESENTMENT.
rancorous *adjective* RESENTFUL.
random *adjective*
1. Having no particular pattern, purpose, organization, or structure: *a random selection of his writings; random ideas; random acquaintanceships.*
   Syns: desultory, haphazard, hit-or-miss, indiscriminate, objectless, purposeless, spot, stray, unconsidered, unplanned.
2. ARBITRARY.
range *noun*
1. An area within which something or someone exists, acts, or has influence or power: *Extra fuel tanks greatly extend a bomber's range. The range of his mind was limited.*
   Syns: ambit, compass, extension, extent, orbit, purview, reach, realm, scope, sphere, sweep.
2. GRASP.
3. KEN.
4. NEIGHBORHOOD.
range *verb*
1. ARRANGE.
2. GO.
3. LINE.
4. ROVE.
rangy *adjective* GANGLING.
rank[1] *noun*
1. CLASS.
2. LINE.
3. PLACE.
rank *verb*
1. ARRANGE.
2. CLASS.
rank[2] *adjective*
1. FLAGRANT.
2. MOLDY.
3. OBSCENE.
4. THICK.
rankness *noun* FLAGRANCY.

ransack *verb*
1. LOOT.
2. SCOUR.

rant *verb*
To speak in a loud, pompous, or prolonged manner: *ranted on and on about capital punishment.*
   Syns: bloviate, harangue, mouth, perorate, rave.

ranting *adjective* FURIOUS.

rap¹ *verb*
1. BLAME.
2. CALL DOWN at **call**.
3. TAP¹.

rap out *verb* EXCLAIM.

rap *noun*
1. CONFERENCE.
2. SENTENCE.
3. TAP¹.

rap² *noun* DAMN.

rapacious *adjective*
1. GREEDY.
2. VORACIOUS.

rapacity *noun*
1. GREED.
2. VORACITY.

rape *verb*
1. To compel (another) to participate in or submit to a sexual act: *Enemy soldiers pillaged the town and raped the women.*
   Syns: assault, force, outrage, ravish, violate.
2. SACK².

rapid *adjective* FAST.

rapidity *noun*
1. HASTE.
2. SPEED.

rapport *noun*
1. AGREEMENT.
2. HARMONY.

rapprochement *noun*
RECONCILIATION.

rapt *adjective* ABSORBED.

rapture *noun* HEAVEN.

rare *adjective*
1. Far beyond what is usual, normal, or customary: *a touch of rare wit.*
   Syns: exceptional, extraordinary, remarkable, singular, uncommon, unusual.
2. INFREQUENT.
3. THIN.

rarefied *adjective* THIN.

rarefy *verb* THIN.

rarely *adverb* INFREQUENTLY.

raring *adjective* EAGER.

rascal *noun* MISCHIEF.

rash¹ *adjective*
1. Characterized by unthinking boldness and haste: *rash judgments.*
   Syns: brash, foolhardy, harum-scarum, hasty, headlong, hotheaded, impetuous, impulsive, mad-brained, madcap, mad-headed, precipitant, precipitate, precipitous, reckless, slap-bang (*Informal*), slapdash, temerarious.
2. PRECIPITATE.

rash² *noun* OUTBREAK.

rashness *noun*
1. HASTE.
2. TEMERITY.

rasp *verb* SCRAPE.

raspberry *noun* HISS.

rasping *adjective* HARSH.

raspy *adjective* HARSH.

rat *verb*
1. BETRAY.
2. DEFECT.
3. INFORM.

rat *noun*
1. BETRAYER.
2. DEFECTOR.
3. INFORMER.

rate¹ *verb*
1. CLASS.
2. EARN.
3. ESTIMATE.

rate² *verb* BAWL OUT at **bawl**.

rather *adverb* FAIRLY.

ratification *noun* CONFIRMATION.

ratify *verb* CONFIRM.

ratiocinate *verb* THINK.

ratiocination *noun* LOGIC.

ratiocinative *adjective* LOGICAL.

ration *noun* ALLOTMENT.

rational *adjective*
1. LOGICAL.
2, 3. SANE.

rationale *noun*
1. ACCOUNT.
2. SENSE.

rationality *noun*
1. LOGIC.
2. SENSE.

rationalization *noun* ACCOUNT.

rationalize *verb*
1. ACCOUNT FOR at **account**.
2. JUSTIFY.

rattle *verb*
1. To make or cause to make a succession of short, sharp sounds: *an old refrigerator that rattles; wind rattling the shutters.*
   Syns: brattle (*Chiefly Scot.*), chatter, clack, clatter, clitter.

2. CHATTER.
3. EMBARRASS.
rattled *adjective* EMBARRASSED.
ratty *adjective*
1. ILL-TEMPERED.
2. SHABBY.
3. TESTY.
raucous *adjective* HARSH.
raunchiness *noun* OBSCENITY.
raunchy *adjective* OBSCENE.
ravage *verb*
1. DEVASTATE.
2. SACK².
ravaging *adjective* CONSUMPTIVE.
rave *verb*
1. ENTHUSE.
2. RANT.
ravel *verb* COMPLICATE.
ravenous *adjective*
1. Desiring or craving food: *The smells of cooking made us ravenous. Ravenous wild dogs ran down and ate the deer.*
   Syns: famished, hungry, starving.
2. GREEDY.
3. VORACIOUS.
ravenousness *noun* VORACITY.
raving *adjective* FURIOUS.
ravish *verb* RAPE.
ravishing *adjective* BEAUTIFUL.
raw *adjective*
1. Not cooked: *loves to munch on raw carrots.*
   Syn: uncooked.
2. COARSE.
3. CRUDE.
4. INEXPERIENCED.
5. OBSCENE.
6. RUDE.
rawboned *adjective* THIN.
ray *noun* BEAM.
raze *verb* DESTROY.
razz *noun* HISS.
razz *verb*
1. JOKE.
2. RIDICULE.
razzing *noun* RIDICULE.
reach *verb*
1. To extend, esp. an appendage: *reached out her hand to the child.*
   Syns: outstretch, stretch (out).
2. To succeed in communicating with: *Where can we reach you?*
   Syns: contact (*Informal*), get.
   —*Idioms* get hold of, get in touch with, get through to, get to.
3. ACCOMPLISH.
4. AMOUNT.
5. ARRIVE.
6. EXTEND.

reach *noun*
1. EXPANSE.
2. EXTENT.
3. GRASP.
4. KEN.
5. RANGE.
react *verb* RESPOND.
react to *verb* GREET.
reaction *noun*
1. BEHAVIOR.
2. RESPONSE.
reactionary *also* **reactionist** *adjective*
1. Vehemently, often fanatically opposing progress or reform: *a reactionary backlash to progressive reforms.*
   Syns: die-hard (*also* diehard), ultraconservative.
2. UNPROGRESSIVE.
reactionary *also* **reactionist** *noun*
A person who vehemently, often fanatically opposes progress and favors return to a previous condition: *a reactionary who clung to a belief in the monarchy.*
   Syns: die-hard (*also* diehard), mossback, royalist, ultraconservative.
reactivate *verb* REVIVE.
read *verb*
1. INTERPRET.
2. SHOW.
3. UNDERSTAND.
readiness *noun*
1. DEXTERITY.
2. EASE.
3. PREPARATION.
reading *noun* INTERPRETATION.
ready *adjective*
1. In a state of preparedness: *All systems are ready for liftoff.*
   Syns: go (*Informal*), prepared, primed, set¹, together (*Slang*).
   —*Idioms* all set, booted and spurred, in harness, in the saddle, in working order.
2. EASY.
3. GLAD.
4. SMOOTH.
ready *verb*
1. GIRD.
2, 3. PREPARE.
real *adjective*
1. Having actual reality: *real evidence; real, not imaginary fears.*
   Syns: concrete, substantial, substantive, tangible.
2. ACTUAL.
3. AUTHENTIC.
4. GENUINE.

realistic *adjective*
1. Accurately representing what is depicted or described: *a realistic novel.*
   Syns: lifelike, natural, naturalistic, true-to-life, truthful.
2. Having or indicating an awareness of things as they really are: *realistic about his chances of winning; a realistic evaluation of the company's financial posture.*
   Syns: down-to-earth, hard, hard-boiled, hard-eyed, hardheaded, matter-of-fact, objective, practic, practical, pragmatic (*also* pragmatical), sober, tough-minded, unromantic.
3. GRAPHIC.

reality *noun*
1, 2. ACTUALITY.

realization *noun*
1. EFFECT.
2. FULFILLMENT.
3. INTERPRETATION.

realize *verb*
1. To make real or actual: *By running the marathon she realized a lifelong dream.*
   Syns: actualize, materialize. —*Idioms* bring to pass, carry into effect, carry out (*or* through).
2. ACCOMPLISH.
3. BRING.
4. RETURN.

really *adverb*
1. In truth: *The walls really shook with his bellowing.*
   Syns: absolutely, actually, fairly, indeed, positively, verily (*Archaic*). —*Idiom* for fair.
2. ACTUALLY.

realm *noun*
1. AREA.
2. RANGE.

realness *noun* AUTHENTICITY.

ream *noun* HEAP.

reanimation *noun* REVIVAL.

reap *verb*
1. GATHER.
2. GLEAN.

reaping *noun* HARVEST.

reappear *verb* RECUR.

reappearance *noun* RECURRENCE.

rear[1] *noun*
1. BACK.
2. BOTTOM.
3. TAIL.

rear *adjective* BACK.

rear[2] *verb*
1. BRING UP at **bring**.

2. BUILD.
3. ERECT.

rearmost *adjective* LAST[1].

rearward *adverb*
1. BACK.
2. BACKWARD.

rearward *noun* BACK.

reason *noun*
1. A fact or circumstance that gives logical support to an assertion, claim, or proposal: *What are your reasons for voting as you did?*
   Syns: argument, ground, proof, wherefore, why.
2. ACCOUNT.
3. ARGUMENT.
4. BASIS.
5, 6. CAUSE.
7. LOGIC.
8. SANITY.
9. SENSE.

reason *verb*
To use the faculty of reason: *Man's capacity to reason sets him apart from other animals.*
   Syns: cogitate, deliberate, think.

reasonable *adjective*
1. CONSERVATIVE.
2. LOGICAL.
3. MODERATE.
4. POPULAR.
5. SANE.

reassume *verb* RESUME.

reawaken *verb* REVIVE.

rebate *noun* DEDUCTION.

rebate *verb* DECREASE.

rebel *verb*
To refuse allegiance to and oppose by force a government or ruling authority: *rebelled against the military government.*
   Syns: insurrect, mutineer (*Archaic*), mutinize (*Archaic*), mutiny, revolt, rise (up).

rebel *noun*
A person who rebels: *Dozens of rebels have been jailed by the regime.*
   Syns: insurgent, insurrectionist, mutineer.

rebellion *noun*
Organized opposition intended to change or overthrow existing authority: *a left-wing rebellion against the dictator.*
   Syns: insurgence, insurgency, insurrection, mutiny, revolt, uprising.

rebellious *adjective*
In open revolt against a government or ruling authority: *rebellious mobs barricading the streets.*
   Syns: insurgent, mutinous.

rebirth *noun*
1. CONVERSION.
2. REVIVAL.
rebound *verb*
1. BACKFIRE.
2. BOUNCE.
3. ECHO.
4. RECOIL.
rebound *noun*
1. BOUNCE.
2. ECHO.
rebuff *noun* SNUB.
rebuff *verb* SNUB.
rebuild *verb* RESTORE.
rebuke *noun*
Words expressive of strong disapproval:
*The neighbor's rebuke took him by
surprise.*
Syns: admonishment, admonition,
chiding, reprimand, reproach,
upbraiding.
rebuke *verb*
1. CALL DOWN at **call.**
2. CORRECT.
rebut *verb* REFUTE.
recalcitrance or **recalcitrancy** *noun*
1. DEFIANCE.
2. UNRULINESS.
recalcitrant *adjective*
1. DEFIANT.
2. UNRULY.
recalcitrate *verb* CONTEST.
recall *verb*
1. LIFT.
2. REMEMBER.
3. RETRACT.
recall *noun* MEMORY.
recant *verb* RETRACT.
recantation *noun* RETRACTION.
recanting *noun* RETRACTION.
recap *noun* SUMMARY.
recap *verb* REVIEW.
recapitulation *noun* SUMMARY.
recede *verb*
To move back or away from a point,
limit, or mark: *The flood waters receded;
His hairline is receding.*
Syns: ebb, retract, retreat, retrocede,
retrograde, retrogress.
receivable *adjective* DUE.
receive *verb*
1. To admit to one's possession,
presence, or awareness: *received
visitors graciously; received a present
from an admirer; received instructions.*
Syns: accept, take.
2. ACCEPT.
received *adjective*
1. ACCEPTED.
2. ORTHODOX.

recently *adverb*
1. JUST.
2. LATE.
receptive *adjective*
1. Ready and willing to receive
favorably, as new ideas: *The new
symphony was played to a receptive
audience.*
Syns: acceptant, acceptive, amenable,
open, open-minded, responsive.
2. SENSORY.
receptivity *noun* APPRECIATION.
recess *noun* BREAK.
recess *verb* BREAK.
recession *noun* DEPRESSION.
recidivate *verb* RELAPSE.
recidivation *noun* LAPSE.
recidivism *noun* LAPSE.
reciprocal *adjective* MUTUAL.
reciprocate *verb*
1. To give or take mutually: *She
reciprocated his affection. He accepts
invitations and never reciprocates.*
Syns: requite, return.
2. RETALIATE.
reciprocation *noun* RETALIATION.
reciprocative *adjective* MUTUAL.
recite *verb* DESCRIBE.
reckless *adjective*
1. IRRESPONSIBLE.
2. PRECIPITATE.
3. RASH[1].
recklessness *noun* TEMERITY.
reckon *verb*
1. CALCULATE.
2. COUNT.
3. ESTIMATE.
4. REGARD.
5. SUPPOSE.
reckon on (or **upon**) *verb* DEPEND ON
at **depend.**
reckoning *noun*
1. ACCOUNT.
2. CALCULATION.
3. COUNT.
reclaim *verb*
1. RESCUE.
2. RESTORE.
3. RESUME.
recline *verb*
1. LIE[1].
2. REST[1].
recluse *adjective* SECLUDED.
recluse *verb* SECLUDE.
reclusion *noun* SECLUSION.
recognition *noun*
Favorable notice, as of an achievement:
finally received full recognition as a tenor.
Syns: acknowledgment (*also*
acknowledgement), credit.

recognize *verb*
1. To perceive to be identical with something held in the memory: *recognized his voice even over the telephone.*
   Syn: know.
2. ACKNOWLEDGE.
3. PLACE.

recoil *verb*
1. To jerk backward, as a gun upon firing: *Stand back when the cannon recoils.*
   Syns: rebound, ricochet.
2. FLINCH.

recollect *verb* REMEMBER.

recollection *noun*
1, 2. MEMORY.

recommence *verb* CONTINUE.

recommend *verb*
1. ADVISE.
2. COMPLIMENT.

recommendable *adjective* ADVISABLE.

recommendation *noun*
1. ADVICE.
2. REFERENCE.

recompense *verb*
1. COMPENSATE.
2. PAY.

recompense *noun*
1. COMPENSATION.
2. DUE.

reconcile *verb*
1. To re-establish friendship between: *reconciling old enemies.*
   Syns: conciliate, reunite. —*Idiom* heal the breach.
2. To bring (oneself) to accept: *reconciled herself to the loss of her friend.*
   Syn: resign.
3. ADAPT.
4. HARMONIZE.
5. SETTLE.

reconcilement *noun* RECONCILIATION.

reconciliate *verb* HARMONIZE.

reconciliation *noun*
A re-establishment of friendship or harmony: *effected a reconciliation between the warring countries.*
   Syns: conciliation, rapprochement, reconcilement.

recondite *adjective* DEEP.

recondition *verb*
1. RENEW.
2. RESTORE.

reconditioning *noun* RENEWAL.

reconnaissance *noun* EXPLORATION.

reconnoiter *verb* EXPLORE.

reconsider *verb*
To consider again, esp. with the possibility of change: *Why not reconsider your foolish plan?*
   Syns: re-evaluate, re-examine, rethink, review, think over.

reconstruct *verb* RESTORE.

record *verb*
1. POST.
2. SHOW.

recount *verb* DESCRIBE.

recoup *verb* RECOVER.

recoup *noun* RECOVERY.

recourse *noun* RESORT.

recover *verb*
1. To get back: *hopes to recover her stolen car.*
   Syns: recoup, regain, repossess, retrieve.
2. To regain one's health: *recovering after a long illness.*
   Syns: come around (*or* round), convalesce, gain, improve, mend, perk up, rally, recuperate.
3. RESCUE.
4. RESTORE.

recovery *noun*
1. A return to normal health: *made a quick recovery.*
   Syns: rally, recuperation.
2. The act of getting back or regaining: *The Crusaders' objective was the recovery of the Holy Land.*
   Syns: recoup, repossession, retrieval.
3. COMEBACK.

recreancy *noun* DEFECTION.

recreant *adjective* FAITHLESS.

recreant *noun* DEFECTOR.

recreate *verb*
1. AMUSE.
2. PLAY.

recreation *noun*
1. AMUSEMENT.
2. PLAY.

recrudesce *verb* RETURN.

rectify *verb*
1. CORRECT.
2. SETTLE.

rectitude *noun*
1. CHARACTER.
2. GOOD.
3. HONESTY.

recumbent *adjective* FLAT.

recuperate *verb* RECOVER.

recuperation *noun* RECOVERY.

recur *verb*
1. To happen again or repeatedly: *an area where typhoons recur.*
   Syns: reappear, reoccur, return.
2. RETURN.

recurrence *noun*
A repeated occurrence: *experienced a recurrence of her headaches.*
   Syns: reappearance, reoccurrence, return.

recurrent *adjective*
Happening or appearing at regular intervals: *a recurrent problem.*
   Syns: cyclic (*also* cyclical), isochronal (*also* isochronic, isochronous), periodic (*also* periodical), recurring.
   —*Idiom* as regular as (*or* like) clockwork.

recurring *adjective* RECURRENT.

red-blooded *adjective* LUSTY.

redden *verb* BLUSH.

redeem *verb*
1. COMPENSATE.
2. RESCUE.

red-hot *adjective*
1, 2. HOT.
3. PASSIONATE.

redolence *noun* FRAGRANCE.

redolent *adjective* FRAGRANT.

redouble *verb*
1. DOUBLE.
2. INTENSIFY.

redoubtable *adjective* EMINENT.

redress *verb*
1. AVENGE.
2. COMPENSATE.
   redress *noun* COMPENSATION.

reduce *verb*
1. To lose bodily weight, as by dieting: *Avoid sweets if you want to reduce.*
   Syns: slim (down), trim down.
2. CUT BACK at **cut.**
3. DECREASE.
4. DEMOTE.
5. DEPRECIATE.

reduction *noun*
1. CUTBACK.
2. DECREASE.
3. DEDUCTION.
4. DEMOTION.
5. DEPRECIATION.

redundant *adjective* TAUTOLOGICAL.

reduplicate *verb* COPY.

reduplication *noun* COPY.

re-echo *verb* ECHO.

reek *verb* SMELL.

reeking *adjective* SMELLY.

reel *verb*
1. LURCH.
2. SPIN.

reeling *adjective* DIZZY.

re-evaluate *verb* RECONSIDER.

re-examine *verb* RECONSIDER.

ref *noun* JUDGE.

refer *verb*
1. To direct (a person) elsewhere for help, information, etc.: *will refer the patient to a cardiologist.*
   Syns: send, transfer, turn over.
2. To call or direct attention to (an occurrence, situation, etc.): *I'll never refer to your indiscretion.*
   Syns: advert, allude, bring up, mention, point out, touch on (*or* upon).
3. APPLY.
4. ATTRIBUTE.
5. RESORT TO at **resort.**

referee *noun* JUDGE.
   referee *verb* JUDGE.

reference *noun*
A statement attesting to personal qualifications, character, and dependability: *Include three references with your application.*
   Syns: character (*Archaic*), recommendation, testimonial.

refine *verb*
1. To make or become clear by the removal of impurities: *refining oil into gasoline; refining butter by heating it.*
   Syns: clarify, clean, cleanse, purify.
2. PERFECT.

refined *adjective*
1. Made pure, esp. by a commercial refining process: *a lotion containing refined lanolin.*
   Syns: clarified, purified.
2. CULTURED.
3. DELICATE.

refinement *noun*
1. CLASS.
2. CULTURE.
3. DISCRIMINATION.

refining *adjective* CULTURAL.

reflect *verb*
1. To send back or form an image of: *a pool that reflects nearby buildings.*
   Syns: image, mirror.
2, 3. ECHO.
4. PONDER.
5. THINK.

reflection *noun*
1. Something that is reflected: *a reflection of clouds on the water.*
   Syn: image.
2. An implied criticism: *His trouble cast no reflection on his parents.*
   Syns: reproach, slur.
3. ECHO.
4. THOUGHT.

reflective *adjective* THOUGHTFUL.

reflex *adjective* SPONTANEOUS.
   reflex *noun* ECHO.

reformatory *adjective* CORRECTIVE.
refract *verb* BEND.
refractoriness *noun*
1. OBSTINACY.
2. UNRULINESS.
refractory *adjective*
1. OBSTINATE.
2. UNRULY.
refrain *verb*
To hold oneself back: *Please refrain from applauding.*
   Syns: abstain, forbear, hold off, keep, withhold.
refresh *verb*
1. To impart renewed energy and strength to (a person): *Sleep refreshed me.*
   Syns: freshen, reinvigorate, rejuvenate, renew, restore.
2. RENEW.
refreshing *adjective* TONIC.
refuge *noun*
1. The state of being protected or safeguarded, as from danger or hardship: *a political dissident seeking refuge in Sweden.*
   Syns: asylum, sanctuary, shelter.
2. COVER.
3. HOME.
4. RESORT.
refugee *noun* FUGITIVE.
refulgent *adjective* BRIGHT.
refurbish *verb*
1. MODERNIZE.
2. RENEW.
refurbishing *noun* RENEWAL.
refurbishment *noun* RENEWAL.
refusal *noun*
1. A turning down of a request: *refusal of permission to leave early.*
   Syns: denial, disallowance, rejection, turn-down (*Informal*).
2. NO.
refuse *verb*
1. To be unwilling to grant: *refused him the right to visit the children.*
   Syns: deny, disallow, disapprove, turn down, withhold. —*Idiom* turn thumbs down on.
2. DECLINE.
refute *verb*
To prove or show to be false: *Evidence came to light that refuted the theory.*
   Syns: belie, confute, discredit, disprove, rebut.
regain *verb* RECOVER.
regal *adjective*
1, 2. GRAND.

regard *verb*
1. To look upon in a particular way: *I regard him as a fool.*
   Syns: account, consider, esteem, reckon, view.
2. ADMIRE.
3. LOOK.
regard *noun*
1. CARE.
2. CONCERN.
3. CONSIDERATION.
4. ESTEEM.
5. LOOK.
6. NOTICE.
regards *noun*
Friendly greetings: *Give them our regards.*
   Syn: respects.
regeneration *noun* CONVERSION.
regime *noun* GOVERNMENT.
regimen *noun* TREATMENT.
region *noun* AREA.
register *verb*
1. To come as a realization: *His real meaning finally registered with them.*
   Syns: dawn on (*or* upon), sink in, soak in.
2. POST.
3. SHOW.
register *noun* LIST[1].
regnant *adjective*
1. DOMINANT.
2. PREVAILING.
regress *verb* RELAPSE.
regress *noun* REVERSION.
regression *noun* REVERSION.
regret *verb*
To feel or express sorrow for: *He deeply regrets his treatment of his wife.*
   Syns: deplore, repent, rue, wail (*Archaic*).
regret *noun* DISAPPOINTMENT.
regretful *adjective*
1. APOLOGETIC.
2. REMORSEFUL.
regrets *noun* APOLOGY.
regrettable *adjective* SORROWFUL.
regular *adjective*
1. CLEAN.
2. COMMON.
3. CUSTOMARY.
4. EVEN[1].
5. METHODICAL.
6. SYMMETRICAL.
regulate *verb*
1. ADJUST.
2. GOVERN.
regulation *noun*
1. LAW.
2. RULE.

regulatory *adjective* GOVERNMENTAL.
rehabilitate *verb* RESTORE.
rehearsal *noun* PRACTICE.
rehearse *verb* DESCRIBE.
reign *verb*
1. DOMINATE.
2. GOVERN.
reimburse *verb* COMPENSATE.
rein *verb* RESTRAIN.
reinforce *verb* TIGHTEN.
reinstate *verb*
1, 2. RESTORE.
reintroduce *verb* RESTORE.
reinvigorate *verb* REFRESH.
reinvigorating *adjective* TONIC.
reiterate *verb* REPEAT.
   reiterate *adjective* REPETITIVE.
   reiteration *noun* REPETITION.
   reiterative *adjective* REPETITIVE.
reject *verb* DECLINE.
rejection *noun*
1. DENIAL.
2. NO.
3. REFUSAL.
rejoice *verb*
1. To feel or take joy or pleasure: *The whole city rejoiced at the homecoming of its hero.*
   Syns: delight, exult, joy.
2. CELEBRATE.
rejoicing *noun* CELEBRATION.
rejoin *verb* ANSWER.
rejoinder *noun* ANSWER.
rejuvenate *verb*
1. MODERNIZE.
2. REFRESH.
3. RENEW.
4. RESTORE.
rejuvenation *noun* RENEWAL.
rekindle *verb* REVIVE.
rekindling *noun* REVIVAL.
relapse *verb*
To slip from a higher or better condition to a former, usu. lower or poorer one: *When untended, the garden relapsed into weeds.*
   Syns: backslide, lapse, recidivate, regress, retrogress, revert.
   relapse *noun* LAPSE.
relate *verb*
1. *Informal.* To interact with another or others in a meaningful fashion: *He doesn't relate with young people.*
   Syns: click (*Informal*), communicate (*Informal*), connect (*Informal*).
   —*Idiom* be on the same wavelength.
2. APPLY.
3. ASSOCIATE.
4. DESCRIBE.
5. IDENTIFY.

related *adjective*
Connected by or as if by kinship or common origin: *related to her through my father.*
   Syns: agnate, akin, allied, cognate, connate, connatural, consanguineous (*also* consanguine), kindred.
relation *noun*
1. A logical or natural association between two or more things: *the relation between hard work and success.*
   Syns: connection, correlation, hookup (*Informal*), interconnection, interdependence, interrelation, interrelationship, link, relationship, tie-in.
2. RELATIVE.
relationship *noun* RELATION.
relative *adjective*
1. COMPARATIVE.
2. DEPENDENT.
   relative *noun*
A person connected to another person by blood: *one of my relatives from the old country.*
   Syns: kin, kinsman, kinswoman, relation.
relax *verb*
1. EASE.
2. REST[1].
relaxation *noun* REST[1].
relaxed *adjective*
1. EASYGOING.
2. LOOSE.
release *verb*
1. EMIT.
2. FREE.
3. RID.
released *adjective* FREE.
relegate *verb* ENTRUST.
relent *verb*
1. SUBSIDE.
2. WEAKEN.
relentless *adjective*
1. CONTINUAL.
2. STUBBORN.
relevance *also* **relevancy** *noun*
1. The fact of being related to the matter at hand: *That idea has no relevance to our current situation.*
   Syns: application, bearing, germaneness, pertinence (*also* pertinency).
2. CONCERN.
relevant *adjective*
Related to the matter at hand: *relevant questions; relevant issues.*
   Syns: applicable, apposite, apropos,

germane, material, pertinent. —*Idiom*
to the point.
reliable *adjective* DEPENDABLE.
reliance *noun* CONFIDENCE.
reliant *adjective* DEPENDENT.
relic *noun*
1. RUIN.
2. TRACE.
relief *noun*
1. Assistance, esp. money, food, and
other necessities, given to the needy
or dispossessed: *received relief
following the flood.*
Syns: dole, handout, welfare.
2. Freedom, esp. from pain: *no relief
from her suffering.*
Syns: allayment, alleviation,
assuagement, ease, mitigation.
3. A person or persons taking over the
duties of another: *His relief arrived
early.*
Syn: replacement.
4. HELP.
relieve *verb*
1. To make less severe or more
bearable: *takes medication to relieve
the pain.*
Syns: allay, alleviate, assuage,
comfort, ease, lessen, lighten,
mitigate, palliate.
2. To free from a specific duty by acting
as a substitute: *A new guard will
relieve you at midnight.*
Syns: spell³, take over (for).
3. EXCUSE.
4. RID.
religion *noun*
A system of religious belief: *Many
religions exist in the Orient.*
Syns: creed, denomination, faith,
persuasion, sect.
religious *adjective*
1. DIVINE¹.
2. HOLY.
3. SPIRITUAL.
relinquish *verb*
1. To let (something) go: *relinquished his
ambitions; relinquished my umbrella to
the attendant.*
Syns: abandon, forgo (*also* forego),
hand over, lay down, surrender,
waive, yield.
2. ABDICATE.
relish *verb*
1. ADMIRE.
2. APPRECIATE.
3. EAT UP at **eat.**
4. ENJOY.
relish *noun*
1. DELIGHT.

2. FLAVOR.
3. TASTE.
4. ZEST.
relocate *verb* MOVE.
relocation *noun* REMOVAL.
reluctance *noun* INDISPOSITION.
reluctant *adjective* INDISPOSED.
remain *verb*
To continue to be in a place: *She
remained at home after he left for work.*
Syns: abide, bide, linger, stay¹, stick
around (*Informal*), tarry, wait.
remainder *noun*
1. BALANCE.
2. RUIN.
remainder *adjective* REMAINING.
remaining *adjective*
That remains, esp. after a part has been
removed: *The remaining pie was quickly
polished off.*
Syns: leftover, remainder.
remains *noun*
1. BALANCE.
2. BODY.
3. TRACE.
remark *verb*
1. COMMENT.
2. NOTICE.
remark *noun*
1. COMMENT.
2. NOTICE.
3. WORD.
remarkable *adjective*
1. NOTICEABLE.
2. RARE.
remedial *adjective*
1. CORRECTIVE.
2. CURATIVE.
remedy *noun*
1. Something that corrects or
counteracts: *There are no easy
remedies for inflation.*
Syns: antidote, corrective,
counteragent, countermeasure,
curative, cure.
2. CURE.
remedy *verb*
1. CORRECT.
2. CURE.
remember *verb*
1. To renew (an image or thought) in
the mind: *couldn't remember his
name; couldn't remember what
happened.*
Syns: bethink, mind (*Rare*), recall,
recollect, retain, revive, think (of).
—*Idiom* bring to mind.
2. To care enough to keep (someone) in

mind: *How kind of you to remember me with flowers.*
Syn: think (of).

remembrance *noun*
1. Something that causes one to remember: *kept her dance card as a remembrance of the prom.*
Syns: keepsake, memento, reminder, souvenir, token, trophy.
2. MEMORIAL.
3, 4. MEMORY.

reminder *noun* REMEMBRANCE.

reminiscence *noun*
1. COMMENTARY.
2, 3. MEMORY.

reminiscent *adjective* SUGGESTIVE.

remiss *adjective* NEGLIGENT.

remission *noun*
1. ABEYANCE.
2. FORGIVENESS.

remissive *adjective* LATENT.

remissness *noun* NEGLIGENCE.

remit *verb*
1. DEFER[1].
2. FORGIVE.

remittent *adjective* LATENT.

remnant *noun*
1. BALANCE.
2. END.
3. RUIN.

remonstrance *noun* OBJECTION.

remonstrate *verb* OBJECT[2].

remonstration *noun* OBJECTION.

remorse *noun* PENITENCE.

remorseful *adjective*
Feeling or expressing regret for one's sins or misdeeds: *made a remorseful admission that he had lied.*
Syns: compunctious, contrite, penitent, penitential, regretful, repentant, sorry.

remorsefulness *noun* PENITENCE.

remorseless *adjective*
1. Devoid of remorse: *a remorseless cad.*
Syns: impenitent, unrepentant.
2. GRIM.
3. MERCILESS.

remote *adjective*
1. Small in degree, esp. of probability: *only a remote chance of survival.*
Syns: fat (*Slang*), negligible, off, outside, slender, slight, slim.
2. Far from centers of human population: *a remote outpost deep in the Andes.*
Syns: isolated, insular, lonely, lonesome, obscure, out-of-the-way, removed, secluded, solitary. —*Idiom* off the beaten path (*or* track).

3. COOL.
4. DISTANT.
5. HIGH.

remoteness *noun*
1. DETACHMENT.
2. DISTANCE.

remotion *noun* REMOVAL.

removal *noun*
1. The act or process of moving from one place to another: *removal of the goods from the flooded warehouse to a new facility.*
Syns: move, relocation, remotion.
2. ELIMINATION.

remove *verb*
1. To move (something) from a position occupied: *removed the dirty dishes from the table; removed the troops from the field.*
Syns: take away, take off, take out, withdraw.
2. To take from one's own person: *removed his coat and sat down.*
Syns: doff, douse, take off.
3. ANNIHILATE.
4. DROP.
5. ELIMINATE.
6. GO.
7, 8. MOVE.

remove *noun*
Degree of separation, esp. in time: *It is difficult to judge the administration at this far remove.*
Syn: distance.

removed *adjective*
1. DISTANT.
2. HIGH.
3. REMOTE.
4. SOLITARY.

remunerate *verb*
1. COMPENSATE.
2. PAY.

remuneration *noun*
1. COMPENSATION.
2. PAYMENT.

remunerative *adjective*
1. COMPENSATORY.
2. PROFITABLE.

renaissance *noun* REVIVAL.

renascence *noun* REVIVAL.

rend *verb* TEAR[1].

render *verb*
1. ABDICATE.
2. INTERPRET.
3. REPRESENT.
4. RETURN.
5. TRANSLATE.

rendering *noun* PARAPHRASE.

rendezvous *noun*
1. ENGAGEMENT.
2. HAUNT.
rendezvous *verb* MEET[1].
rendition *noun* INTERPRETATION.
renegade *noun* DEFECTOR.
renew *verb*
1. To make new or as if new again: *renewed the furniture by reupholstering it.*
   Syns: furbish, recondition, refresh, refurbish, rejuvenate, renovate, restore. —*Idiom* give a new look to.
2. To arrange for the extension of: *renew a contract.*
   Syn: extend.
3. CONTINUE.
4. REFRESH.
5. RESTORE.
6. REVIVE.
renewal *noun*
1. The act of making new or as if new again: *urban renewal.*
   Syns: face lifting (*also* facelift), reconditioning, refurbishing, refurbishment, rejuvenation, renovation, restoration.
2. A continuing after interruption: *renewal of United States-Soviet hostilities.*
   Syns: resumption, resurgence, revival.
3. REVIVAL.
renewing *adjective* TONIC.
renitence or **renitency** *noun* RESISTANCE.
renitent *adjective* RESISTANT.
renounce *verb*
1. ABANDON.
2. ABDICATE.
renovate *verb*
1. MODERNIZE.
2. RENEW.
renovation *noun* RENEWAL.
renown *noun*
1. EMINENCE.
2. FAME.
renowned *adjective* EMINENT.
rent[1] *verb* HIRE.
rent[2] *noun*
1, 2. BREACH.
3. TEAR[1].
renunciation *noun* ABDICATION.
reoccupy *verb* RESUME.
reoccur *verb*
1. RECUR.
2. RETURN.
reoccurrence *noun* RECURRENCE.
reopen *verb* CONTINUE.
repair *verb*
1. FIX.

2. GO.
3. RESORT TO at **resort.**
reparation *noun* COMPENSATION.
repartee *noun* RETORT.
repay *verb*
1. AVENGE.
2. COMPENSATE.
3. RETURN.
repeal *verb*
1. ABOLISH.
2. LIFT.
3. REVERSE.
repeal *noun*
1. ABOLITION.
2. REVERSAL.
repeat *verb*
1. To state again: *repeated the oath of office after the Chief Justice.*
   Syns: iterate, reiterate, restate.
2, 3. ECHO.
repel *verb*
1. DISGUST.
2. PARRY.
repellence also **repellency** *noun* ANTIPATHY.
repellent *adjective*
1. ANTIPATHETIC.
2. OFFENSIVE.
repent *verb* REGRET.
repentance *noun* PENITENCE.
repentant *adjective*
1. APOLOGETIC.
2. REMORSEFUL.
repercussion *noun*
1. ECHO.
2. IMPACT.
repetition *noun*
1. The act or process of repeating: *Children often learn by repetition. The repetition of your complaints is annoying.*
   Syns: iteration, reiteration, restatement.
2. ECHO.
repetitious *adjective* REPETITIVE.
repetitive *adjective*
Characterized by repetition: *repetitive statements characteristic of some journalists.*
   Syns: iterative, reiterate, reiterative, repetitious.
rephrase *verb* PARAPHRASE.
replace *verb*
1. To remove (something) and substitute (another) for it: *replaced the broken pane with new glass.*
   Syns: supplant, supersede.
2. RESTORE.

replacement *noun*
1. RELIEF.
2. SUBSTITUTE.
replete *adjective*
1. ALIVE.
2. FULL.
3. SATIATED.
repletion *noun* SATIATION.
replica *noun*
1. COPY.
2. LIKENESS.
replicate *verb* COPY.
replication *noun* COPY.
reply *verb* ANSWER.
reply *noun* ANSWER.
report *noun*
1. A sudden sharp, explosive noise: *From the reports of rifles we knew that hunters must be nearby.*
   Syns: bang, bark, crack, explosion, pop, snap.
2. GOSSIP.
3. REPUTATION.
4. STORY.
report *verb*
1. COMMUNICATE.
2. COVER.
3. DESCRIBE.
4. NOISE.
reportage *noun* COVERAGE.
repose *verb*
1. CONSIST.
2. LIE¹.
3. REST¹.
repose *noun* REST¹.
repository *noun*
1. CONFIDANT.
2. DEPOSITORY.
repossess *verb*
1. RECOVER.
2. RESUME.
repossession *noun* RECOVERY.
reprehend *verb*
1. BLAME.
2. DEPLORE.
reprehensible *adjective*
1. FILTHY.
2. INFAMOUS.
reprehension *noun* BLAME.
represent *verb*
1. To serve as the image of: *The sword represents valor.*
   Syns: body (forth), embody, epitomize, exemplify, illustrate, personify, stand for, symbol, symbolize, typify.
2. To present a lifelike image of: *The painting represents the agony and crucifixion of Christ.*

   Syns: describe, delineate, depict, image, limn, picture, portray, render, show.
3. To serve as an official delegate of: *My lawyer will represent me at the hearing.*
   Syns: speak for, stand for.
4. ACT.
representation *noun*
The act or process of describing in lifelike imagery: *a sculpture that is the representation of the heroism of the defenders of Leningrad.*
   Syns: description, delineation, depiction, picture, portraiture, portrayal.
representative *noun*
1. One who stands for another: *representatives at a political convention.*
   Syns: delegate, deputy.
2. EXAMPLE.
representative *adjective*
1. DESCRIPTIVE.
2. SYMBOLIC.
3. TYPICAL.
repress *verb*
To hold (something requiring an outlet) in check: *repressed my laughter with difficulty; congressional whips repressing dissenting legislators.*
   Syns: choke, gag, hold back, hold down, hush (up), muffle, quench, shush, sit on (*or* upon) (*Informal*), smother, squelch, stifle, strangle, suppress, throttle.
repression *noun*
1. The act of restraining forcefully: *repression of giggles; repression of the Young Turks' arguments.*
   Syns: choking, quashing, quenching, smothering, squelching, stifling, suppression, throttling.
2. SUPPRESSION.
repressive *adjective*
Serving to restrain forcefully: *took repressive measures against the rebels.*
   Syn: suppressive.
reprieve *noun* GRACE.
reprimand *verb* CALL DOWN at **call.**
reprimand *noun* REBUKE.
reprisal *noun* RETALIATION.
reproach *verb* CALL DOWN at **call.**
reproach *noun*
1. REBUKE.
2. REFLECTION.
reprobate *adjective* EVIL.
reprobate *verb*
1. BLAME.
2. DEPLORE.

reprobation *noun* BLAME.
reproduce *verb*
1. *Biol.* To produce sexually or asexually others of one's kind: *Flies reproduce in astronomical numbers.*
   Syns: breed, multiply, procreate, proliferate, propagate, spawn.
2. COPY.
reproduction *noun*
1. *Biol.* The process by which an organism produces others of its kind: *studied the reproduction of the monarch butterfly; a group advocating unrestricted reproduction of the human race.*
   Syns: breeding, multiplication, procreation, proliferation, propagation, spawning.
2. COPY.
reproductive *adjective*
1. *Biol.* Of or pertaining to reproduction: *reproductive cycles.*
   Syns: procreant (*Biol.*), procreative.
2. *Biol.* Employed in reproduction: *reproductive organs.*
   Syns: progenitive (*Biol.*), sexual.
reprove *verb*
1. CALL DOWN at **call.**
2. CORRECT.
repudiate *verb*
To refuse to recognize or acknowledge: *repudiating the black sheep of the family; repudiated his previous testimony.*
   Syns: deny, disacknowledge, disavow, disclaim, disown. —*Idiom* turn one's back on.
repugnance also **repugnancy** *noun* HATE.
repugnant *adjective*
1. CONTRARY.
2. FILTHY.
repulse *verb*
1. DISGUST.
2. PARRY.
repulsion *noun*
1. DISGUST.
2. HATE.
3. HORROR.
repulsive *adjective* OFFENSIVE.
reputable *adjective* HONORABLE.
reputation *noun*
1. Public estimation of someone: *has a bad reputation.*
   Syns: character, name, report, repute.
2. FAME.
3. HONOR.
repute *verb*
To regard or be regarded in an appraising way: *Rasputin was reputed to be the power behind the Romanov throne.*
   Syns: suppose, think.
repute *noun*
1. FAME.
2. HONOR.
3. REPUTATION.
reputed *adjective*
Assumed to be such: *the reputed father of the child.*
   Syns: putative, supposed.
request *verb*
To endeavor to obtain (something) by expressing one's needs or desires: *requested a revised schedule to facilitate production of the book.*
   Syns: ask (for), solicit.
requiescence *noun* REST¹.
require *verb*
1. To oblige to do or not do by force of authority, propriety, or custom: *Men are required to wear ties in this restaurant.*
   Syns: expect, suppose.
2. COMMAND.
3, 4. DEMAND.
5. LACK.
required *adjective*
1. Imposed on one by authority, command, or convention: *English composition is a required course at most colleges. He had to make the required apologies.*
   Syns: called-for, compulsory, imperative, mandatory, necessary, obligatory, requisite.
2. ESSENTIAL.
requirement *noun*
1. CONDITION.
2. DEMAND.
requisite *adjective*
1. ESSENTIAL.
2. REQUIRED.
requisite *noun* CONDITION.
requisition *verb* DEMAND.
requisition *noun* DEMAND.
requital *noun*
1. COMPENSATION.
2. RETALIATION.
requite *verb*
1. AVENGE.
2. COMPENSATE.
3. RECIPROCATE.
rescind *verb*
1. ABOLISH.
2. LIFT.
3. REVERSE.
rescindment *noun* ABOLITION.

rescission *noun*
1. ABOLITION.
2. REVERSAL.

rescue *verb*
1. To extricate, as from danger or confinement: *The Coast Guard rescued the shipwrecked sailors. Commandos rescued the hostages.*
   Syns: deliver, save. —*Idioms* come to the rescue of, snatch from the jaws of death.
2. To extricate from an undesirable state: *Federal funds are needed to rescue the city from bankruptcy. A new president rescued the troubled corporation.*
   Syns: reclaim, recover, redeem, salvage.

rescue *noun*
Extrication from danger or confinement: *a meticulously executed rescue of the shipwrecked sailors.*
Syns: deliverance, delivery, salvage, salvation.

resemblance *noun* LIKENESS.
resemble *verb* FAVOR.
resentful *adjective*
Bitingly hostile: *a resentful, unforgiving person; wrote a resentful letter.*
Syns: acrimonious, bitter, embittered, hard, rancorous, virulent.

resentfulness *noun* RESENTMENT.
resentment *noun*
1. The quality or state of feeling bitter: *Let there be no resentment between us.*
   Syns: acridity, acrimony, bitterness, gall¹, rancor, resentfulness.
2. OFFENSE.

reservation *noun*
1. Public land kept for a special purpose: *an Indian reservation; a reservation for wildlife.*
   Syns: preserve, reserve.
2. PROVISION.
3. QUALM.

reserve *noun*
1. The keeping of one's thoughts and emotions to oneself: *a man of iron reserve.*
   Syns: control, restraint, reticence, self-control, self-restraint, taciturnity, uncommunicativeness.
2. HOARD.
3. RESERVATION.

reserve *verb*
1. BOOK.
2. HOLD.

reserve *adjective* AUXILIARY.
reserved *adjective*
1. Tending to keep one's thoughts and

emotions to oneself: *a reserved banker type.*
Syns: constrained, controlled, incommunicable, noncommittal, restrained, self-controlled, self-restrained.
2. COOL.
3. QUALIFIED.
4. TACITURN.

reserves *noun* RESOURCES.
reservoir *noun* HOARD.
reside *verb*
1. CONSIST.
2. LIVE¹.

residue *noun* BALANCE.
resign *verb*
1. ABDICATE.
2. QUIT.

resignation *noun*
1. ABDICATION.
2. PATIENCE.

resigned *adjective* PATIENT.
resilience *also* **resiliency** *noun*
1. The ability to recover quickly from depression or discouragement: *His innate resilience helped him through the mid-life crisis.*
   Syns: bounce, buoyancy, elasticity.
2. FLEXIBILITY.

resilient *adjective* FLEXIBLE.
resist *verb*
1. To oppose actively and with force: *The rebels resisted the invasion.*
   Syns: combat, duel, fight, withstand. —*Idioms* mount (*or* offer) resistance, put up a fight, stand up to (*or* against).
2. CONTEST.

resistance *noun*
1. The capacity to withstand: *an unusually high resistance to viruses.*
   Syns: immunity, imperviousness, unsusceptibility.
2. The act of resisting: *overcame their resistance to school busing.*
   Syns: opposition, renitence *or* renitency.
3. A clandestine organization of freedom fighters in an oppressed land: *The French Resistance helped the Allies.*
   Syn: underground.

resistant *adjective*
1. Having the capacity to withstand: *was totally resistant to our imprecations; a body very resistant to viruses; a paint resistant to weathering.*
   Syns: immune, impervious, proof, resistive.
2. Tending to resist, as an influence or

idea: *a die-hard conservative resistant to change.*
Syns: renitent, resisting, resistive.
resistant *noun* RESISTER.
resister *noun*
One who resists: *draft resisters.*
Syns: opponent, resistant.
resisting *adjective* RESISTANT.
resistive *adjective*
1, 2. RESISTANT.
resolute *adjective*
1. DECISIVE.
2. FAITHFUL.
3. FIRM¹.
4. SET¹.
resoluteness *noun* DECISION.
resolution *noun*
1. ANALYSIS.
2. COURAGE.
3, 4. DECISION.
5. WILL¹.
resolve *verb*
1. To find a solution for: *resolved the mystery; resolved the problem.*
Syns: clear up, decipher, dope out (*Informal*), explain, figure out, solve, unravel. —*Idiom* get to the bottom of.
2. ANALYZE.
3. DECIDE.
4. SETTLE.
resolve *noun*
1. DECISION.
2. WILL¹.
resonant *adjective*
Having or producing a full, deep, or rich sound: *a resonant baritone.*
Syns: mellow, orotund, plangent, resounding, ringing, rotund, round, sonorous, vibrant.
resort *noun*
1. That to which one turns for help when in desperation: *As a last resort I asked the bank for a loan.*
Syns: expediency (*also* expedience), expedient, recourse, refuge, resort, resource, stopgap.
2. HAUNT.
resort to *verb*
1. To have recourse to when in need: *The government has resorted to censorship. We were unwilling to resort to a loan shark for financial aid.*
Syns: apply, go, refer, repair, run, turn. —*Idiom* fall back on.
2. FREQUENT.
resounding *adjective*
1. EMPHATIC.
2. RESONANT.
resounding *noun* ECHO.

resource *noun* RESORT.
resourceful *adjective*
Able to use the means at one's disposal to meet situations effectively: *a resourceful mind.*
Syns: fertile, ingenious, inventive.
resourcefulness *noun* RESOURCES.
resources *noun*
1. The ability and the means to meet situations effectively: *Her inner resources sustained her during the illness.*
Syns: reserves, resourcefulness, wherewithal.
2. All property or goods having economic value: *It was hard to pinpoint the true extent of the deposed ruler's resources.*
Syns: assets, capital, fortune, means, wealth, wherewithal.
respect *verb*
1. ADMIRE.
2. APPRECIATE.
respect *noun*
1. ESTEEM.
2. PHASE.
respectable *adjective*
1. ACCEPTABLE.
2. CORRECT.
3. DECENT.
4. HONORABLE.
5. SIZABLE.
respectful *adjective* DEFERENTIAL.
respects *noun* REGARDS.
respiration *noun* BREATH.
respire *verb* BREATHE.
respite *noun*
1. BREAK.
2. GRACE.
resplendence or **resplendency** *noun* GLITTER.
resplendent *adjective* GLORIOUS.
respond *verb*
1. To act in return to something, as a stimulus: *The patient is responding to treatment.*
Syn: react.
2. ANSWER.
respond to *verb* GREET.
respondent *noun* ACCUSED.
response *noun*
1. An action elicited by a stimulus: *a patient's adverse response to chemotherapy; a military response to the embargo.*
Syns: reaction, retroaction.
2. ANSWER.
responsibility *noun* DUTY.

responsible *adjective*
1. DEPENDABLE.
2. LIABLE.

responsive *adjective*
1. APPROACHABLE.
2. RECEPTIVE.
3. SENSITIVE.

responsiveness *noun* APPRECIATION.

rest¹ *noun*
1. Freedom from labor, responsibility, or strain: *sat down and took his rest.*
   Syns: ease, leisure, relaxation, repose, requiescence.
2. BREAK.

rest *verb*
1. To take repose by sleeping, lying quietly, or the like: *rested for an hour before dinner.*
   Syns: lie, lie down, recline, repose, stretch out.
2. To take repose by ceasing work or other effort for an interval of time: *We just want to rest during the vacation.*
   Syns: relax, unbend, unwind.
   —*Idioms* live the life of Riley, take it easy.
3. BASE¹.
4. CONSIST.
rest on (or **upon**) *verb* DEPEND ON at depend.

rest² *noun* BALANCE.

restart *verb* CONTINUE.

restate *verb*
1. PARAPHRASE.
2. REPEAT.

restatement *noun*
1. PARAPHRASE.
2. REPETITION.

restitute *verb* RESTORE.

restitution *noun* COMPENSATION.

restive *adjective* EDGY.

restiveness *noun* RESTLESSNESS.

restless *adjective*
1. Affording no quiet, repose, or rest: *spent a restless night before the interview.*
   Syns: uneasy, unsettled.
2. EDGY.

restlessness *noun*
An uneasy or nervous state: *We noticed the restlessness of the cattle.*
Syns: disquiet, disquietude, inquietude, restiveness, uneasiness, unrest.

restoration *noun* RENEWAL.

restorative *adjective*
1. CURATIVE.
2. TONIC.

restorative *noun* TONIC.

restore *verb*
1. To bring back into existence or use: *restore law and order.*
   Syns: reinstate, reintroduce, renew, return, revive.
2. To bring back to a previous normal condition: *restored the Revolutionary house.*
   Syns: rebuild, reclaim, recondition, reconstruct, recover, rehabilitate, rejuvenate, restitute. —*Idiom* restore the first flower (*or* bloom) of.
3. To put (someone) in the possession of a prior position or office: *an emperor restored to the throne.*
   Syns: give back, reinstate, replace, return.
4. MODERNIZE.
5. REFRESH.
6. RENEW.
7. RETURN.
8. REVIVE.

restrain *verb*
To control, restrict, or arrest: *restrained him from starting a fight; restrained my curiosity.*
Syns: bit², brake, bridle, check, constrain, curb, hold back, hold down, hold in, inhibit, keep, keep back, pull in, rein.

restrained *adjective*
1. CONSERVATIVE.
2. QUIET.
3. RESERVED.

restraint *noun*
1. RESERVE.
2. RESTRICTION.

restraints *noun* BONDS.

restrict *verb* LIMIT.

restricted *adjective*
1. Kept within certain limits: *a restricted number of students.*
   Syns: circumscribed, determinate, fixed, limited.
2. Excluding or unavailable to certain groups: *a restricted neighborhood.*
   Syn: segregated.
3. CONFIDENTIAL.
4. LOCAL.
5. QUALIFIED.

restriction *noun*
1. The act of limiting or condition of being limited: *Absolute rulers have power without restriction.*
   Syns: circumscription, confinement, constrainment, constraint, limitation.
2. Something that limits or restricts: *wanted restrictions on presidential power.*

Syns: circumscription, constraint, cramp, limitation, restraint, stricture, trammel.

result *noun*
1. ANSWER.
2. EFFECT.

result *verb* FOLLOW.

result in *verb* CAUSE.

resultant *noun* EFFECT.

resume *verb*
1. To occupy or take again: *The former prime minister resumed power.*
   Syns: reassume, reclaim, reoccupy, repossess, retake, take back.
2. CONTINUE.

resumption *noun* RENEWAL.

resurgence *noun*
1. RENEWAL.
2. REVIVAL.

resurrect *verb* REVIVE.

resurrection *noun* REVIVAL.

resuscitate *verb* REVIVE.

resuscitation *noun* REVIVAL.

retail *verb* SELL.

retain *verb*
1. EMPLOY.
2. HAVE.
3. HOLD.
4. KEEP.
5. REMEMBER.

retake *verb* RESUME.

retaliate *verb*
To return like for like, esp. to return an unfriendly or hostile action with a similar one: *retaliate against an enemy attack.*
   Syns: counter, hit back, reciprocate, retort, strike back.

retaliation *noun*
The act of retaliating: *an insult that provoked retaliation; attacked in retaliation for the attack on the ship.*
   Syns: avengement, avenging, counteraction, counterattack, counterblow, counterstroke, reciprocation, reprisal, requital, retribution, revanche, revenge, vengeance. —*Idioms* an eye for an eye, a tooth for a tooth, blow for blow, like for like, measure for measure, tit for tat.

retard *verb*
1. DELAY.
2. HINDER.

retardation *noun* DELAY.

retarded *adjective* BACKWARD.

rethink *verb* RECONSIDER.

reticence *noun*
1. MODESTY.
2. RESERVE.

reticent *adjective*
1. COOL.
2. TACITURN.

retinue *noun*
A group of attendants or followers: *Several translators joined the President's retinue for the summit conference.*
   Syns: entourage, following, suite, train.

retire *verb*
1. To go to bed: *retired at 11:00.*
   Syns: bed (down), crash (*Slang*), flop (*Slang*), pile in (*Informal*), roll in (*Informal*), turn in (*Informal*).
   —*Idioms* call it a night, hit the hay (*or* sack), meet the sandman.
2. To withdraw from business or active life: *retired after 50 years on the job.*
   Syns: demit, step down. —*Idioms* call it quits, hang up one's spurs, turn in one's badge.
3. To remove from active service: *retire a career officer.*
   Syns: pension (off), superannuate. —*Idioms* put on the retired list, put out to pasture.
4. GO.
5. RETREAT.

retirement *noun*
1. RETREAT.
2. SECLUSION.

retiring *adjective* MODEST.

retort *noun*
1. A spirited, incisive reply: *a master of the quick retort.*
   Syns: comeback (*Slang*), counter, repartee, riposte (*also* ripost).
   —*Idiom* back answer.
2. ANSWER.

retort *verb*
1. ANSWER.
2. RETALIATE.

retouch *verb* TOUCH UP at **touch.**

retract *verb*
1. To disavow (something previously written or said) irrevocably and usu. formally: *The senator retracted his previous denial.*
   Syns: abjure, palinode, recall, recant, take back, withdraw.
2. RECEDE.
3. WITHDRAW.

retraction *noun*
A formal statement of disavowal: *issued a retraction of the ethnic slur and made an apology.*
   Syns: abjuration, palinode, recantation, recanting.

retreat *noun*
1. The moving back of a military force

in the face of enemy attack or after a defeat: *In their hasty retreat the soldiers abandoned their arms.*
Syns: fallback, pullback, pullout, retirement, withdrawal (*also* withdrawment).
2. COVER.
3. HOME.

retreat *verb*
1. To move back in the face of enemy attack or after a defeat: *Napoleon's forces retreating from Moscow.*
Syns: draw back, fall back, retire, withdraw. —*Idioms* beat (*or* sound) a retreat, give ground (*or* place *or* way).
2. BACK.
3. BACK DOWN at **back**.
4. RECEDE.

retribution *noun* RETALIATION.
retrieval *noun* RECOVERY.
retrieve *verb* RECOVER.
retroaction *noun* RESPONSE.
retrocede *verb*
1. BACK.
2. RECEDE.

retrograde *adjective* BACKWARD.
retrograde *verb*
1. BACK.
2. DETERIORATE.
3. RECEDE.

retrogress *verb*
1. BACK.
2. RECEDE.
3. RELAPSE.

retrogression *noun* REVERSION.
retrogressive *adjective* BACKWARD.
return *verb*
1. To go again to a former place: *returned to my birthplace.*
Syns: come back, revert, revisit.
2. To come back to a former condition: *a disease that returned.*
Syns: recrudesce, recur, reoccur, revert.
3. To send, put, or carry back to a former location: *returning empty bottles to the store.*
Syns: give back, restore, take back.
4. To make as income or profit: *My investment returned 15 per cent.*
Syns: bring in, clear, draw, earn, gain, gross, net², pay, produce, realize, repay, yield.
5. To deliver (an indictment or verdict): *returned a verdict of guilty.*
Syns: hand down, render.
6. ANSWER.
7. RECIPROCATE.
8. RECUR.
9, 10. RESTORE.

return *noun*
1. GAIN.
2. RECURRENCE.

reunite *verb* RECONCILE.
revamp *verb*
1. FIX.
2. MODERNIZE.
3. REVISE.

revamping *noun* REVISION.
revanche *noun* RETALIATION.
reveal *verb*
1. To make visible; bring to view: *A cleaning revealed the grain of the wood.*
Syns: bare, disclose, discover (*Archaic*), display, expose, lay open, show, unclothe, uncover, unmask, unveil. —*Idioms* bring to light (*or* view), lay bare, make plain.
2. BETRAY.

revel *verb*
1. To behave riotously: *drunken students reveling until dawn.*
Syns: carouse, frolic, hell (around) (*Informal*), riot, roister, spree. —*Idioms* blow off steam, cut loose, kick over the traces, kick up one's heels, let go, let loose, make whoopee, paint the town red, raise Cain, raise hell, raise ned, whoop it up.
2. CELEBRATE.
3. LUXURIATE.

revel *noun* GAIETY.
revelation *noun*
Something disclosed, esp. something not previously known or realized: *a revelation about drug use among teenagers.*
Syns: apocalypse, disclosure, exposé, exposure, eye opener, unveiling.

reveling *noun* GAIETY.
revelry *noun*
1. CELEBRATION.
2. GAIETY.

revels *noun* CELEBRATION.
revenant *noun* GHOST.
revenge *noun*
1. RETALIATION.
2. VINDICTIVENESS.

revengeful *adjective* VINDICTIVE.
reverberate *verb* ECHO.
reverberation *noun* ECHO.
revere *verb* ADORE.
reverence *noun* ADORATION.
reverence *verb* ADORE.
reverend *noun* PREACHER.
reverent *adjective*
Feeling or showing reverence: *looked at the pope with reverent affection.*

Syns: adorant, adoring, reverential, worshipful.
reverential *adjective* REVERENT.
reverie *noun*
1. DREAM.
2. TRANCE.
reversal *noun*
1. *Law.* The act of reversing or annulling: *a reversal of the decision in the appeals court.*
   Syns: repeal, rescission, revocation.
2. The act of changing or being changed from one position, direction, or course to the opposite: *a reversal of figures resulting in a printer's error.*
   Syns: inversion, transposition (*also* transposal).
3. REVERSED.
reverse *noun*
1. A change from better to worse: *persevering in the face of sharp reverses.*
   Syns: backset, reversal, setback.
   —*Idiom* reverse of fortune.
2. OPPOSITE.
reverse *adjective* OPPOSITE.
reverse *verb*
1. To change to the opposite position, direction, or course: *reversed the empty glasses to fill them; will reverse the photographs in the album.*
   Syns: inverse, invert, transpose, turn (around).
2. *Law.* To annul (a decision or decree): *a judge reversing a decision.*
   Syns: repeal, rescind, revoke.
3. DOUBLE.
4. LIFT.
reversion *noun*
A return to a former, usu. worse condition: *reversion to old eating habits after the diet.*
   Syns: regress, regression, retrogression.
revert *verb*
1. RELAPSE.
2, 3. RETURN.
review *verb*
1. To write a critical report on: *His function is to review new plays.*
   Syns: criticize, critique. —*Idiom* pass (*or* pronounce) judgment on.
2. To recapitulate the salient facts of: *The commentator reviewed the President's address after it was over.*
   Syns: abstract, epitomize, go over, recap, run down, run through, summarize, sum up, synopsize.
3. RECONSIDER.

review *noun*
1. A formal military inspection: *The top brass turned out for the review.*
   Syn: parade.
2. Evaluative and critical discourse: *The new book received rave reviews.*
   Syns: commentary, comment, criticism, critique, notice.
3. ANALYSIS.
reviewer *noun* CRITIC.
revile *verb*
To attack with harsh, often insulting language: *reviled his opponent in a stormy political debate.*
   Syns: abuse, assail, rail at (*or* against), vituperate.
revile *noun* VITUPERATION.
revilement *noun* VITUPERATION.
reviling *noun* VITUPERATION.
reviling *adjective* ABUSIVE.
revise *verb*
To prepare a new version of: *an almanac that is revised each year.*
   Syns: amend, emend, emendate, revamp.
revision *noun*
The act or process of revising: *a complete revision of the dictionary.*
   Syns: amendment, emendation, revamping, rewrite, rewriting.
revisit *verb* RETURN.
revitalization *noun* REVIVAL.
revitalize *verb* REVIVE.
revival *noun*
1. The act of reviving or condition of being revived: *a revival of interest in crafts.*
   Syns: reanimation, rebirth, rekindling, renaissance, renascence, renewal, resurgence, resurrection, resuscitation, revitalization, revivification.
2. RENEWAL.
revive *verb*
1. To cause to come back to life or consciousness: *They revived her with artificial respiration.*
   Syns: bring around, restore, resuscitate, revivify.
2. To rouse from a state of inactivity or quiescence: *revived my interest in Chaucer.*
   Syns: reactivate, reawaken, rekindle, renew, resurrect, revitalize, revivify.
3. REMEMBER.
4. RESTORE.
revivification *noun* REVIVAL.
revivify *verb*
1, 2. REVIVE.

revocation *noun* REVERSAL.
revoke *verb*
1. LIFT.
2. REVERSE.
revolt *verb*
1. DISGUST.
2. REBEL.
revolt *noun* REBELLION.
revolting *adjective*
1. OFFENSIVE.
2. UNSPEAKABLE.
revolution *noun*
1. A momentous or sweeping change: *an invention that caused a revolution in the industry.*
   Syns: cataclysm, convulsion, upheaval.
2. Circular movement around a point or about an axis: *the earth's revolution around the sun; a phonograph record turning at 45 revolutions a minute.*
   Syns: circuit, circulation, circumvolution, gyration, rotation, turn, wheel, whirl.
revolutionary also **revolutionist** *noun* EXTREMIST.
revolutionize *verb*
To bring about a radical change in: *an electronic advance that revolutionized broadcasting.*
   Syns: metamorphose, transform.
revolve *verb*
1. PONDER.
2. TURN.
revulsion *noun*
1. HATE.
2. HORROR.
reward *noun*
1. Something given in return for a service or accomplishment: *received a reward for the brave rescue.*
   Syns: award, dividend, guerdon (*Poetic*), honorarium, plum, prize. —*Idiom* token of appreciation (*or* esteem).
2. A sum of money offered for a special service, as the apprehension of a criminal: *a reward for the return of the lost jewelry.*
   Syns: bonus, bounty.
3. DUE.
reward *verb*
To bestow a reward on: *rewarded her assistant with a day off.*
   Syn: guerdon (*Poetic*).
reword *verb* PARAPHRASE.
rewording *noun* PARAPHRASE.
rhapsodize *verb* ENTHUSE.
rhetoric *noun* ORATORY.

rhetorical *adjective*
1. ORATORICAL.
2. SONOROUS.
rhetorician *noun* ORATOR.
rhodomontade *noun, adjective, & verb*
SEE **rodomontade.**
rhubarb *noun* ARGUMENT.
rhyme *noun* POEM.
rhyme *verb* AGREE.
rhythm *noun*
The regular recurrence of strong and weak elements, such as stressed and unstressed notes in music: *the rhythm of the tides; a lively waltz rhythm.*
   Syns: beat, cadence (*also* cadency), measure, meter, swing.
rhythmical also **rhythmic** *adjective*
Marked by a regular rhythm: *rhythmical clapping at the end of the concert.*
   Syns: cadenced, measured, metrical (*also* metric), pulsating.
rib *verb* JOKE.
ribbing *noun* RIDICULE.
rich *adjective*
1. Possessing a large amount of money, land, or other material possessions: *His investments had made him rich.*
   Syns: affluent, flush, loaded (*Slang*), moneyed, wealthy. —*Idioms* having money to burn, in the money, made of money, rolling in money.
2. FERTILE.
3. HEAVY.
4. LUXURIOUS.
5. PRICELESS.
riches *noun*
A great amount of accumulated money and precious possessions: *the deposed monarch's riches.*
   Syns: fortune, treasure, wealth, worth.
richness *noun* FERTILITY.
rickety *adjective* UNSTABLE.
ricochet *verb*
1. GLANCE¹.
2. RECOIL.
rid *verb*
To free from something objectionable or undesirable: *plans to rid himself of the unwanted responsibility.*
   Syns: clear, disburden, disembarrass, disencumber, release, relieve, shake (off), throw off, unburden.
riddance *noun*
1. DISPOSAL.
2. ELIMINATION.
riddle *noun* MYSTERY.
ride *verb*
1. BAIT.
2. JOKE.

ride out *verb* SURVIVE.
ride *noun* DRIVE.
ridicule *verb*
To make fun of: *The angry fans ridiculed the losing quarterback.*
  Syns: deride, fleer at, gibe at, jeer at, laugh at, mock, quiz (*Brit.*), razz (*Slang*), scoff (at), scout², sneer at, taunt, twit. —*Idioms* laugh out of court, poke fun at.
ridicule *noun*
Words or actions intended to evoke contemptuous laughter: *had to tolerate a storm of ridicule from his colleagues.*
  Syns: derision, mockery, razzing (*Slang*), ribbing (*Slang*), taunt, twitting.
ridiculous *adjective*
1. LAUGHABLE.
2. OUTRAGEOUS.
rife *adjective*
1. ALIVE.
2. PREVAILING.
riffle *verb*
1. BROWSE.
2. SHUFFLE.
riffraff *noun* TRASH¹.
rift *noun*
1. BREACH.
2. CRACK.
rig *noun*
1. DRESS.
2. OUTFIT.
rig *verb* FURNISH.
rigamarole *noun* SEE **rigmarole**.
right *adjective*
1. ACCURATE.
2. APPROPRIATE.
3. CONSERVATIVE.
4. CORRECT.
5. ETHICAL.
6. HEALTHY.
right *noun*
1. That which is morally proper, fitting, or good: *learning the difference between right and wrong.*
  Syns: rightfulness, rightness.
2. BIRTHRIGHT.
3. FACULTY.
right *adverb*
1. DIRECTLY.
2. PRECISELY.
right *verb*
1. To restore to an upright or proper position: *tipped the boat and then righted it.*
  Syns: stand up, upright.
2. CORRECT.
3. FIX.

righteous *adjective*
1. ETHICAL.
2. HONEST.
righteousness *noun*
1. ETHICS.
2. GOOD.
rightful *adjective* TRUE.
rightfulness *noun* RIGHT.
rightist *noun* CONSERVATIVE.
rightist *adjective* CONSERVATIVE.
right-minded *adjective* ETHICAL.
rightness *noun*
1. ACCURACY.
2. ETHICS.
3. GOOD.
4. RIGHT.
right on *adverb* YES.
right-wing *adjective* CONSERVATIVE.
right-winger *noun* CONSERVATIVE.
rigid *adjective*
1. Not changing shape or bending: *a rigid iron bar.*
  Syns: inelastic, inflexible, stiff, unbending, unflexible, unyielding.
2. INFLEXIBLE.
3. SEVERE.
4. STUBBORN.
rigmarole also **rigamarole** *noun* NONSENSE.
rigor *noun*
1. DIFFICULTY.
2. SEVERITY.
rigorous *adjective*
1. ACCURATE.
2. BURDENSOME.
3. CLOSE¹.
4. STRICT.
rim *noun* BORDER.
rim *verb* BORDER.
rimple *noun* FOLD.
rimple *verb* WRINKLE¹.
rind *noun* SKIN.
ring¹ *noun*
1. CIRCLE.
2. COMBINE.
3. GANG.
4. LOOP.
ring *verb* SURROUND.
ring² *verb*
1. To give forth or cause to give forth a clear, resonant sound: *church bells ringing on Sunday morning.*
  Syns: bong, chime, knell, peal, strike, toll², tintinnabulate (*Rare*).
2. TELEPHONE.
ring *noun* CALL.
ringer *noun* DOUBLE.
ringing *adjective* RESONANT.
ringleader *noun* BOSS.

riot *noun*
1. BRAWL.
2. SCREAM.
  riot *verb*
1. BRAWL.
2. REVEL.
  riot away *verb* WASTE.
riotous *adjective*
1. DISORDERLY.
2. PROFUSE.
rip *verb*
1. SLAM.
2. TEAR¹.
  rip off *verb*
1. ROB.
2. SKIN.
3. STEAL.
  rip *noun* TEAR¹.
ripe *adjective*
1. AGED.
2. MATURE.
  ripe *verb* MATURE.
ripen *verb* MATURE.
ripened *adjective* AGED.
rip-off *noun* ROBBERY.
riposte also **ripost** *noun* RETORT.
ripping *adjective* MARVELOUS.
rippling *adjective* LAUGHING.
rise *verb*
1. To move from a lower to a higher
   position: *Hot air rises.*
   Syns: arise, ascend, lift, mount, soar.
2. To become greater in number,
   amount, or intensity: *Living costs
   continue to rise. Nationalistic feeling
   rose higher every day.*
   Syns: build, burgeon, escalate, grow,
   heighten, increase, magnify, mount,
   multiply, soar.
3. To attain a higher status, rank, or
   condition: *rose through the ranks to
   become a general.*
   Syns: advance, ascend, climb (up),
   mount. *—Idiom* go up the ladder.
4, 5. GET UP at **get.**
6. REBEL.
7. STEM.
8. SUCCEED.
  rise *noun*
1. The act of rising or moving upward:
   watched the rise of the floodwaters.
   Syns: ascension, ascent, mounting,
   rising.
2. ASCENT.
3. HILL.
4, 5. INCREASE.
risible *adjective*
1. AMUSING.
2. LAUGHABLE.

rising *noun* RISE.
risk *verb*
1. To expose to possible loss or
   damage: *risked his money in
   commodity futures; risked the cause of
   peace by loose talk.*
   Syns: adventure, compromise, luck
   (it), hazard, venture.
2. ENDANGER.
3. GAMBLE.
4. HAZARD.
  risk *noun*
1. A possibility of danger or harm: *took
   the risk of walking against the traffic
   light.*
   Syns: chance, gamble, hazard.
2. DANGER.
risky *adjective* DANGEROUS.
risqué *adjective* RACY.
rite *noun* CEREMONY.
ritual *noun*
1. A conventional social gesture or act
   without intrinsic purpose: *Small talk
   at cocktail parties is mere ritual.*
   Syns: ceremony, form, formality.
2. CEREMONY.
  ritual *adjective*
Of or characterized by ceremony: *the
ritual incantations of priests.*
   Syns: ceremonial, formal, liturgical.
ritzy *adjective* EXCLUSIVE.
rival *verb*
1. To come near in quality, amount,
   etc.: *a gourmet dinner that rivaled the
   cuisine of a top restaurant.*
   Syns: approach, approximate, border
   (on *or* upon), challenge, verge on.
2. COMPETE.
  rival *noun* COMPETITOR.
rivalry *noun* COMPETITION.
rive *verb*
1. BREAK.
2. TEAR¹.
rivet *verb* GRIP.
road *noun* WAY.
roadway *noun* WAY.
roam *verb*
1. BROWSE.
2. ROVE.
roaming *adjective*
1. ERRANT.
2. NOMADIC.
roar *verb*
1. To speak or say very loudly: *"Who
   goes there?" roared the sentry. The
   mob roared in rage.*
   Syns: bawl, bellow, bluster, call,
   clamor, cry, halloo (*also* halloa),
   holler, shout, yawp (*also* yaup), yell.
2. BLAST.

3. BREAK UP at **break**.
roar *noun*
1. A loud, deep, prolonged sound: *heard a roar of excitement in the stadium.*
   Syns: bawl, bellow, clamor.
2. BLAST.
roaring *adjective*
1. FLOURISHING.
2. LOUD.
roast *verb*
1. BURN.
2. SLAM.
rob *verb*
1. To take property or possessions from (a person, company, etc.) unlawfully and usu. forcibly: *robbing pedestrians in the park; robbed a bank.*
   Syns: bail³ (*Austral.*), heist (*Slang*), hit (*Slang*), hold up, knock off (*Slang*), knock over (*Slang*), rip off (*Slang*), stick up (*Informal*).
2. DEPRIVE.
robbery *noun*
The act or crime of taking another's property unlawfully and by force: *a bank robbery committed in broad daylight.*
   Syns: heist (*Slang*), holdup, rip-off (*Slang*), stickup (*Informal*).
robe *verb* CLOTHE.
robes *noun* HABIT.
roborant *adjective* TONIC.
roborant *noun* TONIC.
robust *adjective*
1. FLOURISHING.
2. LUSTY.
3. MUSCULAR.
rock¹ *noun* BLUNDER.
rock² *verb*
1, 2. AGITATE.
3. SHAKE.
4. TOSS.
rocket *verb*
1. RUSH.
2. SOAR.
rockiness *noun* INDISPOSITION.
rocky *adjective*
1. OBSCENE.
2. SICKLY.
rococo *adjective* ORNATE.
rod *noun* STICK.
rodomontade also **rhodomontade** *noun* BOAST.
rodomontade also **rhodomontade** *adjective* BOASTFUL.
rodomontade also **rhodomontade** *verb* BOAST.
rogation *noun* PRAYER.
Roger *adverb* YES.

rogue *noun* MISCHIEF.
roguery *noun* MISCHIEF.
roguishness *noun* MISCHIEF.
roiled *adjective*
1. ROUGH.
2. TURBID.
roily *adjective*
1. ROUGH.
2. TURBID.
roister *verb* REVEL.
role also **rôle** *noun*
1. FUNCTION.
2. PART.
roll *verb*
1. FLOW.
2. LURCH.
3. LUXURIATE.
4. RUMBLE.
5. TOSS.
6. WRAP UP at **wrap**.
roll in *verb* RETIRE.
roll out *verb* GET UP at **get**.
roll up *verb* ACCUMULATE.
roll *noun* LIST¹.
rollick *verb*
1. GAMBOL.
2. LUXURIATE.
roly-poly *adjective* PLUMP¹.
romance *verb* COURT.
romantic *adjective*
1. IDEALISTIC.
2. SENTIMENTAL.
romanticize *verb* SENTIMENTALIZE.
Romeo *noun* GALLANT.
romp *verb* GAMBOL.
romp *noun* RUNAWAY.
roof *noun* HEIGHT.
rook *verb* CHEAT.
rookie *noun* BEGINNER.
room *noun*
1. Suitable opportunity to accept or allow something: *no room for error.*
   Syns: latitude, leeway, margin, play, scope.
2. PLACE.
room *verb* HARBOR.
roomy *adjective*
Having plenty of room: *a roomy house.*
   Syns: ample, capacious, commodious, spacious.
root¹ *noun*
1. BASIS.
2. CENTER.
3. HEART.
4. ORIGIN.
5. THEME.
root *verb* FIX.
root in *verb* BASE¹.
root out *verb* ANNIHILATE.

root² *verb* APPLAUD.
rootstock *noun* ORIGIN.
roseate *adjective*
  1. ENCOURAGING.
  2. OPTIMISTIC.
rose-colored *adjective*
ENCOURAGING.
roster *noun* LIST¹.
rosy *adjective*
  1. ENCOURAGING.
  2. OPTIMISTIC.
  3. RUDDY.
rot *verb* DECAY.
  rot *noun* DECAY.
rotate *verb*
  1. To do, use, or occur in successive
     turns: *rotated their days off.*
     Syns: alternate, interchange
     (*Archaic*).
  2. TURN.
rotation *noun*
  1. Occurrence in successive turns:
     *worked weekends in rotation with other
     nurses.*
     Syns: alternation, interchange
     (*Archaic*).
  2. REVOLUTION.
rotten *adjective*
  1. BAD.
  2. CORRUPT.
  3. FILTHY.
  4. SHODDY.
rotund *adjective*
  1. PLUMP¹.
  2. RESONANT.
roué *noun* WANTON.
rough *adjective*
  1. Having a coarse, irregular surface:
     rough granite cliffs.
     Syns: asperous, coarse, cragged,
     craggy, harsh, ironbound, jagged,
     ragged, rugged, scabrous, uneven.
  2. Marked by vigorous physical
     exertion: *rugby and other rough
     games.*
     Syns: knockabout, rough-and-
     tumble, rugged, strenuous, tough.
  3. Violently disturbed, as by storms:
     rough seas.
     Syns: agitated, dirty, heavy, raging,
     roiled, roily, stormy, tempestuous,
     tumultuous, turbid, turbulent, ugly,
     violent, wild.
  4. Not perfected, elaborated, or
     completed: *the rough draft of a
     treaty.*
     Syns: preliminary, sketchy,
     tentative, unfinished, unperfected,
     unpolished.

  5. BURDENSOME.
  6, 7. COARSE.
  8. HARSH.
  9. RUDE.
  10. WILD.
rough *verb* SLAP AROUND at **slap.**
rough in *verb* DRAFT.
rough out *verb* DRAFT.
rough up *verb* BATTER.
rough *noun* DRAFT.
rough-and-tumble *adjective* ROUGH.
roughly *adverb* APPROXIMATELY.
roughneck *noun* TOUGH.
roughness *noun* IRREGULARITY.
round *adjective*
  1. Having the shape of a curve
     everywhere equidistant from a fixed
     point: *The world is round.*
     Syns: annular, circular, globoid,
     globular, spherical (*also* spheric),
     spheroidal (*also* spheroidic,
     spheroidical).
  2. Not more or less: *a round dozen.*
     Syns: complete, entire, full, good,
     perfect, whole.
  3. PLUMP¹.
  4. RESONANT.
round *noun*
  1. BEAT.
  2. BEND.
  3. CIRCLE.
  4. ROUTINE.
  5. RUN.
round *adverb*
  1. BACK.
  2. BACKWARD.
  3. THROUGH.
round *verb* BEND.
round off *verb* COMPLEMENT.
round out *verb* COMPLEMENT.
round up *verb* ASSEMBLE.
roundabout *adjective* INDIRECT.
rounded *adjective* BENT.
round-the-clock *also* **around-the-clock**
adjective CONTINUAL.
rouse *verb*
  1. AROUSE.
  2. PROVOKE.
  3. WAKE.
rousing *adjective*
  1. INSPIRING.
  2. STIMULATING.
roustabout *noun* LABORER.
rout¹ *noun* CROWD.
rout² *verb* DEFEAT.
  rout *noun* DEFEAT.
route *verb*
  1. GUIDE.
  2. SEND.

route *noun*
1. BEAT.
2. TICKET.

routine *noun*
1. A course of action to be followed regularly: *a daily routine that includes exercise.*
   Syns: round, track.
2. BIT[1].
3. GRIND.

routine *adjective*
1. Lacking in interest or originality: *a routine comedy.*
   Syns: cut-and-dried, formulaic, standard, stock.
2. ACCUSTOMED.
3. COMMON.

rove *verb*
To move about at random, esp. over a wide area: *tourists roving around in the city.*
   Syns: drift, gad about (*or* around), gallivant, meander, peregrinate, ramble, range, roam, stray (over), traipse, wander.

roving *adjective*
1. ERRANT.
2. NOMADIC.

row[1] *noun* LINE.

row[2] *noun*
1. ARGUMENT.
2. BRAWL.

rowdy *adjective* DISORDERLY.

rowdy *noun* TOUGH.

royal *adjective* GRAND.

royalist *noun* REACTIONARY.

rozzer *noun* POLICEMAN.

rub *noun* CATCH.

rub out *verb*
1. ANNIHILATE.
2. CANCEL.
3. MURDER.

rubberneck *also* **rubbernecker** *noun* TOURIST.

rubble *verb* DESTROY.

rubicund *adjective* RUDDY.

rubric *noun* RULE.

ruck[1] *noun*
1. COMMONALTY.
2. HEAP.

ruck[2] *verb* FOLD.
ruck *noun* FOLD.

ruckle *verb* WRINKLE[1].

ruckus *noun* BRAWL.

ruction *noun* BRAWL.

ruddy *adjective*
1. Of a healthy, reddish color: *ruddy cheeks.*
   Syns: blooming, florid, flush, flushed, full-blooded, glowing, rosy, rubicund, sanguine.
2. DAMNED.

rude *adjective*
1. Lacking good manners: *rude, offensive behavior.*
   Syns: bad-mannered, discourteous, ill-bred, ill-mannered, impolite, ungracious, unmannerly, unpolished.
2. Lacking expert, careful craftsmanship: *a rude hut; a rude sculpture.*
   Syns: crude, primitive, raw, rough, unpolished.
3. COARSE.
4. INHARMONIOUS.
5. UNCIVILIZED.

rudeness *noun* IMPUDENCE.

rudiment
1. BASIS.
2. ELEMENT.

rudimental *adjective* ELEMENTARY.
rudimentary *adjective* ELEMENTARY.

rue *noun* PENITENCE.
rue *verb* REGRET.

rueful *adjective*
1. PITIFUL.
2, 3. SORROWFUL.

ruffian *noun* THUG.

ruffle *verb*
1. AGITATE.
2. ANNOY.

rugged *adjective*
1. BITTER.
2. HARD.
3. HARSH.
4, 5. ROUGH.

ruin *noun*
1. Severe damage or decay rendering something useless or worthless: *Moral turpitude hastened the ruin of the Roman Empire.*
   Syns: decimation, degeneration, destruction, deterioration, devastation, disintegration, undoing.
2. Something that causes total loss or severe impairment of one's health, fortune, honor, hopes, etc.: *Adolf Hitler was the ruin of Germany. Gambling was his ruin.*
   Syns: bane, destroyer, destruction, downfall, ruination, undoing.
3. The remains of something destroyed, disintegrated, or decayed: *the barnacled ruin of a pirate's brigantine; a land dotted with the ruins of past civilizations.*
   Syns: relic, remainder, remnant, vestige, wrack, wreckage.
4. DESTRUCTION.

ruin *verb*
1. To reduce to financial insolvency: *Bad investments ruined him.*
   Syns: bankrupt, break, bust (*Slang*), clean out (*Informal*), impoverish, pauper, sink. —*Idioms* drive to the wall, put (*or* shove) onto the rocks.
2, 3. BREAK.
4. DESTROY.

ruinate *verb* DESTROY.

ruination *noun*
1. DESTRUCTION.
2. RUIN.

ruinous *adjective*
1. Falling to ruin: *A ruinous old fortress was the island's only tourist attraction.*
   Syns: dilapidated, ramshackle, tumble-down. —*Idiom* gone to seed.
2. DESTRUCTIVE.
3. FATAL.

rule *noun*
1. A code or set of codes governing action, procedure, etc.: *the rules of chess; a rule of grammar.*
   Syns: dictate, prescript, regulation, rubric.
2. DOMINATION.
3, 4. GOVERNMENT.
5. LAW.
6. USUAL.

rule *verb*
1. BOSS.
2. CONTROL.
3. DOMINATE.
4. GOVERN.
5. JUDGE.

rule out *verb*
1. EXCLUDE.
2. PREVENT.

ruling *noun*
An authoritative or official decision, esp. one made by a court: *an appellate court ruling; the Supreme Court's ruling on school integration.*
   Syns: decree, determination, edict, judgment, pronouncement.

ruling *adjective*
1. Having pre-eminent significance: *the ruling passion of his life.*
   Syns: ascendant, dominant, predominant, prepotent, prevailing, supreme.
2. DOMINANT.

rum *also* **rummy** *adjective*
ECCENTRIC.

rumble *verb*
1. To make a continuous deep, reverberating sound: *heard the convoy rumbling in the distance.*
   Syns: boom, growl, grumble, roll.

2. MUTTER.

rumble *noun* MUTTER.

ruminate *verb* PONDER.

rumination *noun* THOUGHT.

ruminative *adjective* THOUGHTFUL.

rummage *verb* SCOUR.

rummy[1] *noun* DRUNKARD.

rummy[2] *adjective* SEE **rum.**

rumor *noun* GOSSIP.

rumor *verb* GOSSIP.

rumorer *noun* GOSSIP.

rumormonger *noun* GOSSIP.

rump *noun* BOTTOM.

rumple *verb*
1. TOUSLE.
2. WRINKLE[1].

rumpus *noun*
1. DISTURBANCE.
2. NOISE.
3. VOCIFERATION.

run *verb*
1. To move swiftly on foot so that both feet leave the ground during each stride: *The boy runs like a deer. We ran to the corner.*
   Syns: dash, fly (*Informal*), scamper, scoot, scurry, sprint, tear (*Informal*). —*Idiom* run like the wind.
2. To leave hastily: *hates people who eat and run; robbed the bank and ran.*
   Syns: bolt, clear out (*Informal*), fly, get (*Regional & Informal*), get out, hightail (*Slang*), hotfoot (*Slang*), scram (*Slang*), skedaddle (*Informal*), skiddoo (*Informal*), split (*Slang*), take off (*Slang*), vamoose (*also* vamose) (*Slang*). —*Idioms* beat it, make tracks.
3. To complete a race or competition in a specified position: *He ran third in a field of eight.*
   Syns: come in, finish, place.
4. ADMINISTER.
5. AMOUNT.
6, 7. DRIVE.
8. EXTEND.
9. FLOW.
10, 11. GO.
12. HUNT.
13. MELT.
14. OPERATE.
15. RAM.
16. RESORT TO at **resort.**
17. RUSH.
18. SMUGGLE.
19. WORK.

run across *verb* COME ACROSS at **come.**

run after *verb* PURSUE.
run along *verb* GO.
run around *verb* ASSOCIATE.
run away *verb* ESCAPE.
run down *verb*
1. To lose so much strength and power as to become ineffective or motionless: *I seem to run down at about 4 o'clock in the afternoon.* **Syns:** burn out, give out, play out, poop out (*Slang*).
2. To pursue and locate: *The police were able to run down their missing witness.* **Syns:** hunt down, nose out (*Slang*), trace, track down. —*Idiom* run to earth.
3. BELITTLE.
4. REVIEW.
run dry *verb* DRY UP at **dry.**
run in *verb*
1. ARREST.
2. VISIT.
run into *verb*
1. COME ACROSS at **come.**
2. ENCOUNTER.
run on *verb* CHATTER.
run out *verb*
1. DEFECT.
2. DRY UP at **dry.**
3. FAIL.
4. LAPSE.
run through *verb*
1. BROWSE.
2. EXHAUST.
3. GO.
4. REVIEW.
run up *verb* INCREASE.
run *noun*
1. An unbroken sequence of events: *a run of victories; a run of Broadway hits.* **Syns:** chain, round, series, string, succession, train.
2. BRANCH.
3. CONTINUANCE.
4. SERIES.
runagate *noun* DEFECTOR.
runaway *noun*
1. *Informal.* An easy victory: *The election was a runaway for our candidate.* **Syns:** pushover, romp (*Slang*), walkaway, walkover.
2. FUGITIVE.
runaway *adjective*
1. Out of control: *a runaway train; a runaway mob of angry protesters.* **Syns:** amuck (*also* amok), uncontrolled. —*Idioms* out of hand, running wild.
2. FUGITIVE.

run-down *noun* SUMMARY.
run-down *adjective*
1. Depleted of strength or robust health: *He's run-down from overwork.* **Syns:** debilitated, drained, enervated, enfeebled, weakened.
2. SHABBY.
rung *noun* DEGREE.
run-in *noun*
1. ARGUMENT.
2. BRUSH.
3. FIGHT.
runner *noun*
1. BEARER.
2. SHOOT.
3. SMUGGLER.
running *adjective*
1. ACTIVE.
2. SMOOTH.
run-of-the-mill *adjective* ORDINARY.
run-through *noun* SUMMARY.
runty *adjective* ILL-TEMPERED.
rupture *noun*
1, 2. BREACH.
rupture *verb*
1. BREACH.
2. CRACK.
rural *adjective* COUNTRY.
ruse *noun*
1. DECEPTION.
2. TRICK.
rush *verb*
1. To move swiftly: *rushed home from the airport.* **Syns:** barrel (*Slang*), boil, bolt, bucket, bullet, bustle, dart, dash, dust (*Slang*), festinate, flash, fleet¹, flit, fly, haste (*Poetic*), hasten, hell (*Informal*), highball, hurry, hustle (*Informal*), nip¹ (*Brit. Slang*), pelt², race, rip (*Brit. Slang*), rocket, run, sail, scoot, scour, scurry, shoot, skin (out), speed, stave², tear¹, trot, whirl, whisk, whiz (*also* whizz), wing, zip, zoom. —*Idioms* beeline it, get a move on, get cracking, go like lightning, go like the wind, hotfoot it, make a beeline, make haste, make tracks, shake a leg, step (*or* jump) on it.
2. COURT.
3. FLOW.
rush *noun*
1. CHARGE.
2. FLOW.
3. HASTE.
rush *adjective* CRASH.
rustic *adjective*
1. Of a plain and unsophisticated nature: *the truth in his rustic philosophy; a rustic beauty.*

Syns: artless, homely, homespun, natural, unadorned, unpolished.
2. COUNTRY.

rut *noun*
1. GRIND.
2. HEAT.

ruthless *adjective* UNSCRUPULOUS.

S

sable *adjective* BLACK.

sabotage *noun*
A deliberate and underhanded effort to defeat or do harm to an endeavor: *Production was slowed down by industrial sabotage.*
Syns: subversion, undermining.

sabotage *verb*
To damage, destroy, or defeat by sabotage: *a campaign that was sabotaged by undercover agents.*
Syns: subvert, undermine.

saccharine *adjective*
1. INSINUATING.
2. SWEET.

sack¹ *noun* DISMISSAL.
sack *verb* DISMISS.

sack² *verb*
To rob of goods by force, esp. in time of war: *villages that were sacked by invaders.*
Syns: depredate, despoil, harrow, havoc (*Rare*), loot, pillage, plunder, rape, ravage, spoil (*Obs.*), spoliate.

sacrarium *noun* SANCTUARY.

sacred *adjective*
1. Given over exclusively to a single use or purpose: *a place sacred to the memory of those who fell in battle.*
Syns: consecrated, dedicated, devoted, hallowed.
2. Protected from violation or abuse by custom, law, or feelings of reverence: *a sacred vow.*
Syns: inviolable, sacrosanct.
3. DIVINE.
4. HOLY.

sacredness *noun*
1. HOLINESS.
2. SANCTITY.

sacrifice *noun*
1. A living creature slain and offered to a deity as part of a religious rite: *The priest chose a young goat as a sacrifice.*
Syns: hecatomb, immolation, offering, victim.
2. COST.

sacrifice *verb*
To offer as a sacrifice: *sacrificed two white doves on the altar of the temple.*
Syns: immolate, victimize.

sacrilege *noun*
An act of disrespect or impiety toward something regarded as sacred: *The theft of the holy relics was a sacrilege.*
Syns: blasphemy, desecration, profanation, violation.

sacrilegious *adjective*
Showing irreverence and contempt for something sacred: *sacrilegious mockery.*
Syns: blasphemous, profane.

sacrosanct *adjective*
1. HOLY.
2. SACRED.

sacrosanctity *noun* SANCTITY.

sad *adjective*
1. Tending to cause sadness or low spirits: *a sad tale of family discord.*
Syns: depressing, dismal, gloomy, joyless, melancholy.
2. DEPRESSED.
3. SORROWFUL.

sadden *verb* DEPRESS.

saddened *adjective* DEPRESSED.

saddle *verb*
1. CHARGE.
2. FIX.
3. IMPOSE.

sadness *noun* GLOOM.

safe *adjective*
1. Free from danger, injury, or the threat of harm: *was perfectly safe at home.*
Syns: unharmed, unhurt, uninjured, unscathed. —*Idioms* safe and sound, with a whole skin.
2. Affording protection: *a spot safe from enemy fire.*
Syn: secure. —*Idiom* as safe as houses.

safeguard *verb* DEFEND.
safeguard *noun* DEFENSE.
safeness *noun* SAFETY.

safety *noun*
The quality or state of being safe: *guaranteed the safety of the children.*
Syns: assurance, safeness, security.

sag *verb*
1. SLIP.
2. SLOUCH.
3. WILT.

sag *noun* DEPRESSION.

sagacious *adjective*
1. SANE.
2. WISE¹.
sagacity *noun* DISCERNMENT.
sage *noun*
A usu. elderly man noted for wisdom, knowledge, and judgment: *Many considered Oliver Wendell Holmes a sage.*
    Syns: Nestor, pundit, savant, scholar.
sage *adjective*
1. SANE.
2. WISE¹.
sageness *noun* DISCERNMENT.
sail *verb*
1. FLOW.
2, 3. FLY.
4. RUSH.
sail in (or into) *verb*
1, 2. ATTACK.
sailor *noun*
A person engaged in sailing or working on a ship: *A crew of 11 sailors manned the tanker.*
    Syns: gob¹ (*Slang*), jack (*Informal*), jack-tar (*Informal*), mariner, navigator, salt (*Informal*), sea dog (*Slang*), seafarer, seaman, tar (*Informal*).
salability *noun* SELL.
salableness *noun* SELL.
salary *noun* WAGE(S).
sales clerk *noun* SELLER.
salesperson *noun* SELLER.
salient *adjective* NOTICEABLE.
salivate *verb* DROOL.
salivation *noun* DROOL.
sallow *adjective* PALE.
salmagundi *noun* ASSORTMENT.
salt *noun*
1. LIVING.
2. SAILOR.
salt away *verb*
1. BANK¹.
2. SAVE.
salty *adjective* RACY.
salubrious *adjective* HEALTHFUL.
salutary *adjective*
1. BENEFICIAL.
2. HEALTHFUL.
salutation *noun* GREETING.
salute *verb* GREET.
salute *noun*
1. GREETING.
2. TESTIMONIAL.
salvage *verb* RESCUE.
salvage *noun* RESCUE.
salvation *noun* RESCUE.

salvo *noun*
1. BARRAGE.
2. TESTIMONIAL.
same *adjective*
1. Being one and not another or others; not different in nature or identity: *That is the same seat I had yesterday.*
    Syns: identic (*Archaic*), identical, selfsame, very.
2. CONSISTENT.
3. EQUAL.
sameness *noun*
1. The quality or condition of being exactly the same as something else: *the sameness of the fingerprints.*
    Syns: identicalness, identity, oneness, selfsameness.
2. EQUIVALENCE.
3. MONOTONY.
sample *noun*
1. EXAMPLE.
2. TASTE.
sanctified *adjective* HOLY.
sanctify *verb*
To make sacred by a religious rite: *sanctified the day for the worship of God.*
    Syns: bless, consecrate, hallow.
sanctimonious *adjective* HYPOCRITICAL.
sanctimony also **sanctimoniousness** *noun* HYPOCRISY.
sanction *verb* PERMIT.
sanction *noun*
1. A coercive measure intended to ensure compliance or conformity: *invoked sanctions against the countries that flouted international law.*
    Syns: interdict, interdiction, penalty.
2. PERMISSION.
sanctioned *adjective*
1. ACCEPTED.
2. AUTHORITATIVE.
3. ORTHODOX.
sanctity *noun*
1. The quality or condition of being safe from assault, trespass, or violation: *the sanctity of the home.*
    Syns: inviolability, sacredness, sacrosanctity.
2. HOLINESS.
sanctorium *noun* SANCTUARY.
sanctuary *noun*
1. A sacred or holy place: *the sanctuary of a church.*
    Syns: sacrarium (*Eccles.*), sanctorium, sanctum, shrine.
2. COVER.
3. REFUGE.
sanctum *noun* SANCTUARY.

sane *adjective*
1. Of sound mind; mentally healthy: *a sane person.*
   Syns: compos mentis (*Latin*), lucid, rational. —*Idioms* all there, in one's right mind, of sound mind.
2. Possessing, proceeding from, or exhibiting good judgment and prudence: *a sane decision.*
   Syns: balanced, commonsensible, commonsensical, judicious, levelheaded, prudent, rational, reasonable, sagacious, sage, sapient, sensible, sensical, sound², well-founded, well-grounded, wise¹.

saneness *noun* SANITY.

sang-froid *noun*
1. CALM.
2. NONCHALANCE.

sanguinary *adjective*
1. BLOODY.
2. MURDEROUS.

sanguine *adjective*
1. OPTIMISTIC.
2. RUDDY.

sanguineness *noun* OPTIMISM.

sanguineous *adjective*
1. BLOODY.
2. MURDEROUS.

sanguinity *noun* OPTIMISM.

sanitize *verb* STERILIZE.

sanitized *adjective* STERILE.

sanity *noun*
A healthy mental state: *lost her sanity.*
   Syns: lucidity, lucidness, marbles (*Slang*), mind, reason, saneness, sense, senses, soundness, wit, wits.

sap¹ *noun* DUPE.

sap² *verb* ENERVATE.

sapience *noun* WISDOM.

sapient *adjective*
1. SANE.
2. WISE¹.

sapor *noun* FLAVOR.

sappy *adjective*
1. FOOLISH.
2. SENTIMENTAL.

sarcasm *noun*
Ironic, bitter humor designed to wound: *cruel and devastating sarcasm.*
   Syns: acerbity, causticity, corrosiveness, mordacity, mordancy.

sarcastic *adjective*
Given to or expressing sarcasm: *a sarcastic, sneering critic; sarcastic remarks.*
   Syns: acerb, acerbic, caustic, corrosive, mordant.

sardonic *adjective* CYNICAL.

sashay *verb* STRUT.

sass *verb* TALK BACK at **talk.**

sassy *adjective* IMPUDENT.

satanic also **satanical** *adjective* FIENDISH.

sate *verb* SATIATE.

sated *adjective* SATIATED.

satellite *noun* FOLLOWER.

satiate *verb*
To satisfy to the full or to excess: *The large meal satiated our hunger.*
   Syns: cloy, glut, gorge, sate, surfeit.

satiate *adjective* SATIATED.

satiated *adjective*
Filled to satisfaction or excess: *Satiated with crime stories, readers turned to other amusements.*
   Syns: glutted, gorged, replete, sated, satiate, surfeited.

satiation *noun*
The condition of being full to or beyond satisfaction: *Some dietitians advise stopping eating before the point of satiation.*
   Syns: engorgement, repletion, satiety, surfeit.

satiety *noun* SATIATION.

satiny *adjective* SLEEK.

satire *noun*
A work, as a novel or play, that exposes folly by the use of humor or irony: *wrote an amusing satire on pompous businessmen.*
   Syns: lampoon, lampoonery.

satisfaction *noun* COMPENSATION.

satisfactory *adjective*
1. ACCEPTABLE.
2. CONVINCING.
3. SUFFICIENT.

satisfied *adjective* FULFILLED.

satisfy *verb*
1. To grant or have what is demanded by (a need or desire): *satisfied his appetite for the time being; satisfying a lifelong desire to see Ireland.*
   Syns: appease, fulfill, gratify, indulge.
2. To supply fully or completely: *satisfied all requirements.*
   Syns: answer, fill, fulfill, meet¹.
3. CONVINCE.
4. PLEASE.
5. SETTLE.

satisfying *adjective* GRATEFUL.

satisfyingly *adverb* WELL².

saturate *verb*
1. CHARGE.
2. WET.

saturnine *adjective* GLUM.

satyr *noun* WANTON.

sauce *noun* IMPUDENCE.
  sauce *verb* TALK BACK at **talk**.
saucebox *noun* SMART ALECK.
sauciness *noun* IMPUDENCE.
saucy *adjective* IMPUDENT.
saunter *verb* STROLL.
  saunter *noun* WALK.
savage *adjective*
1. Of or relating to beasts of prey: *a savage lion.*
  Syns: feral, wild.
2. CRUEL.
3. FIERCE.
4. UNCIVILIZED.
savant *noun* SAGE.
save *verb*
1. To reserve for the future: *saved the old baby clothes for future grandchildren; save money each month in a Christmas club.*
  Syns: keep, lay aside, lay away, lay by, lay in, put by, salt away, set by, spare.
2. CONSERVE.
3. ECONOMIZE.
4. RESCUE.
5. STOCKPILE.
saving *adjective* ECONOMICAL.
savoir-faire *noun* TACT.
savor *noun*
1, 2. FLAVOR.
3. QUALITY.
  savor *verb*
1. APPRECIATE.
2. ENJOY.
3. FEEL.
4. SMACK².
savory *adjective* DELICIOUS.
savvy *noun* GRASP.
  savvy *adjective* SHREWD.
  savvy *verb* UNDERSTAND.
saw *noun* PROVERB.
saw off *verb* SUSPEND.
say *verb*
1. To put into words: *The speaker said what was on his mind and then sat down.*
  Syns: articulate, communicate, convey, declare, express, state, tell, utter¹, vent, vocalize, voice. —*Idiom* give vent (*or* voice *or* tongue) to.
2. CLAIM.
3. PRONOUNCE.
  say *noun* VOICE.
saying *noun* PROVERB.
say-so *noun*
1. AUTHORITY.
2. VOICE.

scabrous *adjective*
1. RACY.
2. ROUGH.
scad *noun* HEAP.
scaffold *noun* STAGE.
scaffolding *noun* STAGE.
scalding *adjective* HOT.
scale¹ *verb* SKIN.
scale² *verb* ASCEND.
scaling *noun* ASCENT.
scalp *verb* SKIN.
scamp *noun* MISCHIEF.
scamper *verb* RUN.
scan *verb*
1. BROWSE.
2. SURVEY.
scandal *noun* LIBEL.
  scandal *verb* LIBEL.
scandalize *verb*
1. LIBEL.
2. SHOCK.
scandalmonger *noun* GOSSIP.
scandalous *adjective*
1. LIBELOUS.
2. OUTRAGEOUS.
scant *adjective*
1. BARE.
2. MEAGER.
scantiness *noun* SHORTAGE.
scanty *adjective*
1. INSUFFICIENT.
2. MEAGER.
scapegoat *noun*
One who is made an object of blame: *The manager was a convenient scapegoat for the team's poor performance.*
  Syns: fall guy (*Slang*), goat, patsy (*Slang*), whipping boy.
scarce *adjective*
1. INFREQUENT.
2. INSUFFICIENT.
  scarce *adverb* BARELY.
scarceness *noun* SHORTAGE.
scarcity *noun* SHORTAGE.
scare *verb* FRIGHTEN.
scarecrow *noun* TATTERDEMALION.
scared *adjective* AFRAID.
scaremonger *noun* ALARMIST.
scarify *verb*
1. FRIGHTEN.
2. SLAM.
scary *adjective* FEARFUL.
scathe *verb* SLAM.
scathing *adjective* BITING.
scatological *also* **scatologic** *adjective*
OBSCENE.
scatter *verb*
1. To separate or cause to separate and go in various directions: *At a*

command the children scattered and
found hiding places.
Syns: dispel, disperse, dissipate.
2. LIFT.
3. SPREAD.

scatterbrained *adjective* GIDDY.

scattergood *noun* WASTREL.

scene *noun*
1. The place where an action or event
occurs: *Police arrived on the scene
shortly after the robbery.*
Syns: locale, setting, site, stage.
2. The properties, backdrops, and other
objects arranged for a dramatic
presentation: *When the curtain rose,
the audience applauded the beautifully
designed scene.*
Syns: mise en scène, scenery, set²,
setting.
3. AREA.
4. VIEW.

scenery *noun* SCENE.

scent *noun*
1. FRAGRANCE.
2. LEAD.
3, 4. SMELL.
5. TRAIL.

scent *verb*
1. To fill with a pleasant odor: *Pine
resin scented the air about the
campsite.*
Syns: aromatize, perfume.
2. SMELL.

scented *adjective* FRAGRANT.

schedule *noun*
1. LIST¹.
2. PROGRAM.

schedule *verb*
1. To enter on a schedule: *scheduled a
dental appointment for next Thursday.*
Syns: program, slate.
2. ARRANGE.
3. TIME.

scheduled *adjective* DUE.

schema *noun* DESIGN.

scheme *noun*
1. DESIGN.
2. PLOT.

scheme *verb* PLOT.

scheming *adjective*
1. ARTFUL.
2. CALCULATING.

schism *noun* BREACH.

schismatic *noun* SEPARATIST.

schismatist *noun* SEPARATIST.

schlep *verb* CARRY.

schlocky *adjective* SHODDY.

schmaltz *noun* SENTIMENTALITY.

schmaltzy *adjective* SENTIMENTAL.

schmo also **schmoe** *noun* FOOL.

schmuck *noun* FOOL.

schnozzle *noun* NOSE.

scholar *noun*
1. SAGE.
2. STUDENT.

scholarly *adjective*
1. LEARNED.
2. STUDIOUS.

scholarship *noun* EDUCATION.

scholastic *adjective*
1. LEARNED.
2. PEDANTIC.

scholastic *noun* STUDENT.

schooling *noun* EDUCATION.

science *noun* EDUCATION.

scilicet *adverb* NAMELY.

scintillate *verb* FLASH.

scintillating *adjective* CLEVER.

scintillation *noun* GLITTER.

scion *noun* DESCENDANT.

scoff *verb* RIDICULE.

scold *verb* CALL DOWN at **call.**

scold *noun*
A person, esp. a woman, who habitually
uses loud, abusive language: *If he came
home late, his scold of a wife berated him
unmercifully.*
Syns: battle-ax *or* battle-axe, fishwife,
fury, harpy, shrew, termagant, virago,
vixen, Xanthippe.

scoop *verb* DIG.

scoop up *verb* DIP.

scoot *verb*
1. RUN.
2. RUSH.

scope *noun*
1. GRASP.
2. KEN.
3. RANGE.
4. ROOM.

scorch *verb*
1, 2. BURN.
3. SLAM.

scorch *noun* BURN.

scorching *adjective* HOT.

score *noun*
1. An incision, notch, or slight cut made
with or as if with a knife: *made a
score in the maple trunk to let the sap
run.*
Syns: scotch, scratch, slash.
2. The total number of points made by
a contestant, side, or team in a game
or contest: *a final score of 3–2.*
Syn: tally. —*Idiom* the final count (*or*
result).
3. A harbored grievance demanding

satisfaction: *We have an old score to settle.*
Syn: account.
score *verb*
1. To gain (a point or points) in a game or contest: *scored three aces in the last set.*
Syns: notch, post, tally. —*Idioms* bring home, hang up another, put in one's column.
2. To evaluate and assign a grade to: *scored the test.*
Syns: grade, mark.
3. ACCOMPLISH.
4. PROSPER.
5. SLAM.
scores *noun* CROWD.
scorn *noun* DESPISAL.
scorn *verb* DESPISE.
scotch *noun* SCORE.
Scotch *adjective* ECONOMICAL.
scoundrel *noun* HEAVY.
scour *verb*
1. To make a thorough search of: *I scoured the bookstores for that novel.*
Syns: comb, forage, ransack, rummage, shake down (*Informal*). —*Idioms* beat the bushes, leave no avenue unexplored, leave no stone unturned, look high and low, look up and down, search the high heavens, turn inside out, turn upside-down.
2. RUSH.
3. SCRAPE.
4. SCRUB.
scourge *noun* CURSE.
scourge *verb*
1. AFFLICT.
2. SLAM.
scout¹ *verb* EXPLORE.
scout² *verb*
1. DESPISE.
2. RIDICULE.
scowl *noun*
1. FROWN.
2. GLARE.
scowl *verb*
1. FROWN.
2. GLARE.
scram *verb* RUN.
scramble *verb*
1. To move or climb hurriedly, esp. on all fours: *scrambled over the hills to safety.*
Syn: clamber.
2. CONFUSE.
3. SHUFFLE.
scramble *noun* DISORDER.
scrap¹ *noun*
1. BIT¹.

2. END.
scrap *verb* DISCARD.
scrap² *noun*
1, 2. FIGHT.
scrape *verb*
1. To remove (an outer layer or adherent matter) by rubbing a surface with considerable pressure: *scrape the old paint off the bench.*
Syns: scour, scrub.
2. To bring or come into sliding, abrasive contact, often with a harsh, grating sound: *a chair scraping along the floor.*
Syns: grate, rasp, scratch.
3. To manage with difficulty or so as to barely escape failure: *scraped through college.*
Syn: shave. —*Idiom* get through on a wing and a prayer.
4. SCRIMP.
scrape *noun* PREDICAMENT.
scrappy *adjective*
1. ARGUMENTATIVE.
2. BELLIGERENT.
scratch *noun*
1. MONEY.
2. SCORE.
scratch *verb*
1. CANCEL.
2. SCRAPE.
scratch out *verb* CANCEL.
scrawny *adjective* THIN.
screak also **screek** *noun* SCREAM.
screak also **screek** *verb* SCREAM.
scream *verb*
1. To utter a long, loud, piercing cry, as of pain or fright: *screamed when the bus hit the light pole.*
Syns: screak (*also* screek), screech, shriek, shrill.
2. To have or produce a blatantly startling effect: *His long hair and loud clothes screamed his nonconformity.*
Syns: blare, blaze¹, shout, shriek.
scream *noun*
1. A long, loud, piercing cry or sound: *gave a scream of terror.*
Syns: screak (*also* screek), screech, shriek, shrill.
2. *Slang.* Something or someone uproariously funny or absurd: *a comedy that was a real scream.*
Syns: absurdity, gas (*Slang*), hoot (*Slang*), howl (*Slang*), joke, laugh (*Informal*), panic (*Slang*), riot (*Slang*), screech (*Slang*). —*Idiom* a laugh a minute.
screaming *adjective* PRICELESS.

screech *noun*
1, 2. SCREAM.
screech *verb* SCREAM.
screek *noun & verb* SEE **screak.**
screen *verb*
1. BLOCK OUT at **block.**
2. CENSOR.
3. SHADE.
screened *adjective* SECLUDED.
screwball *noun* CRACKPOT.
screw up *verb* BOTCH.
screw-up *noun* BLUNDER.
screwy *adjective* INSANE.
scribe *verb* WRITE.
scrimp *verb*
To be severely sparing in order to economize: *scrimped for years to buy the house.*
  Syns: pinch, scrape, skimp, stint.
  —*Idioms* pinch pennies, tighten one's belt, tighten the screws.
scriptural *adjective* GRAPHIC.
Scrooge *noun* MISER.
scrub *verb*
1. To rub hard in order to clean: *scrubbing the bathtub.*
  Syn: scour.
2. CANCEL.
3. SCRAPE.
scrubby *adjective* SHABBY.
scruffy *adjective* SHABBY.
scrumptious *adjective* DELICIOUS.
scrunch *verb* STOOP.
scruple *noun*
1. BIT[1].
2. QUALM.
scrupulous *adjective* CAREFUL.
scrupulousness *noun*
THOROUGHNESS.
scrutinize *verb*
1. EXAMINE.
2. WATCH.
scrutiny *noun*
1. EXAMINATION.
2. WATCH.
scuff *verb* SHUFFLE.
scuffle *noun* FIGHT.
scuffle *verb*
1. SHUFFLE.
2. WRESTLE.
scum *noun* TRASH[1].
scurrility *noun* VITUPERATION.
scurrilous *adjective*
1. ABUSIVE.
2. OBSCENE.
scurry *verb*
1. RUN.
2. RUSH.
scuttlebutt *noun* GOSSIP.

sea dog *noun* SAILOR.
seafarer *noun* SAILOR.
seam *noun* JOINT.
seaman *noun* SAILOR.
sear *verb*
1. BURN.
2. DRY UP at **dry.**
sear *noun* BURN.
search *verb*
1. To examine the person or personal effects of in order to find something lost or concealed: *Customs inspectors searched him for narcotics.*
  Syns: fan[1] (*Slang*), frisk, inspect, shake down (*Informal*). —*Idiom* give the once-over to.
2. SEEK.
search *noun* SHAKEDOWN.
season *verb*
1. FLAVOR.
2. HARDEN.
season *noun*
1. HEAT.
2. PERIOD.
3. TIME.
seasonable *adjective* OPPORTUNE.
seasoned *adjective* EXPERIENCED.
seasoning *noun* FLAVORING.
seat *noun*
1. BASE[1].
2. BOTTOM.
3. CENTER.
seat *verb*
1. To cause to take a sitting position: *Seat yourself over there.*
  Syns: sit, sit down.
2. BASE[1].
3. ESTABLISH.
secede *verb*
To break away or withdraw from membership in an association or federation: *seceded from the party because of differences over fundamental issues.*
  Syns: splinter (off), split.
seclude *verb*
1. To put into solitude: *a monk who secluded himself from all worldly influences.*
  Syns: cloister, recluse (*Obs.*), sequester, sequestrate.
2. ISOLATE.
secluded *adjective*
1. Solitary and shut off from society: *led a secluded life in a convent.*
  Syns: cloistered, hermetic, recluse, secluse, sequestered, sequestrate (*Archaic*).
2. Concealed from view: *a secluded garden surrounded by high walls.*

Syns: hidden, screened, secret, sequestered.

3. REMOTE.

secluse *adjective* SECLUDED.

seclusion *noun*

The act of secluding or the state of being secluded: *lived a life of seclusion after her husband's death.*

Syns: reclusion, retirement, sequestration.

second[1] *noun* FLASH.

second[2] *noun* ASSISTANT.

secondary *adjective*

1. DERIVATIVE.

2. MINOR.

3. SUBORDINATE.

secondary *noun* SUBORDINATE.

second-class *adjective* INFERIOR.

second-rate *adjective* INFERIOR.

secrecy *noun*

The habit, practice, or policy of keeping secrets: *believed that secrecy is a key ingredient of foreign-policy successes.*

Syns: concealment, huggermugger *or* hugger-mugger, hugger-muggery, secretiveness, secretness, wraps.

secret *adjective*

1. Existing or operating in a way so as to ensure complete concealment and confidentiality: *secret counterintelligence operations; secret agents.*

Syns: clandestine, cloak-and-dagger, covert, huggermugger *or* hugger-mugger, hush-hush (*Informal*), sub-rosa, undercover.

2. SECLUDED.

secrete *verb* HIDE[1].

secretive *adjective* SLY.

secretiveness *noun* SECRECY.

secretly *adverb*

In a secret way: *secretly planned to attack the smaller country.*

Syns: clandestinely, huggermugger *or* hugger-mugger. —*Idioms* by stealth, on the sly, under cover.

secretness *noun* SECRECY.

sect *noun*

1. FAITH.

2. RELIGION.

sectary *noun*

1. DEVOTEE.

2. SEPARATIST.

section *noun*

1. A particular subdivision of a written work: *The book contained a long section on controlled narcotics.*

Syns: part, passage, segment.

2. A thin piece, esp. of tissue, suitable

for microscopic examination: *frozen sections of cancerous liver.*

Syn: slice.

3. CUT.

4. DIVISION.

section *verb* DIVIDE.

sectional *adjective* TERRITORIAL.

secular *adjective*

1. EARTHLY.

2. PROFANE.

secure *verb*

1. To give a promise of payment to (a creditor): *secure a loan.*

Syns: guarantee, pledge.

2. ATTACH.

3. CAUSE.

4. DEFEND.

5. FASTEN.

6. GET.

7. GUARANTEE.

8. TAKE.

9. TIE.

secure *adjective*

1. CONFIDENT.

2. SAFE.

3. SOUND[2].

4. SURE.

5. TIGHT.

security *noun*

1. DEFENSE.

2. PAWN[1].

3. SAFETY.

4. STABILITY.

sedate *adjective* GRAVE[2].

sediment *noun* DEPOSIT.

sedition *noun* TREASON.

seditious *adjective* TREASONOUS.

seditiousness *noun* TREASON.

seduce *verb*

1. To lure or persuade into a sexual relationship: *a young girl seduced by a notorious roué.*

Syns: debauch, undo.

2. To beguile or draw into a wrong or foolish course of action: *was seduced into gambling by the vision of easy money.*

Syns: allure, entice, inveigle, lure, tempt.

seducer *noun*

1. One that seduces: *Money is a well-known seducer.*

Syns: charmer, enticer, inveigler, tempter.

2. A man who seduces women: *a seducer without a conscience.*

Syns: debaucher, Don Juan.

seduction *noun*

1. The act or an instance of seducing

sexually: *shot the man for the seduction of his sister.*
Syns: debauching, debauchment (*Obs.*).
2. LURE.

seductive *adjective*
Tending to seduce: *the seductive powers of some women; the seductive pull of money.*
Syns: alluring, bewitching, enticing, inviting, siren, sirenic *or* sirenical, tempting, witching.

seductress *noun*
A usu. unscrupulous woman who seduces or exploits men: *Mata Hari was a famous seductress.*
Syns: enchantress, femme fatale (*French*), siren, temptress, vamp, witch (*Informal*).

sedulous *adjective* DILIGENT.
sedulousness *noun* DILIGENCE.
see *verb*
1. To apprehend (images) by use of the eyes: *I could see the sailboat clearly. She sees very well even at ninety.*
Syns: behold, ken (*Archaic*), perceive.
2. To be together socially on a regular basis: *He has been seeing her for a year now.*
Syns: date, take out (*Informal*).
3. EXPERIENCE.
4. FORESEE.
5. IMAGINE.
6. LOOK.
7. NOTICE.
8. UNDERSTAND.
9. VISIT.
see to *verb* TEND[2].
seeable *adjective* VISIBLE.
seed *noun*
1. A fertilized plant ovule capable of germinating: *wheat and barley seeds.*
Syns: kernel, pip, pit, stone.
2. A propagative part of a plant: *looked like tiny seeds on the backs of the fronds.*
Syn: spore.
3. The male fluid of fertilization: *The seed of a prize bull can be sold for a high price.*
Syns: semen, sperm.
4. ANCESTRY.
5. GERM.
6. PROGENY.
seed *verb*
To put (seeds) into the ground for growth: *seed a lawn.*
Syns: pitch, plant, sow.
seedtime *noun* SPRING.
seedy *adjective* SHABBY.

seeing *noun* VISION.
seek *verb*
1. To try to find: *sought the lost shoe; seeking just the right person for the job.*
Syns: cast about (for), hunt up, look for, quest, search (for). —*Idiom* be in search of.
2. AIM.
3. ATTEMPT.
seeker *noun* APPLICANT.
seem *verb* APPEAR.
seeming *adjective* APPARENT.
seemingly *adverb* APPARENTLY.
seemliness *noun* DECENCY.
seemly *adjective* CORRECT.
seep *verb* OOZE.
seer[1] *noun* PROPHET.
seer[2] *noun* WITNESS.
seesaw *verb* LURCH.
seethe *verb*
1. ANGER.
2, 3. BOIL.
4. STEEP[2].
seething *adjective* ANGRY.
see-through *adjective* TRANSPARENT.
segment *noun*
1. CUT.
2. DIVISION.
3. SECTION.
segment *verb* DIVIDE.
segregate *verb* ISOLATE.
segregated *adjective* RESTRICTED.
segregation *noun*
1. The policy or practice of excluding a minority group from full freedom or participation in a society: *the evils of segregation.*
Syns: apartheid, separatism.
2. ISOLATION.
seize *verb*
1. To take quick and forcible possession of: *seized and nationalized all foreign industry; seized the smugglers' boat and impounded it.*
Syns: commandeer, confiscate, expropriate, grab, snatch. —*Idiom* help oneself to.
2. To have a sudden, overwhelming effect on: *was seized with a sneezing fit.*
Syns: catch, strike, take.
3. ARREST.
4. ASSUME.
5. CATCH.
6. GRASP.
seizure *noun*
1. The act of taking quick and forcible possession of: *seizure by customs*

agents of the illicit drug shipment; seizure of all personal property in a communist state.
Syns: commandeering, confiscation, expropriation.
2. A sudden and often acute manifestation of a disease: *has frequent seizures of gout.*
Syns: access, attack, fit, spell.
3. ARREST.
4. CATCH.
5. USURPATION.
seldom *adverb* INFREQUENTLY.
select *verb* CHOOSE.
select *noun* ELECT.
select *adjective*
1. Singled out in preference: *Only a select group of Washington insiders knew the secret.*
Syns: choice, chosen, elect, exclusive.
2. CHOICE.
3. DISCRIMINATING.
selection *noun* CHOICE.
selective *adjective* DISCRIMINATING.
selectiveness *noun* DISCRIMINATION.
selectivity *noun* DISCRIMINATION.
self *noun*
An individual's awareness of what constitutes his or her essential nature and distinguishes him or her from all others: *a strong sense of self.*
Syn: ego.
self-absorbed *adjective* EGOTISTICAL.
self-absorption *noun* EGOISM.
self-assurance *noun* CONFIDENCE.
self-assured *adjective* CONFIDENT.
self-centered *adjective* EGOTISTICAL.
self-centeredness *noun* EGOISM.
self-confidence *noun* CONFIDENCE.
self-confident *adjective* CONFIDENT.
self-contained *adjective* INDEPENDENT.
self-control *noun* RESERVE.
self-controlled *adjective* RESERVED.
self-denying *adjective* SELFLESS.
self-determination *noun* INDEPENDENCE.
self-effacing *adjective* MODEST.
self-esteem *noun* PRIDE.
self-esteeming *adjective* PROUD.
self-forgetful *adjective* SELFLESS.
self-forgetting *adjective* SELFLESS.
selfhood *noun* IDENTITY.
self-importance *noun* EGOTISM.
self-important *adjective* POMPOUS.
selfish *adjective* EGOTISTICAL.
selfishness *noun* EGOISM.
selfless *adjective*
Without concern for oneself: *selfless devotion to duty.*

Syns: self-denying, self-forgetful, self-forgetting, unselfish.
self-possessed *adjective* CONFIDENT.
self-possession *noun*
1. BALANCE.
2. CONFIDENCE.
self-regard *noun* PRIDE.
self-reliance *noun* INDEPENDENCE.
self-reliant *adjective* INDEPENDENT.
self-respect *noun* PRIDE.
self-respecting *adjective* PROUD.
self-restrained *adjective* RESERVED.
self-restraint *noun* RESERVE.
selfsame *adjective* SAME.
selfsameness *noun* SAMENESS.
self-seeking *adjective* EGOTISTICAL.
self-serving *adjective* EGOTISTICAL.
self-sufficiency *noun* INDEPENDENCE.
self-sufficient *adjective*
1, 2. INDEPENDENT.
self-supporting *adjective* INDEPENDENT.
sell *noun*
1. Market appeal: *a product with a lot of sell to it.*
Syns: marketability, marketableness, salability, salableness.
2. DECEPTION.
sell *verb*
1. To offer for sale: *We don't sell lawn mowers.*
Syns: deal in, handle, market, merchandise, merchant, peddle, retail, trade in, vend.
2. BRING.
3. PERSUADE.
sell for *verb*
1. BRING.
2. COST.
sell off *verb*
To get rid of completely by selling, esp. in quantity or at discount: *sold off all the water-damaged stock.*
Syns: close out, dump, sell out, sell up (*Brit.*), unload.
sell out *verb*
1. BETRAYAL.
2. SELL OFF at **sell**.
sell up *verb* SELL OFF at **sell**.
seller *noun*
One who sells: *sellers of books.*
Syns: sales clerk, salesperson.
sellout *noun* BETRAYAL.
semaphore *verb* SIGNAL.
semblance *noun*
1. FAÇADE.
2. SHADE.
semblant *adjective* APPARENT.
semen *noun* SEED.

seminar *noun* CONFERENCE.
sempiternal *adjective* ETERNAL.
sempiternity *noun* ETERNITY.
send *verb*
1. To cause (something) to be conveyed
   to a destination: *sent the package by
   air to Europe.*
   Syns: address, consign, dispatch,
   forward, route, ship, transmit.
2. CARRY AWAY at **carry.**
3. REFER.
send away *verb* DISMISS.
send for *verb* CALL.
send forth *verb* EMIT.
send up *verb* COMMIT.
senectitude *noun* AGE.
senesce *verb* AGE.
senescence *noun* AGE.
senile *adjective*
Exhibiting the mental and physical
deterioration often accompanying old
age: *senile patients unable to care for
themselves.*
Syns: doddering, doddery, doting.
senility *noun*
The condition of being senile: *Old age
does not necessarily mean senility.*
Syn: dotage.
senior *adjective*
1. Of greater age than another: *The
   senior Mr. Walker objected to his son's
   plans.*
   Syns: elder, older.
2. HIGHER.
3. OLD.
senior *noun*
1. A person who is older than another:
   She is my senior by six years.
   Syn: elder.
2. An elderly person: *seniors still able to
   make substantial contributions to
   society.*
   Syns: ancient, elder, golden ager,
   oldster (*Informal*), old-timer
   (*Informal*), senior citizen.
3. SUPERIOR.
senior citizen *noun* SENIOR.
sensation *noun*
1. The capacity for or an act of
   responding to a stimulus: *lost all
   sensation in the arm; a sensation of
   vague uneasiness.*
   Syns: feeling, sense, sensibility,
   sensitivity, sentiment (*Rare*).
2. A condition of intense public interest
   or excitement: *The scandal created an
   international sensation.*
   Syns: brouhaha, hoo-hah (*Slang*),

stir[1], to-do (*Informal*), uproar.
3. MARVEL.
sensational *adjective*
1. Of or pertaining to sensation or the
   senses: *sensational response to a
   stimulus.*
   Syns: sensatory, sensitive, sensory
   (*also* sensorial), sensual.
2. DRAMATIC.
3. MARVELOUS.
sensatory *adjective*
1. SENSATIONAL.
2. SENSORY.
sense *noun*
1. What is sound or reasonable: *There's
   no sense in waiting any longer.*
   Syns: logic, rationale, rationality,
   reason. —*Idiom* rhyme or reason.
2. COMMON SENSE.
3. INTELLIGENCE.
4. MEANING.
5. SANITY.
6. SENSATION.
sense *verb*
1. FEEL.
2. PERCEIVE.
3. UNDERSTAND.
senseless *adjective*
1, 2. MINDLESS.
3. UNCONSCIOUS.
senselessness *noun* FOOLISHNESS.
senses *noun* SANITY.
sensibility *noun*
1. SENSATION.
2. SENSITIVENESS.
sensible *adjective*
1. AWARE.
2. LOGICAL.
3. PHYSICAL.
4. SANE.
5. SENSITIVE.
sensical *adjective* SANE.
sensile *adjective* SENSITIVE.
sensitive *adjective*
1. Able to receive and respond to
   external stimuli: *Frostbitten tissue
   always remains especially sensitive to
   the cold. She is a sensitive person,
   attuned to the moods of others.*
   Syns: impressible, impressionable,
   responsive, sensible, sensile, sentient,
   susceptible, susceptive.
2. ACUTE.
3, 4. DELICATE.
5. EMOTIONAL.
6. SENSATIONAL.
sensitiveness *noun*
The quality or condition of being

emotionally and intuitively sensitive: *sensitiveness to the unspoken needs of others.*
Syns: feeling, sensibility, sensitivity.

sensitivity *noun*
1. SENSATION.
2. SENSITIVENESS.

sensory also **sensorial** *adjective*
1. Transmitting impulses from sense organs to nerve centers: *sensory nerve bundles.*
Syns: afferent, receptive (*Physiol.*), sensatory.
2. SENSATIONAL.

sensual *adjective*
1. Suggesting sexuality: *a sensual belly dance.*
Syns: sexual, sexy (*Slang*), suggestive, voluptuous.
2. MATERIALISTIC.
3. PHYSICAL.
4. SENSATIONAL.
5. SENSUOUS.

sensualism *noun* SENSUOUSNESS.
sensualistic *adjective* SENSUOUS.
sensuality *noun*
1. The quality or condition of being sensual: *the blatant sensuality of the stripper's movements.*
Syns: sexiness (*Slang*), sexuality, suggestiveness, voluptuousness.
2. PHYSICALITY.
3. SENSUOUSNESS.

sensuous *adjective*
Pertaining to, suggestive of, or appealing to sense gratification: *took sensuous pleasure in the gourmet dinner; rich, sensuous velvet.*
Syns: epicurean, sensual, sensualistic, voluptuary, voluptuous.

sensuousness *noun*
The quality or condition of being sensuous: *the sensuousness of the music.*
Syns: sensualism, sensuality, voluptuousness.

sentence *noun*
A judicial decision, esp. one setting the punishment to be inflicted on a convicted person: *a ten-year sentence for assault.*
Syns: judgment, rap[1] (*Slang*).
sentence *verb* CONDEMN.

sentient *adjective*
1. AWARE.
2. EMOTIONAL.
3. SENSITIVE.

sentiment *noun*
1. A general cast of mind with regard to something: *Anti-American sentiment was running high in the Islamic world.*
Syns: attitude, disposition, feeling.
2. BELIEF.
3. EMOTION.
4. SENSATION.

sentimental *adjective*
Affectedly or extravagantly emotional: *sentimental soap operas.*
Syns: bathetic, drippy (*Slang*), gooey (*Informal*), gushy, maudlin, mawkish, mushy (*Informal*), romantic, sappy (*Slang*), schmaltzy (*Slang*), sloppy (*Informal*), slushy (*Informal*), sobby, soft, soppy (*Slang*), soupy (*Informal*), tear-jerking (*Slang*).

sentimentalism *noun*
SENTIMENTALITY.

sentimentality *noun*
The quality or condition of being affectedly or overly emotional: *the cloying sentimentality of the novel.*
Syns: bathos, maudlinism, mawkishness, mush (*Informal*), mushiness (*Informal*), schmaltz (*Slang*), sentimentalism, sloppiness (*Informal*). —*Idiom* sob stuff.

sentimentalize *verb*
To regard or imbue with affected or exaggerated emotion: *vices sentimentalized into virtues.*
Syn: romanticize.

sentry *noun* GUARD.

separate *verb*
1. To terminate a relationship or association by or as if by leaving one another: *They have separated but have not yet filed for divorce. The two partners separated after a very serious and prolonged disagreement about finances.*
Syns: break off, break up, part, split (up). —*Idioms* call it quits, come to a parting of ways, part company.
2. DISCHARGE.
3. DISTINGUISH.
4, 5. DIVIDE.
6. ISOLATE.
7. SORT.

separate *adjective*
1. DISTINCT.
2. INDIVIDUAL.
3. LONE.

separately *adverb*
As a separate unit: *Let's consider each problem separately.*
Syns: apart, discretely. —*Idioms* one at a time, one by one.

separateness *noun* INDIVIDUALITY.
separation *noun*
1. DETACHMENT.

2. DISTINCTION.
3. DIVISION.
4. ISOLATION.

separatism *noun* SEGREGATION.

separatist *noun*
A person who dissents from the doctrine of an established church: *The Pilgrims were separatists from the Church of England.*
   Syns: dissenter, dissident, heretic, nonconformist, schismatic, schismatist, sectary.

sepulcher *noun* GRAVE¹.

sepulture *noun* GRAVE¹.

sequel *noun* EFFECT.

sequence *noun*
1. ARRANGEMENT.
2. EFFECT.
3. ORDER.
4. SERIES.

sequent *adjective* CONSECUTIVE.

sequent *noun* EFFECT.

sequential *adjective* CONSECUTIVE.

sequester *verb*
1. ISOLATE.
2. SECLUDE.

sequestered *adjective*
1, 2. SECLUDED.

sequestrate *verb* SECLUDE.

sequestrate *adjective* SECLUDED.

sequestration *noun*
1. ISOLATION.
2. SECLUSION.

sequin *noun* GLITTER.

serene *adjective* CALM.

serenity *noun* CALM.

serfdom *noun* SLAVERY.

serial *adjective* CONSECUTIVE.

series *noun*
1. A number of things placed or occurring one after the other: *A series of hard winters decimated the deer population.*
   Syns: chain, consecution, course, order, run, sequence, streak (*Informal*), string, succession, suite, train.
2. RUN.

serious *adjective*
1. Marked by sober sincerity: *Be serious and tell me how you really feel. We had a serious talk about business matters.*
   Syns: businesslike, earnest, no-nonsense, serious-minded, sobersided.
   —*Idiom* serious as a judge.
2, 3. GRAVE².
4. GRIEVOUS.

serious-minded *adjective* SERIOUS.

serious-mindedness *noun*
SERIOUSNESS.

seriousness *noun*
1. Sober sincerity: *He told me that in complete seriousness.*
   Syns: earnest, earnestness, serious-mindedness, sobriety.
2. GRAVITY.

sermonize *verb* PREACH.

serpentine *adjective* WINDING.

serve *verb*
1. To work and care for: *a nurse who served her patients well.*
   Syns: attend, do for, minister (to), wait on (*or* upon).
2. To place food before (someone): *The waitress still has not served us.*
   Syn: wait on (*or* upon).
3. To spend or complete (time), as a prison term: *served 25 years for armed robbery.*
   Syns: do (*Informal*), put in (*Informal*).
4. To meet a need or requirement: *a dictionary that will serve you well; a tool that serves my purpose efficiently.*
   Syns: answer, do, suffice, suit.
5. ACT FOR at act.
6. PROFIT.

service *noun*
1. CEREMONY.
2. DUTY.
3. FAVOR.

serviceable *adjective*
1. HELPFUL.
2. PRACTICAL.
3. USABLE.

servile *adjective*
Excessively eager to serve or obey: *The hostess scurried about waiting on us in an unpleasantly servile way.*
   Syns: menial, obsequious, slavish, subservient.

servility *noun* SLAVERY.

servitude *noun* SLAVERY.

serving *noun*
An individual quantity of food: *one serving of peas.*
   Syns: helping, mess, portion.

sesquipedalian *adjective* LONG¹.

set¹ *verb*
1. To deposit in a specified position: *Just set your bag on the floor.*
   Syns: fix, lay¹, place, put, stick.
2. To arrange tableware upon (a table) in preparation for a meal: *set the table for four.*
   Syns: lay¹, spread.
3. ADJUST.
4. AIM.

5. ARRANGE.
6. COAGULATE.
7. ESTIMATE.
8. GAMBLE.
9. HARDEN.
10. LAY¹.
11. POSITION.
12. STATION.

set apart *verb* DISTINGUISH.
set aside *verb* ABOLISH.
set back *verb* DELAY.
set by *verb* SAVE.
set down *verb* LAND.
set off *verb*
1. BALANCE.
2. COMPENSATE.
3. CONTRAST.
4. GRACE.

set out *verb*
1. BEAR.
2. DESIGN.
3. START.

set to *verb* START.
set up *verb*
1. ERECT.
2. FOUND.
3. TREAT.

set *adjective*
1. On an unwavering course of action: *is set on going to Europe.*
   Syns: bent, decided, determined, fixed, intent, resolute.
2. CONFIRMED.
3. FIRM¹.
4. READY.
5. SPECIFIC.

set² *noun*
1. CIRCLE.
2. CLASS.
3. CROWD.
4. GROUP.
5. SCENE.

setback *noun* REVERSE.
setoff *noun* COMPENSATION.
setting *noun*
1, 2. SCENE.

settle *verb*
1. To fall or drift down to the bottom: *The dust settled. Silt settles on the riverbed.*
   Syns: gravitate, sink.
2. To put into correct or conclusive form: *The official settled the matter with a few quick calls.*
   Syns: arrange, attend to, conclude, dispose of, fix.
3. To bring (something) into a state of agreement or accord: *settle an argument.*

Syns: reconcile, rectify, resolve, smooth over, straighten out.
4. To set right by giving what is due: *finally had enough money to settle his debts.*
   Syns: clear, discharge, liquidate, pay (up *or* off), satisfy, square.
5. ARRANGE.
6. CALM.
7. DECIDE.
8. ESTABLISH.
9. LAND.

settled *adjective*
1. CONFIRMED.
2. FIRM¹.

sever *verb* CUT.
several *adjective*
1. Consisting of an indefinitely small number that is more than two or three but less than many: *Several friends stopped by to visit.*
   Syns: divers (*Archaic*), some, sundry, various.
2. DISTINCT.

severe *adjective*
1. Rigorous and unsparing in treating others: *an excellent but severe teacher.*
   Syns: demanding, exacting, rigid, stern, strict, tough, unyielding.
2. Conveying great physical force: *gave him a severe blow to the head.*
   Syns: hard, heavy, hefty, powerful.
3. BITTER.
4. BLEAK.
5. BURDENSOME.
6. GRAVE².
7. GRIEVOUS.

severity *noun*
1. The fact or condition of being rigorous and unsparing: *an ordeal of extraordinary severity.*
   Syns: austerity, harshness, rigor, stringency.
2. INTENSITY.

sexiness *noun* SENSUALITY.
sexual *adjective*
1. EROTIC.
2. REPRODUCTIVE.
3. SENSUAL.

sexuality *noun* SENSUALITY.
sexy *adjective*
1. DESIRABLE.
2, 3. EROTIC.
4. SENSUAL.

shabby *adjective*
1. Showing signs of wear and tear or neglect: *a shabby couch; a shabby old building.*
   Syns: bedraggled, broken-down, decaying, decrepit, dilapidated, dingy,

down-at-heel *or* down-at-the-heel,
faded, mangy, ratty (*Slang*), run-
down, scrubby, scruffy, seedy,
shoddy, sleazy, tacky³ (*Informal*),
tagrag, tattered, threadbare. —*Idioms*
all the worse for wear, gone to seed
(*or* pot), past cure (*or* hope).
2. DISGRACEFUL.
3. FILTHY.

shackle *verb* HAMPER.

shackles *noun* BONDS.

shade *noun*
1. Comparative darkness that results
from the blocking of light rays: *sat in
the shade of an oak tree.*
   Syns: adumbration, penumbra,
   shadow, umbra, umbrage (*Archaic*).
2. The degree of vividness of a color, as
when modified by the addition of
black or white pigment: *a delicate
shade of pink; shades of gray and
black.*
   Syns: gradation, hue, tinge, tint.
3. A slight variation between nearly
identical entities: *not a shade of
difference between the two politicians;
shades of meaning.*
   Syns: gradation, nuance.
4. A slight amount: *a shade of sadness
in the music.*
   Syns: ghost, hair, hint, intimation,
   semblance, shadow, soupçon
   (*French*), strain², streak, suggestion,
   suspicion, tinge, touch, trace, whisker,
   whisper.
5. COLOR.
6. GHOST.
7. TRACE.

shade *verb*
1. To shelter, esp. from light: *A big hat
shaded her face.*
   Syns: inumbrate, screen, shadow.
2. To make dark or darker: *shaded in
the background with pencil.*
   Syns: adumbrate, darken, shadow.
3. *Informal.* To make a slight reduction
in (a price): *The manager of the
bookstore shaded the cost of the books
for students.*
   Syns: shave, trim.

shaded *adjective* SHADY.

shadiness *noun* INDIRECTION.

shadow *noun*
1. GHOST.
2, 3. SHADE.
4. TAIL.

shadow *verb*
1. FOLLOW.
2. OBSCURE.
3, 4. SHADE.

shadowy *adjective*
1. SHADY.
2. UNCLEAR.

shady *adjective*
1. Full of shade: *shady lawns.*
   Syns: bosky, shaded, shadowy,
   umbrous.
2. Casting shade: *shady trees.*
   Syn: umbrageous.
3. Of dubious character: *a shady
operator; a shady business deal.*
   Syns: doubtful, equivocal, fishy,
   questionable, suspect, suspicious,
   uncertain.

shaft *noun*
1. BEAM.
2. STICK.

shake *verb*
1. To cause to move to and fro with
short, jerky movements: *shake the
piggy bank to get out the last few
coins.*
   Syns: jiggle, joggle.
2. To move to and fro in short, jerky
movements: *The dog was shaking like
a leaf at the vet's.*
   Syns: quake, quaver, quiver, shiver,
   shudder, tremble, tremor, twitter.
3. To move to and fro violently: *The
house shook as the jets flew overhead.*
   Syns: quake, rock², tremble, vibrate.
4, 5. AGITATE.
6. DISMAY.
7. DISTURB.
8. LOSE.
9. RID.

shake down *verb*
1. EXTORT.
2. SCOUR.
3. SEARCH.

shake up *verb* FRIGHTEN.

shake *noun* TREMOR.

shakedown *noun*
Informal. A thorough search of a place
or person: *gave the suspect a shakedown.*
   Syns: frisk, once-over (*Informal*),
   search.

shakes *noun* JITTERS.

shakeup *noun*
A thorough or drastic reorganization:
*The top three people in the office were
fired in the company shakeup.*
   Syns: house-cleaning, overhaul.

shakiness *noun*
1. INSTABILITY.
2. UNSTABLENESS.

shaking *adjective* TREMULOUS.

shaky *adjective*
1. INSECURE.

2. TREMULOUS.
3. UNSTABLE.

shallow *adjective*
1. Measuring little from bottom to top or surface: *a shallow river; a shallow bowl.*
   Syns: ebb (*Brit. Regional*), fleet[2] (*Chiefly Regional*), shoal.
2. SUPERFICIAL.

shallow *noun* SHOAL.

sham *noun*
1. ACT.
2. COUNTERFEIT.
3. MOCKERY.

sham *verb* ACT.

sham *adjective*
1. ARTIFICIAL.
2. COUNTERFEIT.

shamble *verb* SHUFFLE.

shambles *noun* BOTCH.

shame *noun*
1. A great disappointment or regrettable fact: *It's a shame she didn't get the job.*
   Syns: bummer (*Slang*), crime (*Informal*), pity. —*Idiom* a crying shame.
2. DISGRACE.

shame *verb* DISGRACE.

shameful *adjective*
1. DEPLORABLE.
2. DISGRACEFUL.

shamefulness *noun* INFAMY.

shameless *adjective*
Characterized by or done without shame: *a shameless display of greed and corruption.*
   Syns: arrant, bald-faced, barefaced, blatant, brassy (*Informal*), brazen, brazenfaced, unabashed, unblushing. —*Idiom* dead (*or* lost) to shame.

shanty *noun* HOLE.

shape *noun*
1. FORM.
2. TRIM.

shape *verb*
1. FORM.
2. MAKE.

shapeless *adjective*
Having no distinct shape: *a shapeless mass of goo.*
   Syns: amorphous, formless, inchoate, unformed, unshaped.

shapely *adjective*
Having a full, voluptuous figure: *a shapely young gymnast.*
   Syns: built (*Informal*), curvaceous, curvesome, curvy, rounded, stacked (*Informal*), well-developed.

shard *noun* END.

share *noun*
1. ALLOTMENT.
2. PART.

share *verb*
1. CONTRIBUTE.
2. DISTRIBUTE.

sharing *noun* PARTICIPATION.

sharp *adjective*
1. Having a fine edge, as for cutting: *a sharp knife.*
   Syns: honed, keen, whetted.
2. Clearly defined; not ambiguous: *a sharp distinction.*
   Syns: clear, distinct, unambiguous, unequivocal, unmistakable.
3. Astute but lacking in ethics or principles: *sharp business practices.*
   Syns: canny, clever, cunning, shifty, slick, sly, wily.
4. Marked by severity or intensity: *a sharp pain in his abdomen.*
   Syns: acute, gnawing, knifelike, lancinating, piercing, shooting, stabbing.
5. ACUTE.
6. CLEVER.
7. FASHIONABLE.
8. INCISIVE.
9. POINTED.
10. PUNGENT.

sharp *verb* SHARPEN.

sharpen *verb*
To give a sharp edge to: *sharpened the knife.*
   Syns: acuminate, edge, hone[1], sharp (*Regional*), whet.

sharper *noun* CHEAT.

sharpness *noun* EDGE.

sharp-witted *adjective* CLEVER.

shatter *verb*
1. BREAK.
2. DESTROY.

shattering *adjective* DESTRUCTIVE.

shave *verb*
1. BRUSH.
2. SCRAPE.
3. SHADE.

shear *verb* CUT BACK at **cut.**

sheath *noun* SKIN.

sheathe *verb* FACE.

sheathing *noun* SKIN.

shed *verb*
1. To send out heat, light, or energy: *The moon shed a ghostly light over the yard.*
   Syns: cast, emit, irradiate, project, radiate, throw.

2. To cast off by natural process: *snakes that shed their skins.*
   Syns: exuviate (*Zool.*), molt, slip, slough² , throw off.

sheen *noun* GLOSS.

sheer¹ *verb*
1. SWERVE.
2. TURN.

sheer² *adjective*
1. FILMY.
2. PURE.
3. STEEP¹.
4. UTTER².

shellac *verb*
1. DEFEAT.
2. OVERWHELM.

shellacking *noun*
1. DEFEAT.
2. TROUNCING.

shell out *verb* SPEND.

shelter *noun*
1. Dwellings in general: *How much of your salary goes for shelter?*
   Syns: housing, lodging, quarterage.
   —*Idiom* a roof over one's head.
2. COVER.
3. REFUGE.

shelter *verb* HARBOR.

shelve *verb* DEFER¹.

shenanigan *noun*
1. PRANK.
2. TRICK.

shepherd *verb* GUIDE.

shield *noun* DEFENSE.

shield *verb* DEFEND.

shift *verb*
1. CHANGE.
2. CONSUME.
3. DISTURB.
4. MANAGE.
5. MOVE.
6. TURN.

shift *noun*
1. CHANGE.
2. CONVERSION.
3. MAKESHIFT.
4. TRANSITION.
5, 6. TURN.

shiftless *adjective* LAZY.

shiftlessness *noun* LAZINESS.

shifty *adjective*
1. DISHONEST.
2. EVASIVE.
3. SHARP.
4. UNDERHAND.

shilly-shally *verb* HESITATE.

shilly-shally *noun* HESITATION.

shimmer *verb* FLASH.

shimmer *noun* GLITTER.

shindig *noun* BLAST.

shine *verb*
1. BEAM.
2. FLOURISH.
3. GLOSS.

shine *noun* GLOSS.

shiner *noun* BLACK EYE.

shining *adjective*
1. BRIGHT.
2. GLOSSY.

shiny *adjective* GLOSSY.

ship *verb* SEND.

shipshape *adjective* NEAT.

shipwreck *verb* WRECK.

shirk *verb*
1. IDLE.
2. NEGLECT.
3. SNEAK.

shiver *verb*
1. BREAK.
2. SHAKE.

shiver *noun* TREMOR.

shivering *adjective* TREMULOUS.

shivers *noun* JITTERS.

shivery *adjective*
1. COLD.
2. TREMULOUS.

shoal *noun*
A shallow part of a body of water: *ran aground in the shoals.*
   Syn: shallow.

shoal *adjective* SHALLOW.

shock *verb*
1. To affect with a strong feeling of moral aversion: *Such shameless behavior shocked him.*
   Syn: scandalize. —*Idiom* stink in one's nostrils.
2. STARTLE.
3. TRAUMATIZE.

shock *noun*
1. Something that jars the mind or emotions: *Her death was a terrible shock to her family.*
   Syns: blow², jolt, trauma.
2. COLLISION.

shocked *adjective*
Overcome with intense feeling, as of amazement, horror, or dismay: *was shocked by the bloodshed and violence of war.*
   Syns: aghast, appalled, confounded, dismayed, dumfounded (*also* dumbfounded), horrified, horrorstruck, thunderstruck.

shocking *adjective*
1. INFAMOUS.
2, 3. OUTRAGEOUS.
4. TERRIBLE.
5. UNSPEAKABLE.

shoddy *adjective*
1. Of decidedly inferior quality: *shoddy workmanship.*
    Syns: base², cheap, cheesy (*Slang*), common, crappy (*Slang*), crummy (*also* crumby) (*Slang*), lousy (*Slang*), paltry, poor, rotten (*Informal*), schlocky (*Slang*), sleazy, tacky² (*Informal*), tatty, trashy.
2. SHABBY.

shoo-in *noun* FAVORITE.

shoot *noun*
A young stemlike growth arising from a plant: *new shoots at the base of the trunk.*
    Syns: bine, offshoot, runner (*Bot.*), sprig, sprout, tendril.

shoot *verb*
1. To discharge a gun or firearm: *shot at a moving target.*
    Syn: fire. —*Idiom* take a shot at.
2. To wound or kill with a firearm: *Do you know who shot him?*
    Syns: gun (down), pick off, plug (*Slang*). —*Idiom* stop in one's tracks.
3. To launch with great force: *shoot rockets toward the moon; shoot arrows with a crossbow.*
    Syns: discharge, fire, hurtle, loose, project, propel. —*Idiom* let fly.
4. FLY.
5. RUSH.

shoot down *verb* DISCREDIT.

shoot up *verb* SOAR.

shooting *adjective* SHARP.

shop *noun* STORE.

shopworn *adjective* TRITE.

shore *noun* SUPPORT.

short *adjective*
1. ABRUPT.
2, 3. BRIEF.
4. INSUFFICIENT.

short *adverb*
1. Without any warning: *stopped the car short.*
    Syns: sudden, suddenly.
2. UNAWARES.

shortage *noun*
The condition or fact of being deficient: *a shortage of fuel.*
    Syns: defect, deficit, deficiency (*also* deficience), failure, insufficiency (*also* insufficience), lack, paucity, poverty, scantiness, scarceness, scarcity, underage¹.

shortcoming *noun*
1. DEFECT.
2. DISADVANTAGE.
3. WEAKNESS.

shorten *verb*
1. To make short or shorter: *had to shorten their stay in Paris; wants to shorten the dress.*
    Syns: abbreviate, curtail, cut back, cut down.
2. TRUNCATE.

shorthanded *adjective*
UNDERHANDED.

short-lived *adjective* TRANSITORY.

short-range *adjective*
1. TACTICAL.
2. TEMPORARY.

short-spoken *adjective* ABRUPT.

short-term *adjective* TEMPORARY.

shot *noun*
1. DROP.
2. OPPORTUNITY.
3. TRY.

shotgun *verb* COERCE.

shoulder *verb*
1. ASSUME.
2. PUSH.

shout *noun*
A loud cry: *a shout for help.*
    Syns: call, halloo (*also* halloa), holler, yell.

shout *verb*
1. To say (something) with a shout: *Fans shouted their approval.*
    Syns: bawl, bellow, cry, holler, vociferate, whoop, yell.
2. ROAR.
3. SCREAM.
4. TREAT.

shove *verb*
1. DRIVE.
2. MUSCLE.
3. POKE.
4, 5. PUSH.

shove off *verb* GO.

shove *noun* PUSH.

shovel *verb*
1, 2. DIG.

show *verb*
1. To make manifest or apparent: *showed prudence by driving carefully.*
    Syns: demonstrate, display, evidence, evince, exhibit, manifest, proclaim.
2. To give a precise indication of, as on a register or scale: *The thermometer shows 18° F.*
    Syns: indicate, mark, read, record, register.
3. APPEAR.
4. DESIGNATE.
5. DISPLAY.
6. PROVE.
7. REPRESENT.
8. REVEAL.

show off *verb* DISPLAY.
show up *verb*
1. APPEAR.
2. ARRIVE.
show *noun*
1. ACT.
2. DISPLAY.
3. EXHIBITION.
4. FAÇADE.
5. SHOWING.
shower *noun* BARRAGE
shower *verb*
1. To give in great abundance: *showered praise on her.*
   Syns: heap, lavish, rain.
2. BARRAGE.
showing *noun*
Performance, as in a competition or test of skill: *made a brilliant showing in the finals.*
   Syn: show.
showy *adjective*
1. Marked by outward, often extravagant display: *a showy diamond-encrusted watch.*
   Syns: flamboyant, ostentatious, pretentious, splashy, splurgy.
2. COLORFUL.
shred *noun*
1. BIT[1].
2. DAMN.
shrew *noun* SCOLD.
shrewd *adjective*
1. Having or showing a clever awareness and resourcefulness in practical matters: *a shrewd bargainer; a shrewd business deal.*
   Syns: astute, cagey (*also* cagy), knowing, perspicacious, savvy (*Slang*), slick, sly (*Chiefly Regional*), smart, wise[1].
2. INCISIVE.
shrewdness *noun* DISCERNMENT.
shriek *noun* SCREAM.
   shriek *verb*
   1, 2. SCREAM.
shrieky *adjective* HIGH.
shrill *adjective* HIGH.
   shrill *noun* SCREAM.
   shrill *verb* SCREAM.
shrilly *adjective* HIGH.
shrimp *noun* NONENTITY.
shrine *noun* SANCTUARY.
shrink *verb*
1. CONTRACT.
2. FLINCH.
shrivel *verb* DRY UP at **dry.**
shroud *verb*
1. BLOCK OUT at **block.**

2. COVER.
3. WRAP.
shrouded *adjective* ULTERIOR.
shrunken *adjective* WASTED.
shuck *verb* DISCARD.
shudder *verb* SHAKE.
   shudder *noun* TREMOR.
shuffle *verb*
1. To drag (the feet) along the floor or ground while walking: *Stop shuffling your feet.*
   Syns: scuff, scuffle, shamble.
2. To mix together so as to change the order of arrangement: *shuffled the cards, then dealt.*
   Syns: jumble, riffle, scramble.
3. EQUIVOCATE.
4. MUDDLE.
shun *verb*
1. AVOID.
2. SNUB.
shush *verb*
1. REPRESS.
2. SILENCE.
shut *verb* CLOSE[1].
shut in *verb* ENCLOSE.
shut out *verb*
1. BLACKBALL.
2. BLOCK OUT at **block.**
3. DISMISS.
shut up *verb*
1. IMPRISON.
2. SILENCE.
shut-eye *noun* SLEEP.
shy[1] *adjective*
1. INSUFFICIENT.
2. MODEST.
   shy *verb* FLINCH.
shy[2] *verb* THROW.
   shy *noun* THROW.
sibilate *verb* HISS.
sibyl *noun* PROPHET.
sibylline *adjective*
1. AMBIGUOUS.
2. PROPHETIC.
sick *adjective*
1. Suffering from or affected with an illness: *She's out sick with the flu.*
   Syns: down, ill, laid up (*Informal*).
2. Out of patience with: *sick of the whole situation.*
   Syns: disgusted, fed up, tired, weary.
   —*Idiom* sick and tired.
3. MORBID.
4. SICKLY.
sicken *verb*
1. CONTRACT.
2. DISGUST.

sickening *adjective*
1. OFFENSIVE.
2. UNSPEAKABLE.

sickly *adjective*
1. Affected or tending to be affected with minor health problems: *He's been sickly all winter.*
    Syns: ailing, indisposed, low, mean² (*Informal*), off-color, offish, poorly, rocky, unwell. —*Idiom* under the weather.
2. Of or associated with sickness: *You're looking a bit sickly these days.*
    Syns: anemic, peaked, peaky, sick.
3. MORBID.

sickness *noun*
1. The condition of being sick: *suffers from a lingering sickness.*
    Syns: affliction, disorder, illness, indisposition, infirmity.
2. DISEASE.

side *noun*
1. One of two or more contrasted parts or places identified by its location with respect to a center: *the north side of the park; seated on both sides of the table.*
    Syns: flank, hand.
2. One of two or more opposing opinions, actions, or attitudes, as in a disagreement: *There's another side to the story.*
    Syn: part.
3. PHASE.

side *verb* FACE.
side with *verb* SUPPORT.
sidekick *noun* FRIEND.
sidesplitting *adjective* PRICELESS.
sidestep *verb*
1. EVADE.
2. SKIRT.

sidle *verb* EDGE.

siege *noun*
1. A prolonged surrounding of an objective by hostile troops: *the siege of Leningrad.*
    Syn: besiegement.
2. An often prolonged period, as of illness: *a month-long siege of hepatitis.*
    Syns: bout, go.

siege *verb* BESIEGE.
siesta *noun* NAP.
siesta *verb* NAP.
sift *verb* SORT.

sigh *verb*
1. To exhale audibly in a long, deep breath, as in sorrow, weariness, or relief: *He sighed when he heard the news.*
    Syn: sough.

2. MURMUR.

sigh *noun*
1. The act or sound of sighing: *heaved a sigh of relief when the plane landed safely.*
    Syn: sough.
2. MURMUR.

sight *noun*
1. HEAP.
2. LOOK.
3. MESS.
4. VIEW.
5. VISION.

sightless *adjective* BLIND.
sightlessness *noun* BLINDNESS.
sightly *adjective* BEAUTIFUL.
sightseer *noun* TOURIST.

sign *noun*
1. Something visible or evident that gives grounds for believing in the existence or presence of something else: *A high forehead is thought to be a sign of intelligence.*
    Syns: evidence, index, indication, indicator, mark, manifestation, signification, stamp, symptom, token, witness.
2. CHARACTER.
3. EXPRESSION.
4. GESTURE.
5. SIGNAL.

sign *verb*
1. To affix one's signature to: *We signed the lease this morning.*
    Syns: autograph, endorse, inscribe, subscribe, undersign. —*Idioms* put one's John Hancock on, set one's hand to.
2. GESTURE.

sign over *verb* TRANSFER.
sign up *verb*
1. APPLY.
2. JOIN.

signal *noun*
An action, motion, or gesture that conveys an idea, an order, or a desire: *gave us the signal to proceed.*
    Syn: sign. —*Idiom* high sign.

signal *verb*
1. To communicate by means of such devices as lights or signs: *signaled the train to move ahead.*
    Syns: flag¹, semaphore.
2. GESTURE.

signal *adjective* NOTICEABLE.
signalize *verb*
1, 2. DISTINGUISH.
3. GESTURE.

significance also **significancy** *noun*
1. IDEA.

2. IMPORTANCE.
3. MEANING.

significant *adjective*
1. EXPRESSIVE.
2. IMPORTANT.
3. PREGNANT.

signification *noun*
1. MEANING.
2. SIGN.

signify *verb*
1. COUNT.
2. MEAN[1].

silence *noun*
1. The absence of sound or noise: *the silence of a starry night.*
   Syns: hush, quiet, quietness, quietude, soundlessness, still, stillness.
2. The avoidance of speech: *maintained a silence on controversial issues.*
   Syns: dumbness, muteness, speechlessness.

silence *verb*
To cause to become silent: *silenced the child with a menacing look.*
Syns: hush, quiet, quieten, shush, shut up, still.

silent *adjective*
1. Marked by, done with, or making no sound or noise: *a silent mountain valley; wept silent tears; silent guns.*
   Syns: hush, hushed, noiseless, quiet, soundless, still, stilly.
2. Not voiced or expressed: *a silent admission of guilt.*
   Syns: tacit, undeclared, unexpressed, unsaid, unspoken, unuttered, unvoiced, wordless.
3. SPEECHLESS.
4. TACITURN.

silhouette *noun* OUTLINE.

silliness *noun* FOOLISHNESS.

silly *adjective*
1. FOOLISH.
2. GIDDY.
3. MINDLESS.

silver-tongued *adjective*
1. ELOQUENT.
2. GLIB.

similar *adjective* LIKE[2].

similarity *noun* LIKENESS.

similitude *noun* LIKENESS.

simmer *verb*
1, 2. BOIL.

simmer down *verb* COMPOSE.

simper *verb* SMIRK.

simper *noun* SMIRK.

simple *adjective*
1. ARTLESS.
2. BACKWARD.

3. BARE.
4. EASY.
5. HUMBLE.
6. INFORMAL.
7. MINDLESS.
8. MODEST.
9. STUPID.

simple *noun* FOOL.

simple-minded *adjective*
1. BACKWARD.
2. STUPID.

simpleton *noun*
1, 2. FOOL.

simplicity *noun*
1. INFORMALITY.
2. MODESTY.

simplify *verb* BOIL DOWN at boil.

simulacrum also **simulacre** *noun* COPY.

simulate *verb*
1. ACT.
2. ASSUME.
3. FAKE.

simulation *noun*
1. ACT.
2. COPY.

simultaneous *adjective*
Existing or occurring at the same moment: *simultaneous translations.*
Syns: coincident, contemporary.

sin *noun*
1, 2. CRIME.
3. EVIL.

sin *verb* OFFEND.

sincere *adjective* GENUINE.

sine qua non *noun* CONDITION.

sinew(s) *noun* STRENGTH.

sinewy *adjective* MUSCULAR.

sinful *adjective* EVIL.

sing *verb*
1. To utter words or sounds in musical tones: *learned to sing in a school chorus.*
   Syns: carol, chant, tune (*Archaic*), vocalize.
2. INFORM.

singe *verb* BURN.

singe *noun* BURN.

singer *noun* VOCALIST.

single *adjective*
1. Without a spouse: *a bar for single people.*
   Syns: lone, sole, spouseless, unattached, unmarried, unwed.
   —*Idiom* footloose and fancy-free.
2. EXCLUSIVE.
3. INDIVIDUAL.
4. LONE.

single out *verb* CHOOSE.

single-handedly *adverb* ALONE.
singleness *noun*
1. UNIQUENESS.
2. UNITY.
singular *adjective*
1. ECCENTRIC.
2. INDIVIDUAL.
3. RARE.
singularity *noun*
1. ECCENTRICITY.
2. INDIVIDUALITY.
3. UNITY.
singularize *verb* DISTINGUISH.
sinister *adjective* MALIGN.
sink *noun*
1. DEPRESSION.
2. PIT.
sink *verb*
1. To go beneath the surface or to the bottom of a liquid: *The Titanic sank in 1912.*
   Syns: founder², submerge, submerse. —*Idiom* go to Davy Jones's locker.
2, 3. DESCEND.
4. DESTROY.
5. DETERIORATE.
6. DROP.
7, 8. FALL.
9. RAM.
10. SETTLE.
sink in *verb* REGISTER.
sinuous *adjective* WINDING.
sip *verb* DRINK.
sip *noun*
1. DRINK.
2. DROP.
sire *noun* FATHER.
sire *verb*
1. FATHER.
2. PRODUCE.
siren *noun* SEDUCTRESS.
siren *adjective* SEDUCTIVE.
sirenic or **sirenical** *adjective*
SEDUCTIVE.
sissified *adjective* EFFEMINATE.
sit *verb*
1. POSE.
2. SEAT.
sit in *verb* SUBSTITUTE.
sit on (or **upon**) *verb* REPRESS.
site *noun*
1. POSITION.
2. SCENE.
site *verb* POSITION.
situate *verb* POSITION.
situation *noun*
1. BEARING.
2. CONDITION.
3. PLACE.
4, 5. POSITION.
sizable also **sizeable** *adjective*
1. Somewhat big: *a sizable inheritance; a sizable piece of land.*
   Syns: biggish, goodly, largish (*also* largeish), respectable.
2. BIG.
sizableness also **sizeableness** *noun*
SIZE.
size *noun*
1. The amount of space occupied by something: *measured the size of the room with a yardstick.*
   Syns: amplitude, dimensions, extent, magnitude, measure, proportions.
2. The quality or state of being large in amount, extent, or importance: *a city that impressed me with its size.*
   Syns: amplitude, bigness, extent, greatness, largeness, magnitude, sizableness (*also* sizeableness).
3. BULK.
size up *verb* ESTIMATE.
sizeable *adjective* SEE **sizable.**
sizeableness *noun* SEE **sizableness.**
sizzle *verb* HISS.
sizzling *adjective* HOT.
skedaddle *verb* RUN.
skein *noun*
1. TANGLE.
2. THREAD.
skeletal *adjective* WASTED.
skeleton *noun* DRAFT.
skeptic *noun*
One who habitually or instinctively doubts or questions: *Political skeptics called into question the administration's policy.*
   Syns: doubter, doubting Thomas, headshaker, Humist, unbeliever.
skeptical *adjective*
1. DOUBTFUL.
2. INCREDULOUS.
skeptically *adverb*
With skepticism: *regarded that plan more than a little skeptically.*
   Syns: askance, dubiously, questioningly. —*Idioms* with a grain of salt, with a note of skepticism, with a skeptical eye.
skepticism *noun* DOUBT.
sketch *noun*
1. A short theatrical piece within a larger production: *a comic sketch in a variety show.*
   Syns: act, skit.
2. DRAFT.
sketch *verb* DRAFT.

sketchy *adjective*
1. ROUGH.
2. SUPERFICIAL.

skew *verb*
1. BIAS.
2. SWERVE.

skid *verb*
1. FALL.
2. SLIDE.

skid *noun* FALL.

skiddoo *verb* RUN.

skill *noun*
1. ABILITY.
2. DEXTERITY.

skilled *adjective*
1. ABLE.
2. ACCOMPLISHED.

skillful *adjective*
1. ABLE.
2. NEAT.

skim *verb*
1. BROWSE.
2. BRUSH.
3. FLY.
4. GLANCE¹.

skim *noun* BRUSH.

skimp *verb* SCRIMP.

skimpy *adjective*
1. INSUFFICIENT.
2. MEAGER.

skin *noun*
1. The tissue forming the external covering of the body: *burned her skin in the sun.*
   Syns: epidermis, integument.
2. The outer covering of a fruit: *the skin of a tangerine.*
   Syns: peel, rind.
3. A thin outer covering of an object: *the skin of an aircraft.*
   Syns: lamina, sheath, sheathing.

skin *verb*
1. To remove the skin of: *skinned an onion.*
   Syns: decorticate, excorticate, peel, scale¹, strip¹.
2. *Slang.* To exploit (another) by charging too much for something: *We really got skinned by that restaurant.*
   Syns: clip¹ (*Slang*), gouge (*Informal*), hold up, nick (*Slang*), overcharge, rip off (*Slang*), scalp (*Informal*), soak (*Slang*), stick (*Slang*). —*Idioms* make someone pay through the nose, see someone coming, take someone for a ride, take someone to the cleaners.
3. FACE.
4. RUSH.

skin-deep *adjective* SUPERFICIAL.

skinflint *noun* MISER.

skinny *adjective* THIN.

skip *verb*
1. To bound lightly: *children skipping around a Maypole.*
   Syns: hop, lope, skitter, spring, trip.
2. CUT.
3. DROP.
4. ESCAPE.
5. GLANCE¹.

skip *noun*
1. A light bounding movement: *ran with skips and jumps across the playground.*
   Syns: hop, spring.
2. CUT.

skirmish *noun* BRUSH.

skirt *verb*
1. To pass around but not through: *skirted the many potholes in the road.*
   Syns: bypass, circumnavigate, circumvent, detour, go around.
2. To evade, as a topic, esp. by circumlocution: *skirted all the touchy issues to avoid confrontations.*
   Syns: burke, bypass, circumvent, get around, hedge, sidestep.
3. BORDER.

skirts *noun*
The periphery of a city or town: *lived on the skirts of a huge metropolis.*
   Syns: environs, fringe, outskirts, suburbs.

skit *noun* SKETCH.

skitter *verb* SKIP.

skittish *adjective*
1. EDGY.
2. GIDDY.

skulk *verb* SNEAK.

skulking *adjective* STEALTHY.

sky *noun* AIR.

sky *verb* SOAR.

sky-high *adjective*
1. LOFTY.
2. STEEP¹.

skyrocket *verb* SOAR.

slab *noun* STICK.

slack *adjective*
1. LOOSE.
2. NEGLIGENT.
3. SLOW.

slack *verb*
1. EASE.
2. NEGLECT.

slacken *verb*
1. EASE.
2. SUBSIDE.
3. WEAKEN.

slackening *noun* WANE.

slackness *noun* NEGLIGENCE.
slam *noun*
A forceful movement causing a loud
noise: *shut the door with a slam; hit his
fist on the table with a slam.*
 Syns: bang, crash, smash, wham.
slam *verb*
1. *Slang.* To criticize harshly and
devastatingly: *The candidate slammed
his opponent for declining to debate.*
 Syns: blister, drub, excoriate, flay,
lash (into), rip (into) (*Informal*), roast
(*Informal*), scarify, scathe, scorch,
score, scourge, slap, slash. —*Idioms*
burn someone's ears, crawl all over,
give someone a roasting, pin
someone's ears back, put someone on
the griddle, put someone on the hot
seat, rake over the coals, read the riot
act to.
2. BANG.
3. HIT.
slammer *noun* JAIL.
slander *noun* LIBEL.
 slander *verb* LIBEL.
slanderous *adjective* LIBELOUS.
slant *verb*
1. BIAS.
2. INCLINE.
3. TEND[1].
slant *noun*
1. INCLINATION.
2. LIGHT[1].
3. POINT OF VIEW.
slanted *adjective* BIAS.
slanting *adjective* BIAS.
slap *noun*
A quick, sharp blow, esp. with the
hand: *gave the naughty child a slap on
the bottom.*
 Syns: box[2], buffet, bust (*Slang*),
chop[1], clip[1] (*Informal*), cuff, smack[1],
smacker, spank, spat (*Informal*).
slap *verb*
1. To hit with a quick, sharp blow of
the hand: *slapped the child for having
tantrums.*
 Syns: blip, box[2], buffet, bust, cuff,
smack[1], spank.
2. SLAM.
slap around *verb*
To be rough or brutal with: *The police
slapped the suspect around during
questioning.*
 Syns: manhandle, mess (up) (*Slang*),
rough (up).
slap-bang *adjective* RASH[1].
slapdash *adjective*
1. CARELESS.
2. RASH[1].

slash *verb*
1. CUT.
2. CUT BACK at **cut.**
3. SLAM.
slash *noun*
1. CUT.
2. CUTBACK.
3. SCORE.
slashing *adjective* BITING.
slate *noun*
1. SCHEDULE.
2. TICKET.
 slate *verb* SCHEDULE.
slattern *noun* SLUT.
slaughter *verb* ANNIHILATE.
 slaughter *noun* MASSACRE.
slaughterer *noun* MURDERER.
slaughterous *adjective* MURDEROUS.
slave *verb* GRIND.
slaver *verb*
1. DROOL.
2. FAWN.
3. FLATTER.
slaver *noun*
1. DROOL.
2. FLATTERY.
slavery *noun*
A state of subjugation to an owner or
master: *sold into slavery.*
 Syns: enslavement, helotry, serfdom,
servility, servitude, thrall, thralldom
or thraldom, villeinage (*also*
villainage), yoke. —*Idioms*
involuntary servitude, the chains (*or*
yoke) of slavery.
slavish *adjective*
1. DIFFICULT.
2. IMITATIVE.
3. SERVILE.
slay *verb*
1. KILL.
2. MURDER.
slayer *noun* MURDERER.
slaying *noun* MURDER.
 slaying *adjective* PRICELESS.
sleazy *adjective*
1. SHABBY.
2. SHODDY.
sled *verb* SLIDE.
sledge *verb* SLIDE.
sleek *adjective*
1. Smooth and lustrous as if polished:
the cat's sleek black fur.
 Syns: satiny, sleeky.
2. Having slender and graceful lines: *a
sleek new convertible.*
 Syns: streamlined, trim.
3. UNCTUOUS.

sleek *verb*
1. DISGUISE.
2. GLOSS.

sleeky *adjective* SLEEK.

sleep *noun*
The natural recurring condition of suspended consciousness by which the body rests: *needed a full eight hours of sleep.*
   Syns: shut-eye (*Slang*), slumber, snooze (*Informal*). —*Idioms* land of Nod, the arms of Morpheus.

sleep *verb*
To be asleep: *slept for twelve hours.*
   Syns: slumber, snooze (*Informal*). —*Idioms* be in the land of Nod, be sunk in sleep, catch some shut-eye, rest in the arms of Morpheus, sleep like a log (*or* rock *or* top), sleep tight.

sleep in *verb*
To sleep longer than intended: *slept in and was late to work.*
   Syn: oversleep.

sleep with *verb* TAKE.

sleeper *noun* HIT.

sleeping *adjective*
1. In a state of sleep: *Sleeping children are beautiful.*
   Syns: asleep, out (*Informal*), slumbering, snoozing (*Informal*), unawake. —*Idioms* dead to the world, fast (*or* sound) asleep, in a sound (*or* wakeless) sleep, out like a light.
2. In a state of temporary inactivity: *a sleeping giant among the unaligned nations.*
   Syns: dormant, inactive.

sleepless *adjective* WAKEFUL.

sleepy *adjective*
1. Ready for or needing sleep: *tired, sleepy children.*
   Syns: dozy, drowsy, nodding, slumberous (*also* slumbery, slumbrous), snoozy (*Informal*), somnolent, soporific.
2. Inducing sleep: *a hot, sleepy day.*
   Syns: hypnotic, narcotic, slumberous (*also* slumbery, slumbrous), somnifacient, somniferous (*also* somnific), somnolent, somnorific, soporific.

sleer *verb* SNEER.

sleight *noun*
1. DECEPTION.
2. DEXTERITY.
3. TRICK.

slender *adjective*
1. REMOTE.
2. THIN.

sleuth *noun* DETECTIVE.

slew also **slue** *noun* HEAP.

slice *verb* CUT.

slice *noun*
1, 2. CUT.
3. SECTION.

slick *adjective*
1. So smooth and glassy as to offer insecure hold or footing: *steps slick with ice.*
   Syns: lubricious, sliddery, slippery, slippy, slithery. —*Idioms* slick as a greased pig, slick as greased glass, slippery as an eel.
2. DEXTEROUS.
3. GLIB.
4. SHARP.
5. SHREWD.

slick *verb*
1. DRESS UP at **dress**.
2. GLIDE.

sliddery *adjective* SLICK.

slide *verb*
1. To pass smoothly, quietly, and undisturbed or as if on a slippery surface: *skaters sliding across a frozen pond; decided to let the matter slide for the moment.*
   Syns: coast, drift.
2. To lose one's balance and fall or almost fall: *slid on the freshly waxed floor.*
   Syns: skid, slip, slither. —*Idiom* take a slide (*or* skid).
3. To ride on a sled in the snow: *The children went sliding on our hill.*
   Syns: sled, sledge (*Brit.*).
4. CRAWL.
5. EASE.
6. GLIDE.
7. SLIP.
8. SNEAK.

slide *noun* FALL.

slight *adjective*
1. LIGHT².
2. REMOTE.

slight *verb*
1. IGNORE.
2. NEGLECT.

slight *noun* NEGLECT.

slighting *adjective* DISPARAGING.

slim *adjective* REMOTE.

slim *verb* REDUCE.

slime *noun*
A viscous, usu. offensively dirty substance: *a swimming pool coated with green slime.*
   Syns: muck, ooze.

slimy *adjective*
Of, pertaining to, or covered with slime: *slimy mud; a slimy, brackish pool.*
   Syns: mucky, oozy.

sling *verb*
1. HANG.
2. THROW.

sling *noun* THROW.

slink *verb* SNEAK.

slink *noun*
1. SNEAK.
2. STEALTH.

slinkiness *noun* STEALTH.

slinking *adjective* STEALTHY.

slinky *adjective* STEALTHY.

slip *noun*
1. ERROR.
2. LAPSE.

slip *verb*
1. To shift or be shifted out of place: *The boxes slipped from my grasp and crashed to the floor.*
   Syn: slide.
2. *Informal.* To decline, as in value or quantity, very gradually: *Stock prices slipped an eighth of a point.*
   Syns: drop off, fall off, sag.
3. To displace (a bone) from a socket or joint: *slipped his shoulder in the soccer game.*
   Syns: dislocate, throw out. —*Idiom* throw out of joint.
4. EASE.
5. ERR.
6. FALL.
7. GLIDE.
8. MISCARRY.
9. SHED.
10. SLIDE.
11. SNEAK.

slip away *verb* ESCAPE.

slip into *verb* DON.

slip on *verb* DON.

slip up *verb* ERR.

slippery *adjective*
1. EVASIVE.
2. SHARP.
3. SLICK.

slippy *adjective* SLICK.

slipshod *adjective*
1. CARELESS.
2. MESSY.

slip-up *noun*
1. ERROR.
2. LAPSE.

slit *verb* CUT.

slit *noun* CUT.

slither *verb*
1. To move sinuously: *A large earthworm slithered in the garden.*

   Syns: snake, undulate.
2. GLIDE.
3. SLIDE.

slithery *adjective* SLICK.

slobber *verb* DROOL.

slobber *noun* DROOL.

slobbery *adjective* MESSY.

slog *verb*
1. GRIND.
2. HIT.
3. PLOD.

slop *verb*
1. PLOD.
2. SLOUCH.
3. SPLASH.

slope *verb* INCLINE.

slope *noun*
1. ASCENT.
2. INCLINATION.

sloped *adjective* INCLINED.

sloping *adjective* INCLINED.

sloppiness *noun* SENTIMENTALITY.

sloppy *adjective*
1. CARELESS.
2. MESSY.
3. SENTIMENTAL.

slosh *verb*
1. SPLASH.
2. WASH.

sloshed *adjective* DRUNK.

slot *noun*
1. PLACE.
2. POSITION.

sloth *noun* LAZINESS.

slothful *adjective* LAZY.

slothfulness *noun* LAZINESS.

slouch *verb*
1. To take on or move with an awkward, slovenly posture: *He slouched into the room and fell into a big chair.*
   Syns: loll, lop², slop, slump.
2. To hang limply, loosely, and carelessly: *a hat with a wide, slouching brim.*
   Syns: droop, flop, loll, lop², sag, wilt.

slouch *noun* WASTREL.

slough¹ *noun* SWAMP.

slough² *verb* SHED.

slovenly *adjective*
1. CARELESS.
2. MESSY.

slow *adjective*
1. Proceeding at a rate less than usual or desired: *slow progress toward peace; slow traffic during rush hour.*
   Syns: dilatory, dragging, flagging, laggard, lagging, poky (*also* pokey) (*Informal*), slow-footed, slow-going,

slow-paced, tardy. —*Idioms* slow as a
swamp turtle, slow as molasses in
January.
2. Characterized by reduced economic
activity: *Car sales have been slow this
year.*
   Syns: down, dull, off, slack, sluggish,
   soft.
3. BACKWARD.
4. STUPID.
slow *verb* DELAY.
slow *adverb*
So as to fall behind schedule: *This clock
runs slow. The train is an hour slow.*
   Syns: behind, behindhand, late.
   —*Idiom* behind time.
slow-footed *adjective* SLOW.
slow-going *adjective* SLOW.
slow-paced *adjective* SLOW.
slowpoke *noun* LAGGARD.
slow-witted *adjective*
1. BACKWARD.
2. STUPID.
slue¹ *verb* SWERVE.
slue² *noun* SEE **slew.**
slug¹ *noun* DROP.
slug² *verb* HIT.
slug³ *noun* WASTREL.
slugabed *noun* WASTREL.
sluggard *noun* WASTREL.
sluggish *adjective*
1. LETHARGIC.
2. SLOW.
sluggishness *noun*
1. LAZINESS.
2. LETHARGY.
slumber *verb* SLEEP.
slumber *noun* SLEEP.
slumbering *adjective* SLEEPING.
slumberless *adjective* WAKEFUL.
slumberous *also* **slumbery, slumbrous**
adjective
1, 2. SLEEPY.
slump *noun*
1. DEPRESSION.
2. FALL.
slump *verb*
1. DROP.
2. FALL.
3. SLOUCH.
slur *verb* LIBEL.
slur *noun* REFLECTION.
slushy *adjective* SENTIMENTAL.
slut *noun*
A vulgar, promiscuous woman who
flouts propriety: *a forward slut in tawdry
finery.*
   Syns: baggage, floozy (*also* floozey)
   (*Slang*), hussy, jade, slattern,

strumpet, tart², tramp, wench,
wanton.
sly *adjective*
1. Trickily secret: *a sly maneuver.*
   Syns: furtive, secretive, surreptitious.
2. ARTFUL.
3. SHARP.
4. SHREWD.
sly *verb* SNEAK.
slyness *noun* INDIRECTION.
smack¹ *verb*
1. HIT.
2. KISS.
3. SLAP.
smack *noun*
1. BLOW².
2. KISS.
3. SLAP.
smack *adverb* PRECISELY.
smack² *verb*
To have a particular flavor or
suggestion of something: *Those
statements smack of treason.*
   Syns: flavor, savor, smell, suggest,
   taste.
smack *noun*
1, 2. FLAVOR.
smacker *noun*
1. BLOW².
2. KISS.
3. SLAP.
small *adjective*
1. Not yet large in size due to
   incomplete growth: *mothers with
   small children.*
   Syn: little.
2. FINE¹.
3. LITTLE.
4. MINOR.
5. NARROW.
6. PETTY.
7. SOFT.
smallest *adjective* MINIMAL.
small-fry *adjective* MINOR.
smallish *adjective* LITTLE.
small-minded *adjective*
1. INTOLERANT.
2. NARROW.
3. PETTY.
smallness *noun* PETTINESS.
small-time *adjective* MINOR.
small-town *adjective* LOCAL.
smarm *verb* SMEAR.
smarmy *adjective* UNCTUOUS.
smart *verb* STING.
smart *noun* PAIN.
smart *adjective*
1, 2. CLEVER.

3. FASHIONABLE.
4. IMPUDENT.

smart aleck *noun*

Informal. One who is obnoxiously self-assertive and arrogant: *smart alecks who heckled the speaker; smart alecks cracking jokes during the love scene.*

   Syns: know-it-all (*Informal*), malapert, saucebox, smarty (*Informal*), smarty-pants (*Slang*), wiseacre (*Informal*), wisecracker (*Slang*), wise guy (*Slang*), wisehead (*Informal*), wiseling (*Archaic*), wisenheimer (*also* weisenheimer) (*Informal*), witling (*Archaic*).

smarten *verb* FIX UP at **fix.**
smarting *adjective* PAINFUL.
smarts *noun* INTELLIGENCE.
smarty *noun* SMART ALECK.
smarty-pants *noun* SMART ALECK.
smash *verb*

1. BREAK.
2. BREAK DOWN at **break.**
3. CLASH.
4. CRASH.
5. DESTROY.
6. HIT.

smash up *verb* CRASH.
smash *noun*

1. CLASH.
2. COLLAPSE.
3. COLLISION.
4. CRASH.
5. SLAM.

smashed *adjective* DRUNK.
smashup *noun*

1. COLLAPSE.
2. CRASH.

smatterer *noun* AMATEUR.
smaze *noun* HAZE.
smear *verb*

1. To spread with a greasy, sticky, or dirty substance: *smeared the bricks with mortar.*
   Syns: bedaub, besmear, butter, clart (*Brit. Regional*), dab[1], daub, plaster, smarm (*Regional*), smudge. —*Idiom* lay it on thick.
2. BLACKEN.
3. DEFEAT.
4. OVERWHELM.

smear *noun*

1. A discolored mark made by smearing: *had a huge smear of axle grease on his jeans.*
   Syns: blot, blotch, dab[1], daub, smirch, smudge, smutch, splotch.
2. An attempt to destroy someone's reputation: *a carefully engineered smear by use of rumors.*

   Syns: mudslinging, vilification.
   —*Idiom* smear campaign.

smell *noun*

1. The sense by which odors are perceived: *Rodents often identify their offspring by means of smell.*
   Syns: nose, olfaction, scent.
2. The quality of something that may be perceived by the olfactory sense: *the mingled smells of food and seawater at the beach.*
   Syns: aroma, odor, scent, snuff[1].
3. AIR.

smell *verb*

1. To perceive with the olfactory sense: *One could smell the smoke for miles.*
   Syns: nose, scent, sniff, snuff[1], whiff. —*Idiom* catch (*or* get) a whiff of.
2. To have or give off a foul odor: *This shrimp smells.*
   Syns: funk[1], reek, stench, stink. —*Idiom* smell to high heaven.
3. SMACK[2].

smeller *noun* NOSE.
smelly *adjective*

Informal. Having an unpleasant odor: *smelly fumes from a soap factory.*
   Syns: fetid, foul, foul-smelling, malodorous, mephitic, noisome, reeking, stinking.

smidgen *noun* BIT[1].
smile *noun*

A facial expression marked by an upward curving of the lips: *gave me a cheery smile.*
   Syn: grin. —*Idiom* broad grin.

smile *verb*

To curve the lips upward in expressing amusement, pleasure, or happiness: *smiled and waved good-bye.*
   Syns: beam, grin. —*Idioms* break into a smile, crack a smile, wreathe one's face in smiles.

smile on (*or* **upon**) *verb* ENCOURAGE.
smirch *noun* SMEAR.
smirk *verb*

To smile in an insincere, knowing way: *men smirking at peepshows.*
   Syn: simper. —*Idiom* grin like a Cheshire cat.

smirk *noun*

An affected, knowing smile: *smirks and giggles in the back of the theater.*
   Syn: simper. —*Idiom* sardonic grin.

smitch *noun* BIT[1].
smite *verb*

1. AFFLICT.
2. HIT.

smitten *adjective* INFATUATED.

smolder *verb* BOIL.

smooch *noun* KISS.

  smooch *verb* KISS.

smooth *adjective*
1. Marked by facility, esp. of expression: *a smooth prose style.*
   Syns: cursive, easy, effortless, flowing, fluent, fluid, graceful, ready, running.
2. EASY.
3. EVEN¹.
4. GENTLE.
5. SUAVE.

  smooth *verb*
1. EVEN¹.
2, 3. PERFECT.

smooth over *verb* SETTLE.

smooth-spoken *adjective* ELOQUENT.

smother *verb*
1. CHOKE.
2. OVERWHELM.
3. REPRESS.

smothering *noun* REPRESSION.

smudge *verb*
1. BLACKEN.
2. DIRTY.
3. SMEAR.

  smudge *noun* SMEAR.

smuggle *verb*
1. To import or export secretly and illegally: *smuggled in cocaine from South America.*
   Syns: bootleg, contraband, run.
   —*Idiom* run contraband.
2. To bring in or take out secretly: *Friendly diplomats smuggled the hostages out of the country.*
   Syns: sneak, spirit.

smuggler *noun*
A person who engages in smuggling: *arms smugglers operating out of Northern Ireland.*
   Syns: bootlegger, contrabandist, runner.

smut *noun* OBSCENITY.

  smut *verb*
1. BLACKEN.
2. STAIN.

smutch *verb* DIRTY.

  smutch *noun* SMEAR.

smutty *adjective*
1. DIRTY.
2. OBSCENE.

snack *noun* BITE.

snafu *verb*
1. BOTCH.
2. CONFUSE.

  snafu *noun*
1. BOTCH.
2. DISORDER.

snag *noun*
1. BAR.
2. CATCH.

snake *verb*
1. CRAWL.
2. SLITHER.
3. SNEAK.
4. WIND².

snaky *adjective* WINDING.

snap *verb*
1. To make a light, sharp noise: *The lock snapped shut.*
   Syns: clack, clacket (*Regional*), click.
2. To grasp at (something) eagerly, forcibly, and abruptly with the jaws: *sharks snapping at the bloody bait.*
   Syns: catch, nip¹, snatch, strike.
3. To speak abruptly and sharply: *He snapped at me for no reason at all.*
   Syns: bark, snarl². —*Idioms* bite someone's head off, snap someone's head (*or* nose) off.
4. BREAK DOWN at **break.**
5, 6. CRACK.

  snap *noun*
1. A light, sharp noise: *the snap of a light switch.*
   Syns: clack, click.
2. BIT¹.
3. BITE.
4. BREEZE.
5. DRIVE.
6. JERK.
7. REPORT.

  snap *adjective*
1. EASY.
2. EXTEMPORANEOUS.

snappish *adjective*
1. ILL-TEMPERED.
2. IRRITABLE.

snappy *adjective*
1. FASHIONABLE.
2. IRRITABLE.
3. SPIRITED.
4. VIGOROUS.

snare *verb* CATCH.

  snare *noun* LURE.

snarl¹ *noun*
1. DISORDER.
2. TANGLE.

  snarl *verb*
1. COMPLICATE.
2. CONFUSE.
3. ENTANGLE.

snarl² *verb* SNAP.

snatch *verb*
1. CATCH.
2. KIDNAP.
3. SEIZE.

4. SNAP.
5. STEAL.
snatch *noun* CATCH.
sneak *verb*
1. To move silently and furtively: *tried to sneak out of the room when my back was turned; a cat burglar sneaking onto the roof.*
   Syns: creep, glide, gumshoe (*Slang*), lurk, mouse, prowl, pussyfoot, shirk, skulk, slide, slink, slip, sly, snake, steal.
2. SMUGGLE.
sneak *noun*
One who behaves in a stealthy, furtive way: *Her sneak of a husband was deceiving her.*
   Syns: slink, sneaker, weasel.
sneaker *noun* SNEAK.
sneakiness *noun*
1. INDIRECTION.
2. STEALTH.
sneaking *adjective*
1. STEALTHY.
2. UNDERHAND.
sneakish *adjective* STEALTHY.
sneaky *adjective*
1. STEALTHY.
2. UNDERHAND.
sneer *noun*
A facial expression conveying scorn or derision: *He responded to my idea with a sneer.*
   Syns: fleer, snicker (*also* snigger).
sneer *verb*
1. To smile or laugh scornfully or derisively: *The audience sneered at the politician's promises.*
   Syns: fleer, sleer (*Brit. Regional*), snicker (*also* snigger). —*Idiom* curl one's lip.
2. DESPISE.
sneer at *verb* RIDICULE.
snicker *also* **snigger** *verb*
1. GIGGLE.
2. SNEER.
snicker *also* **snigger** *noun*
1. GIGGLE.
2. SNEER.
sniff *verb* SMELL.
snigger *verb & noun* SEE **snicker.**
snippety *adjective* ABRUPT.
snippy *adjective* ABRUPT.
snit *noun* STATE.
snitch *verb*
1. INFORM.
2. STEAL.
snitch *also* **snitcher** *noun* INFORMER.

snob *noun*
One who despises people or things he regards as inferior, esp. because of social or intellectual pretension: *That snob thinks all American movies are trash.*
   Syns: elitist (*also* élitist), high-hat (*Slang*), snoot (*Informal*).
snobbish *adjective*
Characteristic of or resembling a snob: *a snobbish attitude.*
   Syns: elitist (*also* élitist), high-hat (*Slang*), snobby, snooty (*Informal*), uppity (*also* uppish) (*Informal*).
snobby *adjective* SNOBBISH.
snoop *verb*
Informal. To look into or inquire about curiously, inquisitively, or in a meddlesome fashion: *snooping into their private business, looking for gossip.*
   Syns: nose (around), poke, pry.
   —*Idiom* stick one's nose into.
snoop *noun*
Informal. A person who snoops: *an office snoop who repeated all the latest gossip.*
   Syns: busybody, meddler, prier (*also* pryer), snooper (*Informal*).
snooper *noun* SNOOP.
snoopiness *noun* CURIOSITY.
snoopy *adjective* CURIOUS.
snoot *noun*
1. NOSE.
2. SNOB.
snooty *adjective* SNOBBISH.
snooze *verb* SLEEP.
snooze *noun* SLEEP.
snoozing *adjective* SLEEPING.
snoozy *adjective* SLEEPY.
snort *noun* DROP.
snout *noun* NOSE.
snowball *verb*
1. EXPLODE.
2. INCREASE.
snub *verb*
1. To slight (someone) deliberately: *dared to address him familiarly and was roundly snubbed.*
   Syns: cold-shoulder (*Informal*), cut, rebuff, shun, spurn. —*Idioms* give someone the cold shoulder, turn a cold shoulder on, turn one's back on, slam the door on.
2. IGNORE.
snub *noun*
A deliberate slight: *gave me a snub right in front of the boss.*
   Syns: cold shoulder (*Informal*), cut, rebuff, spurn.

snuff¹ *verb* SMELL.
snuff *noun* SMELL.
snuff² *verb* EXTINGUISH.
snuff out *verb* ANNIHILATE.
snug *adjective*
1. COMFORTABLE.
2. NEAT.
3. TAUT.
snuggle *verb*
To lie or press close together, usu. with another person or thing: *The cat snuggled on the blanket.*
Syns: cuddle, nestle, nuzzle.
soak *noun* DRUNKARD.
soak *verb*
1. DRINK.
2. SKIN.
3. STEEP².
soak in *verb* REGISTER.
soak up *verb*
1. ABSORB.
2. DRINK.
soaked *adjective* WET.
soar *verb*
1. To rise abruptly and precipitously: *The price of gold has soared.*
Syns: rocket, shoot up, sky, skyrocket, upsoar.
2, 3. RISE.
soaring *adjective* TALL.
sob *verb* CRY.
sobby *adjective* SENTIMENTAL.
sober *adjective*
1. GRAVE².
2. REALISTIC.
3. TEMPERATE.
soberness *noun* TEMPERANCE.
sobersided *adjective* SERIOUS.
sobriety *noun*
1. GRAVITY.
2. SERIOUSNESS.
3. TEMPERANCE.
sociable *adjective*
1. COMPANIONABLE.
2. GRACIOUS.
3, 4. SOCIAL.
social *adjective*
1. Of, characterized by, or inclined to living together in communities: *a social being.*
Syns: gregarious, sociable.
2. Spent, marked by, or enjoyed in the company of others: *a pleasant social afternoon.*
Syns: companionable, convivial, sociable.
3. COMPANIONABLE.
4. SOCIETAL.

socialize *verb*
1. To place under government or group ownership or control: *socialize the steel industry.*
Syns: communalize, nationalize.
2. To fit for companionship with others, esp. in attitude or manners: *socializing small children.*
Syns: acculturate, civilize.
3. To take part in social activities: *The team members socialize together off the field.*
Syn: mingle.
societal *adjective*
Of or pertaining to the structure, organization, or functioning of society: *pressures for societal change.*
Syns: social, societary.
societary *adjective* SOCIETAL.
society *noun*
1. People of the highest social level: *was formally presented to New York society at a ball.*
Syns: aristocracy, aristoi, blue blood, crème de la crème (*French*), elite (*also* élite), flower, gentility, gentry, haut monde (*French*), patriciate, quality, upper class, upper crust (*Informal*), who's who.
2. COMPANY.
3. PUBLIC.
4. UNION.
sock *noun*
1. BLOW².
2. WALLOP.
sock *verb* HIT.
sock away *verb* BANK¹.
sodden *verb* WET.
sodden *adjective*
1. DRUNK.
2. WET.
soft *adjective*
1. Yielding easily to pressure or weight; not firm: *soft butter; a soft pillow.*
Syns: mushy, pappy, pulpous, pulpy, quaggy, spongy, squashy, squelchy, squishy, yielding.
2. Not irritating, strident, or loud: *a soft voice.*
Syns: hushed, low, low-key (*also* low-keyed), quiet, small, subdued.
3. COMFORTABLE.
4, 5. GENTLE.
6. LIGHT².
7. SENTIMENTAL.
8. SLOW.
9. STUPID.
10. TOLERANT.

soften *verb*
1. MODERATE.
2. PACIFY.
3. WEAKEN.

softheaded *adjective* FOOLISH.

softhearted *adjective* GENTLE.

soft-pedal *verb*
Informal. To make less emphatic or obvious: *soft-pedaled our contributions in an attempt to take most of the credit for herself.*
Syns: de-emphasize, play down, tone down.

soft-soap *verb*
1. COAX.
2. FLATTER.

soggy *adjective*
1. STICKY.
2. WET.

soil *verb*
1. BLACKEN.
2. DIRTY.
3. TAINT.

soiled *adjective* DIRTY.

soily *adjective* DIRTY.

soiree also **soirée** *noun* PARTY.

sojourn *verb* STAY¹.

sojourn *noun* STAY¹.

solace *verb* COMFORT.

solace *noun* COMFORT.

soldier *noun* FIGHTER.

soldierly *adjective* MILITARY.

sole *adjective*
1. EXCLUSIVE.
2. LONE.
3. SINGLE.

solecism *noun* CORRUPTION.

solely *adverb*
1. To the exclusion of anyone or anything else: *I work solely at night.*
Syns: alone, but, entirely, only.
2. ALONE.

solemn *adjective* GRAVE².

solemness *noun* GRAVITY.

solemnity *noun* GRAVITY.

solemnize *verb* CELEBRATE.

solicit *verb* REQUEST.

solicitous *adjective*
1. ATTENTIVE.
2. EAGER.

solicitously *adverb* CONSIDERATELY.

solid *adjective*
1. CONVINCING.
2. DEPENDABLE.
3. FIRM¹.
4, 5. SOUND².
6. SURE.
7. UNANIMOUS.

solidarity *noun* UNITY.

solidify *verb* HARDEN.

solidity *noun*
1. SOUNDNESS.
2. THICKNESS.

solitary *adjective*
1. Set away from all others: *a solitary Norman watchtower on the English coast.*
Syns: alone, apart, detached, isolate, isolated, lone, removed.
2. ALONE.
3. COOL.
4. LONE.
5. REMOTE.

solitude *noun* ALONENESS.

solo *adverb* ALONE.

solution *noun* ANSWER.

solve *verb*
1. RESOLVE.
2. WORK.

somatic *adjective* BODILY.

somber also **sombre** *adjective*
1. GLOOMY.
2. GRAVE².

somberness *noun* GRAVITY.

sombre *adjective* SEE **somber**.

some *adjective* SEVERAL.

somebody *noun* DIGNITARY.

someone *noun* DIGNITARY.

something *noun* THING.

sometime *adjective* LATE.

somnifacient *adjective* SLEEPY.

somnifacient *noun* SOPORIFIC.

somniferous also **somnific** *adjective* SLEEPY.

somnolent *adjective*
1, 2. SLEEPY.

somnorific *adjective* SLEEPY.

sonance *noun* SOUND¹.

sonant *adjective* VOCAL.

songster *noun* VOCALIST.

songstress *noun* VOCALIST.

sonorous *adjective*
1. Characterized by language that is elevated and sometimes pompous in style: *sonorous phrases that stirred the crowd.*
Syns: aureate, bombastic, declamatory, fustian, grandiloquent, highfalutin *or* hifalutin (*also* highfaluting) (*Informal*), high-flown, high-sounding, magniloquent, orotund, rhetorical.
2. RESONANT.

soothe *verb*
1. CALM.
2. COMFORT.
3. PACIFY.

soothsay *verb* PROPHESY.

soothsayer *noun* PROPHET.

sooty *adjective* BLACK.

sop *verb*
1. DRINK.
2. WET.

sophism *noun* FALLACY.

sophistic *adjective* FALLACIOUS.

sophisticate *verb* ADULTERATE.

sophisticated *adjective*
1. Experienced in the ways of the world; lacking natural simplicity: *tried to appear sophisticated but was really very naive.*
   Syns: cosmopolitan, worldly, worldly-wise.
2. INTELLECTUAL.

sophistry *noun* FALLACY.

soporific *noun*
Something that induces sleep: *a soporific prescribed by the doctor.*
   Syns: hypnotic, narcotic, opiate, somnifacient.

soporific *adjective*
1, 2. SLEEPY.

sopping *adjective* WET.

soppy *adjective*
1. SENTIMENTAL.
2. WET.

sorceress *noun* WITCH.

sorcery *noun* MAGIC.

sordid *adjective*
Having or proceeding from low moral standards: *His life was a sordid affair.*
   Syns: base[2], contemptible, despicable, ignoble, low, low-down, mean[2], squalid, vile.

sore *adjective*
1. ANGRY.
2. PAINFUL.

sorehead *noun* GROUCH.

soreness *noun*
1. IRRITATION.
2. PAIN.

sorrow *noun* GRIEF.

sorrow *verb* GRIEVE.

sorrowful *adjective*
1. Causing sorrow or regret: *a sorrowful and shameful death.*
   Syns: doleful, dolorous, grievous, lamentable, lugubrious, mournful, regrettable, rueful, sad, woeful (*also* woful).
2. Full of or expressive of sorrow: *a sorrowful smile.*
   Syns: doleful, dolorous, lugubrious, mournful, plaintive, rueful, woebegone (*also* wobegone), woeful (*also* woful).

sorry *adjective*
1. APOLOGETIC.
2. DISAPPOINTING.
3. FILTHY.
4. REMORSEFUL.

sort *noun* KIND[2].

sort *verb*
1. To set apart (one kind or type) from others: *sort the wheat from the chaff; sorting out good ideas from bad.*
   Syns: separate, sift, winnow.
2. ARRANGE.
3. ASSORT.

sort out *verb* ASSORT.

sortilege *noun* MAGIC.

sot *noun* DRUNKARD.

sough *verb*
1. MURMUR.
2. SIGH.

sough *noun*
1. MURMUR.
2. SIGH.

soul *noun*
1. *Theol.* The essential being of a person, regarded as immaterial and immortal: *consigned his soul to God.*
   Syn: spirit.
2, 3. HEART.
4. HUMAN BEING.
5. SPIRIT.

sound[1] *noun*
1. The sensation caused by vibrating wave motion that is perceived by the organs of hearing: *What was that sound?*
   Syns: noise, sonance.
2. HEARING.

sound *verb*
1. APPEAR.
2. APPROACH.
3. FEEL OUT at **feel.**

sound[2] *adjective*
1. Not easily moved or shaken: *a house with a sound foundation.*
   Syns: firm[1], secure, solid, stable, sturdy, sure.
2. Based on good judgment, reasoning, or evidence: *sound logic.*
   Syns: cogent, just, solid, tight (*Slang*), valid.
3. CONVINCING.
4. GOOD.
5. HEALTHY.
6. SANE.

soundless *adjective* SILENT.

soundlessness *noun* SILENCE.

soundness *noun*
1. The condition of being free from defects or flaws: *tested the machine for soundness.*

Syns: firmness, integrity, solidity, stability, strength, wholeness.
2. HEALTH.
3. SANITY.
4. STABILITY.

soup *noun* PREDICAMENT.

soupçon *noun*
1. SHADE.
2. TRACE.

soupy *adjective* SENTIMENTAL.

sour *adjective*
1. Having a taste characteristic of that produced by acids: *a very sour lemon.* *Syns:* acerb, acerbic, acetous (*also* acetose), acid, acidulous, dry, tart[1].
2. BITTER.
3. GLUM.

sour *verb* EMBITTER.

sour *adverb*
1. HARD.
2. WRONG.

source *noun*
1. CONTACT.
2. ORIGIN.

sourpuss *noun* GROUCH.

souse *noun* DRUNKARD.

souse *verb*
1. DIP.
2. WET.

soused *adjective*
1. DRUNK.
2. WET.

souvenir *noun* REMEMBRANCE.

sovereign *adjective*
1. EXCELLENT.
2. FREE.

sovereignty *noun* FREEDOM.

sow *verb* SEED.

space *noun*
1. BIT[1].
2. DISTANCE.
3. EXPANSE.

spaced-out *adjective* DRUGGED.

spacious *adjective*
1. BROAD.
2. ROOMY.

spade *verb*
1, 2. DIG.

span *noun*
1. EXTENT.
2. PERIOD.
3. TERM.

spangle *verb* FLASH.

spangle *noun* GLITTER.

spank *verb* SLAP.

spank *noun* SLAP.

spanner *noun* WRENCH.

spare *verb*
1. ECONOMIZE.
2. EXCUSE.
3. FAVOR.
4. SAVE.

spare *adjective*
1. MEAGER.
2. SUPERFLUOUS.
3. THIN.
4. TIGHT.

sparing *adjective* ECONOMICAL.

spark *noun*
1. BLINK.
2. GERM.

spark *verb* COURT.

sparkle *verb* FLASH.

sparkle *noun*
1, 2. GLITTER.

sparkling *adjective*
1. CLEVER.
2. EXUBERANT.

sparse *adjective* MEAGER.

spasm *noun* THROE.

spat *noun*
1. ARGUMENT.
2. SLAP.

spate *noun*
1. FLOOD.
2. FLOW.

spatter *verb*
1. LIBEL.
2. SPLASH.
3. SPOT.

spawn *verb*
1. GENERATE.
2. PRODUCE.
3. REPRODUCE.

spawning *adjective* FERTILE.

spawning *noun* REPRODUCTION.

speak *verb*
1. To express oneself in speech: *couldn't speak because of laryngitis; spoke to each parent who attended the play.* *Syns:* talk, utter[1], verbalize, vocalize. —*Idioms* break silence, open one's mouth (*or* lips), put in (*or* into) words, wag one's tongue.
2, 3. ADDRESS.
4. CONVERSE[1].
5. TALK.

speak for *verb* REPRESENT.

speaker *noun*
1. One who delivers a public speech: *a moving and effective speaker.* *Syns:* speechifier, speechmaker, talker.
2. A person who speaks on behalf of another or others: *The speaker for the governor made the announcement.* *Syns:* mouth (*Informal*), mouthpiece (*Informal*), spokesman, spokesperson, spokeswoman.

special *adjective*
1. Of, relating to, or intended for a distinctive thing or group: *a special medication for arthritis; a special entrance for the physically handicapped.*
   Syns: especial, individual, particular, specific.
2. SPECIFIC.

specialty *noun*
1. BRANCH.
2. FORTE.

species *noun* KIND[2].

specific *adjective*
1. Fixed and distinct from others: *had no specific purpose in mind.*
   Syns: express, set[1], special.
2. DEFINITE.
3. SPECIAL.

specificate *verb* STIPULATE.

specification *noun* PROVISION.

specify *verb*
1. DESIGNATE.
2. NAME.
3. STIPULATE.

specimen *noun* EXAMPLE.

specious *adjective*
1. FALLACIOUS.
2. FALSE.

speciousness *noun* FALLACY.

speck *noun* BIT[1].
speck *verb* SPECKLE.

speckle *verb*
To mark with many small spots: *a white horse speckled with brown spots.*
   Syns: bespeckle, dapple, dot, fleck, freckle, mottle, pepper, speck, sprinkle, stipple.

spectacle *noun* DISPLAY.

spectacular *adjective*
1. DRAMATIC.
2. STAGGERING.

spectator *noun* WATCHER.

specter *noun* GHOST.

spectral *adjective* GHASTLY.

spectrum *noun* GHOST.

speculate *verb*
1. GAMBLE.
2. THINK.

speculation *noun*
1. GAMBLE.
2. THEORY.
3. THOUGHT.

speculative *adjective*
1. THEORETICAL.
2. THOUGHTFUL.

speculator *noun*
1. One who speculates for quick profits: *stock-market speculators.*
   Syns: adventurer, gambler, operator.
2. BETTOR.

speech *noun*
1. The faculty, act, or product of speaking: *a sore throat that made speech difficult; terms that occur in speech more than writing.*
   Syns: discourse, talk, utterance, verbalization, voice. —*Idiom* oral communication.
2. A usu. formal oral communication to an audience: *a valedictory speech at graduation.*
   Syns: address, allocution, declamation, lecture, oration, prelection, talk.
3. LANGUAGE.

speechifier *noun* SPEAKER.

speechless *adjective*
1. Temporarily unable or unwilling to speak, as from shock or fear: *was speechless in her confusion and surprise.*
   Syns: dumb, mum, mute, silent, tight-lipped, wordless.
2. DUMB.

speechlessness *noun* SILENCE.

speechmaker *noun* SPEAKER.

speed *noun*
1. Rate of motion or performance: *drove at a moderate speed; working at breakneck speed.*
   Syns: celerity, clip[1] (*Informal*), pace, quickness, rapidity, swiftness, tempo, velocity.
2. HASTE.

speed *verb*
1. RUSH.
2. SPEED UP at **speed**.

speed up *verb*
To increase the speed of: *We speeded up the loading so as to be done by quitting time.*
   Syns: accelerate, expedite, hasten, hurry, quicken, speed, step up.

speediness *noun* HASTE.

speedy *adjective*
1. FAST.
2. QUICK.

spell[1] *verb* MEAN[1].
spell out *verb* EXPLAIN.

spell[2] *verb* CHARM.

spell[3] *noun*
1. BIT[1].
2. TURN.
spell *verb* RELIEVE.

spellbind *verb*
1. CHARM.
2. GRIP.

spend *verb*
1. To distribute (money) as payment: *The studio spent a million dollars to promote the film.*
   Syns: disburse, expend, fork out (*Informal*), give, lay out (*Informal*), outlay, pay, shell out (*Informal*).
2. To use time in a particular way: *spent summers at the beach; spent the day calculating her taxes.*
   Syns: pass, put in.
3. EXHAUST.
4. GO.

spendthrift *adjective* EXTRAVAGANT.
spendthrift *noun* WASTREL.
sperm *noun* SEED.
spew *verb* ERUPT.
sphere *noun* RANGE.
spherical also **spheric** *adjective* ROUND.
spheroid also **spheroidic, spheroidical** *adjective* ROUND.
spic-and-span *adjective* NEAT.
spicy *adjective* RACY.
spiel *verb* CHATTER.
spill *verb*
1. BETRAY.
2. FALL.
3. SPRAWL.
spill *noun* FALL.
spin *noun* DRIVE.
spin *verb*
1. To rotate rapidly: *spun the top; car wheels spinning on the ice.*
   Syns: gyrate, pirouette, swirl, twirl, whirl.
2. To have the sensation of turning in circles: *left the tavern with his head spinning.*
   Syns: reel, swim, swirl, whirl.
spin out *verb* LENGTHEN.
spindling *adjective* GANGLING.
spindly *adjective* GANGLING.
spin-off *noun* DERIVATIVE.
spiny *adjective*
1, 2. THORNY.
spiral *verb* WIND².
spirit *noun*
1. The vital principle or animating force within living beings: *understood life as matter infused with spirit.*
   Syns: anima, animus, atman (*Hinduism*), pneuma, psyche, soul, vitality. —*Idioms* breath (*or* essence) of life, divine spark, élan vital, life force, vital force.
2. A lively, emphatic, eager quality or manner: *She played the piece with spirit. The children had been drained of spirit by their oppressive guardian.*

Syns: animation, bounce, brio, dash, élan, esprit, ginger (*Informal*), life, liveliness, oomph (*Slang*), pep (*Informal*), verve, vigor, vim, vivacity, zip (*Informal*).
3. COURAGE.
4. GHOST.
5. HEART.
6. SOUL.
7. TEMPER.
spirit *verb* SMUGGLE.
spirit away *verb* KIDNAP.
spirited *adjective*
1. Full of or characterized by a lively, emphatic, eager quality: *The mild disagreement grew into a spirited debate.*
   Syns: fiery, high-spirited, mettlesome, peppery, snappy (*Informal*), vibrant.
2. LIVELY.
spiritless *adjective*
1. DEPRESSED.
2. DULL.
3. LANGUID.
spirits *noun* MOOD.
spiritual *adjective*
1. Of or concerned with the spirit rather than the body or material things: *looked to music and literature for spiritual nourishment.*
   Syns: numinous, otherworldly, unworldly.
2. Of or relating to a church or to an established religion: *the medieval popes' temporal and spiritual power.*
   Syns: ecclesiastical, church, churchly, religious.
3. IMMATERIAL.
spirituous *adjective* HARD.
spirt *noun & verb* SEE **spurt**.
spite *noun*
1. MALEVOLENCE.
2. VINDICTIVENESS.
spiteful *adjective*
1. MALEVOLENT.
2. VINDICTIVE.
spitefulness *noun*
1. MALEVOLENCE.
2. VINDICTIVENESS.
splash *verb*
1. To hurl or scatter liquid upon: *splashed the counter with soup as he ladled it out; dove into the pool without splashing.*
   Syns: bespatter, dash, slop, slosh, spatter, splatter, swash.
2. WASH.
splashy *adjective* SHOWY.

splatter *verb*
1. SPLASH.
2. SPOT.
spleen *noun* TEMPER.
splendid *adjective*
1. EXCELLENT.
2. GRAND.
3. MARVELOUS.
splendor *noun* GLORY.
splendorous or **splendrous** *adjective*
GLORIOUS.
splinter *verb*
1. BREAK.
2. SECEDE.
split *noun*
1. CRACK.
2. CUT.
3. DIVISION.
split *verb*
1. CRACK.
2. CUT.
3. DIVIDE.
4. GO.
5. RUN.
6. SECEDE.
7. SEPARATE.
8. TEAR¹.
split-up *noun* DIVISION.
splotch *noun* SMEAR.
splotch *verb* SPOT.
splurgy *adjective* SHOWY.
splutter *verb* CRACKLE.
spoil *verb*
1. BABY.
2. BOTCH.
3. DECAY.
4. DEVASTATE.
5. SACK².
spoilage *noun* DECAY.
spoiled *adjective* BAD.
spoils *noun*
1. PATRONAGE.
2. PLUNDER.
spoken *adjective*
1. ORAL.
2. VOCAL.
spokesman *noun* SPEAKER.
spokesperson *noun* SPEAKER.
spokeswoman *noun* SPEAKER.
spoliate *verb*
1. DEVASTATE.
2. SACK².
sponge *noun*
1. DRUNKARD.
2. PARASITE.
spongy *adjective* SOFT.
sponsor *noun*
1. One who assumes financial responsibility for another: *became a generous sponsor of fledgling businessmen.*
   Syns: angel, backer, guarantor, guaranty, surety, underwriter.
2. PATRON.
sponsor *verb* PATRONIZE.
sponsorship *noun* PATRONAGE.
spontaneity *noun* EASE.
spontaneous *adjective*
1. Acting or happening without apparent forethought, prompting, or planning: *The two suddenly embraced in a spontaneous gesture of affection.*
   Syns: automatic, impulsive, instinctive, reflex, unpremeditated.
2. VOLUNTARY.
spook *noun*
1. GHOST.
2. SPY.
spook *verb* GHOST.
spoor *noun* TRAIL.
sporadic *adjective*
1. INFREQUENT.
2. INTERMITTENT.
spore *noun* SEED.
sport *noun*
1, 2. PLAY.
sport *verb*
1. DISPLAY.
2. PLAY.
sporting *adjective*
1. FAIR.
2. SPORTSMANLIKE.
sportiveness *noun* MISCHIEF.
sportsmanlike *adjective*
According to the rules: *a sportsmanlike fight; sportsmanlike play.*
Syns: clean, fair, sporting.
spot *noun*
1. BIT¹.
2. PLACE.
3, 4. POINT.
5. POSITION.
6. PREDICAMENT.
7. STAIN.
spot *verb*
1. To mark or soil with spots: *The blood dripped from her finger and spotted her dress.*
   Syns: bespatter, blotch, spatter, splatter, splotch.
2. CATCH.
3. DISCERN.
4. FIND.
spot *adjective* RANDOM.
spotless *adjective* CLEAN.
spotty *adjective* UNEVEN.
spousal *adjective* MARITAL.
spousal *noun* WEDDING.

spouse *noun*
A husband or wife: *Employees may bring their spouses to the company Christmas party.*
   Syns: consort, mate, partner. —*Idiom* better half.

spouseless *adjective* SINGLE.

sprain *verb* TURN.

sprat *noun* SQUIRT.

sprawl *verb*
1. To sit or lie with the limbs spread out awkwardly: *staggered home exhausted and sprawled on the couch.*
   Syns: drape, loll, spread-eagle, straddle.
2. To grow or spread in a disorderly or planless fashion: *handwriting that sprawled across the page; a crowd sprawling out of the stadium.*
   Syns: spill, straggle.
3. FALL.

sprawl *noun* FALL.

spread *verb*
1. To extend over a wide area: *a poisonous gas that spreads quickly.*
   Syns: diffuse, disperse, distribute, radiate, scatter, strew.
2. To move or arrange so as to cover a larger area: *spread the blanket on the grass; a bird spreading its wings for flight.*
   Syns: expand, extend, fan out, open (out *or* up), outstretch, unfold.
3. To cause to become widely known: *spread the news.*
   Syns: advertise (*also* advertize), blaze (around), blazon, broadcast, bruit (about), circulate, diffuse, disseminate, noise about (*or* abroad), propagate.
4. COMMUNICATE.
5. GET ABOUT at **get**.
6. SET¹.

spread over *verb* COVER.

spread *noun*
1. EXPANSE.
2. EXPANSION.
3. FEAST.

spread-eagle *verb* SPRAWL.

spree *noun* BINGE.

spree *verb* REVEL.

sprig *noun* SHOOT.

sprightliness *noun* ENERGY.

sprightly *adjective*
1. CLEVER.
2. ENERGETIC.
3. LIGHT².
4. VIGOROUS.

spring *verb*
1. BOUNCE.

2. DESCEND.
3. JUMP.
4. JUMP.
5. SKIP.
6. STEM.

spring *noun*
1. The season of the year during which the weather becomes warmer and plants revive: *We're going to Paris this spring.*
   Syns: seedtime, springtide, springtime.
2. BIRTH.
3, 4. BOUNCE.
5. CAUSE.
6. JUMP.
7. ORIGIN.
8. SKIP.
9. YOUTH.

spring *adjective*
Of, occurring in, or characteristic of the season of spring: *a spring thaw; spring cleaning.*
   Syn: vernal.

springiness *noun*
1. BOUNCE.
2. FLEXIBILITY.

springtide *noun*
1. SPRING.
2. YOUTH.

springtime *noun*
1. SPRING.
2. YOUTH.

springy *adjective* FLEXIBLE.

sprinkle *verb*
1. To scatter or release in drops or small particles: *sprinkled shredded coconut over the pudding.*
   Syns: besprinkle, dust, powder.
2. SPECKLE.

sprint *verb* RUN.

sprout *noun* SHOOT.

spruce *verb*
1. FIX UP at **fix**.
2, 3. TIDY.

spruce *adjective* NEAT.

spry *adjective*
1. NIMBLE.
2. VIGOROUS.

spume *noun* FOAM.

spume *verb* FOAM.

spumy *adjective* FOAMY.

spunk *noun* COURAGE.

spur *verb*
1. PRECIPITATE.
2. PROVOKE.

spur *noun* STIMULUS.

spurious *adjective*
1. ARTIFICIAL.

2. COUNTERFEIT.
3. FALLACIOUS.
4. ILLEGITIMATE.
spuriousness *noun* FALLACY.
spurn *verb*
1. DECLINE.
2. SNUB.
spurn *noun* SNUB.
spur-of-the-moment *adjective*
EXTEMPORANEOUS.
spurt also **spirt** *noun*
A sudden, swift stream of ejected
liquid: *a spurt of blood.*
   Syns: jet[2], squirt.
spurt also **spirt** *verb*
To eject or be ejected in a thin, swift
stream: *Blood spurted from the ruptured
artery.*
   Syns: jet[2], squirt.
sputter *verb* CRACKLE.
spy *noun*
A person who secretly observes others
to obtain information: *A spy planted in
the enemy high command smuggled out
regular reports.*
   Syns: operative, spook (*Informal*).
   —*Idiom* secret (*or* undercover) agent.
spy *verb*
1. To observe or listen in secret to
obtain information: *spied on the
thieves by hiding in a closet.*
   Syn: eavesdrop.
2. CATCH.
squabble *noun* ARGUMENT.
squabble *verb*
1. ARGUE.
2. BRAWL.
squab *adjective* STOCKY.
squabby *adjective* STOCKY.
squalid *adjective*
1. FILTHY.
2. SORDID.
squander *verb* WASTE.
squander *noun* EXTRAVAGANCE.
square *noun*
Slang. An old-fashioned person who is
reluctant to change or innovate: *Some
kids think that ballroom dancing is for
squares.*
   Syns: antediluvian, fogy, fossil,
fuddy-duddy, mossback, stick-in-the-
mud (*Informal*). —*Idiom* back
number.
square *adjective*
1. Having four equal sides and four
right angles: *a square plot of land.*
   Syn: quadrate.
2. CONVENTIONAL.
3, 4. EVEN[1].
5. FAIR.

square *verb*
1. ADAPT.
2. AGREE.
3. EQUALIZE.
4. SETTLE.
square *adverb*
1. DIRECTLY.
2. PRECISELY.
squash *verb*
1, 2. CROWD.
3. CRUSH.
4. SUPPRESS.
squashy *adjective* SOFT.
squat *verb*
To sit on one's heels: *The boy squatted
as he prepared to shoot his marble.*
   Syn: hunker (down).
squat *adjective* STOCKY.
squawk *verb* OBJECT[2].
squawk *noun* OBJECTION.
squawky *adjective* HARSH.
squeal *verb*
1. INFORM.
2. YELP.
squeal *noun* YELP.
squealer *noun* INFORMER.
squeeze *verb*
1. To subject to compression: *The tight
collar squeezed my throat.*
   Syns: compress, constrain, constringe,
constrict.
2. To extract from by applying
pressure: *squeeze the juice from
oranges.*
   Syns: crush, express, press.
3, 4. CROWD.
5. EMBRACE.
6. EXTORT.
squeeze *noun*
1. CONSTRICTION.
2. EMBRACE.
squeezing *noun* CONSTRICTION.
squelch *verb*
1. REPRESS.
2. SUPPRESS.
squelching *noun* REPRESSION.
squelchy *adjective* SOFT.
squiggle *verb* WIGGLE.
squinch *verb*
1. FLINCH.
2. SQUINT.
squinch *adjective* SQUINTY.
squint *verb*
To peer with the eyes partly closed:
squinted at the fine print.
   Syn: squinch. —*Idioms* look asquint,
screw up one's eyes.
squint toward (*or* at) *verb* TEND[1].

squint *noun*
1. The condition of not having the visual axes parallel: *The ophthalmologist recommended special eye exercises to rectify the child's squint.*
   Syns: cross-eye, strabismus.
2. BENT.

squint-eyed *adjective* SQUINTY.

squinty *adjective*
Marked by or affected with a squint: *eyes squinty from sun and snow.*
   Syns: cross-eyed, squinch, squinny, squint-eyed, strabismal *or* strabismic.

squirm *verb*
1. WIGGLE.
2. WRITHE.

squirrel *verb* HOARD.

squirt *verb* SPURT.

squirt *noun*
1. *Informal.* An insignificant but arrogant and obnoxious young person: *had to tell the little squirt to get lost.*
   Syns: pup, puppy, sprat, twerp (*also* twirp) (*Slang*).
2. SPURT.

squishy *adjective* SOFT.

squiz *noun* GLANCE[1].

stab *verb* RAM.

stab *noun*
1. DIG.
2, 3. PRICK.
4. TRY.

stabbing *adjective* SHARP.

stability *noun*
1. Reliability in withstanding pressure, force, or stress: *tested the stability of the fuselage in the wind tunnel; a man lacking stability of character.*
   Syns: firmness, security, soundness, stableness, steadiness, strength.
2. SOUNDNESS.

stabilize *verb*
1. To make stable: *tried in vain to stabilize the country on the verge of anarchy.*
   Syn: steady.
2. BALANCE.

stable *adjective*
1. SOUND[2].
2. STEADY.
3. SURE.

stableness *noun* STABILITY.

stack *noun* HEAP.

stack *verb* HEAP.

stack up *verb* COMPARE.

stacked *adjective* SHAPELY.

staff *noun* STICK.

stage *noun*
1. A temporary framework with a floor, used by workmen: *a window-washing stage.*
   Syns: platform, scaffold, scaffolding.
2. The raised platform on which theatrical performances are given: *the stage in Lincoln Center.*
   Syns: the boards, proscenium.
3. ACTING.
4. DEGREE.
5. PERIOD.
6. SCENE.

stage *verb*
1. To produce on the stage: *staged a new performance every month.*
   Syns: act (out), do, dramatize, enact, give, perform, present[2], put on.
2. HAVE.

stagger *verb*
1. To overwhelm with surprise, wonder, or bewilderment: *The murder just staggered us.*
   Syns: boggle, bowl over, dumfound (*also* dumbfound), flabbergast, floor.
2. HESITATE.
3. LURCH.
4. MANAGE.
5. MUDDLE.

staggering *adjective*
1. Of such a character as to overwhelm: *staggering acrobatic feats; staggering corruption.*
   Syns: mind-boggling (*Slang*), mind-blowing (*Slang*), overwhelming, spectacular, stunning.
2. TOWERING.

staginess *noun* THEATRICALISM.

stagnation *noun* INACTION.

staid *adjective* GRAVE[2].

stain *verb*
1. To soil with foreign matter: *trousers stained with engine oil.*
   Syns: bestain, discolor, smut.
2. BLACKEN.
3. COLOR.
4. CORRUPT.

stain *noun*
1. A mark of discredit or disgrace: *That scandal is a stain on American politics.*
   Syns: attaint (*Archaic*), bar sinister, black eye, blemish, blot, onus, spot, stigma, taint, tarnish. —*Idioms* black mark, blot on the escutcheon.
2. COLOR.

stainless *adjective* CLEAN.

stake *noun*
1. BET.
2. INTEREST.

stake *verb*
1. BET.
2. FINANCE.

stale *adjective*
1. FLAT.
2. OLD-FASHIONED.
3. TRITE.

stalemate *noun* TIE.

stalk *verb*
1. HUNT.
2. STRIDE.

stalwart *adjective* STRONG.

stamina *noun* ENDURANCE.

stammer *verb*
1. To intrude involuntary repetitions and pauses into one's speech: *a nervous child who stammered and then fell silent.*
   Syns: hammer (*Brit. Regional*), stutter.
2. LURCH.

stammer *noun*
A speech impediment marked by involuntary repetitions and pauses: *has suffered from a pronounced stammer since childhood.*
Syns: stutter, stuttering.

stamp *noun*
1. IMPRESSION.
2. KIND².
3. SIGN.

stamp *verb*
1. ENGRAVE.
2. TRAMP.
3. TRAMPLE.

stamp out *verb* ANNIHILATE.

stance *noun*
1, 2. POSTURE.

stand *noun* BLIND.

stand *verb*
1. ENDURE.
2. TREAT.

stand behind *verb* SUPPORT.

stand for *verb*
1, 2. REPRESENT.

stand in *verb* SUBSTITUTE.

stand out *verb*
1. BULGE.
2. GLARE.

stand up *verb*
1. BEAR UP at **bear**.
2. GET UP at **get**.
3. RIGHT.
4. WASH.

stand up for *verb* SUPPORT.

standard *noun*
1. A means by which individuals are compared and judged: *Standards of public morality have clearly changed.*

The early American Presidents set a high standard.
Syns: benchmark, criterion, gauge (*also* gage), mark, measure, test, touchstone, yardstick.
2. FLAG¹.
3. MODEL.

standard *adjective*
1. AUTHORITATIVE.
2. ROUTINE.

standby *adjective* AUXILIARY.

stand-in *noun* SUBSTITUTE.

standing *noun*
1. FACE.
2. PLACE.

stand-off *noun* TIE.

standoffish *adjective* COOL.

standout *adjective* OUTSTANDING.

standpoint *noun*
1. LIGHT¹.
2. POINT OF VIEW.

standstill *noun* STOP.

star *noun* LEAD.

starch *noun* VIGOR.

starchy *adjective* STIFF.

star-crossed *adjective* UNFORTUNATE.

stare *verb* GAZE.

stare *noun* GAZE.

stark *adjective* EMPTY.

starry-eyed *adjective* IDEALISTIC.

start *verb*
1. To go about the initial step in doing (something): *starts every concert with a Bach fugue; is starting a new curriculum-development program.*
   Syns: approach, begin, commence, embark, enter, get off (*Informal*), inaugurate, initiate, kick off (*Informal*), launch, lead off (*Informal*), open, set out, set to, take on, take up, undertake. —*Idioms* get going, get the show on the road.
2. BEGIN.
3. FLINCH.
4. FOUND.
5. JUMP.

start *noun*
1. ADVANTAGE.
2. BEGINNING.
3. BIRTH.
4. JUMP.

startle *verb*
1. To cause to experience a sudden, momentary shock: *The cold shower startled him awake.*
   Syns: jolt, shock.
2. FRIGHTEN.
3. JUMP.
4. SURPRISE.

startle *noun* JUMP.

startling *adjective*
Causing momentary shock: *a startling sight.*
   Syns: astonishing, astounding, electrifying, jolting, surprising.
starving *adjective* RAVENOUS.
stash *verb*
   1. HIDE[1].
   2. HOARD.
   3. KEEP.
stasis *noun* BALANCE.
state *noun*
   1. An organized geopolitical unit: *France is one of the Western European states.*
      Syns: country, land, nation, polity. —*Idiom* body politic.
   2. *Informal.* A condition of excited distress: *Don't get into a state because of this delay.*
      Syns: fume, snit (*Slang*), sweat (*Informal*), swivet (*also* swivvet), tizzy (*Slang*).
   3. CONDITION.
state *verb*
   1. To declare by way of a systematic statement: *Einstein stated his theory of relativity in a rather short paper.*
      Syns: enounce, enunciate.
   2. AIR.
   3. ASSERT.
   4. SAY.
stately *adjective*
   1, 2. GRAND.
statement *noun*
   1. ACCOUNT.
   2. ASSERTION.
   3. EXPRESSION.
   4. STORY.
   5. WORD.
station *noun*
   1. An assigned position: *a sentry station; a duty station.*
      Syns: post, posting.
   2. BASE[1].
   3. PLACE.
station *verb*
To appoint and send to a particular place: *guards stationed on the border; airmen stationed on the DEW Line.*
   Syns: assign, post, set[1].
stationary *adjective*
   1. FIXED.
   2. MOTIONLESS.
stature *noun* MERIT.
status *noun*
   1. BASIS.
   2. CONDITION.
   3. FACE.

   4. HONOR.
   5. PLACE.
statute *noun* LAW.
staunch *adjective*
   1. FAITHFUL.
   2. SURE.
stave[1] *noun* STICK.
stave off *verb* PREVENT.
stave[2] *verb* RUSH.
stay[1] *verb*
   1. To remain as a guest or lodger: *stayed with relatives instead of going to a hotel.*
      Syns: sojourn, visit.
   2. DEFER[1].
   3. KEEP.
   4. REMAIN.
   5. STOP.
stay with *verb* KEEP.
stay *noun*
   1. A remaining in a place as a guest or lodger: *a six-week stay with relatives.*
      Syns: sojourn, visit.
   2. DELAY.
   3. STOP.
   4. WAIT.
stay[2] *noun* SUPPORT.
stead *noun* PLACE.
steadfast *adjective*
   1. FAITHFUL.
   2. FIXED.
steadfastness *noun* FIDELITY.
steadiness *noun* STABILITY.
steady *adjective*
   1. Consistently reliable, esp. due to resistance to outside pressures: *a steady hand on the wheel; a steady job held for 20 years.*
      Syns: stable, steady-going.
   2. EVEN[1].
   3. FAITHFUL.
steady *verb*
   1. BALANCE.
   2. STABILIZE.
steady-going *adjective* STEADY.
steal *verb*
   1. To take (another's property) without permission: *accused him of stealing her bicycle.*
      Syns: cop (*Slang*), filch, hook (*Slang*), lift (*Informal*), nip[1] (*Slang*), pilfer, pinch (*Slang*), purloin, rip off (*Slang*), snaffle (*Chiefly Brit. Regional*), snatch, snitch (*Slang*), swipe (*Slang*), thieve. —*Idioms* make off with, walk off with.
   2. SNEAK.
steal *noun*
   1. BARGAIN.
   2. LARCENY.

stealer *noun* LARCENER.

stealing *noun* LARCENY.

stealth *noun*
The act of proceeding slowly, deliberately, and secretly to escape observation: *the stealth of a cat burglar.*
  Syns: furtiveness, slink, slinkiness, sneakiness, stealthiness.

stealthiness *noun* STEALTH.

stealthy *adjective*
So slow, deliberate, and secret as to escape observation: *The mugger cast stealthy glances to the right and left and then attacked.*
  Syns: catlike, feline, furtive, skulking, slinking, slinky, sneaking, sneakish, sneaky.

steam *noun*
1. DRIVE.
2. ENERGY.

steam up *verb* ANGER.

steamroller *verb* OVERWHELM.

steel *verb* GIRD.

steep¹ *adjective*
1. So sharply inclined as to be almost perpendicular: *a steep cliff.*
  Syns: abrupt, arduous, bold, breakneck, precipitate, precipitous, sheer².
2. Vastly exceeding a normal limit, as in cost: *steep gold prices this year.*
  Syns: dizzy, dizzying, sky-high, stiff, stratospheric, towering, unconscionable.

steep² *verb*
To saturate (something) with a liquid: *steeped the tea bags in hot water.*
  Syns: seethe, soak.

steer *verb*
1. CONDUCT.
2. GUIDE.
3. MANEUVER.

steer *noun* TIP³.

stem *verb*
To have as a source: *customs stemming from the past.*
  Syns: arise, come, derive, emanate, flow, issue, originate, proceed, rise, spring, upspring.

stem *noun* THEME.

stench *verb* SMELL.

stentorian *adjective* LOUD.

stentorious *adjective* LOUD.

step *verb*
1. DANCE.
2. WALK.

step down *verb* RETIRE.

step up *verb* SPEED UP at **speed.**

step *noun*
1. DEGREE.
2. TREAD.

step-by-step *adjective* GRADUAL.

stereotype *noun* CLICHÉ.

stereotyped *adjective* TRITE.

stereotypic also **stereotypical** *adjective* TRITE.

sterile *adjective*
1. Free or freed from microorganisms: *keeping the operating room sterile.*
  Syns: sanitized, sterilized.
2. Lacking originality: *a sterile play devoid of action and new ideas.*
  Syns: uncreative, unimaginative, uninspired, uninventive, unoriginative.
3. BARREN.
4. BORING.

sterility *noun*
1. The state or condition of being unable to reproduce sexually: *Excess exposure to radiation can cause sterility.*
  Syns: barrenness, infecundity, infertility, sterilization.
2. The state or condition of being free from microorganisms: *Sterility must be maintained in operating rooms.*
  Syn: sterilization.

sterilization *noun*
1. The act or an instance of making one incapable of reproducing sexually: *enforced sterilization of prisoners; sterilization of farm animals.*
  Syns: castration, gelding, mutilation, unsexing.
2, 3. STERILITY.

sterilize *verb*
1. To render incapable of reproducing sexually: *had the cat sterilized.*
  Syns: alter, castrate, change, fix, geld, neuter, unsex.
2. To render free of microorganisms: *sterilized the instruments in an autoclave.*
  Syns: decontaminate, disinfect, sanitize.

sterilized *adjective* STERILE.

stern *adjective* SEVERE.

stew *verb*
1. BOIL.
2. BROOD.
3. FUSS.
4. WORRY.

stew *noun* AGITATION.

stewardly *adjective* ECONOMICAL.

stewed *adjective* DRUNK.

stick *noun*
1. A fairly long, straight piece of solid

material used esp. as a support in
walking: *The old man was bent over
his stick.*
   Syns: cane, staff, stave[1]. —*Idiom*
walking stick.
2. A relatively long, straight, rigid piece
of metal or other solid material: *a
stick of pig iron; a stick of candy; a
stick of wood.*
   Syns: bar, rod, shaft, slab.

stick *verb*
1. BOND.
2. CATCH.
3. CHEAT.
4. IMPOSE.
5. NONPLUS.
6. RAM.
7. SET[1].
8. SKIN.

stick around *verb* REMAIN.
stick out *verb*
1. BULGE.
2. GLARE.

stick up *verb* ROB.
stick-at-nothing *adjective*
UNSCRUPULOUS.
stick-in-the-mud *noun* SQUARE.
stickup *noun* ROBBERY.
sticky *adjective*
1. Having the property of adhering:
sticky icing.
   Syns: adhesive, claggy (*Regional*),
cloggy, gluey, gooey (*Informal*),
gummy, tacky[1].
2. Damp and warm: *a sticky day in the
delta country.*
   Syns: humid, mucky, muggy, soggy,
sultry.
3. DIFFICULT.
4. TIGHT.

sticky-fingered *adjective* LARCENOUS.
stiff *adjective*
1. So rigidly constrained, formal, or
awkward as to lack all grace and
spontaneity: *a stiff, uncomfortable
interview; a person who was stiff and
ill at ease with others.*
   Syns: buckram, cardboard, starchy,
stilted, wooden.
2. INFLEXIBLE.
3. RIGID.
4. STEEP[1].

stiff *noun*
1. BODY.
2. DRUNKARD.
3. MISER.

stiff *verb* STIFFEN.
stiffen *verb*
1. To make stiff or stiffer: *stiffen a collar
with starch.*

   Syn: stiff.
2. HARDEN.
3. TENSE.

stiff-necked *adjective* OBSTINATE.
stifle *verb*
1. CENSOR.
2. CHOKE.
3. MUFFLE.
4. REPRESS.

stifling *adjective* AIRLESS.
stifling *noun* REPRESSION.
stigma *noun*
1. *Med.* A mark on the skin indicative
of a disease, as typhus: *a
hemorrhaging stigma.*
   Syn: petechia.
2. STAIN.

stigmatize *verb*
To mark with disgrace or infamy: *a
family stigmatized by congenital insanity;
an administration stigmatized by scandal.*
   Syn: brand. —*Idiom* give a bad name
to.

still *adverb*
1. Without noise: *He lay still and
watched the attack.*
   Syn: quiet —*Idiom* still (*or* quiet) as
a mouse.
2. In spite of a preceding event or
consideration: *values that are age-old
but still valid.*
   Syn: yet. —*Idioms* be that as it may,
still and all, still and on (*Scot.*).
3. ADDITIONALLY.
4. EVEN[1].

still *adjective*
1. Motionless and undisturbed: *the still
waters of a secluded lagoon.*
   Syns: calm, halcyon, placid, quiet,
stilly (*Poetic*), untroubled.
2. AIRLESS.
3. MOTIONLESS.
4. SILENT.

still *verb*
1. CALM.
2. SILENCE.

still *noun* SILENCE.
stillness *noun*
1. An absence of motion or disturbance:
an ominous stillness before the storm.
   Syns: calm, hush, lull, placidity,
quiet.
2. SILENCE.

stilly *adjective*
1. SILENT.
2. STILL.

stilted *adjective* STIFF.
stimulant *noun* STIMULUS.
stimulate *verb*
1. ACTIVATE.

2. ENCOURAGE.
3. INSPIRE.
4. PROVOKE.

stimulating *adjective*
1. Serving to enliven: *a stimulating debate on foreign policy; a stimulating night of good theater.*
   Syns: animating, enlivening, quickening, rousing, stimulative, vitalizing, vivifying.
2. TONIC.

stimulation *noun*
1. ENCOURAGEMENT.
2. STIMULUS.

stimulative *adjective* STIMULATING.
stimulator *noun* STIMULUS.

stimulus *noun*
1. Something that causes and encourages a given response: *laissez-faire economic policies serving as a stimulus to free enterprise.*
   Syns: catalyst, fillip, impetus, impulse, incentive, motivation, prod, push, spur, stimulant, stimulation, stimulator.
2. Something that incites esp. a violent response: *Rumors of police brutality constituted the main stimulus for the riot.*
   Syns: goad, incitation, incitement, instigation, provocation, trigger.

sting *noun*
1. EDGE.
2. KICK.
3. PRICK.

sting *verb*
1. To feel or cause to feel a sensation of heat or discomfort: *Smoke made my eyes sting. Alcohol stings an open wound.*
   Syns: bite, burn, smart.
2. CHEAT.
3. IRRITATE.

stinging *adjective* BITING.

stingy *adjective*
1. Ungenerously or pettily reluctant to spend money: *too stingy to pay his employees a living wage.*
   Syns: cheap, close¹, close-fisted, costive, hardfisted, mean², miserly, narrow (*Regional*), niggard, niggardly, parsimonious, penny-pinching, penurious, pinching, tight, tightfisted.
2. MEAGER.

stink *verb* SMELL.

stinking *adjective*
1. DRUNK.
2. SMELLY.

stint *verb* SCRIMP.
stint *noun*
1. TASK.
2. TURN.

stipend *noun* WAGE(S).
stipple *verb* SPECKLE.

stipulate *verb*
To make specific: *The contract stipulates the obligations of all parties.*
   Syns: detail, particularize, specificate, specify.

stipulation *noun* PROVISION.

stir¹ *verb*
1. To impart movement to: *A slight smile stirred her lips. The breeze stirred my hair.*
   Syn: move.
2. To make a slight movement: *The child stirred in his sleep. He wouldn't stir from the TV set.*
   Syns: budge, move.
3. AROUSE.
4. FIRE.
5. GENERATE.
6. INSPIRE.
7. MIX.
8. WAKE.

stir *noun*
1. Agitated, excited movement and activity: *an angry stir in the crowd.*
   Syns: bustle, flurry, whirl, whirlpool.
2. DISTURBANCE.
3. MOTION.
4. SENSATION.

stir² *noun* JAIL.
stirred *adjective* AFFECTED¹.

stirring *adjective*
1. AFFECTING.
2. INSPIRING.

stitch *noun* PAIN.

stock *adjective*
1. ORDINARY.
2. ROUTINE.

stock *verb* CARRY.
stock *noun*
1. FAMILY.
2. HOARD.

stockpile *verb*
1. To accumulate and set aside for future use: *The air force stockpiled nuclear weapons for use in case of war.*
   Syns: lay up, save (up), store (up).
2. HOARD.

stockpile *noun* HOARD.
stock-still *adjective* MOTIONLESS.

stocky *adjective*
Short, heavy, and solidly built: *The coach made him a shot-putter, since he was too stocky to run races.*
   Syns: blocky, chunky, dumpy, squab,

squabby, squat, stodgy, stubby,
stumpy.

stodgy *adjective*
1. STOCKY.
2. THICK.

stole *noun* WRAP.

stolid *adjective* APATHETIC.

stolidity *noun* APATHY.

stomach *noun* APPETITE.

stomach *verb* ENDURE.

stomp *verb*
1. TRAMP.
2. TRAMPLE.

stone *noun* SEED.

stoned *adjective*
1. DRUGGED.
2. DRUNK.

stonyhearted *adjective* COLD-
BLOODED.

stooge *noun* PAWN².

stool *verb* INFORM.

stoolie *noun* INFORMER.

stool pigeon *noun* INFORMER.

stoop *verb*
1. To incline the body: *an old man
stooped over his cane.*
Syns: bend, bow, hump, hunch,
scrunch.
2. CONDESCEND.
3. DESCEND.

stop *verb*
1. To prevent the occurrence or
continuation of a movement, action,
or operation: *The governor stopped the
execution. Stop that noise!*
Syns: arrest, belay (*Naut.*), cease,
check, discontinue, halt¹, stay¹,
surcease (*Archaic*). —*Idioms* bring to
a standstill, call a halt to, put a stop
to.
2. To come to a cessation: *The snow has
finally stopped. Work on the project
stopped last week. The guard yelled for
us to stop, and we froze in our tracks.*
Syns: belay (*Rare*), cease, desist,
discontinue, halt¹, lay off (*Slang*),
leave off, quit, surcease (*Archaic*).
—*Idiom* come to a standstill (*or*
stop).
3. ABANDON.
4. BREAK.
5. BREAK UP at **break.**
6. FILL.
7. TIE UP at **tie.**
8. VISIT.

stop *noun*
1. The act of stopping: *The skier made a
gradual stop at the bottom of the hill.*
Syns: arrest, cessation, check, cut-off,

halt¹, stay¹, stoppage. —*Idiom*
screeching halt.
2. The condition of being stopped:
*Work on the dam has been at a total
stop for a year.*
Syns: cessation, halt¹, stoppage,
standstill. —*Idiom* dead (*or* full) stop.
3. BAR.
4. END.

stopgap *noun*
1. MAKESHIFT.
2. RESORT.

stoppage *noun*
1, 2. STOP.
3. TIE-UP.

store *noun*
1. A retail establishment where
merchandise is sold: *a clothing store.*
Syns: emporium, outlet, shop.
2. DEPOSITORY.
3. HOARD.

store *verb*
1. KEEP.
2. STOCKPILE.

storehouse *noun* DEPOSITORY.

storm *verb* ATTACK.

storm *noun* BARRAGE.

storm and stress *noun* UNREST.

stormy *adjective*
1. ROUGH.
2. TURBULENT.

story *noun*
1. A recounting of past events: *war
stories.*
Syns: account, chronicle, description,
history, narrative, report, statement,
version.
2. FICTION.
3. ITEM.
4. LIE².
5. PLOT.
6. YARN.

storyteller *noun* LIAR.

stout *adjective*
1. BRAVE.
2. BULKY.
3. FAT.
4. STRONG.

stouthearted *adjective* BRAVE.

strabismal *or* **strabismic** *adjective*
SQUINTY.

strabismus *noun* SQUINT.

straddle *verb*
1. SPRAWL.
2. STRIDE.

straggle *verb* SPRAWL.

straggler *noun* LAGGARD.

straight *adjective*
1. Not diluted or mixed with other

substances: *Straight bourbon,
bartender.*
Syns: full-strength, neat, plain, pure,
unblended *or* unblent, undiluted,
unmixed. —*Idiom* right off the top.
2. CONVENTIONAL.
3. DIRECT.
4. EVEN[1].
5. FIRM[1].
6. FRANK.

straight *adverb*
1. DIRECTLY.
2. PRECISELY.

straighten *verb* TIDY.

straighten out *verb* SETTLE.

straightforward *adjective*
1. DIRECT.
2. FRANK.
3. PLAIN.

straight-from-the-shoulder *adjective*
FRANK.

straight-shooting *adjective*
1. HONEST.
2. PLAIN.

strain[1] *verb* LABOR.

strain *noun*
1. EFFORT.
2. PRESSURE.

strain[2] *noun*
1. MELODY.
2. SHADE.
3. STREAK.

strained *adjective* FORCED.

strait-laced *adjective* GENTEEL.

strake *verb* STREAK.

strand *noun* THREAD.

strange *adjective*
1. ECCENTRIC.
2. FOREIGN.
3. FUNNY.

stranger *noun* FOREIGNER.

strangle *verb*
1. CHOKE.
2. REPRESS.

strapped *adjective* POOR.

strapping *adjective* ABLE-BODIED.

stratagem *noun*
1. DECEPTION.
2. TRICK.

strategy *noun* DESIGN.

stratospheric *adjective*
1. HIGHEST.
2. STEEP[1].

straw *noun* DAMN.

stray *verb*
1. DEVIATE.
2. DIGRESS.
3. ROVE.

stray *adjective*
1. ERRATIC.
2. RANDOM.

streak *noun*
1. An intermixture of a contrasting or
unexpected quality, esp. in a person's
character: *He's got a real mean
streak.*
Syns: strain[2], stripe, vein.
2. SERIES.
3. SHADE.

streak *verb*
To mark with a line or band of different
color or texture: *Lightning streaked the
sky.*
Syns: strake, striate, stripe, variegate.

stream *noun* FLOW.

stream *verb*
1, 2. FLOW.

streamer *noun* FLAG[1].

streamlined *adjective* SLEEK.

street *noun* WAY.

streetwalker *noun* PROSTITUTE.

strength *noun*
1. The state or quality of being
physically strong: *You could sense the
strength in his legs and arms.*
Syns: brawn, might, muscle, potency
(*also* potence), power, powerfulness,
puissance, sinew(s), thew(s), vigor,
vigorousness.
2. ENERGY.
3. FORCE.
4. SOUNDNESS.
5. STABILITY.

strengthen *verb*
1. CONFIRM.
2. GIRD.
3. TIGHTEN.
4. TOUGHEN.

strenuous *adjective*
1. ENERGETIC.
2. ROUGH.

stress *noun*
1. EMPHASIS.
2. PRESSURE.

stress *verb* EMPHASIZE.

stretch *verb*
1. EXTEND.
2. EXAGGERATE.
3. HANG.
4. LENGTHEN.
5. REACH.

stretch out *verb*
1. LIE[1].
2. REST[1].

stretch *noun*
1. BIT[1].
2. DISTANCE.
3. EXPANSE.

4. EXTENT.
5. TERM.
6. TIME.

stretch *adjective* EXTENSIBLE.
stretchable *adjective* EXTENSIBLE.
strew *verb* SPREAD.
striate *verb* STREAK.
strict *adjective*
1. Conforming completely to established rule: *a strict construction of the Constitution.*
 Syns: exact, rigorous, uncompromising.
2. CLOSE[1].
3. SEVERE.

stricture *noun*
1. CONSTRICTION.
2. RESTRICTION.

stride *verb*
1. To walk with long steps, esp. in a vigorous manner: *strode into the office and demanded to see the manager.*
 Syns: march[1], stalk.
2. To sit with a leg on each side of: *stride the fence.*
 Syns: bestride, straddle.

strident *adjective*
1. HARSH.
2. VOCIFEROUS.

strife *noun*
1. COMPETITION.
2, 3. CONFLICT.

strike *verb*
1. To cease working in support of demands made upon an employer: *The miners decided to strike for higher pay.*
 Syn: walk out. —*Idiom* go on strike.
2. AFFECT[1].
3. AFFLICT.
4. ATTACK.
5. HIT.
6. OCCUR.
7. RING[2].
8. SEIZE.
9. SNAP.

strike back *verb* RETALIATE.
strike out *verb*
1. BEAR.
2. CANCEL.

strike *noun*
1. ATTACK.
2. DISCOVERY.

striking *adjective* NOTICEABLE.
string *noun*
1. LINE.
2. PROVISION.
3. RUN.
4. SERIES.

string *verb* THREAD.
string up *verb* HANG.

stringency *noun*
 SEVERITY.

strip[1] *verb*
1. To remove all the clothing from: *stripped and searched each suspect; quickly stripped and jumped into the pool.*
 Syns: denude, disrobe, unclothe, undress.
2. BARE.
3. DEPRIVE.
4. DEVASTATE.
5. SKIN.

strip[2] *noun* BAND[1].
stripe *noun*
1. BAND[1].
2. KIND[2].
3. STREAK.

stripe *verb* STREAK.
stripped *adjective* NUDE.
strive *verb*
1. ATTEMPT.
2. LABOR.

striving *noun*
1. COMPETITION.
2. EFFORT.

stroll *verb*
1. To walk at a leisurely pace: *We strolled about the gardens as we talked.*
 Syns: amble, meander, mosey (*Informal*), perambulate, promenade, ramble, saunter, wander.
2. BROWSE.

stroll *noun* WALK.
strong *adjective*
1. Having great physical strength: *It takes two strong men to move a piano.*
 Syns: brawny, lusty, mighty, potent, powerful, puissant.
2. Capable of exerting considerable effort or of withstanding considerable stress or hardship: *a strong national economy; strong woolen fabric.*
 Syns: hardy, stalwart, stout, sturdy, tough.
3. Having a high concentration of the distinguishing ingredient: *a strong drink.*
 Syns: concentrated, potent, stiff.
4. DEEP.
5. FORCEFUL.
6. HARD.
7. HIGH.
8. SURE.

strong-arm *verb*
1. INTIMIDATE.
2. MUSCLE.

strong-arm *adjective* FORCIBLE.
struck *adjective* AFFECTED[1].
structure *noun* BUILDING.

struggle *verb* CONTEND.
struggle *noun*
1. BATTLE.
2. EFFORT.
strumpet *noun* SLUT.
strut *verb*
To walk with exaggerated or unnatural motions expressive of self-importance or self-display: *Modeling her new outfit, she strutted about like a peacock.*
    Syns: flounce, peacock, sashay (*Informal*), swagger, swank, swash.
stubborn *adjective*
1. Firmly, often unreasonably immovable in purpose or will: *stubborn adherence to an unworkable plan.*
    Syns: adamant, adamantine, brassbound, die-hard (*also* diehard), inexorable, inflexible, iron, obdurate, relentless, rigid, unbendable, unbending, uncompliant, uncompromising, unswayable, unyielding. —*Idiom* stubborn as a mule (*or* ox).
2. Difficult to alleviate or cure: *a stubborn cold.*
    Syns: obstinate, persistent, pertinacious.
3. OBSTINATE.
stubbornness *noun* OBSTINACY.
stubby *adjective* STOCKY.
stuck-up *adjective* EGOTISTICAL.
student *noun*
One who is being educated: *college students.*
    Syns: educand, learner, pupil, scholar, scholastic (*Obs.*).
studied *adjective* ADVISED.
studious *adjective*
1. Devoted to study or reading: *a studious young man who preferred books to sports.*
    Syns: bookish, scholarly.
2. ADVISED.
3. DILIGENT.
study *noun*
1. ADVISEMENT.
2. EXAMINATION.
3. PRACTICE.
4. TRANCE.
study *verb*
1. To apply one's mind to the acquisition of knowledge: *studying for an exam.*
    Syns: con, lucubrate.
2. CONSIDER.
3. EXAMINE.
stuff *noun*
1. BELONGINGS.

2. HEART.
3. MATERIAL.
4. NONSENSE.
5. TIMBER.
stuff *verb* CROWD.
stuffed *adjective* FULL.
stuffy *adjective*
1. AIRLESS.
2. BORING.
3. GENTEEL.
4. POMPOUS.
stumble *verb*
1. To catch the foot against something and lose one's balance: *stumbled on an electric cord and nearly fell.*
    Syn: trip. —*Idioms* lose one's footing, make a false step.
2. BLUNDER.
3. ERR.
4. LURCH.
5. MUDDLE.
stumble on (or **upon**) *verb* COME ACROSS at **come.**
stumble *noun* BLUNDER.
stump *verb*
1. LUMP¹.
2. NONPLUS.
stump *noun* DARE.
stumpy *adjective* STOCKY.
stun *verb* PARALYZE.
stunner *noun*
1. BEAUTY.
2. MARVEL.
stunning *adjective* STAGGERING.
stunt *noun*
1. FEAT.
2. TRICK.
stupefy *verb*
1. DAZE.
2. DULL.
3. PARALYZE.
stupendous *adjective*
1. FABULOUS.
2. GIANT.
stupid *adjective*
1. Lacking in intelligence: *too stupid to grasp her meaning.*
    Syns: blockheaded, dense, dimwitted, doltish, dumb (*Informal*), feeble-minded, half-witted, hebetudinous, obtuse, simple, simple-minded, slow, slow-witted, soft (*Informal*), thick, thickheaded, thick-witted.
2. LETHARGIC.
stupor *noun*
1. DAZE.
2. LETHARGY.
sturdy *adjective*
1. ABLE-BODIED.
2. MUSCULAR.

3. SOUND[2].
4. STRONG.
Sturm und Drang *noun* UNREST.
stutter *verb* STAMMER.
stutter *noun* STAMMER.
stuttering *noun* STAMMER.
style *noun*
1. A distinctive way of expressing oneself: *He wrote the script in a disjointed style.*
   Syns: fashion, manner, mode, tone, vein.
2. BEARING.
3. FASHION.
4. NAME.
5. WAY.
style *verb*
1. CALL.
2. NAME.
stylish *adjective* FASHIONABLE.
stylize *verb* CONVENTIONALIZE.
stymie *verb* FRUSTRATE.
suave *adjective*
Effortlessly gracious and tactful in social manner: *a suave reply calculated to display his wit without arousing envy.*
   Syns: bland, smooth, urbane.
sub *noun* SUBSTITUTE.
subaltern *noun* SUBORDINATE.
subdivide *verb* BRANCH.
subdivision *noun*
1. BRANCH.
2. DIVISION.
subdue *verb*
1. BREAK.
2. DEFEAT.
3. MODERATE.
subdued *adjective*
1. QUIET.
2. SOFT.
subject *adjective*
1. DEPENDENT.
2. LIABLE.
3. SUBORDINATE.
subject *noun*
1. What a speech, piece of writing, or artistic work is about: *She chose the colonial prison system as the subject of her paper.*
   Syns: argument, point, matter, text, theme, topic. —*Idiom* subject matter.
2. AREA.
3. CITIZEN.
subject *verb*
1. ENSLAVE.
2. EXPOSE.
subjective *adjective* ARBITRARY.
subjugate *verb* ENSLAVE.
sublimation *noun* EXALTATION.

sublime *adjective*
1. EXALTED.
2. GLORIOUS.
3. GRAND.
submerge *verb*
1. DIP.
2. FLOOD.
3. OBSCURE.
4. SINK.
submerse *verb*
1. DIP.
2. SINK.
submission *noun*
1. OBEDIENCE.
2. PROPOSAL.
3. SURRENDER.
submissive *adjective*
1. OBEDIENT.
2. PASSIVE.
submit *verb*
1. To commit to the consideration or judgment of another: *submitted his report to the authorities.*
   Syn: turn in.
2. DEFER[2].
3. PROPOSE.
4. SUCCUMB.
5. SURRENDER.
subordinate *noun*
One belonging to a lower class or rank: *The supervisors kept a tight rein on their subordinates.*
   Syns: inferior, junior, secondary, subaltern, underling.
subordinate *adjective*
In a position of subordination: *a subordinate territory of a major power.*
   Syns: collateral, dependent (*also* dependant), secondary, subject, subservient.
sub-rosa *adjective* SECRET.
subscribe *verb*
1. CONTRIBUTE.
2. SIGN.
subscribe to *verb* APPROVE.
subscriber *noun* DONOR.
subsequent *adjective*
1. CONSECUTIVE.
2. FURTHER.
3. FUTURE.
4. LATER.
subsequential *adjective*
1. CONSECUTIVE.
2. LATER.
subservient *adjective*
1. SERVILE.
2. SUBORDINATE.
subside *verb*
To become less active or intense: *The storm gradually subsided.*

Syns: abate, bate, die (down), ease off, ebb, fall, fall off, lapse, let up, moderate, relent, slacken, wane.

subsidiary *noun*
A local unit of a business or an auxiliary controlled by such a business: *A small subsidiary of the multinational corporation is located here.*
Syns: affiliate, branch, division.

subsidiary *adjective* AUXILIARY.

subsidize *verb* FINANCE.

subsidy *noun* GRANT.

subsist *verb*
1. BE.
2. EXIST.
3. LIVE[1].

subsistence *noun* LIVING.

substance *noun*
1. BODY.
2. HEART.
3. IMPORT.
4. MATERIAL.
5. MATTER.
6. THRUST.

substandard *adjective* INFERIOR.

substantial *adjective*
1. HEAVY.
2. IMPORTANT.
3. PHYSICAL.
4. REAL.

substantiate *verb*
1. BACK.
2. CONFIRM.
3. EMBODY.
4. PROVE.

substantiation *noun*
1. CONFIRMATION.
2. EMBODIMENT.

substantive *adjective* REAL.

substitute *noun*
One that takes the place of another: *a guest lecturer who is a substitute for a professor on sabbatical.*
Syns: alternate, fill-in, pinch hitter (*Informal*), replacement, stand-in, sub (*Informal*), surrogate.

substitute *verb*
1. To act as a substitute: *When the minister was sick, a church elder would substitute for him.*
Syns: fill in, pinch-hit (*Informal*), sit in, spell, stand in, supply.
2. CHANGE.

substitution *noun* CHANGE.

substratum *noun* BASE[1].

subsume *verb* CONTAIN.

subterfuge *noun* DECEPTION.

subterrane *adjective* UNDERGROUND.

subterranean *adjective*
UNDERGROUND.

subterrene *adjective* UNDERGROUND.

subterrestrial *adjective*
UNDERGROUND.

subtle *adjective*
1. DELICATE.
2. FINE[1].

subtract *verb* DEDUCT.

suburbs *noun* SKIRTS.

subvention *noun* GRANT.

subversion *noun* SABOTAGE.

subvert *verb*
1. OVERTHROW.
2. SABOTAGE.

succedent *adjective* CONSECUTIVE.

succeed *verb*
1. To turn out well: *The lower crime rate indicates that the campaign to make the streets safer has succeeded.*
Syns: click (*Slang*), come off, come through, go, go over, pan out (*Informal*), work out.
2. To gain wealth or fame: *sure to succeed as an architect.*
Syns: arrive, get ahead, get on, rise. —*Idioms* go far, go places, make good, make it.
3. FOLLOW.

succeeding *adjective* CONSECUTIVE.

success *noun*
The achievement of something desired, planned, or attempted: *His efforts to enter a good college ended in success.*
Syns: arrival, successfulness. —*Idiom* flying colors.

successfulness *noun* SUCCESS.

succession *noun*
1. ORDER.
2. RUN.
3. SERIES.

successional *adjective* CONSECUTIVE.

successive *adjective* CONSECUTIVE.

succinct *adjective* BRIEF.

succor *verb* HELP.

succor *noun* HELP.

succumb *verb*
1. To give in from or as if from a gradual loss of strength: *succumbed to the disease after a valiant struggle.*
Syns: bow, capitulate, fold (*Informal*), submit, surrender, yield.
2. COLLAPSE.
3. DIE.
4. SURRENDER.

sucker *noun* DUPE.

suck in *verb* INVOLVE.

sudden *adjective* ABRUPT.

sudden *adverb* SHORT.

sudoriferous *adjective* SWEATY.

suds *noun*
1. FOAM.
2. GLOOM.

sudsy *adjective* FOAMY.

sue *verb*
1. To institute or subject to legal proceedings: *sued to regain custody of the child; suing the newspaper for libel.*
   Syns: action (*Law*), law (*Chiefly Regional*), litigate, prosecute. —*Idiom* bring suit (against).
2. ADDRESS.
3. APPEAL.
4. COURT.

suet *noun* FAT.

suffer *verb*
1. ENDURE.
2. EXPERIENCE.
3. GRIEVE.
4. PERMIT.

sufferable *adjective* BEARABLE.

suffering *noun* MISERY.

suffering *adjective* MISERABLE.

suffice *verb* SERVE.

sufficiency *noun* ENOUGH.

sufficient *adjective*
1. Being what is needed without being in excess: *We had just sufficient fuel to get us across the desert.*
   Syns: adequate, comfortable (*Informal*), competent, decent, enough, satisfactory, sufficing.
2. ACCEPTABLE.

sufficient *noun* ENOUGH.

sufficing *adjective* SUFFICIENT.

suffocate *verb* CHOKE.

suffuse *verb*
1. CHARGE.
2. FILL.

sugar *verb* SWEETEN.

sugarcoat *verb*
1. COLOR.
2. SWEETEN.

sugary *adjective*
1. INSINUATING.
2. SWEET.

suggest *verb*
1. HINT.
2. IMPLY.
3. PROPOSE.
4. SMACK².

suggestion *noun*
1. A feeling, thought, idea, etc., associated in one's mind or imagination with someone or something specific: *What suggestion does the word "home" bring to mind?*
   Syns: association, connection, connotation.
2. HINT.

3. PROPOSAL.
4. SHADE.
5. TRACE.

suggestive *adjective*
1. Tending to bring something, as a memory, mood, or image, subtly or indirectly to mind: *music suggestive of an autumn woodland scene.*
   Syns: allusive, evocative, impressionistic, reminiscent.
2. INSINUATING.
3. PREGNANT.
4. RACY.
5. SENSUAL.

suggestiveness *noun* SENSUALITY.

suit *noun*
1, 2. APPEAL.
3. COURTSHIP.
4. LAWSUIT.

suit *verb*
1. To be appropriate or suitable to: *A less strident tone would suit you better.*
   Syns: become, befit, behoove, beseem (*Archaic*).
2. ADAPT.
3. FIT.
4. FLATTER.
5. PLEASE.
6. SERVE.

suitable *adjective*
1. CONVENIENT.
2. ELIGIBLE.
3, 4. JUST.

suitableness *noun* QUALIFICATION.

suite *noun*
1. RETINUE.
2. SERIES.

suited *adjective* APPROPRIATE.

suitor *noun*
1. APPEALER.
2. BEAU.
3. SUPPLICANT.

sulk *verb*
To be sullenly aloof or withdrawn, as in silent resentment or protest: *Angry at the slight, he sulked for the rest of the day.*
   Syns: mope, pet², pout.

sulky *adjective* GLUM.

sullen *adjective*
1. DARK.
2. GLUM.

sully *verb* BLACKEN.

sultry *adjective*
1. HOT.
2. STICKY.

sum *verb* ADD.

sum up *verb* REVIEW.

sum *noun*
1. SUMMARY.

2. SYSTEM.
3. TOTAL.
4. WHOLE.
summarize *verb* REVIEW.
summary *noun*
A condensation of the essential or main points of something: *a summary of the day's news.*
    Syns: recap, recapitulation, run-down, run-through, sum, summation, summing-up, wrap-up.
summary *adjective* BRIEF.
summate *verb* ADD.
summation *noun*
1. ADDITION.
2. SUMMARY.
3. TOTAL.
summer *noun*
The season occurring between spring and autumn: *going to camp in the summer.*
    Syn: summertime.
summertime *noun* SUMMER.
summing-up *noun* SUMMARY.
summit *noun*
1. CLIMAX.
2. HEIGHT.
summon *verb*
1. ASSEMBLE.
2. CALL.
sumptuousness *noun* GLITTER.
sunder *verb* BREAK.
sundries *noun* ODDS AND ENDS.
sundry *adjective*
1. GENERAL.
2. SEVERAL.
3. VARIOUS.
sunny *adjective*
1. CHEERFUL.
2. CLEAR.
sunrise *noun* DAWN.
sunup *noun* DAWN.
sup *verb* DRINK.
sup *noun* DRINK.
super *adjective*
1. EXCELLENT.
2. MARVELOUS.
super *adverb* UNDULY.
superabundance *noun* EXCESS.
superabundant *adjective* PROFUSE.
superannuate *verb*
1. OBSOLESCE.
2. RETIRE.
superb *adjective*
1. BEST.
2. EXCELLENT.
3. GLORIOUS.
4. GRAND.
5. MARVELOUS.

superbness *noun* EXCELLENCE.
supercilious *adjective* ARROGANT.
superciliousness *noun* ARROGANCE.
supererogative *adjective* WANTON.
supererogatory *adjective*
1. SUPERFLUOUS.
2. WANTON.
superficial *adjective*
1. Lacking in intellectual depth or thoroughness: *the superficial job television does in covering the news.*
    Syns: cursory, one-dimensional, shallow, sketchy, skin-deep, uncritical.
2. APPARENT.
superfluity *noun*
1. EXCESS.
2. SURPLUS.
superfluous *adjective*
Being more than is needed, desired, or appropriate: *carried a raincoat that proved superfluous.*
    Syns: de trop (*French*), excess, extra, spare, supererogatory, surplus.
superhuman *adjective*
SUPERNATURAL.
superintend *verb*
1. ADMINISTER.
2. SUPERVISE.
superintendence *noun*
1. ADMINISTRATION.
2. CARE.
superintendent *noun* BOSS.
superior *adjective*
1. ARROGANT.
2. BETTER¹.
3. CHOICE.
4. EXCELLENT.
5, 6. HIGHER.
superior *noun*
One who stands above another in rank: *Servicemen must salute their superiors.*
    Syns: better¹, elder, higher-up, senior.
superiority *noun*
1. ADVANTAGE.
2. ARROGANCE.
3. EXCELLENCE.
superlative *adjective* BEST.
supernatural *adjective*
1. Of, coming from, or relating to forces or beings that exist outside the natural world: *invoked the supernatural aid of the goddess.*
    Syns: extramundane, extrasensory, metaphysical (*also* metaphysic), miraculous, preternatural, superhuman, superphysical, supersensible, transcendental, unearthly.
2. PRETERNATURAL.

superphysical *adjective*
SUPERNATURAL.
superscribe *verb* ADDRESS.
superscription *noun* ADDRESS.
supersede *verb* REPLACE.
superseded *adjective* OBSOLETE.
supersensible *adjective*
SUPERNATURAL.
supervene *verb* FOLLOW.
supervenient *adjective* ACCIDENTAL.
supervise *verb*
  1. To direct and watch over the work
     and performance of others: *supervised
     a team of investigators.*
     Syns: boss, overlook, oversee,
     superintend.
  2. CONDUCT.
supervision *noun* CARE.
supervisor *noun* BOSS.
supplant *verb*
  1. To take the place of (another) against
     the other's will: *In the party caucus
     several committee chairmen were
     supplanted by young challengers.*
     Syns: cut out, displace, usurp.
  2. REPLACE.
supple *adjective*
  1. FLEXIBLE.
  2. MALLEABLE.
supplement *noun*
  1. ATTACHMENT.
  2. COMPLEMENT.
supplement *verb* COMPLEMENT.
supplemental *adjective*
  1. AUXILIARY.
  2. COMPLEMENTARY.
suppleness *noun* FLEXIBILITY.
supplicant *noun*
One who humbly entreats: *The
supplicants fell on their knees and begged
for mercy.*
  Syns: beggar, prayer, suitor,
  supplicator.
supplicate *verb*
  1. APPEAL.
  2. PRAY.
supplication *noun*
  1. APPEAL.
  2. PRAYER.
supplicator *noun* SUPPLICANT.
supply *verb*
  1. GIVE.
  2. SUBSTITUTE.
support *verb*
  1. To aid the cause of by approving or
     favoring: *A majority of the voters
     supported his candidacy.*
     Syns: advocate, back, champion, get
     behind, plump for, side with, stand
     behind, stand up for, uphold.

—*Idioms* align oneself with, go to bat
for, stick up for, take the part of.
  2. To sustain the weight of: *columns
     designed to support the roof.*
     Syns: carry, hold, maintain, uphold.
  3. To supply with the necessities of life:
     *Besides her own family, she supported
     her husband's elderly mother.*
     Syns: keep, maintain, provide for.
     —*Idiom* take care of.
  4. BEAR.
  5. ENDURE.
  6. PATRONIZE.
  7. SUSTAIN.
support *noun*
  1. A means or device that keeps
     something erect, stable, or secure:
     *used the railing as a support as he
     lifted himself up.*
     Syns: brace², buttress, crutch, prop,
     shore, stay², underpinning.
  2. HELP.
  3. LIVING.
supporter *noun*
  1. FOLLOWER.
  2. PATRON.
supportive *adjective* HELPFUL.
suppose *verb*
  1. To take for granted without proof: *I
     suppose that he is feeling guilty.*
     Syns: assume, posit, postulate,
     premise, presume, presuppose, reckon
     (*Informal*).
  2. GUESS.
  3. REPUTE.
  4. REQUIRE.
supposed *adjective*
  1. Presumed to be true, real, or genuine,
     esp. on inconclusive grounds: *He
     argued that deficit spending, the
     supposed cause of inflation, was in fact
     not the culprit.*
     Syns: conjectural, hypothetical (*also
     hypothetic*), suppositional,
     suppositious.
  2. PRESUMPTIVE.
  3. REPUTED.
supposition *noun*
  1. ASSUMPTION.
  2. GUESS.
  3. THEORY.
suppositional *adjective* SUPPOSED.
suppositious *adjective* SUPPOSED.
suppress *verb*
  1. To bring to an end forcibly as if by
     imposing a heavy weight: *The czar's
     forces easily suppressed the rebellion.*
     Syns: crush, extinguish, put down,
     quash, quell, quench, squash, squelch.
     —*Idiom* put the lid on.

2. CENSOR.
3. REPRESS.

suppression *noun*
1. Sudden punitive action: *suppression of narcotics trafficking.*
   Syns: clampdown (*Informal*), crackdown, repression.
2. REPRESSION.

suppressive *adjective* REPRESSIVE.
supremacy *noun* DOMINANCE.
supreme *adjective*
1. IDEAL.
2. RULING.
3. ULTIMATE.

surcease *verb*
1, 2. STOP.

sure *adjective*
1. Having no doubt: *I'm sure that you will succeed.*
   Syns: assured, certain, confident, positive, undoubting.
2. Such as could not possibly fail or disappoint: *a sure winner; a sure sign of illness.*
   Syns: certain, infallible, surefire, unerring, unfailing.
3. Firmly settled or positioned: *a sure footing on the slope; a sure friendship.*
   Syns: fast, firm¹, secure, solid, stable, staunch, strong. *—Idioms* firm as Gibraltar, solid as a rock.
4. CERTAIN.
5. DEFINITE.
6. SOUND².

sure-enough *adjective* ACTUAL.
surefire *adjective* SURE.
sureness *noun*
The fact or condition of being without doubt: *denying the rumor with absolute sureness.*
   Syns: certainty, certitude, confidence, conviction, surety.

surety *noun*
1. GUARANTEE.
2. SECURITY.
3. SPONSOR.
4. SURENESS.

surface *noun*
1, 2. FACE.

surfeit *noun*
1. EXCESS.
2. SATIATION.

surfeit *verb* SATIATE.
surfeited *adjective* SATIATED.
surge *verb* FLOW.
surly *adjective*
1. GLUM.
2. ILL-TEMPERED.

surmise *verb* GUESS.
surmise *noun*
1. ASSUMPTION.
2. GUESS.

surmount *verb* TRIUMPH.
surpass *verb*
1. To be greater or better than: *This year's wheat crop surpassed last year's by two million bushels.*
   Syns: beat (*Informal*), best, better¹, exceed, excel, outdo, outmatch, outshine, outstrip, pass, top, transcend. *—Idioms* go beyond, go one better.
2. EXCEED.

surpassing *adjective*
1. OUTSTANDING.
2. ULTIMATE.

surplus *noun*
1. An amount or quantity beyond what is needed, desired, or appropriate: *With their earnings they paid their bills and split the surplus as profit.*
   Syns: excess, fat, glut, overage, overflow, overmuch, overrun, overstock, oversupply, superfluity.
2. EXCESS.

surplus *adjective* SUPERFLUOUS.
surprise *verb*
1. To impress strongly by what is unexpected or unusual: *Truman's electoral victory in 1948 surprised most political observers.*
   Syns: amaze, astonish, astound, startle. *—Idioms* catch (*or* take) unawares, take aback.
2. AMBUSH.
3. TAKE.

surprising *adjective* STARTLING.
surrender *verb*
1. To undergo capture, defeat, or ruin: *France surrendered to the Nazis in 1940.*
   Syns: collapse, fall, go down, go under, submit, succumb, topple.
2. ABDICATE.
3. GIVE OVER at give.
4. RELINQUISH.
5. SUCCUMB.

surrender *noun*
1. The act of submitting or surrendering to the power of another: *The defeat forced the surrender of the entire army.*
   Syns: capitulation, submission.
2. ABDICATION.
3. DELIVERY.

surreptitious *adjective* SLY.
surrogate *noun* SUBSTITUTE.
surround *verb*
To shut in on all sides: *A crowd*

surrounded the movie star. The city is surrounded by suburbs.

Syns: begird, beset, besiege, circle, compass, encircle, enclose, encompass, envelop, environ, gird, girdle, hedge (in), hem (in, about, *or* around), ring[1].

surroundings *noun*

1, 2. ENVIRONMENT.

surveillance *noun* LOOKOUT.

survey *verb*

1. To view broadly or from a height: *surveyed the city from the top of a skyscraper.*
Syns: look over, overlook, oversee, scan.
2. EXAMINE.
3. WATCH.

survey *noun*

1. A general or comprehensive view or treatment: *a course that offers a survey of world literature.*
Syn: overview.
2. ANALYSIS.

survive *verb*

1. To exist in spite of adversity: *None of his family survived the Holocaust. A passing ship rescued the few crewmen who survived.*
Syns: come through, last[2], persist, pull through, ride out, weather.
2. OUTLAST.

susceptibility *noun* EXPOSURE.

susceptible *adjective*

1. EASY.
2. INCLINED.
3. LIABLE.
4. SENSITIVE.

susceptive *adjective* SENSITIVE.

suspect *verb* DISTRUST.

  suspect *adjective* SHADY.

suspend *verb*

1. To stop suddenly, as a conversation, activity, relationship, etc.: *The two sides suspended negotiations after a deadlock occurred.*
Syns: break off, cease, discontinue, interrupt, saw off (*Slang*), terminate.
2. DEFER[1].
3. HANG.

suspended *adjective* HANGING.

suspension *noun*

1. ABEYANCE.
2. BREAK.
3. DELAY.

suspicion *noun*

1. DISTRUST.
2. DOUBT.
3. FEELING.
4. HINT.
5. SHADE.

suspicious *adjective*

1. DISTRUSTFUL.
2. SHADY.

sustain *verb*

1. To keep from yielding or failing during stress or difficulty: *At such desperate times her faith sustained her.*
Syns: bolster, buoy up, prop, support, uphold.
2, 3. BEAR.
4. MAINTAIN.

sustenance *noun*

1, 2. FOOD.
3. LIVING.

susurration *noun* MURMUR.

swaddle *verb* WRAP UP at **wrap.**

swagger *verb* STRUT.

swain *noun* BEAU.

swallow *verb*

1. To cause to pass from the mouth into the stomach: *chewed and swallowed his food calmly.*
Syns: down, ingest, take.
2. BELIEVE.
3. CONSUME.
4. ENDURE.

swallow *noun*

An act of swallowing: *took a swallow of coffee.*
Syns: gobble, gulp, ingestion.

swamp *noun*

A usu. low-lying area of soft, waterlogged ground and standing water: *birds that breed in the seclusion of tropical swamps.*
Syns: fen, marsh, marshland, mire, morass, muskeg, quag, quagmire, slough[1], swampland, wetland.

swampland *noun* SWAMP.

swank *verb* STRUT.

  swank *also* **swanky** *adjective*

1. EXCLUSIVE.
2. FASHIONABLE.

swap *also* **swop** *verb* CHANGE.

  swap *also* **swop** *noun* CHANGE.

swarm *verb*

1. POUR.
2. TEEM[1].

swarm over *verb* INVADE.

  swarm *noun* CROWD.

swarthy *adjective* DARK.

swash *verb*

1. SPLASH.
2. STRUT.
3. WASH.

swat *noun* BLOW[2].

  swat *verb* HIT.

swathe *verb* WRAP UP at **wrap.**

sway *verb*
1. To move back and forth or from side to side, as if about to fall: *swayed dizzily at the top of the stairs.*
   Syns: teeter, totter, waver, weave, wobble.
2. AFFECT[1].
3. DISPOSE.
4. GOVERN.
5. INFLUENCE.
6. SWING.
sway *noun*
1. AUTHORITY.
2. DOMINATION.
3. INFLUENCE.
swayed *adjective* AFFECTED[1].
swear *verb*
1. To use profane or obscene language: *swore like a trooper; swore at the other motorist.*
   Syns: bedamn, blaspheme, curse, cuss (*Informal*), damn, execrate, imprecate. —*Idioms* call names, use language.
2. PLEDGE.
3. TESTIFY.
swear off *verb* ABANDON.
swear *noun*
A profane or obscene term: *uttered a stream of swears.*
   Syns: blasphemy, curse, cuss (*Informal*), cussword (*Informal*), epithet, expletive, invective, oath, swearword.
swearword *noun* SWEAR.
sweat *verb*
1. To excrete moisture through the pores of the skin: *sweating as he jogged.*
   Syns: lather, perspire.
2. LABOR.
sweat out *verb* ENDURE.
sweat *noun*
1. Moisture excreted through the pores of the skin: *wiping the sweat from her forehead.*
   Syns: lather, perspiration.
2. LABOR.
3. STATE.
sweating *adjective* SWEATY.
sweaty *adjective*
Producing or covered with sweat: *left the gym all hot and sweaty.*
   Syns: perspiring, sudoriferous, sweating.
sweep *noun*
1. EXPANSE.
2. RANGE.
sweep *verb* FLOURISH.
sweeping *adjective* GENERAL.

sweet *adjective*
1. Having or suggesting the taste of sugar: *a sweet icing.*
   Syns: saccharine, sugary.
2. ADORABLE.
3. ATTRACTIVE.
sweet *noun* DARLING.
sweeten *verb*
1. To make superficially more acceptable or appealing: *sweetened his demands with the promise of a reward for obedience.*
   Syns: candy, gild, honey, sugar, sugarcoat.
2. PACIFY.
sweetheart *noun* DARLING.
sweet-talk *verb*
1. COAX.
2. FLATTER.
swell *verb* INCREASE.
swell *adjective*
1. EXCELLENT.
2. MARVELOUS.
swelled head *noun* EGOTISM.
swellheaded *adjective* EGOTISTICAL.
swelling *noun* BUMP.
swelter *verb* BURN.
sweltering *adjective* HOT.
swerve *verb*
1. To turn aside sharply from a straight course: *swerved to avoid hitting a pedestrian.*
   Syns: chop[2] (*Naut.*), cut, sheer[1], skew, slue[1], veer, yaw.
2. DEVIATE.
swift *adjective* FAST.
swiftness *noun*
1. HASTE.
2. SPEED.
swig *verb* DRINK.
swig *noun* DRINK.
swill *verb* GULP.
swill *noun* DRINK.
swim *noun* PLUNGE.
swim *verb* SPIN.
swindle *verb* CHEAT.
swindle *noun* CHEAT.
swindler *noun* CHEAT.
swing *verb*
1. To move rhythmically back and forth suspended or as if suspended from above: *ship's lanterns swinging like pendulums.*
   Syns: oscillate, sway.
2. To turn or cause to turn in place, as on a hinge or fixed point, tracing an arclike path: *a door swinging open; swung the tone arm carelessly across the record surface.*
   Syns: pivot, wheel.

3. To change one's attitudes, policies, or the like: *swung from one position to another in the debate on abortion.*
   Syns: vacillate, waver.
4. EFFECT.
5. HANG.
6. TURN.

swing *noun*
1. FREEDOM.
2. HANG.
3. RHYTHM.

swipe *verb* STEAL.

swirl *verb*
1. To move or cause to move like a rapid rotary current of liquid: *water swirling over the dam; difficulties that swirled about her.*
   Syns: eddy, gurge, whirl, whorl.
2, 3. SPIN.

swish *verb*
1. HISS.
2. WASH.

swish *adjective*
1. EFFEMINATE.
2. FASHIONABLE.

switch *verb*
1, 2. CHANGE.
3. WAG¹.

switch *noun* CHANGE.
swivel *verb* TRAVERSE.
swivet also **swivvet** *noun* STATE.
swoon *verb* BLACK OUT at **black.**
swoon *noun* BLACKOUT.
swoop *noun* PLUNGE.
swop *verb & noun* SEE **swap.**
sybarite *noun*
A person devoted to pleasure and luxury: *an unlikely breed of sybarites spawned by the 1849 Gold Rush.*
   Syns: epicure (*Archaic*), hedonist, voluptuary.

sybaritic or **sybaritical** *adjective*
Characterized by or devoted to pleasure and luxury as a lifestyle: *sybaritic tastes; a sybaritic young woman.*
   Syns: epicurean, hedonic, hedonistic.

sycophant *noun*
One who flatters another excessively: *Beware of sycophants and yes-men.*
   Syns: adulator, apple-polisher (*Informal*), courtier, flatterer, truckler.

syllabus *noun* PROGRAM.

symbol *noun*
1. An object associated with and serving to identify something else: *scales as the symbol of justice.*
   Syns: attribute, emblem.
2. CHARACTER.

symbol *verb* REPRESENT.

symbolic also **symbolical** *adjective*
Serving as a symbol: *a gift symbolic of our appreciation; the mark symbolic of division in arithmetic.*
   Syns: emblematic (*also* emblematical), indicative, representative.

symbolize *verb* REPRESENT.

symmetrical also **symmetric**
1. Characterized by or displaying symmetry, esp. correspondence in scale or measure: *a symmetrical floor plan; adjoining buildings that are symmetrical.*
   Syns: balanced, commensurable, commensurate, proportional, proportionate, regular.
2. Having components pleasingly combined: *statuary symmetrical with the layout of the gardens.*
   Syns: accordant (to *or* with), balanced, concordant, congruous, harmonious.

symmetry *noun* PROPORTION.

sympathetic *adjective*
1. Feeling or expressing sorrow: *a sympathetic note.*
   Syns: commiserative, compassionate.
2. FRIENDLY.
3. PITYING.
4. UNDERSTANDING.

sympathize *verb*
1. To understand or be sensitive to another's feelings or ideas: *We sympathized with his difficult position.*
   Syn: empathize.
2. FEEL.
3. IDENTIFY.

sympathy *noun*
1. A very close relationship between persons, esp. one resulting in mutual understanding or affection: *the sympathy that often strengthens marriages in later and quieter years.*
   Syn: empathy.
2. PITY.

symphonic *adjective* HARMONIOUS.
symptom *noun* SIGN.
synchronic also **synchronical** *adjective* CONTEMPORARY.
synchronous *adjective* CONTEMPORARY.
syncope *noun* BLACKOUT.
syndicate *noun* COMBINE.
synergetic *adjective* COOPERATIVE.
synergy *noun* COOPERATION.
synopsis *noun*
A short summary prepared by cutting down a larger work: *gave her a synopsis of the novel.*

Syns: abridgment, abstract, brief, condensation, epitome.
synopsize *verb* REVIEW.
synthesize *verb* HARMONIZE.
synthetic *adjective*
1, 2. ARTIFICIAL.
3. PLASTIC.
system *noun*
1. An organized array of individual elements and parts forming and working as a unit: *The universe is a cosmic system.*
Syns: entity, integral, integrate, sum, totality, whole.
2. COMPLEX.
3. METHOD.
4. WAY.
systematic also **systematical** *adjective*
1. BUSINESSLIKE.
2. METHODICAL.
systematize *verb*
1. ARRANGE.
2. METHODIZE.

T

tab *noun*
1. ACCOUNT.
2. COST.
3. COUNT.
tabby *noun* GOSSIP.
table *noun*
An orderly, columnar display of data: *a table of census figures.*
Syns: chart, tabulation.
table *verb* DEFER¹.
taboo also **tabu** *noun* FORBIDDANCE.
taboo also **tabu** *adjective* FORBIDDEN.
tab(s) *noun* WATCH.
tabu *noun & adjective* SEE **taboo.**
tabulation *noun* TABLE.
tacit *adjective*
1. IMPLICIT.
2. SILENT.
taciturn *adjective*
Not speaking freely or openly: *a taciturn Yankee farmer.*
Syns: close¹, close-mouthed, reserved, reticent, silent, tight-lipped, uncommunicative.
taciturnity *noun* RESERVE.

tack *noun*
1. APPROACH.
2. TURN.
tackle *noun* OUTFIT.
tackle *verb*
1. ASSUME.
2. ATTACK.
tacky¹ *adjective* STICKY.
tacky² *adjective*
1. Lacking style and good taste: *tacky behavior.*
Syns: inelegant, tasteless, unbecoming.
2. Quite outmoded: *tacky old clothes from the 1950's.*
Syns: dowdy, frumpish, out-of-date.
3. GAUDY.
4. SHABBY.
5. SHODDY.
tact *noun*
The ability to say and do the right thing at the right time: *Tact is needed in dealing with high-strung people.*
Syns: address, diplomacy, savoir-faire (*French*), tactfulness.
tactful *adjective* DELICATE.
tactfulness *noun* TACT.
tactic¹ *noun*
1. A method of deploying troops and equipment in combat: *used the tactic of encirclement to cut off the enemy.*
Syn: maneuver.
2. MOVE.
tactic² *adjective* TACTILE.
tactical *adjective*
Designed or implemented so as to gain a limited, temporary advantage: *took tactical rather than strategic measures to settle the crisis.*
Syn: short-range.
tactile *adjective*
1. Of, pertaining to, or arising from the sense of touch: *a tactile reflex.*
Syns: tactic², tactual.
2. TANGIBLE.
tactility *noun*
1. TANGIBILITY.
2. TOUCH.
tactless *adjective*
Lacking sensitivity and skill in dealing with others: *took a tactless approach in the interview; tactless remarks made by a heavy-handed critic.*
Syns: brash, clumsy, impolitic, indelicate, maladroit, undiplomatic, unpolitic, untactful.
tactual *adjective* TACTILE.
tag *verb*
1. CALL.
2. DOG.

3. MARK.
4. TICKET.

tag *noun*
1. NAME.
2. TICKET.

tag end *noun* TAIL.

tagrag *adjective* SHABBY.

tail *noun*
1. The hindmost part of something: *marched at the tail of the platoon.*
   Syns: end, rear[1], tag end, tail end.
2. *Informal.* An agent assigned to observe and report on another: *Counterintelligence assigned a tail to the suspected spy.*
   Syns: shadow, watcher.
3. TRAIN.

tail *verb* FOLLOW.

tail off *verb* DECREASE.

tail end *noun* TAIL.

tailor *verb* ADAPT.

tailor-made *adjective*
1. CONVENIENT.
2. CUSTOM.

tailor-make *verb* ADAPT.

taint *verb*
1. To make morally impure: *a young child's morals tainted by delinquents.*
   Syns: contaminate, corrupt, defile, infect, pollute, soil.
2. BLACKEN.

taint *noun* STAIN.

taintlessness *noun* PURITY.

take *verb*
1. To go aboard (a means of transport): *took the six o'clock train.*
   Syns: board, catch.
2. To gain possession of, esp. after a struggle or chase: *took the thief after a high-speed pursuit.*
   Syns: bag (*Slang*), capture, catch, get, nail (*Slang*), net[1], secure.
3. To come upon, esp. suddenly or unexpectedly: *The attackers took the enemy by surprise.*
   Syns: catch, hit on (*or* upon), surprise.
4. To engage in sexual relations with: *Abraham took his slave girl.*
   Syns: bed, copulate (with), couple with, have, mate (with), sleep with.
   —*Idioms* go to bed with, make love to (*or* with), take to bed.
5. ACCEPT.
6. ASSUME.
7. ATTRACT.
8. BRING.
9. CAPTURE.
10. CHEAT.

11. CONTRACT.
12. DEDUCT.
13. DEMAND.
14. DERIVE.
15. ENDURE.
16. FUNCTION.
17. INTERPRET.
18. RECEIVE.
19. SEIZE.
20. SWALLOW.
21. UNDERSTAND.

take after *verb* FAVOR.

take away *verb* REMOVE.

take back *verb*
1. RESUME.
2. RETRACT.
3. RETURN.

take down *verb*
1. To take (something) apart: *take down a Christmas tree; take down a rifle and clean it.*
   Syns: disassemble, dismantle, dismember, dismount.
2. LOWER[2].

take in *verb*
1. ACCEPT.
2. CONTAIN.
3. DECEIVE.
4. UNDERSTAND.

take off *verb*
1. To rise up in flight: *The jet took off with a roar.*
   Syn: lift (off).
2. DEDUCT.
3. GO.
4. IMITATE.
5, 6. REMOVE.
7. RUN.

take on *verb*
1. ADOPT.
2. ASSUME.
3. EMPLOY.
4. ENGAGE.
5. FUSS.
6. START.

take out *verb*
1. REMOVE.
2. SEE.

take over *verb*
1. ASSUME.
2. OCCUPY.
3. RELIEVE.

take to *verb* LIKE[1].

take up *verb*
1. ACCEPT.
2. ASSUME.
3. CONTINUE.
4. DEAL.
5. ELEVATE.

6. START.

take *noun*
1. *Slang.* The amount of money collected as admission, esp. to a sporting event: *Today's take amounts to $10,000.*
Syns: gate, gate money. —*Idioms* box-office receipts, gate receipts.
2. ATTEMPT.
take-in *noun* DECEPTION.
takeoff *noun*
1. The act of rising in flight: *The plane crashed during takeoff.*
Syn: liftoff.
2. A usu. amusing caricature of another: *did a takeoff on the President.*
Syns: imitation, parody.
taking *adjective*
1. ATTRACTIVE.
2. COMMUNICABLE.
tale *noun*
1. LIE².
2. YARN.
tale *verb* COUNT.
talebearer *noun* GOSSIP.
talebearing *adjective* GOSSIPY.
talent *noun*
An innate capability: *a talent for music; a talent for mathematics.*
Syns: aptitude, aptness, bent, faculty, flair, genius, gift, head, inclination, instinct, knack, turn.
talented *adjective* GIFTED.
taletelling *adjective* GOSSIPY.
talisman *noun* CHARM.
talk *verb*
1. To articulate (something) in words: *talk treason.*
Syns: speak, utter¹, verbalize. —*Idiom* put into words.
2. ADDRESS.
3. CONFER.
4. CONVERSE¹.
5. GOSSIP.
6. INFORM.
7. SPEAK.
talk back *verb*
To utter an impertinent rejoinder: *talked back when his parents refused him the car.*
Syns: sass (*Informal*), sauce (*Informal*), talk up. —*Idiom* give someone some lip.
talk down *verb*
1. BELITTLE.
2. CONDESCEND.
talk into *verb* PERSUADE.
talk over *verb* DISCUSS.
talk up *verb*
1. ADVERTISE.

2. TALK BACK at **talk**.
talk *noun*
1. The act or process of dealing with another to reach an agreement: *the American-North Vietnamese peace talks.*
Syns: negotiation, parley.
2. CONVERSATION.
3, 4. SPEECH.
talkative *adjective*
Given to conversation: *a very talkative person.*
Syns: chatty, conversational, free-spoken, gabby, garrulous, loquacious, multiloquent, talky.
talker *noun*
1. CONVERSATIONALIST.
2. SPEAKER.
talky *adjective* TALKATIVE.
tall *adjective*
1. Extending to a great height: *tall mountains.*
Syns: elevated, high, lofty, soaring, towering.
2. DIFFICULT.
3. HIGH.
tally *verb*
1. ADD.
2. AGREE.
3. COUNT.
4. SCORE.
tally *noun*
1. COUNT.
2. SCORE.
tallying *noun* AGREEMENT.
tame *adjective*
1. DOMESTIC.
2. GENTLE.
tame *verb*
1. DOMESTICATE.
2. GENTLE.
3. MODERATE.
tamper *verb*
1. To handle something idly, ignorantly, or destructively: *Someone tampered with the TV set and spoiled the reception.*
Syns: fiddle, fool, meddle, mess, monkey (*Informal*), tinker.
2. FIX.
tangent *noun* DIGRESSION.
tangential *adjective* DIGRESSIVE.
tangibility *noun*
The quality or condition of being discernible by touch: *The tangibility of the reward excited them.*
Syns: palpability, tactility, tangibleness, touchability, touchableness.

tangible *adjective*
1. Discernible by touch: *tangible objects.*
   Syns: palpable, tactile, touchable.
2. PHYSICAL.
3. REAL.
tangibleness *noun* TANGIBILITY.
tangle *noun*
1. Something that is intricately and often bewilderingly complex: *a tangle of interlocking corporations; a tangle of freeways; a marital tangle.*
   Syns: entanglement, jungle, knot, labyrinth, maze, mesh, morass, skein, snarl¹, web. —*Idiom* cat's cradle.
2. ARGUMENT.
tangle *verb*
1. CATCH.
2. COMPLICATE.
3. ENTANGLE.
tangled *adjective* COMPLEX.
tank up *verb* DRINK.
tantalize *verb*
To excite (another) by exposing something desirable while keeping it out of reach: *tantalized the dog with raw meat.*
   Syns: bait, tease, torment. —*Idiom* make one's mouth water.
tantalizing *adjective*
Enticingly in sight, yet often out of reach: *had a tantalizing vision of an oasis.*
   Syns: mouthwatering, teasing.
tantamount *adjective* EQUAL.
tantrum *noun* TEMPER.
tap¹ *verb*
1. To make a noise by striking: *tapped at the door and called her name.*
   Syns: bob (*Obs.*), knock, rap¹.
2. APPOINT.
tap *noun*
An audible blow: *heard the tap of a pencil on the desk; a tap at the door.*
   Syns: bob (*Obs.*), knock, rap¹.
tap² *verb*
1. To monitor (telephone calls) with a concealed listening device connected to the circuit: *got a court order to tap the suspect's phone.*
   Syns: bug, wiretap.
2. DRAIN.
taper off *verb* DECREASE.
tar *noun* SAILOR.
tardiness *noun* LATENESS.
tardy *adjective*
1. LATE.
2. SLOW.
target *noun*
1. One that is fired at, attacked, or abused: *The arrow fell short of its target. His pomposity made him a target of satirists.*
   Syns: butt, mark.
2. INTENTION.
target *verb*
To make a target of: *The terrorists targeted the war hero as their prime victim.*
   Syn: mark. —*Idiom* draw a bead on.
tariff *noun* TAX.
tarnish *verb*
1. BLACKEN.
2. INJURE.
tarnish *noun* STAIN.
tarry *verb*
1. DELAY.
2. PAUSE.
3. REMAIN.
tart¹ *adjective* SOUR.
tart² *noun* SLUT.
tartuffe also **tartufe** *noun* HYPOCRITE.
tartuffery *noun* HYPOCRISY.
tartuffian *adjective* HYPOCRITICAL.
task *noun*
1. A piece of work that has been assigned: *His task is to prepare the publicity campaign.*
   Syns: chore, duty, job, stint.
2. A difficult or tedious undertaking: *Writing letters is a real task for me.*
   Syns: chore, effort, job, onus, taskwork.
3. MISSION.
task *verb* WORK.
taskmaster *noun* BOSS.
taskwork *noun* TASK.
taste *verb*
1. EXPERIENCE.
2. FEEL.
3. SMACK².
taste *noun*
1. A limited or anticipatory experience: *had a taste of success.*
   Syns: foretaste, sample.
2. A liking or personal preference for something: *a taste for luxury.*
   Syns: appetite, fondness, inclination, partiality, predisposition, relish, weakness.
3. The faculty or sense of discerning what is aesthetically pleasing or appropriate: *a house designed with taste and imagination.*
   Syn: tastefulness.
4. APPETITE.
5. APPRECIATION.
6. FLAVOR.
7. TRACE.

tasteful *adjective*
1. Showing good taste: *a tasteful and pleasing combination of colors.*
   Syns: aesthetic *or* esthetic, artistic, tasty (*Rare*).
2. DELICIOUS.
3. QUIET.

tastefulness *noun* TASTE.

tasteless *adjective*
1. COARSE.
2. FLAT.
3. TACKY[2].

tasty *adjective*
1. DELICIOUS.
2. TASTEFUL.

tatterdemalion *noun*
A person wearing ragged or tattered clothing: *a shabby tatterdemalion begging for food.*
   Syns: ragamuffin, scarecrow.

tatterdemalion *adjective* TATTERED.

tattered *adjective*
1. Torn into or marked by shreds or tatters: *tattered clothing.*
   Syns: ragged, raggedy, tatterdemalion.
2. SHABBY.

tatters *noun*
Torn and ragged clothing: *dressed in tatters.*
   Syn: rags.

tattle *verb*
1. GOSSIP.
2. INFORM.

tattle *noun*
1, 2. GOSSIP.

tattler *noun*
1. GOSSIP.
2. INFORMER.

tattletale *noun*
1. GOSSIP.
2. INFORMER.

tatty *adjective* SHODDY.

taunt *verb*
1. BAIT.
2. RIDICULE.

taunt *noun* RIDICULE.

taut *adjective*
1. Stretched tightly: *a taut anchor line.*
   Syns: close[1], snug, tense, tight.
2. NEAT.

tauten *verb* TENSE.

tautological *adjective*
Characterized by excessive and obfuscatory wordiness: *long-winded and tautological arguments.*
   Syns: circumlocutional, circumlocutionary, circumlocutious, circumlocutory, pleonastic, redundant, roundabout.

tawdry *adjective* GAUDY.

tax *noun*
1. A compulsory contribution, usu. of money, that is required of persons or groups of persons for the support of a government: *a tax on gasoline.*
   Syns: assessment, duty, impost, levy, tariff.
2. BURDEN.

tax *verb*
1. ACCUSE.
2. CALL DOWN at **call**.
3. CHARGE.
4. WORK.

taxing *adjective*
1. BURDENSOME.
2. DEMANDING.
3. TIRING.

TB also **T.B.** *noun* TUBERCULOSIS.

teach *verb* EDUCATE.

teachable *adjective* EDUCABLE.

teacher *noun* EDUCATOR.

teaching *noun*
1. DOCTRINE.
2. EDUCATION.

team *noun* FORCE.

teamwork *noun* COOPERATION.

tear[1] *verb*
1. To separate or pull apart by force: *tore my stocking on a nail.*
   Syns: cleave, rend, rip, rive, split.
2. PULL.
3. RUN.
4. RUSH.

tear down *verb*
1. BREAK DOWN at **break**.
2. DESTROY.
3. LIBEL.

tear *noun*
1. A hole made by tearing: *mended the tears in the fabric.*
   Syns: rent[2], rip.
2. BENDER.

tear[2] *noun*
A drop of the clear liquid secreted by the glands of the eyes: *A tear trickled down her cheek.*
   Syn: teardrop.

tear *verb*
To fill with tears: *eyes that were tearing and smarting from the smoke.*
   Syn: water.

teardrop *noun* TEAR[2].

tearful *adjective*
Filled with or shedding tears: *a sad and tearful child.*
   Syns: lachrymose, teary, weeping, weepy. —*Idiom* in (*or* to) tears.

tear-jerking *adjective* SENTIMENTAL.

tears *noun* CRY.
teary *adjective* TEARFUL.
tease *verb*
1. ANNOY.
2. TANTALIZE.
teasing *adjective* TANTALIZING.
technic *noun* TECHNIQUE.
technicality *noun* DETAIL.
technique *noun*
1. The degree of skill exhibited in any performance: *a faultless technique on the piano.*
   Syns: command, technic.
2. APPROACH.
3. ART.
4. WAY.
techy *adjective* SEE **tetchy.**
tedious *adjective* BORING.
tediousness *noun* MONOTONY.
tedium *noun*
1. BOREDOM.
2. MONOTONY.
tee-hee *verb & noun* SEE **tehee.**
teem¹ *verb*
1. To overflow with: *a street teeming with pedestrians.*
   Syns: abound, bristle, crawl, flow, formicate, pullulate, swarm.
2. POUR.
teem² *verb* POUR.
teeming *adjective* ALIVE.
teeny also **teensy** *adjective* TINY.
teeter *verb*
1. LURCH.
2. SWAY.
teetotalism *noun* TEMPERANCE.
tehee or **tee-hee** *verb* GIGGLE.
tehee or **tee-hee** *noun* GIGGLE.
telephone *verb*
To communicate with (someone) by telephone: *She's telephoned me twice today.*
   Syns: buzz (*Informal*), call, dial (*Informal*), phone, ring² (*Informal*).
   —*Idioms* get someone on the horn, give someone a buzz (*or* call *or* ring).
tell *verb*
1. BETRAY.
2. COMMAND.
3. COMMUNICATE.
4. DISTINGUISH.
5. INFORM.
6. SAY.
tell off *verb*
1. BAWL OUT at **bawl.**
2. COUNT.
telling *adjective* CONVINCING.
telltale *noun* GOSSIP.
tellurian *adjective* EARTHLY.

telluric *adjective* EARTHLY.
temerarious *adjective* RASH¹.
temblor *noun* TREMOR.
temerity *noun*
1. Foolhardy boldness or disregard of danger: *had the temerity to challenge the dictator's authority.*
   Syns: brashness, chutzpah (*Slang*), rashness, recklessness.
2. PRESUMPTION.
temper *noun*
1. A tendency to become angry or irritable: *was widely known for his temper.*
   Syns: choler, irascibility, irascibleness, spleen, temperament.
   —*Idioms* low boiling point, short fuse.
2. An angry outburst: *flew into a temper.*
   Syns: conniption (*Informal*), fit, huff, passion, tantrum.
3. A prevailing quality, as of thought, behavior, or attitude: *The temper of the early 1920's was one of optimism.*
   Syns: climate, mood, spirit, tone.
4. DISPOSITION.
5. MOOD.
temper *verb* MODERATE.
temperament *noun*
1. DISPOSITION.
2. TEMPER.
temperamental *adjective*
1. CAPRICIOUS.
2. MOODY.
temperance *noun*
1. The practice of refraining from use of alcoholic liquors: *believed that temperance was next to godliness.*
   Syns: abstinence, dryness, nephalism, soberness, sobriety, teetotalism.
2. MODERATION.
temperate *adjective*
1. Exercising moderation and self-restraint in appetites and behavior: *is temperate in his tastes, unlike his high-living brother.*
   Syns: abstemious, abstentious, abstinent, continent, sober.
2. CONSERVATIVE.
3. MILD.
4. MODERATE.
tempestuous *adjective*
1. ROUGH.
2. TURBULENT.
tempo *noun* SPEED.
temporal *adjective*
1. EARTHLY.
2. MATERIALISTIC.
3. PROFANE.
4. TRANSITORY.

temporary *adjective*
1. Intended, used, or present for a limited time: *temporary repairs; temporary employees.*
   Syns: impermanent, interim, provisional, short-range, short-term.
2. Temporarily assuming the duties of another: *temporary chairman.*
   Syns: acting, ad interim (*Latin*), interim, pro tem, pro tempore (*Latin*).
3. TRANSITORY.

tempt *verb*
1. To beguile or draw into a wrong or foolish course of action: *was tempted to destroy the records.*
   Syns: allure, entice, inveigle, lure, seduce. —*Idiom* lead astray.
2. COURT.

temptation *noun* LURE.

tempter *noun* SEDUCER.

tempting *adjective*
1. ATTRACTIVE.
2. SEDUCTIVE.

temptress *noun* SEDUCTRESS.

tenable *adjective*
1. Capable of being defended against armed attack: *an outpost that is no longer tenable.*
   Syns: defendable, defensible.
2. JUSTIFIABLE.

tenacious *adjective*
1. OBSTINATE.
2. TIGHT.

tend[1] *verb*
To have a tendency or inclination: *tends to stammer when excited.*
   Syns: incline, lean[1] (to *or* toward), slant, squint toward (*or* at), trend.

tend[2] *verb*
1. To have the care and supervision of: *tending the sheep in the pasture.*
   Syns: attend, care for, look after, mind, minister to, see to, watch.
   —*Idioms* keep an eye on, look out for, take care (*or* charge) of, take under one's wing.
2. TILL.

tendency *noun*
1. BENT.
2. THRUST.

tendentious *adjective* BIASED.

tendentiousness *noun* BIAS.

tender[1] *adjective* GENTLE.

tender[2] *noun* OFFER.
   tender *verb* OFFER.

tenderfoot *noun* BEGINNER.

tenderhearted *adjective* GENTLE.

tendril *noun* SHOOT.

tenebrific *adjective* GLOOMY.

tenebrosity *noun* DARK.

tenebrous *adjective* DARK.

tenet *noun* DOCTRINE.

tenor *noun* THRUST.

tense *verb*
To make or become tense: *My muscles tensed when I heard the knock at the door.*
   Syns: stiffen, tauten, tighten.

tense *adjective*
1. EDGY.
2. TAUT.

tension *noun* PRESSURE.

ten-strike *noun* HIT.

tentative *adjective*
1. CONDITIONAL.
2. HESITANT.
3. ROUGH.

tenuous *adjective*
Having little substance or significance; not solidly based: *tenuous reasoning.*
   Syns: feeble, flimsy, insubstantial, unsubstantial.

tenure *noun*
The holding of something, such as a position: *a three-year tenure in office.*
   Syns: incumbency, occupancy, occupation.

tepid *adjective*
Lacking warmth, interest, enthusiasm, or involvement: *her tepid approval of the plans.*
   Syns: halfhearted, lukewarm, unenthusiastic.

tergiversate *verb*
1. DEFECT.
2. EQUIVOCATE.

tergiversation *noun*
1. AMBIGUITY.
2. DEFECTION.
3. EQUIVOCATION.

tergiversator *noun* DEFECTOR.

term *noun*
1. A limited or specific period of time during which something happens, lasts, or extends: *a term of two years as chairman.*
   Syns: duration, span, stretch, time.
2. A sound or combination of sounds that symbolizes and communicates a meaning: *used the term in its most common sense.*
   Syns: expression, word.
3. LIFE.
4. PERIOD.
5. PROVISION.

term *verb*
1. CALL.
2. NAME.

termagant *noun* SCOLD.
terminal *adjective*
1, 2. LAST¹.
terminate *verb*
1. CLOSE¹.
2. DISMISS.
3. QUIT.
4. SUSPEND.
termination *noun*
1. DISMISSAL.
2, 3. END.
terminology *noun* LANGUAGE.
terminus *noun*
1. BORDER.
2. END.
terms *noun* BASIS.
terpsichorean *noun* DANCER.
terrain *noun*
1. The character, natural features, and
   configuration of land: *rocky, hilly
   terrain.*
   Syn: topography. —*Idiom* the lay of
   the land.
2. AREA.
3. TERRITORY.
terrene *adjective*
1. EARTHLY.
2. EARTHY.
terrestrial *adjective*
1. EARTHLY.
2. EARTHY.
terrible *adjective*
1. Very bad: *a terrible blunder.*
   Syns: appalling, awful, dreadful,
   fearful, frightful, ghastly, horrendous,
   horrible, shocking.
2. FEARFUL.
3. INTENSE.
terrific *adjective*
1. EXCELLENT.
2. HORRIBLE.
3. MARVELOUS.
terrify *verb* FRIGHTEN.
terrifying *adjective* HORRIBLE.
territorial *adjective*
Pertaining to or restricted to a
particular territory: *a territorial problem
concerning land development.*
Syn: sectional.
territory *noun*
1. A particular area used for or
   associated with a specific individual
   or activity: *a salesman's territory;
   cattle territory.*
   Syns: country (*Informal*), terrain, turf
   (*Slang*).
2. AREA.
terror *noun* FEAR.
terrorist *noun* ALARMIST.

terrorize *verb* FRIGHTEN.
test *noun*
1. A set of questions or exercises
   designed to determine knowledge or
   skill: *Tests were given at intervals
   during the course.*
   Syns: catechism, catechization, exam
   (*Informal*), examination, quiz.
2. An operation employed to resolve an
   uncertainty: *ran tests to determine the
   effects of weightlessness on the human
   body.*
   Syns: experiment, experimentation,
   trial.
3. A procedure that ascertains
   effectiveness, value, proper function,
   or other quality: *The long hike was a
   test of our endurance.*
   Syns: assay, essay, proof, trial, try-
   out (*Informal*).
4. STANDARD.
test *verb*
1. To subject to a test of knowledge or
   skill: *tested the children's literacy
   levels.*
   Syns: check, examine.
2. To subject to a procedure that
   ascertains effectiveness, value, proper
   function, or other quality: *He tested
   his headlights to be sure they were
   working.*
   Syns: assay, check, essay, examine,
   prove, try, try out. —*Idioms* bring to
   test, make trial of, put to the test (*or
   proof*).
3. To engage in experiments: *scientists
   involved in testing new alloys; tested
   out the new theory.*
   Syns: experiment, try out.
test *adjective* PILOT.
testament *noun* CONFIRMATION.
testifier *noun* WITNESS.
testify *verb*
1. To give evidence or testimony under
   oath: *A witness testified that he saw
   the defendant at the scene of the crime.*
   Syns: attest, depone (*Archaic*),
   depose (*Law*), swear, witness (*Obs.*).
   —*Idioms* bear witness, take the stand.
2. CERTIFY.
3. CONFIRM.
4. INDICATE.
testimonial *noun*
1. A formal token of appreciation and
   admiration for a person's high
   achievements: *a banquet as a
   testimonial to the hero.*
   Syns: salute, salvo, tribute.
2. CONFIRMATION.
3. REFERENCE.

testimony *noun*
1. A formal declaration of truth or fact given under oath: *A court reporter recorded the testimony.*
   Syns: deposition (*Law*), witness (*Obs.*).
2. CONFIRMATION.

testy *adjective*
1. Easily annoyed: *a frustrated, testy man.*
   Syns: choleric, hot-tempered, irascible, peppery, quick-tempered, ratty (*Chiefly Brit.*), tetchy (*also* techy), touchy.
2. ILL-TEMPERED.

tetchy *also* **techy** *adjective* TESTY.

text *noun* SUBJECT.

texture *noun*
1. A distinctive, complex underlying pattern or structure: *the texture of city life.*
   Syns: contexture, fabric, fiber, web.
   —*Idiom* woof and warp.
2. ESSENCE.

thalassic *adjective* MARINE.

thank *verb*
To feel and express gratitude to: *I thank you for helping out.*
   Syn: bless.

thankful *adjective* GRATEFUL.

thankfulness *noun* APPRECIATION.

thankless *adjective*
1. Not showing or feeling gratitude: *a thankless sponger.*
   Syns: unappreciative, ungrateful, unthankful, unthanking.
2. Not apt to be appreciated: *a thankless task.*
   Syns: unappreciated, ungrateful, unthankful.

thanks *noun*
1. APPRECIATION.
2. GRACE.

thanksgiving *noun* GRACE.

thaumaturgic *adjective* MAGIC.

thaumaturgy *noun* MAGIC.

thaw *verb* MELT.

theatrical *also* **theatric** *adjective*
1, 2. DRAMATIC.

theatricalism *noun*
Showy mannerisms and behavior: *a grand gesture symptomatic of his theatricalism.*
   Syns: dramaticism, staginess, theatricality, theatricalness.

theatricality *noun* THEATRICALISM.

theatricalness *noun* THEATRICALISM.

theatricals *noun* THEATRICS.

theatrics *noun*
Overemotional, exaggerated behavior calculated for effect: *a child who used hysteria and theatrics to get what he wanted.*
   Syns: dramatics, histrionics, melodramatics, theatricals.

theft *noun* LARCENY.

thematic *adjective*
Of, constituting, or relating to a theme or themes: *found a thematic tie-in between the two poems.*
   Syn: topical.

theme *noun*
1. *Ling.* The main part of a word to which affixes are attached: *The word "eat" is the theme on which the derivative "eater" is based.*
   Syns: base^1, root^1, stem.
2. COMPOSITION.
3. SUBJECT.

theorem *noun* LAW.

theoretical *also* **theoretic** *adjective*
1. Concerned with or restricted to a theory or theories: *theoretical mathematics.*
   Syns: abstract, academic, speculative.
2. Existing only in concept and not in reality: *constructed a theoretical model of a society devoid of class conflict.*
   Syns: abstract, hypothetical (*also* hypothetic), ideal, transcendent, transcendental.
3. DOCTRINAIRE.

theory *noun*
1. A belief used as the basis for action: *Unstructured classroom activities resulted from the theory that children require free expression to learn.*
   Syns: hypothesis, supposition.
2. Abstract reasoning: *the theory that the Romanovs survived execution.*
   Syns: conjecture, perhaps, speculation.
3. ASSUMPTION.

therapeutic *adjective* CURATIVE.

therapy *noun* TREATMENT.

thesis *noun*
1. A systematic, thorough written presentation of an original point of view: *a doctoral thesis.*
   Syn: dissertation.
2. A hypothetical, controversial proposition: *His thesis is that big government is the root of inflation.*
   Syns: contention, contestation.
3. ASSUMPTION.

thespian *noun* ACTOR.

thespian *adjective* DRAMATIC.

theurgy *noun* MAGIC.
thew(s) *noun* STRENGTH.
thick *adjective*
1. Relatively great in extent from one surface to the opposite: *cut himself a thick slice of bread.*
   Syn: fat.
2. Having all parts near to each other: *The pile in the carpet is thick.*
   Syns: close[1], compact[1], crowded, packed, tight.
3. Having so many constituent particles in suspension as to be condensed, often viscous: *a thick white sauce.*
   Syns: gelatinous, heavy, stodgy.
4. Growing profusely: *thick jungle vegetation.*
   Syns: dense, heavy, lush, luxuriant, profuse, rank[2].
5. FAMILIAR.
6. HEAVY.
7. IMPLAUSIBLE.
8. STUPID.
thick *noun*
The most intensely active central part: *the thick of the fighting; caught in the thick of the controversy.*
   Syns: eye, midst.
thickbodied *adjective* HEAVY.
thicken *verb*
To make thick or thicker, esp. through evaporation or condensation: *thickened the gravy by adding flour and heating it.*
   Syns: condense, inspissate.
thickhead *noun* DULLARD.
thickheaded *adjective* STUPID.
thickness *noun*
The quality, condition, or degree of being thick: *measured the thickness of the wall.*
   Syns: compactness, density, solidity.
thickset *adjective* HEAVY.
thick-witted *adjective* STUPID.
thief *noun* LARCENER.
thieve *verb* STEAL.
thievery *noun* LARCENY.
thieving *noun* LARCENY.
thieving *adjective* LARCENOUS.
thievish *adjective* LARCENOUS.
thin *adjective*
1. Having little flesh or fat on the body: *became weak and thin during her illness.*
   Syns: angular, attenuate, bony, fleshless, gaunt, lank, lanky, lean[2], meager, rawboned, scrawny, skinny, spare, slender, twiggy, weedy.
   —*Idioms* all skin and bones, lean as a rake, thin as a rail.

2. Marked by great diffusion of component particles: *the thin air in the high Sierras.*
   Syns: rare, rarefied.
3. DILUTE.
4. IMPLAUSIBLE.
thin *verb*
1. To make physically thin or thinner: *a body thinned from malnutrition and malaria.*
   Syns: extenuate (*Archaic*), gaunt, lean (down).
2. To become diffuse: *At 50,000 feet the air thins markedly.*
   Syns: attenuate, rarefy.
3. DILUTE.
thing *noun*
1. One that exists independently: *discerned three things on the horizon, one of which moved.*
   Syns: being, entity, existence, existent, individual, object[1], something.
2. An irrational preoccupation: *He has a thing about cleanliness.*
   Syns: fetish, fixation (*Psychol.*), mania, obsession.
3. ACT.
4. EVENT.
5. FASHION.
6. FORTE.
7. GADGET.
8. KICK.
9. MATTER.
10. OBJECT[1].
thingamabob also **thingumabob** *noun* GADGET.
thingamajig also **thingumajig** *noun* GADGET.
things *noun*
1. BELONGINGS.
2. EFFECTS.
thingumabob *noun* SEE **thingamabob**.
thingumajig *noun* SEE **thingamajig**.
think *verb*
1. To use the powers of the mind, as in conceiving ideas, drawing inferences, and making judgments: *took time and thought carefully before answering.*
   Syns: cerebrate, cogitate, ratiocinate, reflect, speculate. —*Idioms* put on one's thinking cap, use one's head.
2. BELIEVE.
3. FEEL.
4. IMAGINE.
5. REASON.
6. REMEMBER.
7. REPUTE.
think of *verb*
1. HEAR OF at **hear**.

2, 3. REMEMBER.

think over *verb*
1. CONSIDER.
2. PONDER.
3. RECONSIDER.

think through *verb* PONDER.

think up *verb* INVENT.

thinkable *adjective* EARTHLY.

thinker *noun*
1. A person who seeks reason and truth by thinking and meditation: *Aristotle was a great thinker.*
   Syn: philosopher.
2. MIND.

thinking *adjective* THOUGHTFUL.

third-degree *verb* INTERROGATE.

thirst *noun* APPETITE.

thirst *verb* LUST.

thirsting *adjective* EAGER.

thirsty *adjective*
1. Needing or desiring drink: *The hike left us hungry and thirsty.*
   Syns: athirst, dry, parched.
2. DRY.
3. EAGER.

thistly *adjective* THORNY.

thorn *noun*
1. One that makes another totally miserable by causing sharp pain and irritation: *His wife had been a thorn in his life for many years.*
   Syns: pain, trial. —*Idioms* pain in the neck, pea in the shoe, thorn in the flesh (*or* side).
2. PRICK.

thorn *verb* ANNOY.

thorny *adjective*
1. Full of sharp, needlelike protuberances: *a thorny shrub; a thorny marine animal.*
   Syns: briery (*also* briary), echinate, prickly, spiny, thistly.
2. So replete with interlocking points and complications as to be painfully irritating: *the thorny problems of energy and inflation.*
   Syns: nettlesome, prickly, spiny, vexatious. —*Idiom* set with thorns.

thorough *adjective*
1. Covering all aspects with painstaking accuracy: *a thorough physical examination; a thorough search.*
   Syns: all-out, complete, exhaustive, full-dress, intensive, thoroughgoing, thoroughpaced, whole-hog (*Slang*).
2. DETAILED.
3. UTTER².

thoroughbred *adjective*
1. Of pure breeding stock: *thoroughbred horses.*

Syns: full-blooded, highbred, pureblooded, purebred.
2. NOBLE.

thoroughfare *noun* WAY.

thoroughgoing *adjective*
1. THOROUGH.
2. UTTER².

thoroughness *noun*
Attentiveness to detail: *edited the manuscript with great thoroughness.*
   Syns: care, meticulousness, pains, painstaking, scrupulousness.

thoroughpaced *adjective* THOROUGH.

thought *noun*
1. The act or process of thinking: *gave the matter much thought before reaching a decision.*
   Syns: brainwork, cerebration, cogitation, deliberation, meditation, reflection, rumination, speculation.
2. IDEA.

thoughtful *adjective*
1. Of, characterized by, or disposed to thought: *a quiet, thoughtful child; a thoughtful pause before she began to play the music.*
   Syns: cogitative, contemplative, deliberative, meditative, museful, pensive, reflective, ruminative, speculative, thinking. —*Idiom* in a brown study.
2. ATTENTIVE.
3. INTELLECTUAL.
4. MINDFUL.

thoughtfulness *noun*
CONSIDERATION.

thoughtless *adjective*
1. Devoid of consideration for others' feelings: *a thoughtless person; a thoughtless remark.*
   Syns: inconsiderate, ungracious, unthinking, unthoughtful.
2. CARELESS.

thoughtlessness *noun*
1. A lack of consideration for others' feelings: *The thoughtlessness of his behavior is appalling.*
   Syns: disregard, inconsiderateness, inconsideration, unthoughtfulness.
2. ABANDON.

thought-out *adjective* ADVISED.

thraldom *noun* SEE **thralldom.**

thrall *noun* SLAVERY.

thralldom *or* **thraldom** *noun*
SLAVERY.

thrash *verb*
1. To swing about or strike at wildly: *The wounded shark thrashed in the water. The delirious child thrashed about in his sleep.*

Syns: flail, thresh, toss. —*Idiom* toss and turn.
2. To beat (plants) with a machine or by hand to separate the grain from the straw: *thrashed the wheat.*
   Syn: thresh.
3, 4. BEAT.
5. DEFEAT.
6. OVERWHELM.
thrash out *verb* DISCUSS.
thrashing *noun*
1. BEATING.
2. DEFEAT.
3. TROUNCING.
thread *noun*
1. A very fine, continuous strand: *polyester thread; threads trailing behind the tropical fish.*
   Syns: fiber, fibril (*also* fibrilla), filament.
2. Something drawn or spun out like a fine, continuous filament: *tried to follow the thread of the plot; lost the thread of the conversation.*
   Syns: skein, strand.
thread *verb*
To put (objects) onto a fine, continuous filament: *beads threaded into a necklace.*
   Syn: string.
threadbare *adjective*
1. SHABBY.
2. TRITE.
threads *noun* DRESS.
threat *noun*
1. An expression of the intent to hurt or punish another: *The loan shark used threats of hideous beatings to collect his due.*
   Syns: intimidation, menace.
2. An indication of impending danger or harm: *the threat of a recession.*
   Syns: forewarning, thundercloud. —*Idioms* gathering clouds, storm clouds.
3. One regarded as an imminent danger: *considered the other woman a threat to the marriage; felt that Soviet military presence in the Middle East was a threat to the oil fields.*
   Syn: menace. —*Idioms* clear and present danger, sword of Damocles.
threaten *verb*
1. To give warning signs of (impending peril): *economic indicators threatening recession. The company threatens to go under.*
   Syns: forebode, forewarn.
2. To be imminent: *Civil Defense has announced that a typhoon threatens.*

Syns: hang (over), impend, loom, lower[1] (*also* lour), menace, overhang.
3. INTIMIDATE.
threatening *adjective*
Expressing, indicating, or warning of an impending danger or misfortune: *gave me a threatening look; a threatening letter; threatening clouds.*
   Syns: menacing, minatory, overhanging.
threesome *noun* TRIO.
thresh *verb*
1, 2. THRASH.
threshold *noun* VERGE.
thrift *noun* ECONOMY.
thriftiness *noun* ECONOMY.
thriftless *adjective* IMPROVIDENT.
thrifty *adjective* ECONOMICAL.
thrill *noun*
1. A strong, pleasant feeling of excitement or stimulation: *got a thrill out of bobsledding.*
   Syns: bang (*Slang*), boot[1], high (*Slang*), kick (*Slang*), lift, wallop (*Informal*).
2. TREMOR.
thrill *verb* CARRY AWAY at **carry.**
thrilled *adjective*
Feeling a very strong emotion: *too thrilled by the day's events to sleep.*
   Syns: atingle, excited, fired up, turned-on (*Slang*), worked up.
thrive *verb*
1. FLOURISH.
2. PROSPER.
thriving *adjective* FLOURISHING.
throb *verb* BEAT.
throb *noun* BEAT.
throe *noun*
1. A violent, excruciating seizure of pain: *the throes of a heart attack.*
   Syns: grip, paroxysm, spasm.
2. A condition of anguished struggle and disorder: *in the throes of a devastating civil war.*
   Syns: convulsion, paroxysm.
3. PAIN.
throng *noun* CROWD.
throng *verb* POUR.
throttle *verb*
1. CHOKE.
2. REPRESS.
throttling *noun* REPRESSION.
through *adverb*
1. From one end to the other: *worked furiously the whole day through.*
   Syns: around, over, round, throughout.

2. To an end or conclusion: *Let's see this thing through.*
   Syn: over.

through *adjective*
1. No longer effective, capable, or valuable: *He's through as a ballplayer.*
   Syns: done, done for, finished, kaput (*Slang*), washed-up. —*Idioms* at the end of the road (*or* line), over the hill, past one's prime.
2. Having no further relationship: *You and I are through.*
   Syns: done, finished, washed-up.
3. COMPLETE.
4. DIRECT.

throughout *adverb* THROUGH.

throw *verb*
1. To send through the air with a motion of the hand or arm: *threw the ball to the catcher.*
   Syns: cast, fire, fling, heave, hurl, pitch, shy², sling, toss.
2. CONFUSE.
3. DROP.
4. SHED.
5. TRIP.

throw away *verb*
1. DISCARD.
2. WASTE.

throw off *verb*
1. EMIT.
2. LOSE.
3. RID.
4. SHED.

throw out *verb*
1. DISCARD.
2. EJECT.
3. SLIP.

throw over *verb* ABANDON.

throw *noun*
An act of throwing: *a throw of 60 feet.*
   Syns: cast, fling, heave (*Informal*), hurl, pitch, shy², sling, toss.

thrust *noun*
1. The thread or current of thought uniting or occurring in all the elements of a text or discourse: *the socialistic thrust of the new policy statement.*
   Syns: aim, drift, intent, purport, substance, tendency, tenor.
2. PUSH.

thrust *verb*
1. DRIVE.
2. POKE.
3. RAM.

thud *verb*
To make a dull sound by or as if by striking a surface with a heavy object:

horses' hoofs thudding down the cobblestone street.
   Syns: clomp, clump, clunk.

thug *noun*
A person who treats others violently and roughly, esp. for hire: *The mobster sent his thugs to teach the welsher a lesson.*
   Syns: ape (*Slang*), goon (*Slang*), gorilla (*Slang*), hood (*Slang*), hoodlum, hooligan, ruffian.

thumb *verb* BROWSE.

thump *noun* BEAT.

thunder *noun* BLAST.
   thunder *verb* BLAST.

thundercloud *noun* THREAT.

thunderstruck *adjective* SHOCKED.

thwack *noun* BLOW².

thwart *verb* FRUSTRATE.
   thwart *adjective* TRANSVERSE.

tic *noun* TREMOR.

tick *noun* FLASH.
   tick off *verb* ENUMERATE.

ticker *noun* HEART.

ticket *noun*
1. An identifying or descriptive slip: *a price ticket.*
   Syns: label, marker, tag.
2. A list of candidates proposed or endorsed by a political party: *the Republican state ticket.*
   Syns: line-up (*also* lineup), slate.
3. A means or method of entering into or achieving something desirable: *Hard work is the ticket to success.*
   Syns: key, route, secret.

ticket *verb*
To attach a ticket to: *She's ticketing the new merchandise.*
   Syns: label, tag.

tickle *verb* DELIGHT.

tickled *adjective* GLAD.

ticklish *adjective*
1. CAPRICIOUS.
2. DELICATE.

tidbit *noun* DELICACY.

tide *noun* FLOW.

tidings *noun* NEWS.

tidy *verb*
1. To make or keep (an area) clean and orderly: *tidied the room for weekend houseguests.*
   Syns: clean (up), clear (up), neaten, police, spruce (up), straighten (up).
2. To make neat and trim; make presentable: *used their bathroom in order to tidy up.*
   Syns: freshen (up), groom, neaten, spruce (up), trig (up *or* out), trim.

tidy *adjective*
1. ACCEPTABLE.
2. BIG.
3. NEAT.

tie *verb*
1. To make fast or firmly fixed by means of a cord, rope, etc.: *tied the package with twine; tied her shoes.*
   Syns: bind, fasten, knot, secure, tie up.
2. EQUAL.

tie down *verb* HAMPER.

tie up *verb*
1. To cause to cease regular activity: *a wreck that tied up traffic.*
   Syns: idle, immobilize, stop. —*Idiom* bring to a screeching halt.
2. To cause to be busy or in use: *He's tied up until noon. All the office telephones were tied up.*
   Syns: engage, monopolize, occupy.
3. TIE.

tie *noun*
1. An equality of scores, votes, or performances in a contest: *The teams played to a tie. The first game was a tie.*
   Syns: deadlock, draw, stalemate, stand-off. —*Idiom* dead heat.
2. ATTACHMENT.
3. BOND.

tie-in *noun* RELATION.

tier *noun*
1. CLASS.
2. LINE.

tie-up *noun*
A cessation of normal activity caused by an accident, strike, etc.: *a traffic tie-up.*
   Syn: stoppage.

tiff *noun* ARGUMENT.

tiff *verb* ARGUE.

tiger *noun* FIEND.

tight *adjective*
1. Hard to deal with or get out of: *in a tight spot.*
   Syns: rough, sticky, tricky.
2. Affording little room for movement: *tight quarters.*
   Syns: close[1], confining, cramped, crowded, narrow.
3. Persistently holding to something: *a tight embrace.*
   Syns: fast, firm[1], secure, tenacious.
4. Characterized by an economy of artistic expression: *a tight writing style.*
   Syns: compact[1], lean[2], spare.
5. CLOSE[1].
6. DRUNK.

7. FAMILIAR.
8. NEAT.
9. SOUND[2].
10. STINGY.
11. TAUT.
12. THICK.

tighten *verb*
1. To make or become tight or tighter: *tightened wage and price controls.*
   Syns: reinforce, strengthen.
2. TENSE.

tightfisted *adjective* STINGY.

tight-laced *adjective* GENTEEL.

tight-lipped *adjective*
1. SPEECHLESS.
2. TACITURN.

tightwad *noun* MISER.

till *verb*
To prepare (soil) for the planting and raising of crops: *farmers tilling their fields.*
   Syns: cultivate, culture, dress, labor (*Archaic*), tend[2], work.

tilt *noun*
1. Any competition or test of opposing wills likened to the sport in which knights fought with lances: *her frequent legal tilts with corporate management.*
   Syns: joust, tournament, tourney.
2. INCLINATION.

tilt *verb*
1. CONTEND.
2. INCLINE.
3. LURCH.

tilted *adjective* INCLINED.

tilting *adjective* INCLINED.

timber *noun*
1. The basic substance or essential elements of character that qualify a person for a specified role: *Without doubt she's presidential timber.*
   Syns: material, stuff.
2. BEAM.

timbre *noun* TONE.

time *noun*
1. A term of service, as in the military or in prison: *put in his time in the army; did time for armed robbery.*
   Syns: hitch, stretch.
2. A span designated for a given activity: *harvest time.*
   Syns: period, season.
3. AGE.
4. BIT[1].
5. OCCASION.
6. TERM.
7. TURN.

time *verb*
1. To set the time for (an event or

occasion): *timed her absence so as not to interrupt our progress.*
Syn: schedule.

2. To record the speed or duration of: *timed the horse's workouts; timed the television show.*
Syn: clock.

time-honored *adjective* ORTHODOX.

timeless *adjective*
1. AGELESS.
2. CONTINUAL.

timely *adjective*
1. OPPORTUNE.
2. PUNCTUAL.

time-out *noun* BREAK.

time(s) *noun* AGE.

timetable *noun* PROGRAM.

timeworn *adjective*
1. OLD.
2. TRITE.

timid *adjective*
1. HESITANT.
2. MODEST.

tincture *noun* COLOR.

tinge *noun*
1, 2. SHADE.
3. TINT.

tinker *verb*
1. FIDDLE.
2. TAMPER.

tinsel *adjective* GAUDY.

tint *noun*
1. A shade of a color, esp. a pale or delicate variation: *a tint of red in her hair.*
Syns: cast, hue, tinge, tone.
2. SHADE.

tint *verb* COLOR.

tintinnabulate *verb* RING².

tiny *adjective*
Extremely small: *a tiny speck of soot in her eye.*
Syns: diminutive, dwarf, lilliputian, midget, miniature, minute, peewee, pint-size (*also* pint-sized), pygmy (*also* pigmy), teeny (*also* teensy), wee, weeny (*Informal*).

tip¹ *noun* POINT.

tip² *verb* INCLINE.

tip³ *noun*
1. An item of advance or inside information given as a guide to action: *a tip on the stock market; gave her a tip that she should buy gold ingots.*
Syns: pointer, steer, tip-off (*Informal*).
2. GRATUITY.

tip-off *noun* TIP³.

tipped *adjective* INCLINED.

tipple *verb* DRINK.

tippler *noun* DRUNKARD.

tipster *noun* INFORMER.

tipsy *adjective* DRUNK.

tiptop *adjective* EXCELLENT.

tirade *noun*
A long, violent, or blustering speech, usu. of censure or denunciation: *had to listen to her father's frequent tirades.*
Syns: diatribe, fulmination, harangue, jeremiad, obloquy, philippic.

tire *verb*
1. BORE.
2. FATIGUE.

tire out *verb* EXHAUST.

tired *adjective*
1. SICK.
2. TRITE.

tiredness *noun* EXHAUSTION.

tired out *adjective* EXHAUSTED.

tireless *adjective*
Having or showing a capacity for protracted effort, regardless of difficulty or frustration: *tireless efforts to resolve the labor dispute.*
Syns: indefatigable, inexhaustible, unflagging, untiring, weariless.

tiresome *adjective* BORING.

tiring *adjective*
1. Causing fatigue: *a long, tiring walk; an extraordinarily lengthy and tiring lecture on entomology.*
Syns: exhausting, fatiguing, taxing, wearying.
2. BORING.

tissue *noun* WEB.

titan *noun* GIANT.

titan *adjective* GIANT.

titanic *adjective* GIANT.

title *noun*
1. CLAIM.
2. INTEREST.
3. OWNERSHIP.
4. POSSESSION.
5. PUBLICATION.

title *verb* NAME.

titter *verb* GIGGLE.

titter *noun* GIGGLE.

tittle *noun* BIT¹.

tittle-tattle *noun* GOSSIP.

tittle-tattle *verb* GOSSIP.

tizzy *noun* STATE.

to-and-fro *noun* HESITATION.

toast *noun*
The act of drinking to someone: *He proposed a toast to the queen's health.*
Syn: pledge.

toast *verb* DRINK.

tocsin *noun* ALARM.

today *adverb* NOW.

today *noun* NOW.

to-do *noun*
1. DISTURBANCE.
2. FUSS.
3. SENSATION.

tog *verb* DRESS.

tog out *verb* DRESS UP at **dress**.

tog up *verb* DRESS UP at **dress**.

together *adverb*
1. In, into, or as a single body: *six people singing together in perfect harmony.*
    Syns: ensemble (*French*), jointly.
    —*Idioms* as one, in one breath, in the same breath, in unison, with one accord, with one voice.
2. At the same time: *The bells rang out together.*
    Syns: concurrently, simultaneously, synchronously. —*Idioms* all at once, all together.

together *adjective* READY.

togs *noun* DRESS.

toil *verb*
1. GRIND.
2. LABOR.
3. PLOD.

toil *noun* LABOR.

toilworn *adjective* HAGGARD.

token *noun*
1. EXPRESSION.
2. PAWN¹.
3. REMEMBRANCE.
4. SIGN.

tolerable *adjective*
1. ACCEPTABLE.
2. BEARABLE.

tolerance *noun*
Forbearing or lenient treatment: *tolerance of his brother's boorish manners.*
    Syns: charitableness, charity, forbearance, indulgence, leniency (*also* lenience), toleration.

tolerant *adjective*
1. Not strict or severe: *tolerant and understanding parents.*
    Syns: charitable, clement, easy, forbearant (*Archaic*), forbearing, indulgent, lax, lenient, merciful, soft.
2. BROAD.

tolerate *verb*
1. ENDURE.
2. PERMIT.

toleration *noun* TOLERANCE.

toll¹ *noun*
1. A fixed amount of money charged for a privilege or service: *a toll of 50¢ to use the new bridge.*
    Syns: charge, exaction, fee.
2. COST.

toll² *verb* RING².

tomb *noun* GRAVE¹.

tome *noun* BOOK.

tomfool *noun* FOOL.

tomfool *adjective* FOOLISH.

tomfoolery *noun*
1. FOOLISHNESS.
2. NONSENSE.
3. PRANK.

tommyrot *noun* NONSENSE.

tonality *noun* TONE.

tone *noun*
1. A sound of distinct pitch and quality: *the unmistakable tone of a violin.*
    Syns: timbre, tonality. —*Idiom* tone color.
2. A particular vocal quality that indicates some emotion or feeling: *asked in an angry tone why I had gone.*
    Syns: accent, inflection, intonation. —*Idiom* tone of voice.
3. AIR.
4. COLOR.
5. TEMPER.
6. TINT.

tone down *verb*
1. MODERATE.
2. SOFT-PEDAL.

toney *adjective* SEE **tony**.

tongue *noun* LANGUAGE.

tongue-lash *verb* BAWL OUT at **bawl**.

tonic *noun*
A medicine that restores or increases vigor: *a spring tonic of sulfur and molasses.*
    Syns: bracer, pick-me-up (*Informal*), restorative, roborant.

tonic *adjective*
Producing or stimulating physical, mental, or emotional vigor: *The mountain air proved very tonic.*
    Syns: bracing, energizing, invigorating, refreshing, reinvigorating, renewing, restorative, roborant, stimulating.

tonish *adjective* FASHIONABLE.

tony *also* **toney** *adjective* FASHIONABLE.

tool *noun*
1. A device used to do work or perform a task: *the tools needed to repair a car.*
    Syns: implement, instrument, utensil.
2. DUPE.
3. PAWN².

tool *verb* DRIVE.

toothsome *adjective* DELICIOUS.
top *noun*
1. BEST.
2. FACE.
3. HEIGHT.

top *adjective*
1. Of, being, located at, or forming the top: *the top shelf; typing at top speed.*
   Syns: highest, loftiest, topmost, uppermost.
2. EXCELLENT.
3. MAXIMUM.
4. PRIMARY.

top *verb*
1. To put a topping on: *Top the sundae with a cherry.*
   Syns: cap, crown, top off.
2. SURPASS.

top off *verb*
1. CLIMAX.
2. TOP.

top-drawer *adjective* HIGHEST.
topflight *adjective* EXCELLENT.
topic *noun* SUBJECT.
topical *adjective* THEMATIC.
topmost *adjective*
1. MAXIMUM.
2. TOP.

topnotch *adjective* EXCELLENT.
topography *noun* TERRAIN.
topple *verb*
1. FALL.
2. OVERTHROW.
3. OVERTURN.
4. SURRENDER.

toppling *noun* FALL.
top-quality *adjective* CHOICE.
top-ranking *adjective* HIGHEST.
topsy-turviness *noun* DISORDER.
topsy-turvy *adjective* CONFUSED.
torch *verb* LIGHT[1].
torment *verb*
1. AFFLICT.
2. HAUNT.
3. TANTALIZE.
4. TORTURE.

torment *noun* HELL.
tormenting *adjective*
Extraordinarily painful or distressing: *a tormenting wait outside the operating room.*
   Syns: agonizing, excruciating, harrowing, torturous.
torpedo *verb* DESTROY.
torpid *adjective* LETHARGIC.
torpidity *noun* LETHARGY.
torpidness *noun* LETHARGY.
torpor *noun*
1. INACTION.
2. LETHARGY.

torrent *noun* FLOOD.
torrid *adjective*
1. HOT.
2. PASSIONATE.

torridness *noun* HEAT.
tort *noun* CRIME.
tortuous *adjective*
1. INDIRECT.
2. WINDING.

torture *verb*
1. To subject (another) to extreme physical cruelty, as in punishing: *prisoners tortured by their captors.*
   Syns: crucify, rack, torment. —*Idiom* put on the rack (*or* wheel).
2. AFFLICT.

torture *noun* HELL.
torturous *adjective* TORMENTING.
Tory *noun* CONSERVATIVE.
Tory *adjective* CONSERVATIVE.
toss *verb*
1. To move vigorously from side to side or up and down: *a small boat tossed by the waves; toss in one's sleep.*
   Syns: heave, pitch, rock[2], roll.
2. To throw (a coin) in order to decide something: *Let's toss to see which team will kick off.*
   Syns: flip, toss up. —*Idioms* call heads or tails, call the coin.
3. AGITATE.
4. THRASH.
5. THROW.
6. WRITHE.

toss about *verb* DISCUSS.
toss around *verb* DISCUSS.
toss down *verb* DRINK.
toss off *verb* DRINK.
toss up *verb* TOSS.
toss *noun* THROW.
tot[1] *noun*
1. CHILD.
2. DROP.

tot[2] *verb* ADD.
total *noun*
1. A number or quantity obtained as a result of addition: *Losses reached a new total.*
   Syns: aggregate, amount, sum, summation, totality, tote[2]. —*Idiom* sum total.
2. WHOLE.

total *adjective*
1. UTTER[2].
2. WHOLE.

total *verb*
1. ADD.
2. AMOUNT.
3. DESTROY.

totalitarian *noun* DICTATOR.
totalitarian *adjective*
1. ABSOLUTE.
2. AUTHORITARIAN.
totalitarianism *noun*
1. ABSOLUTISM.
2. TYRANNY.
totality *noun*
1. COMPLETENESS.
2. SYSTEM.
3. TOTAL.
4. WHOLE.
totalization *noun* ADDITION.
totalize *verb* ADD.
tote[1] *verb* CARRY.
tote[2] *noun* TOTAL.
tote *verb* ADD.
totter *verb*
1. LURCH.
2. SWAY.
tottering *adjective* UNSTABLE.
tottery *adjective* INSECURE.
touch *verb*
1. To bring into contact with, esp. by means of the hands or fingers, so as to give or receive a physical sensation: *The doctor gently touched the wound.*
   Syns: feel, finger, handle, palp, palpate.
2. ADJOIN.
3. AFFECT[1].
4. COMPARE.
5. CONTACT.
touch down *verb* LAND.
touch off *verb*
1. EXPLODE.
2. GENERATE.
touch on (or **upon**) *verb* REFER.
touch up *verb*
To improve by making minor changes or additions: *touched up his speech to make it more lively.*
   Syns: polish, retouch.
touch *noun*
1. An act of touching: *felt a gentle touch on her shoulder.*
   Syns: feeling, palpation.
2. The faculty or ability to perceive tactile stimulation: *the sense of touch.*
   Syns: feel, feeling, tactility.
3. A particular sensation conveyed by means of physical contact: *the soft touch of velvet.*
   Syns: feel, feeling.
4. A situation allowing exchange of ideas or messages: *tried in vain to get in touch with her.*
   Syns: communication, contact, intercommunication.

5. CONTACT.
6. SHADE.
7. TRACE.
touchability *noun* TANGIBILITY.
touchable *adjective* TANGIBLE.
touchableness *noun* TANGIBILITY.
touch-and-go *adjective* DELICATE.
touched *adjective*
1. AFFECTED[1].
2. INSANE.
touching *adjective*
1. ADJOINING.
2. AFFECTING.
touchstone *noun* STANDARD.
touchy *adjective*
1. DELICATE.
2. TESTY.
tough *adjective*
1. BURDENSOME.
2. DEMANDING.
3. DIFFICULT.
4. FIRM.
5. HARD.
6. OBSTINATE.
7. ROUGH.
8. SEVERE.
9. STRONG.
tough *noun*
A rough, violent person who engages in destructive actions: *neighborhood toughs breaking windows.*
   Syns: mug, punk (*Slang*), roughneck, rowdy, toughie (*also* toughy).
tough out *verb* ENDURE.
toughen *verb*
1. To become or cause to become tough or strong: *The soles of her feet toughened from going barefoot.*
   Syn: strengthen.
2. HARDEN.
toughie *also* **toughy** *noun* TOUGH.
tough-minded *adjective* REALISTIC.
tour *noun*
1. CIRCLE.
2. TURN.
tour de force *noun*
1. FEAT.
2. MASTERPIECE.
tourist *noun*
One who travels for pleasure: *saw a group of tourists snapping pictures.*
   Syns: excursionist, rubberneck (*also* rubbernecker) (*Slang*), sightseer, tripper (*Chiefly Brit.*).
tournament *noun* TILT.
tourney *noun* TILT.
tousle *also* **touzle** *verb*
To put (the hair or clothes) into a state of disarray: *The wind tousled the child's curls.*

Syns: disarrange, dishevel, disorder, mess (up), muss (up), rumple.

tout *verb* PROMOTE.

tow *verb* PULL.

toward *adjective* BENEFICIAL.

tower above *verb* DOMINATE.

towering *adjective*
1. Awesomely or forbiddingly intense: *in a towering fury.*
   Syns: overpowering, overwhelming, staggering.
2. LOFTY.
3. OUTSTANDING.
4. STEEP¹.
5. TALL.

towheaded *adjective* FAIR.

toxic *adjective* POISONOUS.

toxicant *adjective* POISONOUS.

toxin *noun* POISON.

toy *noun*
1. An object for children to play with: *Toys and games are sold on the third floor.*
   Syn: plaything.
2. NOVELTY.

toy *verb*
1. COURT.
2. FIDDLE.
3, 4. FLIRT.

trace *noun*
1. A mark or remnant that indicates the former presence of something: *traces of an ancient civilization.*
   Syns: relic, remains, vestige.
2. A barely perceivable indication of something: *not a trace of scandal.*
   Syns: breath, dash, hint, shade, soupçon (*French*), suggestion, taste, touch, whiff.
3. SHADE.
4. TRACK.

trace *verb*
1. RUN DOWN at **run**.
2. TRACK.

track *noun*
1. A visible sign or mark of the passage of someone or something: *tire tracks in the mud.*
   Syns: print, trace, tread.
2. ROUTINE.
3. TRAIL.

track *verb*
1. To follow the traces or scent of, as in hunting: *tracked the bear for miles before treeing it.*
   Syns: trace, trail.
2. FOLLOW.
3. TRAVERSE.

track down *verb* RUN DOWN at **run**.

tract *noun*
1. AREA.
2. LOT.

tractable *adjective* OBEDIENT.

traction *noun* PULL.

trade *noun*
1, 2. BUSINESS.
3. CHANGE.
4. PATRONAGE.

trade *verb* CHANGE.

trade in *verb* SELL.

trademark *noun* MARK.

trader *noun* DEALER.

tradesman *noun* DEALER.

trading *noun* BUSINESS.

tradition *noun*
1. HERITAGE.
2. LORE.

traditional *adjective* CONVENTIONAL.

traditionalist *also* **traditionalistic** *adjective* CONSERVATIVE.

traffic *noun*
1. BUSINESS.
2. PATRONAGE.

trafficker *noun* DEALER.

tragedy *noun* DISASTER.

trail *verb*
1. To hang or cause to hang down and be pulled along behind: *The dog raced away, its leash trailing.*
   Syns: drag, draggle, train.
2. DELAY.
3. DOG.
4, 5. FOLLOW.
6. TRACK.

trail *noun*
1. Evidence of passage left along a course followed by a hunted animal or fugitive: *He crossed a stream to throw the pursuers off his trail.*
   Syns: scent, spoor, track.
2. TRAIN.

train *noun*
1. Something that follows or is drawn along behind: *a wedding gown with a long train.*
   Syns: tail, trail.
2. RETINUE.
3. RUN.
4. SERIES.

train *verb*
1. AIM.
2. EDUCATE.
3. TRAIL.

training *noun*
1. EDUCATION.
2. PRACTICE.

traipse *verb* ROVE.

trait *noun* QUALITY.

traitor *noun* BETRAYER.
traitorous *adjective*
1. FAITHLESS.
2. TREASONOUS.
traitorousness *noun* TREASON.
trammel *noun* RESTRICTION.
 trammel *verb*
 1. CATCH.
 2. HAMPER.
tramp *verb*
1. To walk with loud, heavy steps: *I was awakened by a neighbor tramping up the stairs.*
 Syns: trample, tromp, stamp, stomp.
2. TRAMPLE.
 tramp *noun* SLUT.
trample *verb*
1. To step on heavily and repeatedly so as to crush, injure, or destroy: *Occasionally a bull will trample and gore a matador.*
 Syns: stamp, stomp, tramp, tread, tromp.
2. TRAMP.
 trample on *verb* TYRANNIZE.
trance *noun*
1. The condition of being so lost in solitary thought as to be unaware of one's surroundings: *sat gazing at the fire in a trance.*
 Syns: abstraction, muse, reverie, study.
2. DAZE.
tranquil *adjective* CALM.
tranquility *noun* SEE **tranquillity.**
tranquilize also **tranquillize** *verb* CALM.
tranquillity or **tranquility** *noun* CALM.
tranquillize *verb* SEE **tranquilize.**
transaction *noun* BARGAIN.
transcend *verb* SURPASS.
transcendent *adjective*
1. OUTSTANDING.
2. THEORETICAL.
3. ULTIMATE.
transcendental *adjective*
1. SUPERNATURAL.
2. THEORETICAL.
transfer *verb*
1. To change the ownership of (property) by means of a legal document: *persuaded large landholders to transfer their unused acres to the national forest system.*
 Syns: alien, alienate (*Law*), assign (*Law*), cede, convey (*Law*), deed, grant, make over, sign over.
2. CONVERT.

3. GIVE.
4, 5. MOVE.
6. REFER.
 transfer *noun*
 1. DELIVERY.
 2. GRANT.
transfiguration *noun* CHANGE.
transfigure *verb* CONVERT.
transfix *verb* GRIP.
transform *verb*
1. CONVERT.
2. REVOLUTIONIZE.
transformation *noun*
1. CHANGE.
2. CONVERSION.
transfuse *verb* CHARGE.
transgress *verb*
1. OFFEND.
2. VIOLATE.
transgression *noun*
1. BREACH.
2. CRIME.
transient *adjective* TRANSITORY.
transit *noun*
1. TRANSITION.
2. TRANSPORTATION.
 transit *verb* CROSS.
transition *noun*
The process or an instance of passing from one form, state, or stage to another: *transition from an agricultural to an industrial economy.*
 Syns: changeover, passage, shift, transit.
transitory *adjective*
Lasting or existing only for a short time: *the transitory Arctic summer.*
 Syns: ephemeral, evanescent, fleeting, fugacious, fugitive, momentary, passing, short-lived, temporal, temporary, transient.
translate *verb*
1. To express in another language, while systematically retaining the original sense: *translated the Italian into English with the help of a dictionary.*
 Syns: construe, put, render.
2. CONVERT.
3. PARAPHRASE.
translation *noun*
1. CHANGE.
2. PARAPHRASE.
translucent *adjective* TRANSPARENT.
transmigrant *noun* EMIGRANT.
transmigrate *verb*
1. EMIGRATE.
2. MIGRATE.
transmigration *noun* EMIGRATION.
transmigratory *adjective*
MIGRATORY.

transmit *verb*
1, 2. COMMUNICATE.
3. CONDUCT.
4. HAND DOWN at **hand**.
5. PASS.
6. SEND.

transmogrify *verb* CONVERT.

transmutation *noun* CHANGE.

transmute *verb* CONVERT.

transparent *adjective*
1. Admitting light so that objects beyond can be seen: *transparent glass*.
   Syns: clear, crystal-clear, crystalline, limpid, see-through, translucent.
2. CLEAR.
3. FILMY.

transpire *verb*
1. COME.
2. COME OUT at **come**.
3. OOZE.

transport *verb*
1. BANISH.
2. CARRY.
3. CARRY AWAY at **carry**.
transport *noun*
1. HEAVEN.
2. TRANSPORTATION.

transportable *adjective* MOBILE.

transportation *noun*
The moving of persons or goods from one place to another: *A central mountain range hampers transportation between the east and west coasts*.
   Syns: carriage, conveyance, transit, transport.

transposal *noun* SEE **transposition**.

transpose *verb*
1. CONVERT.
2. REVERSE.

transposition also **transposal** *noun*
1. CHANGE.
2. REVERSAL.

transubstantiate *verb* CONVERT.

transude *verb* OOZE.

transversal *adjective* TRANSVERSE.

transverse *adjective*
Situated or lying across: *transverse beams visible above the room*.
   Syns: crossing, crosswise, thwart, transversal, traverse.
transverse *verb* CROSS.

trap *noun*
1. LURE.
2. MOUTH.
3. PITFALL.
4. POLICEMAN.
trap *verb* CATCH.

trash¹ *noun*
1. A group of persons regarded as the lowest class: *racism promulgated by trash*.
   Syns: dregs, hoi polloi, rabble, ragtag (*also* ragtag and bobtail), riffraff, scum. —*Idioms* dregs of society, lumpen proletariat, other half, scum of the earth, tag and rag, the great unwashed.
2. NONSENSE.
trash *verb*
Slang. To injure or destroy (property) maliciously: *A gang of youths trashed the store*.
   Syns: vandalize, wreck.

trash² *verb* PLOD.

trashy *adjective* SHODDY.

trauma *noun*
1. *Path.* Marked tissue damage, esp. when produced by physical injury: *trauma in the lower lumbar region*.
   Syns: traumatism, wound.
2. SHOCK.

traumatic *adjective*
Causing trauma: *a traumatic injury sustained in the collision*.
   Syn: traumatizing.

traumatism *noun* TRAUMA.

traumatize *verb*
To inflict physical or mental injury or distress on: *victims traumatized by the plane crash*.
   Syns: shock, wound.

traumatizing *adjective* TRAUMATIC.

travail *noun*
1. BIRTH.
2. LABOR.
travail *verb* LABOR.

travel *verb*
1. GET ABOUT at **get**.
2. GO.
3. JOURNEY.

traveling *adjective* MOBILE.

traversal *noun* DENIAL.

traverse *verb*
1. To descend, as a ski slope, by crossing and recrossing laterally: *traversed the hill and then began to parallel*.
   Syn: zigzag.
2. To journey over (a specified distance): *traversed 400 miles a day*.
   Syns: cover, do, make, pass, track.
3. To move, as a gun, laterally: *The gunner traversed the tank's cannon and raked the farmhouse with withering fire*.
   Syns: pivot, swivel.
4. CONTEST.
5. CROSS.

6. DENY.

7. EXAMINE.

traverse *adjective* TRANSVERSE.

traverse *noun* BAR.

travesty *noun* MOCKERY.

travesty *verb* IMITATE.

treacherous *adjective*

1. DANGEROUS.

2. DOUBLE.

3. FAITHLESS.

treacherousness *noun* TREACHERY.

treachery *noun*

1. Willful betrayal of fidelity, confidence, or trust: *The treachery of a double agent compromised the lives of the resistance fighters.*
   Syns: perfidiousness, perfidy, treacherousness, treason (*Rare*).
   —*Idioms* dirty work at the crossroads, Judas kiss, knife in the back.

2. BETRAYAL.

tread *noun*

1. The act or manner of going on foot: *heard his heavy tread on the stairs.*
   Syns: footfall, footstep, step.

2. TRACK.

tread *verb*

1. TRAMPLE.

2. WALK.

treadmill *noun* GRIND.

treason *noun*

1. Willful violation of allegiance to one's country: *was hanged for treason.*
   Syns: sedition, seditiousness, traitorousness.

2. TREACHERY.

treasonable *adjective* TREASONOUS.

treasonous *adjective*

Involving or constituting treason: *aiding and abetting the enemy and other treasonous activities.*
   Syns: Iscariotic *or* Iscariotical, seditious, traitorous, treasonable.

treasure *noun*

1. Someone or something considered exceptionally precious: *That editor is a real treasure.*
   Syns: diamond, gem, pearl, prize.

2. HOARD.

3. RICHES.

treasure *verb*

1. APPRECIATE.

2. CHERISH.

3. HOARD.

treasure-house *noun* TREASURY.

treasury *noun*

A place where one keeps one's valuables: *the king's treasury deep in the bowels of the fortress.*
   Syn: treasure-house.

treat *verb*

1. To pay for the food, drink, or entertainment of (another): *He treated me to dinner and a concert.*
   Syns: blow[1] (*Slang*), set up (*Informal*), shout (*Austral.*), stand (*Informal*). —*Idioms* go (*or* stand) treat, pick up the tab for.

2. To give medical aid to: *was treated by a cardiologist.*
   Syn: doctor.

3. DEAL.

4. DEAL WITH at **deal.**

treat *noun* DELICACY.

treatise *noun* DISCOURSE.

treatment *noun*

The systematic application of remedies to effect a cure: *treatment prescribed by a physician; dietary treatment for obesity.*
   Syns: care, regimen, therapy.

treaty *noun*

A formal, usu. written settlement between nations: *an arms-limitation treaty.*
   Syns: accord, agreement, concord, convention, pact.

treble *adjective* HIGH.

trek *verb* JOURNEY.

tremble *verb*

1, 2. SHAKE.

trembler *noun* SEE **tremblor.**

tremble(s) *noun* JITTERS.

trembling *adjective* TREMULOUS.

tremblor *or* **trembler** *noun* TREMOR.

tremendous *adjective*

1. FEARFUL.

2. GIANT.

3. MARVELOUS.

tremendousness *noun*
ENORMOUSNESS.

tremor *noun*

1. A shaking of the earth: *a tremor measuring eight points on the Richter scale.*
   Syns: earthquake, quake, shake, temblor (*Regional*), tremblor *or* trembler.

2. A nervous shaking of the body: *A tremor ran through his body as he watched the massacre from a hiding place.*
   Syns: quaver, quiver, shiver, shudder, thrill, tic, twitch.

tremor *verb* SHAKE.

tremulous *also* **tremulant, tremulent** *adjective*

Marked by or affected with tremors: *the*

tremulous hands of a patient with Parkinson's disease.
Syns: aquake, aquiver, ashake, ashiver, quaking, quaky, quivering, quivery, shaking, shaky, shivering, shivery, trembling.

trenchant *adjective* INCISIVE.

trend *noun* FASHION.

trend *verb* TEND[1].

trendy *adjective* FASHIONABLE.

trepidation *noun* FEAR.

trespass *verb*
1. BREAK IN at **break**.
2. OFFEND.

trespass *noun*
1. BREACH.
2. CRIME.

triable *adjective* LITIGABLE.

trial *noun*
1. *Law.* The examination and deciding upon evidence, charges, and claims in court: *testified at the trial.*
   Syn: hearing (*Law*).
2. A state of pain or anguish that tests one's resiliency and character: *The death of her parents was a great trial for her.*
   Syns: crucible, ordeal, tribulation, visitation. —*Idioms* crown of thorns, fiery ordeal, time of trial, trial by fire, trial and tribulation.
3. ATTEMPT.
4. BURDEN.
5. EFFORT.
6, 7. TEST.
8. THORN.

trial *adjective* PILOT.

tribe *noun* FAMILY.

tribulation *noun* TRIAL.

tribunal *noun* COURT.

tribute *noun*
1. COMPLIMENT.
2. TESTIMONIAL.

trice *noun* FLASH.

trick *noun*
1. An indirect, usu. cunning means of gaining an end: *used every trick in the bag to win the election.*
   Syns: artifice, device, feint, gimmick (*Slang*), jig (*Slang*), maneuver, play, ploy, ruse, shenanigan (*Informal*), sleight, stratagem, wile.
2. A clever, dexterous act: *magicians' tricks.*
   Syns: feat, stunt.
3. DECEPTION.
4. HANG.
5. PRANK.
6. TURN.

trick *adjective*
So weak or defective as to be liable to fail: *a trick lock; a trick knee.*
   Syns: tricky, undependable, unreliable.

trick *verb* DECEIVE.

trick out *verb* DRESS UP at **dress**.

trick up *verb* DRESS UP at **dress**.

trickery *noun* INDIRECTION.

trickiness *noun* INDIRECTION.

trickle *verb* DRIP.

trickle *noun* DRIP.

trickster *noun* CHEAT.

tricky *adjective*
1. ARTFUL.
2. DELICATE.
3. TIGHT.
4. TRICK.

trifle *noun* NOVELTY.

trifle *verb*
1. FIDDLE.
2, 3. FLIRT.
4. IDLE.

trifle away *verb* WASTE.

trifles *noun* TRIVIA.

trifling *adjective*
1. LAZY.
2. PETTY.

trig *adjective*
1. FASHIONABLE.
2. FULL.
3. NEAT.

trig *verb* TIDY.

trigger *noun* STIMULUS.

trigger *verb* TRIP.

triggerman *noun* MURDERER.

trillion *noun* HEAP.

trim *verb*
1. ADORN.
2. BEAT.
3. CHEAT.
4. CUT BACK at **cut**.
5. DEFEAT.
6. SHADE.
7. TIDY.

trim down *verb* REDUCE.

trim *adjective*
1. NEAT.
2. SLEEK.

trim *noun*
1. A state of sound readiness: *got into trim for the race.*
   Syns: condition, fettle, fitness, form, kilter, order, shape (*Informal*).
2. ADORNMENT.

trimming *noun*
1. ADORNMENT.
2. DEFEAT.

trine *noun* TRIO.

trinity also **trinuity** *noun* TRIO.

trinket *noun* NOVELTY.

trio *noun*
A group of three individuals: *a trio of generals conspiring to overthrow the government; a trio of musicians.*
   Syns: threesome, trine, trinity (*also* trinuity), triple, triumvirate, triune, troika.

trip *verb*
1. To put (a mechanical device or process) in motion by releasing an activating mechanism: *trip a light switch.*
   Syns: throw, trigger.
2. ERR.
3. JOURNEY.
4. SKIP.
5. STUMBLE.

trip *noun*
1. A setting out or venturing forth: *a trip to the French Quarter.*
   Syns: excursion, jaunt, junket, outing.
2. BLUNDER.
3. ERROR.
4. HALLUCINATION.
5. KICK.

triple *noun* TRIO.

tripper *noun* TOURIST.

tristful *adjective*
1. DEPRESSED.
2. PENSIVE.

trite *adjective*
Without freshness or appeal due to overuse: *Trite expressions spoiled the writing.*
   Syns: banal, bathetic, bromidic, cliché, commonplace, corny (*Slang*), hackneyed, musty, platitudinous, shopworn, stale, stereotyped, stereotypic (*also* stereotypical), threadbare, timeworn, tired, warmed-over, well-worn, worn-out.

triturate *verb* CRUSH.

triumph *verb*
1. To get the better of: *triumphed over all obstacles.*
   Syns: best, conquer, master, overcome, prevail (*over or against*), surmount, worst.
2. DEFEAT.
3. EXULT.

triumph *noun*
1. CONQUEST.
2. EXULTATION.

triumphal *adjective* VICTORIOUS.

triumphant *adjective*
1. EXULTANT.
2. VICTORIOUS.

triumvirate *noun* TRIO.

triune *noun* TRIO.

trinuity *noun* SEE **trinity**.

trivia *noun*
1. Unimportant matters or concerns: *the trivia of daily living.*
   Syns: minutiae, trifles, triviality.
   —*Idioms* small change, small potatoes.
2. FROTH.

trivial *adjective*
1. LITTLE.
2. PETTY.

triviality *noun*
1. FROTH.
2. PETTINESS.
3. TRIVIA.

trivialness *noun* PETTINESS.

troika *noun* TRIO.

tromp *verb*
1. TRAMP.
2. TRAMPLE.

troop *verb*
1. ASSOCIATE.
2. POUR.

troop *noun*
1. ASSEMBLY.
2. BAND².

trophy *noun*
1. A memento received as a symbol of excellence or victory: *The Oscar is a much-sought-after trophy.*
   Syns: award, prize.
2. REMEMBRANCE.

tropic *adjective* TROPICAL.

tropical *adjective*
Of or relating to the tropics: *a tropical climate in South America.*
   Syn: tropic.

trot *noun*
1. A person's steady, easy gait that is faster than a walk but slower than a run: *The child came across the yard at a trot.*
   Syns: jog, lope.
2. WITCH.

trot *verb*
1. To move with a steady, easy gait faster than a walk but slower than a run: *The football players trotted around the field to warm up.*
   Syns: jog, lope.
2. RUSH.

troth *noun* ENGAGEMENT.

trouble *noun*
1. A condition or situation characterized by danger, distress, or annoyance: *Walking alone at night in the city is just asking for trouble. He didn't watch what he said and got in trouble.*

Syns: difficulty, Dutch (*Informal*),
hot water (*Slang*).
2. CARE.
3. DISTRESS.
4. EFFORT.
5. INCONVENIENCE.
trouble *verb*
1. HAUNT.
2. INCONVENIENCE.
3. WORRY.
troubled *adjective* ANXIOUS.
troublesome *adjective*
1. Hard to treat, manage, or cope with:
*a troublesome hitter who usually gets
on base.*
Syns: mean² (*Slang*), pesky,
vexatious, wicked (*Slang*).
2. DISTURBING.
3. INCONVENIENT.
4. VEXATIOUS.
trounce *verb*
1. DEFEAT.
2. OVERWHELM.
trouncing *noun*
A severe defeat: *The voters gave the
incumbent a trouncing.*
Syns: drubbing (*Slang*), dusting,
lambasting (*Slang*), licking (*Slang*),
shellacking (*Slang*), thrashing.
troupe *noun* BAND².
truancy *noun* CUT.
truce *noun*
A temporary cessation of hostilities by
mutual consent of the contending
parties: *called for a truce so the wounded
could be removed from the area.*
Syns: armistice, cease-fire. —*Idiom*
cooling-off period.
truckle *verb* FAWN.
truckler *noun* SYCOPHANT.
truculence also **truculency** *noun*
1. BELLIGERENCE.
2. CRUELTY.
truculent *adjective*
1. BELLIGERENT.
2. BITING.
3. FIERCE.
trudge *verb* PLOD.
true *adjective*
1. Being so legitimately: *the true heir to
the throne; the true victor of the
contest.*
Syns: legitimate, rightful.
2. ACCURATE.
3. ACTUAL.
4, 5. AUTHENTIC.
6. FAITHFUL.
7. GENUINE.
8. HONEST.

truelove *noun* DARLING.
true-to-life *adjective* REALISTIC.
truism *noun* CLICHÉ.
trump *noun*
Something, esp. something held in
reserve, that gives one a decisive
advantage: *The attorney decided to use
his trump and call the witness' bluff.*
Syns: ace², clincher (*Informal*).
—*Idioms* ace in the hole, trump card.
trump *verb*
To outmaneuver (an opponent), esp.
with the aid of some extra resource: *The
incumbent President trumped the other
candidate by sending federal aid to the
cities on the eve of the election.*
Syns: finesse, one-up (*Slang*).
truncate *verb*
To make short or shorter by or as if by
cutting: *a speech that was truncated to fit
into the allotted time.*
Syns: abbreviate, abridge, brief, crop,
lop¹, shorten.
trust *noun*
1. CARE.
2. COMBINE.
3. CONFIDENCE.
trust *verb*
1. BELIEVE.
2. DEPEND ON at **depend.**
3. ENTRUST.
trustless *adjective* UNDEPENDABLE.
trustworthy *adjective*
1. AUTHENTIC.
2. DEPENDABLE.
trusty *adjective* DEPENDABLE.
truth *noun*
1. Freedom from deceit or falseness: *a
claim having the ring of truth.*
Syns: truthfulness, veracity, verity.
2. VERACITY.
truthful *adjective*
1. Consistently telling the truth: *so
truthful that she had our absolute
confidence.*
Syns: veracious, veridical.
2. REALISTIC.
truthfulness *noun*
1. AUTHENTICITY.
2. TRUTH.
truthless *adjective* FALSE.
truthlessness *noun* MENDACITY.
try *noun*
1. A brief trial: *I'll give the task a try*
Syns: crack (*Slang*), fling (*Informal*)
go (*Informal*), shot, stab, whack
(*Informal*), whirl (*Informal*).
2. ATTEMPT.
try *verb*
1. ATTEMPT.

2. TEST.

try out *verb*
1, 2. TEST.

trying *adjective* BURDENSOME.

try-out *noun* TEST.

tryst *noun* ENGAGEMENT.

tubby *adjective* PLUMP[1].

tubercular *adjective*
Pertaining to or afflicted with
tuberculosis: *tubercular therapy;
tubercular patients.*
   Syns: consumptive (*Path.*), phthisic
(*also* phthisical) (*Path.*), tuberculous.

tuberculosis *noun*
A contagious disease producing lesions
esp. of the lungs: *pains and a cough that
suggested tuberculosis.*
   Syns: consumption, phthisis (*also*
phthisic) (*Path.*), TB (*also* T.B.),
white plague.

tuberculous *adjective* TUBERCULAR.

tucker *verb* EXHAUST.

tuckered *adjective* EXHAUSTED.

tug *verb*
1. JERK.
2. LABOR.
3. PULL.

tug *noun* JERK.

tuition *noun* EDUCATION.

tumble *verb*
1. COME ACROSS at **come.**
2. DISORDER.
3, 4. FALL.
5. OVERTHROW.

tumble *noun*
1. DISORDER.
2, 3. FALL.
4. HEAP.

tumble-down *adjective* RUINOUS.

tumescent *adjective* INFLATED.

tumid *adjective* INFLATED.

tumult *noun*
1. AGITATION.
2. BRAWL.
3. DISTURBANCE.
4. NOISE.

tumultuous *adjective*
1. ROUGH.
2. TURBULENT.

tune *noun*
1. AGREEMENT.
2. HARMONY.
3. MELODY.

tune *verb*
1, 2. ADJUST.
3. HARMONIZE.
4. SING.

tuneful *adjective*
1, 2. MELODIOUS.

turbid *adjective*
1. Having sediment or foreign particles
stirred up or suspended: *turbid water.*
   Syns: muddy, roiled, roily.
2. Heavy, dark, or dense, esp. with
impurities: *atmosphere made turbid by
smoke from factories.*
   Syns: hazy, murky (*also* mirky).
3. ROUGH.

turbulence *noun*
1. AGITATION.
2. DISTURBANCE.

turbulent *adjective*
1. Marked by unrest or disturbance: *the
turbulent times just before and after
the revolution; a turbulent love affair.*
   Syns: stormy, tempestuous,
tumultuous.
2. ROUGH.

turf *noun* TERRITORY.

turgid *adjective* INFLATED.

turkey *noun* FOOL.

turmoil *noun*
1. AGITATION.
2. DISORDER.
3. UNREST.

turn *verb*
1. To move or cause to move in circles
or around an axis or center: *a
weather vane turning in the breeze.*
   Syns: circle, gyrate, revolve, rotate,
wheel.
2. To spade or dig (soil) to bring the
undersoil to the surface: *turn the
earth before planting.*
   Syns: break, plow, turn over.
3. To injure (a bodily part) by
twisting: *turn an ankle.*
   Syns: sprain, wrench.
4. To change the direction or course
of: *turn the bicycle into the driveway.*
   Syns: avert, deflect, divert, pivot,
sheer[1], shift, swing, veer.
5. AIM.
6. APPLY.
7. BECOME.
8. BEND.
9. CHANGE.
10. DULL.
11. DECAY.
12. DEFECT.
13. RESORT TO at **resort.**
14. REVERSE.
15. UPSET.

turn aside *verb* PREVENT.

turn down *verb*
1. DECLINE.
2. REFUSE.
3. VETO.

turn in *verb*
1. RETIRE.
2. SUBMIT.
turn off *verb*
1. HANG.
2. OFFEND.
turn on *verb* INTEREST.
turn on (or **upon**) *verb* DEPEND ON at
depend.
turn out *verb*
1. FURNISH.
2. GET UP at **get**.
turn over *verb*
1. ENTRUST.
2. GIVE.
3. PONDER.
4. TURN.
5. OVERTURN.
turn up *verb*
1. ARRIVE.
2. UNCOVER.
turn *noun*
1. An often sudden change or
departure, as in a trend: *a new turn of
events since yesterday.*
Syns: shift, tack, twist.
2. A limited, often assigned period of
activity, duty, or opportunity: *I took
a turn at the wheel while Frank rested.
We took turns washing the dishes.*
Syns: bout, go, hitch, innings, shift,
spell³, stint, time, tour, trick, watch.
3. BEND.
4. BENT.
5. CIRCLE.
6. CONSTITUTIONAL.
7. MOVEMENT.
8. REVOLUTION.
9. TALENT.
turncoat *noun* DEFECTOR.
turn-down *noun* REFUSAL.
turned-on *adjective*
1. DRUGGED.
2. ELATED.
3. THRILLED.
turnkey *noun* JAILER.
turnout *noun*
1. DRESS.
2. OUTFIT.
turpitude *noun* CORRUPTION.
tussle *noun* FIGHT.
tussle *verb* WRESTLE.
tutelage *noun* EDUCATION.
tutor *verb* EDUCATE.
tutoring *noun* EDUCATION.
twaddle *noun*
1. BABBLE.
2. NONSENSE.
twang *noun* FLAVOR.

twelvemonth *noun* YEAR.
twerp also **twirp** *noun* SQUIRT.
twiddle *verb* FIDDLE.
twiggy *adjective* THIN.
twilight *noun* EVENING.
twin *adjective*
Consisting of two identical or similar
related things, parts, or elements: *the
twin evils of drink and lust.*
Syns: double, dual, paired.
twin *noun* MATE.
twine *verb* WIND².
twinge *noun* PAIN.
twinkle *verb*
1, 2. BLINK.
3. FLASH.
twinkle *noun*
1. BLINK.
2. FLASH.
twinkling *noun* FLASH.
twirl *verb* SPIN.
twirp *noun* SEE **twerp**.
twist *verb*
1. DEFORM.
2. DISTORT.
3. WIND².
twist *noun*
1. TURN.
2. WRINKLE².
twisting *adjective*
1. CROOKED.
2. WINDING.
twit *verb* RIDICULE.
twitch *verb* JERK.
twitch *noun*
1. JERK.
2. TREMOR.
twitchy *adjective* EDGY.
twitter *verb* SHAKE.
twitting *noun* RIDICULE.
two bits *noun* PEANUTS.
two-faced *adjective*
1. DOUBLE.
2. HYPOCRITICAL.
two-facedness *noun* HYPOCRISY.
two-fisted *adjective* HEAVY.
twofold *adjective*
1, 2. DOUBLE.
twosome *noun* PAIR.
type *noun* KIND².
typical also **typic** *adjective*
1. Having the nature of, constituting, or
serving as a type: *a piece of jewelry
typical of Fabergé; typical weather for
this part of the country.*
Syns: archetypal, archetypic (*also*
archetypical), classic, classical,
model, paradigmatic, prototypal,

prototypic *or* prototypical,
quintessential, representative.
2. COMMON.
3. DISTINCTIVE.

typically *adverb* USUALLY.

typify *verb* REPRESENT.

tyrannical *also* **tyrannic** *adjective*
1. ABSOLUTE.
2. AUTHORITARIAN.

tyrannize *verb*
1. To exercise absolute power, esp.
arbitrarily or cruelly: *The occupying
army tyrannized the vanquished.*
Syn: trample on. —*Idiom* grind
someone's face in the dirt (*or* mud).
2. BOSS.

tyrannous *adjective* ABSOLUTE.

tyranny *noun*
Absolute power, esp. when exercised
unjustly or cruelly: *fascist tyranny.*
Syns: autocracy, despotism,
dictatorship, totalitarianism.

tyrant *noun*
1. AUTHORITARIAN.
2. DICTATOR.

tyro *noun*
1. AMATEUR.
2. BEGINNER.

U

ubiquitous *adjective* UNIVERSAL.

ugliness *noun*
1. The quality or condition of being
ugly: *the ugliness of ghetto squalor.*
Syns: frightfulness, hideousness,
unsightliness.
2. MESS.

ugly *adjective*
1. Extremely displeasing to the eye: *An
ugly scar disfigured his face.*
Syns: hideous, ill-favored, ill-looking,
unsightly. —*Idioms* enough to stop a
clock, ugly as sin.
2. ILL-TEMPERED.
3. OFFENSIVE.
4. ROUGH.

ugly *noun* MESS.

uh-huh *adverb* YES.

ulterior *adjective*
1. Lying beyond what is obvious or

avowed: *The President tried to discern
the Soviets' ulterior motives.*
Syns: buried, concealed, covert,
hidden, obscured, shrouded. —*Idiom*
under cover (*or* wraps).
2. FURTHER.

ultimate *adjective*
1. Of the greatest possible degree,
quality, or intensity: *His death was
the ultimate proof of his patriotism.*
Syns: supreme, surpassing,
transcendent, unsurpassable.
2. ELEMENTAL.
3. EXTREME.
4. LAST¹.
5. MAXIMUM.

ultimate *noun* MAXIMUM.

ultimate *verb* CLOSE¹.

ultimately *adverb* AT LAST at last¹.

ultra *adjective* EXTREME.

ultra *noun* EXTREMIST.

ultraconservative *adjective*
REACTIONARY.

ultraconservative *noun*
REACTIONARY.

ululate *verb* HOWL.

ululation *noun* HOWL.

umbra *noun*
1. GHOST.
2. SHADE.

umbrage *noun*
1. OFFENSE.
2. SHADE.

umbrageous *adjective* SHADY.

umbrous *adjective* SHADY.

ump *noun* JUDGE.

umpire *verb* JUDGE.

unabashed *adjective* SHAMELESS.

unable *verb* UNFIT.

unabridged *adjective* COMPLETE.

unacceptable *adjective*
OBJECTIONABLE.

unaccompanied *adjective* ALONE.

unaccountable *adjective*
1. INEXPLICABLE.
2. MYSTERIOUS.

unacquainted *adjective* IGNORANT.

unadorned *adjective*
1. BARE.
2. RUSTIC.

unadulterated *adjective*
1. NATURAL.
2. PURE.

unadvantageous *adjective*
UNFAVORABLE.

unaffected *adjective*
1. ARTLESS.
2. COLD.
3. GENUINE.

unafraid *adjective* BRAVE.
unalterable *adjective*
1. INFLEXIBLE.
2. IRREVOCABLE.
unambiguous *adjective*
1. DEFINITE.
2. SHARP.
unanimity *noun*
The quality or condition of being in complete mutual agreement: *The unanimity of their disapproval was disconcerting.*
   Syns: accord, consensus, unanimousness.
unanimous *adjective*
Being in or characterized by complete agreement: *unanimous in wanting to return home; a unanimous opinion of the court.*
   Syns: concurrent, solid. —*Idioms* as one, of one mind, with one voice.
unanimousness *noun* UNANIMITY.
unappeasable *adjective* VORACIOUS.
unappetizing *adjective* UNPALATABLE.
unappreciable *adjective*
IMPERCEPTIBLE.
unappreciated *adjective* THANKLESS.
unappreciative *adjective* THANKLESS.
unapproachable *adjective*
1. COOL.
2. INACCESSIBLE.
unapt *adjective*
1. IMPROPER.
2. INEFFICIENT.
unassuming *adjective* HUMBLE.
unattached *adjective* SINGLE.
unattainable *adjective*
1. IMPOSSIBLE.
2. INACCESSIBLE.
unattractive *adjective* PLAIN.
unavailing *adjective* FUTILE.
unavoidable *adjective* CERTAIN.
unawake *adjective* SLEEPING.
unaware *adjective* IGNORANT.
  unaware *adverb* UNAWARES.
unawares *adverb*
Without adequate preparation: *The sudden accusation caught her unawares.*
   Syns: aback, short, unaware. —*Idioms* by surprise, off base.
unbalance *verb* DERANGE.
  unbalance *noun* INSANITY.
unbalanced *adjective* INSANE.
unbearable *adjective*
Not capable of being endured or tolerated: *had to flee the unbearable heat.*
   Syns: impossible, insufferable, insupportable, intolerable,

unendurable, unsufferable, unsupportable.
unbecoming *adjective*
1, 2. IMPROPER.
3. TACKY[2].
unbefitting *adjective*
1, 2. IMPROPER.
unbelief *noun* DISBELIEF.
unbelievable *adjective*
1. FABULOUS.
2. IMPLAUSIBLE.
3. INCREDIBLE.
unbelieve *verb* DISBELIEVE.
unbeliever *noun* SKEPTIC.
unbelieving *adjective* INCREDULOUS.
unbend *verb* REST[1].
unbendable *adjective* STUBBORN.
unbending *adjective*
1. FIRM[1].
2. GRIM.
3. RIGID.
4. STUBBORN.
unbiased *adjective*
1. FAIR.
2. NEUTRAL.
unbind *verb* UNDO.
unblamable *adjective* EXEMPLARY.
unblemished *adjective*
1. CLEAR.
2. GOOD.
3. INNOCENT.
unblended or **unblent** *adjective*
STRAIGHT.
unblushing *adjective* SHAMELESS.
unbodied *adjective* IMMATERIAL.
unbounded *adjective*
1. ENDLESS.
2. UTTER[2].
unbridled *adjective* ABANDONED.
unbroken *adjective*
1. CLEAR.
2. GOOD.
unburden *verb* RID.
uncalled-for *adjective*
1. UNNECESSARY.
2. WANTON.
uncandor *noun* INSINCERITY.
uncanny *adjective* WEIRD.
uncaring *adjective* UNSYMPATHETIC.
unceasing *adjective* CONTINUAL.
unceremonious *adjective* INFORMAL.
unceremoniousness *noun*
INFORMALITY.
uncertain *adjective*
1, 2. AMBIGUOUS.
3. CAPRICIOUS.
4. CHANGEABLE.
5. DEBATABLE.
6. DOUBTFUL.

7. HESITANT.
8. INDEFINITE.
9. SHADY.

uncertainty *noun*
1. DOUBT.
2. VAGUENESS.

unchangeable *adjective* INFLEXIBLE.

unchanging *adjective*
1. CONSISTENT.
2. EVEN[1].

uncharitable *adjective*
UNSYMPATHETIC.

unchaste *adjective* IMPURE.

uncivil *adjective*
1. DISRESPECTFUL.
2. UNCIVILIZED.

uncivilized *adjective*
1. Not civilized: *an uncivilized people.*
   Syns: barbarian, barbaric, barbarous, primitive, rude, savage, uncivil, uncultivated, wild.
2. COARSE.

unclad *adjective* NUDE.

unclasp *verb* UNDO.

unclean *adjective*
1. DIRTY.
2, 3. IMPURE.

uncleanliness *noun* DIRTINESS.

uncleanly *adjective*
1. DIRTY.
2. IMPURE.

uncleanness *noun*
1. DIRTINESS.
2. IMPURITY.

unclear *adjective*
1. Not clearly perceived or perceptible: *an unclear view through the smog; an unclear recollection.*
   Syns: blear, bleary, cloudy, dim, faint, foggy, fuzzy, hazy, indefinite, indistinct, misty, obscure, shadowy, undistinct, vague, vaporous (*also* vapory).
2, 3. AMBIGUOUS.

unclearness *noun* VAGUENESS.

unclose *verb* OPEN.

unclothe *verb*
1. REVEAL.
2. STRIP[1].

unclothed *adjective* NUDE.

unclouded *adjective* CLEAR.

uncomely *adjective* PLAIN.

uncomfortable *adjective*
1. Causing discomfort: *a lumpy, uncomfortable mattress.*
   Syns: comfortless, uncomforting, uncomfy (*Informal*).
2. AWKWARD.

uncomforting *adjective*
UNCOMFORTABLE.

uncomfy *adjective* UNCOMFORTABLE.

uncommitted *adjective* NEUTRAL.

uncommon *adjective*
1. INFREQUENT.
2. RARE.

uncommunicative *adjective*
1. COOL.
2. TACITURN.

uncommunicativeness *noun*
RESERVE.

uncompassionate *adjective*
UNSYMPATHETIC.

uncompelled *adjective* VOLUNTARY.

uncompensated *adjective* UNPAID.

uncompliant *adjective*
1. DISOBEDIENT.
2. STUBBORN.

uncomplimentary *adjective*
DISPARAGING.

uncomprehending *adjective* BLIND.

uncomprehensible *adjective*
INCOMPREHENSIBLE.

uncompromising *adjective*
1. FIRM[1].
2. STRICT.
3. STUBBORN.

unconceivable *adjective*
IMPLAUSIBLE.

unconcern *noun* APATHY.

unconcerned *adjective*
1. APATHETIC.
2. CARELESS.
3. DETACHED.

unconditional *adjective*
1. Without limitations or mitigating conditions: *an unconditional surrender.*
   Syns: absolute, unconditioned, unqualified, unreserved.
2. IMPLICIT.

unconditioned *adjective*
UNCONDITIONAL.

unconfined *adjective* LOOSE.

uncongenial *adjective*
1. ANTIPATHETIC.
2. INHARMONIOUS.

unconquerable *adjective* INVINCIBLE.

unconscionable *adjective*
1. OUTRAGEOUS.
2. STEEP[1].
3. UNSCRUPULOUS.

unconscious *adjective*
1. Lacking consciousness: *knocked unconscious by the punch.*
   Syns: cold (*Informal*), insconscious, insensible, senseless. —*Idiom* out like a light.
2. IGNORANT.

unconsequential *adjective* PETTY.

unconsidered *adjective*
1. PETTY.
2. RANDOM.

unconspicuous *adjective*
INCONSPICUOUS.

unconstrained *adjective* ABANDONED.

uncontrollability *noun* UNRULINESS.

uncontrollable *adjective* UNRULY.

uncontrollableness *noun*
UNRULINESS.

uncontrolled *adjective*
1. ABANDONED.
2. RUNAWAY.

unconventional *adjective* UNUSUAL.

unconvincing *adjective* IMPLAUSIBLE.

uncooked *adjective* RAW.

uncorporal *adjective* IMMATERIAL.

uncorrupted *adjective* INNOCENT.

uncountable *adjective*
INCALCULABLE.

uncouple *verb* DETACH.

uncoupling *noun* DETACHMENT.

uncouth *adjective* COARSE.

uncover *verb*
1. To find by investigation: *a reporter who uncovered the true facts of the murder.*
   Syns: dig up (*or* out), turn up, unearth. —*Idiom* bring to light.
2. BARE.
3. BETRAY.
4. EXPOSE.
5. REVEAL.

uncovered *adjective* OPEN.

uncreative *adjective* STERILE.

uncritical *adjective* SUPERFICIAL.

unctious *adjective* UNCTUOUS.

unctuous *adjective*
1. Affectedly and self-servingly earnest: *The ambassador had an oozing, unctuous manner.*
   Syns: fulsome, oily, oleaginous, sleek, smarmy, unctious.
2. FATTY.

uncultivated *adjective*
1. COARSE.
2. UNCIVILIZED.
3. WILD.

uncut *adjective* COMPLETE.

undamaged *adjective* GOOD.

undaunted *adjective* BRAVE.

undecided *adjective*
1. AMBIGUOUS.
2. DOUBTFUL.
3. INDEFINITE.

undecisive *adjective* RESISTANT.

undeclared *adjective*
1. IMPLICIT.
2. SILENT.

undefiled *adjective* INNOCENT.

undemonstrated *adjective* UNTRIED.

undemonstrative *adjective* COOL.

undeniable *adjective*
1. ACTUAL.
2. CERTAIN.

undependable *adjective*
1. Not to be depended on: *an undependable bridge needing maintenance; undependable weather.*
   Syns: trustless, unreliable, untrustworthy.
2. TRICK.

under *adjective* MINOR.

underage[1] *noun* SHORTAGE.

underage[2] *adjective* MINOR.

undercover *adjective* SECRET.

underdeveloped *adjective*
BACKWARD.

underdog *noun* UNFORTUNATE.

undergo *verb* EXPERIENCE.

underearth *adjective* UNDERGROUND.

underground *adjective*
Located or operating beneath the earth's surface: *wells that tap underground pools of fresh water.*
   Syns: hypogeal (*also* hypogean, hypogeous), subterrane, subterranean, subterrene, subterrestrial, underearth.

underground *noun* RESISTANCE.

underhand *adjective*
Marked by treachery or deceit: *such underhand business practices as profiteering and false advertising.*
   Syns: devious, disingenuous, duplicitous, guileful, indirect, shifty, sneaking, sneaky, underhanded.

underhanded *adjective*
1. Lacking the requisite workers or players: *an underhanded typing pool.*
   Syns: shorthanded, undermanned.
2. UNDERHAND.

underhandedness *noun*
INDIRECTION.

underline *verb* EMPHASIZE.

underlined *adjective* EMPHATIC.

underling *noun* SUBORDINATE.

underlying *adjective*
1. ELEMENTAL.
2. RADICAL.

undermanned *adjective*
UNDERHANDED.

undermine *verb*
1. ENERVATE.
2. SABOTAGE.

undermining *noun* SABOTAGE.

undermost *adjective* BOTTOM.

underneath *noun* BOTTOM.

underpinning *noun*
1. BASE[1].
2. SUPPORT.

underprivileged *adjective* DEPRESSED.

underprivileged *noun* UNFORTUNATE.

underscore *verb* EMPHASIZE.

underscored *adjective* EMPHATIC.

underside *noun* BOTTOM.

undersign *verb* SIGN.

understand *verb*
1. To perceive and recognize the meaning of: *The teacher spoke slowly and simply so that all could understand him.*
   Syns: accept, apprehend, catch, catch on (*Informal*), compass, comprehend, conceive, dig (*Slang*), fathom, follow, get (*Informal*), grasp, ken (*Scot.*), make out, read, savvy (*Slang*), see, sense (*Informal*), take, take in, twig.
   —*Idiom* get the picture.
2. KNOW.

understandable *adjective*
Capable of being readily understood: *mumbled in a way that his audience found scarcely understandable.*
   Syns: comprehensible, fathomable, intelligible, knowable.

understanding *adjective*
Cognizant of and comprehending the needs, feelings, problems, and views of others: *an understanding counselor.*
   Syns: empathic (*also* empathetic), sympathetic.

understanding *noun*
1. AGREEMENT.
2. GRASP.
3. INTELLIGENCE.

understood *adjective* IMPLICIT.

undertake *verb*
1. ASSUME.
2. ATTEMPT.
3. PLEDGE.
4. START.

undertaking *noun*
1. ATTEMPT.
2. PROJECT.

undertone *noun* HINT.

underwriter *noun* SPONSOR.

undescribable *adjective* UNSPEAKABLE.

undesigned *adjective* UNINTENTIONAL.

undesirable *adjective*
1. OBJECTIONABLE.
2. UNWELCOME.

undesired *adjective* UNWELCOME.

undetected *adjective* UNFOUND.

undetermined *adjective*
1, 2. INDEFINITE.

undeveloped *adjective* BACKWARD.

undevised *adjective* UNINTENTIONAL.

undiluted *adjective*
1. PURE.
2. STRAIGHT.

undiplomatic *adjective* TACTLESS.

undisciplined *adjective* UNRULY.

undiscovered *adjective* UNFOUND.

undisguised *adjective* FRANK.

undisputable *adjective* CERTAIN.

undissembling *adjective* PLAIN.

undistinct *adjective* UNCLEAR.

undistinguishable *adjective* IMPERCEPTIBLE.

undistinguished *adjective* HUMBLE.

undivided *adjective* CONCENTRATED.

undo *verb*
1. To free from ties or fasteners: *She gently undid the bow and opened the package.*
   Syns: disengage, loose, loosen, slip, unbind, unclasp, unfasten, unloose, unloosen, untie.
2. CANCEL.
3. DESTROY.
4. ENERVATE.
5. OPEN.
6. SEDUCE.

undoing *noun*
1, 2. RUIN.

undomesticated *adjective* WILD.

undoubted *adjective* AUTHENTIC.

undoubting *adjective*
1. IMPLICIT.
2. SURE.

undress *noun* NUDITY.

undress *verb* STRIP[1].

undressed *adjective* NUDE.

undue *adjective* EXCESSIVE.

undulate *verb*
1. SLITHER.
2. WAVE.

unduly *adverb*
Too much: *unduly conceited.*
   Syns: over, overmuch, super (*Informal*).

undying *adjective* IMMORTAL.

unearth *verb* UNCOVER.

unearthly *adjective*
1. FOOLISH.
2. SUPERNATURAL.
3. WEIRD.

unease *noun* ANXIETY.

uneasiness *noun*
1. ANXIETY.
2. RESTLESSNESS.

uneasy *adjective*
1. ANXIOUS.
2. AWKWARD.

3. EDGY.
4. RESTLESS.
uneducated *adjective* IGNORANT.
unemotional *adjective*
1. COLD.
2. DRY.
unemployed *adjective*
1. IDLE.
2. WORKLESS.
unending *adjective*
1. CONTINUAL.
2. ENDLESS.
unendurable *adjective* UNBEARABLE.
unenlightened *adjective*
1, 2. IGNORANT.
unenthusiastic *adjective* TEPID.
unequal *adjective*
1. INADEQUATE.
2. UNFAIR.
unequaled *adjective* UNIQUE.
unequivocal *adjective*
1. DEFINITE.
2. SHARP.
3. UTTER².
unerring *adjective* SURE.
unessential *adjective* UNNECESSARY.
unethical *adjective*
1. CORRUPT.
2. UNSCRUPULOUS.
uneven *adjective*
1. Lacking consistency or regularity in quality or performance: *an uneven novel, at times flat and at times moving.*
   Syns: on-again-off-again, patchy, spotty, unsteady, variable.
2. IRREGULAR.
3. ROUGH.
unevenness *noun* IRREGULARITY.
unexampled *adjective* UNIQUE.
unexceptional *adjective* ORDINARY.
unexplainable *adjective*
1. INEXPLICABLE.
2. MYSTERIOUS.
unexposed *adjective* UNFOUND.
unexpressed *adjective*
1. IMPLICIT.
2. SILENT.
unexpressible *adjective* UNSPEAKABLE.
unexpurgated *adjective* COMPLETE.
unfailing *adjective*
1. CONSISTENT.
2. SURE.
unfair *adjective*
Not fair, right, or just: *unfair housing laws.*
   Syns: inequitable, injust (*Obs.*), unequal, unjust.

unfairness *noun* INJUSTICE.
unfaithful *adjective* FAITHLESS.
unfaithfulness *noun* FAITHLESSNESS.
unfamiliar *adjective*
1. IGNORANT.
2. NEW.
unfamiliarity *noun* IGNORANCE.
unfasten *verb* UNDO.
unfastened *adjective* CLEAR.
unfathomable *adjective*
1. INCOMPREHENSIBLE.
2. MYSTERIOUS.
unfavorable *adjective*
1. Tending to discourage, retard, or make more difficult: *weather unfavorable for hang-gliding; an unfavorable economic climate.*
   Syns: adverse, disadvantageous, negative, unadvantageous, unsatisfactory, untoward.
2. BAD.
unfeasible *adjective* IMPOSSIBLE.
unfeeling *adjective*
1. COLD-BLOODED.
2. DEAD.
unfeigned *adjective* GENUINE.
unfinished *adjective* ROUGH.
unfit *adjective*
1. Not suited to a given purpose: *a house unfit for human habitation; an aircraft unfit for flight.*
   Syns: ill-suited, inappropriate, inapt, unsuitable, unsuited.
2. INADEQUATE.
3. INCOMPETENT.
unfit *verb*
To make incapable, as of doing a job: *a heart condition unfitting him to be a pilot.*
   Syns: disable, disqualify, unable, unqualify.
unfitness *noun* IMPROPRIETY.
unfitting *adjective* IMPROPER.
unflagging *adjective* TIRELESS.
unflappable *adjective* COOL.
unflawed *adjective* PERFECT.
unflexible *adjective* RIGID.
unfold *verb*
1. DEVELOP.
2. SPREAD.
unfolding *noun* DEVELOPMENT.
unforbearing *adjective* INTOLERANT.
unforced *adjective* VOLUNTARY.
unforgivable *adjective* INEXCUSABLE.
unformed *adjective* SHAPELESS.
unfortunate *adjective*
1. Involving or undergoing chance misfortune: *an unfortunate turn of events; an unfortunate marriage.*

Syns: hapless, ill-fated, ill-starred, luckless, misfortunate, star-crossed, unhappy, unlucky, untoward.

2. Characterized by inappropriateness and gracelessness, esp. in expression: *an unfortunate, ill-timed remark.*
Syns: awkward, ill-chosen, inappropriate, inept, infelicitous, unhappy.

3. DEPLORABLE.

unfortunate *noun*
A person living under very unhappy circumstances: *social workers trying to help the world's unfortunates.*
Syns: loser, miserable, underdog, underprivileged, wretch. —*Idiom* poor devil.

unfound *adjective*
Not found: *hitherto unfound Egyptian tombs.*
Syns: undetected, undiscovered, unexposed.

unfounded *adjective* BASELESS.

unfoundedly *adverb*
Without basis or foundation in fact: *was unfoundedly charged with theft.*
Syns: groundlessly, unwarrantedly.

unfrequented *adjective* LONELY.

unfriendly *adjective* HOSTILE.

ungainly *adjective* AWKWARD.

ungovernable *adjective* UNRULY.

ungovernableness *noun*
UNRULINESS.

ungoverned *adjective* ABANDONED.

ungraceful *adjective* AWKWARD.

ungracious *adjective*
1. RUDE.
2. THOUGHTLESS.

ungraciousness *noun* UNWELCOME.

ungrateful *adjective*
1, 2. THANKLESS.

unguarded *adjective* INSECURE.

unhandy *adjective*
1. AWKWARD.
2. INCONVENIENT.

unhappiness *noun*
1. GLOOM.
2. MISERY.

unhappy *adjective*
1. DEPRESSED.
2, 3. UNFORTUNATE.

unharmed *adjective* SAFE.

unharmonious *adjective*
1, 2. INHARMONIOUS.

unhealthy *adjective*
1. CORRUPT.
2. MORBID.
3, 4. UNWHOLESOME.

unheard-of *adjective* OBSCURE.

unheeding *adjective* MINDLESS.

unhesitating *adjective* IMPLICIT.

unhinge *verb*
1. DERANGE.
2. UPSET.

unhorse *verb* OVERTHROW.

unhospitable *adjective* FORBIDDING.

unhurried *adjective* DELIBERATE.

unhurt *adjective*
1. GOOD.
2. SAFE.

unicity *noun* UNIQUENESS.

unification *noun*
1. A bringing together into a whole: *The USSR is a vast nation resulting from the unification of many autonomous republics.*
Syns: coalition, consolidation, union, unity.
2. COMBINATION.

unified *adjective* ALLIED.

uniform *adjective*
1. EVEN[1].
2. LIKE[2].

unify *verb*
1. HARMONIZE.
2. INTEGRATE.

unimaginable *adjective* INCREDIBLE.

unimaginative *adjective*
1. DULL.
2. STERILE.

unimpaired *adjective* GOOD.

unimpeded *adjective* CLEAR.

unimportance *noun* INDIFFERENCE.

unimportant *adjective* LITTLE.

unimpressionable *adjective*
INSENSITIVE.

uninformed *adjective* IGNORANT.

uninhibited *adjective* ABANDONED.

uninitiate *noun* AMATEUR.

uninjured *adjective*
1. GOOD.
2. SAFE.

uninspired *adjective*
1. DULL.
2. STERILE.

unintelligent *adjective* MINDLESS.

unintelligible *adjective*
1. AMBIGUOUS.
2. INCOMPREHENSIBLE.

unintended *adjective*
UNINTENTIONAL.

unintentional *adjective*
Not intended: *an unintentional delay; an unintentional gaffe.*
Syns: inadvertent, undesigned, undevised, unintended, unmeant, unplanned, unpremeditated, unthinking, unwitting.

uninterested *adjective*
1. APATHETIC.
2. DETACHED.
uninteresting *adjective* BORING.
uninterrupted *adjective* CONTINUAL.
uninvited *adjective* UNWELCOME.
uninviting *adjective* FORBIDDING.
uninvolved *adjective* NEUTRAL.
union *noun*
1. A group of people united in a relationship and having some interest, activity, or purpose in common: *a trade union; a union of draft resisters.*
   Syns: association, club, confederation, congress, federation, fellowship, fraternity, guild, league, order, organization, society.
2. ALLIANCE.
3. COMBINATION.
4. JOINT.
5. UNIFICATION.
6. UNITY.
unique *adjective*
1. Without equal or rival: *an artist unique in creativity.*
   Syns: alone, apart, incomparable, matchless, nonpareil, only, peerless, unequaled (*also* unequalled), unexampled, unmatched, unparalleled, unrivaled (*also* unrivalled).
2. LONE.
uniqueness *noun*
The quality or condition of being unique: *the uniqueness of the diamond.*
   Syns: oneness, singleness, unicity, uniquity.
uniquity *noun* UNIQUENESS.
unit *noun* FORCE.
unite *verb*
1. BAND².
2. COMBINE.
unity *noun*
1. The condition of being one: *argued the unity of God and nature.*
   Syns: oneness, singleness, singularity.
2. An identity or coincidence of interests, purposes, or sympathies among the members of a group: *believed that there was strength in unity.*
   Syns: oneness, solidarity, union.
3. HARMONY.
4. UNIFICATION.
universal *adjective*
1. So pervasive and all-inclusive as to exist in or affect the whole world: *a universal fear of nuclear war; universal truths.*
   Syns: catholic, cosmic, cosmopolitan, ecumenical, global, pandemic, planetary, worldwide.
2. Ever present in all places: *believed in a universal divine spirit guiding men.*
   Syns: omnipresent, ubiquitous.
3. GENERAL.
universal *noun* LAW.
universalize *verb*
To make universal: *rules governing the treatment of POW's universalized by the Geneva Convention.*
   Syn: generalize.
universe *noun*
1. The totality of all existing things: *studied the beginnings and the continuing development of the universe.*
   Syns: cosmos, creation, macrocosm, macrocosmos, megacosm, nature, world.
2. MANKIND.
unjust *adjective* UNFAIR.
unjustifiable *adjective* INEXCUSABLE.
unjustness *noun* INJUSTICE.
unkempt *adjective* MESSY.
unknowing *adjective* IGNORANT.
unlade *verb* UNLOAD.
unlawful *adjective*
1. Contrary to accepted, esp. moral conventions: *an unlawful love.*
   Syns: illicit, lawless, wrongful.
2. CRIMINAL.
3. ILLEGAL.
4. ILLEGITIMATE.
unlawfulness *noun* ILLEGALITY.
unlearned *adjective*
1. IGNORANT.
2. UNSCHOLARLY.
unlike *adjective* DIFFERENT.
unlikely *adjective* DOUBTFUL.
unlikeness *noun* DIFFERENCE.
unlimited *adjective*
1. ENDLESS.
2. UTTER².
unload *verb*
1. To remove the cargo or load from: *longshoremen unloading cargo from a freighter.*
   Syns: disburden, discharge, unlade.
2. To unburden oneself of by pouring out (one's troubles): *He unloaded all of his marital problems on me.*
   Syn: dump.
3. SELL OFF at sell.
unloose *verb* UNDO.
unloosen *verb* UNDO.
unlovely *adjective* PLAIN.
unluck *noun* MISFORTUNE.
unluckiness *noun* MISFORTUNE.

unlucky *adjective*
1. DISAPPOINTING.
2. FATEFUL.
3. UNFORTUNATE.

unmanageability *noun* UNRULINESS.

unmanageable *adjective*
1. AWKWARD.
2. UNRULY.

unmanliness *noun* COWARDICE.

unmanly *adjective*
1. COWARDLY.
2. EFFEMINATE.

unmannered *adjective* PLAIN.

unmannerly *adjective* RUDE.

unmarked *adjective* CLEAR.

unmarred *adjective* GOOD.

unmarried *adjective* SINGLE.

unmask *verb* REVEAL.

unmatched *adjective* UNIQUE.

unmeant *adjective* UNINTENTIONAL.

unmerciful *adjective* MERCILESS.

unmindful *adjective* MINDLESS.

unmistakable *adjective*
1. SHARP.
2. UNSUBTLE.

unmitigated *adjective* UTTER².

unmixed *adjective*
1. PURE.
2. STRAIGHT.

unmovable *adjective* FIXED.

unmoved *adjective* UNSYMPATHETIC.

unmoving *adjective* FIXED.

unmusical *adjective* INHARMONIOUS.

unnamed *adjective* ANONYMOUS.

unnatural *adjective*
1. ABNORMAL.
2. PRETERNATURAL.

unnecessary *adjective*
Not necessary: *unnecessary roughness in football; avoided making unnecessary trips in the car.*
    Syns: inessential, needless, nonessential, uncalled-for, unessential, unneeded, unrequired.

unneeded *adjective* UNNECESSARY.

unnegotiable *adjective*
IMPRACTICABLE.

unnerve *verb* ENERVATE.

unnoticeable *adjective*
1. IMPERCEPTIBLE.
2. INCONSPICUOUS.

unobjectionable *adjective*
ACCEPTABLE.

unobservable *adjective*
IMPERCEPTIBLE.

unobstructed *adjective* CLEAR.

unobtrusive *adjective*
1. INCONSPICUOUS.
2. QUIET.

unoccupied *adjective* UNRESERVED.

unoffensive *adjective* HARMLESS.

unordinary *adjective* UNUSUAL.

unoriginative *adjective* STERILE.

unostentatious *adjective* MODEST.

unostentatiousness *noun* MODESTY.

unpaid *adjective*
1. Contributing one's time without pay: *unpaid hospital volunteers.*
    Syns: uncompensated, unrecompensed, unremunerated, unsalaried.
2. DUE.

unpalatable *adjective*
1. So unpleasant in flavor as to be inedible: *sent the unpalatable meal back to the kitchen.*
    Syns: distasteful, unappetizing, unsavory.
2. BITTER.

unparalleled *adjective* UNIQUE.

unpardonable *adjective*
INEXCUSABLE.

unperceptive *adjective* BLIND.

unperfected *adjective* ROUGH.

unpitying *adjective* UNSYMPATHETIC.

unplanned *adjective*
1. RANDOM.
2. UNINTENTIONAL.

unpleasant *adjective*
Not pleasant or agreeable: *an unpleasant odor; in an unpleasant mood.*
    Syns: bad, disagreeable, displeasing, offensive.

unpleasantness *noun* ARGUMENT.

unpolished *adjective*
1. COARSE.
2. ROUGH.
3, 4. RUDE.
4. RUSTIC.

unpolitic *adjective* TACTLESS.

unpracticed *adjective*
1. INEXPERIENCED.
2. UNTRIED.

unprecedented *adjective* NEW.

unpredictable *adjective* CAPRICIOUS.

unprejudiced *adjective*
1. FAIR.
2. NEUTRAL.

unpremeditated *adjective*
1. SPONTANEOUS.
2. UNINTENTIONAL.

unpresuming *adjective* HUMBLE.

unpretentious *adjective*
1. HUMBLE.
2. INFORMAL.
3. MODEST.

unpretentiousness *noun* MODESTY.

unprincipled *adjective*
1. CORRUPT.
2. UNSCRUPULOUS.

unprocessed *adjective* CRUDE.

unproductive *adjective* BARREN.

unprogressive *adjective*
Clinging to obsolete ideas: *unprogressive views about minority rights.*
   Syns: backward, benighted, reactionary (*also* reactionist).

unprotected *adjective*
1. HELPLESS.
2. INSECURE.
3. OPEN.

unproved *adjective* UNTRIED.

unqualified *adjective*
1. INADEQUATE.
2. INCOMPETENT.
3. UNCONDITIONAL.
4. UTTER².

unqualify *verb* UNFIT.

unquestionable *adjective*
1. AUTHENTIC.
2. CERTAIN.
3. DECIDED.

unquestioning *adjective* IMPLICIT.

unravel *verb* RESOLVE.

unreachable *adjective* INACCESSIBLE.

unreal *adjective* IMAGINARY.

unrealistic *adjective* IDEALISTIC.

unrealizable *adjective* IMPOSSIBLE.

unreason *noun*
The absence of reason: *demands based purely on unreason, not rationality.*
   Syns: irrationality, unreasonableness.

unreasonable *adjective*
1. Not governed by or predicated on reason: *an unreasonable demand; an unreasonable expectation.*
   Syns: illogical, irrational, unreasoned.
2. OUTRAGEOUS.

unreasonableness *noun* UNREASON.

unreasoned *adjective* UNREASONABLE.

unreceptiveness *noun* UNWELCOME.

unrecompensed *adjective* UNPAID.

unrefined *adjective*
1. COARSE.
2. CRUDE.

unrehearsed *adjective*
EXTEMPORANEOUS.

unrelenting *adjective* GRIM.

unreliable *adjective*
1. TRICK.
2. UNDEPENDABLE.

unrelieved *adjective* UTTER².

unremitting *adjective*
1. CONTINUAL.
2. INSISTENT.

unremunerated *adjective* UNPAID.

unrepentant *adjective* REMORSELESS.

unrequired *adjective* UNNECESSARY.

unreserved *adjective*
1. Not spoken for or occupied: *unreserved seats; unreserved computer time.*
   Syns: free, open, unoccupied.
2. IMPLICIT.
3. OUTGOING.
4. PLAIN.
5. UNCONDITIONAL.
6. UTTER².

unresolved *adjective* INDEFINITE.

unresponsive *adjective*
1. APATHETIC.
2. DULL.
3. FRIGID.

unresponsiveness *noun* APATHY.

unrest *noun*
1. A state of uneasiness and usu. resentment brewing to an eventual explosion: *Stringent new laws fomented unrest throughout the country.*
   Syns: ferment, storm and stress, Sturm und Drang, turmoil.
2. RESTLESSNESS.

unrestrained *adjective*
1. ABANDONED.
2. LOOSE.

unrestraint *noun*
1. ABANDON.
2. EASE.

unrestricted *adjective* OPEN.

unrivaled *adjective* UNIQUE.

unroll *verb* PLAY OUT at **play.**

unromantic *adjective* REALISTIC.

unruffled *adjective*
1. CALM.
2. COOL.

unruliness *noun*
1. The quality or condition of being unruly: *the unruliness of classroom troublemakers.*
   Syns: fractiousness, obstreperousness, recalcitrance *or* recalcitrancy, refractoriness, uncontrollability, uncontrollableness, ungovernableness, unmanageability, wildness.
2. DEFIANCE.
3. DISOBEDIENCE.

unruly *adjective*
1. Not submitting to discipline or control: *an unruly student who was expelled; an unruly mob.*
   Syns: fractious, indocile, indomitable, obstreperous, recalcitrant, refractory, uncontrollable, undisciplined,

ungovernable, unmanageable,
untoward, wild.
2. DEFIANT.
3. DISOBEDIENT.
4. DISORDERLY.

unsafe *adjective*
1. DANGEROUS.
2. INSECURE.

unsaid *adjective*
1. IMPLICIT.
2. SILENT.

unsalaried *adjective* UNPAID.
unsalutary *adjective* UNWHOLESOME.
unsatisfactory *adjective*
1. BAD.
2. UNFAVORABLE.

unsavory *adjective* UNPALATABLE.
unscathed *adjective* SAFE.
unscholarly *adjective*
Lacking the requisite scholarship or
instruction: *an unscholarly approach to
the writing of history.*
Syns: unlearned, unstudious.

unschooled *adjective* IGNORANT.
unscrupulous *adjective*
1. Lacking scruples or principles: *an
unscrupulous courtier who stopped at
nothing to gain power.*
Syns: conscienceless, ruthless, stick-
at-nothing, unconscionable, unethical,
unprincipled.
2. CORRUPT.

unseasonable *adjective*
Not suitable for or characteristic of the
season: *unseasonable weather for
January.*
Syn: untimely.

unseasoned *adjective*
INEXPERIENCED.
unseeing *adjective* BLIND.
unseemliness *noun* IMPROPRIETY.
unseemly *adjective*
1, 2. IMPROPER.

unselfish *adjective*
1. GENEROUS.
2. SELFLESS.

unserviceable *adjective*
IMPRACTICABLE.
unsettle *verb*
1. AGITATE.
2. DISORDER.
3. UPSET.

unsettled *adjective*
1. AMBIGUOUS.
2. ANXIOUS.
3. CHANGEABLE.
4. DUE.
5. INDEFINITE.
6. RESTLESS.

unsettling *adjective* DISTURBING.
unsex *verb* STERILIZE.
unsexing *noun* STERILIZATION.
unshaped *adjective* SHAPELESS.
unsightly *adjective* UGLY.
unsigned *adjective* ANONYMOUS.
unsightliness *noun* UGLINESS.
unskilled *adjective*
1. AMATEURISH.
2. INEFFICIENT.

unskillful *adjective*
1. Clumsily lacking in the ability to do
or perform: *an unskillful attempt to
dance the hula.*
Syns: awkward, bumbling, clumsy,
gauche, heavy-handed, inept,
maladroit.
2. AMATEURISH.
3. INEFFICIENT.

unsleeping *adjective* WAKEFUL.
unsoiled *adjective* CLEAN.
unsophisticate *noun* INNOCENT.
unsophisticated *adjective* ARTLESS.
unsought *adjective* UNWELCOME.
unsound *adjective*
1. ERRONEOUS.
2. FALSE.
3. INFIRM.
4. INSANE.
5. UNWISE.

unsoundness *noun* INFIRMITY.
unsparing *adjective* GENEROUS.
unspeakable *adjective*
1. That cannot be described:
unspeakable happiness.
Syns: incommunicable, indefinable,
indescribable, ineffable, inenarrable,
inexpressible, undescribable,
unexpressible, unutterable. —*Idioms*
beyond description (*or* words),
defying description.
2. Too awful to be described:
unspeakable acts of genocide.
Syns: abominable, frightful,
nauseating, revolting, shocking,
sickening.

unspoken *adjective*
1. IMPLICIT.
2. SILENT.

unstability *noun*
1. INSTABILITY.
2. UNSTABLENESS.

unstable *adjective*
1. Not physically steady or firm: *an
unstable ladder.*
Syns: rickety, shaky, tottering,
unsteady, wobbly.
2. CAPRICIOUS.
3. CHANGEABLE.
4. INSECURE.

unstableness *noun*
1. The quality or condition of being physically unsteady: *The unstableness of the scaffolding frightened the painters.*
   Syns: instability, precariousness, shakiness, unstability, unsteadiness.
2. INSTABILITY.

unstained *adjective* INNOCENT.
unsteadiness *noun* UNSTABLENESS.
unsteady *adjective*
1. CAPRICIOUS.
2. CHANGEABLE.
3. INSECURE.
4. UNEVEN.
5. UNSTABLE.

unstinting *adjective* GENEROUS.
unstirred *adjective* UNSYMPATHETIC.
unstudied *adjective* ARTLESS.
unstudious *adjective* UNSCHOLARLY.
unsubstantial *adjective*
1. IMMATERIAL.
2. IMPLAUSIBLE.
3. INFIRM.
4. TENUOUS.

unsubtle *adjective*
Easily seen through due to a lack of subtlety: *The host gave the drunken guest a very unsubtle hint to leave.*
   Syns: broad, clear, obvious, patent, plain, unmistakable.

unsuccess *noun* FAILURE.
unsuccessful *adjective* FUTILE.
unsuccessfulness *noun* FAILURE.
unsufferable *adjective* UNBEARABLE.
unsuitability *noun* IMPROPRIETY.
unsuitable *adjective*
1. IMPROPER.
2. UNFIT.

unsuitableness *noun* IMPROPRIETY.
unsuited *adjective* UNFIT.
unsullied *adjective*
1. CLEAN.
2. INNOCENT.

unsupportable *adjective*
UNBEARABLE.
unsure *adjective*
1. AMBIGUOUS.
2. DOUBTFUL.
3. INDEFINITE.
4. INSECURE.

unsurmountable *adjective*
INSUPERABLE.
unsurpassable *adjective* ULTIMATE.
unsurpassed *adjective* BEST.
unsusceptibility *noun* RESISTANCE.
unsusceptible *adjective* INSENSITIVE.
unswayable *adjective* STUBBORN.
unswerving *adjective* CONCENTRATED.

unsympathetic *adjective*
1. Not sympathetic: *The old miser was unsympathetic toward charitable causes.*
   Syns: uncaring, uncharitable, uncompassionate, unmoved, unpitying, unstirred, untouched.
2. ANTIPATHETIC.

unsystematic *adjective* DISORDERLY.
untactful *adjective* TACTLESS.
untainted *adjective* INNOCENT.
untamed *adjective* WILD.
untangle *verb* CLEAR.
untaught *adjective* IGNORANT.
untested *adjective* UNTRIED.
unthankful *adjective*
1, 2. THANKLESS.

unthanking *adjective* THANKLESS.
unthinkable *adjective*
1. IMPOSSIBLE.
2. INCREDIBLE.

unthinking *adjective*
1. THOUGHTLESS.
2. UNINTENTIONAL.

unthoughtful *adjective*
THOUGHTLESS.
unthoughtfulness *noun*
THOUGHTLESSNESS.
untidy *adjective*
1. CARELESS.
2. MESSY.

untie *verb* UNDO.
untighten *verb* EASE.
untimely *adjective*
1. EARLY.
2. INCONVENIENT.
3. UNSEASONABLE.

untiring *adjective* TIRELESS.
untouched *adjective* UNSYMPATHETIC.
untoward *adjective*
1. IMPROPER.
2. UNFAVORABLE.
3. UNFORTUNATE.
4. UNRULY.

untried *adjective*
1. Not tested or proved: *remedies as yet untried.*
   Syns: undemonstrated, unpracticed, unproved, untested.
2. INEXPERIENCED.

untroubled *adjective* STILL.
untrue *adjective*
1. ERRONEOUS.
2. FAITHLESS.

untrusting *adjective* DISTRUSTFUL.
untrustworthy *adjective*
UNDEPENDABLE.
untruth *noun*
1. FALLACY.
2. LIE².

untruthful *adjective*
1. DISHONEST.
2. FALSE.
untruthfulness *noun* MENDACITY.
unusable *adjective*
1. IMPRACTICABLE.
2. USELESS.
unused *adjective* IDLE.
unusual *adjective*
1. Not usual or ordinary: *a necklace of unusual design.*
   Syns: atypical (*also* atypic), novel, offbeat (*Informal*), unconventional, unordinary, unwonted.
2. ECCENTRIC.
3. INFREQUENT.
4. RARE.
unusually *adverb*
In a manner or to a degree that is unusual: *The child is unusually gifted. It is an unusually oppressive day.*
   Syns: exceptionally, extraordinarily.
unutterable *adjective* UNSPEAKABLE.
unuttered *adjective*
1. IMPLICIT.
2. SILENT.
unvarnished *adjective* BARE.
unvarying *adjective* EVEN[1].
unveil *verb*
1. BETRAY.
2. REVEAL.
unveiling *noun* REVELATION.
unveracity *noun* MENDACITY.
unveridical *adjective* DISHONEST.
unversed *adjective* INEXPERIENCED.
unvoiced *adjective* SILENT.
unwanted *adjective*
1. OBJECTIONABLE.
2. UNWELCOME.
unwarranted *adjective* BASELESS.
unwarrantedly *adverb*
UNFOUNDEDLY.
unwashed *adjective* LOWLY.
unwed *adjective* SINGLE.
unwelcome *adjective*
1. Not welcome or wanted: *an unwelcome phone call late at night.*
   Syns: undesirable, undesired, uninvited, unsought, unwanted, unwished-for.
2. OBJECTIONABLE.
unwelcome *noun*
Lack of cordiality and hospitableness: *Upon entering the room we felt a strong sense of unwelcome.*
   Syns: inhospitableness, inhospitality, ungraciousness, unreceptiveness.
unwell *adjective* SICKLY.

unwholesome *adjective*
1. Not sustaining or promoting health: *unwholesome foods.*
   Syns: insalubrious, insalutary, unhealthy, unsalutary.
2. Morally detrimental: *fell into an unwholesome way of life.*
   Syns: contaminating, contaminative, corrupting, demoralizing, unhealthy.
3. MORBID.
4. OFFENSIVE.
unwholesomeness *noun* IMPURITY.
unwieldy *adjective* AWKWARD.
unwilling *adjective* INDISPOSED.
unwillingness *noun* INDISPOSITION.
unwind *verb*
1. PLAY OUT at **play**.
2. REST[1].
unwise *adjective*
Not wise: *impoverished by some unwise investments; unwise decisions.*
   Syns: ill-advised, ill-considered, ill-judged, impolitic, improvident, imprudent, injudicious, unsound.
unwished-for *adjective* UNWELCOME.
unwitting *adjective*
1. IGNORANT.
2. UNINTENTIONAL.
unwonted *adjective* UNUSUAL.
unworkable *adjective*
1. IMPOSSIBLE.
2. IMPRACTICABLE.
unworkmanlike *adjective*
INEFFICIENT.
unworldly *adjective* SPIRITUAL.
unwritten *adjective* ORAL.
unyielding *adjective*
1. FIRM[1].
2. GRIM.
3. INFLEXIBLE.
4. RIGID.
5. SEVERE.
6. STUBBORN.
up *adjective* EQUAL.
up *verb* RAISE.
up-and-comer *noun* COMER.
up-and-coming *adjective* COMING.
upbeat *adjective*
1. OPTIMISTIC.
2. POSITIVE.
upbraid *verb* CALL DOWN at **call**.
upbraiding *noun* REBUKE.
upcoming *adjective* COMING.
update *verb* MODERNIZE.
upgrade *verb*
1. IMPROVE.
2. PROMOTE.
upgrading *noun*
1. ADVANCEMENT.
2. IMPROVEMENT.

upheaval *noun* REVOLUTION.
uphill *adjective* DIFFICULT.
uphold *verb*
1. ELEVATE.
2, 3. SUPPORT.
4. SUSTAIN.
upkeep *noun* LIVING.
uplift *verb*
1. ELATE.
2. ELEVATE.
3. EXALT.
uplift *noun* ELATION.
uplifted *adjective*
1. ELATED.
2. ELEVATED.
up on *adjective* FAMILIAR.
upper class *noun* SOCIETY.
upper crust *noun* SOCIETY.
uppermost *adjective* TOP.
upper story *noun* HEAD.
upperworks *noun* HEAD.
uppish *adjective* SEE **uppity**.
uppitiness *noun* PRESUMPTION.
uppity also **uppish** *adjective*
1. PRESUMPTUOUS.
2. SNOBBISH.
upraise *verb*
1. ELEVATE.
2. ERECT.
upraised *adjective*
1. ELEVATED.
2. ERECT.
uprear *verb* ERECT.
upright *adjective*
1. ERECT.
2. HONEST.
3. VERTICAL.
upright *verb* RIGHT.
uprightness *noun*
1. GOOD.
2. HONESTY.
uprise *verb*
1, 2. GET UP at **get**.
uprisen *adjective* ELEVATED.
uprising *noun* REBELLION.
uproar *noun*
1. BRAWL.
2. DISTURBANCE.
3. NOISE.
4. SENSATION.
5. VOCIFERATION.
uproot *verb* ANNIHILATE.
upset *verb*
1. To disturb the health or physiological functioning of: *Heavy meals upset my stomach.*
   Syns: derange, disorder, turn, unhinge, unsettle.
2. AGITATE.

3. DISORDER.
4. DISRUPT.
5. OVERTURN.
upset *noun*
1. The act or an example of upsetting: *an upset in our plans.*
   Syns: disordering, disorganization, disruption.
2, 3. AGITATION.
upset *adjective* UPSIDE-DOWN.
upsetting *adjective* DISTURBING.
upshot *noun* EFFECT.
upside *adjective* MAXIMUM.
upside-down *adjective*
1. Overturned completely: *an upside-down car in the ditch.*
   Syns: inverted, upset, upturned.
2. CONFUSED.
upsoar *verb* SOAR.
upspring *verb*
1. GET UP at **get**.
2. STEM.
upstanding *adjective*
1. ERECT.
2. HONEST.
upsurge *verb* INCREASE.
upswing *noun* INCREASE.
up tight also **uptight** *adjective* EDGY.
up-to-date *adjective* CONTEMPORARY.
up-to-the-minute *adjective*
CONTEMPORARY.
upturn *noun* INCREASE.
upturned *adjective* UPSIDE-DOWN.
urban *adjective* CITY.
urbane *adjective*
1. CULTURED.
2. SUAVE.
urbanity *noun* ELEGANCE.
urbanize *verb* CITIFY.
urge *verb*
1. To impel to action: *We urged the President to be more decisive. My conscience urged me to tell the truth at last.*
   Syns: exhort, press, prick, prod, prompt, propel.
2. INSIST.
urgence *noun* INSISTENCE.
urgency *noun* INSISTENCE.
urgent *adjective* BURNING.
urging *noun* INSISTENCE.
usable *adjective*
1. In a condition to be used: *Does he really think this manuscript is usable?*
   Syns: employable, serviceable, utilizable.
2. OPEN.
usage *noun*
1. CONSUMPTION.

2. CONVENTION.

3. CUSTOM.

4. EXERCISE.

use *verb*

1. To put into action or use: *Use the utmost caution at intersections. He used the money to pay off debts. I used the brakes as quickly as possible. We want to use her talents to our advantage.*
 Syns: actuate, apply, employ, exercise, exploit, implement, practice, utilize. —*Idioms* bring into play, bring to bear, make use of, put into practice, put to use.

2. ABUSE.

3. GO.

4. OPERATE.

use up *verb*

1. DEPLETE.

2. EXHAUST.

use *noun*

1. The quality of being suitable or adaptable to an end: *found a use for the extra chair; a lazy person of no use to us.*
 Syns: account, advantage, avail, benefit, profit, usefulness, utility.

2. CONSUMPTION.

3. CUSTOM.

4. DUTY.

5. EXERCISE.

used to *adjective* ACCUSTOMED TO at accustomed.

useful *adjective*

1. BENEFICIAL.

2. CONVENIENT.

3. PRACTICAL.

usefulness *noun* USE.

useless *adjective*

1. Having no useful purpose: *A dead battery is useless in starting a car.*
 Syns: ineffectual, inutile, unusable, worthless.

2. FUTILE.

3. IMPRACTICABLE.

uselessness *noun* FUTILITY.

user *noun* CONSUMER.

usher *verb* GUIDE.

usher in *verb*

1. To make known the presence or arrival of: *Falling leaves usher in autumn. The doorkeeper ushered in the President as members of Congress applauded.*
 Syns: announce, herald, introduce, presage, proclaim.

2, 3. INTRODUCE.

usual *noun*

A regular or customary matter, condition, or course of events: *Fair weather is the usual here.*
 Syns: commonplace, ordinary, rule.

usual *adjective*

1. COMMON.

2. CUSTOMARY.

usually *adverb*

1. In an expected or customary manner: *August is usually warm here.*
 Syns: consistently, customarily, naturally, normally, typically.
 —*Idioms* as usual, per usual.

2. For the most part: *He is usually out of town once a week.*
 Syns: commonly, frequently.

usualness *noun*

The quality or condition of being usual: *the usualness of rain in the tropics.*
 Syns: ordinariness, prevalence.

usurp *verb*

1. ASSUME.

2. SUPPLANT.

usurpation *noun*

The act of taking something for oneself: *usurpation of authority by mutinous sailors.*
 Syns: appropriation, arrogation, assumption, pre-emption (*also* preemption, preëmption), seizure.

utensil *noun* TOOL.

utilitarian *adjective* PRACTICAL.

utility *noun* USE.

utilizable *adjective* USABLE.

utilization *noun*

1. APPLICATION.

2. DUTY.

utilize *verb* USE.

utmost *adjective*

1, 2. EXTREME.

3. MAXIMUM.

utopian *noun* DREAMER.

utopian *adjective* IDEALISTIC.

utter¹ *verb*

1. PRONOUNCE.

2. SAY.

3. SPEAK.

4. TALK.

utter² *adjective*

Completely such, without qualification or exception: *an utter fool; a room in utter chaos; had utter confidence in his ability.*
 Syns: absolute, all-out, arrant, blooming (*Slang*), complete, consummate, crashing, damned, dead, downright, flat, flat-out, out-and-out, outright, perfect, positive (*Informal*), pure, sheer², thorough, thoroughgoing,

total, unbounded, unequivocal,
unlimited, unmitigated, unqualified,
unrelieved, unreserved.

utterance *noun*
1. EXPRESSION.
2. SPEECH.
3. VOICING.
4. WORD.

uttered *adjective*
VOCAL.

utterly *adverb*
PURELY.

uttermost *adjective*
1, 2. EXTREME.

V

vacancy *noun*
1, 2. EMPTINESS.

vacant *adjective*
1. Lacking intelligent thought or
content: *a vacant mind; vacant
rhetoric.*
   Syns: empty, empty-headed, vacuous.
2, 3. EMPTY.
4. IDLE.

vacate *verb*
1. CANCEL.
2. EMPTY.

vacation *noun*
A regularly scheduled period spent
away from work or duty, often in
recreation: *teachers enjoying their long
summer vacation.*
   Syns: furlough, holiday, leave².

vacillant *adjective*
HESITANT.

vacillate *verb*
1. HESITATE.
2. SWING.

vacillating *also* **vacillatory** *adjective*
HESITANT.

vacillation *noun* HESITATION.

vacillatory *adjective* SEE **vacillating.**

vacuity *noun*
1, 2. EMPTINESS.
3. HOLE.
4. NOTHINGNESS.

vacuous *adjective*
1. EMPTY.
2. VACANT.

vacuum *noun*
1, 2. EMPTINESS.

vagabond *adjective* NOMADIC.

vagary *noun* FANCY.

vagrant *adjective* NOMADIC.

vague *adjective*
1. AMBIGUOUS.
2. INDEFINITE.
3. UNCLEAR.

vagueness *noun*
The quality or state of being
ambiguous: *suggestions impractical due
to their vagueness.*
   Syns: ambiguity, ambiguousness,
cloudiness, equivocalness,
indefiniteness, obscurity, uncertainty,
unclearness.

vain *adjective*
1. Unduly preoccupied with one's own
appearance: *A vain man, he would
pluck out his gray hairs as soon as he
noticed them.*
   Syns: conceited, narcissistic.
2. EMPTY.
3. FUTILE.

vainglorious *adjective* EGOTISTICAL.

vainglory *noun* EGOTISM.

vainness *noun* EGOTISM.

valedictory *adjective* PARTING.

valiance *or* **valiancy** *noun*
1. COURAGE.
2. HEROISM.

valiant *adjective* BRAVE.

valid *adjective*
1. AUTHENTIC.
2. SOUND².

validate *verb*
1. CONFIRM.
2. PROVE.

validation *noun* CONFIRMATION.

validity *noun* AUTHENTICITY.

valor *noun*
1. COURAGE.
2. HEROISM.

valorous *adjective* BRAVE.

valorousness *noun* HEROISM.

valuable *adjective*
Of great value: *valuable Georgian silver.*
   Syns: costly, inestimable, invaluable,
precious, priceless, worthy. —*Idioms*
beyond price, of great price.

valuate *verb* ESTIMATE.

valuation *noun*
1. ESTIMATE.
2. WORTH.

value *noun*
1. MEANING.
2. MERIT.
3. WORTH.

value *verb*
1. ADMIRE.
2. APPRECIATE.
3. ESTIMATE.

valueless *adjective* WORTHLESS.

vamoose also **vamose** *verb* RUN.

vamp *noun* SEDUCTRESS.

vampire *noun* FIEND.

vandalize *verb* TRASH[1].

vanish *verb* DISAPPEAR.

vanished *adjective*
No longer in use, force, or operation: *the vanished languages of ancient peoples.*
  Syns: dead, defunct, extinct, lost.

vanity *noun* EGOTISM.

vanquish *verb* DEFEAT.

vantage *noun*
1, 2. ADVANTAGE.

vapid *adjective* INSIPID.

vapidity *noun* INSIPIDITY.

vaporize *verb* EVAPORATE.

vaporous also **vapory** *adjective*
1. FILMY.
2. UNCLEAR.

variable *adjective*
1. CAPRICIOUS.
2. CHANGEABLE.
3. UNEVEN.

variance *noun*
1. CONFLICT.
2. VARIATION.

variant *noun* VARIATION.

variant *adjective*
1. CHANGEABLE.
2. DIFFERENT.

variation *noun*
1. The condition or fact of varying: *A wind shift can bring a sharp variation in temperature.*
  Syns: difference, variance.
2. One that is slightly different from others of the same kind or designation: *Several variations of hopscotch are played in this neighborhood.*
  Syns: variant, variety, version.
3. CHANGE.

varicolored *adjective*
MULTICOLORED.

varied *adjective* VARIOUS.

variegate *verb* STREAK.

variegated *adjective*
1. MULTICOLORED.
2. VARIOUS.

variety *noun*
1. The quality of being made of many different elements, forms, kinds, or individuals: *a monotonous life without variety; the variety of cultural expression in a great metropolis.*
  Syns: diverseness, diversity, heterogeneity, multifariousness, multiformity, multiplicity, polymorphism (*Biol.*), variousness.
2. ASSORTMENT.
3. KIND[2].
4. VARIATION.

various *adjective*
1. Consisting of a number of different kinds: *various books on the shelves; dresses of various colors.*
  Syns: assorted, divers, diverse, diversified, heterogeneous, miscellaneous, mixed, motley, multifarious, sundry, varied, variegated.
2. CHANGEABLE.
3. DIFFERENT.
4. DISTINCT.
5. SEVERAL.
6. VERSATILE.

variousness *noun* VARIETY.

varnish *verb* COLOR.

vary *verb*
1. CHANGE.
2, 3. DIFFER.
4. GO.

vast *adjective* GIANT.

vastness *noun* ENORMOUSNESS.

vatic also **vatical** *adjective*
PROPHETIC.

vaticinal *adjective* PROPHETIC.

vaticinate *verb* PROPHESY.

vaticination *noun* PROPHECY.

vault[1] *noun* GRAVE[1].

vault[2] *verb* JUMP.

vault *noun* JUMP.

vaunt *verb* BOAST.

vector *noun* HEADING.

veer *verb*
1. SWERVE.
2. TURN.

vehemence *noun* INTENSITY.

vehement *adjective* INTENSE.

veil *noun* FAÇADE.

veil *verb*
1. COVER.
2. WRAP.

vein *noun*
1. MOOD.
2. STREAK.
3. STYLE.

velocity *noun* SPEED.

venal *adjective*
1, 2. CORRUPT.
3. CORRUPTIBLE.

vend *verb*
1. PEDDLE.
2. SELL.

veneer *noun* FAÇADE.
 veneer *verb* COLOR.
venerable *adjective* OLD.
venerate *verb*
 1. ADORE.
 2. HONOR.
veneration *noun* ADORATION.
vengeance *noun* RETALIATION.
vengeful *adjective* VINDICTIVE.
vengefulness *noun* VINDICTIVENESS.
venial *adjective* PARDONABLE.
venom *noun* POISON.
venomous *adjective*
 1. MALEVOLENT.
 2. POISONOUS.
vent *verb*
 1. AIR.
 2. DISCHARGE.
 3. EMIT.
 4. SAY.
 vent *noun*
 1. EXPRESSION.
 2. HOLE.
ventilate *verb*
 1, 2. AIR.
ventilation *noun* CONFERENCE.
venture *noun*
 1. ADVENTURE.
 2. PROJECT.
 venture *verb*
 1, 2. GAMBLE.
 3. HAZARD.
 4. PRESUME.
 5. RISK.
venturer *noun* ADVENTURER.
venturesome *adjective*
 ADVENTUROUS.
venturous *adjective*
 1. ADVENTUROUS.
 2. DANGEROUS.
veracious *adjective*
 1. ACCURATE.
 2. TRUTHFUL.
veracity *noun*
 1. Correspondence with fact or truth:
 *No one doubted the veracity of the
 prediction.*
 Syns: accuracy, correctness,
 exactitude, exactness, fidelity, truth.
 2. TRUTH.
verbal *adjective*
 1. Pertaining to, consisting of, or having
 the nature of words: *a verbal war
 between the two candidates.*
 Syn: wordy.
 2. LITERAL.
 3. ORAL.
verbalism *noun* WORDING.
verbalization *noun* SPEECH.

verbalize *verb*
 1. SPEAK.
 2. TALK.
verbatim *adjective* LITERAL.
verbose *adjective* WORDY.
verboseness *noun* WORDINESS.
verbosity *noun* WORDINESS.
verboten *adjective* FORBIDDEN.
verge *noun*
 1. A transitional interval beyond which
 some new action or different state of
 affairs is likely to begin or occur: *two
 nations on the verge of war.*
 Syns: borderline (*also* border line),
 brink, edge, point, threshold.
 2. BORDER.
 verge *verb*
 1. ADJOIN.
 2. BORDER.
 verge on *verb* RIVAL.
veridical *adjective*
 1. ACCURATE.
 2. TRUTHFUL.
verification *noun* CONFIRMATION.
verify *verb*
 1. CONFIRM.
 2. PROVE.
verily *adverb*
 1. EVEN[1].
 2. REALLY.
verisimilitude *noun*
 Appearance of truth or authenticity:
 *statistics that lend verisimilitude to the
 story.*
 Syns: color, plausibility.
verity *noun* TRUTH.
vernacular *noun*
 1. DIALECT.
 2, 3. LANGUAGE.
vernal *adjective* SPRING.
versant *adjective* FAMILIAR.
versatile *adjective*
 Having many aspects, uses, or abilities:
 *a versatile athlete who excels in all track
 events; a versatile building material.*
 Syns: all-round (*also* all-around),
 ambidextrous, many-sided,
 multifaceted, protean, various.
verse *noun* POEM.
versed *adjective*
 1. EXPERIENCED.
 2. FAMILIAR.
versicolor *also* **versicolored** *adjective*
 MULTICOLORED.
version *noun*
 1. PARAPHRASE.
 2. STORY.
 3. VARIATION.

vertical *adjective*
At right angles to the horizon or to level ground: *careful to make the doorposts vertical.*
   Syns: perpendicular, plumb, upright.

vertiginous *adjective*
1. DIZZY.
2. GIDDY.

vertigo *noun* DIZZINESS.

verve *noun*
1. SPIRIT.
2. VIGOR.

very *adverb*
To a high degree: *very cold; very pleased to see her.*
   Syns: awfully (*Informal*), dreadfully (*Informal*), eminently, exceptionally, extra, mighty (*Informal*), most, muchly, notably, pure (*Chiefly Regional*).

very *adjective*
1. MERE.
2. PRECISE.
3. SAME.

vesper *noun* EVENING.

vestige *noun*
1. TRACE.
2. RUIN.

vestments *noun* HABIT.

vet *noun* VETERAN.

veteran *noun*
One who has had long experience in a given activity or capacity: *a veteran of 20 years' service on the police force.*
   Syns: old-timer (*Informal*), vet.
   —*Idiom* old hand.

veteran *adjective*
1. EXPERIENCED.
2. PRACTICAL.

veto *verb*
To prevent or forbid authoritatively: *The board vetoed the plan.*
   Syns: blackball, negative, nix (*Slang*), turn down. —*Idiom* turn thumbs down on.

vex *verb* ANNOY.

vexation *noun*
1, 2. ANNOYANCE.
3. BOTHER.

vexatious *adjective*
1. Troubling the nerves or peace of mind, as by repeated vexations: *had a vexatious habit of cracking his knuckles.*
   Syns: aggravating (*Informal*), annoying, bothersome, galling, irksome, irritating, nettlesome, plaguy (*also* plaguey) (*Informal*), provoking, troublesome, vexing.

2. THORNY.
3. TROUBLESOME.

vexing *adjective* VEXATIOUS.

viable *adjective* POSSIBLE.

vibrant *adjective*
1. RESONANT.
2. SPIRITED.

vibrate *verb* SHAKE.

vice *noun* CORRUPTION.

vicinity *noun*
1. ENVIRONMENT.
2. LOCALITY.
3. NEIGHBORHOOD.

vicious *adjective*
1. CRUEL.
2. EVIL.
3. FIERCE.
4. MALEVOLENT.

viciousness *noun* CRUELTY.

vicissitude *noun* DIFFICULTY.

victim *noun*
1. One that is made to suffer injury, loss, or death: *The plague claimed millions of victims.*
   Syns: casualty, prey.
2. DUPE.
3. SACRIFICE.

victimize *verb*
1. CHEAT.
2. SACRIFICE.

victor *noun*
1. CONQUEROR.
2. WINNER.

Victorian *adjective* GENTEEL.
Victorian *noun* PRUDE.

victorious *adjective*
Pertaining to, having the nature of, or experiencing triumph: *a victorious entry into the conquered city; victorious teams.*
   Syns: conquering, triumphal, triumphant.

victory *noun* CONQUEST.

videlicet *adverb* NAMELY.

vie *verb*
1. COMPETE.
2. CONTEND.

view *noun*
1. That which is or can be seen: *stepped out on the porch to enjoy the ocean view.*
   Syns: lookout, outlook, perspective, prospect, scene, sight, vista.
2. BELIEF.
3. FACE.
4. INTENTION.
5. LOOK.
6. POINT OF VIEW.

view *verb*
1. EXAMINE.

2. LOOK.
3. REGARD.
viewable *adjective* VISIBLE.
viewer *noun* WITNESS.
viewpoint *noun*
1. LIGHT[1].
2. POINT OF VIEW.
vigil *noun*
1. LOOKOUT.
2. WAKE.
vigilance *noun* LOOKOUT.
vigilant *adjective* ALERT.
vigor *noun*
1. A quality of active mental and
physical forcefulness: *the vigor of
early manhood; the vigor of a bright,
inquisitive mind.*
Syns: dash, starch, verve,
vigorousness, vitality. —*Idiom* vim
and vigor.
2. DRIVE.
3. ENERGY.
4. FORCE.
5. SPIRIT.
6. STRENGTH.
vigorous *adjective*
1. Disposed to action: *a vigorous fellow
who found retirement a bore.*
Syns: active, brisk, brisky, driving,
dynamic (*also* dynamical), energetic,
enterprising, lively, peppy, snappy
(*Informal*), sprightly, spry, zippy.
2. ENERGETIC.
3. FORCEFUL.
4. LUSTY.
vigorously *adverb* HARD.
vigorousness *noun*
1. STRENGTH.
2. VIGOR.
vile *adjective*
1. FILTHY.
2. INFAMOUS.
3. OFFENSIVE.
4. SORDID.
vilification *noun* SMEAR.
vilify *verb* LIBEL.
vilifying *adjective* LIBELOUS.
villain *noun* HEAVY.
villainage *noun* SEE **villeinage.**
villainous *adjective* CORRUPT.
villainy *noun* INFAMY.
villeinage *also* **villainage** *noun*
SLAVERY.
vim *noun*
1. ENERGY.
2. SPIRIT.
vincible *adjective* VULNERABLE.
vinculum *noun* BOND.

vindicate *verb*
1. ASSERT.
2. AVENGE.
3. CLEAR.
4. DEFEND.
5. JUSTIFY.
vindictive *adjective*
Disposed to seek revenge: *a bitter,
vindictive man.*
Syns: revengeful, spiteful, vengeful,
wreakful (*Archaic*).
vindictiveness *noun*
The quality or condition of being
vindictive: *actions motivated by pure
vindictiveness.*
Syns: revenge, spite, spitefulness,
vengefulness.
vintage *noun*
Informal. A period of origin: *a good
vintage for that wine; a car of 1942
vintage.*
Syn: year.
vintage *adjective*
1. Characterized by enduring excellence,
appeal, and importance: *vintage
paintings of the Cubist period.*
Syns: classic, classical.
2. DISTINCTIVE.
3. OLD-FASHIONED.
violate *verb*
1. To spoil or mar the sanctity of: *an
altar violated by vandals.*
Syns: defile, desecrate, profane.
2. To fail to fulfill (a promise) or
conform to (a regulation): *violated his
sacred oath; violated the traffic laws.*
Syns: breach, break, contravene,
transgress.
3. To deprive of virginity: *a young girl
violated by an older man.*
Syns: defile (*Obs.*), deflorate,
deflower.
4. RAPE.
violation *noun*
1. BREACH.
2. CRIME.
3. SACRILEGE.
violence *noun*
1. FORCE.
2. INTENSITY.
violent *adjective*
1. FORCIBLE.
2. INTENSE.
3. ROUGH.
VIP *noun* DIGNITARY.
virago *noun* SCOLD.
virgin *noun* INNOCENT.
virginal *adjective* INNOCENT.
virile *adjective* MANLY.

virtual *adjective* IMPLICIT.

virtue *noun*
1. A special feature or quality that confers superiority: *The virtue of the faculty lies in its diversity.*
   Syns: beauty, distinction, excellence, merit, perfection.
2. CHASTITY.
3. GOOD.
4. MERIT.

virtuous *adjective*
1. CHASTE.
2. EFFECTIVE.

virtuousness *noun*
1. CHASTITY.
2. GOOD.

virulent *adjective*
1. Extremely destructive or harmful: *virulent rumors.*
   Syns: baneful, deadly, malignant, noxious, pernicious, pestilent, pestilential.
2. POISONOUS.
3. RESENTFUL.

virus *noun* POISON.

visage *noun*
1. EXPRESSION.
2, 3. FACE.

vis-à-vis *noun* COUNTERPART.

visceral *adjective*
1. INNER.
2. INSTINCTIVE.

viscerous *adjective* INNER.

viscid *adjective* VISCOUS.

viscidity *noun* VISCOSITY.

viscose *adjective* VISCOUS.

viscosity *noun*
The physical property of being viscous: *measured the viscosity of the oil.*
Syn: viscidity.

viscous *adjective*
Having a heavy, gluey quality: *Unrefined oil is viscous.*
Syns: glutinous, mucilaginous, viscid, viscose.

visibility *noun*
The quality, condition, or degree of being visible: *Visibility was zero because of fog.*
Syn: visuality.

visible *adjective*
1. Capable of being seen: *Yellow headlights are visible even in fog.*
   Syns: perceivable, perceptible, seeable, viewable, visual.
2. APPARENT.

vision *noun*
1. The faculty of seeing: *Her vision has deteriorated since the accident.*
   Syns: eyes, eyesight, light[1] (*Poetic*), seeing, sight.
2. Unusual or creative discernment or perception: *We need a leader who is a man of vision.*
   Syns: far-sightedness, foresight, prescience.
3. DREAM.
4. PROPHECY.

vision *verb* IMAGINE.

visionary *adjective*
1. Characterized by foresight: *a visionary film about the aftereffects of nuclear war.*
   Syns: far-sighted, prescient.
2. DREAMY.
3. IDEALISTIC.

visionary *noun* DREAMER.

visit *verb*
1. To go to or seek out the company of in order to socialize: *visited relatives.*
   Syns: call, come by, come over (*Informal*), drop by, drop in, look in, look up, pop in, run in, see, stop (in or by). —*Idiom* pay a visit.
2. CONVERSE[1].
3. INFLICT.
4. STAY[1].

visit *noun*
1. An act or an instance of going or coming to see another: *She paid a visit to her aunt.*
   Syns: call, visitation.
2. STAY[1].

visitant *noun*
1. COMPANY.
2. GHOST.

visitation *noun*
1. TRIAL.
2. VISIT.

visitor *noun*
1. ARRIVAL.
2. COMPANY.

vista *noun* VIEW.

visual *adjective*
1. Serving, resulting from, or pertaining to the sense of sight: *visual cues; visual images; visual acuity.*
   Syns: optic, optical.
2. VISIBLE.

visuality *noun* VISIBILITY.

visualize *verb* IMAGINE.

vital *adjective*
1. ALIVE.
2. DEADLY.
3. ESSENTIAL.
4. LUSTY.

vitality *noun*
1. FORCE.

2. SPIRIT.
3. VIGOR.
vitalizing *adjective* STIMULATING.
vitiate *verb*
1. ABOLISH.
2. CORRUPT.
3. FALL.
4. INJURE.
vitiated *adjective* CORRUPTED.
vitriolic *adjective* BITING.
vituperate *verb* REVILE.
vituperation *noun*
Harsh, often insulting language: *a family row characterized by much vituperation.*
   Syns: abuse, billingsgate, contumely, invective, obloquy, railing, revile (*Obs.*), revilement, reviling, scurrility.
vituperative *adjective*
1. ABUSIVE.
2. BITING.
vivacious *adjective*
1. EXUBERANT.
2. LIVELY.
vivacity *noun* SPIRIT.
vivid *adjective*
1, 2. COLORFUL.
3. GRAPHIC.
vivifying *adjective* STIMULATING.
vivify *verb* QUICKEN.
vixen *noun* SCOLD.
vocabulary *noun*
1. An alphabetical list of words often defined or translated: *The vocabulary includes idioms and two-word verbs.*
   Syns: dictionary, lexicon, wordbook.
2. All the words of a language: *The vocabulary of Russian is very expressive.*
   Syns: lexicon, word-hoard, word-stock.
3. LANGUAGE.
vocal *adjective*
1. Produced by the voice: *a vocal prayer.*
   Syns: articulate, oral, sonant, spoken, uttered, voiced.
2. *Phon.* Characterized by, containing, or functioning as a vowel or vowels: *vocal as opposed to consonant sounds.*
   Syns: vocalic, vowel.
3. OUTSPOKEN.
vocalic *adjective* VOCAL.
vocalism *noun* VOICING.
vocalist *noun*
A person who sings: *a vocalist who performs at weddings.*
   Syns: singer, songster, songstress, voice.
vocalization *noun* VOICING.

vocalize *verb*
1. SAY.
2. SING.
3. SPEAK.
vocation *noun*
1. An inner urge to pursue an activity or perform a service: *the vocation of the priesthood.*
   Syns: calling, mission.
2. BUSINESS.
vociferant *adjective* SEE **vociferous.**
vociferate *verb* SHOUT.
vociferation *noun*
Offensively loud and insistent utterances, esp. of disapproval: *Gas rationing was greeted by widespread public vociferation.*
   Syns: clamor, hullabaloo (*also* hullaballoo), outcry, rumpus, uproar.
   —*Idiom* hue and cry.
vociferous *also* **vociferant** *adjective*
Offensively loud and insistent: *vociferous complaints from the demoralized staff.*
   Syns: blatant, boisterous, clamorous, loudmouthed, multivocal, obstreperous, strident.
vogue *noun* FASHION.
voice *noun*
1. The right or chance to express an opinion or participate in a decision: *was allowed no voice in choosing his replacement.*
   Syns: say, say-so (*Informal*), suffrage.
2. EXPRESSION.
3. SPEECH.
4. VOCALIST.
voice *verb* SAY.
voiced *adjective* VOCAL.
voiceless *adjective* DUMB.
voicing *noun*
The use of the speech organs to produce sounds: *a loud voicing of hitherto unspoken resentment.*
   Syns: articulation, utterance, vocalism, vocalization.
void *adjective*
1, 2. EMPTY.
void *noun*
1. EMPTINESS.
2. GAP.
3. HOLE.
4. NOTHINGNESS.
void *verb*
1. ABOLISH.
2. DISCHARGE.
3. EMPTY.
volatile *adjective* CAPRICIOUS.
volatilize *verb* EVAPORATE.
volition *noun* WILL[1].

volitional *adjective* VOLUNTARY.
volley *noun* BARRAGE.
volume *noun*
1. BOOK.
2. BULK.
3. PUBLICATION.
voluminous *adjective*
1. FULL.
2. HEAVY.
3. MANY.
voluntarily *adverb*
Of one's own free will: *voluntarily gave up his seat to the old lady.*
    Syns: voluntary, willingly. —*Idioms* of one's own accord, on one's own volition.
voluntary *adjective*
1. Done by one's own choice: *voluntary enlistment into the army; voluntary labor.*
    Syns: free, spontaneous, uncompelled, unforced, willful (*Obs.*).
2. Of or relating to free exercise of the will: *voluntary sacrifices; voluntary acts.*
    Syns: volitional, willing.
3. DELIBERATE.
voluntary *adverb* VOLUNTARILY.
voluntary *noun* VOLUNTEER.
volunteer *noun*
Someone who offers his or her services freely: *unpaid political volunteers.*
    Syn: voluntary.
volunteer *verb* OFFER.
voluptuary *noun* SYBARITE.
voluptuary *adjective* SENSUOUS.
voluptuous *adjective*
1. SENSUAL.
2. SENSUOUS.
voluptuousness *noun* SENSUALITY.
voracious *adjective*
1. Having an insatiable appetite for an activity or pursuit: *a voracious reader.*
    Syns: avid, edacious, omnivorous, rapacious, ravenous, unappeasable.
2. GREEDY.
voracity *noun*
The quality or condition of being voracious: *The hungry wolf consumed its fallen prey with frightening voracity.*
    Syns: avidness, edacity, gulosity, rapacity, ravenousness.
votary *noun* DEVOTEE.
vote *verb* ELECT.
voter *noun* ELECTOR.
vouch *verb* CERTIFY.
vouchsafe *verb*
1. CONDESCEND.
2. GRANT.

vow *noun* PROMISE.
vow *verb* PLEDGE.
vowel *adjective* VOCAL.
vulgar *adjective*
1. COARSE.
2. LOWLY.
vulgarian *noun* BOOR.
vulgarism *noun* CORRUPTION.
vulnerability *noun* EXPOSURE.
vulnerable *adjective*
1. Open to attack and capture because of a lack of protection: *a strategic position vulnerable to counterattack.*
    Syns: assailable, attackable, pregnable, vincible.
2. LIABLE.
vulnerableness *noun* EXPOSURE.
vying *noun* BATTLE.
vying *adjective* COMPETITIVE.

W

wacky *also* **whacky** *adjective*
1. FOOLISH.
2. INSANE.
wad *noun*
1. FORTUNE.
2. HEAP.
3. LUMP[1].
waffle *verb* EQUIVOCATE.
wag[1] *verb*
To move to and fro vigorously and usu. repeatedly: *The dog wagged its tail.*
    Syns: lash, switch, waggle, wave.
wag[2] *noun* JOKER.
wage *verb*
To engage in (a war or campaign): *waged war on two fronts; waging an antipoverty campaign.*
    Syns: carry on, carry out, conduct, prosecute.
wager *verb*
1. BET.
2. GAMBLE.
wager *noun*
1. BET.
2. GAMBLE.
wage(s) *noun*
1. Payment for work done: *an hourly wage of $8.50; high union wages.*
    Syns: earnings, emolument, fee, hire,

pay, salary, stipend. —*Idioms* pay
envelope, pay packet (*Brit.*).
2. DUE.
waggle *verb*
1. FLAP.
2. WAG[1].
3. WIGGLE.
wail *verb*
1. BAWL.
2. CRY.
3. HOWL.
4. REGRET.
wail *noun* HOWL.
wailing *noun* CRY.
wait *verb*
1. DEFER[1].
2. PAUSE.
3. REMAIN.
wait on (or **upon**) *verb*
1, 2. SERVE.
wait *noun*
An act or the time of waiting: *had a
two-hour wait in the doctor's office.*
   Syns: stay[1], waiting.
waiting *noun* WAIT.
waive *verb*
1. ABDICATE.
2. DEFER[1].
3. RELINQUISH.
waiver *noun* ABDICATION.
wake *verb*
To cease sleeping: *woke at six in the
morning.*
   Syns: arouse, awake, awaken, rouse,
   stir[1], waken.
wake *noun*
A watch over the body of a dead person
before burial: *laid in a plentiful supply of
food and drink for the wake.*
   Syn: vigil.
wake *adjective* WAKEFUL.
wakeful *adjective*
1. Not in a state of sleep: *a wakeful,
   fretting baby.*
   Syns: awake, unsleeping, wake, wide-
   awake.
2. Marked by an absence of sleep: *had a
   wakeful, restless night.*
   Syns: sleepless, slumberless.
3. ALERT.
waken *verb*
1. AROUSE.
2. WAKE.
wale *noun* WELT.
walk *noun*
1. An act of walking, esp. for pleasure:
   *With time between trains, he checked
   his luggage and took a walk.*
   Syns: amble, perambulation,
   promenade, ramble, saunter, stroll.

2. CONSTITUTIONAL.
walk *verb*
To go on foot: *walked to and fro in deep
thought.*
   Syns: ambulate, foot (it), hoof
   (*Informal*), pace, step, tread.
walk out *verb* STRIKE.
walk out on *verb* ABANDON.
walkaway *noun*
1. BREEZE.
2. RUNAWAY.
walkover *noun*
1. BREEZE.
2. RUNAWAY.
wall *noun*
1. A solid structure that encloses an
   area or separates one area from
   another: *We knocked down a wall
   between two bedrooms to make a large
   studio for our son.*
   Syns: barrier, partition.
2. BAR.
wall *verb*
1. To separate with or as if with a wall:
   *We have walled off part of our yard for
   a patio.*
   Syns: fence (off), partition.
2. BAR.
3. ENCLOSE.
wallop *verb*
1. HIT.
2. OVERWHELM.
wallop *noun*
1. *Informal.* The capacity to create a
   powerful effect: *Today's editorial
   really packs a wallop.*
   Syns: impact, punch (*Informal*), sock
   (*Slang*).
2. BLOW.
3. COLLISION.
4. THRILL.
walloping *adjective* GIANT.
wallow *verb*
1. To move about in an indolent or
   clumsy manner: *two drunks wallowing
   in the snow.*
   Syns: flounder, welter.
2. BLUNDER.
3. LUXURIATE.
waltz *verb* BREEZE.
wampum *noun* MONEY.
wan *adjective*
1. HAGGARD.
2. PALE.
wan *verb* PALE.
wander *verb*
1. BROWSE.
2. DIGRESS.
3. ROVE.
4. STROLL.

wandering *adjective*
1. ERRANT.
2. ERRATIC.
3. NOMADIC.

wane *verb*
1. FADE.
2. SUBSIDE.

wane *noun*
The act or process of becoming less active or intense: *popularity that was on the wane.*
   Syns: abatement, ebb, letup, slackening.

wangle *verb*
Informal. To make, achieve, or get through contrivance or guile: *How did you wangle an interview with such a reclusive man?*
   Syns: engineer, finagle (*also* fenagle (*Informal*), finesse, worm.

want *verb*
1. CHOOSE.
2. LACK.

want *noun*
1. ABSENCE.
2. DEMAND.
3. POVERTY.

wanting *adjective*
1. ABSENT.
2. DEFICIENT.
3. EMPTY.
4. INSUFFICIENT.

wanton *adjective*
1. Sexually promiscuous: *a wanton woman.*
   Syns: easy, fast, libertine, light², loose, whorish. —*Idiom* of easy virtue.
2. Not required, necessary, or warranted by the circumstances of the case: *wanton killing; the wanton destruction of Sheridan's army.*
   Syns: gratuitous, supererogative, supererogatory, uncalled-for.
3. ABANDONED.

wanton *noun*
1. An immoral or licentious man: *a toothless old wanton still chasing young girls.*
   Syns: lecher, libertine, profligate, rake¹, roué, satyr. —*Idiom* dirty old man.
2. SLUT.

wantonness *noun* ABANDON.

war *noun*
1. COMPETITION.
2. CONFLICT.

ward *noun*
1. DEFENSE.
2. DEPENDENT.
3. GUARD.

ward *verb* PREVENT.

ward off *verb* PARRY.

warden *noun*
1. GUARDIAN.
2. JAILER.

warder *noun* JAILER.

wares *noun* GOODS.

warfare *noun*
1. COMPETITION.
2. CONFLICT.

wariness *noun* CAUTION.

warlike *adjective*
1. BELLIGERENT.
2. MILITARY.

warm *adjective*
1. APPROACHABLE.
2. ENTHUSIASTIC.

warmed-over *adjective* TRITE.

warmhearted *adjective* FRIENDLY.

warmth *noun* HEAT.

warn *verb*
To notify (someone) of imminent danger or risk: *warned them about the cyclone's approach.*
   Syns: alarm, alert, caution, forewarn.

warning *noun*
1. Advice to beware, as of a person or thing: *disregarded her friend's warnings.*
   Syns: admonishment, admonition, caution, caveat, forewarning, monition.
2. ALARM.
3. EXAMPLE.

warning *adjective* CAUTIONARY.

warp *verb*
1. BIAS.
2. CORRUPT.
3. DISTORT.

warrant *noun*
1. BASIS.
2. GUARANTEE.
3. LICENSE.
4. PAWN¹.
5. WORD.

warrant *verb*
1. CALL FOR at **call**.
2. CONFIRM.
3, 4. GUARANTEE.

warranty *noun* GUARANTEE.

warring *adjective* BELLIGERENT.

warrior *noun* FIGHTER.

wary *adjective*
1. Trying attentively to avoid danger, risk, or error: *a wary driver.*
   Syns: careful, cautious, chary, circumspect, gingerly, prudent.

2. ALERT.
3. ECONOMICAL.

wash *verb*
1. To make moist: *flowers washed by dew; cheeks washed by tears.*
   Syns: bathe, dampen, moisten.
2. To flow against or along: *waves that washed the rocks.*
   Syns: bathe, lap, lave, lip.
3. To move along with or be carried away by the action of water: *The skiff washed down the stream in the storm.*
   Syns: drift, float.
4. To flow or move with a low, slapping sound: *could hear water washing about the floor of the ship's engine room.*
   Syns: burble, gurgle, lap, slosh, splash, swash, swish.
5. *Informal.* To prove valid under scrutiny: *Her alibi doesn't wash.*
   Syns: hold up, prove out, stand up.
   —*Idioms* hold water, pass muster, ring true.

wash out *verb* FAIL.
wash up *verb* GO.
washed-up *adjective*
1, 2. THROUGH.
washout *noun* FAILURE.
washy *adjective*
1. DILUTE.
2. INSIPID.
waspish *adjective*
1. ILL-TEMPERED.
2. IRRITABLE.
waste *verb*
1. To use up foolishly or needlessly: *wasted gas by joyriding; a poorly insulated house that wastes energy.*
   Syns: consume, devour, expend, squander.
2. To spend (money) excessively and usu. foolishly: *wasted their inheritance gambling.*
   Syns: blow¹ (*Slang*), blue (*Brit. Slang*), consume, dissipate, fool away, fritter away, riot away, squander, throw away, trifle away.
3. CONSUME.
4. DEVASTATE.
5. FADE.
6. IDLE.
7. LOSE.
8. MURDER.
waste *noun*
1. BARREN.
2. EXTRAVAGANCE.
wasted *adjective*
Physically haggard: *the wasted remains of famine victims.*

Syns: cadaverous, emaciated, gaunt, shrunken, skeletal. —*Idiom* all skin and bones.
wasteful *adjective* EXTRAVAGANT.
wastefulness *noun* EXTRAVAGANCE.
wasteland *noun* BARREN.
waster *noun* WASTREL.
wasting *adjective* CONSUMPTIVE.
wastrel *noun*
1. A person who spends money or resources wastefully: *a wastrel who squandered his fortune on clothes and cars.*
   Syns: prodigal, profligate, scattergood, spendthrift, waster.
2. A self-indulgent person who spends time avoiding work or other useful activity: *joined his fellow wastrels for the daily visit to the poolroom.*
   Syns: bum, dolittle, do-nothing, drone¹, fainéant, good-for-nothing, idler, lazybones (*Slang*), loafer, ne'er-do-well, no-good, slouch, slug³ (*Informal*), slugabed, sluggard.
   —*Idiom* Weary Willie.

watch *verb*
1. To look at or on attentively or carefully: *The guard watched the prisoner closely. He demonstrated the wrestling hold while we watched.*
   Syns: eye, observe, scrutinize, survey.
   —*Idiom* keep an eye on.
2, 3. LOOK.
4. TEND².
watch out *verb* LOOK OUT at **look**.
watch *noun*
1. The act of observing, often for an extended time: *The guards kept a 24-hour watch on the prisoner.*
   Syns: eye, observance, observation, scrutiny, tab(s).
2. GUARD.
3. LOOKOUT.
4. TURN.
watcher *noun*
1. Someone who observes: *Kremlin watchers tried to predict new Soviet moves.*
   Syns: beholder, by-sitter, bystander, looker-on, observer, spectator.
2. TAIL.
watchful *adjective*
1. ALERT.
2. CAREFUL.
water *verb*
1. DILUTE.
2. TEAR².
watered *adjective* DILUTE.
watered-down *adjective* DILUTE.

waterish *adjective*
1. DILUTE.
2. INSIPID.
3. PALE.

waterless *adjective* DRY.

Waterloo *noun* FALL.

watershed *noun* BASIN.

watery *adjective*
1. DILUTE.
2. INSIPID.
3. PALE.

wave *verb*
1. To have or cause to have a curved or sinuous form or surface: *hair that waves naturally; waved her hair with a hot iron.*
   Syns: curl, curve, undulate.
2, 3. FLAP.
4. FLOURISH.
5. WAG¹.

waver *verb*
1. HESITATE.
2. SWAY.
3. SWING.

wavering *adjective* HESITANT.

wavering *noun* HESITATION.

wax *verb*
1. BECOME.
2. INCREASE.

waxen *adjective* PALE.

way *noun*
1. A course affording passage from one place to another: *historic houses on both sides of the way.*
   Syns: avenue, boulevard, drive, freeway, highway, path, road, roadway, street, thoroughfare.
2. The manner in which something is done: *demonstrated various ways of tackling in football; a circuitous way of expressing himself.*
   Syns: fashion, method, mode, modus, modus operandi (*Latin*), style, system, technique, wise².
3. BEHAVIOR.
4. CUSTOM.
5. DISTANCE.

waylay *verb* AMBUSH.

wayward *adjective* CONTRARY.

weak *adjective*
1. DILUTE.
2. FAINT.
3. IMPLAUSIBLE.
4. INEFFECTUAL.
5. INFIRM.
6. INSECURE.

weaken *verb*
1. To moderate or change a position or course of action as a result of

pressure: *did not weaken in spite of public opinion.*
   Syns: ease off, relent, slacken, soften, yield. —*Idiom* give way (*or* ground).
2. DILUTE.
3. ENERVATE.
4. FADE.

weakened *adjective* RUN-DOWN.

weakening *noun* FAILURE.

weakling *noun* BABY.

weakly *adjective* INFIRM.

weakly *adverb* FAINTLY.

weak-minded *adjective*
1. BACKWARD.
2. MINDLESS.

weakness *noun*
1. A liking or personal preference for something: *A love of rich food is my weakness.*
   Syns: failing, fault, foible, frailty, infirmity, shortcoming. —*Idiom* weak point.
2. INFIRMITY.

weal¹ *noun* WELFARE.

weal² *noun* WELT.

wealth *noun*
1. HEAP.
2. RESOURCES.
3. RICHES.

wealthy *adjective* RICH.

wear *verb*
1. BITE.
2. FATIGUE.

wear away *verb* BITE.

wear down *verb* FATIGUE.

wear out *verb*
1. EXHAUST.
2. FATIGUE.

wearied *adjective* EXHAUSTED.

weariful *adjective*
1. BORING.
2. EXHAUSTED.

weariless *adjective* TIRELESS.

wearily *adverb*
In a weary way: *yawned and sat down wearily.*
   Syn: heavily.

weariness *noun* EXHAUSTION.

wearisome *adjective* BORING.

weary *adjective*
1. BORING.
2. EXHAUSTED.
3. SICK.

weary *verb*
1. BORE.
2. FATIGUE.

wearying *adjective* TIRING.

weasel *noun* SNEAK.

weasel *verb* EQUIVOCATE.

weather *verb* SURVIVE.
weave *verb*
1. LURCH.
2. SWAY.
3. WIND².

web *noun*
1. An open fabric woven of strands that are interlaced and knotted at usu. regular intervals: *a light, filmy web of lace.*
   Syns: mesh, net¹, netting, network.
2. A group of things that are linked or interconnected as if by weaving: *a web of lies.*
   Syns: network, tissue.
3. TANGLE.
4. TEXTURE.

web *verb* CATCH.
wed *verb*
1. COMBINE.
2. MARRY.

wedded *adjective* MARITAL.
wedding *noun*
The act or ceremony by which two people become husband and wife: *an outdoor wedding.*
   Syns: bridal, espousal, marriage, nuptial, spousal.

wedlock *noun* MARRIAGE.
wee *adjective* TINY.
weeny *adjective* TINY.
weep *verb*
1. CRY.
2. DRIP.
3. OOZE.

weeping *adjective* TEARFUL.
weeping *noun* CRY.
weepy *adjective* TEARFUL.
weigh *verb*
1. CHARGE.
2. COUNT.
3. PONDER.

weigh down *verb* DEPRESS.
weigh on (or **upon**) *verb* HAUNT.
weighed *adjective* ADVISED.
weight *noun*
1. The greatest part or portion: *the weight of the evidence.*
   Syns: bulk, mass, preponderance (also preponderancy).
2. BURDEN.
3. HEAVINESS.
4. INFLUENCE.
5. IMPORTANCE.
6. MUSCLE.

weight *verb* CHARGE.
weightiness *noun*
1. GRAVITY.
2. HEAVINESS.
3. IMPORTANCE.

weightless *adjective* LIGHT².
weighty *adjective*
1. BURDENSOME.
2. FAT.
3. GRAVE².
4. HEAVY.
5. IMPORTANT.
6. INFLUENTIAL.

weird *adjective*
1. Of a mysteriously strange and usu. frightening nature: *a weird premonition of disaster.*
   Syns: eerie (*also* eery), uncanny, unearthly.
2. ECCENTRIC.
3. FUNNY.

weirdie *also* **weirdy, weirdo** *noun* CRACKPOT.
weisenheimer *noun* SEE **wisenheimer.**
welcome *adjective*
1. AGREEABLE.
2. GRATEFUL.

welcome *noun* GREETING.
welcome *verb*
1. ACCEPT.
2. GREET.

welcoming *adjective* APPROACHABLE.
welfare *noun*
1. A state of health, happiness, and prospering: *A government ought to seek the welfare of all its citizens.*
   Syns: advantage, benefit, good, prosperity, weal¹, well-being.
2. RELIEF.

welkin *noun* AIR.
well¹ *noun* ORIGIN.
well *verb* FLOW.
well² *adverb*
1. In the manner desired: *The program is going well.*
   Syn: satisfyingly.
2. COMPLETELY.
3. CONSIDERABLY.
4. CONSIDERABLY.

well *adjective*
1. ADVISABLE.
2. HEALTHY.

well-being *noun* WELFARE.
well-born *adjective* NOBLE.
well-bred *adjective*
1. COURTEOUS.
2. CULTURED.

well-developed *adjective* SHAPELY.
well-fixed *adjective* PROSPEROUS.
well-founded *adjective* SANE.
well-groomed *adjective* NEAT.
well-grounded *adjective* SANE.
well-heeled *adjective* PROSPEROUS.

well-known *adjective* FAMOUS.
well-liked *adjective* FAVORITE.
well-mannered *adjective* COURTEOUS.
well-off *adjective* PROSPEROUS.
well-timed *adjective* OPPORTUNE.
well-to-do *adjective* PROSPEROUS.
well-worn *adjective* TRITE.
welt *noun*
1. A ridge or bump raised on the flesh by a lash or blow: *The beating left raw welts on the boy's back and shoulders.*
  Syns: wale, weal², wheal, whelk (*Path.*).
2. BLOW².
welter *verb* WALLOW.
wench *noun* SLUT.
wend *verb* GO.
wet *adjective*
Covered with or full of liquid: *removed her wet bathing suit.*
  Syns: drenched, soaked, sodden, soggy, sopping, soppy, soused.
wet *verb*
To make thoroughly wet: *wetted the sponge.*
  Syns: douse, drench, saturate, soak, sodden, sop, souse.
wetland *noun* SWAMP.
whack *verb*
1. BANG.
2. HIT.
whack *noun*
1. BLOW².
2. TRY.
whacky *adjective* SEE **wacky.**
wham *noun* SLAM.
wham *verb* HIT.
whatnot *noun* NOVELTY.
wheal *noun* WELT.
wheedle *verb* COAX.
wheel *noun*
1. CIRCLE.
2. REVOLUTION.
wheel *verb*
1. DRIVE.
2. SWING.
3. TURN.
whelk *noun* WELT.
whelm *verb*
1, 2. FLOOD.
wherefore *noun* REASON.
wherewithal *noun*
1, 2. RESOURCES.
whet *verb* SHARPEN.
whiff *noun* TRACE.
whiff *verb* SMELL.

while *noun*
1. BIT¹.
2. EFFORT.
  while *verb* IDLE.
whilom *adjective* LATE.
whim *noun* FANCY.
whimper *verb* WHINE.
whimsey *noun* SEE **whimsy.**
whimsical *adjective*
1. ARBITRARY.
2. CAPRICIOUS.
3. FANCIFUL.
whimsy also **whimsey** *noun* FANCY.
whim-whams also **wim-wams** *noun* JITTERS.
whine *verb*
1. To cry with soft, intermittent, often plaintive sounds: *The frightened kitten began to whine pitifully.*
  Syns: pule, whimper.
2. COMPLAIN.
whip *verb*
1, 2. BEAT.
3. DEFEAT.
whipping *noun*
1. BEATING.
2. DEFEAT.
whipping boy *noun* SCAPEGOAT.
whir *verb* HUM.
whir *noun* HUM.
whirl *verb*
1. RUSH.
2, 3. SPIN.
4. SWIRL.
whirl *noun*
1. DRIVE.
2. REVOLUTION.
3. STIR¹.
4. TRY.
whirlpool *noun* STIR¹.
whisk *verb*
1. BEAT.
2. HISS.
3. RUSH.
whisker *noun* SHADE.
whisper *verb*
1. CONFIDE.
2. MURMUR.
3. MUTTER.
  whisper *noun*
1. MURMUR.
2. SHADE.
whispering *noun* GOSSIP.
whit *noun*
1. BIT¹.
2. DAMN.
white plague *noun* TUBERCULOSIS.
whitewash *verb*
1. COLOR.
2. EXTENUATE.

whiz also **whizz** verb
1. HISS.
2. HUM.
3. RUSH.

whiz also **whizz** noun
1. EXPERT.
2. HUM.

whole adjective
1. Including every constituent or individual: *The whole town backed the mayor.*
   Syns: all, complete, entire, gross, total.
2. COMPLETE.
3. CONCENTRATED.
4. GOOD.
5. HEALTHY.
6. ROUND.

whole noun
1. An amount or quantity from which nothing is left out or held back: *spent the whole of our cash reserve.*
   Syns: aggregate, all, entirety, gross, sum, total, totality. —*Idioms* kit and caboodle; lock, stock, and barrel; the works.
2. SYSTEM.

wholehearted adjective IMPLICIT.
whole-hog adjective THOROUGH.
wholeness noun
1. COMPLETENESS.
2. HEALTH.
3. SOUNDNESS.

wholesome adjective
1. CLEAN.
2. HEALTHFUL.
3. HEALTHY.

wholly adverb
1. COMPLETELY.
2. PURELY.

whoop verb SHOUT
whoopee noun GAIETY.
whoosh verb HISS.
whop noun BLOW².
whopper noun
1. GIANT.
2. LIE².

whopping adjective GIANT.
whore noun PROSTITUTE.
whorish adjective WANTON.
whorl verb SWIRL.
who's who noun SOCIETY.
why noun REASON.
wicked adjective
1. EVIL.
2. MALEVOLENT.
3. TROUBLESOME.

wickedness noun
1. CORRUPTION.
2. EVIL.
3. INFAMY.

wide adjective
1. BROAD.
2. FULL.

wide-awake adjective
1. ALERT.
2. WAKEFUL.

widen verb
1. BROADEN.
2. EXTEND.

wideness noun WIDTH.
wide-ranging adjective GENERAL.
wide-reaching adjective GENERAL.
widespread adjective
1. COMMON.
2. GENERAL.
3. PREVAILING.

width noun
The extent of something from side to side: *measured the width of the windowpane.*
   Syns: breadth, broadness, wideness.

wield verb
1. EXERCISE.
2. HANDLE.

wig verb BAWL OUT at **bawl.**
wiggle verb
To move or proceed with short, irregular motions up and down or from side to side: *He wiggled his toes to be sure the new shoes were roomy.*
   Syns: squiggle, squirm, waggle, worm, wriggle, writhe.

wild adjective
1. In a primitive state; not domesticated or cultivated: *wild countryside; wild animals.*
   Syns: agrestal (*also* agrestial), native, natural, rough, uncultivated, undomesticated, untamed.
2. ABANDONED.
3. FAST.
4. FRANTIC.
5. ROUGH.
6. SAVAGE.
7. UNCIVILIZED.
8. UNRULY.

wild noun
An uninhabited region left in its natural state: *a resourceful backpacker, at home in the wild.*
   Syns: backland, bush, wilderness, wildness.

wilderness noun
1. BARREN.
2. WILD.

wildness noun
1. ABANDON.

2. UNRULINESS.
3. WILD.
wile *noun* TRICK.
  wile *verb* IDLE.
wiliness *noun* ART.
will¹ *noun*
1. The mental faculty by which one deliberately chooses or decides: *He stood hesitant in a paralysis of will.*
  Syn: volition.
2. The power to make choices and set goals and to act upon them firmly in spite of opposition or difficulty: *lacked the will to carry his theories into practical social action.*
  Syns: decision, determination, resolution, resolve. —*Idiom* will power.
3. Unrestricted freedom to choose: *wandered about at will.*
  Syns: choice, discretion, pleasure.
4. LIKING.
  will *verb* CHOOSE.
will² *verb* LEAVE¹.
willful *adjective*
1. ARBITRARY.
2. DELIBERATE.
3. OBSTINATE.
4. VOLUNTARY.
willfulness *noun* OBSTINACY.
willies *noun* JITTERS.
willing *adjective*
1. Disposed to accept or agree: *asked her for one last dance, and she was willing.*
  Syns: acquiescent, agreeable, fain (*Archaic*), game (*Informal*), inclined, minded, ready.
2. VOLUNTARY.
willingly *adverb* VOLUNTARILY.
will-o'-the-wisp *noun* ILLUSION.
willy-nilly *adverb* HELPLESSLY.
wilt *verb*
1. To become limp, as from loss of freshness: *Cut wildflowers wilt quickly.*
  Syns: droop, flag², sag.
2. SLOUCH.
wily *adjective* ARTFUL.
wim-wams *noun* SEE **whim-whams**.
win *verb*
1. CAPTURE.
2, 3. EARN.
4. GET.
win over *verb* CONVINCE.
win *noun* CONQUEST.
wince *verb* FLINCH.
wind¹ *noun*
A natural movement or current of air: *seeds that are scattered and blown by the wind.*

  Syns: air, blow, breeze, gale (*Archaic*), gust, zephyr.
wind *verb* AIR.
wind² *verb*
1. To move or proceed on a repeatedly curving course: *A staircase wound its way up the tower. The river wound slowly through the plain.*
  Syns: coil, corkscrew, curl, entwine, meander, snake, spiral, twine, twist, weave, wreathe.
2. INSINUATE.
wind up *verb* CLOSE¹.
windiness *noun* WORDINESS.
winding *adjective*
Repeatedly curving in alternate directions: *a winding footpath down a mountain.*
  Syns: anfractuous, flexuous (*also* flexuose), meandering, meandrous, serpentine, sinuous, snaky, tortuous, twisting.
windless *adjective* AIRLESS.
window-dressing *also* **window dressing** *noun* FAÇADE.
wind-up *noun*
1, 2. END.
windy *adjective*
1. AIRY.
2. INFLATED.
wing *noun* BRANCH.
  wing *verb*
1. FLY.
2. RUSH.
wink *verb*
1, 2. BLINK.
wink at *verb* BLINK AT at **blink.**
wink *noun*
1, 2. BLINK.
3. FLASH.
winner *noun*
1. One that wins a contest or competition: *the winner of the tennis match.*
  Syn: victor.
2. CONQUEROR.
winning *adjective* ATTRACTIVE.
winnow *verb*
1. BLOW¹.
2. SORT.
winsome *adjective* ATTRACTIVE.
wintry *adjective* FRIGID.
wiped-out *adjective* DRUGGED.
wipe out *verb*
1. ANNIHILATE.
2. CANCEL.
3. ELIMINATE.
4. MURDER.
wiretap *verb* TAP².

wisdom *noun*
1. Deep, thorough, or mature understanding: *an old judge famous for his wisdom.*
   Syns: insight, profundity, sagaciousness, sagacity, sageness, sapience.
2. COMMON SENSE.
3. KNOWLEDGE.

wise¹ *adjective*
1. Possessing or showing sound judgment and keen perception: *a wise elder statesman.*
   Syns: discerning, knowing, sagacious, sage, sapient.
2. AWARE.
3. IMPUDENT.
4. LEARNED.
5. SANE.
6. SHREWD.

wise² *noun* WAY.
wiseacre *noun* SMART ALECK.
wisecrack *noun* CRACK.
wisecracker *noun* SMART ALECK.
wise guy *noun* SMART ALECK.
wisehead *noun* SMART ALECK.
wiseling *noun* SMART ALECK.
wisenheimer also **weisenheimer** *noun* SMART ALECK.

wish *verb*
1. CHOOSE.
2. DESIRE.

wishy-washy *adjective* INSIPID.
wistful *adjective* PENSIVE.

wit *noun*
1. DISCERNMENT.
2. HUMOR.
3. INTELLIGENCE.
4. JOKER.
5. SANITY.

witch *noun*
1. A woman who practices magic: *The witch turned the handsome prince into a frog.*
   Syns: enchantress, hag, hex, lamia, sorceress.
2. An ugly, frightening old woman: *children scared by the evil-looking old witch.*
   Syns: bag (*Slang*), bat² (*Slang*), beldam (*also* beldame), biddy (*also* biddie) (*Slang*), crone, drab², drone, hag, trot (*Archaic*).
3. SEDUCTRESS.

witch *verb* CHARM.
witchcraft *noun* MAGIC.
witchery *noun*
1. ATTRACTION.
2. MAGIC.

witching *noun* MAGIC.
witching *adjective*
1. Pertaining to magic: *the witching hour.*
   Syns: bewitching, magic (*also* magical).
2. SEDUCTIVE.

withdraw *verb*
1. To pull back in: *The cat withdrew its claws.*
   Syns: draw in, retract.
2. DETACH.
3. GO.
4. REMOVE.
5. RETRACT.
6. RETREAT.

withdrawal also **withdrawment** *noun*
1. DEPARTURE.
2. RETREAT.

withdrawn *adjective* COOL.

wither *verb*
1. To render (another) speechless or incapable of action: *He withered me with a baleful look.*
   Syn: petrify.
2. DRY UP at dry.
3. LANGUISH.

withhold *verb*
1. HOLD.
2. REFRAIN.
3. REFUSE.

with-it *adjective* FASHIONABLE.
withstand *verb* RESIST.
witless *adjective*
1. INSANE.
2. MINDLESS.

witling *noun* SMART ALECK.
witness *noun*
1. Someone who sees something occur: *a witness to murder.*
   Syns: eyewitness, seer², viewer.
2. One who testifies, esp. in court: *a witness for the defense.*
   Syns: attestant, deponent (*Law*), testifier.
3. SIGN.
4. TESTIMONY.

witness *verb*
1. CERTIFY.
2. INDICATE.
3. TESTIFY.

wits *noun* SANITY.
witticism *noun* JOKE.
wittiness *noun* HUMOR.
witting *adjective* DELIBERATE.
witty *adjective*
1. CLEVER.
2. HUMOROUS.

wizard *noun* EXPERT.

wizardly *adjective* MAGIC.
wizardry *noun* MAGIC.
wizen *verb* DRY UP at **dry.**
wobble *verb*
1. LURCH.
2. SWAY.
wobbly *adjective*
1. HESITANT.
2. INSECURE.
3. UNSTABLE.
wobegone *adjective* SEE **woebegone.**
woe *noun*
1. CURSE.
2. DISTRESS.
3. GRIEF.
4. MISERY.
woebegone also **wobegone** *adjective*
1. MISERABLE.
2. SORROWFUL.
woeful also **woful** *adjective*
1. MISERABLE.
2, 3. SORROWFUL.
wolf *noun* PHILANDERER.
wolf *verb* GULP.
womanish *adjective* EFFEMINATE.
womanishness *noun* EFFEMINACY.
womanity *noun* FEMININITY.
womanize *verb* PHILANDER.
womanizer *noun* PHILANDERER.
womankind *noun* FEMININITY.
womanliness *noun* FEMININITY.
womanly *adjective* FEMININE.
womanness *noun* FEMININITY.
womenfolk *noun* FEMININITY.
wonder *noun*
1. The emotion aroused by something awe-inspiring or astounding: *viewed the northern lights with wonder.*
 Syns: admiration (*Archaic*), amaze (*Archaic*), amazement, awe, dread, marveling, wonderment.
2. DOUBT.
3. MARVEL.
4. MIRACLE.
wonder *verb*
To have a feeling of great awe and rapt admiration: *wondered at the beauty and engineering excellence of the Great Pyramid.*
 Syn: marvel.
wonderful *adjective*
1. FABULOUS.
2. MARVELOUS.
wonderment *noun*
1. MARVEL.
2. WONDER.
wondrous *adjective* FABULOUS.

wont *adjective* ACCUSTOMED TO at **accustomed.**
wont *verb* ACCUSTOM.
wont *noun* CUSTOM.
woo *verb* COURT.
wooden *adjective*
1. DULL.
2. STIFF.
woolgathering *adjective* DREAMY.
woolly *adjective* HAIRY.
wooziness *noun* DIZZINESS.
woozy *adjective* DIZZY.
word *noun*
1. Something said: *May I say a word about that? Remember: not a word about this to anyone!*
 Syns: comment, remark, statement, utterance.
2. A statement that expresses a commitment on the part of its maker as to its truthfulness or to the fulfillment of its conditions: *gave my word that I had not revealed his identity.*
 Syns: assurance, guarantee, warrant.
 —*Idioms* solemn word, word of honor.
3. COMMAND.
4. COMMUNICATION.
5. GOSSIP.
6. NEWS.
7. TERM.
word *verb* PHRASE.
wordage *noun* WORDING.
wordbook *noun* VOCABULARY.
word-for-word *adjective* LITERAL.
word-hoard *noun* VOCABULARY.
wordiness *noun*
Words or the use of words in excess of those needed for clarity or precision: *Instead of getting to the point, he obscured his meaning with wordiness.*
 Syns: prolixity, prolixness, verboseness, verbosity, windiness.
wording *noun*
Choice of words and the way in which they are used: *complex wording in a contract.*
 Syns: diction, parlance, phrase, phraseology, phrasing, verbalism, wordage.
wordless *adjective*
1. IMPLICIT.
2. SILENT.
3. SPEECHLESS.
word-of-mouth *adjective* ORAL.
words *noun* ARGUMENT.
word-stock *noun* VOCABULARY.

wordy *adjective*
1. Using or containing an excessive number of words: *a halting, wordy apology that made everyone impatient.*
   Syns: diffuse, longwinded, periphrastic, pleonastic, prolix, verbose.
2. VERBAL.

work *noun*
1. The technique, style, and quality of working: *did excellent work on the watch; the exquisite work of Fabergé.*
   Syns: craftsmanship, workmanship.
2. BUSINESS.
3. COMPOSITION.
4. LABOR.
5. PUBLICATION.

work *verb*
1. To force to work: *The overseer worked the slaves unmercifully.*
   Syns: drive, labor, task, tax. —*Idiom* crack the whip.
2. To function effectively: *The car doesn't work half the time.*
   Syns: function, go, operate, run.
3. To handle in a way so as to mix, form, and shape: *worked the dough into a ball.*
   Syns: knead, manipulate.
4. To arrive at an answer to (a mathematical problem): *worked two problems.*
   Syns: figure out (*Informal*), solve, work out.
5. FUNCTION.
6. INSINUATE.
7. LABOR.
8. OPERATE.
9. TILL.

work out *verb*
1. ARRANGE.
2. EXERCISE.
3. SUCCEED.
4. WORK.

work up *verb* PROVOKE.

workable *adjective*
1. MALLEABLE.
2. POSSIBLE.

workaday *adjective* EVERYDAY.

workday *adjective* EVERYDAY.

worked up *adjective* THRILLED.

worker *noun*
1. EMPLOYEE.
2. LABORER.

workhand *noun* LABORER.

working *noun* BEHAVIOR.

working *adjective*
1. ACTIVE.
2. EMPLOYED.

workingman *noun* LABORER.

workless *adjective*
Out of work: *workless coal miners.*
   Syns: jobless, unemployed.

workman *noun* LABORER.

workmanship *noun* WORK.

works *noun*
A building or complex in which an industry is located: *the Krupp works.*
   Syns: mill, plant.

world *noun*
1. AREA.
2. EARTH.
3. ENVIRONMENT.
4. HEAP.
5. MANKIND.
6. UNIVERSE.

worldly *adjective*
1. EARTHLY.
2. MATERIALISTIC.
3. PROFANE.
4. SOPHISTICATED.

worldly-wise *adjective*
SOPHISTICATED.

worldwide *adjective* UNIVERSAL.

world-without-end *adjective* ENDLESS.

world-without-end *noun*
1. ENDLESSNESS.
2. IMMORTALITY.

worm *verb*
1. CRAWL.
2. INSINUATE.
3. WANGLE.
4. WIGGLE.

worn *adjective*
1. EXHAUSTED.
2. HAGGARD.

worn-down *adjective* EXHAUSTED.

worn-out *adjective*
1. EXHAUSTED.
2. TRITE.

worried *adjective* ANXIOUS.

worry *verb*
1. To be troubled: *I worry about his sanity.*
   Syns: cark, pother, stew. —*Idioms* bite one's nails, play with the worry beads, worry one's head over.
2. To cause anxious uneasiness in: *The patient's high fever worried the doctors.*
   Syns: ail, cark, concern, distress, trouble.
3. ANNOY.
4. BROOD.

worry *noun* ANXIETY.

worrywart *noun* PESSIMIST.

worsen *verb* DETERIORATE.

worsening *noun* DETERIORATION.

worship *verb*
1, 2. ADORE.
  worship *noun* ADORATION.
worshipful *adjective* REVERENT.
worst *verb*
1. DEFEAT.
2. TRIUMPH.
worth *noun*
1. A measure of those qualities that determine merit, desirability, usefulness, or importance: *the innate worth of the individual; a book of little worth or interest; a Caucasian rug of great worth.*
  Syns: account, valuation, value.
2. MERIT.
3. RICHES.
worthless *adjective*
1. Lacking all worth and value: *worthless costume jewelry; a worthless occupation.*
  Syns: drossy, good-for-nothing, inutile, no-good, nothing (*Slang*), valueless.
2. USELESS.
worthy *adjective*
1. ADMIRABLE.
2. ELIGIBLE.
3. HONORABLE.
4. VALUABLE.
wound *noun* TRAUMA.
wound *verb*
1. HURT.
2. TRAUMATIZE.
wow *noun* HIT.
wrack *noun*
1. DESTRUCTION.
2. RUIN.
  wrack *verb* DESTROY.
wraith *noun* GHOST.
wrangle *verb*
1. ARGUE.
2. BRAWL.
  wrangle *noun* ARGUMENT.
wrap *verb*
1. To cover and tie (something), as with paper and string: *wrap a box for mailing.*
  Syns: do up, package.
2. To surround and cover completely so as to obscure: *Fog wrapped the lonely moors.*
  Syns: cloak, clothe, enfold (*also* infold), enshroud, envelop, enwrap, invest, shroud, veil.
wrap up *verb*
1. To cover completely and closely, as with clothing or bandages: *Infants were formerly wrapped up in strips of linen called swaddling clothes.*
  Syns: enfold (*also* infold), enswathe, envelop, enwrap, invest, roll, swaddle, swathe.
2. To put on warm clothes: *They wrapped up in furs.*
  Syns: bundle (up), hap² (*Regional*).
3. CLOSE¹.
wrap *noun*
1. A garment wrapped about a person: *a mink wrap.*
  Syns: cloak, hap² (*Regional*), stole.
2. WRAPPER.
wrapped up *adjective* ABSORBED.
wrapper *noun*
The material in which something is wrapped: *foil candy wrappers.*
  Syns: wrap, wrapping (*also* wrappings).
wrapping *also* **wrappings** *noun* WRAPPER.
wraps *noun* SECRECY.
wrap-up *noun*
1, 2. END.
3. SUMMARY.
wrath *noun* FURY.
wrathful *adjective* ANGRY.
wrathfulness *noun* FURY.
wreak *verb* INFLICT.
wreathe *verb* WIND².
wreck *verb*
1. To damage, disable, or destroy (a seacraft): *The violent storm in the Irish Sea wrecked the racing yachts.*
  Syns: cast away, pile up, shipwreck.
2. BLAST.
3. DESTROY.
4. TRASH¹.
wreck *noun*
1. COLLAPSE.
2. CRASH.
3. DESTRUCTION.
wreckage *noun*
1. BREAKAGE.
2. DESTRUCTION.
3. RUIN.
wrench *verb*
1. To alter the position of by a sharp, forcible twisting or turning movement: *wrenched the steering wheel to the right; wrenched the child from the deep water.*
  Syns: wrest, wring, wry.
2. DISTORT.
3. EXTORT.
4. JERK.
5. TURN.
wrench *noun*
1. A tool with jaws for gripping and twisting: *opened the pipe with a big wrench.*

Syn: spanner (*Chiefly Brit.*).
2. JERK.

wrest *verb*
1. EXTORT.
2. WRENCH.

wrestle *verb*
1. To contend with an opponent, esp.
by attempting to throw him:
*heavyweights wrestling in amateur
competition; wrestled the skyjacker to
the ground and disarmed him.*
Syns: grapple, scuffle, tussle. —*Idiom*
go to the mat with.
2. CONTEND.

wretch *noun* UNFORTUNATE.

wretched *adjective*
1. FILTHY.
2, 3. MISERABLE.

wretchedness *noun* MISERY.

wriggle *verb* WIGGLE.

wring *verb*
1. EXTORT.
2. WRENCH.

wrinkle¹ *verb*
To make irregular folds in, esp. by
pressing or twisting: *The overloaded
washer wrinkled all the clothes.*
Syns: crimp, crimple, crinkle,
crumple, rimple, ruckle (*Brit.*),
rumple.

wrinkle *noun*
1. FOLD.
2. LINE.

wrinkle² *noun*
Informal. A clever, unexpected new trick
or method: *a strategy with some new
wrinkles guaranteed to increase sales.*
Syns: angle (*Slang*), gimmick (*Slang*),
kick, kicker, twist.

write *verb*
1. To form letters, characters, or words
on a surface with an instrument:
*wrote the equation on the blackboard
with chalk; wrote a message on the
card.*
Syns: engross, indite, inscribe, scribe.
—*Idiom* put in writing.
2. COMPOSE.
3. PUBLISH.

write down *verb* DEPRECIATE.

write off *verb*
To put out of one's mind as a loss or
failure: *wrote off the incident as an
exercise in futility.*
Syn: discount.

writhe *verb*
1. To twist and turn, as in pain,
struggle, or embarrassment: *The
patient writhed in a convulsion.*

Syns: agonize, squirm, toss.
2. WIGGLE.

written *adjective* GRAPHIC.

wrong *adjective*
1. AMISS.
2. ERRONEOUS.
3. EVIL.
4. FALSE.
5. INSANE.

wrong *adverb*
Not in the right way or on the proper
course: *Our plans went wrong at the last
minute.*
Syns: afield, amiss, astray, badly, sour
(*Informal*). —*Idiom* off the mark.

wrong *noun*
1. CRIME.
2. EVIL.
3, 4. INJUSTICE.

wrong *verb*
To do a wrong to; treat unjustly:
*wronged and injured those who had
trusted him.*
Syns: aggrieve, oppress, outrage,
persecute.

wrongdoing *noun*
1. CRIME.
2. MISBEHAVIOR.

wrongful *adjective*
1. CRIMINAL.
2. ILLEGAL.
3. UNLAWFUL.

wry *adjective* CYNICAL.
wry *verb* WRENCH.

Xanthippe *noun* SCOLD.
x out *verb* CANCEL.

yahoo *noun* BOOR.
yak *noun* CHATTER.
yak *verb* CHATTER.

yank *verb* JERK.

yank *noun* JERK.

yap *verb* YELP.

yap *noun* YELP.

yard *noun* COURT.

yardstick *noun* STANDARD.

yarn *noun*

Informal. An entertaining and often oral account of a real or fictitious occurrence: *told the children yarns about his adventures.*
　　Syns: anecdote, fable, story, tale.
　　—Idiom tall story (*or* tale).

yaup *verb & noun* SEE **yawp.**

yaw *verb*

1. LURCH.
2. SWERVE.
3. YAWN.

yawn *verb*

1. To open the mouth wide with a deep inward breath, as when tired or bored: *yawning and nodding in front of the fire.*
　　Syns: gape, yaw (*Regional*).
2. To open wide: *The chasm yawned at our feet.*
　　Syns: gap (*Regional*), gape.

yawn *noun* BOREDOM.

yawning *adjective*

Open wide: *a yawning gulf.*
　　Syns: abysmal, abyssal, cavernous, gaping.

yawp *also* **yaup** *verb*

1. COMPLAIN.
2. GAZE.
3. ROAR.
4. YELP.

yawp *also* **yaup** *noun* YELP.

yea *adverb* YES.

yea *noun* YES.

yeah *also* **yeh** *adverb* YES.

year *noun*

1. A period of time of approx. 12 months, esp. that period during which the earth completes a single revolution around the sun: *spent a year in London.*
　　Syn: twelvemonth.
2. VINTAGE.

yearn *verb*

1. DESIRE.
2. FEEL.

yearner *noun* ASPIRANT.

yearning *noun* DESIRE.

years *noun* AGE.

yeast *noun*

1. CATALYST.
2. FOAM.

yeh *adverb* SEE **yeah.**

yell *verb*

1. ROAR.
2. SHOUT.

yell *noun* SHOUT.

yellow *adjective* COWARDLY.

yellow-bellied *adjective* COWARDLY.

yellow-belly *noun* COWARD.

yellowness *noun* COWARDICE.

yelp *verb*

To utter a shrill, short cry: *a dog that yelped at strangers; yelped with pain.*
　　Syns: squeal, yap, yawp (*also* yaup), yip.

yelp *noun*

A shrill, short cry: *gave a yelp of surprise.*
　　Syns: squeal, yap, yawp (*also* yaup), yip.

yen *noun* DESIRE.

yenta *noun* GOSSIP.

yep *also* **yup** *adverb* YES.

yes *adverb*

It is so; as you say or ask: *Yes, he was here yesterday.*
　　Syns: absolutely, agreed, all right, aye (*also* ay), certainly, O.K. *or* OK (*Informal*), okeydoke (*also* okeydokey) (*Slang*), right on (*Informal*), Roger (*Informal*), uh-huh (*Informal*), yea (*Archaic*), yeah (*also* yeh) (*Informal*), yep (*also* yup) (*Slang*).

yes *noun*

1. An affirmative vote or voter: *The yeses were in the majority, and the bill became law.*
　　Syns: aye (*also* ay), yea.
2. ACCEPTANCE.

yesterday *noun* PAST.

yesteryear *noun* PAST.

yet *adverb*

1. EARLIER.
2. EVEN[1].
3. STILL.

yield *verb*

1. ABDICATE.
2. BEAR.
3. DEFER[2].
4. GIVE IN at **give.**
5. RELINQUISH.
6. RETURN.
7. SUCCUMB.
8. WEAKEN.

yield *noun*

1. The amount or quantity produced: *a high yield of corn per acre.*
　　Syns: output, product, production.
2. HARVEST.

Z

yielding *adjective*
1. PASSIVE.
2. SOFT.

yip *noun* YELP.

yip *verb* YELP.

yoke *noun*
1. BOND.
2. SLAVERY.

yoke *verb* COMBINE.

yore *noun* PAST.

young *adjective*
Being in an early period of growth or development: *a young country full of the pioneer spirit.*
Syns: green, immature, infant, juvenile, youthful.

young *noun*
1. Young people collectively: *had a great influence on the young.*
Syns: juvenility, youth.
2. The offspring, as of an animal, bird, etc., that are the result of one breeding season: *a lioness with her young.*
Syns: brood, litter.

youngster *noun* CHILD.

youth *noun*
1. The time of life between childhood and maturity: *In her youth she lived in Europe.*
Syns: greenness, juvenescence, juvenility, prime (*Rare*), spring, springtide, springtime, youthfulness. —*Idiom* salad days.
2. YOUNG.

youthful *adjective* YOUNG.

youthfulness *noun* YOUTH.

yowl *verb*
1. BAWL.
2. CRY.
3. HOWL.

yowl *noun* HOWL.

yummy *adjective* DELICIOUS.

yup *adverb* SEE **yep.**

zaftig or **zoftig** *adjective* PLUMP[1].

zany *adjective*
1. AMUSING.
2. FOOLISH.

zany *noun* JOKER.

zap *verb*
1. KILL.
2. MURDER.

zeal *noun* ENTHUSIASM.

zealot *noun* ENTHUSIAST.

zealous *adjective* ENTHUSIASTIC.

zealousness *noun* ENTHUSIASM.

zenith *noun* CLIMAX.

zephyr *noun*
1. BREEZE.
2. WIND[1].

zero *noun* NONENTITY.

zero in *verb* AIM.

zest *noun*
Spirited enjoyment: *ate and drank with zest.*
Syns: gusto, relish.

zigzag *verb* TRAVERSE.

zilch *noun*
1. NONENTITY.
2. NOTHING.

zillion *noun* HEAP.

zip *noun*
1. ENERGY.
2. SPIRIT.

zip *verb*
1. BREEZE.
2. RUSH.

zippy *adjective* VIGOROUS.

zoftig *adjective* SEE **zaftig.**

zonked *adjective*
1. DRUGGED.
2. DRUNK.

zoom *verb* RUSH.